THE ENFORCEMENT OF EU LAW AND VALUES

The Enforcement of EU Law and Values

Ensuring Member States' Compliance

Edited by

ANDRÁS JAKAB

Director of the Institute for Legal Studies at the Centre for Social Sciences of the Hungarian Academy of Sciences, Budapest; Professor in Constitutional and European Law at Pázmány Péter Catholic University, Budapest

and

DIMITRY KOCHENOV

Chair in EU Constitutional Law, University of Groningen

OXFORD
UNIVERSITY PRESS

OXFORD
UNIVERSITY PRESS

Great Clarendon Street, Oxford OX2 6DP,
United Kingdom

Oxford University Press is a department of the University of Oxford. It furthers the University's objective of excellence in research, scholarship, and education by publishing worldwide. Oxford is a registered trade mark of Oxford University Press in the UK and in certain other countries

First Edition published in 2017
Impression: 1

Published in the United States of America by Oxford University Press
198 Madison Avenue, New York, NY 10016, United States of America

British Library Cataloguing in Publication Data
Data available

Library of Congress Control Number: 2016954563

ISBN 978–0–19–874656–0

Printed and bound by
CPI Group (UK) Ltd, Croydon, CR0 4YY

To Norbert Reich

Avant-propos

During the many years that this book was in preparation, we had the luck of benefiting from the assistance, advice, and support of a number of remarkable colleagues, including Leonardo Álvarez Álvarez, Eszter Bodnár, Bojan Bugarič, Aleksejs Dimitrovs, Federico Fabbrini, Tamás Győrfi, Tamás Hoffmann, Miklós Hollán, Balázs Horváthy, Ester Herlin Karnell, Mónika Papp, Michael Meyer-Resende, Kim Lane Scheppele, Gábor Sulyok, Jonathan Tomkin, Anna Tsiftsoglu, David Wineroither, and Andrej Zwitter. Most importantly, however, we would like to thank the authors of the book for their engaging scholarship, constant support, and, importantly with a volume as large as this one, their infinite patience. We are grateful also to the scholars whose work did not pass peer review and was thus not included in this volume.

The idea of the present volume grew out of a conference organized by the Hungarian Academy of Sciences, with the generous support of the Swedish, Dutch, French, and US embassies in Budapest, on 'The Enforcement of EU Law against Member States' on 21 May 2013, which made it clear that the EU cannot do much in terms of the enforcement of values. This is when the work on this volume started. The initial structure was penned at a café not far from the Academy and the authors' workshop followed in one year's time, where the drafts were discussed in-depth. We are thankful to Mattias Kumm who hosted the authors' workshop at WZB in Berlin and to all the scholars who attended without submitting chapters.

Alec Swann, Elinor Shields, and Natasha Flemming of Oxford University Press made this book a delight to work on. Pázmány Peter Catholic University, Budapest and Stichting voor Bevoordering van Europees Recht, Groningen contributed financial support to the linguistic revisions of the manuscript. Last but not least, this collection would not have been possible without the dedication and help of a number of our assistants, including Eva Kappelhof (Groningen), Justin Lindeboom (London), Harry Panagopoulos (Brussels), Jacquelyn Veraldi (Groningen), and especially, Bálint Gárdos (Budapest), who was at the lead of the hands-on work on this book. Thank you.

To our deep regret, one of the key contributors to this volume, Professor Norbert Reich passed away during the final stages of the work on this project. We dedicate this book to his memory as a token of our profound respect of his optimistic and jovial spirit, overwhelming dedication to the study of the law, and the depth and breadth of his scholarly achievement, which has inspired both of us since our university days.

AJ and DK

Budapest / Princeton, May 2016

Contents

III. COMPARATIVE OUTLOOK

IV. CASE STUDIES IN THE CONTEXT OF EU LAW

Contents

List of Abbreviations

ACP	African, Caribbean, and Pacific
AFSJ	Area of Freedom, Security and Justice
AG	Advocate General of the Court of Justice of the EU
ALBA	Alianza Bolivariana para los Pueblos de Nuestra America (Bolivarian Alliance for the Peoples of Our America)
AMR	Alert Mechanism Report
ASEAN	Association of Southeast Asian Nations
AU	African Union
BayVerwGH	*Bayerischer Verwaltungsgerichtshof* (Bavarian Administrative Court)
BGB	*Bürgerliches Gesetzbuch* (German Civil Code)
BGH	*Bundesgerichtshof* (Federal Court of Justice of Germany)
BL	Basic Law (Basic Law for the Federal Republic of Germany)
BVerfG	*Bundesverfassungsgericht* (German Federal Constitutional Court)
BVerfGE	*Entscheidungen des Bundesverfassungsgerichts* (Decisions of the German Federal Constitutional Court)
CAN	Andean Community
CAP	Common Agricultural Policy
CARICOM	Caribbean Community
CCR	Constitutional Court Ruling
CEEC	Central and Eastern European Countries
CELAC	Community of Latin American and Caribbean States
CEPEG	European Commission for the Efficiency of Justice
CFR	Charter of Fundamental Rights
CHGOM	Commonwealth Heads of Government Meeting
CM	Committee of Ministers of the Council of Europe
CMAG	Commonwealth Ministerial Action Group
CoE	Council of Europe
CPT	Committee for the Prevention of Torture
CSCE	Committee on Security and Cooperation in Europe
CSLS	Council of State, Legislation Section (Belgium)
CTC	UN Counter-Terrorism Committee
CUP	Cambridge University Press
CUP	Candidacy of Popular Unity
EAC	East African Community
EC Bull	EC Bulletin
ECB	European Central Bank
ECHR	European Convention on Human Rights
ECJ	Court of Justice of the EU
ECN	European Competition Network
ECOWAS	Economic Community of West Africa
ECtHR	European Court of Human Rights
EFSF	European Financial Stability Facility
EFSM	European Financial Stability Mechanism
EIB	European Investment Bank
EMU	Economic and Monetary Union
EP	European Parliament
EPG	Eminent Persons Group
EPP	European Peoples' Party
ESM	European Stability Mechanism
ESM Treaty	Treaty establishing the European Stability Mechanism
EU	European Union

EUSA	European Union Studies Association
FEIE	Exhange of Information and Enforcement
FPÖ	Freedom Party of Austria
FRA	Fundamental Rights Agency
GATT	General Agreement on Tariffs and Trade (1947)
GC	General Court of the European Union
GDP	Gross Domestic Product
GUAM	Georgia, Ukraine, Azerbayan, and Moldova
IACHR	Inter American Court of Human Rights
IADC	Inter-American Democratic Charter
IAEA	International Atomic Energy Agency
ICAO	International Civil Aviation Organization
ICJ	International Court of Justice
ICLQ	International and Comparative Law Quarterly
ILO	International Labour Organization
IMF	International Monetary Fund
IMPEL	EU Network for the Implementation and Enforcement of Environmental Law
JHA	Justice and Home Affairs
LG	*Landgericht* (State Court of Justice: Germany)
Mercosur	*Mercado Común del Sur* (Southern Common Market)
MFN	Most favoured nation
MoU	Memorandum of Understanding
MSC	Mediation and Security Council
MTO	Medium-Term Objective
NATO	North Atlantic Treaty Organization
NCA	National Competition Authority
NJO	National Judicial Office (Hungary)
NRP	National Reform Programmes
OAS	Organization of American States
OAU	Organization of African Unity
ODIHR	Office for Democratic Institutions and Human Rights
OFT	Office of Fair Trading
OIF	*Organisation internationale de la Francophonie* (International Organisation of La Francphonie)
OJ	Official Journal of the EC
OLAF	European Anti-fraud Office
OLCC	Organic Law on the Constitutional Court (Spain)
OMC	Open Method of Coordination
OMT	Outright Monetary Transactions
OSCE	Organization for Security and Cooperation in Europe
OUP	Oxford University Press
PACE	Parliamentary Assembly of the Council of Europe
PDCR	Parliamentary Documents of the Chamber of Representatives (Belgium)
PDS	Parliamentary Documents of the Senate (Belgium)
PIF	Pacific Islands Forum
PPP	Purchasing Power Parity
QMV	Qualified Majority Voting
RQMV	Reversed Qualified Majority Voting
SAC	State Audit Commission (Hungary)
SAC	Statute of Catalonia
SADC	Southern African Development Community
SASRS	Special Act on the Sixth Reform of the State 2014 (Belgium)
SCP	Stability and Convergence Programmes
SGP	Stability and Growth Pact

SICA	*Sistema de la Integración Centroamericana* (Central American Integration System)
SIRA	Special Institutional Reform Act 1980 (Belgium)
SJ	Solicitors' Journal
TEU	Treaty on European Union
TFEU	Treaty on the Functioning of the European Union
TSCG	Treaty on Stability, Coordination and Governance in Economic and Monetary Union
UDI	Unilateral Declaration of Independence
UK	United Kingdom
UKIP	United Kingdom Independence Party
UN	United Nations
UNASUR	*Unión de Naciones Suramericanas* (Union of South American Nations)
UPU	Universal Postal Union
US	United States
WEO	World Economic Outlook
WGI	World Bank Worldwide Governance Indicators
WTO	World Trade Organization
WTO DSB	WTO Dispute Settlement Body
WTO DSU	WTO Dispute Settlement Understanding

List of Contributors

Fabian Amtenbrink is Vice Dean and Professor of EU Law at the Erasmus School of Law, Erasmus University Rotterdam, and Visiting Professor at the College of Europe, Bruges.

Carlino Antpöhler is Research Fellow at the Max Planck Institute for Comparative Public Law and International Law, Heidelberg.

Matej Avbelj is Dean and Associate Professor of European Law at the Graduate School of Government and European Studies, Kranj.

Leonard Besselink is Head of the Department of Public Law and Chair of Constitutional Law at the Faculty of Law, University of Amsterdam.

Armin von Bogdandy is Director at the Max Planck Institute for Comparative Public Law and International Law in Heidelberg.

Morten Broberg is is Professor of Law and Jean Monnet Chair (2012–15), Faculty of Law, University of Copenhagen and is a Visiting Fellow (2016–17), Department of Politics and International Studies, University of Cambridge.

Carlos Closa is Professor at the Institute of Public Goods and Policies (IPP) at the Spanish National Research Council (CSIC).

Irène Couzigou is Lecturer at the University of Aberdeen Law School.

Katalin Cseres is Associate Professor of Law at the Amsterdam Centre for European Law and Governance, University of Amsterdam.

Laurence W Gormley is Professor of European Law and Jean Monnet Professor, University of Groningen, Faculty of Law and Visiting Professor at the College of Europe, Bruges.

Dirk Hanschel holds the Chair of German, European and International Public Law at the University of Halle-Wittenberg, Germany.

Michael Ioannidis is Senior Research Fellow at the Max Planck Institute for Comparative Public Law and International Law, Heidelberg.

Giulio Itzcovich is Associate Professor of Philosophy of Law in the Department of Legal Science at the University of Brescia, Italy, and a permanent fellow of the Tarello Institute for Legal Philosophy at the University of Genoa.

András Jakab is Director of the Institute for Legal Studies at the Centre for Social Sciences of the Hungarian Academy of Sciences, and Professor in Constitutional and European Law at Pázmány Péter Catholic University Budapest.

Dimitry Kochenov is Chair in EU Constitutional Law at the University of Groningen, Faculty of Law.

Konrad Lachmayer holds a Research Chair at the Institute for Legal Studies of the Centre for Social Sciences at the Hungarian Academy of Sciences, and is a Research Fellow at Durham Law School.

Élisabeth Lambert Abdelgawad is CNRS Research Professor at SAGE, Université de Strasbourg.

Adam Łazowski is Professor of EU Law at the Westminster Law School, University of Westminster, London.

Alberto López-Basaguren is Professor of Constitutional Law, University of the Basque Country, Bilbao.

Franz C Mayer is Chair of Public Law, European Law and Public International Law, Comparative Law, Law and Politics at Bielefeld University.

Jan-Werner Müller is a Professor of Politics at Princeton University.

Norbert Reich (†) was Emeritus Professor at the University of Bremen and Visiting Professor at the University of Groningen, Faculty of Law.

René Repasi is researcher at the Department for International and European Union Law of the Erasmus University Rotterdam and scientific coordinator of the European Research Centre for Economic and Financial Governance (EURO-CEFG).

Céline Romainville is Professor in Constitutional Law and a member of the Research Centre on State and Constitution, Université de Louvain, Louvain-la-Neuve.

Oana Ştefan is a Senior Lecturer in EU Law at Dickson Poon School of Law, King's College, London.

Zoltán Szente is Professor of Constitutional Law at the University of National Public Service, Budapest and holds a Research Chair at the Institute for Legal Studies of the Centre for Social Sciences at the Hungarian Academy of Sciences

Antonello Tancredi is Professor of International Law at the Department of Law, University of Palermo.

Mark Tushnet is William Nelson Cromwell Professor of Law at Harvard Law School.

Marc Verdussen is Professor in Constitutional Law and a member of the Research Centre on State and Constitution, Université de Louvain, Louvain-la-Neuve.

Pål Wennerås is Advocate at the Office of the Attorney General, Norway.

Jacques Ziller is Professor of EU Law at the University of Pavia.

Table of Cases

SUPRANATIONAL AND INTERNATIONAL COURTS

Court of Justice of the European Union (CJEU)

European Court of Justice (ECJ)

General Court

European Court and Commission of Human Rights (ECtHR)

International Court of Justice

Permanent Court of International Justice

World Trade Organisation Dispute Settlement Body

NATIONAL COURTS OF THE MEMBER STATES

Belgium

Constitutional Court of Belgium (Cour Constitutionnelle)

German Federal Constitutional Court (Bundesverfassungsgericht)

Landgericht (State Court of Justice)

Hungary

The Competition Council of the Hungarian Competition Authority (Gazdasági Versenyhivatal)

The Constitutional Court of Hungary (Magyarország Alkotmánybírósága)

Ireland

High Court of Ireland

Spain

The Constitutional Court of Spain

The Supreme Court of Spain

The High Court of Justice of Catalonia

United Kingdom

UK House of Lords

NATIONAL COURTS OF THE THIRD COUNTRIES

Canada

Supreme Court of Canada

United States

Supreme Court of the United States

Introductory Remarks

András Jakab and Dimitry Kochenov

The current crisis of the EU is not confined to migration and the EMU. A potentially much more worrisome trend of developments is observable in parallel, showcasing the apparent inability of the Union to be effective in ensuring that all its Member States comply with the principles and values underlying the integration project in Europe.[1] An array of countries ranging from Hungary and Greece to Poland illustrates this point. While the values in question are spelled out in the Treaties in an overwhelmingly clear fashion, trying to come up with clear examples of their successful enforcement by the Union should problems arise would leave one at a loss: such examples might not exist, the importance of the values in question notwithstanding. Article 2 TEU, lying at the heart of what the Union is about, speaks for itself:

> The Union is founded on the values of respect for human dignity, freedom, democracy, equality, the rule of law and respect for human rights, including the rights of persons belonging to minorities. These values are common to the Member States in a society in which pluralism, non-discrimination, tolerance, justice, solidarity and equality between women and men prevail.

And while the conversation among the scholars, civil servants, and politicians about whether this provision is enforceable via the 'conventional' means of ensuring compliance with EU law—beyond the special procedure contained in Article 7 TEU—is ongoing,[2] the backsliding Member States—to use Jan-Werner Müller's oft-quoted characterization[3]—entrench their 'illiberal democracies' further and further, bringing into question the adequacy of the response from the European institutions.[4] The promise of the Union, namely that its supranational law can legitimately be expected to provide an additional guarantee that the core values on which Europe is built would not be undermined in any of the Member States,[5] thus remains unfulfilled, posing one of the greatest—if not the most important—challenges for the Union today, never mind the large amount of contestants for this position of dubious honour, from Brexit to the refugee flows.[6]

Defiance in the face of the EU, including not only the letter and the spirit of the *acquis sensu stricto*, but also seemingly the very values on which the Union is built, has thus come to affect the Union profoundly. Crucial in this respect is precisely the failure of the law as it

[1] A von Bogdandy and P Sonnevend (eds), *Constitutional Crisis in the European Constitutional Area: Theory, Law and Politics in Hungary and Romania* (Hart 2015).

[2] See e.g. the contributions in C Closa and D Kochenov (eds), *Reinforcing Rule of Law Oversight in the European Union* (CUP 2016).

[3] J-W Müller, 'Safeguarding Democracy inside the EU: Brussels and the Future of Liberal Order' (2013) Working Paper No 3 (Transatlantic Academy).

[4] P Oliver and J Stefanelli, 'Strengthening the Rule of Law in the EU: The Council's Inaction' (2016) 54 *Journal of Common Market Studies* 1075; J Sargentini and A Dimitrovs, 'The European Parliament's Role: Towards the New Copenhagen Criteria for the Existing Member States?' (2016) 54 *Journal of Common Market Studies* 1085.

[5] W Sadurski, *Constitutionalism and Enlargement of Europe* (OUP 2012).

[6] A von Bogdandy and M Ioannidis, 'Systemic Deficiency in the Rule of Law: What It Is, What Has Been Done, What Can Be Done' (2014) 51 *Common Market Law Review* 59.

stands to capture the essence of the problem at hand and offer workable solutions to it. It is indispensable in this context to adopt a much broader view of enforcement and compliance than the one the literature has embraced so far:[7] the stakes are too high to overstate the importance of traditions. In broadening the focus it is the knowledge of the natural limitations of the supranational law and practice as applied to this day which should play the central role, rather than the narrow focus on the enforcement of the *acquis* as such. Regrettably, adherence to the *acquis*, however strict, does not bring with it respect of Article 2 TEU values, as scholars and politicians used to hope. That said, there is no denying of course that the importance of the classical enforcement of the *acquis* and the key procedures for this purpose available in the EU remains indispensable for the proper functioning of the Union.[8]

This collective volume builds precisely on the realization that a logical step forward is indispensable alongside the enforcement of EU law centred on a black letter understanding of the *acquis*, to move towards the analysis of the enforcement of EU values underlying the integration exercise which, although they might not be part of the classical understanding of the *acquis sensu stricto*, supply the bedrock on which the Union rests and thus cannot be ignored when we speak seriously about compliance. The book thus offers a multifaceted assessment of the phenomenon of defiance and boasts a much broader focus than usual, covering examples from the history of what can be presented as the failure to comply with EU law and values, and also turning to theoretical and comparative analysis to dissect the essence of the ongoing crisis, with a view to offering solutions which will indicate how to cope with the problem outlined in the years to come.

Defiance is not a new phenomenon, to which numerous examples from the history of EU law testify, but precisely what amounts to defiance is often a matter of perspective and should necessarily be subjected to historical evaluation. This emerges with great clarity in this work, from the story of the *Bundesverfassungsgericht*'s attitude vis-à-vis EU law (is it defiance to demand human rights protection of a nascent constitutional system?), to the French Empty Chair policy which led to the Luxembourg compromise—which, as Jacques Ziller clearly shows in his contribution, has been misused as an example of defiance in countless textbooks and is not, actually, what it seems at the first sight. The FPÖ crisis in Austria more than ten years ago offers a similarly complex story, which the literature has equally somewhat over-simplified, this book suggests. Other examples, however, are more telling and straightforward. To present contemporary Hungary as compliant with Article 2 TEU values would be unfair to the very idea of the values the Union is built upon. The same, but for different reasons, is the case with Greece and some other Balkan Member States. While defiance can definitely be part of a cunning plan designed by politicians pretending that the concept of the Rule of Law has no meaning—such as in the case of *Prawo i Sprawiedliwość* (*PiS*, 'Law and Justice') ruling Poland today, which is now the subject of the first investigation by the Commission of the possible failure by a Member State to comply with EU values in the history of the Union[9]—defiance can also be a result of the weakness of the state, and general mismanagement and corruption coupled with a severe economic downturn. A yet more ordinary example of non-compliance with

[7] For a classical account, see F Snyder, 'The Effectiveness of European Community Law: Institutions, Processes, Tools and Techniques' (1993) 56 *Modern Law Review* 19.

[8] See, for meticulous treatments of this subject, M Cremona (ed), *Compliance and the Enforcement of EU Law* (OUP 2012); H-W Mickliz and A Wechsler (eds), *The Transformation of Enforcement* (Hart 2015); S Drake and M Smith (eds), *New Directions in the Effective Enforcement of EU Law and Policy* (Edward Elgar 2016).

[9] D Kochenov and L Pech, 'Better Late than Never?: The Analysis of the Commission's First Activation of the Rule of Law Mechanism against Poland' (2016) 54 *Journal of Common Market Studies* 1062.

Fig. 1 Spectrum of defiance

supranational law is a simple failure to implement a directive correctly and on time, or otherwise infringing the provisions of the *acquis*—either with economic free-riding in mind or not. Crucially, it is only in the latter two cases, it seems, that the EU's procedures to deal with the failures to comply are effective. Figure 1 shows this spectrum of defiance.

The book you are holding is acutely aware of the fact that popular wisdom about defiance is often misleading and passing a judgment about compliance requires a serious assessment of the situation on the ground as well as the consequences of the suspicious policies at all levels in the complex, layered legal system concerned. Such judgment also requires consideration of the fact that presenting infringement proceedings coupled with Article 260 TFEU sanctions, *Francovich* accountability, Article 7 TEU, and the individualized enforcement via the preliminary rulings route as an effective set of EU's measures to ensure compliance of the Member States with EU law cannot withstand any serious scrutiny, once the problems on the ground and the actual effectiveness of these tools are assessed. In this sense, the broad spectrum of possible causes of failures to comply with the law always have to be borne in mind when approaching defiance. This spectrum ranges from the conscious dismantlement of the Rule of Law, *Fidesz* and *PiS*-style, to a Member State's inability to act due to internal failures, relatively innocent economic free riding, and, finally, non-compliance as a result of simple mistakes and ordinary delays. The breadth of the spectrum of non-compliance needs to be matched by the breadth of the spectrum of the effective tools available to the Union and its Member States to end defiance and deviations from the law. Sadly, as this book demonstrates with abundant clarity, this match, in the context of EU law, is nowhere to be found.

In the search for possible solutions to this problem, this volume includes a range of proposals building on the realization of the mismatch outlined above, aiming to remedy the Union's far-reaching vulnerabilities in dealing with the biggest chunk of the defiance spectrum, including its most dangerous extremes. In addition to looking at all the tools to ensure compliance already available in EU law, including specific sectoral compliance and defiance concepts, ranging from the EMU and competition law to the experiments with soft law, the book moves to the assessment of what *could* be done to break out of the current *impasse*.

A critical look at the law as it stands with an eye on the possible future improvements is more effective when comparative material is at hand. Besides looking forward, the volume thus also looks around, in an attempt to learn from the other multilayered legal systems out there, from complex states to international organizations: compliance is an issue constantly walking hand-in-hand with the very idea of the law, which is why a selection of chapters offer a detailed overview of how the spectrum of defiance is approached outside the EU's legal system *sensu stricto*. Indeed, virtually every federation or constitutional state with a functioning machinery of guarantees aimed at ensuring compliance with the Rule of Law could provide an array of telling examples of how important it is to deal with defiance in the face of the enforcement of key principles, values, and the law, as well as to offer (at least a hint) to possible solutions to the problems outstanding in the EU's context. This volume takes the richness of Member State-level EU examples into account, also drawing on the experience of the US legal system and that of international legal contexts, including the Council of Europe, the UN and the WTO, as well as the experience of the integration projects on other continents. All the examples at hand demonstrate with clarity that the EU is definitely not alone in facing the current challenges on the non-compliance spectrum.

This volume thus builds on the richness of this legal–political context, focusing on responding to Member State defiance by legal and not fully legal means. The main emphasis lies with the assessment of the adequacy of the enforcement mechanisms, taking not only *acquis* enforcement, but also values enforcement into account. To this end, it embraces a comparative perspective, while also learning from EU integration history. The material is organized in four parts.

Part I discusses the pros and cons of adopting a broad view of compliance, to include principles and values alongside the *acquis*. The three chapters included in this Part largely focus on the theoretical issues of defiance in the context of multilayered legal orders, introducing the most important legal-theoretical trends in dealing with the problem of non-compliance in the EU and focusing in particular on the legitimacy issues springing from the attempts to deal with non-compliance, as well as the need to ensure that the principle of the constitutional autonomy of the Member States is fully respected and that the array of the problematic issues tackled is not confined to the *acquis*, but also covers the values on which the Union is built.

Part II, dedicated to the EU's mechanisms for ensuring compliance, has a dual structure, focusing on all the key compliance mechanisms in operation in the EU today and—building on Part I's key finding, that ensuring *acquis* compliance might actually not be sufficient to ensure and police compliance with values—also includes an array of chapters advocating concrete improvements to be introduced into the Union's compliance system to ensure that at least some of its current deficiencies are addressed. The analysis of all the key tools available to the Union for dealing with deviant Member States—including both actual and potential tools—is thus included. Particular emphasis is placed on the assessment of the effectiveness of such tools. All the key areas of law-enforcement are covered, including the most important proposals for how the current system could be reformed—including the Copenhagen Commission of Jan-Werner Müller and the reversal of *Solange* by Armin von Bogdandy—to ensure that the picture is complete.

Part III offers a comparative perspective on the enforcement of law and values in multilayered legal systems, covering both national and international enforcement. Both dimensions are potentially instructive for the EU, as the problems faced by the Union and the legal systems under scrutiny are very much alike. Moreover, they often concern the same states, as different layers of the law are not infrequently co-extensive to each other and overlap in terms of the jurisdictions where they apply. The examples brought by the international dimension focus on the enforcement of WTO law, the law of regional organizations outside of Europe, as well as of International and ECHR law—with a particular focus on the judgments of the European Court of Human Rights. The national dimension is as broad in scope, covering a number of multilayered jurisdictions in an attempt to see how far their rich experience in dealing with non-compliance with the law and the values on which the respective legal systems built could inform EU law's approach to resolving the outstanding enforcement issues in EU law. The tools ensuring compliance with the values offered in Part III are thus extraordinarily varied, ranging from an option to move in the National Guard, which is the US approach to basic constitutional values enforcement as discussed by Mark Tushnet in his chapter, to the suspension of defiant states' membership in international organizations analysed by Carlos Closa. In the EU, Germany, Belgium, and Spain are chosen as case studies. Part III does not make a secret of the fact that the supranational or international enforcement of the law and underlying values is and is bound to remain an exception of sorts, unnecessary in properly functioning states. Also in the EU, therefore, involving values is bound to be only an issue of last resort, a safety valve, making too frequent recourse to which would extend enforcement beyond cases of outright Article 2 TEU violations, unquestionably counter-productive.

Part IV, the final Part, assembles an array of telling case studies along the spectrum of understanding and misunderstanding and the depth of non-compliance and defiance vis-à-vis the values and the law as described above. Helping make sure that we learn from the past mistakes, Part IV offers a detailed analysis of how the EU managed (or failed) to resolve the crises related to the enforcement of law and values in the past. Not only does it become apparent from the chapters included that some of the famous crises are in fact quite far-reaching examples of unhelpful misunderstandings—such as France and Austria—we also learn that those crises which are 'real' as it were have not been solved at all. The chapters dealing with the contemporary situation in the problematic Member States thus outline the state of the art in dealing with the ongoing constitutional crises by the EU, only to show that the Union's involvement leaves very much to be desired.

The variation among the case studies chosen provides clear examples drawing on each of the particular types along the spectrum of non-compliance discussed above. Of particular importance are the case studies dealing with the developments which seemingly call into question the very essence of EU's values, i.e. where the apparent deviation from Article 2 TEU has been triggered by fully legitimate democratic outcomes, making these cases trickier to deal with in the light of the legitimacy problems outlined in Part I as well as the capacity problems outlined in Part II. The last chapter of this volume provides a detailed assessment of a *sui generis* case of the UK. Not an example of outright defiance, the study of the UK by Adam Łazowski demonstrates the far-reaching effects of a deep-rooted general scepticism about integration in the context of the defiance-induced crisis of the integration project. Although the volume was submitted to the Press immediately after the Brexit referendum, the outcome of the plebiscite does not alter the core findings of Łazowski's analysis, updated to reflect Brexit in full at the proofing stage. It is very regrettable that the dynamic nature and the fast pace of the developments on the ground prevented us from including an analysis of the recent events in Poland: the landscape changed so quickly there that any analysis would have been well outdated by the time of publication.

Let us be clear: many more Member States are bound to follow Poland, Hungary, and others down the slippery slope of backsliding and undermining the values enshrined in Article 2 TEU. This is precisely why a broader and more inclusive approach to ensuring compliance and combatting defiance which avoids fetishizing the law on the books and moves on in search of new institutional, legislative, and judicial solutions is absolutely indispensable. To pretend that occasionally turning your back on values is bound to be exceptional and thus does not merit a systemic institutional treatment would not be far removed from an exercise in wishful thinking. The EU deserves more than that: clear, reliable, and effective ways of dealing with the outstanding problems will have to be found.

PART I

THEORETICAL ISSUES

1

The *Acquis* and Its Principles

The Enforcement of the 'Law' versus the Enforcement of 'Values' in the EU

*Dimitry Kochenov**

1. Values and principles in Article 2 TEU

Let us start with a disclaimer. Although it is universally accepted that 'moral and political values are central to the public law enterprise',[1] while the EU Treaty speaks in Article 2 TEU about the 'values' of the Union, it is absolutely clear that what is meant by 'values' in this context is actually 'principles'—fundamental principles—of EU law. This was the actual wording before the Lisbon revision of the relevant Treaty provision.[2] Through the enforcement of the 'values' of Article 2 TEU in the context of EU law, a reference is thus made to something more important than a set of vague extravagant proclamations, unlike what 'values' would sometimes imply in other constitutional contexts. Contrary to a classical understanding, where values, in the words of Pierre Schlag, are like little divinities, replacing theological arguments in now-secular law,[3] EU values, at least some of them, seem to be quite different in legal nature. A clear distinction should thus be made between Article 2 TEU values on the one hand, and the familiar national-level aspirational provisions on the other, such as, say, the 'Repubblica [. . .] fondata sul lavoro' of the Italian constitution, or 'the Most Holy Trinity' of the Irish.

The elements of Article 2 TEU, including democracy, the Rule of Law, and the protection of fundamental rights, go as deep as 'the very foundations of [EU] legal order'.[4] Indeed, 'Principles' would be the established way of referring to the foundational, enforceable, and legally meaningful assumptions informing every aspect of the functioning of a given legal system, such as democracy and the Rule of Law.[5] It is thus necessary to see beyond the dual

* I am grateful to Tamás Győrfi, Giulio Itzcovich, András Jakab, and Kim Lane Scheppele for useful comments and engagement with the earlier drafts of this text.

[1] P Cane, 'Theory and Values in Public Law', in P Craig and R Rawlings (eds), *Law and Administration in Europe: Essays in Honour of Carol Harlow* (OUP 2003) 3, 4.

[2] Art 6 EC. Compare F Dorssemont, 'Values and Objectives', in N Bruun et al. (eds), *The Lisbon Treaty and Social Europe* (Hart 2012) 45. For a principled legal-theoretical criticism of the introduction of values into the text of the Treaties, see J Lacroix, 'Does Europe Need Common Values?' (2009) 8 *European Journal of Political Theory* 141.

[3] P Schlag, 'Values' (1994) 6 *Yale Journal of Law and Humanities* 219, 225.

[4] For a crisp analysis of this concept, see N Lavranos, 'Revisiting Article 307 EC: The Untouchable Core of Fundamental European Constitutional Law Values and Principles', in F Fontanelli et al. (eds), *Shaping Rule of Law through Dialogue: International and Supranational Experiences* (Europa Law 2010) 119.

[5] See, for the core contributions, ML Fernández Esteban, *The Rule of Law in the European Constitution* (Kluwer Law International 1999); also U Everling, 'The European Union as a Federal Association of States and Citizens', in A von Bogdandy and J Bast (eds), *Principles of European Constitutional Law* (2nd edn, Hart/CH Beck 2010) 701; M Zuleeg, 'The Advantages of the European Constitution', in A von Bogdandy and J Bast (eds), *Principles of European Constitutional Law* (2nd edn, Hart/CH Beck 2010) 763, at 772–9. The EU Institutions' own accounts of what is meant by the Rule of Law beyond the tautology of 'being bound by law' present a most diverse account, which found expression in the EU's external action: L Pech, 'Promoting the Rule of Law Abroad', in D Kochenov and F Amtenbrink (eds), *The European Union's Shaping of the International Legal Order* (CUP 2013) 108.

The *Acquis* and Its Principles: The Enforcement of the 'Law' vs. the Enforcement of 'Values' in the European Union. First Edition. Dimitry Kochenov. © Dimitry Kochenov 2017. Published 2017 by Oxford University Press.

confusion introduced by the Treaty of Lisbon.[6] The first confusion, as already stated, is terminological. Should the above not be convincing, a basic consistency argument would do: given that the Rule of Law in one example is clearly a 'principle' in the CFR, which has the force of primary law of the EU, locating it among the 'values' in TEU is clearly a mistake. Moreover, it has always been recognized as a principle, at least since the oft-cited ECJ decision in *Les Verts*.[7] The second confusion is theoretical: legal scholarship knows clear differences between values (which are very roughly, desirable ideals) and principles (which are, again very roughly, binding rules).[8] It is not among my intentions in this chapter to engage with the extensive and beautiful literature on both, as my goals are much more practical and down-to-earth and are thus far removed from the jurisprudential realm. This basic distinction is clear without a legal-philosophical digression. Regrettably, however, in the context of the Lisbon Treaty this misclassification results in an apparent synonymization of the two.

It is clear, however, as Laurent Pech has persuasively argued, that the unfortunate wording of Article 2 TEU does not deprive the Rule of Law of the legal value of a core legal principle in the context of EU law.[9] The same obviously applies to democracy and the protection of fundamental rights.[10] Human rights in the EU are not 'the Most Holy Trinity'. We should thus be very careful when taking the Treaty's own categorizations at face value: the wording on the crucial issue of principles is misleading. In this sense, I will argue that the distinction made by Giulio Itzcovich elsewhere in this volume between 'the government by laws and the government by values' does not fit the context of the EU's Article 2 TEU as neatly as one would expect.[11] Knowing this, it is much easier to argue and be persuasive that the values of Article 2 TEU should not be excluded from the core conversation about the enforcement of EU law. As this chapter will demonstrate, indeed, the failure to enforce the values of the Union will most likely result in the undermining of the core *acquis* going to the heart of EU law and is not solely confined to the internal market.

2. Enforcement of values and the structure of the argument

Article 2 TEU is quite special in the sense that it can be enforced via Article 7 TEU—a purely political procedure far removed from the classical *acquis*-enforcement approaches to be found elsewhere in the Treaties.[12] Whether the values are actually part of the *acquis* of the Union and whether the Union possesses the general competence to intervene in the 'value' as opposed to the '*acquis*' domains are questions which some, surprisingly, still seem to

[6] For an analysis, see L Pech, '"A Union Founded on the Rule of Law": Meaning and Reality of the Rule of Law as a Constitutional Principle of EU Law' (2010) 6 *EU Constitutional Law Review* 359.

[7] Case 294/83 *Partie Ecologiste 'Les Verts' v Parliament* [1986] ECLI:EU:C:1986:166, 23. See also Opinion 1/91 *EEA Agreement* [1991] ECLI:EU:C:1991:490.

[8] My mundane view of principles for the purpose of this distinction is informed in part by A Jakab, 'Concept and Function of Principles', in M Borowski (ed), *On the Nature of Legal Principles* (Steiner 2009) 145 (and the literature cited therein).

[9] L Pech (n 6).

[10] c.f. E Sharpston, 'Citizenship and Fundamental Rights – Pandora's Box or a Natural Step towards Maturity?', in P Cardonnel et al. (eds), *Constitutionalising the EU Judicial System* (Hart 2012).

[11] It should be noted that Itzcovich's critique of governing by values, when the latter are understood not to refer simply to the principles of the law, is solid and convincing. On a similar critique in the realm of private law, see e.g. MW Hesselink, 'Private Law and the European Constitutionalisation of Values' (2016) *Amsterdam Law School Research Paper* No 26.

[12] See L Besselink in Chapter 8 of this volume; B Bugarič, 'Protecting Democracy inside the EU: On Article 7 TEU and the Hungarian Turn to Authoritarianism', in C Closa and D Kochenov (eds), *Reinforcing the Rule of Law Oversight in the European Union* (CUP 2016); W Sadurski, 'Adding Bite to a Bark: The Story of Article 7, EU Enlargement, and Jörg Haider' (2010) 16 *Columbia Journal of European Law* 385.

consider open.[13] In other words: is Article 7 TEU the only way to enforce Article 2 TEU or not? Numerous arguments for[14] and against[15] a permissive approach to the enforcement of EU values by for instance applying Articles 258, 260 TFEU and other enforcement procedures[16] to the domain of Article 2 TEU are well documented.[17] In the face of this perceived uncertainty, the general caution of including Article 2 TEU among the provisions of the Treaties to be enforced by the EU institutions via the classical procedures going beyond the exceptional—and hitherto dormant—Article 7 TEU[18] persist, notwithstanding the fact that the clearly enforceable nature of Article 2 TEU is widely acknowledged.[19] Considering the nature of the values of Article 2 TEU, which are in fact the principles of EU law, confining their enforcement to Article 7 TEU would seem too narrow a reading, a conclusion which has come to be the prevalent view in the literature today—from Christophe Hillion to Kim Lane Sheppele.[20] The Commission also agrees, expressly listing standard enforcement procedures as useful tools of Rule of Law enforcement in its pre-Article 7 procedure.[21]

Consequently, pretty much all the discussion of the enforcement of EU law has until very recently been ignoring a crucially important element of the puzzle of the effectiveness of EU law: values. Unlike in the case of the *acquis sensu stricto*, the high level of the Member States' compliance with the values of Article 2 TEU has been simply presumed, thus seemingly not requiring the opening of the Pandora's box of the values enforcement debate.[22] The literature has been focusing instead on the transposition of the Directives and compliance with Court decisions among other aspects of the complex enforcement landscape[23]—an established tradition which numerous chapters in this volume equally follow.[24]

[13] The Council Legal Service's take on this matter is the most extreme example of how restrictively the values are approached: the Commission was suspected of breaching the principle of conferral based on its declared readiness to serve its Treaty-assigned role in the context of Art 7 TEU in a transparent and orderly manner via a so-called 'Rule of Law Mechanism' (European Commission, 'A New EU Framework to Strengthen the Rule of Law', Strasbourg, 11 March 2014, COM(2014) 158 final): Council of the EU, Opinion of the Legal Service 10296/14, of 14 May 2014, esp. para 28. For analysis and critique, see D Kochenov and L Pech, 'Monitoring and Enforcement of the Rule of Law in the European Union: Rhetoric and Reality' (2015) 11 *EU Constitutional Law Review* 512.

[14] C Closa, 'Reinforcing the Rule of Law: Normative Arguments, Institutional Proposals and Procedural Limitations', in Closa and Kochenov (n 12).

[15] JHH Weiler, 'Epilogue: Living in a Glass House: Europe, Democracy and the Rule of Law', in Closa and Kochenov (n 12); J Cornides, 'The European Union: Rule of Law or Rule of Judges?' (2013) *EJIL Analysis* (blog) http://www.ejiltalk.org/the-european-union-rule-of-law-or-rule-of-judges/, accessed 12 October 2016.

[16] Such as Art 259 TFEU, for instance: D Kochenov, 'Biting Intergovernmentalism: The Case for the Reinvention of Article 259 TFEU to Make It a Viable Rule of Law Enforcement Tool' (2015) 7 *The Hague Journal of the Rule of Law* 153.

[17] e.g. A von Bogdandy and M Ioannidis, 'Systemic Deficiency in the Rule of Law: What It Is, What Has Been Done, What Can Be Done' (2014) 51 *Common Market Law Review* 59.

[18] For the criticism of the deployment by the Commission of the 'Pre-Article 7 Procedure' against Poland in January 2016—the only example of a move by an EU institution which could result in the invocation of Art 7 TEU to date, see D Kochenov and L Pech, 'Better Late than Never? On the Commission's Rule of Law Framework and Its First Activation' (2016) 54 *Journal of Common Market Studies* 1062.

[19] Most notably by J-C Piris, *The Lisbon Treaty* (CUP 2010) 71; C Hillion, 'Overseeing the Rule of Law in the EU: Legal Mandate and Means', in Closa and Kochenov (n 12).

[20] Hillion (n 19); KL Scheppele, 'The Case for Systemic Infringement Actions', in Closa and Kochenov (n 12).

[21] See, COM(2014) 158 final.

[22] For notable recent exceptions, see Besselink in Chapter 8, von Bogdandy et al. in Chapter 12, and Müller in Chapter 13 of this volume; von Bogdandy and Ioannidis (n 17); contributions to Closa and Kochenov (n 12).

[23] The two main types of non-compliance this literature has been traditionally outlining since Francis Snyder's seminal contribution, which included failure to comply with the judgments of the ECJ and failure to transpose Directives in a timely and correct fashion, do not touch upon the essence of the key problem the EU is facing today: non-compliance with values. F Snyder, 'The Effectiveness of European Community Law: Institutions, Processes, Tools and Techniques' 56 (1993) *Modern Law Review* 19; L Conant, 'Compliance and What EU Member States Make of It', in M Cremona (ed), *Compliance and the Enforcement of EU Law* (OUP 2012) 1 (for a great contemporary overview from the traditional perspective). Compare D Piqani, 'The Role of National Constitutional Courts in Issues of Compliance', in Cremona (n 23) 132; J Tallberg, 'Paths to Compliance: Enforcement, Management, and the European Union' (2002) 56 *International Organisation* 609.

[24] See, to a different degree, Gormley in Chapter 4, Wennerås in Chapter 5, and Reich in Chapter 7 of this volume.

Such an exclusive focus of the *acquis* is only justifiable if the presumptions of adherence to Article 2 TEU are correct and reflect the actual state of the Union and the Member States.[25] Increasingly voluminous evidence is emerging, however, that such presumptions could actually be baseless,[26] which makes ensuring that the values are complied with an issue of key importance. The box has to be open, after all. Indeed, should compliance with values not be made real throughout the EU, insisting on the enforcement of the *acquis* can produce profoundly adversarial effects, actually resulting in undermining the Rule of Law, instead of bringing about positive outcomes.[27] Bieber and Maiani are thus absolutely right to point out that 'the assumption of compliance must be sustainable, and credible means and procedures to detect and terminate breaches must be in place'[28]—this is precisely what the EU has to ensure in the nearest future.

The goal of this chapter is to problematize the current lack of focus on compliance with the values in the general EU law enforcement literature, notwithstanding the emergence of a notable body of work which considers the problems posed by the lack of working mechanisms of the enforcement of values in detail. Echoing the conviction clearly held by the authors of the value-enforcement proposals, which this chapter presents and discusses—and thus joining a chorus of (still) largely dissenting voices in the sea of key EU law enforcement literature—the chapter argues that the enforcement of values should occupy a key place in the story of the enforcement of EU law. To this end, in addition to providing an overview of the role played by the values of EU law and tracing some of the history of values-aware thinking in EU law (section 3), the chapter surveys the key approaches to the enforcement of values proposed by scholars (section 4),[29] followed by a critical analysis of the implications of not taking the outstanding values enforcement problem seriously (section 5).

3. The values in the context of the *acquis*

The EU received its core values at its inception. Achieving peace and prosperity, the immediate goals of the Union still with us since the times of the Schuman declaration, had a strong implied liberty component. Dictatorships and any countries which were not 'free' were not welcome to join the Union.[30] Notwithstanding the fact that democracy and the Rule of Law were not part of the black letter law of the Communities for a long time, both have clearly been regarded as important unwritten principles, eventually getting codified thanks to the pre-accession strategy in the context of the preparation of the 'big-bang' enlargement to the East of the continent.[31] It is this process, alongside the political initiatives of the institutions and the *obiter dicta* in the case law of the Court of Justice

[25] D Kochenov, 'The EU and the Rule of Law – Naïveté or a Grand Design?', in M Adams et al., *Constitutionalism and the Rule of Law: Bridging Idealism and Realism* (CUP 2017); R Bieber and F Maiani, 'Enhancing Centralized Enforcement of EU Law: Pandora's Toolbox?' (2014) 51 *Common Market Law Review* 1057.

[26] A von Bogdandy and P Sonnevend (eds), *Constitutional Crisis in the European Constitutional Area: Theory, Law and Politics in Hungary and Romania* (Hart 2015).

[27] D Kochenov, 'EU Law without the Rule of Law. Is the Veneration of Autonomy Worth It?' (2015) 34 *Yearbook of European Law* 51.

[28] Bieber and Maiani (n 25). See also, R Bieber and F Maiani, 'Sans solidarité point d'Union européenne' (2012) 48 RTD eur 265; von Bogdandy and Ioannidis (n 17); Closa (n 14).

[29] In doing this, the chapter draws of the analysis I included in the report co-authored for the European Parliament (EP): P Bárd et al., 'An EU Mechanism on Democracy, the Rule of Law, and Fundamental Rights: Assessing the Need and Possibilities for the Establishment of an EU Scoreboard on Democracy, the Rule of Law and Fundamental Rights', EP Research Paper PE 579328 (Brussels, 2016).

[30] D Kochenov, *EU Enlargement and the Failure of Conditionality: Pre-Accession Conditionality in the Fields of Democracy and the Rule of Law* (Kluwer Law International 2008) chapters 1 and 2.

[31] For the whole story, see ibid.

which resulted in the distillation of the core elements of the principle of the Rule of Law and other 'values' in the context of EU constitutionalism.[32]

The founding fathers of the Union were not as naïve as they might seem today, notwithstanding the fact that dealing with the actual adherence to the values has traditionally been approached as a national, not a supranational concern. The membership of the Union as such, with all the perceived constraints it brings, was supposed to guarantee compliance with the basic values through the day-to-day operation of the emerging *droit de l'intégration*.[33] Clearly, and somewhat ironically, for a long time the Union itself posed a more serious threat to the values of the Member States than the Member States' own political and eventually legal problems did, as attested to by the *Solange* saga, for instance:[34] the Union had to reinvent itself under pressure from the Member States to take human rights into account,[35] only to re-emerge as an organization vaguely compatible with some key principles of modern constitutionalism.[36] This was a huge step forward compared with the assumptions informing the early case law of the ECJ, including that human rights are none of the Union's concern.[37] Characteristically, no Treaty change was required, since the core functioning of the Union was in danger.[38] Not a single Member State revolted against the idea of the Union taking human rights on board—which undoubtedly amounted to a profound reinterpretation if not the *de facto* rewriting of the Treaties. The Rule of Law—even if a slightly tautological one[39]—followed suit, only to be joined by an official story of democracy, after the paper dust of the democratic deficit debate settled somewhat.[40]

a. Ad hoc articulation of values in the pre-accession context

There was a traditional difference, however, in how the Union would treat its founding members as opposed to the Member States joining later. Perusal of the literature of the day demonstrates that there were burning concerns with the *new* Member States' ability to undermine the Union through either a failure to adhere to the basic principles of democracy and the Rule of Law, or through entering the Union only to dismantle or undermine what has been created from within. Both would amount to an assault on EU values. The realization of these two dangers resulted in the gradual articulation of EU customary law on enlargement, which would only allow democratic states adhering to the Rule of Law to

[32] Pech (n 6). On the analysis of this distillation process and its outcomes, see, D Kochenov, 'The EU Rule of Law: Cutting Paths through Confusion' (2009) 2 *Erasmus Law Review* 5.

[33] P Pescatore, *Le droit de l'intégration. Emergence d'un phénomène nouveau dans les relations internationales selon l'expérience des Communautés Européennes* (AW Sijthoff 1972).

[34] FC Mayer, 'Multilevel Constitutional Jurisdiction' in A von Bogdandy and J Bast (eds), *Principles of European Constitutional Law* (2nd edn, Hart/CH Beck 2010) 400, 410–20.

[35] B de Witte, 'The Past and Future of the European Court of Justice in the Protection of Human Rights' in P Alston (ed), *The EU and Human Rights* (OUP 1999); JHH Weiler and NJS Lockhart, '"Taking Rights Seriously" Seriously' (I and II) (1995) 32 *Common Market Law Review* 52 and 579.

[36] As a result, human rights now make an important part of EU law, even though human rights protection as such is generally viewed as lying outside of the scope of EU law: a rare activity of the EU coming without a proper competence to act. C.f. Alston (ed) (n 35).

[37] Case 1/58 *Stork v High Authority* [1959] ECLI:EU:C:1959:4.

[38] c.f. On the possibility of a 'Cassandra scenario' of inter-court dialogue: M Kumm, 'Who Is the Final Arbiter of Constitutionality in Europe? Three Conceptions of the Relationship between the German Federal Constitutional Court and the European Court of Justice and the Fate of the European Market Order of Bananas' (1999) 36 *Common Market Law Review* 360.

[39] G Palombella, 'Beyond Legality – before Democracy: Rule of Law Caveats in a Two-Level System', in Closa and Kochenov (n 12).

[40] For the official democracy story, see K Lenaerts and JA Gutiérrez-Fons, 'EU Citizenship: Hopes and Fears' in D Kochenov (ed), *EU Citizenship and Federalism: The Role of Rights* (CUP 2017).

accede long before these requirements made it into the text of the Treaties.[41] Applications from totalitarian states, like Franco's Spain or the Kingdom of Morocco, were either politely turned down or left without any consideration. These rejections, alongside the academic doctrine of the time,[42] were the first articulations of the shared values the Union and the Member States are built upon besides the formulation of the initial invitation preceding the creation of the Union, which was addressed to 'free European states', freedom being interpreted in the literature as a requirement of adherence to democracy and the Rule of Law coupled with a capitalist economy.[43] These essential foundations gradually came to play the role of vital principles of EU law and ended up recognized as such in the primary law of the Union.

The two different potential value-problems which became acute in the enlargement context are still with us today. The first, which was already being discussed in the literature before the accession of the UK, concerned a new democratic Member State undermining the integration project from within. The second, which is as old as the first, concerned a non-democratic state not abiding by the Rule of Law, undermining the Union by failing to adhere to its basic (then unwritten) principles. The Union had to deal with both in the context of the application and evolution of its pre-accession policy. The core approach chosen in this context was an *ex ante* one: targeting the likely problems before the accession of the new Member States to the Union. The insufficiency of this approach is now clear in the context of both problems it aimed to solve. This insufficiency is attested to by the uncooperative behaviour of some Member States and the backsliding of others, no matter how seriously both had been scrutinized by the Union before they became part of it.

The nascent *ex post* approach, first tried ad hoc in Austria[44] and now articulated in Article 7 TEU and the pre-Article 7 procedure recently launched against Poland,[45] has been criticized in the literature for its political rather than legal essence and the difficulty of its deployment, requiring reinforcement of the *ex post* approach and upgrading the tools to defend Article 2 TEU compliance in the EU's arsenal.

b. A democratic Member State undermining the Union from within

The first problem out of the two outlined above is still acute, not caught sufficiently by the duty of loyalty. The UK 'vetoing' the banking union package at the height of the euro-crisis or the undermining of EU policies in the neighbourhood by Greece are clear reminders of this fact.[46] For an open-minded observer this is not a problem at all, potentially merely pointing instead towards the existence of political space in the precise articulation of EU law. Surely, EU law—even the four freedoms—can roll back, if not entirely, then in part, to reflect the political will of the Member States. It is clear, however, that it was precisely this political space of negotiation and renegotiation which the founding *Herren der Verträge* were aiming to eliminate.[47] Given that the *acquis* is largely about the rigidity of the

[41] Kochenov (n 30) chapter 1.

[42] e.g. P Soldatos and G Vandersanden, 'L'admission dans la CEE—Essai d'interprétation juridique' (1968) *Cahiers de droit européen* 628; J-P Puissochet, *The Enlargement of the European Communities. A Commentary on the Treaty and the Acts Concerning the Accession of Denmark, Ireland and the United Kingdom* (AW Sijthoff 1975).

[43] Soldatos and Vandersanden (n 42).

[44] See Lachmayer in Chapter 25 of this volume; Sadurski (n 12).

[45] Kochenov and Pech (n 18).

[46] E Basheska and D Kochenov, 'Thanking the Greeks: The Crisis of the Rule of Law in EU Enlargement Regulation' (2015) 39 *Southeastern Europe* 392.

[47] These efforts crystalized in the formulation of the first principle of EU enlargement law: the prohibition to renegotiate or permanently alter the existing *acquis*. This principle resulted in the rejection of the first UK application for membership. For a detailed analysis, see Kochenov (n 30).

objectives of integration and the sanctification of the internal market, the elements of which are not open for reconsideration,[48] it was only logical that scholars proposed seeking binding commitments from the incoming Member States concerning the need to uphold the goals of integration. Judge Pescatore was among the proponents of the idea:

> Aux nouveaux venus, [...] il faut demander non seulement de définir leur position à l'égard des objectifs d'ores et déjà définis et consacrés par des engagements fermes. Il faut les interroger aussi sur leurs intentions en ce qui concerne les chances d'une evolution ultérieure vers l'union politique.[49]

Given the core of what EU economic integration stands for, including perfecting the internal market edifice and the sacred commandments of the four freedoms, concerns about the key objective of the internal market are as valid today as they were in the seventies.[50] It is clear that David Cameron's pre-Brexit referendum 'renegotiation' is exactly what Pescatore, Puissochet, and others were worried about;[51] Brexit, however, is not, as long as it does not damage the EU's *acquis*.[52]

The first problem has thus not yet been solved so far, but we are still in the shadow of the proposed solutions to it: it seems that the internal market cannot be changed, not only not through renegotiation (a theoretical possibility of an overwhelming and radical overhaul of the Union aside) but also not democratically,[53] and is not necessarily an apolitical force of the good,[54] which poses a serious qualification in any text characterizing the EU as such as a democracy, particularly in the age of austerity.[55] The Union thus emerges as a democracy of means, not a democracy of ends.

c. Member States' backsliding undermining the Union

Solving the second problem equally met with challenges. Most importantly, these concerned the insufficient adherence of some Member States to the core principles of the Union. Attempts to solve this problem are of fundamental importance to us, as they triggered the very formal inclusion of values in the Treaty text, thus giving unwritten principles a clear textual articulation in what is now Article 2 TEU.[56] The early nineties marked a time when the hitherto unwritten principles of enlargement law—the basic values

[48] G Davies, 'Social Legitimacy and Purposive Power: The End, the Means and the Consent of the People', in D Kochenov et al. (eds), *Europe's Justice Deficit?* (Hart 2015); G Peebles, '"A Very Eden of the Innate Rights of Man"? A Marxist Look at the European Union Treaties and Case Law' (1997) 22 *Law and Social Inquiry* 581, 605.

[49] Pescatore (n 33) 29. See also Puissochet (n 42).

[50] For a grand overview, see C Barnard, *The Substantive Law of the EU: The Four Freedoms* (OUP 2013).

[51] C O'Brien, 'Cameron's Renegotiation and the Burring of the Balance of Competences Review' (2014) http://ukandeu.ac.uk/camerons-renegotiation-and-the-burying-of-the-balance-of-competencies-review/, accessed 12 October 2016.

[52] See Łazowski in Chapter 28 of this volume.

[53] Davies (n 48); A Somek, 'Europe: Political, Not Cosmopolitan' (2014) 20 *European Law Journal* 142.

[54] P Allott, 'European Governance and the Re-branding of Democracy' (2002) 27 *European Law Review* 60; C O'Brien, 'I Trade Therefore I Am: Legal Personhood in the European Union' (2013) 50 *Common Market Law Review* 1643; P Caro de Sousa, 'Quest for the Holy Grail – Is a Unified Approach to the Market Freedoms and European Citizenship Justified?' (2014) 20 *European Law Journal* 499. C Joerges and M Weimer, 'A Crisis of Executive Managerialism in the EU: No Alternative?' in G de Búrca et al. (eds), *Critical Perspectives on Global Governance. Liber Amicorum David M. Trubek* (Hart 2014) 297; M Bartl, 'Internal Market Rationality, Private Law and the Direction of the Union: Resuscitating the Market as the Object of the Political' (2015) 21 *European Law Journal* 572; D Kochenov, 'Neo-Mediaeval Permutations of Personhood in Europe', in L Azoulai et al. (eds), *Ideas of the Person and Personhood in European Union Law* (Hart 2016).

[55] AJ Menéndez, 'The Existential Crisis of the European Union' (2013) 14 *German Law Journal* 453.

[56] Indeed, this could be characterized as one of the key legacies of EU enlargements in the field of EU constitutionalism. See W Sadurski, *Constitutionalism and Enlargement of Europe* (OUP 2012).

the candidate countries were supposed to adhere to—came to be distilled in writing.[57] Crucially, they came to be applied both in the external (pre-accession) and the internal context of EU law.

Following the decision to enlarge to the East of the continent of 1993, the EU formulated the Copenhagen Criteria for the candidate countries to fulfil, including democracy, the Rule of Law, the protection of human rights, and respect for and protection of minorities.[58] The general wording of the criteria, coupled with the *de facto* elimination of any *ratione materiae* constraints on the set of issues the EU could examine in the context of the required pre-accession adaptation of the candidate countries' constitutional structure and operation resulted in a reinterpretation of the international agreements then in force to produce values-compliance and, even more importantly for us, produced a whole cottage industry within the European Commission which ultimately released thousands of pages of reports assessing *all* the areas of law in the candidate countries to ensure that these complied with EU demands.[59] This corpus of documents allowed the Commission to formulate the essential components of the values which were then made binding on the candidate countries.[60] It is based on this corpus that we know that they had to adhere to democracy, the Rule of Law, and human rights protection, as well as what each of these elements implied in practice.[61] Although the Commission's engagement was a resounding failure in that it stopped far short of shaping any sufficiently general and clear rules which would govern the EU's pre-accession engagement with democracy and the Rule of Law, and were marked by inconsistent, self-contradictory, oblivious, and inconsequential application of its own newly created rules,[62] the values were now definitely part of positive *koiné* of EU law and later entered the Treaties as such. Indeed, this is probably the core effect of the Eastern enlargement for the constitutional essence of the Union.[63]

Upon joining the Union, the *carte blanche* the Union endowed itself with in the course of enlargement preparation was bound to expire. The morning when the acceding states woke up as Member States, the majority of the pre-accession constraints[64] on how they should shape their statehood, from civil service law to the training and appointment rules for the judiciary, as well as the number of readings particular bills should receive in Parliament were gone, along apparently with the EU's ability to intervene directly should serious Rule of Law/democracy backsliding occur.

Following this change in the EU's role, the need to come up with effective means to deal with the backsliding Member States became only more acute—and not merely with regard to the new Member States. Moreover, from a theoretical possibility backsliding turned into an acute reality in a number of the Member States. Given that the presumption that the values of Article 2 TEU do not form a part of ordinary *acquis*, remained popular, the core

[57] D Kochenov, 'Behind the Copenhagen Façade. The Meaning and Structure of the Copenhagen Criterion of Democracy and the Rule of Law' (2004) 8(10) *European Integration Online Papers* 1.

[58] The criteria read as follows:

> Membership requires that the candidate country has achieved stability of institutions guaranteeing democracy, the rule of law, human rights and respect for and protection of minorities, the existence of a functioning market economy as well as the capacity to cope with competitive pressure and market forces within the Union. Membership presupposes the candidate's ability to take on the obligations of membership including adherence to the aims of political, economic and monetary union.

See C Hillion, 'The Copenhagen Criteria and Their Progeny' in C Hillion (ed), *EU Enlargement: A Legal Approach* (Hart 2004).

[59] For analyses, see M Maresceau, 'Quelques réflexions sur l'application des principes fondamentaux dans la stratégie d'adhésion de l'UE' in J Raux, *Le droit de l'Union européenne en principes: Liber amicorum en l'honneur de Jean Raux* (LGDJ 2006) 69; Kochenov (n 30).

[60] Kochenov (n 30). [61] ibid. [62] ibid. [63] Sadurski (n 56).

[64] See Kochenov (n 30) for a detailed analysis.

instrument left for the solution of the problem to hand is Article 7 TEU, which contains a procedure not limited to violations of the *acquis*. Much has been written about this instrument and scholars and the institutions seem to agree that triggering it is excessively difficult, while its purely political nature and with no role left for the ECJ to play potentially undermines the effectiveness of Article 2 TEU and the practical legal significance of the values shared between the EU and the Member States. The agreement is so clear that the Commission actually inaugurated a 'pre-Article 7 Procedure'[65] to overcome some of the perceived shortcomings of the instrument. The Procedure's activation against Poland, boasting of no results demonstrates with clarity that the procedure is not a game-changer in the value-enforcement debate.[66]

d. Deep-rooted vulnerabilities of the Union in the domain of values

The Union's vulnerabilities when it comes to safeguarding its values are of a fundamental nature and pose a very serious threat to the success of the whole integration project. Given the perceived novel nature of the threat—as adherence to the values of Article 2 TEU had simply been taken for granted before recent years marked by the 'backsliding' of several Member States[67]—simply falling back on the old time-tested approaches is not an option: academic literature had until recently focused exclusively on the Union's *own* adherence to the Rule of Law[68] and the candidate countries' record in this area, assuming that any, indeed, *all* serious Rule of Law deficiencies within each EU Member State would be dealt with by the relevant national authorities. The problems we are currently facing were thus largely unforeseen in 'a Community based on the rule of law',[69] all the instruments described above notwithstanding. Academics and policymakers have however quickly caught up with the issue of 'Rule of Law backsliding' in the EU and formulated an array of proposals on how to deal with the outstanding problems.

4. The core proposals to ensure that values are enforced alongside the *acquis*

The majority of proposals focus on institutional action, either within the context of the Union, or with the involvement of outside actors and institutions. In addition to the legally articulated ways there is of course always a possibility of ad hoc actions, akin to the kind which marked the EU's involvement in Austrian politics fifteen years ago in reaction to the building of a governing coalition in that state, which involved FPÖ, an extreme right nationalist party, which was still unusual in the political context of the time, but now looks to some degree like a strange exaggeration.[70] The legality of such ad hoc actions, especially in the presence of specific Treaty provisions aiming at achieving the same effects, is of dubious nature, given the abundance of procedures in the Treaties designed specifically to deal with the situation at hand, including, but not limited to the two procedures of Article 7 TEU.[71]

[65] European Commission (n 13). [66] See Kochenov and Pech (n 18).

[67] The term was coined by Jan-Werner Müller: J-W Müller, 'Safeguarding Democracy inside the EU: Brussels and the Future of Liberal Order' (2013) Working Paper No 3 (Washington DC: Transatlantic Academy).

[68] See, most importantly, L Pech, 'The Rule of Law as a Constitutional Principle of the European Union' (2009) Jean Monnet Working Paper No 04/09 (NYU Law School); Fernández Esteban (n 5).

[69] Case 294/83 *Les Verts v Parliament* [1986] ECLI:EU:C:1986:166, para 23.

[70] GN Toggenburg, 'La crisi austriaca: delicati equilibrismi sospesi tra molte dimensioni' (2001) 2 *Diritto pubblico comparato ed europeo* 735; Lachmayer in Chapter 25 of this volume.

[71] See, for a meticulous analysis, Hillion (n 19); Besselink in Chapter 8 of this volume.

In this vast sea of academic proposals, seven stand out in particular. They offer contrasting visions and due to the complexity of the problems we confront, none appears sufficient on its own to solve these problems, but they nonetheless offer EU policymakers plenty of food for thought. Most importantly, there is enormous potential to deploy different elements of these proposals in combination. While the majority among them attempts to offer short-term solutions and are thus deployable immediately (at least according to their creators), several unquestionably require Treaty change, which is clearly an unfeasible option in the current legal–political climate.

The emphasis on the actual *enforcement* of values is present in the proposals to a varying degree, since not all of them come equipped with a fine-tuned sanctioning mechanism in addition to the possibility to use the exiting instruments, such as the shaming of the backsliding Member State, the suspension of the participation of that state in the Union institutions via Article 7 TEU, or, alternatively, recourse to the financial penalties via Article 260 TFEU: all much criticized in the literature and for very good reasons.[72]

The key proposals briefly discussed below include the following:

a. Systemic infringement procedure;
b. Biting intergovernmentalism;
c. Reverse *Solange*;
d. The Copenhagen Commission;
e. The 'exit card';
f. Peer-review and 'Horizontal *Solange*';
g. Outsourcing monitoring and enforcement to non-EU institutions.

a. Systemic infringement procedure

Kim Lane Scheppele's 'systemic infringement procedure' proposal deserves to be examined first.[73] In a nutshell, this proposal aims to ensure the most effective use of existing infringement procedures, which have been deployed relatively successfully by the Commission in the context of the enforcement of EU law since the founding of the Communities. The proposal makes a sound attempt to address the shortcomings of the existing EU law enforcement machinery aiming to upgrade its ability to deal with any potential and actual serious breaches of EU values. This is done in two fundamental steps, covering both the procedure for identifying the breach of values and the enforcement of compliance.

Firstly, Scheppele suggests enabling the bundling up of infringements so as to empower the Commission to present a whole infringement package to the Court of Justice, rather than pursuing single instances of non-compliance on a case-by-case basis. The crucial underlying assumption in this approach is that pursuing numerous infringements simultaneously amounts to more than just the sum of its parts, as it should enable the Commission to present a clear picture of systemic non-compliance as regards Article 2 TEU. In this way—especially if Article 2 TEU is coupled with the duty of loyalty laid down

[72] e.g. Wennerås in Chapter 5 of this volume; M Smith, 'The Evolution of Infringement and Sanction Procedures. Of Pilots, Diversions, Collisions, and Circling', in A Arnull and D Chalmers (eds), *The Oxford Handbook of European Law* (OUP 2015) 350; B Jack, 'Article 260(2) TFEU: An Effective Judicial Procedure for the Enforcement of Judgments?' (2013) 19 *European Law Journal* 420; P Wennerås, 'Sanctions against Member States under Article 260 TFEU: Alive, but not Kicking?' (2012) 49 *Common Market Law Review* 145; M Smith, 'Inter-institutional Dialogue and the Establishment of Enforcement Norms: A decade of Financial Penalties under Article 228 EC (now Article 260 TFEU)' (2010) 16 *European Public Law* 547.

[73] Scheppele (n 20).

in Article 4(3) TEU,[74] the Court could for instance hold that the Rule of Law has been breached by a Member State on the basis of multiple single breaches of EU law bundled together and submitted by the Commission in one go. Even more, multiple individual breaches might even not be required, as long as a complex pattern of developments described in the case testifies to a violation of EU's values. While it is often assumed that Article 2 TEU lacks justiciability, combining it with Article 4 TEU could potentially solve this problem, with jurisdiction stemming from the overwhelming demonstration of the seriousness of breach. Moreover, this 'bundling approach' would not in fact be entirely new, although it has only been used so far with respect to a systemic breach of the EU *acquis*,[75] even if involving a provision of the CFR on at least one occasion.[76] Scheppele's proposal should therefore be commended for offering a creative route to enforcing Article 2 TEU on the basis of an existing and well-tried procedure by merely altering the mode and scope of its application by stepping from dwelling strictly in the field of the *acquis* of the Union into the area of values.

The second part of Scheppele's proposal is just as important and is designed to deal with the limited effectiveness of financial sanctions as a tool to ensure compliance. The proposal is simple: rather than imposing financial sanctions, the EU should seek to subtract any EU funds that the relevant Member State is entitled to receive. Although some secondary legislation would likely be needed to make this part of the proposal a reality,[77] it is definitely an approach to be considered very seriously. While the effectiveness of this change may not work with respect to countries which do not depend on EU funds, it may well be effective with respect to Member States particularly dependent on EU funds, such as Hungary. While both elements of the proposal are legally solid, its weakest point is the second part, not the first. Given that sanctions are usually particularly ineffective in bringing about regime change, any country which is not merely becoming autocratic, but is *already* there is most unlikely to change its ways under financial pressure.[78] Scheppele's proposal is thus unable to cover all the spectrum of defiance outlined in the introduction to this volume. This problem is generally applicable to virtually all the proposals for consideration below, however: not much can be done with money against an autocratic government which is particularly nasty and absolutely determined. Some other tools should be found. There is a second important weak spot, however: the Commission's approach to reading Article 258 TFEU and applying this instrument seems to be hostile to taking EU values into account when bringing a case. This resulted in a number of missed opportunities—the judicial retirement case with regard to Hungary, which was a glorified loss in terms of the Rule of Law, rather than a win, being one of the examples of this.[79] The proposal, however legally sound, is unlikely to be employed in practice, unless the Commission changes its

[74] 'Pursuant to the principle of sincere cooperation, the Union and the Member States shall, in full mutual respect, assist each other in carrying out tasks which flow from the Treaties. The Member States shall take any appropriate measure, general or particular, to ensure fulfilment of the obligations arising out of the Treaties or resulting from the acts of the institutions of the Union [...]'.

[75] e.g. Case C-494/01 *Commission v Ireland (Irish Waste)* [2005] ECLI:EU:C:2005:250.

[76] http://europa.eu/rapid/press-release_IP-15-6228_en.htm, accessed 12 October 2016.

[77] A certain change in the ECJ's approach to the calculation of penalties under Article 260 TFEU, in particular the criterion of the 'ability to pay', could also be in need of some reconsideration, but the current approach is unlikely to form an overwhelming obstacle to the implementation of the proposal: D Kochenov, 'On Policing Article 2 TEU Compliance – Reverse *Solange* and Systemic Infringements Analyzed' (2014) 33 *Polish Yearbook of International Law* 145.

[78] N Tocci, *Can the EU Promote Democracy and Human Rights through the ENP? The Case for Refocusing on the Rule of Law* in M Cremona and G Meloni (eds), *The European Neighbourhood Policy: A Framework for Modernisation?*, (2007) EUI Working Paper LAW 21, 29. See also Kochenov (n 77) 168.

[79] See for an analysis, Szente in Chapter 26 of this volume.

counterproductive and artificially narrow approach to the scope of Article 258 TFEU and the enforcement of values more generally.

b. Biting intergovernmentalism

'Biting intergovernmentalism'[80] builds on the idea of utilizing the systemic infringement procedure explained above, but offers a potentially more sensible way to deploy the procedure, while not expecting the Commission to change its ways. In this sense, biting intergovernmentalism is deployable immediately. The core idea consists in bringing systemic infringement cases based on Article 259 TFEU, rather than Article 258 TFEU. The former provision allows the Member States themselves to bring their Treaty-violating peers to Court. The presumption behind the provision is that all the members of the Union are equally interested—just like the institutions—in ensuring sustained compliance with the Treaties by their peers. Importantly, no demonstration of direct concern is needed to meet the standing requirements: the mere fact of a breach of EU law is sufficient.[81]

Under Article 258 TFEU the Commission enjoys absolute discretion in bringing Article 258 TFEU cases.[82] Given that the Commission might choose at any moment not to bring a case even where there is a clear breach, or, which would be even more counterproductive in the context of values enforcement, to bring a case based merely on the violation of the rules of the *acquis sensu stricto*, getting twenty-seven additional potential litigators on board is hugely important. True, the Commission is the first point of contact for a Member State bringing a case under Article 259 TFEU—the provision even allows the Commission to take over. What is crucial in this context, however, is that the initiating Member State is not bound by the Commission's exercise of discretion. This concerns both the Commission's decision *not* to take over the case and the Commission's selection of arguments on the basis of which to proceed once the case has been taken over. In both instances the Member State concerned with the failure to abide by the Treaties evident from the state of affairs in one (or more) of its peers is free to bring the latter to Court construing the case as it sees fit.[83]

This is the first great advantage of the biting intergovernmentalism proposal over a simple systemic infringement action brought by the Commission: the Commission's limited reading of the scope of infringement proceedings cannot deprive biting intergovernmentalism of its effectiveness, making the deployment of systemic infringement proposal straightforward and available immediately.

There is a second advantage, however: the Union is constantly criticized for 'creeping competences' and 'power grabs', allowing Member States which fail to comply with the values of Article 2 TEU to misrepresent the Commission's systemic infringement action under Article 258 TFEU as a blunt attempt to violate Member State sovereignty by a power-hungry Union. The same argument is difficult to make when another Member State is bringing a systemic infringement action, which gives the biting intergovernmentalism proposal a political edge. With regard to the actual enforcement of values once a

[80] Kochenov (n 16).

[81] This is the case since Art 259—just like 258 TFEU—is not intended to protect the claimants' rights. Rather, the provisions aim to ensure general compliance with EU law: e.g. Case C-431/92 *Commission v Germany* [1995] ECLI:EU:C:1995:260, para 21. Compare L Prete and B Smulders, 'The Coming of Age of Infringement Proceedings' (2010) 47 *Common Market Law Review* 9, 13.

[82] e.g. Opinion of AG Tizzano in Joined cases C-466 and 476/98 *Commission v UK et al.* [2002] ECLI:EU:C:2002:624, para 30. Compare Prete and Smulders (n 81) 14.

[83] See e.g. Case 141/78 *France v UK* [1979] ECLI:EU:C:1979:225. For an overview of relevant practice, see, most importantly, Prete and Smulders (n 81) 27 (and the references cited therein).

non-compliant Member State has been found in breach under Article 259 TFEU, the standard procedure financial sanctioning procedure will then need to be applied.

c. 'Reverse *Solange*'

One of the most widely discussed proposals is based on AG Poiares Maduro's Opinion in *Centro Europa 7*, and was popularized by Armin von Bogdandy.[84] Similarly to the two proposals discussed above, the existing law and institutional structure of the Union are relied upon to address the Rule of Law crises in the EU, and no Treaty change is therefore required. The core idea focuses on grave violations of fundamental rights. Once the seriousness of rights violations in a given Member State is particularly grave, this allows the Union courts (including that same Member State's courts in their capacity as enforcers of EU law) to intervene. The gravity of the violation would create jurisdiction.[85]

This proposal is known as 'Reverse *Solange*' as it purports to espouse the logic of the *Budesverfassungsgericht* (*BVerfG*) in the *Solange I* and *Solange II* cases.[86] In these two cases, the *BVerfG* reserved to itself the final say on matters of EU law in situations where EU law could threaten the core of human rights protection established by the German Basic Law. Although the *BVerfG* has never actually acted on its threat, its *Solange* jurisprudence led the Court of Justice to reconsider its earlier stance (in *Stork*) regarding human rights protection in the early 1960s and hold that respect for human rights is one of the key conditions governing the lawfulness of EU acts.

The essence of Armin von Bogdandy's proposal is to 'reverse' the *Solange* approach by allowing the Court of Justice to move within the domain of the national law with a view to protecting EU values. The authors of the proposal presume that such a jurisdictional move would only be possible in truly exceptional cases of systemic non-compliance, suggesting that in a situation where human rights would be systemically violated in a 'captured' Member State, national courts should be empowered to make a preliminary reference under Article 267 TFEU in order to invite the Court of Justice to consider the legality of national actions in the light of Article 2 TEU, which the Court is not currently entitled to do.

While normatively defensible, this proposal however suffers from several shortcomings, as it emerges as most probably unworkable both in theory and in practice. Most importantly, it does not even address the key issues related to the lack of compliance with Article 2 TEU in some Member States. This is due firstly to the proposal's heavy reliance on national courts, whereas the judiciary is normally the first institution which illiberal forces would seek to capture, as the Hungarian example itself shows. Tellingly, Poland followed suit very closely, as obstructing the work of the Constitutional Tribunal was among the priorities of the new government. If national courts are packed and decapitated,[87] one can hardly expect

[84] Opinion of the Advocate General, Case C-380/05 *Centro Europa 7* [2007] ECR I-349, para 14 et seq. For an academic articulation, see A von Bogdandy et al., 'Reverse *Solange* – Protecting the Essence of Fundamental Rights against EU Member States' (2012) 49 *Common Market Law Review* 489; A von Bogdandy et al., 'A European Response to Domestic Constitutional Crisis: Advancing the Reverse-*Solange* Doctrine', in von Bogdandy and Sonnevend (n 26); von Bogdandy et al. in Chapter 12 of this volume. For criticism, see e.g. J Croon Gestefeld, 'Reverse *Solange* – European Citizenship as a Detour on the Route to Fundamental Rights Protection against National Infringements', in Kochenov (n 40); Kochenov (n 77).

[85] In this sense the proposal is in line with the case law of the Court of Justice, which finds jurisdiction based on the gravity of consequences caused by the deprivation of rights, see e.g. D Kochenov, 'A Real European Citizenship; A New Jurisdiction Test; A Novel Chapter in the Development of the Union in Europe' (2011) 18 *Columbia Journal of European Law* 56.

[86] *BVerfGE* 37, 271 (1974); *BVerfGE* 73, 378 (1986); *BVerfGE* 89, 155 (1993).

[87] e.g. ECtHR *Baka v Hungary* (Grand Chamber) [2016] Application No. 20261/12. c.f. TT Koncewicz, 'On Institutions, Democracy Constitutional Self-Defence and the Rule of Law' (2016) 53 *Common Market Law Review* 1753.

them to play any effective role in promoting Article 2 TEU compliance in the captured state of which they are part.

More importantly, however, the requirement of systemic non-compliance makes the implementation of the proposal practically impossible: the threshold is simply too high.[88] Ultimately, the presumption that the logic of trying not to give up *existing* jurisdiction—the original driver behind the *BVerfG*'s *Solange*—and the logic behind claiming *new* powers by the ECJ—which is the driver behind the Reverse *Solange* proposal—are comparable, seems to underplay significantly the fundamental differences between the two.[89] As a consequence, the so-called 'Reverse *Solange*' seems misnamed.

The last point of criticism to put forward would be that not all backsliding in Rule of Law terms implies grave and persistent human rights violations. Quite the contrary seems to be true: a well-executed dismantlement of the Rule of Law and the constitutional checks and balances can happen—or at least go through crucial initial stages—without bald violations of human rights.[90] Once the main jurisdictional argument made in Reverse *Solange* is considered outside of its rights context, however, it is very similar in essence to the one employed in the context of the systemic infringements proposal: the graveness of violation as such combined with their demonstrable character allows for intervention. For the reasons above, however, it is abundantly clear that systemic infringement procedures—either via Article 258 TFEU, or Article 259 TFEU—are overwhelmingly preferable to Reverse *Solange*: they are not limited in their deployment to human rights, the thresholds are more manageable and formulated more clearly, and they do not rely on the national institutions in the backsliding Member States.

The problem of enforcement *sensu stricto* is as acute with Reverse *Solange* as with other proposals discussed: it comes down to Article 260 TFEU again, the effectiveness of which is not beyond doubt.

d. The Copenhagen Commission

None of the proposals mentioned above suggested the creation of a new EU body, unlike Jan-Werner Müller's, which refers to a 'Copenhagen Commission' he proposes creating. This new body would ensure regular monitoring and the enforcement of compliance of current EU Member States with Article 2 TEU. This proposal does not therefore, unlike the previous proposals, rely on existing law and structures.[91]

The creation of a special Copenhagen Commission is potentially very attractive, as it would be an important step towards establishing a 'swift and independent monitoring mechanism and an early-warning system', which the Tavares Report also wanted to see in place.[92] The new institution would build on the Copenhagen criteria idea, going back to the 1993 European Council in Copenhagen, which established the political conditions for

[88] The example used in the proposal itself is 'the refusal to abide by the decision of the European Court of Human Rights': von Bogdandy et al. (n 84) 513.

[89] See Kochenov, 'On Policing Article 2 TEU Compliance' (n 77).

[90] C Closa et al. 'Reinforcing Rule of Law Oversight in the European Union' (2014) RSCAS EUI Working Paper No 25, 1.

[91] Müller in Chapter 13 of this volume; J-W Müller, 'Why the EU Needs a Democracy and Rule of Law Watchdog' (2015) 2 *Aspen Review* http://www.aspeninstitute.cz/en/article/2-2015-why-the-eu-needs-a-democracy-and-rule-of-law-watchdog/, accessed 12 October 2016.

[92] Proposing a new mechanism to enforce Article 2 TEU effectively. EP resolution of 3 July 2013 on the situation of fundamental rights: standards and practices in Hungary (pursuant to the EP resolution of 16 February 2012) (2012/2130(INI)), commonly referred to by the name of its Rapporteur 'the Tavares Report' http://www.europarl.europa.eu/sides/getDoc.do?type=TA&reference=P7-TA-2013-0315&language=EN&ring=A7-2013-0229, accessed 12 October 2016.

membership of the Union, including the respect for democracy, the Rule of Law, and the protection of fundamental rights, which had to be complied with by all the countries willing to join.

Unlike the previously examined proposals, which are mostly related to mending the holes in the EU's Article 2 TEU enforcement by relying on the existing tools already in place, the creation of a special organ with a new mechanism would clearly amount to a systemic mid to long-term solution, which is no doubt preferable, as it would potentially allow turning the EU into a full-fledged militant democracy.[93] To this end, it is possible for instance, also to involve the Fundamental Rights Agency of the Union (FRA) more in the matters of Article 2 TEU compliance, which will most likely require only the amendment of some secondary legislation.[94]

The proposal is however of a long-term nature, thus potentially unable to address immediate challenges, as the creation of any new EU body of this nature would no doubt require the approval, as well as full participation, of the Member State already experiencing problems with Article 2 TEU compliance. Moreover, questions remain as to the desirability of further complicating the institutional structure of the Union, as well as, fundamentally, the mechanics of the actual *enforcement* of the decisions of the Copenhagen Commission.

e. The 'exit card'

A more radical proposal still, which would definitely require Treaty change, has been advanced by Carlos Closa.[95] It suggests the introduction of a provision akin to Article 8 of the Statute of the Council of Europe and a number of other international organizations,[96] on the basis of which the EU could force a chronically non-compliant EU Member State out.[97] Such a new provision would complement Article 50 TEU, which currently permits voluntary withdrawal from the Union.[98] As outlined by Closa,[99] the idea is not to start throwing countries out of the Union, but to ensure an additional level of credibility for the sanctions which the EU can adopt on the basis of either Article 7 TEU or Article 260 TFEU.

The option to force an EU country out would be even more radical than the so-called 'nuclear option' laid down in Article 7 TEU and which, as previously noted, has never been used. It may be that the sheer possibility of being 'kicked out' of the EU would be of stronger persuasive value for the non-compliant Member State in question than the mere possibility of losing voting rights in Council.[100] The crucial problem with this proposal is that it can only be deployed in the long-term and unquestionably requires Treaty change. Moreover, such a proposal will have truly far-reaching implications for the concept of EU citizenship.[101] Viewed from the citizens' standpoint, ejecting a Member State facing severe troubles in the field of the Rule of Law and human rights could potentially demonstrate the Union's inability to guarantee actual Article 2 TEU compliance and protect the citizens of

[93] J-W Müller, 'The EU as a Militant Democracy, or: Are There Limits to Constitutional Mutations within the Member States' (2014) 165 *Revista de Estudios Políticos* 141.

[94] GN Toggenburg and J Grimheden, 'The Rule of Law and the Role of Fundamental Rights: Seven Practical Pointers', in Closa and Kochenov (n 12).

[95] Closa et al. (n 90).

[96] For a meticulous assessment, see Closa in Chapter 22 of this volume.

[97] Compare to Abdelgawad in Chapter 19 of this volume.

[98] For analyses, see P Nicolaides, 'Withdrawal from the European Union: A Typology of Effects' (2013) 20 *Maastricht Journal* 209; A Łazowski, 'Withdrawal from the European Union and Alternatives to Membership' (2012) 37 *European Law Review* 523.

[99] See, Closa et al. (n 90).

[100] What Article 7 TEU provides in terms of sanctions.

[101] D Kochenov, 'The Essence of EU Citizenship Emerging from the Last Ten Years of Academic Debate: Beyond the Cherry Blossoms and the Moon' (2013) 62 *International and Comparative Law Quarterly* 97.

the 'captured' state. Building upon the presumption that this option would enter the Treaties on the assumption that it is never to be used, like the Council of Europe's own Article 8 of the Statute, adding the possibility of ejecting a Member State is definitely helpful, as it will dispel the unfortunate sense that Article 7 TEU is the last resort measure and should thus not be made effective use of. Enriching EU law with a Member State ejection option is thus likely to be a positive development, notwithstanding the fact that, strictly speaking, it will not help solve the problems of the non-compliant Member State.

f. Peer-review and Horizontal *Solange*

Peer-review and 'Horizontal *Solange*' options are profoundly interconnected as, similarly to the biting intergovernmentalism proposal, they attempt to involve the Member States, not the Union institutions, as much as possible in solving a Rule of Law crisis. Unlike biting intergovernmentalism, however, the deployment of these two options is either potentially inconsequential (peer-review) or potentially too costly in terms of ensuring the proper functioning of the law of the Union (Horizontal *Solange*). One could be branded as a 'positive' version of the other.

The positive proposal was made by Ernst Hirsch Ballin and a team of researchers in the Netherlands and focuses on mutual peer-review of the Member States' compliance with the Rule of Law.[102] To a degree the Council pays heed to this proposal.[103] Peer review would allow the EU to avoid a number of problems at the core of all the other proposals under review: namely, it would not require any clear definition of the scope of EU law and the *acquis*, since peer review would be done based on agreements between the Member States outside of the framework of EU law. Although there is an obvious problem with detaching Article 2 TEU compliance from the EU legal system, the peer-review solution could be implemented swiftly. Moreover, the EU's organs could no doubt help by providing necessary information—the FRA is the first which springs to mind in this regard.[104] The obvious drawback of the proposal is the presumption that naming and shaming works, while we know from experience that it often does not, which explains for instance the inclusion of Article 260 TFEU into the Treaties: initially the Court did not have a legal ability to fine non-compliant Member States. The Treaties were amended in the face of the reality that Member States failing to comply with EU law would ignore Court decisions calling on them to respect the law.[105] It is indeed difficult to expect fundamental change from an illiberal national government as a result of other governments stating that *tout n'est pas rose* there. The problem of enforcement persists.

The 'negative' proposal allows the Member States rather than the EU to enforce sanctions against a non-compliant government by *de facto* disapplying EU law in bilateral relations with the 'guilty' state. This approach, recently analysed by Iris Canor, has been branded 'Horizonal *Solange*'.[106] Although the idea is not new, such treatment of non-

[102] See the Report prepared by Ernst Hirsch Ballin et al. for the Adviesraad Internationale Vragstukken (AIV): AIV, 'The Rule of Law: Safeguard for European Citizens and Foundation for European Cooperation' (2014) Report No 87, 35. See also E Hirsch Ballin, 'Mutual Trust: The Virtue of Reciprocity Strengthening the Acceptance of the Rule of Law through Peer Review', in Closa and Kochenov (n 12).

[103] Council of the EU, Press Release No 16936/14, 3362nd Council meeting, General Affairs (Brussels, 16 December 2014) 20–1. For a critical analysis, see P Oliver and J Stefanelli, 'Strengthening the Rule of Law in the EU: The Council's Inaction' (2016) 54 *Journal of Common Market Studies* 1075.

[104] Toggenburg and Grimheden (n 94).

[105] K Lenaerts et al. (JT Nowak (ed)), *EU Procedural Law* (OUP 2013).

[106] I Canor, 'My Brother's Keeper? Horizontal *Solange*: "An Ever Closer *Distrust* among the Peoples of Europe"' (2013) 50 *Common Market Law Review* 383.

compliant Member States profoundly undermines the very foundations of EU law, which is *not* based on reciprocity.[107] It strikes therefore at the core of the *acquis* and is thus unattractive for both normative and pragmatic reasons. In essence, it has the potential to throw the EU's internal market into chaos by opening up a Pandora's box of mutual accusations and immediate retaliation by the Member States—precisely what the EU has been so successful in outlawing over so many decades. Should the value enforcement problem not be addressed effectively by other means, however, Horizontal *Solange* is bound to be considered seriously by Member States disturbed by the democratic and Rule of Law backsliding of their peers.

g. 'Outsourcing' the Monitoring/Enforcement of EU Values

The President of the Venice Commission, Gianni Buquicchio, put another noteworthy proposal forward.[108] He suggested that the EU should avail of the expertise of his institution. The Venice Commission, which is not an EU organ, belonging to the Council of Europe system instead, has built up a solid reputation on the issues of the Rule of Law both in the context of its protection and promotion in EU countries and elsewhere in Europe.[109] All the Member States are represented in it.

The Venice Commission proposal did not come as a surprise to those interested in the enforcement of EU values, as this body of legal experts has traditionally played an important role in ensuring compliance with the Rule of Law in current EU Member States.[110] Given the established tradition of fruitful cooperation between the EU and the Venice Commission, which is already a reality, deepening the relations between the two offered a promising path. Buquicchio's offer does however raise two fundamental problems for the EU: one of a practical nature, the other of a normative nature.

From a practical perspective, we must note that the Venice Commission, although it obviously possesses an impressive track record and admirable expertise, cannot boast any enforcement machinery to ensure Article 2 TEU compliance where it is most needed. In other words, outsourcing Rule of Law questions to the Council of Europe would not solve the key issue: how to guarantee actual change in the non-compliant Member States.

From a normative perspective, it is important to stress that Article 2 TEU established the core values on which both the Union and the Member States are built. Outsourcing Article 2 TEU issues thus potentially amounts to sending a signal of the EU's inability to deliver on its core promise. For this reason alone, taking up the kind offer from the Venice Commission would seem to be inappropriate as it would most likely further undermine the EU's authority in this fundamental area. In the light of the Venice Commission's inability to enforce compliance with the Rule of Law standards it formulates, taking up the offer, in addition to being inappropriate, would also be of little use.

[107] Joined cases 90 and 91/63 *Commission v Belgium and Luxembourg* [1964] ECLI:EU:C:1964:80.

[108] See his speech at the Assizes de la Justice (2014). K Tuori, 'From Copenhagen to Venice', in Closa and Kochenov (n 12).

[109] See, esp., European Commission for Democracy through Law (The Venice Commission), *Report on the Rule of Law*, Strasbourg, CDL-AD (2011)003rev., 4 April 2011. J Nergelius, 'The Role of the Venice Commission in Maintaining the Rule of Law', in von Bogdandy and Sonnevend (n 26).

[110] See e.g. its important opinions on Hungary at: http://www.venice.coe.int/WebForms/documents/by_opinion.aspx, accessed 12 October 2016.

5. Complexities behind the simple solutions: concluding remarks

When the *acquis* functions well in a situation where not all the Member States of the EU are in full compliance with the foundational values of the Union, the 'proper functioning of EU law' can even be dangerous, since the presumption of mutual trust which EU law forces on the Member States will make building firewalls between states failing to comply with the values of democracy and the Rule of Law and the fully values-compliant Member States virtually impossible, even if the 'Reverse *Solange*' logic might in the end be a necessary response to the outstanding challenges coming from the blatantly non-compliant Member States. Numerous convincing arguments have been cited in favour of EU intervention in the domain of values.[111] It is clear, however, that such intervention cannot take the tested *acquis*-inspired route pretending that a meticulous policing of the *acquis* will solve the values problems. It will not. Indeed, the enforcement of values is a different matter compared with the enforcement of the *acquis sensu stricto*—a crucial difference for which both the design and the day-to-day practice of functioning of EU law is to blame.[112]

The majority of the enforcement literature falls short of tackling the core compliance problems in the EU today, since while the overwhelming focus is on the *acquis*, the values of the Union are virtually never taken into account. Even the most innovative accounts of enforcement, presenting justice in the EU as a service, for instance,[113] do not pay sufficient attention to the need to ensure that the basic values of Article 2 TEU are adhered to. Viewed against the lacunae in the literature on enforcement, all the values' enforcement proposals set out above, however realistic each of them can actually be, demonstrate a fundamentally important break with the dangerously short-sighted tradition approaching the issues of enforcement in the context of EU law solely with the Union *acquis* in mind. Poland, Hungary, and indeed potentially any other Member State in the future, could serve as vivid illustrations of the fact that the currently dominant approach to the enforcement of EU law in the literature is counterproductive. A different approach, akin to Jan-Werner Müller's conceptualization of the EU's possible future as a militant democracy, is absolutely indispensable at this stage.

The natural goal of the most important enforcement work at this point is then necessarily directly related to extending the debate about the essence of the law and the practice of ensuring compliance beyond the ambit of the *acquis* to the sphere of values. Only a system able to react to a Member State's constitutional departures from Article 2 TEU can aspire to acquire a real constitutional nature. Indeed, any enforcement of compliance not taking the values into account can be harmful, acting on the presumption of the existence of a particular type of constitutionalism[114] in all the Member States without inquiring whether this is indeed the case.[115]

Should this premise be accepted as valid—and numerous examples from the backsliding Member States seem to require us to accept it as such—new challenges arise. This is true even notwithstanding the view of the 'values' of Article 2 TEU as 'principles' of EU law defended in the disclaimer opening this chapter. Bringing the values closer to the *acquis* does not solve the core problem of EU law related to its value-enforcement re-articulation, which this chapter advocates, and as the new trend in the literature it documents makes

[111] e.g. Closa (n 14). [112] Kochenov (n 25).

[113] A Wechsler and B Tripković, 'Enforcement in Europe as a Market of Justice', in H-W Micklitz and A Wechsler (eds), *The Transformation of Enforcement* (Hart 2015).

[114] V Perju, 'Proportionality and Freedom – An Essay on Method in Constitutional Law' (2012) 1 *Global Constitutionalism* 334.

[115] Kochenov (n 27).

apparent. Indeed, viewed in the context of values enforcement, compliance cannot simply mean the 'correspondence of behaviour with legal rules', as Benedict Kingsbury has rightly claimed, and should connect with the meaning of justice espoused by the legal system in question.[116] Should we agree with Kingsbury, a vision of justice going beyond simple compliance with the *acquis* and accepting in full the pre-set objective of the internal market is indispensable for the EU,[117] in order to move the compliance debate in the direction of values. This is true no matter which specific enforcement technique the EU is to choose. We also have to admit that private enforcement, however glorified in the EU, has not been overwhelmingly effective.[118] Building a legal system with an overwhelming reliance on the narrative of its depoliticized goodness and entrusting the policing of compliance to private actors does not work well anymore: we are not only incapable of facing the (values) compliance problems effectively. The narrative of the 'goodness' of the Union also does not work as smoothly to justify the law and explain why compliance is necessary.[119] Worse still, the EU also comes to be viewed as a potent generator of injustice and a vehicle of oppression.[120] The realization of the importance of these dynamics triggered a new critical trend in the literature, focusing on the contexts of justice and injustice in the EU.[121] The justice debate in the Union is ongoing and the approaches to justice differ,[122] as the criticism of the current state of affairs from the justice perspective becomes harsher every day.

It seems logical in this context that connecting the internal aspirations of the EU legal system with the idea of justice is not a luxury problem: the EU is facing the justice dilemma in the context of the democratic and Rule of Law backsliding of the Member States, for which it was entirely unprepared. It is this backsliding, not so much the justice debates per se, which makes adherence to the classical *acquis*-centred approach to enforcement and compliance impossible, requiring the rethinking of the jurisdictional boundaries of the Union and of the enforcement tools the Union should have at its disposal, as well as the modalities of the deployment of such tools. The trouble is, the dominant narrative of the 'apolitical' process of the construction of the internal market cannot possibly justify the EU's actions in the sphere of values, requiring the Union to come up with much more convincing and realistic justifications for the *acquis*.

[116] Professor Kingsbury's claim, although made in the context of a discussion of compliance in International Law, clearly applies to the EU's legal context too. See B Kingsbury, 'The Concept of Compliance as a Function of Competing Conceptions of International Law' (1998) 19 *Michigan Journal of International Law* 345, 346.

[117] A Williams presented a crystal-clear description of the limitations of the EU's values landscape, where compliance with the *acquis* seems to be prone to taking the upper hand without any deeper considerations: A Williams, 'Taking Values Seriously: Towards a Philosophy of EU Law' (2009) 29 *Oxford Journal of Legal Studies* 549.

[118] See e.g. Broberg in Chapter 6 and Reich in Chapter 7 of this volume; T Lock, 'Is Private Enforcement of EU Law through State Liability a Myth?' (2012) 49 *Common Market Law Review* 1675, esp 1699; M Dougan, 'The Vicissitudes of Life on Coalface: Remedies and Procedures for Enforcing Union Law before the National Courts' in P Craig and G de Búrca (eds), *The Evolution of EU Law* (2nd edn, OUP 2011) 407.

[119] c.f. JHH Weiler, 'The Schuman Declaration as a Manifesto of Political Messianism' in J Dickson and P Eleftheriadis (eds), *Philosophical Foundations of European Union Law* (OUP 2012).

[120] S Douglas-Scott, 'Justice, Injustice and the Rule of Law in the EU' in Kochenov et al. (eds) (n 48) 51; C O'Brien, '*Civis capitalist sum*: Class as the New Guiding Principle of EU Free Movement Rights' (2016) 53 *Common Market Law Review* 937.

[121] 'Editorial comments: The *Critical Turn* in *EU Legal Studies*' (2015) 52 *Common Market Law Review* 881 (and the literature cited therein).

[122] e.g. the debate in Kochenov et al. (eds) (n 48); A Williams, *The Ethos of Europe* (CUP 2009); F de Witte, *Justice in the EU* (OUP 2015).

2

On the Legal Enforcement of Values. The Importance of the Institutional Context

Giulio Itzcovich

1. Premise. Government by laws and government by values

The expression 'enforcement of values' may strike one as somewhat obscure and problematic. In what sense is a value the kind of normative standard that can be 'enforced'? We know that values can be accepted, acknowledged, embraced, proclaimed, and promoted. Moral agents and public institutions are capable of recognizing that something is valuable (to them or per se) and provides reasons for acting or for refraining from acting in certain valuable or valueless ways. Moreover, we can follow, fulfil, satisfy, and comply with values: after having recognized that a state of affairs is valuable, moral agents and public institutions can act upon that belief and have recourse to that value in order to determine their duties or to assess other people's behaviour. However, accepting a value and acting accordingly are not identical to enforcing that value; voluntary compliance and coercive enforcement are clearly distinct concepts. I may well recognize a certain standard of conduct as binding on me without intending to compel other people to accept it.

Thus, when we speak of the enforcement of values by the EU institutions, or within the EU by its Member States, we are not referring to the ability of the EU as a whole to live up to the standards it sets to itself. Rather, we are referring to the EU's ability to compel other subjects—namely the Member States, the citizens of the EU, and perhaps individuals and institutions external to the EU—to comply with certain standards. Moreover, we are referring to the capability of the EU and of the Member States to react to the violation of those standards with coercive measures. In fact, values cannot just be accepted and fulfilled, embraced and satisfied: they can also be imposed. And coercive imposition might be the correct way of rendering the meaning of 'enforcement of values': the question would thus be how the EU and its Member States could compel observance of certain standards of conduct they believe to be of the utmost value.

However, this last formulation helps us to highlight why the idea of the enforcement of values by political and legal institutions might sound problematic. The obvious answer to how the EU and the Member States can compel observance of certain values is by issuing laws, provided that these laws fall within their competence and fulfil the values in question. Among the principles that the EU and the Member States embraced and proclaimed most solemnly we find the Rule of Law ('The Union is founded on the values of [...] the rule of law', according to Article 2 TEU), and the Rule of Law demands 'government under the forms of law and law in the form of clearly identifiable rules', among other things.[1] In a community based on the Rule of Law, no direct enforcement of values should ever be acceptable. Values as

[1] B Brown and N MacCormick, 'Law, Philosophy of' in E Craig (ed) *Routledge Encyclopedia of Philosophy* (Routledge 1998), http://www.rep.routledge.com/articles/law-philosophy-of/v-1/, accessed 13 October 2016.

such should be binding on those who accept them, but in order for values to be properly 'enforced', that is, to be coercively imposed upon somebody who does not embrace them voluntarily, they should first be transformed into valid laws according to the rules which govern the legislative process. Coercion should be effected exclusively by means of legal provisions which have been properly enacted by the established authorities, and the individuals directly concerned by the 'enforcement of values'—more precisely, the enforcement of laws which entrench values—should have the right to independent judicial review.

Therefore, when we speak of the ability of the EU to enforce its values, we are neither referring to the ability of the EU voluntarily to live up to the standards it sets itself, nor to the EU's ability to enforce its laws and have them applied to recalcitrant Member States, or by the courts and public officials of the Member States. We are referring to something distinct, but to what precisely?

One possible answer—certainly not the only one[2]—is that the enforcement of values concerns the choice of the methods used by the courts, and possibly by other officials, in determining the meaning of the rules they apply and in justifying the conclusions they reach. According to this understanding, the question of the enforcement of values is nothing but the questions of the standards on which independent courts, having doubts about the meaning and scope of the existing laws, rely to adjudicate hard cases.

Courts enforce laws, not values. The EU institutions and the institutions of the Member States cannot and should not enforce non-legally binding moral values. However, it can often happen that in order to justify their interpretive decisions on the content of a law, courts have recourse to standards of construction different from the literal meaning of the text, the intentions of the legislator, the objective purposes of the law, the coherence of a system, settled case law, etc; they can also make reference to the extra-legal consequences of the decision, and to the moral rights of the parties. In assessing the practical consequences of their decisions and in determining what is morally right and fair for the parties, courts might engage in explicit moral reasoning. They openly ground their decisions in moral principles and—in this limited sense—it can be said that they 'enforce values'. Thus the question arises: under what condition is it appropriate for a court to rely on its best moral reasoning to adjudicate a hard case, that is, a case not clearly settled by existing law?

This question, as is well known, has received a variety of answers. My aim in this chapter is neither to review that normative debate on legal interpretation, nor to argue for or against a given solution. Instead, I will argue that any sensible answer to the question of the role of explicit moral reasoning in adjudication must take into account a broad set of institutional facts. Whether the court aiming to 'enforce values' is the ECJ or whether it is a domestic constitutional court is an important distinction for many reasons, and in what follows I will try to explore these reasons and argue for their relevance.

I will proceed as follows. First, I will maintain that the current debate on the role of moral reasoning in adjudication is related to a set of institutional processes such as the global spread of constitutionalism, the diffusion of written constitutions and declarations of human rights, the growing importance of rights claims in adjudication, and the processes of globalization and Europeanization (section 2). To put it briefly: the idea of the legal enforcement of values emerges because the legal systems of many countries recognize a great deal of value-laden legal provisions: rights declarations and constitutional principles

[2] In the context of EU legal scholarship, the expression usually refers to enforcement of the 'values' of Article 2 TEU. As Kochenov rightly notes elsewhere in this volume, the wording is unfortunate: Article 2 TEU 'values' are in fact binding legal principles, that is, 'laws' as opposed to values.

the application of which seems to entail the need for having recourse to moral considerations instead of formally established rules and arguments from authority.

Second, I will distinguish two positions in the debate on the role of moral reasoning in adjudication, which I will label 'normative legal positivism' and 'neoconstitutionalism'. By normative legal positivism and neoconstitutionalism, I intend two opposite perspectives on the standards to be followed when interpreting and applying the law, particularly in the case of value-laden, open-ended legal provisions such as those establishing human rights and constitutional principles. I will argue that the choice between the two rival approaches must necessarily consider a variety of contingent legal, political, and social factors: we cannot accept or reject a normative theory of legal interpretation without first having analysed and assessed the institutional context in which the interpretation is performed. A purely theoretical-normative approach—one which explains and defends the ethical premises of legal positivism and neoconstitutionalism in order to support the choice of one over the other—would therefore be insufficient (sections 3 to 5).

Finally, I will try to clarify some methodological and substantive consequences which can be drawn from the nexus that binds together the choice of interpretive method with the greater or lesser trust we have in the interpreter (section 6).

2. The spread of rights

The debate on the proper criteria for interpreting human rights declarations and other open-ended and value-laden legal provisions has become increasingly topical in recent years as a consequence of a number of developments which are often expressed with formulas such as the advent of the 'constitutional state' (*Verfassungsstaat, Estado constitucional de derecho*) and the processes of 'constitutionalization', 'integration', and 'globalization' of the legal orders. These developments concern the content of positive law and the system of law-applying institutions as well as the theories and ideologies which prevail in the legal community about the best conception of democracy and the separation of powers, the role of the judiciary, the nature of the constitution, and the nature of international law, among other things. Various authors have described in different ways the characteristics of the constitutional state which influence the solution to the problems of legal interpretation. Aside from the cultural factor, such as the growing importance of 'neoconstitutionalist' theories of legal interpretation which I will highlight in the next section, the following three institutional factors seem particularly significant.

(i) *The constitutionalization of fundamental rights*. The first process is the global spread of written, rigid and justiciable constitutions which contain declarations of rights and entrench 'values' in the form of indeterminate legal provisions.[3] Bills of rights are framed in a language that is solemn, ethically inspired, concise, and generic:[4] their application to concrete cases often implies the adoption of highly controversial value choices. Judicial review of legislation therefore entails that the judiciary is empowered to 'determine issues of profound moral and political importance, on the basis of very limited textual guidance resulting in legal decisions that may last for decades and are practically almost impossible to change by regular democratic processes'.[5]

[3] T Ginsburg, 'The Global Spread of Constitutional Review' in GA Caldeira et al. (eds), *The Oxford Handbook of Law and Politics* (OUP 2008) 81–98; AS Sweet and J Mathews, 'Proportionality Balancing and Global Constitutionalism' (2008) 47 *Columbia Journal of Transnational Law* 73.

[4] A very common observation. See e.g. E-W Böckenförde, *Staat, Verfassung, Demokratie* (Suhrkamp 1991) 116, on the 'lapidary and, technically speaking, thoroughly fragmentary character of the provisions on fundamental rights'.

[5] A Marmor, *Interpretation and Legal Theory* (2nd edn, Hart 2005) 141.

Moreover, the legal culture in many jurisdictions has developed techniques for the application of rights, such as the balancing test and the proportionality principle, that allow the judiciary to exercise a penetrating and yet flexible review of the activities of other branches of government.[6] These techniques are premised on the notion that fundamental rights and constitutional principles are not categorical and absolute norms. Thus, it is often held that fundamental rights and constitutional principles must be applied in a case-sensitive way, fulfilled gradually and to various degrees, and must be concretized and balanced in various manner, from time to time, based on the circumstances of the controversies. In order to avoid that clearly defined rules prove to be over- or under-inclusive of future cases, many courts around the world refrain from constructing a system of rules, and instead apply fundamental rights and constitutional principles as generic and defeasible directives bound to enter into conflict one with the other in concrete cases. This understanding of fundamental rights and these techniques for their application seem to imply the necessity of having recourse to moral reasoning instead of purely formal legal arguments.

(ii) *Diffusion and judicialization of fundamental rights*. Not only the legislator but also private individuals might be required to respect fundamental rights according to the interpretations given by the courts. In the 'horizontal' relations between individuals, there is a widespread trend toward the growing presence and relevance of controversies framed in terms of rights different from the traditional property and contract rights. The courts of many countries adjudicate on violations of human dignity, on civil and political rights such as the right to privacy, to the physical and mental integrity of the person, freedom of speech and of association, and on economic and social rights such as the right to health. The courts apply human rights and the principle of equality to a variety of situations, such as family and work relations that in the past belonged to the private or social sphere that was subject to private law and not to constitutional law.

Thus, the violation of fundamental rights stops being the extreme case of 'legal injustice' potentially capable of sweeping away the legitimacy of public authority and justifying the appeal, if not to tyrannicide, to the right of revolution and to civil disobedience. Violations of fundamental rights no longer call into question the ground of political obligation and become, conversely, quite ordinary and frequent events that can come across in a large amount of cases and that the court system of the constitutional state manages on a daily basis. At first sight paradoxically, the increasing importance of fundamental rights is accompanied by their trivialization, as fundamental rights turn into a common currency used to describe and decide even the most routine and mundane conflicts of interests.[7]

(iii) *Internationalization of rights*. Since the second half of the twentieth century, universal and regional conventions for human rights protection have multiplied and have established a body of law that is often applicable not only to states, but also to

[6] In the extensive literature on balancing and proportionality, recent contributions include K Möller, *The Global Model of Constitutional Rights* (OUP 2012); M Cohen-Eliya and I Porat, *Proportionality and Constitutional Culture* (CUP 2013); J Bomhoff, *Balancing Constitutional Rights: The Origins and Meanings of Postwar Legal Discourse* (CUP 2013); L Lazarus et al. (eds), *Reasoning Rights: Comparative Judicial Engagement* (Hart 2014); G Huscroft et al. (eds), *Proportionality and the Rule of Law: Rights, Justification, Reasoning* (CUP 2014).

[7] This remark can be found in some early criticisms of the constitutionalization process, such as that of C Schmitt, *Die Tyrannei der Werte* (3rd edn, Duncker & Humblot 2011). On 'rights inflation' see J Gerards, 'The Prism of Fundamental Rights' (2012) 8 *European Constitutional Law Review* 173, at 178 ff.; M Kumm, '*Internationale Handelsgesellschaft*, *Nold* and the New Human Rights Paradigm' in M Maduro and L Azoulai (eds), *The Past and Future of EU Law: The Classics of EU Law Revisited on the 50th Anniversary of the Rome Treaty* (Hart 2010) 106–18.

international organizations and even to private actors, such as transnational corporations and individuals.[8] It is sometimes held that the point of these Treaties is not to establish mutual obligations between the contracting parties—obligations that would be interpreted strictly, having regard for the sovereignty of the states—but to create an effective system of individuals' rights protection, which justifies evolutive, extensive, and teleological interpretation in order to ensure the full implementation of human rights.[9]

Thus, states are placed under the influence of legal interpretations rendered by courts belonging to different planes of a 'multilevel system' of fundamental rights protection.[10] As there are no hierarchical relations between the various courts that participate in such a system, the free competitions between courts in the interpretation and application of rights creates the opportunity for constitutional conflicts and the consequent necessity of preventing and managing such conflicts through legal argumentation and pragmatic accommodation (the so-called 'dialogue' on the protection of fundamental rights[11]).

To sum up, we have three institutional processes that, although interrelated, can be analytically distinguished and that together explain the crucial importance in contemporary legal culture of the issue on the enforcement of 'values' through legal interpretation. (1) The spread of written, rigid, justiciable constitutions containing declarations of rights (rights constitutionalization); (2) The horizontal application of fundamental rights to private law relations and, more generally, the centrality of rights in today's legal practice (rights diffusion); and (3) The birth of international human rights law and, especially in Europe, the development of a multilevel system of rights protection (rights' internationalization, globalization, and Europeanization).

3. Normative theories of legal interpretation

The trends toward rights' constitutionalization, diffusion, and globalization feed a wide debate on the role and justification of judicial review and rights discourse.

Many political theorists have envisaged a shift from aggregative democracy to deliberative democracy. The former is considered, following Schumpeter, as a procedure for arriving at political decisions by means of 'competitive struggle for the people's vote':[12] democracy is an institutional arrangement for selecting the political leadership by aggregating the preferences of the voters. By contrast, deliberative democracy is inspired by the regulative ideal of a universal consensus achieved through public reason and resembles a form of collective moral conversation on the founding principles of the political community. Within that theoretical framework, the judges have been thought of as being capable of acting as 'political theorists' that clarify and develop the fundamental choices of values of a given political community,[13] and courts have been depicted as 'guardian[s] of deliberative

[8] On the expansion of international human rights, see e.g. A Peters, 'Membership in the Global Constitutional Community' in J Klabbers et al. (eds), *The Constitutionalization of Intenational Law* (OUP 2009) 167 ff.

[9] See e.g. ICJ, *Reservations to the Genocide Convention* (Advisory Opinion) 1951 ICJ Reports 15 at 23; European Commission of Human Rights, *Austria v Italy* (Pfunder's case) App No 788/60 11 January 1961 (1962) 4 Yearbook 116 at 138; Case C-26/62, *Van Gend en Loos* (1963) ECR 1 at 12. For further references, see F Mégret, 'The Nature of Obligations' in D Moeckli et al. (eds), *International Human Rights Law* (2nd edn, OUP 2014) 96–118; E Bjorge, *The Evolutionary Interpretation of Treaties* (OUP 2014).

[10] On constitutional pluralism and adjudication, see e.g. G Martinico, *The Tangled Complexity of the EU Constitutional Process: The Frustrating Knot of Europe* (Routledge 2012); P Popelier et al. (eds), *The Role of Constitutional Courts in Multilevel Governance* (Intersentia 2012).

[11] See AS Sweet, 'Constitutional Dialogues: Protecting Human Rights in France, Germany, Italy and Spain' in SJ Kenney et al. (eds), *Constitutional Dialogues in Comparative Perspective* (Macmillan 1999) 8–41.

[12] J Schumpeter, *Capitalism, Socialism and Democracy*, (3rd edn, HarperCollins 2008) 269.

[13] D Robertson, *The Judge as a Political Theorist: Contemporary Constitutional Review* (Princeton University Press 2010).

democracy' and 'exemplar[s] of public reason': institutions that enrich the deliberative quality of democracy by 'call[ing] some issues from the battleground of power politics to the forum of principles'.[14]

Moreover, some deliberative democracy theorists have imagined that rights could work as a sort of *lingua franca* by means of which different countries and political cultures communicate with one another in the international arena as well as in the state's constitutional setting:[15] rights could be the engine and the object of global deliberative processes,[16] the vehicle of 'transnational judicial conversation'[17] within an emerging 'global community of courts'.[18]

Other political theorists, however, have criticized constitutionalization by holding that fundamental rights are nothing but the expression of particular political and cultural identities—namely a Western, secular, individualistic, male, and neoliberal identity[19]—or by holding that constitutionalization is the way certain political and economic *élites* react to the erosion in their popular support by delegating powers to the courts so that they can preserve their declining hegemony.[20] Thus, there has been talk of an 'age of right'[21] and a 'rights revolution',[22] but also of 'legal globalism',[23] the 'global expansion of judicial power',[24] 'judicial democracy',[25] 'juridical *coup d'état*',[26] and 'insatiable rights'.[27]

A parallel debate is taking place in jurisprudence: a debate that must not be too sharply distinguished from theoretical-political reflection on the transnational process of rights constitutionalization. Here too judicial review and the protection of fundamental rights are viewed as either a dynamic that strengthens and completes democracy or that endangers democracy and evacuates it of any meaning. This disagreement is reflected in different approaches to the problems of legal interpretation. Which criteria ought to be followed in applying value-laden and open-ended legal provisions such as those establishing fundamental rights and constitutional principles? What should be the role of moral reasoning in adjudication? As far as the enforcement of values through legal interpretation is concerned, it is possible to distinguish between two positions that are premised on different assessments of the processes of rights' constitutionalization, diffusion, and globalization. I propose to call them 'neoconstitutionalism' and 'normative legal positivism'.

[14] R Dworkin, *A Matter of Principle* (Harvard University Press 1985) 71.

[15] M Ignatieff, *Human Rights as Politics and Idolatry* (Princeton University Press 2001) 95 ('the shared vocabulary from which our arguments can begin'); J Tasioulas, 'The Moral Reality of Human Rights' in Th Pogge (ed), *Freedom from Poverty as a Human Right: Who Owes What to the Very Poor?* (OUP 2007) 75–101, p. 75 ('an ethical *lingua franca*').

[16] A Buchanan, 'Human Rights and the Legitimacy of the International Legal Order' (2008) 14 *Legal Theory* 39, 67.

[17] Ch McCrudden, 'A Common Law of Human Rights? Transnational Judicial Conversations on Constitutional Rights' (2000) 20 *Oxford Journal of Legal Studies* 499.

[18] A-M Slaughter, 'A Global Community of Courts' (2003) 44 *Harvard Journal of International Law* 191.

[19] For a recent overview of these criticisms, see R Cruft et al., 'The Philosophical Foundations of Human Rights. An Overview' in *Philosophical Foundations of Human Rights* (OUP 2015) 31 ff.

[20] R Hirschl, *Towards Juristocracy: The Origins and Consequences of the New Constitutionalism* (Harvard University Press 2004).

[21] N Bobbio, *L'età dei diritti* (Einaudi 1990).

[22] ChR Epp, *The Rights Revolution: Lawyers, Activists, and Supreme Courts in Comparative Perspective* (Chicago University Press 1998).

[23] D Zolo, 'The Rule of Law: A Critical Reappraisal' in P Costa and D Zolo (eds), *The Rule of Law. History, Theory and Criticism* (Springer 2007) 54.

[24] CN Tate and T Vallinder (eds), *The Global Expansion of Judicial Power* (New York University Press 1995).

[25] C Guarnieri and P Pederzoli, *La democrazia giudiziaria* (Il Mulino 1997).

[26] AS Sweet, 'The Juridical Coup d'État and the Problem of Authority' (2007) 8 *German Law Journal* 915.

[27] A Pintore, 'Insatiable Rights' (2001) 14 *International Journal for the Semiotics of Law* 277.

It is important to bear in mind that authors that embrace legal positivism may from a theoretical or methodological viewpoint,[28] without any contradiction, reject normative legal positivism and adopt a neoconstitutionalist stance with regard to the criteria to be followed in interpreting the law.[29] The distinction between legal positivism and neoconstitutionalism has been made in various ways and the relation between the two is the object of a wide discussion in legal theory.[30] It is hardly possible to find a set of theoretical assumptions that all neoconstitutionalists accept and define their position. Every characterization of neoconstitutionalism is bound to be conventional and approximate. The use of these labels is here justified only by their capability of grouping together certain stances on legal interpretation that present a strong 'family resemblance' one with the other.

Neoconstitutionalism gives a positive if not enthusiastic assessment of the tendencies to rights constitutionalization, diffusion, and internationalization that constitute the institutional premises of the debate on the enforcement of values via legal interpretation. According to this approach, the constitutional state represents an achievement that deserves to be safeguarded, where it is present, and to be spread and adopted, where it is lacking. The state should acknowledge the binding force of fundamental rights not only toward the public administration, as the old liberal state (*liberaler Rechtsstaat*) did, but also toward the democratically elected legislator. According to some, the binding force of fundamental rights should be acknowledged also toward private individuals, so that the private sphere might be sheltered against the 'wild powers'[31] of the market and the family. There are things no authority can ever do to people (Dworkin's 'rights as trumps',[32] Ferrajoli's 'sphere of the undecidable',[33] Garzón Valdés's *coto vedado*[34]). Considerations related to parliament's sovereignty, on the constitutional plane, and to state's sovereignty, on the international plane, cannot defeat the duty to respect, protect, and fulfil human rights.

As far as legal interpretation is concerned, neoconstitutionalism maintains that fundamental rights' positivization entails that judges cannot limit themselves to investigate the intentions of the legislator or to comply with the settled case law and social conventions. When the judge is called on to decide on the alleged violation of a fundamental right, formal arguments based on authority and on tradition are insufficient, and so are lexicographical surveys of linguistic usages, historiographical investigations of the intentions of long-time deceased people (the framers), and opinion polls of present-day citizens. On the contrary, it is necessary to engage in sound moral reasoning that takes seriously the rights of the individuals: enforcing fundamental rights implies a readiness at least to question the legitimacy of the existing laws and social morality. The judge will have, for instance, to

[28] On the distinction between mythological legal positivism (detached, scientific approach to the law), theoretical legal positivism (various theories on the essential features of the law) and ideological legal positivism (existence of a moral duty to obey the law), see N Bobbio, *Giusnaturalismo e positivismo giuridico* (Laterza 2011) 87 ff.

[29] e.g. Marmor (n 5) 159 ('the courts should strive to interpret the constitution according to their best possible understanding of the moral/political issues involved, striving to reach the best possible moral decision under the current circumstances'); J Raz, 'On the Authority and Interpretation of Constitutions: Some Preliminaries' in L Alexander (ed), *Constitutionalism: Philosophical Foundations* (CUP 1998) 152 ff. (constitutional courts strike the balance between reasons for constitutional continuity and fidelity to the law and reasons for change and innovation in order to reach a morally justified decision).

[30] For an introduction to the debate, see T Mazzarese (ed), *Neocostituzionalismo e tutela (sovra)nazionale dei diritti* (Giappichelli 2002); M Carbonell (ed), *Neoconstitucionalismo(s)* (Trotta 2003); S Pozzolo (ed), *Neconstitucionalismo, derecho y derechos* (Palestra 2011).

[31] L Ferrajoli, *Poteri selvaggi. La crisi della democrazia italiana* (Laterza 2011).

[32] R Dworkin, *Taking Rights Seriously* (Harvard University Press 1977).

[33] L Ferrajoli, *Principia iuris* (Laterza 2007), vol. 1, 819 ff., and vol. 2, 19, 44, 92, *passim*.

[34] EG Valdés, 'Rapresentación y democracia' (1989) 6 *Doxa* 143.

subordinate the policies of the legislator to the principles of public morality entrenched in the constitution, to set out the best theory of what the constitutional principles require in the case at hand, to evaluate the relative weight of the principles identified as relevant for the decision, and to strike a balance between the reasons for institutional continuity and the reasons for change. The constitution itself, by including fundamental rights and principles, requires the judge to engage in these kinds of deliberations.[35]

Legal positivism, as a descriptive theory of law, must obviously account for all the trends toward rights' constitutionalization, diffusion, and internationalization that are the starting point of neoconstitutionalism. However, when they move from description to assessment, some legal positivists—certainly not all of them, and not even the majority—consider with caution or concern such trends and assume a stance that is, if not openly conservative,[36] akin to what in literature is known as normative legal positivism, rule formalism, political or popular constitutionalism.[37]

The basic idea is that allowing the judges to expose (and impose) a theory of justice through legal interpretation means providing a non-representative and non-accountable élite with the power to determine the fundamental standards of civil life. But the standards of civil life cannot be abandoned to a normative theory of justice that the judges should guard and to which they would have privileged access; those standards are the ever-unstable outcome of a conflict of ideas, values, and interests in which every citizen should be allowed to participate on a footing of equal dignity and respect. In order for those standards to be consistent with the moral freedom and the political equality of all citizens, they must result from a political process that is open to a plurality of voices, and in which the judges should not have the last word.

With regard to legal interpretation in general and to the interpretation of fundamental rights declarations in particular, normative legal positivists prescribe the use of a variety of standards. They can deny the existence of any specificity of constitutional interpretation in respect of statutory interpretation and, based on that assumption, they can reject the theoretical premises of some neoconstitutionalist theories, such as the distinction between rules and principles, and reject their interpretive methods, such as recourse to extensive, evolutive, or consistent interpretation and recourse to balancing judgments.[38] Alternatively, normative legal positivists can recommend fidelity to the intentions of the framers or

[35] See e.g. Ferrajoli (n 33) vol. 1, pp. 39 ff., on the 'critical and normative' role assumed by legal knowledge as consequence of constitutionalization. The same idea is shared by critics of legal positivism, such as R Dworkin, *Freedom's Law* (Harvard University Press 1996) 7 ff., and G Zagrebelsky, *Il diritto mite. Legge diritti giustizia* (Einaudi 1992) 163 ff.; by inclusive legal positivists, such as W Waluchow, *Inclusive Legal Pluralism* (OUP 1994) 113 ff.; as well as by exclusive legal positivists, such as J Raz, *The Authority of Law: Essays on Law and Morality* (2nd edn, OUP 2009) 49, and *Between Authority and Interpretation* (OUP 2009) 196, arguing that when the constitution uses moral concepts, it empowers the judges to develop and modify the law on the basis of moral considerations, which nonetheless continue to be external to the law.

[36] Apart from Carl Schmitt's *Die Tyrannei der Werte*, in the German legal scholarship, see Böckenförde (n 4) 53 ff., and 115 ff.

[37] JAG Griffith, 'The Political Constitution' (1979) 42 *Modern Law Review* 1; J Waldron, *Law and Disagreement* (OUP 1999); LD Kramer, *The People Themselves: Popular Constitutionalism and Judicial Review* (OUP 2004); A Tomkins, *Our Republican Constitution* (Hart 2005); M Tushnet, *Weak Courts, Strong Rights* (Princeton University Press 2008); R Bellamy, *Political Constitutionalism: A Republican Defence of the Constitutionality of Democracy* (CUP 2007). For a critical discussion, see M Goldoni, 'Political constitutionalism and the value of constitution making' (2014) 27 Ratio Juris 387. For similar views, see A Pintore, *I diritti della democrazia* (Laterza 2003); JC Bayón, 'Derechos, democracia y constitución' (2000) 1 *Discusiones* 65, http://www.cervantesvirtual.com/obra/derechos-democracia-y-constitucion, accessed 13 October 2016.

[38] R Guastini, *Distinguendo. Studi di teoria e metateoria del diritto* (Giappichelli 1996) 115 ff. and 237 ff.; E Forsthoff, *Rechtsstaat im Wandel* (Kohlhammer 1964) 147–75.

to the original public meaning of the text,[39] or they can recommend deference toward the will of the current legislator, therefore self-restraint and respect for the constitutional interpretations reflecting a general consensus of the fellow citizens or of their representatives.[40]

These directives are obviously not equivalent one with the other. The will of the framers might not correspond to the constitutional interpretations of the current legislator; originalism and textualism do not necessarily imply self-restraint and respect for the margin of appreciation of other authorities. Nonetheless, all these directives coincide in assuming the possibility of a tension between judicial review and democracy or, in the case of the conservative criticism, a tension between judicial review, on the one side, and legal certainty and social and institutional stability, on the other. Normative legal positivism looks with some concern at such a tension and therefore does not recommend the judges to decide according to their best moral judgment. As the responsibility for the decision must not lie on the moral reasoning of the judge, legal positivism goes in search of criteria external to the consciousness of the adjudicator—such as the letter and spirit of the law, the will of the framers, the will of present-day legislator, the social morality—on the basis of which to justify the enforcement (or non-enforcement) of rights and of other value-imbued legal provisions.

4. Noble dreams and nightmares

No matter how we want to conceive the 'success' of neoconstitutionalism and legal positivism as normative theories of adjudication—as an effective rights protection or as the realization of a certain idea of democracy—that success cannot but depend on the legal, political, and social situation in which those theories happen to operate; a variety of conditions external to the theories, which the theories do not control directly, affect the possibility of achieving their objectives.

If we assume different background conditions, we can imagine opposite extreme outcomes of the two theories—let us call them the 'noble dream' and the 'nightmare' scenarios[41]—and maintain that for the interpreter the choice between neoconstitutionalism and normative legal positivism necessarily depends not only on the intrinsic desirability of their dreams and undesirability of their nightmares, but also on their plausibility and probability in the given situation. If the noble dream of neoconstitutionalism (or of legal positivism) seems to be, in a particular context, totally fantastic and unrealizable, and its nightmare seems to be a real possibility that must be avoided, then legal positivism (or neoconstitutionalism) will be preferable for prudential, pragmatic reasons, that is, for reasons other than the principled considerations internal to the theories and explicitly formulated by the theories (such as, for instance, some conception of authority, rights, democracy, the constitution, the role of the judiciary, and so on).

[39] On the US debate on originalism, see G Huscroft and BW Miller (eds), *The Challenge of Originalism: Theories of Constitutional Interpretation* (CUP 2011); FB Cross, *The Failed Promise of Originalism* (Stanford University Press 2013).

[40] On public opinion's consensus and the legitimacy of judicial review, see B Friedman, *The Will of the People: How Public Opinion Influenced the Supreme Court and Shaped the Meaning of the Constitution* (Farrar, Straus, and Giroux 2009). On the margin of appreciation doctrine, see J Gerards, 'Pluralism, Deference and the Margin of Appreciation Doctrine' (2011) 17 *European Law Journal* 80; G Itzcovich, 'One, None and One Hundred Thousand Margins of Appreciations. Notes on the Lautsi Case' (2013) 13 *Human Rights Law Review* 287.

[41] The terminology comes from HLA Hart, *Essays in Jurisprudence* (OUP 1983) 123–44, who however applies it to the theories of legal interpretation and not to their practical outcomes.

With an effort of synthesis and trying to do justice both to legal positivism and to neoconstitutionalism, I think that the noble dream and the nightmare of the two theories can be rendered in the following way.

(i) The noble dream of neoconstitutionalism is that the judicial application of fundamental rights and constitutional principles is not, at least not necessarily or in most cases, irrational, unfounded, and unpredictable; it is not the expression of the subjective preferences of the judge, or of judges as a group. On the contrary, the judicial 'enforcement of values' might represent the best possible approximation either to an objective morality that in principle can be known by an impartial observer, such as the judge, or to a social morality widely shared by reasonable people like the judges.

According to the noble dream, through the legal process and the gradual development of the case law it is possible to do justice to the parties in the objectively right way, or at least in a socially acceptable way. Moreover, it is possible not only to protect individuals' rights, but also to enrich the democratic debate making it more participatory and inclusive. Social and political movements and civil society associations can make use of the language of rights not only as a means of political claims, but also as vehicle of legal claims: through public interest litigation, the legal process, and the system of courts can be channels of political participation. Arguments that otherwise would not receive adequate consideration, or that would not even reach the public sphere, are publicly expressed by the parties to the legal proceedings and are carefully pondered by a personally disinterested judge. The courts and the legal scholarship engage in an ongoing debate on the developments of constitutional adjudication, and in that way they constitute a forum of normative reflection and political deliberation that is parallel to, different from but not worse than, that of party politics. The process of common reflection on constitutional interpretation taking place within the legal community complements representative democracy. It introduces new normative contents that deserve to be taken into account, opens policy-making to minority interests that otherwise would be excluded, corrects the legislative process when its outcomes are defective, and prevents the risk that liberticidal and tyrannical laws determine the self-destruction of democracy.

(ii) The noble dream of normative legal positivism is that it is possible to have a political regime that, by distinguishing jurisdiction and legislation, bestows the former to a judiciary that is professional, independent, politically non-accountable, and yet respectful of the prerogatives of the other branches of government. Moreover, the legislative power can be entrusted to a democratic political process that is consistent with the equal moral dignity of the citizens, that is, with their equal right to make their voice be heard and to count in the adoption of collective decisions. According to the noble dream of legal positivism, the best chances for the fulfilment and the development of rights are not to be found in an idealized image of legal reasoning and constitutional courts, but lie in the resources of the ordinary legislative process and of a civil society that is lively and capable of organizing itself politically. Rights claims are neither the description of the objective morality nor of a widely accepted social morality; they are the expression of conflicts between specific interests and views. Such conflicts can receive an adequate mediation through the legislative process and the democratic policy-making, without being entrusted to the care of a non-representative and not democratically accountable aristocracy of the robe. In a pluralist society, the application of rights and other value-laden legal provisions cannot be objective and generally shared; disagreement is inevitable[42] as the law is not, and cannot

[42] Waldron (n 37) 105 ff., p. 163.

be, a substitute for politics.[43] In order for political decisions to be regarded as legitimate, we need to establish procedures that allow the citizens to participate in politics on a roughly equal basis. Legitimacy cannot depend on the substantive justice of political decisions, but on the fact that political decisions are the outcome of procedures that rest on political equality, and on the fact that political decisions are open to contestation and easily modifiable by means of the ordinary legislative process. There is no way of preventing democracies making mistakes from time to time, but the free competition between political parties is the best way for managing and at the same time guaranteeing the pluralism of contemporary societies.

From the debate on constitutionalization and legal interpretation, it is also possible to extract the nightmares of legal positivism and neoconstitutionalism, that is, the scenarios of extreme failure of the two theories.

(iii) The nightmare of neoconstitutionalism is obviously some variation of 'government by judiciary',[44] the 'jurisdictional state',[45] and the dictatorship of a 'judicial oligarchy'[46] or 'guardian bureaucracy'[47] practicing an immoral, unpredictable, and antidemocratic 'Kadi justice'.[48]

The judicial application of fundamental rights and other open-ended constitutional provisions might reveal itself as arbitrary and unacceptable from the viewpoint of critical morality (an immoral justice). Alternatively, it might reveal itself unstable and surprising, when it is inconsistent with the social morality expressed in the legal precedents, in the legislative decisions, and in the ethical convictions widely accepted in the community (an unpredictable justice). Finally, the judicial application of fundamental rights might reveal itself the predictable but unilateral expression of the personal convictions of the judges, that is, of the sectional social morality of a professional group or of a specific court of justice (an antidemocratic justice).

In the neoconstitutionalist nightmare, a politically non-accountable authority establishes in an almost definitive way what is right and wrong relying on its own moral appreciation of the controversy. By voicing their private morality, or the social morality of their professional group, the judges of the nightmare pretend to rule not only on what is legal or illegal, but also on what is morally acceptable or inacceptable, politically possible or illegitimate. Moreover, the diktats of the hierocratic community of the constitution's interpreters do not enrich the public debate but, on the contrary, they deprive democratic politics of any salient content: the space of politics is reduced to that of the administration of the existing system within the confines of the legal principles entrenched in the constitution and interpreted by the courts.

In one possible version of the nightmare, politics reacts to the hegemonic claims of the judiciary in a way that endangers the fundamental principles of the constitutional state and the rule of law. For instance, judgments provoke popular or 'populist' hostility toward the courts and politics succeeds in delegitimizing the judiciary, curtailing its independence, and effectively controlling it; or the recipients of the ruling do not comply with them and the

[43] Griffith (n 37) 16.

[44] LB Boudin, 'Government by Judiciary' (1911) 26 *Political Science Quarterly* 238, 267; E Lambert, *Le gouvernement des juges et la lutte contre la législation sociale aux États-Unis* (Giard 1921).

[45] '[A] mere non-political community [...] in which the deciding judge in the legal dispute has the last word, rather than the norm-setting lawmaker': C Schmitt, *Legality and Legitimacy* (trans. J Seitzer, Duke University Press 2004) 7, 4.

[46] GE Roe, *Our Judicial Oligarchy* (Huebsch 1912).

[47] FM Marx, *The Administrative State* (University of Chicago Press 1957) 55.

[48] M Weber, *Economy and Society*, ed G Roth and C Wittich (University of California Press 1978) 823, 976, 1116, *passim*, uses the expression *Kadi Justiz* to refer to formally irrational, personalised, ad hoc adjudication.

judgments remain unimplemented and unenforced, and this causes legal uncertainty and a crisis of legitimacy of the political system.

(iv) In the scenario of the legal positivist nightmare, the application of fundamental rights by the judges and the officials functions as a well-oiled machine that carries into inexorable execution the perverse or senseless decisions of a tyrannical or unintelligible power, in the presence of a civil society that is alienated, passivized, indifferent, or complicit. As a virtuous and active civil society is lacking, the inclusive capacity of democratic politics proves to be illusory: in the nightmare of legal positivism civil society is depoliticized and silent, fragmented and resigned, or even actively evil, illiberal, and racist, mobilized for the conquest of power.

Faced with the nightmare of legal positivism, those who care for the protection of individuals' rights cannot rely only on the democratic resources of the legislative process. The legislator might be unresponsive or openly hostile to the interests of 'discrete and insular minorities'[49] that are not capable of forming effective political coalitions and that therefore cannot make their voice heard in the legislative process. The legislator might be prisoner of a moral majority that aims to force everybody to follow its precepts and that has no interest in the rights of people involved in private choices with public consequences (abortion, same-sex marriage, in-vitro fertilization, etc.). The legislator might react to a real or perceived threat to national security with exceptional public order measures that jeopardize democratic politics. Finally, the legislator might simply have forgotten to enact an appropriate provision, to make a necessary exception, or to eliminate an unjustified difference in treatment.

In all these cases, as well as in others,[50] when the legislator is the expression of the arrogance of the powerful, or the expression of the fear by the powerless, or when it is only incapable of foreseeing the consequences of its laws, the nightmare of legal positivism tells us that anybody would like to have a 'judge in Berlin', reasonable and courageous, willing to do the right thing and 'enforce values'.

5. Enforcement of values and institutional context

The hyperbolic nature of the noble dreams and nightmares presented in the preceding paragraph is evident. The point is that the construction of these extreme scenarios shows that the choice between neoconstitutionalism and normative legal positivism—between enforcement of values and strict constructionism, between *Wertjurisprudenz* and *Gesetzespositivismus*—does not depend only on the strength of the principled arguments in their support; the degree of desirability of the noble dream and undesirability of the nightmare is not the only relevant consideration. The choice between the two theories depends also on the greater or lesser plausibility of these scenarios in the context where the interpretive choice takes place. Prudential considerations related to the trust we have, or do not have, in the interpreters of the constitutions and to the foreseeable consequences on the social and institutional settings are therefore relevant for the choice of the criteria to be adopted in

[49] The so-called 'Carolene Products Footnote' by Justice Stone in *United States v Carolene Products Co* 304 US 144 (1938), 152 note 4. On that standard of review, see JH Ely, *Democracy and Distrust: A Theory of Judicial Review* (Harvard University Press 1980) 75 ff.

[50] Another nightmare scenario of normative legal positivism is evoked by PP Portinaro, 'Beyond the Rule of Law: Judges' Tyranny or Lawyers' Anarchy?' in P Costa and D Zolo (n 23) 353 ff., 363: rather than the danger of judicial hegemony (the 'judges' tyranny'), contemporary democracy face the threat of the 'lawyers' anarchy': 'the supremacy of lawyers' partisan and mercenary "expertocracies" that take strategic advantage of the opportunities and resources of a litigation society'.

interpreting the constitution and the rights declarations. Any choice presupposes an institutional context on the background and can be justified only once that context has been analysed and assessed. There might well be a space for a 'pure' theory of legal interpretation, that is, for a theory that does not take into account the context, but the normative claims of such a theory cannot but be very limited.

Apart from the greater or lesser plausibility of the noble dreams and nightmares, it seems that in order to take a stance on the controversy between neoconstitutionalism and normative legal positivism, we must first assess the level of development of the processes of constitutionalization, rights' diffusion and internationalization that represent the institutional premises of the debate on the enforcement of values through legal interpretation. As already stated, neoconstitutionalism is based on a positive assessment of such processes and normative legal positivism on a negative assessment, or at least a sceptical one, which minimizes their importance for legal theory.

Moreover, the choice on the interpretive criteria depends on social, political, and institutional factors such as the following:

(i) The social composition and ideological orientation of the judiciary. *Who are the judges that might enforce values through legal interpretation?* Is it possible to recognize some coherent policy pursued by the judiciary, or by specific courts, and if so, how should we characterize and assess it? Do judges deserve trust? Moreover, which kind of trust do they ask for? Are they public officials legitimized through legal expertise demanding independence from the political power, or are they public communication professionals, voices in the democratic debate, claiming to be representative of civil society, responsive to its needs, and morally responsible?

(ii) The distribution of opportunities of access to justice. *Who can go before the judge?* Which interests succeed in obtaining an adequate consideration and protection in the legal process? Is there any group being systematically disadvantaged? Is the court system sufficiently accessible and effective for those who have an interest in the enforcement of the law?

(iii) The position of the judiciary vis-à-vis the authorities whose acts are subject to its control and who should implement its rulings. *To whom does the judge address?* Is the target a democratically elected legislator, another national or international judge, a state or group of states, or an international or supranational bureaucracy? How likely is it for the judgment to encounter compliance problems and refusal to enforcement?

(iv) The stability and integration of the reference political system. *Where and when does the interpretation take place?* In a (unitary or federal) state or in a (international or supranational) organization? In a period of normal politics[51] or in a revolutionary situation, in an emergency, or during a constitutional transition?

(v) Finally, any stance on the normative criteria for legal interpretation should take into account not only the political and factual context but also the legal context: the normative framework in which interpretation takes place, the object and the standards of the judicial review, its procedures and warranties. In other words, *what is the judge interpreting?* Which rules and principles belong to the legal order where the judge is placed and that the judge applies? Is the judge interpreting the Bill of Rights or the Italian Fascist Labour Charter, a democratic constitution, or the constitution of an authoritarian state? Is the judge interpreting an international treaty like the ECHR, or the treaties establishing an international or supranational organization like the EU? Which act is subject to judicial review: the

[51] B Ackerman, *We The People: Foundations* (Harvard University Press 1991) 230 ff.

legislation enacted by a democratically elected legislator, the agreements reached by states through international negotiation and cooperation, or the regulations adopted by some international or supranational body? Are the principles that the judge must apply the civil, political, and social rights of twentieth-century democratic constitutionalism, or are they the basic principles of the common market, such as the freedom of movement of capital, people, goods and services, equality as fair and undistorted competition, mutual recognition of national regulations, etc?

The debate on the enforcement of values through legal interpretation makes sense only against the background of the legal, political, and social context where it takes place. It is certainly true that legal theory can rely on an implicit analysis and assessment of the context, allocate such analysis and assessment to other disciplines, and avoid thematizing them every time. But the analysis and assessment are nonetheless necessary, because we cannot say anything meaningful on the proper criteria of legal interpretation if we have not first clarified who the judge interpreting the law is, who he is addressing, upon the request of whom, which powers he possesses, what he is interpreting, and under which circumstances.

6. Conclusion

> Therefore, we find ourselves, even if at our own cost, in the best condition to realise how extremely changeable legal ideologies are, as their progressive or reactionary orientation depends on the historical circumstances in which they are endorsed and on the parties that embrace them.
>
> Norberto Bobbio[52]

The conclusion of the preceding paragraph is that the only meaningful answer that legal theory can provide to questions such as 'How should we interpret the constitution and the declarations of rights? Which are the best criteria for legal interpretation? What should be the role of explicit moral reasoning in adjudication?' is 'It depends'. It depends on the degree of development of the rights' constitutionalization, diffusion, and globalization processes, it depends on the way we evaluate the chances and the risks of judicial review in the present context, it depends on who interprets what and under which circumstances. This is a sceptical conclusion on the normative power of a general theory of law but—one might object—it is also an obvious thesis, one that no one would reject and that is therefore lacking in significant effects on the method and subject of legal theory.

It is certainly true that that thesis has already been advanced in the theory of legal interpretation.[53] On closer inspection, it is only a specific application to the field of legal interpretation of the proposition, characteristic of legal realism, according to which a purely normative consideration of legal and jurisprudential issues is insufficient and must be complemented by the assessment of additional factors. These factors are different from the rules and principles directly involved in the legal or jurisprudential issue at hand, as they pertain to the context of the legal decision.

However, although it does not claim to be entirely original, the proposition that it does not make sense to accept or reject a normative theory without having first analysed and

[52] Bobbio (n 28) 5.

[53] e.g. M Troper, *Pour une théorie juridique de l'État* (Presses Universitaires de France 1994) 291, arguing that the constraints on constitutional interpretation are not normative but empirical and depend on the institutional context; CR Sunstein and A Vermeule, 'Interpretation and Institutions' (2003) 101 *Michigan Law Review* 885, criticizing several theories of legal interpretation for their indifference to institutional structure and constraints; SJ Shapiro, *Legality* (Harvard University Press 2011) 331 ff., holding that the attitudes of trust and distrust presupposed by the law are central to the choice of interpretive methodology.

assessed the institutional context where interpretation takes place, is neither obvious because non-controversial, not is it irrelevant. On the contrary, that proposition (i) has been explicitly rejected by one leading legal theorist, (ii) has been implicitly rejected or ignored by many others, and (iii) has important methodological consequences for the theory of constitutional interpretation.

(i) A conscious opponent of the idea that institutional context matters is Ronald Dworkin.

True enough, Dworkin did not pretend to elaborate a general theory of law in the sense of a theory that is applicable to every legal system. As opposed to 'semantic' theories that assume the existence of a social consensus on the facts that make legal propositions true, Dworkin's theory is 'interpretive [...] of a particular stage of a historically developing practice [...] Interpretive theories are by their nature addressed to a particular legal culture, generally the culture to which their authors belong.'[54] This has led some theorists to speak about '*particular* jurisprudence'.[55]

However, nobody could ever deny that in Dworkin's theory, no matter how general or particular it is, the analysis of the institutional context does not play any role. To illustrate his theory of law as integrity, Dworkin relies on the thought experiment of Justice Hercules, which explicitly disregards not only the institutional context, but also the limited intellectual capabilities that the judge can invest in the decision ('an imaginary judge of superhuman intellectual power and patience who accepts law as integrity'[56]). Dworkin refuses to consider the issues of normative theory of interpretation as institutional issues for the (questionable) reason that his theory of the moral reading is applicable to the legislator as well as to the courts because it addresses anybody who wants to interpret the constitution in the best way. Therefore, according to Dworkin, the issues of constitutional interpretation should not be approached by taking into consideration the possible consequences of the general adoption of a certain interpretive method.[57]

(ii) An implicit opponent is Scott Shapiro. In fact, he urges the interpreters to respect the 'economy of trust' inscribed or presupposed by the law, but does not take into consideration the possibility that political and social factors, external to the law, suggest the adoption of interpretive methods not envisaged by the Plane.[58] Moreover, following a line of argument that is quite common in English-speaking analytical jurisprudence, he holds that the debates in legal philosophy, such as the debate on the nature of law, 'can make a profound practical difference', because the solution to interpretive disagreements might depend on them: 'there is often no way to resolve specific disagreements about *the* law without first resolving disagreements about *the nature of law* in general'.[59]

We should reject this line of argument. The justification of theoretical reflection cannot be found in its practical consequences because such consequences are—and for the foregoing reasons should be—quite limited.

(iii) The thesis here advanced does not only have the obvious consequence that there must be stringent limitations to what a general theory of legal interpretation can usefully

[54] R Dworkin, *Law's Empire* (Hart 1986) 102.

[55] B Leiter, *Naturalizing Jurisprudence: Essays on American Legal Realism and Naturalism in Legal Philosophy* (OUP 2007) 162, borrowing the expression from HLA Hart's 'Postscript' in *The Concept of Law* (2nd edn, OUP 1994) 240 f.

[56] Dworkin (n 54) 239. See also Dworkin (n 54) 381.

[57] Dworkin (n 35) 34. The reason is questionable as it takes for granted that it is desirable that different institutions and individuals (the legislator, the courts, the public officials, and the citizens) adopt the same normative theory of constitutional interpretation. If the judges were generally incapable or evil, as is the case in the neoconstitutionalist nightmare, we would rather be inclined to advise against the adoption of Dworkin's moral reading.

[58] Shapiro (n 53). [59] ibid, 28 f.

say on the normative plane. The thesis also has a more interesting consequence concerning the way we should approach legal interpretation 'in action' before the courts.

I would express the point in the following way. Obviously it is possible, and it might often be interesting and useful as well, to criticize the arguments put forward by courts in judgments, and it is possible to do that from a variety of different perspectives: from a legal technical perspective, from the perspective of a moral criticism to the case law, from that of the economic analysis of law, from the viewpoint of the internal logical consistency of the reasoning, etc. However, it does not make sense to assume that the judge must express all the arguments, or even the best arguments, in support of the decision. I am not referring here to the 'unmentionable' reasons, that is, the motives exercising a causal influence on the judge's thought process that cannot be openly stated without rendering illegitimate the decision (e.g., what the judge had for breakfast, his dislike for the parties to the proceeding, etc.). Neither do I refer only to the extra-legal reasons which, although in the abstract relevant for someone, cannot be expressed without the legal community deeming them as inappropriate and devoid of justificatory force in the context of the legal process (e.g., the teachings of the Catholic Church, the programme of a political party, the defence of national identity, the moral progress of mankind, etc.). Rather, I am referring to all those reasons that, although relevant for the decision and endowed with justificatory force in the legal process (e.g., the need to protect fundamental rights or to fulfil the democratic principle), could be appropriate to omit because of the institutional consequences that their use might have.

In a great variety of institutional contexts, there can be several good reasons for saying less than one could do; it can be reasonable for judgments to be brief, poor in theory, lacking candour, assertive and dogmatic, not much persuasive, and irrelevant for the general public debate. If the assessment of the institutional context and of the trust that it is appropriate (not) to have in the constitution's interpreters suggest the acceptance of normative legal positivism, legal argumentation should not be subject to excessive and unrealistic expectations.

In those cases where the assessment of the context of interpretation suggests the opportunity of adopting the views of normative legal positivism, a judgment can be good—although this might seem paradoxical—not just despite its being badly written, but because of it. A judgment can be good because it is written by a judge that does not speak in first person, does not aim to express the true moral values or to be representative of civil society, and does not claim to advance the best justification of the legal system in which he works and of the legal principles that he applies; a judge that is aware of the risk that a diffuse, widely argumentative, solemn, or inspired legal reasoning—a reasoning aimed at persuading or at teaching—can irritate the political system and provoke unsuccessful attempts at emulation or at contrast in the legal community.[60]

[60] For instance, institutional considerations might suggest a constitutional court such as the *Bundesverfassungsgericht* to contain the wide-ranging theoretical inspiration of some of its decisions on European integration (*Maastricht-Urteil*, *BVerfGE* 89, 155, of 12 October 1993; *Lissabon-Urteil*, *BVerfGE* 123, 267, of 30 June 2009) and to limit itself to reviewing compliance with the procedural requirements set out in Article 23 German Basic Law for the changes to the European Treaties (in particular, the enactment of a constitutional amendment). The method of the 'treatise-judgments' might in fact be imitated by courts that are even more cautious, if not hostile, toward European integration than the *Bundesverfassungsgericht*, and this might create a domino effect and disrupt the political process in a hardly resolvable way (as opposed to politicians, constitutional courts cannot sit around a table and have a direct negotiation, and cannot vote and decide by majority). Once that the 'treatise-judgments', each one formulating its guidelines of constitutional policy, have multiplied all over the twenty-eight Member States of the EU, the process of negotiation and ratification, which is not easy, would become even more complicated and uncertain.

3

Pluralism and Systemic Defiance in the EU

Matej Avbelj

1. Introduction

The project of European integration has traditionally had its ups and downs. The years of success and progress are followed by the times of crisis. The latest crisis has, however, spanned a whole decade and has affected the constitutional, political, and economic dimensions of the EU. This is no big surprise. After all, the European project is crisis driven. It started as a reaction to one of the gravest crises of humanity, the Second World War, and it has since not only lived through but also resolved a number of smaller and bigger crises. In so doing, the EU has remained faithful to its modernist character and has striven, time and again, progressively to ensure the realization of its key values. However, recently the crisis has moved to an area where it had not previously been very common: it has affected the core values of the Union: democracy and the Rule of Law.

The first example of such a crisis, admittedly, had already appeared fifteen years ago in the form of Haider's Austria.[1] The reaction of the EU and its Member States to the national coalition which included a political party with at least a dubious democratic and human rights record was somehow both clumsy, due to its ad hoc character, and inadequate in terms of its lacking legal basis and meaningful outcomes.[2] As such, it has therefore been assessed mainly critically.[3] However, the Austrian crisis was considered exceptional, something that is unlikely to be repeated and was institutionally and academically laid to rest other than prompting a minor but not unimportant amendment in the Treaty of Nice to current Article 7 TEU.[4] Yet only a decade later, this expectation has turned out false. Rather than a one-off event, in hindsight the Austrian example appears to be a harbinger of what is now happening, perhaps even systematically. As the most notorious Hungarian,[5]

[1] See Lachmayer in Chapter 25 of this volume; for an earlier debate see GN von Toggenburg, 'La crisi austriaca: delicate equilibrismi sospesi tra molte dimensioni' (2001) *Diritto pubblico comparato ed europeo* 735.

[2] For an overview, see P Cramer and P Wrange, 'The Haider Affair, Law and European Integration' (2000) 28 *Europarattslig tidskrift* 28.

[3] See e.g. W Sadurski, *Constitutionalism and the Enlargement of Europe* (OUP 2012) 84 ff.

[4] The Treaty of Nice introduced a new paragraph 1 providing a legal basis for a preventive monitoring action, see Cramer and Wrange (n 2). See also Lachmayer in Chapter 25 of this volume.

[5] The debate has been extensive. Other than Zoltan in Chapter 26 of this volume, see e.g. J-W Müller, 'The Hungarian Tragedy' (2011) *Dissent Magazine* 5; G Halmai et al., *Opinion on Hungary's New Constitutional Order: Amicus Brief for the Venice Commission on the Transitional Provisions of the Fundamental Law and the Key Cardinal Laws* (2012), http://lapa.princeton.edu/hosteddocs/hungary/Amicus_Cardinal_Laws_final.pdf, accessed 12 October 2016; KL Scheppele, 'The Unconstitutional Constitution' (2 January 2012) *New York Times*, http://krugman.blogs.nytimes.com/2012/01/02/the-unconstitutional-constitution, accessed 12 October 2016; see the vibrant debate at Verfassungsblog, *Hungary—Taking Action*, http://www.verfassungsblog.de/en/category/focus/hungary-taking-action/, accessed 12 October 2016; M Dawson and E Muir, 'Hungary and the Indirect Protection of EU Fundamental Rights and the Rule of Law' (2013) 14 *German Law Journal* 1959; B Bugarič, 'Protecting Democracy and the Rule of Law in the European Union: The Hungarian Challenge' (2014) LSE 'Europe in Question' Discussion Paper Series No 79/2014; A von Bogdandy and P Sonnevend (eds), *Constitutional Crisis in the European Constitutional Area* (Hart, forthcoming).

less publicized Romanian,[6] and mostly unknown Slovenian[7] cases demonstrate, the EU is, at least according to the dominant narrative, facing a backlash in terms of its fundamental values.[8] Political and constitutional developments, failed transitions—mostly, but not exclusively in its new Member States—according to several concerned voices amount to a systemic defiance of the EU's most basic values.[9]

The purpose of this chapter is neither to repeat nor to evaluate the well-known narratives about constitutional backsliding, illiberal turns, and the resurgence of authoritarianism in the EU Member States in question. My aim is to place these developments in a more rigorous theoretical framework in order to elucidate what constitutes systemic defiance in a pluralist EU and how this systemic failure could be remedied while preserving the EU's pluralist structure. I argue that the identification of the alleged systemic defiance by selected EU Member States is contingent on our assumptions about the system at hand, of which these states partake, and on the expectations, even requirements, which flow from this system. The chosen conception of a system then, in turn, also results in the normative prescription of the most suitable remedies for the removal of the perceived systemic problems.[10]

In what follows, this chapter is going to shed light on systemic defiance from a pluralist perspective. It will proceed in four steps. First, I will explain what exactly is meant by pluralism here and what normative advantages are expected to flow from it. Secondly, I will outline my pluralist take on the EU. This will enable me, thirdly, to examine what counts as systemic defiance in a pluralist constellation and what special challenges the latter poses to the identification and remedying mechanisms. By way of conclusion, the chapter will address the question of the extent to which pluralism is at all a viable theoretical framework for addressing the challenges of systemic defiance in the EU. I will argue that if Member States are truly committed to pluralism, this creates a virtuous circle in which their shared normative spirit of pluralism endogenously creates an environment conducive to a sound national constitutional development that naturally precludes the emergence of systemic defiance. In the absence of a genuine commitment to pluralism, the opposite will be true.

2. Pluralism and the pluralist conception of the EU

This chapter proceeds from a normative assumption that the EU is best conceived of in a pluralist form and that any means of addressing the systemic defiance inside the EU must

[6] See also V Perju and KL Scheppele, 'Separating Law and Politics in Romania' (12 July 2012) *New York Times*, http://krugman.blogs.nytimes.com/2012/07/12/guest-post-separating-law-and-politics-in-romania/?_php=true&_type=blogs&_r=0, accessed 12 October 2016; KL Scheppele, *Romania Unravels the Rule of Law* (5 July 2012) *New York Times*, http://krugman.blogs.nytimes.com/2012/07/05/guest-post-romania-unravels-the-rule-of-law/, accessed 12 October 2016.

[7] M Avbelj, 'Failed Democracy: The Slovenian Patria Case – (Non)Law in Context' (2014) unpublished, http://papers.ssrn.com/sol3/papers.cfm?abstract_id=2462613, accessed 12 October 2016, originally published in Slovenian in the journal as M Avbelj, 'Zadeva Patria – (ne)pravo v kontekstu' (2014) 26 *Pravna praksa*.; B Bugarič, 'Crisis of Constitutional Democracy in Post-Communist Europe: "Lands In-between" Democracy and Authoritarianism' (unpublished article, on-file with the author); for a more economic explanation, see R Špruk, 'After 20 Years of Slovenian Status-Quo: the Failure of Gradualism in Slovenia's Post-Socialist Transition' (2012) unpublished, http://mpra.ub.uni-muenchen.de/36268/1/MPRA_paper_36268.pdf, accessed 12 October 2016.

[8] See e.g. J-W Müller, 'Eastern Europe Goes South: Why Democracy is Disappearing in the EU's Newest Member States' (2014) 93 *Foreign Affairs* 2.

[9] See the notes *supra* 6–9.

[10] c.f. C Closa et al., 'Reinforcing Rule of Law Oversight in the European Union' (2014) EUI RSCAS Working Paper 25/2014, who appear to be proceeding from 'the supranational understanding of the Union as a federal legal-political organism, requiring to intervene in defense of the rights and freedoms, which it directly endows the citizens with'.

be such to preserve its pluralist structure. Choosing pluralism[11] is a normative choice[12] informed by a belief that the pluralist structure of the EU most accurately corresponds to what the EU currently is (the descriptive dimension), most persuasively explains how and why the EU currently functions as it does (the explanatory dimension), and also comes with the most appealing normative outcomes and prescriptions for the EU's functioning now and in the future (the normative dimension). However, before outlining this pluralist structure of the EU,[13] it is necessary to explain what exactly I mean by pluralism and why it should be adopted as a paradigm for framing the EU in the first place.

Pluralism is a normative framework for an ordered plurality. Plurality stands for differences and diversity, for the right to be different and to do things one's own way. Plurality is thus an expression of autonomy, first individual and then collective. Autonomy is another word for self-realization or self-fulfilment of each and every individual as she sees fit within the context of an equal right for others. This right, however, emanates from the core value of pluralism, which is concurrently its normative point of departure and its outcome.[14] This is the value of human dignity.[15] Each and every individual has, by way of her very humanity, equal human dignity. This endows her with the said right of self-fulfilment in her own chosen way. As there are many (a plurality of) individuals, there is—as a result of respect for their equal human dignity—many (a plurality) of actual and potential ways of self-fulfilment, many conceptions of a good life. As humans, we therefore necessarily live in a world which is pluralist and therefore diverse. The respect for human dignity mandates that this is good and that plurality should consequently be preserved and even fostered. However, plurality is not the same as pluralism. Pluralism is more than plurality; it is a connected plurality.[16]

Pluralism requires that different entities forming a plurality should be preserved by mutually recognizing this right for each other, but they must simultaneously develop the normative spirit of pluralism underlined by the ethics of a dialectic open self. This is to say that the various entities forming a plurality must commit not only to the preservation of this plurality, but also to the common whole—they have to see themselves as part of the same framework, as if they were travelling in the same boat.[17] Rather than social homogeneity, it is then this normative spirit of pluralism, with a monistic foundation of human

[11] On political pluralism, see G Sartori, 'Understanding Pluralism' (1997) 8 *Journal of Democracy* 58; on moral, philosophical, value pluralism, see J Gray, 'Pluralism and Toleration in Contemporary Political Philosophy' (2000) 48 *Political Studies* 323; for an overview of debates on legal pluralism, see J Griffiths, 'What is Legal Pluralism' (1986) 24 *Journal of Legal Pluralism and Unofficial Law* 1, also, M Delmas-Marty, *Le pluralisme ordonné* (Seuil 2006) 13.

[12] For a view that pluralism as a matter of fact does not even exist in the EU, see G Letsas, 'Harmonic Law: The Case Against Pluralism' in J Dickson and P Eleftheriadis (eds), *Philosophical Foundations of European Union Law* (OUP 2012) 77; for a critique along similar lines, see P Elefetheriadis, 'Pluralism and Integrity' (2010) 23 *Ratio Juris* 365.

[13] For other approaches to a mainly constitutionally pluralist EU, see N MacCormick, 'The Maastricht Urteil' (1995) 1 *European Law Journal* 265; N MacCormick, *Questioning Sovereignty: Law, State and Nation in the European Commonwealth* (OUP 1999); M Avbelj and J Komárek (eds), *Constitutional Pluralism in the EU and Beyond* (Hart 2012); M Poiares Maduro, 'Contrapuntcual Law: Europe's Constitutional Pluralism in Action' in N Walker (ed), *Sovereignty in Transition* (Hart 2003); M Kumm, 'The Jurisprudence of Constitutional Conflict: Constitutional Supremacy in Europe before and after the Constitutional Treaty' (2005) 11 *European Law Journal* 102; N Krisch, *Beyond Constitutionalism—The Pluralist Structure of Postnational Law* (OUP 2012).

[14] T Isiksel, 'Global Legal Pluralism as Fact and Norm' (2013) 2 *Global Constitutionalism* 3, 160, who critiques pluralism for being contingent on other values and not a value in itself. While this is true, there are hardly any values which are entirely self-dependent.

[15] See C McCrudden, *Understanding Human Dignity* (OUP 2014).

[16] For a distinction between pluralism and plurality, see N Walker, 'Constitutionalism and Pluralism in Global Context' in M Avbelj and J Komárek (eds), *Constitutional Pluralism in the EU and Beyond* (Hart 2012).

[17] See e.g. J Tully, *Strange Multiplicity, Constitutionalism in an Age of Diversity* (CUP 1995) and the use of the metaphor of the Spirit of the Haida Gwaii.

dignity, which provides the fibre of cohesiveness required for the viability of any social entity no matter how tiny or small, let alone for polity building.[18] In short, pluralism is understood here as a paradigm which derives from human dignity and is designed to ensure human dignity's preservation and flourishing. It is advanced as a paradigm which can achieve these objectives better than any other normative approach. For this reason, I have relied on it in conceptualizing the EU.

Because of its contested nature and the correspondingly many conceptions of the EU, the latter has long been considered either as a legally and politically unidentified project[19] or as a *sui-generis* entity between an international organization and a federal state which does not really fit any of the well-established constitutional forms. As this *non-liquet* take on the fundamental question of the EU's character is clearly—theoretically and practically—unsatisfactory, I have responded to it by arguing that the EU is best conceived of in pluralist terms as a union.[20] This is a special neither federal nor confederal non-statist entity, founded upon a hybrid Treaty–Constitution agreement between the Member States for an unlimited period. Its constitutional form consists of three dimensions: the legal-institutional, the sociopolitical, and the philosophical.[21]

In legal-institutional terms, the EU is not a constitutional federal quasi-state entity, but a pluralist entity: a union—neither a federal state nor a confederacy.[22] It is composed of three layers: the Member States, the supranational level (the union *stricto sensu*, hereinafter the EU) and the common whole—the EU *lato sensu* (the Union), which encompasses the two aforementioned layers in a pluralist unity, without consuming their autonomy. Indeed, the Member States in the Union remain autonomous legal and political entities. They are autonomous constitutional sites and the same can be said of the supranational level. Moreover, they are both sovereign: Member States in a territorial sense, the EU in a functional sense, which entails that the Union features a pluralist sovereignty.[23]

The Union as such does not have a constitution. The Member States of course preserve their constitutions, and the supranational level can consider its own founding document a constitutional text too. But the supranational constitution is not the constitution of the Union as a common whole. It regulates the autonomous supranational order, but not the equally autonomous national legal orders. This means that there is no principle of supremacy in the pluralist Union. There is primacy, a relational principle through which the supranational and national legal orders are legally bound in a coherent heterarchical, rather than a hierarchical common whole.[24]

In sociopolitical terms the EU is not a single polity, but a composition of a plurality of polities. The national polities are fully fledged. They exercise a genuine political authority over their citizens. The latter's status is not only formal (legally constructed); rather, they

[18] M Avbelj, 'Theory of European Union' (2011) 36 *European Law Review* 818.

[19] As J Delors put it in his Luxembourg speech on 9 September 1985, http://www.cvce.eu/content/publication/2001/10/19/423d6913-b4e2-4395-9157-fe70b3ca8521/publishable_en.pdf, accessed 12 October 2016.

[20] Avbelj (n 18).

[21] For a more in-depth discussion, see M Avbelj, 'Can European Integration be Constitutional and Pluralist – Both at the Same Time?', in M Avbelj and J Komárek (eds), *Constitutional Pluralism in the EU and Beyond* (Hart 2012).

[22] Other scholars have, admittedly in varying ways, also engaged with the concept of the union. See e.g. M Forsyth, *Unions of States* (Leicester University Press 1981); C Schönberger, 'Die Europäische Union als Bund, Zugleich ein Beitrag zur Verabschiedung des Staatenbund-Bundesstaat-Schemas' (2005) 129 *Archiv des öffentliches Rechts* 81; S Fabbrini, *Compound Democracies* (OUP 2007); O Beaud, *Théorie de la fédération* (Presses universitaires de France 2009); A Glencross, *What Makes the EU Viable?* (Palgrave Macmillan 2009); R Schütze, *From Dual to Cooperative Federalism* (OUP 2009); and R Schütze, 'On "Federal" Ground: The European Union as an (Inter)national Phenomenon' (2009) 46 *Common Market Law Review* 1069.

[23] c.f. M Avbelj, 'Theorizing Sovereignty and European Integration' (2014) 27 *Ratio Juris* 344.

[24] M Avbelj, 'Supremacy or Primacy of EU Law – (Why) Does it Matter?' (2011) 17 *European Law Journal* 744.

see themselves in sociological terms as members of their national polity, engaged indirectly and/or directly in its public, political life, from which the national polity draws its democratic legitimacy. However, the supranational level also has a polity status, or at least one in the making. Its legal and political authority is undoubted, whereas its community dimension is still evolving through the concept and practice of EU citizenship. EU citizenship is indeed a fundamental status of the Member States' nationals in the supranational realm.[25] Its gist is to provide a legal and social fabric for the functioning of the supranational democracy, e.g. for legitimating the actions of the EU institutions. EU citizenship also comes with a number of rights whose chief purpose is to protect the individuals against the actions of the EU institutions in the supranational affairs and to be free of discrimination on the basis of nationality when they exercise their free movement rights in the Member States.[26]

It has to be stressed here that the national and supranational levels exist as distinct entities in sociopolitical terms. The supranational level is charged with particular objectives and endowed with enumerated powers for their achievement, whereas the residual competences remain with the Member States. Pluralism in sociopolitical terms entails that the Member States have the right to develop autonomously, in accordance with their own understanding of what constitutes a good constitutional polity.[27] To paraphrase Weiler, they have the right to make their own fundamental choices within their own fundamental boundaries.[28] However, the same holds true for the supranational level.

As Neil Walker has argued, the EU and the Member States are different epistemic sites,[29] which is—from the pluralist perspective—something that is good and ought to be preserved. This also indicates that there is no single common good in the EU, but there are many common goods, which is the good that all constituent entities ought to be committed to and shall work together to preserve. Furthermore, a pluralist Union also means that in case of conflict there is no third, neutral, or ultimate point of view from which the differences between the Member States *inter se* and between the supranational level could be reconciled.[30]

Finally, from a philosophical dimension, the unifying factor of the Union is not uniformity, but pluralism itself, correctly understood. As stressed above, pluralism is not a mere plurality, it is a connected plurality. It requires the mutual recognition of different entities (plurality) and simultaneously imposes on them a commitment to the common whole that they form. This commitment must be genuine, but it cannot be unlimited. Each entity, as a distinct epistemic site, has its own irreducible epistemic core,[31] its own way of comprehending and social being, which cannot always be reconciled with the value claims

[25] For an overview, see D Kostakopoulou, 'The Evolution of European Citizenship' (2008) 7 *European Political Science* 285 and more recently: K Lenaerts, '"*Civis europeus sum*": From the Cross-Border Link to the Status of Citizen of the Union' (2011) 3 *Journal on Free Movement of Workers in the European Community* 6; D Kochenov, 'The Essence of EU Citizenship Emerging from the Last Ten Years of Academic Debate: Beyond the Cherry Blossoms and the Moon?' (2013) 62 *International and Comparative Law Quarterly* 97.

[26] See e.g. C Schönberger, 'European Citizenship as Federal Citizenship, some Citizenship Lessons of Comparative Federalism' (2007) 19 *European Review of Public Law* 63.

[27] I have described this as a polity's public order, see M Avbelj, 'Security and Transformation of the EU Public Order' (2013) 14 *German Law Journal* 2057.

[28] JHH Weiler, 'Fundamental Rights and Fundamental Boundaries: On Standards and Values in the Protection of Human Rights', in N Nuewahl and A Rosas (eds), *The European Union and Human Rights* (Martinus Nijhoff 1995) 52; 'Fundamental boundaries are about the autonomy and self-determination of the communities.'

[29] N Walker, 'The Idea of Constitutional Pluralism' (2002) 65 *Modern Law Review* 361.

[30] ibid, 338.

[31] See N Walker, 'Late Sovereignty in the European Union', in Walker (ed), *Sovereignty in Transition* (Hart 2003) 28. German literature speaks of the '*integrationsfester Kern der staatlichen Verfassung*', see M Nettesheim, 'German report on European Law and National Constitutions' in Lord Slynn and M Andenas (eds), *FIDE XX*

of the other constitutive entities as well as of the common whole, if plurality is to be preserved. A pluralist Union is thus, thanks to plurality, inherently open, therefore unstable, but simultaneously also very strong if this openness is recognized, cherished, and exercised with an eye on the claims of the other entities as well as on the wellbeing of the whole.

3. Systemic defiance from a pluralist perspective

Having outlined the pluralist vision of the EU, how does it bear on the identification of the so-called systemic defiance by its Member States and how could the latter be removed or remedied, while preserving the EU's pluralist structure? This question is motivated by an introductory assumption that a theoretical lens through which a social object is approached determines, to an important extent, its contours as well as the answers to the challenges this social object is confronted by. In other words, a constitutional approach to the questions of systemic defiance will engender different answers as an international or a pluralist approach.[32] However, even before measuring the persuasiveness of these different answers, we must ensure that the debate is structured around a shared concept. We should therefore aim at an abstract definition of systemic defiance,[33] unaffected in its abstraction by any particular theory of the nature of European integration.

Proceeding in this way, systemic defiance in its most general terms can be described as a type of violation of EU law which is especially grave,[34] so that it affects the fundamental requirements of the EU. The fundamental requirements can be imagined in two forms: procedural and substantive. Procedural requirements are about faithfulness to the normative ethos of pluralism which, in the absence of constitutional hierarchy and the related societal monistic glue, holds the Union together and calls for a dual commitment: to the plurality, e.g. in form of the preservation of Member States as autonomous constitutional sites, and to the common integrity of the EU—both at the same time. Substantive requirements, however, determine the substantive constitutional quality of the Member States, the supranational level and the Union *lato sensu*. This substantive quality is described through the values, stipulated mainly in Articles 2 and 3 TEU, but which can also be found in the Charter of Fundamental Rights, as well as in the case law of the CJEU referring to the general principles of law common to the Member States.[35] Most

Congress London 2002 vol 1: National Reports European Union Law and National Constitutions, (British Institute of International and Comparative Law 2002) 130.

[32] For an illustration, see the exchange between various scholars on VerfassungsBlog, http://www.verfassungsblog.de/rescue-package-fundamental-rights-comments-peter-lindseth/#.U8ZJoZR_vst, accessed 12 October 2016.

[33] The need for a shared concept of 'systemic deficiency' was also identified by A von Bogdandy and M Ioannidis, 'Systemic Deficiency in the Rule of Law: What it is, What has been Done, What Can be Done?' (2014) 51 *Common Market Law Review* 96. By demonstrating that the concept of systemic deficiency is already present in the positive law and practice of the EU (Art 7 TEU [2010] OJ C83/01, CJEU asylum jurisprudence), the Council of Europe, and in general international law, they define systemic deficiency as the deficiency 'which is spread throughout and affect the entire system', which in more practical terms marks the threshold point at which 'a legal system fails to exercise its core function, to support reliable expectations'.

[34] The notion of gravity of violation is loose, lax, and inevitably context-dependent. You know it when you see it. As also noted by A von Bogdandy and M Ioannidis (n 33), who confirm this by referring to the CJEU jurisprudence in the field of asylum protection whereby it was claimed that the identification of a systemic deficiency in asylum protection depends on the 'duration and gravity of deficiency', at 33, referring to Joined Cases C-411/10 and C-493/10 *NS v Secretary of State for the Home Department and ME and Others v Refugee Applications Commissioner and Minister for Justice, Equality and Law Reform* [2011] ECLI:EU:C:2011:865.

[35] For an overview, see T Tridimas, *The General Principles of EU Law* (OUP 2006); also M Avbelj, 'European Court of Justice and the Question of Value Choices' (2004) NYU Law School Jean Monnet Working Paper 06/2004.

important among them number respect for human dignity, freedom, democracy, equality, the Rule of Law and human rights.[36] These values are considered by many as universal, which assumes their shared substantive core whose violation is therefore not context dependent.[37] Nevertheless, as this chapter centres on systemic defiance in the EU focusing on the deviationist behaviour of its Member States, it will be concerned with how these values are protected in the EU, therefore context specific, and how they can be violated by the Member States.

In abstract terms, a systemic defiance denotes a behaviour of Member States which violates the procedural and substantive fundamentals of the EU. In practice, these violations can occur through national actions of two sorts. It can be distinguished into actions which are directed either outwardly: towards the EU law; or inwardly, affecting the constitutional structure of the Member States. This chapter will be concerned exclusively with the latter type of infringements, while the former are discussed in other chapters.[38] As these will demonstrate, contrary to the long-dominant narrative following which the Treaty provides a complete system of remedies[39] designed to address the direct violations of EU law, which keeps their occurrence small in number and therefore relatively unproblematic,[40] the truth about the respect of EU law in the Member States might be very different.

While the prevailing opinion has been that the Member States have developed, by and large, and certainly more than is the case under international law, a habit of 'obedience to EU law',[41] this perception has mostly been generated due to the limited focus, centring only on the surface, which consists of the cases brought to the CJEU either by the Commission or the national courts through the preliminary ruling procedure. What is happening beneath the surface, at the heart of the national legal orders, is however much less well known. As argued in particular by Baquero, there are numerous occasions when EU law is violated passively, by simply disregarding the need for its correct application.[42] Such actions and omissions by national judicial and administrative and legislative organs are much more difficult to detect, especially if left unchallenged by the parties who possess a legal interest in the correct application of EU law, but which are perhaps even ignorant of their very existence. Furthermore, even in the cases where a direct violation is established by the CJEU and the Member States pays its fine, practice shows that there is no guarantee

[36] Art 2 TEU.

[37] D Kochenov 'The Issue of Values', in R Petrov and P Van Elsuwege (eds), *The Application of EU Law in the Eastern Neighbourhood of the European Union* (Routledge 2014).

[38] See Gormley in Chapter 4, Wennerås in Chapter 5, Broberg in Chapter 6, Reich in Chapter 7, and Amtenbrink and Repasi in Chapter 9 of this volume.

[39] C-294/83 *Parti écologiste Les Verts* v *European Parliament* [1986] ECLI:EU:C:1986:166, para 23; for criticism, see W Van Gerven, 'Of Rights, Remedies and Procedures' (2000) 37 *Common Market Law Review* 501; A Arnull, 'The Principle of Effective Judicial Protection in EU Law: An Unruly Horse?' (2011) 36 *European Law Review* 51; AH Türk, *Judicial Review in EU Law* (Edward Elgar 2009); LW Gormley, 'Judicial Review: Advice for the Deaf' (2005) 29 *Fordham International Law Journal* 4, 655; R Barents, 'The Court of Justice after the Treaty of Lisbon' (2010) 47 *Common Market Law Review* 709; for a broader overview see also, K Lenaerts et al. (eds), *European Union Procedural Law* (OUP 2014).

[40] Judging at least from the CJEU statistics available at: http://curia.europa.eu/jcms/jcms/Jo2_7032/, accessed 16 October 2016, which reveals a consistent decline in the use of Art 258 TFEU ([2012] OJ C326/01) infringement proceedings. However, due to the Commission's discretionary power to bring a case before the Court, the number of actual violations of EU law cannot be determined on this ground alone.

[41] The concept is most often associated with HLA Hart, *The Concept of Law* (OUP 1994); for its application in EU scholarship see JHH Weiler, 'The Transformation of Europe' (1991) 100 *Yale Law Journal* 2403.

[42] See, J Baquero Cruz, 'The Legacy of the Maastricht-Urteil and the Pluralist Movement' (2008) 14 *European Law Journal* 419, where he refers to his other works: J Baquero Cruz, 'La procédure préjudicielle suffit-elle à garantir l'efficacité et l'uniformité du droit de l'Union européenne?', in L Azoulai and L Burgorgue-Larsen (eds), *L'autorité de l'Union européenne* (Bruylant 2006), 241; and J Baquero Cruz, 'De la cuestión prejudicial a la casación europea: Reflexiones sobre la eficacia y launiformidad del Derecho de la Unión' (2005) 13 *Revista Española de Derecho Europeo* 35.

that the formally compliant Member State will actually *de facto* align its laws and practice with the requirements of EU law.[43]

By contrast, the inwardly oriented actions of the Member States affect the soundness of national constitutional orders and take various forms of national constitutional conflicts and fully blown crises. Their number has grown in recent years, but the EU keeps struggling to find an appropriate response to them. This is unsurprising, as the pluralist structure of the EU already poses two challenges at the level of identification of the cases of alleged systemic defiance.

The first challenge is epistemic. It holds that in a pluralist EU one must be aware of the various epistemic starting points from which a given phenomenon, to be potentially qualified as systemic defiance, is perceived and evaluated. This means that the same empirical phenomena can be known and understood differently. Already, in terms of description we can therefore count on some epistemic margin of error, resulting in uneven identification of a case of systemic defiance. Furthermore, in a pluralist EU these different epistemes are located within their own legal jurisdictions and sociopolitical contexts. National constitutional crises therefore have various faces and, despite several similarities, the reasons behind their occurrence and their actual detrimental effects vary from one state to the next.[44] As these crises are reported from Member State to Member State, or to the supranational level, these reports travel across jurisdictions and therefore across different contexts. The descriptions, explanations, and assessments of these crises depend on the narrators who report on them usually from within their respective national contexts, and the audience, usually outside this context, who receives and distils these reports. Much can get lost in translation across different epistemic sites between the narrators and the audience. Simultaneously, a lot can be added to the reports, thanks to normative biases of different sorts, which are especially present in the politically deeply divisive issues of the alleged cases of systemic defiance. The presence of plurality of epistemes, as a result, calls for caution and self-reflexivity in identifying a particular situation in a Member State as systemically defiant.

The second challenge in the way of identifying a case of systemic defiance is the pluralist structure of the EU itself. The EU ought to be legally pluralist since it is socially pluralist. Legal orders as forms shield different understandings of the substance of values in the constituent entities of the Union. Pursuant to a pluralist understanding, there is no value unity or uniformity in the Union. A great majority of its fundamental constitutional values are shared, but they are not identical or homogeneous across the Union. Even if nominally the same, they are—due to each entity's distinctive episteme—understood and practiced differently. In other words, pluralism allows each entity of a pluralist construction to strike its own balance of fundamental values, to develop its own scheme of justice.[45] The core of

[43] Greece is thus often anecdotally quoted as a country which complies with the CJEU rulings by paying the court mandated penalties but without actually bringing its legislation in line with EU law. For an overview, see TA Börzel et al., 'Recalcitrance, Inefficiency, and Support for European Integration: Why Member States Do (Not) Comply with European Law' (2007) Center for European Studies Working Paper 151/2007, http://www.people.fas.harvard.edu/~ces/publications/docs/pdfs/Borzel_CES_151.pdf, accessed 12 October 2016.

[44] The Hungarian example has been described as constitutional backsliding into authoritarian or illiberal constitutionalism. The Romanian case has been compared to it, but downplayed in terms of its less encompassing scope, making it less prone to turn into a proper dictatorship. On the other hand, the Slovenian example is best described as a diminished form of democracy, where under the guise of impeccable formal adherence to the Rule of Law and democracy, a *de-facto*, informally captured and therefore failed constitutional democracy lurks. See in particular, Perju and Scheppele (n 6) and others available at: http://lapa.princeton.edu/newsdetail.php?ID=63, accessed 16 October 2016; see also Bugarič (n 7).

[45] To paraphrase Rawls, a scheme of justice draws together its political and social institutions as one system of cooperation, which is publicly known to rely on principles of justice that all polity members consider just and therefore generally comply with it; J Rawls, *Political Liberalism* (CUP 1993) 35.

these values even form the so-called 'constitutional identity' of a Member State, which is now explicitly safeguarded by EU law.[46] This means that the Member States are entitled, even by EU law, to be different, to do things their own way. They have the right to a substantive margin of appreciation, as it were.

Accordingly, since the Union is a pluralist entity, not all departures from the EU's laws or values and not each and every example of constitutional conflict in the Member States can be considered systemic defiance. Furthermore, in a pluralist constellation there is also no ultimate authority to decide for all the entities involved on a single correct balance of fundamental values or on the ultimate suitability of a given constitutional settlement. This again speaks in favour of a fine-tuned approach to the alleged cases of systemic defiance. From a pluralist perspective the identification of a particular conduct as systemically defiant therefore calls for some self-restraint. In the same way, however, it should be followed by remedying the case of systemic defiance once identified.

Two reasons dictating a circumspect remedial approach are especially worth pointing out here:[47] the legal–jurisdictional reason and the reason related to democratic legitimacy. Starting with the former, since the Union is a pluralist entity composed of autonomous constitutional sites, boundaries, jurisdictions, and competences matter. They do so not merely because of the formal reasons (e.g. because the Treaty says so), but because they are a guarantee and a sign of respect for autonomous development: for a veritable self-government. This means that systemic defiance, once identified, can be approached only through the legal and political means provided for by the Treaty. The legal–jurisdictional dimension namely requires respect for the principle of conferral of competences.[48]

The EU can therefore act only when it is authorized, and in so doing it must closely respect the principles of subsidiarity and proportionality. Furthermore, for the EU to act, there must be a link between the national breach and EU law. The cases of national inwardly oriented actions are difficult to address precisely because their link with EU law is remote and tenuous. As EU law in principle does not apply in purely national circumstances,[49] to trigger EU action the case of systemic defiance must involve an external dimension. A national constitutional crisis would therefore need to cause some negative externalities: be it to the other Member States, to the EU at the supranational level, or to the EU citizens.

Finally, in pursuing its remedial measures the EU must be cognizant of its democratic dimension. According to the mainstream perception, the EU has traditionally suffered from a democratic deficit.[50] Its legitimacy for intervening in national cases of alleged

[46] Art 4(2) TEU: 'The Union shall respect the equality of Member States before the Treaties as well as their national identities, inherent in their fundamental structures, political and constitutional, inclusive of regional and local self-government. It shall respect their essential State functions, including ensuring the territorial integrity of the State, maintaining law and order and safeguarding national security. In particular, national security remains the sole responsibility of each Member State'.

[47] Von Bogdandy and Ioannidis are also aware of 'the numerous legal problems with the measures adopted to address systemic deficiencies, in particular fundamental rights concerns as to democratic legitimacy' (n 33) 94.

[48] Art 4(1) TEU.

[49] What counts as a purely internal, national situation, excluding the application of EU law, cannot be easily identified from the Court's, admittedly, incoherent and somehow fuzzy case law, whose clarity has only worsened with the move from the internal market to the non-economic EU citizenship dimension. Nevertheless, the borderline between the application of national and EU law, even if blurred, remains and must be heeded—especially from the pluralist perspective—to respect the vertical allocation of powers between EU law and national law. See Lenaerts (n 25); K Lenaerts, 'Federalism and the rule of law: Perspectives from the European Union Court of Justice' (2011) 33 *Fordham International Law Journal* 1338; also N Nic Shuibhne, 'Free Movement of Persons and the Wholly Internal Rule: Time to Move on?' (2002) 39 *Common Market Law Review* 731.

[50] According to Closa et al. (n 10) 26 'two primordial features of any functioning democracy are missing—the grand principles of accountability and representation'; see also, W Sadurski, 'Democratic Legitimacy of the

systemic defiance is therefore limited.[51] In contrast with classical federal states, such as the US or Germany, the locus of democratic legitimacy in the EU is still at the national rather than at the supranational level.[52] This means that the supranational level in the EU is, as a matter of democratic legitimacy, more constrained in terms of the scope and nature of the corrective mechanisms which can be applied against the recalcitrant Member States.

These pluralist caveats in identifying and remedying the cases of systemic defiance disappear, of course, if we approach the EU from a constitutional perspective. In this mode the EU is still conceived of as a kind of multilevel, but ultimately monist structure.[53] Accordingly, the supranational level of the EU, like the federal level in federal states, possesses both the competences and legitimacy for intervening in the 'recalcitrant' Member States. The rationale behind this constitutional approach pretty much follows the rationale that has undergirded the 'incorporation' of the Bill of Rights in the US.[54] While the Bill of Rights was originally adopted with the aim of binding the federal level only, it was later selectively, but *de facto* 'incorporated', e.g. used against the states through the Fourteenth Amendment's procedural and substantive due process clause.[55]

In so doing, and distinct from a pluralist entity, within the scope of the incorporated rights the federal government and the states are bound by the same, e.g. federal, standards of human rights protection.[56] The rights protection is thus constitutionalized, made uniform top-down and is—as has also not been uncommon to propose in the field of EU law[57]—tied to the essential status of US citizens. Moreover, since the locus of democratic legitimacy, the people, in a federal state exists at a federal level, such a monistic constitutionalization has also come to be regarded as justified in democratic terms. Finally, for all these reasons a federal state such as the US also possesses, as a means of a last resort, a concrete repressive mechanism, the police and the army, to bring a recalcitrant State back to compliance.[58] Obviously, none of this exists in the EU, conceived of in pluralist terms. And neither would it, was the EU a mere international organization. In that case the Member States would simply fall back on the principles of sovereign equality and

European Union: A Diagnosis and Some Modest Proposals' (2012) 32 *Polish Yearbook of International Law* 9; M Avbelj, 'Can the new European Constitution Remedy the EU Democratic Deficit?' (10 March 2005) Open Society Institute, https://www.opensocietyfoundations.org/briefing-papers/can-new-european-constitution-remedy-eu-democratic-deficit, accessed 12 October 2016; following JHH Weiler, 'The Transformation of Europe' (1991) 100 *Yale Law Journal* 2455 in stressing the distinction between the practically non-existent formal, but very much present social democratic deficit.

[51] For a particularly strong warning in this regard see Closa et al. (n 10) 29: '[The EU] should simultaneously hurry up and put its own democratic house in order lest it be reminded that those living in glass houses should be careful when throwing stones.'

[52] But compare with A Jakab, 'Full Parliamentarisation of the EU without Changing the Treaties: Why We Should Aim for It and How Easily It Can be Achieved?' (2011) NYU Law School Jean Monnet Working Paper 03/2012, 19 ff.

[53] For an overview of constitutional accounts of the EU, see M Avbelj, 'Questioning EU Constitutionalisms?' (2008) 9 *German Law Journal* 26.

[54] See e.g. AR Amar, 'The Bill of Rights as a Constitution' (2010) 100 *Yale Law Journal* 1136.

[55] 'No state shall make or enforce any law which shall abridge the privileges or immunities of citizens of the United States; nor shall any state deprive any person of life, liberty, or property, without due process of law; nor deny to any person within its jurisdiction the equal protection of the laws'.

[56] Contrast this with the CJEU permitting greater discretion to the Member States when human rights protection is at stake, see e.g. C-112/00 *Eugen Schmidberger, Internationale Transporte und Planzüge v Republik Österreich* [2003] ECLI:EU:C:2003:333 and Case C-36/02 *Omega Spielhallen- und Automatenaufstellungs-GmbH v Oberbürgermeisterin der Bundesstadt Bonn* [2004] ECLI:EU:C:2004:614.

[57] See e.g. D Kochenov, 'A Real European Citizenship: A New Jurisdiction Test. A Novel Chapter in the Development of the Union in Europe' (2011) 11 *Columbia Journal of European Law* 59 ff.

[58] For an excellent presentation of a variety of ways of 'regulating' the States by the national federal authorities in the USA, see Tushnet in Chapter 18 of this volume.

non-intervention and their constitutional crises, no matter how severe, would be considered as purely domestic affairs.

Having said all this, the implications for addressing and resolving systemic defiance in a pluralist setting are the following.[59] Where a Member State's internal constitutional conflict amounts to systemic defiance, the EU should first approach it with a degree of trust that a national polity is able to resolve it by itself. This is a reflection of the Member State's constitutional autonomy. If a Member State fails to act, the Union can, and depending on the gravity of the situation even should, proceed to taking measures. However, this must be done in accordance with the law and, more broadly, in accordance with the pluralist character of the Union.

Any EU intervention must be taken while recalling that the Union too lacks legal powers, that its democratic legitimacy is not unquestioned,[60] that there should be no uniform constitutional model across the Union and that even the most fundamental constitutional values might legitimately be understood and practiced differently in different Member States. A pluralist vision therefore rejects the extension of the EU's competences beyond its enumerated powers. Indeed, there should be no more room for integration by stealth, as was practiced in the 1960s and 1970s.[61] As the Union is a pluralist entity, the Member States have to be taken seriously. The textual constraints to which they have subjected the EU institutions should be heeded. This includes, for example, Article 51 Charter of Fundamental Rights. If a constitutional approach supports the Charter's incorporation and proposing to widen its application beyond its textual confines to make it fully enforceable against the Member States,[62] the pluralist does not.

The Court too should be aware of its institutional limits and avoid unprincipled, case-specific departures from its established jurisprudence.[63] The Commission should act in accordance with the law, especially when applying interim sanctions suspending payments from cohesion funds. Any action taken by the EP should be conducted with the political divisiveness of the situation in mind and simultaneously by remaining faithful to the core values of the Union, which should be elevated above short-term partisan interests.[64] Any measures taken by EU institutions should be guided by the principles of subsidiarity and proportionality. They should match the gravity of the alleged national violation. The measures should be intensified incrementally: ranging from the least to the most intrusive. Assembling these measures on a continuum, they can consist of soft diplomatic, dialogical

[59] This draws on my earlier contribution to Verfassungsblog, M Avbelj, 'The Hungarian Dilemma from a Pluralist Perspective' (*VerfassungsBlog*, 8 May 2013), http://www.verfassungsblog.de/the-hungarian-dilemma-from-a-pluralist-perspective/#.U9eH_fl_sgU, accessed 12 October 2016.

[60] Recently Somek has argued that 'the Union looks quite disastrous when approached from the perspective of political self-determination', see A Somek, 'Europe: Political, not Cosmopolitan' (2014) 20 *European Law Journal* 142.

[61] See D Thym, 'Rescue Package for Fundamental Rights: Comments by D Thym' (*VerfassungsBlog*, 23 February 2012), http://www.verfassungsblog.de/en/rescue-package-for-fundamental-rights-comments-by-daniel-thym, accessed 12 October 2016; also A Menon and S Weatherill, 'Democratic Politics in a Globalizing World: Supranationalism and Legitimacy in the European Union' (2007) LSE Working Paper 13/2007.

[62] See Jakab in Chapter 14 of this volume.

[63] One such example is C-34/09 *Gerardo Ruiz Zambrano v Office national de l'emploi* [2011] ECLI:EU:C:2011:124.

[64] An example of good practice is a Tavares report on the situation of fundamental rights: standards and practices in Hungary (pursuant to the European Parliament resolution of 16 February 2012, 2012/2130(INI)), http://www.europarl.europa.eu/sides/getDoc.do?pubRef=-//EP//TEXT+REPORT+A7-2013-0229+0+DOC+XML+V0//EN, accessed 12 October 2016.

measures, and benchmarking,[65] political pressure, initiation of legal proceedings,[66] actual filing of applications before the CJEU, court penalties,[67] economic sanctions in form of withheld payments from EU funds[68] or in form of withholding tranches in the EU economic adjustment programmes,[69] and suspension of voting rights pursuant to Article 7 TEU.[70] Perhaps further sanctions could be provided for after a Treaty change.[71] Not all of them should necessarily be of general application, but could be more specifically tailored to the needs or requirements of particular Member States, as is already the case with Romania, Bulgaria,[72] to a certain extent with Croatia,[73] and of course with the countries in the EU bailout programmes.[74] Last but not least, the possibility of expelling an utterly rogue Member State should not be excluded.[75]

It is clear that the pluralist vision already allows for an integrated legal and political approach to sanctioning a recalcitrant Member State today, without any Treaty amendment.[76] The Commission's proposal for a new EU framework to strengthen the Rule of Law goes in that direction.[77] In legal terms, Kim Lane Scheppele's proposal could be quoted as one of such, at least in theory, well thought through mechanism. She has argued for a 'systemic infringement action'.[78] This would enable the Commission in cases of national systemic defiance which could not be addressed through the present piecemeal and often protracted individual infringement actions, to bundle together a number of individual

[65] See e.g. the so-called EU Justice Scoreboard designed to permit a comparative evaluation of the EU Member States' judicial systems across a variety of criteria: European Commission, The EU Justice Scoreboard: a Tool to Promote Effective Justice and Growth, http://ec.europa.eu/justice/effective-justice/files/justice_scoreboard_communication_en.pdf, accessed 12 October 2016.

[66] Be it directly on the basis of Art 258 TFEU [2012] OJ C326/01 read with Art 260 TFEU [2012] OJ C326/01, or indirectly using the preliminary ruling procedure of Art 267 TFEU [2012] OJ C326/01.

[67] For an overview and a rather sceptical analysis of the CJEU's fining measures, see B Jack, 'Article 260(2) TFEU: An Effective Judicial Procedure for the Enforcement of Judgments' (2013) 19 ELJ 404. See also Wennerås in Chapter 5 of this volume.

[68] See most recently, V Gulyas, 'Hungary Under Commission Scrutiny on EU Funds' (28 August 2014) *The Wall Street Journal*, http://blogs.wsj.com/emergingeurope/2014/04/28/hungary-under-commission-scrutiny-on-eu-funds/, accessed 12 October 2016; or against Croatia due to its *Lex Perković* case, see N Nielsen, 'EU tells Croatia to change law or face sanctions' (21 August 2013) *EU Observer*, http://euobserver.com/justice/121162, accessed 12 October 2016.

[69] See e.g. European Commission, Financial Assistance to Greece, http://ec.europa.eu/economy_finance/assistance_eu_ms/greek_loan_facility/, accessed 12 October 2016.

[70] For a broad analysis of the potentials and limits of Art 7 TEU, see C Pinelli, *Protecting the Fundamentals: Article 7 of the Treaty on the European Union and Beyond* (Foundation for European Progressive Studies, 2012). However, as has been noted by von Bogdandy and Ioannidis (n 33) 85, Art 7 TEU is not really well suited to addressing cases of systemic defiance, since it is insufficiently inclusive. Moreover, it has never been used and the Commission appears reluctant to put it into action.

[71] Closa et al. (n 10) 8, admit that while the chances for bringing about the Treaty amendments are really scarce, they nevertheless believe that the amendments should be considered with all seriousness in the future.

[72] The former two countries are subject to the cooperation and verification mechanism, see von Bogdandy and Ioannidis (n 33) 85. See also, MA Vachudova and A Spendzharova, 'The EU's Cooperation and Verification Mechanism: Fighting Corruption in Bulgaria and Romania after EU Accession' (2012) *European Policy Analysis* 1.

[73] See in particular, Art 36, Act concerning the conditions of accession of the Republic of Croatia and the adjustments to the Treaty on European Union, the Treaty on the Functioning of the European Union and the Treaty Establishing the European Atomic Energy Community [2012] OJ L112/21.

[74] See e.g. I Katsaroumpas, 'EU Bailout Conditionality as a De Facto Mode of Government: A Neo-Liberal 'Black Hole' for the Greek Collective Labour Law System?' (2013) 4 *CritQ* 345; P Tsoukala, 'Euro Zone Crisis Management and the New Social Europe' (2013) 20 *Columbia Journal of European Law* 31.

[75] As proposed e.g. by C Closa in Closa et al. (n 10) 20.

[76] For an in-depth analysis of actual and potential legal bases and procedures to tackle the national cases of systemic defiance, see Closa et al. (n 10) Part 1.

[77] See Communication of the Commission to the European Parliament and the Council on A New European Framework to strengthen the Rule of Law, COM(2014) 158 final, Brussels 11 March 2014.

[78] KL Scheppele, 'Making Infringement Procedures More Effective: A Comment on Commission v Hungary' (*VerfassungsBlog*, 30 April 2014), http://www.verfassungsblog.de/en/making-infringement-procedures-more-effective-a-comment-on-commission-v-hungary, accessed 12 October 2016.

infringements demonstrating the Member State's systemic violation either of the principle of sincere cooperation[79] or even of the fundamental values of the Union, contained in Article 2 TEU. With the exception of the latter part of the proposal—which is in my mind untenable because, due to its wording, Article 2 is not directly applicable and consequently enforceable against the Member States—Scheppele's creative procedural proposal remains within the language of the Treaty, introduces new potential avenues for enforcing compliance, and is therefore compatible with the pluralist vision of the EU.

The same can be said of Jan-Werner Müller's political proposal for creating a Copenhagen Commission charged with protecting the Europe's *acquis normatif*.[80] Composed of bureaucrats, members of the judiciary and peers (statesmen), it would be entrusted with a mandate of offering comprehensive and consistent political judgments.[81] These would assess national compliance with the minimal criteria of Rule of Law and democracy, also known as the Copenhagen criteria,[82] and exert political peer-pressure on the recalcitrant Member States. Despite facing criticism for duplication of existing institutions,[83] such as the Venice Commission, this political proposal is a welcome one. Not only is it fully compatible with the dialogical requirement of pluralism, as it stems from the dialectic open-self, it also comes as an inevitable complement to the legal dimension for those occasions when the legal solutions run out, or as we shall see below, are not even available.

4. Pluralism: its strengths and weaknesses

Having outlined the pluralist vision of the EU and its suggested approach to the cases of systemic defiance, a critical observer might arrive at the conclusion that pluralism's advocated self-restraint not only inhibits an efficient approach to recalcitrant Member States, but even provides the latter with a pretext for successfully escaping responsibility for their violations, even of the most fundamental EU values. As we have seen, the Member States can avail themselves of the epistemic margin of error, they can rely on the substantive margin of appreciation inherent to the pluralist Union, and they can appeal in their defence against supranational intervention to the principles of conferral, subsidiarity, proportionality and, last but not least, the lack of democratic underpinnings to the supranational institutions.

However, in reality no such conclusion is warranted. The pluralist nature of the EU leaves no room for pretexts for the recalcitrant Member States. Pluralist insistence on the respect for national constitutional autonomy, for the national pluralist-self, cannot be misused or even abused to legitimate national measures corrosive of the EU fundamental values under the guise of pluralism. In short, pluralism cannot be defied pluralistically. A pluralist European integration assumes that its Member States are well-ordered societies.[84] After all, this is what the entire process of pre-accession conditionality is dedicated

[79] Art 4(3) TEU. [80] See Müller in Chapter 13 of this volume. [81] ibid. [82] ibid.

[83] J Komárek, 'The EU Is More Than A Constraint On Populist Democracy' (*VerfassungsBlog*, 25 March 2013), http://www.verfassungsblog.de/the-eu-is-more-than-a-constraint-on-populist-democracy, accessed 12 October 2016.

[84] Not necessarily well ordered in a Rawlsian sense whereby 'everyone accepts and knows that the others accept the same principles of justice and that the basic social institutions generally satisfy and are generally known to satisfy these principles', but in the sense that the conventional standards of Rule of Law and democracy are well established. For Rawls' concept of a well-ordered society, see J Rawls, *A Theory of Justice* (Harvard University Press 1971), 5.

to.[85] A pluralist European integration can therefore only exist if its Member States are *ab initio* committed to pluralism.

If so, a Member State will not rely on a pluralist structure and invoke its autonomy in order to conceal or to defend its internal constitutional misgivings. Pluralism leaves no room for complacency, for self-sufficiency, for self-closure, but it requires the ethics of a dialectic open-self. In other words, any Member State which in defence of its own autonomy, invokes the pluralist structure of the Union, can only do so after it has given effect to pluralism within its own constitutional polity. In the circumstances of constitutional crisis within a Member State, the various parties, but especially those in power (the government, the ruling coalition), have to be able to enter into a meaningful dialogue with those holding opposing views, as well as if need be, with their counterparts in the Union, and justify their respective positions. In this process of justification, the conflicting sides within a Member State as well as the Member State with regard to the EU institutions must genuinely consider the counter-arguments, be open to reconsider their own positions and amend them.

In that way, if Member States are truly committed to pluralism, this creates a virtuous circle in which their shared normative spirit of pluralism endogenously creates an environment conducive to a sound national constitutional development which naturally precludes the emergence of systemic defiance. This is a special virtue of pluralism which—unlike constitutionalism which in a statist-federalist manner imposes (or creates an impression of imposition) of the 'foreign' constitutional values top-down—grows these values bottom-up. However, as the historical experience of failed unions teaches us,[86] pluralism is a demanding and unstable normative order. It requires a lot of self-discipline and commitment. If this is not present or if it fades away, if a country gives up on the normative spirit of pluralism, as is patently the case when systemic defiance occurs, what can be done then?

Three alternatives appear to be available: pluralism can be reintroduced into a Member State endogenously or exogenously, and if these two alternatives fail: a Member State can be expelled from the Union. Of course, it is also possible to do nothing, but this is not really a meaningful alternative. From a pluralist perspective, the first alternative is the most attractive. Pluralism, defined as a connected plurality whose connection hinges on the commitment to this plurality and to the common whole, is truly, perhaps even only, viable if it is endogenous. The commitment constitutive of normative spirit of pluralism must be genuine, it must be truly internalized by the participating entities and their members. A non-genuine commitment, a commitment which is forced from the outside, which is exogenous, is a contradiction in terms. It is not a commitment, but more or less reluctant obedience. This demonstrates what has in recent years been proven time and again in the practice of international relations, that pluralism, as a prerequisite for a modern democratic state based on the Rule of Law—that is for a well-ordered society—cannot be simply exported from one polity into another.[87]

Pluralism is thus a very vulnerable and frail state of society. If it is present, it sets in motion through social practices all other virtuous elements of a well-ordered society; however, if it is lacking or even absent, then it is hard and laborious to bring it about.

[85] For its critique see D Kochenov, *EU Enlargement and the Failure of Conditionality: Pre-accession Conditionality in the Fields of Democracy and the Rule of Law* (Kluwer Law International 2008).

[86] M Avbelj, 'Theory of European Union' (2011) 36 *European Law Review* 818.

[87] The literature critiquing the export of democracy, especially to the Middle East or to the Balkans, is vast. See e.g. CC Coyne, *After War: The Political Economy of Exporting Democracy* (Stanford University Press 2008).

The EU Member States, whose internal constitutional crises bring them on the verge of systemic defiance, are almost unexceptionally those whose still recent totalitarian historical legacy has caused the virtual elimination of their in any case limited pluralist social capital. These are, as I have described them elsewhere,[88] simply not normal countries. In the absence of pluralism, they have been able to meet the formal criteria for the membership in the EU, but substantively they remain half-built democracies, destined to swing from the leftist to the rightist semi-authoritarianism and back.

These countries therefore need time before they can develop into well-ordered societies. However, they need time which is spent wisely and not wasted without anything being done. In the absence of pluralism, the structures that do not favour pluralism work hard to ossify the system, to capture and hijack the state, and to lock it into the status quo for the time to come. To prevent systemic defiance, the EU would therefore need to devise policies and mechanisms which would strengthen the endogenous development of pluralism in its troubled Member States. These mechanisms can combine a range of tools, on the one hand sanctioning those who threaten pluralism, while rewarding those who foster it on the other. These rewards should, however, be less political and institutional than pecuniary, in order to stimulate pluralism at its social root by supporting civil society. No matter how unorthodox this might sound, the EU would need to recognize that since its pre-accession screening mechanisms have succeeded only partly, it is therefore required, as a result to address the democratic (and Rule of Law) deficits not at the supranational but at the national level.[89]

What has just been suggested contrasts significantly with the court-centred approaches to recalcitrant Member States typically favoured by legal scholars. One of the most resounding proposals of this kind has recently been made by von Bogdandy and his team. They have advanced a 'reverse *Solange*' approach.[90] According to this proposal, the Member States are presumed to be well-ordered societies and therefore free of the EU's interference as long as they do not cause systemic violations. In that case, the presumption is rebutted and the systemic defiance should be addressed through individuals relying on the essence of their status as EU citizens, turning to the national courts and the CJEU.[91] However, this proposal overlooks[92] that nowhere can systemic defiance be resolved through courts which have proverbially lacked both purse and sword, let alone achieving this in post-totalitarian countries in which the judiciary has been one of the arms of the regime and is usually one of the culprits of systemic defiance.[93]

Not all problems in a polity, especially those of systemic character, can be solved through the law, let alone by the courts. The law has its inherent limits.[94] As I have argued elsewhere,[95] the values and objectives of Article 2 TEU, which are threatened in cases of

[88] Matej Avbelj, 'Transformation in the Eye of the Beholder' in M Bobek (ed), *Central European Judges under the European Influence* (Hart 2015).

[89] I have long argued that the alleged EU democratic deficit is in fact national at root, see Avbelj (n 50).

[90] A von Bogdandy et al., 'Reverse *Solange* – Protecting the essence of fundamental rights against EU Member States' (2012) 49 *Common Market Law Review* 489.

[91] ibid, 490.

[92] In a subsequent article von Bogdandy and Ioannidis acknowledge that the reverse *Solange* approach is indeed inappropriate for the cases of systemic deficiency; von Bogdandy and Ioannidis (n 33) 84.

[93] Again, this conclusion might vary from one country to another, and does not apply to Hungary, as was kindly brought to my attention by A Jakab.

[94] Or to paraphrase MacCormick, who has also stressed, albeit in a somewhat different context that 'not all legal problems can be solved legally', see MacCormick (n 13) 265. See also M Avbelj, 'The Inherent Limits of Law – the Case of Slovenia' (*VerfassungsBlog*, 6 December 2013), http://www.verfassungsblog.de/the-inherent-limits-of-law-the-case-of-slovenia, accessed 12 October 2016.

[95] Avbelj (n 94).

systemic defiance, can never be restored through the courts, neither national nor supranational. For law is not some almighty, metaphysical force, but is made and enforced by people of flesh and blood. The actual realization of the values of Article 2 TEU depends on the critical mass of institutional actors enforcing them with their own integrity. Hart and Dworkin, perhaps unintentionally, meet at this point. To have the democracy and the Rule of Law proper, the institutional actors (indeed everyone) have to integrate their underlying values as part of their internal point of view, turning them into their rule of recognition.[96] But they will only be able and willing to do so, if they are themselves men and women of integrity.[97] As Joseph Weiler once wrote: democracy of vile persons will be vile.[98] And so will be the law, I can add.

In the absence of the endogenous social capital of pluralism, the alternative to hand is to opt for a completely exogenous solution of a federal sort: to constitutionalize human rights protection in the Union, developing uniform standards and their top-down imposition by legal and political means. However, this is not very likely to happen in the EU as it presently stands, but if it did occur, it would mark the end of its pluralist nature. This alternative therefore, for obvious reasons, does not enjoy the support of a pluralist account. Finally, giving up on a Member State which has decided to pursue its own non-pluralist systemically defiant course and excluding it from the Union, is also not an attractive solution. It means preserving the pluralist structure of the EU in its shrunken form, but leaving the people in an expelled Member State in the hands of their rouge regime.[99] This is certainly not the normative spirit of pluralism at its best and it does not contribute to the flourishing of the human dignity of the individuals in an excluded Member State.[100]

Having said all this, alternative number one is obviously the most optimal solution. But this comes with a sobering conclusion too: if pluralism is not endogenous, it basically does not exist. Therefore, if the EU is to remain a pluralist entity—the EU and the Member States—in particular those in the deviationist camp—should be aware of the fragility of its pluralist construction and act accordingly. If they do not, the system will either be constitutionalized top-down or disintegrate. Either way, something of great importance to the European project will be lost.

5. Conclusion

In this chapter I have approached the questions of systemic defiance in the EU through the prism of pluralism. This was a normative choice motivated by the advantages expected to stem from an EU conceived of in pluralist terms. I have therefore argued that any approach to cases of systemic defiance in the EU should be devised so that the EU's pluralist character is preserved. Admittedly, this leaves us in many respects with our hands tied when it comes both to identifying as well as remedying cases of systemic defiance. At the same time, the pluralist perspective allows for an integral approach to remedying systemic defiance in the EU, drawing together legal, political, and economic means. But all these measures are

[96] Hart (n 41).

[97] On Law as integrity, see R Dworkin, *Law's Empire* (Harvard University Press 1986); on integrity in general, see L McFall, 'Integrity' (1987) 98 *Ethics* 1.

[98] JHH Weiler, 'In Defence of the Status Quo: Europe's Constitutional Sonderweg', in JHH Weiler and M Wind (eds), *European Constitutionalism Beyond the State* (CUP 2003) 18.

[99] Hungary appears to be openly treading such a path: http://www.nytimes.com/2014/08/02/opinion/a-test-for-the-european-union.html?_r=0, accessed 12 October 2016.

[100] For a similarly sceptical approach to this alternative, see Closa et al. (n 10).

unlikely to succeed if the defiant Member States have suppressed that critical degree of pluralism necessary for the building of a well-ordered society.

I believe that most of the remedial attempts and the discussions surrounding them have failed to recognize this problem. They have all rushed at the symptoms, at the visible pathological outcomes caused by the national constitutional conflicts and crises, without looking for the deeper societal causes which have provoked these problems in the first place. In addressing the particular cases of Member States, at least the academic debate started with a presumption that while previously they had all been normal states, now—with this or that particularly authoritarian government in place—the backsliding has begun. It was this unwarranted assumption that has prompted many academic observers and institutional stakeholders not to ask the right questions, which has consequently resulted in the absence of the right answers. Before devising new legal, political, economic, perhaps even broader institutional means for dealing with the recalcitrant Member States, it is therefore necessary to inquire into the real causes for a Member State's recalcitrance.

My assumption, judging also from my personal experience with a *de facto* failed Slovenian democracy,[101] is that the recalcitrant Member States—most, if not all, ex-communist countries—simply lack the very pluralist preconditions for developing a genuine democracy and the Rule of Law. Throughout their history these countries were never marked by pluralism and liberalism, and even to the extent that they were, those elements were extinguished during their communist period. To ensure that these Member States stop being a potentially permanent source of systemic defiance, the EU would need to develop a comprehensive approach to fostering pluralism and the other societal prerequisites of the Rule of Law and democracy on the ground within them. Making this step is of utmost importance. Due to the deterioration of the geostrategic situation at the EU's eastern borders, the EU faces real threats that the elites in its failing, backsliding, and captured states align with those who would enable them to preserve their desired status quo. In the worst-case scenario this would turn the recalcitrant Member States into Trojan horses within Europe.[102]

Simultaneously, at least some of the old Member States, which are much more consolidated democracies and live much more closely, but of course not entirely, up to the ideal of a well-ordered society, have started to face their own systemic problems related to the Rule of Law and democracy. These are mainly due to their diminishing economic power, which is moving to the global East, resulting in the deteriorating position of the middle class which has traditionally formed the backbone of democracy. The decline of the middle class is combined with a simultaneous increase in the number of migrants coming to these countries, both legal and illegal, which brings additional, often irritating, diversity in the polity and moreover, puts further pressure on their welfare states' anyhow dwindling resources. As a result, violent incidents against minorities are becoming ever more frequent[103] and, more critically, the classical political parties are giving way to the

[101] See Avbelj (n 7).

[102] As also noted by J-W Muller, 'Moscow's Trojan Horse' (Foreign Affairs, August 2014), http://www.foreignaffairs.com/articles/141825/jan-werner-mueller/moscows-trojan-horse, accessed 12 October 2016.

[103] Recall the violence and outright discriminative practices against the Roma in France, Italy, Hungary, and Slovakia, see e.g. O Parker, 'Roma and the Politics of EU Citizenship in France: Everyday Security and Resistance' (2012) 50 *Journal of Common Market Studies* 475; M Dawson and E Muir, 'Individual, Institutional and Collective Vigilance in Protecting Fundamental Rights in the EU: Lessons from the Roma' (2011) 48 *Common Market Law Review* 751; K Halasz, 'The Rise of the Radical Right in Europe and the Case of Hungary: Gypsy crime defines national identity?' (2009) 52 *Development* 490; P Colacicchi, 'Ethnic Profiling and Discrimination against Roma in Italy: New Developments in a Deep-Rooted Tradition' (2008) 2 *Roma Rights Quarterly* 35. Other minorities, in particular, Muslims, Jews, gays, and immigrants have been increasingly subject to violence too, see DC Speedie and

representatives of both sides of the political extreme.[104] The robustness of democracy and of the institution of the Rule of Law is therefore on the wane even in the old Member States.

This shows that the EU is facing a real dilemma in the decline of democracy and of the Rule of Law as we have traditionally known them. This decline has always been there in some of its Member States, only hidden behind the veil of formal compliance with the EU standards,[105] while in others it is taking new forms and shapes due to the changing regional and global geo-economic circumstances which inevitably have their particular local repercussions.[106] The EU as a common whole—the supranational level and the Member States—should take this negative trend seriously and approach it at its roots before it is too late. Selective and again only formal focus on some, particularly recalcitrant Member States, is inadequate when the problems are much deeper, context-dependent in their causes and outcomes, but essentially pervasive. This calls for a joined, concentrated, deliberate, strategic, and comprehensive approach which considers the actual sociological state of democracy and of the Rule of Law in the EU Member States afresh. Simply assuming that these are, by and large, well-ordered societies, will not do. This rather perpetuates the complacent status quo. Perhaps the opposite is true. And if it is, it needs to be tackled pluralistically—combining the endogenous with exogenous positive forces for the success of the common whole. Is pluralism at all viable in such circumstances? It better be. If it is not, this means that the core value of human dignity will be deprived of the normative framework through which I believe it can be realized best.

J Otterson Mollick, 'The Rise of Extremism in a Disunited Europe' (17 January 2014) *Carnegie Council*, http://www.carnegiecouncil.org/publications/articles_papers_reports/0186.html, accessed 12 October 2016.

[104] e.g. Front National in France, Golden Dawn in Greece, Freedom Party in Austria, Party for Freedom in the Netherlands, Jobbik in Hungary, UK Independence Party, etc. See, for an overview, P Hockenos, *Free to Hate: The Rise of the Right in Post-Communist Eastern Europe* (Routledge 2013); K von Beyme (ed), *Right-Wing Extremism in Western Europe* (Routledge 2013); A Mammone et al. (eds), *Varieties of Right-Wing Extremism in Europe* (Routledge 2013).

[105] Slovenia is the most notable example of this, see e.g. Bugarič (n 7); for a similar observation on other Central and Eastern European Countries, see J Rupnik and J Zielonka, 'Introduction: The State of Democracy 20 Years On: Domestic and External Factors' (2013) 27 *East European Politics & Societies* 3.

[106] For a brief, but insightful analysis, see Speedie and Otterson Mollick (n 103).

PART II

INSTRUMENTS AND METHODS: ESTABLISHED AND PROPOSED

4

Infringement Proceedings

Laurence W Gormley

1. Introduction

Infringement proceedings are at once the classic method of supervision and the Swiss cheese in the armoury of the European Commission. Like Swiss cheese, they look attractive, have an initially diverting taste, but on closer examination, being full of holes, are not quite what one might first imagine. Within the context of the discussion about the enforcement of the Union's values, the questions whether infringement proceedings can be used for this purpose, and whether a concept of systematic infringements would be possible or desirable, are two questions which will be examined in this contribution, after the stage has been set through some observations on infringement proceedings and how they work.

2. Some general observations

The mechanism itself, now set out in Articles 258 and 259 TFEU,[1] bolstered by the fines and/or penalties provisions of Article 260 TFEU,[2] is clear, but reveals already a hole in the cheese. While the apparent obligation to issue a reasoned opinion if the Commission considers that a Member State has failed to fulfil an obligation under the Treaties might appear to be unconditional, the discretionary nature of the following step, bringing the matter to the Court of Justice, demonstrates that infringement proceedings are discretionary.[3] It logically follows, therefore, that the Commission cannot be forced to commence infringement proceedings.[4] Although it is possible for one Member State to bring an infringement procedure against another under Article 259 TFEU,[5] this is extremely rare indeed.[6] The Member States tend to leave the initiative almost entirely to the Commission,

[1] As to the special procedures involving direct access to the Court of Justice, see Arts 108(2); 114(9), and 348, 2nd para TFEU. As to the powers of the Board of Directors of the EIB on compliance by Member States with their obligations under the Statute of the EIB, see Art 271(a) TFEU; as to the powers of the Governing Council of the ECB in relation to national central banks, see Art 271(d) TFEU.

[2] As to which, see Wennerås in Chapter 5 of this volume.

[3] See e.g. Case 7/68 *Commission v Italy* [1968] ECLI:EU:C:1968:51, 428; Case 415/85 *Commission v Ireland* [1988] ECLI:EU:C:1993:891, para 9; Case 247/87 *Star Fruit Company SA v Commission* [1989] ECLI:EU:C:1989:58, para 12; Case C-207/97 *Commission v Belgium* [1999] ECLI:EU:C:1999:17, para 24.

[4] See e.g. Case 48/65 *Alfons Lüttike GmbH et al. v Commission* [1966] ECLI:EU:C:1966:8, 27; Case C-371/89 *Emrich v Commission* [1990] ECLI:EU:C:1990:158, paras 6–7.

[5] The Member State must first bring the matter to the attention of the Commission, which hears each side orally and in writing and may in effect take the matter over itself by issuing a reasoned opinion, and subsequently bring the matter to the Court in the normal manner. If within three months of the matter being brought before the Commission, no reasoned opinion has been issued, the matter may be brought to the Court of Justice despite there being no reasoned opinion. In effect the Commission has the opportunity to take the matter over, and if it does not then the Member State can go to the Court after the three-month period. A Member State may also use the special procedures of Arts 108(2); 114(9), and 348 TFEU, where appropriate.

[6] See Case 141/78 *France v United Kingdom* [1979] ECLI:EU:C:1979:225; Case 388/95 *Belgium v Spain* [2000] ECLI:EU:C:2000:244; Case C-145/04 *Spain v UK* [2006] ECLI:EU:C:2006:543, and Case C-364/10 *Hungary v Slovakia* [2012] ECLI:EU:C:2012:630.

which is very well-suited for this task, given that it is an impartial body.[7] Although no less an authority than Advocate General Roemer has observed that the object of the procedure is not to attach moral blame, but to clarify the legal position to enable the Member State concerned to stay on the path of legality,[8] it is no secret that some Member States really do not share this view of infringement proceedings: national sensitivities can resemble toes which are easily trodden on (or as it is put in Dutch, some Member States just have very long toes). Infringement proceedings are brought in the interest of the public order of the EU.[9]

3. The workings of the procedure

As is well known, the procedure under Article 258 TFEU is divided into an administrative stage and a judicial stage. The administrative stage offers the opportunity to the Member State of justifying its behaviour or its legislation; it also gives the Commission an opportunity to persuade the Member State to climb down (more or less) gracefully of its own volition.[10] At the same time, it complies with the principle of *audi alteram partem* and allows the dispute to be clearly delimited before it reaches the Court.

Before the formal stages are reached there will have been considerable contacts with the Member State concerned. Until the late 1980s contacts were more ad hoc than systematic: when a complaint file was opened, as a result of a complaint from a company or a trade body, or from a private individual or an individual trader, or perhaps from a trading standards or consumer protection organization, written contacts would take place with the Member State via its Permanent Representation in Brussels; sometimes there would be contacts by phone and meetings might be organized with the complainant or with the authorities of the Member state concerned. Sometimes recalcitrant Member States just ignored the Commission's requests for information, and a tedious round of letters and even telexes ensued. It often took time to get results, although the Commission could and did act quickly where it was necessary.[11] In the early 1980s the concept of package meetings started to develop. These had the advantage of ensuring that all dossiers in a particular area could be discussed, although the potential for horse-trading never seemed to be far away. But the old patchwork approach was increasingly ineffective in a vastly enlarged EU. The treatment of complaints has now become much more formalized: in 1999 the Commission even published a form for complainants in infringement proceedings;[12] in 2002, largely in response to pressure from the European Ombudsman in relation to a particular

[7] PJG Kapteyn and P VerLoren van Themaat, *Introduction to the Law of the European Union and the European Communities* (5th edn, Kluwer Law International 2008) 441.

[8] See Case 7/71 *Commission v France* [1971] ECLI:EU:C:1971:121, para 1034 'concerned not with guilt and morality but simply with clarification of the legal position'; See also AG Gand in Case 77/69 *Commission v Belgium* [1970] ECLI:EU:C:1970:34, para 247 'the authority of your judgment will give the various powers concerned a clearer understanding of the extent of their obligations in respect of the Community'.

[9] JV Louis in *Miscellenea W J Ganshof van der Meersch* (Bruylant 1972) Vol. II 225 at 237 (referring to the public order of the Communities).

[10] See e.g. Joined Cases 142 and 143/80 *Amministrazione delle Finanze dello Stato v Essevi SpA et al.* [1981] ECLI:EU:C:1981:121, para 15.

[11] As one Member State found to its surprise when trying to introduce new trade barriers during the transitional period following its accession in the early 1980s, the Commission's staff are not all on leave during the summer period, and reaction from the Commission was swift. In the celebrated Dundalk procurement saga, the Commission was quick to seek interim measures as soon as possible (granted *ex parte* but strangely refused *inter partes*; the Commission won the substantive case, though), see Case 45/87 *Commission v Ireland* [1988] ECLI:EU:C:1988:435 (and, as to the interim measures, Case 45/87 R *Commission v Ireland* [1987] ECLI:EU:C:1987:86 and [1987] ECLI:EU:C:1987:132).

[12] [1999] OJ C119/5. The use of the form is not compulsory.

complaint,[13] it published a Communication on the handling of relations with complainants,[14] and this was updated in 2012.[15]

If the Commission's services are of the view that a Member State has failed to fulfil its obligations and the Member State has given no or no satisfactory justification, a proposal may be made that formal infringement proceedings should be commenced. The Secretariat General, the Legal Service and the Directorate or Directorates General concerned will discuss the matter and make a recommendation. This will usually be handled in a periodic special meeting of the members of the Commissioners' cabinets dealing with infringement proceedings, although it can be dealt with at any meeting of the chefs de cabinet (initially, in either case, at staff level and if necessary at 'HEBDO' by the chefs themselves).[16] These meetings are sometimes used as the prime forum for horse-trading and for political interests to be laid firmly on the table, even to the extent of 'give me this one, and I'll give you that one'. More than one cabinet responsible for the area concerned lost credibility with its peers by frankly doing the bidding of the Member State from which its member of the Commission comes, instead of actually following the advice of the services that proceedings should be commenced against that Member State. But the ostensible purpose of the meeting is to make the proposal: if there is agreement then the matter will be on the Commission's agenda as an 'A point' and will be approved without discussion; if there is no consensus, much depends on how the cabinet of the Commissioner responsible wishes to proceed, although its view may not be decisive: the matter may be referred back to the services, or the dossier may even be closed as a result of a 'deal', or the matter may be placed on the Commission's agenda as a 'B point'. In this latter case there will be discussion and a decision may or may not emerge, sometimes at the cost of much horse-trading.

If the Commission does decide to initiate infringement proceedings (and, to be fair, it usually follows the advice of the services), the letter of formal notice will be drafted in the unit handling the case; the draft will be sent to any other Directorates General involved in the matter for their agreement, and to the Legal Service for its opinion. If all concerned agree and the opinion is favourable, if necessary after tweaking, the letter is prepared for signature. Usually the letter will be signed by the member of the Commission holding the portfolio concerned, or the lead portfolio if there are several Directorates General involved. The letter is sent to the Foreign Minister of the Member State concerned, via its Permanent Representation. This letter is of key importance, as it sets out the Commission's stall, putting the Member State in a position to prepare its defence.[17] This is an essential procedural requirement.[18] It is possible to raise additional points in a supplementary letter of formal notice, but this is a relatively rare event.[19] The letter of formal notice will set out a

[13] See European Ombudsman Press Release 3/2001 of 5 February 2001. See also C Harlow and R Rawlings, *Process and Procedure in EU Administration* (Hart 2014) 188.

[14] COM(2002) 141 final.

[15] COM(2012) 154 final. As to complaints and the EU Pilot scheme, see section 5 below.

[16] S Grohs in M Cremona (ed), *Compliance and the Enforcement of EU Law* (OUP 2012) 65. While massive quarterly package meetings on infringements were customary some years ago, infringement meetings are now held monthly, and more effectively.

[17] Case 211/81 *Commission v Denmark* [1982] ECLI:EU:C:1982:437, para 8. The Court has held 'in a consistent line of decisions that the scope of [infringement proceedings] is delimited both by the preliminary administrative procedure provided for by [Article 258 TFEU] and by the conclusions set out in the application and that the commission's reasoned opinion and its application must be founded on the same grounds and submissions', Case 166/82 *Commission v Italy* [1984] ECLI:EU:C:1987:451, para 16. See also the approach in Case C-494/01 *Commission v Ireland* [2005] ECLI:EU:C:2005:250, paras 27–39.

[18] e.g. Case 293/85 *Commission v Belgium* [1988] ECLI:EU:C:1988:40, para 14; Case C-306/91 *Commission v Italy* [1993] ECLI:EU:C:1993:161, paras 22–6).

[19] If in the meantime a reasoned opinion has been sent, a new reasoned opinion, taking account of the reply, if any, to the supplementary letter, will also be necessary before the action can be brought to the Court, see e.g. Case 211/81 *Commission v Denmark* [1982] ECLI:EU:C:1982:437, paras 10–11.

period within which the Member State is to make its observations known to the Commission;[20] in default of any observations or any satisfactory observations, the Commission states in the letter that it expressly reserves the right to issue a reasoned opinion in the matter.

It may be that the Member State then climbs down and undertakes to change its laws or practices as appropriate. The dossier will not, however, be closed simply on a promise to act. If the Member State satisfactorily justifies the action or inaction concerned, then the Commission will close the file on the matter. More frequently it will be necessary to go to the reasoned opinion stage.

The reasoned opinion is an important document because it sets out the default of the Member State which the Commission will seek to have established if it takes the case to the Court of Justice. The adoption procedure by the Commission is similar to that described for the letter of formal notice. Once the Commission has decided to send a reasoned opinion[21] the Legal Service draws up the draft, usually drawing very heavily on the letter of formal notice. The reasoned opinion will also take account of any reply by the Member State to the letter of formal notice and will seek to rebut any arguments advanced by the Member State. The draft is sent to the Directorate or Directorates General concerned for agreement, and, after any changes, the agreed draft is sent to the cabinet of the Member of the Commission responsible by the lead Directorate General, with a copy to the Secretariat General which then prepares the formal version for signature by the relevant member of the Commission. Again, the reasoned opinion is addressed to the Minister of Foreign Affairs of the Member State concerned and sent via the Permanent Representation. The reasoned opinion is more formal in nature and concludes by requiring the Member State to take the steps necessary to comply with the reasoned opinion within a particular time. This will usually be two months,[22] and the Commission expressly reserves the right to bring the matter to the Court of Justice in the absence of any or any satisfactory compliance after the end of that period. If the Member State fails to climb down, the matter is usually then taken to the Court. Sometimes, however, in the exercise of its discretion, the Commission may feel that it is not yet opportune to commence proceedings immediately. Perhaps if a general election is just about to take place in a Member State, the Commission might well delay commencing proceedings so that the dispute does not become a political football or factor in the election process. During the recent financial crises with, in particular, Greece, it was common knowledge that many, if not all of the infringement proceedings were put on 'hold' to avoid alienating Greek public opinion still further.

[20] Deadlines may be short, but they must be reasonable, taking account of the circumstances of the case, Case 293/85 *Commission v Belgium* [1988] ECLI:EU:C:1988:341, 352. Very short periods may be justified, especially where it is necessary to remedy the breach urgently, or where the Member State is fully aware of the Commission's views before the procedure starts, ibid. The Court made this point clearly in Case 293/85 as it had two references for preliminary rulings on the same problem: it handed down its judgments in Case 309/85 *Barra v Belgian State et al.* [1988] ECLI:EU:C:1988:42 and Case 24/86 *Blaizot v University of Liège et al.* [1988] ECLI:EU:C:1988:43 on the same day as that in Case 293/85 and was thus able to ensure that the substance of the dispute could be resolved, while at the same time reminding the Commission to be reasonable in its dealings with national administrations. See further, HG Schermers and D Waelbroeck, *Judicial Protection in the European Union* (6th edn, Kluwer Law International 2001) 615–16; K Lenaerts et al., *EU Procedural Law* (OUP 2014) 191, and S Andersen, *The Enforcement of EU Law* (OUP 2012) 50–1.

[21] The decision to issue a reasoned opinion must be the subject of collective deliberation by the Commission (as must the decisions to send the letter of formal notice and to bring infringement proceedings to the Court), and the information on which the decision is based must be available to the Commission. However, the college does not itself have to formally decide on the wording of the acts giving effect to that decision or put them in their final form, C-191/95 *Commission v Germany* [1998] ECLI:EU:C:1998:441, para 48.

[22] The observations in n 20 above as to deadlines apply in respect of this deadline as well.

The Commission's discretion whether to commence proceedings and when, and against which Member State is clear,[23] and the fact that it may have been aware of the problem for a long time[24] or that there has been some time between the letter of formal notice and the reasoned opinion will not prevent the action from being admissible,[25] save where the pre-litigation procedure has dragged on so long that it is more difficult for the Member State concerned to refute the Commission's arguments, thus infringing the rights of the defence.[26] It is for the defendant Member State to provide evidence that this is the case: a mere assertion will not suffice.[27]

When the case gets to the Court, the request is that the Court find that the Member State has failed to fulfil its obligations in the matter concerned and has not put an end to it by the date fixed for compliance with the reasoned opinion.[28] Sometimes the Member State climbs down while the case is before the Court; in these circumstances the Commission will usually simply withdraw the action, although it is entitled to pursue the matter to judgment if it wishes. This was made clear in Case 39/72 *Commission v Italy*,[29] in which the Court also noted that a judgment finding that there had been an infringement 'may be of substantive interest as establishing the basis of a responsibility that a Member State can incur as a result of its default, as regards other Member States, the Community or private parties.'[30] The Court was clearly already well aware of the potential of damages as a remedy

[23] See the judgments cited in n 3. If the Commission fails to act against other Member States this will not release the defendant Member State from its obligations to comply with EU law, Joined Cases 52 and 53/65 *Germany v Commission* [1966] ECLI:EU:C:1966:32, para 172. The Commission may start proceedings against one Member State and then bring proceedings against others (it can sometimes be difficult to persuade the Commission to take on a huge number of Member States at once, so salami tactics may be appropriate), see e.g. Case C-235/89 *Commission v Italy* [1992] ECLI:EU:C:1992:73, paras 797 and 799–804 (report for the hearing); and Case 30/90 *Commission v United Kingdom* [1992] ECLI:EU:C:1992:74, paras 850–5 (report for the hearing).

[24] As with the *Reinheitsgebot* for beer in Germany: the legislation had been in place for many years before the Commission took action, but this was rightly not raised by the German government as an obstacle to the admissibility of the action, see Case 178/84 *Commission v Germany* [1987] ECLI:EU:C:1987:126; another example is the Volkswagen law litigation: Case C-112/05 *Commission v Germany* [2007] ECLI:EU:C:2007:623. See also Case C-359/93 *Commission v Netherlands* [1995] ECLI:EU:C:1995:14, paras 12–14. But in deciding on interim measures, delay may tilt the balance against the Commission: Case 87/94 R *Commission v Belgium* [1994] ECLI:EU:C:1994:166, paras 38–42.

[25] See e.g. Case C-317/92 *Commission v Germany* [1994] ECLI:EU:C:1994:212, para 4; Case C-207/97 *Commission v Belgium* [1999] ECLI:EU:C:1999:17, paras 23–7; Case C-333/99 *Commission v France* [2001] ECLI:EU:C:2001:73, para 25. See also L Prete and B Smulders, 'The Coming of Age of Infringement Proceedings' (2010) 47 *Common Market Law Review* 9, 15–17.

[26] See e.g. Case C-96/89 *Commission v Netherlands* [1991] ECLI:EU:C:1991:213, para 16; Case C-207/97 *Commission v Belgium* [1999] ECLI:EU:C:1999:17, paras 25–7; Case C-187/98 *Commission v Greece* [1999] ECLI:EU:C:1999:535, para 39; Case C-333/99 *Commission v France* [2001] ECLI:EU:C:2001:73, para 25. In the latter case the action was commenced some seven years after the Member State has sent the Commission its observations on the reasoned opinion).

[27] See e.g. Case C-96/89 *Commission v Netherlands* [1991] ECLI:EU:C:1991:213, para 16; Case C-207/97 *Commission v Belgium* [1999] ECLI:EU:C:1999:17, paras 25–7; Case C-187/98 *Commission v Greece* [1999] ECLI:EU:C:1999:535, para 39.

[28] See e.g. Case C-362/90 *Commission v Italy* [1992] ECLI:EU:C:1992:158, para 10; Case C-525/03 *Commission v Italy* [2005] ECLI:EU:C:2005:648, para 14.

[29] Case 39/72 *Commission v Italy* [1973] ECLI:EU:C:1973:13, paras 9–11. As that great jurist Gerhard Bebr recognized, this judgment is important, see G Bebr, *Development of Judicial Control of the European Communities* (Martinus Nijhoff 1981) 297–8, yet it is inexplicably often overlooked: it follows the well-known judgment on premiums for slaughtering cows in Case 93/71 *Leonesio v Ministry for Agriculture and Forestry of the Italian Republic* [1972] ECLI:EU:C:1972:39. See also e.g. Case 103/84 *Commission v Italy* [1986] ECLI:EU:C:1986:229, para 8; Case 283/86 *Commission v Belgium* [1988] ECLI:EU:C:1988:325, para 6; Case C-249/88 *Commission v Belgium* [1991] ECLI:EU:C:1991:121, para 41; Case C-317/92 *Commission v Germany* [1994] ECLI:EU:C:1994:212, paras 3–5; Case C-209/02 *Commission v Austria* [2004] ECLI:EU:C:2004:61, paras 16–19.

[30] Case 39/72 *Commission v Italy* [1973] ECLI:EU:C:1973:13, para 11. See also e.g. Case 309/84 *Commission v Italy* [1986] ECLI:EU:C:1986:73, para 18; Case 103/84 *Commission v Italy* [1986] ECLI:EU:C:1986:229, para 9; Case 154/85 *Commission v Italy* [1987] ECLI:EU:C:1987:292, para 6; Case 240/86 *Commission v Greece* [1988] ECLI:EU:C:1988:173, para 14; Case C-249/88 *Commission v Belgium* [1991] ECLI:EU:C:1991:121, para 41; Case C-119/00 *Commission v Luxembourg* [2001] ECLI:EU:C:2001:351, para 17; Case C-168/03 *Commission v Spain*

for breach of Community law by the Member States long before the judgment in *Francovich*.[31] An acknowledgement by a Member State of the infringement and a mere promise by the Member State to remedy it (hoping that the Commission might then drop the case) will not justify a stay of proceedings.[32]

If the Court finds that the Member State has indeed failed to fulfil its obligations, a declaratory judgment is the result. The Court of Justice gives no guidance as to what steps the Member State must take to put an end to the infringement (although there are occasionally suggestions that this might be helpful).[33] Sometimes the steps will be obvious: repeal the offending instrument or change the practice that has been found incompatible with EU law. But it is up to the Member State to decide what to do, and the obligation incumbent on them to act is one that actually arises from the moment of delivery of the judgment finding that there has been an infringement of EU law: the Court requires the process of compliance (now under Article 260(1) TFEU) to be initiated at once and to be completed as soon as possible.[34]

4. Failures concerning directives

Many infringement proceedings are of a routine nature, concerning failure to implement directives adequately or at all, and/or failure to notify the Commission of the measures

[2004] ECLI:EU:C:2004:525, para 24. A national court would have to take account of the finding of infringement, although the rights which individuals may invoke do not derive from the judgment in the infringement proceedings, but from the substantive Treaty or other provisions having direct effect in the internal legal order of the Member States; see Joined Cases 314–316/81 and 83/82 *Procureur de la République et al. v Waterkeyn et al.* [1982] ECLI:EU:C:1982:430, paras 15–16.

[31] Joined Cases C-6/90 and 9/90 *Francovich and Bonifaci v Italy* [1991] ECLI:EU:C:1991:428. Given that infringement proceedings and actions for damages by litigants before national courts have very different purposes and take place in different fora, it is unsurprising that the Court of Justice has held that an action for damages does not require that the Court has previously found that the Member State had committed an infringement, see e.g. Case C-445/06 *Danske Slagterier v Bundesrepublik Deutschland* [2009] ECLI:EU:C:2009:178, paras 37–9, citing earlier case law).

[32] Case C-243/89 *Commission v Denmark* [1993] ECLI:EU:C:1993:257, para 30; C-414/03 *Commission v Germany* [2005] ECLI:EU:C:2005:134, paras 8–9. See also e.g. Case C-366/00 *Commission v Luxembourg* [2002] ECLI:EU:C:2002:101, paras 10–12. Particularly when a Member State has been guilty of infringing conduct over many years before the complainant actually brought the case to the Commission's attention, withdrawing the action on a mere promise would be remarkably ill-advised and the Commission is clearly right to refuse to do so, otherwise there is a serious risk of having to start all over again from square one, as some Member States in particular can be totally disingenuous in their promises. The old adage 'Put not your trust in princes' comes to mind (Psalm 146, v. 3; King James Version).

[33] See the discussion in Andersen (n 20) 55 and HAH Audretsch, *Supervision in European Community Law* (2nd edn, North Holland 1986) 114–23 and 130, but the Court will refrain from making prescriptive statements (save where it is obvious, e.g. that a Member State must require repayment of an unlawfully granted State aid), although it may indicate or imply possible solutions.

[34] e.g. Case 131/84 *Commission v Italy* [1985] ECLI:EU:C:1985:447, para 7; Case 169/87 *Commission v France* [1988] ECLI:EU:C:1988:393, para 14; Case C-334/94 *Commission v France* [1996] ECLI:EU:C:1996:90, 1343 (non-compliance for more than twenty years!). See already the inspired discussion by G Bebr (n 29) 293–304. Failure to change legislation will usually lead to further action, and compliance in the form of circulars is manifestly not acceptable because circulars can be withdrawn at the whim of the administration and offer no legal certainty. On the very odd occasion, though, the Commission may conclude that there are better ways of furthering European integration than standing on ceremony: after the famous judgment in Case 121/85 *Conegate Ltd v HM Customs and Excise* [1986] ECLI:EU:C:1986:114 the British government instructed customs officers not to seize items of the type to which the judgment related; it would have been open to the UK to ban the goods altogether (domestic production and sale, not just imports) rather than amend the prohibition on imports; the Commission followed the advice of its services that in the absence of any evidence that the instruction was not being followed, it was sensible to accept what the UK government had done, avoiding potentially lurid headlines in the gutter press: the file was duly closed. As to the consequences of failure to comply with judgments in infringement proceedings, see Wennerås in Chapter 5 in this volume.

adopted.[35] With 447 late transposition infringements in 2012 there was a marked decline compared with 2011 (1185) and 2010 (855); there were 418 such cases open at the end of 2012, a 45 per cent decrease as against the 763 such cases open at the end of 2011; the cause of the decline is attributable to there being fewer directives adopted in 2012 than in previous years.[36] In 2015 there were 543 late transposition proceedings launched, up from 478 in 2013, but down from 585 in 2014. There were 518 late transposition cases still open at the end of 2015, a 19 per cent increase on the 421 cases at the end of 2014. In 2015 there were 56 directives to transpose, as against 67 in 2014.[37]

In respect of late transposition of directives, the Commission now has the quicker route of incentivizing earlier compliance, namely the stick of financial sanctions under Article 260(3) TFEU. In 2011 the Commission referred the first late transposition infringement to the Court, requesting such sanctions: five Member States were involved in nine such cases that year: Germany and Poland were each involved in three cases, and Austria, Greece, and Italy in one each. In 2012 the Commission used the procedure on thirty-five occasions against twelve Member States: Poland (ten cases), Slovenia (five), the Netherlands and Finland (four each), Belgium and Cyprus (three each), while Germany, Bulgaria, Slovakia, Luxembourg, Portugal, and Hungary each had one such case.[38]

In 2014 the Commission took three Member States to the Court, seeking the imposition of daily penalties: Belgium, Finland, and Ireland (which was hit with two cases, one of which was withdrawn). All these cases involved the energy sector. While the Commission also decided to take cases involving other areas to the Court, the Member States finally adopted the transposition measures required before the applications were actually filed, complying at the eleventh hour. So far, the Commission has not proposed that the Court should impose lump sum payments, feeling that the penalty payment would prove sufficient to achieve the objective of giving Member States a stronger incentive to transpose directives by the due date. Although all cases brought to the Court of Justice seeking penalties for non-transposition since 2011 were by the end of 2014 withdrawn due to complete transposition, this means in effect that some Member States are still reaping the benefits of non-compliance for long after the transposition period has expired.[39] This is completely incompatible with the uniform application of EU law at the same time throughout the Union, and in many instances actually distorts competition by maintaining in force legislation which gives local industry an advantage over competitors in other Member States who have to comply with requirements imposed by the date set at European level.[40] While the Commission has noted that in 2014 and in 2015, Member States increased their efforts to complete transposition before the Court of Justice delivered its

[35] The requirements the Court makes in regard to implementation are conveniently summarized in Case C-427/07 *Commission v Ireland* [2009] ECLI:EU:C:2009:457, paras 54 and 55.

[36] 30th Annual Report on the monitoring of EU Law (2012), COM(2013) 726 final, 2.

[37] 33rd Annual Report on the monitoring of EU law (2015), COM(2016) 463 final, 27. Of the sixty-seven directives due to be transposed in 2014, seven in the environmental field were repealed in 2013 and some Member States were given transitional periods, 32nd Annual Report on the Monitoring of EU Law (2014), COM(2015) 329 final, 17.

[38] 30th Annual Report (n 36) 5.

[39] 32nd Annual Report (n 37) 20. In 2015 the Commission announced in Press Release IP/15/54499 on 26 February 2015 that the completion of transposition and consequent withdrawal of the court proceedings in Case C-320/13 *Commission v Poland* [2015] ECLI:EU:C:2015:221 at a very late stage in the Court proceedings (after the Advocate General had given his Opinion) has led the Commission to consider revising its policy on the implementation of Art 260(3) TFEU so as to ensure more effective and timely transposition of directives by the Member States.

[40] The Commission's Annual Reports on the application of EU law give much useful information on the areas in which there are problems, and on the detailed situation of each Member State, see http://ec.europa.eu/atwork/applying-eu-law/infringements-proceedings/annual-reports/index_en.htm, accessed 20 October 2016.

judgments, in 2014 eight cases with a proposal for daily penalties still remained open (some cases had been started in earlier years): against Austria and Poland (two each), and one case each against Belgium, Finland, the Netherlands, and Ireland.[41] At the end of 2015 four cases involving a proposal for financial penalties remained open: one case each against Greece and Luxembourg, and two against Poland.[42] Several cases were sent to the Court in 2015: two against Poland, and one each against Germany, Greece, Luxembourg, and Slovenia, although the latter case was withdrawn after transposition ensued. One Member State avoided proceedings by completing transposition after the Commission had decided to go to the Court of Justice, but before proceedings were actually initiated.[43]

There are various informal networks through which timely compliance can be encouraged, such as IMPEL, the EU Network for the Implementation and Enforcement of Environmental Law;[44] the European Competition Network,[45] and the Forum for the Exchange of Information on Enforcement (FEIE)[46] which operates under the auspices of the European Chemicals Agency established under the REACH Regulation.[47] The Commission's increasing use of Transposition and Implementation Plans should facilitate easier—and even guided—implementation of directives by the Member States.[48]

5. Complaints

Complaints are certainly still a fertile basis for infringement proceedings, although the priority given to bringing infringement proceedings as a result of a complaint has actually varied over the years. Sometimes, particularly after the Commission's famous Communication on the Consequences of the *Cassis de Dijon* judgment[49] and after the adoption of the White Paper on Completing the Internal Market,[50] there is a surge in complaints. At other times there is a political feeling that complainants should seek redress in the national courts, and that the Commission should concentrate on getting its legislative agenda through the EP and the Council; at these moments complaints may be perhaps too easily fobbed off. The mood is presently positive towards dealing with complaints, stimulated to an extent by the improved internet presentation of means to ensure that citizens and businesses are properly informed of their rights under EU law. The SOLVIT network,[51] with a one-stop-shop point of contact in each Member State has been quite effective in offering a low-threshold approach to the resolution of internal market problems, although a number of fundamental problems have been identified.[52] Connection of SOLVIT to the Commission's internal tool for registering complaints on the application of EU law (CHAP) has sought to meet some of these problems (particularly the speedier handling of complaints), although understaffing of some national contact points and disagreements

[41] 32nd Annual Report (n 37) 21. [42] 33rd Annual Report (n 37) 30. [43] ibid.

[44] See http://impel.eu, accessed 12 October 2016.

[45] See http://ec.europa.eu/competition/ecn/, accessed 12 October 2016.

[46] See http://echa.europa.eu/about-us/who-we-are/enforcement-forum, accessed 12 October 2016.

[47] Reg. 1907/2006 ([2007] OJ L396/1). [48] See e.g. 32nd Annual Report (n 37) 24.

[49] [1980] OJ C256/2 (the *Cassis de Dijon* judgment is Case 120/78 *Rewe-Zentral AG v Bundesmonopolverwaltung für Branntwein* [1979] ECLI:EU:C:1979:42). See further, LW Gormley, 'Cassis de Dijon and the Communication from the Commission' (1981) 6 *European Law Review* 454 (discussing also other comments on the Communication).

[50] COM(85) 310 Final. See R Bieber et al. (eds), *1992: One European Market?* (Nomos 1988) and LW Gormley, 'Some Reflections on the Internal Market and the Free Movement of Goods' (1989) 1 *Legal Issues of European Integration* 9.

[51] See http://ec.europa.eu/solvit/, accessed 12 October 2016. SOLVIT is one of the services within the Commission's 'Your Europe' portal: http://europa.eu/youreurope/index_en.htm, accessed 12 October 2016.

[52] See Commission Staff Working Document SWD (2012) 33/F1 and Commission Recommendation on the principles governing Solvit [2013] OJ L249/10.

between contact points in the different Member States about the interpretation of EU law have not helped.

The systematization of the complaints procedure in many areas of internal market law through EU Pilot has proved remarkably successful, although it is also used for own-initiative files and files triggered by inquiries as well as complaints.[53] If the matter is not resolved amicably (and the average resolution rate in 2014 and in 2015 was 75 per cent) the matter moves out of EU Pilot into the formalized infringement procedure process.

6. Bagging several flies in one swat

Usually the infringement proceedings will concern a specific infringement—sometimes a specific incident—but it may well be that there have been continuing incidents which give rise to the infringement proceedings, or even a spate of various incidents. Thus the possibility of an umbrella proceeding is an important weapon in the Commission's armoury. Where an infringement relates to a group of acts, the Court requires that each individual act concerned must have been drawn to the attention of the Member State involved in the letter of formal notice, so that the Member State has a chance to respond, and the action before the Court will be admissible only in respect of those acts for which this has been done.[54] The Court has declared admissible infringement proceedings which in part relate to a string of specific incidents (which had been dealt with in the administrative phase) and in part to a general and continuous approach by the national authorities to which specific incidents testified, even when some of those incidents were not included in the administrative proceedings prior to going to Court.[55] While compliance with a judgment funding an infringement relating to particular incidents may be relatively straightforward, compliance with a finding of 'general and persistent' infringement or a 'structural and general' infringement may be more difficult to ensure.[56] Advocate General Geelhoed has opined that a structural infringement 'suggests that there is a more general practice or a pattern of non-compliance which is also likely to keep recurring.'[57] He observed further that:

[53] 1,208 new EU Pilot files were opened in 2014 (423 as a result of complaints; 8 through inquiries, and 777 new own-initiative files); this marked a return to the level in 2011 (1201), whereas the figures for 2012 and 2013 were 1405 and 1502 respectively: see 32nd Annual Report (n 37) 10–11. In 2015 only 881 new EU Pilot files were opened, of which 295 resulted from complaints and 578 were own-initiative files: see 33rd Annual Report (n 37) 19–20.

[54] Case 309/84 *Commission v Italy* [1986] ECLI:EU:C:1986:73, paras 14–16.

[55] Case C-494/01 *Commission v Ireland* [2005] ECLI:EU:C:2005:250, para 27. See also Case C-248/05 *Commission v Ireland* [2007] ECLI:EU:C:2007:629, paras 63–70; C-331/07 *Commission v Greece* [2009] ECLI:EU:C:2009:247 (available only in French and Greek, para 32); Case C-160/08 *Commission v Germany* [2010] ECLI:EU:C:2010:230, paras 106–12.

[56] The terms 'general and persistent' infringement and a 'structural and general' infringement seem to be interchangeable, see Case C-494/01 *Commission v Ireland* [2005] ECLI:EU:C:2005:250, paras 127 136, 139, 151, 170–1, 174, 184, 194 (all 'general and persistent') and Case C-135/05 *Commission v Italy* [2007] ECLI:EU:C:2007:250, paras 22 and 45 ('structural and general' and 'general and persistent' respectively). As to 'structural and general' infringements, see AG Geelhoed in Case C-494/01 *Commission v Ireland* [2005] ECLI:EU:C:2005:250, paras 19 and 43–8. See also P Wennerås, 'A New Dawn for Commission Enforcement under Articles 226 and 228 EC: General and Persistent (GAP) Infringements, Lump Sums and Penalty Payments' (2006) 43 *Common Market Law Review* 31. As to systemic deficiencies in asylum procedures and the reception conditions of asylum seekers, see Joined Cases C-411/10 & C-493/10 *N.S.* [2011] ECLI:EU:C:2011:865, paras. 94 and 106 and Case C-4/11 *Bundesrepublik Deutschland v Puid* [2013] ECLI:EU:C:2013:740, para 36. As to flagging up systemic problems in human rights judgments, see the Resolution adopted by the 114th session of the Committee of Ministers of the Council of Europe on 12 May 2004 (Res (2004) 3), https://search.coe.int/cm/Pages/result_details.aspx?ObjectID=09000016805dd190, accessed 12 October 2016.

[57] In Case C-494/01 *Commission v Ireland* [2005] ECLI:EU:C:2005:250, para 44.

> In short, a general and structural infringement may be deemed to exist where the remedy for this situation lies not merely in taking action to resolve a number of individual cases which do not comply with the Community obligation at issue, but where this situation of non-compliance can only be redressed by a revision of the general policy and administrative practice of the Member State in respect of the subject governed by the Community measure involved. Restricting the remedial action to identified cases of non-compliance would after all leave other situations of non-compliance intact until they too have been identified and challenged either by the Commission in new infringement proceedings or by persons affected at national level in proceedings before the national courts. In the meantime, a situation contrary to that envisaged by the Community measure persists.[58]

Koen Lenaerts has observed that the concept of general and persistent or structural and general breaches of EU law has been interrelated to some extent with the Court's approach to administrative practice as an infringement; he rightly notes, however, that they are not the same.[59] The broader finding of an infringement has particularly featured in the environmental law field, but there is absolutely no reason to confine it to that field. On the basis that the Commission is the enforcer of Member States' obligations under EU law through infringement proceedings,[60] and taking account of the general obligations of Union loyalty under Article 4(3) TEU, there is no reason to confine the Commission's substantive remit to bring infringement proceedings in any respect. Thus it is not only incidental or even repetitive misconduct relating to substantive duties or the enforcement of rights that can be enforced through infringement procedures, but also compliance with and respect for general principles of EU law, whether stated in the EU Treaties or in secondary EU law, or developed in the case law of the Court of Justice.

In this context discussions about the interaction between political remedies and legal remedies become particularly important, and nowhere more so than in relation to respect for the Rule of Law. These principles form an essential part of the *acquis de l'Union*. That the EU is a Union based on the Rule of Law has now been loudly proclaimed at Treaty level.[61] The Union's values are 'part and parcel of the very essence of the EU.'[62] The central question is whether compliance with the requirement to respect the values of Article 2 can be the subject of infringement proceedings under Articles 258 or 259 TFEU, or whether only the political route of Article 7 FEU is available. The first reaction to this question is that the existence of a particular political remedy should not as such stand in the way of the availability of a legal remedy. A 'serious and persistent breach' by a Member State of the values referred to in Article 2 TEU may result in the suspension of certain of a Member State's rights (including but clearly not limited to voting rights in the Council) deriving from the application of the Treaties to that Member State.[63] There is no role mentioned for the Court of Justice in this process—no requirement that the Court must first have found an infringement of Article 2 TEU. The absence of the Court from this process clearly confirms the difference between legal mechanisms and purely political mechanisms.

[58] In Case C-494/01 *Commission v Ireland* [2005] ECLI:EU:C:2005:250, para 48.

[59] Lenaerts et al. (n 20) 167.

[60] Save in the cases envisaged in Art 271(a), (d) TFEU.

[61] Art 2 TEU includes the Rule of Law as one of the foundational values of the EU. The Court of Justice has long stressed that the EU is based on the Rule of Law, see e.g. Case 294/83 *Parti écologiste 'Les Verts' v European Parliament* [1986] ECLI:EU:C:1986:166, para 22; Case C-15/00 *Commission v European Investment Bank* [2003] ECLI:EU:C:2003:396, para 75; Case C-50/00 P *Unión de Pequeños Agricultores v Council* [2002] ECLI:EU:C:2002:462, para 38; Case C-229/05 P *Osman Ocalan, on behalf of the Kurdistan Workers' Party (PKK) and Serif Vanly, on behalf of the Kurdistan National Congress (KNK) v Council* [2007] ECLI:EU:C:2007:32, para 109; C-274/12 P *Telefónica SA v Commission* [2013] ECLI:EU:C:2013:852, para 56.

[62] J-C Piris, *The Lisbon Treaty* (CUP 2010) 72.

[63] Art 7(3) TEU.

However, a judgment of the Court in an individual case—whether an infringement proceeding or on a reference for a preliminary ruling—or, more probably in a series of cases, and/or a judgment or series of judgments from the ECtHR in areas in which the values of the Union and the values and case law of the ECtHR overlap or interact may well prove a strong enough trigger to persuade a sufficient number of Member States, or the EP or the Commission to trigger the Article 7 TEU process. This might be the softer determination of the existence of 'a clear risk of a serious breach of the values referred to in Article 2' or the harder determination of the existence of 'a serious and persistent breach'. Thus a practical but informal role for the Court of Justice (and/or the ECtHR) in triggering the process of Article 7 TEU can be envisaged.

The innovative aspect of the proposal by Scheppele for a systematic infringement procedure[64] is not actually in suggesting that an infringement procedure can have a systematic element, but in suggesting its use in relation to Article 2 TEU. If the Commission were to be able to bundle a series of concrete individual infringements and meet the general and persistent or structural and general test as well, it would be perfectly possible to imagine the Court being willing to issue a more globally worded finding of a failure to fulfil obligations than merely confining itself to a listing of the individual infringements. However, the Court may well be more inclined to confine itself to specifics.

A finding of an infringement of Article 2 is unlikely, however, to be made in isolation from an infringement of a concrete obligation expressed in the EU Treaties, secondary legislation, or long-standing case law on general principles of law. Both attacks by the Commission against the present Hungarian government's policy of removing those in judicial or quasi-judicial functions who display an unwelcome degree of judicial independence have concerned very specific infringements: in Case C-286/12 *Commission v Hungary*[65] relating to age discrimination concerning compulsory retirement of judges, and in Case C-288/12 *Commission v Hungary*[66] the dismissal of the data protection officer. It would be highly unlikely that the Commission would seek a judgment solely finding an infringement of the values of Article 2 (even though the present Hungarian government manifestly disrespects the independence of the judiciary in many ways) on the basis of some already pronounced judgments in individual cases. If ever political action were to be a realistic likelihood, the case law finding infringements, and the evidence of reaction by Hungary to that case law, could be evidence to swing the political balance of opportunity in favour of invoking Article 7 TEU.

Hungary is, however, not the only problem Member State, as recent extraordinary events in Poland in relation to the Constitutional Tribunal demonstrate. After launching a dialogue on 13 January 2016, and after many fruitless discussions at the level of officials and at the political level, on 1 June 2016 the Commission adopted an Opinion on the Rule of Law in Poland, relating to three specific matters: (1) the appointment of judges to the Constitutional Tribunal and the lack of implementation of the judgments of the Constitutional Tribunal of 3 and 9 December 2015 relating to those matters; (2) the Law of 22 December 2015 amending the Law on the Constitutional Tribunal, the judgment of the Constitutional Tribunal of 9 March 2016 relating to that law, and the respect of the judgments handed down by the Constitutional Tribunal since 9 March 2016; and (3) the effectiveness of the Constitutional review of new legislation adopted and enacted in 2016,

[64] See KL Scheppele, 'Enforcing the Basic Principles of EU Law through Systemic Infringement Procedures', in C Closa and D Kochenov (eds), *Reinforcing Rule of Law Oversight in the European Union* (CUP 2016).

[65] Judgment of 6 November [2012] ECLI:EU:C:2012:687.

[66] Judgment of 8 April [2014] ECLI:EU:C:2014:237.

including legislation such as the new media law.[67] While some concerns were addressed, many were not. The result was that on 27 July 2016 the Commission adopted Recommendation 2016/1374 regarding the Rule of Law in Poland.[68] The recommendation dealt with concerns relating to (1) the appointment of judges to the Constitutional Tribunal and the lack of implementation of the judgments of the Constitutional Tribunal of 3 and 9 December 2015 relating to those matters; (2) the lack of publication in the Official Journal and of implementation of the judgment of 9 March 2016 and of the judgments rendered by the Constitutional Tribunal since 9 March 2016, and (3) the effective functioning of the Constitutional Tribunal and the effectiveness of Constitutional review of new legislation, in particular in view of the law on the Constitutional Tribunal adopted by the *Sjem* (the Polish parliament) on 22 July 2016. The conduct of the Polish government in these matters has been nothing less than disgraceful, and speaks volumes about the attitude of certain elements in the political class in Poland to the Rule of Law, the independence of the judiciary, and governance of state broadcasting. There is, though, considerable judicial solidarity with the Constitutional Tribunal in Poland: the Commission noted (in recital 26 to the recommendation) that the General Assembly of the Supreme Court of Poland adopted a resolution on 26 April 2016 attesting that the rulings of the Constitutional Tribunal are valid, even if the Polish government refuses to publish them in the Official Journal.

The practical difficulty with bundling in relation to Article 2 is collecting enough incidents together to demonstrate a general and persistent or structural and general breach of a value in time to be able to offer a real remedy for the incidents.[69] Cumulating specific incidents may well lead to a multi-faceted finding of infringements (as has been seen in relation to environmental protection above): the individual instances are confirmed as infringements and the cumulative effect is assessed as a different infringement[70] (presumably also involving Article 4(3) TEU, which would have to have been pleaded from the outset), but quite what the concrete steps that the Member State would have to take to comply with the judgment may be very uncertain.

While Scheppele's use of bundling to obtain a finding of a breach of Article 2 TEU is a stimulating suggestion, in political terms it is novel, or even courageous. The Commission has traditionally been unwilling to bring a general non-compliance action solely based on what is now Article 4(3) TEU, and it is submitted that there would be similar reluctance to act solely for non-compliance with Article 2 TEU.

It may be going too far to expect the Commission to attack non-compliance with a value through infringement proceedings. It may also be difficult for the Court of Justice to be willing to bite the bullet and find a general and systematic infringement of one of the values mentioned in Article 2 TEU; the only real chance of it doing so would be in conjunction with a series of individual infringements that are evidence of a general policy. It is already evident that Article 7 is extremely difficult to activate, though this is not surprising as Member States are reluctant to see the mote in another's eye while remaining unwilling to

[67] See Commission Press Release IP/16/1828, and Commission Fact Sheet MEMO/16/2017.

[68] [2016] OJ L217/53. The recommendation documents extensively the events in Poland and the dialogue between the Commission and the Polish government.

[69] Given that the Hungarians had already appointed a new data protection officer, the unlawfully dismissed previous officer was really left to whistle for damages. Courts packed with political allies of a government may not be expected to be sympathetic!

[70] See AG Geelhoed in Case C-494/01 *Commission v Ireland* [2005] ECLI:EU:C:2005:250, para 19; D Kochenov, 'On Policing Article 2 Compliance – Reverse *Solange* and Systematic Infringements Analyzed' (2013) 33 *Polish Yearbook of International Law* 145, 164–5.

see the beam in their own.[71] The Commission proposed in March 2014 a new EU Framework to strengthen the Rule of Law,[72] which would deal with situations where the authorities of a Member State were taking measures or tolerating situations which were likely to systematically and adversely affect the integrity, stability, or the proper functioning of the institutions and the safeguard mechanisms established at national level to secure the Rule of Law.[73] But this appeared at first to be nothing much, having apparently found an unfavourable reaction in the Council's Legal Service, and in any event the framework was designed only in the context of trying to prevent the need to have recourse to Article 7 TEU: nowhere was there a threat to activate infringement procedures in relation to the perceived threats to the value of the Rule of Law.[74] Given that the Commission has now taken formal steps in relation to Poland through the adoption of the opinion and the recommendation referred to above, it may be that the new Framework will start to show its worth. If the Polish government does not climb down, the Commission will have to be prepared to continue to take further action in the third stage of the Rule of Law framework process[75] if it is to be taken seriously in this field.

Values are inherently more fuzzy and less tangible than clear obligations to act or not to act in a certain way, and a Member State may protest lip-service to values while infringing concrete obligations. There is also the question of degree: at what point does the balance tilt? Hungary is not the only Member State in which the authorities seek to influence the judiciary, although it has gone to extraordinary lengths by any standards. In the UK lower courts or tribunals have been discouraged from making references under Article 267 TFEU (particularly in immigration cases); access to justice has been made more difficult by raising court costs in civil and administrative litigation (which has also happened in the Netherlands) in order to dissuade frivolous claims, a not entirely unmeritorious aim; criminal courts charges were being now being routinely imposed on those convicted of crimes, even when was is manifestly disproportionate to do so because of a wholly misconceived policy by the then Justice Secretary (Grayling).[76] Did this policy start to indicate an undermining of the value of the Rule of Law? Member States are obliged to 'provide sufficient remedies to ensure effective legal protection in the fields covered by Union law.'[77] To what extent does a failure to do so involve a breach of the value of the Rule of Law; could slashing the legal aid budget be deemed a breach of the obligation and of the value? Finding a breach of the obligation, in so far as the act of the Member State hinders access to justice in cases involving EU law, is more likely than a finding that the value has been infringed.

[71] Matthew 7, v. 3; King James Version. [72] COM(2014) 158 final/2, 11 March 2014.

[73] ibid, point 4.1.

[74] While polemical, rather than academic in nature, I Butler's opinion column 'European Commission refuses to uphold rule of law' https://euobserver.com/opinion/131100, accessed 12 October 2016, is instructive.

[75] See point 4.2 of the Framework (n 72). The Commission monitors the follow-up given by the Member State concerned to the recommendation; there may be further dialogue, 'which could, for example, focus on whether certain practices which raise concerns continue to occur, or on how the Member State implements the commitments it has made in the meantime to resolve the situation'. The Commission, in its recommendation to Poland (n 68), gave a three-month period for a solution of the problems identified. While the recommendation concludes in point 77 by saying that the Commission is ready to pursue a constructive dialogue with the Polish government, point 4.2 of the Framework indicates that in the event of inadequate follow-up, the Commission will assess the possibility of activating one of the mechanisms set out in Article 7 TEU.

[76] Fortunately Grayling's successor (Gove) backtracked in the face of massive criticism, and the charge was abolished with effect from Christmas Eve 2015, see https://www.theguardian.com/law/2015/dec/03/michael-gove-scraps-criminal-courts-charge, accessed 12 October 2016.

[77] Art 19(1) TEU, 2nd para.

7. Concluding observations

Infringement proceedings have long been an important weapon in ensuring that EU law is properly applied and respected in the Member States of the EU. The practical likelihood of infringement proceedings solely or in part being based on an infringement of a Union value expressed in Article 2 TEU is, it is submitted, in the present state of EU law, somewhat remote. That is not to say that it would not be a good thing, but the reality of the situation is that Member States sign up to all sorts of values, and respect them in many cases not even by paying them lip service. This is reminiscent of the adage that in the EU's external relations agreements, the more prominence given in the text to respect for fundamental rights, the greater the degree to which they would be ignored by the non-member State concerned. Absent a sea change from the Court holding that the values in Article 2 are enforceable at the behest of individuals—and it is clear that under the existing understanding of the conditions for direct effect they are not (they are simply a statement relating to the foundations of the Union)—the likelihood of the Commission acting via the infringement proceedings route in relation to Article 2 TEU seems little more than zero.

Nevertheless, the general picture as to infringement proceedings in other areas is rather more encouraging, and, subject to political considerations, such as not inflaming Greek public opinion by bringing infringement proceedings during a crisis, the Commission has done much good work in encouraging Member States to work towards resolving problems instead of simply adopting the view that thumb to nose is the highest form of European virtue. Non-compliance may be seen by some as a form of resistance, but more often than not it does not serve the real long-term interests of the Member State, merely the short-term interest of politicians concerned to secure their re-election.

5

Making effective use of Article 260 TFEU

Pål Wennerås

1. Introduction

Much has been written on Article 260 TFEU, and the refrain continues along the lines that it is a potentially effective instrument for securing compliance with EU law which has yet to materialize.[1] Some have started to question whether pecuniary sanctions can ever be an effective tool and have eyed the political procedure in Article 7 TEU with a glimmer of hope.[2] But since money talks and the conditions in Article 7 TEU are onerous, it seems premature to discard the value of Article 260 TFEU just yet. But what then is the problem and is it possible to do anything about it? That is the topic of this chapter, which examines the design of the system and its application by the Commission and the Court.

2. Control and enforcement

The principle of sincere cooperation in Article 4(3) TEU requires the Union and the Member States to assist each other in carrying out tasks which flow from the Treaties. This entails inter alia that the Member States must sanction infringements of EU rules through penalties which are effective, proportionate, and have a deterrent effect, an obligation which the Court has emphasized is of fundamental importance.[3] The deterrent effect of sanctions presupposes, moreover, a system of control which is capable of detecting and establishing the infringements in the first place.[4] Article 260 TFEU reflects the countervailing obligation on the EU institutions to impose penalties on Member States infringing EU law.[5] But this system does not necessarily meet the standards required by Article 4(3) TEU, neither with regard to effective control nor expedient enforcement. It is true that the Lisbon Treaty introduced some improvements, most notably by providing in Article 260(3) TFEU that belated transposition of directives can already be sanctioned in infringement proceedings under Article 258 TFEU. But all other infringements of EU law are still subject to the procedure in Article 260(2) TFEU. This means that the Court of Justice cannot impose sanctions before a Member State has failed to comply with a previous judgment declaring that it has infringed EU law. Furthermore, this applies only to judgments declaring a failure to fulfil obligations under Article 258 TFEU.

[1] P Wennerås, 'A new dawn for Commission enforcement under Articles 226 and 228 EC: General and persistent (GAP) infringements, lump sums and penalty payments' (2006) 43 *Common Market Law Review* 1413; L Prete and B Smulders, 'The coming of age of infringement proceedings' (2010) 47 *Common Market Law Review* 9; I Kilbey, 'The interpretation of Article 260 TFEU (ex 228 EC)' (2010) 35 *European Law Reports* 370; P Wennerås, 'Sanctions against Member States under Article 260 TFEU: Alive, but not kicking?' (2012) 49 *Common Market Law Review* 145; and B Jack, 'Article 260(2) TFEU: An Effective Judicial Procedure for the Enforcement of Judgments' (2013) 19 *European Law Journal* 404.

[2] Jack (n 1) 413.

[3] e.g. Case C-304/02 *Commission v France* [2005] ECLI:EU:C:2005:444, para 67.

[4] ibid, para 70.

[5] ibid, First Opinion of AG Geelhoed, para 87, c.f. paras 29 and 73.

Making Effective Use of Article 260 TFEU. First Edition. Pål Wennerås © Pål Wennerås 2017. Published 2017 by Oxford University Press.

This presents two structural flaws. First, most will agree that the Commission does not have the requisite monitoring powers and resources adequately to control the compliance of twenty-eight Member States, let alone the means needed effectively to bring a representative number of infringement proceedings before the Court.[6] A significant proportion of infringements of EU law will therefore never be established under Article 258 TFEU, which in turn diminishes the deterrent effect of Article 260(2) TFEU. Secondly, the period before an infringement is liable to attract sanctions is too long to be a genuine deterrent. The Commission must first detect the infringements and assemble sufficient facts to initiate a case under Article 258 TFEU, and then go through the administrative and judicial phase of that procedure. Thereafter, but only after giving the Member State reasonable time to comply with the judgment declaring an infringement,[7] the Commission must repeat that procedure in a second set of proceedings under Article 260(2) TFEU. The Lisbon Treaty has dispensed with the reasoned opinion,[8] but this only shortens the administrative phase by a few months[9] and the machinery slows down again when the case reaches the Court.[10] All in all, an infringement may have persisted for more than twenty years before the Court hears a case concerning sanctions.[11]

These structural flaws need to be remedied. One option is to amend the Treaty and make the rule in Article 260(3) TFEU applicable to all infringements. A less cumbersome and probably more effective alternative, discussed below, is to explore whether Article 260(2) TFEU could be construed less narrowly.

3. The scope of Article 260(1)–(2) TFEU

a. Judgments falling within the scope of Article 260(1) TFEU

Case law tells us that Article 260(2) TFEU constitutes a special procedure for the enforcement of judgments.[12] Consequently, the Court has stated that only a failure of a Member State to fulfil obligations which has been declared well founded on the basis of Article 258 TFEU may be dealt with under that procedure.[13] The first limb of that statement, prima facie limiting Article 260(2) TFEU to enforcement of judgments rendered under Article 258 TFEU, is not precise. The Court has for instance imposed sanctions for failing

[6] This is essentially what the Commission itself has said in various proposals for supplementary tools, see e.g. Proposal for a Council Regulation creating a mechanism whereby the Commission can intervene in order to remove certain obstacles to trade (COM(1997) 619); Proposal for a Council Regulation on the conservation and sustainable exploitation of fisheries resources under the Commission Fisheries Policies (COM(2002) 185); and S Andersen, *The Enforcement of EU Law* (OUP 2012) 128–30. The enforcement deficit is particularly pronounced with regard to lacking application and enforcement of EU law by the Member States. This is exacerbated by the fact that in some areas of EU law, such as the environment, the Commission lacks inspection powers, see P Wennerås, *The Enforcement of EC Environmental Law* (OUP 2007) 253–6.

[7] What amounts to reasonable or sufficient time depends on the circumstances of the case, taking into account the complexity and duration of the operations needed to comply with the judgment, see e.g. Case C-278/01 *Commission v Spain* [2003] ECLI:EU:C:2003:635, para 30; and, *mutatis mutandis*, Case C-32/05 *Commission v Luxembourg* [2006] ECLI:EU:C:2006:749, paras 37–40.

[8] Case C-610/10 *Commission v Spain* [2012] ECLI:EU:C:2012:781, para 43.

[9] The Commission reckons that this amendment will shorten the pre-litigation procedure from between 12–24 months to 8–18 months, see 'Communication from the Commission – Implementation of Article 260(3) of the Treaty' [2011] OJ C12/1, para 3.

[10] Although the length of proceedings dropped for a few years, the average length of direct actions has now risen to approximately two years, see CJEU, 'Annual Report' (2013), 98.

[11] e.g. Case C-610/10 *Commission v Spain* [2012] ECLI:EU:C:2012:781, para 122. See also Case C-496/09 *Commission v Italy* [2011] ECLI:EU:C:2011:740.

[12] Case C-304/02 *Commission v France* [2005] ECLI:EU:C:2005:444, para 92.

[13] Case C-457/07 *Commission v Portugal* [2009] ECLI:EU:C:2012:521, para 47; and Case C-95/12 *Commission v Germany* [2013] ECLI:EU:C:2013:676, para 23.

to comply with judgments rendered under Article 108(2) TFEU, whereby the Commission may bring state aid cases directly before the Court.[14] The same must apply to judgments issued under Articles 114(9) and 348(2) TFEU, which allow for a similar procedure for certain national measures distorting trade and competition.[15]

More importantly, there is nothing in the wording of Article 260(1) TFEU restricting it to judgments rendered in infringements proceedings under Article 258 TFEU and Articles 108(2), 104(9), and 348(2) TFEU. Unlike Article 260(3) TFEU, Article 260(1) TFEU covers all judgments in which the Court of Justice has found that a Member State has 'failed to fulfil its obligations under the Treaties'.[16] This could include various kinds of judgments[17] and most importantly preliminary rulings under Article 267 TFEU. There are several arguments against this proposition, however. In contrast to infringement proceedings, the preliminary reference procedure neither gives the Court jurisdiction to apply EU law to a specific case nor to decide upon the compatibility of national law with EU law.[18] All the Court does, it says, is rule on the interpretation of EU law in order to allow the national court to assess the compatibility of national rules.[19] Furthermore, there are no parties to preliminary reference proceedings and the ruling is only directly binding on the referring court.[20]

While these objections have merit, it should be underscored that it is not a question of all or nothing. It is certainly true that many, perhaps most, preliminary rulings leave the final assessment to the national court. Such judgments evidently fall outside the scope of Article 260(1) TFEU. The same goes for the *erga omnes* effects in Member States other than the one from which the request for a preliminary ruling originated. What requires closer scrutiny are those preliminary rulings which in fact pass judgment on the legality of national measures. It is noteworthy that the national court often provides sufficient information about the facts of the case and the interpretation of national law to allow the Court to rule on the legality of the national measures, and it regularly does so. This includes restrictions to free movement,[21] equal treatment,[22] state aid,[23] whether a national measure constitutes a sufficiently serious breach to incur state liability,[24] and in particular, since there is often little or no margin of discretion involved, whether a national measure conflicts with secondary EU legislation.[25] The operative part of the judgment will state that EU law precludes a national measure 'such as that at issue in the main proceedings', but the legal consequences are the same as if it had explicitly referred to the national act.

[14] See e.g. Case C-496/09 *Commission v Italy* [2011] ECLI:EU:C:2011:740; and Case C-610/10 *Commission v Spain* [2012] ECLI:EU:C:2012:781.

[15] Similar Case C-292/11 P *Commission v Portugal* [2014] ECLI:EU:C:2014:3, Opinion of AG Jääskinen, para 82.

[16] ibid.

[17] e.g. judgments rendered by the Court of Justice in annulment proceedings (prior to transfer of competence to the General Court). Consider for instance dismissal of challenges to Commission state aid decisions on the grounds that the aid was, indeed, unlawful, e.g. Case C-480/98 *Spain v Commission* [2000] ECLI:EU:C:2000:559, para 21.

[18] See e.g. Case 6/64 *Costa v ENEL* [1964] ECLI:EU:C:1964:66; Joined Cases C-134/91 and Case C-135/91 *Kerafina* [1992] ECLI:EU:C:1992:434, para 16; and Case C-577/08 *Brouwer* [2010] ECLI:EU:C:2010:449, para 27.

[19] e.g. Case C-130/93 *Lamaire* [1994] ECLI:EU:C:1994:281, para 10.

[20] e.g. Case 69/85 *Wünsche* [1986] ECLI:EU:C:1986:104, paras 13–14.

[21] e.g. Case C-228/98 *Dounias* [2000] ECLI:EU:C:2000:65; Case C-341/05 *Laval* [2007] ECLI:EU:C:2007:809; Case C-346/06 *Rüffert* [2008] ECLI:EU:C:2008:189; and Case C-421/09 *Humanplasma* [2010] ECLI:EU:C:2010:760.

[22] e.g. Case C-206/00 *Mouflin* [2001] ECLI:EU:C:2001:695; and Case C-173/13 *Leone* ECLI:EU:C:2014:2090.

[23] e.g. Case C-143/99 *Adria-Wien Pipeline* [2001] ECLI:EU:C:2001:598; and Joined Cases C-261/02 and 262/02 *van Calster* [2003] ECLI:EU:C:2003:571.

[24] e.g. Case C-392/93 *British Telecom* [1996] ECLI:EU:C:1996:131, paras 41–5; Case C-319/96 *Brinkman* [1998] ECLI:EU:C:1998:429, para 26; and Case C-224/01 *Köbler* [2003] ECLI:EU:C:2003:513, paras 101 and 124.

[25] e.g. Case C-160/01 *Mau* [2003] ECLI:EU:C:2003:280; Case C-429/09 *Fuß* [2010] ECLI:EU:C:2010:717; Case C-244/13 *Ogierakhi* [2014] ECLI:EU:C:2014:2068; and Case C-318/13 *X* [2014] ECLI:EU:C:2014:2133.

This follows from the fact that the operative part must be interpreted in light of the main body of the judgment,[26] which identifies the national measure and explains why it is unlawful. The Court has therefore acknowledged that certain preliminary rulings make it 'apparent that national legislation is incompatible with EU law'[27] or 'clear that the conduct in question constituted an infringement'.[28] Such findings are binding on the referring court in accordance with Article 267 TFEU, but the principle of sincere cooperation in Article 4(3) TEU extends the binding effect to all national authorities.[29] Following a judgment from which it is apparent that national legislation is incompatible with EU law, the competent authorities are thus obliged to take the measures necessary to ensure that EU law is complied with in that state.[30] This includes setting aside the legislation in question, making sure that beneficiaries under the EU rules obtain their rights and, where appropriate, making reparation for loss and damage caused as a result of the breach of EU law.[31] If national authorities allow an infringement to persist despite a preliminary ruling from which it is clear that the conduct constituted an infringement, they will have committed a sufficiently serious breach of EU law to incur state liability.[32] It is precisely because of the 'consequences which might result for a Member State from a preliminary ruling' that the Court may limit the temporal effects of the judgment.[33] The consequences of a preliminary ruling from which it is 'apparent' or 'clear' that a Member State has failed to fulfil its obligations are thus the same as those stemming from a judgment explicitly declaring so under Article 258 TFEU, and it is difficult to see why the two should be distinguished for the purposes of Article 260(1) TFEU.[34]

The only reason for doing so would be right of defence. The procedure in Article 258 TFEU allows the Member State to present its case against the complaints set out by the Commission. These safeguards do not exist in the preliminary reference procedure. It should be added, however, that the Member State is often party to the national proceedings and can in any event submit observations to the Court.[35] Furthermore, the Court will only pass judgment on the lawfulness of national measures under Article 267 TFEU if it has the necessary information to do so.[36] And if the Court does render a ruling from which it is 'apparent' or 'clear' that a Member State has failed to fulfil its obligations under the Treaties, the fact remains that the national authorities must take the necessary measures to comply with the judgment. It would thus be inconsistent to treat such judgments differently from those rendered under Article 258 TFEU. Acknowledging that sanctions could be imposed for a failure to comply with such judgments, on the other hand, is consonant with the wording of Article 260(1) TFEU and the objectives underpinning the procedure in Article 260(2) TFEU. This would also engage the vigilance of individuals to protect their rights in the supervision of EU law[37] and thus conform to the rationale underlying the doctrines of direct effect, supremacy, and state liability. The Court may very

[26] e.g. Case 135/77 *Bosch* [1978] ECLI:EU:C:1978:75, para 4; and Case C-95/12 *Commission v Germany* [2013] ECLI:EU:C:2013:676, para 40.

[27] See e.g. Joined Cases C-231/06 to C-233/06 *Jonkman and Others* [2007] ECLI:EU:C:2007:373, para 38.

[28] Case C-118/00 *Larsy* [2001] ECLI:EU:C:2001:368, para 44.

[29] See e.g. Joined Cases C-231/06 to C-233/06 *Jonkman and Others* [2007] ECLI:EU:C:2007:373, para 37.

[30] ibid, para 38. [31] ibid, paras 38–40.

[32] Case C-118/00 *Larsy* [2001] ECLI:EU:C:2001:368, para 44.

[33] e.g. Case C-262/12 *Association Vent De Colère! Fédération national and Others* [2013] ECLI:EU:C:2013:851, para 42.

[34] e.g. Case C-304/02 *Commission v France* [2005] ECLI:EU:C:2005:444, Second Opinion of AG Geelhoed, para 5.

[35] Article 23 of the Statutes of the Court of Justice.

[36] See e.g. Case C-392/93 *British Telecom* [1996] ECLI:EU:C:1996:131, para 41.

[37] Case 26/62 *van Gend & Loos* [1963] ECLI:EU:C:1963:1.

well hesitate in taking this last step, but the Commission should at least present it with an opportunity to do so.

b. The procedure under Article 260(2) TFEU

The enforcement procedure in Article 260(2) TFEU concerns a failure to fulfil obligations which the Court has declared 'well founded'.[38] The first step is to ascertain the scope of the failure to fulfil obligations, as defined by the Court,[39] and next to identify the measures which are necessary to comply with the judgment. A judgment stating that a Member State has failed to fulfil an obligation under EU law may cover several infringements necessarily included and subsidiary to that finding.[40] Incorrect or incomplete transposition is covered by a failure to notify measures transposing a directive, either completely[41] or partially.[42] An omission to enforce EU law through penalties which are effective, proportionate, and a deterrent is secondary to a finding that there was no system of controls in place.[43] A judgment declaring that national rules are discriminatory may likewise constitute grounds for sanctioning insufficient legislative amendments as well as the flawed application of the amended rules.[44] Member States may also incur sanctions for failing to nullify the unlawful consequences of an infringement,[45] e.g. ensuring that workers acquire rights which they had been deprived of,[46] providing redress for traders affected by an unlawful product approval scheme,[47] rescinding contracts contrary to public procurement directives,[48] recovering unlawful state aid,[49] and cleaning up illegal waste sites.[50]

While the obligations under Article 260(1) TFEU and the corresponding potential for sanctions under Article 260(2) TFEU are potentially far-reaching, they ultimately depend on the ambit of the infringements proceedings.[51] Consider the practical scenario of a Member State which has transposed a directive but which consistently fails to apply and/or enforce the transposition measures. Instead of bringing proceedings under Article 258 TFEU for each and every infringement, the Commission could lump them together in one case and ask the Court to declare that the Member State has infringed the relevant EU rules in a general and persistent manner.[52] Such a judgment extends beyond the specific infringements relied upon by the Commission and means that the Member State must take

[38] Case C-457/07 *Commission v Portugal* [2009] ECLI:EU:C:2009:531, para 47; and Case C-95/12 *Commission v Germany* [2013] ECLI:EU:C:2013:676, para 23.

[39] Case C-292/11 P *Commission v Portugal* [2014] ECLI:EU:C:2014:3, para 41.

[40] See, *mutatis mutandis*, Case C-117/02 *Commission v Portugal* [2004] ECLI:EU:C:2004:266, para 55; Case C-456/03 *Commission v Italy* [2005] ECLI:EU:C:2005:388, para 40; and Case C-32/05 *Commission v Luxembourg* [2006] ECLI:EU:C:2006:749, para 56.

[41] Case C-366/89 *Commission v Italy* [1993] ECLI:EU:C:1993:330. See also, to this effect, Case C-456/03 *Commission v Italy* [2005] ECLI:EU:C:2005:388, para 40; and Case C-32/05 *Commission v Luxembourg* [2006] ECLI:EU:C:2006:749, para 56.

[42] Case C-177/04 *Commission v France* [2006] ECLI:EU:C:2006:173, paras 33–6.

[43] Case C-304/02 *Commission v France* [2005] ECLI:EU:C:2005:444, paras 69–70.

[44] e.g. Case C-119/04 *Commission v Italy* [2006] ECLI:EU:C:2006:489, paras 39–40.

[45] e.g. Case 6/60 *Humblet* [1960] ECLI:EU:C:1960:48; Case C-201/02 *Wells* [2004] ECLI:EU:C:2004:12, paras 64–5; Case C-212/04 *Adeneler and Others* [2006] ECLI:EU:C:2006:443, para 102; and Case C-180/04 *Vassalo* [2006] ECLI:EU:C:2006:518, para 38.

[46] Case C-119/04 *Commission v Italy* [2006] ECLI:EU:C:2006:489, para 29.

[47] Case C-457/07 *Commission v Portugal* [2009] ECLI:EU:C:2009:531, paras 96–100.

[48] Case C-503/04 *Commission v Germany* [2007] ECLI:EU:C:2007:432, paras 28–30.

[49] Case C-369/07 *Commission v Greece* [2009] ECLI:EU:C:2009:428, para 42.

[50] Case C-196/13 *Commission v Italy* [2014] ECLI:EU:C:2014:2407, paras 52–3; and Case C-378/13 *Commission v Greece* [2014] ECLI:EU:C:2014:2405, paras 25–30.

[51] e.g. Case C-456/03 *Commission v Italy* [2005] ECLI:EU:C:2005:388, para 35.

[52] See Case C-494/01 *Commission v Ireland* [2005] ECLI:EU:C:2005:250.

the necessary measures to end and prevent infringements of this generic kind.[53] The potency of this instrument was illustrated in an action brought against Italy in the waste sector. The Court declared in 2007, based on several thousands of illegal tips found throughout the national territory, that Italy had generally and persistently infringed various provisions of Council Directive 75/442 on waste.[54] The Commission subsequently brought proceedings under Article 260(2) TFEU on the grounds that Italy had failed to close and clean up illegal tips, although not necessarily restricted to the ones which had been identified in the first case. Italy protested that other sites fell outside the scope of the first judgment and the Advocate General found the approach 'questionable',[55] whereas the Court correctly noted that 'such sites must be regarded as necessarily encompassed by the general and persistent failure to fulfil obligations established in the first action brought under [Article 258 TFEU]'.[56] The Court proceeded to impose a considerable penalty payment and the highest lump sum to date, underscoring the seriousness of a general and persistent infringement of EU law.[57]

But success stories like this are unfortunately few and far between. Although the Court refined the doctrine of general and persistent infringements in *Irish Waste* and pretty much gave the Commission all the tools it needs to bring such actions effectively,[58] it still seldom does so. Many of the subsequent actions have also been dismissed because of insufficient substantiation of the scale, duration, and widespread nature of the infringement.[59] This is surprising given that these conditions are clearly set out in the case law and some actions have drawn scathing criticism from the Court.[60] It is challenging to establish general and persistent infringements, however, and some failures are to be expected. But the Commission should be careful of adopting a laissez-faire approach which may undermine its credibility and the Court's support for this instrument.

There is also room for improvement in cases involving individual infringements. The main problem, which also explains the limited use of the doctrine on general and persistent infringements, is the Commission's piecemeal manner of addressing a failure to achieve the result required by EU law. One example is the tendency to split belated transposition of directives into several distinct infringements, thus requiring multiple infringement proceedings.[61] Another weakness lies in the inclination to focus on the unlawfulness of national measures rather than on the ultimate failure to attain the result required. Consider

[53] Wennerås (n 1). [54] Case C-135/05 *Commission v Italy* [2007] ECLI:EU:C:2007:250.

[55] Case C-196/13 *Commission v Italy* [2014] ECLI:EU:C:2014:2407, Opinion of AG Kokott, paras 78 et seq.

[56] Case C-196/13 *Commission v Italy* [2014] ECLI:EU:C:2014:2407, para 33.

[57] ibid, paras 100 and 119.

[58] See Case C-494/01 *Commission v Ireland* [2005] ECLI:EU:C:2005:250; and Wennerås (n 1).

[59] e.g. Case C-34/11 *Commission v Portugal* [2012] ECLI:EU:C:2012:712, paras 41–50; Case C-68/11 *Commission v Italy* [2012] ECLI:EU:C:2012:815, paras 49–57; Case C-160/08 *Commission v Germany* [2010] ECLI:EU:C:2010:230, paras 113–23; Case C-416/07 *Commission v Greece* [2009] ECLI:EU:C:2009:528, paras 44–9 and 97–100; Case C-342/05 *Commission v Finland* [2007] ECLI:EU:C:2007:341, paras 32–9; Case C-156/04 *Commission v Greece* [2007] ECLI:EU:C:2007:316, paras 44–53; Case C-287/03 *Commission v Belgium* [2005] ECLI:EU:C:2005:282, paras 24–33; Case C-441/02 *Commission v Germany* [2006] ECLI:EU:C:2006:253, paras 44–56.

[60] Case C-34/11 *Commission v Portugal* [2012] ECLI:EU:C:2012:712, para 48; and Case C-68/11 *Commission v Italy* [2012] ECLI:EU:C:2012:815, para 54.

[61] In the context of Directive 91/676, see e.g. Case C-195/97 *Commission v Italy* [1999] ECLI:EU:C:1999:100 and Case C-127/99 *Commission v Italy* [2001] ECLI:EU:C:2001:597; Case C-71/97 *Commission v Spain* [1998] ECLI:EU:C:1998:455 and Case C-416/02 *Commission v Spain* [2005] ECLI:EU:C:2005:511. As regards Directive 92/43 on conservation of natural habitats and wild fauna and flora, see e.g. Case C-83/97 *Commission v Germany* [1997] ECLI:EU:C:1997:606 and Case C-98/03 *Commission v Germany* [2006] ECLI:EU:C:2006:3; Case C-256/98 *Commission v France* [2000] ECLI:EU:C:2000:192 and Case C-241/08 *Commission v France* [2010] ECLI:EU:C:2010:114; Case C-329/96 *Commission v Greece* [1997] ECLI:EU:C:1997:333 and Case C-103/00 *Commission v Greece* [2002] ECLI:EU:C:2002:60. See also Case C-526/08 *Commission v Luxembourg* [2010] ECLI:EU:C:2010:379, Opinion of AG Kokott, para 69.

for instance the long-running saga involving Portuguese legislation making damages for breach of EU public procurement rules conditional on fault. The Commission's application stated that Portugal had thereby failed to transpose Council Directive 89/665, but the action was subsequently limited to a failure to repeal the national provisions[62] and this was all that the judgment stated.[63] It was thus the persistent failure to repeal the law which next led the Court to impose a penalty payment under Article 260(2) TFEU.[64] A dispute arose thereafter as to whether the amending legislation fulfilled the requirements of the Directive and thus whether the penalty payment kept running. Portugal eventually brought successful annulment proceedings against the Commission's decision saying so. The General Court noted that, according to the terms of the judgment, the penalty payment stopped running when the law in question had been repealed.[65] Whether the amended legislation achieved the result required by the Directive would have to be addressed in new infringement proceedings under Article 258 TFEU. This revolving door might have been avoided if the Commission's action had been more broadly drafted, as it originally had been.[66]

Another problem concerns the manner in which a case is reasoned. A practical example concerns instances where two or more provisions of national law are interlinked and can be assessed independently or jointly. This may be illustrated by the *Volkswagen* case, which concerned a specific company law designed to ensure public control. Paragraph 2(1) of the law thus capped shareholder voting rights to 20 per cent and paragraph 4(3) provided a blocking minority for any shareholder with 20 per cent of the shares. The Commission considered that these provisions constituted independent infringements of Article 56 EC [Article 63 TFEU], but the Court chose to assess them together and found that they jointly infringed EU law.[67] The German authorities repealed paragraph 2(1) of the law, whereupon the Commission required sanctions under Article 260(2) TFEU for failing to repeal paragraph 4(3) as well. This was dismissed by the Court as the previous judgment was based on the cumulative effects of the provisions.[68] That is not to say that paragraph 4(3) of the law necessarily complied with Article 63 TFEU, but only that such an independent assessment had not been made in the previous judgment.[69] Had the Commission wanted to pursue the matter, it would thus have had to bring new infringement proceedings and, potentially, another set of proceedings under of Article 260(2) TFEU.[70]

c. The relationship between Articles 258 and 260(2) TFEU

The cases above illustrate the importance of obtaining broad and clear judgments under Article 258 TFEU in order to successfully tackle persistent infringement in subsequent actions under Article 260 TFEU. There is no escaping, however, that it will occasionally be doubtful whether an infringement falls within the scope of a previous judgment declaring a failure to fulfil obligations. Such cases may thus tempt the Commission to err on the safe

[62] See comment in Case C-292/11 P *Commission v Portugal* [2014] ECLI:EU:C:2014:3, Opinion of AG Jääskinen, paras 39–40.

[63] Case C-275/03 *Commission v Portugal* [2004] ECLI:EU:C:2004:632.

[64] Case C-70/06 *Commission v Portugal* [2008] ECLI:EU:C:2008:3.

[65] Case T-33/09 *Portugal v Commission* [2011] ECLI:EU:C:2011:127, paras 69–89; and Case C-292/11 P *Commission v Portugal* [2014] ECLI:EU:C:2014:3, paras 41–57.

[66] See, to this effect, Case C-292/11 P *Commission v Portugal* [2014] ECLI:EU:C:2014:3, Opinion of AG Jääskinen, para 39–40.

[67] Case C-112/05 *Commission v Germany* [2007] ECLI:EU:C:2007:623, paras 8, 30, and 56.

[68] Case C-95/12 *Commission v Germany* [2013] ECLI:EU:C:2013:676, para 45.

[69] ibid, Opinion of Advocate General Wahl, paras 21 and 54.

[70] ibid, para 54.

side and bring new infringement proceedings under Article 258 TFEU rather than risk an unsuccessful action under Article 260(2) TFEU.

These issues surfaced in *Commission v Luxembourg*.[71] The Member State argued that the complaint had already been settled by the Court in previous infringement proceedings and that the principle of *res judicata* prevented new proceedings under Article 258 TFEU. If the Commission had considered that it had failed to comply with that judgment, Luxembourg added, it should have taken action under Article 260(2) TFEU instead. The Court emphasized at the outset that the case had been brought under Article 258 TFEU.[72] The question whether Article 260(2) TFEU was applicable, the Court continued, arose only if the complaints were identical in fact and in law to those put forward in the previous case.[73] It next dismissed that the principle of *res judicata* prevented the action under Article 258 TFEU as the cases were not identical in fact and in law.[74] The Court concluded that the question of the applicability of Article 260(2) TFEU thus did not arise.[75]

The judgment is somewhat ambiguous. It could be read as saying not only that identity in fact and in law prevent new proceedings under Article 258 TFEU, but also that such circumstances are prerequisites for bringing proceedings under Article 260 TFEU. This would not make much sense, however. The subject matter of the procedure under Article 260(2) TFEU is not the original infringement, but whether the Member State thereafter failed to take the necessary measures to comply with the judgment declaring that infringement.[76] The procedure in Article 260(2) TFEU will therefore necessarily revolve around matters of fact and law which differ from previous infringement proceedings under Article 258 TFEU. It seems that the point the Court was making in *Commission v Luxembourg* is rather that a complaint which is not identical in fact and in law to a previous case can be brought under Article 258 TFEU and if the Commission has done so, 'the question of the applicability of Article 228 EC [Article 260(2) TFEU] does not arise'. This is a convoluted way of saying that the Commission may, subject to the principle of *res judicata*, choose to use the procedure under Article 258 TFEU regardless whether Article 260 TFEU could have been applied.

Furthermore, the limits imposed by the principle of *res judicata* appear questionable after *Commission v Spain*.[77] The Court had in previous proceedings under Article 108(2) TFEU dismissed a complaint concerning a failure to recover state aid. The factual premise relied on turned out to be false, however. The Commission brought new proceedings under Article 108(2) TFEU and argued that the principle of *res judicata* did not prevent the action due to factual developments which had occurred after the first judgment. The Court emphasized instead that the reference date for the assessment of facts was far later in the present case than in the first judgment.[78] Accordingly, the Court said, it could not reasonably be claimed that the two cases had the same subject matter.[79] But if it is sufficient that a failure to fulfil obligations is examined at different times, which this reasoning indicates, the principle of *res judicata* would hardly ever hinder new proceedings under Article 258 TFEU.[80]

[71] Case C-526/08 *Commission v Luxembourg* [2010] ECLI:EU:C:2010:379. [72] ibid, para 23.
[73] ibid. [74] ibid, paras 24–35. [75] ibid, para 37.
[76] See, to this effect, Case C-503/04 *Commission v Germany* [2007] ECLI:EU:C:2007:432, paras 15–16; and Joined Cases C-514/07 P, C-528/07 P and C-532/07 P *Sweden and Others/API v Commission* [2010] ECLI:EU:C:2010:541, para 118.
[77] Case C-529/09 *Commission v Spain* [2013] ECLI:EU:C:2013:31.
[78] ibid, paras 69–76. [79] ibid, para 77.
[80] Similar Case C-526/08 *Commission v Luxembourg* [2010] ECLI:EU:C:2010:379, Opinion of AG Kokott, para 39.

The application of Article 260 TFEU was not an option for the Commission in the Spanish case nor, it seems, in the case concerning Luxembourg. But the combined effect of the general reasoning in these judgments suggests that the Commission is pretty much free to initiate proceedings under Article 258 TFEU irrespective of whether the procedure under Article 260 TFEU could have been applied. This may appear logical, since the Commission is not obliged to bring either kind of proceedings in the first place. A pick and choose approach would nevertheless conflict with the system established by Articles 258 and 260(2) TFEU, which presupposes that the latter procedure is *lex specialis*.[81] Furthermore, it would undermine the deterrent effect of Article 260(2) TFEU.[82] This is exacerbated by the difficulty of collecting sanctions, which could add another set of proceedings before a failure to fulfil obligations is properly enforced.

d. Collecting penalty payments

The challenge posed by collecting penalty payments is similar to that discussed above, namely resolving whether a failure to fulfil obligations falls within the scope of a previous judgment. The difference is that the Treaty does not provide a specific system for resolving disputes at this third stage of enforcement. The Commission has thus taken it upon itself to assess whether and when a Member State has taken the necessary measures to comply with a judgment imposing a penalty payment, whereupon it adopts a decision stipulating the amount due. The legality of such a decision was challenged under Article 256 TFEU in the Portuguese case discussed above. It will be recalled that the General Court held that the periodic penalty payment ended when the Member State had repealed the legislation which had been declared unlawful, while the legality of the amending legislation had to be assessed in new infringement proceedings under Article 258 TFEU.[83] The Court of Justice basically agreed with that assessment[84] and more importantly added some general remarks on how such conflicts must be resolved in the future. This clarification came as a response to the Commission's argument that it must be able to assess whether measures adopted by a Member State are sufficient to comply with a judgment imposing a penalty payment. The logical corollary, according to the Commission, was that the General Court must be able to do the same in its review of the Commission's decision. The Court of Justice affirmed at the outset that the Commission has a power of appraisal and that it is competent to issue decisions collecting fines.[85] That power could not, however, be exercised in a manner prejudicial to the exclusive jurisdiction of the Court of Justice under Articles 258 and 260 TFEU. Hence, neither the Commission nor the General Court are competent to review whether a Member State has complied with a judgment imposing sanctions under Article 260(2) TFEU where that requires assessment of national legislation or practice which has not yet been examined by the Court of Justice.[86]

What this judgment essentially says is that the Commission must bring the matter to the Court of Justice where there is reasonable doubt as to whether and when a Member State complied with a judgment imposing a penalty payment. It also thwarts suggestions that the Commission could collect penalty payments by halting EU contributions, either by

[81] See, to this effect, e.g. Case C-503/04 *Commission v Germany* [2007] ECLI:EU:C:2007:432, paras 15–16. See also Case C-177/04 *Commission v France* [2006] ECLI:EU:C:2006:173, Opinion of AG Geelhoed, paras 43 and 48; and Case C-503/04 *Commission v Germany* [2007] ECLI:EU:C:2007:432, Opinion of AG Trstenjak, para 40.

[82] C-177/04 *Commission v France* [2006] ECLI:EU:C:2006:173, Opinion of AG Geelhoed, para 45.

[83] Case T-33/09 *Portugal v Commission* [2011] ECLI:EU:C:2011:127, paras 69–72.

[84] Case C-292/11 P *Commission v Portugal* [2014] ECLI:EU:C:2014:3, paras 42–3.

[85] ibid, paras 47 and 53.

[86] ibid, paras 48–54.

virtue of its general budgetary powers[87] or through new secondary legislation specifically designed for this purpose.[88] The need for renewed involvement by the Court of Justice in ascertaining the claim clearly frustrates the temporal (and arguably main) benefit of such setoffs.[89] The judgment does not explicitly say that the Commission may resolve disputes through another set of proceedings under Article 260(2) TFEU, but the wording and objectives of that provision accommodate such a course of action.[90] If the Court finds that the Member State has failed to comply with a judgment imposing sanctions, it may render a new judgment establishing with the force of *res judicata* what the Member States owes as a penalty payment. Furthermore, should the infringement persist at the time of the second hearing under Article 260(2) TFEU, the Court may impose a further lump sum and a higher penalty payment effective from the date of the judgment.[91] This should provide sufficient deterrent effect to prevent the need for frequent repeat proceedings under Article 260(2) TFEU.

4. The scope of Article 260(3) TFEU

Article 260(3) TFEU is a new instrument introduced by the Lisbon Treaty. It permits the imposition of penalties earlier, at the stage of the infringement proceedings under Article 258 TFEU, for a failure to 'notify measures transposing a directive adopted under a legislative procedure'.[92] This means that belated transposition of directives not adopted under a legislative procedure falls outside its scope.[93] More importantly, the Commission's Communication on Article 260(3) TFEU suggests that it is limited to a failure to notify complete transposing measures in time, while the correctness of the transposition measures must be dealt with in 'ordinary' infringement proceedings under Article 258 TFEU.[94] This interpretation carries over the Commission's unfortunate practice of bringing separate infringement proceedings for incomplete and incorrect transposition.[95] The consequence of this standpoint is that the Commission may have to bring three cases to compel Member States to transpose directives in time: first seeking a judgment declaring a failure to notify completed transposition measures and imposing sanctions under Article 260(3) TFEU, then bringing another case under Article 258 TFEU for the incorrect transposition

[87] P Craig and G de Burca, *EU Law* (5th edn, OUP 2011) 434.

[88] KL Scheppele, 'What Can the European Commission Do When Member States Violate Basic Principles of the European Union? The Case for Systemic Infringement Actions' (2013) http://ec.europa.eu/justice/events/assises-justice-2013/files/contributions/45.princetonuniversityscheppelesystemicinfringementactionbrusselsversion_en.pdf, accessed 12 October 2016. Setoffs have thus far not been a pressing issue, however; see e.g. D Kochenov, 'On policing Article 2 TEU Compliance – reverse Solange and systemic infringements analyzed' (2013) 33 *Polish Yearbook of International Law* 145, 167–8.

[89] Another issue is that the Commission can withhold EU contributions as a means of enforcement complementary to sanctions under Article 260(2) TFEU. There are several instruments which provide for suspension of financial commitments which are sufficiently linked to an infringement pursued by the Commission under Article 258 TFEU, see e.g. Case C-385/13 P *Italy v Commission* [2014] ECLI:EU:C:2014:2350.

[90] Case C-292/11 P *Commission v Portugal* [2014] ECLI:EU:C:2014:3, Opinion of AG Jääskinen, paras 81–9.

[91] Similarly, ibid, paras 83–5.

[92] The background is the widespread problem of untimely transposition of directives, which threatens the uniform application of EU law and has exacted a high toll on the Commission's enforcement resources, see SEC (2005) 1658, para 20.

[93] That is to say, administrative acts implementing secondary legislation without modifying the scope of its basic obligations. The delimitation of directives which respectively may be adopted under an administrative and legislative procedure is not always straightforward; see e.g. Case C-22/88 *Vreugdenhil and Others* [1989] ECLI:EU:C:1989:277; and Case C-303/94 *Parliament v Council* [1996] ECLI:EU:C:1996:238.

[94] Communication from the Commission—Implementation of Article 260(3) TFEU [2011] OJ C12/1, para 19.

[95] Case C-526/08 *Commission v Luxembourg* [2010] ECLI:EU:C:2010:379, Opinion of AG Kokott, para 69.

measures and finally requiring sanctions under Article 260(2) TFEU for a failure to comply with the second judgment.

Such an approach, if that is indeed what the Commission contemplates, appears flawed. Transposition means absorbing the content of a directive into national law in sufficiently clear and precise terms and creating the legal and administrative framework for its proper application and enforcement.[96] These transposition measures must be notified to the Commission within the time schedule set out in the directive, and they must be complete *and* correct to permit the ongoing process of application and enforcement.[97] This is why incorrect transposition of a directive is necessarily included and subsidiary to a finding that a Member State has failed to transpose a directive in time.[98] The Court therefore sometimes explicitly states that the Member State failed to ensure 'correct and complete transposition' of a directive within the prescribed period.[99] The Commission's position is also contradictory to the purpose behind Article 260(3) TFEU, which is to dispense with a second set of proceedings under Article 260(2) TFEU. All this goes to show that the only sensible reading of Article 260(3) TFEU is that the Commission needs only to bring *one* case for a failure to transpose a directive in time and a penalty payment will run until the Member State has notified complete *and* correct transposition measures.[100]

5. Sanctions under Article 260(2) TFEU

a. Penalty payments

The aim of the penalty payment is to induce a Member State to end a breach of obligations.[101] The relevant question is therefore whether the infringement persists at the time of the Court's examination.[102] If it does, the Court has always found it 'appropriate' to impose a penalty payment, although not required to do so. The amount is determined by the duration of the infringement, its degree of seriousness, and the ability of the Member State to pay.[103] The effects on private and public interests and the urgency of getting the Member States to fulfil its obligations are also considered when applying those criteria[104] and the degree of seriousness in particular.[105]

The Court has held that a Member State's gross domestic product and its number of votes in the Council appropriately reflect its ability to pay, while keeping the variation between the Member States within a reasonable range.[106] These factors are revised by the Commission on a yearly basis, albeit based on statistics established two years prior to each

[96] e.g. Case C-494/01, *Commission v Ireland* [2005] ECLI:EU:C:2005:250, Opinion of AG Geelhoed, paras 24–6.

[97] ibid, para 27. See also, to this effect, e.g. Case C-8/81 *Becker* [1982] ECLI:EU:C:1982:7, para 17–20.

[98] See, to this effect, Case C-366/89 *Commission v Italy* [1993] ECLI:EU:C:1993:330; and Case C-177/04 *Commission* v *France* [2006] ECLI:EU:C:2006:173, paras 33–6.

[99] e.g. Case 294/09 *Commission* v *Ireland* [2010] ECLI:EU:C:2010:200, para 15; and Case C-431/10 *Commission v Ireland* [2011] ECLI:EU:C:2011:227, para 11.

[100] For a different view, see Nils Wahl and Luca Prete, 'Between Certainty, Severity and Proportionality: Some Reflections on the Nature and Functioning of Article 260(3) TFEU' (2014) 6 *European Law Reporter* 170, 174 et seq.

[101] Case C-304/02 *Commission v France* [2005] ECLI:EU:C:2005:444, para 80; and Case C-177/04 *Commission v France* [2006] ECLI:EU:C:2006:173, para 59.

[102] Case C-304/02 *Commission v France* [2005] ECLI:EU:C:2005:444, para 21, c.f. para 20; and Case C-119/04 *Commission v Italy* [2006] ECLI:EU:C:2006:489, paras 45–6.

[103] Case C-387/97 *Commission v Greece* [2000] ECLI:EU:C:2000:356, para 92.

[104] ibid. [105] Case C-304/02 *Commission v France* [2005] ECLI:EU:C:2005:444, para 105.

[106] e.g. Case C-304/02 *Commission v France* [2005] ECLI:EU:C:2005:444, para 109; and Case C-177/04 *Commission v France* [2006] ECLI:EU:C:2006:173, para 75.

update. The Commission considers that two years is the minimum required to gather stable macroeconomic data.[107] The Court has in contrast held that the benchmark is the inflation and GDP at the time of its examination of facts. Hence, some judgments rely on data submitted by the Member States indicating a lower ability to pay than the figures provided by the Commission.[108] Case law does not specify how much weight is given to the ability to pay, or to other criteria for that matter. However, a finding that a Member State's ability to pay has 'to a certain degree been diminished in the context of the economic crisis' is presumably significant.[109] Such cases have regularly attracted lower sanctions than the Commission's proposals.[110] If the Member State is also receiving economic assistance from the EU, it is understandable that the Court might hesitate from imposing significant sanctions which the EU in effect would have to finance. This could nevertheless mean that irresponsible economic policy (which may have conflicted with EU stability requirements) earns Member States much lower sanctions than more prudent Member States. Ability to pay is therefore a delicate matter which must be balanced against the other relevant criteria.[111]

The seriousness of the infringement is examined objectively. The Court does not accept any excuses for failing to comply with its judgments, save perhaps *force majeure*[112] and other instances where it would be 'absolutely impossible' for the Member State to take the requisite measures in time.[113] The degree of seriousness and in particular the effects on public and private interests is assessed by taking into account the importance of the EU rules infringed. Non-compliance with the Treaty provisions on free movement and state aid is considered particularly serious,[114] and the same goes for infringements of secondary legislation concerning the protection of human health, the environment, and the common fisheries policy.[115] The scale and impact of the infringement is also relevant,[116] and a 'general and persistent' infringement of EU law is deemed especially serious.[117] The Court does not explicitly go into whether the Member State is at fault, but it appears to influence the assessment. The cases which have been deemed the most serious concerned instances where the national authorities had plainly ignored the Court's judgments and, in one instance, had even continued to enforce the unlawful measures by way of penalties.[118]

[107] Communication from the Commission C(2014) 6767 final p. 2.

[108] Case C-279/11 *Commission v Ireland* [2012] ECLI:EU:C:2012:834, paras 78–9 and Case C-374/11 *Commission v Ireland* [2012] ECLI:EU:C:2012:827, para 44.

[109] ibid (concerning imposition of a lump sum). See also Case C-496/09 *Commission v Italy* [2011] ECLI:EU:C:2011:740; Case C-407/09 *Commission v Greece* [2011] ECLI:EU:C:2011:196; and Case C-374/11 *Commission v Ireland* [2012] ECLI:EU:C:2012:827.

[110] Case C-279/11 *Commission v Ireland* (n 108) and Case C-374/11 *Commission v Ireland* (n 108).

[111] See, *mutatis mutandis*, the reasoning employed in competition cases, e.g. Case C-499/11 P *Dow Chemical and Others* [2013] ECLI:EU:C:2013:482, paras 86–91.

[112] e.g. Case C-121/07 *Commission v France* [2008] ECLI:EU:C:2008:695, para 72 with further references.

[113] See to this effect, Case C-496/09 *Commission v Italy* [2011] ECLI:EU:C:2011:740.

[114] e.g. Case C-121/07 *Commission v France* [2008] ECLI:EU:C:2008:695, para 78; Case C-369/07 *Commission v Greece* [2009] ECLI:EU:C:2009:428, paras 118–20; and Case C-496/09 *Commission v Italy* [2011] ECLI:EU:C:2011:740, paras 60–2.

[115] Case C-387/97 *Commission v Greece* [2000] ECLI:EU:C:2000:356, para 94; and Case C-278/01 *Commission v Spain* [2003] ECLI:EU:C:2003:635, para 57; and Case C-304/02 *Commission v France* [2005] ECLI:EU:C:2005:444, para 105.

[116] Regarding aggravating circumstances, see e.g. Case C-304/02 *Commission v France* [2005] ECLI:EU:C:2005:444, para 105; Case C-70/06 *Commission v Portugal* [2008] ECLI:EU:C:2008:3, para 42; Case C-568/07 *Commission v Greece* [2009] ECLI:EU:C:2009:342, para 34; and Case C-109/08 *Commission v Greece* [2009] ECLI:EU:C:2009:346, para 36. Regarding less serious circumstances, see e.g. Case C-177/04 *Commission v France* [2006] ECLI:EU:C:2006:173, paras 65–6; and Case C-369/07 *Commission v Greece* [2009] ECLI:EU:C:2009:428, para 122.

[117] e.g. Case C-304/02 *Commission v France* [2005] ECLI:EU:C:2005:444, para 105; and Case C-196/13 *Commission v Italy* [2014] ECLI:EU:C:2014:2407, para 100.

[118] Case C-304/02 *Commission v France* [2005] ECLI:EU:C:2005:444, paras 105–6; Case C-610/10 *Commission v Spain* [2012] ECLI:EU:C:2012:781, para 130; Case C-109/08 *Commission v Greece* [2009] ECLI:EU:C:2009:346, para 35; and Case C-196/13 *Commission v Italy* [2014] ECLI:EU:C:2014:2407, para 101.

The duration of the infringement refers to the lapse of time from delivery of the first judgment until the Court assesses the facts in the second proceedings.[119] Although it is settled case law that duration is significant, it is not clear why this is so. The penalty payment is a coercive instrument and the main issue is to determine the degree of pressure needed to persuade the Member State to end the infringement.[120] The seriousness of the infringement and the ability to pay are relevant in this context, not the duration of the previous behaviour. The Court not only considers the length of time which has passed, and other factors include the complexity and nature of the measures needed to comply with the judgment as well as the extent to which the obligations were clearly defined in the relevant EU rules.[121] The clarity of the Court's judgments does not seem relevant, even though this sometimes poses the greatest challenge for the Member State.[122]

The fine is calculated according to the Commission's Communication (2005) and updated guidelines, by employing a set unit amount (currently EUR 650) which is multiplied by the degree of seriousness (1–20), the duration of the infringement (1–3), and a coefficient reflecting the Member State's ability to pay.[123] The Court has recognized that methodology, although emphasizing that it is not bound by the scale for the relevant coefficient or the criteria for determining the concrete coefficient.[124] While the Court initially followed the Commission's methodology quite rigidly,[125] it has since refrained from stipulating concrete coefficients. The judgments instead describe the relative gravity of the different criteria, e.g. that the duration of the infringement is 'very considerable',[126] 'exceptionally long',[127] or just stating the length of the infringement.[128] Perhaps the Court found it burdensome to specify coefficients in each and every case. Another explanation is scepticism as to whether the Commission's methodology is helpful in identifying what the Court considers to be appropriate amounts. This is supported by the fact that the Court usually imposes radically lower fines than the Commission demands. Most penalty payments are at least halved and often cut further.[129] The two latest judgments depart from this pattern, however. They concerned 'general and persistent' infringements of EU waste regulation committed by well-known offenders in this field and attracted high penalties.[130] Italy received about the same penalty payment as proposed by the Commission while Greece in fact got a higher penalty payment. Considering the case law as a whole, it appears that the discrepancy between the Court and the Commission primarily concerns different views on the seriousness of the infringements. The Court seems to take a fairly relaxed view of 'minor' and 'ordinary' failures to fulfil obligations, whereas it is ready to slam exceptional

[119] e.g. Case C-177/04 *Commission v France* [2006] ECLI:EU:C:2006:173, para 71.

[120] e.g. Case C-196/13 *Commission v Italy* [2014] ECLI:EU:C:2014:2407, para 96.

[121] e.g. Case C-278/01 *Commission v Spain* [2003] ECLI:EU:C:2003:635, paras 53–4; and Case C-177/04 *Commission v France* [2006] ECLI:EU:C:2006:173, para 72.

[122] See, *mutatis mutandis*, Case C-177/04 *Commission v France* [2006] ECLI:EU:C:2006:173, Opinion of AG Geelhoed, para 70.

[123] Commission Communication (SEC (2010) 923/3), 4.

[124] See to this effect, Case C-177/04 *Commission v France* [2006] ECLI:EU:C:2006:173, para 70.

[125] e.g. Case C-278/01 *Commission v Spain* [2003] ECLI:EU:C:2003:635, paras 52–60; and Case C-304/02 *Commission v France* [2005] ECLI:EU:C:2005:444, paras 107–13.

[126] Case C-496/09 *Commission v Italy* [2011] ECLI:EU:C:2011:740, para 59.

[127] Case C-610/10 *Commission v Spain* [2012] ECLI:EU:C:2012:781 para 121.

[128] Case C-576/11 *Commission v Luxembourg* [2013] ECLI:EU:C:2013:773, para 52.

[129] e.g. Case C-610/10 *Commission v Spain* [2012] ECLI:EU:C:2012:781; Case C-374/11 *Commission v Ireland* [2012] ECLI:EU:C:2012:827; Case C-533/11 *Commission v Belgium* [2013] ECLI:EU:C:2013:659; Case C-576/11 *Commission v Luxembourg* [2013] ECLI:EU:C:2013:773.

[130] Case C-196/13 *Commission v Italy* [2014] ECLI:EU:C:2014:2407; and Case C-378/13 *Commission v Greece* [2014] ECLI:EU:C:2014:2405.

ones.[131] The Commission, on the other hand, considers that common infringements are serious and is perhaps less strict in relative terms with regard to the gravest breaches. They should attempt to find some middle ground. The Commission is right to view ordinary and thus common infringements as serious, but it would probably benefit from distinguishing cases more than it currently does.

The amount is not the only thing which determines the coercive effect of a penalty payment. The frequency of a payment and whether the rates are flat or decreasing are equally important.[132] In cases involving legislative amendments, the penalty payment usually consists of a flat daily amount running from the date of the Court's judgment until the infringement ceases.[133] Cases involving a failure to achieve a particular result or an unlawful administrative practice have been treated differently. Since the effects of remedial measures may not be ascertained immediately, the Court has often found it appropriate to impose a biannual or annual penalty payment.[134] This is 'in certain specific cases', yet is in fact becoming commonplace, combined with rates which decrease with the Member State's progress.[135] The common denominator in these cases is that significant improvement can be achieved in the short term and that the Commission can easily monitor the Member States' progress, e.g. achieving conformity with limit values for bathing waters,[136] recovery of state aid,[137] and closing and cleaning up illegal waste sites.[138] These modifications are consonant with the objective of the penalty payment and the principle of proportionality, i.e. to coerce the Member State into compliance rather than penalizing it. The consequence is nevertheless that the Member State may incur quite low penalty payments or escape them altogether, which undermines the deterrent effect of Article 260(2) TFEU.[139] This objection loses its force if the Court simultaneously imposes lump sums which are capable of ensuring deterrence, but this is seldom the case.

b. Lump sums

A lump sum is a dissuasive measure designed to prevent repetition of similar infringements of EU law.[140] It may therefore be imposed where the Member State has failed to take the necessary measures to comply with a judgment within the time limit set in the Commission's formal notice (previously the reasoned opinion) and thus regardless of whether the infringement has ended when the case reaches the Court.[141] Member States could otherwise avoid sanctions by terminating the infringement shortly before the proceedings under

[131] See also Case C-241/11 *Commission v Czech Republic* [2013] ECLI:EU:C:2013:423, Opinion of AG Jääskinen, para 8.

[132] The starting point of the penalty payment is the delivery of the Court's judgment. An exception was made, however, in a case where it was uncertain whether the infringement had in fact ended at the time of the Court's examination of facts, see Case C-369/07 *Commission v Greece* [2009] ECLI:EU:C:2009:428, para 125.

[133] Case C-177/04 *Commission v France* [2006] ECLI:EU:C:2006:173, para 77; and Case C-70/06 *Commission v Portugal* [2008] ECLI:EU:C:2008:3, para 52.

[134] Case C-278/01 *Commission v Spain* [2003] ECLI:EU:C:2003:635, paras 43–6; Case C-304/02 *Commission v France* [2005] ECLI:EU:C:2005:444, paras 111–12; and Case C-496/09 *Commission v Italy* [2011] ECLI:EU:C:2011:740, paras 53–5.

[135] Case C-196/13 *Commission v Italy* [2014] ECLI:EU:C:2014:2407, paras 106–10.

[136] Case C-278/01 *Commission v Spain* [2003] ECLI:EU:C:2003:635, paras 47–51.

[137] Case C-496/09 *Commission v Italy* [2011] ECLI:EU:C:2011:740, paras 48–52.

[138] Case C-196/13 *Commission v Italy* [2014] ECLI:EU:C:2014:2407, paras 108–10; and Case C-378/13 *Commission v Greece* [2014] ECLI:EU:C:2014:2405, paras 61–6.

[139] e.g. Case C-304/02 *Commission v France* [2005] ECLI:EU:C:2005:444, para 97. See also the doubts harboured by the Court in Case C-196/13 *Commission v Italy* [2014] ECLI:EU:C:2014:2407, para 80.

[140] Case C-121/07 *Commission v France* [2008] ECLI:EU:C:2008:695, paras 56 and 69.

[141] ibid.

Article 260(2) TFEU.[142] Furthermore, since the penalty payment and the lump sum pursue different objectives (coercion and deterrence) and complement each other, the Court held in *French Fisheries II* that the sanctions may be cumulated where the infringement persists at the time of the Court's examination.[143]

The Court has nevertheless underscored that a lump sum shall not be imposed as a matter of course, but depends on all the relevant factors concerning the nature of the infringement and the conduct of the Member State.[144] Accordingly, the Court refrained from imposing a lump sum in the four cases following *French Fisheries II*.[145] The Commission emphasized in the next case, again involving France, that the Member State had been held in violation of the relevant EU rules on numerous occasions[146] and that measures necessary to ensure compliance were often deferred until just prior to the Court's examination of the facts.[147] The Court tersely agreed that 'where a Member State repeatedly engages in unlawful conduct in such a manner in a specific sector, this may be an indication that effective prevention of future repetition of similar infringements of Community law may require the adoption of a dissuasive measure, such as a lump payment'.[148] The Commission has since requested a lump sum in every action under Article 260(2) TFEU and the Court has always obliged.[149]

The criteria determining the amount of a lump sum are the same as those applying to a penalty payment, i.e. the seriousness of the infringement, its duration, and the ability to pay.[150] The weighting of the respective factors is different, however. The most significant distinction concerns the importance of the effects on public and private interests.[151] The Court has stated that adverse effects on such interests constitute the primary justification for imposing a lump sum, in particular where the breach has persisted for a long time.[152] A finding of significant effects will therefore often entail relatively high lump sums[153] and vice versa.[154] This means that the Commission is not only required to prove that the infringement persisted until its letter of formal notice, but also to provide evidence of its effects until then or, if applicable, at the time of the hearing.[155] Appraising the conduct of

[142] SEC (2005) 1658, point 10.1.

[143] Case C-304/02 *Commission v France* [2005] ECLI:EU:C:2005:444, paras 80–2.

[144] e.g. Case C-568/07 *Commission v Greece* [2009] ECLI:EU:C:2009:342, para 44.

[145] Case C-177/04 *Commission v France* [2006] ECLI:EU:C:2006:173, paras 62–3; Case C-119/04 *Commission v Italy* [2006] ECLI:EU:C:2006:489; Case C-503/04 *Commission v Germany* [2007] ECLI:EU:C:2007:432, paras 40–1; and Case C-70/06 *Commission v Portugal* [2008] ECLI:EU:C:2008:3.

[146] Case C-121/07 *Commission v France* [2008] ECLI:EU:C:2008:695.

[147] ibid, paras 66–8.

[148] ibid, para 69. See also Case C-496/09 *Commission v Italy* [2011] ECLI:EU:C:2011:740, paras 89–91.

[149] Case C-568/07 *Commission v Greece* [2009] ECLI:EU:C:2009:342; Case C-109/08 *Commission v Greece* [2009] ECLI:EU:C:2009:346; Case C-369/07 *Commission v Greece* [2009] ECLI:EU:C:2009:428; Case C-496/09 *Commission v Italy* [2011] ECLI:EU:C:2011:740; Case C-407/09 *Commission v Greece* [2011] ECLI:EU:C:2011:196; Case C-610/10 *Commission v Spain* [2012] ECLI:EU:C:2012:781; Case C-279/11 *Commission v Ireland* [2012] ECLI:EU:C:2012:834; Case C-374/11 *Commission v Ireland* [2012] ECLI:EU:C:2012:827; Case C-270/11 *Commission v Sweden* [2013] ECLI:EU:C:2013:339; Case C-241/11 *Commission v Czech Republic* [2013] ECLI:EU:C:2013:423; Case C-533/11 *Commission v Belgium* [2013] ECLI:EU:C:2013:659; Case C-95/12 *Commission v Germany* [2013] ECLI:EU:C:2013:676; Case C-576/11 *Commission v Luxembourg* [2013] ECLI:EU:C:2013:773.

[150] See e.g. Case C-496/09 *Commission v Italy* [2011] ECLI:EU:C:2011:740, paras 146–8; and Case C-533/11 *Commission v Belgium* [2013] ECLI:EU:C:2013:659, para 53.

[151] See to this effect, Case C-378/13 *Commission v Greece* [2014] ECLI:EU:C:2014:2405, para 78.

[152] e.g. Case C-121/07 *Commission v France* [2008] ECLI:EU:C:2008:695, para 58.

[153] e.g. Case C-496/09 *Commission v Italy* [2011] ECLI:EU:C:2011:740, para 95, c.f. para 63; and Case C-184/11 *Commission v Spain* [2014] ECLI:EU:C:2014:316, para 80, c.f. paras 73–4.

[154] e.g. Case C-279/11 *Commission v Ireland* [2012] ECLI:EU:C:2012:834, para 74; Case C-270/11 *Commission v Sweden* [2013] ECLI:EU:C:2013:339, para 50; and Case C-241/11 *Commission v Czech Republic* [2013] ECLI:EU:C:2013:423, paras 53–4.

[155] e.g. Case C-270/11 *Commission v Sweden* [2013] ECLI:EU:C:2013:339, para 50.

the Member State, which is akin to an assessment of fault,[156] also plays a more important role when determining the amount of a lump sum. This criterion originated from the aggravating circumstance that some Member States were responsible of repeatedly unlawful conduct.[157] Since then, however, the Court has increasingly emphasized a Member State's conduct as a mitigating factor, e.g. underscoring that the Member State had not failed to comply with a judgment before, that it had cooperated in good faith with the Commission, that substantial investments to ensure compliance had been made, and that the Member State had initiated the process of compliance promptly, and the Court has even emphasized the complexity, cost, and duration required to comply with its judgment.[158] Finally, it appears that the Court gives greater weight to ability to pay when determining the amount of a lump sum.[159]

The Commission's calculation of lump sums is similar to the method for calculating penalty payments, but there are some differences. First, the Commission has calculated a 'minimum lump sum' for each Member State on the basis of its gross domestic product and its voting rights in the Council. Minimum lump sums are, according to the Commission's guidelines, set 'irrespective of aggravating circumstances and represent the minimum necessary to avoid purely symbolic amounts which would have no deterrent effect and could undermine, rather than strengthen, the authority of Court judgments'.[160] The Commission also calculates a lump sum based on the facts of the case. A daily amount is set by multiplying a standard flat rate by the coefficient for seriousness (1–20) and by an 'n' factor reflecting the ability to pay, which is then multiplied by the number of days the infringement persisted after the judgment which established the failure to fulfil obligations.[161] This lump sum is requested by the Commission whenever it is higher than the minimum lump sum, which is invariably the case and often by a significant margin.

The Court has not referred to the minimum lump sum as a kind of minimum benchmark nor does it seem to engage in any genuine calculation of the lump sum. The deliberations usually consist of some sparse remarks on the relevant criteria, coupled where appropriate with a reference to its assessment of the penalty payment, and the outcome is a round sum based on a 'fair assessment'.[162] The amount is almost always significantly lower than the Commission's proposal. In the judgments rendered after the adoption of the Lisbon Treaty, the Court has cut the proposed lump sums by half and often significantly more,[163] sometimes coming close to the minimum lump sum in the Commission's guidelines.[164] And if that was not enough to question whether the Court is in fact disregarding the Commission's methodology, the judgment in *Commission v the Czech*

[156] e.g. Case C-241/11 Commission *v* Czech Republic [2013] ECLI:EU:C:2013:423, Opinion of Advocate General Jäaskinen, paras 49–61.

[157] Case C-121/07 *Commission v France* [2008] ECLI:EU:C:2008:695, paras 66–9.

[158] Case C-270/11 *Commission v Sweden* [2013] ECLI:EU:C:2013:339, para 55; Case C-241/11 *Commission v Czech Republic* [2013] ECLI:EU:C:2013:423, para 51; Case C-533/11 *Commission v Belgium* [2013] ECLI:EU:C:2013:659, paras 59–60; and Case C-576/11 *Commission v Luxembourg* [2013] ECLI:EU:C:2013:773, paras 61–2.

[159] See e.g. Case C-496/09 *Commission v Italy* [2011] ECLI:EU:C:2011:740; and Case C-374/11 *Commission v Ireland* [2012] ECLI:EU:C:2012:827.

[160] SEC (2005) 1658, point 20. [161] ibid, points 21–4.

[162] e.g. Case C-568/07 *Commission v Greece* [2009] ECLI:EU:C:2009:342, paras 57–61.

[163] e.g. Case C-496/09 *Commission v Italy* [2011] ECLI:EU:C:2011:740; Case C-610/10 *Commission v Spain* [2012] ECLI:EU:C:2012:781; Case C-279/11 *Commission v Ireland* [2012] ECLI:EU:C:2012:834; Case C-374/11 *Commission* v *Ireland* [2012] ECLI:EU:C:2012:827; Case C-270/11 *Commission v Sweden* [2013] ECLI:EU:C:2013:339; Case C-533/11 *Commission* v *Belgium* [2013] ECLI:EU:C:2013:659; Case C-184/11 *Commission v Spain* [2014] ECLI:EU:C:2014:316; Case C-196/13 *Commission v Italy* [2014] ECLI:EU:C:2014:2407; and Case C-378/13 *Commission v Greece* [2014] ECLI:EU:C:2014:2405.

[164] e.g. Case C-279/11 *Commission v Ireland* [2012] ECLI:EU:C:2012:834; Case C-374/11 *Commission* v *Ireland* [2012] ECLI:EU:C:2012:827; and Case C-270/11 *Commission v Sweden* [2013] ECLI:EU:C:2013:339.

Republic surely does.[165] The minimum lump sum for the Czech Republic was EUR 1,768,000 and the Commission had proposed a lump sum of EUR 3,364,395 based on a coefficient for seriousness of 8 (of 1–20).[166] The Advocate General considered that a coefficient of 1 or 2 was more appropriate, but noted that neither would yield an amount exceeding the minimum lump sum.[167] He therefore questioned such thresholds as they excluded the application of the lowest coefficients in most cases, save very persistent infringements.[168] The Advocate General eventually arrived at a round sum which was lower than the minimum lump sum but slightly higher than if a coefficient of 2 had been employed, namely EUR 1 million.[169] The Court (in Grand Chamber) set the lump sum to EUR 250,000 without further ado.[170] This result is incompatible with the Commission's methodology for calculating lump sums as well as the concept of minimum lump sums. The case was admittedly special insofar as the infringement had very limited effects on private and public interests,[171] but the Commission's analytical framework should be appropriate for all cases. This aspect of the Commission's fining policy, even more so than the method for calculating penalty payments, is therefore in need of some fine-tuning in light of the Court's case law.

That the Commission got it wrong does not mean that the Court got it right, however. The Commission probably is, and rightly so, frustrated by the Court's fining policy. It is, firstly, difficult to ascertain how the Court arrives at its lump sums. The Commission has been deservedly criticized for some inconsistency in its application of the coefficient for seriousness,[172] but that only goes to show that its practice is amenable to review. The Court's case law, on the other hand, hardly provides any benchmarks for its fining policy. This may in turn present a risk of arbitrariness.[173] It is certainly true that imposition of fines is not a mathematical exercise and that the deterrent effect may be undermined if the economic risks posed by infringements could be calculated accurately.[174] There is a limit to such arguments, however.

Secondly, the lump sums imposed by the Court are plainly too low.[175] The primary reason is the Court's preoccupation with the effects on public and private interests, which explains the symbolic sum imposed in the Czech case. Another reason is the emphasis placed on the Member State's conduct and the weight given to mitigating circumstances. The Court also seems hesitant to impose significant lump sums on Member States experiencing economic difficulty. The first and (partially) the second factor are reminiscent of the state liability doctrine, and it should be recalled that the Court emphasized in *French Fisheries II* that a 'a penalty payment and/or a lump sum is not intended to compensate for damage caused by the Member State concerned, but to place it under economic pressure which induces it to put an end to the breach established'.[176] This applies particularly to a lump sum. The purpose of this instrument is to dissuade repetition of similar infringements

[165] Case C-241/11 *Commission v Czech Republic* [2013] ECLI:EU:C:2013:423.
[166] ibid, Opinion of AG Jääskinen, paras 84 and 87.
[167] ibid, paras 89–91. [168] ibid, para 94. [169] ibid, para 96.
[170] Case C-241/11 *Commission v Czech Republic* [2013] ECLI:EU:C:2013:423, paras 50–5.
[171] ibid, para 53.
[172] Case C-241/11 *Commission v Czech Republic* [2013] ECLI:EU:C:2013:423, Opinion of Advocate General Jääskinen, paras 45–8.
[173] e.g. Kilbey (n 1).
[174] See, in the context of competition law, e.g. Case C-499/11 P *Dow Chemical and Others* [2013] ECLI:EU:C:2013:482, para 89; and WPJ Wils, 'The European Commission's 2006 Guidelines on Antitrust fines: A Legal and Economic Analysis' (2007) 30 *World Competition* III B.
[175] Similar T Hartley, *The Foundations of European Union Law* (7th edn, OUP 2010), 343 and 345 with further references.
[176] Case C-304/02 *Commission v France* [2005] ECLI:EU:C:2005:444, para 91.

of EU law[177] rather than, as has been suggested, punishing a Member State based on its relative culpability.[178] The extent to which the infringement damaged public and private interests and the conduct of the Member State should therefore, as in competition cases,[179] not constitute the main factors determining the appropriate amount of the fine. The Court should rather focus on duration, the nature of the infringement and above all on finding the appropriate fining level to prevent similar infringements from recurring.[180] Perhaps the Court harbours the same view as one Advocate General, namely that 'from a budgetary perspective, the unexpected forfeiture of an amount that could be regarded as "trifling" has an undoubted deterrent effect for the Member States'.[181] If so, there are quite a lot of competition lawyers who will start sharpening their pencils and query why the same logic does not hold true for companies infringing EU law.

The Court is willing to take off its gloves for the most serious infringements, however. A general and persistent infringement in the field of human health and environment, which added to the list of similar breaches, recently earned Italy a lump sum of EUR 40 million.[182] This is the highest lump sum thus far, albeit still only about half of what the Commission requested.

6. Sanctions under Article 260(3) TFEU

The imposition of sanctions under Article 260(3) TFEU differs in some respects from the main rule in Article 260(2) TFEU. The Commission is not obliged to propose financial penalties under Article 260(3) TFEU and the Court may not impose sanctions exceeding the amount specified by the Commission. This is worrisome since the Commission indicated in its Communication on Article 260(3) TFEU that it would normally propose only a penalty payment and reserve the lump sum for instances where this sanction is 'warranted by the circumstances of the case'.[183] Such a policy presents a risk that the Member State will wait to notify the requisite transposition measures until imminently prior to the Court's examination of the facts and thus escape sanctions.[184] That risk has materialized. The Commission has currently brought fourteen claims for penalty payments in accordance with Article 260(3) TFEU, all of which were withdrawn after the Member States notified the relevant measures prior to the Court's hearing.[185] The Commission

[177] e.g. Case C-610/10 *Commission v Spain* [2012] ECLI:EU:C:2012:781, para 142; and Case C-279/11 *Commission v Ireland* [2012] ECLI:EU:C:2012:834, para 66.

[178] Case C-241/11 *Commission v Czech Republic* [2013] ECLI:EU:C:2013:423, Opinion of AG Jääskinen, paras 31–2 and 49–52.

[179] Regarding the effects of the infringement, see e.g. Case T-410/03 *Hoechst* [2008] ECLI:EU:T:2008:211, paras 343–5; and Case T-208/06 *Quinn Barlo* [2011] ECLI:EU:T:2011:701, para 189. Regarding conduct during the administrative procedure, see e.g. Case C-287/98 P *SCA Holding* [2000] ECLI:EU:C:2000:468, para 36; Joined Cases C-189/02 P, C-202/02 P, C-205/02 P to C-208/02 P, and C-213/02 P *Dansk Rørindustri and Others* [2005] ECLI:EU:C:2005:408, para 403;Case T-340/03 *France Telecom* [2007] ECLI:EU:T:2007:22, para 277.

[180] Compare in the field of competition e.g. Case T-38/02 *Danone* [2005] ECLI:EU:T:2005:367, paras 168–170 with further references.

[181] Case C-241/11 *Commission v Czech Republic* [2013] ECLI:EU:C:2013:423, Opinion of AG Jääskinen, para 94.

[182] Case C-196/13 *Commission v Italy* [2014] ECLI:EU:C:2014:2407. For a similar infringement, see Case C-304/02 *Commission v France* [2005] ECLI:EU:C:2005:444.

[183] Communication from the Commission—Implementation of Article 260(3) TFEU [2011] OJ C12/1, para 21.

[184] P Wennerås, 'Sanctions against Member States under Article 260 TFEU: Alive, but not kicking?' (2012) 49 *Common Market Law Review* 145, 168.

[185] Case C-386/13 *Commission v Cyprus* [2014] ECLI:EU:C:2014:2257; Case C-241/13 *Commission* v *Estonia* [2014] ECLI:EU:C:2014:2137; Case C-240/13 *Commission v Estonia* [2014] ECLI:EU:C:2014:2136; Case *Commission* v *Bulgaria* [2013] ECLI:EU:C:2013:621; Case C-111/13 *Commission v Finland* [2013] ECLI:EU:C:2013:881; Case C-109/13 *Commission v Finland* [2013] ECLI:EU:C:2013:880; Case C-545/12 *Commission v Cyprus* [2013] ECLI:EU:C:2013:329; Case C-532/12 *Commission v Luxembourg* [2013] ECLI:EU:C:2013:158; Case C-407/12

should therefore amend its policy and regularly start requesting lump sums, as it does under Article 260(2) TFEU.[186] It is true that the Commission's actions have been successful insofar as the threat of penalty payments compelled the Member States to end their infringements. But lump sums are included in Article 260(3) TFEU to deter Member States from failing to transpose directives in the first place. This is underscored by the fact that a lump sum may already be imposed at the stage of infringement proceedings.

If the Commission continues to turn the other cheek, however, it may be that the Court will take it upon itself to ensure that Article 260(3) TFEU has a deterrent effect. That provision admittedly states that the Court may impose a lump sum or penalty payment 'not exceeding the amount specified by the Commission'. It may be construed, however, as merely requiring deference with regard to the amounts specified by the Commission, while not preventing the Court from assessing the appropriateness of imposing sanctions which the Commission has not specified.[187] The Commission likewise initially refrained from requesting lump sums under Article 260(2) TFEU, a policy which the Court gave short shrift in *French Fisheries II*. The appropriateness of imposing a financial penalty and the choice of penalty most suited to the circumstances of the case, the Court said, can be appraised only in the light of the findings made by the Court and therefore fall outside the political sphere.[188] The Court also considered that, once the Commission has exercised its discretion as to the initiation of infringement proceedings, the case is subject to a judicial procedure in which political considerations are irrelevant.[189]

7. Conclusion

The objectives underpinning Article 260 TFEU can only be attained if the threat of sanctions is effective, proportionate, and a deterrent. This presupposes a credible risk of detection, that a sufficient number of infringements can be brought before the Court and that sanctions are imposed expeditiously.[190] These requirements are largely satisfied with regard to belated transposition of directives. The only dark cloud on the horizon is the Commission's narrow interpretation of Article 260(3) TFEU with regard to incorrect transposition, but we may hope that it will alter its position or that the Court will correct it.

The situation is more precarious for all other infringements of EU law. The Commission neither has the monitoring powers nor the resources necessary to supervise compliance with the EU Treaties effectively, let alone the application and enforcement of secondary legislation. This means that it is not able to bring enough cases under Article 258 TFEU to bring the deterrent potential of Article 260(2) TFEU to fruition. Add to this that infringements may last for more than twenty years before the Court is in a position to impose sanctions, even with the shortening of the pre-litigation phase, and it is plain to see that Article 260(2) TFEU is not having a satisfactorily deterrent effect. This could be remedied, however, if the Court were to recognize that certain preliminary rulings fall within the

Commission v Slovenia [2013] ECLI:EU:C:2013:216; Case C-406/12 *Commission v Slovenia* [2013] ECLI:EU:C:2013:215; Case C-331/12 *Commission v Poland* [2013] ECLI:EU:C:2013:214; Case C-330/12 *Commission v Poland* [2013] ECLI:EU:C:2013:213; Case C-329/12 *Commission v Germany* [2014] ECLI:EU:C:2014:2034; and Case C-245/12 *Commission v Poland* [2013 ECLI:EU:C:2013:584.

[186] The Commission has warned that the approach may be adjusted 'depending on what the Member States do'; see Communication from the Commission—Implementation of Article 260(3) TFEU [2011] OJ C12/1, para 21 et seq.

[187] For a different view, see Wahl and Prete (n 100) 185.

[188] Case C-304/02 *Commission v France* [2005] ECLI:EU:C:2005:444, para 90. [189] ibid.

[190] See, *mutatis mutandis*, Case C-304/02 *Commission v France* [2005] ECLI:EU:C:2005:444, para 37.

scope of Article 260(1) TFEU and thereby employ the vigilance of individuals to protect their rights in the supervision of EU law.[191]

The effectiveness of Article 260 TFEU would also benefit from a reformed mindset on the part of the Commission and the Court. Most lawyers prefer to limit their activities in a manner which maximizes their chance of success. Judges like to solve the matter at hand on narrow grounds, thus allowing for latitude in future cases. This is all very well in general, but it undermines the effectiveness of Article 260 TFEU. It is therefore paramount that the Commission and the Court strive to identify a failure to fulfil obligations clearly and generally, in particular by focusing on the objectives and results required by EU law rather than the means employed by the Member States.

Establishing infringements effectively is not enough, however. It must be coupled with persuasive sanctions. The penalty payments imposed by the Court are relatively low, but they are probably sufficient to compel the Member States to end their infringement. However, coercion is not really an optimal approach; what is needed is deterrence. The Commission should consider amending its methodology for calculating lump sums in order to gain more influence in the fining process and the Court ought to draw from the reasoning employed when fining companies in competition cases, in particular the paragraphs on deterrence.

None of these adjustments require Treaty amendment and they could be beneficial for all. The Commission and the Court do not take pleasure in proposing and imposing sanctions, and the Member States surely do not enjoy receiving them. A better functioning system would reduce the need for such a heavy-handed response.

[191] Case 26/62 *van Gend & Loos* [1963] ECLI:EU:C:1963:1.

6

Preliminary References as a Means for Enforcing EU Law

Morten Broberg

1. Introduction

The preliminary reference procedure which we find today in Article 267 TFEU enables national courts to apply to the Court of Justice of the European Union to obtain a ruling on the interpretation or validity of an EU legal act. Even though the Court has held that Article 267 is not a remedy available to the parties to a case before a national court,[1] in practice the provision has become a highly important means for private parties' enforcement of EU law; perhaps even *the* most important one. Indeed, the preliminary reference procedure is sometimes referred to as 'indirect enforcement'.[2]

The Court of Justice is not competent to invalidate a national law. Therefore, if a Member State court refers a preliminary question as to whether a national law is invalid for incompatibility with EU law, the Court of Justice will rephrase the question so that it reads whether EU law 'precludes' a national law such as that of the Member State. If the Court of Justice answers the rephrased question in the affirmative, the Member State is obliged to amend its national law,[3] so in practice there is no real difference between the original question and the rephrased one. In this chapter we will examine to what extent and how the preliminary reference procedure can be used as a means for private parties to enforce EU law against the Member States.

2. Private parties' access to the preliminary reference procedure

a. Overview

Today it is far from uncommon for a private party to use the preliminary reference procedure as one of the main means for enforcing EU law against a Member State.[4] For example, the Sunday trading case law, where British retailers fought to be able to trade on Sundays, to a considerable extent relied on the preliminary reference procedure.[5] Similarly, Professor Jens Kristiansen has shown how Danish trade unions instituted proceedings against the Danish State on the basis that Danish law contravened EU law—and with the clear objective of having preliminary questions referred to the Court of Justice. Indeed, when a Danish court declined to make a reference in one case, the applicant trade union

[1] Case C-344/04 *IATA and ELFAA* [2006] ECLI:EU:C:2006:10 and Case C-496/04 *Slob v Productschap Zuivel* [2006] ECLI:EU:C:2006:570.

[2] S Andersen, *The Enforcement of EU Law—The Role of the European Commission* (OUP 2012) 32.

[3] See further section 4 below.

[4] See Case C-158/80 *Rewe Handelsgesellschaft v Hauptzollamt Kiel* [1981] ECLI:EU:C:1981:16, paras 44 and 46.

[5] See H-W Micklitz, *The Politics of Judicial Co-Operation in the EU—Sunday Trading, Equal Treatment and Good Faith* (CUP 2005) 274, 462–3, and 466–7.

Preliminary References as a Means for Enforcing EU Law. First Edition. Morten Broberg.
Published 2017 by Oxford University Press.

decided to withdraw the main case.[6] In this section we will first consider how private parties can establish a case which can form the basis of a preliminary reference. We will then examine to what extent Member State laws, directly or indirectly, preclude private parties from using the preliminary reference procedure.

b. Private parties 'creating' a case to form the basis for a preliminary reference

For a private party to use the preliminary reference procedure as a means to enforce EU law against a Member State, there needs to be an existing case which can form the basis for such reference. Moreover, the Court of Justice only has jurisdiction to answer a preliminary reference if the question is relevant to deciding the dispute before the national court,[7] and if the referring court itself can use the preliminary ruling to decide this dispute.[8] Broadly speaking, there are three different ways of 'creating' these cases. The most obvious way is where the private party litigates against the public authorities: indeed today, approximately two-thirds of all preliminary references stem from proceedings between a private entity and a public authority.[9] A second way to create such case is where a (real) conflict arises between two private parties: for instance if one party invokes a Member State measure and the other party invokes a conflicting EU measure. The third—less straightforward—way to create a case is where two parties have a joint interest in having a legal issue referred for a preliminary ruling and where the conflict arises between these two parties. Below, we will examine these three situations in turn.

Where the private party wishes to establish a conflict vis-à-vis a Member State, it is immaterial whether the private party is the plaintiff or the defendant. Even if it is obvious that the private party deliberately 'created' the actual conflict to be able to have the Court of Justice render a preliminary ruling to force the referring court to enforce EU law against the Member State in question, the Court of Justice will not consider the case as contrived. Indeed, the *raison d'être* of the preliminary ruling procedure is to ensure the uniform application of EU law throughout the EU, so if anything, this type of case should be encouraged, not discouraged. Accordingly, the Court of Justice also accepts test cases under the preliminary ruling procedure where the actual subject of the case is so trivial that questions of principle are the only motivation for the litigation.

Whilst instituting legal proceedings against public authorities can appear to be the most obvious way for private parties to use the preliminary reference procedure as a means of enforcing EU law against a Member State, the Member State is free to preclude a preliminary ruling by simply accepting the private party's claim in the main proceedings. Indeed, the Member State may 'close the case' by agreeing to honour the private party's actual claim while making it clear that it does not agree to the legal reasoning put forward in support of it. The Member State may even decide to honour the private party's claim after the national court has made a preliminary reference—which will under normal circumstances lead to the Court of Justice declining to answer the preliminary question(s).

It can prove difficult for a private party to create a conflict vis-à-vis a Member State in a number of situations. This is particularly true where the contested Member State laws

[6] J Kristiansen *Aftalemodellen og dens europæiske udfordringer—Om rollefordelingen mellem overenskomstparterne, Folketinget og domstolene,* (Jurist- og Økonomforbundets Forlag 2013) 195.

[7] See e.g. Case C-343/90 *Lourenço Dias v Director da Alfândega do Porto* [1992] ECLI:EU:C:1992:327.

[8] See e.g. Case C-428/93 *Monin Automobiles* [1994] ECLI:EU:C:1994:192.

[9] Of the 428 preliminary reference introduced before the Court of Justice in 2014 (c.f. the 2014 Annual Report), 297 originated from main proceedings between a private and a public party.

regulate relations among private parties. If a private party unilaterally establishes a conflict against another private party in order to create a case to form the basis for a preliminary reference on the conformity of a Member State's administration/laws with EU law, this will resemble situations where the conflict is directly between the private party and the Member State as such. The fact that the conflict appears to have been created primarily to provide a basis for a preliminary reference will not in itself lead the Court of Justice to consider it not to be a 'real dispute' which can form the basis for a preliminary reference.[10] In this respect it does not matter that one of the parties is trying to achieve an outcome it has been unable to achieve by lobbying for legislative changes. For example, in *Badeck*, the Court of Justice had no objection to dealing with a reference for a preliminary ruling where the main proceedings were brought by forty-six members of the *Landtag*—ie the regional assembly—of Hesse in Germany in proceedings for an abstract review of legality, a '*Normenkontrollverfahren*'.[11]

In principle, the situation becomes more sensitive if two or more parties jointly create a conflict to provide a basis for a preliminary reference. Nevertheless, the Court of Justice will also be prepared to answer preliminary references in cases where the parties in the main proceedings jointly agree that the national court's making a preliminary reference will be useful for the resolution of their dispute. Indeed, even if the parties were ready to settle their dispute without involving the courts, but decided to bring legal proceedings solely to (try to) obtain a preliminary ruling to have their *inter-partes* legal situation clarified, this will not alone cause the Court of Justice to find the preliminary reference inadmissible. Even if the two conflicting parties agree on what, to their mind, should be the correct answer to the preliminary question, this does *not* (in itself) mean that the Court of Justice will consider the dispute to be artificial or collusive (contrived).[12] In other words, the last-mentioned situation could also form a sufficient legal basis for a preliminary reference.[13]

Nonetheless, the Court of Justice has made it clear that the preliminary reference procedure is not intended as a means for parties in proceedings before the Member State courts to obtain answers to abstract or hypothetical questions from the Court in Luxembourg. This means that if it is obvious that the dispute before the referring court is contrived and consequently does not concern genuine disagreements between the parties to the main proceedings, the Court has shown itself ready to find the reference inadmissible on the basis that it does not have jurisdiction to answer the preliminary questions in this situation.[14] We should not, however, exaggerate the importance of the principle of contrived cases, also known as the *Foglia* principle. Thus, while the Court of Justice has been consistent in maintaining that the principle as such shall be upheld, it has simultaneously shown considerable restraint when it comes to its actual application. Firstly, the Court will only apply the *Foglia* principle where both parties to the main proceedings are party to the contrivance of the dispute. Secondly, if the referring court has agreed to hear the case, the Court of Justice will not render a preliminary reference inadmissible on the basis that the dispute in the main proceedings is contrived unless it is manifestly apparent from the facts set out in the order for reference that the dispute is in fact fictitious.[15]

[10] See e.g. Case C-6/64 *Flaminio Costa v ENEL* [1964] ECLI:EU:C:1964:66.

[11] Case C-158/97 *Badeck and Others* [2000] ECLI:EU:C:2000:163. See also Case C-292/04 *Meillicke and Others* [2007] ECLI:EU:C:2007:132.

[12] c.f. Case C-144/04 *Mangold* [2005] ECLI:EU:C:2005:709, para 38.

[13] See e.g. Case C-97/98 *Jägerskiöld* [1999] ECLI:EU:C:1999:515.

[14] Case C-104/79 *Foglia I* [1980] ECLI:EU:C:1980:73 and Case C-244/80 *Foglia II* [1981] ECLI:EU:C:1981:302.

[15] See e.g. Case C-451/99 *Cura Anlagen* [2002] ECLI:EU:C:2002:195 and Case C-47/90 *Delhaize* [1992] ECLI:EU:C:1992:250.

The Court of Justice's restraint in applying the *Foglia* principle is also reflected in the fact that if a case is between a parent company and a subsidiary this in itself does not mean that the Court will consider the dispute to be contrived.[16] Similarly, arguments that the plaintiff in the main proceedings lacks a legal interest in challenging a national provision, or arguments that a national practice is not a matter for the Court of Justice to decide on but instead is a matter for the national court, are also unlikely to render the reference inadmissible.[17]

From the above it follows that it is highly unlikely that the Court of Justice will find a dispute to be contrived and thereby render a reference for a preliminary ruling to be inadmissible under the *Foglia* principle. Nonetheless, we should not completely discount the importance of this principle since it has established the basis upon which the Court of Justice examines its own jurisdiction to determine whether or not to accept a preliminary reference, depending on whether the case in the main action concerns a real or a contrived case.

c. National law precludes the preliminary reference

In order for a private party to create the basis for a preliminary ruling, the party must be able to bring legal proceedings before a national court. In this regard, as a clear main rule, the private party must comply with national procedural rules. Accordingly, if the party does not have *locus standi*, if the case is time-barred, or if for other procedural reasons a case cannot be brought before the national court, this will normally preclude the possibility of creating the basis for a preliminary ruling. It could also be that the most obvious way of having a question brought before a Member State court is by infringing a national rule and thereby provoking administrative or criminal proceedings to be instituted.[18] Obviously, the risk of facing this type of proceedings could deter many private parties from pursuing this route.[19]

Along the same lines, where a private party has instituted proceedings before a Member State court, EU law does not preclude national procedural rules which prevent the private party from invoking certain arguments—even if the coincidental consequence of these national procedural rules is that it will not be possible to have the national court to make a preliminary reference. On the other hand, if the national procedural rules effectively prevent a national court from making a reference for a preliminary ruling, the Court of Justice will set aside these procedural rules.[20]

Similarly where a lower national court is to consider the constitutionality of a national provision, several Member States require the lower court to refer this question to the country's constitutional court. If, however, the case also involves aspects of EU law, the Court of Justice has ruled that the obligation to refer to the constitutional court cannot

[16] See e.g. Case C-379/98 *PreussenElektra* [2001] ECLI:EU:C:2001:160.

[17] See e.g. Case C-309/02 *Radlberger Getränkegesellschaft* [2001] ECLI:EU:C:2004:799, para 26.

[18] In Case C-432/05 *Unibet* [2007] ECLI:EU:C:2007:163, the Court of Justice held that 'If [...] [Unibet] was forced to be subject to administrative or criminal proceedings and to any penalties that may result *as the sole form of legal remedy for disputing the compatibility of the national provision at issue with Community law*, that would *not be sufficient* to secure for it [effective judicial protection of its rights under Community law]' (emphasis added).

[19] See Case C-263/02 P *Commission of the European Communities v Jégo-Quéré & Cie SA*, Opinion AG Francis Jacobs [2003] ECLI:EU:C:2003:410, para 43 and c.f. para 34 of the Court's ruling in the same case, as well as with the Court's subsequent ruling in Case C-432/05 *Unibet* [2007] ECLI:EU:C:2007:163, para 64.

[20] c.f. Case C-312/93 *Peterbroeck* [1995] ECLI:EU:C:1995:437, 11–21. See also Case C-599/10 *SAG ELV Slovensko and Others* [2012] ECLI:EU:C:2012:191, para 19 along with Case C-137/08 *VB Pénzügyi Lízing* [2010] ECLI:EU:C:2010:659, paras 26–35.

preclude the lower court from making a reference for a preliminary ruling.[21] This is so since only the national court before which a case is brought has jurisdiction to determine whether there should be a reference to the Court of Justice.[22]

Even though lower national courts are generally bound by the rulings (and interpretations) handed down by superior national courts, this cannot preclude the lower court from making a preliminary reference.[23] Even where a superior national court had already ruled on the need for making a reference for a preliminary ruling in another case concerning the same problem and decided that a reference was not necessary, a lower national court is not bound by this.[24] The preliminary ruling by the Court of Justice, in a case before a lower national court, will be binding on the national courts even if it conflicts with an earlier ruling of a superior national court.[25] In other words, the lower national court making the preliminary reference will be obliged to set aside the earlier ruling of the superior national court if this is necessary to comply with the Court of Justice's ruling.

3. Inducing a national court to refer

Even though only the Member State court hearing the actual dispute is competent to decide whether to make a preliminary reference,[26] this does not mean that private parties have no opportunities to induce the national courts to make a reference.[27] There are (at least) three ways for a private party to do this. First, by putting forward convincing arguments that a reference will be useful or perhaps even necessary to decide the case. Secondly, a private party may design the case in such a way that the EU law element is decisive. Lastly, a private party can design the case so that the national court will be obliged to refer under EU law.

Where a private party invokes EU law against the laws or practices of a Member State, the primary objective is often simply to have these laws or practices overturned and thereby win the actual dispute. In these situations the actual case is unlikely to have been 'designed' to generate a preliminary reference. In order to induce the national court to make a preliminary reference, the parties will therefore have to put forward convincing arguments in support of the need for a preliminary ruling. If the national court finds that the case does not fall within one of the situations where EU law requires a preliminary reference to be made and if the national court takes the view that there is no need to make such reference, it

[21] Case C-348/89 *Mecanarte* [1991] ECLI:EU:C:1991:278, paras 41–6; Case C-106/77 *Simmenthal* [1978] ECLI:EU:C:1978:49, para 24.

[22] Case C-555/07 *Kücükdeveci* [2010] ECLI:EU:C:2010:21, paras 52–6; Joined Cases C-188/10 and C-189/10 *Melki and Abdeli* [2010] ECLI:EU:C:2010:363, paras 31–57 and, with regard to the main proceedings in this case, decisions by the Conseil constitutionnel (décision du 12 mai 2010, n° 2010-605 DC) and by the Conseil d'État (arrêt du 14 mai 2010, n° 312305).

[23] Case C-166/73 *Rheinmühlen* [1974] ECLI:EU:C:1974:3, paras 3–11; and Case C-146/73 *Rheinmühlen* [1974] ECLI:EU:C:1974:12, para 32. See also Case C-378/08 *Raffinerie Mediterranee (ERG) SpA* [2010] ECLI:EU:C:2010:126, and Case C-210/06 *Cartesio* [2008] ECLI:EU:C:2008:723, paras 88–9.

[24] Regarding appeals against a national court's decision to make a preliminary reference, see M Broberg and N Fenger, *Preliminary References to the European Court of Justice* (OUP 2014) 327–36.

[25] Case C-396/09 *Interedil* [2011] ECLI:EU:C:2011:671, paras 34–40; and Case C-173/09 *Elchinov* [2010] ECLI:EU:C:2010:581, paras 21–32.

[26] This has been clearly reflected in the Court of Justice's *Recommendations to national courts and tribunals in relation to the initiation of preliminary ruling proceedings*, [2012] OJ C338/1. See e.g. Case C-251/11 *Huet* [2012] ECLI:EU:C:2012:133, paras 22–6.

[27] In Joined Cases C-143/88 and C-92/89 *Zuckerfabrik Süderdithmarschen* [1991] ECLI:EU:C:1991:65, para 16, the Court of Justice held that 'the legal protection guaranteed by [EU] law includes the right of individuals to challenge [. . .] the legality of [EU regulations] before national courts and *to induce those courts to refer questions to the Court of Justice for a preliminary ruling*' (emphasis added). It would seem peculiar if the same approach were not adopted where the case concerned the legality of Member State measures under EU law.

is free not to refer to the Court of Justice, even if both parties to the case agree that a reference should be made.[28]

Under Article 6 ECHR, national courts, whose decisions are not open to appeal under domestic law are required to give reasons, based on the applicable law and the exceptions to making a preliminary reference laid down in the case law of the Court of Justice, for their refusal to refer a preliminary question on the interpretation of EU law. In this situation the national court of last instance must set out its reasons for considering the question irrelevant, the provision having already been interpreted by the Court of Justice, or the correct application of EU law being so obvious as to leave no scope for reasonable doubt (*acte clair*). If a national court fails to give reasons when refusing to refer, the refusal to refer may be considered arbitrary and thus in contravention of Article 6(1) ECHR.[29]

Sometimes lawyers, more or less explicitly, 'design' the dispute in such a way that of itself it induces the national court to make a preliminary reference. The most obvious way of doing this is by making it immediately apparent that the case concerns the interpretation of EU law. Thus, two private parties may agree to design the dispute so that it turns upon the correct interpretation of EU law.[30] Similarly, there are examples of preliminary references in the Court of Justice's case law where the only objective was to obtain a ruling on whether a Member State's laws or practices were in conformity with EU law.[31]

A party (or parties) can also design the case in such a way that, under EU law, the national court will be obliged to make a preliminary reference. Three situations can be distinguished. Firstly, where a national court of last instance is required to rule on the interpretation of EU law to decide the dispute and where this interpretation is not obvious (ie the case is not one of *acte clair* or *acte éclairé*). Secondly, where the ruling of a national court entails that an EU legal measure will be rendered invalid. And thirdly, where the national court's intended ruling will depart from the Court of Justice's established interpretation.

The first situation can often be created by structuring the dispute in such a way that there will be no right of appeal from the national court whilst it is necessary to have a question of EU law clarified to adjudicate on the dispute. If the losing party does not have a right to a legal review of the decision allowing for a possibility of a reference for a preliminary ruling by the reviewing national court, the national court is under an obligation to make a preliminary reference (presupposing the case is not one of *acte clair* or *acte éclairé*).[32]

The second situation is more difficult to design because it would not be enough to argue that an EU legal measure is invalid. Only if the national court were inclined to agree that the EU legal measure was invalid would the national court be under a duty to make a preliminary reference.[33]

The third situation is based on the fact that it is for the Court of Justice to establish authoritatively the correct interpretation of EU law. This means that if the Court has ruled

[28] See e.g. judgment of 16 April 1999 (1 O 186, *Zeitschrift für Wirtschaftsrecht* 1999, summarized in *Reflets* 2/1999) and the decision of 17 July 2009 by the Spanish Supreme Court, summarized in JH Jans et al. (eds), *National Courts and EU Environmental Law* (Europa Law Publishing 2013).

[29] *Dhahbi v Italy* App No 17120/09 (ECtHR 8 April 2014).

[30] In Case C-379/98 *PreussenElektra* [2001] ECLI:EU:C:2001:160, para 44, the German government argued that the case was contrived precisely because the two private parties to the case apparently had designed the dispute so that it turned on a specific EU law issue. However, the Court of Justice did not hold in favour of the German government.

[31] Case C-421/09 *Humanplasma v Austria* [2010] ECLI:EU:C:2010:760 and Case C-71/85 *State of the Netherlands v Federatie Nederlands Vakbeweging* [1986] ECLI:EU:C:1986:465, para 2.

[32] e.g. *Costa v ENEL* (n 10).

[33] Case C-119/05 *Ministero dell'Industria, del Commercio e dell'Artigianato v Lucchini SpA* [2007] ECLI:EU:C:2007:434, para 53.

on the validity or correct interpretation of an EU act, the national courts are obliged to follow this. As a consequence, a national court may not depart from a clear ruling or a clearly established practice of the Court of Justice without first making a preliminary reference to ask the Court whether it is possible to make such derogation in a situation such as the one that the referring court is faced with.[34] It follows that in order for a private party to induce a national court to make a preliminary reference in this way, the private party will need to design the case so that it is possible to argue that the reference is needed to depart from a clear ruling or an established practice by the Court of Justice. Even though there may be circumstances where this is possible, it is nevertheless a rather uncertain strategy.[35]

a. Influencing the formulation of the preliminary questions

Since a preliminary reference is a remedy which is exclusively available to the Member State courts, a national court can choose to make a reference even if both parties object.[36] On the other hand, the national court may involve the parties in the preparation of the preliminary reference if it so wishes. Indeed, the Court of Justice supports the parties being heard before the drafting of the reference is completed.[37] In some Member States the courts allow the parties to play important roles in the process leading to the submission of the preliminary reference—sometimes going as far as allowing the parties to draft the preliminary reference jointly (presentation of both facts and law as well as the actual questions to be asked) whilst the national court itself may limit its own involvement to verifying and submitting the reference. This is for instance the case in Denmark, Ireland, and the UK. In contrast, in some of the other Member States the courts draft the preliminary reference themselves without allowing the parties any real influence.[38] It follows that the possibility of influencing the preliminary reference in general and the formulation of the preliminary questions in particular depend on the actual court hearing the case.

b. Influencing the reference during the procedure before the Court of Justice

Parties to the main proceedings and interveners in these proceedings are entitled to submit observations to the Court of Justice with regards to a preliminary reference from the national court.[39] This applies to the submission of written observations as well as to the oral pleadings of the preliminary reference proceedings before the Court of Justice. While the parties are under no obligation to take part in the proceedings, the submission of observations offers a possibility, albeit a limited one, to influence the Court.

[34] For an illustration of this, see Tribunal Constitucional. Sala Segunda. Sentencia 58/2004, (April 2004) Recurso de amparo 4979/1999, summarized in *Reflets* 2/2004.

[35] See e.g. Case C-400/95 *Larsson* [1997] ECLI:EU:C:1997:259—and compare with the subsequent ruling in Case C-394/96 *Brown* [1998] ECLI:EU:C:1998:331.

[36] *Garland v British Rail Engineering Ltd* together with Case 12/81 *Eileen Garland v British Rail Engineering Limited* [1982] ECLI:EU:C:1982:44.

[37] c.f. Court of Justice, 'Recommendations to national courts and tribunals in relation to the initiation of preliminary ruling proceedings' [2012] OJ C338/1, 19. See also 'Notes for the Guidance of Counsel' available at the Court of Justice's website: http://curia.europa.eu/jcms/upload/docs/application/pdf/2008-09/txt9_2008-09-25_17-37-52_275.pdf, accessed 12 October 2016, Section 7 *in fine*, where the Court of Justice clearly (albeit implicitly) acknowledges that the text of the order for reference may be proposed by counsel to the parties to the main proceedings.

[38] We can find examples of this approach at the Austrian Administrative Court, the Belgian Council of State, the German Federal Administrative Courts, the French Council of State, and the Supreme Court of Spain.

[39] Art 23(2) of the Court's Statute as well as Arts 96(1)(a) and 97 of its Rules of Procedure. See e.g. Case C-108/96 *Dennis Mac Quen* [1996] ECLI:EU:C:2001:67.

The starting point is that those entitled to submit observations during the preliminary reference procedure before the Court of Justice cannot amend or expand, or for that matter narrow, the content of the question;[40] they can only submit suggestions with regard to the interpretation of the content of the reference and the answers to the questions referred.[41] This is likely to be an advantage for the parties to the main proceedings since it means that they may influence the formulation of the questions *put by the referring court*—typically without interference from others—and whereupon they may reasonably expect the Court of Justice to decline subsequent attempts to rephrase the questions. This restrictive approach to rephrasing is particularly clear with regards to cases where the national court has restricted a reference to a legal problem derived from a *specific rule under national law*.[42] In contrast, when it comes to identifying the applicable *EU rules* the Court has shown itself more willing (partly or fully) to rephrase the preliminary questions.[43] Hereby the Court will sometimes answer questions that differ from those originally put by the referring court.[44] Such rephrasing primarily take place at the Court's own initiative and less frequently due to observations made by the parties to the main proceedings.[45] It is normally only done at a stage where the preliminary ruling is being drafted, i.e. after the presentation of written and oral observations. In other words, if the parties to the main proceedings want the Court of Justice to consider certain additional arguments, as a rule they must persuade the referring court to make a fresh preliminary reference.[46]

Under Article 267, it is for the referring court to present the facts of the case including the relevant national rules. Only exceptionally will the Court of Justice be willing to consider supplementary information presented to it during the preliminary procedure—and in even more exceptional cases will it base its judgment on an understanding of the facts (including national law) which conflicts with the one presented by the referring court.[47] Nevertheless, the Court of Justice allows the parties to supplement the facts provided in the national court's order for reference to some extent.[48] The Court of Justice is particularly open to including contextual information which can clarify the general background to a problem before it, as long as this new information does not cast doubt on the facts presented in the order for reference in relation to the actual dispute.[49] In

[40] See e.g. Case C-605/12 *Welmory sp z oo v Dyrektor Izby Skarbowej w Gdańsku* [2014] ECLI:EU:C:2014:2298, para 33; Case C-602/10 *SC Volksbank România SA* [2012] ECLI:EU:C:2012:443, paras 46–51; Case C-316/10 *Danske Svineproducenter II* [2011] ECLI:EU:C:2011:863, paras 29–34.

[41] This is particularly the case when the party concerned has not been able to persuade the referring court to expand, amend, or limit the scope of the questions referred, c.f. Case C-373/08 *Hoesch Metals and Alloys GmbH* [2010] ECLI:EU:C:2010:68, paras 57–60 and Case C-305/05 *Ordre des Barreaux francophones et germanophone* [2007] ECLI:EU:C:2007:383, paras 17–19.

[42] For an exception, see e.g. Case C-569/08 *Internetportal und Marketing* [2010] ECLI:EU:C:2010:311, paras 27–30.

[43] See Case C-657/11 *Belgian Electronic Sorting Technology NV v Bert Peelaers and Visys NV* [2013] ECLI:EU:C:2013:516, para 29; Case C-437/09 *AG2R Prévoyance v Beaudout Père et Fils SARL* [2011] ECLI:EU:C:2011:112, para 26; and Case C-70/09 *Alexander Hengartner and Rudolf Gasser v Landesregierung Vorarlberg* [2010] ECLI:EU:C:2010:430, para 27.

[44] e.g. Case C-486/08 *Zentralbetriebsrat der Landeskrankenhäuser Tirols* [2010] ECLI:EU:C:2010:215; and Joined Cases C-267/91 and C-268/91 *Keck and Mithouard* [1993] ECLI:EU:C:1993:905, para 10.

[45] Case C-321/03 *Dyson* [2007] ECLI:EU:C:2007:51, paras 22–6. See also Broberg and Fenger (n 24) 359–62.

[46] Case C-236/02 *J Slob v Productschap Zuivel* [2004] ECLI:EU:C:2004:94, para 29.

[47] See Case C-135/10 *Società Consortile Fonografici (SCF)* [2012] ECLI:EU:C:2012:140, paras 65–9; Case C-232/09 *Danosa* [2010] ECLI:EU:C:2010:674, paras 31–7; contrast with Case C-182/08 *Glaxo Wellcome GmbH & Co* [2009] ECLI:EU:C:2009:559, paras 32–3; Case C-88/99 *Roquette Frères* [2000] ECLI:EU:C:2000:652, paras 16–19.

[48] See Art 23 of the Court's Statute as well as 'Notes for the Guidance of Counsel', February 2009, section 9, available at: http://curia.europa.eu/jcms/upload/docs/application/pdf/2008-09/txt9_2008-09-25_17-37-52_275.pdf, accessed 12 October 2016. For an example, see Case C-251/83 *Haug-Adrion* [1984] ECR 4277, [1984] ECLI:EU:C:1984:397, paras 8–10.

[49] Broberg and Fenger (n 24) 365.

contrast, the Court of Justice only very rarely admits corrections of a national court's interpretation of national law. This is true even when the referring court's interpretation is disputed by the Member State government which issued the national rules in question.[50]

4. Effects of a preliminary ruling

A preliminary reference is a request from a Member State court to the Court of Justice in a situation where the referring court needs assistance to decide an actual case. Initially, legal observers therefore took the view that a preliminary ruling was only binding on the referring court (and on other courts hearing the case in the main proceedings on appeal). Today there is no doubt that a preliminary ruling has general significance. The Court of Justice provides an authoritative interpretation of EU law—and in practice this interpretation is binding *erga omnes*, i.e. on all and in all respects. Indeed, it is precisely the fact that preliminary rulings have this *erga omnes* effect which makes them so powerful when it comes to the enforcement of EU law.

With regard to private parties' enforcement of EU law against Member States through the preliminary procedure, it is particularly important that the Court of Justice has ruled that following a preliminary ruling from which it is apparent that national legislation is incompatible with EU law, it is for the authorities of the Member State concerned to take the general or particular measures necessary to ensure that EU law is complied with. This particularly entails amending national law so as to comply with EU law as soon as possible, and so that the rights which individuals derive from EU law are given full effect.[51]

Not only the Member States are bound by the Court of Justice's preliminary rulings, as they are given general validity and binding force throughout the EU.[52] This accords well with the fact that preliminary rulings are declaratory in nature; ie they explain the correct interpretation of existing EU law from the day of its entry into force.[53] The Court of Justice itself also treats its own preliminary rulings as binding authority similar to its rulings in cases based on direct actions.[54]

The *erga omnes* effect of preliminary rulings means that when interpreting EU law, all national courts are obliged to apply not only the operative part of a preliminary ruling, but also its *ratio*. This obligation applies to all national courts regardless of whether they sit as courts of last instance.[55]

In reality there does not seem to be any difference between the referring court being directly bound by a preliminary ruling as such and other actors such as EU institutions, Member States, and private parties being so bound; in practice the preliminary rulings are equally binding on all these other actors. Indeed, as already observed this is the principal

[50] e.g. Joined Cases C-128/10 and C-129/10 *Naftiliaki Etaireia Thasou* [2011] ECLI:EU:C:2011:163, paras 35–41.

[51] Joined Cases C-231/06 to C-233/06 *Emilienne Jonkman* [2007] ECLI:EU:C:2007:373, para 41.

[52] K Lenaerts et al., *Procedural Law of the European Union* (Sweet & Maxwell 2006) 195 ff; and A Trabucchi, 'L'effet "erga omnes" des décisions préjudicielles rendues par la Cour de justice des Communautés européennes' (1974) 10 *Revue trimestrielle du droit européen* 56. See e.g. Case C-66/80 *ICC* [1981] ECLI:EU:C:1981:102, paras 9–18.

[53] In special situations the Court of Justice may decide to attach a temporal limitation to the binding effect of a preliminary ruling. This however is merely the exception which proves the rule.

[54] c.f. Case C-445/05 *Werner Haderer* [2007] ECLI:EU:C:2007:344, para 18; Case C-465/93 *Atlanta* [1995] ECLI:EU:C:1995:369, para 46; Case C-422/05 *Commission v Belgium* [2007] ECLI:EU:C:2007:342, para 62. Note also that the *acte éclairé* doctrine is based on the idea that, inter alia, preliminary rulings constitute binding authority.

[55] Trabucchi (n 52) 56; but compare AG Toth, 'The Authority of Judgments of the European Court of Justice: Binding Force and Legal Effects' in F Jacobs (ed), *Yearbook of European Law 1984* (Clarendon 1986) 61, 66.

reason why the preliminary ruling procedure can constitute an efficient means of enforcing EU law against the Member States.

5. Ensuring the right of defence

The fact that the preliminary reference procedure is not strictly an enforcement measure is reflected in various ways. First, a preliminary reference presupposes that proceedings are brought before the Member State courts so that the national court can refer a preliminary question. It is far from every lawyer (not to mention European citizen) who will be aware of the possibility of using the preliminary reference procedure in support of a claim. In addition, it can require quite considerable resources to pursue. Perhaps this is why several preliminary references spring from cases brought by pressure groups wishing to enforce EU law against the Member States.[56] Fahey has thus pointed out that '[i]n Ireland, agricultural organisations and farm related bodies have single-handedly comprised the most litigious bodies employing the preliminary reference mechanism to challenge national and [Union] legislation'.[57] Similarly, Professor Kristiansen has pointed out that in Denmark trade unions have consciously used the preliminary reference procedure as an efficient means of enforcing labour rights and that this is an important reason why a large part of the preliminary references from Danish courts are concerned with labour issues.[58] Pressure groups presumably play equally important roles in the use of the preliminary reference procedure in several other Member States.

The apparently important role played by pressure groups in using the preliminary reference procedure as an enforcement measure also means that areas where no strong pressure groups are active could be neglected. For example, this could explain why Danish courts submit surprisingly few preliminary references in the social policy field. Similarly, even though there are several strong pressure groups in the field of environmental protection, they appear to be faced with considerable obstacles when trying to challenge Member State actions—which could explain the lower than expected number of preliminary rulings in this field.[59]

Whereas private parties can reasonably view the preliminary reference as an important, albeit peculiar, remedy for enforcing EU law, the Court of Justice has, as we have seen, explicitly ruled that the preliminary reference does not constitute a remedy available to private parties; the preliminary reference procedure is a remedy exclusively available to the Member State courts. Nevertheless, the Court of Justice has not been completely unequivocal in this regard. Thus, in *Jégo-Quéré*,[60] with particular regard to private parties' access to judicial review of the legality of acts of the EU institutions, the Court observed that by what is now Articles 263 TFEU and 277 TFEU, read with what is now Article 267 TFEU, 'the Treaty has established a complete system of legal remedies and procedures designed to ensure review of the legality of acts of the institutions, and has entrusted such review to the

[56] See e.g. the ruling by the High Court of Ireland in *Digital Rights Ireland Ltd v Minister for Communication & Others* [2010] IEHC 221 (5 May 2010), available at: http://www.bailii.org/ie/cases/IEHC/2010/H221.html, accessed 12 October 2016.

[57] E Fahey, *Practice and Procedure in Preliminary References to Europe: 30 Years of Article 234 EC Case Law from the Irish Courts* (First Law 2007) 108.

[58] J Kristiansen *The growing conflict between European uniformity and national flexibility—The case of Danish flexicurity and European harmonisation of working conditions* (Djoef Publishing 2015) 208 ff. and 265 f.

[59] See Jans et al. (eds) (n 28) 176–83.

[60] Case C-263/02 P *Commission of the European Communities v Jégo-Quéré & Cie SA* [2004] ECLI:EU:C:2004:210.

[Union] Courts.'[61] It went on to explain that '[it is] for the Member States to establish a system of legal remedies and procedures which ensure respect for the right to effective judicial protection [ie that individuals have access to the national courts]'.[62] Indeed, not only the Member States but also the Member State courts are under an obligation to allow individuals access to the national courts to enforce their rights under EU law.[63] That the preliminary reference procedure constitutes a means for protecting European citizens was reiterated by the Court of Justice in its *Opinion 1/09 (European and Community Patents Court)*.[64]

Perhaps the above can be simplified to the observation that while the Court of Justice maintains that the preliminary reference procedure is a remedy only available to Member State courts, it simultaneously acknowledges that this procedure is of utmost importance to the ability of EU citizens to defend their rights under EU law effectively.[65]

In the opinion of the present author there can be no doubt that the preliminary reference procedure has been—and continues to be—crucial for the development of Union law as well as for the ability of European citizens to defend their rights under EU law. Nevertheless, the preliminary reference procedure should not be immune to criticism. Accordingly, the preliminary reference procedure carries an important drawback when it comes to its suitability as an enforcement measure: the fact that it has only been created to enable the Member State courts to obtain advice on the interpretation or validity of EU law means that it has not been designed also to provide the procedural rights of private parties and Member States to establish a fully effective defence.[66]

Therefore, in order for an individual to persuade a national court to make a preliminary reference, this individual necessarily must ensure that a case is brought before such a court. Often, however, the only real possibility of achieving this is by infringing a Member State rule, thereby inducing the Member State authorities to institute proceedings against the person in breach—possibly criminal proceedings. Moreover, even if an individual manages to get a case heard by a national court, this does not necessarily mean that the national court will make a preliminary reference. The national court may consider that a ruling by the Court of Justice is not necessary for the national court to decide the matter. It may also be that the national court could consider a ruling by the Court of Justice necessary, but takes the view that such a ruling can be obtained without making a preliminary reference in the case in question—for instance because it decides to make a preliminary reference in another, but similar case before it, or because the question has been made in a direct action that is pending before the Court of Justice.[67] The problem in such circumstances would be that only the parties to the main proceedings would have the right to plead before the Court of Justice. Other parties who may be affected equally by the preliminary ruling would be precluded from taking part in the procedure before the Court.[68]

It is not only private parties who may find the preliminary reference procedure inadequate as a means of enforcing EU law against a Member State. Member States may also

[61] ibid, para 30. [62] ibid, para 31. [63] ibid, para 32.

[64] Opinion 1/09 *(European and Community Patents Court)* [2011] ECLI:EU:C:2011:123, paras 84 and 86.

[65] Already R Joliet made this clear in his article 'La protection juridictionelle des particuliers contre les manquements étatiques' (1994) 4 *Revue française de droit administratif* 647.

[66] See in this respect Case C-362/12 *Test Claimants* [2013] ECLI:EU:C:2013:834, para 44.

[67] See HG Schermers and D Waelbroeck, *Judicial Protection in the European Communities* (Kluwer 1992) 318 regarding the Danish *Just* Case. c.f. the approach taken by the French *Conseil d'État, Section du contentieux, avis* of 4 February 2000, M Mouflin, req. nº 213321, reported in (2000) *Revue française de droit administratif* 468.

[68] Moreover, where the main proceedings are between two private parties, a party relying on national law can also find that a preliminary ruling which in effect sets aside the national law infringes the principle of legal certainty. See in this regard Case C-441/14 *Ajos*.

come up against difficulties. Thus, if the Commission considers that a Member State infringes EU law, the Commission can initiate infringement proceedings. Normally, the Commission will first raise the matter with the relevant Member State. If this does not lead to a solution, the Commission may send a 'reasoned opinion' to the Member State—enabling the latter to address the points of criticism raised by the Commission. Only after having taken these steps may the Commission bring the dispute before the Court of Justice. This pre-litigation stage is an important means for ensuring the Member State's right to defend itself, or as the Court of Justice explained:

> the purpose of the pre-litigation procedure is to give the Member State concerned an opportunity, on the one hand, to comply with its obligations under EU law and, on the other, *to avail itself of its right to defend itself properly* against the objections formulated by the Commission. The subject-matter of proceedings under Article 258 TFEU is therefore delimited by the pre-litigation procedure prescribed by that provision. The proper conduct of that procedure constitutes *an essential guarantee required by the FEU Treaty* not only in order to protect the rights of the Member State concerned, but also in order to ensure that any contentious procedure will have a clearly defined dispute as its subject-matter.[69]

Moreover, when the infringement action reaches the Court of Justice, it follows the standard rules for contentious proceedings, with an application followed by a defence, possibly followed by a reply and a rejoinder. Only thereafter will there normally be an oral hearing.

In contrast, in preliminary references the Member State may not even be aware of the case until it is notified of it by the Court of Justice: this may be particularly problematic in situations where the national laws of one Member State are challenged before a national court of another Member State. Moreover, written pleadings before the Court of Justice are exchanged only once and simultaneously—thereby preventing the Member State in question from replying in writing to new aspects (claims) raised as part of the written procedure. In those cases where the Court of Justice decides to rephrase one or more of the preliminary questions, this effectively undermines the possibility of submitting observations—as has been recognized by the Court itself.[70] To make matters worse, there is no guarantee of an oral hearing: if the Court of Justice finds that the written pleadings and observations provide it with sufficient information to rule on the preliminary reference, it may decide not to hold one.[71]

Perhaps the best way to address the challenges identified above would be to introduce two rounds of written proceedings in non-urgent preliminary reference cases: a first round where admissibility, the facts, and the specific legal questions to be answered are clearly established, followed by a second round where those entitled are invited to provide written observations on the facts and on the legal questions established. During the first round the parties to the main proceedings, the Member State of the referring court and the European Commission should be entitled to provide observations. The first round should be closed by a joint statement from the reporting judge and the Advocate General (if necessary, after having heard the referring court), unequivocally setting out the facts and the legal questions to be answered. The second round should be followed by an oral hearing unless the Court of Justice considers this to be superfluous. Moreover, when the reporting judge and the Advocate General jointly establish the facts and the legal questions to be answered, they

[69] Case C-525/12 *Commission v Germany* [2014] ECLI:EU:C:2014:2202, para 21 (emphasis added).
[70] Case C-605/12 *Welmory* [2014] ECLI:EU:C:2014:2298, para 34.
[71] c.f. Art 76(2) of the Court's Rules of Procedure. See also Broberg and Fenger (n 24) 368–87.

could also be given the power to decide whether the case merits an opinion from the Advocate General. To my mind, preliminary reference cases rarely benefit appreciably from Advocate General opinions, so dispensing with them in the vast majority of preliminary reference cases would mean the proposed 'additional round' would be unlikely materially to extend the total time spent answering preliminary references.

6. Concluding remarks

In the 1963 ruling of *Van Gend & Loos* the Dutch government observed 'that if a failure by a state to fulfil its [Union] obligations could be brought before the Court by a procedure other than those under [Articles 258 and 259 TFEU] the legal protection of that state would be considerably diminished'.[72] Nevertheless, in the years which followed, the preliminary ruling procedure has developed into arguably the most important measure for enforcing EU law against Member States. Indeed, today the preliminary reference procedure has attained such importance as an enforcement measure that the prospect of a reference to the Court of Justice can of itself induce a Member State party to proceedings before a national court to settle the dispute. While from a Rule-of-Law point of view, the importance of the preliminary ruling procedure can be broadly viewed as positive, it is equally clear that the preliminary reference procedure has not been designed in a way which duly reflects that it is often used as an enforcement measure. In order to address this deficiency, a modest proposal for amendments to the procedures of the Court of Justice is put forward to better safeguard the legitimate interests of both Member States and private parties.

[72] Case C-26/62 *Van Gend en Loos* [1963] ECLI:EU:C:1963:1.

7

Francovich Enforcement Analysed and Illustrated by German (and English) Law

Norbert Reich

1. The objective of this chapter

Can the so-called '*Francovich*' liability of Member States contribute to enforcement? As will be recalled, the case before the ECJ concerned the right to damages of dismissed Italian employees occasioned by the non-implementation of Directive 80/987/EEC on compensation of workers in the event of bankruptcy of their employer.[1] Italy had already been condemned for non-observance of a prior ECJ judgment. The *Francovich* judgment of 19 November 1991 developed in bold terms the principle of state liability for breaches of EU law as a new, hitherto unrecognized general principle of EC/EU law:

> The full effectiveness of Community rules would be impaired and the protection of the rights that they grant would be weakened if individuals were unable to obtain redress when their rights are infringed by a breach of Community law for which a Member State can be held responsible. The possibility of obtaining redress from a Member State is particularly indispensable where, as in this case, the full effectiveness of Community rules is subject to prior action on the part of the State and where, in the absence of such action, individuals cannot enforce before the national courts the rights conferred upon them by Community law. It follows that the principle whereby the State must be held liable for loss and damage caused to individuals as a result of breaches of Community law for which the State can be held responsible is inherent in the system of the Treaty.[2]

Later case law has clarified the scope and conditions of state liability, which are now part of positive Union law: there is no need to go into detail here. The ECJ has clarified that all state bodies—not only the administration but also the legislature[3] and the judiciary[4] can be subject to *Francovich* liability. The conditions for liability are threefold—as consistently confirmed in a succession of cases. Firstly, the Union act which was not implemented must have intended to confer rights on individuals (direct effect is unnecessary) and these rights must have been identifiable with sufficient precision. This is usually a matter for the ECJ to decide. Secondly, the breach by the Member State must have been 'sufficiently serious' (suffisamment caracterisée—hinreichend qualifiziert). This will ultimately be determined by the competent national court, and the ECJ will give indications as to the seriousness to a differing degree—discussed below. And thirdly, a direct causal link under Member State law must be found between the breach and the damage.[5]

[1] Directive 80/987 EEC of the Council of the European Communities on employer insolvency [1980] OJ L283/23.

[2] Joined Cases C-6 and C-9/90 *Andrea Francovich and Danila Bonifaci and Others v Italian Republic* [1991] ECLI:EU:C:1991:428, para 33.

[3] Joined Cases C-46 and C-48/93 *Brasserie du Pêcheur SA v Federal Republic of Germany and The Queen v Secretary of State for Transport ex parte Factortame Ltd and Others* [1996] ECLI:EU:C:1996:79.

[4] Case C-224/01 *Gerhard Köbler v Republik Österreich* [2003] ECLI:EU:C:2003:513.

[5] First held in *Brasserie du Pêcheur* (n 3) para 51.

Francovich Enforcement Analysed and Illustrated by German (and English) Law. First Edition. Norbert Reich.

2. Two conflicting theoretical approaches and one empirical analysis

To overcome the somewhat haphazard approach of citing national—in my case German and to some extent English—cases pointing in one or other direction regarding the relevance of *Francovich* liability to enforcement, this chapter is based on two contrasting approaches. The first is the thorough study by Takis Tridimas analysing all subsequent ECJ case law relating to *Francovich*.[6] The second is the study based on an economic theory of deterrence advanced by Hans-Bernd Schäfer.[7] Lock also conducted a comparative empirical study of the case law in German and UK courts, which will be referred to briefly in section 3.[8]

a. Evidence of the deterrent effect—the Tridimas study

Tridimas bases himself on the thirty-five cases decided by the ECJ in the aftermath of *Francovich*. Following his analysis, *Francovich* is based on the federal division of powers of the ECJ and national courts. The first is competent to define the protective scope of the allegedly breached EU provision. The second element, the so-called seriousness of the breach, does not depend on fault or negligence, but on the amount of discretion a state institution (legislature, administration, or judiciary) has or lacks in implementing EU law.[9] It will, however, be shown later that an element of fault enters through the back door, at least in German practice.

Tridimas very convincingly distinguishes three types of cases depending on how the ECJ approaches answering the question of the seriousness of the breach: outcome cases, where the Court itself provides the answer for the national court; guidance cases, where the Court provides more or less specific guidelines; and deference cases, where the Court leaves the decision on 'seriousness' to the national court. The third element, direct causation, seems to have attracted little attention so far: the ECJ has been quite deferential to national law.

Tridimas also notes that the remedy has been used 'to serve mostly commercial interests. This, in turn, suggests that other groups of rights protected by EU law (social, consumer, environmental, etc) may lack the incentives to use the remedy'.[10] According to Weatherill it is partly correct that there is a lack of 'incentives' for applying the remedy in social, consumer, environmental, etc cases, but there are also several different elements which combine to reduce the incentives.[11] First, that the applicants in social, consumer, and environmental cases may not have an identifiable 'right' within the meaning of *Francovich*. Secondly, even if they do, the loss will be spread among a large number of claimants, making it difficult for one to sue (and class/representative actions are yet another problem). Third, it may even be hard to show that any loss was caused to the applicant at all—e.g. a

[6] T Tridimas, 'State Liability in Damages: vingt ans après' (17 November 2011) unpublished paper presented at the conference 'Celebrating 20 years of *Francovich* in the European Union' at the British Institute of International and Comparative Law, London.

[7] H-B Schäfer, 'Kann Staatshaftung für legislatives Unrecht Parlamente anspornen, höherrangiges Recht stärker zu beachten?', in P Behrens et al., *XII Travemünder Symposion zur ökonomische Analyse des Recht* (Mohr Siebeck 2012) 73.

[8] T Lock, 'Is Private enforcement of EU law through State Liability a Myth? An Assessment 20 years after *Francovich*' (2012) 49 *Common Market Law Review* 1675.

[9] *Brasserie du Pêcheur* (n 3), para 79.

[10] Trimidas (n 6).

[11] S Weatherill, 'Reflections on EC Law's "Implementation Imbalance" in the Light of the Ruling in Hedley Lomas', in L Krämer et al., *Law and Diffuse Interests in the European Legal Order: Liber Amoricum Norbert Reich* (VIEW/Nomos Verlagsgesellshaft 1997) 31; and S Weatherill, 'Addressing problems of Imbalanced Implementation in EC Law: Remedies in an Institutional Perspective' in C Kilpatrick et al., *The Future of Remedies in Europe* (Hart 2000) 87.

case of general environmental pollution. Fourth, the applicant is likely to be small and relatively weak, lacking the means to sue a public authority. This point will be qualified later, in particular when the ECJ refers to *Francovich* liability when a Directive on social protection (consumer or worker protection) has not been correctly implemented in contractual relations, a direct horizontal effect cannot be established, and a *contra legem* interpretation must be ruled out. Tridimas concludes his analysis:

> [...] the value of the right to reparation is mostly prospective and indirect rather than remedial. This is for two reasons. First, although it is impossible to quantify state liability has a high deterrence value it is reasonable to assume that such value is evenly spread among all classes of rights protected by EU law. Secondly it provides the forum for the delineation of constitutional boundaries [...][12]

b. Schäfer: economic analysis of the deterrence or the absence thereof by state liability rules

There has been intense debate in the economic analysis of law (EAL) to analyse the relationship between deterrence and compensation rules. Even without being specialists in this debate, we can discern that the question always vacillates between the seemingly conflicting phenomena of 'over' versus 'under'-deterrence, e.g. regarding provisions on state liability in general[13] or infringements of antitrust law.[14] Optimal enforcement rules try to avoid both extremes in the interests of the efficient allocation of resources. State liability has so far not been analysed in EAL terms, possibly because its public nature prevents it from having any effect on resource allocation in competitive markets.

The economic analysis presented by Schäfer goes a step beyond the classical EAL approach and links deterrence to the budgetary implications of liability, whether concerned with businesses or state institutions.[15] Business liability can be said to have a deterrent effect because it directly relates to its overall market success in maximizing profits and reducing or avoiding losses, provided the optimal deterrence criteria are met. The liability of state institutions, on the contrary, in particular in a Parliamentary setting, imposes costs only on the taxpayer, but does not allow for positive or negative incentives on the behaviour of responsible political agents. It must be regarded as a 'passing-on' mechanism. There is no evidence that the introduction of *Francovich* liability minimizes EU-incompatible legislation. The EAL model of deterrence can on the contrary establish 'perverse' incentives to shield the State from liability, by changing laws or even the constitution, as was evidenced in the German laws exempting banking supervision agencies from liability heard in the *Peter Paul* litigation.[16]

The problem with Schäfer's approach is that he concentrates on the behaviour of individual political agents, determined by financial incentives or risks, but not on the political costs of decisions contradicting EU law and thereby occasioning liability. The public outcry after *Dillenkofer*[17] certainly had a deterrent effect on state institutions

[12] Trimidas (n 6).
[13] G Dari-Mattiacci et al., 'State Liability' (2010) 18 *European Review of Private Law* 773.
[14] S Keske, *Group Litigation in European Competition Law* (Intersentia 2010).
[15] Schäfer (n 7).
[16] Case C-222/02 *Peter Paul, Cornelia Sonnen-Lütte, Christel Mörkens v Bundesrepublik Deutschland* [2004] ECLI:EU:C:2004:606.
[17] Joined Cases C-178/94, C-179/94, C-188/94, C-189/94, and C-190/94 *Erich Dillenkofer, Christian Erdmann, Hans-Jürgen Schulte, Anke Heuer, Werner, Ursula and Trosten Knor v Bundesrepublik Deutschland* [1996] ECLI: EU:C:1996:375.

required to implement EU law. This was the experience with later *Francovich*-style litigation in Germany, which typically attracted considerable attention both in the public and in the administrative discourse: government will usually do anything to avoid such negative reactions by insisting on strict implementation of—mostly secondary—EU law. On the other hand, risk avoidance by legislative manipulation cannot be discounted, as the *Peter Paul* litigation showed (see section 3(b)). However, and this must be levelled against Schäfer, such an exemption from liability always depends on whether it can survive the ECJ's strict scrutiny. In EU law, unlike US law, there is no presumption of 'sovereign immunity', as Schäfer himself argues.

c. Some empirical data on litigation in Germany and England by Lock

Lock compares the success rate of *Francovich*-type litigation in German and English courts, from which most references to the ECJ originated.[18] Thirty-seven cases were brought in Germany, but only eight succeeded (22 per cent success rate); the UK saw twenty-five cases of which nine succeeded (28 per cent success rate). About two-thirds of the cases concerned issues surrounding the transposition of Directives.[19] Again, in around two-thirds of cases the litigation failed because of the absence of a 'sufficiently serious breach'.[20] The author concludes:

> Both the statistical findings and the analysis of national court decisions [...] suggest that Member State liability is not a successful means of enforcing Union law...This article has attempted to answer the question why Member State liability is so rarely successful. It is suggested that a number of factors come into play, on the basis of which the limits of Member State liability as a private enforcement mechanism can be shown [...] It is particularly difficult to establish a sufficiently serious breach outside the clear cut categories of non-transposition cases and of cases where the breach persisted despite it having been established by the Court.[21]

In his opinion, *Francovich* liability should not be regarded as an enforcement mechanism, but rather as a 'remedy providing compensation for individual claimants where they happen to fulfil the strict requirements laid down by the Court [...]'[22]

3. The leeway left to national law in determining the 'seriousness of the breach'

a. The starting point: *Brasserie du Pêcheur*

As will be recalled, in the aftermath of the well-known *Bier* case condemning the German '*Reinheitsgebot*' as an unjustified restriction of free movement,[23] the question arose whether the French producer could claim compensation for not being able to market its product in Germany. The question appeared before the ECJ in *Brasserie du Pêcheur*, where the theory of state liability found its definite contours and where the Court made an interesting distinction between the German rules conditioning the use of the denomination 'Bier' to conformity with the *Reinheitsgebot*—which was found to be obviously illegal under pre-existing ECJ case law and incapable of justifying trade restrictions—and the prohibition of additives and stabilizers, which was originally argued to be in the interest of public health, despite this not ultimately being upheld.

[18] Lock (n 8). [19] ibid, 1685. [20] ibid, 1689. [21] ibid, 1700. [22] ibid, 1702.

[23] Case C-178/84 *Commission of the European Communities v Federal Republic of Germany* [1987] ECLI:EU:C:1987:126.

This rather sophisticated distinction between the motives behind the German *Reinheitsgebot* legislation was eagerly taken up by the *Bundesgerichtshof* (BGH) in a subsequent case turning on the 'sufficiently serious breach'.[24] Since the German *Biersteuergesetz*, condemned by the ECJ, was originally justified on health grounds (despite being misunderstood, one might add) and not on monopolizing the denomination 'Bier', the German legislator's breach was said to be excusable and thus 'not sufficiently serious'. This was quite an unexpected outcome and left the French brewery without any compensation despite its year-long fight, supported by the Commission and the logic of the earlier *Cassis de Dijon* case,[25] against this German trade restriction. Obviously, *Francovich* liability did not have any deterrent effect on the German legislator—quite the contrary, it allowed an *ex post* justification based on fictitious health protection arguments.

b. Conflicting consumer policy-objectives: *Dillenkofer* versus *Peter Paul*

Whether *Francovich* liability can be regarded as an element of 'enforcement' remains unanswered in German law. Anecdotal evidence in both directions appears prevalent. There are cases which seem to confirm this statement, in particular *Dillenkofer*,[26] where the Parliament was initially unable—due to special interest lobbying—to implement Article 7 Package Holiday Directive 90/314/EC.[27] After the ECJ's judgment—followed by a judgment of the *Landgericht* (LG) Bonn finding the government liable to compensate stranded passengers to the tune of DM 20 to 30 million,[28] the *Bundestag* (the lower house of Parliament in Germany) was very quick to enact legislation implementing Article 7 of the Directive to avoid further state liability by introducing a mandatory insurance scheme to be paid and handed out to package holiday passengers. The scheme seems to have worked well so far, thus avoiding any direct government liability. This precedent was used by the government in implementing the Consumer Sales Directive[29] into the *Bürgerliches Gesetzbuch* (BGB—German Civil Code) in 2001–2002, which was then met with fierce resistance from academia and the legal profession, even though the case for ultimate *Francovich* liability because of late or non-implementation was hard to make. The government did not want to risk being compelled again to pay compensation for not having implemented an important piece of EU consumer protection law in time, even though in my opinion the risk was greatly exaggerated.

In contrast, in the *Peter Paul* case[30] Germany was to a large part saved from liability for the incorrect supervision of subsequently bankrupt banks which had not adhered to the deposit guarantee scheme of Directive 94/19. The LG Bonn applied *Francovich* with regard to the sums of compensation under the non-implemented guarantee scheme (EUR 20,000) and referred the question of general liability for Germany's or its banking authorities' breach of their supervising obligations under EU banking legislation to the ECJ. The ECJ denied liability because bank customers did not come under the protective ambit of the EU banking supervision directives, thus saving Germany from the risk of substantive liability beyond the limits of the deposit scheme. It also authorized an exemption provision in the

[24] BGH 134, 30 NJW [1997] 123.

[25] Case C-120/78 *Rewe-Zentral AG v Bundesmonopolverwaltung für Branntwein* [1971] ECLI:EU:C:1979:42.

[26] *Dillenkofer* (n 17).

[27] Directive 90/314/EC of the Council of the European Communities, Package Travel Directive [1990] OJ L158/59.

[28] Lock (n 8) 1686.

[29] Directive 99/44/EC of the European Parliament and of the Council, Consumer Sales Directive [1999] OJ L171/12.

[30] *Peter Paul* (n 16).

German implementing legislation concerning liability of its supervisory authorities (similar to the UK *Three Rivers District Council* case).[31] This seems to set a negative precedent for other breaches to be found to fall under EU-imposed supervisory obligations, such as in medicines, medical devices, and pesticides. Obviously, *Francovich* liability will play no role in the enforcement of supervisory duties vis-à-vis 'le grand public'. Whether this will change with the more recent, much stricter supervisory requirements cannot be predicted, at least where liability exceeds the sums guaranteed by deposit or insurance schemes—provided, one might add, that they have been implemented correctly.

c. A social-policy objective: *Fuß II*

In the litigation concerning maximum working time under Directives 93/104/EC[32] and 2003/88/EU[33] the Court took a much clearer stand concerning not only the protective, but also the preventive objective of *Francovich* liability.[34] The case concerned a fire-fighter whom the responsible agency of the city of Halle had refused to acknowledge as having working time capped at a maximum of forty-eight hours under Article 6(b) Directive 2003/88/EU, and who had been transferred to control room duty without his consent. The Court stressed the social policy objective of the Working Time Directive.[35]

In the subsequent case, *Fuß II*, the plaintiff asked for compensation for the damage caused.[36] Neither EU nor German law at the time contained any rules on compensation. The Court referred to the principle of state liability inherent in the system of EU Treaties. Article 6(b) Directive 2003/88/EU is intended to confer rights on individuals and has direct effect because of the employee's weaker position. With regard to the seriousness of the breach, it held that it had all the information necessary to reach an outcome. The breach occurred in 'obvious disregard' of the Court's case law and must therefore be regarded as a 'sufficiently serious breach of EU law'.[37]

The judgment serves to enforce the Court's controversial case law concerning the definition of the maximum forty-eight hour working week, which includes duty on-call or on stand-by,[38] and on the other hand to deter any employer from deviating from the Court's rulings, at least insofar as public employers are concerned, as in the case of Mr Fuß. The German administrative courts, however, had a problem finding a legal basis for compensation, but the Federal Administrative Court developed an autonomous right to compensation as part of a *beamtenrechtlichen Ausgleichsanpruch* (compensation for civil servants).[39] If compensation in kind is not possible, financial compensation based on equity (*Billigkeitsanspruch*) must be paid.[40]

Private employers were not directly concerned by this case law, but a certain 'spill-over' effect cannot be denied. The state is liable under *Francovich* if its legislation does not follow

[31] *Three Rivers District Council v Governor and Company of the Bank of England* [2001] UKHL 16, [2002] 2 *Weekly Law Reports* 1220; critique R Condon, '*Francovich*: Liability for Systemic Regulatory Failure' in H-W Micklitz et al. (eds), *European Regulatory Private Law—The Paradigms Tested* (2014) EUI Working Papers Law No 4, 57 at 67, http://cadmus.eui.eu/bitstream/handle/1814/31137/LAW_2014_04_ERPL_07corr.pdf?sequence=3, accessed 12 October 2016, preferring the 'sufficiently serious breach' criteria.

[32] Directive 93/104/EC of the Council of the European Union, Working Time Directive [1993] OJ L307/18.

[33] Directive 2003/88/EU of the European Parliament and of the Council, Working Time Directive [2003] OJ L299/9.

[34] Case C-243/09 *Günter Fuß v Stadt Halle (Fuß I)* [2010] ECLI:EU:C:2010:609.

[35] ibid, para 47.

[36] Case C-429/09 *Günter Fuß v Stadt Halle (Fuß II)* [2010] ECLI:EU:C:2010:717.

[37] ibid, para 55.

[38] N Reich, *General Principles of EU Civil Law* (Intersentia 2014) 2.3.

[39] *Bundesverwaltungsgericht* judgment of 26 July 2012, *BVerwGE* 143, 381.

[40] ibid, para 36.

the Court imperatives on defining and monitoring maximum working hours. It therefore clearly serves as an element of law enforcement, also in employment relations governed by civil law.[41]

d. German courts coping with the 'seriousness' of the breach

A detailed study by the reporting judge of the BGH Senate which handles state liability, including *Francovich* litigation, concluded that the litmus test left to national law was the *seriousness of the breach*.[42] He mentioned a number of cases brought against Germany concerning Directive 94/62/EC on packaging and packaging waste,[43] Directive 2001/29/EC on copyright in the information society,[44] and several Council decisions concerning fees due for veterinarian examinations, all of which failed at the seriousness hurdle, despite a simple breach (*einfacher Verstoß*) having been found. The BGH relied on the amount of discretion left to the German legislator by EU law, or to the unclear legal situation itself. The only case to the contrary was the protracted *Danske Slagterier* litigation,[45] where the ECJ had already effectively ruled on seriousness, which was more or less carried over by the subsequent judgment of the BGH.[46]

In his abovementioned paper, the reporting judge Dörr wrote that the seriousness of the breach (*Qualifizierung des Verstoßes*) will frequently be compatible with the requirement of a 'vorsätzliche oder fahrlässige Verletzung der Amtspflicht' (intentional or negligent breach of official duty) in the sense of Section 839 I BGB, the basic German provision concerning state liability. Moreover, the defence of *error iuris* seems relevant in this context. The leading monograph by Ossenbühl is, however, somewhat more cautious.[47] This reappearance of a subjective element of fault, which was so strongly rejected in *Brasserie* is certainly quite surprising, which can be shown in the following detailed analysis of the recent *Gibraltar* judgment of the BGH.[48]

e. German betting legislation—the recent *Gibraltar* case

The case—referring to administrative action taken by the Bavarian city of Landshut, confirmed by the Bavarian administrative courts by interim order of the *Bayrische Verwaltungsgerichtshof* (*BayVerwGH*)[49]—concerns an action for compensation by a Gibraltar company and its German agent, which were prohibited from offering sporting bets between 2005 and 2006. The claim failed because the breach was found not to be 'sufficiently serious' by the BGH.

The BGH took great pains to justify its refusal by making detailed reference to the case law of the ECJ and a parallel case of the *Bundesverfassungsgericht* (*BVerfG*).[50] According to the opinion of the BGH, only the ECJ judgments of 8 September 2010 concerning the

[41] For success rates at German courts, see Lock (n 8) fn 61.
[42] C Dörr 'Der unionsrechtliche Staatshaftungsanspruch in Deutschland zwanzig Jahre nach *Francovich*' (2012) 3 *Europäische Zeitschrift für Wirtschaftsrecht* 86.
[43] Directive 94/62/EC of the European Parliament and Council on packaging and packaging waste [1994] OJ L365/10.
[44] Directive 2001/29/EC of the European Parliament and Council, Copyright Directive [2001] OJ L167/10.
[45] Case C-445/06 *Danske Slagterier v Bundesrepublik Deutschland* [2009] ECLI:EU:C:2009:178.
[46] BGH 4.6.2009 [2009] *Europäische Zeitschrift für Wirtschaftsrecht* 865.
[47] F Ossenbühl and M Cornils, *Staatshaftungsrecht* (6th edn, Verlag CH Beck 2012) 610.
[48] BGH 18.10.2012 [2013] *Europäische Zeitschrift für Wirtschaftsrecht* 194.
[49] *BayVerwGH* 6.12.2006 24 AS 06.2604. [50] *BVerfG* 28.3.2006 1 BvR 1054/01.

restrictive regulations on betting of the *Land Schleswig Holstein*[51] and *Hessen*,[52] removed any doubt about the incompatibility of the betting monopoly under the so-called 'Staatsvertrag' of 2003, in force until 31 December 2007 by virtue of a transitional period granted by the abovementioned judgment of the *BVerfG*. The German state monopoly over lotteries and sports betting was criticized by the ECJ, as will be recalled, as not combating in a 'consistent and systematic manner' the risks to the public and the consumer inherent in games of chance. Through marketing campaigns, the public authorities increased the supply and thereby incited the public to gambling and betting activities rather than preventing them. Other games of chance such as casinos and automated games were subject only to an authorization scheme and had been expanding greatly, despite their increased addiction risk. In its *Winner-Wetten* judgment of the same day,[53] the ECJ insisted that the grace period to the end of 2007 granted to the German Länder regulation had no influence over the status of legality of the German betting monopoly.

To justify its refusal to grant compensation to the Gibraltar betting company and its German agent (who in the meantime became insolvent) the BGH argued that the incoherence of the German monopoly only became clear in the judgments of 8 September 2010, that is after the final prohibition order of the *BayVerwGH*. Even though the 'coherence' in combatting consumer addiction criterion to evaluate state betting monopolies against the free movement provisions of the EU had already been used in the *Gambelli* judgment of 6 November 2003,[54] the German monopoly differed from the impugned Italian regulation and could not serve as a precedent for clearly condemning the German regulations at the time of the Gibraltar proceedings. The BGH writes somewhat sophisticatedly:

> Coherence in the sense of the relevant facts of the litigation, namely that games of chance, which do not come under the state monopoly, have a greater potential for addiction than those falling under the monopoly, was not even hinted at in Gambelli. This was decisive only in the ECJ judgments of 8 September [...] Therefore, the Gambelli judgment could not be regarded as giving rise to a – at least sufficiently serious – unjustified infringement of the freedom to provide services (author's translation).[55]

This looks like a clever argument—the ECJ is to blame, not the Bavarian authorities and administrative courts—but it misses the point. The relevant criteria under EU and also German constitutional law as developed in the *BVerfG* judgment of 28 March 2006—ie before the final order of the *BayVerwGH* of 6 December 2006—was clearly the absent appropriateness and necessity of the German state monopoly to combat consumer addiction to betting. This was denied by the *BVerfG* itself under German law, with an *obiter dictum* on EU law with the same meaning. In its abovementioned judgment the *BVerfG* wrote, citing *Gambelli*:

> In this respect, the requirements of German constitutional law are parallel to the requirements of European law formulated by the European Court of Justice. According to the case-law of the European Court of Justice, the prevention of arranging betting in other Member States is compatible with Community law only if a state monopoly really serves the goal of reducing the opportunities for gambling, and the financing of social activities with the help of a levy on

[51] Case C-46/08 *Carmen Media Group Ltd v Land Schleswig-Holstein and Innenminister des Landes Schleswig-Holstein* [2010] ECLI:EU:C:2010:505.

[52] Case C-316/07 *Markus Stoß, Avalon Service-Online-Dienste GmbH and Olaf Amadeus Wilhelm Happel v Wetteraukreis and Kulpa Automatenservice Asperg GmbH, SOBO Sport & Entertainment GmbH and Andreas Kunert v Land Baden-Württemberg* [2010] ECLI:EU:C:2010:504.

[53] Case C-409/06 *Winner Wetten GmbH v Bürgermeisterin der Stadt Bergheim* [2010] ECLI:EU:C:2010:503.

[54] Case C-243/01 *Piergiorgio Gambelli and Others* [2003] ECLI:EU:C:2003:597.

[55] BGH (n 46).

> the earnings from authorised gambling is only a useful accompanying effect, but not the real reason for the restrictive policy pursued [. . .]The requirements of Community law are therefore the same as those of the Basic Law.[56]

The only difference is the 'grace period' granted to the legislator (the German Länder being competent to conclude and to modify the '*Staatsvertrag*') by the *BVerfG*—an extension clearly violating EU law unless expressly authorized by the ECJ, as was held in the subsequent *Winner-Wetten* judgment.[57] The BGH used the extension period granted by the *BVerfG* as a sort of defence against the Gibraltar claim, thereby implicitly rejecting the priority argument of EU law. It is true that when the *BayVerwGH* decided its order of 6 December 2006, it was caught between EU and German law; the only way out would have been a reference to the ECJ, as done by the *Verwaltungsgericht* Köln in the case leading to *Winner-Wetten*. Even though, as the BGH correctly argues,[58] the *BayVerwGH* was not under an obligation in interim proceedings to make a reference as a court of last instance under Article 234(4) EC (now Article 267(4) TFEU), it should have done so to avoid a potential liability claim.[59]

Another problem results from the specific federal situation in Germany, where the Länder are competent to regulate sports betting activities, which they had done under the impugned Staatsvertrag, while other types of games of chance—such as bets on horse racing, casinos, and automated games—come under criminal and trade law subject to federal competence, and where only an authorization regime applies. The BGH relied on this fact to argue extensively that the Land Bayern was not under an obligation to modify its part of the Staatsvertrag.

As a result, the plaintiff's claim was caught in the intricacies of German constitutional law, which clearly violated EU law and should not serve as a defence. The restrictive attitude of the BGH inserts a subjective fault element in the form of an excusable *error iuris* into the criteria for a 'sufficiently serious' violation of EU law as a condition of a successful damages action under the *Francovich* doctrine. We recall, however, that *error iuris non nocet*, an error about existing EU law by the defendant state is no excuse under *Brasserie* but only an element to determine the seriousness of the breach.

4. Causation, co-responsibility, and national law

a. The starting point in *Brasserie du Pêcheur*

An example of the implicit recognition of the good faith principle in state liability cases is the rule on 'co-responsibility' as a limitation to a right derived from EU law, for instance as a defence against a claim of damages against a Member State that has breached EU law. In *Brasserie*, the Court insisted on the principle of full compensation including 'pure' economic loss, and including the payment of interest. Member States may however require that the injured party be reasonably diligent in limiting the extent of the loss or damage, otherwise that party risks the loss or reduction of its claim. The more recent *Danske-Slagterier* justified a requirement of national law that an individual not be able to obtain reparation for loss or damage which he has wilfully or negligently failed to avert by utilizing a legal remedy, 'provided that utilisation of that remedy can reasonably be required of the injured party, a matter which is for the referring court to determine in light of all the

[56] *BVerfG* (n 50) 144. [57] *Winner Wetten* (n 53) para 60. [58] *BayVerwGH* (n 49) 33.
[59] See, on the functioning of Art 267 TFEU, Broberg in Chapter 6 of this volume.

circumstances of the main proceedings'[60]—an element which the follow-up judgment of the BGH denied. However, the claim for compensation which was remanded to the *Oberlandesgericht Köln* for fact finding ultimately failed because of the absence of a causal link between breach and damage.[61] As a paradoxical result of the highly complex and protracted litigation, the Danish exporters of pig meat changed their marketing practice and later exported only the meat of castrated pigs to Germany.

b. The protective element in *Fuß II*

In *Fuß II* the Court was asked whether an employee asking for compensation because his rights under Article 6(2) Directive 2003/88/EC[62] had been denied him, must make a 'prior application' to the employer to secure compliance with that provision. The Court flatly denied such a condition for damages, despite recognizing the duty of the victim to mitigate its damages by showing 'reasonable diligence' to limit loss.

The Court explained that the objective of the Directive was to protect the worker as the weaker party, which rules out such an obligation.[63] The German courts followed suit.

c. Other defences, in particular prescription

In *Palmisani* the ECJ stated that compensation must be commensurate with the loss or damage sustained to ensure effective protection for the rights of individuals.[64] National law may lay down the conditions for liability, including time limits, but they must meet the principles of *equivalence* (they must not be less favourable than those relating to similar domestic claims) and of *effectiveness* (they must not be so framed as to make it virtually impossible or excessively difficult to obtain reparation). The ECJ had no problem with the one-year time limit from the perspective of effectiveness because it constitutes 'an application of the fundamental principle of legal certainty'.[65] More problematic was the fulfilment of the principle of equivalence, since under Italian law claims for compensation for non-contractual liability are subject to a five-year prescription period. However, the ECJ was not sure whether these actions related to the same subject matter as those covered by the special rules on a one-year limit and therefore capable of being subject to the equivalence test. This was a matter for the national court to decide.

Danske Slagterier was also concerned with German prescription rules under Section 852 (1) BGB by analogy, with a three-year period beginning on the date the victim became aware of the damage. The ECJ left it to the national court to decide whether this rule, to be applied by analogy, satisfied the requirement of legal certainty, but in the subsequent judgment the BGH took a different view, favouring the plaintiff and thus avoiding any conflict with the EU law principles of equivalence and effectiveness. Concerning the interruption of prescription, the ECJ did not equate an enforcement action brought by the Commission[66] with an action on the liability of a state official under German law.

[60] *Danske Slagterier* (n 45) para 69. [61] Lock (n 8) fn 134.

[62] Directive 2003/88/EC of the European Parliament and of the Council, Working Time Directive [2003] OJ L299/19.

[63] *Fuß II* (n 36) para 80.

[64] Case C-261/95 *Rosalba Palmisani v Istituto nazionale della previdenza sociale (INPS)* [1997] ECLI:EU:C:1997:351.

[65] *Palmisani* (n 64) para 28. [66] Art 258 TFEU.

5. Liability as a safety net where horizontal direct effect has been denied?

a. State liability as a remedy of last resort?

If the theory of direct effect cannot be invoked by the consumer or employee against an undertaking, despite a directive seeking to grant subjective rights to them, then state liability as a remedy of last resort can arise against the Member State for having failed to implement a directive intending such protection properly or at all. *Francovich* liability appears to be a safety net or a remedy of last resort where the not or incorrectly implemented directive does not permit the conferral rights on consumers or employees directly in their contractual relations with their supplier or employer. In the cases where the horizontal direct effect of a directive is precluded by EU law, the ECJ established that an individual citizen who has suffered damage through a Member State's failure properly to implement a directive has a right to compensation against that State. Starting with *Faccini Dori* the ECJ noted that Italy had not implemented the then valid Doorstep Directive 85/577,[67] allowing a consumer induced into a contract on the street a right of withdrawal.[68] A Directive harmonizing the interpretation of existing law cannot work *contra legem* and therefore could not itself impose obligations on the trader.[69] However, the Italian state could be liable to the consumer for not having implemented the Directive in due time and form, provided that the other requirements of *Francovich* are fulfilled. The Court wrote:

> If the result prescribed by the directive cannot be reached by way of interpretation, is should also be borne in mind that, in terms of the judgment in [...] *Francovich* [...] the Community law requires the Member States to make good any damage caused to individuals through failure to transpose a directive, provided that three conditions are fulfilled [...][70]

This case law was continued in several consumer and employment cases decided later, where consistent interpretation would not lead to a satisfactory result, and where a horizontal direct effect of a protective directive could not be established, e.g. *El Corte Inglés*,[71] *Adeneler*,[72] *Domingez*,[73] and *AMS*,[74] but surprisingly not in *Pfeiffer*.[75]

b. Is *Francovich* really of help both with regard to prevention and to compensation?

The frequent reference of the ECJ to state liability in cases where direct horizontal effect of non-implemented directives cannot be found suggests the existence of a remedy which is seemingly effective at protecting individual rights and furthermore at preventing such violations by the sState concerned from occurring. The Court however does not seem to be aware of the limits to compensation which its *Francovich* case law itself imposed. The Court not only places the burden, risks, and costs of additional proceedings on the victim

[67] Directive 85/577 EEC of the Council of the European Communities, the Doorstep Selling Directive [1985] OJ L372/31.

[68] Case C-91/92 *Paola Faccini Dori v Recreb Srl* [1994] ECLI:EU:C:1994:292, para 8.

[69] ibid, para 24. [70] ibid, para 27.

[71] Case C-192/94 *El Corte Inglés SA v Cristina Blázquez Rivero* [1996] ECLI:EU:C:1996:88, para 22.

[72] Case C-212/04 *Konstantinos Adeneler and Others v Ellinikos Organismos Galaktos (ELOG)* [2006] ECLI:EU:C:2006:443, para 112.

[73] Case C-282/10 *Maribel Dominguez v Centre informatique du Centre Ouest Atlantique and Préfet de la région Centre* [2012] ECLI:EU:C:2012:33, para 43.

[74] Case C-176/12 *Association de médiation sociale v Union locale des syndicats CGT and Others* [2014] ECLI:EU:C:2014:2, para 30.

[75] Case C-397/01 *Bernhard Pfeiffer, Wilhelm Roith, Albert Süß, Michael Winter, Klaus Nestvogel, Roswitha Zeller and Matthias Döbele v Deutsches Rotes Kreuz, Kreisverband Waldshut eV* [2004] ECLI:EU:C:2004:584.

EU law is expected to protect, but also makes its success depend to a great extent on the intricacies of Member State compensation law. This is particularly true of the requirement of *causation between breach and damage*. Consider *Faccini Dori*: the consumer's damage, caused by non-implementation of Directive 85/577/EC, consisted in being bound by a contract she no longer wanted. This was her 'negative interest' in being freed from an onerous contract—a right which cannot be fulfilled by the state, not being a party to the contract. What if the goods or services delivered under the contract conformed with market conditions or normal consumer expectations? It would appear that state liability is not an adequate, or is only a symbolic, remedy in this case, a result which the Court had condemned as insufficient in a somewhat different setting in *Von Colson*.[76]

AMS turned on the threshold for the right of information or consultation applied to employee organizations such as trade unions for the workers in a French social work institution. What damage is suffered from being unable to claim these representation rights from the State? This again seems to result in an obligation which cannot be fulfilled at all (*impossibile nullum est obligatio*) and therefore can cause no damage.

State liability seems to be an inadequate remedy in cases where Sstates have not correctly fulfilled their obligations to implement directives under EU social contract law. An extension of the theory of direct effect would be much more effective, as the case law of the Court on sex and age discrimination clearly shows. This case law works 'negatively' insofar as the discrimination on horizontal relations imposed or allowed by state law breaching EU law will be eliminated by applying general principles of EU civil law.[77] Why take a complex legal detour if the direct application of EU law can achieve much more convincing results?

6. Through the critical 'Looking Glass': The 'implementation imbalance' of *Francovich*

a. *Danske Slagterier* as a recent starting point

Too strict *Francovich* liability could result in social policy interests being sacrificed on the altar of free movement. Consider the abovementioned *Danske Slagterier* case concerning the alleged illegal action of German veterinary inspectorates against imported Danish pig meat from uncastrated male animals, which was said to comply with home country checks but which did not comply with German standards which fixed a threshold of 0.5 μg/g for androstenone to avoid the risk of the meat giving off a pronounced sexual odour when heated. The Danish exporters litigated their case on *Francovich* liability, where the BGH under guidance of the ECJ found a 'sufficiently serious breach', but ultimately failed at the causation hurdle and had to change their marketing practice. Why did they not comply with German standards rather than insisting on problematic Danish inspections, and why did the Court not show more sensitivity to consumer acceptance of products instead of insisting on a rather abstract country of origin principle?

b. *AGM-COS MET*: free movement 'über alles'

Similar conflicts arose in the *AGM-COS MET* case concerning unauthorized warnings by a Finnish official against a dealer of Italian car lifts.[78] I have already critically analysed facts of *AGM-COS MET* and the ECJ's conclusion in a paper which argues that there is on a conflict

[76] Case C-14/83 *Von Colson and Kamann v Land Nordrhein-Westfalen* [1984] ECLI:EU:C:1984:153.
[77] Reich, *General Principles of EU Civil Law* (n 38) 4.14.
[78] Case C-470/03 *AGM-COS MET Srl v Suomen valtio and Tarmo Lehtinen* [2007] ECLI:EU:C:2007:213.

between EU free movement principles and product safety issues.[79] The unclear relationship between market access and product warnings concerned two questions of law. Firstly the admissibility of product warnings against a potentially dangerous imported product (a vehicle lift from Italy) bearing the 'CE' conformity mark, which were based on the producer's instructions that a car should be driven onto the vehicle lift only when facing forwards, while the relevant European standard allegedly required that lifts be capable of being mounted both forwards and backwards. Secondly the liability of the Finnish state for unauthorized public product criticism by an employee, Mr Lehtinen (the co-defendant).

The balancing of the conflicting legal interests—free movement for the producer and safety as a citizen's right protected by the state and its officials—was limited to the interpretation of secondary law, namely the Machinery Directive[80]—where the case demonstrates remarkable differences in reasoning between the AG and the Court.

The Court took the following steps to bring the case within the scope of the relevant Directive, thereby prejudicing the questions of state liability. First, it considered how far the Italian producer could invoke the internal market clause of Article 4 of the Directive in his favour. This presupposes that he fulfilled the Directive's basic safety requirements in the sense of Article 5, that an adequate certification procedure has been performed by an authorized body, and that the 'CE' conformity mark had been placed on the product. According to the order for reference by the Finnish court, this was the case. Second, the 'CE' mark creates a presumption of conformity for the producer giving him a Community right to market entry.[81] There is no need to refer to primary law because Directive 98/37/EC creates 'vertical direct effect' against any state action. This subjective, directly effective right is affected in the sense of the *Dassonville* formula by any 'state measure directly or indirectly, actually or potentially, hindering intra-Community trade'.[82] There should be no doubt that product warnings from a public authority can have this effect. Third, the presumption of conformity can be rebutted, but only within the safeguard procedure of Article 7 of the Directive; there are no other principles to be applied in addition.[83]

This 'product safety by procedure', in which the Member State, the producer and the Commission participate, but not the potential victims and their associations, demonstrates a fundamental problem clearly evidenced but not solved by the Court in *AGM-COS MET*: what happens if the conditions for the presumption are no longer fulfilled, but the State concerned does not take measures for whatever reasons by not invoking the safeguard procedure? Advocate General Kokott and the Court took a strikingly different view in this respect: the AG, in answering the second question of the referring court, pointed out that the vehicle lift did not comply with the safety requirements of the relevant European standard because '[f]or structural design purposes vehicle position on load carrying devices shall be considered in both directions'.[84]

The Court however rejected this question as irrelevant without even mentioning the product's substantive non-conformity.[85] It thus avoided the central point of the litigation, namely the decisive level of safety of a product according to the relevant European standards: the producer cannot simply rely on his own judgment concerning safety by

[79] N Reich, 'AGM-COS MET or: Who is protected by EC safety regulation?' (2008) 31 *European Law Reports* 85.

[80] Directive 98/37/EC of the European Parliament and of the Council, Machinery Directive [1998] OJ L207/1.

[81] *AGM-COS MET* (n 78) para 86.

[82] Case C-8/74 *Procureur du Roi v Benoît and Gustave Dassonville* [1974] ECLI:EU:C:1974:82, para 60.

[83] *AGM-COS MET* (n 78) para 53.

[84] Case C-470/03 *AGM-COS MET* [2005] ECLI:EU:C:2005:693, Opinion of AG Kokott, para 22.

[85] *AGM-COS MET* (n 78) para 74.

requiring that the vehicle lift be used only in one direction without considering that there may be situations where a vehicle is driven in the opposite direction for reasons which the producer cannot possibly exclude, therefore the safety devices must be designed in such a way that they guarantee stability for the raised car in both directions. The AG convincingly cites the recommendations of the committees which coordinate certifying bodies, insisting on an 'interpretation on which restrictions on driving direction and the use of loading tables are not compatible with the Directive's safety requirements'.[86]

The case therefore culminated in the question of the consequences under Community law where the conditions for the presumption of safety are no longer present, because the vehicle lift does not comply with the relevant EU safety standards, even if the competent national authority did not take action under the Directive's safeguard procedure, despite one of its employees (the technical expert and second defendant Mr Lehtinen), in open opposition to his superiors, continuing to warn against the risks of the vehicle lift because the producer's operating instructions restricted its use in a manner contrary to the EU standard.[87] Such contradictions require clarification of the importance of the safeguard procedure under EC law, which was only done incidentally in the judgment.

The Court interprets the safeguard clause in conjunction with the free movement rule of Article 4 in such a way that it confers upon the producer a subjective, directly effective right against state measures (such as product warnings) restricting or impeding his market access. This right can only be limited by state measures complying with the required procedural steps and without the possibility of an official interfering through unauthorized action. The safeguard procedure is not only an option—and perhaps even an obligation—for action for the Member State concerned to protect the safety of its citizens, but also simultaneously a prohibition on action if no measures under Article 7 are taken.[88] The responsibility of Member States for the safety of EU products according to recital 19 of the Preamble to Directive 98/37/EC will at the same time be created and limited by the safeguard procedure. This preempts the competence of lower and local Member State health and safety bodies.

Another important question raised by the case which had not yet been answered by the Court concerned the state's liability for unauthorized statements of its officials interfering with the producer's subjective right to freely market its products within the internal market. The criteria developed by the AG and the Court, emphasizing not so much the state's internal competence structure but the public's perception, probably conform with general principles of international law which the AG mentions expressly.[89]

> The decisive factor for attributing the statements of an official to the State is whether the persons to whom the statements are addressed can reasonably suppose, in the given context, that they are positions taken by the official with the authority of his office.[90]

This had to be determined by the national court as a matter of fact. Both the AG and the Court list a number of criteria for how to determine this perception.[91]

State liability requires, as has been pointed out earlier, the fulfilment of the criterion of 'sufficiently serious breach', where the Court usually leaves a large margin of discretion to the state but seems to have taken a more rigid approach in *AGM-COS MET*. This 'sufficiently serious breach' depends on the interpretation of the safeguard clause: if it

[86] *AGM-COS MET* Opinion of AG Kokott (n 84) para 66. [87] ibid, para 31.
[88] *AGM-COS MET* Opinion of AG Kokott (n 84) para 137 and *AGM-COS MET* (n 78) para 82.
[89] *AGM-COS MET* Opinion of AG Kokott (n 84) paras 84–6.
[90] *AGM-COS MET* (n 78) para 57.
[91] Respectively *AGM-COS MET* Opinion of AG Kokott (n 84) para 105 and *AGM-COS MET* (n 78) para 58.

only contains an authorization to act, then a warning by a unauthorized official will not be regarded as fulfilling these requirements per se; only if the producer had actually conformed to the safety requirements for the stability and capacity of vehicle lifts which the co-defendant Lehtinen repeatedly alleged were not met would the test have been met. Since the conformity requirement can also be rebutted in liability proceedings, the breach could no longer be regarded as 'sufficiently serious' because it only concerned the procedure not the substance of the matter. Ultimately, the Mr Lehtinen's warnings were justified, even if not stemming from legitimate authority. In my view Mr Lehtinen's lack of competence under *national law* cannot be invoked in favour of the producer.

If, on the other hand, we agree with the opinion of the Court that the safeguard procedure also contains a prohibition against action in favour of the EU producer, which must therefore be strictly and formally observed in the interest of the free movement of goods, then a mere violation of the procedural requirements suffices to imply a 'sufficiently serious breach'.[92] As a consequence of this stance, the Court forces Member States to adhere strictly to the requirements of the safeguard procedure even for obviously unsafe products. At the same time, it prevents a critical public assessment of safety risks in which State officials may also participate by virtue of their expertise and public responsibility. Such an interpretation of the safeguard procedure excludes the protection of the consumer or worker who may be injured by dangerous, non-conforming products, but results in privileging the producer who sets his own definition of 'safety' against the state-of-the-art, if the competent authority does not exercise her discretion under EC law.

c. *Hedley Lomas* privileging non-conforming states? The 'implementation imbalance' in EU law

Hedley Lomas concerned the systematic refusal of the British authorities to issue licences for the export to Spain of live animals for slaughter.[93] The authorities had formed the view that Spanish slaughterhouses did not correctly apply Directive 74/577/EEC against cruelty to animals. The exporter, Hedley Lomas, brought a *Francovich* claim against the UK and won because of an unjustified, sufficiently serious breach of Article 36 EEC (now Article 35 TFEU). UK 'self-help' could not justify enforcing the Directive against the supposedly uncompliant Spanish authorities.

In a thorough and critical analysis of this case Weatherill pointed to an '*implementation imbalance*' in the proceedings:[94] even though there appeared to be evidence that Spain had indeed breached Directive 74/577/EEC by not ensuring that the provisions on slaughter were effectively implemented, the Commission did not bring an enforcement action. However, UK animal protection non-governmental organizations (NGOs) had no right to force the Commission to take action nor did they have any *Francovich*-like remedies for the under-enforcement of secondary EU law.[95] Weatherill writes:

> The nature of 'individual rights' that are subject to protection at national level requires elucidation in the context of the need to address the implementation imbalance. Whereas the trader's ability to rely on, for example Art. 30 EEC (now Art. 34 TFEU) before national courts to

[92] *AGM-COS MET* (n 77) para 82.

[93] Case C-5/94 *The Queen v Ministry of Agriculture, Fisheries and Food, ex parte: Hedley Lomas (Ireland) Ltd* [1996] ECLI:EU:C:1996:205.

[94] Weatherill, 'Reflections on EC Law's "Implementation Imbalance"' (n 11) and Weatherill, 'Addressing problems of Imbalanced Implementation' (n 10).

[95] Weatherill, 'Reflections on EC Law's "Implementation Imbalance"' (n 11) 43.

> challenge obstacles to trade in goods is clear and illustrated by a vast body of case law, the same cannot be said of the individual's ability to invoke Community law to challenge under-implementation of the law of market regulation. Finding 'rights' to markets freed of unsafe products or to environmental protection in line with EC Directives is jurisprudentially difficult.[96]

Weatherill warns that '*Francovich* should not be over-estimated as a method for addressing the implementation imbalance'.[97] As a result, in *Hedley Lomas* 'free trade won', at the expense of protecting animals against cruel slaughter practices expressly forbidden by secondary EU law.[98]

7. Conclusion

This study leaves the critical observer of EU law puzzled: *Francovich* liability can be regarded as an element of enforcement of EU law, but this is limited in scope in an objective and subjective sense. It requires a 'sufficiently serious'—i.e. clear and unambiguous—breach of Union law by the competent state bodies—criteria applied rather restrictively by state courts in Germany and, as far as I have evidence, the UK. This is also true in cases where business interests are in question, such as in *Gibraltar*. A similar situation occurred in *Danske Slagterer*, where compensation ultimately failed on causation grounds. The usually rather complex litigation is of no help in enforcing EU law.

Concerning the enforcement of social rights, the situation is somewhat more complex, whether in general or specifically under German law. Instances of the obvious disregarding of secondary law in requiring the establishment of guarantee funds for consumers, as in *Dillenkofer* and *Peter Paul*, or the enforcement of the social rights of public officials, as in *Fuß II*, demonstrate the courts' remarkable willingness to use *Francovich* against Member States 'creatively'. In contrast, *Francovich* liability is a remedy of limited success against incompliant states in cases of insufficient protection of social rights guaranteed by secondary contract law (*Faccini Dori, Adeneler*). *Francovich* liability may even provoke an 'implementation imbalance' preferring business interests over social rights, as in *AGM-COS MET* and *Hedley Lomas*—cases which have no parallel in Germany but which certainly deter public action against Member States which do not comply with their EU obligations without the EU institutions having taken action. As a result, *Francovich* liability cannot substitute for absent enforcement actions by the Commission or Member States when they are competent and required to act.

[96] ibid, 46. [97] ibid, 47. [98] ibid, 50.

8

The Bite, the Bark, and the Howl

Article 7 TEU and the Rule of Law Initiatives

Leonard Besselink

In this chapter I analyse Article 7 TEU on sanctions against Member States for certain potential and actual breaches of the values enshrined in Article 2 TEU, and the related 'Rule of Law initiatives'.

The debates over Article 7 TEU and the Rule of Law initiatives, so this chapter argues, reveal a twofold boundary issue: that of the legal delimitation of the procedures and powers under Article 7, and that of the fuzzy boundaries of the Member State political orders as distinct from the EU political order. The very identity of the foundational values of the Union and of the Member States makes it impossible to delimit the scope of EU law from that of Member State orders when it comes to guaranteeing these values. This also explains the politically highly sensitive nature of doing so. Defining the contours of the ensuing problems—mainly the question what is the scope of the powers under the various procedures and when are they triggered—requires a precise legal reconstruction of Article 7 TEU and its development.

Historically, this development takes the form of a backward shift from the issue of sanctions to their preconditions and of powers under prior procedures. The initial point was the introduction of the sanctions; then—in the aftermath of the *Haider* affair—the issue shifted from sanctions to preventative measures at an earlier stage (the type of breach and the issue of which institutions should have a say, and the desirability of a 'preventive mechanism'). The 'monitoring powers' preceding the 'preventive mechanism' have become the focus of the most recent controversies over the Commission's 'Rule of Law Initiative' and the Council's counter-initiative, the 'Rule of Law Dialogue', which steps even further back from 'monitoring' to a mere conversation within the Council. The structure of the analysis follows this retrograde development. It starts with a discussion of the sanctions and procedures. It ends with a discussion of the Commission's and the Council's respective initiatives, asserting that these should more correctly be viewed as integral parts of the procedure under Article 7, rather than be situated outside it.

1. Article 7 TEU

Article 7 TEU concerns compliance with the values enumerated in Article 2 TEU, which are common to the Member States and on which the Union is based, namely 'the values of respect for human dignity, freedom, democracy, equality, the rule of law and respect for human rights, including the rights of persons belonging to minorities', the promotion of which is the aim of the Union (Articles 3(1) and 13(1) TEU).[1]

[1] See also Arts 21(2), 32(1), 42(5), and 49(1) TEU; the Preamble to Protocol No 24 (Lisbon), and the Preamble to the Charter.

The Bite, the Bark and the Howl: Article 7 TEU and the Rule of Law Initiatives. First Edition. Leonard Besselink.

These values constitute, one may say, the constitutional identity of the Union insofar as it coincides with the identity common to the Member States. This provision is therefore sometimes referred to as the 'homogeneity' clause.[2] As the *commonality* of values is the very essence of what is to be protected, the duty for the EU to respect the national identity inherent in a Member State's political and constitutional structure (Article 4(2) TEU) cannot logically be affected by Article 7 TEU, nor can an infringement of the values of Article 2 be justified by reference to the national identity clause.[3]

The sanctions for a 'serious and persistent breach' of the fundamental values provided for in Article 7(3) consist in the suspension of 'certain of the rights deriving from the application of the Treaties to the Member State in question, including the voting rights of the representative of the government of that Member State in the Council'.

Historically, this is the core of the provision. Only with the Nice Treaty was the first paragraph of the present Article 7 inserted, concerning a determination that there is 'a clear risk of a serious breach' by a Member State of the values referred to in Article 2. It was introduced to permit monitoring of Member States and prevent the actual occurrence of a 'serious and persistent breach'.[4] Therefore, Article 7 has a three part structure:

(1) the determination of 'a *clear risk of a serious* breach';
(2) the determination of 'a *serious and persistent* breach' (which is not dependent on having a prior 'clear risk' determination); and
(3) the decision to impose sanctions (which is dependent on a determination of a 'serious and persistent breach').

We discuss this procedure below, both as to its meaning and its procedural characteristics. But true to the retrograde form of the analysis announced, we will first discuss the sanctions and the procedure leading to their imposition.

2. What sanctions?

Article 7(3) TEU is unclear as to the substance of the sanctions which can be imposed. These concern the suspension of 'certain rights deriving from the application of the Treaties to the Member State in question'. There is a surprising paucity in the literature as to what those 'certain rights' might be, except for voting rights in the Council as mentioned in Article 7(3). So this issue must be a matter of speculation.

3. What rights can and cannot be suspended?

The use of the expression 'certain rights' implies both that the rights suspended are specified in the decision on the imposition of sanctions, and that not all rights can be suspended. Hence, Article 7(3) TEU excludes the possibility of suspension of membership

[2] F Schorkopf, *Homogenität in der Europäischen Union, Ausgestaltung und Gewährleistung durch Art. 6 Abs, I und Art 7 EU* (Duncker & Humblot 2000); R Miccù and V Altripaldi (eds), *L'omogeneità costituzionale nell'Unione Europea* (CEDAM 2003).

[3] Convincingly, Cesare Pinelli, 'Protecting the Fundamentals: Article 7 of the Treaty on the European Union and Beyond' (2012) Foundation for European Progressive Studies, 7, http://www.feps-europe.eu/assets/9a4619cf-1a01-4f96-8e27-f33b65337a9b/protecting%20the%20fundamentals.pdf, accessed 12 October 2016. I do not agree, however, that the view expressed in the text entails that Art 4(2) TEU excludes elements of national identity common to the Member States.

[4] An overview of the history of Art 7 TEU is Wojciech Sadurski, 'Adding Bite to a Bark: The Story of Article 7, EU Enlargement, and Jörg Haider' (2010) 16 *Columbia Journal of European Law* 382.

or the cessation of membership. It is up to the Member State who is the target of sanctions to decide whether to leave the Union—it cannot be compelled to leave. Accordingly, even in the case in which a Member State persistently refuses to mend its ways and restore its compliance with the fundamental values of the EU, the EU cannot force it to leave.

This is different under the counterpart of Article 7 TEU in the TEU's human rights sibling, the Statute of the Council of Europe's (Article 8). This provision was triggered after the colonels' coup in Greece by Max van der Stoel's reports on Greece to the Consultative Assembly,[5] which led to the withdrawal of Greece from the Council of Europe on 12 December 1969, before actual decisions under Article 8 of the Statute were taken.[6]

This experience suggests that a similar scenario could unfold in the event of large scale sanctions under Article 7(3) TEU: should a Member State targeted by EU sanctions be unwilling to comply, it may well withdraw.

Could sanctions include such measures as were taken by the fourteen Member State governments in February 2000, subsequent to Haider's FPÖ becoming a coalition partner in Austria in 1999? These sanctions aimed at creating a *cordon sanitaire* around the Austrian coalition government, and took the form of bilateral diplomatic measures: the suspension of bilateral diplomatic contacts except on a 'technical level', freezing of bilateral contacts with other high officials, and no support for Austrian candidates for positions in international organizations.[7]

These measures fall short of being a suspension of 'rights deriving from the application of the Treaties'. Rather they concern the benefits of diplomatic intercourse. Moreover, the sanctions against Austria were not EC/EU sanctions, but bilateral sanctions of fourteen Member States against Austria that were not supposed to interfere with obligations under European law. They might, however, have been allowed as EU sanctions under the present Article 7(3) TEU to the extent that if more severe steps are allowed—the suspension of rights—then less severe ones are also allowed—'suspension' of (non-rights related) factual benefits.

There is little other historical precedent on which one might rely in speculating on the nature of the sanctions under Article 7(3) TEU.

It is plausible that these types of sanctions taken under Article 7 against a Member State would justify the infringement of the principle of loyal cooperation and other possible infringements of EU law resulting from the enforcement of and compliance with sanctions.

In principle, sanctions could concern any 'right deriving from the application of the Treaties' for the Member State concerned. This implies that rights under *secondary* law can be suspended with regard to that Member State, secondary law being 'the application of the Treaties'. This is made explicit in the preamble to the European Arrest Warrant Framework Decision, which states that, being based on a high level of confidence between Member States, its implementation may be suspended only in the event of a serious and persistent

[5] It is wrong to say that Art 8 Statute CoE has never been activated; EU Commission in A New EU Framework for the Rule of Law (n 15), 6.

[6] The 'Greek case' was brought by Denmark, Norway, and Sweden, joined by the Netherlands, to the European Commission of Human Rights; the Assembly found this procedure too burdensome and slow, given clear evidence that the Greek regime did not intend to restore democracy and the full enjoyment of human rights. Max Sørensen considered this a missed opportunity for building a human rights practice of the European Commission, but Max van der Stoel found awaiting the slow evidence gathering and procedure of the Commission to be counterproductive and called successfully for political intervention; see T van Boven, *Human Rights From Exclusion to Inclusion: Principles and Practice* (F Coomans et al. eds, Kluwer Deventer 2000) 52–3.

[7] Statement by the Portuguese Presidency of the EU, 31 January 2000, http://www.cvce.eu/content/publication/2009/12/16/8a5857af-cf29-4f2d-93c9-8bfdd90e40c1/publishable_en.pdf, accessed 12 October 2016.

breach by one of the Member States of the principles of Article 2 TEU pursuant to Article 7 TEU.[8]

Another sanction which has been discussed concerns the suspension of EU funding to the Member State under any of the relevant instruments of secondary law.[9]

There is only one express limitation to sanctions governing the actions of the Council, contained in the wording of Article 7(3) TEU: sanctions must 'take into account the possible consequences of such a suspension on the rights and obligations of natural and legal persons'. This does not exclude the suspension of rights or the disapplication of rights which do not primarily target the government of the state in question, so sanctions might concern deviations from *any* of the Treaty rights. 'Taking into account the consequences for the rights and obligations of natural and legal persons' does not imply that sanctions must exclusively target the Member State executive, and it suggests that sanctions must be proportionate.

The judgment of the Court of Justice on sanctions imposed by the EU in *Bosphorus* confirms this as regards *fundamental* rights (right to property). When assessing the proportionality of an EU sanction the fact that a natural or legal person's fundamental rights can be affected—also of those who have nothing whatsoever to do either with the causes or objectives of the sanctions—was found not to be decisive. The Court held that if the aim of EU sanctions is 'putting an end to [. . .] massive violations of human rights', this objective is sufficient justification for a substantial interference with fundamental rights of persons who are in no way responsible for such violations.[10]

So if a 'serious and persistent breach' of the fundamental EU values under Article 7 TEU is similar to 'massive violations of human rights', this can justify the far-reaching curtailment of the fundamental rights of arbitrary natural and legal persons, as was the case in *Bosphorus*. If this is a correct inference, the somewhat paradoxical situation arises that fundamental rights infringements justify fundamental rights infringements: the sanctions acquire the nature of *talio*. Clearly, the *Bosphorus* case concerned an extreme situation which we cannot imagine easily to occur within the Union. Article 7 TEU is written to address less severe violations than the outrages against human rights which occurred in the conflict in the former Yugoslavia, although very serious infringements can and do occur, if we consider for instance Member State complicity in the extraordinary renditions with a view to 'enhanced interrogation' of suspected terrorists.[11]

4. Five actors and their roles

There are five actors on the stage when it comes to deciding on sanctions:

- the *Council*, who, after hearing the Member State concerned, determines by qualified majority whether and what sanctions are imposed (Article 7(3) TEU);

[8] Council (EU), Framework Decision of 13 June 2002 on the European arrest warrant and the surrender procedures between Member States [2002] OJ L190/1, Recital 10.

[9] Thus the German, Dutch, Danish, and Finnish foreign ministers in their letter to the Commission President on the protection of the Rule of Law in the EU of 6 March 2013, see n 22. B Bugarič, 'Protecting Democracy and the Rule of Law in the European Union: The Hungarian Challenge' LEQS Paper 79/2014, 16, http://ssrn.com/abstract=2257935, accessed 12 October 2016, mistakenly claims: 'If other, primarily financial sanctions, are added, it is more likely that the Article 7 system will become more effective. Needless to say, an amendment of the treaty to that purpose is required in all cases'.

[10] Case C-84/95 *Bosphorus Hava Yollari Turizm v Ticaret AS v Minister for Transport, Energy and Communications and others* [1995] ECLI:EU:C:1996:312, paras 22–3 and 26.

[11] c.f. *Al Nashiri v Poland* (ECtHR, App No 28761/11); *Husayn (Abu Zubaydah) v Poland* (ECtHR, App No 7511/13); EP resolution on the alleged use of European countries by the CIA for the transportation and illegal detention of prisoners [2006] OJ C287E/309.

- the *European Council*, which unanimously determines the prerequisite existence of a 'serious and persistent breach' of the values of Article 2 after inviting the Member State involved to submit its observations (Article 7(2) TEU);
- either at least *one third of the Member States* or the *Commission* can trigger the European Council's determination—these two actors also have the right of initiative; and finally there is
- the *EP* which has to consent to the determination of the 'serious and persistent breach' by the European Council.

The voting arrangement of Article 354 TFEU determines that the Member State targeted does not participate in the vote, and does not count either for determining the votes required or for the calculation of the number of Member States.

It is clear that within the procedure, the determination of the existence of a 'serious and persistent breach' is the most convoluted element. It involves a proposal from either the Commission or one third of the Member States, following which the European Council needs to decide by unanimity after obtaining the consent of the EP. So the European Council acts together with the EP, and an initiating role for the Commission is not mandatory.

The fact that this determination is made not by the Council but by the European Council indicates that it is considered the most important step in the whole procedure. Although this step in the procedure could be dominated by the Member States both in the European Council and potentially as initiators, the determination requires interplay between both the states and the Union inasmuch as the EP must consent (and also the Commission can take the initiative).

The role of the EP can in fact be somewhat greater than Article 7 suggests. The Parliament does not have a formal right of initiative under paragraphs 2 and 3, but the Rules of Procedure of the Parliament explicitly provide for the possibility of a vote on a proposal to call on the Commission or Member States to submit a proposal under paragraph 2, or on the Council to act under paragraph 3.[12] The Parliament clearly wants to be involved more actively than Article 7 suggests. In practice we see frequent—but unsuccessful—appeals by MEPs to activate the procedure in concrete cases.

After the determination of a serious and persistent breach, the actual sanctions are determined by the Council, acting on its own by a reinforced qualified majority.[13] No initiative is needed, nor the consent of the Parliament. So, after a determination of a 'serious and persistent breach', the actual determination of sanctions is the most 'intergovernmental' of decisions—no other EU institution than the Council is involved. However, this is not the intergovernmentalism of the old 'second' and 'third pillar' from the days of the Maastricht Union: the decision is taken by qualified majority.

The procedure is of a highly political nature. The political actors dominate; a Commission initiative is not strictly necessary. The Court of Justice has not been given an explicit role in the procedure under Article 7: *de lege ferenda*, it could be imagined that the Council would be competent to impose sanctions following a suitable finding by a court. In practice, if for instance members of government of an EU Member State were prosecuted or convicted before the International Criminal Court, this might trigger determinations and sanctions under Article 7 TEU. But this is not the law as it stands. Since the Treaty of Nice,

[12] Rule 83, Rules of Procedure, EP, July 2014.

[13] Art 354 TFEU refers to the qualified majority of Art 238(3)(b), i.e. at least 72 per cent, instead of the normal number of participating Council members, comprising 65 per cent of the population.

Article 7 is no longer completely excluded from its jurisdiction,[14] but its jurisdiction is explicitly restricted to procedural issues only.

5. The preventive function of the first paragraph of Article 7

As we have already seen, the EU Treaty originally only provided for the determination of a serious and persistent breach and the imposition of sanctions by the Council. Imposing sanctions after the determination of a serious and persistent breach as only means to enforce compliance with the common constitutional values might be too great a step ever to be taken, and therefore impracticable. As Sadurski put it: the Article 7 mechanism in its original form was no more than a bark in practice; or more accurately, a bite without a previous bark, which is not how it should be—except for really mean dogs. What was considered desirable was the creation of earlier and lesser intervention, since the existent power to impose sanctions could only be a last resort.

That was precisely why the Nice Treaty introduced the 'preventive mechanism' that we now find in Article 7(1):

> 1. On a reasoned proposal by one third of the Member States, by the European Parliament or by the European Commission, the Council, acting by a majority of four fifths of its members after obtaining the consent of the European Parliament, may determine that there is a clear risk of a serious breach by a Member State of the values referred to in Article 2. Before making such a determination, the Council shall hear the Member State in question and may address recommendations to it, acting in accordance with the same procedure.
>
> The Council shall regularly verify that the grounds on which such a determination was made continue to apply.

This provision intended to create powers for the EU to *prevent* the occurrence of an actual serious and persistent breach. So there is a certain relation between the preventive mechanism of paragraph 1 and the sanctions mechanism of paragraphs 2 and 3. Nevertheless, the preventative procedure under paragraph 1 is—for the very reason of being preventive in nature—considered to constitute a *separate* and *different* mechanism from the sanctions procedures under paragraphs 2 and 3.[15] Biting and barking are two different ways of responding to a Rule of Law crisis.

Part of the 'preventive mechanism' is the possibility of issuing recommendations to the relevant Member State. The formulation since Lisbon is different from the previous formulation:

Prior to Lisbon	Since Lisbon
... the Council [...] may determine that there is a clear risk of a serious breach by a Member State of principles mentioned in Article 6(1), and address appropriate recommendations to that State. Before making such a determination, the Council shall hear the Member State in question	*Before making such a determination, the Council shall hear the Member State in question and may address recommendations to it, acting in accordance with the same procedure.*

[14] The Amsterdam Treaty omitted Art 7 from the justiciable provisions enumerated in Art 46 TEU; Nice amended it to include: '(e) the purely procedural stipulations in Article 7, with the Court acting at the request of the Member State concerned within one month from the date of the determination by the Council provided for in that Article'. See Case T-337/03 *Luis Bertelli Gálvez v Commission* [2004] ECLI:EU:T:2004:106. Interestingly, in Case T-280/09 *Morte Navarro v Parliament* [2010] ECLI:EU:T:2010:28 inadmissibility was not based on this provision, but on the proper motivation of the EP to reject a petition to start investigations into the alleged infringement of Art 6(1) TEU (pre-Lisbon).

[15] Commission Communication to the Council and the EP on Art 7 of the TEU 'Respect for and promotion of the values on which the Union is based' COM(2003) 606 final, at 4 et seq.

A major but little noticed difference resides in the moment at which the Council can address recommendations to a Member State. The textual change suggests that prior to Lisbon, recommendations could only be issued together with or after the determination of the existence of a 'clear risk of serious breach'. The text since Lisbon clearly suggests that recommendations can be made *before* the existence of such a risk has been determined, albeit under the same procedure as for that determination. This suggests Union competence prior to the risk determination.

A point of controversy has become the question whether paragraph 1 confers the power to monitor the situation in a Member State. The letter of the law suggests that such monitoring powers are explicitly granted to the Council *after* the determination of a 'serious risk'. But whether monitoring of Member States is also allowed *prior* to the determination of a 'serious risk' has become controversial.

Given the fact that decision making in the Council will need a solid factual basis for the determination process, the logical assumption is that the monitoring powers are inherent in the powers of the Council and the right of initiative of the Parliament, Commission, and Member States. This was also evident in the literature at the time.[16]

The Commission explicitly adopted this view in its Communication on Article 7 TEU of 15 October 2003.[17] As we will see below, this common sense has recently become disputed by the Council. In 2003 the Commission expressed the view that by introducing the concept of 'clear risk',

> Article 7 of the Union Treaty provides a means of sending a warning signal to an offending Member State before the risk materialises. It also places the institutions under an obligation to maintain constant surveillance, since the 'clear risk' evolves in a known political, economic and social environment and following a period of whatever duration during which the first signs of, for instance, racist or xenophobic policies will have become manifest. [...]
>
> Apart from the fact that the Union policies themselves help to secure respect for and promotion of common values, the legal and political framework for the application of Article 7 as described above, based on prevention, requires practical operational measures to ensure thorough and effective monitoring of respect for and promotion of common values.[18]

6. The Rule of Law Initiative: origin and reception

Even though the preventive procedure was devised as a more feasible mechanism, Rule of Law policy and politics moved in an opposite direction. The main use of Article 7 was that actually using it is unthinkable. Barroso described Article 7 as 'the nuclear option'.[19] This has received continuous criticism by NGOs and others who felt it resulted in misplaced complacency, and moreover by applying this metaphor the Commission essentially deprives the Union from its practical use. The Commission exhibited this complacency in its conclusion of the 2003 Communication, stating that it 'is convinced that in this Union of values it will not be necessary to apply penalties to Article 7 of the Union Treaty and

[16] A von Bogdandy, 'The European Union as a Human Rights Organization? Human Rights and the Core of the European Union' (2000) 37 *Common Market Law Review* 1318, and G De Burca, 'Beyond the Charter: How Enlargement has Enlarged the Human Rights Policy of the European Union' (2004) 27 *Fordham International Law Journal* 713.

[17] COM(2003) 606 final (n 15) at 3: '[T]he amended Article 7 confers new powers on the Commission in its monitoring of fundamental rights in the Union and in the identification of potential risks. The Commission intends to exercise its new right in full and with a clear awareness of its responsibility'.

[18] COM(2003) 606 final (n 15), at 7 and 8 respectively.

[19] State of the Union 2012 Address, 10.

Article 309 of the EC Treaty'.[20] By merely saying we cherish certain constitutional values, however, we do not automatically observe them in practice. Hence, the Commission launched its 'Rule of Law Initiative' in a Communication of March 2014, setting out 'A new EU Framework to strengthen the Rule of Law'.[21]

Commission President Barroso announced this initiative in his State of the Union speech in 2012, expressing the wish to develop a broader set of instruments to occupy the ground between mere political persuasion and the use of Article 7. This was also followed up in the Council with a debate in the General Affairs Council, taking note of a German/Dutch/Danish/Finnish initiative calling for Rule of Law instruments with a key role for the Commission,[22] and the Home Affairs Council in 2013, which seemed not unsympathetic to the idea of developing such tools.[23] The EP joined with a number of reports, urging the development of further instruments.[24]

The Commission introduced a Justice Scoreboard in 2013, which monitors the quality of the judiciary in the Member States on a range of indicators, such as caseload in relation to duration of case handling, perceived independence, etc.[25] This was justified on the strength of the argument that the quality of judicial systems contribute to the investment climate and hence influences trade and economic growth and development, and the Commission proposed its inclusion in the European Semester.[26] The Justice Scoreboard uses data provided by the Council of Europe Commission for the Evaluation of the Efficiency of Justice (CEPEJ), with the addition of sources from the World Bank and other international organizations, albeit with an unexplained and unspecified and hence non-transparent methodology.[27]

[20] COM(2003) 606 final (n 15), at 12; for criticism, e.g. Amnesty International, 'Response to the European Commission Communication on Article 7 of the Treaty on European Union' (December 2003), http://www.amnesty.eu/static/documents/AI_response_to_EC_Comm_on_Article_7_of_Treaty_on_EU.doc, accessed 12 October 2016.

[21] Communication from the Commission to the European Parliament and the Council, 'A new EU Framework to strengthen the Rule of Law' COM(2014) 158 final.

[22] Letter from Guido Westerwelle, Guido Westerwelle, Villy Søvndal, and Erkki Tuomioja to José Manuel Barroso (6 March 2013), http://www.rijksoverheid.nl/bestanden/documenten-en-publicaties/brieven/2013/03/13/brief-aan-europese-commissie-over-opzetten-rechtsstatelijkheidsmechanisme/brief-aan-europese-commissie-over-opzetten-rechtsstatelijkheidsmechanisme.pdf, accessed 12 October 2016, 2.

[23] Council (EU), Press Release (22 April 2013), http://www.consilium.europa.eu/uedocs/cms_Data/docs/pressdata/EN/genaff/136915.pdf, accessed 12 October 2016; and Council Conclusions of June 2013, http://www.consilium.europa.eu/uedocs/cms_data/docs/pressdata/en/jha/137404.pdf, accessed 12 October 2016.

[24] R Tavares, 'Report on the situation of fundamental rights: standards and practices in Hungary (pursuant to the EP resolution of 16 February 2012)' 2012/2130(INI) http://www.europarl.europa.eu/sides/getDoc.do?type=REPORT&reference=A7-2013-0229&language=EN, accessed 12 October 2016; Louis Michel, 'Report on the situation of fundamental rights in the European Union (2012)' 2013/2078(INI), http://www.europarl.europa.eu/sides/getDoc.do?pubRef=-//EP//TEXT+REPORT+A7-2014-0051+0+DOC+XML+V0//EN, accessed 12 October 2016; and K Göncz, 'Report on evaluation of justice in relation to criminal justice and the rule of law' 2014/2006(INI) http://www.europarl.europa.eu/sides/getDoc.do?pubRef=-//EP//TEXT+REPORT+A7-2014-0122+0+DOC+XML+V0//EN, accessed 12 October 2016.

[25] Commission, 'The EU Justice Scoreboard' COM (2013) 160 final, http://ec.europa.eu/justice/effective-justice/files/justice_scoreboard_communication_en.pdf, accessed 12 October 2016; scoreboards for 2014 and 2015 have also been published: Commission, Commission, 'The 2014 EU Justice Scoreboard' COM(2014) 155 final, http://ec.europa.eu/justice/effective-justice/files/justice_scoreboard_2014_en.pdf, accessed 12 October 2016; and Commission 'The 2015 EU Justice Scoreboard' COM(2015) 116 final, http://ec.europa.eu/justice/effective-justice/files/justice_scoreboard_2015_en.pdf, accessed 12 October 2016.

[26] This has happened in the meantime, and recommendations on judicial systems have been made in some country-specific recommendations in this framework, e.g. the recommendations to Slovakia, which has many problems with the quality of the judiciary and has the lowest perceived judicial independence in Europe, see Commission, 'Country Report Slovakia 2015' (Staff Working Document) COM(2015) 85 final, http://ec.europa.eu/europe2020/pdf/csr2015/cr2015_slovakia_en.pdf, accessed 12 October 2016, 35–6.

[27] The Commission has also begun publishing anti-corruption reports in 2013 and 2014, see http://ec.europa.eu/dgs/home-affairs/what-we-do/policies/organized-crime-and-human-trafficking/corruption/anti-corruption-report/index_en.htm, accessed 12 October 2016.

The Rule of Law Framework, developed in the Commission Communication, aims to fill the gap between triggering Article 7 TEU and the normal instruments for infringement proceedings under the TFEU, which had to be resorted to during the Roma crisis in France and the constitutional reform crisis in Hungary.

The framework provides a three-step approach and is triggered in situations where the authorities of a Member State are taking measures or are tolerating situations which are likely to *systematically* and adversely affect the integrity, stability or the proper functioning of the institutions and the safeguard mechanisms established at national level to secure the rule of law.[28]

To distinguish the situations in which the Framework is triggered, the emphasis is on the 'systemic' effects of a situation or of certain measures; it is not triggered in the case of individual infringements of fundamental rights or miscarriages of justice.[29]

The three steps envisaged are:[30]

- Commission assessment and confidential dialogue with a view to resolving the issues:
  - Where there is a systemic threat to the Rule of Law, the Commission initiates a dialogue with the Member State concerned, by sending a public 'Rule of Law opinion' and substantiating its concerns, giving the Member State concerned the opportunity to respond.
- Commission recommendation:
  - Unless the matter has already been resolved satisfactorily in the meantime, the Commission issues a 'Rule of Law recommendation' addressed to the Member State concerned, if it finds that there is objective evidence of a systemic threat and that the authorities of that Member State are not taking appropriate action to redress it. The recommendation may include specific indications on ways and measures to resolve the situation. The 'main content' of the recommendation will be made public by the Commission.
- A follow-up stage to the recommendation:
  - In this third stage, the Commission monitors the follow-up provided by the Member State concerned to the recommendation addressed to it. If there is no satisfactory follow-up to the recommendation by the Member State concerned 'within the time limit set', the Commission will assess the possibility of activating one of the mechanisms set out in Article 7 TEU.

7. The Council on the Rule of Law Initiative

The Commission's communication presenting the Framework has been received critically by the Council, leading to the latter's own Rule of Law Initiative: the Rule of Law Dialogue.

No doubt, an important role was played by the Council Legal Service's opinion of 27 May 2014, which presented an analysis of the Commission's Rule of Law Framework, concluding that the Framework is incompatible with the Treaties.[31] The opinion takes the view that:

[28] Framework (n 21) 6.

[29] Compare A von Bogdandy and M Ioannidis, 'Systemic Deficiency in the Rule of Law: What it is, what has been done, what can be done' (2014) 51 *Common Market Law Review* 59.

[30] Framework (n 21) 6–8.

[31] Council Legal Service, 'Opinion on the Commission's Communication on a new EU Framework to strengthen the Rule of Law' (Document 10296/14, 27 May 2014) http://data.consilium.europa.eu/doc/document/ST-10296-2014-INIT/en/pdf, accessed 12 October 2016.

> there is no legal basis in the Treaties empowering the institutions to create a new supervision mechanism of the respect of the rule of law by the Member States, additional to what is laid down in Article 7 TEU, neither to amend, modify or supplement the procedure laid down in this Article. Were the Council to act along such lines, it would run the risk of being found to have abused its powers by deciding without a legal basis.[32]

This view is based on the principle of conferred powers of Article 5 TEU, under which 'competences not conferred upon the Union in the Treaties remain [with] the Member States'. The lack of a legal basis for the Framework is the core of the analysis, basically because:

> [r]espect of the rule of law by the Member States cannot be, under the Treaties, the subject matter of an action by the institutions of the Union irrespective of the existence of a specific material competence to frame this action, with the sole exception of the procedure described at Article 7 TEU. Only this legal basis provides for a Union competence to supervise the application of the rule of law, as a value of the Union, in a context that is not related to a specific material competence or that exceeds its scope. [...] [T]hat Article does not set a basis to further develop or amend [the] procedure [set out in Article 7 itself].[33]

The opinion then continues to discuss the absence of a power to address recommendations beyond what is stipulated in Article 7.

In the view of the Council Legal Service the lack of a legal basis vitiates the whole Framework. The opinion does point out that the *Member States* are allowed to agree on arrangements additional to Article 7 TEU:

> This solution is that Member States – and not the Council – agree on a review system of the functioning of the rule of law in the Member States, which may allow for the participation of the Commission and of other institutions if necessary, and on the consequences that Member States might engage to draw from such review. The possibility for the Union to use the powers provided for in Article 7 TEU and Articles 258, 259 and 260 TFEU must be unaffected by such agreement among the Member States. [...]
>
> Such a peer review approach, with a possible involvement of the institutions if so decided, could find its legal basis in an intergovernmental agreement designed to supplement the law of the Union and to ensure effective respect of the values on which the Member States have founded the Union, without by doing so conferring on the Union competences whose transfer the Treaties have not foreseen.[34]

After what must be understood as the negative opinion of its Legal Service concerning the Commission's Rule of Law Initiative, the Council launched its own 'initiative [which] focuses more specifically on the respect for Rule of Law that is an essential element of the EU's identity'.[35] Instead of a separate intergovernmental agreement supplementing the EU Treaty, as the legal service had suggested, it decided that it would hold a 'constructive dialogue' between all Member States in thematic sessions once a year. This dialogue is conducted on the basis of equality and aims:

> to encourage the culture of 'respect for rule of law' [...] *within the framework of the Treaties*, [...], in respect of the principles of objectivity, non-discrimination, equal treatment, on a non-partisan and evidence-based approach [...] without prejudice to the principles of conferred competences as well as the respect of national identities of Member States' (emphasis added).[36]

[32] Framework (n 21) 7. [33] ibid, 5. [34] ibid, 7.

[35] Council Document 16862/14, 12 December 2014, http://data.consilium.europa.eu/doc/document/ST-16862-2014-INIT/en/pdf, accessed 12 October 2016, 1, para 3.

[36] Framework (n 21) 6.

The Council considers the annual dialogue to be 'complementary' to other EU institutions and international organizations. The dialogue will be prepared 'by the COREPER (Presidency)'. The Council will evaluate the experience acquired in the dialogue by the end of 2016.

8. Monitoring powers: within or outside the framework of Article 7?

The precise extent of the differences between Commission and Council concerning the legal basis of the Rule of Law Initiative is unclear. The Council Legal Service opinion is explicit in its conclusion that Article 7 'does not set a basis to further develop or amend' the procedure contained therein and in particular that Commission recommendations on the Rule of Law require a legal basis that is absent. The fact that the Council has reverted to a mere 'dialogue' prepared by COREPER might suggest that the Council implicitly went along with its Legal Service, although it is by no means clear that the Council has endorsed the opinion.

With the exception of one point, the Council Legal Service opinion is unclear as to *what* exactly the 'new supervision mechanism' is which is 'additional' to Article 7 TEU, 'amends, modifies or supplements' the procedure under this provision and lacks a legal basis. In other words, what kind of monitoring falls outside the scope of Article 7?

The one point on which the opinion seems clear is the power of the Commission to issue a 'rule of law recommendation': the required legal basis for such recommendations is missing. The opinion bases this on two considerations:

> The first one is that the non-binding nature of a recommendation does not allow the institutions to act by issuing such type of acts in matters or subjects on which the Treaties have not vested powers [in] them. (See Case C-233/02 *France v. Commission*, ECR 2004 p. I-2781, paragraph 40.)
>
> The second is that even if recommendations are not intended to produce binding effects and are not capable of creating rights that individuals can rely on before a national court, they are not without any legal effect. (See Case C-207/01, *Altair*, ECR 2003 p. I-8894, paragraph 41.) As a consequence the legality and interpretation of recommendations may be the object of proceedings before the Court of Justice, via preliminary rulings or actions for damages.[37]

This part of the opinion is premised on the idea that Rule of Law recommendations are outside the scope of Article 7. The Commission has aided this approach by taking as its point of departure that its Rule of Law initiative is 'complementary' to Article 7, which can be understood as 'being located outside the scope' of Article 7. This is the implicit assumption in the Legal Service's opinion. For if, on the contrary, we were hypothetically to assume that the Commission's Rule of Law initiative is *within* the remit of Article 7, the Legal Service's considerations, in particular the case law of the Court of Justice cited, could not apply: Article 269 TFEU would prohibit the Court from giving preliminary rulings and receiving actions for damages.

Another indicator that the Legal Service assumed that the Framework is outside the remit of Article 7 is that the opinion passes over the explicit power of the *Council* under the 'preventive mechanism' of Article 7(1) TEU to address recommendations to the Member State involved. From the attribution of this power of recommendation to the Council one can infer that the *Commission* has no power to issue such recommendations under

[37] Council Legal Service, 'Opinion on the Commission's Communication on a new EU Framework', 5, para 19.

Article 7. The Legal Service's first argument on the legal importance of recommendations could be an argument in line with this inference. (The second argument does not apply within the scope of Article 7, as we have just seen.)

The opinion does not actually argue that all elements of the Commission's Framework are outside the remit of Article 7; this is assumed only implicitly. But is the assumption that systematic Rule of Law monitoring is outside the scope and framework of Article 7 correct?

There are good reasons to think that it is not. The starting point must be the explicit wording of Article 7 concerning the stage prior to applying the 'sanctions mechanism', which is to say the 'preventive mechanism' of paragraph 1. It is indeed often overlooked, both in the Council's documents and in the literature,[38] that the Council's powers to issue recommendations exists already *prior* to the determination of a 'clear risk' of a serious breach, which, as we saw above, was a clarification (or perhaps 'novelty') in the Lisbon Treaty's formulation of Article 7(1). It is no wild assumption that the preliminary power to address recommendations to Member States on the Rule of Law within the framework of Article 7(1) necessarily implies the power to monitor Member State behaviour. If such an implied power did not exist, the Council would risk issuing recommendations that are not based in established fact. This would be totally contrary to established principles of EU law. It is absurd to assume that the Council can only act as a talking shop in which views are exchanged which lead to recommendations addressed to a Member State, given that these recommendations are supposed to prevent—and in the case of non-compliance lead to—the actual use of such severe powers for sanctioning a systemic breach as are granted in Article 7. Council recommendations and subsequent determinations of a 'clear risk' of a serious breach would be based on hearsay only, instead of on objective verification. It would run counter to the institutional architecture if the Council could not involve the Commission in an assessment aimed at verification, and be at odds with the consistent calls of the Council to the Commission to develop tools for assessing compliance with the Rule of Law and the other values of Article 2.[39]

The conclusion must be that for the Council to be able to use its powers under the 'preventive mechanism', there must be implied monitoring powers, which either the Council itself can use, or for which it can invoke the assistance of the Commission.

It is not only the Council which must have implied monitoring powers. The same must necessarily be true for those who can initiate (Parliament, Commission, and a Council minority of a third of the Member States) the determination of a 'clear risk' of a serious breach and must come with a '*reasoned* proposal'. Without possessing monitoring powers, a proposal could hardly be reasoned. The adjective 'reasoned' is used only in the context of the initiative for triggering the preventive mechanism, and is a decisive argument to conclude that there must be powers of monitoring included in the right to initiative.

A further question is what the scope of monitoring powers implicit in Article 7 must be in order to remain within its boundaries.

Here, the Council Legal Service opinion perpetrates a rhetorical trick by changing 'monitoring' into 'supervision', thus suggesting the submission of the Member States to the Commission. It does so both with regard to the existing Article 7 procedures and with regard to the Commission initiative. This language suggests an inherent inequality between the supervisory Commission and the subjected Member State involved, and plays on

[38] e.g. H von Heinegg, 'Artikel 7' in C Vedder and WH von Heinegg (eds), *Europäisches Unionsrecht, Handkommentar* (Nomos 2012) 90; alternatively, H-J Blanke, 'Article 7' in H-J Blanke and S Mangiameli (eds), *The Treaty on European Union (TEU): A Commentary* (Springer 2012) 363.

[39] Especially the Council Conclusions on fundamental rights and the Rule of Law (n 23) 4, paras 9–11.

Member States' sensitivities at not being treated equally. It again invokes the mantra, repeated in many Council documents on the Rule of Law and Article 7, that any mechanism should be non-discriminatory and treat all Member States in the same way. Hence the Council initiative's stress on the peer-review character of its own 'Rule of Law Dialogue'. Indeed, the idea that it is other Member States conducting this dialogue instead of the Commission is to reinforce the 'peer' aspect of the review.

It would be incorrect, however, to conclude that monitoring and dialogue conducted by other institutions than the Council and its members are excluded. As we noted above, the framework of Article 7 is *not* merely intergovernmental and gives significant powers to the Commission and Parliament, notably the right of initiative and the right of consent. But this does not turn their monitoring activity into 'supervision' as a hierarchical device to which Member States are subjected. The principles of non-discrimination between Member States and their equality in monitoring can be achieved by basing monitoring on the principle of general monitoring of all Member States and the application of transparent and uniform criteria and methodologies. These are for good reason chosen as the basis of the Commission's Rule of Law Initiative,[40] although the criticism can rightly be made that too many aspects of diplomatic confidentiality are written into it.

Monitoring must in essence be gathering information, which might be provided by Member States directly to Commission and Parliament, but may also be collected from many other sources which can provide relevant information, usually from the Member States. These include sources already available to the Union institutions, including the FRA, and available from other organizations, such as Council of Europe monitoring exercises (including the Venice Commission, the Human Rights Commissioner, the Parliamentary Assembly, the Committee of Ministers, and the ECtHR), OCSE, the ILO, and the UN (including the supervisory committees of the various UN conventions). The amount of information relevant to monitoring under Article 7 is indeed so great that it might be useful to systematically organize it within a platform established specifically for this purpose.[41]

A subsequent step must be the processing of information in the form of some kind of engagement with the relevant Member States. The Council suggests that it is the privileged forum to do so, but this is questionable in light of the Commission's and Parliament's role in both the preventive and sanctioning mechanism. It is true that the preventive mechanism of Article 7(1) explicitly solely grants the Council the power to issue formal recommendations prior to the determination of a 'clear risk'. The power of initiative on the basis of a reasoned proposal for the other institutions would be pretty meaningless if there were no other role for them than mere information gathering.

To avoid a multiplicity of opinions expressed at an early stage prior to the formal engagement of the two mechanisms, some orderly way of proceeding would be desirable. An inter-institutional agreement might be necessary to achieve this, which could be based on the experience with existing monitoring procedures in which more than one institution has a role to play.[42] The current lack of coordination and actual inter-institutional rivalry displayed in the context of the Commission's and Council's respective Rule of Law

[40] Framework (n 21) 7.

[41] See the Netherlands Advisory Council on International Affairs, 'The rule of law: Safeguard for European Citizens and Foundation for European Cooperation', (Report No 87, January 2014), http://aiv-advies.nl/download/57da03fa-3410-4aba-af05-663cb780df72.pdf, accessed 12 October 2016, 32.

[42] Compare the cooperation and verification monitoring of Bulgaria and Romania, and the monitoring introduced in the context of the Schengen Acquis, in Council Regulation (EU) 1053/2013 of 7 October 2013 establishing an evaluation and monitoring mechanism to verify the application of the Schengen acquis [2013] OJ L295, 27–37.

initiatives clearly exhibit the risk that institutions can be played off against each other, thus frustrating the operability of the preventive and sanctioning mechanisms of Article 7.

9. The fuzzy boundaries between the Union and Member State political orders

The boundary issues of Article 7 regarding the possibility of Rule of Law monitoring—determining which activity remains within the framework of Article 7 and which lacks a legal basis—are not the only issues. There is a more profound explanation for the sensitivity of matters surrounding Article 7. This is the permeability of the boundaries of the Union's order itself in relation to those of the constitutional orders of the Member States. This permeability is ingrained in the nature of Article 2, which the Article 7 mechanisms aim to protect. Article 2 sums up the values on which the Union is founded and which are common to the Member States. From the Union perspective, these values are not restricted to the Union's specific competences or the operation of Union law; from the Member State perspective, these values do not target the specific operation or realization of the Union and its laws in the Member States. They are foundational values which are at the basis of the exercise of *all* public authority both by the Union and by the Member States. The compliance mechanisms of Article 7 refer, therefore, necessarily not solely to the activity of the Union within the Member State, nor to Member State activity concerning the implementation of Union law or the Union's specific competence. That is why Article 7 is generally considered the only provision conferring a power to the Union over matters which relate to Member State activity which can be *outside* the scope of EU law. As this activity concerns values which are also the values of the Member State concerned, we are in a situation that is doubly sensitive: on the one hand, this is due to the constitutional nature of the Member State activity and on the other hand, due to the Union acting with regard to Member State activity which can be completely outside the scope of Union law in the strict sense.

This sensitivity explains the Council's slamming on the brakes as soon as it approaches Rule of Law monitoring of Member State action. A good illustration is the manner in which the Council understood its Legal Service's opinion on a crucial point.

The opinion is at first sight somewhat opaque and contradictory, focusing on Articles 2 and 7 respectively when it comes to Member State action within and outside the scope of EU law. I will quote two paragraphs here. The first might seem to suggest that Rule of Law monitoring can only concern Member State actions within the scope of Union law, whereas the second paragraph states the contrary, i.e. the Union can—exceptionally—act with respect to Member State acts which are otherwise outside the scope of Union law:

> [16] Article 2 TEU does not confer any material competence upon the Union but, similarly to the Charter provisions, lists certain values that ought to be respected by the institutions of the Union and by its Member States *when they act within the limits of the powers conferred on the Union in the treaties*, and without affecting their limits. Therefore, a violation of the values of the Union, including the rule of law, may be *invoked against a Member State only when it acts in a subject matter for which the Union has competence* based on specific competence-setting Treaty provisions.
>
> [17] Respect of the rule of law by the Member States cannot be, under the Treaties, the subject matter of an action by the institutions of the Union irrespective of the existence of a specific material competence to frame this action, *with the sole exception of the procedure described at Article 7 TEU*. Only this legal basis provides for a Union competence to supervise the application

of the rule of law, as a value of the Union, in a context that is *not related to a specific material competence* or that exceeds its scope.[43] (emphasis added)

The first quoted paragraph may, however, also be construed as saying that the Union cannot invoke a violation of the values of Article 2 unless it has been granted the competence to do so. The second paragraph quoted can then be read as saying that such a competence is granted in Article 7.

The Council, however, summarized the two paragraphs to read: 'In essence, under this opinion, the Rule of Law applies as a value of the EU in the areas in which the EU has competence and EU monitoring mechanisms are possible to this extent'.[44] The two paragraphs are understood to mean that Rule of Law monitoring is possible *only* when a Member State is acting *within* the scope of EU law. That is not what the Legal Service actually said in the second of its paragraphs quoted. It held that Article 7 'provides for a Union competence to supervise the application of the rule of law, as a value of the Union, in a context that is *not related to a specific material [Union] competence*'.

The Council's interpretation goes against standard views expressed in the literature and in the case law.[45] These views need to be developed further to understand what the Council is doing when it attempts to set it aside in its new interpretation of Article 7.

In the standard account, the Union can act under Article 7 with regard to Member State acts which are not necessarily undertaken within the scope of EU law. This is precisely why an alleged infringement of the values of Article 2 is regarded as not being or not merely being the object of the ordinary infringement proceedings under Article 258 and following TFEU: these are restricted to acts and omissions of Member States within the scope of EU law, whereas serious breaches of the values of Article 2 are not necessarily so.[46] In short, Article 7 can be considered a special procedure for situations in which there is a risk of a serious breach or an actual persistent and serious breach of the foundational values of the Union by a Member State *outside* the scope of EU law in the strict sense.

I have been using the expression 'the scope of EU law in the strict sense'. The paradox is that if the Union is competent to act on Member State behaviour *outside* the scope of EU law—ie in the narrower sense of all EU law other than Articles 2 and 7 TEU—this brings that behaviour *within* the scope of Union law in a broader sense (ie including Articles 2 and 7). The reason is the very nature of what Article 2 claims: the values it lists are common to the Member States and form the very foundation of the Union, so the common constitutional values of the *Member States* constitute the foundation of the *Union*. Member State constitutional values and the founding constitutional values of the Union cannot be strictly separated: they are commensurate, the Union and the Member States have a common constitutional identity. The Union and the Member State orders are inextricably linked, bound up with each other, intertwined, and enmeshed. This in turn is caused by the

[43] Council Legal Service (n 37), paras 16 and 17. [44] Council Document (n 35) para 12.

[45] Famously, Advocate General Maduro in Case C-380/05 *Centro Europa 7 Srl v Ministero delle Comunicazioni e Autorità per le garanzie nelle comunicazioni* [2008] ECLI:EU:C:2008:59, paras 17–23; A Duxbury, 'Austria and The European Union: The Report Of The 'Three Wise Men' (2000) 1 *Melbourne Journal of International Law* 169, 170; Mangiameli (n 38) 351, with further references; von Bogdandy and Ioannidis (n 29) 65 and 67. In Case C-505/13 *Yumer*, Order of the Court of 17 July 2014, paras 22–4, the Court distinguished claims of compatibility of Member State action with Art 2 TEU from that with the Charter; in Case C-28/14 *Ryszard Pańczyk*, Order of the Court, 12 June 2014, para 16, the Court was asked on the compatibility with Art 2 TEU and several other provisions of the Charter, but ignored the question about Art 2 and found that it was outside the scope of the Charter; in Case T 512/12 *Front Polisario*, 15 December 2015, paras 159 ff. at 164–5, the General Court seemed to accept that Art 2 TEU is justiciable as standard for EU acts, but found that in the context of external economic relations the institutions enjoy a wide discretion that prevented the matter of the conclusion of an international agreement with application to an illegally occupied territory to regard the 'founding values of the Union'.

[46] COM(2003) 606 final (n 15) 5, para 1.1; Mangiameli (n 38) 355.

nature of the values concerned: they are not specific from one Member State to another, but foundational to the individual Member State constitutional orders as well. They are foundational, but from the Union's perspective they also *ought to be* foundational: they are prerequisites for Union membership. A failure to heed those foundational values is for that very reason sanctionable by suspension of the rights deriving from membership.

The Council's stance that Article 2 and 7 are *only* applicable to Member State action within the scope of EU law in the strict sense is therefore a misconstruction. Otherwise, a Member State could respect human dignity, freedom, equality, the Rule of Law, human rights—including the rights of persons belonging to minorities—and be a democracy *only* when acting within the narrower confines of EU law, but then still persistently and seriously breach those values and denigrate human dignity, stifle freedom, crush equality, deny the Rule of Law, trample human rights, and act as a dictatorship in gross denial of minority rights outside the scope of EU law narrowly construed. That would seem to be as untenable as it is improbable, given the entwining of the national and Union legal orders in the practical exercise of public authority.

The conclusion on the contrary must be that the values of Article 2 affect both national and the Union identities, with the consequence that, when threatened at the national level, they are also threatened at the EU level.[47]

10. Final remarks

The analysis of Article 7 and the Commission's Rule of Law initiative and the Council's Rule of Law Dialogue initiative show that the legal possibilities offered under Article 7 are insufficiently explored, both by the institutions and in the literature. As a consequence, we see the debate recoiling from sanctions, towards prevention and prior monitoring powers in the Commission's and the Council's Rule of Law 'initiatives', the latter even hesitating to monitor. Deficiencies in the legal analysis facilitate this, some ignoring the nature of the 'preventive mechanism' of Article 7 altogether by holding that Article 7 concerns *a posteriori* procedures.[48] Both the literature and the institutions seem to overlook the power to issue recommendations under Article 7 *prior* to the establishment of a 'clear risk' of serious breach of Article 2, and the powers of initiative and the monitoring powers necessarily entailed by both the power to issue Council recommendations at that stage and the right to initiative are swept under the carpet or flatly denied. Thus the bite and the bark may end up being a howl, or even less.

No doubt the developments sketched in the preceding analysis reflect the dynamics in the relations between the Member States and the Union as regards the control and authority over their constitutional foundations. But this calls for further reflection.

Authors suggest that the whole kerfuffle over Article 7 is caused by the political nature of the procedure, the decisive role of the Council, and the high threshold posed by the voting requirements for formal determinations to be made. At one level we can say, as we have done above, that this on the one hand again overlooks the significant powers preceding such determinations and the moderating influence that the roles of the EP, Commission, and Member States can play in such overly politicized decision making. On the other hand, the involvement of institutions which are not accountable before directly elected bodies

[47] Pinelli (n 3) 7.

[48] A Faure-Atger and S Carrera, 'L'affaire des Roms: A Challenge to the EU's Area of Freedom, Security and Justice' (September 2010) CEPS, Liberty and Security in Europe, http//www.ceps.eu/system/files/book/2010/09/Carrera%20%26%20Faure%20Atger%20on%20Roma%20Affair.pdf, accessed 12 October 2016.

would seriously undermine the democratic quality and legitimacy of the relevant procedures. This brings us to a different level of insight, namely that these procedures concern the very foundations of political order in Europe, which precede the legal institutions established on their basis. The political nature of Article 7 is inherently and indissolubly connected to the political and constitutional nature of Article 2.

The quality of the polity is determined by its constitutive values. These are common and identical between the Union and the Member States. Upholding the quality of the values in practice means upholding the quality of the exercise of public authority both in the Union and in the Member States. This identical communality creates an unbreakable bond of mutuality in upholding those values and in the reasons for doing so, of which citizens are the beneficiaries. The objective of and the whole process underlying Article 7 is therefore not a matter of politics holding the Union hostage, nor of muzzling the Member State democracies which require 'containment'. The identity of their foundational values necessarily also implies that it is mistaken to think of guaranteeing their constitutive foundations only by reference to behaviour which is within the scope of Union law, and not to behaviour outside that scope narrowly understood. When it comes to its foundational values the Union is about *any* political behaviour touching on those values. The only way forwards is the insight expressed in Article 2 TEU: that the EU and the Member States are each and both together based on identical values, the guarantee of which is as necessary for the Union as for the Member States.

9

Compliance and Enforcement in Economic Policy Coordination in EMU

Fabian Amtenbrink and René Repasi

1. Introduction

Arguably in no area of EU law has the enforcement of the European regulatory framework against (alleged) recalcitrance of Member States been more heatedly debated in recent times than in the context of the EMU and namely fiscal policy coordination and the economic adjustment programmes in the euro area. In seeking explanations for the over-indebtedness of several euro area Member States and the rather fragile economic situation in others, having observed the consequences of the breakdown of the financial markets, attention quickly turned to the legal framework governing economic policy coordination in the euro area and its application in practice as a viable explanation for the state of affairs.

While a reform of Regulations 1466/97 and 1467/97—which form the core of the Stability and Growth Pact—aimed at reinforcing the multilateral surveillance and excessive deficit procedure was begun in 2005, it was only in the face of the European economic and financial crisis and the near default of several euro area Member States that a sense of urgency for the reform of economic governance and more generally the fiscal stability of the euro area emerged.[1] The declared aim of the reform of the system was to provide for 'stronger national ownership of commonly agreed rules and policies', to create 'a more robust framework at the level of the Union for the surveillance of national economic policies', and moreover 'to make the enforcement of budgetary surveillance in the euro area more effective'.[2] Put differently, it can be argued that the reform was aimed at achieving a higher degree of compliance and better enforcement.

This chapter critically examines this new economic policy coordination regime and specifically the secondary Union law rules in the shape of the Six Pack and Two Pack,[3]

[1] Council Regulation 1466/97 on the strengthening of the surveillance of budgetary positions and the surveillance and coordination of economic policies [1997] OJ L209/1, as amended by Council Regulation 1055/2005 [2005] OJ L174/1; Council Regulation 1467/97 on speeding up and clarifying the implementation of the excessive deficit procedure [1997] OJ L209/6, as amended by Council Regulation 1056/2005 [2005] OJ L174/5.

[2] Recitals 3 and 13 to the Preamble of Regulation 1173/2011.

[3] The Six Pack consists of five Regulations and one Directive: Regulation 1173/2011 on the effective enforcement of budgetary surveillance in the euro area [2011] OJ L306/1; Regulation 1174/2011 on enforcement measures to correct excessive macroeconomic imbalances in the euro area [2011] OJ L306/8; Regulation 1175/2011 amending Council Regulation 1466/97 on the strengthening of the surveillance of budgetary positions and the surveillance and coordination of economic policies [2011] OJ L306/12; Regulation 1176/2011 on the prevention and correction of macroeconomic imbalances, [2011] OJ L306/25; Council Regulation 1177/2011 amending Regulation 1467/97 on speeding up and clarifying the implementation of the excessive deficit procedure [2011] OJ L306/33; Council Directive 2011/85/EU on requirements for budgetary frameworks of the Member States [2011] OJ L306/41. The Two Pack consists of Regulation 472/2013 on the strengthening of economic and budgetary surveillance of Member States in the euro area experiencing or threatened with serious difficulties with respect to their financial stability [2013] OJ L140/1, and of Regulation 473/2013 on common provisions for monitoring and assessing draft budgetary plans and ensuring the correction of excessive deficit of the Member States in the euro area [2013] OJ L140/11.

which make up the core of the new European fiscal surveillance framework, as well as the TSCG and the ESM Treaty against the background of these aims.[4] To this end an analytical framework for the assessment of the current legal framework is developed in section 2, thereby drawing insights from international law and international relations compliance literature. Section 3 thereafter operationalizes this analytical framework by categorizing and analysing the main legal mechanisms in place to ensure compliance with the Union's objectives geared towards ensuring fiscal stability in EMU.[5] By focusing on the Member State's compliance with one specific, core policy area of European integration this contribution distinguishes itself both from mainstream EU compliance literature that zooms in on the implementation of secondary Union law in the shape of directives by Member States or, very broadly, studies the adherence of Member States with (the total body of) (written) Union law, as well as from legal works that traditionally focus on enforcement arrangements.[6] Section 4 offers a qualitative evaluation of the potential of the current economic policy coordination framework to ensure (better) compliance based on the findings of section 2 and 3. Finally, section 5 makes some concrete proposals on how the current system can be improved upon considering the theoretical findings on compliance and places this in the broader context of the future of EMU as perceived by the main Union institutions in the 2015 Five Presidents' Report.

2. Member State compliance—a theoretical framework

A growing number of contributions analyse the observance of Member States with EU rules, thereby building on a strand of mainly international law and international relations literature studying the compliance with and enforcement of international principles and rules.[7] These studies focus primarily on the non-implementation of secondary Union law, whereby inter alia specifically the number of cases of belated or non-implementation of EU directives[8] or very broadly the number of infringement proceedings[9] are used as a proxy to measure the degree of (non-)compliance with a particular legal instrument or with the (written) body of Union law as such.

Yet, as has been pointed out in the introduction to this chapter, non-compliance may also be examined in a particular policy field, such as EMU, where the failure of the Maastricht legal framework on economic policy coordination laid down in primary and secondary Union law has formed one main justification for the major overhaul of the system. Applying compliance theories to economic policy coordination in the EMU may help better to understand not only the shortcomings of the original Maastricht legal framework, but also the potential of the new economic governance regime effectively to remedy the situation. Indeed, relaxing the strictly legal perspective opens the way for one which does not focus primarily on the enforceability of the existing framework at the Union level in a strict legal sense, thereby studying the nature of the rules and procedures in place, but rather considers the behaviour of the Member States vis-à-vis the European legal

[4] T/SCG/en 1; T/ESM 2012/en 1. [5] For an explanation of the term 'fiscal stability' see section 3.

[6] See on the enforceability of the new economic governance regime: R Bieber and F Maiani, 'Enhancing Centralized Enforcement of EU Law: Pandora's Toolbox?' (2014) 51 *Common Market Law Review* 1057.

[7] O Treib, 'Implementing and complying with EU governance outputs' (2014) 9.1 *Living Reviews in European Governance* 1; TA Börzel et al., 'Why Do State not Obey the Law? Lessons from the European Union' (EUSA Conference, Nashville, March 27–30 2003); TA Börzel et al., 'Obstinate and Inefficient: Why Member States Do Not Comply With European Law' (2010) 43 *Comparative Political Studies* 1363.

[8] See Art 288 TFEU.

[9] See Art 258 and 260 TFEU. See e.g. J Tallberg, 'Paths to Compliance: Enforcement, Management, and the European Union' (2002) 56 *International Organization* 543.

regime more broadly. This allows the factoring in of additional (non-legal) variables which acknowledge the actual causes of non-compliance and the different strategies, both with regard to the instruments applied and the level at which they take effect, to achieve compliance before (*ex ante*) and after (*ex post*) a rule breach has occurred.[10]

a. Compliance and enforcement: a view from international law and international relations

A dictionary definition of compliance amounts to 'the state or fact of according with or meeting rules or standards'.[11] Not far off this explanation, Raustiala and Slaughter define compliance in the country context as 'a state of conformity or identity between an actor's behaviour and a specified rule'.[12] Enforcement can be defined as 'the act of compelling observance of or compliance with a law, rule, or obligation'.[13] As such, enforcement constitutes one of several elements potentially contributing to the achievement of compliance, rather than a competing concept. As hinted earlier, this is an important difference in approach to the more conventional legal analyses which closely focus on enforcement as the key element. This understanding of compliance as the leading or overarching concept is also reflected in the international law and in the international relations discourse, as the review and synopsis of the latter by Börzel et al. (2003) highlight. These authors provide a very valuable reference point for the construction of an analytical framework by differentiating between four types of compliance mechanisms (Table 9.1), each representing a particular strand of compliance literature.[14] What the discussed compliance mechanisms all have in common is that they seek to identify causes for non-compliance and, linked to that, strategies to address them.

In contrast to what might be expected in a strictly legal analysis, the starting point for understanding the various compliance mechanisms in the relevant literature is the classification of the behaviour of a country as voluntary or involuntary. According to this, a state is either considered *voluntarily* to refuse to comply as it is 'not willing to bear the cost of compliance', such as for example in the shape of necessary amendments of the domestic legal order, or *involuntarily* to fail to comply as a result of a lack of 'capacity, i.e. the material resources (technology, expertise, administrative manpower, financial means, etc)', uncertainty 'about the required compliance behaviour since the rule is imprecise and ambiguous',[15] a lack of government autonomy as a result of potent 'institutional and partisan veto players',[16] or 'unavoidable or unanticipated time lags between commitment and performance'.[17]

Based on this basic classification of state behaviour and the different causes identified to contribute to non-compliance, Börzel et al. (2003) establish different compliance strategies discussed in the literature, including:

[10] On the different approaches in the international law and international relations discourse on compliance with regard to legally binding and other rules, see K Raustiala and A-M Slaughter, 'International Law, International Relations and Compliance' in W Carlsnaes et al. (eds), *Handbook of International Relations* (Sage 2002) 538–58, 539.

[11] See https://www.oxforddictionaries.com/definition/english/compliance, accessed 12 October 2016.

[12] Raustiala and Slaughter (n 10) 539, with further references to earlier literature.

[13] See http://www.oxforddictionaries.com/definition/english/enforcement, accessed 12 October 2016.

[14] Börzel et al. (n 7).

[15] ibid, 19. It should be noted that the authors consider cases in which 'states object that their (refraining from) action constitutes a rule violation in the first place' to be involuntary non-compliance, rather than an act of voluntary non-compliance.

[16] The effect of veto players is referred to in a subsequent publication: Börzel et al. (n 7) 7.

[17] Raustiala and Slaughter (n 10) 543, with further references.

Table 9.1 Theoretical approaches in the compliance literature according to Börzel et al. (2003)[18]

	Voluntary non-Compliance	Involuntary non-Compliance
Sanctioning (negative/positive)	'Sticks' Monitoring and sanctioning (compliance through enforcement)	'Carrots' Capacity building and contracting (compliance through management)
Socialization	Precaution and learning (compliance through persuasion)	Legal internalization (compliance through litigation)

- *compliance through enforcement*: the focus rests on the monitoring of the behaviour and the sanctioning of *voluntary non-compliance* by a state, thereby increasing the costs of non-compliance;
- *compliance through management*: aimed at capacity building at the state level to address *involuntary non-compliance*;
- *compliance through persuasion*: rather than to sanction, this approach is aimed at 'increasing acceptance of the norm in question as a standard of appropriate behaviour', as well as socialization aimed at 'changing "actor's preferences"' to prevent or counter *voluntary non-compliance*;
- *compliance through internalization*: this approach seeks to address *involuntary non-compliance* through the 'internalization of international norms and rules into the domestic legal system' through adjudication and dispute settlement.[19]

Furthermore, these authors differentiate compliance mechanisms based on their aim, namely sanctioning or socialization, resulting in the overall framework presented in Table 9.1.

In a subsequent publication Börzel et al. (2010) refined this general analytical framework somewhat based on the same basic differentiation of voluntary and involuntary non-compliance, identifying *enforcement*, *management*, and *legitimacy* as the three major compliance mechanisms deriving from a similar literature review.[20] Resembling the central elements of what Francke, with reference to Max Weber,[21] refers to as 'a community organized around rules, compliance is secured—to whatever degree it is—at least in part by perception of a rule as legitimate by those to whom it is addressed', legitimacy is defined by these authors as 'the extent to which rule addressees accept the legitimacy of the rule of law' and 'comply out of a normative belief that a rule or institution ought to be obeyed rather than because it suits their instrumental self-interest'.[22] As such, this approach closely resembles the compliance through persuasion approach referred to by Börzel et al. (2003) in their earlier publication, while at the same time placing more emphasis on the function of the legitimacy of a rule in socializing states into compliance.

b. Towards an analytical framework for economic policy coordination in EMU

The schematic synthesis of the compliance approaches by Börzel et al. (2003, Table 9.3) and subsequently Börzel et al. (2010) provide the basic elements for the building hereafter of a

[18] Presented there as Table 9.2 entitled 'Theoretical approaches in the compliance literature'.

[19] Börzel et al. (n 7) 18–19. On the debate of the role of international courts, including the ECJ, in compliance with international rules, see Raustiala and Slaughter (n 10) 541–2, with further references.

[20] Börzel et al. (n 7) 5 et seq.

[21] M Weber, *Society and Economy* (University of California Press 1978) 215.

[22] T Franck, 'Legitimacy in the International System' (1988) 82 *American Journal of International Law* 705, 706 and 709; Börzel et al. (n 7) 8.

framework based on which the current law applicable to economic policy coordination can be assessed. The analytical value of this framework for this study of economic policy coordination in the EMU is then explored further.

While fully recognizing the importance of the differentiation between voluntary and involuntary non-compliance for determining the most effective compliance mechanism, the narrow definition of what amounts to voluntary non-compliance is not entirely unproblematic. Börzel et al. (2010) discuss blocking by institutional and partisan veto players in the context of compliance through management, which suggests that this constellation can be considered as an example of a voluntary or involuntary lack of capacity or inability.[23] However, it remains unclear why the lack of political will which results from the influence of regular institutional and partisan veto players should not be attributed to government and thus, should not be considered to constitute deliberate defiance. In fact, it may well be that these parties are not willing to bear the (political) costs of compliance and consider the costs of non-compliance tolerable. What is more, if the approach of assigning mechanisms for achieving compliance to the categories of voluntary and involuntary non-compliance is followed, it is impossible to see how management aimed at capacity building could overcome resistance by veto players. Indeed, raising the costs of non-compliance and, potentially even more so, increasing compliance through persuasion seem—at least from a theoretical perspective—more promising strategies in such a constellation. Therefore, for the purposes of this study the category of involuntary non-compliance will be restricted to cases of incapacity or inability which are not directly linked to the formation of political will, thereby somewhat broadening the category of voluntary non-compliance.

Following the suggestion by Raustiala and Slaughter—who concluded from a review of the compliance literature that there is too much focus on *ex post* mechanisms—we argue that a distinction between *ex ante* and *ex post* compliance mechanisms can enhance the analytical framework for the assessment of the existing economic governance structure in EMU.[24] Whereas *ex ante* mechanisms are aimed at preventing cases of voluntary and involuntary non-compliance, *ex post* mechanisms are aimed at dealing with non-compliance. This situation-based categorization arguably permits a more realistic mapping of existent compliance structures for a regulatory system that is mainly constructed around the dealing with the observance and non-observance of a statutory legal regime, such as in the EMU. At the same time, the differentiation between sanctioning and socialization proposed by Börzel et al. (2003) will not be followed.[25] Firstly, the main function of this differentiation seems to be to describe the nature of the compliance mechanism, though it remains open what additional analytical insights this may offer. What is more, the categorization of the compliance mechanisms into negative and positive sanctioning and socialization, as proposed by these authors, may prove difficult to defend on closer inspection. While compliance either through monitoring and enforcement or management are considered in the former category, compliance through persuasion and internalization are considered means for the socialization of countries into the norms and rules of a given legal order (see Table 9.1).[26] However, at least from a legal perspective, it is problematic to bring the managerial approach within the bounds of sanctions, which has certain authoritative connotations, while compliance through management is summarized in the relevant literature as being 'non-confrontational, forward-looking and facilitative in nature'.[27]

[23] Börzel et al. (n 7) 7. See also Table 9.1.

[24] Raustiala and Slaughter (n 10) 552.

[25] See Table 9.1.

[26] Whereas Börzel et al. (n 7) do not make this categorization, due to the close links between the concepts, compliance through persuasion and legitimacy can arguably be considered in the same category.

[27] Raustiala and Slaughter (n 10) 543.

What is more, in the context of the EU a further analytical layer can be introduced focusing on the level at which the compliance mechanism is situated and the actors involved in precipitating compliance. The top-down perspective takes the supranational European level order as a point of departure, whereby, at the European level, Union institutions are tasked to ensure the observance of European law in the national legal order.[28] Actions by the supranational institutions are based on rules and procedures above the Member States domestic legal order. As such, this perspective coincides with compliance through sanctioning, management, and persuasion, all of which in the EU context are initiated and pursued by Union institutions. The bottom-up perspective takes the national legal order of the Member States as a reference point. Here, compliance relies on actors other than the supranational institutions, in particular private actors. Compliance mechanisms which lean on private actors employ the possibilities of influencing a state's behaviour by domestic means and affect the (potentially) non-compliant state from the inside. They aim at internalizing the objectives and rules which must be complied with in the domestic order of the state concerned. By internalizing the objective and the rules linked therewith, the initially external (international/European) interests becomes the state's own interests.[29] As such, this perspective coincides with the compliance through internalization mechanism referred to in section 2.a. In this context, Koh distinguishes three types of internalization: *social*, *political*, and *legal* internalization.[30] According to this author, social internalization refers to the public legitimacy of a norm, which leads to 'widespread general obedience to it', thus closely resembling what is discussed by Börzel et al. (2003) as compliance through persuasion and subsequently by Börzel et al. (2010) as a legitimacy compliance mechanism.[31] While political internalization requires political elites to accept an international norm and include it in national government policy, legal internalization stands for the incorporation of an international rule into the domestic legal order 'through executive action, judicial interpretation and legislative action'.[32]

These three subcategories facilitate a broader understanding of 'compliance through internalization' by making clear that compliant behaviour of national governments is not only ensured by means of legal enforcement, but also by social and political processes. Yet, in contrast to the presently suggested distinction between top-up and bottom-down, Koh does not distinguish the different sources of the processes that lead to internalization. Such differentiation is, however, vital to properly assessing the quality of the compliance mechanisms foreseen by a supranational legal order. Political internalization, for instance, can be achieved either through supranational institutions that are able to persuade a national government to accept an international norm, or through national non-governmental organizations or other private actors which push the government to internalize the international norm. If compliance is achieved without any involvement of supranational institutions or processes, the supranational level cannot be given any credit for this. Applying this distinction, political internalization triggered by supranational institutions is understood as 'compliance through persuasion' (top-down) whilst the same result provoked by other actors corresponds to 'compliance through internalization' (bottom-up).

When Koh refers to social internalization as the legitimacy of the international rule itself, this resembles mechanisms which aim at 'compliance through persuasion' (top-down)

[28] More generally, in the international sphere, this may also be a group of states to which a (potentially) non-compliant state belongs.

[29] HH Koh, 'Why Do Nations Obey International Law' (1997) 106 Yale LJ 2599, 2651; Börzel et al. (n 7) 19.

[30] Koh (n 28) 2656. [31] See section 2.a. above. [32] Koh (n 28) 2656 et seq.

rather than 'compliance through internalization' (bottom-up). This is because the legitimacy of a norm derives from the legal order to which this norm belongs and not from the legal order that has to comply with this norm. An internalization of an international norm resulting from a government considering it as legitimate is hence, by definition, triggered by the international legal order (top-down). In addition to what has been observed by Koh, *economic* internalization may form another type of internalization that focuses on processes that lead to compliant behaviour in a national government without involving supranational institutions. Economic internalization occurs when market actions push a government to accept and to apply an international rule as a standard for government policy.

Table 9.2 compiles the insights from the compliance literature and the above reflections into a single analytical framework, which resembles the desirable situation with regard to economic policy coordination in EMU. This framework is hereafter used in section 3 to analyse the as-is state and, thereafter, in section 4 to assess the latter against the desirable situation.

Table 9.2 Analytical framework for compliance in economic policy coordination

	Voluntary non-compliance (lack of political will)		**Involuntary non-compliance (lack of capacity)**	
Perspective	**Top → down**	**Bottom → up**	**Top → down**	**Bottom → up**
Ex ante	Compliance through persuasion	Compliance through internalization	Compliance through management	Compliance through internalization
Ex post	Monitoring and sanctioning	Compliance through internalization	Compliance through management	Compliance through internalization

3. In search of compliance mechanisms in economic policy coordination

In order to evaluate the mechanisms in EU law aiming at achieving compliance with EU economic policy objectives, this section applies the analytical framework for compliance in economic policy coordination developed in section 2 to the current, reformed, economic governance rules. A preliminary, yet anything but straightforward question in this context is how the complex web of primary and secondary Union law, as well as the relevant rules deriving from the two intergovernmental treaties can be examined in a comprehensive and comprehensible way.

The operationalization is determined by the subject matter of the analysis, the EMU legal framework. This framework defines the objectives and the rules which have to be complied with. It specifies the role and powers of the Union institutions. These ensure 'top-down' compliance. In doing so, the EMU legal framework adopts, by definition, a 'top-down' perspective, as described in section 2.b above. In contrast, the EMU legal framework appears not to contain rules to ensure 'bottom-up' compliance. To be employed, 'bottom-up' compliance mechanisms rely on other actors than the Union institutions. These mechanisms draw on 'internalized', thus national rules and on directly applicable Union rules. In the absence of directly applicable Union rules in the EMU legal framework, the latter may only indirectly prompt the national legal regime to provide for 'bottom-up' compliance mechanisms. It follows that in analysing the current legal framework, as a first step, a distinction should be made between 'top-down' and 'bottom-up' compliance mechanisms.

As a second step, within the basic categories of 'top-down' and 'bottom-up' compliance, a further subdivision can be made based on the objectives set by the EMU legal framework. This follows from the fact that compliance mechanisms can hardly be analysed *in abstracto*, but only in relation to and in the context of the objective and the rules which must be complied with. In a final step, existing compliance mechanisms for each identified objective can be divided into two categories based on whether they are geared towards preventing non-compliance or towards addressing cases of non-compliance. Put differently, a distinction can be drawn between *ex ante* and *ex post* compliance mechanisms.

Legitimacy as a source of compliance through persuasion is addressed as a cross-cutting theme both with regard to the legitimacy of the policy objective itself and the rules linked to it, and with regard to national and European Parliamentary involvement in the application of the compliance mechanisms.

The objectives set by the EMU legal framework on economic policy coordination can first be derived from the guiding principles in Article 119(3) TFEU, which the Member States and the Union must observe, namely 'stable prices, sound public finances and monetary conditions and a sustainable balance of payments'. Arguably ultimately aiming at ensuring 'fiscal stability', these guiding principles constitute optimization commands (*Optimierungsgebote*).[33] Fiscal stability is achieved through economic policy, budgetary policy, and monetary policy. Whereas the latter is exclusively a matter for the Union, the first two in principle fall within the Member States' remaining competences.[34] However, the scope of these competences is anything but clear-cut, as can be derived already from a study of primary Union law.[35] Article 5(1) TFEU, which establishes a coordinating competence for the Union in economic policy matters, also explicitly refers to 'specific provisions' that apply to those Member States whose currency is the Euro. Article 119(1) TFEU states that 'the activities of the Member States and the Union shall include, as provided in the Treaties, the adoption of an economic policy that is based on the close coordination of Member States' economic policies, on the internal market and on the definition of common objectives, and conducted in accordance with the principle of an open market economy with free competition'. Moreover, according to Article 120 TFEU 'Member States shall conduct their economic policies with a view to contributing to the achievement of the objectives of the Union'. Consequently, when coordinating Member States' economic and budgetary policies, the compliance mechanisms foreseen in the EU legal framework have to strike a delicate balance between the Member States' remaining competences and the need for European intervention in order to implement the guiding principles of EMU in Article 119(3) TFEU. As will become clear from the following analysis, the current legal framework foresees a sliding scale in this regard, as the intensity

[33] For the purpose of this chapter 'fiscal stability' is used as the generic term for the overall objective for Member States' economic policies in the EMU. It follows the terminology used by the German Federal Constitutional Court in its Maastricht judgment calling EMU a 'stability community' (*Stabilitätsgemeinschaft*), see *BVerfGE* 89, 155 at 205. It is presently employed to clearly distinguish the stability required by the EMU from the stability required for the financial markets. With regard to the latter, EU institutions sometimes use the term 'financial stability' in both instances, whereas we would argue that the latter term should only be applied in the broader context of financial market regulation. Hereafter, where the Union legislator explicitly refers to 'financial stability' in terms of 'fiscal stability', the term 'financial stability' will nevertheless be used to avoid confusion with the legal terminology.

[34] Arts 3(1)(c), 5(1), 119(1), and 120 TFEU.

[35] See also on the issue of the scope of competence, R Bieber, 'The Allocation of Economic Policy Competences in the European' in L Azoulai (ed), *The Question of Competence in the European Union* (OUP 2014) 86–100.

in which the national economic policies are engaged with increases with the degree to which a Member State's fiscal stability becomes at risk.

Arguably, the legal framework is geared towards the achievement of five basic economic policy objectives. Firstly, as stated by Regulation 472/2013, Member States have to safeguard their 'financial stability' and, to the extent that these Member States use the euro as their currency, the 'financial stability' of the euro area as a whole. This obligation has also been emphasized by the ECJ in *Pringle*.[36] Secondly, according to Article 126(1) TFEU, Member States[37] must avoid excessive government deficits.[38] Thirdly, inherently incorporated in the obligation to avoid excessive deficits, Member States must pursue sound budgetary policies.[39] Fourthly, Regulation 1176/2011 commands Member States to prevent and correct excessive macroeconomic imbalances. Finally, Article 121(1) TFEU calls upon Member States to coordinate their economic policies with a view to contribute to the objectives of Union, as defined in Article 3 TEU and the broad guidelines adopted by the Council.

Certainly, these five objectives should not be considered in isolation, as they are economically intertwined. Some economic policies could result in macroeconomic imbalances which increase government deficits and debts in excess of what Article 126(1) TFEU allows. Such excessive deficits may eventually result in serious difficulties in terms of the 'financial stability' of a country, hampering its access to the financial markets.

a. 'Top-down' compliance mechanisms

The assessment of the 'top-down' compliance mechanisms will, considering the above-identified macroeconomic interactions, begin with economic policy convergence, followed by the duty to avoid macroeconomic imbalances and to pursue sound budgetary policies, before turning to the avoidance of excessive deficits and the safeguarding of fiscal stability.

I. Assurance of economic policy convergence

According to Article 121(1) TFEU, Member States must conduct their economic policies as a matter of common concern. To do so, their policies have to be consistent with the broad guidelines for the economic policies of the Member States and for the Union. These broad guidelines implement the EU economic policy strategy 'Europe 2020'.[40] Member States have to submit national reform programmes in which they outline which national policy measures they took to align their economic policies with the broad guidelines. These programmes should not be confused with the Convergence and Stability Programmes, discussed below in section 3.a.III., which Member States are obliged to submit as part of the multilateral surveillance procedure on the pursuit of sound budgetary policies.

The broad guidelines are adopted in the form of legally non-binding recommendations by the Council based on a conclusion by the European Council, which discusses the draft guidelines submitted by the Council upon a recommendation by the Commission. The Council must inform the EP of its recommendation.

[36] C-370/12 *Pringle* [2012] ECLI:EU:C:2012:756, para 135.
[37] Except for the UK, see No 4 of Protocol (No 15) on certain provision relating to the UK.
[38] As defined in Protocol (No 12) on the excessive deficit procedure annexed to the TEU and TFEU.
[39] C-370/12 *Pringle* [2012] ECLI:EU:C:2012:756, para 135.
[40] Commission, 'Europe 2020. A strategy for smart, sustainable and inclusive growth' (Communication) COM (2010) 2020 final.

In addition to these policy guidelines which involve the Council, the Commission, and the EP, the Heads of State or Government of twenty-three Member States (including all the euro area Member States) adopted the 'Euro Plus Pact', which outlines concrete economic policy commitments and the implementation of which is to be monitored by the 'Heads of State or Government on the basis of a series of indicators covering competitiveness, employment, fiscal sustainability and financial stability'.[41] The 'Euro Plus Pact' is a legally non-binding intergovernmental 'soft law document'[42] and can only be modified by consensus among its participants.

i. Ex ante *compliance mechanisms*

The *ex ante* compliance mechanism follows the 'open method of coordination' (OMC) as defined by the European Council in Lisbon in 2000. The OMC consists of fixing guidelines combined with specific timetables, the establishing of quantitative and qualitative indicators and benchmarks as a means of comparing best practice, the translation of these guidelines into national and regional policies, and periodic monitoring, evaluation, and peer review, organized as mutual learning processes.[43] The OMC follows the principles of learning from best practice and the application of peer pressure to reform undesirable practices. Compliance under the OMC is supposed to be ensured through discussions among all parties under an obligation to comply.

With the adoption of the 'Six Pack' regulations, the evaluation of national reform programmes has become part of the 'European semester for economic policy coordination'.[44] Hence, national reform programmes will be discussed in the Council along with the stability and convergence programmes under Regulation 1466/97 and the results of the macroeconomic imbalances assessment by the European Commission. The Council may adopt country-specific recommendations containing proposals for modifications of a Member State's economic policies. These recommendations are legally not binding and are not enforceable as such. At the same time they do not entitle Member States to any kind of EU assistance.

The mechanism to ensure *ex ante* compliance of Member State economic policies with the broad guidelines falls into the category of 'compliance through persuasion'. By organizing a dialogue, the acceptance of the broad guidelines by Member States is supposed to be increased.

Parliaments are involved at both the European and the national levels. The degree of Parliamentary involvement at national level in the adoption of the national reform programmes is entirely up to the respective national (constitutional) arrangements, as Union law is silent on this point. There is a broad range of ways by which national parliaments can in principle be involved, starting from the absence of any consultation of the national parliament, Committee and Plenary debates, to a formal adoption of a national reform programme.[45] Moreover, it should be recalled that national reform programmes do not constitute legal acts and hence national parliaments in their capacity as legislators remain in principle free to adopt laws which are not consistent with the broad economic guidelines.

[41] Annex I to the Conclusions of the European Council of 24–25 March 2011, EUCO 10/1/11.

[42] K Tuori and K Tuori, *The Eurozone Crisis—A Constitutional Analysis* (CUP 2014) 113.

[43] Lisbon European Council 23–24 March 2000, Presidency Conclusions, Bulletin of the European Union 2000, No. 3, I.18, No. 37.

[44] Art 2a Regulation 1466/97.

[45] For an overview of the involvement of national parliaments in the 'European semester', see M Hallerberg et al., *An Assessment of the European Semester,* study commissioned by the EP, Brussels 2012.

The EP is involved via the 'Economic Dialogue' that was introduced along with the 'Six Pack' regulation.[46] This dialogue is modelled on the 'Monetary Dialogue' with the ECB, which has been in place since 1999.[47] The purpose of the 'Economic Dialogue' is 'to enhance the dialogue between the institutions of the Union, in particular the EP, the Council, and the Commission, and to ensure greater transparency and accountability'.[48] In order to achieve this goal 'the competent committee of the EP may invite the President of the Council, the Commission and, where appropriate, the President of the European Council or the President of the Eurogroup to appear before the committee to discuss'[49] matters relating to the EU economic governance. With respect to economic policy convergence, the EP may discuss information provided by the Council on the broad economic policy guidelines, the Annual Growth Survey published at the beginning of the annual surveillance cycle, as well as any conclusions drawn by the European Council on orientations for economic policies.[50] Furthermore, the Council and the Commission have to 'regularly inform' the EP.[51] The 'Economic Dialogue' is thus envisaged as a forum in which the compliance of Member States with the economic policy guidelines by the Union institutions is discussed and subject to political review.[52]

ii. Ex post *compliance mechanisms*

If a Member State's economic policies are not consistent with the broad guidelines, the Commission may address a warning to the Member State concerned.[53] The Council may, furthermore, address recommendations to the latter that may be made public. These mechanisms can be classified as 'compliance through monitoring and sanctioning'. Neither the TFEU nor secondary Union law provide for any further *ex post* compliance mechanisms.

The EP accompanies the *ex post* compliance mechanisms in the framework of the 'Economic Dialogue'. It discusses with the relevant Union institutions and bodies the results of the multilateral surveillance procedure.[54]

II. Prevention and correction of macroeconomic imbalances

Regulation 1176/2011 has introduced a new objective into the EMU legal framework on economic policy coordination, as Member States must prevent and if necessary correct excessive macroeconomic imbalances before divergences become entrenched. 'Imbalances' are defined in Article 2(1) Regulation 1176/2011 as 'any trend giving rise to macroeconomic developments which are adversely affecting, or have the potential adversely to affect, the proper functioning of the economy of a Member State or of the economic and monetary union, or of the Union as a whole'. They are tracked by the European Commission on the basis of a scoreboard, which is drawn up by the same institution.[55] The scoreboard features numerous economic indicators relating to external imbalances and competitiveness, such as the current account balance, the net international investment position, and the real effective exchange rate, as well as relating to internal

[46] Art 2ab Regulation 1466/97. [47] See Rule 126, Rules of Procedure of the EP [2005] OJ L44/1.
[48] Art 2ab(1) Regulation 1466/97.
[49] ibid. The 'competent committee' is currently the 'Committee for Economic and Monetary Affairs' (ECON).
[50] Art 2ab(1)(a)–(c) Regulation 1466/97. [51] Art 2ab(4) Regulation 1466/97.
[52] C Fasone, 'The Struggle of the European Parliament to Participate in the New Economic Governance' (2012) EUI Working Paper RSCAS 2012/45, at 11 et seq. http://cadmus.eui.eu/bitstream/handle/1814/23429/RSCAS_2012_45.pdf?sequence=, accessed 12 October 2016.
[53] Art 121(4) TFEU. [54] Art 2ab(1)(e) Regulation 1466/97. [55] Art 4 Regulation 1176/2011.

imbalances, such as housing prices, private sector debt, and unemployment rates.[56] In its concrete assessment, the Commission is not supposed to apply this scoreboard 'mechanically', as for example according to Article 3(2) Regulation 1176/2011 'the assessment of Member States showing large current-account deficits may differ from that of Member States that accumulate large current-account surpluses'. As becomes clear from Article 2a(2)(e) Regulation 1466/97, the macroeconomic imbalances procedure forms an integral part of the 'European semester for economic policy coordination'.

i. Ex ante *compliance mechanisms*

Regulation 1176/2011 establishes an 'alert mechanism' according to which the Commission has annually to prepare an 'Alert Mechanism Report' (AMR) on macroeconomic imbalances.[57] The AMR constitutes 'a screening device for economic imbalances, published at the start of each annual cycle of economic policy coordination.'[58]As a follow-up, the Commission may undertake an in-depth review for each Member State which it considers affected, or at risk of being affected, by imbalances.[59] Based on this in-depth review, countries are classified according to the seriousness of the situation observed, including countries which have no imbalances, countries with imbalances that require monitoring and decisive policy action, countries with imbalances that require specific monitoring and decisive policy action, countries with excessive imbalances that require specific monitoring and decisive policy action, and countries with excessive imbalances that require decisive policy action and the activation of the imbalance procedure.[60] If the Commission considers that a Member State is experiencing imbalances on the basis of this report, the Council adopts recommendations, which are then published. These recommendations are legally non-binding and, moreover, do not entitle Member States to any kind of assistance from the EU.

The *ex ante* compliance mechanism with a view to preventing macroeconomic imbalances falls into the category of 'compliance through persuasion'. The publication of a report and the subsequent dialogue with Member States aims to increase the acceptance of the policy measures to prevent macroeconomic imbalances.

ii. Ex post *compliance mechanisms*

A Member State fails to realize the objective of preventing macroeconomic imbalances if it is affected by excessive macroeconomic imbalances. According to Article 2(2) Regulation 1176/2011, imbalances have to be considered excessive if they are severe, which includes (but apparently not exclusively) 'imbalances that jeopardize or risks jeopardizing the proper functioning of the economic and monetary union'. The existence of such excessive macroeconomic imbalances is established by a Council recommendation based on Article 121(4) TFEU and includes a deadline for the submission of a corrective action plan by the Member State concerned, which is assessed and endorsed by the Council. The European Commission monitors the implementation of this corrective action plan. If the corrective action plan is not properly implemented, the Commission presents a

[56] Commission, 'Scoreboard for the surveillance of macroeconomic imbalances' (February 2012) European Economy Occasional Papers 92; Commission 'Completing the Scoreboard for the MIP: Financial Sector Indicators' (Staff Working Document) COM(2012) 389 final.

[57] Art 3(1) Regulation 1176/2011.

[58] Commission, 'Report from the Commission to the European Parliament, the Council, the European Central Bank and the European Economic and Social Council, Alert Mechanism Report 2015', COM(2014) 904 final, at 3.

[59] Art 5 Regulation 1176/2011.

[60] Commission, 'Macroeconomic Imbalances. Main Findings of the In-Depth reviews 2015' (June 2015) European Economy Occasional Papers 228, section 5 (on country-specific findings).

recommendation establishing non-compliance to the Council. When adopting this recommendation, reversed qualified majority voting (RQMV) applies, a novel feature introduced with the 'Six Pack' legislation.[61] In a nutshell, RQMV foresees that a Commission recommendation will be deemed to have been adopted by the Council unless the latter decides by a qualified majority to reject the recommendation within ten days of the Commission's adoption thereof, or otherwise adopts an amended decision. This decision must be accompanied by a Council recommendation setting new deadlines, which must be adopted by a positive qualified majority.[62] According to Article 3 Regulation 1174/2011, if a euro area Member State does not comply, the Council can impose sanctions in the form of interest-bearing deposits or an annual fine. The Council decision is adopted in application of the RQMV rule. At the time of writing no sanctions had yet been applied in practice.

Another *ex post* compliance mechanism comes in the shape of Regulation 1303/2013 on the common provisions for the European Structural and Investment Funds.[63] According to its Article 23(9), the Council may suspend part or all of the commitments or payments for Member State programmes financed by one of the European Structural and Investment Funds. This mechanism is triggered when the Council adopts two successive recommendations in the same imbalance procedure on the grounds that a Member State has submitted an insufficient corrective action plan or where the Council adopts two successive decisions in the same imbalance procedure on the grounds that a Member State has not taken the recommended corrective action.[64]

These *ex post* compliance mechanisms aiming at correcting excessive macroeconomic imbalances consist of adopting decisions and recommendations, establishing programmes by the Member State concerned which cover only national measures, as well as sanctions in the event of non-compliance. They can therefore be classified as 'compliance through monitoring and sanctioning'.

The role of national parliaments is addressed by recital 25 of Regulation 1176/2011, which requires that 'the Council and the Commission should fully respect the role of national parliaments' when applying the regulation. National parliaments should in particular be involved in the adoption of the corrective action plan, even though the regulation itself does not require national parliamentary involvement. What must be recalled in this context is that the corrective action plans do not constitute legally binding acts and that national parliaments in their capacity as legislators therefore in principle remain free to adopt laws which are not in line with the corrective action plans. National parliaments therefore remain in a position to overrule a corrective action plan.

At the European level, the macroeconomic imbalances procedure is included in the 'Economic Dialogue' of the EP.[65] The Parliament may discuss with the responsible Union institutions and bodies the opening of an excessive imbalance procedure, the assessment of the national corrective action plan, a decision, and recommendations concerning a Member State's non-compliance with its corrective action plan, and the application of sanctions

[61] For criticism on the legality of the introduction of RQMV against the background of the amended Art 136(1) TFEU: M Ruffert, 'The European Debt Crisis and European Union Law' (2011) 48 *Common Market Law Review* 1777, 1800 et seq., with further references.

[62] Art 10(4) Regulation 1176/2011.

[63] Regulation 1303/2013 of the EP and of the Council laying down common provisions on the European Regional Development Fund, the European Social Fund, the Cohesion Fund, the European Agricultural Fund for Rural Development and the European Maritime and Fisheries Fund and laying down general provisions on the European Regional Development Fund, the European Social Fund, the Cohesion Fund and the European Maritime and Fisheries Fund [2013] OJ L347/320.

[64] Art 23(9)(b)–(c) Regulation 1303/2013.

[65] Art 14 Regulation 1176/2011 and Art 6 Regulation 1174/2011.

in case of non-compliance. In this context, an interesting feature of the 'Economic Dialogue' is the possibility for the EP to 'offer the opportunity' to a Member State which is the subject of a decision or recommendation in the context of a macroeconomic imbalances procedure to participate in an exchange of views'[66] at committee level. However, the exchange of views is done with the Member State's executive, rather than with the national parliament.

The EP is also involved in the adoption and any future modification of the legal framework itself, since Regulations 1174/2011 and 1176/2011 were adopted on the basis of Article 121(6) TFEU, which—since the Treaty of Lisbon—refers to the ordinary legislative procedure. Both regulations foresee a continous review of the effects of their application.[67]

III. *Pursuit of sound budgetary policies*

In addition to the macroeconomic imbalances procedure, the assessment of Member State stability or convergence programmes also forms part of the 'European semester for economic policy coordination'.[68] The pursuit of sound budgetary policies is inherent to the duty to avoid excessive government deficits laid down in Article 126(1) TFEU, as compliance with this provision requires sound budgetary policies. Compliance is determined on the basis of stability programmes for euro area Member States and of convergence programmes for all other Member States.[69] Sound budgetary policies are to be assumed, if the budget is 'close to balance or in surplus position'.[70] In order to reach this objective, Member States have to define a 'differentiated medium-term objective for their budgetary position' (MTO). In accordance with Article 2a Regulation 1466/97 the MTO has to be 'within a defined range between −1% of GDP and balance or surplus, in cyclically adjusted terms, net of one-off and temporary measures'. If a Member State fails to reach its MTO, it has to define an adjustment path to achieve this MTO in its stability or convergence programme. The two core criteria for the assessment of compliance with the objective to pursue sound budgetary policies are the MTO and the adjustment path towards it.

The intergovernmental TSCG tightens the budgetary rules laid down in Regulation 1466/97 further for the Contracting Parties.[71] The lower limit for the MTO is reduced to −0.5 per cent of GDP.[72] A significant observed deviation from this tightened MTO or the adjustment path towards it automatically triggers a mechanism aiming at correcting the deviations over a defined period of time.[73] This correction mechanism has to be implemented in national law 'through provisions of binding force and permanent character, preferably constitutional'.[74] Deviation from the MTO is permitted only in exceptional circumstances which are defined as unusual events 'outside the control of the Contracting Party concerned which has a major impact on the financial position of the general government or to periods of severe economic downturn [...] provided that the temporary deviation of the Contracting Party concerned does not endanger fiscal sustainability in the medium-term'.[75] Moreover, where the government debt is 'significantly' below the 60 per cent threshold and where the risks in terms of long-term sustainability of public finances

[66] Art 2ab(3) Regulation 1466/97. [67] Art. 7 Regulation 1174/2011 and Article 16 Regulation 1176/2011.
[68] Art 2a(2)(c) Regulation 1466/97 [69] Arts 3 and 7 Regulation 1466/97.
[70] Art 2a(1) Regulation 1466/97.
[71] All EU Member States with the exception of Croatia, the Czech Republic, and the UK.
[72] Art 3(1)(a) TSCG. [73] Art 3(1)(d) TSCG. [74] Art 3(2) TSCG.
[75] Arts 3(1)(c) and 3(3)(b) TSCG.

are low, a structural deficit of 'at most 1.0%' is allowed.[76] Finally, according to Article 6, Contracting Parties are obliged to report *ex ante* on their public debt issuance plans to the Council and to the Commission with 'a view to better coordinating the planning of their national debt issuance'. The latter obligation was taken over by the Two Pack legislation, including the Eurogroup as addressee of the report on national debt issuance plans.[77] In light of the two fundamental approaches that categorize compliance mechanisms—top-down and bottom-up—the TSCG emerges as a somewhat special legal instrument in adopting both a top-down and a bottom-up approach. With regard to the latter it can be observed that the legal obligation to provide for a debt break in national (constitutional) law constitutes an instrument of legal internalization.[78]

i. Ex ante *compliance mechanisms*

The Commission examines Member State stability and convergence programmes for whether they pursue sound budgetary policies. If a Member State fails to achieve its MTO, it may still be deemed to pursue sound budgetary policies if the adjustment path towards the MTO is considered economically persuasive. This is notably the case when the annual improvement in a Member State's cyclically-adjusted budgetary balance amounts to 0.5 per cent of GDP as a benchmark.[79] If, however, a Member State's debt level exceeds the 60 per cent threshold, the annual improvement has to exceed 0.5 per cent of GDP.[80] When assessing a Member State's budgetary policies, particular attention must be paid to 'the implementation of major structural reforms' or pension reforms.[81]

The *ex ante* compliance mechanisms to ensure sound budgetary policies fall into the category of 'compliance through persuasion'. The duty to produce stability and convergence programmes on the part of the Member States and their assessment by the Council and the European Commission, followed by a dialogue with the Member States, aims to increase the acceptance of the policy measures to ensure sound budgetary policies.

Parliaments are involved at both the European and the national levels. Similar to the observations on the involvement of parliaments in section 3.a.I.i. the degree of parliamentary involvement at national level in the adoption of the stability or convergence programmes is entirely up to the respective national (constitutional) arrangements, as Union law is silent on this point. Moreover, the national parliaments in their capacity as legislators remain free to adopt laws which are not in line with these programmes. At the European level, the compliance mechanisms relating the pursuit of sound budgetary policies form part of the 'Economic Dialogue' of the EP. According to Article 2ab(1)(d) Regulation 1466/97, the results of multilateral surveillance carried out under this regulation are subject to discussion between the EP and the responsible Union institutions and bodies. Furthermore, since the amendment of Article 121(6) TFEU by the Treaty of Lisbon, the EP is involved in the adoption and in any future modification of the legal framework itself, as Regulation 1466/97 is based on Article 121(6) TFEU, which refers to the ordinary legislative procedure.

ii. Ex post *compliance mechanisms*

The observance of sound budgetary policies is considered to have failed if there is an actual or expected significant departure from the adjustment path towards the MTO.[82] In such a situation the Commission addresses a warning to the Member State concerned.

[76] Art 3(1)(d) TSCG. [77] Art 8(1) Regulation 473/2013.

[78] With regard to the constitutional debt break as bottom-up mechanism, see further section 3.b.

[79] Art 5(1) and Art 9(1) Regulation 1466/97. [80] ibid. [81] ibid.

[82] Art 6(2) and Art 10(2) Regulation 1466/97.

The Council adopts a recommendation containing the necessary policy measures and sets a deadline for action. If the Member State fails to take appropriate actions, the Council may, upon recommendation of the Commission, adopt a decision establishing non-compliance. In the event that the Council does not adopt the decision and the non-compliance persists, the Commission may again recommend to the Council one month after its previous recommendation to adopt a decision establishing that no effective action has been taken. When adopting this decision, RQMV applies. A sanctioning regime is foreseen for euro area Member States, which in the context of the multilateral surveillance procedure takes the shape of interest-bearing deposits.[83] RQMV also applies when deciding these sanctions.[84] At the time of writing no sanctions had yet been applied in practice.

The *ex post* compliance mechanism consists of adopting recommendations and decisions by the Council and sanctions in the event of non-compliance. It can therefore be classified as 'compliance through monitoring and sanctioning'.

The EP is involved in the mechanism for restoring compliance via the 'Economic Dialogue'. According to Article 2ab(1)(g) Regulation 1466/97, it discusses 'recommendations addressed to Member States in the event of significant deviation and the report made by the Council to the European Council as defined in Article 6(2) and Article 10(2) of this Regulation'. Member States that are the subject of a Council recommendation based on these provisions may also be invited by the EP to participate in an exchange of views at committee level,[85] which is an exchange with the Member State's executive rather than with the national parliament.

IV. *Avoidance of excessive government deficits*

The objective of avoiding excessive government deficits is enshrined in Article 126(1) TFEU. The criteria for the assessment of an excessive government deficit are defined by Protocol 12 on the excessive deficit procedure, Regulation 1467/97, and a communication by the European Commission.[86]

Merely exceeding the reference values, as defined by Article 126(2) TFEU read with Protocol 12, does not in itself constitute an excessive government deficit. An overall assessment of the economic and budgetary situation of the Member State concerned is required, which may justify the excess of the reference values in economic terms. Possible exonerating factors are 'financial contributions to fostering international solidarity and achieving the policy goals of the Union, the debt incurred in the form of bilateral and multilateral support between Member States in the context of safeguarding financial stability, and the debt related to financial stabilization operations during major financial disturbances',[87] as well as the implementation of pension reforms.[88]

i. Ex ante *compliance mechanisms*

Excessive deficits can arise from unsound budgetary policies and macroeconomic imbalances. The prevention of excessive deficits is therefore the core purpose of the compliance

[83] Art 4(1) Regulation 1173/2011.
[84] Art 4(2),(3) Regulation 1173/2011.
[85] Art 2ab(3) Regulation 1466/97.
[86] Commission, 'Making the best use of the flexibility within the existing rules of the Stability and Growth Pact' (Communication) COM(2015) 12 final.
[87] Art 2(3) Regulation 1467/97.
[88] Art 2(5) Regulation 1467/97.

mechanisms bundled in the 'European semester'. The latter can therefore be considered as an *ex ante* compliance mechanism for avoiding excessive deficits.

Furthermore, Regulation 473/2013 introduces a timeline for euro area Member States into the 'European semester', which concerns draft national budgetary plans. These draft budgets have to be consistent with recommendations adopted by the Council on national reform programmes and on stability programmes as well as in the context of the macroeconomic imbalances procedure.[89] The draft budgetary plans have to be submitted to the Commission and to the Eurogroup for the forthcoming year by 15 October[90] to enable the Commission to form an opinion on these plans for publication the year thereafter.[91] The Commission has no veto right over the draft budgetary plans, but may issue a warning if it considers a draft budgetary plan to be in 'serious non-compliance' with the budgetary policy obligations under the Stability and Growth Pact. In such a situation, the Commission has to request a revised draft budgetary plan.[92] Interestingly, non-compliance with this obligation to present a revised draft budgetary plan is not addressed in Regulation 473/2013.

The 'European semester', including the obligation to submit draft budgetary plans for euro area Member States, is supposed to ensure *ex ante* compliance with the objective of avoiding excessive deficits. This can be classified as 'compliance through persuasion'. Together with the opinion issued by the European Commission on the draft budgetary plans, the 'European semester' seeks to increase the acceptance of the policy measures needed to prevent excessive deficits.

At the same time national parliaments remain the main actors in adopting the national budgetary plans, as they cannot be overruled by Union institutions, even if the latter consider the national budgetary plan to be in contradiction with EU rules or specifications. National parliaments may also invite the Commission to present its opinion to their parliament.[93] At the European level, the European Commission's opinion on draft national budgetary plans and its overall assessment of the budgetary situation and the prospects in the euro area, as well as the specifications of the content of the draft budgetary plans, are all part of the 'Economic Dialogue' of the EP with the responsible Union institutions and bodies.[94] Furthermore, as observed for other objectives above, the EP is involved in the adoption and in any future modification of the part of the legal framework which concerns the euro area Member States, since Regulation 473/2013 is based on Article 121(6) TFEU in conjunction with Article 136 TFEU, which refers to the ordinary legislative procedure.[95] On the contrary, Regulation 1467/97 is based on Article 126(14) TFEU, which requires only the consultation of the EP.

ii. Ex post *compliance mechanisms*

The procedure for the determination of the breach of the obligation to avoid excessive government deficits consists of three steps beginning with the Commission's monitoring of the budgetary situation of the Member States.[96] Upon establishing that at least one of the reference values is exceeded, the Commission prepares a report taking into account any mitigating factors for the Member State concerned.[97] If the Commission concludes that an excessive deficit exists notwithstanding, it drafts a proposal for the Council which must formally decide by qualified majority excluding the Member State concerned, after

[89] Art 4(1) Regulation 473/2013. [90] Art 6 Regulation 473/2013. [91] Art 7 Regulation 473/2013.
[92] Art 7(2) Regulation 473/2013. [93] Art 7(3) Regulation 473/2013.
[94] Art 15 Regulation 473/2013. [95] Art. 16(1) Regulation 473/2013 includes a review clause.
[96] Art 126(2) TFEU. [97] Art 126(3) TFEU and Art 2(3) Regulation 1467/97.

conducting its own assessment of the economic and budgetary situation in the Member State concerned, whether the deficit is excessive.[98]

Once an excessive deficit is established, the Council adopts a recommendation to the Member State concerned on measures to remedy the excessive deficit.[99] If a Member State previously already had to lodge an interest-bearing deposit due to unsound budgetary policies, as noted in section 3.a.III.ii., the Commission may recommend to the Council to require the Member State concerned to lodge a non-interest bearing deposit amounting to 0.2 per cent GDP of the preceding year. The same applies in cases where the Commission finds that a Member State has not complied with the budgetary policy obligations laid down in Regulation 1467/97 in a 'particularly serious' manner.[100] The Commission recommendations are adopted as Council decisions using the RQMV rule. Furthermore, according to Article 23(9) Regulation 1303/2013 on the common provisions of the European Structural and Investment Funds, the Council may suspend part of or all programme commitments or payments for the Member State concerned where the Council decides that the Member State has not taken effective action to correct its excessive deficit.[101] Such a suspension has already been applied once in the case of Hungary.[102] Article 126(10) TFEU explicitly excludes the application of the infringement procedures pursuant to Article 258 and 259 TFEU, which then also excludes the application of financial sanctions foreseen in Article 260(2) TFEU as a compliance mechanism.[103]

Based on the reports by the Member States on the action taken, as well as any other publicly announced decisions by that country, the Council, by means of a qualified majority vote, can establish that the Member State concerned has failed to take effective action in response to its recommendations.[104] Once such a decision concerning a euro area Member State is taken,[105] pursuant to Article 126(8) TFEU, the Council may decide by qualified majority vote to give notice to the Member State to take measures to remedy the situation within a specified time limit.[106] Subsequent to this Council decision, the Commission may recommend to the Council to adopt a decision imposing a fine, amounting to 0.2 per cent of the Member State's GDP. The Council decision is adopted using the RQMV rule.[107] The Council and the Commission monitor the implementation of any action taken. In the event of persistent non-compliance, the Council may decide to apply sanctions against the Member State concerned in the form of fines.[108] Fining decisions must be taken by positive qualified majority, excluding the Member State concerned. There is thus no automatism in the application of sanctions.

Additional requirements arise from the Two Pack and TSCG for participating Member States subject to an excessive deficit procedure. Firstly, according to Article 4 TSCG, they are obliged to reduce their government debt at an average rate of 0.05 per cent per year as a

[98] Art 126(6) TFEU and Art 3(3) Regulation 1467/97. It should be noted that other Member States subject to separate excessive deficit procedures are not banned from voting.

[99] Art 126(7) TFEU and Art 3(3) Regulation 1467/97.

[100] Art 5(1) Regulation 1173/2011.

[101] Art 23(9)(a) Regulation 1303/2013.

[102] Council Implementing Decision 2012/156/EU suspending commitments from the Cohesion Fund for Hungary with effect from 1 January 2013 [2012] OJ L78/19, lifted by Council Implementing Decision 2012/323/EU [2012] OJ L165/46.

[103] In the context of Art 126(1)–(9) TFEU. As is rightly observed by Bieber and Maiani (n 6) 1066.

[104] Art 126(8) TFEU and Art 4 Regulation 1467/97.

[105] Pursuant to Art 139(2)(b) TFEU, Art 126(9)–(11) TFEU and thus the sanctioning regime does not apply to non-euro area Member States (Member States with a derogation).

[106] Art 5(1) Regulation 1467/97.

[107] Art 6(1) Regulation 1173/2011. This sanction should not be confused with the one foreseen by Art 126(11) TFEU.

[108] Art 126(11) TFEU, Art 11 Regulation 1467/97.

benchmark if it exceeds the reference value of 60 per cent.[109] Moreover, they have to put in place budgetary and economic partnership programmes which must feature 'the policy measures and structural reforms that are needed to ensure an effective and lasting correction of the excessive deficit, as a development of its national reform programme and its stability programme, and fully taking into account the Council recommendations on the implementation of the integrated guidelines for the economic and employment policies of the Member State concerned.'[110] The programmes have to be submitted along with a report on the action that a Member State has taken in response to the Council's recommendation under Article 126(7) TFEU. The monitoring of the implementation of these plans lies in the hands of the Council and the Commission.[111]

The TSCG attempts to extend the new RQMV to the excessive deficit procedure. According to Article 7 TSCG, euro area Member States 'commit to supporting the proposals or recommendations submitted by the European Commission where it considers that a Member State [. . .] is in breach of the deficit criterion [. . .]', unless a QMV decision is taken in the Council opposing the Commission's proposal or recommendation. This reference to 'commitment' has to be understood as a political rather than a legally binding commitment of the Contracting Parties of the TSCG on how to use their voting powers in the Council and on how to establish a majority in analogy to the 'Luxembourg compromise' of 1966[112] or the 'Ioannina compromise' of 1994.[113]Any other interpretation would imply that the TSCG effectively modifies the voting rules established in Article 126 TFEU in conjunction with Article 16(3) TEU, which would only be possible with an amendment of primary Union law pursuant to Article 48 TFEU.[114]

It is somewhat perplexing that the scope of Article 7 TSCG on the application of RQMV in the excessive deficit procedure has not been extended to the 'debt criterion', especially since Regulation 1177/2011 has resulted in the amendment of Regulation 1467/947, now also exacting the financial sanctions regime foreseen in the case of non-compliance with the debt criterion.[115] The latter suggests that this criterion is still considered of somewhat lesser importance, something that has already been observed in the pre-crisis legal framework.[116] This is possibly because it is assumed that debts levels will no longer rise if excessive deficits are prevented, or because there was basically no political consensus at the time of the drafting of the TSCG.

Overall, the *ex post* compliance mechanism aiming at correcting excessive deficits in the event of non-compliance can be classified as 'compliance through monitoring and sanctioning'.

National parliaments in their capacity as legislators are not involved at any stage of the *ex post* compliance mechanism. They are, however, also not bound by the commitments of their national governments and can overrule any objections raised by the Council. As regards the adoption of the economic partnership programme, the degree of parliamentary involvement at national level is entirely up to the respective national (constitutional) arrangements, as Union law is silent on this point. As has been observed with the other

[109] This requirement must be understood as a reduction of the differential with respect to the reference value, as defined by Art 2(1a) Regulation 1467/97. Art 4 TSCG has to be understood in this way due to its reference to Art 2 Regulation 1467/97. See in this regard, R Repasi, 'Völkervertragliche Freiräume für EU-Mitgliedstaaten' (2013) *Europarecht* 45, at 70 et seq.

[110] Art 9(1) Regulation 473/2013 and 5(1) TSCG.

[111] Art 9(6) Regulation 473/2013 and 5(2) TSCG.

[112] Bulletin EEC 3/1966, p. 9.

[113] [1994] OJ C105/1.

[114] Repasi (n 108), at 69 et seq.

[115] Art 12(1) Regulation 1467/97 (as amended).

[116] Critical of the pre-crisis legal situation, F Amtenbrink and J De Haan, 'Economic Governance in the European Union - Fiscal policy discipline versus flexibility' (2003) 40 *Common Market Law Review* 1075, 1100.

objectives above, a broad range of national parliamentary involvement is conceivable. National parliaments were involved in the formal adoption of the TSCG since, as an international treaty, it had to be ratified by all Contracting Parties in accordance with their respective national constitutional requirements in order to enter into force.

At the European level, any decision or recommendation adopted on the basis of Article 126 TFEU,[117] as well as the Council's opinion on the economic partnership programme and the assessment whether effective action has been taken,[118] are part of the 'Economic Dialogue' between the EP and the responsible Union institutions and bodies. As an intergovernmental agreement, the EP was not involved in the drafting and adoption of the TSCG. Nevertheless, Article 13 TSCG, with reference to the Protocol on the role of national parliaments, addresses the EP in the sense that the latter and the national parliaments of the Contracting Parties may organize a conference of representatives from the relevant committees to discuss budgetary policies and other issues covered by the TSCG. Furthermore, under Article 16 TSCG, the necessary steps are supposed to be taken within five years of the entry into force of the TSCG 'with the aim of incorporating the substance of [the] Treaty into the legal framework of the European Union', based on 'an assessment of the experience with its implementation'. Such an initiative would then require the formal involvement of the EP. Finally, as has been observed above, Regulation 473/2013 was adopted in accordance with the ordinary legislative procedure, whilst Regulation 1467/97, being based on Article 126(14) TFEU, only requires consultation of the EP.

V. *Safeguarding the fiscal stability of the euro area and in the Member States*

The inclusion of the objective to safeguard the fiscal stability of the euro area as a whole and of its Member States is a result of the economic and financial crisis. Previously, it was assumed that fiscal stability would be ensured as long as the Member States avoid excessive deficits. But the economic and financial crisis has revealed the fundamental problem with this assumption. How should a situation be addressed, in which a Member State that does not want to avoid or is incapable of avoiding excessive deficits encounters difficulties to refinance itself on the open market? This question points towards the 'Achilles heel' of the entire economic policy coordination system: a system originally designed on the premise that Member States would always act economically soundly in order to secure access to open market refinancing. The drafters of the original legal framework had not foreseen any mechanisms to deal with a situation where open market refinancing would no longer be possible in practice. Such a situation constitutes a threat to the fiscal stability of the Member State and even the stability of the euro area as a whole, as the situation in Greece has highlighted during the crisis.

i. Ex ante *compliance mechanisms*

Threats to the fiscal stability of a Member State or to the sustainability of its public finances are arguably prevented by avoiding excessive deficits and through the pursuit of sound budgetary policies. Public finances are protected if public spending does not have to be geared towards compensating for macroeconomic imbalances or for wrong economic policies. The 'European semester' and the excessive deficit procedure, as well as the common budgetary timeline for euro area countries, are therefore *ex ante* mechanisms

[117] Art 2a(1) Regulation 1467/97. [118] Art 15(1)(d) Regulation 473/2013.

foreseen by the EMU legal framework on economic policy coordination to safeguard the fiscal stability of the Member States and of the euro area as a whole.

In addition to the 'European semester' *ex ante* compliance mechanisms, the ESM Treaty provides for 'precautionary financial assistance'.[119] This assistance 'aims at helping ESM Members whose economic conditions are still sound to maintain continuous access to market financing by reinforcing the credibility of their macroeconomic performance while ensuring an adequate safety-net.'[120] Such assistance is granted by means of a credit line and is subject to the conclusion and implementation of a MoU containing policy conditions.

A special kind of *ex ante* compliance mechanism can be found in Article 14 Regulation 472/2013, in the shape of 'post-programme surveillance'. This mechanism comes into play once the serious difficulties with fiscal stability have been resolved, while the Member State concerned at the same time has not yet repaid at least 75 per cent of the financial assistance received from other Member States, the EFSM, the EFSF, or the ESM.[121] This 'post-programme surveillance' aims at preventing the reoccurrence of serious fiscal stability difficulties and can therefore be classified as an *ex ante* compliance mechanism. It covers reporting duties for the Member State concerned, biannual reviews conducted by the Commission in liaison with the ECB, and recommendations adopted by the Council under RQMV, containing corrective measures for the Member State concerned.

Ex ante compliance with the objective of safeguarding fiscal stability organized within the 'European semester' can be classified as 'compliance through persuasion'. The 'European semester' seeks to increase the acceptance of the policy measures that are needed in order to prevent difficulties with respect to fiscal stability. The same can be observed for 'post-programme surveillance'. The 'precautionary financial assistance' provided by the ESM takes effect before serious fiscal stability difficulties occur. Such assistance comprising financial support to a Member State, aims at achieving *ex ante* 'compliance through management'.

In addition to the previously described parliamentary involvement in the 'European semester', national parliaments and the EP are part of a mechanism for the exchange of information and views with regard to the 'post-programme surveillance'. The European Commission has to communicate its assessment to these parliaments and, if invited by a parliament, has to participate in an exchange of views.[122]

ii. Ex post *compliance mechanisms*

Once serious difficulties with the fiscal stability of a Member State are found, the European Commission may decide to subject the Member State concerned to enhanced surveillance.[123] This enhanced surveillance involves an obligation on the Member State's authorities to closely cooperate with the European supervisory authorities and where appropriate, the International Monetary Fund (IMF), in order to remedy the source or potential sources of the difficulties. According to Regulation 472/2013 the Member State concerned may request financial assistance from one or several other Member States, third countries, the EFSM, the ESM, or the EFSF.[124] In practice, a request for financial assistance is filed with the ESM. In such a case the Member State will not only be subject to enhanced surveillance, but also has to prepare a macroeconomic adjustment programme, which must be approved

[119] Art 14 ESM Treaty.

[120] Art 1 European Stability Mechanism Guideline on Precautionary Financial Assistance, http://esm.europa.eu/pdf/ESM Guideline on precautionary financial assistance.pdf, accessed 12 October 2016.

[121] It does not cover financial assistance received from the IMF or third countries.

[122] Art 14(3)(2) and 14(5) Regulation 472/2013. [123] Art 2 Regulation 472/2013.

[124] Art 1(1)(b) Regulation 472/2013.

by the Council by qualified majority on a proposal from the Commission.[125] This programme should not be confused with the MoUs, which must be concluded by the Member State concerned in order to receive financial assistance from the ESM.[126] However, any such MoU must be consistent with the macroeconomic adjustment programme.[127] In addition to the adoption of a macroeconomic adjustment programme containing national measures to remedy the difficulties, a Member State with insufficient administrative capacity or significant problems in the implementation of the programme may seek technical assistance from the Commission.[128]

No further consequences are foreseen by Regulation 472/2013 in the case of non-compliance with the macroeconomic adjustment programme. This is different from non-compliance with an MoU under the ESM Treaty. Such MoUs contain policy reform commitments which must be complied with to remain eligible for financial assistance under the ESM.[129] In case of non-compliance, the ESM may discontinue financial assistance, potentially pushing the Member State concerned into sovereign default. This danger is an efficient factor to ensure *ex post* compliance, as practical experience suggests. In July 2015, Greece decided to sign a new MoU in order to receive financial assistance from the ESM even though large parts of the substance of the MoU were rejected by a referendum of the Greek people beforehand. Furthermore, under Regulation 1303/2013 on the common provisions of the European Structural and Investment Funds, the Council may suspend part or all of the programme commitments or payments of the Member State concerned if it decides that a Member State is not complying with the macroeconomic adjustment programme.[130]

The *ex post* compliance mechanism of Regulation 472/2013 aiming at remedying serious fiscal stability difficulties can be classified as 'compliance through monitoring and sanctioning'. Furthermore, the European Commission may be requested to support the Member State concerned with technical assistance. In the past the EFSM and EFSF, and currently the ESM, provide Member States with financial assistance. Both instruments require measures which are additional to the national ones undertaken by the Member State concerned. They therefore reach beyond 'monitoring' and can thus be classified as 'compliance through management'.

Parliaments are involved at several stages of the *ex post* compliance mechanisms aiming at restoring fiscal stability. With regard to the 'enhanced surveillance' pursuant to Regulation 472/2013, the European Commission is obliged to inform the competent committees of the EP and the parliament of the Member State concerned about the measures taken within this 'enhanced surveillance'[131] and must send an assessment of the 'enhanced surveillance' to the EP every quarter of a year.[132] On request, the Commission has to participate in an exchange of views with the competent committee of the EP, as well as with the national parliament concerned. In contrast to the negotiation of an MoU under the ESM Treaty, the EP is significantly involved in the negotiation of a macroeconomic adjustment programme in accordance with Regulation 472/2013. The European Commission must 'orally inform the Chair and Vice-Chairs of the competent committee of the EP of the progress made in the preparation of the draft macroeconomic adjustment

[125] Art 7 Regulation 472/2013.

[126] Namely, the MoU on Economic and Financial Policies, the MoU on Specific Economic Policy Conditionality, and the Technical MoU, which are negotiated with the Commission 'in liaison with the ECB and, wherever possible, together with the IMF' (Art 13(3) ESM Treaty).

[127] Art 7(2)(2) Regulation 472/2013.

[128] Art 7(8) Regulation 472/2013.

[129] Art 3 and 12 ESM Treaty.

[130] Art 23(9)(e) Regulation 1303/2013.

[131] Art 3(1)(2) Regulation 472/2013.

[132] Art 3(5)(2) Regulation 472/2013.

programme'.[133] The information received must, however, be treated confidentially. The same procedure applies to the Commission's conclusions drawn from monitoring the macroeconomic adjustment programme.[134] In the course of the implementation of the macroeconomic adjustment programme, the Commission must appear, if invited, before the national parliament, and the EP may offer the opportunity to the Member State concerned and to the Commission to participate in an exchange of views. It is finally worth mentioning that the EP was involved in the adoption of Regulation 472/2013, and therefore in any future amendment, since this regulation is based on Article 121(6) TFEU in conjunction with Article 136 TFEU, which refers to the ordinary legislative procedure.

Parliamentary involvement is significantly limited when it comes to the ESM. The ESM does not include the EP in any of its decision-making processes. National parliaments are only mentioned in Article 30(5) ESM Treaty, according to which the ESM Board of Governors must make its annual report 'accessible to the national parliaments'. In practice, national parliaments are at least involved in the implementation of MoUs. The latter in fact requires enacting laws which implement the commitments made by the Member State concerned, in accordance with the national legislative procedures. Whilst this implies a formal involvement of national parliaments, it can hardly be considered substantial parliamentary participation. This is because the consequence of a failure to adopt the legislation required to give effect to the MoU in the national legal order is the freezing of financial assistance by the ESM, which could lead to sovereign default. 'Rubberstamping' laws implied by an MoU therefore appears to be the only viable option for national parliaments. Coupling an MoU with a macroeconomic adjustment programme under Article 7(2)(2) Regulation 472/2013 can, furthermore, not be considered as outweighing this lack of genuine parliamentary input in the context of the ESM Treaty. Yet according to Article 13(3) ESM Treaty, the 'MoU shall be fully consistent with the measures of economic policy coordination provided for in the TFEU, in particular with any act of EU law, including any opinion, warning, recommendation or decision addressed to the ESM Member concerned'. This suggests that the Commission is obliged to take the contents of the macroeconomic adjustment programme into account when negotiating an MoU. Consequently, European Parliamentary involvement in the latter is also important for the MoU as part of the financial assistance granted under the ESM. At the same time, we must critically note that the European Parliamentary involvement is limited to the role of recipient of information, which it cannot even use in a public debate, as the information must be treated as confidential.[135]

b. 'Bottom-up' compliance mechanisms

In contrast to the 'top-down' compliance mechanisms, mechanisms which ensure compliance through internalization seek to influence a Member State's behaviour at the domestic level and affect the (potentially) non-compliant state from the inside. In doing so, as is observed in section 2.b., this mechanism 'makes use of symbolic structures, standard operating procedures, and other internal mechanisms to maintain "habitual obedience" with the internalized norm'.[136]

Among the subcategories of 'compliance through internalization' established in section 2.b., mechanisms aiming at compliance through legal and economic internalization can be identified in the area of EMU economic policy coordination. Legal internalization

[133] Art 7(1)(5) Regulation 472/2013.
[134] Art 7(4)(3) Regulation 472/2013.
[135] Art 7(1)(5) Regulation 472/2013.
[136] Börzel et al. (2003) (n 7) 19.

can be found with regard to the objectives of pursuing sound budgetary policies and of avoiding excessive government deficits. Economic internalization can be identified in relation to all EMU economic and budgetary policy objectives in the shape of a mechanism that aims at making use of the investment behaviour of private financial market actors into national government bonds. As both legal and economic internalization in EMU apply across several policy objectives, the following presentation of mechanisms aiming at compliance through internalization does not distinguish between several objectives, as it was done with regard to the 'top-down' mechanisms, but rather between the kinds of processes (legal or economic) through which the 'bottom-up' mechanisms seek to achieve compliance.

I. *Legal internalization*

Legal internalization in EU law refers to directly applicable EU provisions and to the implementation of EU secondary law in the shape of directives into national law. The latter requires the transposition of 'the result to be achieved' set by the EU directive into legally binding rules in the national legal order.[137] The former relates to the individual who is empowered through directly applicable EU rules and who invokes them in a national court deciding on a breach of these EU rules by the Member State concerned. This compliance mechanism relies therefore on the individual seeking enforcement of EU rules within a national legal order and on the Member State observing its own national rule of law. When a national court decides in favour of an individual, EU rules prevail over the non-compliant Member State and can be enforced against the Member State by the same national legal instruments as any other national rule. The direct applicability of EU law allows these rules to become an integral part of the national legal order. A Member State is thus compliant because it obeys the judgments of its own national courts, even though the latter apply EU law. In short, compliance is ensured because the objectives with which the Member State has to comply have become part of that state's internal affairs.

Such legal internalization can be found in Article 3(1)(e) TSCG. According to this provision, a significant observed departure from a tightened MTO or the adjustment path towards it automatically triggers a mechanism aimed at correcting the departure over a defined period. This correction mechanism has to be implemented in national law, as is already observed in section 3.a.III., 'through provisions of binding force and permanent character, preferably constitutional'. Non-compliance with this requirement can result in a proceedings before the ECJ pursuant to Article 8(1) TSCG, which describes a procedure that to some extent resembles the infringement procedures under Articles 258 and 259 TFEU.[138]

Moreover, Directive 2011/85/EU on the requirements on Member States to provide budgetary frameworks sets certain rules for national budgets, such as 'numerical fiscal rules'[139] and the establishment of 'independent bodies or bodies endowed with functional autonomy vis-à-vis the fiscal authorities',[140] which have to carry out 'reliable and independent analysis' on which an 'effective and timely monitoring of compliance with

[137] Art 4(3) TEU and Art 288(3) TFEU.

[138] Art 258 TFEU could not be directly applied, since it covers only infringements of the obligations under the EU Treaties. Art 8 TSCG constitutes a 'special agreement' in accordance with Art 273 TFEU. The procedure has to be initiated by another Member State.

[139] Art 5 Directive 2011/85/EU.

[140] These 'independent bodies' are e.g. in the Netherlands the 'Centraal Planbureau' (CPB); in Austria the 'Fiskalrat'; in France the 'Haut Conseil des Finances Publiques'; in Germany the 'Unabhängiger Beirat beim Stabilitätsrat'; in Portugal the 'Conselho das Finanças Públicas'.

(country specific numerical fiscal) rules' can be based.[141] In addition to this obligation, Article 5 Regulation 473/2013 requires euro area Member States to confer upon 'independent bodies' the task of 'monitoring compliance' with numerical fiscal rules incorporating an MTO and implementing Directive 2011/85, as well as the task of providing public assessments in cases relating to significant observed departures from an MTO, their correction, and the application of exceptions for temporary departures from an MTO.

II. Economic internalization

Legal internalization addresses only a small part of the mechanisms aiming at ensuring 'compliance through internalization'. This is because there are only few EU directives and no directly applicable norms in the area of economic policy coordination. The effect of the other relevant internalization process in this area, economic internalization, becomes apparent when considering financial market transactions. In general, the core compliance mechanism for the coordination of Member State economic and budgetary policies is the rise and fall of interest rates on government bonds. If financial market actors perceive a Member State's economic and budgetary policies to be unsustainable, they demand higher interest rates, i.e. risk premium, to purchase government bonds issued by that state. Conversely, if a Member State's economic and budgetary policies are perceived as sustainable, its bonds only require low rates to attract investment. To achieve this effect, Member States have to be placed on the financial markets on an equal footing with any other private debtor. There should therefore be no monetary financing of Member States' budgets, no privileged access for Member States to financial institutions, and no other Member State or Union should become liable for a Member State's commitments. The underlying assumption of these prohibitions, which have found their way into primary Union law through Arts 123–125 TFEU, is that interest rates should reflect the sustainability of a Member State's economic and budgetary policies. Certain market reactions can even be triggered at the EU level through publication of certain Council recommendations. At this point, the 'top-down' compliance mechanisms meet compliance through internalization. As a consequence of the rises or falls in the interest rates on government bonds, Member States decide to continue or alter their economic and budgetary policies to avoid rising internal budget costs. Financial markets are thereby supposed to precipitate compliance through internalization.[142]

4. Assessment of the Union legal framework on economic policy coordination

Table 9.3 offers an overview of the economic policy coordination framework as it emerges from the analysis in section 3. What derives from this is that subjecting the highly complex regulatory framework ultimately geared towards ensuring fiscal stability through an analysis based on the compliance model developed in section 2 (Table 9.2) allows for an unobstructed view at the actual nature of the mechanisms provided by primary and secondary Union law and the relevant intergovernmental treaties to ensure compliance. Considering insights from the compliance literature, the present analysis casts doubts on the efficacy of the current legal regime in ensuring compliance. These doubts are further fuelled by anecdotal evidence from the system's actual operation in the run-up to the economic and financial crisis, as the current legal framework arguably does not address all shortcomings of the original framework.

[141] Art 6(1)(b) Directive 2011/85/EU.

[142] As to the tenability of these assumptions in the face of practical experience, see section 4.b.

Table 9.3 Economic policy coordination legal framework

	European semester			Avoidance of excessive deficits	Fiscal stability
	Convergent economic policies	Avoidance of macroeconomic imbalances	Sound budgetary policies		
Ex ante	National Reform Programmes (NRP)	Alert mechanism MS specific in-depth review by the Commission (based on 'scoreboard')	Stability and Convergence Programmes (SCP) (definition of adjustment path towards the MTO)	European semester TSCG: 'Golden Rule' in national law	European semester Avoidance of excessive deficits Post-programme surveillance ESM precautionary financial assistance
	Increase/decrease of interest rates on government bonds according to the degree of compliance (condition: MS are on an equal footing with any other private debtor ⇒ Articles 123, 124 and 125 TFEU)				
Ex post	(1) Warning by the COM (2) Recommendations by the Council (3) Publication of the recommendation	(1) Recommen-dations by the Council (2) Corrective action plan by MS (3) Monitoring implementation (4) Sanctions: interest-bearing deposit/annual fine (Regulation 1174/2011)	(1) Warning by the COM (2) Recommendations by the Council (3) Publication of the recommendation (4) Sanctions (Regulation 1173/2011) TSCG: Automatic correction mechanism in national law	Article 126(7)-(11) TFEU (1) Recommendations by the Council (2) Publication of the recommendation (3) Setting a time limit (4) Sanctions TSCG: Automatic correction mechanism in national law	Enhanced surveillance: • Reports • Macroeconomic adjustment programme • Technical assistance from the COM Financial assistance from the ESM/EFSM: • MoU (monitored by creditors COM, ECB, IMF) • Payments
	Increase/decrease of interest rates on government bonds according to the degree of compliance (condition: MS are on an equal footing with any other private debtor ⇒ Article 123, 124, 125 TFEU)				

a. On the near absence of compliance mechanisms aiming at involuntary non-compliance

In Table 9.4, the compliance mechanisms summarized in Table 9.3, as they were detected in the current, reformed, economic governance legal framework,[143] are translated into the categories of compliance mechanisms, as they were established by the analytical framework for compliance in economic policy coordination.[144] In doing so, Table 9.4 reveals some interesting patterns in the EU's approach to compliance. The legal framework for all economic policy objectives is *ex ante* geared towards compliance through persuasion, whereas only with regard to the avoidance of excessive deficits could a mechanism be identified that can specifically be assigned to legal internalization. With the notable exception of the objective of fiscal stability, for situations of actual non-compliance the legal framework relies on monitoring and sanctioning as the main mechanism for inducing Member States to change their behaviour. Specific legal internalization can only be detected for the objective of sound budgetary polices and for the avoidance of excessive deficits. However, economic internalization can be identified across all objectives, at both the *ex ante* and *ex post* stages. This refers to the market-induced compliance mechanism where the rise and fall of interest rates on government bonds reflects the sustainability of a Member State's economic and budgetary policies.

In return, Table 9.5 takes the opposite perspective on the compliance mechanisms detected in the current, reformed, economic governance legal framework under section 3 than Table 9.4. It reproduces Table 9.2 on the analytical framework for compliance in economic policy coordination[145] and replaces the categories of compliance mechanisms by the compliance mechanisms summarized in Table 9.3. In doing so, Table 9.5 reveals how the legal instruments in place correspond to an overwhelming extent to mechanisms that compliance theories propose for voluntary non-compliance situations, while few instruments can be found which correspond to mechanisms that compliance theories propose for involuntary non-compliance situations. With the exception of the ESM precautionary financial assistance in case of threats to fiscal stability, there are no instruments geared towards preventing non-compliance through the application of management mechanisms. Indeed, from an *ex post* perspective, only the financial assistance granted by the EFSF and

Table 9.4 Compliance mechanisms based on economic objectives

	European semester				
	Convergent economic policies	**Avoidance of macroeconomic imbalances**	**Sound budgetary policies**	**Avoidance of excessive deficits**	**Fiscal Stability**
Ex ante	Persuasion Internalization	Persuasion	Persuasion	Persuasion Internalization	Persuasion Management
Ex post	Monitoring & Sanctioning Internalization	Monitoring & Sanctioning	Monitoring & Sanctioning Internalization	Monitoring & Sanctioning Internalization	Management Management

[143] See section 3. [144] See section 2.b. [145] See section 2.b.

Table 9.5 Compliance mechanisms based on nature of non-compliance

	Voluntary non-compliance (lack of political will)		Involuntary non-compliance (lack of capacity)	
Perspective	**Top → down**	**Bottom → up**	**Top → down**	**Bottom → up**
Ex ante	*Persuasion* • European semester • Excessive deficits • Fiscal Stability	*Internalization* • Markets • TSCG	*Management* • Fiscal stability	*Internalization* (–)
Ex post	*Monitoring and Sanctioning* • European semester • Excessive deficits • Fiscal stability	*Internalization* • Markets • TSCG	*Management* • Fiscal stability	*Internalization* (–)

ESM, and the enhanced surveillance in the event of serious fiscal stability difficulties for a Member State or the euro area as a whole under Regulation 472/203 can be considered as compliance through management. Compliance through management mechanisms thus only come into play when all other safeguards built into the system have apparently failed and financial assistance remains the only remedy to rescue the situation.

Recalling also the earlier observation on the great reliance of the current framework on monitoring and sanctioning, this regulatory approach runs contrary to one of the main findings of compliance studies, that enforcement is one, but certainly not the only mechanism for achieving compliance. In fact, in the case of involuntary non-compliance which cannot be attributed to a lack of political will, monitoring and sanctioning is not only unlikely to remove the obstacles which cause non-compliance, but may actually trigger political resistance against a system perceived as unreasonable. This decreases any persuasive power which the existing legal framework may have. These shortcomings are very relevant, as non-compliance with the legal regime for economic policy coordination cannot by necessity be exclusively attributed to the lack of political will of a Member State.

One situation in which non-compliance can be caused by a lack of capacity is an exogenous 'asymmetric shock'[146] hitting one or more euro area countries. An economic shock is considered 'asymmetric' in the euro area, if such an event affects one Member State more than another.[147] In a currency union, monetary policy does not provide a solution to the asymmetric shock. Monetary policy measures which might help an affected country will harm unaffected countries. Consequently, the affected Member State will use fiscal policy to cushion itself from the shock.[148] This can lead to an increase in the government deficit of the affected Member State and trigger doubts among private investors about the solvency of this state. In such a situation the non-compliance with budgetary policy objectives is not based on a lack of political will to comply with those objectives, but on a lack of capacity due to the fiscal policy measures needed to correct the asymmetric shock.

Another example which proves that involuntary non-compliance is not just a theoretical category is lack of administrative capacity. If the national tax administration is, for

[146] Exogenous shocks are caused by changes in the general environment or market developments. A Belke and D Gros, 'Asymmetric Shocks and EMU: Is there a Need for a Stability Fund?' (1998) *Intereconomics* 274, 277 also referring to 'exogenous asymmetric shocks'.

[147] ibid, 274.

[148] P De Grauwe, *Economics of Monetary Union* (OUP 2016) 10 et seq.

example, unable to raise taxes effectively, the affected state's non-compliance is, in relation to this particular question, due to a lack of capacity rather than a lack of political will.

b. The failure of compliance through internalization

As explained in section 2, involuntary non-compliance can be addressed by mechanisms aiming at 'compliance through management' and at 'compliance through internalization'. The conspicuous absence of mechanisms to achieve compliance through management aimed at addressing involuntary non-compliance could therefore be compensated by efficient mechanisms which precipitate compliance through internalization. Yet clear bottom-up compliance mechanisms aiming at internalization in the case of involuntary non-compliance are also missing in the legal framework pertaining to economic policy coordination. In fact, it may be argued that there are signs that the EU is creating such mechanisms outside the legal framework of economic policy coordination. A prominent example of an initiative to enhance the economic capacity of Member States by financial market operators can be observed in the establishment of a European Fund for Strategic Investments (EFSI) which creates an EU guarantee and an EU guarantee fund, with the involvement of the European Investment Bank, as part of a strategy to mobilize finance for investment, to help investment reach the real economy, to improve the investment environment in the Union, aiming at boosting competitiveness and economic recovery.[149]

In contrast to involuntary non-compliance, mechanisms aiming at 'compliance through internalization' can be found with regard to voluntary non-compliance. Here, compliance through economic internalization is mainly achieved by the rise and fall of interest rates on government bonds, which is supposed to trigger modification of a Member State's economic and budgetary policies. Yet, a closer examination of the evolution of sovereign bond yields for euro area countries in the period from the introduction of the euro in 1999 to the present reveals that this mechanism did not function properly. The interest rate on German government bonds with a maturity of ten years was recorded at 3.7 per cent in January 1999, followed by 3.56 per cent in January 2005 and 3.02 per cent in January 2011. In comparison, the long-term interest rates on Greek government bonds was 6.32 per cent in January 1999, followed by 3.69 per cent in January 2005 and 11.73 per cent in January 2011. For Spanish government bonds the rate was 4.07 per cent in January 1999, followed by 3.59 per cent in January 2005 and 5.38 per cent in January 2011.[150] The yield curves show a rapid convergence of yields on euro area sovereign bonds after the introduction of the euro towards the German level. Until the collapse of Lehman Brothers in September 2008, the yield curves of all euro area Member States were basically at the same low level independently of the sustainability of a Member State's economic and budgetary policy.[151] From that moment on the yield spreads between euro area sovereign bonds widened dramatically. This development reached its peak in June 2012, with an interest rate of 27.82 per cent on Greek government bonds compared to 1.30 per cent on German government bonds.[152]

What becomes apparent from this development is that for a long period, financial markets did not take the sustainability of a Member State's economic and budgetary

[149] Regulation 2015/1017 on the European Fund for Strategic Investments, the European Investment Advisory Hub and the European Investment Project Portal and amending Regulations 1291/2013 and 1316/2013—the European Fund for Strategic Investments [2015] OJ L169/1.

[150] Data from the ECB Statistical Data Warehouse.

[151] J Kilponen et al., 'Sovereign Risk, European Crisis-Resolution Policies, and Bond Spreads' (2015) *International Journal of Central Banking* 285, 289.

[152] Data from the ECB Statistical Data Warehouse.

policies (sufficiently) into account when calculating their risk premium. That financial markets were actually aware of the economic weaknesses of certain Member States can be construed from the fact that with the outbreak of the crisis, the interest rates of those Member States which had accumulated deficits during the calm times or whose national economies were particularly vulnerable to the financial crisis increased immediately.[153] These market reactions highlight the fact that the financial markets were unable or unwilling to exert market incentives for Member States to modify their economic and budgetary policies. Instead of indicating risky economic and budgetary policies, arguably the markets assumed that all euro area sovereign bonds could be equated to a '*de facto* Eurobond' with a default risk at German level, as the aforementioned yield curves illustrate.

With regard to legal internalization, an attempt has been made with the TSCG to use this mechanism to achieve compliance, in particular through the requirements of the introduction into national law of a balanced budget rule and automatic correction mechanisms in case of its violation. Table 9.6 shows the state of implementation of both rules into national law,[154] and the actual structural balance of 2015 according to a forecast made by the European Commission in its 'European Economic Forecast' of autumn 2014.[155] The overview highlights how even though all the Contracting Parties obliged to implement both the balanced budget rule and automatic correction mechanisms[156] had included these rules into their national laws, only three of the Contracting Parties are forecasted to meet the lower structural deficit criterion of 0.5 per cent of GDP in 2015.

The comparison of the forecast structural balance two years after the entry into force of the TSCG with the state of its implementation demonstrates that the mere adoption of national rules does not lead to internalization in the sense of turning an externally set supranational policy objective into an internal national government policy goal. The German Council of Economic Experts already observed in its annual report 2012/2013 that in the past (prior to the TSCG) 'the introduction of such fiscal rules was accompanied by a political willingness to consolidate government budgets, whereas their introduction by way of the Fiscal Compact was largely driven by political pressure, since the euro area states cannot apply for ESM financial support unless they ratify the Fiscal Compact. It remains to be seen whether the introduction of national fiscal rules under such circumstances will have a similarly positive impact on budget consolidation.'[157] Based on these considerations, it appears indeed doubtful whether legal internalization in the EMU context works in the same way as it did in internal market matters. This becomes particularly clear in cases of involuntary non-compliance. If a Member State is not capable of complying with the EU rules for economic reasons, this will not change merely because these rules have been implemented into national law. As regards the lack of political will, an economically capable but politically unwilling Member State will not adopt different corrective actions to remedy a significant departure from its MTO merely because it is required to do so by

[153] J Kilponen et al. (n 150) 290.

[154] See HT Burret and J Schnellenbach, 'Implementation of the Fiscal Compact in the Euro Area Member States' (2013, partly updated 2014) German Council of Economic Experts Working Paper 08/2013; E Bova et al., 'Fiscal Rules at Glance' (2015) Update of IMF Working Paper 12/273.

[155] European Commission, European Economic Forecast, Autumn 2014.

[156] According to Art 14(5) TSCG, these obligations only enter into force for Contracting Parties which are not part of the euro area 'as from the day when the decision abrogating that derogation or exemption takes effect, unless the Contracting Party concerned declares its intention to be bound at an earlier date by all or part of the provisions in Titles III and IV of this Treaty'. Such declaration was made by Denmark and Romania.

[157] German Council of Economic Experts, Annual Report 2012/2013, at para 180.

Table 9.6 Structural balance (forecast 2015) and state of implementation of the TSCG

	Structural balance (forecast 2015)	**Implementation of TSCG into national law**
Austria	−1.0%	Ordinary law
Belgium	−2.2%	Ordinary law
Bulgaria *(declaration, Article 14(5))*	−3.4%	Ordinary law
Cyprus	−1.3%	Ordinary law (but superior to simple laws)
Denmark *(declaration, Article 14(5))*	−1.2%	Ordinary law
Estonia	−0.7%	Ordinary law
Finland	−1.1%	Ordinary law
France	−2.9%	Ordinary law
Germany	0.6%	Constitution
Greece	1.6%	Implemented on 15 July 2015[158]
Hungary *(no declaration, Article 14(5))*	−2.8%	
Ireland	−3.3%	Ordinary law
Italy	−0.8%	Constitution
Latvia	−1.6%	Ordinary law
Lithuania	−1.6%	Constitution
Luxembourg	0.4%	Ordinary law
Malta	−2.9%	Ordinary law
Netherlands	−0.8%	Ordinary law
Poland *(no declaration, Article 14(5))*	−2.5%	
Portugal	−1.7%	Ordinary law (but superior to simple laws)
Romania *(declaration, Article 14(5))*	−2.5%	Ordinary law
Slovakia	−1.3%	Constitution
Slovenia	−2.2%	Constitution
Spain	−2.3%	Constitution
Sweden *(no declaration, Article 14(5))*	−1.1%	

national law. Lack of political will or a Member State's incapacity to comply constitute barriers to legal internalization, rather than challenges that the latter is capable of overcoming. In short, economic policy coordination arguably reveals the limits of 'legal internalization' as a means to address voluntary and involuntary non-compliance.

c. On the limits of the present legal framework to address voluntary non-compliance

Leaving aside the issue of the application of monitoring and sanctioning instruments as compliance mechanisms in case of involuntary non-compliance, past experience with the enforcement of the multilateral surveillance and excessive deficit procedure begs the question of the extent to which this mechanism can function in the future as a mechanism for effectively addressing voluntary non-compliance. Moreover, the value of persuasion mechanisms to achieve compliance can also be doubted, given current arrangements on the involvement of national parliaments and of the EP.

[158] Required by Art 3(3) Council Implementing Decision 2015/1181 on granting short-term Union financial assistance to Greece [2015] OJ L192/15.

I. Monitoring and enforcement

If the number of excessive deficit procedures decided upon by the Council is viewed as a proxy for the compliance of euro area and non-euro area Member States with the rule laid down in Article 126 TFEU, the record was anything but picture perfect before November 2009, when the European Commission acknowledged the effects of the global financial crisis for the EU and adopted its European Recovery Plan.[159] As early as 2005, with Germany (1/2003),[160] France (6/2003),[161] and Italy (7/2005),[162] three of the four largest European economies in terms of GDP had been subject to excessive deficit procedures. With the Netherlands (6/2004)[163] and Greece (7/2004)[164] added to this list, five of the twelve Member States which had adopted the single currency before 2009 had failed to comply with the Union objective to avoid excessive deficits.[165]

It is thus unsurprising that the limited compliance with the excessive deficit rules by some of the largest euro area members and the actual enforcement of these rules by the EU institutions were pointed out in academic work prior to the breakout of the economic and financial crisis. Evidence mainly from the first five years of the system's operation points to a rather uncommitted application of the legal regime. This had already been observed in the application of the multilateral surveillance procedure when in February 2002 the Council decided not to put a European Commission recommended application of the early warning mechanism for Germany and Portugal to the vote and, moreover, to close the procedure, pointing out that both countries had expressly committed themselves to avoiding excessive deficits.[166] The rather lax approach to the excessive deficit rule and the application of the procedure was highlighted in late 2003. Back then the Council failed to reach the required qualified majority to establish Germany's and France's non-compliance with the Council recommendation for deficit reduction and to adopt country-specific recommendations on concrete measures. Instead, the Council decided on generic conclusions, which stated that the excessive deficit procedure was to be held in abeyance for the time being for the two countries in question, and which included recommendations for correcting the excessive deficit.[167] The unlawfulness of these recommendations outside the procedural framework provided by primary and secondary Union law was confirmed by the ECJ, which annulled the Council recommendations in a case brought by the European Commission.[168] The ECJ did not, however, follow the Commission's submission that the Council had effectively taken a decision not to continue the excessive deficit procedure when failing to reach the required qualified majority for decisions in the context of Article 126 TFEU. According to the Court, 'failure by the Council to adopt acts provided for in Article 104(8) and (9) EC [now Article 126(8) and (9) TFEU] that are recommended by the Commission cannot be

[159] Communication from the Commission to the European Council, 'A European Economic Recovery Plan' COM(2008) 800 final.

[160] [2003] OJ L34/16. [161] [2003] OJ L165/29. [162] [2005] OJ L266/57.

[163] [2005] OJ L47/26. [164] [2004] OJ L389/25.

[165] Added to that are Hungary (7/2004) and Slovakia (7/2004), two Member States with a derogation but are also subject to the economic surveillance regime, which breached the excessive deficit rule.

[166] F Amtenbrink and J de Haan, 'Economic governance in the European Union: Fiscal policy discipline versus flexibility' (2003) 40 *Common Market Law Review* 1075, 1090; 2407th Council meeting, ECOFIN, Brussels (12 February 2002) Doc No 6108/28.

[167] 2546th Council meeting, ECOFIN, Brussels (25 November 2003) 14492/1/03 REV 1 (en).

[168] Case C-27/04 *Commission v Council* [2004] ECLI:EU:C:2004:436. For a detailed assessment, see B Dutzler and A Hable, 'The European Court of Justice and the Stability and Growth Pact – Just the Beginning?' (2005) 9 (5) *European Integration Online Papers*, http://eiop.or.at/eiop/texte/2005-005a.htm, accessed 12 October 2016.

regarded as giving rise to acts open to challenge for the purposes of Article 230 EC [now Article 263 TFEU]'.[169]

By making the application of each procedural step subject to a qualified majority decision the drafters of the original primary Union framework had effectively politicized the excessive deficit procedure. While this may or may not be desirable from a democratic point of view, this approach has opened the door for political bargaining and an inconsistent application of the procedure. The system of peer review reduced the effectiveness of the excessive deficit procedure as a compliance mechanism. Indeed, this observation seems to verify the hypothesis by Börzel et al. (2010) that politically and economically more powerful states may be more resilient to external pressure and not as vulnerable to reputational or material damage, diminishing the value of mechanisms relying on compliance through enforcement.[170]

Practice will show whether the introduction of RQMV throughout economic policy coordination will result in a more stringent application of the excessive deficit rules and, for that matter, the multilateral surveillance and macroeconomic imbalances procedure, rather than only accentuate the differences between the veto players at the supranational level in cases where the Commission's views are rejected by the Council. In the opinion of Bieber and Maiani, who refer in this context to the application of sanctions at the outset of the excessive deficit procedure, the introduction of RQMV could have positive affects as it results in a 'more easy' adoption of sanctions, which 'might therefore have a stronger deterrent effect.'[171] Be that as it may, it would in any event be premature to refer to an automated enforcement procedure. Arguably the same can be observed for the application of sanctions in the case of non-compliance with the Council recommendations pursuant to Article 126(11) TFEU and Article 12 Regulation 1467/97. The absence of any examples of an application of the pre-crisis sanctioning regime raises doubts about the practical value of this enforcement mechanism, which are arguably not addressed by RQMV. First and foremost, the political and economic efficacy of financial sanctions in the case of excessive deficits can be questioned, as it has been done with regard to the original legal framework[172] and with regard to the reformed legal framework.[173] In fact, the lenient application of the excessive deficit procedure may not only be due to political reluctance among the peers to apply the legal regime stringently, but may also highlight reservations with regard to the suitability of sanctions as a mechanism to force a Member State into compliance in the case of severe economic difficulties. Short of empirical evidence for such a correlation, this may also explain the relatively long duration of the ongoing excessive deficit procedures, as becomes clear from setting the time of the Council decision on the existence of an excessive deficit off against the deadline fixed for correction. As of 1 September 2015, in eight of the nine ongoing procedures with current deadlines for correction, the original Council decision on the existence of an excessive deficit had been taken before 2011, and in seven cases even before 2010. The oldest current Council decision dates from June 2008

[169] Case C-27/04, para 34. Whether this behaviour can amount to a failure to act in the sense of Art 265 TFEU, as is hinted at by the ECJ, is debatable.

[170] Börzel et al. (n 7) 5–6.

[171] Bieber and Maiani (n 6) 1071.

[172] F Amtenbrink et al., 'Stability and Growth Pact: Placebo or Panacea? (II)' (1997) 8 *European Business Law Review* 233, 236–7; Amtenbrink and De Haan (n 114) 1089 et seq. on the political economy of fiscal policy coordination.

[173] D Adamski, 'National power games and structural failures in the European macroeconomic governance' (2012) 49 *Common Market Law Review* 1319, 1342.

and concerns the UK. A similar picture emerges when observing past records of completed procedures.[174] The significance of the duration of these procedures becomes especially apparent when compared to the relatively strict timeframe envisaged in Regulation 1467/97.

II. Parliamentary involvement

An important feature of the assessment of the potential effectiveness of compliance mechanisms aiming at voluntary non-compliance, such as 'monitoring and sanctioning' and 'persuasion', is parliamentary involvement. When addressing voluntary non-compliance, mechanisms aiming at preventing or remedying such non-compliance seek to influence the political will of the non-compliant Member State. The political will of a state is formed through the popular vote in parliamentary elections and, between elections, through parliamentary votes representing the electorate's policy preferences. The persuasive power of compliance mechanisms aiming at influencing political will therefore increase when they not only involve national governments but also national parliaments. The latter's involvement in the mechanisms aiming at addressing voluntary non-compliance are, however, as has been shown above, very limited in the domain of economic policy coordination. While national parliaments retain, within the scope of Union coordination competences, the power to adopt laws, they are formally not involved in the undertaking of policy commitments by the national government within the coordination framework. There is no EU obligation for national parliaments to adopt, for instance, national reform programmes, stability or convergence programmes, corrective action plans, macroeconomic adjustment programmes, or memoranda of understanding. This lack of parliamentary involvement affects the efficiency of the compliance mechanisms in two ways: First, there is an absence of political commitment, i.e. ownership, by the national legislator to comply with the policy action recommended by the Union institutions. Second, the more severe a country's fiscal stability difficulties become, the fewer options national parliamentarians have apart from simply 'rubberstamping' policy conditions set by the Union institutions. However, the latter can present such conditions as 'diktats' from the supranational institutions to voters, which will amplify a Member State's political resistance to Union policy objectives, rather than create voluntary commitment.

It can certainly be argued that the lack of national parliamentary involvement may be compensated for by a stronger European Parliamentary involvement. This is because in addition to national parliaments, citizens also directly elect the EP and are represented by the latter.[175] In the EMU economic policy coordination framework, which is characterized by a shared division of tasks between the European and the national level, a citizen is thus represented twice. In their capacity as Member State nationals, citizens are represented by their national parliament and, in their capacity as Union citizens, they are represented by the European Parliament. Against this background, European Parliamentary involvement could thus at least contribute to the legitimacy of the EMU economic policy coordination insofar as the Union is concerned and, through that, increase acceptance of Union action at the Member State level. However, the EP's participation in decision making in economic policy coordination is rather limited. While it has adopted rules governing the macroeconomic imbalances procedure, the pursuit of sound budgetary policies and the reinforced

[174] An overview of the current and past procedures can be found at http://ec.europa.eu/economy_finance/economic_governance/sgp/corrective_arm/index_en.htm, accessed 12 October 2016.

[175] Art 10(2) TEU.

coordination of euro area countries as a co-legislator, the EP cannot hold the responsible Union institutions and bodies effectively to account in the application of these rules. It is a simple recipient of information without the tools to attach consequences to a negative assessment of the performance of the Unions institutions or bodies in EMU matters. The provision remains silent on the possible consequences of the EU institutions and bodies not cooperating with the EP. Again, against the background of the experience with the 'Monetary Dialogue', the effectiveness of the 'Economic Dialogue' in ensuring 'greater transparency and accountability' is at least not self-evident.[176]

Furthermore, the EP is completely omitted from the euro area's most 'intrusive' instrument with regard to the Member States' economic and budgetary policy, the ESM.

In sum, the limited national and European Parliamentary involvement cannot contribute substantially to an increase in the popular acceptance of the mechanisms for dealing with voluntary non-compliance. Accordingly, the absence of more meaningful parliamentary involvement could contribute to the ineffectiveness of the existing compliance mechanisms which precede the application of the ESM and the public refinancing of a Member State's government debt, meaning that Member States accept Union policy conditions as a last resort.

5. Conclusion and outlook

The extent and scope of the measures adopted in response to the economic and financial crisis are unique in the history of European integration. With the ultimate aim of ensuring fiscal stability in the Member States and the EU as a whole, a highly complex framework of partly complementary and partly overlapping rules which are only partly legally binding and, which are, for the time being, only partially situated inside the Union law framework, has been established. Assessing such complex legal arrangements systematically calls for an analytical basis which not only recognizes the position and role of the various actors involved, but also the factors which can influence their behaviour. Compliance theories as they are discussed in the field of international law and international relations offer a promising starting point in this regard, as they do not make enforcement the central and only object of study, but rather focus on the notion of compliance. In taking the actual cause of the behaviour of a state as the point of departure, compliance theories offer more tailor-made answers to how to deal with non-compliance in different situations than any legal study of the enforcement of an existing legal framework could provide.

Considering the economic policy coordination in the euro area and namely recent events surrounding several euro area Member States, the differentiation in terms of the proposed compliance mechanisms between Member States which lack political resolve (voluntary non-compliance) and those which lack the capacity to comply with a given rule (involuntary non-compliance) is very relevant. Indeed, involuntary non-compliance is arguably more than just a theoretical category invented by Member States to distract from the true reason for their non-compliance, ie a lack of political will. Yet, the current legal framework for economic policy coordination relies heavily on monitoring and the threat of sanctions to achieve compliance and, in doing so, does not consider the causes of non-compliance structurally. Consideration of the overall macroeconomic situation of a Member State in the context of the decision on the existence of an excessive deficit only leads to a non-application of 'monitoring and sanctioning', but does not contribute to capacity building.

[176] F Amtenbrink and K van Duin, 'The European Central Bank before the European Parliament: Theory and Practice after 10 Years of Monetary Dialogue' (2009) 34 *European Law Review* 561.

Indeed, the latter does not feature prominently in involuntary non-compliance. Moreover, the conditionality foreseen by Regulation 1303/2013 on the common provisions for the European Structural and Investment Funds, according to which the Council may suspend part or all of the commitments or payments for programmes in case of non-compliance, may only deepen the economic problems of a Member State in case of involuntary non-compliance. In its basic construction, the cohesion funds actually aim at capacity building in Member States. When it comes to involuntary non-compliance, in which a Member State's lack of capacity to comply is the reason for non-compliance, the suspension of payments only aggravates the economic difficulties of the Member State concerned and will thus not remedy the non-compliance.

Mechanisms to achieve compliance through internalization and thus bottom-up compliance mechanisms are unavailable for involuntary non-compliance. At the same time, it can be argued that the economic internalization mechanisms foreseen by the drafters of the legal framework, which assign a crucial role to financial market actors to influence the Member State economic and budgetary policies, have not succeeded in preventing the crisis. Yet even where compliance theory would opt in favour of monitoring and sanctioning, doubts can be raised about the ability of the mechanisms foreseen in the current legal framework effectively to address voluntary non-compliance.

These main findings point towards the need for an extension of the mechanisms for achieving compliance through management in order to address involuntary non-compliance before threats to fiscal stability materialize. Sanctions will not produce the desired results in case of involuntary non-compliance. When it comes to voluntary non-compliance, the legitimacy of the economic and budgetary policy objectives and of the rules linked thereto can be improved by strengthening the involvement of the European and national parliaments to increase the persuasive power of the legal framework. Finally, sanctions aiming at influencing the political will of a Member State after a rule breach should in future be applied consistently and systematically. The inability of the current legal framework to properly address and to remedy voluntary non-compliance is closely linked to the fact that the sanctions in place were never applied. This is mainly because the Council has a wide margin of political discretion in adopting decisions and recommendations in the economic policy coordination which results in a political reluctance to apply sanctions to non-compliant Member States. It remains to be seen whether RQMV will make a difference in this regard. Yet it may be more convincing to equip the European Commission with the necessary decision-making powers to apply sanctions to voluntarily non-compliant Member States.

The building of EMU remains an ongoing project, as becomes clear from the proposals made in the 2015, the 'Five Presidents report' by the presidents of the European Commission (Jean-Claude Juncker), the EP (Martin Schulz), the European Council (Donald Tusk), the ECB (Mario Draghi), and the Eurogroup (Jeroen Dijsselbloem) for 'completing Europe's Economic and Monetary Union'.[177] The report proposes the establishment of national 'competitive authorities', to track 'performance and policies in the field of competitiveness'.[178] This points towards legal internalization through national authorities. However, the present analysis has revealed the shortcomings of legal internalization in EMU matters. It can be observed from the implementation of the balanced budget rule and the automatic correction mechanisms required by the TSCG that compliance did not increase after the mere transposition of these rules into national law. A lack of political

[177] J-C Juncker et al., *Completing Europe's Economic and Monetary Union* (2015).

[178] ibid, 7 et seq.

will or the incapacity of a Member State to comply with objectives set by the EMU legal framework cannot be overcome by legal internalization. These findings have implications for the ultimate effectiveness of the 'Five Presidents report' proposals. Furthermore, the existing compliance mechanism geared towards persuasion in the shape of the 'European semester' is supposed to be strengthened by restructuring the process into two successive stages (a European and a national one) and by a 'more systematic' use of 'periodic reporting on implementation, regular peer reviews, or a 'comply-or-explain' approach'.[179] The more concrete proposal to establish a 'European Fiscal Board' can be classified as a further element contributing to compliance through persuasion.[180] Considering the existing shortcomings, none to these measures will solve the main problems of non-compliance. They do not address involuntary non-compliance and improve compliance through persuasion only to a small extent. However, the report also proposes to introduce 'in the longer term' a 'fiscal stabilization function for the euro area' in order to 'improve the cushioning of large macroeconomic shocks and thereby make EMU overall more resilient'.[181] Fiscal stabilizers would be activated before threats to fiscal stability arise, and they could contribute to addressing involuntary non-compliance at an earlier stage. As such, this proposal addresses the current lack of sufficient instruments to tackle involuntary non-compliance through management at an early stage, before fiscal stability is at risk.

Finally, the report also deals with the legitimacy shortcomings in the EMU legal framework.[182] It suggests strengthening the 'Economic Dialogue' by including plenary debates with the European Commission in the EP on the Annual Growth Survey and Country-Specific Recommendations. In this context, however, no proposals can be found as to how to empower the EP with instruments to attach consequences to a negative assessment of the Commission's performance in economic policy coordination. The same applies to the dialogue between the Commission and national parliaments. 'As a rule', the report states, 'national Parliaments should be closely involved in the adoption of National Reform and Stability Programmes'.[183] Arguably the implementation of the proposals made in the report will not result in a major improvement in parliamentary involvement resulting in stronger accountability of responsible Union institutions and bodies. On the contrary, the report proposes a strengthening of the Eurogroup, which is not accountable to any parliamentary body in the 'European semester'. These measures are not likely to increase the legitimacy of the economic policy coordination framework and will not thus contribute to the increase of its persuasive power on voluntarily non-compliant Member States.

[179] ibid, 9, 22. [180] ibid, 14, 23. [181] ibid, 14. [182] ibid, 17 et seq. [183] ibid, 17.

10

Rule of Law Values in the Decentralized Public Enforcement of EU Competition Law

Katalin J Cseres

1. Introduction

The decentralized enforcement system of Articles 101 and 102 TFEU introduced by Regulation 1/2003 in 2004 has often been designated as a success and an effective way to enforce EU law. The decentralized enforcement system has been praised for effectively easing the Commission's workload by delegating enforcement powers to national competition authorities (NCAs), national courts, and introducing a fundamental role for networked governance. Decentralized enforcement appears to work smoothly, and it has increased the Europeanization of competition rules across the Member States, while also developing a shared sense of competition policy and culture among the Member States. The decentralized public enforcement of EU competition law has often been considered as a model of economic governance for other policy areas.

However, there is also a certain degree of scepticism, especially in scholarly discourse,[1] which questions the success of this enforcement model. The Commission has also acknowledged that NCAs encounter difficulties in carrying out their work. Accordingly, late in 2015 the Commission started a public consultation on how to empower NCAs to be more effective enforcers.[2]

The aim of the decentralization of EU competition law enforcement was to ensure effective enforcement on the one hand, and to simplify its administration to the greatest possible extent on the other.[3] At the same time, it has been argued that to ensure the effectiveness of Articles 101 and 102 TFEU is in fact a manifestation of substantive legitimacy as laid down in Article 3 TEU: the enforcement system is legitimate if it achieves its objectives—to guarantee that competition in the internal market is not distorted.[4] Article 2 TEU enshrines procedural legitimacy and requires that the enforcement of the competition rules necessary for the functioning of the internal market must occur in accordance with Rule of Law principles.[5] In other words, the decentralized enforcement

[1] G Monti, 'Independence, Interdependence and Legitimacy: the EU Commission, National Competition Authorities, and the European Competition Network' (2014) EUI Working Paper Law No 01, http://cadmus.eui.eu/bitstream/handle/1814/29218/LAW_2014_01.pdf?sequence=1, accessed 12 October 2016; G Monti, 'Managing decentralized antitrust enforcement: *Toshiba*' (2014) 51 *Common Market Law Review* 261; KJ Cseres 'Competition Law Enforcement Beyond the Nation-State: A Model for Transnational Enforcement Mechanisms?' in H-W Micklitz and A Wechsel (eds), *The Transformation of Enforcement* (Hart 2015) 319–39.

[2] European Commission, 'Empowering the national competition authorities to be more effective enforcers', http://ec.europa.eu/competition/consultations/2015_effective_enforcers/index_en.html, accessed 20 October 2016.

[3] Council Regulation (EC) 1/2003 of 16 December 2002 on the implementation of the rules on competition laid down in Articles 81 and 82 of the Treaty [2003] OJ L1/1.

[4] R Nazzini, 'Fundamental Rights beyond Legal Positivism: Rethinking the *Ne Bis in Idem* Principle in EU Competition Law' (2014) 2 *J Antitrust Enforcement* 270, 282–3.

[5] ibid, 282.

of EU competition rules have to be effective to be legitimate and it must achieve this goal by guaranteeing Rule of Law values.[6]

The aim of this chapter is to evaluate critically the functioning of the decentralized public enforcement of EU competition law. This analysis will focus on the effectiveness of the decentralized enforcement which relies on Rule of Law principles. It has been argued that Rule of Law principles are a prerequisite for effective competition law enforcement:[7] the key component of such principles is that the enforcement authorities apply clear legal prohibitions to particular facts with sufficient transparency, uniformity, and predictability.[8]

Assessing the effectiveness of the decentralized enforcement framework will also take account of the problems of multilevel governance which have emerged as a result of the decentralization of enforcement powers and the creation of parallel competences for the Commission and national actors which made it essential to guarantee uniform and consistent application of the EU competition rules.[9] Centrifugal pulls from the Member States towards their national legal systems and centripetal pushes from the Commission create uniformity and consistency in this multilevel system. Analysing these bottom-up and top-down approaches allows us to analyse decentralized enforcement as a specific governance model.

2. Decentralizing enforcement

Until 2004 the Commission had a central role in the enforcement of EU competition law. Under the enforcement framework of Regulation 17/62 the Commission had a monopoly on the application of Article 101(3) TFEU and enjoyed a considerable margin of discretion in applying the conditions its provided. This hierarchical enforcement system seemed justified in the light of the fact that many Member States lacked 'proper' competition law and enforcement regimes until the 1980s or even late 1990s. Competition law in many Member States was not regarded as an economic policy tool of primary importance.[10] This meant that the relationship between EU and national laws had no practical relevance and any possible conflict between EU and national regimes remained without significant legal or economic consequences.[11] In that respect EU competition law and policy was atypical compared to other areas of EU law, such as consumer law, where enforcement has generally

[6] Article 2 TEU contains the values the EU is founded on. The Rule of Law is one of them.

There is now a consensus on the core meaning of the Rule of Law, that it essentially entails compliance with the following legal principles. Legality, which implies a transparent, accountable, democratic, and pluralistic process for enacting laws; legal certainty; prohibition of arbitrariness of the executive powers; independent and impartial courts; effective judicial review, including respect for fundamental rights; and equality before the law.

European Commission Communication on Article 7 of the Treaty on European Union. Respect for and promotion of the values on which the Union is founded, COM(2003) 606 final, at 4. See also D Kochenov and L Pech, 'Upholding the Rule of Law in the EU: On the Commission's "Pre-Article 7 Procedure" as a Timid Step in the Right Direction', http://www.robert-schuman.eu/en/european-issues/0356-upholding-the-rule-of-law-in-the-eu-on-the-commission-s-pre-article-7-procedure-as-a-timid-step>, accessed 12 October 2016.

[7] The law should be sufficiently specific and its enforcement predictable and fair. ME Stucke, 'Does the Rule of Reason Violate the Rule of Law?' (2009) 42 *UC Davis Law Review* 1417.

[8] P Marsden, 'Checks and balances: EU competition law and rule of law' (2009) 5 *Competition Law International* 24; E Fox, 'Rule of Law, Standards of Law, Discretion and Transparency' (2014) 67 *SMU Law Review* 795.

[9] Council Regulation (EC) 1/2003 (n 3).

[10] RJ Van den Bergh and PD Camesasca (2001), *European Competition Law and Economics: A Comparative Perspective* (Intersentia 2001), 125–6; DJ Gerber, *Law and Competition in Twentieth Century Europe: Protecting Prometheus* (Clarendon 1998); KJ Cseres, 'The impact of Regulation 1/2003 in the new Member States' (2010) 6 *Competition Law Review* 145.

[11] M Botta, 'Testing the decentralization of competition law enforcement: Comment on Toshiba' (2013) 38 *European Law Review* 114.

been subject to a multilevel governance system,[12] ie EU substantive rules are enforced through national procedure laws in accordance with national procedural autonomy. In 2004 this 'first supranational policy in the European Union'[13] was fundamentally changed by Regulation 1/2003.[14] Regulation 1/2003 delegated enforcement powers to NCAs and national courts to relieve the Commission of its increasing administrative burden and make the enforcement of EU rules more effective.

The transformation of EU competition law enforcement[15] resulted in a multilevel governance model, where a mix of substantive EU provisions and national procedural laws and institutional designs are applied and enforcement is shared by the Commission and twenty-eight NCAs. Regulation 1/2003 created a system of parallel competences between the Commission and NCAs and national courts and obliged the national actors to apply EU and national competition laws simultaneously. Decentralized enforcement thus became subject to similar problems of multilevel governance as other fields of EU law, such as the enforcement gap between substantive and procedural rules or the problem of accountability for acts which are the result of this mixed enforcement system.[16] Such a multilevel system considerably challenges the uniform and consistent application of EU law and creates uncertainty for national actors how to apply and not to apply Treaty provisions. In order to safeguard uniform and consistent application of Articles 101 and 102 TFEU,[17] various legal provisions were laid down in Regulation 1/2003 and cooperation mechanisms between the Commission and the NCAs were introduced in the framework of the European Competition Network (ECN).[18]

While these mechanisms accelerated a remarkable Europeanization[19] of competition rules,[20] much of the effectiveness of the decentralized enforcement now depends on the success of these coordination mechanisms in safeguarding uniform and consistent application while the legitimacy of shared enforcement depends on its compliance with Rule of Law values.[21]

[12] Governance can be understood as a shift from 'government' to 'governance', a diffusion and fragmentation of governmental arrangements with the decentring of the state; I Maher, 'Regulation and modes of governance in EC competition law; what's new in enforcement?' (2007) 31 *Fordham International Law Journal* 1720; I Maher, 'Competition Law in the International Domain: Networks as a New Form of Governance' (2002) 29 *Journal of Law and Society* 116. In the EU context, governance has to be understood in the multilevel context of EU institutions, Member States, and growing participation of private actors.

[13] L McGowan and S Wilks, 'The first supranational policy in the European Union: Competition policy' (1995) 28 *European Journal of Political Research* 149.

[14] Council Regulation (EC) 1/2003 (n 3).

[15] See Cseres (n 1) on the transformation of EU competition law.

[16] F Cengiz, 'Regulation 1/2003 Revisited' (2009) 42 *TILEC Discussion Paper* 26, 30.

[17] Council Regulation (EC) 1/2003 (n 3).

[18] Commission Notice on cooperation within the Network of Competition Authorities [2004] OJ C101/43.

[19] Europeanization is understood as 'the reorientation or reshaping of politics in the domestic arena in ways that reflect policies, practices or preferences advanced through the EU system of governance'. I Bache and A Jordan, 'Europeanization and Domestic Change' in I Bache and A Jordan (eds), *The Europeanization of British Politics* (Palgrave Macmillan 2006) 30.

[20] For example, when candidate countries join the EU and its competition law regime, external incentives and conditionality end their function, as governance modes and the mechanisms within the ECN become crucial.

[21] The effectiveness of EU law enforcement had been defined in literature by 'the degree to which both the formal transposition and the practical application of supranational measures at the national level correspond to the objectives specified in the European legislation'. The main factors of effective competition law enforcement lie in effective administrative organization, clearly worded national law provisions, and the extent to which European rules are successfully transposed into the existing institutional and regulatory traditions of the Member States. O Treib, 'Implementing and complying with EU governance outputs' (2006) 1 *Living Reviews in European Governance*, http://www.livingreviews.org/lreg-2006-1, accessed 20 October 2016. C Knill and A Lenschow, 'Coping with Europe: the impact of British and German administrations on the implementation of EU environmental policy' (1998) 5 *Journal of European Public Policy* 595.

At the same time, the transformation of EU competition law enforcement reflects the diffusion and fragmentation of governance.[22] Regulation 1/2003 introduced several hybrid modes of governance. The regulation itself is a hierarchical tool of EU governance. European competition law is legislated through directly applicable Treaty provisions and regulations and thus directly enters national legal regimes. The shift to a decentralized architecture introduced networked governance, a fundamental role for information sharing, and increased participation of private actors (leniency, private actions) which reflect the modes of new governance.[23]

Accordingly, the following sections will first analyse the legal framework and jurisprudence on the parallel application of EU and national competition rules, including a critical analysis of how NCAs interpret the idea of an 'effect on trade' between Member States as the core criterion of parallel application. Then the way case allocation and the various coordination mechanisms are construed and applied in practice are examined in order to evaluate the effective functioning of the decentralized architecture. The third section further analyses the multilevel enforcement framework and the implications of the mixed enforcement system for effective law enforcement. Then the fourth section evaluates the so-called 'voluntary' harmonization process and the role of the Commission. The chapter closes with conclusions.

3. Parallel application of EU and national competition law

The parallel application of EU and national competition laws was already recognized by the CJEU in *Walt Wilhelm*.[24] In this ruling the CJEU specifically recognized the supremacy of EU competition law over national competition law,[25] but it accepted that national courts apply national competition legislation and EU competition rules in parallel. The Court argued that EU law and national competition law may apply in parallel,[26] as competition rules at the European and national levels 'view restrictions on competition from different angles'[27] and later added that their areas of application do not coincide.[28] In 2004 this dictum was incorporated in Article 3(1)[29] of Regulation 1/2003, which went even further by

[22] I Maher, 'Regulation and Modes of Governance in EC Competition Law: What's New in Enforcement?' (2007) 31 *Fordham International Law Journal*; Y Svetiev, 'Networked Competition Governance in the EU: Delegation, Decentralization or Experimentalist Architecture?' in C Sabel and J Zeitlin (eds), *Experimentalist Governance in the EU* (OUP 2010).

[23] Soft-law instruments such as Notices and Guidelines had been part of the enforcement regime of EU competition law since the 1960s. I Maher, 'Functional and Normative Delegation to Non-Majoritarian Institutions: The Case of the European Competition Network' (2009) 7 *Comparative European Politics* 414.

[24] Case 14/68 *Walt Wilhelm v Bundeskartellamt* [1969] ECLI:EU:C:1969:4, para 4.

[25] Of course, the precedence of EU law had already been recognized in Case C-6/64 *Costa v Enel* [1964] ECLI:EU:C:1964:66. Case 14/68 *Walt Wilhelm v Bundeskartellamt* [1969] ECLI:EU:C:1969:4; The ruling in *Walt Wilhelm* only dealt with the principle of supremacy for cases in which the Commission found a violation of Art 101(1) TFEU. The Court has not given a clear answer to the question whether NCAs and national courts could prohibit agreements granted exemption by the Commission under Art 101(3) TFEU, either individually through Art 101(3) TFEU or through a Block Exemption Regulation.

[26] *Walt Wilhelm* (n 24), para 3; Case C-137/00 *Milk Marque and National Farmers' Union* [2003] ECLI:EU:C:2003:429, para 61; Joined Cases C-295/04 to C-298/04 *Manfredi and Others* [2006] ECLI:EU:C:2006:461, para 38.

[27] *Walt Wilhelm* (n 24) para 3; *Manfredi and Others* (n 26) para 38; Case C-550/07P *Akzo Nobel Chemicals and Akcros Chemicals v Commission* [2010] ECLI:EU:C:2010:512, para 103; C-17/10 *Toshiba Corporation and Others* [2012] ECLI:EU:C:2012:72, para 81.

[28] Case C-505/07 *Compañía Española de Comercialización de Aceite* [2009] ECLI:EU:C:2009:591, para 52.

[29] Art 3(1) defines the principle of simultaneous application of national and EU competition law with the limitation posed in Art 3(2): Member States may not adopt and apply on their territory stricter national competition laws which prohibit agreements, decisions by associations of undertakings or concerted practices which may affect trade between Member States but which do not restrict competition within the meaning of Art

imposing an obligation on NCAs to apply Articles 101 and 102 TFEU in parallel to their national competition rules when an 'effect on trade between Member States' could be established. Moreover, Article 3(2) Regulation 1/2003 introduced a strict supremacy standard obliging Member States to comply with EU interpretations of Articles 101 and 102 TFEU when applied in parallel to national rules. In other words, stricter national competition laws are not objectionable as such, as long as they are not applied to agreements, concerted practices, and decisions of associations of undertakings which fall within the jurisdictional scope of EU competition rules in breach of Article 3(2). Article 3 acted as a radical intervention in the domestic legal systems of the Member States and has further strengthened the already ongoing convergence of competition rules towards the EU Treaty provisions.[30] This convergence will be discussed in section 4 below. What is of relevance here is the fact that under Regulation 1/2003, NCAs and the Commission have concurrent jurisdictions and there are neither territorial limitations to their enforcement powers nor a prohibition of parallel proceedings between the Commission under EU law and the NCAs under national law.[31]

Most importantly, this envisaged system of parallel application of EU and national competition rules raises a number of significant legal questions which NCAs face in practice.

First of all, when is the criterion of 'effect on trade' fulfilled and how should this notion be interpreted? The Court's case law provides a broad interpretation, which leaves a wide margin of discretion for the NCAs. How do NCAs decide whether they have to apply EU competition law (as well) or not? Second, decentralized enforcement is fundamentally based on and influenced by how case allocation and coordination between NCAs and between an NCA and the Commission is done. While the Commission's Notice on cooperation[32] provides clear guidelines for case allocation, the NCAs' practice and recent case law raise much uncertainty. In fact, the NCAs and the Commission have broad discretionary powers concerning case allocation and even subdividing investigations. Third, parallel application involves a system of 'shared' or 'mixed' enforcement of EU and national law and actors. How does this shared enforcement system comply with Rule of Law values, most importantly the principle of *ne bis in idem*? Fourth, is the parallel application of EU and national law as established in *Walt Wilhelm* still valid regarding the far-reaching harmonization and convergence between the EU and national laws concerning both substantive and procedural rules? And finally, does the decentralized enforcement of EU competition law guarantee effective, consistent, and uniform application of EU law?

These legal questions will be examined in the following sections.

101(1), or which fulfil the conditions of Art 101(3), or which are covered by a Regulation for the application of Art 101(3). Commission Staff Working Paper of 29 April 2009 accompanying the Report on the functioning of Regulation 1/2003, SEC(2009) 574 final, paras 141, 142, 152. Supremacy of EU competition law over national competition law has been established by *Walt Wilhelm* (n 24), but only for cases where an exemption under Art 101(3) has been granted. See also more recently *Toshiba* (n 27).

[30] It should be recalled that this convergence was ongoing before Regulation 1/2003 came into force. Many EU Member States abandoned their ineffective competition regulation based on the so-called administrative control model during the 1980s and 1990s and adopted a competition law system similar to the rules laid down in Articles 101 and 102 TFEU and the EU Merger Regulation. In the Member States the basic conditions for free competition were introduced by the legal reforms between 1989 and 1991. From 1990 on, new national competition laws were enacted and thus the enforcement of competition law could begin. RJ Van der Bergh and PD Camasesca, *European Competition Law and Economics: A Comparative Perspective* (Intersentia 2001), 125–6. See more details in Cseres (n 11).

[31] Nazzini (n 4) 275.

[32] Commission Notice on cooperation within the Network of Competition Authorities [2004] OJ C101/43.

4. Effect on trade concept

Ever since the CJEU's judgment in *Consten and Grundig*[33] in 1966, the 'effect on trade' has been applied in EU competition law as an autonomous EU law criterion which must be assessed separately in each case. It is a jurisdictional criterion which defines the scope of application of EU competition law. While the criterion is applied in all Treaty provisions concerning substantive competition rules, i.e. Articles 101, 102, 106, and 107 TFEU, the EU Courts and the Commission has most extensively interpreted this notion in the field of Articles 101 and 102 TFEU.[34]

As a significant first filter to defining the 'boundary'[35] between the application of national and EU competition law, the EU Courts have developed a broad interpretation for the idea of an 'effect on trade' in order to enlarge the scope of application of EU competition rules. Accordingly, agreements or practices which have 'an influence, direct or indirect, actual or potential, on the pattern of trade between Member States'[36] have been considered to fall within Articles 101 and 102 TFEU. While the Courts later refined this concept by introducing the doctrine of appreciability in *Völk*, i.e. 'an agreement falls outside the prohibition in Article [101] when it has only an insignificant effect on the markets, taking into account the weak position which the persons concerned have on the market of the product in question,'[37] the concept of 'effect on trade' has continued to be broadly interpreted by the EU Courts in their subsequent case law.[38] Moreover, the Courts have refrained from providing any quantitative criteria for what should be considered an 'appreciable' effect on trade between Member States While the CJEU has so far merely stated that 'an agreement of undertakings falls outside the prohibition in that provision, however, if it has only an insignificant effect on the market',[39] it has not formulated what qualifies as an 'appreciable' effect on interstate trade.[40] This leaves a considerable margin of discretion to the NCAs to decide how to interpret the notion of 'effect on trade' in individual cases.[41]

Even though the Commission published a Notice on the concept of effect on trade[42] in 2004, in which it offered for the first time a quantitative indication of when agreements are in general unlikely to be capable of appreciably affecting trade between Member States, the 'non-appreciable affectation of trade' rule (NAAT-rule), these guidelines only provide

[33] Joined Cases 56/64 and 58/64 *Consten and Grundig* [1966] ECLI:EU:C:1966:41; see also Case 56/65 *Société Technique Minièr* [1966] ECLI:EU:C:1966:38.

[34] For a discussion of the 'effect on trade' concept in EU state aid law, see for example C-D Ehlermann and A Vallery, 'Giving Meaning to the Condition of Effect on Trade: The Court's Judgment in Xunta de Galicia, a Missed Opportunity?' (2005) 4 *European State Aid Law Quarterly* 709; A Biondi and P Eeckhout, 'State aid and obstacles to trade', in A Biondi et al. (eds), *Law of State Aid in the European Union* (OUP 2003), 103–16; see also the most recent *de minimis* Commission Regulation in state aid 1407/2013, OJ L352/1, 24 December 2013, previous versions were adopted in 1996, 2001, and 2006.

[35] Case C-22/78 *Hugin Kassaregister AB* [1979] ECLI:EU:C:1979:138.

[36] *Consten and Grundig* (n 33) para 341; *Société Technique Minière* (n 33) para 38.

[37] Case C-5/69, *Völk/Vervaecke* [1969] ECLI:EU:C:1969:35. Accordingly, EU competition law is only applicable to agreements and practices which are capable of appreciably affecting trade between Member States, in other words, agreements and practices capable of having a minimum level of cross-border effects within the EU.

[38] Botta et al. refer to the broad interpretation of the elements 'indirect' in Case 193/83 *Windsurfing* [1986] ECLI:EU:C:1986:75; and the 'potential' effect in Case C-359/01 *British Sugar* [2004] ECLI:EU:C:2004:255 and Joined Cases C-125, 133, 135 and 137/07P *Erste Group Bank Ag and Others* [2009] ECLI:EU:C:2009:576. M Botta et al., 'The assessment of the effect on trade by the national competition authorities of the "new" Member States: Another legal partition of the Internal Market?' (2015) 52 *Common Market Law Review* 1247.

[39] *Völk/Vervaecke* (n 37) para 7; most recently in Case C-226/11 *Expedia Inc v Autorité de la concurrence and Others* [2012] ECLI:EU:C:2012:795, para 16.

[40] Botta et al. (n 38) 1255. [41] ibid, 1256.

[42] Guidelines on the effect on trade concept contained in Articles 81 and 82 of the Treaty, 2004/C 101/07, point 52.

guidance and do not bind either the national courts or the authorities of the Member States in their application of the effect on trade concept Articles 101 and 102 TFEU.[43]

Establishing such a broad jurisdictional scope used to be relevant when many of the Member States in the EEC and later EC had no or only ineffective competition law regimes. As many EU Member States abandoned their ineffective competition system during the 1980s and 1990s and adopted new competition laws similar to the rules laid down in Articles 101 and 102 TFEU, the relevance of a broad concept of 'effect on trade' has changed. In fact, the interpretation of the idea of an 'effect on trade' by the NCAs became critical to the effective and uniform functioning of the decentralized enforcement of Articles 101 and 102 TFEU for the following reasons.

If an 'effect on trade' between Member States is established by an NCA, then the NCA and national courts are obliged to apply Articles 101 and 102 TFEU in parallel to national competition rules. Furthermore, under Article 11(3) and (4) Regulation 1/2003 they are obliged to inform the Commission and the ECN of the initiation of investigation and also of the envisaged decision. If the 'effect on trade' criterion is established, it also means that the Commission has the prerogative of bringing the Article 101 and 102 investigations of the NCAs to an end by opening its own proceedings against the same violation.[44] In other words, on the basis of Article 11(6) the Commission can relieve an NCA of its competence for reasons of coherent application.

However, if the NCAs apply a narrow interpretation of the 'effect on trade' doctrine and do not thus establish its presence in individual cases, all the above obligations do not apply and thus also the significant mechanisms which were laid down with the aim of safeguarding uniform and consistent application of Articles 101 and 102 TFEU remain inactive. In addition, as Botta et al. argued, if NCAs apply only national competition law they may adopt decisions which would not be possible under Regulation 1/2003. We need only think of the CJEU's judgment in *Tele2 Polska*,[45] where the Court ruled that NCAs, in this case from Poland, cannot adopt a non-infringement decision on the basis of Article 5 of Regulation 1/2003. In cases where only national competition law is applied, the NCAs may also be subject to different procedural guarantees than the procedural guarantees developed by the EU Courts under Regulation 1/2003.[46] There remain significant differences across Member States on the rights of defence of undertakings and on third party rights in competition law proceedings.[47]

Botta, Svetlicinii, and Bernatt[48] analysed the interpretation of the 'effect on trade' doctrine in six Central and Eastern European Member States and found that on the one hand, not all of these NCAs systematically conduct an analysis of this idea in their decisions and on the other hand, that some of them adopted a narrow interpretation in contrast with

[43] Guidelines on the effect on trade concept contained in Articles 81 and 82 of the Treaty, 2004/C 101/07, point 3. See also *Expedia* (n 39) para 29.

[44] Article 11(6) Regulation 1/2003; see also Opinion of AG Mazák of 7 December 2010 in Case C-375/09 *Prezes Urz ę du Ochrony Konkurencji i Konsumentów v Tele2 Polska sp z o.o, now Netia SA w Warszawie* [2011] ECLI:EU:C:2011:270, para 47.

[45] See *Tele2 Polska* (n 44).

[46] For example, the lack of professional legal privilege or third party access to the competition law procedure in Poland if the NCA applies Polish competition law alone, while the *AKZO* doctrine (C-550/07 *AKZO*) applies when it employs Arts 101 and 102 TFEU. See Botta et al. (n 38) 1251. M Bernatt, 'Convergence of procedural standards in the European competition proceedings' (2012) 8 *The Competition Law Review* 260–267

[47] There are further differences in criminal sanctions, liability in groups of undertakings, liability of associations of undertakings, succession of undertakings, prescription periods and the standard of proof, the power to impose structural remedies, as well as the ability of NCAs formally to set enforcement priorities. See also K Ost, 'From Regulation 1 to Regulation 2: National Enforcement of EU Cartel Prohibition and the Need For Further Convergence' (2014) 5 *Journal of European Competition Law and Practice* 125.

[48] Botta et al. (n 38).

the CJEU's case law.[49] Tóth reports on the inconsistent way the Hungarian NCA has applied the 'effect on trade' doctrine.[50] While the Hungarian NCA has often acknowledged the existence of 'effect on trade' between Member States, it has analysed the respective case under Hungarian competition rules while extensively relying on EU case law on the respective legal issues.[51] However, while these decisions may be in line with EU law in terms of the substantive competition law issues, the procedural rules which frame the decision making can still differ. Taccani reviewed Italian, French, German, and UK interpretations and he shows that while Italian NCAs and courts seem to apply a broad interpretation, other jurisdictions have applied a more restrictive interpretation of the notion.[52] Even though these are not complete overviews of the twenty-eight NCAs' practices, they still signal the uncertainty and the inconsistency governing the application of this doctrine. The fact that Member States enjoy a wide margin of discretion in interpreting this notion means that they may be enforcing national competition laws more actively than EU rules.

The next section will analyse another key element of the decentralized enforcement system, namely the way the Commission and the NCAs coordinate their actions.

5. Case allocation and coordination mechanisms

As mentioned above, one of the key challenges of the decentralized enforcement system is how to maintain uniform and consistent application of the Treaty rules among the various EU and national actors. The NCAs and the Commission enjoy wide discretion concerning case allocation and while EU law should have primacy, parallel proceedings are not prohibited by Regulation 1/2003. In order to coordinate the enforcement of Articles 101 and 102 TFEU among the various enforcers, Article 11(3)–(4) of Regulation 1/2003 obliges NCAs to inform the Commission of cases where an effect on trade between the Member States has been established and thus provide not only information on ongoing cases and envisaged decisions but also to give the Commission the possibility to veto such decisions (Article 11(6)) if it considers it necessary. Article 16 of Regulation 1/2003 is also aimed at maintaining consistency between national and EU competition laws as well as at guaranteeing uniform application of the two sets of rules. Moreover, Regulation 1/2003 established the ECN for close cooperation between the European Commission and national authorities. The ECN lays down the rules for case allocation and other cooperation mechanisms for NCAs when they apply Articles 101 and 102 TFEU.

The ECN is a highly juridified network with detailed rules defined in Regulation 1/2003 and in the Notice on cooperation within the Network of Competition Authorities. The ECN is characterized by formalism to safeguard consistent application of the law, and by a quasi-hierarchical structure where the Commission plays a central role. Unlike other European regulatory networks, the ECN did not emerge as an initiative of the Member

[49] ibid.

[50] T Tóth, 'The reception and application of EU competition rules in Hungary: an organic evolution', in M Varjú and E Várnay (eds), *The Law of the European Union in Hungary: Institutions, Processes and the Law* (HVG-ORAC 2014) 241–87, 253–6.

[51] See decisions of the Hungarian Competition Council: VJ-51/2005, Vj-69/2005, VJ-83/2005, VJ-180/2004, VJ-1/2008.

[52] I Taccani, 'The scope of EU and national competition law', in B Cortese (ed), *EU competition law, between public and private enforcement* (2014) 55 *Kluwer International Competition Law Series* 63–77. The broad interpretation of the Italian practice may be related to the fact that Italians apply only EU Law to cases falling under the prohibition of Arts 101–102. That might also explain the wide interpretation.

States, but was centrally designed and established by the Commission.[53] The two main pillars of the ECN are case allocation and information exchange. Information sharing within the ECN is based on formal obligations. On the basis of Articles 11(3) and (4) of Regulation 1/2003, Member States share information about their investigations and about the decisions to be taken. They may also share confidential information, though respecting the safeguards guaranteeing fundamental rights (Articles 11 and 12(1)).[54] While the ECN has been formally established with a vertical division of enforcement powers between the Commission and the NCAs, it has proved far more horizontal in practice.[55] In fact, the Commission's reports on the functioning of Regulation 1/2003 show that case allocation does not form the core of the ECN's work. Few cases have been reallocated[56] and sharing information about specific cases has been only sporadic.[57]

Beyond these statistics and despite the fact that the ECN was created to avoid multiple proceedings and subdivision of investigations, there are recent examples from the case law which show that the NCAs and the Commission may find it efficient to allocate different aspects of the same case to different authorities.[58] In *Orange*, for example, in relation to an alleged infringement of Article 102 TFEU in the market for internet connectivity services, the General Court (GC) confirmed the Commission's powers to investigate practices which had been previously investigated by an NCA. While Orange argued that the Commission's inspections concerned identical practices to those investigated by the French Competition Authority, thus in violation of the *ne bis in idem* principle, the GC held that as the French NCA had not found an infringement and as NCAs are not empowered to determine that Articles 101 or 102 TFEU have not been infringed (*Tele2Polska*) the Commission could adopt decisions on Articles 101 and 102 TFEU even if they contradict findings by NCAs.[59] This case confirms the wide discretion the NCAs and the Commission enjoy in how they allocate cases and as Nazzini pointed out, raises a fundamental issue for the rights of defence, as the parties under investigation may only challenge such decisions *ex post*.[60]

In an earlier case, *Toshiba*, the CJEU had the opportunity in to clarify important questions on case allocation, the parallel enforcement of national and EU law and the compatibility of this multilevel enforcement system with the Rule of Law.[61] In *Toshiba* the CJEU was asked to interpret Article 11(6) of Regulation 1/2003 and the *ne bis in idem* principle concerning a parallel investigation of a cartel by the Commission and the Czech

[53] For example, the creation of the European Electricity Regulation Forum or the European Gas Regulation Forum were established as informal fora of sectoral public and private actors, who met infrequently and had no formal powers or organization. Later, informal groups of national independent regulatory authorities were established, such as the Independent Regulators Group for telecommunications or the Forum of European Securities and the Council of European Energy Regulators that were networks set up by up by national regulatory authorities. D Coen and M Thatcher, 'Network Governance and Multi-level Delegation: European Networks of Regulatory Agencies' (2008) 28 *Journal of Public Policy* 49.

[54] They may conduct inspections of premises or other fact-finding activities on behalf of another NCA investigating a case (Art 22 (1)).

[55] I Maher and O Stefan, 'Competition Law in Europe: The Challenge of a Network Constitution', in OD Prosser and T Rawlings (eds), *The Regulatory State: Constitutional Implications* (OUP 2010) 188.

[56] Commission Staff Working Paper (n 29) points 214–24. Interestingly, there is much less information provided on specifically case allocation in the ten years report. European Commission, Commission Staff Working Document—Enhancing competition enforcement by the Member States' competition authorities: institutional and procedural issues (2014) SWD 231/2, 9 July 2014, http://ec.europa.eu/competition/antitrust/legislation/swd_2014_231_en.pdf, accessed 20 October 2016, points 237–45.

[57] Monti (n 1) 70.

[58] Case T-64/12 *Henkel AG* [2013] ECLI:EU:T:2013:116. Case T-128/11 *LG Display* [2011] ECLI:EU:T:2014:88. Case T-402/13 *Orange* [2013] ECLI:EU:T:2014:991.

[59] *Orange* (n 58). [60] Nazzini (n 4) 278.

[61] See *Toshiba* (n 27) and Case C-68/12 *Protimonopolný úrad Slovenskej republiky* (cartel of banks) [2013] ECLI:EU:C:2013:71.

NCA. While the Czech NCA was investigating the case before the Czech Republic's accession to the EU, there was no question of the *ne bis in idem* principle raised on the facts. While similarly to *Orange*, the Court's judgment in *Toshiba* illustrates that a stricter interpretation of the *ne bis in idem* principle[62] should be adopted, there are also broader implications to the judgment. In *Toshiba* the CJEU confirmed the *Walt Wilhelm* dictum and justified parallel proceedings by stating that the Commission's investigation merely suspends an NCA's investigation, but does not remove it.[63]

The Court's ruling has been criticized as contradicting the development of national competition laws, largely converging with the EU Treaty provisions and the various legal rules and mechanisms established by Regulation 1/2003 and the accompanying Notices which safeguard uniform and consistent application.[64] The main aim of the decentralized enforcement system was to avoid parallel proceedings and establish a single best-placed NCA to investigate a given case. In *Walt Wilhelm* the Court still argued that parallel proceedings were justified on the basis of the fact that EU and national completion laws had different objectives and the relationship between EU and national competition laws had not been regulated.[65] However, by now the competition laws of the EU Member States have considerably converged towards the rules under Articles 101 and 102 TFEU, as also acknowledged by the Court in *Allianz Hungária*.[66] Accordingly, the parallel investigations and the Court's ruling in *Walt Wilhelm* seem to have lost their validity in the decentralized enforcement system. In view of that, the Court's ruling that the Commission's investigation merely suspends the investigation of the NCA but does not remove it raises the question of why an NCA would continue an investigation once the Commission has investigated the cross-border or EU-wide effects of the same case. In fact, this way the same act by the same undertakings may be investigated and prosecuted twice and thus violate the principle of *ne bis in idem*.[67]

Case allocation thus seems to be functioning ineffectively as the low number of cases allocated and the CJEU's ruling in *Toshiba* demonstrate. Moreover, the way it operates now actually undermines Rule of Law principles, such as *ne bis in idem*, and the legitimacy of parallel proceedings. These concerns have been overlooked by the Commission as it stated in its latest report on the functioning of Regulation 1/2003 that the ECN responded effectively to stakeholder concerns about the 'risk of diverging outcomes in a system with multiple enforcers' and '[T]he results achieved within the ECN in the last decade confirm that the fears of some commentators that NCAs would be operating in isolation from each other and from the Commission and develop "national" versions of the EU competition rules were unfounded.'[68] However, at present the decentralized system as practiced by the NCAs and in the Court's interpretations is developing exactly in the opposite direction, namely as standalone variations of national enforcement in isolation of the EU law sphere. A recent example is *Booking.com*, where several NCAs coordinated their investigations, but

[62] The EU courts apply a threefold test in EU competition law when they interpret the *ne bis in idem* principle: identity of the facts, identity of the offender, and identity of the legal interest protected. Joined Cases C-204/00 P, C-205/00 P, C-211/00P, C-213/00P, C-217/00P and C-219/00P *Aalborg Portland and others* [2004] ECLI:EU:C:2004:6, para 338. AG Kokott argued in *Toshiba* that the Court should adopt a criterion only on the identity of the facts as this is the criterion the EU courts apply in other fields of EU law and which the ECtHR applies under Article 4, Protocol 7 to the ECHR. Opinion of AG Kokott of 8 September 2011 in *Toshiba* (n 27).

[63] *Toshiba* (n 27) para 79.

[64] Monti (n 1); Nazzini (n 4).

[65] *Toshiba* (n 27) para 5, referring to Article 103(2)(e) TFEU.

[66] Case C-32/11 *Allianz Hungária Biztosító Zrt* [2012] ECLI:EU:C:2013:160, paras 21–2; see also Case C-345/14, *SIA for Latvia* [2015] ECLI:EU:C:2015:784, paras 12–14.

[67] Monti (n 1) 275, Nazzini (n 4) 300.

[68] Commission Staff Working Document 231 (n 56), point 229.

all ultimately decided to continue in their own jurisdictions.[69] Such national solutions may also be 'encouraged' by domestic legislation which restrict the NCAs' sanctions only to domestic effects of anticompetitive practices, such as the case is in Germany.[70]

While witnessing such a 'nationalization' of enforcement, there are also indications that the decentralized enforcement system has in fact preserved important characteristics of hierarchical governance and thus the Commission's central role.[71] Hierarchical governance is present in the form of directly applicable legislative instruments such as the Treaty provisions and regulations, which directly enter national legal regimes. There is also strong top-down pressure from the Commission to the Member States to align national competition rules to the EU law provisions.[72] The traditional forms of governance are further strengthened by a large body of case law, the traditional application of economic analysis, and the active involvement of the epistemic community of competition lawyers.[73]

The ECN has also preserved a key role for the Commission. First, in the legislative framework of the ECN the Commission's role has been established as *primus inter pares*, guarding the uniform application of EU rules.[74] While it has been argued[75] that the ECN functions as a successful 'joint enterprise' between the Member States and the Commission, in practice the Commission still plays a fundamental role. It may not make use of its legislative prerogatives on the basis of Article 11(6) to relieve an NCA of its competence for reasons of coherent application,[76] but it does play an influential role. The Commission sets the agenda of the plenary meetings and even though the NCAs are invited to approve it and to add items,[77] the NCAs stated that agenda setting is a powerful tool and even though

[69] See for example http://www.bundeskartellamt.de/SharedDocs/Meldung/EN/Pressemitteilungen/2015/23_12_2015_Booking.com.html, accessed 20 October 2016; Editorial comments (2015) 51 CMLR 1191–1200; B Csépai, '*Toshiba* v *Commission*: Parental Liability of a Minority Shareholder' (2016) 7 *Journal of European Competition Law & Practice* 115.

[70] The jurisdiction of the German Federal Cartel Office is limited by the effects test in Art 130(2) of the German Act against Restraints of Competition. See also the OFT's guidance as to the appropriate amount of a penalty (OFT 423, September 2012) para 2.10. 'In cases concerning infringements of Article 101 and/or Article 102, the OFT *may*, in determining the starting point, take into account effects in another Member State of the agreement or conduct concerned. Where it does so, the OFT will take into account effects in another Member State through its assessment of relevant turnover. The OFT *may* consider turnover generated in another Member State if the relevant geographic market is wider than the UK and the express consent of the relevant Member State or NCA, as appropriate, is given in each particular case.' (emphasis added).

[71] S Wilks, 'Agency Escape: Decentralization or Dominance of the European Commission in the Modernization of Competition Policy?' (2005) 18 *Governance* 431.

[72] This feature was a core characteristic of the accession process of new Member States in 2004, 2007, and 2013, where the candidate countries had to align their competition law regime to that of the EU due to EU conditionality.

[73] F Van Waarden and M Drahos, 'Courts and (epistemic) communities in the convergence of competition policies' (2002) 9 *Journal of European Public Policy* 928; Maher, 2007 (n 12) 1730.

[74] Regulation 1/2003 granted the Commission new enforcement powers and extended some of its existing ones. Art 9 Regulation 1/2003 grants the Commission the power to accept commitments from the parties under investigation in Art 101 and 102 procedures and makes these commitments binding. Regulation 1/2003 also extended its search powers during sector inquiries. It has given it the prerogative to bring Arts 101 and 102 investigations of NCAs to an end by opening its own proceedings against the same violation. Art 11(6) Regulation 1/2003; see also Opinion of AG Mazák of 7 December 2010 in *Tele2 Polska* (n 44) para 47.

[75] Commission Staff Working Paper (n 29); Commission Staff Working Document—Ten Years of Antitrust Enforcement under Regulation 1/2003, SWD(2014) 230/2, 9 July 2014, http://ec.europa.eu/competition/antitrust/legislation/swd_2014_230_en.pdf, accessed 20 October 2016, paras 229–44; H Kassim and K Wright, 'The European Competition Network: a European Regulatory Network with a Difference' (Dublin 17–19 June 2010) Paper presented to the Third Biennial Conference of ECPR Standing Group on Regulatory Governance, http://regulation.upf.edu/dublin-10-papers/2E3.pdf, accessed 12 October 2016; Svetiev (n 22); DMB Gerard, 'The ECN—network antitrust enforcement in the European Union', in D Geradin and I Lianos, *Research Handbook on EU Competition Law* (Edward Elgar 2013), 181.

[76] Commission Staff Working Paper (n 29) para 28; Report on the functioning of Regulation 1/2003; and Commission Staff Working Paper accompanying the Report on the functioning of Regulation 1/2003 (n 75).

[77] Kassim and Wright (n 75).

discussions are not dominated by the Commission, its officials take part in working groups and subgroups which do take a very active role.[78]

The ECN has often been characterized as an experimentalist governance model[79] because it employs new governance modes, such as consultations, negotiations, and soft-law instruments. It has been argued that there is a certain 'can-do-ness'[80] in the work of the ECN and that it has been functioning without any major conflicts or serious political or judicial challenges since its conception.[81] Nevertheless, we need to evaluate this success in the light of the fact that the ECN was primarily designed as a policy enforcement network, but now functions much more in the capacity of a policy-making network through informal discussions and mutual policy learning among the NCAs. Hence its function in the shared enforcement sphere between the Commission and Member States seems to be very limited in practice.

These facts and the analysis of case allocation clearly challenge public views on the success of the decentralized enforcement system[82] and support those commentators who argue that in fact recentralization has taken place.[83] Formulated differently, the Commission's role is being recentralized, while the national actors pull towards their domestic locus of authority instead of engaging in coordination. The next section will investigate how.

6. Multilevel governance under Regulation 1/2003

As mentioned above, uniform and consistent application of EU competition rules became crucial in the multilevel architecture of EU competition law enforcement. While the previous section assessed the various mechanisms for case allocation and coordination to achieve this goal, this section will examine which harmonization processes emerged and how these processes are geared from the bottom up by the Member States, and from top down by the Commission.

First, Regulation 1/2003 contains some basic rules on the powers of the NCAs but leaves national procedures and institutional designs unaddressed. Article 5 lists their powers when they apply Articles 101 and 102 TFEU by actually listing the type of decisions the NCAs can take in such cases. Article 5 is a very basic provision and does not formally regulate or harmonize the procedural rules to be followed by the NCAs or the ECN.[84] This

[78] This information has been received through conducting semi-structured interviews with NCAs in CEECS in 2013.

[79] Svetiev concluded that the ECN leaves substantial scope for the emergence of experimentalist governance mechanisms. His analysis focuses on the ECN's Model Leniency Programme and conducts a textual analysis of the programme where he identifies the presence of experimentalist governance. Svetiev (n 22).

[80] Maher (n 12); European Commission, Annual Report on Competition Policy (2005) http://ec.europa.eu/competition/publications/annual_report/2005/en.pdf, accessed 20 October 2016, 14, 69.

[81] This alleged success rests on peer esteem, trust, confidentiality, and credibility among the ECN members and is strengthened by a strong epistemic community of lawyers, officials, and academics. *Waarden and Drahos* (n 73) 928; Maher (n 23) 425.

[82] A Italianer, 'The ECN, convergence and enforcement of EU competition law: achievements and challenges' (3 October 2014 Vilnius) Lithuanian Presidency European Competition Day, http://ec.europa.eu/competition/speeches/text/sp2013_08_en.pdf, accessed 20 October 2016; WPJ Wils, 'Ten Years of Regulation 1/2003 – A Retrospective' (2013) 4 *Journal of European Competition Law & Practice* 293; B Lasserre, 'The future of the European Competition Network' (16 May, 2013) Keynote speech, Vth Intertic conference on antitrust policy, http://www.autoritedelaconcurrence.fr/doc/intervention_BrunoLasserre_ECN_rome_mai13.pdf, accessed 12 October 2016; interview of the President of the *Bundeskartellamt* and the Chairman of the ICN, Andreas Mundt, to Concurrences Competition Law Journal; 'Focus, implementation, inclusiveness – The impact of the ICN' (2013), http://www.bundeskartellamt.de/SharedDocs/Interviews/EN/Concurrence-ImpactICN_neu.html, accessed 20 October 2016; Kassim and Wright (n 75).

[83] Monti (n 1); S Wilks, 'Agency Escape: Decentralization or Dominance of the European Commission in the Modernization of Competition Policy?' (2005) 18 *Governance* 431.

[84] Commission Staff Working Paper (n 29), para 200.

means that the NCAs apply the same substantive rules, but in divergent procedural frameworks and may impose different sanctions. These procedural differences had been addressed to some extent in Articles 11 and 12 of Regulation 1/2003 through the cooperation of the NCAs within the ECN.[85]

With regard to the institutional setup of NCAs, under Article 35 of Regulation 1/2003, each Member State had a clear obligation to designate a competition authority responsible for the application of Articles 101 and 102 TFEU before 1 May 2004.[86] The authorities chosen could be administrative or judicial in nature. The only requirement was that they have to be designated to guarantee that the provisions of Regulation 1/2003 are effectively complied with.[87] Beyond Article 35 of Regulation 1/2003, neither further requirements nor additional formal rules have been formulated on the powers and procedures to be followed by the NCAs.[88] Only recently has the independence of NCAs been gaining relevance in EU law.[89] EU law has traditionally focused on independence from market players[90] and it is this very feature which the Courts had established as a core element in regulated markets.[91] While European legislation has become detailed with respect to the concept of independence, the EU judiciary has not formulated any general principles on the independence of regulatory authorities.[92] Accordingly, EU law requires regulators to be independent from political institutions, yet without laying down the criteria for independence that regulatory authorities must meet.[93] Regulation 1/2003 does not specify any kind of requirements on the formal independence of NCAs.[94] However, political independence from central

[85] ECN's Working Group on cooperation issues and due process monitor this voluntary convergence among the Member States. Individual Reports provide an overview of the different systems and procedures for antitrust investigations within the ECN (2012), http://ec.europa.eu/competition/ecn/documents.html, accessed 20 October 2016.

[86] Article 35(1) Regulation 1/2003: 'The Member States shall designate the competition authority or authorities responsible for the application of Articles 81 and 82 of the Treaty in such a way that the provisions of this regulation are effectively complied with. The measures necessary to empower those authorities to apply those Articles shall be taken before 1 May 2004. The authorities designated may include courts'.

[87] Point 2 of the Notice on cooperation within the NCA provides that 'Under general principles of Community law, Member States are under an obligation to set up a sanctioning system providing for sanctions which are effective, proportionate and dissuasive for infringements of EC law'. See also Case C-176/03 *Commission v Council* [2005] ECLI:EU:C:2005:542, paras 46–55.

[88] Albeit that their competences were set out very roughly in Arts 5 and 6 Regulation 1/2003. Although national procedural rules had to provide for the admission of the Commission as *amicus curiae* in national procedures, NCAs need to be empowered to conduct examinations in accordance with Regulation 1/2003, and Member States have to report to the Commission. The Commission retains broad supervisory powers which allows it to intervene in proceedings before national authorities and which in fact enables it to act as 'primus inter pares'. See Art 11(6).

[89] Commission Staff Working Document 231 (n 56).

[90] The Commission had already introduced in 1988 in Article 6 Directive 88/301 on competition in the markets in telecommunications terminal equipment, an obligation on the Member States to entrust the regulation of terminal equipment to a body independent from market parties active in the provision of telecoms services or equipment. This requirement of independence has also been implemented in the second liberalization package in the energy and telecoms sector.

[91] See the judgments in Case C-202/88 *France v Commission* [1991] ECLI:EU:C:1990:64, paras 51–2; Case C-18/88 *RTT v GB-Inno-BM* [1991] ECLI:EU:C:1991:474, paras 25–6; Case C-82/07 *Comisión del Mercado de las Telecomunicaciones* [2008] ECLI:EU:C:2008:143.

[92] The latest package of liberalization Directives of 2009 mentions a general principle of independence towards the legislative and executive organs. Art 35 Directive 2009/72 on electricity compels Member States to make the regulatory authority 'functionally independent from any other public or private entity' and give it the autonomy to decide 'independently of any public body'. Art 39 Directive 2009/73 for gas formulates the same obligation. Directive 2009/140 on electronic communications states that 'national regulatory authorities responsible for *ex-ante* market regulation or for the resolution of disputes between undertakings [...] shall act independently and shall not seek or take instructions from any other body in relation to the exercise of these tasks assigned to them under national law implementing Community law'.

[93] CJ Hanretty, P Larouche, and AP Reindl, 'Independence, Accountability and Perceived Quality of Regulators' (2012) *CERRE Report*.

[94] Case C-53/03 *Syfait* [2005] ECLI:EU:C:2005:333, paras 31–6.

government is not guaranteed in all countries, a fact that can be problematic as competition authorities have to use their expertise independently from political and market actors.[95] It is not surprising that the Commission is now calling for more independence for NCAs in order to enhance further the enforcement of EU competition law.[96]

Articles 5 and 35 of Regulation 1/2003 imposed very rudimentary obligations on the Member States and allow for legal diversity in national procedures and institutional designs. This approach is in line with the general principle of subsidiarity, as enshrined in Article 5 TEU, and respects the Member States' procedural autonomy. This freedom is however not unlimited. Article 4(3) TEU requires the Member States to take all appropriate measures to ensure fulfillment of the obligations arising out of the EU Treaty and facilitate the achievement of the Community's tasks.[97] The diversity of the NCAs' institutional design is largely determined by country-specific traditions.[98]

Given this diverse procedural and institutional landscape, it has been questioned whether the decentralized enforcement system where NCAs operate under different national procedural rules and impose a variety of sanctions and remedies, could jeopardize effective EU law enforcement.

Recent cases such as *VEBIC*,[99] *Tele2 Polska*,[100] *Orange*,[101] and *Schenker*[102] clearly signal that there are fundamental legal puzzles which arise when NCAs apply Articles 101 and 102 TFEU under domestic procedural rules.[103] Accordingly, it has been argued that consistent

[95] The most recent and comprehensive study on the issue of the formal independence of NCAs is likely to be the work of Guidi, who finds extensive variations in the independence of the NCAs. However, Guidi's study raises the question of how an NCA's *de iure* independence reflects its *de facto* independence. M. Guidi, 'Does independence affect regulatory performance? The case of national competition authorities in the European Union' (2011) 64 *European University Institute Working Papers*; M Guidi, 'Delegation and varieties of capitalism: Explaining the independence of national competition agencies in the European Union' (2014) 12 *Comparative European Politics* 343.

[96] Commission Staff Working Document 231 (n 56).

[97] Moreover, they should 'abstain from any measure which could jeopardise the attainment of the objectives of this Treaty'. The ECJ has also developed the doctrine of useful effect in EU competition law on the basis of this loyalty principle. According to this doctrine, the Member States may not introduce legislation or take decisions which would deprive the competition rules of their useful effect. This doctrine has no explicit legal basis. In the former EC Treaty this doctrine was founded on Art 3(1)(g) (now implemented in Protocol No 27 on the internal market and competition) read in conjunction with Art 10 (now Art 4(3) TEU) and Arts 81 and 82 EC (now Arts 101 and 102 TFEU). Case 267/86 *Van Eycke v ASPA* [1988] ECLI:EU:C:1988:427, para 16.

[98] The Reports of the ECN's Working Group on cooperation issues and due process provide an overview of the different systems and procedures for antitrust investigations within the ECN (31 October 2012); http://ec.europa.eu/competition/ecn/decision_making_powers_report_en.pdf, accessed 20 October 2016, 6–7; K Ost, 'From Regulation 1 to Regulation 2: National Enforcement of EU Cartel Prohibition and the Need for Further Convergence' (2014) 5 *Journal of European Competition Law & Practice* 125.

[99] See Case C-439/08 *Vlaamse federatie van verenigingen van Brood- en Banketbakkers, Ijsbereiders en Chocoladebewerkers (VEBIC) VZW* [2010] ECLI:EU:C:2010:739, para 56: 'Article 35(1) requests that the NCAs are designated in such a way that the provisions of Regulation 1/2003 are effectively complied with. Agencies must ensure that the Treaty competition provisions are applied effectively in the general interest'. See PJMM Van Cleynenbreugel, 'Institutional assimilation in the wake of EU competition law decentralization' (2012) 8 *The Competition Law Review* 285.

[100] *Tele2 Polska* (n 44); Case C-360/09 *Pfleiderer AG v Bundeskartellamt* [2011] ECLI:EU:C:2011:270; Case C-681/11 *Bundeswettbewerbsbehörde and Bundeskartellanwalt v Schenker & Co AG and Others* [2013] ECLI:EU:C:2013:404; Case C-557/12 *Kone AG, Otis GmbH, Schindler Aufzüge und Fahrteppen GmbH and Others v OBB-Infrastruktur AG* [2014] ECLI:EU:C:2014:1317, para 32.

[101] *Orange* (n 58). In this case the GC confirmed and further clarified the powers of the Commission to investigate practices that had been investigated earlier by an NCA. The GC confirmed that the Commission's unannounced inspection on Orange's premises in relation to an alleged infringement of Art 102 TFEU in the market for internet connectivity services did not violate the principle of *ne bis in idem*, paras 30–1.

[102] See also *Schenker* (n 100) para 46.

[103] See also as Advocate General Kokott argued:'[i]n those circumstances, it is of fundamental importance that the uniform application of competition rules in the [EU] be maintained. Not only the fundamental objective of equal conditions of competition for undertakings on the single market but also the concern for uniform protection of consumer interests in the entire [EU] would be undermined if in the enforcement of the competition rules of

policy enforcement requires a certain degree of harmonization of procedures, resources, and independence of the NCAs.[104] The form this harmonization is expected to take has been described so far as 'voluntary'. However, this chapter questions this qualification and will argue that it is rather a process initiated from the top down.

7. 'Voluntary' harmonization

Regulation 1/2003 did not formally intervene with the procedures of NCAs over and above Articles 5 and 35 of Regulation 1/2003 and the rules applicable to cooperation mechanisms.[105] As mentioned above, Article 3(2) of Regulation 1/2003 introduced a strict supremacy standard and has reinforced the already ongoing convergence of substantive competition rules towards the EU Treaty provisions. Accordingly, most Member States also began to harmonize certain rules in their procedures to take Regulation 1/2003 and the accompanying soft-law instruments, most notably the leniency Notice, into account.[106] This convergence took place through implementing similar procedural rules as those of the Commission's. The underlying reason for these legal transplants[107] could be that once these rules and enforcement methods work effectively and efficiently in the hands of the Commission, they will also prove successful in the hands of the NCAs.

Later, the Commission examined the existing procedural divergences across Member States and decided to harmonize national rules on procedures further.[108] First, in 2009 the Commission put forward the consideration of soft harmonization or the adoption of certain minimum standards through legislative rules.[109] Then in 2012 the ECN's Report on decision-making powers revealed a high level of convergence among the NCAs, which was considered as a basis for further harmonization of the NCAs' procedures for competition law enforcement.[110] In 2013 this convergence of national competition law procedures

Articles [101 and 102 TFEU] significant disparities occurred between the [NCAs] and courts of the Member States. For that reason, the objective of a uniform application of Articles [101 and 102 TFEU] is a central theme which runs throughout Regulation No 1/2003'. Opinion of AG Kokott of 19 February 2009 in Case C-8/08 *T-Mobile Netherlands and Others* [2009] ECLI:EU:C:2009:343, 85. See judgment of that case, paras 85 and 86. Also N Petit, 'The Principles of Equivalence and Effectiveness as a Limit to National Procedural Autonomy' (5–8 March 2014) *ENTraNCE*, https://antitrustlair.files.wordpress.com/2014/07/the-principles-of-equivalence-and-effectiveness-n-petit-final.pdf, accessed 12 October 2016.

[104] F Cengiz, 'Regulation 1/2003 Revisited' (2009) 42 *TILEC Discussion Paper* 17; C Gauer, 'Does the Effectiveness of the EU Network of Competition Authorities Require a Certain Degree of Harmonisation of National Procedures and Sanctions?', in CD Ehlermann and I Atanasiu (eds), *European Competition Law Annual 2000: The Modernisation of EC Antitrust Policy* (Hart 2001), 187–201; F Jenny, 'Does the Effectiveness of the EU Network of Competition Authorities Depend on a Certain Degree of Homogeneity within its Membership?' in Ehlermann and Atanasiu (n 104), 208–10.

[105] The Commission stated that in important respects, the Regulation reconciled the requirements of substantive coherence with the existing procedural diversity amongst NCAs. Commission Staff Working Paper (n 29) para 200.

[106] Results of the questionnaire on the reform of Member States' national competition laws after EC Regulation No. 1/2003 (2013), http://ec.europa.eu/competition/ecn/convergence_table_en.pdf, accessed 20 October 2016.

[107] Convergence between different legal rules towards an efficient model may take place as a result of a legal transplant or as an outcome of a competitive process between different legal formants. In the first case, legal transplants are implemented because they proved to be efficient in other legal systems. In the second case, convergence towards efficiency is the result of the interaction between different legal formants. So while legal transplants are governed by a hierarchy, the second scenario is governed by competition among legal formants: U Mattei et al., 'A. Comparative Law and Economics', in B Bouckaert and G De Geest (eds), *Encyclopedia of Law and Economics* (Edward Elgar 2000) 508–11.

[108] Commission Staff Working Paper (n 91) para 207. See also ECN Investigative Powers Report and Decision Making Powers Report (2002) http://ec.europa.eu/competition/ecn/documents.html, accessed 12 October 2016.

[109] Commission Staff Working Paper (n 29) para 207. See ECN Investigative Powers Report and Decision Making Powers Report' (31 October 2012), http://ec.europa.eu/competition/ecn/documents.html, accessed 12 October 2016.

[110] ECN Investigative Powers Report and Decision Making Powers Report (n 109).

was summarized in the ECN's Recommendations on key investigative and decision-making powers.[111]

The 'voluntary' convergence thus grew into an ECN's Working Group on cooperation issues and due process, which monitors convergence among the Member States and provides an overview of the different systems and procedures for competition law investigations within the ECN.[112]

National rules still differ on fundamental aspects of the procedures such as setting priorities, inspecting non-business premises, powers to inspect, requesting information, or taking commitment decisions, imposing behavioural or structural remedies, procedural rights of parties under investigation, e.g. different scope of the privilege against self-incrimination for undertakings, and the enforcement measures and sanctions related to non-compliance with decisions, e.g. some NCAs do not have the power to impose fines directly in case of non-compliance with a commitment decision.[113]

These are differences that significantly affect the scope of investigative and decision-making powers of the NCAs.[114] Moreover, in the area of sanctions such as fines and the nature of sanctions there are also differences across the national laws.[115] Most importantly, it has been the ECN that served as a major catalyst in encouraging Member States and/or NCAs to ensure greater convergence. In view of the divergences identified in the above Reports a set of ECN Recommendations were issued to promote voluntary convergence. The Commission's dominant role in this so-called 'voluntary' harmonization process, which takes place within the framework of the ECN is undeniable. This convergence steers national procedural rules towards the Commission's procedural model.[116] The best example of this is the ECN Model Leniency Programme,[117] which closely resembles the Commission's leniency programme,[118] but illustrative examples are also the review process of Article 102 TFEU and sector specific regulations.[119]

However, the effectiveness of the transplanted rules was not always successful in the different institutional frameworks of the Member States. For example in the Central and Eastern European Member States, where agencies often had to divide resources between several legislative competences and, crucially, depended on institutional capacity.[120] The

[111] ECN Recommendation on Investigative Powers, Enforcement Measures and Sanctions in the context of Inspections and Requests for Information (2013), http://ec.europa.eu/competition/ecn/recommendation_powers_to_investigate_enforcement_measures_sanctions_09122013_en.pdf, accessed 20 October 2016; Commission Staff Working Document 231 (n 56).

[112] Commission Staff Working Document 231 (n 56).

[113] Commission Staff Working Document 231 (n 56), paras 45–6

[114] See also K Ost, 'From Regulation 1 to Regulation 2: National Enforcement of EU Cartel Prohibition and the Need For Further Convergence' (2014) 5 *Journal of European Competition Law and Practice* 125.

[115] Commission Staff Working Document 231 (n 56), paras 62–77.

[116] The 'voluntary' convergence takes place within the ECN's Working Group on cooperation issues and due process, which monitors convergence among the Member States and provides an overview of the different systems and procedures for competition law investigations within the ECN. Documents available at http://ec.europa.eu/competition/ecn/documents.html, accessed 20 October 2016.

[117] ECN Model Leniency Programme (2006) http://ec.europa.eu/competition/ecn/model_leniency_en.pdf, accessed 12 October 2016; and its 2012 revision, http://ec.europa.eu/competition/ecn/mlp_revised_2012_en.pdf, accessed 12 October 2016.

[118] European Commission, Amendments to the Commission Notice on Immunity from fines and reduction of fines in cartel cases (Communication) (2015) OJ C256/1.

[119] Commission Staff Working Paper (n 29) paras 248–9.

[120] This has been confirmed by the most recent example of Croatia; M Kapural, 'New kid on the block-Croatia's path to convergence with EU competition rules' (2014) 5(4) *Journal of Competition Law & Practice* 218.
The NCAs did not enforce the transplanted rules due to constraints to their administrative capacity and to the enforcement tools not having always delivered the expected results. This is for example the case with regard to the power to investigate private premises. This investigative tool has not yet been used in the Czech Republic, Estonia,

ECN Model Leniency Programme,[121] which has often been praised as a success story of the ECN's cooperation mechanism and as a proof of experimental governance, illustrates this in the CEECs. The first programmes adopted proved to be unproductive due to insufficient transparency or uncertainty about eligibility. Many programmes have therefore been revised recently and have now slowly begun to operate, with a few cases in each country.[122]

In sum, Regulation 1/2003 posed a challenge to the uniform application of EU law. When NCAs apply Articles 101 and 102 TFEU, they employ their national procedural rules and impose the remedies and sanctions which are available in their respective legal systems. Consequently, the enforcement of EU competition rules has come to rely on the effective administrative enforcement of EU competition rules through national administrative procedures. While there is a certain degree of 'voluntary' harmonization towards the Commission's procedural model, the above findings confirm the presence of top-down processes rather than bottom-up ones and thus hierarchical governance mechanisms.

8. Conclusion

The goal of the decentralized enforcement system was to make EU competition law enforcement more effective by delegating enforcement powers to NCAs and national courts. An enforcement system of parallel competences between the European Commission and the Member States was created to share the administrative workload of enforcing EU competition law. Rules for case allocation and close cooperation were laid down in the ECN framework to achieve uniform and consistent application of Articles 101 and 102. This decentralized enforcement system is operated by the Commission and the twenty-eight NCAs on the basis of EU and national rules. Its operation appears to have been a success. However, analysing some of the fundamental legal and governance issues in this mixed enforcement system suggests that it has yielded a less positive end result.

This chapter has critically examined how the parallel application of EU and national competition laws is established in Article 3 of Regulation 1/2003 and how it is applied by the NCAs. The 'effect on trade' doctrine and the case allocation and cooperation mechanisms were investigated in particular detail. Establishing an 'effect on trade' between Member States is a fundamental first criterion to trigger the enforcement of EU competition rules. This notion has been consistently interpreted broadly by the Courts and thus provides a wide margin of discretion for the Member States in their application. While there has been little empirical evidence so far of the application of the 'effect on trade' doctrine by the Member States, the few overviews show a diverse interpretation practice across the Member States. Some Member States have applied a narrow interpretation, which could lead to more national cases and thus to outcomes which are beyond the reach of EU law and the fundamental procedural guarantees available in EU law. Some Member States apply this doctrine very inconsistently and thus create a wide margin of discretion for

Hungary, Romania, Slovenia, and the Slovak Republic, and in Bulgaria it does not exist at all. Commission Staff Working Paper (n 29) para 202.

[121] ECN Model Leniency Programme (n 117) and its 2012 revision (n 117).

[122] The Czech NCA applied its leniency programme for the first time in 2004 for a cartel agreement in the energy drinks market. Poland had its first leniency case in a 2006 cartel agreement but had largely revised its 2004 leniency programme in 2009 due to several shortcomings in the previous model. There are also marker systems in the Czech Republic, Hungary, and Slovakia. However, the decision to grant a 'marker' in the Czech Republic is completely at the discretion of the NCA. See M Zahradnik and H Madárová, 'Slovakia' in *International Comparative Legal Guide to: Cartels & Leniency 2009* (Global Legal Group 2009) 214; A Braun and D Bicková, 'Czech Republic', in ibid, 54; G Bacher and J Budai, 'Hungary' in ibid, 102. In Hungary, leniency was applied in a few cartel cases, yet only one of them has since been closed by the NCA, in 2007 (Vj-81/2006).

themselves in whether to use EU or national law. These practices clearly show that there is uncertainty, inconsistency, and perhaps even unwillingness in the application of EU competition rules. This can certainly have a negative influence on the decentralized enforcement of these rules as well as negatively impact the rights of defence. The case allocation practice also shows a gap between the rules of cooperation and their actual application. According to the Commission's statistics, there have been few instances of case allocation and the sharing of information about specific cases has been scarce. The ECN actually functions more as a policy-making forum than as a platform for enforcement cooperation. Moreover, the Court's case law and most importantly its ruling in *Toshiba* has increased this uncertainty, rather than answering questions on case allocation, parallel enforcement, and the application of the principle of *ne bis in idem*. These developments reinforce the possibility that Member States will develop local competition enforcement cultures in isolation instead of in cooperation with other national actors and the Commission, while the opposite would have been the goal under the decentralized framework. Moreover, the fact that the decentralized architecture has preserved the Commission's role as *primus inter pares* and its role, for example, in the harmonization processes within the ECN, which tend to skew the decentralized system towards hierarchical governance rather than experimentalist governance, contradicts the positive views of the decentralized enforcement as a 'joint enterprise'. In fact, they point to re-centralization of power at the Commission level and remote decentralization at Member State level, without meaningful vertical or horizontal cooperation mechanisms. While this might be a worrying development in itself as it endangers the transparency and predictability and thus fundamental Rule of Law principles, its legal implications as represented in the uneven protection of procedural rights and guarantees for parties are also alarming. It is alarming not least because competition law enforcement has often been considered as a model for other fields of economic governance. In that sense, the decentralized enforcement of EU competition law serves as a relevant example in the EU's learning process on informal network governance as a means to enhance the harmonization of national laws and law enforcement. This model cautions that 'bottom-up' processes need to be encouraged and strengthened to nurture effective enforcement policies, disseminate best practices but also safeguard consistency among Member States. A delicate balance between effectiveness and consistent law enforcement needs to be established in the shared enforcement sphere between the EU and national levels.

11

Soft Law and the Enforcement of EU Law

Oana Ştefan

1. Introduction

Soft law, or 'rules of conduct which, in principle, have no legally binding force but which nevertheless may have practical effects'[1] and also legal effects,[2] is a concept which was first developed in public international law.[3] Closely connected in the literature to the challenges imposed on traditional law making methods by globalization, it has become increasingly relevant in the context of the growing importance of non-State actors on the international plane and,[4] in particular, with the growth of international institutions.[5] In the EU context, soft law consists of recommendations and opinions—instruments deprived of legally binding force in accordance with Article 288 TFEU. However, other instruments not mentioned in that article can also be considered soft law—communications, notices, or guidelines. Until 1968, recourse to soft law instruments was exceptional; later, and especially after the establishment of the internal market, they became quite frequent in the European Commission's activities.[6] Today, soft law instruments account for over 10 per cent of EU law.[7]

It has been argued that international soft law comes in an 'infinite variety'; EU soft law is no exception. The number of soft law instruments, as well as of the fields in which they are issued, has increased significantly since 1989, especially following the Maastricht Treaty[8] and the construction of the second and third pillars. Senden classifies soft law into three categories on functional and purposive criteria. The first category (preparatory/informative instruments) includes acts which put forward various proposals for future action. The second category (interpretative/decisional) includes instruments which interpret hard law provisions, or which indicate how the EU institutions consider they should exercise their

[1] F Snyder, 'The Effectiveness of European Community Law: Institutions, Processes, Tools and Techniques' (1993) 56 *Modern Law Review* 19, 64. The definition is susceptible to cover both international and EU soft law (M Cini, 'The Soft Law Approach: Commission Rule-Making in the EU's State aid Regime' (2001) 8 *Journal of European Public Policy* 192, 194).

[2] I thank Professor Snyder for suggesting this completion to his initial definition of soft law during the 6th International Workshop for Young Scholars, 'The Evolution of European Courts: Institutional Change and Continuity', Dublin, 16–17 November 2007.

[3] I Seidl-Hohenveldern, 'International Economic Soft Law' (1979/II) 163 *Recueil des Cours de l'Academie de Droit International* 165, 173–7.

[4] U Mörth, *Soft Law in Governance and Regulation: An Interdisciplinary Analysis* (Edward Elgar 2004) 4.

[5] C Chinkin, 'Normative Development in the International Legal System' in D Shelton (ed), *Commitment and Compliance: The Role of Non-Binding Norms in the International Legal System* (OUP 2000) 28.

[6] S. Leclerc, 'Les communications de la Commission et le marché intérieur. A propos de l'arrêt rendu par la Cour de justice des Communautés européennes le 20 mars 1997 dans l'affaire C-57-95, Rec. (1997), p I-1640 à I-1652' (1998) 34 *Cahiers de Droit Européen* 161, 163.

[7] A von Bogdandy et al., 'Legal Instruments in European Union Law and their Reform: a Systematic Approach on an Empirical Basis' (2004) 23 *Yearbook of European Law* 91, 112. Only recommendations, opinions, and resolutions are included in this count. The notices, guidelines, frameworks, etc issued by the Commission in areas such as competition law or State aid account for 1.4 per cent more. See ibid, 119.

[8] TEU, at Maastricht on 7 February 1992 (entered into force 1 November 1993) [1992] OJ C191/1.

discretion.[9] The third category (steering instruments) comprises those legal and/or political instruments which are intended to steer or guide action in a not legally-binding way, thereby adding to existing acts.[10] In addition, entire 'soft' regulatory mechanisms have been developed at an EU level. Starting with the economic policy area, a 'model of soft policy coordination'[11] was institutionalized in sectors such as employment and social policy, inspired by methodologies developed at the OECD level.[12] The Lisbon Summit of March 2000 codified this model as the 'Open Method of Co-ordination' (OMC).[13] The OMC is a dynamic mode of governance, whose structure and objectives have transformed over time, since the launch of the Lisbon strategy in 2000, its reshuffling in 2005, and the transition into the Europe 2020 project in 2010.[14] It consists of fixing guidelines for the Union, and timetables to achieve goals in certain policy fields. It also entails establishing indicators and benchmarks for the Member States to compare best practices. The OMC presupposes translating the European guidelines into national policies, and involves monitoring, evaluation, and peer review to foster mutual learning.[15]

Soft law is an essentially composite phenomenon and a single analytical narrative to categorize such instruments cannot be easily achieved. It is beyond the aims of this chapter to delve into soft law taxonomies and their critique;[16] it suffices for now to acknowledge that the vast variety of instruments is bound to determine a variety in enforcement mechanisms. Furthermore, as expressed in the international relations literature, the effects that soft law can have in the absence of legally binding force remain rather uncertain, which makes the enforceability of such instruments problematic.[17]

At least at first glance, it would appear that enforcing soft law must be different to enforcing hard law. The EU legal studies literature generally contrasts soft law and hard law arising 'from the treaties, regulations and the Community method'[18] and taking the form of Article 288 TFEU regulations, directives, and decisions.[19] Hard law is endowed with binding legal force, produces general and external effects, is adopted by the Union institutions according to specific procedures, and has a legal basis in the Treaty.[20] Conversely, due to its lack of legally binding force and emphasis on persuasion and guidance rather than on enforcement by a coercive authority, soft law is considered an instrument of 'governance'.[21] Governance is a new way to govern which 'departs from the traditional

[9] L Senden, *Soft Law in European Community Law* (Hart 2004) 140. [10] ibid, 157.

[11] K Jacobsson, 'Between Deliberation and Discipline: Soft Governance in the EU Employment Policy' in Mörth (n 4) 82.

[12] L Tholoniat, 'The Career of the Open Method of Coordination: Lessons from a "Soft" EU Instrument' (2010) 33 *West European Politics* 93, 96.

[13] Lisbon European Council, Presidency Conclusions (23–24 March 2000) Part I, para 5.

[14] C de la Porte and P Pochet, 'Why and how (still) study the Open Method of Co-ordination (OMC)?' (2012) 22 *Journal of European Social Policy* 336, 338.

[15] Presidency Conclusions (n 13) para 37.

[16] For various taxonomies see KC Wellens and GM Borchardt, 'Soft Law in European Community Law' (1989) 14 *European Law Reports* 267, 298–301, Senden (n 9) 140–57, D Chalmers et al., *European Union Law: Texts and Materials* (CUP 2006) 137–8.

[17] Ch Chinkin, 'The Challenge of Soft Law: Development and Change in International Law' (1989) 38 *International and Comparative Law Quarterly* 850, 862–5.

[18] DM Trubek et al., '"Soft Law", "Hard Law", and the EU Integration' in G de Búrca and J Scott (eds), *Law and New Governance in the EU and the US* (Hart 2006) 65.

[19] F Beveridge and S Nott, 'A Hard Look at Soft Law' in P Craig and C Harlow (eds), *Lawmaking in the European Union* (Kluwer Law International 1998) 285; L Senden and S Prechal, 'Differentiation in and Through Community Soft Law' in B de Witte et al. (eds), *The Many Faces of Differentiation in EU Law* (Intersentia 2001) 185, take the view that only regulations and directives can be considered hard law.

[20] Senden (n 9) 45.

[21] O Treib et al., 'Modes of Governance: Towards a Conceptual Clarification' (2007) 14 *Journal of European Public Policy* 1, 14.

model where collectively binding decisions are taken by elected representatives within parliaments and implemented by bureaucrats within public administrations'.[22]

Though soft law appears to stand in stark contradiction to traditional hard law, practice has nonetheless shown that the various sources of law hardly ever exist in isolation from each other and that it is difficult to determine at the outset the individual or relative impact of the hard or the soft element on policy development.[23] In a judgment concerning the Stability and Growth Pact (SGP),[24] the ECJ held that the discretion of the Council to take decisions was limited by recommendations issued by the European Commission in the framework of the system of multilateral surveillance, thus increasing the importance of SGP's soft dimension.[25] This judgment illustrates that soft law is not simply politics and that 'even where there is no immediate sanction other than peer pressure and the prospect of further decisions, soft law has practical and legal effects that cannot be bypassed'.[26]

Furthermore, soft law is in itself used as a tool to enforce higher norms—or hard law, to the point that distinguishing between enforcement of hard law, enforcement of soft law, and the soft law itself becomes extremely problematic. As argued by Snyder, soft law is a mechanism through which the effectiveness of EU law in all its facets—compliance, enforcement, and implementation—can be ensured.[27] For instance, soft law is often used to explain the existing hard (and other soft) law in a specific sector, to clarify provisions drafted openly or indeterminately.[28] Accordingly, through its informative function, soft law plays an important role in enhancing the links between the institutions and individuals, natural or legal persons, and ultimately contributes to the proper enforcement of hard law. In fact, soft law itself is used to enforce a vast array of values, from transparency to legal certainty to legitimacy and the involvement of the citizens in decision making.

This informative role of soft law makes it fit for non-judicial forms of enforcement. Soft law appears unsuitable for adjudication because court enforcement of soft law instruments can come at the expense of legal certainty.[29] Klabbers points out that use of soft law instruments in court is undesirable.[30] He argues that whenever dealing with soft law, the domestic and international courts try to 'recast it into the more accepted sources of international law: treaties and custom,'[31] and that soft law becomes 'completely indistinguishable from hard law' whenever applied, complied with, or violated.[32] However, the reality of judicial practice requires a more nuanced view, with European courts recognizing certain legal effects for soft law instruments. Some argue that in a 'new governance' context, the role of the courts needs to be redefined: courts are not enforcers of legal rules but rather 'a source of communicating ideas and experience [. . .] without being specifically prescriptive in relation to any particular form'.[33]

This chapter aims to present several challenges raised by the process of enforcement of European soft law. Section 2 briefly reviews various strategies to determine what enforcement

[22] ibid, 3.

[23] I Maher, 'Economic Policy Coordination and the European Court: Excessive Deficits and ECOFIN Discretion' (2004) 29 *European Law Reports* 831.

[24] Case C-27/04 *Commission v Council* [2004] ECLI:EU:C:2004:436.

[25] Maher (n 23) 838–40.

[26] ibid, 841.

[27] Snyder (n 1).

[28] M Gardenes Santiago, 'Las comunicaciones interpretativas de la Comision: concepto y valor normativo' (1992) 19 *Revista de Instituciones Europeas* 933, 939–40.

[29] Chinkin (n 17) 862–5.

[30] See J Klabbers, 'Informal Instruments Before the European Court of Justice' (1994) 31 *Common Market Law Review* 997; J Klabbers, 'The Redundancy of Soft Law' (1996) 65 *Nordic Journal of International Law* 167; J Klabbers, 'The Undesirability of Soft Law' (1998) 67 *Nordic Journal of International Law* 381.

[31] Klabbers, 'The Redundancy of Soft Law' (n 30) 174.

[32] ibid, 177.

[33] Joanne Scott and Susan Sturm, 'Courts as Catalysts: Rethinking the Judicial Role in New Governance' (2007) 13 *Columbia Journal of European Law* 565, 572.

could mean in a soft law context. Even though soft law instruments are deprived of legally binding force, this does not mean that coercive means of enforcement are automatically excluded, as proven empirically on a number of occasions. The chapter looks at a series of examples which demonstrate how soft law is enforced through flexible (section 3), but also more coercive means (section 4), before concluding that ensuring the enforcement of soft law is done through hybrid methods which only reflect the hybridity of regulation in Europe (section 5). The chapter will show how hybridity of regulation is reflected in the hybridity of enforcement mechanisms, with soft law itself becoming an enforcement tool for higher, binding norms, or values. Finally, section 6 reflects on whether, in the coercive enforcement of soft law, fundamental Rule of Law values are still preserved.

2. Enforcement theories: between compliance and deterrence

In his seminal article on the effectiveness of European law, Snyder considered enforcement, implementation, and compliance as facets of effectiveness.[34] According to other accounts, enforcement is part of regulatory implementation. Yeung distinguishes compliance with the 'collective goals underpinning a regulatory scheme' from 'compliance with regulatory standards'.[35] The two are distinct, as compliance with certain standards (which, for example, might be poorly designed) may not always lead to more general compliance alongside the goals of regulation. Yeung therefore suggests that implementation refers to compliance with general regulatory goals, and thus encompasses 'institutional design, standard setting and the monitoring and enforcement of regulatory standards'.[36] Enforcement can be seen as involving 'activities pursued by third parties that are aimed at securing compliance with a set of regulatory norms'.[37] These activities can imply incentives, recourse to courts, or the threat or use of sanctions.[38] For Shavell, the fundamental dimensions of law enforcement concern the stage of legal intervention, the form of sanctions (monetary or non-monetary), and the choice between private and public law enforcement.[39] Each of these dimensions is accompanied by various factors which can contribute towards an optimal level of law enforcement. It is interesting to note that in Shavell's model, the optimal level of law enforcement varies with the function of the particular regulatory sector—tort, criminal law, tax, etc.

The relationship between compliance, implementation, enforcement, and effectiveness is relevant to our discussion, especially as enforcement has a specific coercive meaning in European studies, while 'compliance' is the generic term.[40] Alternatively, by definition and in accordance with Article 288 TFEU, soft law instruments are deprived of legally binding force, making any type of coercion rather problematic, at least in principle. It is thus hard to conceive of soft law being enforced as hard law through traditional mechanisms laid down in the EU Treaties, such as infringement proceedings brought by the Commission. In fact, as we learn from the international relations literature, courts cannot get too involved in this enforcement process and should instead look for other 'soft means of enforcement' such as

[34] Snyder (n 1) 26. [35] K Yeung, *Securing Compliance—A Principled Approach* (Hart 2004) 11.

[36] ibid, 12.

[37] P Verbruggen, 'Gorillas in the closet? Public and private actors in the enforcement of transnational private regulation' (2013) 7 *Regulation and Governance* 512, 515.

[38] Snyder (n 1) 27.

[39] S Shavell, 'The Optimal Structure of Law Enforcement' (1993) 36 *Journal of Law & Economics* 255, 257–9.

[40] M Cremona (ed) *Compliance and the Enforcement of EU Law* (OUP 2012) xxxix.

negotiations, monitoring, or follow-up agencies.[41] The generic term 'compliance' appears more useful for this discussion.[42]

Some authors consider that instead of focusing on enforcement, a better perspective will be obtained by looking at the wider compliance picture, including deterrent means of law enforcement, as well as normative and social motivations and rules awareness.[43] It is thus useful to understand enforcement strategies in a broad sense, including two main streams: a deterrence and a compliance strategy. The deterrence strategy relies on coercion, putting forward a 'confrontational style of enforcement and the sanctioning of the rule-breaking behaviour'.[44] It is done through monitoring and sanctioning to increase the costs of deviation.[45] This increase in costs is achieved either by imposing duties on those who breach the law, on third parties, or by denying rights to violators and/or granting rights to others.[46] On the other hand, enforcement through compliance focuses on cooperation, persuasion, and advice.[47] Compliance is achieved because states undertake commitments in the interests of efficiency and norms, and occurs through clear and transparent norms, economic and political capacity building, and rules interpretation.[48]

It is of course a commonplace that various hybrid combinations of these two strategies are needed, depending on the context, in order to ensure efficient and effective regulation.[49] A sophisticated, flexible, and business-friendly approach to enforcement has been proven in certain cases to be more conducive to compliance than a strict enforcement strategy.[50] Formality of enforcement has been occasionally considered to have a positive effect on compliance with regulatory norms, whereas coercive enforcement has been generally assessed as counterproductive.[51] Similarly, enforcement agencies can be differentiated in their deterrence/compliance dimensions—some focus on correcting behaviour or punishment, while others use legalistic or cooperative approaches to enforcement.[52] The regulatory strategies adopted by agencies can vary between formal (or systematic) and cooperative (or facilitative), with flexibility generally being induced by political circumstances, and with agencies adopting blurred strategies to respond to conflicting external requirements.[53] Ayres and Braithwaite combined the deterrence and the compliance strategies within the 'enforcement pyramid', showing how if softer strategies fail, more constraining (or deterring) strategies can be put in place by enforcers.[54]

These two different enforcement methodologies are also combined in the EU, on a multi-level plane, at the EU and the national level.[55] While the expectation might be that flexible compliance strategies would be the norm with soft law, empirical evidence shows

[41] Chinkin (n 17) 862–3. [42] Cremona (n 40) xl.

[43] S Winter and P May, 'Motivation for Compliance with Environmental Regulations' (2001) 20 *Journal of Policy Analysis and Management* 675.

[44] N Gunningham, 'Enforcement and Compliance Strategies' in R Baldwin et al. (eds), *The Oxford Handbook of Regulation* (OUP 2010) 121.

[45] L Conant, 'Compliance and What EU Member States Make of It' in Cremona (n 40) 7–8.

[46] OA Hathaway and SJ Shapiro, 'Outcasting: Enforcement in Domestic and International Law' (2011) Faculty Scholarship Series, Paper 3850 http://digitalcommons.law.yale.edu/cgi/viewcontent.cgi?article=4846&context=fss_papers, accessed 12 October 2016, 270–3.

[47] Gunningham (n 44) 121. [48] Conant (n 45) 7–8. [49] Gunningham (n 44) 141.

[50] R Burby et al., 'Building Code Enforcement Burdens and Central City Decline' (2000) 66 *Journal of American Planning Association* 143.

[51] Winter and May (n 43) 688–90.

[52] J Braithwaite et al., 'An Enforcement Taxonomy of Regulatory Agencies' (1987) 9 *Law and Policy* 323.

[53] P May and R Burby, 'Making Sense Out of Regulatory Enforcement' (1998) 20 *Law and Policy* 157, 175–7.

[54] I Ayres and J Braithwaite, *Responsive Regulation: Transcending the Deregulation Debate* (OUP 1992). On the application of this framework, see for instance C Scott, 'Non-judicial Enforcement of Transnational Private Regulation' in F Cafaggi (ed), *Enforcement of transnational regulation: ensuring compliance in a global world* (Edward Elgar 2012).

[55] Cremona (n 40) xl–xli.

that deterrence is sometimes also very relevant, with the European Commission, the EU Courts, and national authorities using a broad range of mechanisms to give full effect to soft law.

3. Compliance mechanisms

As argued by Cremona, the basis of compliance procedures is the principle of loyal cooperation enshrined in Article 4(3) TEU.[56] The cooperation between Member States and European institutions in the achievement of the Treaty goals is considered a constitutional principle of EU law and a cornerstone of European integration.[57] Cooperation between national authorities and international organization institutions is frequent in drafting or implementing policies and is a general principle of international public authority.[58] Observance of soft law instruments is an expression of the *voluntary* nature of the cooperation between the Member States and the Commission. The Court reached this conclusion while corroborating former Article 211 EC (now Article 17(1) TEU) with Article 288 TFEU. Article 211 EC provided that the Commission could formulate recommendations and deliver opinions on matters dealt with in the EC Treaty. The Court considered that 'express conferral of the power to adopt acts having no binding legal effect shows that voluntary compliance with the rules of the Treaty and non-binding acts of the institutions is an essential element in the achievement of the goals of the Treaty'.[59]

Research shows that legal orders can sometimes draw on mechanisms aimed at amplifying emotions to ensure compliance with soft law. Such mechanisms rely on feelings such as respect for authority, the fear of being challenged in a court of law or the fear of not benefiting from a certain advantage, shame, but also pleasure, surprise, and empathy.[60] One of the most celebrated functions of the 'new' governance, including soft law, is that not legally binding material can result in transformations in the behaviour and practices of the Member States and the Union institutions. Hence, 'formally non-binding agreements can gradually become politically, socially, and morally binding for the actors involved'[61] by the intervention of certain devices other than the legal force of an act, such as those related to knowledge and meaning making. These are flexible, not constraining mechanisms, which should stimulate common knowledge of the challenges, objectives, and policy goals. While placing social and time pressure on Member States, they are effective in fostering cooperation.

As a study in the employment sector shows, these devices have a strong sociological character and include a common discourse, the symbols of a common project, strengthening socialization through repeated meetings, mobilizing actors and their partnerships through networks, and iterative processes.[62] Such compliance mechanisms appear sometimes to be more important than soft law itself.[63] Far from attempting to instil compliance

[56] ibid, xl.

[57] Conclusions of the 2000 FIDE Congress, cited in J Temple-Lang, 'The duties on co-operation on national authorities and courts under Article 10 EC: two more reflections' (2001) 26 *European Law Reports* 84, 85.

[58] A von Bogdandy, 'General Principles of International Public Authority: Sketching a Research Field' in A von Bogdandy et al. (eds), *The Exercise of Public Authority by International Institutions*, vol 210 (Springer 2010) 727.

[59] Case T-113/89 *Nefarma and Others v Commission* [1990] ECLI:EU:T:1990:82, para 79; Case T-116/89 *Vereniging Prodifarma e.a. v Commission* [1990] ECLI:EU:T:1990:85, para 85.

[60] A Flückiger, 'Pourquoi respectons-nous la soft law? Le rôle des émotions et des techniques de manipulation' (2009) XLVII-144 *Revue européenne des sciences sociales* 73, 81–95.

[61] K Jacobsson, 'Soft Regulation and the Subtle Transformation of States: the Case of EU Employment Policy' (2004) 14 *Journal of European Social Policy* 355, 359.

[62] Jacobsson (n 11) 90–8. [63] ibid, 98.

with one-size-fits-all policy recommendations, the European Employment Strategy aims at ensuring mutual learning and adaptation to national circumstances. Zeitlin and Vanhercke conducted interviews to establish the effectiveness of the social dimension of the European Semester, and discovered that mutual learning, joint exploration, and consensus-building towards a common view on social issues all emerged in the process of multilateral surveillance of the implementation of Country Specific Reports.[64] Important socialization functions are thus performed, as also shown by the older example of the European Political Coordination, which helped the Member States to get used to 'consulting each other on major international issues, to profiting from each other's advice and to paying due attention to each other's concerns'.[65] It thus appears that in the long run, states can integrate norms and practices established by way of soft law into their national orders.

According to theories drawn from comparative politics, another mechanism which fosters compliance is mobilization, with litigation being used strategically to generate incentives to comply.[66] It was noted that soft law could make a very good 'starting point for a litigation strategy, for collective bargaining or for mobilising support for future measures of hard law'.[67] In this context, Beveridge and Nott offer important data supporting the fact that the Commission recommendation and code of practice on sexual harassment had a positive impact on the British workplace. The influence of these soft law instruments in litigation was crucial because the national courts referred to them regularly, requiring employers and trade unions to treat sexual harassment more seriously. Soft law provides interest groups with the necessary knowledge about 'the pre-legal stages of policy formulation and legal developments' and also with an alternative method through which socially marginalized groups can achieve results that they would not have been able to achieve through hard law.[68] By avoiding problems such as the lack of legal basis or the impossibility of achieving the necessary majority for the passage of hard legislation, marginalized groups can use soft law to challenge dominant ideologies.[69]

What we see in all these compliance cases is not only that soft law instruments deprived of legally binding force ultimately have practical relevance for Member States and individuals, but also that soft law is a tool to enforce certain important values. Soft law can lead to policy change but it also induces subtler changes at the level of discourse, understanding, and policy principles.[70] Compliance with soft law is ultimately compliance with its underlying principles, and so the discussion on the enforcement of soft law becomes very much a discussion about enforcing the values promoted through soft law instruments.

4. Deterrence mechanisms

In a recent report on social policy, Zeitlin and Vanhercke showed how deterrence mechanisms were ineffective in securing compliance with the Country Specific Reports within the social limb of the European Semester. Such mechanisms included sanctions under the Macroeconomic Imbalances Procedure (which have not been imposed on any Member States) and reprogramming/suspension of structural funds, and their effectiveness varied across the Member States, depending on differences between Member State interests and national practices.[71] Furthermore, as pointed out by Judge Lenaerts in a public speech,

[64] J Zeitlin and B Vanhercke, 'Socializing the European Semester? Economic Governance and Social Policy Coordination in Europe 2020' (2014) 7 *Swedish Institute for European Policy Studies* 58–60.

[65] R Dehousse and JHH Weiler, 'EPC and the Single Act: from Soft Law to Hard Law?' in M Holland (ed), *The Future of European Political Cooperation* (Macmillan 1991) 132.

[66] Conant (n 45) 7–11. [67] Beveridge and Nott (n 19) 309. [68] ibid, 293. [69] ibid, 296.

[70] Jacobsson (n 11) 89. [71] Zeitlin and Vanhercke (n 64) 56–7.

sanctions under the Excessive Imbalances Procedure of the Macroeconomic Imbalances Procedure were difficult to apply within the scope of the Treaties, given the non-binding character of recommendations.[72]

As research on the Lisbon Agenda and the OMC shows, courts appear reluctant to refer to instruments issued from soft-governance methods.[73] The situation is similar for standalone soft law instruments issued in the social sphere, which do not necessarily accompany hard law.[74] However, there is some evidence in other sectors, such as competition and State aid, that soft law can be enforced through the traditional judicial route.[75] First, soft law could be considered binding at the discretion of the enacting institution. Second, negotiated soft law can bind Member States.

With regards to the former, in judgments such as *BASF*, Commission decisions have been considered to be 'vitiated of illegality'[76] because of the misapplication of the leniency notice.[77] In *Kronofrance*[78] the Court annulled a Commission decision because it failed correctly to apply the adjustment factors for the maximum amount of aid calculations laid down in the multi-sectoral framework on aid for large investment projects.[79] All these outcomes were possible because the Court acknowledged *binding effects* for soft law instruments. The case law recognized that soft law can have binding effects which fetter the discretion of the European Commission as early as the 1990s.[80] The principle was repeated in many other cases, where individuals used soft law as a sword against European administration.[81] An important amount of case law has been generated by the leniency notice and the guidelines on fines, issued in the antitrust field, where the applicants were contesting the amount of fine imposed for cartels, arguing that the guidance from the Commission had not been applied correctly. In the seminal *Dansk Rørindustri*,[82] the ECJ noted that by publishing the antitrust Guidelines on fines,[83] the European Commission imposed a limit on the exercise of its discretion, and soft law was not precluded from producing legal effects.[84]

It is worth pausing briefly to reflect on how the Court reached this conclusion in *Dansk*. It will be recalled that soft law is by definition not legally binding: thus, its legal effects cannot stem directly from the intrinsic properties of the instrument to generate rights and obligations—as is the case with hard law. The Court needed to construct a mechanism

[72] K Lenaerts, 'Economic Integration, Solidarity and Legitimacy: The EU in Times of Crisis', closing remarks to Euroforum Colloquium on Europe 2020: Academics and Policymakers in Dialogue, cited by Zeitlin and Vanhercke (n 64) 57.

[73] S Smismans, 'From harmonization to co-ordination? EU law in the Lisbon governance architecture' (2010) 18 *Journal of European Public Policy* 504.

[74] T Hervey, '"Adjudicating in the Shadow of the Informal Settlement?": The Court of Justice of the European Union, "New Governance" and Social Welfare' (2010) 63 *Current Legal Problems* 92.

[75] O Ştefan, *Soft Law in Court: Competition Law, State Aid and the Court of Justice of the European Union* (Kluwer Law International 2013).

[76] Case T-15/02 *BASF v Commission* [2006] ECLI:EU:T:2006:74, para 541.

[77] Commission Notice on the non-imposition or reduction of fines in cartel cases [1996] OJ C207/4.

[78] Case T-27/02 *Kronofrance v Commission* [2004] ECLI:EU:T:2004:348, para 109.

[79] Multisectoral framework on regional aid for large investment projects [1998] OJ C107/7.

[80] Case T-7/89 *Hercules Chemicals v EC Commission* [1991] ECLI:EU:T:1991:75, confirmed on appeal in Case C-51/92 *Hercules Chemicals v Commission* [1999] ECLI:EU:C:1999:357.

[81] Case C-351/98 *Spain v Commission* [2002] ECLI:EU:C:2002:530, para 53; Case C-409/00 *Spain v Commission* [2003] ECLI:EU:C:2003:92, para 71; Case T-417/05 *Endesa v Commission* [2006] ECLI:EU:T:2006:219, para 204.

[82] Joined Cases C-189, 202, 205, 208 & 213/02 *Dansk Rørindustri and Others v Commission* [2005] ECLI:EU:C:2005:408, para 211.

[83] Guidelines on the method of setting fines imposed pursuant to Article 15 (2) of Regulation No 17 and Article 65 (5) of the ECSC Treaty [1998] OJ C9/3.

[84] But see the recent Opinion of Advocate General Wahl in Case C-526/14 *Kotnik* [2016] ECLI:EU:C:2016:570, not yet reported paras 38 and 39. In his view, the legal effects of soft law should only be confined to situations where it acts 'merely as a limit on the exercise of [European Commission's] discretion'.

indirectly to recognize the legal effects of soft law[85] and, implicitly, to enable its enforcement. In the words of the ECJ, by publishing guidelines on fines, the institution imposes a limit on the exercise of its discretion and cannot depart from those rules or else risk being found in breach of the general principles of law, such as equal treatment or the protection of legitimate expectations, where appropriate.[86] The Court here established a direct link between the principle of legitimate expectations and equal treatment, on the one hand, and the legal effects of the guidelines on fines, on the other. Such a link and mechanism for recognizing the effects of soft law has been employed in many other cases, mainly in competition[87] and State aid.[88]

With regards to the second situation, negotiated soft law (such as many guidelines in the State aid sector) are binding on those Member States which agreed to it. The Court noted in *CIRFS* that in relation to a soft law instrument concerning the textiles sector, 'the rules set out [by the Commission] in the discipline and *accepted* by the Member States themselves have the effect [...] of [...] subjecting [State aid] to the *obligation* of prior notification'.[89] Accordingly, acceptance by Member States is required for the soft law instrument to produce binding effects. *IJssel-Vliet*, a Dutch preliminary ruling case, concerned the legal effects of the Guidelines on aid in the fisheries sector.[90] In its reasoning, the Court first considered the Treaty obligation of cooperation on the Commission and the Member States to keep under constant review the systems of aid, provided for in Article 108(1) TFEU. It identified the guidelines on fisheries as an element of that obligation. Second, the Court analysed whether this cooperation had materialized and concluded that the Netherlands had agreed to the provisions thereof following an exchange of letters. Consequently, the guidelines created a framework of cooperation in accordance with Article 108(1) TFEU from which neither the Commission nor the Member States could be released.

Enforcement of soft law can also occur through decisions of the European Commission, which is sometimes under a *duty* to enforce soft law at the national level. In *CIRFS*, the Court condemned the Commission for not opening proceedings against France, a Member State which had failed in its obligation to notify aid granted in the area of synthetic fibres—as it should have done in accordance with several soft law instruments.[91] In *Commission v Luxembourg* the Commission commenced an Article 258 TFEU action as the Grand Duchy of Luxembourg had failed to notify its annual reports on State aid in the agriculture sector for the period 2000–2001 in time, as it should have done in accordance with Commission guidelines.[92] The Court emphasized that the binding effect that State aid soft law instruments have on the Member States which accepted them was established in previous case

[85] O Ştefan, 'Hybridity Before the Court: A Hard Look at Soft Law in the EU Competition and State Aid Case Law' (2012) 37 *European Law Reports* 49, 62–4.

[86] *Dansk Rørindustri* (n 82) para 211.

[87] Case C-167/04 *JCB Service v Commission* [2006] ECLI:EU:C:2006:594, paras 207–8; Joined Cases T-259/02 to T-264/02 and T-271/02 *Raiffeisen v Commission* [2006] ECLI:EU:T:2006:396, para 222; Order in Case T-11/06 *Romana Tabacchi v Commission* [2006] ECLI:EU:T:2011:560, para 64; Opinion of Advocate General Bot in Case C-76/06 *Britannia Alloys v Commission* [2007] ECLI:EU:C:2007:326; para 46; Case T-73/04 *Le Carbone-Lorraine v Commission* [2008] ECLI:EU:T:2008:416, paras 70–2.

[88] Joined Cases C-465/09P to C-470/09P *Diputación Foral de Vizcaya v Commission* [2011 ECLI:EU:C:2011:372, para 120; Case T-21/06 *Germany v Commission* [2009] ECLI:EU:T:2009:387, para 51; Opinion of Advocate General Ruiz-Jarabo Colomer in Case C-415/07 *Lodato Gennero v INPS and SCCI* [2009] ECLI:EU:C:2009:220, para 36; Case C-75/05P and C-80/05P *Germany v Kronofrance* [2008] ECLI:EU:C:2008:482, para 60.

[89] Case C-313/90 *CIRFS v Commission* [1993] ECLI:EU:C:1993:111, para 35. Emphasis added.

[90] Case C-311/94 *IJssel-Vliet v Minister van Economische Zaken* [1996] ECLI:EU:C:1996:383.

[91] *CIRFS v Commission* (n 89) para 51.

[92] Information from the Commission—Community Guidelines for State aid in the agriculture sector [2000] OJ C28/2.

law,[93] and noted the failure of the Member State to comply with the obligations imposed by Community law.

The European Commission can constrain a recalcitrant Member State to agree to a certain soft law instrument by threatening to issue a hard law decision. For example, in State aid cases, a lot of soft law instruments are issued through negotiations between the Commission and the Member States. As seen in the previous section, the EU Court judged on a number of occasions that once these instruments are accepted by a Member State, they can impose binding obligations[94] and that guidelines which are not accepted by Member States cannot bind them.[95] However, if a Member State does not agree to a certain communication or notice, the Commission can coerce acceptance by threatening to open formal investigations into national aid measures which fall in the ambit of the said instrument. This technique was used on several occasions to obtain the agreement of Spain and Germany to a motor vehicle aid framework,[96] as well as the agreement of Germany to the 2007–2013 guidelines on regional aid.[97]

The support of the Court of Justice is, however, essential in securing compliance through this route, leading to hybrid judicial–administrative enforcement mechanisms. When the Commission responded to Germany's official statement of intention not to apply the motor vehicle aid framework by warning that it would initiate proceedings against all German aid schemes in the motor vehicles industry, Germany argued that the Commission could not introduce new restrictions on existing aid schemes as this would impinge upon Member State independence in establishing regional and general aid schemes. The Commission disagreed and backed up its position by referring to the fact that soft law had been judicially endorsed in the *Deufil* case.[98] In this judgment, the Court of Justice discussed at length an aid code for the synthetic fibres industry, mentioning that it was an instrument intended to set out the course of conduct that the Commission would follow in a particular sector, as well as the fact that a code of conduct could not, in any circumstances depart from Treaty provisions. The Commission generalized the language of the Court in its German decision, pointing out that it was clear from *Deufil* that it could require Member States to comply with certain rules by means of soft law instruments, while still remaining within the boundaries imposed by the Treaty. Snyder observes that the Commission extracted from the *Deufil* judgment 'significant principles which, expressed in key paragraphs of the judgment, encompass not only the particular case, but also potential future situations'.[99] Accordingly, when dealing with soft law, the Court and the Commission influence each other 'such that the result of each institution's decisional processes are incorporated as an input into the decisional processes of the other'.[100]

The mechanism for recognizing binding legal effects of soft law for national authorities is specific and much narrower than the mechanism through which soft law is enforced against the enacting institution or the agreeing Member State. Only negotiated soft law has judicially recognized binding legal effects for Member States and these effects are

[93] Case C-69/05 *Commission v Luxembourg* [2006] ECLI:EU:C:2006:32, para 9 (French version only).

[94] *CIRFS v Commission* (n 89); *IJssel-Vliet v Minister van Economische Zaken* (n 90).

[95] Case C-242/00 *Germany v Commission* [2002] ECLI:EU:C:2002:380, para 35. See also Case T-176/01 *Ferriere Nord v Commission* [2004] ECLI:EU:T:2004:336, para 134.

[96] Cini (n 1) 201–2.

[97] M Blauberger, 'Of "Good" and "Bad" Subsidies: European State Aid Control through Soft and Hard Law' (2009) 32 *West European Politics* 719, 729–30.

[98] Case 310/85 *Deufil v Commission* [1986] ECLI:EU:C:1987:96.

[99] F Snyder, 'Soft Law and Institutional Practice in the European Community' in Stephen Martin (ed), *The Construction of Europe: Essays in Honour of Emile Noël* (Kluwer 1994) 213 citing Snyder (n 1) 50.

[100] Snyder (n 99) 204.

connected by the courts to a specific duty of cooperation provided for in the Treaty, such as Article 108 TFEU in the area of State aid. In *Grimaldi* the ECJ urged national judges to 'take into consideration'[101] soft law whenever deciding on cases; however, no further explanation was offered regarding exactly what this statement entailed. Some explanations with regards to the legal effects of soft law have been brought in subsequent cases.[102] *Grimaldi* was considered to be 'reminiscent of *Von Colson*',[103] which suggests that it introduces a duty of consistent interpretation in relation to soft law instruments. National courts would thus be under a duty to interpret national law in the light of the wording of soft law instruments issued at the European level. Conversely, it was argued that the reading of this judgment should be less strict, and that national courts are required to take soft law into consideration only when it helps to clarify the meaning of Community or national law.[104] In any case, there is some evidence that national courts do take soft law seriously, as shown by the recent *Gauweiler* case law.[105] Indeed, it is remarkable to note that the German Constitutional Court decided to send a preliminary reference revolving around the interpretation of a press release from the ECB.[106]

Arguments that national authorities should observe soft law on the basis of principles such as legitimate expectations or legal certainty have been rejected by the Court so far. National procedural autonomy appears to prevail in this regard. In the *Pfleiderer* case the Court admitted that soft law can produce effects on the practice of national authorities; nonetheless, such effects could not be given legal weight in judicial proceedings.[107] Furthermore, in *Expedia* the Court held that the national authorities and courts were not bound by the provisions of the Notice on agreements of minor importance that do not fall under the EU antitrust rules, and that they had complete discretion to take the thresholds mentioned therein into consideration when deciding on whether agreements between undertakings breached or not EU competition law.[108] The national authorities' disregard of the *de minimis* notice could interfere with principles such legitimate expectations and legal certainty.[109]

Such a conclusion accords importance to the principle of national procedural autonomy: national authorities cannot see their discretion limited by a soft law instrument exterior to them. However, this has serious consequences from the point of view of individual rights, as legitimate expectations and legal certainty appear to have variable content in the multilayered system of EU competition law enforcement. On the one hand, if the case is dealt with by the European Commission, individuals are entitled to expect an application of EU soft law, or at least to a statement of reasons as to why such instruments were not applied in their case. On the other hand, at the national level, the discretion of national

[101] Case C-322/88 *Grimaldi* [1989] ECLI:EU:C:1989:646, para 18.

[102] See Case C-207/01 *Altair Chimica v Commission* [2003] ECLI:EU:C:2003:451, para 41; *Lodato* (n 88) para 32; Joined Cases 253/78 and 1 to 3/79 *Procureur de la République and Others v Bruno Giry and Guerlain SA and Others* [1980] ECLI:EU:C:1980:188, para 13; Case 99/79 *Lancôme v Etos* [1980] ECLI:EU:C:1980:193, para 11.

[103] A Arnull, 'The Legal Status of Recommendations' (1990) 15 *European Law Reports* 318; Chalmers et al. (n 16) 388.

[104] See the debate in Senden (n 9) 387–93 and 391.

[105] Case C-62/14 *Gauweiler and Others* [2015] ECLI:EU:C:2015:400. For a typology of potential engagement of national courts to EU soft law, see Zlatina Georgieva, 'Soft Law in EU Competition Law and its Judicial Reception in Member States: A Theoretical Perspective' (2015) 16(2) *German Law Journal* 224. Georgieva also finds empirical evidence showing that national courts do engage with EU soft law: Zlatina Georgieva, 'The Judicial Reception of Competition Soft Law in the Netherlands and the UK' (2015) *TILEC Discussion Paper* No 2015-025, available at SSRN, https://ssrn.com/abstract=2707556, accessed 20 October 2016.

[106] ECB, Press release, Technical features of Outright Monetary Transactions, 6 September 2012, available at: http://www.ecb.europa.eu/press/pr/date/2012/html/pr120906_1.en.html, accessed 20 October 2016.

[107] Case C-360/09 *Pfleiderer v Bundeskartellamt* [2011] ECLI:EU:C:2011:389, para 23.

[108] Case C-226/11 *Expedia* [2011] ECLI:EU:C:2012:795, para 31.

[109] ibid, para 32.

competition authorities (NCAs) seems to prevail over individual expectations, and national procedural autonomy is given precedence over fundamental Rule of Law values. There appears thus to be some sort of hierarchy between the different principles of law invoked in connection to soft law. The different ways in which the Court deals with cases argued at the EU and at the national levels show that the result differs with the function of the prevailing legal principle invoked. This can lead to the conclusion that the courts do not really enforce soft law, but the legal principles and values soft law is expected to foster.

From a Rule of Law point of view, the discussion above is even more significant if we consider the theories put forward by academics that, through coercive enforcement, soft law might translate into legally binding material, thus hard law. This transformation could occur by judicial intervention, circumventing legitimate decision making routes. Snyder pointed out that the Court could decide that 'the putatively soft law has hard legal consequences' which would blur the distinction between soft and hard law,[110] with Hofmann agreeing and arguing that the EU Courts can endow Commission guidelines with certain hard features.[111] Moreover, following up from the *Deufil* saga discussed above, soft law based partly on a court judgment is transformed into hard law by administrative decision.[112] Transformation of soft law into hard law can arguably occur even if the Court does not expressly acknowledge binding effects of these instruments. Österdahl pointed out that the repeated references to soft law instruments by the Advocates General (AGs) and by both Courts of the EU (especially the ECJ) might contribute to their 'hardening', even if they are qualified as not legally binding.[113]

Two interrelated difficulties can be drawn from the discussion of coercive enforcement of soft law, and they will be dealt with in turn in the following sections. First, it appears that hard legal principles constrain the behaviour of the European Commission, which cannot depart from published soft law; furthermore, the menace of a hard law decision might compel Member States to comply with soft law. Hard and soft law are thus merged along with deterrence and compliance strategies, and it appears difficult to establish clear-cut distinctions between these categories. Second, certain Rule of Law values could be threatened given the potentially important effects recognized for material issued outside the usual legitimacy checks and balances, but also given that the effects of soft law appear to vary at the different levels of enforcement—European or national.

5. Hybridity of enforcement as a consequence of a hybrid regulatory framework

According to the international relations literature, the main differentiating features between hard and soft law lie in the capacity of the norm to prescribe legally binding commitments, the clarity and precision of its terms, and its enforceability. Abbott et al. synthesized these characteristics in the rationalist concept of 'legalization,' understood as 'a particular form of institutionalization characterized by three components: obligation, precision, and delegation'.[114] Obligation implies that the individuals or Member States are legally bound by a certain provision; precision requires clarity with respect to the

[110] Snyder (n 1) 65.

[111] H Hofmann, 'Negotiated and Non-Negotiated Administrative Rule-Making: the Example of EC Competition Policy' (2006) 43 *Common Market Law Review* 153, 165.

[112] Snyder (n 99) 216.

[113] I Österdahl, 'The ECJ and Soft Law: Who's Afraid of the EU Fundamental Rights Charter?' in U Mörth (ed), *Soft Law in Governance and Regulation: an Interdisciplinary Analysis* (Edward Elgar 2004) 51.

[114] KW Abbott et al., 'The Concept of Legalization' (2000) 54 *International Organization* 401.

conduct to follow; and delegation means that the implementation, interpretation, application of the rules and conflict resolution is to be entrusted to third parties. The intensity of these three characteristics can vary and legalization is a continuum, ranging from lower to higher degrees of obligation, precision, and delegation. According to this view, soft law should be situated at the lower end of the spectrum and an increasing degree of obligation, precision, and delegation will move soft law up towards the hard category. In a recent development of Abbott et al.'s theory, Terpan introduces enforcement as a defining characteristic of soft law instead of delegation, and eliminates the precision criterion.[115] A soft law instrument would then be an instrument where the intensity of obligation or enforcement is weak. With regards to enforcement, Terpan distinguishes hard enforcement through courts or supranational institutions, such as the WTO mechanisms of implementation, monitoring, and dispute settlement. On the other hand, soft enforcement entails non-constraining mechanisms such as surveillance and monitoring. Enforcement thus becomes a defining feature of soft law, but it can vary across soft law instruments, with some being enforced softly while others are enforced the hard way.

Following Abbott et al. and Terpan's accounts, soft law can be—and is supposed to be—enforced. The difference from hard law lies in the intensity of the enforcement, or indeed in the intensity of the other ingredients. There is, therefore, no specificity attached to the enforcement of soft law. Provided that the obligation (or precision) is weak, enforcement mechanisms can, at least theoretically, be similar to those which apply to hard law. However, taking the coercive enforcement through courts described in the previous section as an example, we may reasonably wonder whether the guidelines and notices retain their 'soft' character or if they transform into legally binding material. In other words, strong enforcement might be indicative of a high degree of obligation in the first place. Such empirical evidence casts doubts on distinguishing soft from hard law according to the criteria identified by Abbott et al. and Terpan. What is more, obligation, precision, and delegation (or enforcement) cannot contribute to an understanding of soft law, since the possible combinations between them are multiple.[116] More importantly, from a constructivist point of view, these criteria are static and fail to encapsulate the mechanisms through which 'a sense of obligation might be generated'.[117] As concluded by research in EU employment policy, 'formally non-binding agreements can gradually become politically, socially and morally binding for the actors involved'.[118] Thus, in the long run, states integrate norms and practices established by way of soft law into their national orders. We can further argue that soft law is itself under a continuous process of transformation determined by how states deal with it.

Such transformative potential for soft law shows that attempting to distinguish between soft and hard fails to encapsulate the complexity of regulation in the EU, and also the intertwining of deterrence and compliance enforcement mechanisms. On the subject of the regulatory framework, more complex models, underlining the interactions between soft and hard law, are more appropriate to the study of European governance.[119] Combining rationalist and constructivist accounts, Trubek et al. put forward a theory of hybridity to

[115] F Terpan, 'Soft Law in the European Union – The Changing Nature of EU Law' (2015) 21 *European Law Journal* 68.

[116] Mörth (n 4) 6.

[117] M Finnemore and SJ Toope, 'Alternatives to "Legalization": Richer Views of Law and Politics' (2001) 55 *International Organization* 743, 748.

[118] Jacobsson (n 61) 359.

[119] K Armstrong, 'The Character of EU Law and Governance: From "Community Method" to New Modes of Governance' (2011) *Current Legal Problems* 1.

explain the 'coexistence and engagement of law and "new" governance' (including soft law),[120] and 'to explore different ways of securing their fruitful interaction'.[121] The model was further refined by de Búrca and Scott, who identified several types of hybridity, showing how new governance (or soft law) can serve as a compliance/enforcement mechanism for traditional (hard) law, and vice versa.[122] Trubek and Trubek narrowed down the definition of hybridity, considered to be the 'transformation of both law and governance, their integration in a single system in which the functioning of each element is necessary for the successful operation of the other'.[123] They offer the EU Water Framework Directive as an example of transformation hybridity. Although binding on the Member States, the Framework Directive employs 'more open-ended standards instead of detailed rules while setting in motion horizontal and deliberative processes designed to craft both non-binding guidance and detailed and binding rules'.[124] It was argued that by combining new governance tools and traditional community method mechanisms, the Water Framework Directive achieved results that were not possible under either system working alone.[125]

Hybridity occurs *ex ante*, as a conscious decision of the regulators, but also *ex post*, during the implementation process.[126] An example of consciously designed hybridity is the fiscal coordination system which draws on broad economic policy guidelines and multilateral surveillance, while relying on the hard law of the excessive deficit procedure.[127] *Ex post* hybridity is illustrated by the initiatives to combat discrimination at the EU level, through both a Race Directive and an action plan against discrimination. While the Directive contained the requirement to pass national legislation to combat discrimination, the action plan established the necessary framework to exchange ideas between regulators on challenges and best practices. The two systems were conceived to function independently, but they became increasingly integrated during implementation.[128]

Similarly, in competition law, as seen in the previous section, the courts admit legally binding effects on the basis of a mechanism based on general principles of law (such as legitimate expectations, legal certainty, transparency),[129] which have a different legal nature than notices, guidelines, or communications. Indeed, such principles have a constitutional nature:[130] they are entrenched within the Rule of Law, a founding value of the EU according to Article 2 TEU. The source of inspiration of general principles of law is essentially hard and pertains to the constitutional traditions common to the Member States,[131] the international treaties to which the Member States are signatories or in which they have collaborated,[132] and the European Treaties.[133] The breach of these principles may trigger serious consequences, such as the suspension of rights of the defiant

[120] Trubek et al. (n 18) 93.

[121] G De Burca and J Scott, 'Introduction: New Governance, Law and Constitutionalism' in G De Burca and J Scott (eds), *Law and New Governance in the EU and the US* (Hart 2006) 6.

[122] ibid, 6–10.

[123] DM Trubek and LG Trubek, 'New Governance and Legal Regulation: Complementarity, Rivalry and Transformation' (2007) 13 *Columbia Journal of European Law* 539, 543.

[124] ibid, 551. [125] ibid, 557. [126] ibid, 549–50.

[127] I Maher, 'Economic governance: Hybridity, accountability and control' (2006) 13 *Columbia Journal of European Law*,679; Trubek et al. (n 18) 93.

[128] Trubek and Trubek (n 123) 558–9. [129] Ştefan (n 75) 229 ff.

[130] P Craig, 'Substantive Legitimate Expectations in Domestic and Community Law' (1996) 55 *Cambridge Law Journal* 289, 304; J Schwarze, *European Administrative Law* (Sweet & Maxwell 2006) cxliii.

[131] Case 11/70 *Internationale Handelsgesellschaft GmbH v Einfuhr- und Vorratsstelle für Getreide und Futtermittel* [1970] ECLI:EU:C:1970:114, para 4.

[132] Case 4/73 *Nold KG v Commission* [1974] ECLI:EU:C:1974:51, para 13.

[133] Case C-6/90 *Francovich and Bonifaci v Italy* [1991] ECLI:EU:C:1991:428, para 35.

state (Article 7 TEU), the non-contractual liability of the Community (Article 340 TFEU), and it can be a ground for annulment under Article 263 TFEU.[134] Competition law thus offers another example of *ex post* hybridity in Trubek and Trubek's terms, as courts integrate soft law and traditional legal principles during the enforcement stage.

This theory of hybridity does not only apply at the level of the regulatory framework, but has clear implications for enforcement, which becomes hybrid as well. To take the example of coercive enforcement through courts, Armstrong pointed out that adjudication pertains to more than simply applying the rules and often involves complex assessments of interests and values which could ultimately encourage litigants to rely on new forms of governance and cooperation.[135] Indeed, courts could thus shape the necessary link between the realm of governance and that of command-and-control, by inculcating within governance structures Rule of Law values and principles.[136] It follows that courts could actively influence the deliberation processes by determining the standards for review of soft law and encouraging the most principled approaches towards soft law. As conceptualized by Hervey, the relationship between courts and governance could be represented along a continuum ranging from 'mutual ignorance; through separation, either with hierarchy, or in parallel; to hybrid forms of mutual transformation'.[137]

Ignorance of new forms of governance (and soft law) can appear to be the norm from a traditional legal perspective[138] with Smismans providing some evidence that this is the case in OMC processes related to macroeconomic and employment policy coordination.[139] In the social welfare sector, Hervey found parallel or hierarchical relationships between adjudication and governance. Courts can reject the logics of governance if they are considered contrary to the hierarchically superior legal requirements. On the other hand, courts can endorse a 'new governance' position if it illustrates traditional law principles.[140] Korkea-aho observed a stronger impact of soft law on adjudication in the context of implementation of the Water Framework Directive through soft mechanisms based on networks and consensual enforcement. Empirical evidence showed that soft enforcement mechanisms could streamline legal actions, by offering the information and the administrative resources needed to lead effective infringement proceedings. Furthermore, managing implementation through networks reduces case load, as problems are solved by the participants without judicial intervention.[141] Hybrid interactions between adjudication and soft law are also present in competition law.[142] The Court's argumentation based on legal principles is often inserted by the Commission into the preamble of new soft law instruments[143] and then back again by EU Courts in their judgments,[144] completing a kind of 'virtuous circle'.[145]

[134] On these points, see also A Arnull, *The European Union and Its Court of Justice* (2nd edn, OUP 2006) 336; and T Hartley, *The Foundations of European Community Law* (OUP 2007) 143.

[135] Armstrong (n 119) 27. [136] Scott and Sturm (n 33) 567. [137] Hervey (n 74) 138.

[138] ibid, 144. [139] Smismans (n 73). [140] Hervey (n 74) 63.

[141] E Korkea-aho, 'Watering Down the Court of Justice? The Dynamics between Network Implementation and Article 258 TFEU Litigation' (2014) 20 *European Law Journal* 649. On reconceptualizing the role of courts in a new governance context, see also E Korkea-aho, *Adjudicating New Governance: Deliberative Democracy in the European Union* (Palgrave 2015).

[142] Ştefan (n 75) 219–27.

[143] For example: Guidelines on the method of setting fines imposed pursuant to Article 23(2)(a) Regulation No 1/2003 [2006] OJ C210/2, para 3; Commission Notice on the determination of the applicable rules for the assessment of unlawful State aid [2002] OJ C119/22.

[144] See on the guidelines on fines *BASF v Commission* (n 76) para 250. See on the notice on unlawful State aid Case T-357/02 *Freistaat Sachsen and Others v Commission* [2007] ECLI:EU:T:2011:376, para 118.

[145] A Sweet, 'Judicialization and the Construction of Governance' (1999) 31 *Comparative Political Studies* 147, 158–9.

6. Soft law (coercive) enforcement and Rule of Law values?

Yeung identifies effective outcomes as the predominant value of regulatory goals enforcement.[146] These outcomes include efficiency, clarity, and predictability, and flexibility, responsiveness, and timeliness.[147] Constitutional values, on the other hand, constrain the pursuit of these outcomes, and require that decision making should be authorized by law, be certain and stable, accountable and transparent, procedurally fair and proportionate, consistent and rational.[148] Yeung warned that a switch from constraining, 'hard' mechanisms of judicial enforcement towards softer forms based on negotiation and informal advice from the regulators could clash with constitutional principles and Rule of Law values. Transparency, due process, and accountability are under threat and Yeung advocates against viewing law in a shallow instrumental fashion when constructing enforcement or compliance mechanisms.[149] Section 4 has briefly showed that coercive enforcement can also raise Rule of Law problems with regards to soft law.

First, it appears that courts and administrative authorities recognize overly important effects for instruments issued outside the legitimacy checks and balances. Although cheap, fast, and flexible, the procedures for the adoption of soft law generally tend to circumvent more costly, but legitimate, decision making. Therefore, recourse to soft law could enhance the discretion of Community institutions to the detriment of Member States competences.[150] As early as 1968, the EP warned about the dangers associated with the proliferation by the Council of acts not mentioned in the Treaty, notably the circumvention of decision-making formalities in the consultation of the Parliament and the right of initiative of the Commission.[151] National authorities also expressed concerns at the high number of soft documents not mentioned in the Treaty. In its 1992 report, the French *Conseil d'État* condemned the profusion of Council decisions and resolutions, as well as Commission communications.[152]

Despite the fact that Parliament's involvement in the decision-making process has increased by means of soft law measures such as inter-institutional agreements,[153] it was noted that its position is not necessarily strengthened because its bargaining power remains the same: the outcome of the final negotiations on legislation can depart from the content of the inter-institutional agreement.[154] Even though the preparatory and informative soft law instruments fulfil an important function in the pre-legislative stage because it is by these means that the Parliament is informed and consulted on future legislation,[155] many other soft law instruments are concluded without Parliamentary involvement.[156]

The problem of stakeholder and expert participation in the decision-making process is at times even more acute in the case of soft law instruments, 'since consultative procedures are less rigorously adopted and structured in relation to rules whose binding nature is

146 Yeung (n 35) 8. 147 ibid, 51. 148 ibid.

149 K Yeung, 'Better regulation, administrative sanctions and constitutional values' (2013) 33 *Legal Studies* 312.

150 Snyder (n 99) 201–3.

151 Résolution du Parlement européen du 8 mai 1969, sur les actes de la collectivité des États membres de la Communauté ainsi que les actes du Conseil non prévus par les traités adoptée à la suite du rapport fait au nom de la Commission juridique par M. Burger [1969] OJ C63/18.

152 Conseil d'État, Rapport Public 1992, collection 'Études et documents', *Documentation française* 44, 1993, Paris, 22–23, quoted in Leclerc (n 6) 163.

153 F Snyder, 'Interinstitutional Agreements: Forms and Constitutional Limitations' in G Winter (ed), *Sources and Categories of European Union Law: A Comparative and Reform Perspective* (Nomos 1996) 459.

154 See the discussion in Isabella Eiselt and Peter Slominski, 'Sub-Constitutional Engineering: Negotiation, Content, and Legal Value of Interinstitutional Agreements in the EU' (2006) 12 *European Law Journal* 209.

155 Senden (n 9) 483. 156 Hofmann (n 111) 172.

uncertain'.[157] Although it is true that the Commission undertakes lengthy public consultations before publishing soft law, empirical research in the environmental sector shows that these consultations are not always systematic, and there is little information as to how they occur.[158] Furthermore, the Commission practice of forcing Member States to agree to soft law issued in the State aid sector (as illustrated by the motor vehicles example discussed in section 4), is questionable from both transparency and legitimacy perspectives.

Second, as shown by *Expedia* and *Pfleiderer*, the intensity of the coercive enforcement of soft law varies in accordance with the level at which they are invoked—European or national. This creates important individual rights concerns. The fact that in a multilayered structure like the EU the individual has different identities and belongs to multiple polities seems to translate into a weakening of their rights at the various levels in the structure. Of course, at a first glance, national procedural autonomy and the discretion of the national authorities appears difficult to reconcile with imperatives such as ensuring consistent application of EU law or fostering legitimate expectations and legal certainty.

However, this conundrum is not that difficult to solve, as suggested by Advocate General Kokott, but is sadly not followed by the Court in *Expedia*. She noted that, even if not bound by the *de minimis* notice, national authorities and courts should 'consider the Commission's assessment' and also 'give reasons which can be judicially reviewed for any divergences'.[159] In this scenario, national authorities can depart from EU soft law in order to accommodate national specificities[160] or particular economic circumstances which need to be assessed on a case-by-case basis.[161] However, if they decide not to rely on EU soft law, they would either need to give reasons for this or issue their own general soft law by laying down guidelines on national practice.[162]

The criticisms of the use of soft law in courts are therefore undoubtedly serious. On the one hand, they translate into claims that the ECJ is fostering illegitimate decision making and thus widens the democratic deficit of the EU. On the other hand, engagement with soft law might demonstrate that the courts look beyond the formal lack of legal effects and also scrutinize non-legally binding material. However, this is not always the case, as research has found. For example, judicial engagement with instruments issued in the framework of Lisbon/Europe 2020 is scarce, and there is no conclusive evidence of courts acting as guardians of procedural standards and principles of good administration in relation to processes such as the OMC.[163] Furthermore, the courts fail to acknowledge the far-reaching consequences that guidance addressed by the Commission to the Member States authorities can have on the legal situation of individuals. In *PTC* the Polish telecommunications authority applied such EU guidance to assess the market power of an operator and as a consequence, imposed regulatory obligations in the case. While the ECJ acknowledged that the guidance could affect the situation of individuals, it stated that since it was only addressed to the national authorities, it could not provide obligations for individuals that could be of relevance in a court of law.[164] In similar circumstances, Scott argued that the Court does not go far enough and ignores many of the legal effects of soft law, thus often

[157] R Baldwin, *Rules and Government* (Clarendon Press 1995) 284.

[158] J Scott, 'In Legal Limbo: Post-legislative Guidance as a Challenge for European Administrative Law' (2011) 48 *Common Market Law Review* 329, 336.

[159] Opinion in *Expedia* (n108) para 39. [160] ibid, para 42. [161] ibid, para 41.

[162] ibid, fn 40. [163] Smismans (n 73) 517–19.

[164] O Ştefan, 'European Union Soft Law: New Developments Concerning the Divide Between Legally Binding Force and Legal Effects' (2012) 75 *Modern Law Review* 879.

depriving such instruments of judicial scrutiny.[165] Legal certainty also loses, given the differences in enforcement at the European and national level.

7. Conclusion

While enforcement of soft law could seem a *contradictio in terminis* at first glance, it appears from the above study that it is a reality at the European level. The difficulty of establishing a taxonomy of enforcement of soft law stems from the vast variety of soft law instruments issued by the European institutions. What is certain is that enforcement mechanisms vary in intensity, from non-constraining to deterrent, sometimes in various hybrid combinations which only reflect the hybrid character of regulation in the EU. Non-constraining mechanisms, such as those meant to enhance learning and the development of a common discourse, are effective in ensuring compliance with soft law. Enforcement through highly deterrent mechanisms brings to the forefront the legitimacy deficit from which such instruments are thought to suffer, and increases the need to deal with this important problem of 'new' governance in the EU.

Establishing clear-cut boundaries between soft law and hard law, as well as between the enforcement of soft and hard law, is difficult. Given that soft law is a tool for enhancing the effectiveness of European law, it can be considered a mechanism through which hard law is enforced. Hybridity of regulation translates into hybrid enforcement methods, and as seen in competition and State aid, courts rely increasingly on general principles of law and values to ensure compliance with soft law instruments. Enforcement of soft law through the principles and values it represents is sometimes difficult, given that the same instrument can help foster several principles at the same time, such as legal certainty and procedural autonomy. In such contexts, a delicate balance between these varying principles needs sometimes to be struck. While courts cannot be the main enforcers of soft law, they should adopt a less rigid approach, and be ready to acknowledge the full spectrum of practical effects of soft law. The role of the courts needs to change to ensure more intensive oversight of material deprived of legally binding force and issued outside traditional procedures involving legitimacy checks and balances.

[165] Scott (n 158) 342–3.

12

Protecting EU values

Reverse *Solange* and the Rule of Law Framework

Armin von Bogdandy, Carlino Antpöhler, and Michael Ioannidis

1. Introduction: Manifold instances of constitutional crises

Some of the Member States of the EU are threatening the fundamental principles enshrined in Article 2 TEU. The Polish reforms of its Constitutional Tribunal and Public Service Broadcasters are the most recent problems in a long list of concerns. Authoritarian tendencies, threatening democracy and human rights, are evident in Hungary.[1] In Bulgaria, Greece, Italy, and Romania,[2] systemic corruption and the weakness of some domestic institutions threaten the Union's fundamental Rule of Law principle. The financial crisis has aggravated some of the deficiencies in the system. The fact that to date there are only a few EU remedies adds to the sense of crisis. While the EU promotes good governance around the world[3] and scrutinizes candidate countries in terms of democracy, rule of law, and fundamental rights,[4] there is a lack of effective instruments to enforce EU values *within* the Union, that is to say, in its Member States. Of course, Article 7 TEU provides for a preventive and a sanctioning mechanism to address threats against EU values. However, many see these mechanisms as totally impractical.[5] Until recently, the defence of the Union's fundamental values has therefore been largely left to national and international institutions.

This situation is, firstly, deeply troubling for the individuals affected. Moreover, it is of systemic concern. The legitimacy of a Union which is unable to protect its foundational values is undermined. Such situations might also, from a functionalist perspective, threaten

[1] Regarding the situation in Hungary, see L Sólyom, 'The Rise and Decline of Constitutional Culture in Hungary', 5–31; and P Sonnevend et al., 'The Constitution as an Instrument of Everyday Party Politics: The Basic Law of Hungary', 33–109, both in A von Bogdandy and P Sonnevend (eds), *Constitutional Crisis in the European Constitutional Area* (Hart 2015).

[2] On recent developments in Romania, see B Iancu, 'Separation of Powers and the Rule of Law in Romania: The Crisis in Concepts and Contexts', 153–69 and C Tanasoiu, 'Romania in the European Union: Political Developments and the Rule of Law after Accession', 171–190, both in von Bogdandy and Sonnevend (n 1). See also V Perju, 'Defiance as Corruption – Romania and Bulgaria'; and M Ioannidis 'Weak Members and Defiance of EU law: The Case of Greece', both in Jakab and Kochenov (n 1).

[3] Art 21 TEU.

[4] Art 49 TEU. This is not to say that pre-accession scrutiny is devoid of all incoherence and flaws, see in more detail D Kochenov, *EU Enlargement and the Failure of Conditionality* (Kluwer Law International 2008).

[5] We take a different position. See A von Bogdandy, 'How to protect European Values in the Polish Constitutional Crisis', http://verfassungsblog.de/how-to-protect-european-values-in-the-polish-constitutional-crisis/, accessed 12 October 2016. For a conventional view, see W Sadurski, 'Adding Bite to a Bark: The Story of Article 7, EU Enlargement, and Jörg Haider' (2009–2010) 16 *Columbia Journal of European Law* 385, 423. Art 7 TEU can, however, be used as a legal basis for a mechanism below the threshold of the Art 7 mechanism (see Besselink in Chapter 8 of this volume). For an argument proposing the use of Art 7 in the Hungarian situation, see B Bugarič, 'Protecting Democracy inside the EU: On Article 7 TEU and the Hungarian Turn to Authoritarianism', in C Closa and D. Kochenov (eds), *Reinforcement of the Rule of Law Oversight in the European Union* (CUP 2016, forthcoming).

mutual confidence and trust as well as the premise that the Union can rely on the fact that the polities of its Member States function properly. All these are foundations of European integration.

This problem triggered fresh thinking on how the EU could monitor and enforce its fundamental values. Various suggestions have been made regarding the legal basis and the organizational characteristics of possible mechanisms to be used for this purpose, both in the political and academic discourse.[6] In this chapter we discuss the instruments currently on the table regarding the enforcement of EU values, exposing their strengths and weaknesses in legal and practical terms.[7] We will also offer an evaluation of the first use of the Rule of Law Framework. So far, most of the proposed instruments have been presented in isolation. This is particularly true of the proposed 'Copenhagen Commission' and the 'Reverse *Solange*' mechanism. This chapter presents and normatively assesses the ideas proposed and discusses how to combine the various instruments which so far have been considered separately. We argue that the most apt European response to systemic deficiencies is to combine judicial mechanisms, including the Reverse *Solange* mechanism, as well as a complementary political approach. In developing the political mechanism, we focus in particular on the Rule of Law Framework and its recent first activation. We propose to consider supplementing it with a 'Systemic Deficiency Committee'. The proposal combines important insights from the proposal for a Copenhagen Commission by Jan-Werner Müller and the Rule of Law Framework already in place. The fusion enhances both the proposal and the Framework. In light of these new instruments, Article 7(1) TEU could become an important tool in protecting European values.

2. The Reverse *Solange* doctrine

The Reverse *Solange* doctrine aims to empower individuals to challenge domestic exercises of public authority which deprive him or her of the substance of a fundamental right in cases of systemic deficiency.[8] The core idea is to open up 'respect for human rights' provided by Article 2 TEU for individual legal actions via Union citizenship.[9] In *Ruiz Zambrano* the ECJ held that 'Article 20 TFEU precludes national measures which have the effect of depriving citizens of the Union of the genuine enjoyment of the substance of the rights conferred by virtue of their status as citizens of the Union'.[10] We argue that the substance referred to includes essential fundamental rights.[11]

[6] For a review, see C Closa et al., 'Reinforcing Rule of Law Oversight in the European Union' (2014) EUI Working Papers No 15, 2–3, 4; L Moxham and J Stefanelli, 'Safeguarding the Rule of Law, Democracy and Fundamental Rights: A Monitoring Model for the European Union' (Bingham Centre for the Rule of Law, 2013), http://biicl.org/files/6758_main_report_15_11_2013_commission_consultation.pdf, accessed 12 October 2016.

[7] This chapter draws on A von Bogdandy et al., 'Reverse *Solange* – Protecting the essence of fundamental rights against EU Member States' (2012) 49 *Common Market Law Review* 489–519; A von Bogdandy and M Ioannidis, 'Systemic deficiency in the rule of law: What it is, what has been done, what can be done' (2014) 51 *Common Market Law Review* 59–96.

[8] The original proposal was developed in von Bogdandy et al. (n 7) and was further advanced in A von Bogdandy et al., 'Reverse *Solange* – A European Response to Domestic Constitutional Crisis: Advancing the Reverse-Solange Doctrine' in von Bogdandy and Sonnevend (eds) (n 1) 248–67.

[9] This is an approach which was already considered as having some merit in *Van Gend en Loos* 'the vigilance of individuals concerned to protect their rights' and their willingness to turn to domestic courts (ECJ, Case C-26/62 *Van Gend en Loos* [1963] ECLI:EU:C:1963:1, para 24).

[10] Case C-34/09 *Ruiz Zambrano* [2011] ECLI:EU:C:2011:124, para 42.

[11] For earlier proposals in this direction: Case C-380/05 *Centro Europa 7* [2008] ECLI:EU:C:2008:59; Opinion of AG Maduro, ECLI:EU:C:2007:505, para 17ff.; D Halberstam, 'Constitutional Heterarchy: The Centrality of Conflict in the European Union and the United States' in J Dunoff and J Trachtman (eds), *Ruling the World* (CUP 2009), 326, 353.

So far, the ECJ has not had the opportunity to decide on a case suitable for developing this approach. Indeed, it has adopted a rather limited approach regarding the substance of Union citizenship and has refrained from connecting citizenship and fundamental rights per se.[12] At the same time, it has expanded the scope of Article 51 CFR. We argue that the Reverse *Solange* doctrine is a more appropriate mechanism to protecting fundamental rights in extreme situations, while at the same time, respecting Article 51 CFR and the national identities of Member States.[13]

In essence, a serious violation by a Member State, even in purely internal situations,[14] can be considered as constituting an infringement of the substance of Union citizenship. The seriousness criterion is key to preserving European constitutional pluralism as protected by Article 4(2) TEU. Hence, beyond the scope of Article 51(1) CFR, Member States should remain autonomous with respect to fundamental rights protection *as long as* ('solange') it can be presumed that they secure the *essence* of the fundamental rights enshrined in Article 2 TEU. However, in the event of a violation which is considered systemic, this presumption is rebutted and individuals may rely on their status as Union citizens to seek redress before national courts.[15] In the original proposal, non-compliance with a judgment of the ECtHR was offered as an example to engage such a rebuttal.

Recent jurisprudence in EU fundamental rights law, *Åkerberg Fransson* in particular,[16] does not alter or erode the pertinence of this doctrine. The advantage of the Reverse *Solange* doctrine is its ability to protect fundamental rights in circumstances where its use becomes necessary, while respecting the constitutional identities of Member States, for which an autonomous understanding of constitutional rights is often essential. The reasoning in *Åkerberg Fransson* is not entirely convincing in this respect. The case law has shown that the scope of European fundamental rights is partially overstretched in ordinary cases where it appears doubtful whether European protection is needed.[17] At the same time, the more restrictive jurisprudence in the aftermath of *Åkerberg Fransson*[18] highlights the danger that systemic deficiencies in fundamental rights protection violating the core of the Union's values might still be outside the scope of EU fundamental rights protection. The Reverse *Solange* doctrine is limited to systemic deficiencies. It leaves ordinary problems to the domestic institutions. With systemic deficiencies, however, the strong enforcement

[12] Case C-434/09 *McCarthy* [2011] ECLI:EU:C:2011:277, para 49; Case C-256/11 *Dereci* [2011] ECLI:EU:C:2011:734, para 66; Case C-40/11 *Iida* [2012] ECLI:EU:C:2012:691, para 71; Case C-87/12 *Ymeraga* [2013] ECLI:EU:C:2013:291, para 36; Case C-86/12 *Alokpa and Moudoulou* [2013] ECLI:EU:C:2013:645, para 32. On the more limited approach and the need for a constitutional citizenship, see D Sarmiento and E Sharpston, 'European Citizenship and its New Union: Time To Move On?' in D Kochenov (ed) *EU Citizenship and Federalism: The Role of Rights* (CUP 2016, forthcoming).

[13] von Bogdandy et al. (n 8) 241.

[14] In the Union citizenship case law the cross-border element has become increasingly blurred over time (See Case C-148/02 *Garcia Avello* [2003] ECLI:EU: C:2003:539, para 26; Case C-200/02 *Zhu and Chen* [2004] ECLI:EU:C:2004:639, para 26; Case C-135/08 *Rottmann* [2010] ECLI:EU:C:2010:104, para 42. In detail D Kochenov, 'A Real European Citizenship: The Court of Justice Opening a New Chapter in the Development of the Union in Europe' [2011/2012] 18 *Columbia Journal of European* Law 55.

[15] This is inspired by the German Federal Constitutional Court, which no longer exercises its competence to control EU secondary law as long as the Union ensures 'essentially similar' fundamental rights protection as the German Basic Law, meaning that it 'generally safeguard[s] the essential content of fundamental rights' (*BVerfGE* 73, 339, 376 [1986] *Solange II*).

[16] Case C-617/10 *Åkerberg Fransson* [2013] ECLI:EU:C:2013:105.

[17] See the German Federal Constitutional Court on the anti-terror database *BVerfGE* 133, 277, DE:BVerfG:2013:rs20130424.1bvr121507, paras 88–91.

[18] Case C-333/13 *Dano* [2014] ECLI:EU:C:2014:342, para 88; Case C-198/13 *J Hernández* et al. [2014] ECLI:EU:C:2014:2055, para 33 ff.; D Sarmiento, 'Who's afraid of the Charter? The Court of Justice, national courts and the new framework of fundamental rights protection in Europe' (2013) 50 *Common Market Law Review* 1267.

mechanisms of European judgments with direct effect and the authority of the domestic judiciary can be used and relied upon.

a. Insights from the debate so far

When we first presented our proposal, we discussed and rebutted three possible rejoinders: the *ultra vires* objection, the approach's limited protection of third-country nationals, and its effects on the ECtHR.[19] The Reverse *Solange* proposal sparked a rich debate.[20] Interesting insights can be drawn from that discussion. For example, it is noteworthy that all the authors share a sense of dissatisfaction with the current state of affairs. Their common ground is the need for change in order to have better and broader fundamental rights protection under EU law.

Three points reappeared in a number of comments: it was argued that the essence of fundamental rights is too vague a concept to be applied in practice. Furthermore, it was questioned whether it is convincing to rely on domestic courts in times of crisis. Additionally, many comments questioned our proposed increased legal integration, i.e. our court-centredness. Instead, it was argued, more political mechanisms are needed to address the problem. It is indeed correct that the Reverse *Solange* doctrine, relying on courts, ought to

[19] von Bogdandy et al. (n 7) 489, 514–18.

[20] See the contributions by M Avbelj, 'The Hungarian Dilemma from a Pluralist Perspective'; C Franzius, 'Sinn und Unsinn einer Kopenhagen-Kommission'; D Halberstam, 'Rescue Package for Fundamental Rights'; A Jakab, 'Supremacy of the EU Charter in National Courts in Purely Domestic Cases'; D Kochenov, 'The EU in its most serious crisis ever (and that's not the Euro crisis)'; J Komárek, 'The EU is More Than a Constraint on Populist Democracy'; M Kumm, 'Rettungsschirm für Grundrechte'; P Lindseth, 'Rescue Package for Fundamental Rights'; AK Mangold, 'Rettungsschirm für Grundrechte'; JW Müller, 'The Idea of Democracy Protection in the EU Revisited'; K Nicolaidis, '"What" versus "Who": Europe's Rule of Law Agenda Revisited'; W Sadurski, 'Rescue Package for Fundamental Rights'; P Sonnevend, 'Rescue Package for Fundamental Rights'; D Thym, 'Rettungsschirm für Grundrechte'; R Uitz, 'Rescue Package for Fundamental Rights'; A Wiener, 'Rescue Package for Fundamental Rights'; F de Witte 'Less Constraint of Popular Democracy, more Empowerment of Citizens', all in M Steinbeis et al. (eds), *Gebändigte Macht: Verfassung im europäischen Nationalstaat* (Nomos 2015); M van den Brink, 'The Origins and the Potential Federalising Effects of the Substance of Rights Test' in D Kochenov (ed), *EU Citizenship and Federalism: The Role of Rights* (CUP 2016, forthcoming); Bugarič, (n 5); J Croon-Gestefeld, 'Reverse Solange – Union Citizenship as a Detour on the Route to European Rights Protection Against National Infringements', in D Kochenov (ed), *EU Citizenship and Federalism: The Role of Rights* (CUP 2016, forthcoming); I Del Vecchio, 'Koinè constituionale e cittadinanza europea' (2015) 2 *Diritto E Società* 423; C Franzius, 'Grundrechtsschutz in Europa – Zwischen Selbstbehauptungen und Selbstbeschränkungen der Rechtsordnungen und ihrer Gerichte' (2015) 75 *Zeitschrift für ausländisches öffentliches Recht und Völkerrecht* 405; C Franzius, *Recht und Politik in der transnationalen Konstellation* (Campus 2014) 234 ff.; M Hilf and F Schorkopf, 'Art. 2 EUV', in E Grabitz et al. (eds), *Das Recht der Europäischen Union* (CH Beck 2016) para 53; SI Sánchez, 'Fundamental Rights and Citizenship of the Union at Crossroads: A Promising Alliance or a Dangerous Liaison?' (2014) 20 *European Law Journal* 477; P Iosifidis and I Katsirea, 'Public Service Broadcasting in Greece in the Era of Austerity' (2014) EUI Working Paper RSCAS No 42, 9 ff., http://cadmus.eui.eu/bitstream/handle/1814/31872/RSCAS_2014_42.pdf?sequence=1, accessed 12 October 2016; M Klatt, *Die praktische Konkordanz von Kompetenzen. Entwickelt anhand der Jurisdiktionskonflikte im europäischen Grundrechtsschutz* (Mohr Siebeck 2014) 395–406; D Kochenov, 'On Policing Article 2 TEU Compliance – Reverse *Solange* and Systemic Infringements Analyzed' (2013) 33 *Polish Yearbook of International Law* 145; D Kostakopoulou, 'Co-Creating European Union Citizenship: Institutional Process ad Crescive Norms' (2012–2013) 15 *Cambridge Yearbook of European Legal Studies* 271; K Krūma, *EU Citizenship, Nationality and Migrant Status* (Martinus Nijhoff 2014) 422 ff.; W Michl, *Die Überprüfung des Unionsrechts am Maßstab der EMRK. Individualgrundrechtsschutz im Anwendungsbereich des Unionsrechts unter den Vorzeichen des Beitritts der EU zur EMRK* (Mohr Siebeck 2014) 8, 38–41; C Ohler, 'Grundrechtliche Bindungen der Mitgliedstaaten nach Artikel 51 GRCh' (2013) 22 *Neue Zeitschrift für Verwaltungsrecht* 1435; LP Lea, 'A demokrácia és pluralizmus értéke az európai média jogban' (2014) *Iustum Aequum Salutare* 114 ff.; C Pinelli, 'Protecting the Fundamentals' (2002) Foundation for European Progressive Studies Working Paper 9; AM Russo, 'La cittadinanza "sostanziale" dell'UE alla luce della proposta del gruppo di Heidelberg: verso una "reverse *Solange*"?' (2014) 1 *Federalismi* 1; Sarmiento and Sharpston (n 12); A Voßkuhle, 'The Cooperation Between European Courts: The Verbund of European Courts and its Legal Toolbox', in A Rosas et al. (eds), *The Court of Justice and the Construction of Europe: Analyses and Perspectives on Sixty Years of Case-law* (TMC Asser Press 2013) 81, 94–7; W Weiß, 'Grundrechtsschutz durch den EuGH: Tendenzen seit Lissabon' (2013) *Europäische Zeitschrift für Wirtschaftsrecht EuZW* 288.

be complemented by other, more political mechanisms. This, however, does not render the involvement of the courts dispensable. Courts have a particular capacity to protect the rights of individuals.

The first objection concerns the implementation of that doctrine. Some argue that the *essence* of fundamental rights is too vague a concept to be applied judicially.[21] Indeed, a proposal resting on the idea of an essence of fundamental rights which has not been applied broadly to date needs to be spelled out. So far, we have concentrated on the theoretical viability of the *essence* of the concept and the theoretical reasons for its revival.[22] However, we have also shown how it could be applied in the case of media freedom, which provides an example of how the essence of fundamental rights can be concretized.[23] The ECJ has held that media freedom is a 'fundamental pillar for a democratic society',[24] part of a detailed catalogue of rights contained in the essence of fundamental rights which can be drawn from ECtHR case law and Commission practice in the accession procedure. The ECtHR has repeatedly held that 'there is little scope [. . .] for restrictions on political speech or on debate on questions of public interest'.[25] Only the political aspects of media freedom can therefore belong to the essence of the fundamental right.[26] Of course, further precision is valuable to help manage the criterion better in the courts. For example, the protection of journalists' sources is particularly crucial for media freedom and has given rise to numerous court proceedings. According to the ECtHR, any encroachment upon this right requires the 'most careful scrutiny'.[27] In a number of states, the exceptions to the protection of journalist sources are broad and vague, and *ex ante* judicial control is also often lacking.[28] This is contrary to the foreseeability criterion contained in Article 10(2) ECHR and likely to infringe on the essence of the right. The broad exceptions especially augment the danger of preventing sources from interacting with the press since they fear their disclosure.[29] This 'chilling effect' could hinder the media from fulfilling its function as a 'public watchdog'.[30] On the basis of the ECtHR's case law, a too broad or too vague obligation on journalists to disclose their sources is likely to violate the essence of media freedom. While the threshold for European interference is indeed vague, there is ample material to substantiate the essence doctrine in a way which can inform decisions in concrete cases.

A second objection regards the reliance on domestic courts. It is argued that the doctrine 'is fully dependent on the good will of the national courts'.[31] The Reverse *Solange* doctrine

[21] Sadurski (n 20); Sonnevend (n 20); Thym (n 20); and Kochenov (n 20) 154.

[22] J von Bernstorff, 'Kerngehaltsschutz durch den UN-Menschenrechtsausschuss und den EGMR' (2011) 50 *Der Staat* 165.

[23] The High Level Group on Media Freedom and Pluralism, appointed by then Vice-President of the Commission Neelie Croes has taken up the idea to link the substance of citizenship and media freedom (V Vīķe-Freiberga et al., 'A free and pluralistic media to sustain European democracy' [January 2013] 21, https://ec.europa.eu/digital-agenda/sites/digital-agenda/files/HLG%20Final%20Report.pdf, accessed 12 October 2016).

[24] Case C-368/95 *Familiapress* [1997] ECLI:EU:C:1997:325, para 26; Case C-112/00 *Schmidberger* [2003] ECLI:EU:C:2003:333, para 79; c.f. K Stern, 'Art. 11 CFREU', in P Tettinger and K Stern (eds), *Kölner Gemeinschaftskommentar zur Europäischen Grundrechte-Charta* (CH Beck 2006), paras 6–10; Weiler qualifies the freedom of expression as a fundamental right with a transcendent universal core of protected speech (JHH Weiler, 'Fundamental Rights and Fundamental Boundaries', in JHH Weiler, *The Constitution of Europe* (CUP 1999), 102, 105 ff.).

[25] *Sürek/Özdemir v Turkey* Joined App no 23927/94 and 24277/94 (ECtHR (GC), 8 July 1999), para 46; *Wingrove v the United Kingdom* ECHR 1996-V, para 58.

[26] See *Scharsach v Austria* ECHR 2003-XI, para 30; in detail JA Frowein and W Peukert, *Europäische Menschenrechtskonvention* (3rd edn, Engel 2009), Art 10 para 27.

[27] *Goodwin v UK* ECHR 1996-II, para 40.

[28] *Kruslin v France* App nos 11105/84 and 11801/85 (ECtHR, 24 April 1990), para 33.

[29] *Financial Times Ltd and others v the United Kingdom* App No 821/03 (ECtHR, 15 March 2010), para 70.

[30] *Goodwin v UK*, para 39 (n 28); *Financial Times Ltd and Others v the United Kingdom*, para 59 (n 30).

[31] Closa et al. (n 6) 17. Similarly, Croon-Gestefeld (n 21).

indeed involves the domestic courts. We see it as part of its strength that domestic enforcement mechanisms can be used. However, it would be flawed to perceive the doctrine as relying on national courts alone, as Closa, Kochenov, and Weiler suggest. The Reverse *Solange* doctrine is envisaged as an integral part of EU law. Accordingly, it can be enforced through all existing enforcement mechanisms, including infringement proceedings by the Commission according to Article 258 TFEU. Strengthening infringement proceedings in the field of systemic deficiencies is moreover an idea shared with the systemic infringement proceedings proposal by Scheppele.[32] While it would indeed not be convincing to rely on domestic courts alone, they can contribute to mitigating—if not navigating—constitutional crises. The critics seem to have a situation in mind where all domestic courts are barred from preliminary references due to political pressure. A situation where every single court is brought into line seems unlikely and past experience shows that brave courts do exist.

b. The way forward—A complementary political approach

The third point of disagreement is whether to rely on the judiciary[33] or rather on the political realm.[34] A number of scholars express misgivings at finding 'a purely legal remedy to an essentially political problem'.[35] This critique gives the opportunity to stress that Reverse *Solange* does not aim at substituting the political process, but rather at complementing it. A complex problem such as a domestic constitutional crisis cannot be remedied by relying merely on the judiciary. Instead, the particular strengths of every institution are needed. It cannot be denied that protecting individual rights is the very business of courts[36] and arguably the one thing they, as opposed to the political branches of government, are better equipped to do.[37] Moreover, though a constitutional crisis is unlikely to be solved by courts on their own,[38] they might contribute to its resolution. A judgment could trigger domestic political developments while addressing the grievances of the affected individual effectively: by means of the direct effect of Union law, judgments of the ECJ enjoy strong domestic enforceability.

However, activating the Reverse *Solange* doctrine in a critical situation does not preclude political action. Different instruments should complement one another. The focus on individual rights permits forceful intervention to protect an affected individual, but does not alter a more general status quo per se. Furthermore, developments in a Member State may threaten a number of constitutional principles. While a court is particularly apt to assess threats to fundamental rights, it might be less effective when it comes to the protection of other principles such as democracy or the Rule of Law.[39] The Reverse *Solange* doctrine has accordingly been focused on the sphere of fundamental rights.[40] When the

[32] KL Scheppele, 'Enforcing the Basic Principles of EU Law through Systemic Infringement Actions' in Closa and Kochenov (n 5).

[33] Halberstam (n 20); Kochenov (n 20); Kumm (n 20); Wiener (n 20); Franzius (n 20).

[34] The more politicized approach is advocated by: Lindseth (n 20); Mangold (n 20); Sadurski (n 20); Sonnevend (n 20); Thym (n 20); Uitz (n 20).

[35] Sadurski (n 20). [36] Franzius (n 20).

[37] JH Ely, *Democracy and Distrust. A Theory of Judicial Review* (Harvard University Press 1980) 105; Halberstam (n 11) 326, 338 ff.; c.f. U Haltern, *Verfassungsgerichtsbarkeit, Demokratie und Mißtrauen. Das Bundesverfassungsgericht in einer Verfassungstheorie zwischen Populismus und Progressivismus* (Duncker & Humblot 1998) 204 ff.; See the critique of C Möllers, 'Legalität, Legitimität und Legitimation des Bundesverfassungsgerichts' in M Jestaedt, et al. (eds), *Das entgrenzte Gericht. Eine kritische Bilanz nach sechzig Jahren Bundesverfassungsgericht* (Suhrkamp 2011), 281, 406 ff.

[38] Mangold (n 20). [39] Closa et al. (n 6) 12; Müller (n 20).

[40] For an application to the process of constitution making: von Bogdandy et al., 'A European Response to Domestic Constitutional Crisis', in von Bogdandy and Sonnevend (n 1).

discussion is extended to systemic deficiencies in general, it becomes even more obvious that political mechanisms are needed. In the following sections we will discuss such mechanisms and suggest some ideas for how to develop them.

3. The Council's Rule of Law dialogue

The Council has responded to calls[41] for another way to deal with systemic threats to the Article 2 TEU values. The 2014 Tripartite Council Presidency Work Programme stipulates to 'closely accompany the future developments [...] to strengthen the Rule of Law which seeks to resolve future systemic threats to the Rule of Law in Member States before the conditions for activating the mechanism foreseen in Article 7 TEU would be met'.[42] In December 2014 the Council and the Member States 'commit[ted] themselves to establish a dialogue within the Council to promote and safeguard the rule of law in the framework of the Treaties'.[43] That dialogue will be held once a year in the Council. There may be further thematic discussion. The Member States have agreed on a number of principles to inform the implementation of the dialogue in the Council's practice. Of note is the principle of equal treatment among Member States. As this principle is evident from EU primary law (e.g. Article 4(2) TEU), its explicit reiteration highlights the fear of some Member States of being bullied by others. Furthermore, the dialogue is expected to be non-partisan and evidence-based.

However, experience with enforcement through peer pressure within the EU raises doubts regarding the effectiveness of the new dialogue-based mechanism, as the rare use of the infringement proceedings between Member States illustrate.[44] Indeed, the role of the Commission as 'Guardian of the Treaties' rests on the insight that supervision by the Member States is insufficient. Indeed, the Council, the voice of the Member States, has so far been conspicuously silent in dealing with systemic threats. No action has been taken in the case of Poland, for instance. With regards to Hungary and Romania, it seems that the European party system works: domestic parties have managed to avoid isolation in their respective European party. Doubts over the adequacy of the dialogue are also supported by the process leading to the Council statement. While the four Ministers of Foreign Affairs' letter called for a new mechanism, the wording in the programme which was put into effect is more cautious: it calls on the Member States to 'closely accompany future developments'. The Council conclusions also refrain from using the term 'mechanism'. Given this 'watering down' had already happened at the stage of deciding on the general contours of the framework, it seems unlikely that Member States will agree on the highly contentious issue

[41] Of particular importance is the letter sent to the Commission by then Foreign Minister of Denmark, Finland, Germany, and the Netherlands. It can be found on the homepage of the Dutch government (http://www.rijksoverheid.nl/bestanden/documenten-en-publicaties/brieven/2013/03/13/brief-aan-europese-commissie-over-opzetten-rechtsstatelijkheidsmechanisme/brief-aan-europese-commissie-over-opzetten-rechtsstatelijkheidsmechanisme.pdf, accessed 12 October 2016). The letter was preceded by an initiative of a larger group of Ministers of Foreign Affairs, the so-called Future of Europe Group, who called for 'a new, light mechanism [...] enabling the Commission to draw up a report in the case of concrete evidence of violations of the values under Article 2 of the TEU' (http://www.auswaertiges-amt.de/cae/servlet/contentblob/626322/publicationFile/171844/120918-Abschlussbericht-Zukunftsgruppe.pdf, accessed 12 October 2016).

[42] Eighteen-month work programme of 17 June 2014, prepared by the Italian Presidency with the future Latvian and Luxembourg Presidencies and the High Representative, endorsed by the General Affairs Council (11258/1/14).

[43] Press Release, 3362nd Council meeting of 16 December 2014, 16936/14, 20 ff.

[44] N Wunderlich, 'Art. 259 AEUV' in H von der Groeben, J Schwarze and A Hatje, *Europäisches Unionsrecht* (7th edn, Nomos 2015) para 4.

of the actual existence of a systemic threat in a Member State, as the Hungarian experience has shown.[45]

4. The Commission's Rule of Law Framework

In 2014 the Commission established a Rule of Law Framework to support the enforcement of EU values. In January 2016 Commissioner Timmermans officially notified the Minister of Justice of Poland, Mr Ziobro, that from that point on the Commission would consider the issue of Poland's recent constitutional and other legal revisions under the 'EU Framework to strengthen the Rule of Law' (Rule of Law Framework).[46] In the following section, we argue that the Framework is generally a meaningful step towards developing responses to systemic deficiencies in national laws and policy. There are however some weaknesses regarding its institutional setup. Recent practice vis-à-vis Poland confirms this assessment: the application was a step in the right direction, but the situation is very complex and it will require great political skill and legal imagination to make the Framework a success. Accordingly, we propose that the Framework should be supplemented by a Systemic Deficiency Committee.

a. Basic features of the Rule of Law Framework

In a communication to the EP and the Council in March 2014, the Commission announced 'a new EU Framework to strengthen the Rule of Law'.[47] Although this act does not authorize the adoption of binding measures, it substantially strengthens the EU's role in safeguarding the Rule of Law—and might also cover other aspects of the EU's fundamental values. The new mechanism is to be used in advance of the preventive and sanctioning mechanisms provided for by Article 7 TEU[48] and is designed for situations which threaten the Article 2 TEU values, without the existence of a 'clear risk of serious breach' or 'serious and persistent breach' having yet been established.

When the Framework was activated for the first time, many media reports focused on the possibility that this initiative might lead the EU to apply the sanctions under Article 7 TEU—often wrongly termed as 'nuclear'. However, that is far beyond what is politically likely at the moment. The real issue is the deployment of the new Rule of Law Framework as a more conducive alternative, hopefully backed by the support of European public opinion.

There are three noteworthy and salient features regarding this instrument. The first feature is its scope. At first glance, the new mechanism is not designed to protect all the Article 2 TEU values; rather, it is explicitly dedicated to the Rule of Law. However, the Commission adopts a broad reading of the Rule of Law. The Framework, building on the work of the Venice Commission[49] and the case law of the ECJ, cites six principles it

[45] F Hoffmeister, 'Enforcing the EU Charter of Fundamental Rights in Member States: How far are Rome, Budapest and Bucharest from Brussels?' in von Bogdandy and Sonnevend (eds) (n 1).

[46] The letter was leaked by the *Financial Times*, http://blogs.ft.com/brusselsblog/2016/01/13/timmermans-calls-for-talks-as-row-over-polish-media-law-rumbles-on/, accessed 12 October 2016.

[47] Commission, 'A new EU Framework to strengthen the Rule of Law' (Communication from the Commission to the European Parliament and the Council) COM(2014) 158 final, 19 March 2014, 2, http://ec.europa.eu/justice/effective-justice/files/com_2014_158_en.pdf, accessed 12 October 2016.

[48] Commission COM(2014) 158 (n 47) 3.

[49] European Commission for Democracy through Law (Venice Commission), The Rule of Law CDL-AD (2011) 003 rev, Study no 512/2009, http://www.eods.eu/library/VC.Report%20on%20the%20rule%20of%20law%20english.pdf, accessed 12 October 2016.

considers as part of the Rule of Law: 'legality', 'legal certainty', 'prohibition of arbitrariness of the executive powers', 'independent and impartial courts', 'effective judicial review including respect for fundamental rights', and 'equality before the law'.[50] Moreover, for the purposes of the framework 'legality' includes 'a transparent, accountable, democratic and pluralistic process for enacting laws'.[51] It thus appears that the new mechanism is to protect not only the Rule of Law in the narrow sense, but also democracy and human rights as a whole.[52]

This general orientation towards a 'thick' concept of the Rule of Law is in principle reaffirmed in the decision to submit Poland to the Framework, which notes that the Rule of Law is a constitutional principle with both formal and substantive components.[53] Nevertheless, when it comes to the actual reprimands against Polish reforms, priority is accorded to the formal dimension. In his letter of 13 January 2016, Frans Timmermans makes Poland especially accountable for disregarding the decisions of the Polish Constitutional Tribunal. Freedom and pluralism of the media, as questions of democracy and fundamental rights, do form part of the critique, but they take a back seat. It would be unfortunate however if the scope of the Framework were developed to exclude other threats to the European constitutional order, such as democracy and human rights.[54]

A second feature of the Framework is that it explicitly builds on the presumption that Member States abide by the Rule of Law. Individual breaches of fundamental rights or an isolated miscarriage of justice are not enough to trigger action against a Member State under the Framework.[55] Action is reserved for extreme cases which are 'likely to systematically and adversely affect the integrity, stability or the proper functioning of the institutions and the safeguard mechanisms established at national level to secure the rule of law'.[56] The Commission uses the term 'systemic breakdown' when referring to such cases.[57] It considers that such problems justify proactive steps, even if the thresholds of 'clear risk of a serious breach' or 'serious and persistent breach' set by Article 7 TEU are not reached.

However, the Commission's early steps do not address why the situation in Poland could amount to a 'systemic' threat to EU values. The letter to Poland, formally announcing the activation of the Framework, makes no single reference to 'systemic'. Moreover, Frans Timmermans in his introductory remarks to the Discussion of the EP, referred to this element by simply saying that '[g]iven the central position of the Constitutional Tribunal within the Polish judicial system, we risk seeing the emergence of a systemic threat to the Rule of Law'. This treatment of the component of 'systemic' is unsatisfactory for two reasons.

First, the general reference to 'the central position of the Constitutional Tribunal' is too cursory to offer a reasoned justification why the reforms enacted by Poland qualify as a systemic threat. Second, according to the clear wording of the Framework, a simple 'risk' of the emergence of systemic threat is not sufficient to trigger its activation—the systemic character of the threat needs to be present and immediate. As we have shown elsewhere, the

[50] Commission COM(2014) 158 (n 47) 4. [51] ibid.

[52] ibid. Similarly, see Closa, Kochenov, and Weiler (n 6) 12, who also use a broad notion of the Rule of Law.

[53] Frans Timmermans, Readout by First Vice-President Timmermans of the College Meeting (13 January 2016) Speech 16/71, http://europa.eu/rapid/press-release_SPEECH-16-71_en.htm, accessed 12 October 2016.

[54] For the importance of a broad understanding of the rule of law, see also Democracy Reporting International, 'Towards a New Deal for Democracy in Europe' (June 2014) Briefing Paper 49, http://democracy-reporting.org/files/bp_49_16_june_1.pdf, accessed 12 October 2016.

[55] Commission COM(2014) 158 (n 47) 6. [56] ibid.

[57] European Commission, Press Release (11 March 2014), http://europa.eu/rapid/press-release_IP-14-237_en.htm, accessed 12 October 2016.

systemic component to the violation of the Rule of Law is indeed fundamental for the legality of the Framework, since it demarcates the scope of action between the EU and Member States under Article 2 TEU.[58] Moreover, if the Commission's activity is to induce any government to reconsider its policy, it needs to rely on European public opinion—and to mobilize European public opinion, the Commission must indicate the systemic nature of the threat to common values. In our previous work, we shaped this general term using theoretical and comparative considerations.[59] The Commission should do more to clarify its understanding of the concept—not least because this is required by the Rule of Law to which the Commission is also subject: the application of any rule must be reasoned, in particular in such sensitive issues.

The third characteristic of the new mechanism is the central role of the Commission. Compared to its function under Article 7 TEU, where the Commission only has the right to activate the preventive and the sanctioning mechanisms, the new framework foresees important powers. The Commission may initially send the Member State concerned a 'Rule of Law opinion' and engage it in a dialogue with a view to remedying the problem. If that does not lead to a satisfactory resolution, the Commission may proceed to the second stage and issue a 'Rule of Law recommendation', addressed to the Member State concerned. In this recommendation, the Commission may set a fixed time limit and even include specific indications on appropriate measures. The Commission is also responsible for monitoring compliance with the recommendation. If the Member State does not adequately respond to the Commission's concerns and there is no satisfactory follow-up to the recommendation, it will 'assess the possibility of activating one of the mechanisms set out in Article 7 TEU'. More importantly, the Framework foresees a naming-and-shaming mechanism, allowing the Commission to publish both the sending of the recommendation and its main content.[60]

The new mechanism, and the important role it attributes to the Commission in particular, has triggered reactions both in legal and practical terms. The Council Legal Service made public its opinion in the aftermath of the announcement of the new mechanism—in itself a rare occurrence—that the Framework is incompatible with the principle of conferral.[61] According to the Council Legal Service, Article 7 TEU sets out an exclusive procedure for the protection of EU fundamental values; no other action may be taken by the EU institutions. It is thus outside the realm of competences of the Commission to issue recommendations to Member States in relation to Article 2 TEU. We find the Council's arguments to be unconvincing.[62] The Framework may be interpreted as a set of norms which clarify and make transparent how the Commission will proceed before exercising its competence to submit a proposal to activate the Article 7 mechanisms: in other words, it is a set of administrative clarifications. It structures and disciplines the steps that the Commission will adopt as part of its assessment of a threat to the EU's fundamental values. No formal sanction is imposed and the final word continues to be reserved to the Council and the European Council following the steps set out in Article 7 TEU, including the procedural guarantees for the Member State concerned.

[58] von Bogdandy and Ioannidis (n 7) 66. [59] ibid, 62 ff.

[60] Commission COM(2014) 158 (n 47) 8.

[61] Council of the European Union, 'Commission's Communication on a new EU Framework to strengthen the Rule of Law: compatibility with the Treaties' (Opinion of the Legal Service 10296/14 May 2014).

[62] For a thorough assessment, see von Bogdandy and Ioannidis (n 7) 66; A von Bogdandy and M Ioannidis, 'Das systemische Defizit – Merkmale, Instrumente und Probleme am Beispiel der Rechtsstaatlichkeit und des neuen Rechtsstaatlichkeitsaufsichtsverfahrens' (2014) 74 *Zeitschrift für ausländisches öffentliches Recht und Völkerrecht* 293, 324.

The mechanism has been criticized for its likely lack of effectiveness.[63] We believe that such assessments might be premature, considering that the Framework is only a very recent development. We prefer to view this mechanism as a step in the 'right' direction of efficient European means to counter systemic deficiencies. The Framework could exert considerable political pressure on the relevant Member State. Recent practice confirms this optimistic outlook: the activation of the Framework has shown its potential to mobilize European public opinion and orient public discourses to the current condition of EU values. Major EU newspapers have taken up the issue, informed commentary is being produced, and the EP had a promising debate on the issue. The Framework could render the threat of activating Article 7 TEU more realistic. The possible publication of its findings might also contribute to debates on the importance of European responses to systemic deficiencies. We do not believe that engagement in this phased dialogue can easily be ignored by any government, and it will thus have a domestic impact as well as a ripple effect.[64]

While the Framework is a step forward, several doubts remain regarding the dominant role of the Commission. The record of the Commission's activities in recent crises is mixed,[65] and with the Commission's increased politicization, it seems likely that any response to systemic deficiencies can reasonably be criticized as exemplifying partisanship.[66] One consequence of the current Commission actions was a broad spectrum counter-coalition of Eurosceptics who regarded them as a political manoeuvre. To counter such claims, an independent institution should be involved. This body could be, as in the Polish case, the Venice Commission, whose opinion strongly suggests a systemic threat.[67] The Venice Commission, however, might not always prove as helpful as in the Polish case. Firstly, its opinions rely on requests, usually by the state concerned.[68] Secondly, the Commission's standards—with its membership reaching even beyond the Council of Europe—might at times be lower than that required within the EU. Thirdly, a dedicated EU body might be in a better position to establish when a Rule of Law problem acquires a 'systemic' character within the meaning of the Framework. Therefore, we suggest considering the establishment of a dedicated EU institution, a 'Systemic Deficiency Committee', operating as an independent body within the European Commission, building on the proposal of a Copenhagen Commission and supported by the EP.

b. The possible contribution of a Systemic Deficiency Committee

This Committee could institutionally safeguard the effective implementation of the Framework. Of course, proposing an entirely new institution is fraught with all the uncertainties of legal and institutional engineering. However, drawing from our analysis of the status quo, we argue that the Committee could be a plausible step forward. For us, the Systemic

[63] D Kochenov and L Pech, 'Monitoring and Enforcement of the Rule of Law in the EU: Rhetoric and Reality' (2015) 11 *European Constitutional Law Review* 512. For criticism of the effectiveness of the mechanism, see D Kochenov and L Pech 'From bad to worse? On the Commission and the Council's rule of law initiatives', http://verfassungsblog.de/bad-worse-commission-councils-rule-law-initiatives/, accessed 12 October 2016.

[64] Kochenov and Pech, 'From bad to worse?' (n 63).

[65] von Bogdandy et al. (n 6) 489, 490; Closa et al. (n 6) 21 ff.

[66] JW Müller, 'Should the EU Protect Democracy and the Rule of Law inside Member States?' (2015) 21 *European Law Journal* 141, 150.

[67] Venice Commission, 'Opinion on Amendments to the Act of 25 June 2015 on the Constitutional Tribunal of Poland', CDL-AD(2016)001158, Opinion no 833/2015.

[68] Art 3(2) Res (2002)3 adopting the Revised Statute of the European Commission for Democracy through Law (adopted by the Committee of Ministers on 21 Feb. 2002). On the Venice Commission, see W Hoffmann-Riem, 'The Venice Commission of the European Council – Standards and Impact' (2014) 25 *European Journal of International Law* 579.

Deficiency Committee needs to fulfil three criteria if it is to contribute effectively and legitimately to countering systemic deficiencies: first, it needs to have a strong standing in the public sphere. Second, partisanship needs to be avoided, although the mechanism should be political. Third, the Committee should be endowed with a strongly legitimate mandate.

The European capacity to respond to systemic deficiencies has increased in recent years, in particular through the Rule of Law Framework. However, the Commission's activation of the Framework has given rise to doubts of its impartiality. A Systemic Deficiency Committee could help the implementation of the Framework through its stronger institutional independence. The Committee might be built on the example of the 'group of wise men', the high-level group provided for in former Article 7 TEU.[69]

In essence, it should supervise the compliance of Member States with all the values of Article 2 TEU and issue a public report in case of a threat as part of its supervisory jurisdiction. This report should trigger the activation of the Framework by the Commission. Allegations of the Commission's bias or partisanship may accordingly be countered by reference to the independent Committee's report. At the same time, involving an independent institution prior to the Commission would mitigate the fear that the Commission might fail to act for political reasons. Following the Commission's actions vis-à-vis Poland, it remains to be seen whether the Framework will be activated in cases where the threat stems from a party which is a member of the two big European parties. The Committee would also add value in comparison to judicial protection. It has a broader mandate than individual rights and can examine the situation in a given Member State more broadly. It would be able to examine whether the overall situation in a Member State is politically acceptable in light of the values of Article 2 TEU. While this involves questions of legality, it is a more encompassing standard. Supplementing the Framework and the Reverse *Solange* approach with a new Committee promises to make the European response to systemic deficiencies more effective and legitimate.

I. Institutional structure

The Committee should contribute to publicizing the European dimension of domestic systemic deficiencies. This should inform the composition of the Committee. Here, we overlap with Müller's proposal for a 'Copenhagen Commission',[70] who advocates a new independent institution composed of eminent figures. Such a body would also reflect the 'committee of independent eminent persons', established by Regulation 1141/2014 to advise the Authority for European Political Parties and European Political Foundations on alleged breaches of EU values by a European political party or a European political foundation.[71]

[69] The group was eventually deleted from the Treaties as it was regarded as being self-evident that the Council could involve independent experts (F Schorkopf, 'Art 7 EUV', in E Grabitz, M Hilf, and M Nettesheim (eds), *Das Recht der Europäischen Union* (Beck 2016) para 9). For the history of the involvement of experts, see Sadurski (n 5) 405–9.

[70] Müller (n 66) 151. JW Müller, 'Protecting the Rule of Law (and Democracy!) in the EU: The Idea of a Copenhagen Commission' in Closa and Kochenov (n 5). The proposal for a Copenhagen Commission was supported by the EP's Tavares Report (European Parliament Report on the Situation of fundamental rights: standards and practices in Hungary pursuant to the European Parliament resolution of 16 February 2012, 2012/2130[INI]).

[71] Art 11 Regulation (EU, Euratom) No 1141/2014 of the European Parliament and of the Council of 22 October 2014 on the statute and funding of European political parties and European political foundations [2014] OJ L317, 1. On this parallel, see F Schorkopf, 'Wertesicherung in der Europäischen Union. Prävention, Quarantäne und Aufsicht als Bausteine eines Rechts der Verfassungskrise?' (2016) *Europarecht* 148, 154.

Among the suitable candidates for the Committee are former heads of important domestic and European institutions. This includes former presidents of domestic parliaments and courts as well as stateswomen and statesmen, ministers and the like. The former presidents of European institutions and European judges and Commissioners also appear equally suitable. Important European public intellectuals might also be involved. The diversity of backgrounds may strengthen the impact of the Committee. Former judges might for example be more familiar with the intricacies of the factual assessment while former politicians might contribute more powerfully to increasing public awareness of the systemic deficiencies. The members would combine personal authority with the authority of the office they formerly held. Members will be expected to have retired from active politics and the Committee should to be pluralist in terms of gender, geographical representation, and political background. The aim of the Committee is to further a political rather than a judicial discourse. Accordingly, the standard which should be applied is political acceptability and not only legality. The Committee should therefore not build on the ECJ, neither should it only be composed of judges from the highest domestic courts. Courts can contribute to mitigating systemic deficiency and judges might also be involved in the Committee. They should, however, not define nor dominate its essential character.

What would a suitable organizational framework look like? We recommend an independent structure for activating the Commission's Rule of Law Framework. We could therefore consider establishing it as a new expert group on systemic deficiencies within the Commission. Expert groups support the Commission in most fields of its activities. Establishing an expert group is part of the organizational prerogatives of the Commission, such as the former EU Network of Independent Experts on Fundamental Rights.[72] It has been involved in human rights monitoring in a phase prior to activating Article 7 TEU.[73] However, a Systemic Deficiency Committee in the shape of an expert group accountable to the Commission is unlikely to be able to discharge the function envisaged here. Many expert groups have been convincingly criticized by scholars, activists, and the EP for being biased.[74] A group of eminent figures appointed by the Commission alone cannot guarantee sufficient independence, plurality, and publicity. It has been proposed to entrust the FRA with the task of overseeing compliance with European fundamental values.[75] So far, it has established a network of domestic administrative agencies and human rights institutions.[76] It seems doubtful that an administrative agency would be able to provide the political judgment and the anticipated awareness raising effect. The FRA's administrative and bureaucratic character hinders it from becoming an institution involved in a process which requires great legitimacy and publicity. Given these problems, we propose setting up a new

[72] For a proposal for activating the network, see Bingham Centre for the Rule of Law 24 (n 6).

[73] European Commission, 'On Article 7 of the Treaty on European Union – Respect for and promotion of the values on which the Union is based (Communication from the Commission to the Council and the European Parliament)', Brussels, COM(2003) 606 final, 15 October 2003, 9, http://eur-lex.europa.eu/legal-content/EN/TXT/?uri=CELEX%3A52003DC0606&from=DE&lang3=choose&lang2=choose&lang1=EN, accessed 12 October 2016.

[74] The EP has blocked the funding for expert groups for the financial year 2015 until their composition is made more balanced. On the questionable legitimacy of expert groups, see A Pilniok, 'Struktur, Funktionen und Probleme der Expertengruppen der Europäischen Kommission: legitime Expertise oder unzulässige Einflussnahme?' (2014) *Europarecht* 62, 69.

[75] Council Regulation (EC) No 168/2007 of 15 February 2007 establishing a European Union Agency for Fundamental Rights [2007] OJ L53, 1. The idea to make use of the FRA was also voiced by the EP (EP resolution of 3 July 2013 on the situation of fundamental rights: standards and practices in Hungary, 2012/2130 [INI], para 80). On the FRA, see A von Bogdandy and J von Bernstorff, 'The EU Fundamental Rights Agency Within the European and International Human Rights Architecture: The Legal Framework and some Unsettled Issues in a New Field of Administrative Law' (2009) 46 *Common Market Law Review* 1035.

[76] von Bogdandy and von Bernstorff (n 75) 1050.

institution on the basis of Article 352 TFEU. Article 7 TEU demonstrates that the protection of the values enshrined in Article 2 TEU falls within the scope of the EU's competences.[77] Establishing a new committee to safeguard against systemic threats to the values thus comes within the ambit of Article 352 TFEU.[78] Moreover, Article 352 TFEU requires that the EU action must be necessary to attain these objectives. This requirement must be fulfilled, given that only an EU body could plausibly determine for the Union whether its foundational values are being respected. The high requirements for using this competence, unanimity in the Council and a majority in the EP, as well as the consent of some national parliaments,[79] adds to its legitimacy. Of course, it will not be easy to muster the required consensus. However, such consensus is far more likely to be achieved as part of an overall bargain on important issues of EU legislation than a treaty amendment according to Article 48 TEU, as it is foreseen in other proposals.

II. Appointment procedure

The procedure for the appointment of the Committee's composition is a very delicate issue. Weiler has rightly pointed out that the democratic shortcomings of the Union itself should not be forgotten.[80] A European committee intervening in domestic political processes might add a European deficiency to a domestic deficiency, if it is not sufficiently legitimized.

Therefore, the regulation should ensure that the Committee builds on the legitimacy of the Council and the EP. This contrasts with another proposal for giving the right of appointment to the new institution to the parliaments alone:[81] twenty-eight members should be chosen by Member States' parliaments and ten by the EP. Of course, parliaments should be involved in alleviating systemic deficiencies beyond merely partisan debates. However, a Committee with thirty-eight members is probably too large to operate effectively: it should consist of a maximum of ten members.[82] Reducing its size is easiest if the appointment is not left to domestic institutions. For the Committee to meet agreed democratic standards it is advisable to align the appointment procedure with the democratic principle contained in Article 10 TEU.[83] Accordingly, the process should rest equally on the EP and the legitimacy of the Council. These two institutions should, accordingly, appoint an equal number of members to the Committee.

The Committee we suggest could take the form of an independent structure within the Commission, similar to the individual independent status of the European Anti-fraud

[77] L Besselink, 'The Bite, the Bark and the Howl: Article 7 TEU and the Rule of Law Initiatives', in Jakab and Kochenov (n 2).

[78] In more detail, see M Rossi, 'Art 352 AEUV', in C Calliess and M Ruffert (eds), *EUV/AEUV* (Beck 2011) paras 37–43.

[79] Art 352(2) TFEU contains an obligation to inform national parliaments. The consent of national parliaments is an additional requirement in Great Britain and Germany (see P Craig, 'The European Union Act: Locks Limits and Legality' (2011) 48 *Common Market Law Review* 1915, 1934 ff.; *BVerfGE* 123, 167, DE:BVerfG:2009: es20090630.2bve000208, para 328 *Lisbon*).

[80] JHH Weiler, 'Epilogue: Living in a Glass House: Europe, Democracy and the Rule of Law' in Closa and Kochenov (n 5).

[81] Decision of the Green Group in the German Parliament of 24 November 2014 'Gemeinsam Grundwerte stärken–Europa stärken!', http://www.gruene-bundestag.de/fileadmin/media/gruenebundestag_de/fraktion/beschluesse/Beschluss_Europa_staerken.pdf, accessed 12 October 2016.

[82] There is no consensus in the social sciences on the optimal size for a group tasked with solving problems or passing judgments, but the most common size tends to be around five: see RW Napier and MK Gershenfeld, *Groups: Theory and Experience* (Houghton Mifflin 1999). It would be difficult however to represent the variety of interests which need to be considered for decisions as important as those of concern here with such a small group. At the other extreme, interaction in groups of more than twelve people is known to be difficult.

[83] J Habermas, *Zur Verfassung Europas, Essay* (Suhrkamp 2011); J Habermas, *The Crisis of the European Union: A Response* (Polity 2013).

Office (commonly known as OLAF).[84] OLAF is designed to exercise the Commission's powers to carry out investigations (including spot checks) to strengthen the fight against fraud, corruption, and any other illegal activity adversely affecting the Community's financial interests.[85] Although it is integrated in the administrative structure of the Commission, it enjoys wide budgetary and administrative autonomy and 'complete independence'.[86] In exercising its powers, the Director-General of OLAF must 'neither seek nor take instructions from the Commission, any government or any other institution or body'.[87] While the field of application and the mandate of the envisaged Systemic Deficiency Committee are different, we can point to OLAF as an example of how the independence of such a body can be guaranteed.

c. Comparison with the proposal of a 'Copenhagen Commission'

The envisaged Committee overlaps significantly with the Copenhagen Commission proposed by Müller. Müller's proposal however can be enhanced in terms of its mandate and institutional implementation. According to Müller, the Copenhagen Commission would constitute an entirely new institution established through treaty revision and equipped with sanctioning powers.[88] Simply handing over the sanctioning powers to an entirely independent body is however questionable. The Copenhagen Commission as proposed by Müller would attain far-reaching competences in a very delicate question which needs great legitimacy, as it is likely to run up against central policies of elected governments. It is doubtful whether such sanctioning powers can be granted to an institution removed from the usual EU accountability mechanisms. Our second objection is more pragmatic. It is highly unlikely that Member States could be convinced to establish a new institution through treaty revision which requires unanimous ratification and thus exceeds even the requirements of Article 352 TFEU. Of course, Article 352 TFEU also requires unanimity in the Council, but that is far easier to achieve than treaty reform.[89]

In sum, establishing a Systemic Deficiency Committee as an expertise-oriented Committee within the Commission would be an important supplement to the Rule of Law Framework. The Polish case has shown that the Framework can contribute to mitigating threats to the Union's constitutional values. At the same time, the heated Polish debate highlighted the need for an impartial assessment of this sensitive situation. The Committee should be composed of eminent figures appointed by the EP and the Council. As foreseen in the Rule of Law Framework, the Systemic Deficiency Committee should build on the already existing expertise of the FRA, the Venice Commission, and the ECtHR in particular.[90]

[84] See in general, C Stefanou et al., *OLAF at the Crossroads: Action Against EU Fraud* (Hart 2011); JFH Inghelram, *Legal and Institutional Aspects of the European Anti-Fraud Office (OLAF) An Analysis with a Look Forward to a European Public Prosecutor's Office* (Europa Law Publishing 2011).

[85] Art 2 (para 1) Commission Decision 1999/352/EC (ECSC, Euratom) of 28 April 1999 establishing the European Anti-Fraud Office OLAF [1999] OJ L136, 20.

[86] Art 3 Commission Decision 1999/352/EC (ECSC, Euratom).

[87] ibid.

[88] Müller (n 66) 151. According to Müller, the European Commission would be required to cut the funding of the relevant Member State on the Copenhagen Commission's recommendation. This seems particularly ill-suited to achieving the desired effect, as the actual capacity to act and the public responsibility for an act should not be separated.

[89] For the immense significance of Art 352 TFEU, see Rossi, (n 78) para 20.

[90] Commission COM(2014) 158 final (n 47) 10. For the involvement of other European institutions, see also C Grabenwarter, 'Inherent Constitutional Tendencies and the Role of the European Court of Human Rights', 257–73; M Hoffmann, 'Central and Eastern European Member States of the EU and the European Convention on Human Rights', 275–89; J Nergelius, 'The Role of the Venice Commission in Maintaining the Rule of Law in Hungary and in Romania', 291–308, all three in von Bogdandy and Sonnevend (n 1).

5. A new role for Article 7(1) TEU

The new instruments also change the perception of Article 7 TEU. So far, the conventional view sees the Article 7 TEU mechanisms—including the freezing of payments—as totally impractical. Much of that is due to Manuel Barroso unwisely calling these mechanisms a 'nuclear option'.[91] That qualification stuck: today, anybody who proposes to use the Article 7 TEU mechanisms appears as irresponsible as someone proposing a nuclear war. However, Article 7 TEU does not devastate entire countries: instead, it supports fundamental values. It is a legal and legitimate instrument, which—as all others—needs to be deployed wisely.

Many consider the Article 7 TEU mechanism impractical in the Polish case because its second paragraph imposes a very high voting threshold. This position, however, overlooks the fact that a first sanction is already provided for under Article 7(1) TEU: the Council can make the determination by four fifths of its members, i.e., twenty-two Member States, that a Member State exhibits 'a clear risk of a serious breach'. This determination is a sanction in itself, bearing high reputational costs both at the domestic and the EU level—and this is why the Polish government wants to avoid it at all costs. The conclusion of a breach under Article 7(1) gains importance if it is preceded by more formalized procedures as discussed in this chapter.

[91] JMD Barroso, State of the Union 2012 Address, 12 September 2012.

13

A Democracy Commission of One's Own, or What it would take for the EU to safeguard Liberal Democracy in its Member States

Jan-Werner Müller

I have argued elsewhere that the EU has the authority to protect liberal democracy in Member States.[1] The question posed in this chapter is whether it actually has the capacity to do so. Authority is one thing; having effective legal instruments and policies at one's disposal is another. At present, the EU is failing to meet this challenge. The chapter proposes a new institution to remedy the EU's current democracy protection deficit, tentatively called the Copenhagen Commission. The idea is to create an EU-specific democracy and Rule of Law watchdog, an institution which in certain respects would be comparable to the Council of Europe's Venice Commission. However, there would also be major differences. If I may continue with the canine analogy suggested by the word 'watchdog': the Copenhagen Commission would not just be able to bark, but would also bite and, not least, sniff around wherever it liked. Put differently, it would have the authority to sanction a Member State government and also to investigate possible dangers to democracy and the Rule of Law on its own.

The chapter proceeds as follows: I shall first critically examine legal and political strategies which have been proposed to rein in what one might regard as 'rogue governments' in the EU—governments, that is, which act in ways which breach the EU's 'fundamental values' of democracy, the Rule of Law and human rights. Before suggesting alternatives to these existing approaches, I would like to step back and ask more abstractly what it would take for democracy and Rule of Law protection to function properly—a question which can and should be asked about models of 'militant democracy' or strategies for 'defending democracy' in general. I argue that one can draw on the long-standing normative and legal debates about democratic self-defence at national level in order better to understand the novel problems posed by democratic self-defence in the supranational realm.[2] I shall claim that all institutions charged with implementing militant democracy have to address what one might call a double epistemological challenge: one challenge is to obtain political knowledge in order to assess risks (the central question being: 'how do we

[1] See in particular, Transatlantic Academy Working Paper 'Safeguarding Democracy inside the EU: Brussels and the Future of Liberal Order' (2013), http://www.transatlanticacademy.org/sites/default/files/publications/Muller_SafeguardingDemocracy_Feb13_web.pdf, accessed 12 October 2016.

[2] For an extended discussion of the dilemmas associated with militant democracy, see my 'Militant Democracy' in M Rosenfeld and A Sajó (eds), *The Oxford Handbook of Comparative Constitutional Law* (OUP 2012) 1253–69; as well as my 'Protecting Popular Self-Government from the People? New Normative Perspectives on "Militant Democracy"' (2016) 19 *Annual Review of Political Science* 249. For institutional aspects from a political science perspective, see G Capoccia, 'Militant Democracy: The Institutional Bases of Democratic Self-Preservation' (2013) 9 *Annual Review of Law and Social Sciences* 207.

A Democracy Commission of One' s Own, or: What it would take for the EU to safeguard Liberal Democracy in its Member States. First Edition. Jan-Werner Müller. Published 2017 by Oxford University Press.

know that something—or someone—constitutes a genuine threat to liberal democracy?'); the other is to arrive at an assessment of the probable consequences of measures of militant democracy (and, in particular, an assessment of the danger that measures to defend democracy themselves actually end up damaging democracy). Which institutions should be in charge of such risk-assessment and the examination of the likely consequences of militant measures? My initial, rather abstract answer to this question is not specific to the EU and might serve as a contribution to the political theory of liberal democracy protection as such: I distinguish bureaucratic expertise, legal opinions as rendered by courts, and peer review as possible ways to generate knowledge for a militant democracy. I shall then seek to specify what it would take for the EU in particular to protect liberal democracy within Member States and elaborate the proposal of a specialized body which can offer legitimate political–legal judgments. I term that institution the 'Copenhagen Commission' (referring back to the EU's Copenhagen criteria for accession to the Union). After expanding on its institutional setup and its powers, I shall finish the chapter by addressing a number of common objections to my proposal. In particular, I shall address three concerns: that such a body would duplicate existing institutions; that it would be seen as yet another instance of EU 'technocracy' which is likely to alienate Union citizens; and that its specific actions would be seen as illegitimate by Member States subject to sanctions. I shall finish with some necessarily speculative thoughts about the conditions under which the proposal might be implemented.

1. What's wrong with what we have now: a brief review

In this section, I shall briefly review existing legal instruments and political strategies which have been proposed to confront EU governments violating the values codified in Article 2 TEU (democracy and the Rule of Law in particular).

First, Article 7 TEU (also discussed by Besselink in Chapter 8 of this volume), the essence of which is a restriction of political participation rights for a Member State government. The idea for such a 'mechanism' had first been advanced by Italy and Austria in the run-up to enlargement of the EU in 2004, mostly because of a concern that newly admitted Eastern Europeans—considered somehow democratically 'immature'—might politically misbehave inside the Union (the irony being that sanctions—though not under Article 7—were of course first applied against Austria in 2000, as recounted in by Lachmayer in Chapter 25 of this volume).[3] In other words, the point was to insulate the rest of the EU from a 'rogue government'.

Today, Article 7 is widely considered a 'nuclear option'; in other words it is deemed unusable. Countries seem too worried that sanctions might also be applied against them one day; there is widespread concern that an Article 7 procedure would lead to an uncontrollable tit-for-tat (I have heard that worry articulated by leading EU actors several times); sometimes regional solidarity (especially, but not only, in Central and Eastern Europe) might also play a role; and then there is the worry that only smaller Member States might ever be sanctioned, whereas larger ones (Berlusconi's Italy comes to mind immediately) will always effectively be above the law.

Quite apart from these more-or-less practical concerns, there is a deeper reason to have reservations about Article 7. After all, Article 7 does not constitute an intervention of any sort in the politics of a Member State; rather, it aims at what one might call a form of moral

[3] W Sadurski, 'Adding Bite to the Bark: The Story of Article 7, E.U. Enlargement, and Jörg Haider' (2009) 16 *Columbia Journal of European Law* 385.

and political *isolationism*. It insulates the rest of the EU (strictly speaking, all EU citizens) from the EU-related decisions of a government which the Member States, the European Commission, and the EP deem to be in breach of fundamental values—but it does nothing directly to change the fact of the breach. Of course, the hope is that a Member State whose rights in the European Council have been restricted on the basis of Article 7 will mend its ways. But in theory, a government could remain in breach forever; most worryingly, while insulated from the rest of the EU, it could gain time to consolidate a political system which violated the principles of democracy and the Rule of Law.

What about the EU Commission as the (supposedly impartial) guardian of the treaties? Put simply, the problem is that the instruments the Commission has at its disposal are often not a good match for the specific political challenges to liberal democracy. Infringement proceedings can of course only be based on EU law—which often fails to cover the relevant areas of democracy and the Rule of Law, other than in the very generally worded Article 2 TEU (which, in the eyes of most lawyers cannot be operationalized: the Commission cannot take a country to court for violating fundamental values). This makes it harder to address systemic problems with democracy and the Rule of Law in a Member State.

The most striking example in this context is the Hungarian government's 2011 *de facto* decapitation of the judicial system by lowering the retirement age of judges from 70 to 62. Under Article 258 TFEU the Commission eventually took Hungary to the European Court of Justice for age discrimination—and won its case (meanwhile, the Hungarian Constitutional Court had also ruled against the government). But the judges were never comprehensively reinstated (the new government loyalists who were appointed have remained in place) and despite its nominal legal success, Europe appeared impotent in getting at the real issue, which was political—to do with checks and balances in particular—and not about discrimination of individuals at all.[4]

True, not all infringement proceedings have to amount to such a mismatch. To the extent that a rogue government seeks to consolidate power through controlling important parts of the economy, the Commission might be in a better position to exert pressure on such a government. Think of the Commission launching infringement proceedings against Hungary because of new taxes relating to advertising and food stores—which are suspected of serving as means for the government to eliminate troublesome (and politically largely uncontrollable) multinational companies from the television and supermarket sectors.[5]

Nevertheless, there remains a worry about what infringement proceedings essentially are and how that essence affects the legitimacy of EU interventions: since the Commission has to resort to indirect strategies, it is also always in danger of being regarded as dissimulating, or as being hypocritical: things are not what they seem to be about (as in: 'it's not competition law, it's political power, stupid!'), a sense which is likely to erode the trust of EU citizens in the impartial guardian of the treaties. In fact, it might give them good reasons to question the Rule of Law in the EU as such, if the perception takes hold that law is instrumentalized for political purposes (laudable as these purposes might be, when it comes to Article 2 TEU).

[4] For further analysis of the problem and a solution within the Treaties as they are, see Kim Lane Scheppele, 'What can the European Commission do when Member States violate basic principles of the European Union' (2013), http://ec.europa.eu/justice/events/assises-justice-2013/files/contributions/45.princetonuniversityscheppelesystemicinfringementactionbrusselsversion_en.pdf, accessed 12 October 2016.

[5] 'The European Commission is cracking down on Hungarian infringements', *Hungarian Spectrum* (2015), http://hungarianspectrum.org/tag/advertising-taxes/, accessed 12 October 2016.

As an alternative to going 'nuclear' or to infringement proceedings, some legal scholars have proposed that national courts, drawing on the jurisprudence of the European Court of Justice, should protect the fundamental *European* rights of Member State nationals who, after all, also hold the status of EU citizens.[6] As long as Member State institutions can guarantee what these scholars have called 'the essence' of fundamental rights of EU citizens, as set out in the CFR of the EU, there is no role for either national courts or the European Court in protecting the specific status of men and women as *Union citizens*. But if such institutions are hijacked by a rogue government, Union citizens can turn to national courts and ultimately the European Court of Justice to safeguard what the Court itself has called the 'substance' of Union citizenship.

In many ways this is an appealing strategy. The goal of this 'Reverse *Solange*'-logic is not merely to bring in the European Court, but to strengthen *national* institutions in times of political crisis. Yet again, though, there are questions about the practical success of such a strategy. Is a rogue government likely to be impressed by rulings from Luxembourg? Will such rulings not take too long? However, there are once more also concerns quite apart from practical ones. The strategy seems to presume that challenges to liberal democracy will always appear in the form of fundamental rights violations. Yet some problems simply cannot be captured—let alone countered—by focusing just on fundamental rights violations (serious as these can be). While some attempts to undermine checks and balances or to make genuine changes of power extremely difficult will eventually result in incidents which can accurately be described as fundamental rights violations, even rulings against a particular government might not in the end result in the restoration of genuine liberal democracy (as in the age discrimination case just described). Abolishing Article 51 CFR, as proposed by Jakab in Chapter 14 of this volume, would do away with the legal contortions required by the Reverse *Solange* approach—but it would not change the fact that dangers to democracy are not all reducible to fundamental rights violations.

We might be tempted to say that we should abandon legal approaches altogether and focus on clearly political responses to what, after all, are clearly political challenges. Article 7 does fit this requirement—it is a distinctly political and comprehensive judgment by EU institutions and, specifically, a country's *peers* in the EU. But given its seeming ineffectiveness, an alternative would be party politics both inside and outside EU institutions. After all, it has often been said that the Euro-crisis has brought about the politicization of Europe, and that it is now time for the Europeanization of politics: citizens of many Member States—possibly all Member States—have woken up to the fact that what occurs elsewhere in Europe has a direct impact on their lives; what we need, then, are ways to internalize these externalities and reach common European policies which can be justified on the basis of pan-European debates and ultimately, genuinely pan-European elections to the EP.

Alas, a less desirable effect of such a Europeanization of politics has also become apparent: at least initially, the conservative European People's Party (EPP) firmly closed ranks around Viktor Orbán in Hungary when the latter, in the eyes of the European Commission and many other actors, was in danger of breaching fundamental EU values; on the other side of the political spectrum, Martin Schulz, President of the EP and one of Orbán's most outspoken critics, defended his fellow Social Democrat Victor Ponta in Bucharest, at least initially, when the latter appeared to embark on a constitutional coup in the summer of 2012.

[6] A von Bogdandy et al., 'Reverse *Solange* – Protecting the Essence of Fundamental Rights against EU Member States' (2012) 49 *Common Market Law Review* 489; see also von Bogdandy et al. in Chapter 12 of this volume.

To be sure, partisanship might not always trump all other considerations: Slovakia's Robert Fico was temporarily ostracized by his fellow European Social Democrats for allying with the radical nationalist Jan Slota; the application of Fico's party to join the pan-European party of the socialists was only reinstated after Fico signed a letter promising to protect minority rights. And it seems that in the EP, at least some members of the EPP did not oppose the Tavares Report which called for continuous monitoring of Hungary, enabling the adoption of the Report in an assembly in which the centre-right has a majority (even if in the 2014 Hungarian national elections the EPP threw its weight behind Orbán's Fidesz party again, with EPP president Joseph Daul actually campaigning for Orbán at Heroes' Square in Budapest); in 2015, there was again reason to believe that EPP members voted for a resolution critical of the Orbán government's approach to migrants and the question of the death penalty.

It seems implausible, then, to render the protection of democracy and the Rule of Law hostage to the ups and downs of partisan politics—a somewhat different point than saying that militant democracy should never be entrusted to political parties, because they would be tempted to outlaw their competitors. True, the questions are deeply political, but they are not the stuff of day-to-day politics and they should not be dealt with by actors who necessarily have precisely to care about day-to-day politics. Threats to democracy and the Rule of Law constitute (one would hope) exceptional circumstances in Europe; they should be dealt with impartially, from a distance, so to speak, and, I shall argue, by a specialized institution.

2. The proposal: a democracy watchdog for the Union

Let us take a few steps back. Just what was the problem again? The challenge is to locate an *agent of credible legal-political judgment* of whether there is a threat to democracy and the Rule of Law. This is a general challenge for political systems committed to militant democracy. Misperceiving threats—and, as a consequence, overreacting with undemocratic or illiberal measures—is arguably a prime cause for one of the well-known 'paradoxes' of militant democracy, namely the danger that a democracy, in trying to defend itself, will destroy or at least undermine itself in the process.

There is a second, related challenge: judgment is also required for an assessment of what measures of militant democracy are likely to succeed. This need is unaffected by the question whether militant democracy should comprehensively change citizens' beliefs and behaviour beyond banning an immediate threat (a maximalist account of militant democracy), or in a more self-limiting way, just aim at a containment of threats.[7]

Finally, I think it desirable that accounts of militant democracy also make a point of saying that beyond sanctions and prohibitions, militant democracy needs to get at the underlying political challenges and concerns which made citizens and politicians turn to anti-democratic principles (and the parties which espouse them) in the first place.[8] Concerns that voters express in voting for what might be deemed anti-democratic parties do not all need to be taken at face value (as in: some people just are racists and there's nothing that can be done about it); there might be ways of responding to the interests of voters without important policy concessions to sinister political forces. True, even in the

[7] See J Quong, 'The Rights of Unreasonable Citizens' (2004) 12 *Journal of Political Philosophy* 314 and AS Kirshner, *A Theory of Militant Democracy* (Yale University Press 2014).

[8] S Rummens and K Abts, 'Defending Democracy: The Concentric Containment of Political Extremism' (2010) 58 *Political Studies* 649.

most enlightened, liberal etc, contemporary democracies there can be citizens who are not racists because they worry about losing their jobs (as the usual, perversely comforting sociological accounts would have it), but because racism is their freely chosen and reflectively affirmed political identity. However, without trying to address the concerns which made militant democratic measures necessary in the first place, one would not even know how large that group might be.[9] In short, then: militant democracy should be capable of generating knowledge about threats, about the consequences of responses to those threats—and ideally, about the factors which might have given rise to threats in the first place.

There are three plausible institutions for tackling the epistemological challenges of militant democracy: first, something like a political police or a specialized administrative agency (in short: judgment by the bureaucracy, or put differently, specialized experts);[10] second, courts (in short: judgment by jurists); and third, peer review (judgment by those in a similar position to the institutions potentially affected by militant democracy). In a domestic context, peer review would usually mean review by other political parties to determine whether an ostensibly anti-democratic party poses a genuine threat. However, where stripping individual citizens of political rights is also an important element of militant democracy, peer review might mean something like citizens' juries passing judgment on their civic peers who might engage in anti-democratic activities—though no such thing has been instituted anywhere, as far as I know.

In fact, in domestic contexts, courts have usually been the main institutions charged with implementing militant democracy. Sometimes courts rely on information provided by something like a political police, but the latter are generally not authorized to restrict rights on their own. Peer review is virtually absent from the domestic repertoire of a militant democracy: as argued above, the worry is that allowing other parties to decide whether to ban a party seems an open invitation to outlaw the political competition (even if in the paradigmatic German context of militant democracy, parties are effectively the first movers, since it is institutions controlled by parties—the executive or the lower or upper parliament—which bring an application to ban a party to the Constitutional Court).

And in the EU? There is a special challenge here, as banning parties or the loss of individual citizens' rights to participate in politics is not really the issue: Member States may decide to take such measures internally, but not the Union as such. At the same time, Article 7 is akin to something like a 'country ban'—not in the sense, of course, in which a domestic party that has been banned will be dissolved (the country will remain the country . . .), but in the sense that a particular government will not be able to participate in the regular political and legislative process in the Union, as long as it remains in breach of fundamental European values. As set out above, the essence of Article 7 is rights restriction (namely the membership rights of the offending Member State), in a manner similar to that in which anti-democrats' rights to free speech and assembly can sometimes be restricted domestically (think of Article 18 of the German Basic Law as an example). Moreover, in certain respects, Article 7 has an advantage over domestic bans and rights restrictions: a Member State does not lose political representation altogether; its citizens can still pursue their legitimate interests as long as the Member State has MEP's in the EP. In a domestic

[9] On the containment of racist and other unreasonable citizens, see Quong (n 7).

[10] This aspect is often overlooked, even though the proposal of a specialized political police goes all the way back to K Loewenstein, 'Militant Democracy and Fundamental Rights I' (1937) 31 *American Political Science Review* 417, and K Loewenstein, 'Militant Democracy and Fundamental Rights II' (1937) 31 *American Political Science Review* 638.

context, on the other hand, losing political rights—such as the right to form parties or even the right to vote—makes it impossible to advance concerns which have nothing to do with anything like a fight against democracy and hence pose normative problems, which prima facie are at least not as severe in the supranational EU realm.[11]

What is utterly different from militant democracy within a state is the fact that Article 7 is based at least partly on the principle of peer review. As mentioned above, peer review plays virtually no role at the domestic level. At the supranational level, some of the same concerns as those often articulated in domestic contexts might be valid: it is not inconceivable that political competition could corrupt Article 7 procedures ('Let's restrict the rights of a Member State which keeps vetoing our great neoliberal policies!')—but all in all, this is not a very likely scenario. What is more likely is that an Article 7 procedure will pit nation-state against nation-state—the very scenario the EU was designed to avoid. After all, a skilful government leader is likely able to frame a conflict between itself and the EU as one of the whole nation being under attack from the outside. Just think of how Wolfgang Schüssel, as Chancellor of Austria in 2000, managed to convince so many people that fourteen countries had illegitimately imposed 'sanctions against Austria' (the very language—also often unthinkingly employed in academic analysis—is telling: the sanctions were against Schüssel's government, not 'against Austria').

Finally, neither a political police nor courts play much of a role in 'EU militant democracy' such as it is (to be sure, the European Commission does and in that sense, at least, there is also an element of 'bureaucracy'—but note that this is different from a bureaucracy specializing in the protection of democracy). Of course, this picture could change if the CJEU were empowered to review national political and legal systems more comprehensively, as in Jakab's proposal.

So where to go from here? Clearly, an institution in charge of something like EU militant democracy should be able to deal with the epistemological challenges outlined above. In particular, what has to be understood and judged properly by such an institution is whether a Member State government is systematically departing from what we could describe as the EU's *normative acquis*—a task which is different both from assessing compliance with EU law and from ascertaining a belief in values (whatever the latter might mean concretely anyway: a Committee on UnEuropean Beliefs and Activities in the EP?). Technical–legal judgment of rule compliance in and of itself is insufficient, and philosophical consensus about values is simply not the issue (at least at this point in the EU's history, all governments continue to profess to faith in democracy and the Rule of Law; there are no self-declared systemic rivals to liberal democracy at this point); nor, as I was trying to argue in the previous section of this chapter, is it all a matter of fundamental rights violations. We are dealing with systemic, mostly constitutional challenges which will require some understanding of context, some sense of proportion, and, not least, some meaningful capacity for comparison of what is actually happening within different political systems (as opposed to the claims about what is happening within these systems by local elites). A simple checklist, as so often used in the EU accession process ('Do the judiciary's offices have computers? Check!'), will not do;[12] somebody needs to look at and understand the whole picture and

[11] Alexander Kirshner has warned that one should not think of anti-democrats as 'ascetic' political actors who think and do nothing but what leads to the destruction of democracy. They might have all kinds of legitimate concerns which have nothing to do with the nature of the political system.

[12] See also K Nicolaïdis and R Kleinfeld, *Rethinking Europe's 'Rule of Law' and Enlargement Agenda: The Fundamental Dilemma* (2012) Sigma Paper No 49/2012; and the acerbic, but entirely justified comment by Alina Mungiu-Pippidi on the Commission's elaborate monitoring procedures depending upon an 'overall "prescription mechanism" according to which countries are evaluated by the number of measures adopted from detailed

also the particular *sequencing* of the creation—and possibly the dismantling—of a liberal-democratic system.[13] As Kochenov has demonstrated, we cannot simply take the Copenhagen criteria off the legal shelf and pretend, on the basis of the experience with the accession processes, that 'protection of liberal-democratic values' is the same as compliance with these very general criteria (let alone compliance with the *acquis*): they were never sufficiently well-defined and were often inconsistently applied.[14] Going back to checklists or to set up 'scoreboards' might give a sense of (false) bureaucratic comfort—but not much more.

Beyond the challenge of judging consequences of militant measures, there is an additional difficulty in the EU as a particular kind of political space. Authority in the Union remains highly diffuse and fragmented, there is not much in the way of a consciousness of a common European political space (let alone a shared public sphere where substantive arguments could be debated seriously across borders), and it can be hard to get and direct something like common political attention. As of now, there is no clear legal or political actor charged with pushing a red button, so to speak, first in order to alarm others about a potential deterioration in democracy and the Rule of Law inside a Member State.

What follows, then, from framing the problem in this way? First, it seems to me that Article 7 ought to be left in place. However, it also ought to be extended. Situations might arise where democracy is not just slowly undermined or partially dismantled, but where the entire edifice of democratic institutions is blown up or comes crashing down, as it were (think of a military coup). However, in such an extreme case, the Union ought actually to have the option of expelling a Member State completely. Under the TEU, states may decide to leave voluntarily, but there is no legal mechanism for removing a country from the Union. True, these all might seem remote scenarios, but especially those who insist on the symbolic value of something like Article 7—by which they might actually mean something not just symbolic, namely its importance as a form of practical *deterrence*—ought to be sympathetic with including the option of complete removal.[15]

This still does not answer the question of *who* a consistent and credible agent of political judgment could be. 'The Commission' might still seem the most plausible answer—especially in light of the fact that the Commission is acquiring new powers for supervising and potentially changing the budgets of Eurozone Member States. But many—possibly all—proposals to increase the legitimacy of the Commission (seen as a necessary complement to such newly acquired authority) contain the suggestion essentially to *politicize* the Commission: ideas to elect the President directly or to turn the Commissioners into a kind of politically uniform cabinet government all would render the body more partisan—*on*

Commission "roadmaps" rather than by indicators measuring real changes on the ground. This is as if a doctor evaluated a patient by the number of prescribed medicines taken, rather than by measuring the patient's fever to check on the effect of the medicines. Both the adequacy and the impact of such measures in each country were presumed rather than demonstrated'. See A Mungiu-Pippidi, 'EU Accession is no "End of History"' (2007) 18 *Journal of Democracy* 8, 15.

[13] Thanks to Renáta Uitz on this point.

[14] D Kochenov, *EU Enlargement and the Failure of Conditionality* (Kluwer 2008). Certainly, the Commission might have learnt some lessons from this experience: its stance on the quality of the judiciary and fundamental rights protection vis-à-vis Serbia (with which accession negotiations began in January 2014) seems considerably stronger than in the past; the Commission now opens these chapters first and proposes to close them last.

[15] It is not that the possibility of complete exclusion has never been discussed in the preparation of the various treaty revisions, but the option of exclusion has been rejected because, as the report of a Reflection Group appointed by the European Council put it, 'this would call into question the irreversibility of membership [in] the Union'. See Sadurski (n 3) 390.

purpose.[16] And such partisanship makes the Commission much less credible as an agent of impartial legal–political judgment.[17] True, this politicization of the Commission would not just have implications for the question of democracy protection: probably a whole range of functions—such as ensuring competition and other forms of regulation—would have to be split off; we would be left with an EU quasi-government and a number of free-standing regulatory agencies.

In any case, the suggestion for now is to create an entirely new institution which could credibly act as a guardian of Europe's *acquis normatif*.[18] It could be called the 'Copenhagen Commission' (as a reminder of the 'Copenhagen criteria', flawed as they may be), analogous to the Venice Commission—a body, in other words, with a mandate to craft comprehensive and consistent legal and political judgments.[19] The hope is that such a body—ideally composed of legal experts and statesmen and stateswomen with a proven track record of political judgment—could become sufficiently visible so as effectively to raise the alarm across whatever there is in the way of a common European political space.

Picking up on the distinction proposed above, we could say that the composition of the body would combine elements of bureaucracy, of courts and even of peer review (as exercised by elder statesmen and stateswomen)—but would not be reducible to any single one of these domestic models of judgment of militant democracy.

Ideally, such a Commission would have the power itself to start investigations and be able to draw on the knowledge of other EU institutions (such as the FRA). It could regularly monitor developments in Member States and thereby build up a storehouse of knowledge as a basis of comparison not just among countries, but also over time. Most importantly, the Copenhagen Commission ought not only to be empowered to investigate the situation, but also to trigger a mechanism which sends a clear signal (not just words)—though short of the measures envisaged in Article 7. Following the advice of the Copenhagen Commission, the European Commission should be required to cut funds for state capital expenditure or impose significant fines.[20] Especially the former might prove to be effective, if the EU budget were to be increased significantly in future years (a measure included in many proposals to tackle the Euro-crisis), or if a country's government depends significantly on EU contributions (as is the case in Hungary, for instance). Moreover, cuts of EU-specific funds would also reinforce the message that a country undermining the Rule of Law is doing something which concerns the Union as a whole—and that the response is a genuinely European one.

[16] Not that the Commission today is truly 'apolitical'—but the fiction that Commissioners lose their party-political identities upon taking office does have some disciplining effect, I would argue. In the scenario envisaged by proponents of the Commission as a *de facto* (and possibly even in name) European government, the whole point is that the body would be—and ought to be—visibly partisan.

[17] There is also the less obvious point that every harsh criticism of a newer Member State can be regarded as falling back on the Commission itself—did they not do the required work before recommending admission? See in this context also T Gallagher, *Romania and the European Union: How the Weak vanquished the Strong* (Manchester University Press 2009).

[18] We could be tempted to think of decentralizing such an agency: having ombudsmen or something analogous to discrimination agencies in each country—the obvious counter-argument being that such actors and agencies would likely be subject to national capture.

[19] I am indebted to Rui Tavares for discussions on this point.

[20] A major problem here is of course that such measures tend to punish populations, and not governments. The present Hungarian government attempted at one point to constitutionalize the principle of visibly passing EU-related fines on to all citizens, clearly hoping that such 'democracy taxes' will increase resentment of Brussels. This danger is also acute if we consider cutting EU cohesion funds—such cuts would clearly hurt those who are already poor. Less obviously, countries suffering from deficiencies in the Rule of Law would already not be able to absorb much such funds—so this kind of sanction might not hurt as much as one might think just by looking at the gross numbers. I am particularly indebted to Kim Lane Scheppele for discussions on this point.

At the same time, all existing tools would remain at the disposal of the relevant actors: Article 7 could still be invoked, the Commission could take a Member State to the European Court of Justice, the Court could try to protect the substance of EU citizenship, and politicians could have serious words with their peers in another Member State, if they felt that the State in question was leaving the broad European road of liberal democracy.

To be clear, the advantage of the Copenhagen Commission would be that it would not be narrowly constrained by EU law in the way that the European Commission and the European Court of Justice are, it would also not shrink from peer review in the way that present-day Member State governments generally seem to do. Member State peer review, as explained above (and unlike in the ever-so-perfect world of academic journals) is not 'blind'; instead, as argued already, it is in all likelihood dominated by power politics and presumably fear of retaliation.

Of course, one might object that all this is precisely the problem with something like an independent Commission: it will act arbitrarily: in particular, it might overreact to establish and extend its own powers, the way so many EU institutions have done, or even turn into something like a *de facto* constitutional court for the EU as a whole.[21] Such concerns are well founded, but do not constitute anything like knock-out arguments against the proposal advanced here. After all, the Copenhagen Commission could not decide what militant democracy in its essence is all about: rights restrictions. Only Article 7 can do this, restricting the right of a Member State government to EU-wide political participation (in that sense, it really is the equivalent of party bans or restrictions to the right to vote and be elected in national contexts). The national equivalent of the work of the Copenhagen Commission—if there is any analogy at all—would be penalties in party financing or something like strict scrutiny of a party by a kind of political police (think of the German *Verfassungssschutz*, the slightly Orwellian sounding 'Office for the Protection of the Constitution'): not something which puts parties out of the game, but a measure which sends a strong signal regarding doubts about the legitimacy of a party's approach to the game which is aimed at changing behaviour, just as much as financial penalties in the EU are aimed at changing behaviour, not at effecting rights restrictions as such. The hope is that governments under the glaring light of European scrutiny might be willing to moderate their actions, just as much as parties about which there is talk of banning might start to be especially careful in their rhetoric and conduct. True, this might simply be hypocrisy. But no form of militant democracy—whether national or supranational—should get into the business of probing what 'people truly believe'—that way lies McCarthyism. Of course, we might still find moderate, that is to say not undemocratic versions of parties about which we nonetheless have deep normative reservations; but in domestic contexts, nobody forces a person to vote for them, and in the supranational realm, there is always the possibility of engaging in transnational political activism to work against a not undemocratic Member State government which one finds normatively troubling.

3. The question of criteria

It is one thing to identify a plausible institution for judgment; it is another to specify criteria on the basis of which judgments can be made. Against the background of the experience with the Copenhagen criteria as well as the recent history of conflicts between Hungary and the European Commission in 2010–2015, we may well wonder whether

[21] I am grateful to Gábor Halmai for drawing my attention to this worry.

Europeans really agree on 'fundamental values' at all. Yes, we could conclude from the empirical record that there is a single *market*, but no single model of liberal democracy—and therefore, so such a line of criticism would continue, all efforts to protect democracy and the Rule of Law in Europe will be somewhat arbitrary. More particularly, even if standards could be specified a little more precisely, there is no *methodology* which could guide judgments about individual cases and help conclusively answer the question whether an EU Member State is violating these standards (although, strictly speaking, something like no methodology would also mean no peer review—and in general, Article 7 would fall victim to this charge as much as a Copenhagen Commission).

I shall offer three responses to this concern, which could be rephrased as: who ought to face the burden of justifying themselves to the rest of the EU, when they embark on significant political changes (and not just individual fundamental rights violations, which could be very serious, but which can generally be dealt with by the Luxembourg and the Strasbourg courts)? First, from an essentially *historical* perspective, I want to say the following: I believe it can be shown that the whole direction of political development in post-war Europe has been towards delegating power to unelected institutions, such as constitutional courts.[22] That development was based on specific lessons that Europeans—rightly or wrongly—drew from the political catastrophes of the mid-century: the architects of the post-war Western European order viewed the ideal of popular sovereignty with a great deal of distrust; after all, how could one trust the peoples who had brought fascists to power or extensively collaborated with fascist occupiers?[23] Less obviously, the elites also had deep reservations about the idea of *parliamentary* sovereignty. After all, had not legitimate representative assemblies handed all power over to Hitler and to Marshal Pétain, the leader of Vichy France, in 1933 and 1940 respectively? Hence parliaments in post-war Europe were systematically weakened, checks and balances were strengthened, and non-elected institutions (constitutional courts are the prime example) were tasked not just with defending individual rights, but with defending democracy as a whole.[24] In short, distrust of unrestrained popular sovereignty, and even of unconstrained parliamentary sovereignty (what a German constitutional lawyer once called 'parliamentary absolutism') are, so to speak, in the very DNA of post-war European politics.[25] And it is fair to say that these underlying principles of what I have elsewhere called 'constrained democracy' were almost always adopted when countries were able to shake off dictatorships and turned to liberal democracy in the last thirty years of the twentieth century: first on the Iberian peninsula in the 1970s, and then in Central and Eastern Europe after 1989. Going out on a conceptual limb, one might even consider this model of democracy as a kind of European 'basic structure', analogous to the basic structure doctrine of the Indian Constitutional Court.[26]

European integration, it needs to be emphasized, was part-and-parcel of this comprehensive attempt to constrain the popular will: it added supranational constraints to

[22] I have made this argument at greater length in *Safeguarding Democracy* (n 1).

[23] This was the core of the case for judicial review in these countries: there were no proven democratic institutions and there were good reasons to believe that many citizens would not take individual rights seriously. Compare J Waldron, 'The Core of the Case Against Judicial Review' (2006) 115 *Yale Law Journal* 1346.

[24] We could add that dignity—and not freedom—is the main value of post-war constitutions.

[25] Of course, this is another way of saying that while 'constitutional pluralism' and 'constitutional tolerance' are found in the EU (and while both of these have an important normative dimension), both are still constrained—a fact which every accession process makes clear. See N Walker, 'The Idea of Constitutional Pluralism' (2002) 65 *Modern Law Review* 31; and JHH Weiler, 'Federalism Without Constitutionalism: Europe's *Sonderweg*', in K Nicolaïdis and R Howse (eds), *The Federal Vision: Legitimacy and Levels of Governance in the United States and the European Union* (OUP 2001) 54–70.

[26] On India, see for instance GJ Jacobsohn, *Constitutional Identity* (Harvard University Press 2010).

national ones[27] (which is not to say that this entire process was master-minded by anyone, or came about seamlessly: of course, the outcomes were contingent and had to do with who prevailed in particular political struggles). This logic was more evident initially with institutions such as the Council of Europe and the ECHR, but the desire to 'lock in' liberal-democratic commitments became more pronounced in a specific EU (or then EEC) context with the transitions to democracy in Southern Europe in the 1970s.

Now, history is not destiny and its supposed lessons do not automatically generate legitimacy. But it seems a reasonable presumption that radical, sudden departures from this post-war model of politics place a special burden of justification on Member State governments embarking on such a departure. This thought applies to Hungary, for instance, where the constitutional court and in general, the non-elected institutions to which Hungary committed after 1989 *in the name of solidifying democracy* have been systematically weakened.[28] But it does not apply to a country like Britain, where *de facto* constraints on—in theory unlimited -parliamentary sovereignty have had a more informal character, at least until recently, and where the observance of such constraints can generally be expected.[29] Accordingly, not all countries in the EU will necessarily converge on constrained democracy. But in judging individual cases, overall context, and in particular an account of *historical trajectories* and *sequencing* are crucial.[30] The whole may well be something quite different than the sum of its parts, which is—to stress the point again—the main reason why 'check-lists' in judging constitutions or political systems in their totality will not do. The Venice Commission made this argument very plain in its opinion on the proposed fourth amendment to the new Hungarian 'Basic Law' in 2013:

> In constitutional law, perhaps even more than in other legal fields, it is necessary to take into account not only a provision's face value, but also to examine its constitutional context. The mere fact that a provision can also be found in the constitution of another country does not mean that it will 'fit' into *any* other constitution. Each constitution is the result of balancing various powers. If a power is granted to one state body, other powers need to be able to control the exercise of this power effectively. The more power an institution has, the more tightly the control mechanisms need to be constructed. Comparative constitutional law cannot be reduced to identifying the existence of a provision in the constitution of another country to justify its democratic credentials in the constitution of one's own country. Each constitution is a complex array of checks and balances and each provision needs to be examined in view of its merits for the balance of powers as a whole.[31]

Let me mention one other way in which a Member State government might reasonably be expected to face a special burden of justification. Of course, all governments try to justify their actions continuously, regardless whether anyone challenges them from Brussels to

[27] One might ask in what way, then, 'constrained democracy' differs from 'guided' or 'defective' democracy. The answer is that in the former, genuine changes in who holds power is possible and all constraints are ultimately justified with regard to strengthening democracy. In the latter no real change is allowed.

[28] On the new Hungarian constitution, see R Uitz, 'Can you tell when an illiberal democracy is in the making? An appeal to comparative constitutional scholarship from Hungary' (2015) 13 *International Journal of Constitutional Law* 279, 286. On the new Hungarian constitution, see also the special section on Hungary's illiberal turn in the (2012) 23 *Journal of Democracy*; and the collection edited by GA Tóth, *Constitution for a Disunited Nation: On Hungary's 2011 Fundamental Law* (Central European University Press 2012).

[29] Clearly, the picture changed somewhat with the Human Rights Act of 1998—though it is worth noting that recently the adherence of the UK to the ECHR has been highly contested. It is not a fanciful scenario at this point that the country will reverse course and create a new 'bill of rights' which *de facto* uncouples the UK from supranational European rights protection.

[30] I am indebted to Renáta Uitz for making me understand the importance of sequencing.

[31] http://www.venice.coe.int/Newsletter/NEWSLETTER_2013_03/1_HUN_EN.html, accessed 12 October 2016.

do so. To govern is not just to talk, but all governing is accompanied by talk, which is to say: public argument. If the claims offered by a Member State government are notably inconsistent with what a government is actually doing, then more pressure should be applied to make that government explain itself. To offer one example: the current Hungarian government has emphasized that the new constitution which came into effect in early 2012 is a thoroughly democratic one—in light, or so it is claimed, of an entirely legitimate European ideal of parliamentary sovereignty, or also majoritarian democracy. Now, whatever one thinks about the ideal of parliamentary sovereignty, the claim that the constitution conforms to this ideal is hardly credible when, as the Venice Commission and many internal and external critics have pointed out, the new Hungarian Basic Law constitutionalizes many policy areas which in other countries would be subject to the vagaries of day-to-day, or at least election-to-election, political contestation.[32] Again, whatever one thinks of such an 'over-constitutionalization', it is hard to see how to square it with the ideal which is being propounded by the defenders of the Basic Law. This kind of inconsistency calls for more justification and, quite possibly, a process of correction.

Finally, let me address the question of criteria for intervention head-on. Many observers have worried that calls for EU intervention might become the stuff of symbolic politics; in particular, there has been a concern that only *small* (and *newer*) Member States will ever be picked on (a concern reinforced, no doubt, by the invocation of 'Copenhagen'). This is a common interpretation of what happened when Jörg Haider's far-right party came to power in Austria in 2000. Leaders like Jacques Chirac and Gerhard Schröder—unable to do anything about Jean-Marie Le Pen's National Front or the neo-Nazi NPD respectively at home—could moralize about small countries at no cost internationally, or so it seemed, while also scoring some points against their domestic opponents.[33] Meanwhile, nobody ever dared to touch Berlusconi's Italy, no matter how much political *bunga-bunga* was going on. Powerful Member States—and especially founding Member States of the EU—appeared to be above European standards.

However, it would be a mistake to conclude from a comparison between the cases of Italy, Austria, Hungary, and Romania that only weaker and newer Member States get picked on, because there are important differences here: teasing them out can also point us to convincing criteria for what would make EU interventions legitimate. First, the problem with the 'Haider Affair' was partly that sanctions were imposed *before* the new government had taken any significant actions. For sure, you can try to justify sanctions as essentially warning shots. But in the case of Austria they appeared more like expressions of displeasure with Haider's past pronouncements (on Nazi employment policies, for instance) than as principled objections to what the new government actually sought to do. This is in marked contrast with the cases of Hungary, Romania, and also Poland: in all these countries the governments had clear track records; what they were doing also had a systematically anti-democratic character and could not be excused as a one-off mistake.

Second, there is a significant difference between Berlusconi's Italy and the three states further east. True, the *Cavaliere* also tried to weaken checks and balances.[34] But the

[32] As the Venice Commission put it in its opinion on the fourth amendment: 'The crucial distinction between ordinary and constitutional politics and the subordination of the former to the latter should not be disregarded, lest democracy and the Rule of Law be undermined in Hungary'.

[33] See also M Merlingen et al., 'The Right and the Righteous? European Norms, Domestic Politics and the Sanctions Against Austria' (2001) 39 *Journal of Common Market Studies* 59. Perhaps not so surprisingly, the evidence suggests that both domestic party-political incentives and an ideational environment favourable to human rights protection had to come together to motivate sanctions.

[34] For certain, Berlusconi's style of government—to the extent that he actually governed—was highly personalistic and plebiscitarian: it involved less a comprehensive restructuring of the state than the creation of a court of

opposition, despite its generally sorry state, remained just about strong enough to resist major constitutional re-crafting: throughout his time in office, Berlusconi was constrained by the fact that he headed a coalition (ie, not single-party) government; the media was not completely dominated by Berlusconi's own empire, contrary to what outside commentators often claimed; and crucially, the judiciary kept putting up a fight and various Italian presidents—Giorgio Napolitano in particular—would block Berlusconi's plans (for instance, to appoint allies—even his personal lawyer—to particular ministries, or to hold new elections when they suited him).[35] Berlusconi also lost popular referenda, especially the 2006 constitutional one, which would have introduced far-reaching changes (and strengthened the office of the prime minister in particular). In short, there were reasonable grounds for thinking that the situation would over time self-correct through internal political struggle. In that context, outside intervention might easily seem illegitimate: it could look like Brussels picking a winner in a domestic fight for power; it would also cut short what we could describe as a 'democratic learning process'[36] through political struggle, thereby preventing the proper development of a democratic political culture.[37]

Our discussion, then, yields at least three general criteria which need to be met for an actual negative opinion by something like the Copenhagen Commission: first, a Member State government has to have a *track record* of violating liberal-democratic political principles. There is no case for preemptive action. Second, that track record should also show a government's general conduct as well as specific policies as having a *systematic* nature: one-off violations might be deeply problematic, but they can generally be dealt with by courts (and they should always be assessed in context). To be sure, mistakes cannot simply be excused by context, but they can be explained, and such explanations might also make it plausible to come to the conclusion that a particular government, despite mistakes, is fundamentally well-intentioned. Third, intervention is about enforcing commitments which were entered into voluntarily in the past. If there is reasonable hope that such commitments can ultimately largely be enforced internally, intervention should wait. *Self-correction* remains the best outcome, but whether it will actually happen is a matter of political judgment.

4. Objections

There are legitimate worries about the kind of new body I am proposing here—what critics might regard as a kind of *deus ex an ideal militant democracy*, or a typical form of ad hoc manoeuvre (the Copenhagen Commission will 'solve' the problems with the present Hungarian government, but create ten new ones on the way…)[38] or, as Komárek put it, when Europe cannot solve a problem, it invents a new institution instead.[39] And indeed, if

devoted followers. See M Viroli, *The Liberty of Servants: Berlusconi's Italy*, trans. A Shugaar (Princeton University Press 2011).

[35] I am grateful to Giovanni Capoccia and Gianfranco Pasquino for information and views on this matter. See also 'The Future of Western Liberal Order: The Case of Italy' (January 2013) *Transatlantic Academy Paper Series*, http://www.transatlanticacademy.org/sites/default/files/publications/PasquinoEtAl_Italy_Jan13_web_Final.pdf, accessed 12 October 2016.

[36] See also P Niesen, 'Anti-Extremism, Negative Republicanism, Civic Society: Three Paradigms for Banning Political Parties', in S Avineri and Z Sternhell (eds), *Europe's Century of Discontent: The Legacies of Fascism, Nazism and Communism* (Magnes Press 2003) 249.

[37] Though we could of course reasonably ask whether Italians should not have figured out by the end of Berlusconi's second stint in office at the very latest that the *Cavaliere's* statecraft was somewhat deficient.

[38] I am grateful to Christoph Möllers on this point.

[39] J Komárek, 'The EU is More than a Constraint on Populist Democracy' (2014), http://www.verfassungsblog.de/en/the-eu-is-more-than-a-constraint-on-populist-democracy/, accessed 12 October 2016. Clearly, the creation

the political will is lacking to initiate an Article 7 procedure or, say, for a revised and more robust mandate for the FRA—what hope is there that a Copenhagen Commission would fulfil the task of democracy protection?

First, some support has in fact been building for a new 'mechanism' which would send an early warning signal—witness the Tavares Report, which explicitly calls for a Copenhagen Commission-style institution, the letter to President Barroso signed by four EU foreign ministers which stressed the need for mechanisms short of Article 7, and, not least, the Commission's 'Rule of Law Mechanism' unveiled in March 2014. Second, irrespective of what is politically possible, it has to be remembered that Article 7 is not particularly good for issuing early warning signals. Building support for Article 7 is likely to take too long, and the FRA at this point simply does not have the right mandate and is unlikely to acquire it. A properly designed Copenhagen Commission would have the right mandate and above all, it would concentrate minds in a highly fragmented political space and in a weak, some would say non-existent, public sphere.[40]

One might still object that the EU would just be duplicating existing institutions. Have the Venice Commission and the ECtHR not done relatively well in addressing the situation created by the Hungarian government, for instance? My answer is that, first, the EU has reached a depth and density of integration which can find no equivalent in the Council of Europe. EU law is also much more specific in areas such as data protection—and the Council and the Venice Commission could not really comment on them. Second, it is worth mentioning that the Council of Europe is an even more fragmented political space (with no shared public sphere at all). Third, the Council also contains members who probably would have a hard time meeting even the fuzziest or most consciously relaxed Copenhagen criteria. The problem of double standards—charges of hypocrisy abound in virtually any discussion of democracy-protecting interventions—would be exacerbated further.

Finally, the ECtHR can only properly address individual rights violations, whereas the Copenhagen Commission should take a more holistic view; the Venice Commission cannot be proactive, whereas the Copenhagen Commission could routinely monitor the situation in Member States and raise an alarm without having to be prompted. It would thus also build up an institutional memory which would make it easier to prevent double standards both in assessing an individual country over time and in comparing different countries.[41] In sum, without wanting in any way to fault the Venice Commission, I want to insist that ultimately, there is no good, principled argument for the Union permanently to 'contract out' core normative concerns.

That leaves two important worries: first, the idea that what is distinctive (and valuable) about the EU is *pluralism*: tolerance instead of homogenization; mutual opening and respectful peer review instead of a centralized institution defining and defending democracy and thereby destroying the precious heterarchy of norms and institutions which has emerged in the Union.[42] We ought to have a longer argument about pluralism, which after

of new bodies in general poses all kinds of challenges. As we know from the experience of establishing European agencies (including the FRA), there is a great danger that Member States will try to exercise tight control over them and effectively 'neuter' any agent for liberal democracy protection, for all the same reasons that makes them reluctant to invoke Article 7.

[40] There is certainly a potential problem here: how would the Commission acquire a high public profile if it is only to raise the alarm in truly serious cases? The best answer might be to inaugurate the Commission with as much pomp and circumstance as possible.

[41] Thanks to Kim Lane Scheppele for this point.

[42] D Halberstam, 'Constitutional Heterarchy: The Centrality of Conflict in the European Union and the United States', in JL Dunoff and JP Trachtman (eds), *Ruling the World? Constitutionalism, International Law, and Global Governance* (CUP 2009) 326–55.

all, is not a first-order value such as liberty and equality, but which, to gain any normative traction, has to be justified with reference to another value or broader political principle: cultural diversity perhaps, or democratic autonomy, or the beneficial moral–psychological effects of living with differences.[43] For my purposes here, it suffices to say that the EU has always been about *pluralism within common political parameters*. After all, the accession process itself has not pursued the aim of maximizing difference or anything like it, but has in fact been meant to ensure sameness in certain regards (democracy, Rule of Law, state capacity, etc). And as long as it has been taking in new members, the EU has been in the business of making definitive judgments on whether a country really is a liberal democracy (even if the Copenhagen criteria might have given a false sense of certainty in this respect), and more broadly, judgments on where the limits of pluralism should be located. In that sense, mandating a distinct and highly visible body by keeping an eye on whether everyone remains a liberal democracy does not constitute a fundamental break with EU principles and practices.

The second worry is as follows: if supposedly technocratic 'new constitutionalism' is partly to blame for 'backsliding' (as Paul Blokker has forcefully argued), then is some form of 'democracy oversight' from on high not just adding to the problem?[44] If constitutionalism never becomes part of lived political experience in newer Member States in particular, but is instead created and enforced by distant bodies of experts, then will more paternalistic 'guardianship' by Brussels not reinforce the lesson that constitutionalism is something that a particular 'we' does not do autonomously, is incapable of internalizing etc? My—perhaps too flippant—answer is this: nothing prevents one from starting a European Citizens' Initiative to express concern about the Rule of Law in a Member State (and also to find allies within the national 'we' in question), nothing prevents a transnational European civil society from what governments will always condemn as 'meddling in internal affairs' (remember the provocations by the German artist Christoph Schlingensief in Vienna in 2000). The alleged 'technocracy' of the Copenhagen Commission and 'grassroots initiatives' are not mutually exclusive; it makes little sense to play popular democracy off against 'liberal technocracy'.

That leaves one issue unresolved, however. I said earlier that an account of militant democracy should ideally include ways to address the underlying factors giving rise to anti-democratic movements. There are no very certain answers to how to address this challenge domestically, except to say that sometimes more moderate parties can take up genuine concerns of citizens without the anti-democratic stance of parties that might initially have given voice to those concerns.[45] This is another way of stating the obvious—that democratic political parties will have to craft answers to the underlying challenges a society faces; and there is, of course, no guarantee that they will be successful. It is much harder to see which European institutions could play such a role (certainly, parties—within their transnational European 'party families'—could try to help each other across borders). The European Commission can of course help countries with 'cohesion funds' etc—and potentially 'reward' people who get rid of their rogue governments. But the fundamental EU principle of subsidiarity sets a limit to such conduct by the European Commission.

[43] See also T Isiksel, 'Global legal pluralism as fact and norm' (2013) 2 *Global Constitutionalism* 160.

[44] P Blokker, *New Democracies in Crisis? A Comparative Constitutional Study of the Czech Republic, Hungary, Poland, Romania, and Slovakia* (Routledge 2013).

[45] T Bale, 'Are Bans on Political Parties Bound to Turn Out Badly? A Comparative Investigation of Three "Intolerant" Democracies: Turkey, Spain, and Belgium' (2007) 5 *Comparative European Politics* 141.

This shortcoming is not fatal to the proposal of a Copenhagen Commission, nor to the idea of a supranational, European militant democracy. But it needs to be acknowledged frankly, and there needs to be more thought on how it could be remedied.

5. Would democracy protection by the EU really be seen as legitimate?

The very last section of this chapter is necessarily more speculative. We have some record of the conflicts between the European Commission and Hungary, Romania, and Poland respectively. But in a more systematic empirical way, we simply do not know whether financial sanctions, for instance, would create a great nationalist backlash, as is often asserted, turning entire counties from being Euro-enthusiasts to Eurosceptics. I would offer two thoughts, though:

First, for Europe to try to 'hold back' or try to be 'neutral' in highly charged domestic conflicts is not costless and, ultimately, is not actually 'neutral'.[46] A reluctance to try to protect liberal democracy in a Member State will betray the hopes of all those citizens of the country in question who put their trust in the Union as some sort of guarantor against new forms of illiberalism or outright authoritarianism. Moreover, any government eager to dismantle checks and balances, for instance, will at some level know that it is heading for a conflict with European institutions—hence it has every incentive to whip up Eurosceptic sentiments, whether the EU actually does much or not. In other words, preemptive nationalism is likely to appear—quite irrespective of any particular approach the Union adopts.

Second, there is little evidence that any of these nationalist campaigns have worked, or for that matter, that strong exercises of EU leverage have generally produced any severe backlashes. Orbán's self-declared 'war of independence' has not proved popular, or so the polls suggest,[47] and even very heavy-handed forms of conditionality by the EU in the past (think of Slovakia in the late 1990s) have not obviously rendered the EU illegitimate in the eyes of the populations of Member States subject to conditionality.

6. Concluding thoughts

Establishing a Copenhagen Commission would in all likelihood require treaty change (unless such an institution were to be established by international treaty among the Member States, an approach which has been employed by some Member States in addressing the Euro-crisis. It might well only be possible to create this Commission when times are calm—which is to say when there is no apparent need for it. In troubled times the rogue government everyone is concerned about would in all likelihood prevent such an institution from being established.

This problem is not unique to the supranational realm. Sceptics about militant democracy will always be tempted to say that countries which can have militant democracy probably do not need it, whereas those which need it cannot have it.[48] Why? Because any

[46] Of course there is always a danger of the EU being regarded as just another partisan actor in the domestic struggle. But this is a matter of double effect: the goal of the EU is not to have the opposition win; what can come across as *de facto* support for the opposition is an unintended effect of actions against the government.

[47] 'Hungarian public opinion on Viktor Orbán's "war of independence"' (2013) *Hungarian Spectrum*, http://hungarianspectrum.wordpress.com/2013/07/11/hungarian-public-opinion-on-viktor-orbans-war-of-independence, accessed 12 October 2016.

[48] I am indebted to Christoph Möllers for this point.

country where the most powerful actors can agree on what the genuine threats to democracy are (irrespective of whether these threats emanate from the right or the left, or from religion or secular ideologies), probably has such a strong democratic consensus that challenges to democracy will fail by themselves. Conversely, in highly polarized and unstable polities characterized by deep moral disagreement, militant democracy might make some sense—but the very fact of polarization and disagreement probably prevent the creation of a militant democracy. Everyone might be too concerned about the abuse of party bans for partisan purposes, for instance, to agree to have such measures available.

So the outlook for a Copenhagen Commission is not good; that very fact tells us something about the not terribly good state Europe is in. Still, whether it can be realized is ultimately a question of political will, which does not just mean the will of politicians, but also European citizens' individual wills.

14

Application of the EU CFR by National Courts in Purely Domestic Cases

András Jakab

1. Political vs judicial enforcement methods

The EU is not just a WTO-type community based on common interests but it is also a community of values.[1] According to Article 2 TEU, these values are human dignity, freedom, democracy, equality, the Rule of Law, and respect for human rights (including the rights of persons belonging to minorities). If the EU does not want to lose its credibility, it has a duty to defend all of these values to the greatest possible extent, at least within Europe, and especially within the EU. The different options of how to enforce these values do not exclude, but rather reinforce each other. Most of these enforcement mechanisms depend on political discretion (isolation of the political party concerned within its European party family, Article 7 TEU, treaty infringement procedures initiated by the Commission), which makes the use of these methods unreliable as guarantees of the abovementioned values. European politicians might (and often actually do) behave opportunistically, they are interested in smoothing such conflicts or even in pretending that they do not exist. European politicians can tend to turn a blind eye to problems of national constitutionalism when faced with a major crisis affecting the EU as a whole which seems to them to be of greater importance. We should of course expect European politicians to believe in the values of constitutionalism, but liberty is at least to a large part based on distrust of politicians. A mechanism which leaves the enforcement of constitutionalism in the hands of politicians is useful but unreliable. Reliable mechanisms are judicially guaranteed and enable those affected to enforce these values.[2]

In this paper I am going to argue that the most promising way to conceptualize the values of European constitutionalism in a judicially enforceable manner is to extend the application of the EU CFR through a creative reinterpretation of its Article 51(1).

[1] Earlier versions of the present chapter have been presented at the seminar 'Reinforcing Rule of Law Oversight in the European Union' at the European University Institute in Florence (16 January 2014), at the conference 'Rolling back the Rollback' at the Central European University in Budapest (7 April 2014), at the workshop 'Enforcing EU Law against Recalcitrant Member States' of the Wissenschaftszentrum in Berlin (10 July 2014), and at the public hearing 'Taking Citizens' concerns seriously: broadening the scope of the EU Charter on Fundamental Rights (Article 51)?' of the EP Committee on Petitions in Brussels (23 February 2016). I am grateful to Paul Blokker, Carlos Closa, Bruno de Witte, Jonas Grimheden, Christophe Hillion, Michael Ioannidis, Dimitry Kochenov, Mattias Kumm, John Morijn, Jan-Werner Müller, Joakim Nergelius, Gianluigi Palombella, Jari Pirjola, Norbert Reich, Martin Scheinin, Kim Lane Scheppele, Eleanor Sharpston, Kaarlo Tuori, Zsófia Varga, and Andre Wilkens for their critical remarks. For interesting discussions on the concept of 'leading cases' I am indebted to Nele Yang.

[2] As the key question of this chapter concerns the relationship between the individual and the government, I will not concentrate on issues relating to the horizontal effect of fundamental rights. On these issues under the CFR, see T von Danwitz and K Paraschas, 'A Fresh Start for the Charter' (2012) 35 *Fordham International Law Journal* 1396, 1423–5.

2. Existing interpretations of Article 51(1) CFR

Probably the most important provision or 'keystone'[3] of the CFR is Article 51(1), which limits its scope with respect to the Member States: it is applicable to them '*only* when they are implementing Union law'.[4] This restrictive formulation not only contradicts the philosophy which would appear to inspire the CFR,[5] but it is also more restrictive than the former case law of the ECJ concerning the applicability of fundamental rights (conceptualized as fundamental principles of law).[6]

The explanatory memoranda (published in the Official Journal)[7] do not really help clarify the situation either:[8]

> As regards the Member States, it follows unambiguously from the case law of the Court of Justice that the requirement to respect fundamental rights defined in a Union context is only binding on the Member States when they act in the scope of Union law (judgment of 13 July 1989, Case 5/88 Wachauf [1989] ECR 2609; judgment of 18 June 1991, ERT [1991] ECR I-2925); judgment of 18 December 1997 (C-309/96 Annibaldi [1997] ECR I-7493). The Court of Justice confirmed this case law in the following terms: 'In addition, it should be remembered that the requirements flowing from the protection of fundamental rights in the Community legal order are also binding on Member States when they implement Community rules...' (judgment of 13 April 2000, Case C-292/97, [2000] ECR 2737, paragraph 37 of the grounds). Of course this rule, as enshrined in this Charter, applies to the central authorities as well as to regional or local bodies, and to public organisations, when they are implementing Union law.

In the literature, there are three main interpretations of Article 51(1). Firstly, a literal and rather restrictive approach would require actual EU law to exist in an area in order to trigger the application of the CFR.[9] This interpretation, however, not only contradicts the former case law of the ECJ (as quoted above in the explanatory memoranda), but it is also in conflict with the CFR itself, as Article 53 explicitly states that the CFR cannot lead to a diminished level of fundamental rights protection.[10] By accepting this interpretation,

[3] K Lenaerts, 'Exploring the Limits of the EU Charter of Fundamental Rights' (2012) 8 *European Constitutional Law Review* 375, 377.

[4] According to P Eeckhout, 'The EU Charter of Fundamental Rights and the Federal Question' (2002) 39 *Common Market Law Review*, it is paradoxical to have a general fundamental rights charter with a limited scope.

[5] R Alonso García, 'The General Provisions of the Charter of Fundamental Rights of the European Union' (2002) Jean Monnet Working Paper No 4, 5, http://jeanmonnetprogram.org/archive/papers/02/020401.pdf, accessed 12 October 2016.

[6] For a detailed comparison with former case law, see X Groussot et al., 'The Scope of Application of Fundamental Rights on Member States' Action: In Search of Certainty in EU Adjudication' (2011) Eric Stein Working Paper (Czech Society for European and Comparative Law) No 1, http://www.era-comm.eu/charter_of_fundamental_rights/kiosk/pdf/EU_Adjudication.pdf, accessed 12 October 2016. For the history of different draft versions of the CFR, see G de Búrca, 'The drafting of the European Union Charter of fundamental rights' (2001) 26 *European Law Reports* 126.

[7] Explanations relating to the CFR [2007] OJ C303/17, 32.

[8] For a critical view on the rather confusing explanations, see LFM Besselink, 'The Member States, the National Constitutions and the Scope of the Charter' (2001) 8 *Maastricht Journal* 68, 76–8. Groussot et al. (n 6) 19 denounce the explanations to Art 51 as 'a mixture of various formulas'.

[9] S Peers, 'The Rebirth of the EU's Charter of Fundamental Rights' (2013) 13 *Cambridge Yearbook of European Legal Studies* 283, 298; Von Danwitz and Paraschas (n 2) 1409; PM Huber, 'Unitarisierung durch Gemeinschaftsgrundrechte – Zur Überprüfungsbedürftigkeit der ERT-Rechtsprechung' [2008] Europarecht 190, 196; M Borowsky, 'Artikel 51 – Anwendungsbereich' in J Meyer (ed), *Charta der Grundrechte der Europäischen Union* (3rd edn, Nomos 2011) 642, 653–4; Z Varga, 'Az Alapjogi Charta alkalmazási köre I' (2013) 5 *Európai Jog* 17, 19. See also P Yowell, 'The Justiciability of the Charter of Fundamental Rights in the Domestic Law of Member States' in PM Huber (ed), *The EU and National Constitutional Law* (Boorberg 2012) 107, 114–23.

[10] C Nowak, 'Grundrechtsberechtigte und Grundrechtsadressaten' in F Sebastian, M Meselhaus, and C Nowak (eds), *Handbuch der Europäischen Grundrechte* (Beck 2006) 212, 244–5.

however, the level of fundamental rights protection would be lower than it was before the CFR.

However, since *Åkerberg Fransson* it seems clear that the former literal interpretation does not reflect the actual legal situation.[11] The judgment clarified the scope of the CFR through interpretation,[12] and accepted the view widely held in the literature that any material link and any *potential* law making suffice for the application of the CFR.[13] This view was also previously promoted by AG Sharpston in *Ruiz Zambrano*:[14]

> Transparency and clarity require that one be able to identify with certainty what 'the scope of Union law' means for the purposes of EU fundamental rights protection. It seems to me that, in the long run, the clearest rule would be one that made the availability of EU fundamental rights protection dependent neither on whether a Treaty provision was directly applicable nor on whether secondary legislation had been enacted, but rather on *the existence and scope of a material EU competence.* To put the point another way: the rule would be that, provided that the EU had competence (whether exclusive or shared) in a particular area of law, EU fundamental rights should protect the citizen of the EU *even if such competence has not yet been exercised.*

This interpretation also asserts, however, that without a link to the scope of a material EU competence,[15] the application of the CFR cannot be engaged.[16] The application of the CFR is thus still viewed as collateral, and its rights are not free-standing rights.[17] This view probably accords both with current ECJ case law[18] and the dominant opinion in the literature,[19] even if some call for further clarification to ease the CFR's application by national judges.[20]

The motivation to have a third and more liberal interpretation suggesting that the CFR also applies outside the scope of EU law emerged from recent events, especially in Hungary, Italy, and Romania.[21] The legal justification for such an interpretation is that Union citizenship must include a minimum guarantee of fundamental rights for cases of systemic failure in a Member State. This Reverse *Solange* approach has been advanced by Armin von

[11] C-617/10 *Åklagaren v Hans Åkerberg Fransson* [2013] ECLI:EU:C:2013:105.

[12] F Fontanelli, '*Hic Sunt Nationes*: The Elusive Limits of the EU Charter and the German Constitutional Watchdog' (2013) 9 *European Constitutional Law Review* 315; A Ward, 'Article 51 – Scope' in S Peers et al. (eds), *The EU Charter of Fundamental Rights. A Commentary* (Hart 2014) 1413, 1433–7. On the conflict between the wide *Fransson* doctrine and the strict approach of the German FCC to Art 51, see D Thym, 'Separation versus Fusion – or: How to Accommodate National Autonomy and the Charter? Diverging Visions of the German Constitutional Court and the European Court of Justice' (2013) 9 *European Constitutional Law Review* 391.

[13] Eeckhout (n 4) 993; H Kaila, 'The Scope of Application of the Charter of Fundamental Rights of the European Union in the Member States' in P Cardonnel et al. (eds), *Constitutionalising the EU Judicial System* (Hart 2012) 291; J Kokott and C Sobotta, 'The Charter of Fundamental Rights of the European Union after Lisbon' (2010) EUI Working Paper No. 6, 7, http://cadmus.eui.eu/bitstream/handle/1814/15208/AEL_WP_2010_06.pdf?sequence=3, accessed 12 October 2016.

[14] C-34/09 *Gerardo Ruiz Zambrano v Office national de l'emploi* [2010] ECLI:EU:C:2010:560, 163, Opinion of AG Sharpston.

[15] On the different definitions of the general concept 'scope of EU law', see S Prechal, 'The Principle of Attributed Powers and the "Scope of EU Law"' in L Besselink et al. (eds), *The Eclipse of the Legality Principle in the European Union* (Wolters Kluwer 2011).

[16] Eeckhout (n 4) 993; Opinion of AG Sharpston (n 14) 173.

[17] Expression borrowed from Groussot et al. (n 6) 22.

[18] Recently confirmed by C-206/13 *Cruciano Siragusa v Regione Sicilia—Soprintendenza Beni Culturali e Ambientali di Palermo* [2014] ECLI:EU:C:2014:126, 24. For an overview of the relevant case law, see M Dougan, 'Judicial Review of Member State Action under the General Principles and the Charter: Defining the "Scope of Union Law"' (2015) 52 *Common Market Law Review* 1201.

[19] Borowsky (n 9) 758–60.

[20] E Hancox, 'The meaning of "implementing" EU law under Article 51(1) of the Charter: *Åkerberg Fransson*' (2013) 50 *Common Market Law Review* 1411; F Fontanelli, 'National Measures and the Application of the EU Charter of Fundamental Rights – Does curia.eu Know iura.eu?' (2014) 14 *Human Rights Law Review* 231, 263–5.

[21] See e.g. http://www.verfassungsblog.de/category/schwerpunkte/rescue-english/, accessed 12 October 2016.

Bogdandy and his colleagues.[22] The approach has been criticized for different reasons: for being too dramatic and stigmatizing (and thus contradicting the principle of mutual respect as provided for in Article 4(3) TEU), rather than concentrating on the actual fundamental rights protection; for requiring a systemic failure of fundamental rights protection, the establishment of which necessarily requires a decision by a political body under current procedures (thus leaving the fundamental rights protection at the mercy of politicians);[23] and also for using the *Solange* formula, which is considered to be a potential face-saving excuse for inaction.[24] In order to avoid these objections (but possibly resulting in others) I am going to develop a different approach in this chapter: an approach which would elevate the CFR, through creative reinterpretation, into a real and fully fledged Bill of Rights in the EU.

3. For a creative reinterpretation of Article 51(1)

If we aim to create a fully fledged value community which benefits all its citizens equally, then the CFR should become full applicable in every case in its own right, even in purely domestic cases in domestic courts and even in the absence of a systemic failure of fundamental rights protection at the domestic level. This would mean that judicial review would be introduced across Europe via the supremacy of EU law (more precisely here: of the CFR). This judicial review would be decentralized in the sense that local courts could exercise it, but its unified application would be ensured by the preliminary procedure: it can, thus, actually also be called semi-centralized judicial review.

The EU could thus become a 'community of fundamental rights' with nobody left behind (by the way, the idea of excluding a Member State because of fundamental rights violations is an appalling and unacceptable denial of a European moral community: the citizens of the excluded country would be left behind to suffer, whereas the rest of Europe would save itself). This would be especially important in cases where, sacrilegiously, violations of fundamental rights are entrenched in constitutions and where constitutional courts have been stuffed with party apparatchiks who do not care about constitutional arguments. Ordinary courts have the advantage that there are many of them in every country, their personnel is consequently difficult to replace on party political lines, and even a single ordinary judge is able to cry for help in the form of a preliminary reference to the ECJ.

a. Doctrinal triggers: Article 2 and 7 TEU vs Union citizenship

The above contradicts both the literal meaning of Article 51(1) and its current interpretation by the ECJ and the majority of the literature.[25] Accordingly, if we want to promote this idea, we need solid doctrinal arguments for doing so. There seem to be two possible, parallel ways to justify such an extensive interpretation of the scope of the CFR: one is to use the concept of Union citizenship, the other is to use Articles 2 and 7 TEU as triggers.

[22] A von Bogdandy et al., 'Reverse *Solange* – Protecting the essence of fundamental rights against EU Member States' (2012) 49 *Common Market Law Review* 489.

[23] For a detailed explanation of the concept and of different procedures, see Armin von Bogdandy and Michael Ioannidis, 'Systemic deficiency in the rule of law: What it is, what has been done, what can be done' (2014) 51 *Common Market Law Review* 59. See also von Bogdandy et al. in Chapter 12 of this volume.

[24] D Kochenov, 'On Policing Article 2 TEU Compliance – Reverse *Solange* and Systemic Infringements Analyzed' (2014) 33 *Polish Yearbook of International Law* 145, 156.

[25] c.f. Groussot et al. (n 6) 23: 'it is simply wrong to affirm that natural and legal persons, following the entry into force of the Lisbon Treaty, have gained the right to institute judicial proceedings on the basis of any provision of the Charter, in any situation, against any national (or EU) public authorities'.

These two justifications are not mutually exclusive, but the second seems more promising to me.

Union citizenship is generally conceived of as a bundle of rights,[26] and as an 'autonomous' legal status it also seems to replace the ideology of cross-border effects, as it triggers the application of EU law even in cases where there is no cross-border element,[27] and it has developed into being able to protect citizens from their own Member States.[28] One step further in the same direction would be to say that Union citizenship triggers the application of the CFR.[29] This approach differs greatly, though, from the traditional one which views the scope of the CFR as defined *ratione materiae* and not *ratione personae*.[30]

An alternative justification for wider application of the CFR—which retains the *ratione materiae* requirement—would be the following: Article 7 TEU provides that a special procedure can be launched in case of 'clear risk of a serious breach' of the core values laid down in Article 2 TEU (which includes the respect for human rights). Article 7 has remained unused since its inception, but if we use the formula developed in *Fransson* ('if it is capable of indirectly affecting EU law')[31] then—by reference to Articles 2 and 7 read together—basically any human rights violations can trigger the application of Article 51(1) CFR.[32]

b. The nature of the conflict situation

A usual problem with any measure adopted by the EU is that it could reinforce the unfortunate perception of conflicting EU and Member State interests and/or values. My above suggestion, however, is different from most suggestions concerning the solution to fundamental rights problems in Member States,[33] as here the conflict will arise between a Member State government and a Member State court (the ECJ being involved only indirectly, via a preliminary reference). Such situations are much more difficult (albeit not impossible) to frame as a righteous struggle against Brussels bureaucracy. In general, external formal sanctions against a state to force it to change domestic human rights

[26] G Palombella, 'Whose Europe? After the constitution: A goal-based citizenship' (2005) 3 *International Journal of Constitutional Law* 357, 377–82.

[27] P Van Elsuwege, 'Shifting the Boundaries? European Union Citizenship and the Scope of Application of EU Law' (2011) 38 *Legal Issues of Economic Integration* 263, analysing Case C-34/09 *Gerardo Ruiz Zambrano v Office national de l'emploi* [2011] ECLI:EU:C:2011:124. See also the Opinion of AG Poiares Maduro in C-135/08 *Janko Rottman v Freistaat Bayern* [2009] ECLI:EU:C:2009:588, para 23.

[28] D Kochenov, 'The Essence of EU Citizenship Emerging from the Last Ten Years of Academic Debate: Beyond the Cherry Blossoms and the Moon?' (2013) 62 *International and Comparative Law Quarterly* 97, 135.

[29] I Iglesias Sánchez, 'Fundamental Rights and Citizenship of the Union at a Crossroads: A Promising Alliance or a Dangerous Liaison?' (2014) 20 *European Law Journal* 464, arguing for an extension of the scope of the CFR to solve the problem of reverse discrimination. Contrast this with F Schulyok, 'The Scope of Application of EU Citizenship and EU Fundamental Rights in Wholly Internal Situations' (2012) 3 *Europarättslig Tijdskrift* 448.

[30] M Safjan, 'Areas of Application of the Charter of Fundamental Rights of the European Union: Fields of Conflict?' (2012) EUI Working Papers No 22, 2, http://cadmus.eui.eu/handle/1814/23294, accessed 12 October 2016. c.f. on the dilemma, F Fontanelli, 'The European Union's Charter of Fundamental Rights two years later' (2011) 3 (3) *Perspectives of Federalism* 40.

[31] On *Åkerberg Fransson* as symbolizing the end of the possibility of dealing with fundamental rights exclusively based on domestic considerations, see D Sarmiento, 'Who's Afraid of the Charter? The Court of Justice, National Courts and the New Framework of Fundamental Rights Protection in Europe' (2013) 50 *Common Market Law Review* 1267, 1303.

[32] c.f. on this possibility briefly, A Rosas, 'When is the EU Charter of Fundamental Rights Applicable at National Level?' (2012) 19 *Jurisprudencija/Jurisprudence* 1269, 1282. The author rejected it partly for practical (caseload) reasons (see 1285).

[33] See e.g. J-W Müller's proposal on a Copenhagen Commission: J-W Müller, 'Safeguarding democracy inside the EU – Brussels and the future of liberal order' (2013) Transatlantic Academy Paper Series 2012/2013 3, http://www.transatlanticacademy.org/sites/default/files/publications/Muller_SafeguardingDemocracy_Feb13_web.pdf, accessed 12 October 2016.

policies are largely inefficient and tend merely to reinforce a siege mentality within the country, while hurting only those social groups which they are aimed to help.[34]

As recently noted by Łazowski, there is a strong contrast between the usage of the CFR by the ECJ and by the European Commission: whereas the former has already referred to the CFR in 150 cases, the latter often uses the CFR in political rhetoric but is reluctant to do so in actual infringement proceedings.[35] We can only speculate about the reasons why the Commission is not eager to refer to the CFR. One possible explanation is simply risk avoidance: the Commission traditionally seems to prefer claims in which the chances of success are very high and there remain uncertainties (fewer nonetheless after the *Fransson* case) about the right interpretation of Article 51(1). Another explanation seems, however, more plausible to me: if the Commission were to offer a narrow interpretation of Article 51(1) it would then be difficult for the ECJ to expand on that; but if the Commission were to offer a broad (or activist) interpretation, then heavy Member State resistance could be expected. So their strategy seems to be to stay deliberately outside of the debate on the interpretation of Article 51(1) and to hope for the best (or even to argue modestly for less, as in the *Fransson* case, where the Commission even argued for the non-applicability of the CFR),[36] and rightly so: the value of the CFR can only be fully realized if the conflict is not between the Commission and the Member States, but rather between Member State courts (and individuals) and Member State governments.

c. Competence creep

An obvious objection against the above is that according to Article 6 TEU and Article 51(2), the CFR cannot expand the competences of the EU.[37] If we interpret both Articles 6 and 51(2) in light of Article 2 TEU, however, then this restriction cannot limit the enforcement of the CFR by the courts. Furthermore, the principle of subsidiarity (also mentioned in Article 51 CFEU) only applies to legislative competence and not to judicial authority.[38] This could be presented as a fresh step towards federalization,[39] but that is rather a side effect and not the actual justification for the above reinterpretation of Article 51(1).[40]

[34] c.f. for such a formal sanction mechanism (systemic infringement procedure) see KL Scheppele, 'Making Infringement Procedures More Effective: A Comment on Commission v Hungary, Case C-288/12 (8 April 2014) (Grand Chamber)' (*Eutopia-law.com*, 29 April 2014), http://eutopialaw.com/2014/04/29/making-infringement-procedures-more-effective-a-comment-on-commission-v-hungary-case-c-28812-8-april-2014-grand-chamber/, accessed 12 October 2016.

[35] A Łazowski, 'Decoding the Legal Enigma: the Charter of Fundamental Rights of the European Union and infringement proceedings' (2013) 14 *ERA Forum* 573.

[36] ibid, 585–6.

[37] On this phenomenon in general, but also specifically on the CFR, see e.g. S Prechal, 'Competence Creep and General Principles of Law' (2010) 3 *Review of European Administrative Law* 5.

[38] Groussot et al. (n 6) 23.

[39] For such worries based on the US experience, see A Knook, 'The Court, the Charter, and the Vertical Division of Powers in the European Union' (2005) 42 *Common Market Law Review* 367. For a comparative perspective, see M Cappelletti, *The Judicial Process in Comparative Perspective* (Clarendon 1989) 395: 'there is hardly anything that has greater potential to foster integration than a common bill of rights, as the constitutional history of the United States has proved'. See also on the centripetal force of any bill of rights, LM Díez-Picazo, 'Notes sur la nouvelle Charte des Droits fondamentaux de l'Union européenne' [2002] *Revue Européenne de Droit Public* 937, 946.

[40] This new interpretation would provide content to the otherwise currently legally useless opt-out protocol (Protocol No. 30 on the Application of the Charter of Fundamental Rights of the European Union to Poland and to the United Kingdom). For a view on the very limited current relevance of Protocol 30, see C Barnard, 'The EU Charter of Fundamental Rights: Happy 10th Birthday?' [2011] *EUSA Review* 5, 8.

d. Efficiency

There are possible objections against the above solution concerning its efficiency, coming from two opposing directions. The first objection refers to the worry that having fundamental rights protection depend on Member State courts might not be efficient to protect fundamental rights, as local courts might lack the necessary training or might simply be corrupt.[41] This is a legitimate concern, but it relates to the whole edifice of preliminary references, which is normally considered as being one of the keys to the success of the ECJ and EU law in general.[42]

The second objection expresses worries about whether the ECJ is actually able to take on the increased caseload which would probably result from a wider application of Article 51(1).[43] This is also a legitimate concern, but then again, it is a general and ongoing issue and it would be extremely dubious to reject fundamental rights cases *because* the ECJ is overloaded with other cases. Avoiding an excessive caseload is not a legal argument.

e. Moral authority

My proposal does not mean that the ECJ would usurp the role of the ECtHR. The two roles are and would remain quite different. First, the ECHR does not have direct applicability and supremacy in many countries, meaning that the domestic jurisdictions differ fundamentally. The ECtHR thus finds itself in a weaker legal situation in most EU Member States, though it is definitely stronger in one respect—its moral authority. To achieve the best outcome in implementing fundamental rights, the virtues of these two courts could be merged if the ECJ relied fully on ECtHR case law wherever possible (c.f. Articles 52(3) and 53). In general, the EU should rely on the authority of the CoE, including the Venice Commission, as otherwise its (economic or other) sanctions might appear to be part of a political or money-saving effort, especially if enforcement is in the hands of the Commission. Relying on the moral authority of the CoE and especially of the ECtHR also helps the ECJ counter potential objections concerning a juridical *coup d'État* by the ECJ,[44] and renders any abusive references to preserving national constitutional identities (Article 4(2) TEU) less plausible.

The ECJ could give teeth to the ECtHR, as it would be able not only to speed up enforcement but also ensure the efficiency of fundamental rights protection: the EU enforcement mechanisms are not just stronger (and financially usually more burdensome), but the EU-law-specific non-application of national law by Member State courts could simply stop the national measures from violating fundamental rights (as opposed to just buying them out, as it is the situation in ECHR cases).

[41] C Closa et al., 'Reinforcing Rule of Law Oversight in the European Union' (2014) EUI RSCAS Working Paper No 25, 21.

[42] For a classic account, see K Alter, 'The European Court's Political Power' (1996) 19 *West European Politics* 458.

[43] Rosas (n 32) 1285; EM Frenzel, 'Die Charta der Grundrechte als Maßstab für Mitgliedstaatliches Handeln zwischen Effektivierung und Hyperintegration' (2014) 51 *Der Staat* 1, 26.

[44] c.f. Eeckhout (n 4) 992; J Cornides, 'The European Union: Rule of Law or Rule of Judges?' (*EJIL-talk*, 11 November 2013), http://www.ejiltalk.org/the-european-union-rule-of-law-or-rule-of-judges/, accessed 12 October 2016. The CoE seems to be better equipped to support any ECJ decision with moral authority than a new expert body, e.g. the Copenhagen Commission as suggested by Müller (n 33). The procedures of such expert bodies can be successful if all parties want to end the conflict and if there is no actual substantive conflict, as in the case of the Austrian Haider affair in 2000. If you face a real conflict on human rights, you had better entrust a judicial body to decide.

f. Formal modification of Article 51(1)?

Some may agree with the purposes of my proposal, but would say that without a formal modification of the CFR (and of the TEU) it would be *contra legem* and thus unacceptable.[45] In general, treaty revisions are cumbersome and slow processes,[46] and treaty revisions which lead to politicians losing some of their discretionary powers are especially difficult. As I have argued in the *Spitzenkandidaten* debate, a reinterpretation of existing treaty provisions is more realistic in such cases,[47] and besides the pragmatic reasons I have also tried to sketch a doctrinal justification for this step above.[48]

4. 'This is just not the law'—or the nature of leading cases and the values of European integration

Whenever I have presented the above argument, there have always been one or two colleagues whose objection has simply been that 'this is just not the law'.[49] I am entirely aware that my interpretative suggestion contradicts the mainstream opinion about what the current status of the law is. However, law is not a physical object which exists independently from us and which we are simply obliged to recognize as is. Law is what courts make of it.[50]

Sooner or later the ECJ is going to receive a preliminary reference from a small rural court in one of the EU Member States (be it a large or small), and will thereby be given the opportunity to make, without exaggeration, one of the biggest leading cases of modern constitutionalism.[51] A European *Marbury v Madison* is yet to come,[52] which will transform the CFR into a real Charter for all European citizens, into a Charter which guarantees their freedoms even when domestic forums fail. The ECJ will have to face this challenge and it should not shy away from the task. Leading cases often seem impossible (or even doctrinally doubtful) at the time in which they were made, but if they comply with the general value system of society of a given time (the *Zeitgeist*) and if they help the judiciary to

[45] V Reding, 'Observations on the EU Charter of Fundamental Rights and the future of the European Union' Speech 12/403 held at the XXV Congress of FIDE (Tallinn, 31 May 2012) 11, http://europa.eu/rapid/press-release_SPEECH-12-403_en.pdf, accessed 12 October 2016; Closa et al. (n 41) 17; N Chronowski, 'Enhancing the scope of the Charter of Fundamental Rights?' (2014) 1 *JURA* 13. For the *ultra vires* argument, see J Kühling, 'Fundamental Rights' in A von Bogdandy and J Bast (eds), *Principles of European Constitutional Law* (Hart 2009) 500–1.

[46] C Closa, *The Politics of Ratification of EU Treaties* (Routledge 2013).

[47] A Jakab, 'Full Parliamentarisation of the EU without Changing the Treaties. Why We Should Aim for It and How Easily It Can be Achieved' (2012) Jean Monnet Working Papers No 3; A Jakab, 'Why the Debate between Kumm and Armstrong is about the Wrong Question' (VerfassungsBlog, 20 June 2014), http://www.verfassungsblog.de/debate-kumm-armstrong-wrong-question, accessed 12 October 2016.

[48] On the phenomenon that the ECJ steps in furthering the integration if politicians are unable reach an agreement, see JHH Weiler, 'The Transformation of Europe' (1991) 100 *Yale Law Journal* 2403.

[49] For a *contra legem* objection explicitly against my suggestion, see e.g. Closa et al. (n 41) 21.

[50] c.f. the constitutional-law proverb: 'The Constitution is what the judges say it is.' C Evans Hughes, *Speech at Elmira* (3 May 1907) cited by B Schwartz, *Constitutional Law* (The Macmillan Company 1972). For a similar view by R Smend, 'Festvortrag zur Feier des zehnjährigen Bestehens des Bundesverfassungsgerichts am 26. Januar 1962' in Federal Constitutional Court, *Das Bundesverfassungsgericht* (CF Müller 1963) 24: 'The Basic Law is now virtually identical with its interpretation by the Federal Constitutional Court'.

[51] As a matter of fact, the ECJ has already been presented with the opportunity to do so, but unfortunately it missed it. See Joined Cases C-488/12 to C-491/12 and C-526/12 *Sándor Nagy v Hajdú-Bihar Megyei Kormányhivatal, Lajos Tiborné Böszörményi, Róbert Gálóczhi-Tömösváry and Magdolna Margit Szabadosné Bay v Mezőgazdasági és Vidékfejlesztési Hivatal and Józsefné Ványai v Nagyrábé Község Polgármesteri Hivatal* ECLI:EU:C:2013/703. But no doubt, new occasions will arise.

[52] We could also argue that *van Gend en Loos* or *Costa v ENEL* were already the *Marbury v Madison* of European integration, so we just need yet another (and not 'the') *Marbury v Madison*. This is a fair observation, but it does not change the actual argument I am making.

enhance these values, then they will later become obvious and unquestionable. The direct effect of directives was considered by many to be a *contra legem* (meaning contrary to the literal interpretation, but *not* meaning illegal) interpretation of the EEC Treaty—until it became a permanent feature of the case law of the ECJ. If we do not want to give Article 51 CFR a meaning which deprives Union citizens of their fundamental rights, then the literal meaning of the provision should be regarded rather as the determination of a minimal, and not a maximal, scope for the CFR.

Every society is held together by certain values which are at least rhetorically unquestionable. In the Middle Ages it was Christianity and heretics faced serious consequences for breaching religious taboos. After the Second World War in Western Europe, and since the end of Communism across Europe, these integrating values have been the secular values of constitutionalism. The twentieth century in Europe can also be interpreted as a history of experimenting and failing with new secular taboo systems, such as nationalism or socialism. By now, democracy and the protection of fundamental rights (c.f. the purposes of the CoE) seem to be the only society-organizing options in Europe. There are, of course, constant debates about the meaning of these concepts;[53] but at the same time, there is a final institutionalized arbiter in Europe for these questions: the ECtHR. To put it another way: the Vatican of today is in Strasbourg. There were and there will be heretic attempts to question these values, but if we want to believe that European integration is to have a chance, then we have to stop these attempts before it becomes too late. If it can happen in one EU Member State, then it can also happen in another, and the European edifice built upon these values will fall apart surprisingly quickly. There are already possibilities in the European constitution which can be used with creative reinterpretation to stop any dangerous tendencies. The ECJ can use the moral authority of the ECtHR to enforce the values of European integration, and via the preliminary procedure it can turn all Member State courts into local agents professing and enforcing these values.

It is of course not enough to refer to values when a court makes a decision. A good lawyer always thinks on two levels: on the one hand, trying to provide a doctrinal justification for the decision (c.f. section 3.a. on the doctrinal triggers), but on the other hand, deciding what is acceptable from a social and/or moral point of view (c.f. the values of European integration).[54] Both of these general preconditions seem to be fulfilled to support a courageous judgment by the ECJ in the present situation.

5. Advice to the ECJ

The history of the ECJ is full of activist moves where decisions were made which were not obvious from the text of the treaties, to say the least.[55] How could the Court get away with this? What are the characteristics of these successful competence expansions?

(1) The arguments used in these cases were normally teleological arguments relying either on the purpose of the whole integration project or on the purpose of specific rules/institutions. This point is actually given for the expansive interpretation of Article 51(1) in light of the above: the purpose is to protect fundamental rights as a fundamental value according to Article 2 TEU. (2) Institutionally, the European Commission would usually

[53] c.f. WB Gallie, 'Essentially Contested Concepts' (1956) 56 *Proceedings of the Aristotelian Society* 167.

[54] On Magnaud, *Le bon juge*, see A Jakab, 'What Makes a Good Lawyer? Was Magnaud Indeed Such a Good Judge?' (2007) 2 *Zeitschrift für öffentliches Recht* 275.

[55] See e.g. K Alter, *Establishing the Supremacy of European Law. The Making of an International Rule of Law in Europe* (OUP 2001).

adopt a position first for the ECJ to later affirm.[56] In our case, this would mean expanding an explicitly stated aim of the Commission to abolish the limits of Article 51(1). This has actually already happened: Viviane Reding, then Commissioner responsible for justice, fundamental rights, and citizenship, explicitly proposed this in her Tallinn speech.[57] (3) The third factor which makes expansions more likely is if political law making appears to be inoperative.[58] This is also obviously true: we can only observe the pretext for real action, e.g. in the form of the so-called 'Rule of Law mechanism'[59]—the necessary majority of the Member States in support of action is obviously missing. (4) A usual method for expanding judicial competences is to establish the competence but not to use it, or to use it in a way which does not lead to conflict with any government. This was famously done in *Marbury v Madison*, but also in *Costa v ENEL* in which 'the ECJ declared the supremacy of EC law' but 'found that the Italian law [...] did not violate EC law'.[60] The first step here should also probably be a *Costa v ENEL* type of decision establishing the full applicability of the CFR without establishing its actual violation. (5) As a second step—once competence has been established in a case without the establishment of a violation—a violation also needs to be established. For this second case, the more obvious a fundamental rights violation is and the more isolated the 'convicted' Member State, the more likely it is that the judgment establishing the violation will be accepted by Member States.[61] We do not need to be pessimistic to predict that such cases are likely to reach the ECJ in the near future. (6) Parallel to (4) and (5), in order to avoid unnecessary involvement in domestic politics concerning questions which are far from obvious, the ECJ also has to develop a margin of appreciation doctrine, similar to the one of the ECtHR.[62] It would cast intervention as being available only in cases which violate the common minimum of fundamental rights protection. It would be similar in its deferential function to the concept of 'systemic deficiency',[63] but deciding on the point would remain with a judicial and not a political body.

To sum up, all the cards are in the hands of the ECJ.[64] The European institutions do not seem to want to stop such a move by the ECJ, and Member States have no means to do so. Member State coalitions against ECJ judgments and visions of judicial Armageddon are highly unrealistic. As Marcus Höreth put it:[65]

> '[...] non-compliance by Member States was not perceived as a threat by the European Justices but rather a welcome opportunity to develop their judicial regime even further. Member-State

[56] E Stein, 'Lawyers, Judge, and the Making of a Transnational Constitution' (1981) 75 *American Journal of International Law* 1.

[57] Reding (n 45) but she wanted to achieve this via a formal Treaty amendment.

[58] Weiler (n 48).

[59] Communication of the Commission to the European Parliament and the Council on A New European Framework to strengthen the Rule of Law, COM(2014) 158, Brussels 11 March 2014.

[60] K Alter, 'Who are the "Masters of the Treaties"? European Governments and the European Court of Justice' (1998) 52 *International Organization* 121, 131.

[61] c.f. Groussot et al. (n 6) 24 fn 104: 'It must be remembered that the US Supreme Court's 'legal coup' took place in rather unique historical circumstances – the persistent segregationist practices in Southern States – which required, in turn, a revolutionary expansion of the scope of the US Bill of Rights'. See also M Cartabia, 'Article 51 – Field of Application' in WBT Mock et al. (eds), *Human Rights in Europe* (Carolina Academic Press 2010) 318–19 on similarities between certain interpretation of Art 51 and the US constitutional law 'doctrine of incorporation'.

[62] On the margin of appreciation doctrine as a special type of deference doctrine, see A Legg, *The Margin of Appreciation in International Human Rights Law* (OUP 2012) 17.

[63] See von Bogdandy et al. in Chapter 12 of this volume.

[64] M Höreth, 'Warum der EuGH nicht gestoppt werden sollte – und auch kaum gestoppt werden kann' in U Haltern and A Bergmann (eds), *Der EuGH in der Kritik* (Mohr Siebeck 2012) 73. On the practical impossibility of the revision of ECJ rulings by Member States see M Höreth, 'The least dangerous branch?' in M Dawson et al. (eds), *Judicial Activism at the European Court of Justice* (Edward Elgar 2013) 32, 39–40.

[65] Höreth (n 64) 43.

non-compliance generates legal actions, followed by new rulings; non-compliance with important new rulings again generates new litigation and new findings of non-compliance, and so on.'

If the European integration process fails, it will not be because of a stronger protection of fundamental rights. It will either be for purely economic reasons or because of anti-constitutionalist and illiberal efforts within some Member States.

With judicial statesmanship, patience for the right cases to emerge and a conscious strategy, a decisive move toward a community of fundamental rights can be achieved in the very near future.[66] For this purpose, the ECJ has to reassert its responsibility in both enhancing European integration and promoting the values of the EU.[67]

[66] Once achieved, some the current characteristics of ECJ judgments will have to be reconsidered, especially their cryptic style and brevity, which will have to become more discursive, and possibly include dissenting opinions in order to be more transparent and give more substantive reasons for the decisions. On the former, see G de Búrca, 'After the EU Charter of Fundamental Rights: The Court of Justice as a Human Rights Adjudicator?' (2013) 20 *Maastricht Journal* 168. The latter is actually not explicitly regulated anywhere; Art 35 of the Statute of the Court only provides for the secrecy of deliberations which does not exclude dissenting or parallel opinions. For a general anti-activist critique concerning the lack of transparency, including the lack of dissenting opinions, see H Rasmussen, 'Plädoyer für ein Ende des judikativen Schweigens' in Haltern and Bergmann (n 64) 113–86. Dissenting opinions are an important method of control restraining a court, see K Kelemen, 'Dissenting Opinions in Constitutional Courts' (2013) 14 *German Law Journal* 1359.

[67] For a sad account of recent disappointing developments showing that the ECJ is actually more and more shying away from the application of the CFR, see X Groussot and G Thor Petursson, 'The EU Charter of Fundamental Rights Five Years on: The Emergence of a New Constitutional Framework?' in S de Vries et al. (eds), *The EU Charter of Fundamental Rights as a Binding Instrument. Five Years on and Growing* (Hart 2015) 153.

PART III
COMPARATIVE OUTLOOK

15

Enforcement of Federal Law against the German *Länder*

Dirk Hanschel

1. Introduction

For the purpose of this analysis, enforcement will be understood as a way to secure compliance by means of coercion in a wide sense.[1] The notion of law enforcement within a federation presupposes a certain preconception of hierarchy and subordination which places the centre above the periphery and empowers it to make demands of the latter.[2] In light of this understanding, this chapter will examine the various legal and political means of federal law enforcement by the Federal Government and by the Federal Constitutional Court. This is contextualized as a form of resolution of vertical power conflicts within federations, as examined elsewhere by this author.[3]

While the concept of intra-federal hierarchy may not be equally valid for all federations,[4] it is quite visible with regard to the German Federal State. There can be no doubt that, even though the two levels have their own spheres of governance as protected by their competences, hierarchy generally rules where conflicts arise. As a consequence, enforcement of federal law plays a major role in the German federation. This corresponds to the notion of Germany as a unitary federal state (Konrad Hesse) and as a system of cooperative and executive federalism.[5]

As the title suggests, this analysis will not include enforcement of federal law by the *Länder* themselves. While such action would usually not entail coercion and hence merely qualifies more generally as implementation, enforcement structures can nevertheless be found within the hierarchy of the *Länder* organization. Accordingly, for instance, a *Land* Ministry can order its lower authorities to implement *Land* law, as much as federal law. The federal context is much weaker in this case. There is, in particular, no juxtaposition or antagonism between the two levels of government, as opposed to the scenario where federal law is enforced *against* the *Länder*.

[1] The author wishes to thank the editors for their insightful comments and his research assistants Katrin Kappler, Anna Stransky, and Vinzent Vogt for their editorial assistance.

[2] J Isensee, '§ 126. Idee und Gestalt des Föderalismus im Grundgesetz', in J Isensee and P Kirchhof (eds), *Handbuch des Staatsrechts* (3rd edn, CF Müller Verlag 2008), vol VI §126 para 129 et seq. describes this as the *status passivus* according to which the *Länder* are the bearers of duties vis-à-vis the Federation and have to obey it within the limits of its competencies.

[3] See D Hanschel, 'Conflict Resolution in Federal States: Balancing Legislative Powers as a Viable Means?' (2008) 19 *Public Law Review* 131; D Hanschel, *Konfliktlösung im Bundesstaat* (Mohr Siebeck 2012).

[4] See for example on the notion of Belgian federalism, which operates without a clear hierarchy between the two levels of government, D Hanschel, 'The Role of Subnational Constitutions in Accommodating Centrifugal Tendencies within European States: Flanders, Catalonia and Scotland Compared' (2014) 6(2) *Perspectives on Federalism* E-244, E-247; P Peeters, 'The Constitutional and Institutional Autonomy of Communities and Regions in Federal Belgium', in M Burgess and GA Tarr (eds), *Constitutional Dynamics in Federal Systems: Sub-National Perspectives* (McGill-Queen's University Press 2012) 164.

[5] See sections 2.b.–d.

When looking at the various forms of law enforcement, it is striking that the enforcement is rarely done by the same branch of government which set the original act requiring implementation. In most cases laws made by the Federal Parliament are subsequently enforced by the Federal Government, be it by using its own instruments or by ultimately resorting to the Federal Constitutional Court. As a consequence of the German system of parliamentary democracy, the Federal Government usually holds the majority of seats in Parliament.[6] This does not mean that it enforces 'its own' laws, since many of these laws will have been passed long before the government of the day came to power. However, the government can change laws which it does not find suitable.[7] As a quintessence, the two powers of the executive and the legislature are substantially closer to each other than they are to the judicature, so that enforcement by the former may be regarded as autonomous and enforcement by the latter heteronomous. This distinction is of particular relevance as the two types of enforcement correspond to different requirements regarding the legitimation of the respective exercise of enforcement power. Whereas heteronomous enforcement asserts impartiality and hence bears a higher degree of *prima facie* legitimacy and authority, autonomous enforcement cannot make the same claim and has accordingly been subjected to stricter limitations under the German Basic Law (BL).[8]

While by its very nature the main focus of this chapter will lie on the legal means of federal law enforcement, it is appropriate to devote some attention to the political dimension as well. Since German federalism is strongly based on consensus and cooperation,[9] this dimension is very important in practice. As the rare use of the Federation-*Länder* dispute (*Bund-Länder-Streit*)[10] before the Constitutional Court demonstrates, actors often try to avoid legal means of conflict resolution, and instead rely on quiet forms of political negotiation. Where antagonism between the Federation and the *Länder* occurs (whether expressed in political or legal terms), it is frequently either motivated by party politics or triggered by matters where specific subnational interests are at stake (as in the case of nuclear power plants, where the 'not in my backyard' factor may play an important role). Even here, negotiations will usually be the primary means to address disputes. At the same time, it is an apt illustration of the strong position of the German Constitutional Court that adjudication on such conflicts may occur, and probably does so more often than in many other federations with a constitutional court.

2. Overview of pertinent features of the German federation

In order to understand federal law enforcement in Germany sufficiently in its context, specific features of the German model of federalism need to be explained, i.e. (1) hierarchy of norms and preemption; (2) the principle of the unitary federal state; (3) the system of executive federalism; and (4) cooperative federalism and the (dis-)entanglement of powers.

a. Hierarchy of norms and preemption

Like most federal states, Germany is guided by a clear principle of hierarchy of norms which places federal law above regional law (Article 31 BL).[11] This rule operates where

[6] On the German system of parliamentary governance, see for instance B Pieroth 'Art 62', in HD Jarass and B Pieroth, *Grundgesetz für die Bundesrepublik Deutschland, Kommentar* (13th edn, C.H. Beck 2014) para 1; HD Jarass, 'Art 20', in ibid, para 15.

[7] On the process of legislation, see Arts 76–78 BL, http://www.bundestag.de/blob/284870/ce0d03414872b427e57fccb703634dcd/basic_law-data.pdf,accessed 12 October 2016.

[8] For a translation of the German BL, see ibid.

[9] See section 2.d.

[10] Art 93(1)(3) BL.

[11] On the principle of hierarchy, see generally J Pietzcker, '§ 134. Zuständigkeitsordnung und Kollisionsrecht im Bundestaat', in Isensee and Kirchhof (n 2), § 134 para 38 et seq.; Hanschel, *Konfliktlösung* (n 3) 72 et seq.

collision occurs between otherwise valid laws passed by the *Länder* and the Federation.[12] It thus only applies in the field of concurrent powers (Article 72, 74 BL) as opposed to exclusive powers (Article 71, 73 BL)[13] and only where the *Länder* legislated first and subsequent federal legislation has displaced their legislation (or in the much rarer cases where the *Länder* were once exclusively competent, but the Federation has since gained a competence through subsequent constitutional amendment). Article 72(2) BL, by contrast, empowers the Federation to preempt concurrent legislation by the *Länder* in certain fields 'if and to the extent that the establishment of equal living conditions throughout the federal territory or the maintenance of legal or economic unity renders federal legislation necessary in the national interest'.[14] This system has been slightly weakened by the recently established ability of *Länder* to deviate from federal legislation in certain areas (Article 72(3) BL).[15] Here, the principle of hierarchy is substituted by the *lex posterior* rule, allowing for a questionable 'ping pong game'[16] between federal and *Land* legislation.[17]

b. The unitary federal state principle (*unitarischer Bundesstaat*)

Konrad Hesse aptly described Germany as a unitary federal state which is characterized by three elements: the concentration of tasks at the federal level, the self-coordination of the *Länder* in the exercise of their tasks, and finally their participation in decision making at the federal level.[18] Unitarianism and federalism, as irreconcilable as they may appear at first glance, are merged in a rather unique fashion, even though a number of other federations may show similar tendencies.[19] This feature of the German federation corresponds to the public's preferences, as the population's appetite for diverging regional practice is quite limited—instead, Germans commonly want their central government to be able to take effective decisions.[20] This corresponds to the fact that public allegiance with particular regions is generally rather weak.[21] Conversely, where regional identity exceeds a more folkloric level, it is sometimes not congruent with the respective *Land* territory, since the historical boundaries of the former German states were redrawn sometimes rather arbitrarily by the Allied Forces after 1945—as, for instance, in North Rhine Westphalia, Rhineland-Palatinate, or Baden-Wuerttemberg.[22] Even in Bavaria, where regional affili-

[12] Pieroth (n 6), Art 31 para 3; Pietzcker (n 11) §134 para 47; Hanschel, *Konfliktlösung* (n 3) 72.

[13] ibid.

[14] On preemption, see Pieroth (n 6) Art 31(3); Hanschel, *Konfliktlösung* (n 3) 72.

[15] Hanschel, *Konfliktlösung* (n 3) 73 et seq.

[16] For the use of this term, see O Klein and K Schneider, 'Art. 72 n.F. GG im Kompetenzgefüge der Föderalismusreform - Ein Überblick zur Erfindung des "generellen Abweichungsrechts", zur Ersetzung der Rahmenvorschriften und sowie zur Eröffnung einer neuen Antragsart im Verfassungsprozess' (2006) *Deutsches Verwaltungsblatt* 1549, 1553; C Calliess, '§ 83: Auswärtige Gewalt', in Isensee and Kirchhof (n 2) § 83 para 27; Hanschel, *Konfliktlösung* (n 3) 73 et seq. and 113 et seq.

[17] Hanschel, *Konfliktlösung* (n 3) 73; Klein and Schneider (n 16) 1553.

[18] See K Hesse, *Der unitarische Bundesstaat* (CF Müller Verlag 1962) 18 et seq.; see also Hanschel, *Konfliktlösung* (n 3) 84.

[19] See Isensee (n 2) §126 para 4; Hanschel, *Konfliktlösung* (n 3) 84.

[20] On the acceptance of the unitary model, see Hesse (n 18) 21.

[21] See N Johnson, 'Territory and Power: Some Historical Determinants of the Constitutional Structure of the Federal Republic of Germany', in C Jeffery (ed), *Recasting German Federalism—The Legacies of Unification* (Pinter 1999) 23 et seq.; K Hahn and M Hölscher, 'Föderalisierung der Bundesrepublik Deutschland', in F Esterbauer et al. (eds), *Föderalismus als Mittel permanenter Konfliktregelung* (Braumüller 1977), 113, 119; H-W Arndt, 'Erneuerter Föderalismus - Thesen zu einer veränderten Balance zwischen Bund und Ländern', in U Männle (ed), *Föderalismus zwischen Konsens und Konkurrenz—Tagungs- und Materialienband zur Fortentwicklung des deutschen Föderalismus* (Nomos 1998), 31; Hanschel, *Konfliktlösung* (n 3) 84.

[22] On the basic structure of the territorial division of Germany, see Hanschel, *Konfliktlösung* (n 3) 299 et seq.

ation is probably the strongest, distinctions apply with regard to the Franconian and Swabian parts of the population. German citizens usually want the government to provide comparable living conditions, including general welfare, health, education, taxation, etc.[23] This is mirrored by Article 72(2) BL which authorizes concurrent federal legislation in areas where it is 'necessary in the national interest' for the 'establishment of equivalent living conditions throughout the federal territory or the maintenance of legal or economic unity'. Article 28 BL further contributes to this notion of uniformity by guaranteeing a minimum standard of homogeneity between the federal and the *Länder* constitutions, with regard to the 'principles of a republican, democratic, and social state, governed by the rule of law' and certain standards regarding regional elections.[24] Whereas Article 72 BL limits the scope of legislative *Länder* powers, Article 28 BL provides substantial limitations to the exercise of this power, in particular with regard to subnational constitutions.[25] When combined, the two provisions help secure the unitary character of the German Federal State. At the same time, they are paramount in securing federal constitutional values (as stipulated in Article 28 BL), which the *Länder* have to respect.[26]

This strong centripetal tendency of the German federation has led Abromeit to conclude that the Federal Republic could be characterized as a disguised unitary state.[27] However, German history (with the exception of the Third Reich) shows that statehood has been simultaneously influenced by both the unitary and the (con-)federalist traditions.[28] The Federal Republic of Germany aptly encapsulates both traditions, without using either one merely as window-dressing.[29] Instead, it has established a balance which provides a certain degree of regional autonomy while ensuring rather effective central governance (with some limitations). Part of that effectiveness stems from the various enforcement mechanisms which the Federal Government has at its disposal. Admittedly, the balance of powers has tilted towards the Federation in the past decades, but recent federalism reforms have at least partially helped to remedy that situation.[30]

[23] On the underlying postulate of social cohesion, see S Oeter, *Integration und Subsidiarität im deutschen Bundesstaatsrecht—Untersuchungen zur Bundesstaatstheorie unter dem Grundgesetz* (Mohr Siebeck 1998), 542; H-J Blanke 'Staatsfinanzen im Föderalismus' (2005) 65 *Zeitschrift für Ausländisches Öffentliches Recht und Völkerrecht* 71, 82; F Ossenbühl, 'Föderalismus nach 40 Jahren Grundgesetz' (1989) 104 *Deutsches Verwaltungsblatt* 1230, 1234; Hanschel, *Konfliktlösung* (n 3) 84 et seq.; on the tension between social equality and federal diversity, see Isensee (n 2) §126 para 269.

[24] On Art 28 BL, on the homogeneity principle, see M Nierhaus, in M Sachs (ed), *Grundgesetz-Kommentar* (7th edn, Verlag CH Beck 2014); A Dittmann, '§ 127: Verfassungshoheit der Länder und bundesstaatliche Verfassungshomogenität', in Isensee and Kirchhof (n 2) §127 para 2 et seq.; Isensee (n 2) §126 para 83; Hanschel, *Konfliktlösung* (n 3) 117 et seq.

[25] See Hanschel, *Konfliktlösung* (n 3) 118.

[26] V Mehde in T Maunz, and G Dürig (eds), *Grundgesetz -Kommentar* (77th edn, Verlag CH Beck 2016) Art 28 para 1 et seq.

[27] H Abromeit, *Der verkappte Einheitsstaat* (Leske and Budrich 1992).

[28] See for instance, D Hanschel, 'German Federalist Thinking and International Law' (2012) 4 *Goettingen Journal of International Law* 363.

[29] For arguments against the unitary view, see for instance U Scheuner, 'Struktur und Aufgaben des Bundesstaates in der Gegenwart', in Scheuner (ed), *Staatstheorie und Staatsrecht. Gesammelte Schriften* (Duncker & Humblot 1978), 415, 427 et seq.; K-H Friauf, 'Strukturprobleme des gesamtdeutschen Bundesstaates', in J Burmeister et al. (eds), *Germania restituta, Wissenschaftliches Symposium anlässlich des 60. Geburtstages von Klaus Stern am 11. Januar 1992, am 7. und 8. Februar 1992 an der Universität zu Köln* (Heymanns 1993), 23, 28; J Sanden, *Die Weiterentwicklung der föderalen Strukturen der Bundesrepublik Deutschland—Staatsrechtliche Studie zu einem postmodernen Ansatz der Bundesstaatsreform* (Duncker & Humblot 2005) 155; Hanschel, *Konfliktlösung* (n 3) 85 et seq.

[30] See Hanschel, *Konfliktlösung* (n 3) 101 et seq.; F Grotz, 'Verfassungsreformen in der Bundesrepublik: 1969 – 1994 – 2006', in C Hönnige et al. (eds), *Verfassungswandel im Mehrebenensystem* (VS Verlag für Sozialwissenschaften 2011) 108 et seq.

c. The system of executive federalism

I. *Main features of executive federalism*

The division of tasks between the Federation and the *Länder* is characterized by the notion of executive federalism: while the Federation is mainly responsible for legislation (with minor powers being vested in the *Länder*, see Article 70 et seq. BL), the *Länder* are generally entrusted with the execution of these laws (Article 83 et seq. BL).[31] The concept of executive federalism expresses a deal between the two levels of government which addresses the conflict between unity and diversity through an entanglement of powers: the *Länder* recognize federal dominance over legislation while participating in its creation through the *Bundesrat*, and asserting the main authority over the execution of the resulting laws.[32]

However, this does not reduce the *Länder* to mere instruments of implementation, since they also have substantial political functions. This is evidenced by the fact that they can pass their own legislation (either originally or in deviation from federal law) and that they may exercise discretion in implementing federal law. The *Länder* administrative authority entails a certain degree of autonomy, as the Federation depends on competent and measured implementation and application of its laws at the regional level.[33] This autonomy is expressed by the various forms of federal law enforcement stipulated under Article 30 in conjunction with Articles 83–91 BL.

II. *Länder administration in their own right (Articles 83, 84 BL)*

According to Article 30 BL, '[e]xcept as otherwise provided or permitted by this Basic Law, the exercise of state powers and the discharge of state functions is a matter for the *Länder*'.[34] Articles 83, 84 BL apply this principle to the executive power where it is the most dominant, whereas the distribution of legislative powers according to Article 70 et seq. (while formally reflecting Article 30 BL) mostly operates in favour of the Federation (in spite of the efforts made in recent federalism reforms).[35] Article 83 BL stipulates that '[t]he *Länder* shall execute federal laws in their own right as far as this BL does not otherwise provide or permit'. Article 84 (1) (1) BL sets out what this *Länder* administration 'in their own right' entails, i.e. 'they shall provide for the establishment of the requisite authorities and regulate their administrative procedures'. Article 84(2) BL empowers the Federation to 'issue general administrative rules', para 3 allows for measures of federal oversight, paragraph 4 deals with violations of federal law through the *Länder* as established by the *Bundesrat* and ultimately the Federal Constitutional Court, and paragraph 5 grants the Federation a limited right to instruct the *Länder* as to how they should carry out their administrative tasks.[36]

[31] H Maurer, 'Die Ausführung der Bundesgesetze durch die Länder' (2010) 50 *Juristische Schulung* 945; W Hertel, 'Formen des Föderalismus – Die Beispiele der USA, Deutschlands und Europas', in W Graf Vitzthum (ed), *Europäischer Föderalismus—Supranationaler, subnationaler und multiethnischer Föderalismus in Europa* (Duncker & Humblot 2000) 29; J Pietzcker, '§ 134. Zuständigkeitsordnung und Kollisionsrecht im Bundestaat', in Isensee and Kirchhof (n 2) §134 para 5.

[32] Hanschel, *Konfliktlösung* (n 3) 83; Isensee (n 2) §126 para 204 et seq.; on the notion of entanglement of powers, see F Scharpf, 'No Exit from the Joint Decision Trap? – Can German Federalism Reform Itself?' (2005) EUI Working Papers RSCAS No 4.

[33] See Isensee (n 2) §126 para 204 et seq.; Hanschel, *Konfliktlösung* (n 3) 83.

[34] ibid.

[35] J Oebbecke, '§ 136: Verwaltungszuständigkeit', in Isensee and Kirchhof (n 2) §136 para 2 with further references; on the reform efforts, see Hanschel, *Konfliktlösung* (n 3) 101 et seq.

[36] ibid; generally on the various powers expressed in Art 84 BL, see Oebbecke (n 35) §136 para 20 et seq.

III. *Länder administration on federal commission (Article 85 BL)*

Conversely, where the *Länder* 'execute federal laws on federal commission, establishment of the authorities shall remain the concern of the *Länder*, except insofar as federal laws with the consent of the *Bundesrat* otherwise provides' (Article 85(1) BL). Here the federal enforcement options are clearly stronger, both with regard to oversight (paragraph 3) and instructions (paragraph 4), as they interfere less with the administrative autonomy of the *Länder*.[37] These instruments will be analysed in detail below,[38] with specific regard to the field of nuclear power (Article 87c BL), which has caused particular controversy. While this field is generally administered by the *Länder* in their own right, Article 87c BL states that federal laws can (with the consent of the *Bundesrat*) turn this into a case of federal commission.[39]

IV. *Federal administration (Article 86 BL)*

Article 83–85 BL should be distinguished from Article 86 BL, which stipulates the rare case of federal administration.[40] Here, *per definitionem*, the Federation 'executes law through its own administrative authorities or through federal corporations or institutions established under public law'. Accordingly, no enforcement of federal law against the *Länder* is required, unless the establishment of the federal agencies is, as a matter of exception, carried out by the *Länder* themselves (see clause 2, second part). There are only few matters of federal administration, and according to Article 83 BL they need to be explicitly listed in the BL. This has occurred with regard to '[t]he foreign service, the federal financial administration, and [...] the administration of federal waterways and shipping' as well as specific federal police authorities (Article 87(1) BL) and national social insurance institutions (Article 87(2) BL). Finally, Article 87(3) BL stipulates more generally that the Federation may establish its own authorities where it has legislative powers. Further specific fields of federal administration are the armed forces (Articles 87a and 87b BL), air and rail transport (Articles 87d and 87e BL), or the establishment of the federal bank (Article 88 BL).[41] In addition, there are mixed cases where parts of the administration are transferred to the Federation, whereas others may be conducted by the *Länder* (e.g. federal rail transport (Article 87e BL) or highways (Article 90 BL) or have been privatized (e.g. the post and telecommunications (Article 87f BL).[42]

d. Cooperative federalism and (dis-)entanglement of powers

The system of executive federalism leads seamlessly to the observation that German federalism requires a high degree of cooperation between the levels of government in order to deal with the juxtaposition and entanglement of powers.[43] This has worked rather well for an extended period, in line with the requirement of the unitary federal state. Cooperation has extended to the law making process, both at federal and regional levels, and to the implementation of the law. However, continuing centralization of legislative powers has exhausted the scope for compensation through cooperation, which corresponded

[37] ibid. [38] See section 3.a.–c.

[39] ibid; generally Art 85 BL, see Oebbecke (n 35) §136 para 55 et seq.

[40] See for instance Pieroth (n 6) Art 86 para 1 et seq., distinguishing between different types of federal administration.

[41] ibid. [42] ibid; generally on Art 87 BL, see Oebbecke (n 35) §136 para 80 et seq.

[43] Hanschel, *Konfliktlösung* (n 3) 83.

with an enhanced vetoing of federal legislation by the *Länder* governors represented in the *Bundesrat*.[44] This combination has been aptly characterized by Scharpf as a political entanglement trap into which the German federation had manoeuvred itself; it coincided with frequent political blockades resulting from the fact that regional elections (often used for protest against the Federal Government) frequently saw the opposition taking office and using the veto points against the Federal Government quite actively.[45] This situation was partially remedied through the federalism reform of 2006, where a process of disentanglement led to stronger legislative powers of the *Länder* and to a simultaneous limitation of their veto rights in the process of federal legislation.[46] As part of that process, veto points were partially replaced by a right to deviate from federal legislation, e.g. in the field of concurrent legislation (Article 73(3) BL) or where a federal law would intrude into the *Länder* administrative authority (Article 84 BL).[47] These changes affected federal law enforcement as they reduced the scope for federal law to be enforced by the Federation whilst increasing the scope for law made and implemented by the *Länder*. However, they did not alter the cooperative character of German federalism as such, as the system of executive federalism by which the *Länder* implement federal law was left untouched.

3. Instruments of federal law enforcement

Within this context there is a whole array of enforcement options ranging from (1) federal instructions to (2) general administrative rules; (3) federal oversight; (4) federal coercion; and (5) federal intervention, as autonomous means by the Federal Government, towards heteronomous enforcement through the German Federal Constitutional Court. These options (as far as they concern enforcement of federal law by the Federation against the *Länder*) and their relationship with each other will be analysed in the next section. From the outset one should state that while the array of options may seem impressive, their use in practice is rather limited, as most conflicts are resolved by political means before they escalate to this stage. Nevertheless, having these options as a backup is important for the Federation as they strengthen its bargaining position in the political discourse with the *Länder*. In addition, experience shows that there are quite a number of situations where such mechanisms need to be used.

a. Enforcement through federal instructions (*Weisungen*)

Instructions are a typical enforcement device available to the Federal Government.[48] In the field of *Länder* self-administration in their own right, Article 84(5) BL allows for 'instructions in particular cases', where a federal law approved by the *Bundesrat* so provides. Conversely, in the field of federal commission, the empowerment is much broader as the

[44] On the functions of the *Bundesrat* through which the *Länder* executive power participates in federal legislation, and on the increasing veto position of the *Länder*, see for instance, Hanschel, *Konfliktlösung* (n 3) 127 et seq. with further references.

[45] Scharpf (n 32) 1 et seq.; Hanschel, *Konfliktlösung* (n 3) 127 et seq.; on the creeping process of centralization, see Sanden (n 29), 361; R Dolzer, 'Das parlamentarische Regierungssystem und der Bundesrat – Entwicklungsstand und Reformbedarf' (1999) 58 *Veröffentlichungen der Vereinigung der Deutschen Staatsrechtslehrer* 15, 32; Oeter (n 23) 469 et seq.; on the political interests guiding voting behaviour in the *Bundesrat*, see Scharpf (n 32) 4; on citizens' motives in regional elections, see Scharpf (n 32) 4; Hanschel, *Konfliktlösung* (n 3) 131 et seq.

[46] See Hanschel, *Konfliktlösung* (n 3) 135 with further references; A Gunlicks, 'German Federalism Reform: Part One' (2007) 8 *The German Law Journal* 111, 117, 120.

[47] Hanschel, *Konfliktlösung* (n 3) 109 et seq.

[48] Oebbecke (n 35) §136 para 37 et seq.

Federation may simply pass any 'instructions' (Article 85(3) BL) and without the need for specific parliamentary empowerment as in the former case. To preserve *Länder* autonomy as far as possible, the instructions shall be issued by the 'competent highest federal authorities' (Article 85(3)(1)) and 'shall be addressed to the highest *Land* authorities unless the Federal Government considers the matter urgent' (Article 85(3)(2)). Finally, '[i]mplementation of the instructions shall be ensured by the highest *Land* authorities' (Article 85 (3)(3). They should be distinguished from administrative regulations in that they are not general, but related to particular situations.[49]

Except for extreme cases of inappropriateness, the *Länder* have to accept federal instructions even where they consider them to be unconstitutional or factually wrong.[50] While the instruction powers were considered as rather unproblematic for a long time, more recent decisions of the Federal Constitutional Court have shown that there is, indeed, room for controversy.[51] These decisions mostly concerned supervision in the field of nuclear power, which does not come as a surprise as there has been a long-standing political controversy regarding this source of energy as illustrated by the Green movement.[52] In the *Kalkar II* decision the Court stated that the Federation can use its power to pass instructions in such a way that it attracts the full assessment and factual assessment powers (*Sachkompetenz*), hence reducing the *Länder* powers to mere execution powers (*Wahrnehmungskompetenz*), i.e. their protected sphere under Article 85 BL.[53] As the Court observes, this option does not require specific justification as an exception, but instead constitutes a regular means of conflict resolution in favour of the common good as defined by the Federation.[54] This means that, from the very outset, the factual assessment power is only vested in the *Länder* to the extent that it is not assumed by the Federation.[55] The fact that the *Land* has to execute the decision and assume responsibility vis-à-vis the citizens, i.e. outside the intra-federal relation, is a mere consequence of the discrepancy of factual assessment and execution powers and therefore does not warrant a different conclusion.[56] It follows from this that within the scope of Article 85 BL, a *Land* cannot normally demand from the Federation to exercise its right to provide instructions in a manner which satisfies substantive legal requirements. It can merely ask the Federation to respect the limitations of its legal powers, hence not to act *ultra vires*.[57] In addition, according to the principle of federal loyalty, the *Länder* will usually have the right to be heard by the Federation before an instruction is passed.[58] Finally, instructions need to be sufficiently clear.[59]

[49] Isensee (n 2) §126 para 131.

[50] Isensee (n 2) §126 para 130; *BVerfGE* 81, 310 (332 et seq.); *BVerfGE* 84, 25 (31); 102, 167 (172). On the Federation's right informally to engage with third parties in the administrative process, see *Biblis A*, *BverfGE* 104, 249.

[51] Hanschel, *Konfliktlösung* (n 3) 209; Dittmann in Sachs (n 24) Art 85 para 21.

[52] See e.g. http://www.bund.net/themen_und_projekte/atomkraft/atomkraft_in_deutschland/anti_akw_bewegung, accessed 12 October 2016.

[53] See *BVerfGE* 81, 310 (332); see furthermore Isensee (n 2) §126 para 130.

[54] *BverfGE* 81, 310 para 332. [55] ibid. [56] ibid, para 333.

[57] For this, see http://www.servat.unibe.ch/dfr/bv081310.html, accessed 12 October 2016, headnote 2; Hanschel, *Konfliktlösung* (n 3) 208 et seq.; Dittmann (n 51) Art 85 para 36 et seq.; see furthermore T Herbst, *Gesetzgebungskompetenzen im Bundesstaat* (Mohr Siebeck 2014) 288.

[58] See http://www.servat.unibe.ch/dfr/bv081310.html, accessed 12 October 2016, headnote 4. This follows equally from the law of administrative procedure and constitutes an important requirement the violation of which can render the instruction formally unlawful, see the recent decision of the German Federal Administrative Court on the shutting down of the Biblis plant, http://www.bverwg.de/presse/pressemitteilungen/pressemitteilung.php?jahr=2014&nr=4, accessed 12 October 2016.

[59] http://www.servat.unibe.ch/dfr/bv081310.html, accessed 12 October 2016, headnote 3. More generally on the limitations of federal enforcement powers, see section 4.

The wide federal discretion resulting from this interpretation of Article 85 BL by the Federal Constitutional Court has clearly strengthened federal enforcement powers vis-à-vis the *Länder*; at the same time it can be criticized for contributing to a creeping process of centralization which the German federation has been subjected to in the past decades.[60] Due to the financial implications of such wide instructive powers, it is not surprising that Article 85 BL was part of the deliberations of the second federalism commission dealing with the reform of fiscal responsibilities.[61] In that context, Burgi suggested that the administration by federal commission provides a mechanism of conflict resolution offering to discuss very controversial political issues whilst allowing for clear decisions in the end.[62] The right to dismiss *Länder* protest even where the legality of instructions is questioned seems surprising, as it limits the *Länder* autonomy quite substantially and appears to be at odds with the Rule of Law.[63] It is doubtful, however, whether the principle of Rule of Law (in the sense of the German *Rechtsstaat*) applies to intra-federal situations.[64] While the Rule of Law is an objective principle that applies to the exercise of all governmental power, it is intended to limit the external exercise of that power vis-à-vis the citizens, not within the internal relationship between different layers of government.[65] The Rule of Law is a guarantor of freedom and hence connected to freedom as guaranteed by fundamental rights, which is not enjoyed by the layers of government in their relation to each other.[66] Instead, this relation is essentially governed by competencies.[67] The inroad into *Länder* autonomy created by this wider interpretation of the federal instruction power is intended, as it avoids lengthy proceedings about the legality of particular means of enforcement where the legal duty of the *Länder* as such to implement a certain piece of legislation is undisputed. This solution corresponds to the German notion of a strong centre at the top of a unitary federal state. In that sense, this field provides a typical example of how German federalism has opted for a centralized model which allows effective decision-making whilst providing limited autonomy to the regions.

At the same time, the *Biblis A* decision of the Federal Constitutional Court shows that there are limits even to the broad federal power to pass instructions where the Federal Government commits grave procedural or substantive legal errors.[68] In the concrete case, however, the Federal Government's conduct, which included contact and informal agreements with others (ie the power plant operator), was still covered by its right to instruct the *Länder* according to Article 85(3) BL, after the Federation had attracted its power to decide upon the matter instead of leaving the power plant operation to the *Länder*.[69] However, the Court cautioned that the principle of federal loyalty requires that this right is exercised with due regard to the *Länder* interests.[70]

Put in a nutshell, the precise duties of *Länder* to obey federal instructions therefore depend on rules regarding competence and procedure and are further informed by the principle of federal loyalty.[71] The latter constitutes a crucial value in itself as it reflects

[60] See Hanschel, *Konfliktlösung* (n 3) 208 et seq. [61] See ibid, 209.

[62] M Burgi, *Stellungnahme zur öffentlichen Anhörung der Kommission von Bundestag und Bundesrat zur Modernisierung der Bund-Länder-Finanzbeziehungen am 8. November 2007* (Verwaltungsthemen, Kommissionsdrucksache 072, 2007) 18.

[63] See on this with a differentiated analysis, W Pauly, *Anfechtbarkeit und Verbindlichkeit von Weisungen in der Bundesauftragsverwaltung* (Duncker & Humblot 1989) 173, 181, suggesting that illegal instructions might, as a matter of principle, be voidable but binding, voidable and non-binding, non-binding and therefore non-voidable, or binding and non-voidable.

[64] As Jarass in Jarass and Pieroth (n 6), Art 20 para 29, points out, it clearly applies to the Federal Governmental power whilst the direct applicability for the *Länder* is disputed. However, this only concerns the relationship between these governments and the citizens, not their relationship with each other.

[65] Isensee (n 2) §126 para 126; ibid, §133 para 76. [66] ibid. [67] ibid. [68] *BVerfGE* 104, 249.

[69] ibid B I. [70] ibid B II. [71] Isensee (n 2) §126 para 130 et seq.

the fundamental decision that cooperation is preferred to confrontation when dealing with intra-federal conflicts, which helps the German federation to reconcile effective unitary governance with substantial regional autonomy.[72] In practice, the Federation often side-tracks formal hurdles by resorting to informal arrangements which enable the *Länder* to contribute to the solution, i.e. to negotiate implementation instead of being subjected to enforcement.[73] This allows for flexible solutions bypassing the formal requirements and hence diluting formal competencies and responsibilities.[74] At the same time, they are quite typical of the German system of cooperative federalism and the entanglement of powers. It is a positive effect of this system to establish joint responsibility for the development of workable solutions.

b. Enforcement through general administrative rules (*allgemeine Verwaltungsvorschriften*)

In addition to instructions, the Federation may establish 'general administrative rules [with the consent of the *Bundesrat*]' under Articles 84(2) and 85(2) BL. Some authors tend to qualify them as instructions of a general nature.[75] However, it seems more appropriate to understand them as a separate instrument, since instructions by their very nature respond to a specific situation, whereas general administrative rules limit *Länder* discretion in federal law implementation in a more general fashion (although they may also be triggered by a particular situation).[76] Their main function is to guide the interpretation of the applicable law and the use of discretion by the *Länder*.[77] The requirement of consent by the *Bundesrat* must not be circumvented by passing instructions, since these cannot serve as instruments to deal with abstract questions of norm implementation.[78] Hence, political conflicts between the Federal Government and the *Bundesrat* regarding the validity of general administrative rules may not be sidestepped by resorting to instructions instead.[79] The fact that general administrative rules may also deal with the establishment of authorities and procedures creates a tension between Article 84(1) and (2) BL. In order not to undermine the former requirements, such rules need to respect at least the limitations of paragraph (1)(2), according to which the *Länder* may deviate.

Having clarified the nature of general administrative rules, the question is to what extent they contribute to enforcement at all. By limiting the interpretative scope and discretion of the *Länder* in implementing federal law, such rules arguably enforce a particular view of the law upon them. As they do not address specific situations of non-compliance, it is difficult to ascertain whether, in a particular case, a *Land* would otherwise have taken a different view, so that the element of coercion may be a more theoretical one. Nevertheless, general administrative rules will often be prompted by an anticipation of divergent *Länder* views and hence by the aim to eliminate deviant behaviour. In that wider sense, they may well be considered acts of enforcement, albeit a much more indirect form than instructions.

[72] H Bauer, *Die Bundestreue—Zugleich ein Beitrag zur Dogmatik des Bundesstaatsrechts und zur Rechtsverhältnislehre* (Mohr–Siebeck 1992) 349 et seq.
[73] Isensee (n 2) §126 para 131. [74] ibid. [75] Oebbecke (n 35) §136 para 38 et seq.
[76] See Isensee (n 2) §126 para 131. [77] Oebbecke (n 35) §136 para 40.
[78] Isensee (n 2) §126 para 131; for a countervailing view see, however, Dittmann (n 51) Art 85 para 20.
[79] ibid.

c. Federal oversight (*aufsichtliche Mittel*)

The Federation supervises implementation of its legislation by the *Länder*.[80] In the field of *Länder* administration in their own right the Federation can employ certain coercion measures according to Article 84(3) and (4) BL in order to ensure that implementation by the *Länder* fulfils legal requirements.[81] To that end, Article 84(3)(2) BL allows the deployment of 'commissioners to the highest *Land* authorities and, with their consent or, where such consent is refused, with the consent of the *Bundesrat*, also to subordinate authorities'. This enables the Federal Government to establish the facts and to prepare further enforcement measures, where appropriate. Paragraph (4)(1) adds that in case of persistent 'deficiencies in the execution of federal laws in the *Länder*' the *Bundesrat*, 'on application of the Federal Government or of the *Land* concerned, shall decide whether that *Land* has violated the law'.[82] The fact that the *Bundesrat* serves as the arbiter in this regard constitutes a suitable compromise as this institution is composed of representatives from the *Länder* governments whilst constituting a federal legislative organ.[83] In turn, its decision may be reviewed by the Federal Constitutional Court according to Article 84(4)(2) BL. However, this procedure is of little practical relevance, as the conflicting parties will usually avoid litigation and agree on a solution beforehand.[84] Furthermore, the pertinent issues will often be dealt with by administrative courts called upon by citizens prior to escalating into a constitutional conflict.[85]

While federal oversight in the field of *Länder* administration in their own right (Article 84 BL) is limited to the legality of administrative action, it extends to the notion of appropriateness in the case of federal commission (Article 85(4) BL).[86] To that end, the Federal Government can (similarly to its rights under Article 84 BL) demand the 'submission of reports and documents and send commissioners to all authorities'.[87] However, in the case of federal commission, no approval by the *Länder* or the *Bundesrat* is required for that measure which reflects the stronger administrative powers that the Federation has in this case.

d. Federal coercion (*Bundeszwang*)

The most powerful federal instrument to force the *Länder* into obedience is coercion as stipulated by Article 37 BL.[88] In light of the cooperative nature of German federalism and due to the generally accepted federal prerogative, this instrument constitutes an *ultima ratio* which has hardly been considered. At the same time, it goes back to a long history of so-called imperial execution (*Reichsexekution*).[89] Article 37(1) BL states that '[i]f a *Land* fails to comply with its obligations under the BL or other federal laws, the Federal Government, with the consent of the *Bundesrat*, may take the necessary steps to compel the *Land* to comply with its duties'.[90] To this end, instructions may be issued 'to all *Länder* and their authorities' (Article 37(2) BL).[91] Within the framework of Article 37 BL, both the

[80] Hanschel, Konfliktlösung (n 3) 208; Oebbecke (n 35) §136 para 44; Dittmann (n 51) Art 84 para 36 et seq.
[81] ibid. [82] ibid. [83] See also Dittmann (n 51) Art 84 para 41.
[84] See Oebbecke (n 35) §136 para 44.
[85] ibid; see furthermore, Leisner (1976) 288; on the whole matter, see Hanschel, *Konfliktlösung* (n 3) 208.
[86] Hanschel, *Konfliktlösung* (n 3) 208. [87] Art 85(4)(2).
[88] See Hanschel, *Konfliktlösung* (n 3) 209; W Erbguth, in Sachs (n 24) Art 37 para 2; Stern, *Das Staatsrecht der Bundesrepublik Deutschland Band I: Grundbegriffe und Grundlagen des Staatsrechts. Strukturprinzipien der Verfassung* (2nd edn, Verlag CH Beck 1984) 715.
[89] Oebbecke (n 35) §136 para 49. [90] ibid, para 53.
[91] See generally, Erbguth (n 88) Art 37 para 2; Oebbecke (n 35) §136 para 49.

Federal Government and the *Bundesrat* have some degree of discretion as to whether and how they react.[92] Apart from issuing instructions, the Federation has further enforcement options. It can react to defiant behaviour by refusing to fulfil its own obligations towards the *Land*, it can execute the action instead of the *Land* (*Ersatzvornahme*), it may establish a commissioner to supervise the implementation of federal law, or arguably even deploy police forces from elsewhere in the country.[93]

Federal coercion was used a number of times during the Weimar Republic but never during imperial times or in the current Federal Republic.[94] This suggests that its current lack of popularity is not only due to the existing alternatives, in particular judicial dispute resolution through the Federal Constitutional Court, but also to the general political culture of cooperation and entanglement.[95] Nevertheless, the instrument of federal coercion serves as an important backup option which demonstrates that the *Länder* cannot ultimately escape the fulfilment of their obligations vis-à-vis the Federation.[96] That includes a warning which has become useful not only in the field of nuclear oversight, but also where *Länder* have failed adequately to implement European law.[97] The legitimacy of federal coercion can be derived from the fact that the Federation needs to be put in a position to maintain the hierarchy of norms and hence the unity of the federal state including its overriding values when being threatened.[98] At the same time, Article 37 BL posits the limit of enforceability of federal law.[99] Should it ever be put to a test, non-compliance by the *Länder* would hence threaten the integrity of Germany as a State.

e. Federal intervention (*Bundesintervention*)

The instrument of federal intervention has a very specific function in that it only applies to clearly specified emergency situations as defined by Articles 35(2), 87a(3), and 91(1) and (2) BL.[100] Whereas Article 35(1) BL merely stipulates a general duty on 'all federal and *Länder* authorities [to] render legal and administrative assistance to one another', paragraph 2 allows a *Land* to ask assistance from the Federal Border Police in order to 'maintain or restore the public security or order' or even from the armed forces in the case of 'grave accident or natural disaster'. In such emergency situations the Federation may, according to paragraph 3, demand the *Land* government to 'place police forces at the disposal of other *Länder*' and deploy Federal Border Police or armed forces to the scene to support the local police.[101] This rather intrusive power, which is justified by the exceptional character of the situation, is subject to scrutiny by the *Bundesrat*, which may demand removal of these measures at any time; in addition, a kind of proportionality test ensures that measures are terminated as soon as they are no longer required to avert the danger (paragraph 3, clause 2).[102]

Furthermore, there are limits as to the kind of measures that the army may employ. This was shown in a decision of the Federal Constitutional Court regarding the

[92] Oebbecke (n 35) §136 para 52.

[93] Hanschel, *Konfliktlösung* (n 3) 209 et seq.; Oebbecke (n 35) §136 para 53 et seq.; see Pieroth (n 6) Art 37 para 4, stating that the deployment of such forces is debated within the literature.

[94] Oebbecke (n 35) §136 para 49.

[95] ibid.

[96] Hanschel, *Konfliktlösung* (n 3) 210; Oebbecke (n 35) §136 para 49; Erbguth (n 88) Art 37 para 3.

[97] Hanschel, *Konfliktlösung* (n 3) 210; Oebbecke (n 35) §136 para 49 with further references.

[98] Hanschel, *Konfliktlösung* (n 3) 210.

[99] ibid.

[100] Hanschel, *Konfliktlösung* (n 3) 211; A Jakab, 'Das Grunddilemma und die Natur des Staatsnotstandes' (2005) 38 *Kritische Justiz* 323, 326 et seq.

[101] ibid.

[102] On the limitations of proportionality as a general principle in intra-federal relations see section 4.b.

Luftsicherheitsgesetz (Aviation Security Act) which authorized the army, per *ultima ratio*, to shoot down an aircraft hijacked by terrorists threatening to use it against human lives on the ground.[103] The Court stated that 'the concept of an "especially grave accident" [within the meaning of Article 35.2 sentence 2 of the Basic Law] also comprises events in which a disaster can be expected to happen with near certainty'.[104] But this 'does not permit the Federation to order missions of the armed forces with specifically military weapons' to react to such a situation.[105] While the Court has been rather generous in defining the scope of this provision, it has been more cautious as regards the means of law enforcement. This needs to be viewed in light of the fact that the rules pertaining to the use of the army are generally very stringent.[106] As a part of that, there is a clear distinction between civil policing activities and the military tasks of the army.[107] Article 35(2)(2) BL constitutes an exception to that dividing line in that it exceptionally empowers the army to help in police matters. This may serve to explain why the Court has confined the available means to those used by the police in such circumstances.[108]

Article 87a BL complements this empowerment by specifying the conditions for the engagement of the army beyond military defence situations.[109] By stipulating that such action may only occur to the 'extent expressly permitted by this Basic Law', paragraph 2 implicitly refers back to Article 35 BL. Furthermore, Article 87a(3) and (4) BL deal with external and internal emergency situations *(äußerer und innerer Notstand)*. The external emergency refers to assistance tasks the army may perform during 'a state of defence or state of tension'. Here, the armed forces have the 'power to protect civilian property and to perform traffic control functions to the extent necessary to accomplish their defence mission'. Moreover, they may be 'authorised to support police measures for the protection of civilian property' for which they shall cooperate with the competent local authorities. However, as the wording of this provision shows, the focus is mostly on supporting the *Länder* authorities as opposed to enforcement actions against them. This needs to be distinguished from the function of the army in times of internal emergency ('an imminent danger to the existence or free democratic basic order of the Federation or of a *Land*') as stipulated in Article 87a(4) in conjunction with Article 91 BL. Where a *Land* is incapable or unwilling to respond to such a danger, the army may provide similar support as during an external emergency. Due to the specific nature of the emergency situation, this empowerment is amended by the right to 'combat organised armed insurgents'. The *Bundesrat* (as under Article 35 BL), but also the *Bundestag*, may terminate such engagement (Article 87a (4) BL). Article 91 BL alone (ie not read in conjunction with Article 87a BL) grants the same federal powers with regard to the deployment of federal border police and the police forces of other *Länder* which under certain circumstances may even be deployed 'under its own orders' (Article 91(2)(1) BL). Furthermore, if the danger extends beyond the boundaries of one *Land*, 'the Federal Government, insofar as is necessary to combat such danger, may issue instructions to the *Land* governments' (Article 91(2)(3) BL).

[103] The specific wording of §14(3) of the Act as translated in the decision of the Court reads as follows: 'The direct use of armed force is permissible only where it must be assumed under the circumstances that the aircraft is intended to be used against human lives, and where this is the only means to avert the imminent danger.'

[104] *BVerfGE* 115, 118 (English version, see http://www.bverfg.de/e/rs20060215_1bvr035705en.html), accessed 12 October 2016 headnote 1.

[105] ibid, headnote 2. [106] See for instance, Pieroth (n 6) Art 87a para 6 et seq. [107] ibid, para 4.

[108] http://www.bundesverfassungsgericht.de/entscheidungen/rs20060215_1bvr035705en.html, accessed 12 October 2016, para 104.

[109] See Hanschel, *Konfliktlösung* (n 3) 211; Pieroth (n 6), Art 87a para 12 et seq., as well as Art 91 para 1 et seq.; J Kokott, in Sachs (n 24) Art 87a para 44 et seq.; K Windthorst, in Sachs (n 24) Art 91 para 31 et seq.

The internal emergency has a stronger enforcement effect vis-à-vis the *Länder* than external emergency. This makes perfect sense: when the Federal Republic is under external stress, e.g. being attacked by another country, it is rather unlikely that this will lead to an internal power struggle between the Federation and the *Länder*. In such a scenario, it is almost self-evident that the federal army (in the absence of regional ones) as well as the federal police or indeed any other support is welcome to deal with that emergency. An internal emergency, by contrast, may either be a situation where a *Land* requests help or one where it rejects the federal legal order and supports or even organizes a rebellion so that it needs to be disciplined by way of federal police or army deployment.

f. Enforcement through the Federal Constitutional Court

I. Specific characteristics of enforcement through the judiciary

In addition to its own mechanisms of law enforcement as discussed above, the Federation can take the failure of *Länder* to obey federal law to court. This has been classified above as heteronomous as opposed to autonomous enforcement. Autonomous law enforcement raises issues of legitimacy as it equips the Federation with powers which the *Länder* do not have, although they can sometimes also defend themselves against federal law enforcement by recourse to the Federal Constitutional Court (within the limitations illustrated below).[110] Heteronomous enforcement through the Court in turn suggests a higher degree of legitimacy, as it involves a seemingly neutral arbiter. However, as the *Marbury v Madison* debate in the US illustrated, questions may be asked as to whether a court which is technically placed at the federal level will always be neutral.[111] Judicial independence, however, and the methods of interpretation, place the Court at a substantial distance from the Government (both in its executive and its legislative functions). That being said, the Court indirectly helped expand the concurrent legislative power of the Federation by essentially declaring the necessity requirements of Article 72(2) BL non-justiciable.[112] However, the constitutional reform of 1994 which strengthened the Court's powers in this regard, led to a much stricter interpretation of this requirement in recent years.[113]

II. Available procedures

The procedures for resolving intra-federal conflicts are listed in Article 93(1) Nr. 2-4 BL. Amongst those is the procedure that specifically deals with conflicts between the two levels of government, namely the so-called Federation-*Länder* dispute (*Bund-Länder-Streitigkeit*) according to Article 93(1) Nr. 3 BL in conjunction with §13 Nr. 7, and §§ 68–70 of the Constitutional Court Procedure Act.[114] The special remedy provided in Article 84(4) BL, according to which 'deficiencies in the execution of federal law' may ultimately be challenged before the Constitutional Court, essentially also follows the rules of this procedure.[115] The Federation-*Länder* dispute has been used relatively rarely, since it entails more onerous requirements than the abstract normative control (*abstrakte Normenkontrolle*) according to Article 93(1) Nr. 2 BL, which allows checking competence

[110] See section 4. [111] See *Marbury v Madison*, 5 US 1 Cranch 137 (1802).
[112] See Hanschel, *Konfliktlösung* (n 3) 196 et seq.
[113] ibid, with references to pertinent Constitutional Court decisions.
[114] See Hanschel, *Konfliktlösung* (n 3) 173 et seq. [115] See Pieroth (n 6) Art 84 para 21.

limitations incidentally.[116] At the same time, Article 93(1) Nr. 3 BL produced a number of high-profile cases which played a major role in the political conflict resolution of the Federal Republic (such as in the case of nuclear power).[117] It may lead the Court to order the *Länder* actively to implement federal law in a particular way or to confirm (or invalidate) an existing enforcement measure by the Federation. Conversely, the abstract norm control procedure examines the compatibility of *Länder* law with the formal and material requirements set up by the federal law, including the BL itself. Vice versa it allows the *Länder* to challenge the validity of federal law as incompatible with the BL, hence posing limits to the enforceability of federal law. A successful federal case does not require the *Länder* to act, but results in an invalidation of *Land* law and hence to a removal of an obstacle to the effectiveness of federal law. The constitutional reform of 1994 added Article 93(1) Nr. 2 a BL as a further subset of abstract norm control, according to which the conditions of Article 72(2) BL regarding concurrent federal legislation may be ascertained. However, this is not a direct instrument of federal law enforcement since this procedure cannot be triggered by the Federal Government, but only by the *Bundesrat* (ie technically a federal institution which, however, represents the *Länder* governments) or by *Land* institutions. Finally, Article 93(1) Nr. 4 BL—which deals with 'other disputes involving public law between the Federation and the *Länder*, between different *Länder* or within a *Land*, unless there is recourse to another court—lacks major importance for constitutional litigation due to the rather far-reaching competence of the Federal Administrative Court.[118]

4. Legal restraints on federal enforcement

The analysis has shown that the instruments of federal law enforcement vary in their intrusiveness and legal preconditions. As a whole, they can be considered as a toolkit provided to the Federation to ensure that its legal unity can always be preserved. However, this does not necessarily mean that the Federation can use these tools randomly. Apart from the specific requirements examined above, the question is which general principles may limit the exercise of federal law enforcement in favour of the *Länder*. In that regard the autonomous status of the *Länder* (*status negativus*), the principle of proportionality, and the principle of federal loyalty shall be examined below.

a. Limitations resulting from the *status negativus* of the *Länder*

While the *Länder*, unlike individuals, are not bearers of individual rights which they can vindicate against the (federal) State, they nevertheless have a defensible autonomous sphere into which the Federation cannot intrude at will. For this concept Isensee aptly uses the term 'status negativus'.[119] This entails a right to competence (*Recht auf Kompetenz*) in the sense that the Federation may only intervene in the *Länder* sphere under the conditions set by the BL.[120] The Federation can only intrude into this autonomous space on the basis of explicit empowerment by the BL.[121] This follows from the basic separation of administrative spheres at both levels of government.[122] The need for specific empowerment

[116] See Hanschel, *Konfliktlösung* (n 3) 173, 189 et seq.; for an overview of recent procedures, see http://www.bundesverfassungsgericht.de/SiteGlobals/Forms/Suche/Entscheidungensuche_Formular.html?nn=5399828&facettedVerfahrensart=bvg&language_=de, accessed 12 October 2016.

[117] Hanschel, *Konfliktlösung* (n 3)173.

[118] ibid, 171; Sturm in Sachs (n 24) Art 93 para 67 et seq.; Voßkuhle, in H von Mangoldt, F Klein and C Starck (eds), *Kommentar zum Grundgesetz* (6th edn, Verlag Franz Vahlen 2010) vol 3, Art 93 para 152.

[119] See Isensee (n 2) §126 para 132. [120] ibid; see ibid, para 131. [121] ibid. [122] ibid.

may not be replaced by mere reliance on the homogeneity rule of Article 28(3) BL, as the latter merely establishes a duty and a task for the Federation, but not a legal title for intervention.[123] Instead, the Federation needs to resort to the various instruments analysed above.[124] As a consequence, the *status negativus* as an expression of *Länder* autonomy may be identified as the first general and more principled limitation to the exercise of federal law enforcement.

b. Limitations resulting from the principle of proportionality

Even where the Federation is legally entitled to do so, it will often not use any of the instruments analysed above if it can solve a conflict by informal political means. Where the Federal Government does not see any alternative to legal enforcement, it will usually start with the less intrusive measures before escalating things further. The question is whether it is legally required to stick to this order. In this context it is submitted that the principle of proportionality as such is not directly applicable, as it is reserved to constellations between the state and the citizens.[125] Admittedly, the various safeguards entailed in the enforcement powers analysed above are guided by similar concerns, so that it appears apt to say that proportionality operates indirectly. However, this safeguard usually applies within one particular measure, not in order to dictate a certain order amongst several ones. Hence, for instance, federal coercion (provided its conditions are met) only permits necessary measures, instead of stipulating when instruments other than coercion should be used first. Initially, the Federal Constitutional Court seemed to suggest that injunctions sought by the Federation against a *Land* are subsidiary to using federal coercion.[126] But that was only one of several reasons why the Court rejected the injunction, and it may have been owed to the specific circumstances of the case. In addition, this view was not upheld in later decisions.[127] As a consequence, the Court can be approached before federal coercion is exercised, which in turn does not mean that this must happen.[128] For political reasons it usually will, however.[129] Coming back to the distinction between autonomous and heteronomous enforcement, the Federal Government will usually be well advised to use Court litigation first. Federal coercion would be more intrusive, since the degree of legitimacy is higher where the Court decides than where the Federal Government enforces its own law.

c. Limitations resulting from the principle of federal loyalty

The Federal Constitutional Court found federal loyalty to be an unwritten constitutional principle and has used this principle in many of its judgments since.[130] This principle, which formed part of some of the Court decisions examined above, is based on the notion of solidarity founded in Article 20 BL, which is rooted in the fact that the Federation and the *Länder* share a common destiny and therefore need to respect each other with a view to

[123] ibid, para 133; Pieroth (n 6) Art 28 para 32. [124] Pieroth (n 6). See section 3.

[125] *BVerfGE* 81, 310 (338); Isensee (n 2) §126 para 126; Isensee (n 2) §133 para 76; for an overview of this controversial issue, see furthermore A Heusch, *Der Grundsatz der Verhältnismäßigkeit im Staatsorganisationsrecht* (Duncker & Humblot 2003); see furthermore the discussion above at section 3.a regarding Rule of Law. On the necessity test stipulated in Art 72(2) BL, see H-W Rengeling, '§ 135. Gesetzgebungszuständigkeit', in Isensee and Kirchhof (n 2) §135 para 26, who convincingly classifies it as an expression of subsidiarity rather than proportionality.

[126] *BVerfGE* 3, 52 (57); Oebbecke (n 35) §136 para 53.

[127] Oebbecke (n 35), § 136 para 53 with further references. [128] ibid. [129] ibid.

[130] *BVerfGE* 1, 299 (315); W Geiger, 'Die wechselseitige Treuepflicht von Bund und Ländern', in A Süsterhenn (ed), *Föderalistische Ordnung* (Rhenania Verlag, 1961), 123; Hanschel, *Konfliktlösung* (n 3) 76 et seq.

securing the functioning of the governing system.[131] The Court has derived a number of requirements from the principle of federal loyalty which characterize the relationship between the two levels of government: One is the duty of friendly conduct towards the Federation *(Pflicht zu bundesfreundlichem Verhalten)*.[132] Another is a fair play requirement imposed on both sides, which in conflict situations ensures that none of them is marginalized.[133] The principle of federal loyalty operates as an unwritten power limitation on both sides, requiring that legal competences are not abused but exercised with moderation.[134] This can operate as a limitation to law enforcement where such enforcement would otherwise amount to an abuse of power. It can also serve as a facilitator. For instance, *Länder* cannot refuse to implement a law by claiming that the Federation itself failed to fulfil a legal duty.[135] Furthermore, procedural duties apply, such as the equal treatment of the *Länder* and the duty to provide information.[136] The former can determine the measure of law enforcement, the latter may serve as a vital precondition to establish whether enforcement measures are in order or not.

In light of the broad scope of this principle, its limitations need to be pointed out clearly. The principle thus rarely stipulates positive obligations for specific action, but mostly acts as a mechanism for restraining excessive behaviour. It is dependent on context and subsidiary as well as accessory to concrete written rules.[137] Nevertheless, the principle plays a major role in defining the relations between the Federation and the *Länder*. In the context of federal law enforcement it mainly restrains the Federation. However, it also clearly stipulates the duty of the *Länder* to cooperate with the Federation, hence avoiding situations from the outset which would lead to enforcement measures. By asking both sides to cooperate, the principle provides the *Länder* with the opportunity to implement the law themselves or to explain to the Federation why they have not done so yet. In addition to such a right to be heard, the principle of federal loyalty would require the Federation, at least where there is no urgency, to give the *Länder* the chance to appeal to the Court before measures of federal coercion are activated.[138]

5. Conclusion

This analysis has shown that the BL equips the Federation with a wide array of instruments for law enforcement against the *Länder*, ranging from various autonomous enforcement measures by the Federal Government, to heteronomous constitutional review by way of Federal–*Länder* dispute. The multitude of instruments, however, stands in contrast to their limited application in practice. This can be explained by two factors: on the one hand the system of executive federalism implies that most federal law is implemented by the *Länder* themselves. This distinct expression of administrative autonomy of the *Länder* (in return for very limited original legislative competencies) protects them against strong federal law

[131] Isensee (n 2) §126 para 154, 160 et seq.; Hanschel, *Konfliktlösung* (n 3) 76 et seq.; for a critical account, see Bauer (n 72) 118 et seq., 176 et seq., 218 et seq.

[132] *BVerfGE* 1, 299 (315); on similar characterisations of the same duty in the literature, see (n 2) §126, para 155.

[133] See Isensee (n 2) §126 para 163 et seq.

[134] See *BVerfGE* 4, 115 (140); 12, 205 (239 et seq.); 14, 197 (215); 34, 9 (20 et seq.); 34, 216 (232); 43, 291 (348); Hanschel, *Konfliktlösung* (n 3) 78.

[135] *BVerfGE* 8, 122 (140); Hanschel, *Konfliktlösung* (n 3) 78.

[136] *BVerfGE* 12, 205 (254 et seq.); 72, 330 (402); see furthermore Hanschel, *Konfliktlösung* (n 3) 78; for a more critical account, see W Rudolf (2008) '§141. Kooperation im Bundesstaat', in Isensee and Kirchhof (n 2), § 141, para 95.

[137] Isensee (n 2) §126 para 113, 166, with references to the Court jurisprudence; Hanschel, *Konfliktlösung* (n 3) 78 et seq.

[138] See Oebbecke (n 35) §136 para 53.

enforcement in many cases. The level of intrusion and the legal requirements for enforcement clearly reflect this. Accordingly, while there are many empowerments, they only grant rather limited and finely-tuned authorization to intrude into the *Länder* sphere. On the other hand, the system of cooperative federalism and entanglement, as well as the notion of a unitary state, produce a general climate of political negotiation and avoidance of legal conflict resolution by enforcement. The few exceptions (which merely confirm the rule) concern issues which are either politically very sensitive and hotly debated amongst political parties (such as nuclear power) or which present a particular regional burden triggering the reflex of 'not in my backyard'. At the same time, the public expectation of rather uniform effective governance and limited acceptance of regional divergence corresponds to a clear idea of hierarchy, preemption, and homogeneity which makes sure that the Federation can assert its authority where required, whilst respecting regional autonomy where appropriate.

Matters get more complex where EU law is enforced within the German federation, which goes beyond the scope of this chapter. The study of federal law enforcement within the German federation may provide interesting lessons as to the similar system of executive federalism (in a broad sense of the word) within the EU,[139] for instance that confrontation can merely be the exception if long-term effective governance is to be preserved. In that sense, a substantial consensus about uniform norms and values with decentralized implementation protected by autonomy (e.g. through subsidiarity or the principle of enumerated powers) and coupled with clearly-defined and limited enforcement options at the central level, can be found in both systems. The difference is that democratic concerns regarding EU governance and the remaining Member State sovereignty strengthen the need for subsidiarity as opposed to the domestic situation where sovereignty is vested in the centre and democratic processes are similar at both levels.

[139] See for instance, P Dann, *Parlamente im Exekutivföderalismus—Eine Studie zum Verhältnis von föderaler Ordnung und parlamentarischer Demokratie in der Europäischen Union* (Springer 2004).

16

The Enforcement of Federal Law in the Belgian Federal State

Céline Romainville and Marc Verdussen

In the Belgian federal system the institutionalization of the bipolarity between the French-speaking population and the Dutch-speaking population produced a kind of institutionalization of defiance in the form of permanent demands from some federate entities for state reform and for greater autonomy. The reshaping of the distribution of competences through periodic state reforms channels to some extent the hints of defiance into a constitutional system which is permanently reinventing itself.

This institutionalization of defiance through state reform processes does not exhaust every hint of defiance. Expressions of defiance can be found, for instance, in the disrespect for the constitutional rules regulating the distribution of powers between federate entities and federal law. In theory, the strong principle of exclusivity of competences prevents defiance of federal law by federate units. Indeed, this principle, combined with the principle of equipollence between norms, prevents situations of defiance by creating a compartmented system of competences where federal law is enforced only by federal institutions and with federal budgets. However, Belgian constitutional law is experiencing an increase in new forms of competences which implies a temperance of the exclusivity of competence by the assumption of a hierarchy between federal law and the laws of federate entities. Indeed, concurrent competences and framework competences imply that federal law has to be enforced by federate entities. In those cases, defiance could arise from a federate entity's disrespect for the prevalence of federal law.

Moreover, the strength of the exclusivity principle, notably in interactions between the different levels of powers, erodes itself in a time of complex policies. A rising number of policy fields are today subjected to parallel regulations, requiring cooperation and agreement between the federal authorities and federate entities. Such cooperative agreements are sometimes necessary for the federal authority to lead its policies effectively. In such a context, defiance will materialize in the form of a blocking or an obstruction of the development or the pursuit of such cooperation and agreement.

When the enforcement of federal law by federate entities is required and not respected, the arbitration of the conflict will be in the hands of the Constitutional Court. The Court is indeed competent to arbitrate the conflict, according to the Belgian Constitution. The latter Court and the latter Constitution do not belong to the federal level as such, but to the 'super entity' formed by the Constitution that the federal and the federate entities are obliged to respect. The Constitutional Court can repeal legislative acts which are not compatible with the Federal Constitution and with the rules governing the distribution of powers. The conflicts in areas where federal law is required to be enforced by federate entities will thus be arbitrated by the Constitutional Court.

If a federate unit flagrantly defies federal law, the Constitutional Court will sanction it. But what if the federate unit persists in its defiance by entrenching its defiance into legislation? What if the disrespect of the decisions of the Constitutional Court is brought to a dramatic level?

After having briefly introduced the dynamics of Belgian federalism, how it channels processes of defiance to some extent through a dismantling of the federal state, and how it avoids the issue of enforcement of federal law by federate entities by reference to the exclusivity and equality principles, this chapter will: (1) analyse the exceptional situations where the enforcement of federal law is clearly provided for through framework competences and parallel competences; (2) analyse expressions of defiance in the framework of cooperative Belgian federalism; (3) turn then to the power of the Constitutional Court to sanction violations of the enforcement of federal law; and (4) finally examine the scenario where defiance is brought to a higher level, with the flagrant and explicit disrespect by the federate entities of the Federal Constitution and of the judgments of the Constitutional Courts (5).

1. The Institutionalization of defiance and the verticality and equality principles

The Belgian Federal system is somewhat organized to channel the defiance of the federate entities through a dismantling process, each reform of the state being the opportunity of transferring new powers to the federate entities, and thereby absorbing a great part of the claims emanating from federate entities which would have ended up, if not heard, in defiant actions and instability (section 1.a).[1] Moreover, Belgian federalism is built on a distribution of powers which is organized in such a way as to diminish seriously the risk of defiance or open conflict (section 1.b.).

a. Channelling of defiance through the structures and dynamics of Belgian federalism

Belgium is generally categorized as representing the model of federalization by disaggregation.[2] Unlike most of federal states, the Belgian Federal State is the result of the metamorphosis of an initially unitary structure. It took shape following a top-down process, namely the disintegration of a sovereign state under pressure from a centrifugal dynamic. Moreover, the formation of the federal structure took place gradually since it is founded on a multinational federalism which itself is the product of a long historical evolution. The transformation towards federalism began in 1970 and proceeded step-by-step. Belgium has gradually become a true federal state, with a high degree of devolution of powers and competences. The permanent reshaping and bargaining of the Belgian constitutional system thus largely incorporates attempts at defiance, and to some extent forestalls them through reforms to the state. Indeed, those reforms can be viewed as mitigating the conflicting interests, demands, and claims and thereby as containing the potential

[1] In a multinational federation the temporality and quality of the responses to expressed demands for minority self-government are clearly an important source of change (when answers later become sources of instability). J McGarry and B O'Leary, 'Federation and managing nations', in M Burgess and J Pinder (eds), *Multinational Federations* (Routledge 2007) 202–3; N Cox, *Constitutional Paradigms and the Stability of States* (Ashgate 2012), 87–119, 234–5.

[2] See M Verdussen, 'La Belgique: un fédéralisme bipolaire mû par une dynamique de dissociation', in M Seymour and G Laforest (eds), *Le fédéralisme multinational. Un modèle viable?* (PIE–Peter Lang 2011) 7; W Swenden, M Brans and L de Winter, 'The politics of Belgium: Institutions and Policy Under Bipolar and Centrifugal Federalism' (2006) 29 *West European Politics* 863.

expressions of defiance towards the federal constitutional system by increasingly acknowledging spheres of autonomy for federate entities. The question which remains open is of course the never-ending nature of this process which, at its term, implies the extinction of the federal state.

Before turning to a more technical analysis, it must be recalled here that the Belgian Federal State has two kinds of federate units (sub-states): the regions and the communities. There are three regions: the Flemish region, the Walloon region, and the Brussels Capital region. There are three communities: the Flemish community, the French community, and the German-speaking community. The regions are responsible for matters such as the natural environment, housing, economic affairs, energy policy, and transport; they have a territorial basis. The communities are responsible for culture, education, and then 'personalized' with a territorial *and* a personal dimension (indeed the decrees of the French and the Flemish communities have the force of law in French-language and in Dutch-language regions respectively, as well as in those institutions established in the bilingual region of Brussels Capital which, on account of their activities, must be considered as belonging exclusively to one community or the other). Communities are superimposed on the regions, which contributes to the complexity of the system. There is thus a double, parallel, territorially overlapping federal system. All the regions and the communities are vested with a distinct legal personality. All are on an equal footing. Each of them is self-governed, having its own Parliament (legislative assembly) and its own government (executive organ). Each of them has the power to enact legislation with the same hierarchical rank as federal law: their legislation has equal force of law. This description of the Belgian federal system would be incomplete without specifying that the institutional framework of the regions and the communities, including the rules allocating competences, is laid down in the Federal Constitution—which is the supreme norm within the Belgian constitutional order—and pursuant to the Constitution, by special-majority laws, which are adopted by the House of Representatives and the Senate with a qualified (special double) majority: the majority of votes cast in each linguistic group in each Chamber, the total of affirmative votes given by the two linguistic groups having to be equal to at least two-thirds of the votes.[3]

Defiance is often said to be also contained by the fact that the Belgian political system provides inclusion for political minorities and participation at nearly all governance levels for political parties. The Belgian system is a consociational democracy. Belgian constitutional law contains numerous provisions requiring consultation, cooperation, participation, and negotiation among the federate entities or representatives of the federate entities. This broad inclusion and participation is grounded on the idea that 'sharing power between segmental elites, instead of excluding minorities from power, is what turns centrifugal tendencies into constructive forces for democratic stability'.[4] However, the channelling of defiance and the transformation of centrifugal tendencies into constructive forces should not be overestimated. The recent electoral results of nationalistic political parties, the deadlocks in 2008 and 2010, obstruction strategies, and strong oppositions between political parties indicate that there is no guarantee that all political parties would always

[3] The main special-majority laws are the Special Institutional Reform Act of 1980 (SIRA), providing the structures and powers of the Flemish region, the Walloon region, the Flemish community, and the French community; the Institutional Reform Act for the German-speaking Community of 1983, providing the structures and powers of the German-speaking community; and the Special Brussels Institutions Act of 1989, providing the structures and powers of the Brussels Capital region.

[4] D Caluwaerts, *Confrontation and Communication. Deliberative Democracy in Divided Belgium* (Peter Lang 2012) 59.

engage within a constructive dialogue, despite the participatory and inclusive mechanisms in place.

b. Exclusion of the enforcement of federal law by the exclusivity and equality principles

Beyond the structure and dynamics of the Belgian Federal State, the exclusivity and equality principles are also viewed as contributing to the avoidance of conflicts between federal and federate entities.

The Belgian Federal State rests on the *equality* of the constituent entities.[5] The federal entity on the one hand, and the federate units (regions and communities) on the other, have equal footing in exercising their functions and powers. Sovereignty is shared, each partner being the master of its domain of activity. In other words, the several levels of power are in watertight compartments. Accordingly, the laws adopted by regions and communities—which are called 'decrees' and as regards the Brussels Capital region, 'ordinances'—are not subordinated to the federal laws. The equality principle's implications include a principle of equipollence between federal and federate norms and an absence of any kind of hierarchy.[6]

In Belgium the equality principle is seen as going hand-in-hand with the principle of *exclusivity* of competences, which also secures the equipollence between the actors in Belgian federalism by preserving a sphere of autonomy, in order to prevent conflicts of competences as far as possible. The idea is simple: only one entity or one category of entities may rule on a given matter.[7] This principle originates in a dualist vision of a strict confinement of hermetic competences.[8] The verticality principle makes the principle of exclusivity a reality within the Belgian system. It states that the competence over a field not only covers the competence to legislate and to enact legislation but also to regulate, to control, and to finance that field.[9] In other words, this principle means that federal competences must be enforced by federal institutions through federal means and within the federal scope. The 'spending power' is thereby qualified in Belgian law as an accessory power which follows a title of competence. Unlike many other federal states, the federal authority does not have as a rule the power to spend money in fields connected with the competences of the communities or of the regions.[10]

In conclusion, as a matter of principles, federal laws are exclusively enforced by federal authorities and in the areas of federal powers. The equality and exclusivity principles exclude in theory an enforcement of federal law by federate entities. Federal law is enforced by the federal authorities, federal institutions, and federal budgets. This is said to avoid situations of defiance by compartmentalizing the entities' different competences and different spheres of authority. In such a system, defiance of federal law is indeed less likely to occur. Thereby, in principle, federate entities do not have to

[5] F Delpérée and M Verdussen, 'L'égalité, mesure du fédéralisme', in J-F Gaudreault-Desbiens and F Gélinas (eds), *The States and Moods of Federalism—Governance, Identity and Methodology* (Yvon Blais 2005) 193.

[6] M Verdussen, 'Il federalismo asimmetrico in Belgio' (2007) *Diritto Pubblico Comparato ed Europeo* 1172.

[7] See Delpérée and Verdussen (n 5) 196–203; Verdussen (n 2).

[8] Verdussen (n 2) 7.

[9] See, Constitutional Court (CC): case 54/96, 3 October 1996, B.5.; case 30/2000, 21 March 2000; and case CA 56/2000, 17 May 2000. See also, Council of State, Legislation Section (CSLS), opinion 30.037-2 (Parliamentary Documents of the Parliament of the French Community of Belgium CCF, session 1999–2000, 95–1).

[10] See: V Vander Geeten, 'Le pouvoir de dépenser en Belgique et au Canada: gage d'efficacité ou entorse au fédéralisme?' (2008) 4 *Revue belge de droit constitutionnel* 335.

respect, implement, or to enforce federal law, each entity having authority in its own sphere of competence.

However, as we will see, this statement requires qualifications. Federal law is not always enforced by federal entities and in federal areas of power. Indeed, the exclusivity principle is regularly aggravated by the fact that, within a federal state, a public authority will quite often identify the necessity to impinge on the sphere of another public authority's competence to conduct a coherent and efficient policy. In a time of complex public problems and of integrated policies, and within such a small state, the complete isolation and confinement of areas and policies is in fact rare and sometimes impossible. The efficient management of some fields requires some flexibility in more than one field.[11] Accordingly, the principle of exclusivity is tempered by some ineluctable corrective mechanisms.[12]

2. Enforcement of federal law by federate entities

There are several corrective mechanisms by which the principle of exclusivity is qualified in Belgian federal law. Those mechanisms are likely to pave the way for expressions of defiance, because they require the enforcement of federal law by federate entities.

Going beyond the complex nature of those mechanisms, we will try here to identify various cases in the distribution of powers where the interaction between different federal entities is assumed and the enforcement of federal law by other federal entities becomes possible and sometimes required. In these legal examples, federal law is enforced through federal legislation giving clear directions for the enactment of legislation by federate entities and/or through the enactment of legislation by federate entities. These legal examples provide space for expressions of defiance, without however providing for specific mechanisms to secure the enforcement of federal law against the will of the federate entities. Indeed, aside from implicit competences, Belgian constitutional law does not provide for clear and explicit legal mechanisms tempering the rigorous nature of the exclusivity principle, for political reasons linked with its bipolarity and with the centrifugal forces that designed it.[13] In particular, concurrent competences are widely ignored by Belgian constitutional law. Because of this refusal clearly and explicitly to embrace the need to moderate the equality and exclusivity principles, the legal mechanisms by which federal law can be enforced against federate entities are complex, subtle, incomplete, often hidden, overlooked and not thought through. As a result, in case of concurrent competences, if a federate entity does not comply with its obligation to respect the acknowledged superiority of federal law, the legal consequences are insufficiently definite, beyond the certainty that recourse to the Constitutional Court can be had on the strength of the violation of the principle of distribution of powers.

We will analyse first the case of concurrent competences (section 2.a.), framework competences (section 2.b.) and implied powers (section 2.c.), before outlining our transversal and general thoughts on the enforcement of federal law by federate entities (section 2.d.).

[11] Verdussen (n 2) 7. [12] Verdussen (n 6).

[13] See H. Dumont, "La Sixième réforme de l'Etat ou l'art de ne pas choisir?", Journal des tribunaux, 2015, n° 6609, p. 497; H. Dumont, M. El Berhoumi and I. Hachez (eds), La sixième réforme de l'État : l'art du ne pas choisir ou l'art du compromis?, (Larcier 2015) §§ 83–96 and Verdussen (n 2) 211–25. For instance, the idea of federal law superiority appears to be unbearable for both communities. The genuine implementation of the subsidiarity principle, finding the most appropriate level of power to deal a given issue, is almost unrealistic in the Belgian context, with the Flemish political world being unwilling to transfer or return powers to the federal level, with the French political parties sometimes being very reluctant to transfer power to federate entities, and with great division on the question of whether regions or communities should be the driving forces of Belgian federalism.

a. Enforcement of federal concurrent laws against communities and regions

A competence is termed 'concurrent' when it may be regulated by different legislatures, provided that federal law prevails over a federate decree or ordinance when they overlap. The concept of 'concurrent' competences implies therefore the existence of a 'rule of conflict' which presumes the superiority of the federal law over federate laws or the intervention of the federal law in federate matters.[14] In theory and because of its—apparent—contradiction with the principles of equality and with the exclusivity principle, the system of concurrent competences is said to have formally been rejected in Belgian constitutional law.[15] And indeed, in 1988 the Belgian Council of State clearly excluded the idea of this system.[16] However, despite this formal exclusion, there are some cases where the distribution of powers reveals a system of concurrent competences.[17]

The most important one relates to taxing power. Article 170 § 1 of the Belgian Constitution provides that '[t]axes to the benefit of the State can only be introduced by a law'. In 2008, the Constitutional Court confirmed that Article 170 § 1 empowered the federal law to adopt fiscal measures without regard for the competences of communities and regions (but 'exception being made of the cases provided by the Constitution and the special-majority law', with this competence being 'subject to the respect of the proportionality principle inherent to each exercise of competences'.[18] Article 170 § 2 establishes that '[t]axes to the benefit of a community or region can only be introduced by a federate law or a rule as described in Article 134. The law determines, with respect to the taxes referred to in the first paragraph, the exceptions that are proved to be necessary'. Following the Belgian Constitutional Court, this provision authorizes the federal law 'to determine which taxes cannot be introduced by communities and regions'.[19] The Court endorsed the idea that 'communities and regions are not allowed to introduce taxes in areas which are already subjected to a federal tax. They can only introduce taxes in "virgin fields"'.[20] From Article 170 § 2 of the Constitution, the Belgian Constitutional Court thus deduced the idea of a 'superiority of the fiscal law on the fiscal decree'. Moreover, the Constitutional Court also recognizes the competence of the federal legislator not only to exclude some fiscal matters from the communities and regions' own fiscal competences but also to ensure that this taxation will not apply to some categories of tax-payers, to limit *ex ante* and *ex post* the implementation of regional taxations.[21]

This mechanism has been qualified as a 'sort of defence mechanism from the State towards other levels of power in order to secure to the State its own fiscal competence'.[22] It was originally perceived as a mechanism needed to organize the state, as if the system of exclusive competence in the taxation field would automatically lead to a horrific imbroglio. This fiscal superiority clearly requires the enactment of federal taxation laws establishing

[14] M Uyttendaele, *Précis de droit constitutionnel belge: regards sur un système institutionnel paradoxal* (3rd edn, Bruylant 2005) 947.

[15] Uyttendaele (n 14) 945; J Vanpraet, *De latente staatshervorming—De bevoegdheidsverdeling in de rechtspraak van het Grondwettelijk Hof en de adviespraktijk van de Raad van State* (die Keure 2011), 62.

[16] Parliamentary Documents of the Chamber of Representatives (PDCR), extraordinary session 1988, 45.

[17] See also for an extensive analysis of a number of proposals related to a formal and broader recognition of concurrent competences in Belgian constitutional law, X Delgrange, N Lagasse, and J van Nieuwenhove, 'De hervorming van de instellingen en de herzieningsverklaring van 2007. Een grondwettelijke verkenning van enkele voorstellen' (2008) 1 *Chroniques de droit public* 3.

[18] CC case 68/2008, 17 April 2008, B.6.4.

[19] CC case 119/2007, 19 September 2007, B.4.1.

[20] See CC case 119/2007, 19 September 2007, B.4.1 (our translation). See also Parliamentary Documents of the Senate (PDS), 1988–1989 No 562–2, 160.

[21] CC case 124/2001, 16 October 2001, B.4.

[22] PDCR, S.E. 1979 10 No 8/4, 4.

exceptions and limitation to the regional and community taxation competence by those latter federate entities.[23]

There are other cases of concurrent competences. Article 6*bis* § 2 (5) SIRA also provides for a case of concurrent competences: if the communities and regions are competent for the scientific research linked with their areas of competence—another example of parallel competences—the federal authority remains competent for the 'programs and actions' which require a homogenous execution at the national or international level (and under the conditions set in a cooperation agreement).[24] The political control we will analyse below also draws on the same idea.

The Sixth Reform of the State of 2014 (adopted in January 2014, aiming to broaden the autonomy of federate entities, reduce the scope of the federal state,[25] and build more homogenous 'power packages') creates or recognizes new cases of concurrent competences (although it officially signs its commitment to the exclusivity principle). For instance, it explicitly states that officials of both the regions and the federal authority can detect infringements of the rules governing the employment of alien workers.[26] On this question, the Special Act of 6 January 2014 (the Special Act on the Sixth Reform of the State (SASRS)) also provides that regions are competent for the 'application of rules regulating the work permits depending on the particular situation of living of the people concerned' while 'monitoring compliance with these rules is the competence of federal authority' and 'the detection of infringement to those rules can also be made by authorized officials for the purpose by the regions'. Those concurrent competences are created in a lacunar constitutional distribution of powers in the field of social security and social assistance which also allows each entity to expand its own powers.[27]

Other mechanisms in Belgian constitutional law find their inspiration in this idea of concurrent competences and in the underlying principle of superiority of federal law over federate entities. In particular, some political controls are established in order to subordinate the action of federate entities to the agreement of the federal government. Those

[23] Uyttendaele (n 14) 945–6.

[24] There is another case of concurrent competence, linked with the discussion on the nature of competences. P Popelier quotes K Rimanque who argues that the constitutive autonomy recognized to the French community and to the Walloon region is concurrent by nature with the priority of the federal entities (see Popelier, 'Sociaal federalisme en bevoegdheidsverdeling in rechtsvergelijkend perspectief – Voorbij het exclusiviteitsbeginsel', in B Cantillon et al., *De gelaagde Welvaartsstaat, Naar een Vlaamse Sociale Bescherming in België en Europa?* (Intersentia 2010) 106.

[25] See generally on this Sixth Reform of the State, J Sautois and M Uyttendaele (eds), *La sixième réforme de l'État. Tournant historique ou soubresaut ordinaire?* (Anthemis 2013); Dumont, El Berhoumi, and Hachez (n 13); M Uyttendaele and M Verdussen (eds), *Dictionnaire de la sixième réforme de l'État* (Bruylant 2015); A Alen et al. (eds), *Het federale België na de Zesde Staatshervorming* (die Keure 2014); J Velaers et al., *De zesde staatshervorming: instellingen, bevoegdheden en middelen* (Intersentia 2014). One of the main transfers effected by the Sixth Reform relates to the question of family allowances. See on this, W Van Eeckhoutte et al. (eds), *La communautarisation des allocations familiales* (la Charte 2013); and W Pas, 'De Brusselse instellingen in het eerste luik van de zesde staatshervorming' (2013) TBP, 2013, 452–62.

[26] Article 6 § 1, IX, 3 SIRA as modified by Article 22 SASRS.

[27] See J Velaers, 'Het sociaal federalisme in België in het licht van de bevoegdheidsverdeling' in Cantillon, Popelier and Mussche (eds), *De gelaagde welvaartsstaat. Naar een Vlaamse sociale bescherming in België en Europa?* (Intersentia 2010) 133–53. In the *zorgverzekering* case (where the Flemish community was recognized as being empowered to create a new health insurance by two judgments of the Constitutional Court (on the basis of its powers regarding social assistance) one cannot however speak about concurrent competences. The Constitutional Court expressly rejected formal concurrence between federal and federate entities (see CC case 33/2001, 13 March 2001, B.3.9.3.) while it clearly promoted the doctrine of the 'double aspect'. See also R Leysen, 'Het Arbitragehof: 15 jaar rechtspraak insociale zaken' (2000) *RDS* 529; and X Delgrange, 'La Cour d'arbitrage momifie la compétence fédérale en matière de sécurité sociale' (2001) 2 *RBDC* 229; see B Cantillon, '*Quo vadis* sociale zekerheid?', in P Popelier et al. (eds), *Belgium: Quo Vadis? Waarheen na de zesde staatshervorming?* (Intersentia 2012) 353–4; J Vanpraet, 'Vers une sécurité sociale flamande complémentaire dans le cadre actuel de répartition des compétences' (2010) 18 *Journal des Tribunaux* 301.

controls are clearly part of the logic of concurrent competences (see section 2.a.), where the main actor is the federal government.

According to Article 11 (2) SIRA, the regional and community legislatures have the power to adopt criminal legislation—to define human acts as criminal and enact penalties—in their respective fields of competences. But if the legislature plans to establish a new penalty, i.e. a penalty not included in the federal Criminal Code, it has to obtain the assent of the federal Council of Ministers. This is to ensure that the federal entity provides a minimum of uniformity in criminal penalties and also to create a guarantee against a potential reestablishment of the death penalty.[28] The absence of such an ascent would paralyse the federate entity: it is designed as a '*tutelle d'approbation*'.

According to Articles 45 and 46 of the Special Brussels Institutions Act of 1989, the ordinances adopted by the Brussels Capital region in some matters are subject to limited political control by the federal authorities, which can cancel a regional ordinance which jeopardizes the role of Brussels as international city and capital of Belgium. The control can be exercised only for this special purpose and only in four defined regional matters. For the same purpose, the federal government may also present to the Conciliation Committee ('*Comité de concertation*') draft rules that the Brussels Capital region should adopt to preserve the international role and function of Brussels. Where no agreement is reached on those suggestions, the federal state can adopt the rules itself.[29]

Article 169 of the Constitution provides a substitution mechanism which the federal authorities can use when there is a failure to perform its international or supranational obligations on the part of a federate unit. According to this article, 'in order to ensure the observance of international or supranational obligations, the authorities mentioned in Articles 36 and 37 can, provided that the conditions stipulated by the law are met, temporarily replace the bodies mentioned in Articles 115 and 121. This law must be adopted by a majority as described in Article 4, last paragraph'. To sum up, the situation considered is one where a region or a community neglects to abide by an international or supranational obligation (for instance, it does not transpose an EU directive, when it is supposed to do so) and, for this reason, the Belgian state is condemned by the European Court of Justice. If this happens, the federal authorities are entitled to address that gap by taking appropriate action.[30]

Overall, and excepting Article 11 (2), it would be utterly false to claim that the above-mentioned political controls are in wide use. Experience has shown that they have never been implemented. In fact, they are a sword of Damocles hanging over the heads of federate units. Some of these mechanisms can be viewed as being based on a will to give some symbolic precedence to federal law.

Finally, it is noteworthy that if a federal authority or a federate entity plan to adopt a law, a decree, or an ordinance in a way which another entity fears being adversely affected by—termed a 'conflict of interest'—the latter may refer the matter to the Conciliation Committee (*Comité de concertation*), which is a body composed of six federal ministers, including the Prime Minister, and six ministers of federate governments, in compliance with the principle of linguistic parity. The deliberation is frozen and the Conciliation Committee has to try to reach a consensus.

[28] M Verdussen, *Contours et enjeux du droit constitutionnel pénal* (Bruylant 1995) 235–9.

[29] Article 46 of the Special Brussels Institutions Act of 1989.

[30] Another case concerns local powers. The Governor of the Province is nominated by the regional governments only if the Council of Ministers agrees to this nomination.

b. Enforcement of federal framework norms by federate entities

In addition to pure concurrent powers, Belgian constitutional law recognizes some instances of federal authority powers to establish frameworks within which other authorities can operate.[31] Within such a framework the federal authority sets fundamental rules or minimum conditions under which the federate entities can act.[32]

When federal authorities receive competences to set frameworks for other authorities' competences, they sketch the main lines of the political decisions available within those latter competences. Such delineation is mandatory on the federate entities. Indeed, as Jürgen Vanpraet emphasized, the Constitutional Court interestingly declared itself competent to control whether the legislation adopted by the communities and regions respects the federal framework.[33]

Framework competences in Belgian constitutional law can originate from case law, for instance regarding the right to family and private life recognized by Article 22 of the Constitution, which provides that '[e]veryone has the right to the respect of his private and family life, except in the cases and conditions determined by the law'. This case law has to be understood in light of the '*matières réservées*' (reserved matters) to the federal authority doctrine: communities and regions cannot act in a matter reserved to the 'law' by the Constitution after 1980.[34] Despite this doctrine, the Constitutional Court has recognized a parallel competence to implement the right to family and private life. The clear will of the constituting power and of the special-majority legislator to harmonize the protection of private life, namely in the treatment of personal data, led judges to set a—federal—framework for the exercise of this competence.[35] The Court states that the federal laws specifying these limitations should thereby be respected by federate entities when their action can have an impact on the respect of the private and family life.[36] In other words, the Federal Act of 1992 on personal data became a 'framework law'. Similar reasoning was applied for the formal motivation of the administrative acts. Since the Constitutional Court's intervention, the federal law on administrative acts is also a framework law which the federate entities have to respect when regulating the formal reasons for their acts.[37]

Considering the evolution of the case law on the distribution of powers regarding constitutional rights and freedoms, the question remains open whether it is possible to extrapolate from this case law and to consider that when the Constitution reserves to the federal law the protection of some elements of constitutional rights and freedoms, it actually gives to the federal legislator a general competence to set a framework within which other legislators would be allowed to intervene. In other words, when it comes to a *matière réservée* in the case of limitations and conditions to fundamental rights and freedom, and taking into account the 'objective dimension' of fundamental rights which

[31] See J Vande Lanotte and G Goedertier, *Overzicht Publiek Recht* (die Keure 2007) 1035–6.

[32] See A Alen, *Handboek van het Belgisch Staatsrecht* (Kluwer 1995) 342. See also the proposals of Delgrange, Lagasse, and Van Nieuwenhove (n 17) in the field of administrative jurisdictions.

[33] Vanpraet (n 15) 64–5.

[34] See Article 19 § 1 (1) SIRA and CC case 29/2011, 24 February 2011, B.4.4. For an historical appraisal of this theory, see Uyttendaele (n 14) 956–65. See also W Pas, 'De door de Grondwet aan de "wet" voorbehouden aangelegenheden. Vroeger en nu', in A Alen (ed), *De vijfde staatshervorming van 2001* (die Keure, 2002) 25–63.

[35] See on those considerations and on the changes in the interpretation of Article 22 of the Constitution, E Degrave, 'L'article 22 de la Constitution et le traitement des données à caractère personnel' (2009) *Journal des Tribunaux* 366.

[36] See CC case 162/2004, 16/2005; and case 15/2008.

[37] See CC case 55/2001, 8 May 2001; and case 128/2001, 18 October 2001.

'permeates' into all areas, matters and powers, is it possible to consider that the federal authority received a framework competence, i.e. the power to fix conditions and limitations to those rights and freedom at the exclusion of other legislators? Are the conclusions reached for Article 22 of the Constitution and for the formal motivation of administrative acts also applicable to Article 191 (which reserves to the federal legislator the possibility to set exceptions to the principle of the equal enjoyment of constitutional rights and freedoms between foreigners and Belgians)?[38] The case law of the Constitutional Court remains unclear.

Beyond the framework competences originating from the constitutional case law, there are other instances of such competences. In the field of 'social action' policy, if the communities are in principle competent, Article 5 § 1 II 2 a-d SIRA reserves to the federal authority a framework competence on four topics. The federal authority has the power to fix the subsistence minimum, and the conditions for granting and financing the right to the subsistence minimum in a federal legislation which must be respected by federate entities. Moreover, the federal authority is competent in matters and the rules on *centres publics d'action sociale* (CPAS—public centres for social action). This implies that the federal authority is the only authority competent to define the scope of competence for the communities in the domain of social assistance given that it defines not only the basic principles relating to the subsistence minimum but also more detailed rules. In this respect communities can only proceed to the granting of supplements to such rights[39] when the federal authority is competent for the rights which protect human dignity and which provide benefit to persons living in poverty.[40] There are other framework competences within the same field linked to 'helping persons'and 'social assistance', namely regarding the policy for rules regulating the help granted to the disabled (Article 5 § 1 II 4 a SIRA) and help to the elderly (Article 5 § 1 II 5 SIRA).

The minimum and maximum competences are a variant of the framework competences. The federal authority establishes the minimum conditions for attaining diplomas following Article 127 of the Constitution.[41] The federal authority is also competent to set the maximum for assistance granted to enterprises (Article 6 § 1 4 e (4) SIRA).[42]

The recent SASRS paradoxically increases the number of framework competences. Communities can regulate the 'accreditations' in the area of health professions but this regulation must be enacted 'in accordance with the conditions of accreditation set by the federal authority'.[43] In the same area, communities can fix quotas to access professions in the health sector, but 'in accordance, where required, with the overall number that the federal authority can fix annually'.[44] The *maisons de justice* (Justice Centres) were brought back within the aegis of the communities' power but the federal authority 'determines their mission' in some cases.[45] The most illuminating case of framework competences relates to the policies for getting the unemployed back into work. The regions receive 'the power of decision and execution in the control of active and passive availability of the unemployed and of the imposition of penalties related thereto' but the federal authority retains the power related to the 'regulatory framework regarding the regulation of adequate employment,

[38] See M Lys, 'Les droits constitutionnels des étrangers', in M Verdussen and N Bonbled, *Les droits constitutionnels en Belgique. Les enseignements jurisprudentiels de la Cour constitutionnelle, du Conseil d'État et de la Cour de cassation* (vol II, Bruylant 2011) 607–34. See also: Uyttendaele (n 14) 946; Vanpraet (n 15) 386.

[39] Opinion 29.847/1, 9 March 2000, PDCR, session 1999–2000; Opinion 50–462/2.

[40] CSLS No 51/1849/002.

[41] See also CC case 44/2005, 23 February 2005.

[42] CC case 2/2006, 11 January 2006, B.4.3. See Vanpraet (n 15) 64–70.

[43] Article 5 § 1 I 7 a SIRA, as replaced by SASRS.

[44] ibid, as replaced by SASRS.

[45] Article 5 § 1 III SIRA, as amended by SASRS.

of active search for work, administrative controls and sanctions, as well as for the implementation of sanctions, without prejudice to the federal jurisdiction'.[46] In the area of road safety, where a matter is brought by the Sixth Reform within a regions' remit, those regions also 'received the power' to 'control the respect of federal technical prescriptions for vehicles in order to be placed in traffic' and to 'control on the technical level [. . .] vehicles on the road in accordance with federal standards'.[47]

Competences of 'execution' are a variant of 'framework competence'. They share the idea that an entity will have to respect the rules or the framework set by another entity. An 'executive competence' is established when one entity is granted the power to execute a rule which was adopted by another entity.[48] The rule adopted by the federal level does not usually settle the essential aspects of the policy: on the contrary, the responsibility to elaborate the detail of the policy is in the hands of the 'executive' entity. In some cases, however, the entities which receive the competence to execute federal norms do not necessarily have substantial decisions to make.[49]

A first example of executive competence is provided by Article 6 §1 IV 3 SIRA, which establishes executive competences for the regions in the field of the employment of alien workers. The federal authority remains competent to set the conditions of employment of alien workers whereas the regions are only able to execute federal norms.[50] A second example, related to the control of the genuine respect for compulsory schooling, is the communities' execution competence under Article 127 § 1 2 a of the Constitution.[51] A third example concerns electoral expenses. The Parliaments of the federate entities are bound to pursue sanctions in application of the federal law regarding the limitation of electoral expenses, pursuant to Article 31 § 5 SIRA with federal law limiting itself to settling the funding limits.

c. Enforcement of federal law by 'intrusion' into communities and regions' competence through the 'implied powers' technique

The third type of competence which assumes a kind of interaction between federal competences and communities and the region's competences are *the implicit competences* (*implied powers*). The basis for implicit competences is provided by Article 10 SIRA. According to this Article, a decree or an ordinance can contain provisions in a matter for which the regions or the communities are not competent, being a matter under federal jurisdiction. There are three conditions for this to be done: the provisions enacted should be considered necessary for the exercise of the powers of the region or the community; the matter should lend itself to a differentiated regime; and the impact of the provisions at issue should only be marginal. Those '*ancillary competences*' create room for an intrusion of the communities' and region's actions into the federal competences.

Article 10 also paves the way towards federal interventions within the sphere of the communities' and regions' competences. Despite the wording of Article 10 SIRA, and certainly because implied powers function as a general principle of Belgian law,[52] the Constitutional Court has recognized the possibility for the federal authority to claim

[46] Article 6 § 1 IX 5 SIRA, as amended by SASRS.
[47] Article 6 § 1 XII 4 SIRA, as modified by SASRS.
[48] See Vande Lanotte and Goedertier (n 31) 1036.
[49] Vanpraet (n 15) 71, No 79.
[50] It is noteworthy that the control of these norms is however a parallel competence (shared by officials of regions and of the federal entity).
[51] See CC case 109/2009, 9 July 2007, B.8.
[52] Vanpraet (n 15) 118.

implied powers and thereby to take laws containing provisions in matters for which it has no competence as long as it respects the three conditions mentioned above.[53]

d. Concluding thoughts on the enforcement of federal law by federate entities

To conclude on the corrective mechanisms to the principles of exclusivity and equality, we can see that some mechanisms of distribution of powers require the enforcement of federal law by federate entities. The Constitutional Court is competent to control the respect for this enforcement by the legislator and to sanction breaches in this respect, given that the respect for the distribution of powers is one of its core competences.

However, the driving forces behind Belgian federalism remain reluctant to acknowledge the superiority of federal law over federate entities and to recognize any kind of hierarchy between the federal and the federate entities. For this reason the legal mechanisms by which federal law is enforced in other federal systems have not really been developed in Belgian constitutional law, even in those cases where such enforcement is perceived as being necessary, or is clearly more accurate in the light of the subsidiarity principle. As a result, Belgian federal law does not contain a clear theory or a general framework relating to the problem of enforcement of federal law against federate entities; it has rather developed a case-by-case approach, by trial and error, a permanent tinkering of unelaborated legal mechanisms which concur to deal with the enforcement of federal law. This situation is likely to pave the way for expressions of defiance, because of the underdevelopment of the rule of conflict which they postulate. This situation is thereby also likely to make the enforcement of federal law more complex.

3. Cooperation with the federal authority and the issue of obstruction

The exclusivity principle is also in Belgium somewhat tempered by the conclusion of cooperative agreements. Federate entities, although exclusively competent in some fields, and sometimes have to conclude cooperative agreements in order to coordinate their actions and policies. A cooperation agreement between the federal entity and one or several regions or communities can undoubtedly be a way to guarantee the implementation of some aspects of federal politics. For this reason, cooperative federalism entails a risk of the federate entities' defiance of federal law when federate units decide to obstruct the development or the enforcement of the cooperative agreements, while those agreements remain necessary for federal law to be implemented. The question of the enforcement of federal law—more specifically cooperative agreements involving the federal level—then becomes crucial.

The cooperation between the constituent units in Belgium is institutionalized and exceptionally formal.[54] The SIRA contains a chapter entitled 'Cooperation between the State, communities and regions'. Much could be said about this cooperation. Suffice it to say here that the federal entity and the federate entities are able, and sometimes obliged, to conclude cooperation agreements whose legal nature is equivalent to legal norms adopted by legislature, when ratified by the latter legislatures. As a rule, the conclusion of a cooperation agreement is optional: it is left to each entity to sign such an agreement in its own field of competences. However, for some matters, such as transport and

[53] See notably, CC case 166/2004, 17 December 2003, B.3.6.

[54] See J Poirier, 'Formal Mechanisms of Intergovernmental Relations in Belgium' (2002) 12 *Regional and Federal Studies* 24.

waterworks, the federal entity, the regions, or the communities—as the case may be—must sign a cooperation agreement. The SASRS emphasizes more clearly the mandatory character of the cooperation agreements in a range of areas.[55]

4. Judicial control of the enforcement of federal law and its limits

Where a cooperative agreement is not respected, or when federal law is not enforced although it should be the Constitutional Court appears as the guarantor of the supremacy exceptionally recognized in the Belgian constitutional system, and thus as the guarantor of the enforcement of federal law when required. If federate entities adopt rules which defy federal law and do no respect its supremacy where that supremacy is established, the Constitutional Court can repeal those rules for infringing the distribution of power system.

Before analysing the competence of the Court in cases federate entities' defiance of federal law, it is interesting to note here that the Court is composed of six Dutch-speaking judges and six French-speaking ones.[56] The institutionalization of bipolarity in the composition of the Constitutional Court implies that by reflecting the major political trends, it currently includes judges linked to the nationalist parties who are not known for being fond of the federal level.

a. Competence of the Court to sanction defiance of the distribution of powers and to enforce federal law

Because of its transformation from a unitary state to a federal state, Belgium was in need of an arbiter in charge of supervising the observance of the constitutional distribution of powers between the federal legislator and the legislators of the regions and the communities. That is why the Constitutional Court was created. It has exclusive jurisdiction to review regulations with force of law—and only those—for compliance with the constitutional rules governing the allocation of powers to the federal authority, the regions, and the communities.[57] It would thereby intervene in cases of violation of the rules described in the second part, where the enforcement of federal law is organized through asymmetrical distribution of powers. It also remains competent to ensure the correct implementation of political controls organized in favour of the federal authorities.[58]

The Constitutional Court is thus responsible for the overall respect of the distribution of power. It is the jurisdiction competent to sanction defiance by federate units of federal law and to enforce the Constitution and federal law when necessary. Because of the incoherencies and the incompleteness of the Belgian system of distribution of powers,

[55] See Article 92*bis* § 3, § 4*bis*, § 4*ter*, § 4*quarter*, § 4*sexies*, § 4*septies*, § 4*nonies*, § 4*decies*, § 4*undecies* as revised by SASRS. See for a broader analysis of the evolutions of cooperation: E Vandenbossche (ed), *Evoluties in het Belgisch coöperatief federalisme/Evolutions dans le fédéralisme coopératif belge* (Die Keure/La Charte 2013).

[56] Articles 31 and 34 §2 (2) Special Act of 6 January 1989. See more broadly on the composition of the Constitutional Court of Belgium, M Verdussen, *Justice constitutionnelle* (Larcier 2012) 139–56.

[57] On the case law of the Constitutional Court regarding the allocation of powers, see S Feyen, *Beyond Federal Dogmatics—The Influence of EU Law on Belgian Constitutional Case-Law Regarding Federalism* (Leuven University Press 2013) 87–183.

[58] See on Article 11 (2) (assent of the Federal Council of Ministers for new penalties): CC case 41/2010, 29 April 2010, B.8.-B.11.2 (the request for assent was not addressed to the Council); case 127/2000, 6 December 2000 (the Court, while arguing that the assent is a rule distributing powers, considered that in this matter the assent was not required); case 213/2004, 21 December 2004 (a conforming assent was granted by the Council of Ministers); case 41/2010, 29 April 2010 (a request for conforming assent was not addressed to the Council). No cases have been reported on Articles 45 and 46 of the Special Brussels Institutions Act of 1989, or on Article 169 of the Constitution.

Belgian judges are forced into actively participating in the elaboration of this system. This is why they feel the need to create new cases of asymmetrical distribution of powers. Indeed, as we have seen, they sometimes elaborate concurrent competences and they 'discover' implied powers or executive powers. This is also the reason for judgments where the Court created obligations to conclude such cooperation agreements, even if this obligation does not exist in the Constitution and special-majority laws.

However, an analysis of the case law of the Constitutional Court, whose creative character is required somewhat by the deficiencies of the distribution of powers system, shows that this case law does not automatically favour the federal level. Vanpraet argues especially that the constitutional case law (in particular of the Constitutional Court) qualifies quite strongly the principle of exclusivity thanks to a broad diffusion within the case law of the 'double aspect' doctrine (*dubbelaspectleer*) (which is broadly recognized in Canadian federal law). This doctrine, theorized by Vanpraet, means that 'two federal or federate entities are equally competent on the basis of two different competence titles and without that one entity exceeds its power'.[59] The double aspect doctrine would be implicitly acknowledged by the Constitutional Court when it invokes the idea of a 'parallel exercise of exclusive powers'. The promotion of this 'double aspect' doctrine would be a 'latent state reform' which, in addition to the formal state reform, is said to be constantly reshaping the competences of each entity. Application of the double aspect doctrine will sometimes favour the federal entity to act within the sphere of competence of federate entities, but usually it favours the strongest entities at the political and economic level, which are in Belgian constitutional law the federate entities.[60] Moreover, the application of this doctrine will, within the Belgian context, almost automatically lead to conflicts of norms, which appear to be almost inherent to every systems of distribution of powers[61] whose conflicts restate the question of the hierarchy of norms and of the efficiency of the conflict settlement procedures. Furthermore, a broader implementation of this doctrine will almost automatically create gaps in the protection of vulnerable persons or overlaps in the establishment of social security protections as well as a great legal uncertainty about the competences of each community. However, the Constitutional Court seems to have rejected the application of the 'double aspect' doctrine in a case on the funding of nurseries by the Brussels Capital region.[62]

b. Competence of the Court in cooperative agreements

The cooperative agreements are part of the norms on the basis of which constitutional review is operated. The Constitutional Court considers itself as having the competence to review the constitutionality of the rules ratifying cooperative agreements.[63] However, it is not clear whether the Constitutional Court also has the power to ensure the implementation of the cooperation agreements. Should the Constitutional Court declare a law, a decree or an ordinance unconstitutional which does not respect a previously concluded cooperation agreement? Is the Constitutional Court competent to enforce the implementation of a cooperation agreement which guarantees the implementation of some aspects of federal policies against the federate entities' legislation, or to sanction a federate unit

[59] See Vanpraet (n 15) 545. [60] ibid, 168. [61] Verdussen (n 2) 7.

[62] See CC case 67/2012, 24 May 2012. In this case, the Constitutional Court did not address the 'double aspect' doctrine explicitly. However, it rejected the arguments of the Brussels Capital region, regarding the exclusivity principle.

[63] CC case 17/94, 3 March 1994, B.1.; and P Coenraets, 'Réflexions sur le contrôle de constitutionnalité des accords de coopération"' (1995) 19 *Administration Publique Trimestrielle* 219.

which persistently obstructs the conclusion or the enforcement of a cooperative agreement? The case law has not yet answered this question, leaving great uncertainties regarding the legal status of cooperation agreements in Belgian constitutional law.[64]

Recently, the Constitutional Court received the jurisdiction to ensure the correct application of the principle of federal loyalty provided by Article 143 of the Constitution, which provides that '[i]n the exercise of their respective responsibilities, the federal authority, the communities and the regions act with respect for federal loyalty, in order to prevent conflicts of interest'. According to the Constitutional Court, this obligation implies 'the obligation to not disturb the balance of the federal building as a whole, when they exercise their powers; it affects more than the simple exercise of powers: it provides a mind-set within which this exercise must be done'.[65] Only time will tell if the Constitutional Court will apply this constitutional principle to declare unconstitutional a law, a decree, or an ordinance which infringes a cooperation agreement.

5. Enforcement of federal law in case of defiance of the decisions of the Constitutional Court

This last part explores the hypothetical scenario where a federate entity defiance of federal law is not stopped by a decision of the Constitutional Court repealing an act by the federate entity which is incompatible with federal law. This scenario encompasses cases where a federate entity fails to respect the Constitutional Court's finding of a violation of the Constitution detrimental to the federal level, by persisting in the application of, or re-enacting the act repealed by the Court.

In such a case, Article 20 of the Special Act of 6 January 1989 on the Constitutional Court provides that suspension may be ordered 'if an appeal has been lodged against a rule which is identical or similar to a rule already nullified by the Constitutional Court and which has been adopted by the same legislative body'. According to the Constitutional Court, this mechanism intends to guarantee 'that the disregarded authority of a judgment of the Constitutional Court could be immediately restored in the case when a legislature, seeing one of its norms repealed, adopts an identical new one'.[66] The measure is quite radical in the sense that the federate rule will be suspended immediately—as soon as the action for suspension is brought before the Court—and then repealed.

We can, however, elaborate on the exceptional circumstances in which defiance could be brought to a higher level. In those situations, a federate entity would flagrantly disregard the authority of the Constitutional Court's judgments. This could happen if the federate entity persists in giving effect to a rule repealed or suspended by the Court, or by endlessly adopting fresh rules of equal or equivalent effect to the repealed one, for instance.

The proceedings preventing and regulating *conflits d'intérêt* could be of interest here. Strictly speaking, conflict of interests proceeding cannot be used for conflicts of competences. However, in our scenario, if the initial problem was indeed a conflict of

[64] See J Poirier, 'Le droit public survivra-t-il à sa contractualisation ? – Le cas des accords de coopération dans le système fédéral belge' (2006) 33 *Revue de Droit de l'ULB* 287; P Dermine, 'Le Traité de stabilité, de coordination et de gouvernance et l'internalisation de la *Golden Rule* par les États membres de l'Union européenne', text presented at the International Conference of the International Association of Constitutional Law, Oslo, June 2014.

[65] See for instance, CC case 7/2012, 11 January 2012, B.11.1.

[66] CC case 67/96, 28 November 1996, B.4. The Court moreover specifies that in such cases the demand must not show that there are serious grounds or that there is a risk of a serious harm which would be difficult to repair. See also cases 6/91, 12/91, 15/92, 55/93, 68/93, 15/96, 67/96, 134/2000, 38/2001, 96/2004, 9/2006, 100/2006, and 156/2006.

competences, it can be said that the federate entity's defiance of the Constitutional Court's judgment transforms it into an act injurious of the interests of the federal entity in having the federate entities respect its competences and, in some case, the interests of the federal entity in having its law enforced over federate entities. In the case of a conflict between the federal legislature and a federate one, the *Comité de concertation* has the final word.

However, here it must be underlined that once we confront a situation in which federate entities decide to transgress the authority of the Constitutional Court, and thereby of an element of the superstructure organizing the Belgian Federal State, we in fact find ourselves in a '*crise de regime*'.

6. Conclusion

According to the principles of exclusivity, equality, and equipollence between all legislative acts of the federal and federate entities, federal law should be enforced only by federal institutions, within the spheres of exclusive federal competences, and with federal budgets.

In the—allegedly—exceptional cases of concurrent and framework competences, federal law is however considered as superior to federate laws. In those cases, federal law has to be enforced by federate entities. The legal means through which this enforcement is effected are usually not completely definite. The same is true for cooperative agreements. While cooperation is often needed, the issue of obstruction of cooperation processes is not resolved. More generally, uncertainties persist because the distribution of powers is subjected to permanent constitutional tinkering driven by the political world and centrifugal forces, but also by the judges and their 'latent state reform'; even if we have seen that the maintenance of this double aspect doctrine is doubtful in light of the most recent case law of the Constitutional Court.

This chapter shows that against all expectations, there are many mechanisms in Belgian constitutional law which provide room for the enforcement of federal law by federate entities. Moreover, this chapter points out that there is a strong review of these mechanisms (except for cooperative agreements): the Constitutional Court is responsible for dealing with the enforcement of federal law against federate entities and the overall respect of the distribution of powers. It has a quite a radical tool to impose its decisions on recalcitrant federate units: it can suspend the effect of acts which are materially identical to acts previously repealed by the Court.

Belgian constitutional law thus provides for mechanisms which assume the supremacy of federal laws in the interests of efficiency, coherence, or federal loyalty. However, as we have seen, those mechanisms are not properly taken into account or implemented in reality, and suffer—or may suffer—from obstruction by the federate entities. As regards the case law of the Constitutional Court, the composition of the Court and the latent state reform it has proved willing to pursue do not always tend to make the enforcement of federal law against federate entities a priority.

The reason for this difference between constitutional law in action and the constitutional law in books is the weakening of the federal level through centrifugal forces found especially among political elites and which exploit the widespread institutionalization of bipolarity in Belgium. The political weakness of the federal level is nurtured by—and in turn nurtures—this widespread institutionalization of bipolarity. National political parties have become divided into regional political parties. As a result, they have strengthened their regional agendas at the expense of the national ones. The absence of national political parties and of a federal electoral district and the actual organization of elections (which follow the regional borders) explain why parliamentary representatives in the federal

Parliament only feel accountable to 'their' French-speaking or Dutch-speaking voters. The institutionalization of bipolarity is also manifest in the federal institutions. The composition and organization of the latter follow the lines of linguistic bipolarity. The 150 members of the federal Chamber of Representatives are distributed into two 'linguistic groups'. The Senate was and is still partly organized on the basis of linguistic and communitarian affiliations. The Council of Ministers is a joint body. Parity between French speakers and Dutch speakers must be respected in the composition of the *Comité de concertation*, of the *Conseil supérieur de la justice* and of the Constitutional Court. Regarding the public sphere, it is also clearly delimited along linguistic lines as, since 1970, the Communities are exclusively competent for media matters: there is no such thing as a federal public sphere in the Belgium federal system. This institutionalized polarization of political life and of the public sphere is major source of distrust of the federal level and of the weakening of this level. The institutionalization of Belgian bipolarity is also evident in the educational system (which is shaped by Communities on the basis of their exclusive competence). As a result, there is no bilingual education system and language education falls within the remit of the communities, which define themselves by reference to a single language.

This is perhaps the great lesson of Belgian federalism at the political level—there being few more structural lessons to learn from this very contingent and haphazard Belgian federalism: the wide institutionalization of bipolarity, structurally weakening the federal level, is a major source of instability for a federal system where 'no democracy can function, it seems, without enough people from all corners of the demos being capable of talking to each other'.[67] Nonetheless, the complex structures of Belgian federalism, which rest on dialogue and compromises, usually function efficiently. However, their future is mortgaged to the risk of deadlocks arising from the sudden and/or radical exacerbation of the institutionalized bipolarity or from the slow-acting obstruction it engenders. This risk is obviously higher in the present context of great political asymmetry—each layer having its own specific government not shared by any other layer.

[67] P Van Parijs, 'On linguistic territoriality and Belgium's linguistic future', in Popelier et al., *Belgium: Quo Vadis?* (n 27) 60.

17

Regional Defiance and Enforcement of Federal Law in Spain

The Claims for Sovereignty in the Basque Country and Catalonia

Alberto López-Basaguren

1. Introduction: regional defiance of federal law in Spain

The primacy of federal law has been guaranteed in Spain without any difficulties. There have been, however, significant episodes whose analysis offers an ideal opportunity to consider the resources available to the Spanish constitutional system in order to impose compliance with federal law. Moreover, it is necessary to analyse other constitutional tools, as last resorts for guaranteeing the unity of the legal system which have not yet been employed but which may be used in the future.

The first issue is the so-called 'Ibarretxe plan'. It initially consisted of the proposal for a 'New Political Statute' for the Basque Country (Ibarretxe plan I), which was rejected by the Lower House of the Spanish Parliament.[1] The second phase of the plan took the form of passing an Act which regulated the holding of a 'consultation' in order to decide the political future of the Basque Country (Ibarretxe plan II).[2]

The second great political challenge concerns the Catalan Parliament's claim to the 'right to decide': a demand for a referendum in which Catalan citizens could decide their political future. This demand began to take shape in the wake of the failure of the fundamental claims for the amendment of the Statute of Catalonia (SAC, 2006), and came to a sudden end with the Constitutional Court's ruling of June 28, which decided on its constitutionality.[3]

[1] The Lower House of Parliament in the plenary session of 1 February 2005, after debate, refused to proceed with the Proposal for a new Political Statute for the Basque Country with 344 votes against, 29 votes for, and 2 abstentions.

[2] Act (Basque Country) 9/2008 of 27 June, on the call for a popular consultation of public opinion in the Autonomous Community of the Basque Country regarding the opening of a negotiation process to achieve peace and political normalization. Regarding the 'Ibarretxe Plan', see A López-Basaguren, 'The Parliament of the Basque Country and the National Issue: The Weaknesses of a Strong Identity' in G Laforest and A Lecours (eds), *The Parliaments of Autonomous Nations* (McGill-Queen's University Press 2016) 44–71.

[3] CCR 31/2010 of 28 June. See A López-Basaguren, 'Current issues around territorial autonomy in Spain' in A López-Basaguren and L Escajedo San Epifanio (eds), *The Ways of Federalism in Western Countries and the Horizons of Territorial Autonomy in Spain* (Springer 2013) 395–419. JM Castellà Andreu, 'Las consultas populares en la Sentencia 31/2010 sobre el Estatuto de Autonomía de Cataluña' in E Álvarez Conde and C Rosado Villaverde (eds), *Estudios sobre la Sentencia 31/2010, de 28 de junio, del Tribunal Constitucional sobre el Estatuto de autonomía de Cataluña* (IDP–Universidad Rey Juan Carlos 2011) 197–324. JM Castellà Andreu, 'Consultas populares no referendarias en Cataluña. ¿Es admisible constitucionalmente un *tertium genus* entre referéndum y e instituciones de participación ciudadana?', in *Monografías de la Revista Aragonesa de Administración Pública,* XIV (2013), 121–55. V Ferreres Comella, 'The Spanish Constitutional Court Confronts Catalonia's "Right to Decide" (Comment on the Judgment 42/2014)' (2014) 10 *European Constitutional Law Review* 571.

Regional Defiance and Enforcement of Federal Law in Spain: The Claims for Sovereignty in the Basque County and Catalonia. First Edition. Alberto López-Basaguren.

Immediately after the Constitutional Court's ruling, the Catalan government proposed a 'fiscal pact', which would guarantee financing of the devolved Catalan body in more favourable terms than those currently in force. The Spanish government rejected this proposal, which increased unrest, with the popular movement in favour of the 'right to decide' assuming an increasingly higher profile: its milestones being the demonstrations on successive bank holidays on 11 September,[4] culminating in the 'participatory process' of 9 November 2014 (9-N).

In the general policy debate in September 2012, Parliament issued a statement urging the government to call a 'consultation' so that 'the Catalan people might freely and democratically determine their collective future'.[5] Following lengthy negotiations between the parties supporting the 'right to decide', in December 2013 an agreement was reached to hold the 9-N 'consultation' and for the question to be put to the voters.[6]

The Catalan *Advisory Council for the National Transition* drew up a Report on the legal possibilities of holding such a 'consultation'.[7] According to these proposals, the Catalan Parliament first attempted to use a consultative referendum provided for in section 92 of the Spanish Constitution,[8] requesting the Spanish Parliament (16 January 2014)—under section 150(2) Constitution[9]—to delegate to the Catalan Parliament the power to authorize, call, and hold a referendum on the future of Catalonia. The request was rejected by the Lower House (8 April 2014). With this road closed, the Catalan Parliament completed the process of passing an Act on non-referendum consultations,[10] immediately proceeding to issue a Decree convening a consultation (Decree 129/2014 of 27 September). The Spanish government challenged both the Act and the Decree before the Constitutional Court, which were eventually annulled.

Once the 'consultation' had been annulled, the Catalan government declared that it was transforming the latter into a 'participatory process', maintaining however the call to participate in the vote on the same date set for the 'consultation', with the same questions and ballot as before: a strategy which the Catalan government adopted to avoid formal decisions and thus prevent—or at least impair—the government's legal recourse before the

[4] September 11 is the official—or national—holiday of Catalonia (*Diada*), in commemoration of the conquest of Barcelona in 1714 by Philip V's troops, in the last throes of the War of Succession (1701–1713). On his accession to the throne, Philip V issued the '*Nueva Planta*—New Settlement—Decrees' (1707–1716), which abolished the institutional arrangement of the various territories of the former Kingdom of Aragon, one of which was Catalonia (whilst those of the Basque Country and Navarra were maintained).

[5] See *Resolució 742/IX del Parlament de Catalunya, sobre l'orientació política general del Govern* (27 September 2012), in *Butlletí Oficial del Parlament de Catalunya* (2 October 2012) IX Legislature, n 390.

[6] A dual question was agreed upon: 1 'Do you wish Catalonia to be a State?' and 2 'Do you wish Catalonia to be an independent State?' Only people who voted 'Yes' to the first question could cast a vote on the second.

[7] JM Castellà Andreu, 'Secesión y referéndum sobre el "derecho a decidir" en Cataluña. Una aproximación desde el Derecho Constitucional', in J Oliver Araujo (ed): *El futuro territorial del Estado español. ¿Centralización, autonomía, federalismo, confederación o secesión?* (Tirant lo Blanch 2014) 451–90.

[8] Section 92 Constitution establishes that 'political decisions of particular significance may be submitted to all citizens in a consultative referendum' (1), which shall be called by the King, on the proposal of the President of the Government, following authorization by the Congress of Deputies (2); an organic law shall regulate the terms and procedures for the different kinds of referendum provided for in the Constitution (3).

[9] According to s 150(2) Constitution, the State can delegate or transfer—by means of an Organic Law—reserved powers to one or more territories, without amending the Statute of autonomy. The Organic Law is a special kind of Act which the Constitution requires to regulate specific matters (s 81(1)): to be passed it needs an absolute majority vote in the Lower Chamber on the full text (s 81(2)).

[10] Act (Catalonia) 10/2014 of 26 September, on non-referendum consultations and other ways of citizens' participation. The Council of Guarantees (*Consell de Garanties Estatutàries*) decided by five votes to four that the Bill was compatible with the SAC: see Opinion 19/2014, of August 19. The *Consell* is a 'consultative' body whose opinions are not binding (CCR 31/2010).

courts.[11] The Spanish government challenged this action before the Constitutional Court, which agreed to hear the appeal and suspended the 'participatory process'.[12] Despite that, the Catalan government maintained the 'participatory process'. Although it left its execution in the hands of volunteers, the Catalan government was at all times responsible for organizing the consultation, officially reporting its results.[13] Against this background, the *President* called early elections to the Parliament for 27 September 2015. He intended—along with the parties which supported independence—to confer upon these elections the significance of a 'plebiscite' in support of independence: if a majority was won in Parliament in support of independence, he would effect a Unilateral Declaration of Independence (UDI). The single candidature (*Junts pel sí—Together for yes*) led by A Mas failed both in its attempt to obtain a majority mandate[14] and to achieve a majority of votes in favour of independence;[15] however, in combination with the representatives obtained by the Candidacy of Popular Unity (CUP), an extremist left-wing pro-independence, guaranteed a parliamentary majority.[16]

The key questions in these two 'sovereignty'-related challenges lay in the legal design of the referendum, the capacity of the autonomous territories to establish, regulate, and hold referenda different from those specifically established in the Constitution and, alternatively, their capacity to create and regulate an instrument such as a 'consultation'—and to hold it—as a legal instrument different from a 'referendum' and consequently not limited by the constitutional provisions affecting the latter: most notably, the need for state authorization established in section 149(1)(32) Constitution.[17]

The third question is the one known as the 'Atutxa case', involving the former President of the Basque Parliament, which enables us to analyse the characteristics of criminal coercion in the event of non-compliance with Court decisions as a form of refusal to comply with federal law. This case is related to the application of the Political Parties Act—Organic Law 6/2002 of 27 June—and more specifically to the decision to declare the 'Batasuna' political party illegal, on account of its connection with the terrorist organization ETA.[18] In order to execute the ruling, by Order 4428/2003 of 24 April the Supreme Court

[11] *President* Mas, Catalan *First Minister*, declared that the key lay in 'deceiving the State': see the newspaper *El Periódico* 26 October 2014.

[12] Constitutional Court Resolution 6540 of 4 November 2014.

[13] According to data provided by the Catalan government, 6,228,531 people were eligible to participate; 2,344,828 people cast the vote—approximately 37.6 per cent of the 'census'—1,897,274 of whom (80.9 per cent of the votes cast and 30.46 per cent of the 'census') voted in favour of Catalonia being an independent state, 234,848 voted in favour of Catalonia being a state but not independent, 22,755 voted in favour of Catalonia being a state but did not answer the second question, 105,245 voted against, 13,201 cast blank votes, and 71,505 votes were classified as 'others'.

[14] *Junts pel sí* (formed by *Convergencia* and *Esquerra Republicana*) obtained sixty-two seats (compared with the seventy-one they obtained when they stood separately in the 2012 elections), of a total of 135 seats that constitute the Parliament, an (absolute) majority therefore requiring 68 seats.

[15] The candidatures that supported the declaration of independence (*Junts pel sí* and CUP) obtained 1,966,508 votes, whilst those that opposed this declaration (*Ciutadans*, Partido Socialista, Partido Popular, *Catalunya si que es pot* and *Unió*) obtained 2,079,746 votes.

[16] CUP obtained ten MPs. but its demands forced the withdrawal of A Mas as candidate to the presidency of the government, and he was replaced by C Puigdemont. CUP has driven the process rapidly towards the 'disconnection' of Catalonia from Spain as a prerequisite to approving the Budget, as well as to supporting the government in the motion of confidence that has been debated in September (2016).

[17] Section 149(1)(32) Constitution establishes that 'authority to hold popular consultations by means of a referendum' is a state competence.

[18] 'Batasuna' was declared illegal by the Supreme Court Ruling 2133/2003 of 27 March. An appeal for the protection of fundamental rights against the Supreme Court's ruling was lodged before the Constitutional Court, which decided—in Rulings 5 and 6 of 16 January 2004—that the Supreme Court decision did not infringe the Constitution. A claim was lodged before the ECtHR, which ruled that Spain had not infringed the ECHR by illegalizing the party: Judgment of June 30, 2009 *Herri Batasuna and Batasuna v Spain* (App Nos 25803/04 and 25817/04).

required the chairs of the various parliamentary chambers in which the party had representatives to dissolve the relevant parliamentary groups. The Bureau of the Basque Parliament refused to do so, on the grounds that this was a competence of the Chamber and that the legal decision impinged on the dignity and autonomy inherent to legislative power and contravened the division of powers. This decision won majority support, with three of the five members of the Bureau voting in favour, including the Speaker, Mr Atutxa. Despite the Supreme Court's injunction that its decision be enforced, with a warning that the Bureau would otherwise commit criminal disobedience, the Bureau stood by its decision, with the support of the Committee of the Spokespersons of the Chamber.

The three Members of the Bureau who cast the vote against the Court's Injunction were judged before the High Court of Justice of the Basque Country and acquitted of the charges of disobedience, but they were later found guilty by the Supreme Court.[19]

Two types of instrument should be analysed along with the questions highlighted by these events. On the one hand, the compulsory enforcement provided in section 155 of the Constitution and on the other, the hypothetical existence of criminal liability arising from non-compliance with federal law, other than the crime of disobedience. It should be borne in mind in this respect that the Public Prosecutor and also some private individuals have already initiated criminal proceedings against the Catalan *President* and two members of his government to examine their responsibility for conducting the 9-N 'participatory process', despite it having been suspended by the Constitutional Court.

2. The scrutiny of regional activity by the courts

Statutes and regulations in the autonomous territories, as well as their administrative decisions, are subject only to the scrutiny of the courts, there being no control of a 'political' nature, neither *ex ante* nor *ex post*.

In this sense, the Constitution establishes (section 153) that the Constitutional Court controls the constitutionality of primary and secondary legislation in the autonomous territories as at a state level through two procedures: appeal of unconstitutionality (direct appeal) under section 161(1) (a), and question of unconstitutionality (request for a preliminary ruling) under section 163. Furthermore, the Constitutional Court is responsible for guaranteeing respect for the distribution of powers between the state and the autonomous territories, even when disputes arise from an administrative regulation or decision, which are resolved through the 'conflict of powers' (*devolved issue*) procedure—section 161(1)(c) Constitution. Meanwhile, the common Courts—with the Supreme Court at their apex—control the general legality of administrative regulations and decisions in the autonomous territories, just as they control similar regulations or acts at a state level.

a. Scrutiny by the Constitutional Court and the privilege of the suspension of the region's challenged act

The Constitutional Court's control of activity in the autonomous territories reveals a particularity of considerable practical significance: section 161(2) of the Constitution

[19] An appeal of annulment was lodged against the Ruling of the High Court of Justice of the Basque Country and the Supreme Court—Ruling 54/2008 of 8 April 8—sentenced Mr Atutxa to a six-month fine of EUR 100 per day and special disqualification from public employment or office for eighteen months, and the other two defendants to a four-month fine, of EUR 100 per day, and special disqualification from public employment or office for a year.

establishes that the state government 'may challenge before the Constitutional Court the provisions and resolutions adopted by the institutions of the Autonomous Communities', which if declared admissible results in 'the suspension of the provision or resolution appealed against'; the suspension must be ratified or lifted by the Constitutional Court within a maximum of five months.

Though prestigious scholars have offered differing interpretations as to the meaning of this provision,[20] there is virtual unanimity regarding the perplexity that it provokes. However, greater still is that provoked by the development of this provision in the OLCC (Organic Law on the Constitutional Court), as far as it formulates (section 76 ff.) a new appeals procedure before the Constitutional Court, with 'proper substance'.[21] In this way, a provision apparently intended exclusively to have a complementary effect on the procedures established in section 161(1) of the Constitution (appeal of unconstitutionality and conflict of powers),[22] has become a general route of appeal before the Constitutional Court against any provision or territorial action whatever its nature, with the effect of immediate suspension.[23]

Initially, the appeal route constructed by the OLCC on the basis of section 161(2) of the Constitution was very seldom used. However, it has been the route the government has systematically used in order to paralyse the actions of the institutions of the Basque Country and Catalonia in the two 'secessionist' processes under analysis here.

The government thus challenged before the Constitutional Court the decision of the Basque government to bring the Proposal for a political statute for the Basque Country to be debated in Parliament. The Constitutional Court dismissed the application for leave to appeal—consequently not resulting in the Proposal's suspension—given that under challenge were merely procedural decisions within the legislative process of amendment of the SBC.[24]

The Spanish government also challenged before the Constitutional Court using the same procedure, the Catalan Parliament's Declaration of sovereignty and of the Catalan people's

[20] F Rubio Llorente and M Aragón Reyes have argued from the beginning that the provision of s 161(2) Constitution should be linked to the 'conflict of powers' (*devolved issues*), as a result of which the suspension could only affect administrative regulations and acts subject to challenge via this procedure; see their 'La Jurisdicción constitucional', in A Predieri and E García de Enterría (eds), *La Constitución española de 1978. Un estudio sistemático* (Civitas 1981) 881–2. Meanwhile, S Muñoz Machado (*Derecho Público de las Comunidades Autónomas* (2nd edn, Iustel 2007) vol II 355 ff. considers that its insertion as the second paragraph of s 161 Constitution, in relation to s 153 Constitution, would lead to a limitation of its effects on appeals regarding the unconstitutionality of primary and secondary legislation. On the academic controversy with regard to this question and the initial jurisprudence of the Constitutional Court, see G Fernández Farreres, 'La impugnación prevista en el artículo 161.2. de la Constitución y el problema de su sustantividad procesal (A propósito de las Sentencias del Tribunal Constitucional 54/1982, de 26 de julio y 16/1984, de 16 de febrero)' (1985) 13 *Revista Española de Derecho Constitucional* 125, 125 ff.

[21] CCR 64/1990 of 5 April. E García de Enterría ('La posición jurídica del Tribunal Constitucional en el sistema español: posibilidades y perspectivas' (1981) 1 *Revista Española de Derecho Constitucional* 35, 63 ff.) justified this development, although he restricted it to questions related to the constitutional limits of territorial autonomy. The Constitutional Court has stated (Decision 415/1989, of July 18) that the suspension 'is a procedural privilege established for the benefit of the government of the nation, which is an exception to the general principle regarding the validity and effectiveness of legal provisions and, due to this privileged and exceptional nature, ratification of the suspension by this Court needs to be justified by the complete or near irreparability of the damage that may be suffered by public or private interests affected as a consequence of its being lifted'.

[22] Even so, this would not have prevented it having negative effects upon the territorial Acts which, for this reason, have been described as 'weakened Acts': R Jiménez Asensio, *La Ley autonómica en el sistema constitucional de fuentes del Derecho* (Marcial Pons 2001) 92 ff.

[23] M Aragón Reyes, 'Artículo 161. Competencias del Tribunal Constitucional' in Ó Alzaga Villaamil (ed), *Comentarios a la Constitución española de 1978* (Edersa 1999) 189–253, 251.

[24] Decision 135/2004 of 20 April. See S Acierno and J Baquero Cruz, 'The Order of the Spanish Constitutional Court on the Proposal to convert the Basque Country into a freely associated community: keeping hands off constitutional politics' (2005) 3 *International Journal of Constitutional Law* 687.

right to decide,[25] a declaration in which it stated that the Catalan people constituted a sovereign political and legal subject and agreed to initiate the process to put into practice the democratic right to decide Catalonia's political future democratically. The challenge was unique in some respects, in that this was a declaratory act of purely political nature by a representative parliamentary chamber. The question arose whether the Constitutional Court could exercise control of the constitutionality of a Statement of this nature.[26]

In its ruling 42/2014 of 25 March the Constitutional Court declared that the Parliamentary Declaration was ideally suited to challenge, insofar as it had legal consequences since, firstly, it could be interpreted as 'acknowledgement in favour of those called upon to carry out the (pro-sovereignty) process' and, secondly, because 'by agreeing to initiate the process to put into practice the right to decide, it requires the execution of specific actions'. With regard to the Statement's content, it indicated that the declaration that Catalonia is a sovereign subject is incompatible with section 2 of the Constitution, from which it follows that an autonomous territory cannot unilaterally call a referendum of self-determination.[27]

However, after this statement, the Constitutional Court proceeded to elucidate on the 'right to decide', which it regarded as conforming to the Constitution, insofar as it is solely—a 'political aspiration attainable only via a process in accordance with constitutional legality with respect to the principles of "democratic legitimacy", "pluralism", and "legality", specifically proclaimed in the Declaration'. According to the Constitutional Court, to the extent that the Constitution does not impose a militant democracy and permits its total reform, in such a way that 'the primacy of the Constitution should not be confused with a demand for positive adhesion to a fundamental law', there is a place for 'conceptions which seek to modify the very foundations of the constitutional order', provided this is carried out via the amendment procedures established in the Constitution and respecting constitutional principles.

These considerations by the Constitutional Court were interpreted by the advocates of the 'right to decide' as support for the legitimacy of their actions and more specifically, as an endorsement of the legitimacy of the staging of the 'consultation' of 9 November.[28] But this was contradicted by the rulings which declared the unconstitutionality of the law on non-referenda consultations and the Decree calling for the consultation.

[25] *Resolució 5/X* of 23 January 2013 (*Butlletí Oficial del Parlament de Catalunya,* X Legislature, n 13, 24.01.2013). Having been deemed admissible, the statement was suspended (Decision of 7 May 2013, ratified by Constitutional Court Decision 156/2013 on 11 July).

[26] An analysis regarding the debate in this process, criticizing the decision to agree to hear the appeal, in E Fossas Espadaler, 'Interpretar la política. Comentario a la STC 42/2014, de 25 de marzo, sobre la Declaración de soberanía y el derecho a decidir del pueblo de Cataluña' (2014) 101 *Revista Española de Derecho Constitucional* 273, 280 ff. and 295 ff. On this Constitutional Court ruling, see also, Ferreres Comella (n 3); JJ Solozábal Echavarría, 'La sentencia sobre la declaración soberanista y el derecho a decidir del pueblo catalán (STC 42/ 2014)' (2015) 50 *El Cronista del Estado Social y Democrático de Derecho* 46, meanwhile, does consider this to be a Statement that can be challenged.

[27] The Constitutional Court went on to state that: 'This conclusion is similar to that formulated by the Supreme Court of Canada in its declaration of August 20, 1998, in which it denied the compatibility of a unilateral Project for secession by one of its provinces with either its Constitution or the tenets of international law'. Brief mention of the *Reference on Quebec Secession* which might lead to error as it mixes different issues: regional capacity to carry out a consultative referendum on sovereignty—which in Canada was not challenged but which is denied in Spain—and the effects of that manifestation of popular will, in order to impose a unilateral secession. Fossas Espadaler (n 26) 287 ff.) is positive in his evaluation of the mention of the Canadian *Reference*, but considers the quotation to be incorrect, as does, Ferreres Comella (n 3) 581.

[28] See the report on Constitutional Court ruling 42/2014 issued by the *Institut d'Estudis Autonòmics* (headed by Prof C Viver Pi-Sunyer): *Informe sobre la Sentencia del Tribunal Constitucional de 25 de marzo de 2014, relativa a la Resolución 5/X del Parlament de Catalunya, por la cual se aprueba la Declaración de soberanía y del derecho a decidir del pueblo de Catalunya*, of 1 April, 2014. Arguing against this opinion, JJ Solozábal Echavarria, 'La sentencia sobre la declaración soberanista y el derecho a decidir del pueblo catalán (STC 42/2014)' (2015) 50 *El Cronista del Estado Social y Democrático de Derecho* 46.

The phase initiated following the elections to the Catalan Parliament of September 2015 is evolving in accordance with the pressure exerted by the CUP on the government of C Puigdemont, who needs those votes to remain in power and approve the Budget. A phase characterized, so far, by taking steps in the direction of UDI, but postponing the decision to an undetermined moment in the future. It is difficult to know how successful this strategy will prove to be. In this sense, the Catalan Parliament passed (9 November 2015) a Resolution on 'the start of the political process as a consequence of the electoral results',[29] in which, considering there to be a majority of seats in favour of independence, it announced the initiation of a constituent process in Catalonia, in which the Parliament, as trustee of the sovereignty of Catalonia will proceed to pass the laws that will signify the 'disconnection' of Catalonia from Spain.

This Resolution was challenged before the Constitutional Court in accordance with the procedure under analysis in this paragraph, subsequently suspended, when admitted to be heard, and, finally, declared null and void by the Constitutional Court,[30] following the same line of interpretation already explained. The Catalan Parliament, however, passed a new Resolution via which it proceeded to create a Select Committee to study the constituent process[31], which was also challenged before the Constitutional Court and suspended, when admitted to be heard. The Constitutional Court[32] declared that it was not appropriate to declare the unconstitutionality of the creation of the Select Committee, insofar as the orientation of its work and its conclusions was not pre-determined, but established that what would be null and void, as contrary to the Constitution, was the activity of the Select Committee insofar as its work would mean non-compliance with the provisions of Constitutional Court Ruling (CCR) 259/2015, which annulled Resolution 5/XI, initiating the constituent process in Catalonia.

But the Parliament of Catalonia, obliged by the demands of the CUP, has passed a new Resolution,[33] ratifying the report submitted by the Select Committee on constituent process (referred to in the Constitutional Court's Procedural Decision—*Auto*—of July 19), affirming the legitimacy of Catalonia to initiate a constituent process, given that all the democratic channels via which to exercise the 'right to decide' are blocked in the Spanish constitutional system. It indicates that the constituent process will have three phases: the first, a participatory process; the second, the disconnection of Catalonia from the Spanish state, with the calling of constituent elections; and the third, popular ratification via referendum of the Catalan constitution. This Resolution has been challenged before the Constitutional Court, which has initiated the process of executing CCR 259/2015.[34] It should be borne in mind, in this sense, that, in the meantime, there has been reform of the Constitutional Court Act (Organic Law 15/2015, of October 15), attributing to the Constitutional Court coercive measures to guarantee the execution of its decisions, amongst which is the possibility of suspending the authorities that do not execute them or imposing on them different types of fines.

[29] *Resolució 1/XI* of 9 November 2015 (*Butlletí Oficial del Parlament de Catalunya*, XI Legislature n 7, 9.11.2015).

[30] CCR 259/2015, of 2 December.

[31] *Resolució 5/XI* of 20 January 2016 (*Butlletí Oficial del Parlament de Catalunya*, XI Legislature n 42, 25.01.2016).

[32] Constitutional Court's Procedural Decision (*Auto*) of 19 July 2016.

[33] *Resolució 263/XI* of 27 July 2016 (*Butlletí Oficial del Parlament de Catalunya*, XI Legislature n 200, 01.08.2016).

[34] Constitutional Court's Procedural Decision (*Providencia*), of 1 August 2016.

b. The unconstitutionality of the regional attempt to hold a 'consultation' on sovereignty

The Spanish government challenged before the Constitutional Court both the Basque consultation Act and the Catalan Acts of consultation via referendum and of non-referenda consultations, invoking section 161(2), as a result of which they were automatically suspended.

The Basque consultation Act (2008) specifically sought to avoid the word 'referendum'. The Basque Parliament attempted to create a 'consultation' which would not be a referendum insofar as it was not one of the *referenda* specifically established in the Constitution and was not legally binding, but merely consultative.[35]

The Constitutional Court (Ruling 103/2008) proceeded, firstly, to define what a referendum is, and to analyse, subsequently, whether what the Basque Act termed a 'consultation' was or was not a 'referendum'.[36] It indicated that a referendum is a form of direct participation in which the electorate is called to express its will with regard to a particular public issue with the guarantees applicable to the electoral process. The Constitutional Court found that the 'consultation' to which the Basque Act refers includes all the elements which define a 'referendum', and therefore is a 'referendum', despite being termed as a 'consultation'. This definition is not contradicted by its being consultative and non-binding. It is indisputable that in the Spanish constitutional system the only referendum of a general nature established is the consultative referendum regulated by section 92 of the Constitution. For all these reasons, the Constitutional Court concluded that the Basque Act was null and void, on the grounds of infringement of section 149(1)(32) Constitution.

The SAC—totally reformed in 2006—introduced a provision (section 122) entitled 'Popular consultations', which establishes the competence of Catalonia—'in the sphere of its powers'—to regulate and hold 'polls, public hearings, participation fora *and any other instrument of popular consultation, except as provided for in s 149(1)(32) of the Constitution*' (emphasis added).

The Catalan Act on popular consultations by referendum—Act 4/2010 of 17 March—sought to develop this new statutory provision, interpreting it as including referenda, though their convention would remain subject to authorization by the state. For this reason, it regulated the capacity of the Catalan institutions to hold a referendum with the aim of 'determining the will of the electorate with regard to political questions of special political significance with the appropriate guarantees of the electoral process' (section 3). The Catalan legislators' aim was not easy to defend: firstly, because the text of the SAC had specifically eschewed the term 'referendum' so as to permit sufficient consensus in the Congress of Deputies for its approval;[37] and secondly, because the instruments specifically referred to in the SAC—polls, public hearings, and participation fora—on one hand, and referenda, on the other, are of such different legal nature that it is not possible to accept that the former include the latter. It is not, in my opinion, that the SA could not incorporate

[35] A López-Basaguren, 'Sobre referéndum y Comunidades Autónomas. La ley vasca de la "consulta" ante el Tribunal Constitucional (Consideraciones con motivo de la STC 103/2008)' (2009) 9 *Revista d'Estudis Autonòmics i Federals* 202; C Aguado Renedo, 'Referéndum autonómico y jurisprudencia constitucional' (2011) 28 *Teoría y Realidad Constitucional* 541.

[36] CCR 103/2008, of 11 September.

[37] The SAC is an Organic Law of the state initiated by the political representatives of the territory (the Parliament, in this case) and which is the subject of negotiation in the Congress of Deputies (Lower House) between a group representing the latter and another from the territorial Parliament, which establishes the definitive text for approval by the Chambers and which is subsequently submitted to the territory's electorate in a referendum.

the referendum instrument in terms similar to those in which section 92 SAC does for the state: the drafting of this provision of the SAC explicitly avoided its inclusion in the context of a Constitution which views referenda with mistrust.[38] Nevertheless, the *Consell de Garanties Estatutàries* of Catalonia considered that the Act was compatible with the Constitution, on the basis of the constitutional provision for political participation, which led it to understand section 149(1) (32) of the Constitution as a provision permitting the holding of referenda by the autonomous territories, the sole condition thereto being the state's competence to authorize their call.[39]

The Constitutional Court (Ruling 31/2010, on the amendment of the SAC), when analysing the constitutionality of section 122 SAC, indicated that the exception referred to in section 149(1) (32) of the Constitution 'cannot be restricted to state authorization for the convening of popular consultations by means of referendum, but must extend to all features of that institution in other words, to its establishment and regulation'. The Catalan Act had been passed a few months before the Constitutional Court ruled on the new SAC. Following the latter, the Catalan legislators' interpretation appeared to have little chance of success.

In a similar vein, a large majority of scholars agree with this interpretation of the constitutional regulation of referenda,[40] although not all of them agree with all the aspects of the Constitutional Court's reasoning. This means in substance that most scholars agree with the opinion that the so-called 'consultations' are just an attempt to establish a referendum under a different name: something which territories do not have the power to do and under no circumstances without the state's authorization.[41] A different question is whether the state is confronting this claim correctly and what it should do.[42]

The Catalan Act on non-referendum popular consultations and other forms of civic participation (2014) followed the route taken by the Basque consultation Act but attempted to avoid the definition of referendum established by the Constitutional Court.[43] To that end, the people eligible to vote did not coincide exactly with those on the electoral register, as it included people aged 16 to 18, citizens of Member States of the EU with a year of continuous residence and other non-EU nationals with three years of continuous residence (section 5). In terms of formalities, a specific register of voters was created for popular

[38] A López-Basaguren, *Acerca de la caracterización del Estatuto de autonomía en una perspectiva federal* (Fundación Giménez Abad 2011).

[39] Opinion 3/2010 of 1 March.

[40] A Bueno Armijo, '"Consultas populares" y "referéndum consultivo": una propuesta de delimitación conceptual y de distribución competencial' (2008) 177 *Revista de Administración Pública* 195–228; A López-Basaguren (n 35); Aguado Renedo (n 35); E Seijas Villadangos, 'Referéndum y consultas populares en los nuevos Estatutos de autonomía', in Sáenz Royo and Contreras Casado (eds.): *La participación política directa: referéndum y consultas populares* (Comuniter 2013) 133–71; JM Castellà Andreu, 'Las consultas populares en la Sentencia 31/2010 sobre el Estatuto de Autonomía de Cataluña'; 'Consultas populares no referendarias en Cataluña' (n 4); JM Castellà Andreu, 'Secesión y referéndum sobre el "derecho a decidir" en Cataluña. Una aproximación desde el derecho constitucional' in Oliver Araujo (dir.) *El futuro territorial del estado español* (Tirant lo Blanc 2014) 451 ff.; E Martín Nuñez, 'The referendum and popular consultations in the Autonomous State' (2012) 4 *Perspectives on Federalism* 134.

[41] The legal defence of the constitutionality of the Catalan Act has mainly been expressed in the reports of the *Advisory Council for the National Transition* and of the *Institut d'estudis autonòmics*, both of which are headed by Prof Carles Viver Pi-Sunyer. Among scholars, see, in the same sense, J Vintró Castells, 'Legality and the referendum on independence in Catalonia' (23 October 2012) *Blog del Institut de Dret Públic*, and M Barceló Serramalera, 'Elements per una proposta de construcció jurídica del dret a decidir' in *Fòrum sobre el Dret a Decidir (II) Els drets de les minories. La construcció jurídica i política del dret a decidir* (Institut d'Estudis Autonòmics 2015) 77 ff. and 'No es un referéndum, es una consulta' (23 September 2014) *Agenda Pública*.

[42] F Rubio Llorente, 'Un referéndum para Cataluña' (8 October 2012) *El País*; A López Basaguren, 'Cataluña: e la nave va' (11 September 2013) and 'El síndrome de Walter Long' (1 July 2014) *El País*; J Tornos Más, 'El problema catalán: una solución razonable' (2014) 42 *El Cronista del Estado Social y Democrático de Derecho* 44.

[43] Castellà Andreu (n 3).

consultations—the objective being not to use the official census (section 6 ff.), as well as a procedure, an 'electoral administration', and a system of guarantees parallel to the official ones, so as not to attribute the competences of development and control of the process to the electoral administration of the official electoral processes (section 13 ff.).

A ruling was issued by the Constitutional Court, unanimously declaring the unconstitutionality of 'popular consultations of a general nature', and the constitutionality of popular consultations limited to a specific sector of citizens.[44] On the basis of the interpretation established in the Basque consultation Act[45] and in the reform of the SAC,[46] it regards 'general consultations' as unconstitutional and null and void as they constitute an actual referendum: they are directed at an electorate which is not distorted by the inclusion of under-18s and foreigners, and yield results which could be considered an expression of the will of the electorate. Their procedure, guarantees, and 'administration' are also of an electoral nature. A 'general consultation' is thus a referendum which fails to satisfy constitutional requirements and violates the powers of the state under section 149(1) (32) Constitution.

On the same date, the Constitutional Court issued a ruling on the Decree convening the consultation for 9 November based upon the provisions in the non-referendum consultations Act declared unconstitutional, thus rendering the call for consultation itself unconstitutional and null and void in similar fashion.[47]

Finally, the Constitutional Court issued a ruling on 15 June 2015 declaring the 'participatory process' held on 9 November 2014 unconstitutional and null and void. The Constitutional Court considered that it is not necessary in this case to analyse whether such a 'participatory process' is or is not a referendum insofar as section 122 SAC limits the capacity of the devolved body to hold any form of 'popular participation' in 'the sphere of its competences'. According to the Constitutional Court, a 'participatory process' is not within the sphere of powers of a devolved body when it refers to issues that 'were decided during the Constitution-making process and which are excluded from the remit of ordinary powers'. In which case, the proposal for an amendment to the Constitution has to be driven by the procedures actually established for this aim in the Constitution.

3. Compulsory enforcement on the regions: an extraordinary constitutional tool (yet to be used)

The Constitution incorporates an instrument of 'federal coercion' (section 155) taken directly from the German Constitution (section 37), but it does not have other forms of intervention found in other systems of territorial autonomy[48] such as the suspension of territorial autonomy, the dissolution of its institutions, or others which were specifically rejected in the constitutional debate.[49] Indeed, the Constitution does not expressly regulate other instruments typical of federal systems with a stronger tradition, such as state intervention within autonomous territories to defend the country against outside aggression or to guarantee peaceful internal coexistence in the style of Article IV section 4 of the US Constitution ('against invasion... [or] domestic violence') or of section 87a (4), in relation to section 91 of the *Grundgesetz* ('imminent danger to the existence or free

[44] CCR 31/2015 of 21 February. [45] CCR 103/2008 of 24 June. [46] CCR 31/2010 of 28 June.

[47] CCR 32/2015 of 21 February.

[48] E Vírgala Foruria, 'La coacción estatal del artículo 155 de la Constitución' (2005) 73 *Revista Española de Derecho Constitucional* 55, 58–9.

[49] X Ballart, *Coerció estatal i autonomies. Estudi de l'article 155 de la Constitució de 1978* (Escola d'Administració Pública de Catalunya 1987) 50 ff.

democratic basic order of the Federation or of a *Land*'). But it should be understood that the power attributed to the state in section 149(1)(29) Constitution—public security—includes these kinds of measures,[50] not to mention those which may be adopted in the event of circumstances justifying the instigation of states of emergency (states of, both, emergency and siege)—section 55(1) in relation to section 116 Constitution.

Section 155 Constitution establishes that when an autonomous territory does not fulfil the obligations imposed upon it by the Constitution or other laws, and acts in a manner which seriously prejudices the general interest of Spain, the government can call on the President of the territory to comply with that obligation. And in the event that this call is not heeded, with the approval of the absolute majority of the Senate, may take the necessary steps to demand 'forced compliance' with those obligations or for the protection of the aforementioned general interest.

Scholar literature, while highlighting the almost literal transposition of the German regulation, has underlined the differences between the Spanish regulation and its model. The first difference lies in the fact that the Constitution establishes that, along with non-fulfilment of the obligations imposed by the Constitution and the law (present in the *Grudgesetz*) there is a second reason which justifies recourse to federal coercion: acting in a manner which seriously prejudices the general interest of Spain. This distinction has a more apparent than real significance in the definition of the circumstances which might legitimize recourse to federal coercion. Initially, it was understood that this might mean unrestricted access to state intervention, with some scholars describing the instrument defined in section 155 Constitution, for this reason, as a 'full powers clause' or 'constitutional dictatorship'.[51] However, time has shown that the concept of 'general interest' must necessarily be understood within the pattern of the Constitution and the laws in which the Constitution's framers and the legislator had already decided how this 'general interest' should be defined.[52]

The second difference between the Spanish and the German Constitutions is to be found in the considerable difference between the Spanish Senate and the German *Bundesrat* with regard to their status as chambers of territorial representation. Although section 69(1) of the Constitution defines the Senate as such, the election of Senators is mostly carried out on a provincial basis, with a very limited number of members elected by the parliaments of the autonomous territories. That is why the significance of the Spanish Senate is radically different from that of the *Bundesrat* as guarantor of the rights and interests of the *Länder* in the application of constitutional provisions regarding federal coercion. The consequence of this is that two virtually identical provisions in terms of their formal drafting ultimately have in their practical application very different characteristics in the application of an extraordinary measure such as federal coercion.

Section 155 of the Constitution consequently supplies the government with a series of measures which grow progressively to guarantee that the authorities of the autonomous territory fulfil constitutional or legal obligations or cease to act in a manner which seriously prejudices the general interest. The first measure is simply a 'request' to the President of an autonomous territory to correct the action at issue: this is what is referred to as the

[50] Muñoz Machado (n 20) 601–2.

[51] P Cruz Villalón, 'La protección extraordinaria del Estado' in Predieri and García de Enterría (n 20) 687–717, 713–14.

[52] S Muñoz Machado, *Derecho Público de las Comunidades Autónomas* vol 1. (2nd edn, Iustel 2007) 595. This is what the Constitutional Court said in Ruling 42/1981 of 22 December, when it stated that the Constitution 'distinguishes between different levels of general interest, according to which the powers have to be conferred'.

'declarative stage'.[53] In the event of the 'request' not being heeded, the Constitution authorizes the government (following Senate authorization, by absolute majority) to adopt measures effecting the 'obligatory compliance', in the execution of which the government may instruct all the authorities in the autonomous territories directly: this is termed the 'enforcement phase'.[54] There is therefore scope for coercive compulsion which places the state in a 'position of superiority',[55] with the deterrent effect of criminal coercion: resistance would constitute criminal disobedience.

There is no doubt that the aim of section 155 Constitution is to guarantee the unity of the legal framework.[56] But there has been debate in scholarly literature over the *ordinary* or *extraordinary* character of federal coercion in Spain.[57] However, according to most scholars, the formality the requirements demanded, the precautions established in the Constitution, and the enormous political significance of recourse to federal coercion show the *extraordinary* character of these measures: a character which was highlighted in the constitutional debate and which has been confirmed in the functioning of the constitutional system since its foundation.[58]

From a political perspective the awareness of this extraordinary (indeed, absolutely extreme) character is generalized, as has been emphasized by the fact that it has never been used and its activation has not been contemplated, not even on the occasion of the challenge represented by the celebration of the 'consultation' of 9 November. There is no doubt that there is a belief that the ordinary means of control of the activity of the autonomous territories by the courts—and the criminal coercion inherent to non-compliance with their decisions—are sufficient to guarantee the rule of law. This does not mean that in the future (with regard to the Catalan claim for sovereignty, for example) its use may not be considered, but today it seems conceivable only in the event that the authorities of an autonomous territory defy clearly, expressly, and intransigently, the definitive resolutions of the highest courts (the Supreme Court and the Constitutional Court) in questions of great political significance.[59]

The fact that 'federal coercion' has not yet been used does not preclude its usefulness, because it would have a far from negligible preventive effect: an effect which, as has been noted,[60] should be its main function.

4. Refusal to comply with federal law and criminal liability

a. Refusal to comply with federal law and criminal disobedience

A consequence of the assignment to the courts of control of the activity of the autonomous territories is the obligation to comply with their resolutions. This idea is expressly

[53] E García de Enterría, *La ejecución autonómica de la legislación del Estado* (Civitas 1983) 167.

[54] García de Enterría (n 53) 167.

[55] CCR 4/1981 of 2 February.

[56] CCR 25/1981 of 2 July.

[57] García de Enterría (n 53) 163 ff., the great authority on Administrative Law in Spain, defended the normality of the instrument regulated in s 155 Constitution, attempting not to 'dramatize' how it was being interpreted and justifying its use in the field of monitoring of implementation of the law of the state by autonomous territories. He argued that s 155 Constitution is not based exclusively (contrary to what most scholars held) on s 37 *Grundgesetz*, but that it is an amalgam of the aforementioned section and s 84. Accordingly, federal coercion (*Bundeszwang*) and federal oversight (*Bundesaufsicht*) appear together in the same sections in the Spanish Constitution. In any case, this understanding has a decidedly minority following in the academic literature.

[58] In this sense, the Constitutional Court has said more than once that s 155 establishes an 'extraordinary tool': CCR 6/1982 of 22 February ('an extraordinary control'); CCR 49/1988 of 22 March ('an extraordinary means of obligation, not appropriate for the resolution of common matters'); CCR 215/2014 of 18 December ('a last reaction against a flagrant breach of obligations imposed by the Constitution').

[59] Vírgala Foruria (n 48).

[60] Ballart (n 49) 92.

reflected in section 118 Constitution. Public authorities and civil servants are particularly bound by this obligation, to the extent that non-compliance would involve criminal liability, as is reflected in the Penal Code (PC), which includes the crime of disobedience (section 410): a crime which is committed when a public authority or civil servant 'openly' refuses to comply with legal resolutions or the decisions or orders of a higher authority. The criminal disobedience carries a 'fine' of three to twelve months and special disqualification from public employment from six months to two years.[61]

According to the PC (section 24), a 'civil servant' is anybody who is officially appointed and exercises public functions. 'Authority', meanwhile, is any person or official body with the capacity to exercise public authority, executive or judicial, independently in a specific field: in other words, exercise a degree of coercive, not merely executive, power,[62] which excludes those who only give effect to a superior's power.[63] This is a broad definition, which attributes to the measures which may be adopted by the government under section 155 Constitution an extraordinary practical efficiency, as it refers to specific individuals who do not necessarily find themselves in the higher echelons of public powers. The requirement that the disobedience be manifested 'openly' means it must be clear and obvious, but does not prevent it from being purely passive or from consisting in creating obstacles or difficulties, which are the expression of a rebellious will.[64]

Regarding the crime of disobedience by non-compliance with court resolutions, the 'Atutxa case' is of considerable significance. The President and two members of the Bureau of the Basque Parliament were accused of the crime of disobedience for refusing to comply with the Supreme Court Order to dissolve the 'Batasuna' parliamentary group, as a result of its being declared an illegal party. The High Court of Justice of the Basque Country acquitted the three defendants (Ruling of 19 December 2006), on the understanding that they had not committed criminal disobedience because when warned that they might be committing this crime, they attempted to obey the Supreme Court's Order, through a House Speaker's Resolution which was however rejected by the Board of Spokespersons whose ratification was needed.

However, an appeal against this Ruling was lodged before the Supreme Court which convicted the defendants. The Supreme Court considered that there had been repeated delay in complying with the Court's Injunction. It describes the defendants' successive responses to the Supreme Court as 'a camouflaged rhetoric in the service of non-compliance'. The Supreme Court indicated that disobedience may be practised not only explicitly but also tacitly or by means of conclusive acts. It understands, in this sense, that the PC requirement that the disobedience occurs 'openly' does not exclude cases of 'reiterated and evident passivity over time without complying with the mandate'. It noted that the Basque Parliament Standing Orders already established (in section 20(3)) the possibility of members of the House ceasing to belong to a parliamentary group—enforcing their transfer to the 'mixed' group: a reason for which the loophole alleged by the defendants did not exist. Execution of the Court Injunction thus required no additional procedure. The Supreme Court denied that parliamentary autonomy can be a barrier

[61] According to s 50 PC, the 'fine' is a financial penalty which, normally, is imposed using the 'days-fine' system, with a duration of between ten days and two years, and a daily rate of between EUR 2 and 400.

[62] A Martínez Arrieta, 'Artículo 24' in C Conde-Pumpido Tourón et al. (eds), *Comentarios al Código Penal* (Bosch 2007) vol 1, 354.

[63] G Quintero Olivares, 'Artículo 24' in G Quintero Olivares (ed), *Comentarios al Código Penal* (5th edn, Thomson-Aranzadi 2008) vol 1, 387.

[64] A Martínez Arrieta, 'Artículo 410' in Conde-Pumpido Tourón et al. (n 62) vol 4, 3070 ff.

against the duty to comply with legal decisions because 'it would lead to unforeseen consequences alien to constitutional values'. In the opinion of the Supreme Court the defendants openly refused to comply with a judicial resolution, and therefore found criminal disobedience punishable under section 410 PC.

Those convicted submitted an appeal for protection before the Constitutional Court,[65] alleging that the Supreme Court's ruling violated their right to equality in the application of the law, the right to a fair trial and to the presumption of innocence. The Constitutional Court rejected their appeal, considering that the Supreme Court had not violated any of the fundamental rights referred to.[66] It considered that the right to equality had not been violated—due to the non-application of what is known as the 'Botín doctrine',[67] because the circumstances were not similar in both cases. Neither was there violation of the right to a fair trial because the ruling reached by the Supreme Court was not based upon facts different to those considered proven in the preceding ruling.[68]

Various criminal proceedings were brought before the High Court of Justice of Catalonia as a consequence of the holding of the 'consultation' of 9 November, against President Artur Mas and various members of his government, for having continued to perform acts directed towards the consultation's achievement subsequent to its suspension by the Constitutional Court. The High Court of Justice of Catalonia had partially agreed to hear these indictments, deciding to open preliminary proceedings in an attempt to determine whether criminal disobedience and abuse of office were committed.[69] Finally, the examining judge held that the then president and two members of his government may have committed crimes of gross disobedience and abuse of office, referred to, respectively, in sections 410(1) and 404 of the PC and eventually decided that a trial had to be heard.[70]

The manner in which the High Court of Justice of Catalonia—and the Supreme Court—resolved this question and subsequently, in the event of an appeal, the Constitutional Court and the ECtHR, would establish the limits of feasibility of the demand for penal liability for acts challenging compliance with Court decisions in political conflicts related to the 'pro-sovereignty' challenge.

[65] Those who consider themselves victims of a violation of any of the fundamental rights proclaimed in the Constitution may request protection from the common courts via a 'privileged' procedure—a preferential and summary appeal—and, if not satisfied, from the Constitutional Court through an appeal for protection—s 53(2) Constitution, read with s 161(1)(b) and s 162(1)(b).

[66] CCR 205/2013 of 5 December.

[67] This is a purely 'procedural' issue, but with significant practical repercussions in cases like this. The Supreme Court Ruling 1045/2007 (Criminal Chamber; 17.12.2007) established the so-called 'Botín doctrine' (named after the late President of Banco Santander), stating that in crimes in which individuals suffer damage it is not acceptable to proceed only on the basis of a 'popular action', if neither the Public Prosecutor nor any aggrieved individual bring charges.

[68] The three individuals convicted have filed a suit before the ECtHR—(App No 41427/14) registered on 5 June 2014, which has not yet been considered by the Court.

[69] The High Court of Justice's decision to hear the charge was decided by the Orders 5, 6, 9, 15, 16, 22, 24, 26 and 28/2015 of 8 January; 41/2015 of 4 February; and 59/2015 of 26 February. The High Court of Justice of Catalonia rejected the complaint against another two members of the government—its spokesperson and the Home Minister—because it considered that their acts were a legitimate consequence of their professional obligations. Previously, when the Catalan Parliament passed its Resolution on the sovereignty of Catalonia—*Resolució 5/X* (n 23)—similar charges were issued but they were rejected by the High Court of Justice of Catalonia—Order 37/2014 of 24 March.

[70] By a Decision (*Auto*) of 28 June 2016 of the examining judge of the High Court of Justice of Catalonia, the way for hearing the trial was opened. Eventually, by a Decision (*Auto*) of 13 October 2016 the same judge decided to open the hearings regarding the charges of gross disobedience and abuse of office, refusing, at the same time, the charges of embezzlement or misuse of public funds proposed by some popular plaintiffs. In the first Decision the judge ruled that the same crimes might have been committed by a fourth member (then) of the government of Catalonia, who (currently) is a Member of the Lower House of the Spanish Parliament, as a result of which he refers the proceedings to the Supreme Court, before which, if appropriate, he should be prosecuted.

b. Another kind of criminal liability? The (hypothetical) case of a Unilateral Declaration of Independence

The possibility has been considered that apart from criminal disobedience, other crimes may have been committed in the 'pro-sovereignty' process, especially in Catalonia. Most notably, this is the case with regard to the President's declaration that, in the event that parties advocating the Independence of Catalonia were obtained, as it happened, a parliamentary majority in the elections of September 2015, they would proceed to approve a UDI.

According to the PC (section 404) a public authority or civil servant commit criminal corruption when, knowingly breaking the law, they make an arbitrary decision in an administrative matter, this being punishable by special disqualification from public office for between seven and ten years. The crime of corruption is intended to guarantee respect for the principle of legality in the exercise of public office. It requires that the civil servant or authority execute an administrative act in which there is some element of decision, but the crime will only be found if the act is malicious, it being necessary in proving its 'arbitrary' character, to show that the illegality was 'blatant and manifest'.[71]

Meanwhile, according to section 433 PC, the crime of embezzlement of public funds is committed by public authorities or civil servants when they assign to uses other than public service the funds put at their disposal by reason of their duties. This crime is punishable by a fine of six to twelve months and suspension from public office from six months to three years, when not motivated by financial gain. However, if those found guilty of embezzlement do not return the funds 'within ten days of initiation of the process' they will be subject to the penalties set out in section 432 PC—their action thus being aggravated by profit-seeking—three to six years' prison and absolute disqualification for six to ten years.[72]

The aforementioned charges also sought the imputation of two extremely serious crimes: that of rebellion, included amongst crimes against the Constitution (sections 472 ff. PC)[73]—and sedition, included among the crimes against public order (sections 544 ff. CP).[74] The High Court of Justice of Catalonia rejected the possibility that the actions leading to the holding of the 'consultation' of 9 November could have constituted these crimes. Given their nature, there would appear to be little doubt as to the correctness of the High Court of Justice's decision. However, might they be committed in the event of the materialization of the promised UDI by the Catalan Parliament?

The crime of rebellion involves rising up 'violently and publically' so as to declare the independence of a part of the national territory. This means that the crime requires not only achieving this end but that it must be pursued via specific means: violent and public uprising. The requirement that the uprising be 'violent' does not require the recourse to

[71] F Morales Prats and MJ Rodriguez Puerta, 'Artículo 433' in Quintero Olivares (n 63) 530 ff. As we have just referred, the examining judge of the High Court of Justice of Catalonia holds that the three members of the government of Catalonia may have committed that crime with regard to the holding of the 'consultation' of November 9.

[72] Morales Prats and Morales García, in Quintero Olivares (n 63) 685 ff. Section 432 PC establishes harsher penalties in the event of the embezzlement 'being particularly serious given the value of the sums stolen and the damage or disruption to public service': four to eight years prison and absolute disqualification for ten to twenty years.

[73] The crime of rebellion carries very serious penalties: for the instigators and ringleaders, prison sentences of fifteen to twenty-five years; those lower in the chain of command, from ten to fifteen years; and mere participants, from five to ten years.

[74] The crime of sedition carries prison sentences of eight to ten years in the case of instigators and main perpetrators, and from ten to fifteen years if they are 'authorities'. In other cases, four to eight years prison.

violence to be effective: rather the simple intention of using it against those who do not abide by the new order will be sufficient.[75]

That said, it seems very rash to predict that in the 'pro-sovereignty' process currently taking place in Catalonia, criminal rebellion might be committed by the parliamentary political forces and authorities of the autonomous territory. Although some scholars consider that such a declaration by a territorial Parliament would be criminal rebellion 'inasmuch as the Constitution does not envisage the possibility of independence of territories', the requirement of being a 'violent and public uprising' in my opinion excludes the mere declaration of independence by the Parliament of Catalonia from the scope of this provision.[76]

With regard to the hypothetical commission of the crime of sedition, the PC (sections 544 ff.) establishes that it is committed by those who, while not amounting the crime of rebellion, rise up 'publically and tumultuously' to prevent, by force or outside legal channels, the application of the laws or prevent any public authority or civil servant from exercising their functions or complying with legal or judicial resolutions. 'Uprising', according to Supreme Court case law, is any 'insurgency, revolt or insurrection'; the public character means it must be open or manifest and must involve 'open hostility', a meaning which must be attributed to the term 'tumultuously', irrespective of whether it is chaotic or organized.[77]

Given these circumstances, it does not seem easy to fit a UDI by the Parliament into the PC crime of sedition if it is purely and simply a declarative act. However, if on the contrary, the authorities of the government of Catalonia sought to act in practice on the UDI, in order to put it into effect, preventing compliance with laws or resolutions of the public authorities or courts adopted in accordance with the constitutional order, those doing so would very probably be entering the realms of the criminal definition of sedition.

It should be borne in mind that in crimes like sedition—as in rebellion—the PC punishes not only its direct committal but similarly other 'imperfect' actions such as inducement, provocation or in the case of the authorities, the failure to oppose it. In this sense, it is important to remember that people linked to the Catalan government have stated that, in the event of the Parliament approving a UDI, it would proceed immediately to 'disconnect' Catalonia from Spain, ignoring the legal demands stemming from the constitutional system.

Were this to happen, the Catalan authorities would again place themselves in a similar situation to that of the 'Revolution of 1934'.[78] It is hard to conceive of such a scenario in the Spain of today, within the EU. But who knows what will happen?

75 JM Tamarit Sumilla, 'Artículo 472' in Quintero Olivares (n 63) 863.

76 A Juanes Peces, 'Artículos 472 a 484' in Conde-Pumpido Tourón et al. (n 62) vol 5 3327.

77 R García Albero, 'Artículos 544 a 549' in Quintero Olivares (n 63) 1038 ff.

78 Of extraordinary interest with regard to these facts are the testimonies of Gaziel (pseudonym of A Calvet): *Tot s'ha perdut* (RBA-La Magrana 2013) and of A Hurtado: *Abans del sis d'octubre (Un dietari)* (Acantilado 2008, 2nd edn).

18

Enforcement of National Law against Subnational Units in the US

Mark Tushnet

1. Key background features

The question of the enforcement of national law against subnational units in the US is of some theoretical interest, but rather little practical importance. This brief chapter is primarily an exposition of the applicable constitutional doctrine in the US, although I offer some general observations about the underlying theory of federalism that generates US constitutional doctrine. For readers outside the US, the primary message is that the constitutional doctrine dealing with this sort of enforcement is quite limited in scope and importance, in contrast to its importance in systems whose constitutions create a less centralized version of constitutional federalism.

The US as a national government has sporadically faced resistance to the enforcement of its law within the nation's subunits, which I will hereafter refer to as 'states' for convenience. Before the Civil War of 1861 to 1865, officials of Southern state governments occasionally contended that the national government lacked constitutional authority to enforce national law within states that resisted such enforcement on constitutional (not policy) grounds. The US Supreme Court rejected that proposition early in its history.[1] The political theory underlying its rejection—a theory associated with South Carolina's John C Calhoun and known as 'interposition'—never gained real traction in political discourse.[2] The Civil War's outcome has been taken as establishing the proposition that states as such have no authority to obstruct enforcement of otherwise valid national law.[3]

The enforceability of national regulations against the states occurs within a constitutional order with two central features. Firstly, direct power over individuals. The national government has the power to require that individuals comply with nationally prescribed regulations. This is so even when complying with the national regulations would otherwise violate state-law rules, even rules prescribed by state-level constitutions. So for example an employer must comply with a national regulation requiring that employers use a specific type of safety equipment in the workplace, even in states where using that type of equipment is banned by state law, even state constitutional law.[4] The fact that the national

[1] *Martin v Hunter's Lessee* 14 US 1 Wheat 304 (1816) US Lexis 333.

[2] For a judicial treatment of the theory, see *Bush v Orleans Parish School Board* 188 F Supp 916 (ED La, 1960). The court there concluded, after an extensive discussion of the theory, that 'interposition resolutions have no legal efficacy'.

[3] The US national government is one of limited powers, and those subject to its directives sometimes win challenges to those directives based on arguments that the statute at issue was not authorized by the powers enumerated in the US Constitution, and of course based on arguments that the statute, though within Congress' enumerated powers, nonetheless violates individual rights protected by the Constitution. Challenges of these types are not the focus of concern in this book, and I will forgo further discussion of them.

[4] See e.g. *McDermott v Wisconsin* 228 US 115 (1913) No 112–113 (holding that a state could not prosecute those who sold syrup properly labelled according to national law but mislabelled as defined by state law).

Enforcement of National Law against Subnational Units in the United States. First Edition. Mark Tushnet. Published 2017 by Oxford University Press.

government can act directly on individuals greatly reduces the need for the national government to act on state governments, or to act through or with the cooperation of state governments. Indeed, the US Supreme Court has cited the fact that the national government can act directly on individuals as a reason for limiting the national government's power to 'commandeer' state governments in the service of national aims.[5]

Secondly, the national government has the power to implement its regulatory authority through national courts with the power to coerce those subject to that authority. The national courts, known in the US as the 'federal' courts, are institutions located within the national government, staffed by judges nominated by the president and confirmed by the Senate. The judges are, in short, employees of the national government. Their power is backed up by the Supremacy Clause of Article VI, which provides that the Constitution and constitutionally valid laws are 'the supreme Law of the Land; and the Judges in every State shall be bound thereby, any Thing in the Constitution or Laws of any State to the Contrary notwithstanding'. And, should a state court judge be tempted to deny national law's supremacy, the US Supreme Court is empowered to review that judge's decision and if it proves necessary, to enter a coercive order enforcing national law against its regulatory target. As with the national power to act directly on individuals, these institutional arrangements substantially reduce the incentives state-level officials have to obstruct national regulations, and for that reason reduce the need for the national government to try to draft recalcitrant state officials to enforce national law.

These two institutional or legal features operate against an important cultural background. The US has a high degree of cultural homogeneity relative to the nations of Europe. There is of course a great deal of demographic, racial, and religious diversity within the US, but that diversity is not strongly correlated with geography. As Barack Obama said in the speech that brought him to national attention, 'We worship an awesome God in the blue states, and we don't like federal agents poking around our libraries in the red states. We coach little league in the blue states and, yes, we've got some gay friends in the red states'.[6] There are regional differences between the Northeast and the South, and among other regions,[7] but officials from the states within each region have localized incentives that weaken their ability to cooperate against the national government.[8] The 'constitutional identity' of the US is not ethno-nationalist but constitutionalist: US citizens are citizens of a nation held together by a common commitment to the national Constitution.

For these reasons, the question of enforceability of national law against state governments is now at the periphery of constitutional concern in the US. The national government has ample tools to accomplish its regulatory goals in the face of state-based resistance. Sometimes issues of symbolic importance arise and very rarely those issues have ramifications as a matter of practical politics if not as a matter of basic constitutional theory. But in the end, issues that are quite important in the European context are substantially less so in the US.

[5] *Printz v United States* 521 US 898 (1997) No 95–1478.

[6] Available at http://www.washingtonpost.com/wp-dyn/articles/A19751-2004Jul27.html and http://perma.cc/Q3VH-KHFV, accessed 12 October 2016.

[7] Conventionally it is said that two states—Alaska and Texas—might have truly distinctive *state* civic cultures. That is not enough to sustain a vibrant political culture of state-based resistance to the US government as a national government.

[8] For a recent argument noting the extent to which local officials have incentives to resist national initiatives by means of cooperating with members of their own political party holding elected national office, see J Bulman-Pozen, 'Partisan Federalism: Examining the Interaction of Party Politics and Federalism' (2014) 127 *Harvard Law Review* 1078.

2. National regulation of state governments

National law regulates state governments in two ways. First, some state activities are precisely equivalent to activities which private entities engage in: state governments employ people, operate transit systems, construct buildings, and the like. When acting in these ways, state governments must comply with the regulations applicable to private entities engaged in similar actions. They may not discriminate in employment on the basis of race or gender, for example, and they must comply with national environmental regulations. However, remedies against state governments engaging in these activities are more limited than those available against private entities. Second, some state activities are those of quasi-sovereign entities and are for that reason not similar to activities any private entity can engage in: notably, state governments enact and enforce state-level laws. The national government's power to compel states in their quasi-sovereign activities is limited, though often the national government can achieve its ends either by acting directly on non-governmental actors or by providing state governments incentives to comply with national regulatory requirements.

a. Regulating state governments when acting 'like' private entities

State and local governments are significant components of the national economy. They employ large numbers of workers, they operate public buildings, they run public transit systems. In those capacities state governments resemble private actors who engage in similar activities. And in those capacities, state governments have no special immunities from compliance with national regulation.[9] Often state governments have enough influence on policy making that they receive special accommodations unavailable to private actors. For example, state emergency services agencies are allowed to provide 'compensatory' time off instead of paying their workers extra for overtime work, an accommodation not available to private corporations.[10] Such accommodations, though, are not required as a matter of constitutional law.

Like all regulated actors, state governments sometimes do not fully comply with national regulations. Private actors who violate national law can be fined in criminal proceedings, ordered to pay damages for past violations, and ordered to comply with the regulations in the future. Remedies against state governments for their violations of national law are more limited, though in the end the limitations probably do not substantially limit the reach of national regulatory power over state governments.

The reason for the limitations is the Eleventh Amendment to the US Constitution, which provides, 'The judicial Power of the United States shall not be construed to extend to any suit in law or equity, commenced or prosecuted against one of the United States by Citizens of another State [. . .].' The US Supreme Court has construed the Eleventh Amendment to embody a principle of state immunity from suit that goes beyond its express terms.[11] So for example, although amendment refers only to 'Citizens of *another* State', the Court held in 1890 that it barred suits in federal courts against states brought by their own citizens.[12] And although the amendment refers to the 'judicial Power *of the United States*', the Court held

[9] See *Garcia v San Antonio Metropolitan Transit Authaurity* 469 US 528 (1954) No 82–1913.

[10] A summary of the rules can be found in HR Hero, 'Fair Labor Standards Act (FSLA)' (2016) available at http://topics.hrhero.com/fair-labor-standards-act-flsa/and http://perma.cc/L28-QU3L, accessed 12 October 2016.

[11] For an overview of Eleventh Amendment doctrine, see LH Tribe, *American Constitutional Law* Vol 1 (3rd edn, Foundation 2000) 519. Tribe provides an extensive list of relevant scholarship at 529, fn 70.

[12] *Hans v Louisiana* 134 US 1 (1890) No 4.

in 1999 that it precluded Congress from requiring that state courts entertain suits against state governments.[13]

Early in the twentieth century the Supreme Court developed a legal fiction that allowed the federal courts to hear cases 'in equity'—that is, to seek injunctions directing that state governments comply with national law or, equivalently, orders directing that state governments comply with national law.[14] The fiction built on earlier jurisprudence, and allowed suits to be brought against state officials whose official duties included compliance with applicable national law—the officials in charge of state employment policy, for example. The Court conceptualized these suits as actions against the officials, not the state, and therefore not barred by the Eleventh Amendment. The rule allows the national courts to direct that state governments comply with the law prospectively. Violations of those orders are enforceable through the ordinary mechanisms available to courts, such as fines for each instance of noncompliance.[15] Typically the national courts issue these orders, although state courts can issue them in theory, and sometimes do in practice.

In contrast to these departures from the Eleventh Amendment's text are doctrines that take the text seriously. For example, because the Eleventh Amendment refers only to 'Citizens', the Court has held that the national government can bring actions for both prospective relief and retrospective relief, or 'damages', such as actions for amounts wrongfully withheld by state officials who failed to comply with national wage-and-hour requirements.[16] Further, because the Amendment refers to suits against 'States', it does not apply to many sub-state jurisdictions, and in particular to most cities. The Court has developed a complex jurisprudence providing criteria for determining when some sub-state institution like a public university or a county is an 'arm of the state' protected by the Eleventh Amendment, or is not and is therefore fully subject to suit.

In addition, legislation enacted pursuant to power conferred on Congress after the adoption of the Eleventh Amendment can 'override' the ban on suits in federal courts against state governments, at least if Congress makes it clear that it desires to open the federal courts to such suits. The most important statutes of this sort are enacted under Congress's power to 'enforce' the Fourteenth Amendment's guarantee that state governments provide everyone with the 'equal protection of the laws'. National nondiscrimination statutes are the primary examples of congressional exercises of this power.[17] Under such statutes, individuals can bring suits against the state for damages resulting from the state's discriminatory actions. Although the Supreme Court has imposed significant restrictions on the scope of Congress's power to enforce the Fourteenth Amendment by requiring that the remedial system be congruent with and proportional to actual violations of the Fourteenth Amendment, the *power* of Congress to enact such statutes is clearly established.[18]

Most national regulation, though, is enacted pursuant to Congress's powers enumerated in Article I of the Constitution, most importantly, the power to 'regulate Commerce [...]

[13] *Alden et al. v Maine* 527 US 706 (1999) No 98-436. States are free to entertain such if they choose to do so.

[14] *Ex parte Young* 209 US 123 (1908) No 10.

[15] These are conceptualized as violations of court orders, not as violations of the underlying national regulations.

[16] *Principality of Monaco v Mississippi* 292 US 313 (1934) No_, original (referring to jurisdiction of the US Supreme Court over such cases).

[17] See e.g. *Nevada Department of Human Resources v Hibbs* 538 US 721 (2003) No 1-1368 on the Family and Medical Leave Act of 1993; *Fitzpatrick v Bitzer* 427 US 445 (1976) No 75-251 on Title VII of Civil Rights Act of 1964.

[18] *City of Boerne v Flores* 521 US 507 (1997) No 95-2074; *Board of Trustees of The University of Alabama et al. v Patricia Garrett et al.* 531 US 356 (2001) No 99-1240.

among the several States'. The Eleventh Amendment applies in full force to such regulations. The overall effect of the Court's interpretation of the Eleventh Amendment is to make it relatively costless for state governments to ignore national regulations if they wish to, up to the moment when they become subject to a prospective order directing that they comply in the future. The ability to violate national law with impunity—up to a point, but not thereafter—is not a trivial matter, but the scheme of the Constitution taken as a whole places state governments under relatively strong duties to comply with national regulations when they engage in activities like those that private actors engage in.

b. Regulating state governments in their quasi-sovereign capacities; the anti-commandeering principle

The situation is somewhat different with respect to actions taken by state governments acting as quasi-sovereign entities—legislating for example, or executing the law. Here the Supreme Court has developed a doctrine holding that the national government cannot 'commandeer' state governments in their sovereign capacities. That is, the national government cannot direct state legislatures to enact laws or state officials to enforce national law. The Supreme Court did not articulate the anti-commandeering doctrine until the late twentieth century. It has been invoked only occasionally with respect to national statutes, and it is quite controversial, with the Court and scholars dividing basically along standard ideological lines: Conservatives favor the doctrine because it limits the reach of the national government, and liberals oppose it for precisely the same reason.[19]

The reason why the Court has employed the anti-commandeering doctrine only occasionally is clear enough. Congress has rarely attempted to commandeer state legislatures. The reason is straightforward. Because the national government has the power to regulate citizens directly, the circumstances in which the national government seeks to require state legislatures to enact statutes, or state officials to enforce national law, are unusual. So for example, in the late twentieth century the national government faced a difficult problem of storing low-level radioactive waste products from various sources, pending the development of a national storage site.[20] Congress sought to shift the obligation for developing interim storage locations to state governments, through a scheme that in effect required state legislatures to enact statutes identifying local storage sites. The Supreme Court, citing the uniqueness of this obligation, held that it violated the anti-commandeering principle.[21] To the extent the Court offered a functional rationale, it involved transparency and political responsibility. Placing a nuclear storage site in any specific location would be controversial. By forcing the state legislature to identify the site, Congress obscured political responsibility: the public might believe that state officials were responsible for picking the site—as in some sense they would be—whereas the real responsibility should be placed on Congress. But again, the very rarity of such efforts shows how much the national government can do by directly regulating individuals.

It should be noted, however, that the existence of the anti-commandeering doctrine perhaps leads Congress to avoid enacting statutes that might be challenged as commandeering. And it might sometimes be the case that direct regulation of individuals is politically infeasible, or that the substitutes for commandeering are less effective in

[19] For an early but still relevant critique of the anti-commandeering doctrine, see VC Jackson, 'Federalism and the Uses and Limits of Law: *Printz* and Principle?' (1998) 111 *Harvard Law Review* 2180. See also Tribe (n 11) 878.

[20] Such a site has been identified, but political and legal considerations have delayed its opening indefinitely.

[21] *New York v United States et al.* 488 US 1041 (1992) No 91–543.

promoting national goals. So while the doctrine has a rather limited scope, its impact might be somewhat broader than initially appears.

Applying the anti-commandeering principle to state executive officials might be more consequential than to apply it to state legislatures. If the national government cannot force state executive officials to enforce national law, the enforcement must be done by national officials themselves, and resource limitations—including limitations on the number of enforcement officials—might reduce the effective scope of national regulation. When Congress enacted a statute requiring that purchasers of guns from licensed dealers undergo a background check, it planned to develop a national system of computerized checks administered by the national government, in which the gun dealers would have to consult a computerized database before selling the weapon. However, pending the development of that system, Congress attempted to require that state police officials perform the background checks. The Supreme Court held that this was an instance of improper commandeering.[22] Yet, almost simultaneously with the Supreme Court's decision, the national system of background checks was put in place, basically eliminating the need to commandeer state police officials. Moreover, state police officials—and state executive officials more generally—interact with national officials routinely. As a result, the state officials are quite often willing to enforce national law, if only to preserve good working relations with national officials.

c. The position of state courts

The anti-commandeering doctrine has other important qualifications. The national government cannot commandeer state legislatures or executive officials in their sovereign capacity, but it can do precisely that with respect to state courts. State judicial institutions must enforce national law through their exercise of sovereign authority. Early in the nation's history some state courts asserted that, because they were branches in a quasi-sovereign government, they could not be forced to exercise judicial power by national law. That claim was rejected in 1816 with *Martin v Hunter's Lessee*, where the Supreme Court held that the Supremacy Clause, quoted above, limited the state courts' sovereign authority with respect to superior national law.[23] And, as also noted above, the state courts' duty can be enforced by the US Supreme Court, which has the authority—rarely exercised—to enter an enforceable judgment in a case appealed to it from a state court, over the objections of that court.

d. Incentives

The anti-commandeering principle is limited by a third doctrine. Although the national government cannot require state governments to exercise their quasi-sovereign authority to do what the national government wants, it can provide those governments with incentives to do so. The incentives take two forms.

First, the national government can 'conditionally preempt' state law. The national power to regulate individuals directly is joined with the Supremacy Clause to imply that national regulations 'preempt'—that is, override—contrary state regulations. But instead of fully preempting state law, Congress can do so conditionally. Conditional preemption has two components. (1) Congress enacts a comprehensive system of regulation applicable to

[22] *Printz v United States* (n 5). [23] *Martin v Hunter's Lessee* (n 1).

individuals directly. (2) It couples that system with provisions saying in effect that states that choose to enact regulations broadly consistent with nationally prescribed criteria may enforce those regulations rather than the national ones, even if the state-devised regulations depart to some extent from the comprehensive national scheme.

Conditional preemption and related techniques, such as the distribution of funds from the national government to state governments on condition that they implement a national policy, are important methods for achieving what has been called cooperative federalism. States have an incentive to enact their own regulations because they thereby gain some input into the regulatory system in application. Of course some states will not accept the offer of conditional preemption because they prefer to see national officials enforce national law, with the accompanying political responsibility.

Conditional preemption is a technique for inducing state governments to enact regulations applicable to individuals. But what of national regulations aimed at inducing states to exercise their quasi-sovereign powers in a manner consistent with the national government's preferences?

The primary incentive the national government can offer is not surprisingly financial.[24] I begin with the simplest example: the national government creates a programme to finance the construction of roads and other infrastructure. It makes funds available to state governments, but only on the condition that they use specified construction methods or—in the actual case—raise the driving age to twenty-one.[25] States remain free to reject the national funds if they find the conditions too burdensome or disagree with them on policy grounds. Often though, state governments will regard the possibility of using national funds as an attractive solution to local fiscal difficulties. According to the Supreme Court, conditional spending programmes like this are constitutional even if they induce state governments to exercise their quasi-sovereign powers—such as legislating a minimum driving age—in ways that Congress could not directly require because of the anti-commandeering doctrine.

The Supreme Court has articulated some modest limits on the conditional spending power. First, the condition—the activity Congress wants to induce the states to engage in—must be broadly related to the underlying purpose of the funding programme. So for example, raising the minimum driving age to twenty-one was designed to reduce the incidence of young people driving while intoxicated, thereby making the roads built with federal funds safer. As the example indicates, the 'relevance' or 'germaneness' requirement, as it is sometimes called, is not terribly restrictive.

Second, and more importantly, the national offer of funding cannot be so attractive as to be coercive—or conversely—the threat to deny funds unless national conditions are met cannot be so substantial as to be coercive. Making sense of the idea that a mere offer can be coercive is quite difficult, and the Court has not done much to help. In one case it held that conditioning the grant of national funds on state compliance with regulations that were

[24] *New York v United States* (n 21) involved a non-financial incentive. The Constitution has been interpreted to prohibit one state from closing its borders to commerce from another state. But the Supreme Court has also held that Congress can authorize a state to do just that. See *Lewis v BT Invement Managers, Inc* 447 US 27 (1980) No 79–45 ('Congress, if it chooses, may exercise this power indirectly by conferring upon the States an ability to restrict the flow of interstate commerce that they would not otherwise enjoy'.) Congress used that power to authorize states with storage sites for low-level nuclear waste to bar the use of those sites for waste produced in states without such a site. So for example, South Carolina, a state with a storage site, could bar the use of that site for waste from New York. That gives New York an incentive to develop its own storage site.

[25] *South Dakota v Dole* 483 US 203 (1987) No 86–260.

unconstitutional independently of the funding scheme was unconstitutional.[26] However, the independent unconstitutionality seems to render the idea of coercion otiose.

More recently, the Supreme Court issued an important decision finding a funding condition coercive.[27] The case involved one portion of the Affordable Care Act, or 'Obamacare'. Prior to the statute's adoption, the national government provided significant funding for state-administered programmes of medical assistance to the poor, but the states paid a significant portion of the cost of care. The statute offered essentially complete national funding for a significant expansion of that system. To induce states to accept the offer of national funding for the expansion, the statute provided that states that did not expand the system would lose not merely the additional funding provided by the statute but all national funding for the existing system. According to Chief Justice Roberts, this amounted to coercion because states had become dependent on national funding for the existing system, and as a practical matter of ordinary politics could not simply forgo all national funding.

Note that the coercion arose from threatening to take away funding on which state governments had become dependent. The threat, that is, was in an important sense retrospective: states had been told earlier that they would get national funds if they complied with conditions specified at that time. They accepted those conditions, and then were, according to the Court's analysis, locked in to the programme forever, even if Congress changed it substantially. As a matter of analysis, the coerciveness of this sort of threat could be vitiated prospectively, if Congress had made it clear from the outset that it retained the power to change or expand the programme however it chose. And indeed, there was a provision in the original programme for funding medical care for the poor saying just that. But according to the Chief Justice, the provision applied only to 'changes' in the existing programme but not to transformations in its essential nature. According to him, the Affordable Care Act was just such a transformation.[28] All agreed that, had Congress expressly repealed the existing programme and then enacted a new one covering both the old one and the expansion provided in the Affordable Care Act, states would be free to accept or reject the federal funds offered on the condition that states operate the full-scale, expanded system.

e. The residual problem of overcoming forceful state resistance to or obstruction of national law

As noted earlier, the outcome of the Civil War discredited constitutional theories that purported to make it lawful for states to 'interpose' themselves between the national government and individuals. Nor do the states have the military resources to resist. The original Constitution recognized that states would organize 'militias'—state-run military cadres that could be deployed to overcome rebellion more quickly than the national government's military forces could under the circumstances prevailing in the late eighteenth century. The original Constitution also recognized, however, that these militias had to be ultimately at the service of the national government so that they could not be turned against that government. It therefore authorized Congress to prescribe the conditions

[26] *United States v Butler* 297 US 1 (1936) No 401.

[27] *National Federation of Independent Businesses v Sibelius, Secretary of Health and Human Services et al.* 567 US (2012) No 11-393 (132 SCt 2566).

[28] Two dissenters argued that the provision authorizing changes was clear enough to cover the expansion provided in the Affordable Care Act, and so the threat to take away existing funding was not coercive.

under which the state-organized militias could be taken over by national military forces.[29]

The modern successor to the original militias is the 'National Guard'. As in the past, the National Guard is ordinarily organized and run by state officials. But the President has the power to 'nationalize' the Guard. The effect of doing so is to place the Guard under the direction of national officials. Because federal statutes generally bar the domestic use of the national army, the President occasionally nationalizes the National Guard when disasters occur, so that he can deploy military assistance from one state to another.

The most notable example of the use of national military force in emergencies, though, was President Dwight Eisenhower's action during the Little Rock school crisis in 1957.[30] The crisis arose when the state's governor Orval Faubus resisted efforts to desegregate the city's schools in compliance with federal court orders. Faubus directed that the schools be closed, and deployed the state's National Guard to prevent desegregation. Faced with a federal injunction against using the Guard in that way, Faubus then withdrew it. Violence erupted when nine African American students tried to attend the previously all-white schools. President Eisenhower responded by invoking a federal statute, adopted in the aftermath of the Civil War when violent resistance to national authority persisted in the defeated South, authorizing him to use federal troops to enforce federal court orders, and sent units of the 101st Airborne Division of the armed forces to protect the students.[31]

Federal troops were deployed in 1961 in Montgomery, Alabama, to prevent violence associated with resistance to desegregation, and in 1962 and 1963 to prevent violence during the desegregation of the University of Mississippi and the University of Alabama. The desegregation crisis is a unique example in modern times of the use of federal force to enforce national law.[32] Importantly, pre-existing statutes structured the national response: those statutes identified quite limited circumstances under which that sort of intervention is lawful.[33] The threat of military intervention exists in the far background any time state officials challenge national authority, but most of those challenges stay in the domain of rhetoric. The threat of military intervention plays no real role in contemporary disputes about enforcing national law.

[29] US Constitution Art I §8 (15) providing Congress with the power 'To provide for calling forth the Militia to execute the Laws of the Union, suppress Insurrections and repel Invasions'.

[30] For a study of the events, see T Freyer, *The Little Rock Crisis* (Greenwood 1984).

[31] The statute is 10 USC §333:

> The President, by using the militia or the armed forces, or both, or by any other means, shall take such measures as he considers necessary to suppress, in a State, any insurrection, domestic violence, unlawful combination, or conspiracy, if it—
>
> (1) so hinders the execution of the laws of that State, and of the United States within the State, that any part or class of its people is deprived of a right, privilege, immunity, or protection named in the Constitution and secured by law, and the constituted authorities of that State are unable, fail, or refuse to protect that right, privilege, or immunity, or to give that protection; or
>
> (2) opposes or obstructs the execution of the laws of the United States or impedes the course of justice under those laws.

[32] Military interventions at the request of local authorities have been more common, particularly around the turn of the twentieth century, when state officials sought federal assistance to suppress what they characterized as 'labor unrest'. In addition, there is some reason to think that even the desegregation interventions were rather choreographed, with state governors signalling to the national government that they would do no more than oppose the interventions rhetorically and symbolically.

[33] See the Comment 'Federal Intervention in the States for the Suppression of Domestic Violence: Constitutionality, Statutory Power, and Policy' (1966) *Duke Law Journal* 414, for a discussion of the relevant statutes.

3. Conclusion

In the US the question of the enforceability of national law against state governments is a matter of some theoretical interest but relatively little practical importance. The reasons for that situation are a combination of institutional and historical conditions.

Institutionally, the fact that the national government has the power to act directly on individuals dramatically reduces its need to enlist state governments in the task of enforcing national law. In addition, the existence of a cadre of national officials located throughout the nation—geographically within the states but institutionally within the national government—makes enforcement by national officials possible in practice. An important element of these national institutions is the system of national courts, again located geographically in every state. Such courts can issue orders requiring compliance with national law. When they do so they trigger core ideas about the Rule of Law in any system, wholly independent of the federal nature of the US legal system.

Historically, the US has moved from a loose confederation to what the founding generation referred to as a compound republic, to a true federal system in which the national government and the state governments derive their legitimacy from the same people, though organized in different ways. Further, the US federal system is one in which the national government has quite substantial powers, reaching deep into the ordinary affairs of life. It can fairly be described as a rather centralized system with some modest federal features. That centralization developed over time. The Union's victory in the Civil War confirmed that the US was indeed a nation, not a confederation or even a strongly federal system. The national government's response to the Great Depression confirmed—in the view of many—that centralization of governance was a crucial feature of modern government. Developments over the succeeding decades, including the national response to the civil rights movement, did much to confirm that judgment. In the last years of the twentieth century and into the twenty-first, uneasiness about the expansion of national power grew somewhat. As noted earlier, a rather high degree of cultural homogeneity in the US reinforces these historical trends. Though one occasionally encounters talk of secession and the like, every responsible public figure in the US acknowledges that state governments cannot lawfully obstruct the enforcement of national law.

This is not to say, of course, that obstruction never occurs. But when it does, it raises ordinary questions about shortfalls in compliance with law of any sort, rather than special questions about the place of state governments within the national government. Not surprisingly, the situation in less well-established federations, and in weak confederations, may well be different. In such systems there might be *legal* questions about the enforcement of federal or confederal law within and against the federation's component states. In the US for nearly all practical purposes, there are no such legal questions.[34]

[34] This chapter was completed before the election of Donald Trump in November 2016. That event raises questions about the argument made here about the cultural homogeneity of the United States. Whether the answers to those questions will affect the law as described here remains to be seen.

19

The Enforcement of ECtHR Judgments

Élisabeth Lambert Abdelgawad

The purpose of Council of Europe (CoE) judicial proceedings is a practical one: '[a] judgment of the European Court of Human Rights (ECtHR) is not an end in itself, but a promise of future change, the starting point of a process which should enable rights and freedoms to be made effective'.[1] Now more than ever, the enforcement of judgments is considered one of the key factors ensuring the credibility of a whole judicial system.[2] Within the European human rights protection system established by the ECHR, the obligation to abide by judgments is very complex and covers, in principle, three aspects: the payment of just satisfaction (decided by the ECtHR in the operative part of the judgment) and if necessary, the adoption of individual measures to assure *restitutio in integrum*, and/or of general measures to avoid repetitive cases.[3] Such individual and/or general measures are very rarely included in judgments and are executed at the discretion of the State addressed, which complies with the judgment in accordance with the principle of liberty of means.[4] It is the responsibility of the Committee of Ministers (CM) under Article 46(1) ECHR, assisted by the Department for the Execution of Judgments (within the Human Rights Directorate of the CoE) to assess whether the measures proposed by the State are sufficient. Compliance is an even more difficult process, as it does not necessarily limit itself to normative (thus quantifiable) changes, but might even demand 'profound changes in political, social and individual patterns of thinking',[5] thus including training sessions, for example.

Following the increasing number of judgments delivered by the ECtHR, the workload of the CM has grown dramatically. Moreover, the last few years have seen a significant growth in the number of cases relating to complex and sensitive issues. By the end of 2015, the number of pending cases before the CM had reached 10,652. The CM also closed its supervision of a record number of 1,537 cases in 2015.[6] However, the real concern is with the increasing number of cases raising structural/systemic or complex issues[7] requiring the

[1] F Tulkens, 'Execution and Effects of Judgments of the European Court of Human Rights: the Role of the Judiciary' in ECtHR, *Dialogue between judges* (CoE 2006).

[2] Report of the Group of Wise Persons to the Committee of Ministers (CM) (2006) 203, 15 November 2006, 25: 'the credibility of the human rights protection system depends to a great extent on execution of the Court's judgments. Full execution of judgments helps to enhance the Court's prestige and the effectiveness of its action and has the effect of limiting the number of applications submitted to it'.

[3] Rule 6, Rules of the Committee of Ministers for the supervision of the execution of judgments and of the terms of friendly settlements.

[4] V Esposito, 'La liberté des États dans le choix des moyens de mise en œuvre des arrêts de la Cour européenne des droit de l'homme' (2003) 55 *Revue Trimestrielle des Droits de l'Homme* 14; E Lambert Abdelgawad, 'L'obligation de moyens dans l'exécution des arrêts', in F Sudre (ed) *Le principe de subsidiarité au sens du droit de la CEDH* (Anthemis 2014).

[5] A Alkoby, 'Theories of compliance with international law and the challenge of cultural difference' (2008) 4 *Journal of International Law and International Relations* 153.

[6] CM, 'Supervision of the execution of judgments and decisions of the European Court of Human Rights' (9th Annual Report 2015) (CoE 2016) 56–7.

[7] As covered by CM/Res(2004) 3 of 12 May 2014, on judgments revealing an underlying systemic problem.

adoption of general measures to avoid a profusion of potentially repetitive cases (1,555 pending cases).[8]

Strictly speaking, States very rarely openly refused (at least after a certain period) to comply with a judgment of the ECtHR, even if there are some such cases.[9] The concern is more about judgments where the State refuses to adopt parts of the required measures (partial compliance is widespread as States usually agree to award just satisfaction but are more reluctant when the Department comes to asking which additional individual or general measures have been adopted),[10] and/or where the State delays the adoption of some reforms. Many judgments (even those handed down by the ECtHR in 1996 or 1998) illustrate this.[11] When States ratified the ECHR, they could hardly have been expected to envisage completely what obligations they would eventually undertake through adverse judgments, and a target of 100 per cent effective and rapid execution seems an unreasonably optimistic expectation. Nevertheless, following the enlargement of the ECHR to forty-seven States and the increasing number of judgments where the ECtHR finds a violation of the Convention, the pressure on the system has increased to an unprecedented level. What is also worrying and even more serious is the defiance of old CoE members such as the UK. This phenomenon is far more detrimental to the authority of the ECtHR and to the whole system than when the same defiance is voiced by new CoE States, notably those with far greater political and economic obstacles.[12]

It is thus of interest to analyse the reasons for such defiance. The CM (representing the State parties) used to explain the length of time needed to execute judgments on the basis of the extent of the reforms which the States concerned had to undertake, and by the internal difficulties which some countries would encounter in implementing the projected reforms (for example, constitutional amendments might be needed).[13] In 2000 the Parliamentary Assembly (with Erik Jurgens as Rapporteur) listed seven reasons underlying such defiance,[14] a list which remains relevant: (1) 'Political reasons'—'the least frequent type', such as in *Loizidou v Turkey*, and *Hirst v UK* would also certainly fit this category; (2) 'Reasons to do with the scale of reforms required': legislative and sometimes even constitutional reforms need time and the government is not always successful in convincing the national parliament of the need for a reform; (3) 'Practical reasons relating to national legislative procedures', notably when there was no opportunity to reopen a case in the national legal

[8] ibid, 61.

[9] Historically, these include *Hakkar v France* App No 43580/04 (ECtHR, 7 April 2009), *Socialist Party v Turkey* App No 21237/93 (ECtHR 25 May 1998) and *Loizidou v Turkey* App No 15318/89 (ECtHR, 23 March 1995). Currently we can refer to *Green v UK* App No 60041/08 (ECtHR, 23 November 2010) and to *Sejdić and Finci v Bosnia-Herzegovina* App No 27996/06 and 34836/06 (ECtHR, 22 December 2009).

[10] The same assessment has been made in the Inter-American System of Human Rights: AA Cançado Trindade, 'Compliance with judgments and decisions – The experience of the Inter-American Court of Human Rights: a reassessment', Proceedings of the Seminar 'Implementation of the judgments of the European Court of Human Rights: a shared judicial responsibility?', *Dialogue between judges*, 31 January 2014 http://www.echr.coe.int/Documents/Dialogue_2014_ENG.pdf, accessed 12 October 2016.

[11] This list is far from being complete: Committee of Ministers (n 6): *İncal v Turkey* App No 22678/93 (ECtHR, 9 June 1998) pending since 1998; *Al-Nashif and Others v Bulgaria* App No 50963/99 (ECtHR, 16 December 1999) pending since twelve years; *Demirel and Others v Turkey* App Nos 4446/08, 35302/08, 47239/08, 44695/09 (ECtHR, 16 March 2010), final since 2003; *McKerr and others v UK* App Nos 28883/95, 24746/94, 30054/96, 37715/97, 43290/98, 29178/95 (ECtHR, 4 May 2001) pending since 2001. *Gongadze v Ukraine* App No 34056/02 (ECtHR, 8 February 2005), from 2006, despite two Interim Resolutions; *Oliveira Modesto and others v Portugal* App No 34422/97 (ECtHR, 8 June 2000) from 2000, despite two Interim Resolutions.

[12] E Bates, 'British sovereignty and the European Court of Human Rights' (2012) 128 *Law Quarterly Review* 382.

[13] For instance, see Reply given by the CM to Written Question no 378 raised by the PACE.

[14] PACE, Execution of judgments of the European Court of Human Rights (Report, 12 July 2000) Doc 8808, 38 et seq.

system; (4) 'Budgetary reasons', which are a reality today for several European countries; (5) 'Reasons to do with public opinion', in particular with cases dealing with ethical or moral issues; (6) 'Casuistic or unclear judgments', this criticism addressed to the ECtHR seems no longer to be an issue; and (7) 'Reasons relating to interference with obligations deriving from other institutions', in particular with the EU.

Moreover, one of the biggest challenges today also lies in the diverse interpretations open to the State and to the Department for the Execution of Judgments in determining the terms of compliance in the implementation of the judgments. It clearly appears from the practice over the last twenty years that the content of what constitutes compliance is challenged by at least four main actors: the applicant (his/her representative and even sometimes NGOs), the government, the Department for the Execution of Judgments, and the CM, and in some exceptional cases the ECtHR may reconsider a case and impose its view of its own motion. As good compliance cannot easily be measured, it is difficult to assess the impact of normative and institutional changes.

Not surprisingly, more efforts have been made over the last twenty years to prevent the defiance of judgments than in sanctioning the effects of such defiance. The focus has been on assisting States to avoid partial or unsatisfactory compliance. Indeed, it has now been recognized that persuasion and acculturation are also fundamental,[15] meaning that greater emphasis is placed on assistance, exchange of good practice, cooperation, and training to help national actors internalize European standards. Accordingly, preventing State defiance has been the main aim of European actors, while sanctions definitely remain a means of very last resort. We will analyse the measures adopted both to prevent and sanction defiance, and also try to sketch possible reforms to improve compliance in the European system of human rights.

1. Preventing Member State refusal to comply

Over the last twenty years the supervision of judgments has evolved towards a 'participatory model of accountability' involving an increasing number of actors.[16] We will focus here only on two of them, as prevention originates mainly in the work of the ECtHR and the Department for the Execution of Judgments.

a. The new role played by the ECtHR: towards more implementation indications in judgments

I. The historically limited competence of the ECtHR to decide on the consequences of its judgments

Historically, the general approach was that the judicial function of the ECtHR was restricted to deciding whether the ECHR had been breached by a State party. The allocation of responsibility (as prescribed by Article 46 ECHR) is a power of the CM, the CM and the States being in better positions than the ECtHR to determine the most appropriate means

[15] In favour of this approach, and in view of cultural diversity, Alkoby (n 5) 154–5.

[16] According to the analysis and distinction drawn by Grant and Keohane with other fields: R Grant and R Keohane, 'Accountability and Abuses of power in World Politics' (2005) 99 *American Political Science Review* 29, who 'distinguish two basic concepts of accountability: delegation and participation', among which they expose a plurality of models. E Lambert Abdelgawad, 'The execution of the judgments of the European Court of human rights: towards a non-coercive and participatory model of accountability' (2009) 69 *Heidelberg Journal of International Law* 3.

in the national legal order by which to abide by an obligation to achieve a particular result. The ECtHR has consistently reaffirmed that its judgments are still essentially declaratory.[17]

However, because of the backlog at the ECtHR and the CM, notably by repetitive cases (caused by poorly executed previous judgments) and structural cases involving complex implementation plans, the ECtHR, relying on the principle of effectiveness, has come to the conclusion that it should get more involved in recommending or even ordering which measures a State must take. As a result, this new policy also facilitates the tasks of the CM, as it puts more pressure on the State to implement a judgment before the deadline prescribed by the ECtHR. Another argument was that the execution of judicial decisions is a component of the right to a fair trial,[18] meaning that the European courts (the ECtHR and the ECJ) have to depoliticize the execution process.[19] The basis for this evolution is the result of the 'implied powers' theory, with the ECtHR relying on Article 46 ECHR as its legal ground.

II. The ECtHR acting as referee

Under Article 41, the ECtHR usually orders the State to pay just satisfaction to the victim, but it needs to state explicitly far more often than it does whether this award of monetary redress is sufficient.[20] Sometimes, however, only one specific measure will ensure *restitutio in integrum*, and the ECtHR will accordingly indicate this to the State to speed up implementation. In the most recent jurisprudence, it appears that it is less the absence of freedom of means but more a particular concern about the violation and the urgency to end a continued violation that encourages the ECtHR to proceed in this way, notably in cases of illegal detention.[21] In *Youth Initiative for Human Rights v Serbia*,[22] having found a violation of Article 10 on account of a refusal to provide access to documents requested by the applicant, the ECtHR ordered the State to provide the requested information for the applicant within three months and refused to make a monetary award for moral damages, given the preceding injunction made to the authorities. In *Oleksandr Volkov v Ukraine*,[23] the ECtHR thought it unhelpful to recommend reopening the case and 'Having regard to the very exceptional circumstances of the case and the urgent need to put an end to the violations of Articles 6 and 8 of the Convention, the ECtHR holds that the respondent State shall secure the applicant's reinstatement in the post of judge of the Supreme Court at the earliest possible date'. However, this strategy can create problems in cases where a State flatly refuses to adopt the indicated measure. If this occurs, the case should come back before the ECtHR with a statement of continued violation of the Article in question,[24] or under Article 46 ECHR,[25] or even cause infringement proceedings to be initiated.

[17] *Al Nashiri v Poland* App No 28761/11 (ECtHR, 24 July 2014) 586: 'choose, subject to supervision by the Committee of Ministers, the means to be used in order to discharge its legal obligation under Article 46 of the Convention, provided that those means are compatible with the conclusions contained in the Court's judgment'.

[18] *Hornsby v Greece* App No 18357/91 (ECtHR, 19 March 1997). *Dubenko v Ukraine* App No 74221/01 (ECtHR, 11 January 2005) 4.

[19] E Lambert Abdelgawad, 'L'exécution des décisions des juridictions européennes (Cour de Justice des Communautés Européennes et Cour Européenne des Droits de l'Homme)' (2006) 52 *Annuaire Français de Droit International* 677.

[20] C Giakoumopoulos, *Conference on the long-term future of the ECtHR*, Oslo 7, 8 April (CoE, PLURICourts 2014) 174, http://www.coe.int/t/DGHL/STANDARDSETTING/CDDH/REFORMECHR/Publications/Proceedings-Oslo-2014.pdf, accessed 12 October 2016.

[21] *Del Rio Prada v Spain* App No 42750/09 (ECtHR, 10 July 2012) and *Aleksanyan v Russia* App No 46468/06 (ECtHR, 22 December 2008) 239.

[22] *Youth Initiative for Human Rights v Serbia* App No 48135/06 (ECtHR, 25 June 2013).

[23] *Oleksandr Volkov v Ukraine* App No 21722/11 (ECtHR, 9 January 2013) 4.

[24] *Verein Gegen Tierfabriken Schweiz (VgT) v Switzerland* App No 32772/02 (ECtHR, 30 June 2009).

[25] *Emre v Switzerland* App No 5056/10 (ECtHR, 11 October 2011).

III. The indication of more or less precise measures: towards a strictly framed principle of subsidiarity

The ECtHR does not consider that there is only one way to abide by a judgment. This policy is thus an exception to the principle of the declaratory nature of its judgments, and needs to be explained. Such an explanation has evolved over the years in various respects: typically to aid the respondent State and the CM better to execute the judgments; more recently to respond to demands put forward in this respect by certain States, or to define the gravity of the violation of the articles in question less explicitly, to indicate the core rights, to highlight systematic or structural violations, or in cases where the ECtHR senses that the State addressed could resist the implementation of the judgment or would need such explanations given the specificities of its domestic judicial traditions. Contrary to the preceding hypothesis, the State thus retains an important amount of flexibility but the ECtHR is alone in being able to express a preference. Sometimes the ECtHR expressly affirms that it cannot indicate the measures to take due to the complexity of the matter, the task then falling to the CM. The complexity of the measures to take can also be aggravated by the evolving nature of the implementation process, such as in the contemporary examples of *Hirsi Jamaa and Others v Italy* or *MSS v Belgium and Greece.*[26] Individual and general measures can be distinguished.

With regard to *individual measures*, the most common scenarios have concerned recommendations in cases of violation of Article 6(1) ECHR to reopen or re-examine an applicant's case.[27] Less frequently, child custody cases under Article 8 ECHR have also provided a basis for such recommendations.[28] This more offensive policy seems to us to come about as a result of an incentive practice adopted by the CM following Recommendation (2000)2.[29] In a slightly different case,[30] noting 'the absence of a competing third-party interest or other obstacle to the restitution of the applicant's ownership',[31] the ECtHR ordered, in addition to a payment of EUR 9,000 for moral damages, 'the full restitution of the applicant's title to the flat and the annulment of her eviction order'[32] within three months, noting equally the importance of the right to housing and the attachment of the applicant to his apartment.

Much more often than individual measures, the ECtHR recommends the adoption of *general measures* expressed in quite variable terms: sometimes the recommendation is stated in the *merits* section,[33] less often in both the *merits* and the operative sections;[34] it is sometimes accompanied by a deadline;[35] finally, the degree of precision may vary considerably. The general measures to take can be set out very vaguely.[36] The aim is to head off

[26] *Hirsi Jamaa and Others v Italy* App No 27765/09 (ECtHR, 23 February 2012), *MSS v Belgium and Greece* App No 30696/09 (ECtHR, 21 January 2011).

[27] *Abbasov v Azerbaidjan* App No 24271/05 (ECtHR, 17 January 2008).

[28] *MD and others v Malta* App No 64791/10 (ECtHR, 17 July 2012).

[29] Committee Of Ministers, Recommendation to member states on the re-examination or reopening of certain cases at domestic level following judgments of the European Court of Human Rights CM/Rec(2000)2 9 January 2000, htttp://wcd.coe.int/ViewDoc.jsp?id=334147, accessed 12 October 2016.

[30] *Gladysheva v Russia* App No 7097/10 (ECtHR, 6 December 2011). [31] ibid, 106. [32] ibid, 4.

[33] *Al Nashiri v Poland* (n 17) 589, 'For the Court, compliance with their obligations under Articles 2 and 3 of the Convention taken together with Article 1 of Protocol No 6 to the Convention requires the Government to seek to remove that risk as soon as possible, by seeking assurances from the US authorities that he will not be subjected to the death penalty'.

[34] *Foundation Hostel for Students of the reformed church and Stanomirescu v Romania* App Nos 2699/03 and 43597/07 (ECtHR, 7 January 2014) 90.

[35] *Torreggiani and Others v Italy* App No 43517/09 (ECtHR 8 January 2013) 4.

[36] Therefore, the Court limits itself to explaining that national law has to be changed, without indicating precisely what changes have to occur. Nevertheless, this reminder helps the CM in the supervision of the case as it

reluctant States which, in the absence of a recommendation or injunction in the judgment, might feel themselves free to consider that no subsequent measures in addition to the payment of just satisfaction should be necessary.

In some other cases, however, the indications of the ECtHR can be much more precise.[37] This degree of precision is based on the adoption by the ECtHR of a *pilot procedure*. The ECtHR thus helps the State and the CM identify structural problems which could create the risk of repetitive cases.[38] The resulting reduction in the flexibility available to the defending State depends also on whether a deadline is set:[39] when substantial structural reforms need to be adopted, the period set is usually between six and twelve months, and this can be re-examined and subsequently extended by the ECtHR at the State's request. These deadlines encourage States to adopt general measures as soon as possible and constitute an important support for the CM's activities. Moreover, the pilot procedure aims 'to identify the dysfunction under national law that is at the root of the violation', 'to give clear indications to the government as to how it can eliminate this dysfunction' and 'to bring about the creation of a domestic remedy capable of dealing with similar cases'.[40] Again, this mechanism can be variable and the liberty of means left to the State will be a function of the option chosen by the ECtHR.

The liberty of means of the State can also be limited when the ECtHR decides on the compliance and effectiveness of the measures (principally general measures) previously adopted by the State, which the ECtHR has long allowed in the overall assessment of the conformity of domestic law with the Convention.[41] In the final scenario, the ECtHR can strongly influence implementation where a friendly settlement or a unilateral declaration does not receive its endorsement because the State failed to state the specific measures or redress it would adopt. These cases, though rare, are extremely important.[42]

IV. The effectiveness of the indications given by the ECtHR

When the ECtHR has recommended or ordered measures under Article 46, States have in principle shown particular conscientiousness in their implementation on the one hand,[43] and on the other hand, the CM has felt obliged to examine cases in a short time frame, being also accountable to the ECtHR.[44] Nearly all the pilot cases have been implemented satisfactorily.[45] Even a transfer from enhanced to standard supervision was decided for one

exerts more pressure on the State. *Tzamalis and Others v Greece* App No 15894/09 (ECtHR, 4 December 2012); *Oleksandr Volkov v Ukraine* (n 23).

[37] In such cases the Court might indicate which provision has to change and how. *Gülay Cetin v Turkey* App No 44084/10 (ECtHR, 5 March 2013).

[38] P Leach et al., *Responding to systematic human rights violations: an analysis of 'pilot judgments' of the European Court of Human Rights and their impact at national level* (Intersentia 2010).

[39] *Aslakhanova and others v Russia* App Nos 2944/06, 8300/07, 50184/07, 332/08, and 42509/10 (ECtHR, 18 November 2012): the imposition of a deadline is independent of the indication of measures to take.

[40] Information note issued by the Registrar, 'The Pilot Judgment Procedure', http://www.echr.coe.int/Documents/Pilot_judgment_procedure_ENG.pdf, accessed 12 October 2016.

[41] *Michelioudakis v Greece* App No 54447/10 (ECtHR, 3 April 2012) 67.

[42] In *Vojtechova v Slovakia* App No 59102/08 (ECtHR, 25 September 2012) concerning a violation of Art 6(1), the applicant had rejected the unilateral declaration, which did not foresee the reopening of the case. It is without doubt that even if no remedial action is defined in the operative part of the judgment, but only in the grounds, the CM should easily be able to impose such action on the State.

[43] *Del Rio Prada v Spain* (n 21), where the applicant was released the day after. *Lindheim and others v Norway* App No 13221/08 (ECtHR, 12 June 2012).

[44] *RR v Hungary* App No 19400/110 (ECHR, 4 December 2012); *Vyerentsov v Ukraine* App No 20372/11 (ECHR, 11 April 2013).

[45] e.g., *Grudic v Serbia* App No 31925/08 (ECtHR, 17 April 2012).

pilot judgment in 2013.[46] Nevertheless, tensions can arise if States raise the principle of subsidiarity and their liberty of means to implement the judgments.[47]

Assistance is also provided by the CM—which is in charge of supervising judgments—and more precisely by the Department for the Execution of Judgments (which is independent).

b. Assistance through the enhanced supervision procedure

Since January 2011 the CM has imposed a surveillance system in two groups, through which 'all cases will be examined under the standard procedure, excepting, because of their specific nature, justified cases that will be examined through sustained procedure' at the initiative of a Member State or the Secretariat.[48] It 'means in particular that the Committee of Ministers entrusts the Secretariat with more intensive and pro-active cooperation with the States concerned'.[49] The following cases are automatically placed under enhanced supervision: 'judgments requiring urgent individual measures, pilot cases, judgments raising structural and/or complex problems as identified by the ECtHR or by the Committee of Ministers, interstate cases'.[50] It is not unusual for States themselves to request extended monitoring of a case in order to be further supported in the preparation of reforms, to facilitate the adoption of legislation when confronted by political obstacles, or to adopt reforms in the face of financial obstacles despite ministerial support.

Notwithstanding the fact that enhanced supervision is supposed to be exceptional, about sixty per cent of pending cases are registered under this procedure, proof that the implementation of judgments is a complex and difficult matter for national authorities. However, some States clearly favour the standard supervision of cases to limit the CM's interventions. The standard procedure is simpler, where '[t]he Committee's involvement [. . .] will be limited to verifying whether or not action plans or action reports have been presented by member states'.[51] This also applies to the control of just satisfaction payments, where the State has to complete a form providing the information required to pay the applicant. The applicant has two months to file a complaint, after which the CM considers the case closed. With regard to other measures, the State must submit an action plan/report explaining the planned reforms and their impacts. If the six-month deadline to issue this report expires and no such document has been sent, the Department sends a reminder letter, an action it took for twenty States in 2015 concerning 103 cases/groups of cases. 'For 90 of these cases/groups of cases, an action plan/report has been sent to the Committee of Ministers before the end of the year'.[52]

Extended control under enhanced—meaning 'result oriented'—supervision, implies more than 'cooperation' between the CM and the defending State. It is defined as 'assistance in the preparation and/or implementation of actions plans; expertise assistance as regards the type of measures envisaged; bilateral/multilateral cooperation programs (e.g. seminars, round-tables) in case of complex and substantive issues'. The process implies numerous exchanges of communications, action plans, and Secretariat *memoranda* regarding the action plans or in light of new events. This process, therefore, is often to help the State

[46] *Ümmühan Kaplan v Turkey* App No 24240/07 (ECtHR, 20 March 2012).

[47] G Gori, 'Compliance', in D Shelton (ed), *The Oxford Handbook of International Human Rights Law* (OUP 2011).

[48] Document prepared by the Department for the Execution of Judgments of the European Court of Human Rights (DG-HL), 'Supervision of the execution of judgments and decisions of the European Court of Human Rights: implementation of the Interlaken Action Plan – Modalities for a twin-track supervision system' CM/Inf/DH(2010)37, 6 September 2010.

[49] ibid, 20. [50] ibid, 8. [51] ibid, 12. [52] 9th Annual Report, 73.

gather what is missing.[53] Formally, this can also be addressed through the submission of a revised action plan more detailed than the first.[54] The Department in charge of supervising the execution of judgments and for preparing the work for the CM will prepare an evaluation of compliance with the expected response to the judgment. The CM can deem measures to be insufficient on the basis of finding similar new applications being brought before the ECtHR (repetitive cases): greater cooperation between the ECtHR and the CM is therefore fundamental. The CM's requests can sometimes be extremely directive, notably in the absence of internal investigations of serious violations of human rights.[55]

Even more interestingly, national authorities may request assistance from various other organs of the CoE.

c. Requests of assistance by the States themselves

The shared responsibility for implementing a judgment assumes that the State is sufficiently equipped to meet its obligations and that all national authorities work in the same direction: this is far from being the case in all forty-seven Member States, where multiple forms of cooperation are established. Assistance occurs through fact-finding missions, a part of the bilateral consultations. This was done for a number of structural cases concerning the duration of proceedings. Furthermore, following the pilot judgment in *Maria Atanasiu and Others*, in remedying the dysfunction in the compensation mechanism for the restitution of goods nationalized in Romania, the assistance was very narrowly focused in that it evaluated a Bill submitted during a tripartite meeting.[56] In certain cases, a cooperation programme with the new Human Rights Trust Fund can be launched to help the State fulfil its obligations.[57] It is true that some States oppose compliance on the grounds of financial constraints. Following *Mahmudiov v Azerbaijan*,[58] the authorities appealed to the Venice Commission for help.[59] The consultations were held at the highest level (Minister of Justice and General Secretary of the CoE).

[53] Illustrative examples include *MSS v Belgium and Greece* (n 26) and *Makaratzic v Greece* App No 50385/99 (ECtHR, 20 December 2004), cases concerning the response to potentially deadly force used by the police in the absence of adequate legislative and administrative framework on the use of firearms.

[54] e.g. *Barbu Anghelescu and other similar cases v Romania* App No 46430/99 (ECtHR, 5 October 2004).

[55] In the Russian cases on anti-terrorist operations in Chechnya, the CM asked the authorities to provide information on the use of DNA tests as part of the investigation into the fate of the persons involved. They also asked for details of the means used to overcome difficulties such as the destruction of archives and other evidence, on the impact of the expiry of the prescribed deadline, and on the conditions in which amnesty law could have been applied. The CM also requested an evaluation of the impact of already adopted measures on the efficiency of internal investigations, accompanied by concrete examples and relevant statistics (*Isayeva v Russia* App No 57950/00 (ECtHR, 24 February 2005) and other cases); see Committee of Ministers (n 6) 80–1.

[56] *Maria Atanasiu and others v Romania* App Nos 30767/05 and 33800/06 (ECtHR, 12 October 2010). High level representatives of the Romanian government recently came to meet with the Department for the Execution of Judgments of the European Court, the Directorate General of Human Rights and Rule of Law, and the Registry of the European Court: CoE, 'Tripartite meeting at the Council of Europe on a draft law to reform the mechanism of compensation or restitution of property nationalised in Romania', http://www.coe.int/t/dghl/monitoring/execution/News/Tripartite_Meeting_Strain_en.asp, accessed 12 October 2016.

[57] CoE, 'Providing support to the implementation of the European Convention on Human Rights at the national level', http://www.coe.int/t/dghl/monitoring/execution/themes/hrtf/intro_hrtf_EN.asp, accessed 12 October 2016. For example, regarding the cases *Sarban v Moldova* App No 3456/05 (ECtHR, 4 October 2005) concerning, among others things, illegal detention and poor prison conditions, following the revision of the Criminal Proceedings Code and training activities, the implementation process was continued in 2012 with the participation of the Republic of Moldova in a cooperation programme on provisional detention financed by the Human Rights Trust Fund: 7th Annual Report, 92–3.

[58] *Mahmudov and Agazade v Azerbaidjan* App No 35877/04 (ECtHR, 18 December 2008), related to defamation (violation of Art 10 ECHR).

[59] The Venice Commission, during its 96th plenary session of 11, 12 October 2013, had to adopt the draft opinion on the new bill against defamation.

d. Prevention through the reinforcement of national structures and expertise in the field of implementation

As compliance not only depends on political willingness but also and even more often on the capacity of national authorities to cope with their commitments, the reinforcement of national structures has become essential.[60] This reinforcement is realized by several routes. Firstly, it is important to mention the recent practice of providing government employees not only to support the work of the Registry of the ECtHR to resolve its backlog, but also to serve in the Department for the Execution of Judgments, which achieves a dual goal: at the European level, reinforcing the human resources available and thus accelerating the number of cases dealt with; and at the national level, these agents on return should be better informed of the procedures and obligations imposed on their State.[61] Secondly, the States are required to establish internal restitutive processes (particularly in compensation) in conformity with the criteria established by the ECtHR. Thirdly, the CM's Recommendation of 2008 requires the establishment of a national coordinator charged with centralising the issues linked to the implementation of judgments and preferably to suitably empower this official.[62] Following the adoption of this Recommendation, the majority of States did not believe it necessary to establish a specific authority, often leaving it to their government Agent but with often minimal power, for example without the ability to suggest legislative amendments. This is why the Parliamentary Assembly of the CoE recently called on the States to '7.[. . .]7.1.3. "consider establishing a national body responsible solely for the execution of the ECtHR's judgments, in order to avoid a conflict of responsibilities with the agent representing the government before the Court."'[63] Elsewhere, and for several years, this same Parliamentary Assembly has tried to persuade States to increase the involvement of national parliaments in the control of the implementation of judgments,[64] which in certain States, notably the UK, Denmark, and the Netherlands, has proved very useful. Following the Brussels Conference and Declaration, the Delegations agreed to exchange good practices and to consider the necessity to amend Recommendation 2008 (2).[65] After the International Conference held in Saint Petersburg, we delivered a comparative report and concluded that very few national systems seem to be well equipped to correctly supplement general measures. Surprisingly, whereas the executive usually plays a major role, many other actors are not sufficiently involved, parliamentarians in particular, but also the ombudsmen, national human rights institutions, and civil society more broadly.[66]

Assistance may nevertheless prove insufficient in some extreme cases. Sanctioning a State's defiance then becomes necessary.

[60] D Anagnostou and A Mungiu-Pippidi, 'Domestic implementation of human rights judgments in Europe: legal infrastructure and government effectiveness matter' (2014) 25 *European Journal of International Law* 205.

[61] This Department recently launched several appeals with the permanent representatives and the procedure is regulated elsewhere by the Committee of Ministers, Resolution establishing Regulations for secondments to the Council of Europe CM/Res(2012)2, 15 February 2012.

[62] Committee of Ministers, Recommendation to member States on efficient domestic capacity for the rapid execution of judgments of the ECtHR CM/Rec(2008)2, 6 February 2008.

[63] PACE, Ensuring the viability of the Strasbourg Court: structural deficiencies in States parties PACE/Res (2013) 1914.

[64] M Suchkova, 'An analysis of the institutional arrangements within the Council of Europe and within certain Member States for securing the enforcement of judgments' (2011) 4 *European Human Rights Law Review* 448.

[65] High-Level Conference on the 'Implementation of the European Convention of Human Rights: our shared responsibility', Brussels Declaration, 27 March 2015, 9.

[66] E Lambert Abdelgawad, 'General Overview of the Member States' Practices', in Embracing National Mechanisms for Effective Implementation of the ECHR, Constitutional Court of the Russian Federation, 22–23 October 2015, 4–41.

2. Sanctioning a State's refusal to abide by a final judgment

In the current system, sanctioning a State's refusal to comply principally comes from the ECtHR, on no specific grounds or according to the new infringement proceedings, but new tools need to be established. Political pressure from the CM has completely failed and must be reconsidered.

a. Judicial sanctions by the ECtHR on no specific grounds

The ECtHR has sanctioned non-compliance with a previous judgment in a number of decisions. There are two categories of such cases, depending on the applicant.

I. Applications brought by the same applicant

When the applicant considers that a State has failed to comply with a previous judgment and is still suffering a violation of his/her rights under the Convention, he/she may bring a fresh application to the ECtHR: a number of cases can be listed under the same application.[67] The applicant must nevertheless persuade the ECtHR of the existence of a new material fact, a condition which is not always fulfilled.[68]

The *VGT v Switzerland* case is highly instructive. Before the Grand Chamber, the government opposed the re-examination of the case on the strength of the basic principle of the separation of powers between the ECtHR and the CM, as provided by Article 46(2) of the Convention.[69] The national authorities also supported the view that if Protocol 14 had entered into force, 'the Court would have been unable to assume jurisdiction in the instant case because Article 46 § 4 of the Convention, as amended by the Protocol, entitled the Committee of Ministers to institute infringement proceedings before the ECtHR only in cases where a State persistently refused to abide by a final judgment, that is, before the final resolution of the Committee of Ministers had been adopted' (para 50). Had the ECtHR been bound by the CM under the new provisions on infringement proceedings, its reasoning would nonetheless have been very similar to what it had been in this judgment. However, what this judgment revealed most clearly is that the judges at the ECtHR do not share the same views. Judge Malinverni, joined by judges Bîrsan, Myjer and Berro-Lefèvre, held in a dissenting opinion that '[e]ven assuming that the Committee of Ministers erred in adopting its resolution prematurely – that is, before knowing the outcome of the application for review – I consider that it is not for the Court but, if need be, for the Committee of Ministers to rectify that error'.[70]

Burdov v Russia is also relevant, as the non-compliance with the previous judgment brought by the same applicant and the increasing number of repetitive cases brought before the ECtHR convinced the latter to launch a pilot procedure. The ECtHR expressly held that the State's refusal to comply was at the root of hundreds of similar applications, and that Russia had a duty to adopt the necessary measures.[71]

[67] e.g. *Wynne v UK* App No 67385/01 (ECtHR, 16 October 2003); *Slimane-Kaïd v France* App No 48943/99 (ECtHR, 27 November 2003); *Wasserman v Russia* App No 21071/05 (ECtHR, 10 April 2008).

[68] *Hertel v Switzerland* App No 53440/99 (ECtHR, 17 January 2002). See also *Mehemi v France* App No (ECtHR, 10 April 2003) where the Court found no violation of the ECHR.

[69] *VgT v Switzerland* (n 24) 49.

[70] Dissenting Opinion, 39.

[71] *Burdov v Russia* App No 33509/04 (ECtHR, 15 January 2009) 122: 'The Court has already found such violations in more than two hundred judgments since the first such finding in the *Burdov* case in 2002. The Court therefore finds it timely and appropriate to consider this second case brought by the same applicant under Article 46 of the Convention', 134: 'The Court notes with grave concern that the violations found in the present judgment

However, this approach has its limits and can be risky. An illustrative example is again the *VGT v Switzerland case*, as the CM had closed the implementation process by issuing a final resolution. Here the ECtHR's position prevailed. Another recent judgment, *Emre v Switzerland* confirms the willingness of the majority of the ECtHR to play a greater role.[72] However, judge Malinverni, in a dissenting opinion in which he was joined by judge Björgvinsson, considered that the judgment of the Federal Tribunal did not establish a new fact and that there was no violation of Articles 8 or 46, since the Swiss authorities had acted within the limits of national discretion.

These cases raise two issues: is the fact that the CM closes a case by final resolution a guarantee that the State complied fully with the judgment? If so, should the adoption of a final resolution make a difference for the ECtHR? The answers to both these questions seem to be negative. The CM concluded in each of its final resolutions that it had completed its tasks under Article 46, but not that the State had complied with the judgment. This latter assessment is made only by the government itself when submitting the final report to the Department and to the CM. Even if the ECtHR is cautious when dealing with matters linked to the implementation of its judgments, its abovementioned approach should be approved, as only the judicial organ has the competence to decide whether an applicant continues to suffer a violation of the ECHR. However, if the ECtHR goes too far, surely there is a risk that States will refuse to implement some of its judgments, which could jeopardize the whole system and the legitimacy of the judicial organ.

II. Repetitive cases: non-compliance and applications brought by other applicants

The right of other individuals to bring cases before the ECtHR because of repetitive violations in connection with a previous judgment which has not been complied with was precisely one of the main arguments put forward to oppose financial sanctions when debating the introduction of infringement proceedings. Member States argued that providing just satisfaction awards to other applicants would open the floodgates to claims and ultimately cost large amounts of money. However, the figures speak for themselves: in 2015, if all the judgments handed down by the ECtHR are taken together, the forty-seven State parties had to pay less than EUR 54 million;[73] in one infringement case alone, the CJEU required a State to pay EUR 58 million (a penalty payment for each period of six months of non-compliance) and a lump sum of EUR 20 million.[74]

Because of the increasing number of structural cases and the difficulties faced by many States to react quickly, many applicants have brought repetitive cases over the past twenty years. Such cases are joined by the CM for supervision of execution. Increasingly many pilot cases sanction non-compliance with one or several previous judgments. For instance, *Rumpf v Germany*[75] is a consequence of non-compliance with *Sürmeli*.[76] The same is true of *Vassilios Athanasiou and Others v Greece*,[77] where the ECtHR referred to an interim resolution adopted by the CM.[78] In more cases, a second finding of violation by the

occurred several years after its first judgment of 7 May 2002, notwithstanding Russia's obligation under Article 46 to adopt, under the supervision of the Committee of Ministers, the necessary remedial and preventive measures, both at individual and general levels'.

[72] *Emre v Switzerland* (n 25). [73] 9th Annual Report, 84.

[74] Case C-304/02 *Commission v France* [2005] ECLI:EU:C:2005:444.

[75] *Rumpf v Germany* App No 46344/06 (ECtHR, 2 September 2010).

[76] *Sürmeli v Germany* App No 75529/01 (EctHR, 8 June 2008).

[77] *Vassilios Athanasiou and Others v Greece* App No 50973/08 (ECtHR, 21 December 2010). [78] ibid, 15.

ECtHR (sometimes using the pilot procedure[79] with or without prescribed time frames) will be at times the only incentive to adopt the required general measures.[80] In such cases the interim resolutions adopted by the CM have proved much less effective.[81] Therefore, it is fundamental that the ECtHR maintains its practice. The introduction of infringement proceedings certainly does not make it redundant.

b. The introduction of infringement proceedings: a complete failure

The proposal to establish 'a Court of Justice with adequate sanctions for the implementation of this Charter' was already on the table in 1948, but did not succeed.[82] In the nineties it became obvious that there was no actually effective mechanism to tackle reluctant States. Interim Resolutions, which were expected to encourage States to abide by the judgments, proved quite ineffective, which partly explains their decreasing number (nineteen since 2010, fifty-three from 2004 to 2009).

Exclusion from the CoE remains one response theoretically open. Under Article 8 of the Statute, '[a]ny member of the Council of Europe which has seriously violated Article 3 may be suspended from its rights of representation and requested by the Committee of Ministers to withdraw under Article 7. If such member does not comply with this request, the Committee may decide that it has ceased to be a member of the Council as from such date as the Committee may determine'. Persistent failure could be interpreted as a serious violation of the 'principles of the rule of law and of the enjoyment [...] of human rights and fundamental freedoms' within the meaning of Article 3 of the Statute. It is true that 'States have a sense of belonging to the international community, and it is their fear of loss of good standing in that community that motivates them to comply'.[83] In reality, this measure turned out to be implausible. The case of *Loizidou v Turkey* led the CM to officially brandish the threat of exclusion for the first time.[84] Eissen suggested 'that a moral reprimand be imposed, or even that an attachment order be made in respect of any sums which the Treasury of the CoE may owe to the state concerned'.[85] Refusing a seat at the CM and/or calling for pressure from other international organisations might be more feasible.

Consequently, '[t]he new Article 46 therefore adds further possibilities of bringing pressure to bear to the existing ones. The procedure's mere existence, and the threat of using it, should act as an effective new incentive to execute the Court's judgments'.[86] Moreover, the additional power granted the CM to ask the ECtHR to interpret a final judgment was aimed at 'facilitating the supervision of its execution'.[87] This has never been done in practice for the convincing reason that as the ECtHR delivers increasingly many judgments, and as the judges have really made an effort to clarify the impact of their

[79] e.g. *Finger v Bulgaria* App No 37346/05 (ECtHR, 10 May 2011).

[80] e.g. *Nevmerzhitsky v Ukraine* App No 54825/00 (pending since 2005), the implementation of which benefited from: *Kharchenko v Ukraine* App No 40107/02 (ECtHR, 10 February 2011).

[81] *Manios v Greece* App No 70626/01 (ECtHR, 11 March 2004).

[82] P Boillat, 'The European Convention on Human Rights at 60: building on the past, looking to the future', http://www.coe.int/t/dc/files/source/Article_Boillat_en.doc, accessed 14 October 2016, 1.

[83] Alkoby (n 5).

[84] Interim Resolution Res/DH(2000)105, 24 July 2000. See also, in *Loizidou v Turkey*, Interim Resolution Res/DH(2001)80, 26 June 2001.

[85] M Eissen, 'La Cour européenne des Droits de l'Homme: de la Convention au règlement' (1959) 5 *Annuaire Français de Droit International* 618. The Venice Commission and the Parliamentary Assembly have also supported this idea.

[86] Explanatory Report to Protocol 14 to the ECHR, 16, http://www.conventions.coe.int/Treaty/EN/Reports/Html/194.htm, accessed 12 October 2016, 100.

[87] ibid, 96.

decisions, there would appear to be no real need to ask the ECtHR to interpret previous decisions.

However, the same argument cannot be supported when considering infringement proceedings. According to the Explanatory Report to Protocol 14, a refusal to comply means a refusal expressed by the State (or implied from its behaviour) to abide by a judgment. The literature welcomed this new tool as something useful even if the very strict way its scope has been defined (a State must 'refuse' to abide by the judgment) may cause it 'to be nothing more than a paper tiger'.[88] In fact, this provision has not yet been used, despite numerous requests being sent by NGOs to the Secretariat of the CM under Rule 9 of the Rules adopted in accordance with Rule 46,[89] with the *Fattulayev* and *Hirst* cases illustrating this new failure to take action.[90] This can either be attributed to the fact that only the CM can seize the ECtHR of a refusal, or to the lack of political will to address such difficulties, especially regarding the relationships between the ECtHR and the CM. Therefore, Article 46 must be amended to clarify the impact of these proceedings and to allow PACE, the Commissioner for Human Rights and the victims (under strict conditions of urgency and/or the seriousness of the case) to initiate infringement proceedings. Within the EU system, half of the infringement proceedings are brought by individuals. With regard to PACE, the Assembly got involved in the process of supervising the implementation of the most serious cases many years ago, and initiated the financial penalties project.[91]

In that vein, the ECtHR should also be made competent to order a State to pay damages to the Human Rights Trust Fund in a spirit of collective responsibility.[92] The EU's infringement proceedings became effective when the power to impose financial penalties was introduced. What would be the point of infringement proceedings in Strasbourg if the ECtHR did not have a similar power? If its role is limited to confirming the CM's view that

[88] K Mujezinovic Larsen, 'Compliance with judgments from the European Court of Human Rights: the Court's Call for Legislative Reforms' (2013) 4 *Nordic Journal of Human Rights* 496.

[89] 'Rule 9, Communications to the Committee of Ministers: 1. The Committee of Ministers shall consider any communication from the injured party with regard to payment of the just satisfaction or the taking of individual measures. 2. The Committee of Ministers shall be entitled to consider any communication from non-governmental organisations, as well as national institutions for the promotion and protection of human rights, with regard to the execution of judgments under Article 46(2) of the Convention'. See L Miara and V Prais, 'The role of civil society in the execution of judgments of the European Court of human rights' (2012) 5 *European Human Rights Law Review* 528. E Lambert Abdelgawad, 'Un nouveau rôle des ONG et des avocats dans la supervision de l'exécution des arrêts de la Cour européenne des droits de l'homme: Appréciation de la pratique des Communications de la Règle 9', in L Berg et al. (eds), *Liber Amicorum V Berger; Cohérence et impact de la jurisprudence de la Cour européenne des droits de l'homme* (Wolf 2013).

[90] *Hirst v UK* App No 74025/01 (ECtHR, 6 October 2005). With regard to *Fatullayev v Azerbaijan* App No 40984/07 (ECtHR, 22 April 2010), see the representative's letter sent on 28 February 2010, http://www.coe.int/t/dghl/monitoring/execution/Documents/Doc_ref_fr.asp, accessed 12 October 2016.

[91] PACE, 'Execution of judgments of the European Court of human rights' PACE/Res 1226(2000), 28 September 2000, 11A and PACE/Rec 1477(2000), 28 September 2000; also Doc 9307, 21 December 2001. See also E Lambert Abdelgawad, 'Le Protocole 14 et l'exécution des arrêts de la Cour européenne des droits de l'homme', in G Cohen-Jonathan and J-F Flauss, *La réforme du système de contrôle contentieux de la Convention européenne des droits de l'homme* (Nemesis 2005).

[92] Para 5 could be amended as follows: 'If the Court finds a violation of Art. 46(1), it may order the State to make a payment into the Human Rights Trust Fund, whose payment will be supervised by the Committee of Ministers'. 'For the other individual and general measures to be implemented, the Committee shall pursue its supervision'. The current last sentence of para 5 should also be amended. Regarding para 4, we propose: 'If the Committee of Ministers or the PACE considers that a High Contracting Party refuses to abide by a final judgment to which it is a Party, the Committee of the Assembly may refer the matter to the Court by a vote of two thirds after serving formal notice on that Party. The question may also be referred to the Court by an applicant to whom a remedy has been awarded but not received within a reasonable period and in case of urgent or serious matters'. See the Contribution of the National Council of Legal Advisers (POLAND) to open a call for information, http://www.coe.int/t/dghl/standardsetting/cddh/reformechr/GT-GDR-F/Online%20table_all%20contributions.asp, accessed 12 October 2016.

the State has not complied with a judgment, it adds no value. The accession of the EU to the ECHR should definitely convince experts and governments to move in this direction.

Finally, the argument against opening infringement proceedings to other actors because of the risk of overwhelming the ECtHR is not very convincing. The same risk existed with the introduction (with Protocol 14) of referral to the Grand Chamber (Article 43). Today, it has become obvious that some States have used precisely the right to have a case referred to the Grand Chamber to avoid its implementation, or at least to have it delayed. One of the best examples is certainly *Green and MT v the UK*,[93] where the applicants ultimately failed to convince the ECtHR.[94]

c. The need for further incentives? Taking States' defiance more seriously

We can now conclude that a State's refusal to comply has not been effectively sanctioned over the past twenty years and that there is a real risk, not only that the ECtHR and CM could be overwhelmed by repetitive cases (which is already the case), but that more States will challenge the authority of the system. Accordingly, additional and more rigorous reforms need to be adopted.[95] They do not all require amendments to the Convention.

The ECtHR should increase the amounts of damages for repetitive cases (a large percentage of pending cases) to exert greater pressure on States which do not adopt general measures in due time. In 2013 the UK offered the view that States must bear the cost of repetitive cases which are time-consuming for the whole system.[96] The ECtHR could also remind the State of the duty to act *ex tunc*, which is to adopt provisional measures if necessary to avoid similar violations. Thus the Department for the Execution of Judgments should assist States in discovering interim tools until general final measures are enacted. Moreover, it has become obvious that the CM does not exploit all the possibilities of its 'tool box', notably when urgent individual measures are required.[97] For instance, the CM could ask States, much more often than it currently does, to adopt measures within a specific period, or to mention the relevant national authorities, or even to prevent reluctant States from sharing certain responsibilities (the chairmanship of some rapporteur groups, the right to vote, etc). The new practice (launched in 2013) by which ministers are invited to join Human Rights (DH) meetings to explain the difficulties of implementing a specific judgment of the ECtHR, should be developed, but it would also be useful simultaneously to convene (depending on the issue) PACE's rapporteur and/or someone from the Committee for the Prevention of Torture (CPT), from the European Commission for the Efficiency of Justice (CEPEJ), or from the Venice Commission, as these organs may have been involved in the case by assisting national institutions, or could be. It is also fundamental to enlarge the role played by the applicants, their representatives, and civil society more broadly, as they are the core actors exercising the right of individual application. Accordingly, when an

[93] *Greens and MT v the United Kingdom* App Nos 60041/08 and 60054/08 (ECtHR, 23 November 2010).

[94] Press release, 11 April 2011, http://www.echr.coe.int/ECHR/FR/Header/Press/Links/archived+news/ArchivesNews_2011.htm, accessed 12 October 2016.

[95] See our contribution to the Conference on the long-term future of the ECtHR, Proceedings, Oslo 7, 8 April 2014 (CoE, PLURICourts, 2014), https://www.coe.int/t/DGHL/STANDARDSETTING/CDDH/REFORMECHR/Publications/Proceedings-Oslo-2014.pdf, accessed 15 October 2016.

[96] GT-GRD-E(2013) 009, 11 July 2013. 'Financial penalties or punitive damages: as noted by the DH-GDR, it is important to distinguish two different concepts: (a) the use of financial penalties to force implementation of a judgment, by way of a punishment for non-implementation; and (b) specifically where the Court is required to spend its limited resources processing repetitive applications as the result of non-execution of a judgment, payments by the respondent State to cover the Court's costs of doing so'.

[97] GT-DH-PR A (2008)002, 'Inventory of tools allowing the Committee to react, if necessary, to situations of slowness in execution', Document prepared by the Department for the Execution of Judgments of the Court, 37.

urgent individual measure has not been adopted by a State, the CM should offer the applicant's representative the opportunity to join a DH meeting. The same should apply for NGOs when general measures have not been adopted. This possibility had been raised by experts and the Department for the Execution of Judgments in 2008.[98]

Moreover, more than sixty per cent of cases pending before the CM concern only four States.[99] Consequently, it appears urgent and natural to adopt specific measures for these States. Should their contribution to the budget of the ECtHR and to the Department for the Execution of Judgments be reconsidered, taking into account a fixed part (according to the current criteria) and a flexible one (taking into account the number of pending cases and/or the number of pending cases under enhanced supervision, and/or the ratio between the number of cases and the population)? The question needs to be addressed.

The counterpart of the principle of subsidiarity is that a clear red line must not be transgressed. It is obvious that the current system should not be made to suffer the consequences of State failures through the already large number of pending cases. The legitimacy and authority of the European system depend on its capacity to respond to State refusals. If the current system (with the CM at its core) does not prove more efficient in the coming months, supervision should be transferred to the ECtHR (at least for the most serious cases), as the involvement of the judicial organ proved much more effective in the past.[100] Therefore, it has become urgent for the CM to play down the use of infringement proceedings and to use other incentive measures.

Within the framework of the ECHR, compliance has revealed itself to be a complex issue, notably for two reasons: first, a judgment can raise structural deficiencies and second, compliance does not only involve normative consequences. Therefore, it has even been difficult in some cases to determine with certainty that a State has fully complied with a judgment. While the EU has relied mainly on a constraint-based model in infringement proceedings, coupled with daily fines, and on a delegation or elite model of accountability to compel states to enforce the judgments of the CJEU promptly, the CoE has opted for a very different approach: that of persuasion, coordination among the various national and European bodies concerned, and accountability of authorities at different levels, in keeping with the participatory model of accountability. While cooperation and dialogue have proved fundamental, this model has also clearly shown its limits and consequences: an increasing number of repetitive cases pending before the ECtHR and the CM. It is time to consider whether the competence of the CM should remain unchanged: Philippe Boillat, Director General of Human Rights and Legal Affairs of the CoE, wondered in 2008 whether we should not 'confer this task on a body with more judicial character, separate from the Committee of ministers or under its delegated authority'.[101] His thoughts remain true.

[98] ibid, 39. GT-GRD-E(2013) 009, 11 July 2013.

[99] Italy, Turkey, Russia, Ukraine: 9th Annual Report 2015, 62.

[100] B Cali and A Koch, 'Foxes Guarding the Foxes? The Perr review of Human Rights Judgments by the Committee of Ministers of the Council of Europe' (2014) 14 *Human Rights Law Review* 301.

[101] P Boillat, 'Summary Conclusions', in Colloquy 'Towards stronger implementation of the European Convention on Human Rights at the national level' (Stockholm, 8 and 9 June 2008), http://www.coe.int/t/dghl/standardsetting/cddh/Publications/Stockholm_Proceedings.pdf, accessed 12 October 2016.

20

Enforcing WTO Law

Antonello Tancredi

1. Introduction

Among the international legal subsystems which can provide guidance about law enforcement against recalcitrant Member States, the WTO is arguably one of the least contiguous to the EU. Indeed, in the WTO legal system, the enforcement of the rules is essentially linked to the power of the parties to resort to countermeasures according to private justice schemes, but under the control of the organization. Retaliation is the ultimate sanction for Member parties conduct inconsistent with the organization's norms. Unlike other international organizations, WTO bodies are not even endowed with the power to suspend or expel a non-complying member. The only way to dissolve membership is withdrawal (regulated by Article XV Agreement Establishing the WTO).

By contrast—as observed by AG Léger in his Opinion delivered in the *Hedley Lomas* case—'[n]othing is more alien to Community law than the idea of a measure of retaliation or reciprocity proper to classical public international law'.[1]

The reason for this stark difference can be found in the fact that, as maintained by the EU Court of First Instance in the *Biret* case '[t]he purpose of the WTO agreements is to govern relations between States or regional organizations for economic integration and not to protect individuals [. . .] the agreements are still founded on the principle of negotiations with a view to entering into reciprocal and mutually advantageous arrangements'.[2]

Again in contrast, according to the ECJ in the leading *Commission v Luxembourg and Belgium* case '[. . .] the Treaty is not limited to creating reciprocal obligations between the different natural and legal persons to whom it is applicable but establishes a new legal order which governs the powers, rights and obligations of the said persons, as well as the necessary procedures for taking cognizance of and penalizing any breach of it. Therefore [. . .] the basic concept of the Treaty requires that the Member States shall not take the law into their own hands'.[3] Accordingly, as subsequently stated by the same ECJ '[i]n the legal order established by the Treaty, the implementation of Community law by the Member States cannot be made subject to a condition of reciprocity'.[4]

[1] Case C-5/94 *The Queen v Ministry of Agriculture, Fisheries and Food, ex parte Hedley Lomas (Ireland) Ltd* [1995] ECLI:EU:C:1996:205, para 27 of the Opinion.

[2] Case T-210/00 *Établissements Biret et Cie SA v Council* [2002] ECLI:EU:T:2002:3, para 72. According to the AG Léger in *Ikea*, the reason why WTO law only aims at regulating relations among States is that its purpose is not 'to create [. . .] a single market similar to that developed within the European Community. Far more modestly, it forms a common institutional framework within which the Contracting Parties negotiate' (Case C-351/04 *Ikea Wholesale Ltd v Commissioners of Customs and Excise* [2007] ECLI:EU:C:2007:547, para 84). For a similar view, in the legal scholarship, see A von Bogdandy, 'Legal Effects of World Trade Organization Decisions Within European Union Law: A Contribution to the Theory of the Legal Acts of International Organizations and the Action for Damages Under Article 288 (2) EC' (2005) 39 *Journal of World Trade* 45, 54.

[3] Joined Cases 90/63 and 91/63 *Commission v Luxembourg and Belgium* [1964] ECLI:EU:C:1964:80, para 631.

[4] Case C-38/89 *Ministère public v Guy Blanguernon* [1990] ECLI:EU:C:1990:11, para 7.

After all, as observed by Jacqué, the dividing line between different enforcement systems rests upon the possibility of making some relationships bilateral and of playing the 'réciprocité-sanction'[5] with reference to a single State party without prejudice to the rights of other States parties, or—as pointed out by Weiler—without prejudice to the *rights* of individuals.[6] Such a move seems easier to conceive (as concerns the bilateralization of the inter-state relationships), or corresponds to an issue *legally* not dominant, albeit very important factually (as concerns the position of individuals) in the WTO, while this is almost inconceivable within the EU legal system.[7]

As is clear from these introductory notes, the main objective of this chapter—which employs a mostly descriptive method—is to provide a brief analysis of the enforcement tools foreseen in the WTO dispute settlement mechanism and to focus in particular on some of the peculiarities which differentiate them from the EU legal system. From this perspective—as partly illustrated by the case law quoted above—*reciprocity*, but also *post-litigation negotiations* between States, seem to be two of the main features which distinguish the nature of the primary norms and the ensuing implementation mechanisms of the WTO legal system vis-à-vis those of the EU. As the analysis will show, the relevance of these elements influences the legal nature of the WTO dispute settlement system, which today remains to a large extent a *mixed* or *hybrid* system,[8] since it combines diplomatic and judicial means of dispute settlement throughout the whole procedure. This conclusion contrasts one of the mantras diffused in the legal scholarship immediately after the entry into force of the Uruguay Round Agreements, namely that the GATT 1947 had undergone a radical transformation from a 'power-oriented' to an eminently 'rule-oriented' system.[9] It also represents a vehicle for the potential fragmentation of the multilateral legal framework governing international trade, which contributes to undermining the idea of uniformity of the obligations arising under the WTO Agreements for all Members.[10]

[5] 'Tout depend de la possibilité de bilatéraliser certaines relations au sein de la Communauté et de faire jouer la réciprocité-sanction à l'égard d'une seule partie sans porter atteinte au droit des autres membres', J-P Jacqué, 'Reciprocité, droit communautaire et droit interne français', in G Lüke et al. (eds), *Rechtsvergleichung, Europarecht und Staatenintegration. Gedächtnisschrift für Léontin-Jean Constantinesco* (Carl Heymanns 1983) 325, 336.

[6] JHH Weiler, 'The Transformation of Europe' (1991) 100 *Yale Law Journal* 2403, 2422 and fn 42, according to whom the reason why the EC legal order is 'a truly self-contained legal regime with no recourse to the mechanism of state responsibility, at least as traditionally understood, and therefore to reciprocity and countermeasures' is twofold: the existence of a 'comprehensive system of compulsory judicial dispute resolution and remedies', and the fact that 'even in an extreme case in which a Member State failed to execute a judgment of the European Court, the recourse to countermeasures would inevitably affect individuals removed from the dispute, militating against the very notion of a "new legal order of international law... the subjects of which comprise not the only Member States but also their nationals"'.

[7] See L-A Sicilianos, *Les réactions décentralisées à l'illicite: des contre-mesures à la légitime défense* (LGDJ 1990), 363–5, according to whom EC obligations 'revêtent un caractère integral et interdépendant dû à l'objet même des traités communautaires et qu'elles sont de surcroît garanties par des mécanismes institutionnels perfectionnés, facteurs qui excluent la possibilité d'y porter atteinte par voie de contre-mesures'.

[8] See for this thesis, P Picone and A Ligustro, *Diritto dell'Organizzazione mondiale del commercio* (CEDAM 2002) 583.

[9] The distinction between 'power-oriented' and 'rule-oriented' systems of dispute settlement was inaugurated, with specific reference to the GATT, by J Jackson, 'The Crumbling Institutions of the Liberal Trade System' (1978) 12 *Journal of World Trade* 93; and J Jackson, 'Governmental Disputes in International Trade Relations: A Proposal in the Context of GATT' (1979) 13 *Journal of World Trade* 1. After the entry into force of the new WTO dispute settlement mechanism, the idea of a radical shift towards a 'rule-oriented' system was maintained by a large number of authors, see for instance E-U Petersmann, 'The Dispute Settlement System of the World Trade Organization and the Evolution of the GATT Dispute Settlement System Since 1948' (1994) 31 *Common Market Law Review* 1157; and T Cottier, 'Dispute Settlement in the World Trade Organization: Characteristics and Structural Implications for the European Union' (1998) 35 *Common Market Law Review* 325.

[10] View upheld, for instance, by G Marceau, 'Conflicts of Norms and Conflicts of Jurisdictions. The Relationship between the WTO Agreement and MEAs and Other Treaties' (2001) 35 *Journal of World Trade* 1081, 1105 ('WTO obligations are always the same for all Members').

2. The enforcement mechanism set up by the WTO DSU

According to Article 22.2 WTO DSU, if the WTO Member whose conduct has been found in breach of WTO substantial obligations fails to bring the WTO-inconsistent measure into compliance with the recommendations and rulings of the DSB within a reasonable period, this member must if requested enter into negotiations with any party having invoked the dispute settlement procedures, with a view to developing mutually acceptable compensation. If an agreement on compensation is not reached within twenty days after the expiration of the reasonable period allowed for compliance, the complaining Member may request authorization of countermeasures in the form of the suspension of concessions or other obligations under the agreements covered.

The DSB (which is a session of the General Council of the WTO, therefore composed of all the representatives of the WTO member parties) under Article 22.6 DSU authorizes countermeasures almost automatically under the 'reversed consensus' rule (namely, unless a negative consensus is reached, which would imply that the complaining Member should vote against its own request). Accordingly, many speak of a 'right' to countermeasures. In case the Member concerned objects to the level of approved countermeasures, the issue is submitted to arbitral proceedings.

When considering the suspension of concessions or other obligations, the complaining Member is guided by the principles of Article 22.3 DSU, i.e. it should first seek to suspend concessions with respect to the same sector as that in which the violation or other nullification or impairment is found; and only if this is impracticable or ineffective have resort to 'cross-sector' or 'cross-agreement' retaliation. If this is the *qualitative* requirement which constrains the freedom of choice of the complaining member on the other hand, the *quantitative* limit is set out in Article 22.4 DSU, according to which the level of countermeasures authorized 'shall be equivalent to the level of the nullification or impairment'.

Countermeasures pursue a dual objective.[11] They serve as an incentive 'to *induce compliance*'.[12] In addition, countermeasures also compensate, but only prospectively, the injury suffered by the complaining Member, and in so doing, aim at partially rebalancing concessions or obligations.[13] Since—as already said—the level of authorized countermeasures must be *equivalent* to the level of nullification or impairment, punitive countermeasures are not allowed by the DSU. Furthermore, since the WTO dispute settlement mechanism is aimed at securing 'the withdrawal of the measures' found illegal, the remedies granted under the DSU are non-retroactive, i.e. they are limited to the harm which occurs after the expiry of the reasonable period granted for implementation (a period often agreed bilaterally),[14] and thus do not provide *restitutio in integrum*.

[11] For further analysis, see D Palmeter and SA Alexandrov, '"Inducing Compliance" in WTO Dispute Settlement', in D Kennedy and JD Southwick (eds), *The Political Economy of International Trade Law: Essays in Honour of Robert E. Hudec* (CUP 2002), 646; G Sheffer and D Ganin, 'Extrapolating Purpose from Practice: Rebalancing or Inducing Compliance', in CP Bown and J Pauwelyn (eds), *The Law, Economics and Politics of Retaliation in WTO Dispute Settlement* (CUP 2010) 73, 82.

[12] WTO, *European Communities—Regime for the Importation, Sale and Distribution of Bananas—Recourse to Arbitration by the European Communities under Article 22.6 of the DSU—Decision by the Arbitrators* (9 April 1999) WT/DS27/ARB, para 6.3. See also *European Communities—Measures Concerning Meat and Meat Products (Hormones)—Original Complaint by Canada—Recourse to Arbitration by the European Communities under Article 22.6 of the DSU—Decision by the Arbitrators* (12 July 1999) WT/DS48/ARB, para 39.

[13] J Tijmes, 'Jurisprudential Developments on the Purpose of WTO Suspension of Obligations' (2014) 13 *World Trade Review* 1.

[14] *European Communities—Measures Concerning Meat and Meat Products (Hormones)—Original Complaint by the United States—Recourse to Arbitration by the European Communities under Article 22.6 of the DSU—Decision by the Arbitrators* (12 July 1999) WT/DS26/ARB, para 38.

Consequently, as has been recently observed, countermeasures 'fall short of ensuring that reciprocal commitments are not disturbed as the result of the commission of an illegality'.[15] In other words, since remedies are prospective, the authors of illegal acts 'pay back' less than the damage they cause, which is rather at odds with Article 3.2 DSU, according to which the WTO dispute settlement system 'serves to preserve the rights and obligations of members under the covered agreements'. Furthermore, this may create incentives to delay implementation, which is in contrast with the idea expressed in Article 22.1 DSU that 'prompt compliance with recommendations or rulings of the DSB is essential in order to ensure effective resolution of disputes to the benefits of all Members'. These features of the WTO dispute settlement system differentiate it clearly from the EU legal system, where—pursuant to Article 260 TFEU—if the Commission considers that a Member State has not taken the necessary measures to comply with a judgment of the Court of Justice, it may return the matter to the Court and propose lump sum and/or penalty payment.

The dispute settlement mechanism established by the DSU is also *exclusive*. In fact, Article 23 DSU rules out other unilateral options not covered by the DSU but available under domestic (for instance, sections 301–10 *US Trade Act*) or general international law.

The sanction regime mechanism, in principle at least, is not an alternative to full compliance. In other words, there is no 'buy option'. A State cannot buy release from obligations, since compensation and suspension are only 'temporary measures' (Article 22.1 DSU), and are not 'preferred to full implementation of a recommendation to bring a measure into conformity with the covered agreements'.

From the WTO's inception (1 January 1995) to 31 October 2014, out of nearly 500 disputes which have been brought to the WTO, the DSB has only authorized eighteen formal requests for countermeasures (two formal requests were made the same day by the same country, Brazil, in the same *US—Upland Cotton* case)[16] related to ten different disputes;[17] the number of implemented measures is even lower (in at least five cases, in fact, the authorized retaliation was never applied).[18] Most of the authorized requests have come from the US (2), Canada (3), the EC (2), and Brazil (4)) but two of them concern the same dispute, as already noted). The first three of these countries belong to the GATT-era 'Quadrilateral' or Quad countries (Canada, the EU, Japan, and the US), i.e. the traditional trade powers of the twentieth century. More generally, as has been observed with reference

[15] PC Mavroidis, 'Dispute Settlement in the WTO (Mind over Matter)' (2015) EUI Working Papers RSCAS No 34, 16.

[16] *United States—Subsidies on Upland Cotton (I and II)—Recourse to Article 4.10 of the SCM Agreement and Article 22.7 of the DSU by Brazil* (9 November 2009) WT/DS267/41; and *Recourse to Article 7.9 of the SCM Agreement and Article 22.7 of the DSU by Brazil* (9 November 2009) WT/DS267/42 and (19 November 2009) WT/DSB/M/276 for the DSB's authorization.

[17] *Overview of the State of Play of WTO Disputes—Annual Report (2014) Addendum* (26 November 2014) WT/DSB/64/Add.1, 143.

[18] *European Communities—Regime for the Importation, Sale and Distribution of Bananas—Recourse to Article 22.7 of the DSU by Ecuador* (8 May 2000) WT/DS27/54 and (18 May 2000) WT/DSB/M/80 for the DSB's authorisation; *Brazil—Export Financing Programme for Aircraft—Recourse by Canada to Article 22.7 of the DSU and Article 4.10 of the SCM Agreement* (1 December 2000) WT/DS46/25 and (12 December 2000) WT/DSB/M/94 for the DSB's authorization; *Canada—Export Credits and Loan Guarantees for Regional Aircraft—Recourse by Brazil to Article 22.7 of the DSU and Article 4.10 of the SCM Agreement* (7 March 2003) WT/DS222/10 and (18 March 2003) WT/DSB/M/145 for the DSB's authorization; *United States—Subsidies on Upland Cotton (I and II)—Recourse to Article 4.10 of the SCM Agreement and Article 22.7 of the DSU by Brazil* (9 November 2009) WT/DS267/41, and *Recourse to Article 7.9 of the SCM Agreement and Article 22.7 of the DSU by Brazil* (9 November 2009) WT/DS267/42 and (19 November 2009) WT/DSB/M/276 for the DSB's authorization; *United States—Measures Affecting the Cross Border Supply of Gambling and Betting Services—Recourse by Antigua and Barbuda to Article 22.7 of the DSU* (13 December 2012) WT/DS285/25 and (28 January 2013) WT/DSB/M/328 for the DSB's authorization.

to the period up to the end of 2013,[19] Canada has been the most assiduous complainant—with seven requests for (authorized or non-authorized) countermeasures—followed by the EU and the US, with six requests each. Among the G20 economies, considering the ratio of complaints over responses in aggregate for WTO disputes from 1995 to 2013, Canada appears to be an offensive trade power, while the US is the most frequent responder.[20]

Those numbers point to a reality that a 'retaliation club' seems to exist among the WTO membership and also highlights some specific weaknesses of the enforcement mechanism established by the DSU.

Firstly, Quad Members have a certain tendency to resist complying swiftly with DSB rulings,[21] thereby forcing offended countries to request the suspension of concessions or other obligations. The efficiency of the mechanism, thus suffers from the Members' dilatory practice—especially the 'big players' in the system—with respect to timely implementation and to difficulties in identifying effective countermeasures. For instance, the US tends to implement recommendations duly and promptly only if the withdrawal of the offending measure does not involve the US Congress and lies within the powers of the executive.[22] In cases such as *US-Antidumping Act of 1916*,[23] and *US-Offset Act (Byrd Amendment)*,[24] the US refused to implement recommendations for many years and has therefore been (at least in the latter case) targeted by countermeasures from the EU and other Members. On the other side of the Atlantic, the saga of the 'banana disputes' over the *EC-Bananas* regime, with a lengthy sequence of half-hearted steps towards implementation,[25] and the *EC-Hormones* dispute,[26] equally provide telling examples of 'feet-dragging', namely of legislative attitudes towards compliance which are open to reproach.

Secondly, it is often—albeit not unanimously[27]—maintained that developing countries are entirely unable to make effective use of possible countermeasures in a way that would be economically practicable. This is mainly due to their insufficient market size and the negative impact that a rise in trade barriers can have on the development of the local economy, and the quality of life of domestic consumers. Consequently, as previously seen, complaining parties not infrequently refrain from imposing countermeasures, even when they have been authorized to retaliate. In this regard, cross-retaliation has proved to be an important tool for WTO Members with smaller bargaining power determined to cause difficulties to more powerful members able to delay full compliance thanks to their economic power in the sector in which the original dispute took place.[28]

[19] See D Bonomo, 'Hitting Where It Hurts: Retaliation Requests in the WTO', available at: http://www.voxeu.org/article/retaliation-wto, accessed 12 October 2016.

[20] ibid.

[21] See on this, WJ Davey, 'Evaluating WTO Dispute Settlement: What Results Have Been Achieved Through Consultations and Implementation of Panel Reports?' in Y Taniguchi et al. (eds), *The WTO in the Twenty-First Century* (CUP 2007) 98, 113.

[22] J Jackson, 'The WTO Dispute Settlement System after Ten Years: the First Decade's Promises and Challenges', in Y Taniguchi et al. (eds) (n 21) 23.

[23] *United States—Anti-Dumping Act of 1916—Recourse by the European Communities to Article 22.2 of the DSU* (11 January 2002) WT/DS136/15.

[24] *United States—Continued Dumping and Subsidy Offset Act of 2000*, authorizations to suspend concession granted at the DSB meetings on 26 November 2004, WT/DSB/M/178; and on 17 December 2004, WT/DSB/M/180.

[25] See S Griller and E Vranes, 'EC-Bananas Case', *Max Planck Encyclopedia of Public International Law* (online edn, OUP 2016).

[26] See M Koebele, 'EC-Hormones Case', ibid.

[27] See H Nottage, 'Evaluating the Criticism that WTO Retaliation Rules Undermine the Utility of WTO Dispute Settlement for Developing Countries', in Bown and Pauwelyn (n 11) 319.

[28] See G Marceau and JA Hamaoui, 'Implementation of Recommendations and Rulings in the WTO System', in L Boisson de Chazournes et al. (eds), *Diplomatic and Judicial Means of Dispute Settlement* (Martinus Nijhoff 2013) 187, 208–9.

Other weaknesses in the system are that the DSU rules on compensation and the suspension of obligations do not envisage payment of compensation to the affected industries; that compensation is costly (since, according to Article 22.1 DSU it 'shall be consistent with the covered agreements', and thus it should be given without discrimination on the basis of the most-favoured-nation principle), it invites 'free riding', and it is a form of *aliud pro alio*, in the sense that it does not concern a measure which has been found WTO-inconsistent; and that remedies are only prospective since, as already noted, no retroactive redress is provided.

3. Reciprocity as an objective of the WTO legal system

As is evident in this description, the WTO implementation mechanism is based on a system of 'organized' countermeasures which displays elements of originality with respect to other international organizations, and the EU most prominently. In the WTO legal system the implementation of the agreements covered is not the result of a collective guarantee. The only thing which is collective is the control of the implementation of the WTO DSB's rulings potentially (and not necessarily) performed by the whole membership sitting in that organ. No organ plays the role of the EU Commission as the guardian of the inner legality of the system, endowed with the power to trigger *ex officio* enforcement proceedings. Accordingly, the level of 'organization' of the reaction is greatly inferior.

Furthermore, Member States are not prohibited from violating the agreements covered in retaliation. They are only required to obtain an automatic authorization, and to submit themselves to the DSB's control concerning their compliance with the *quantum* of the reaction. The *quomodo*, however, is normally left to their discretion.

These aspects of originality of the WTO system can only be explained with the predominantly bilateral (even if 'multilateralizable') and reciprocal character of WTO obligations,[29] unlike the obligations flowing from the EU or the human rights treaties. The essentially sinalagmatic nature of most obligations entered into by the WTO Members—a feature which however admits of some well-identified exceptions (such as Article 4 Agreement on Subsidies and Countervailing Measures and Article XXIII of the General Agreement on Trade in Services)—was remarked on by the WTO Appellate Body in the *Japan—Alcoholic Beverages* case, where it was pointed out that '[t]he *WTO Agreement* is a treaty – the international equivalent of a contract. It is self-evident that in an exercise of their sovereignty, and in pursuit of their own respective national interests, the Members of the WTO have made a bargain'.[30]

On the other hand, when reference has been made to the existence of '*erga omnes per se*'[31] obligations (for instance, with reference to the prohibition of granting and maintaining an export subsidy), this notion has been invoked incorrectly or technically imperfectly.[32]

[29] Reciprocity may be defined 'as the status of a relationship between two or more States (State) under which a certain conduct by one party is in one way or another juridically dependent upon that of the other party. Such conduct will in most instances, but not necessarily, amount to identical or equivalent treatment' (B Simma, 'Reciprocity', *Max Planck Encyclopedia of Public International Law* (online edn, OUP 2016) para 2). When the treatment is identical, reciprocity is formal; when the treatment is equivalent, reciprocity is substantial.

[30] *Japan—Taxes on Alcoholic Beverages—Report of the Appellate Body* (1 November 1996) WT/DS8/AB/R, WT/DS10/AB/R, WT/DS11/AB/R, 15.

[31] See, for instance, *United States—Tax Treatment for 'Foreign Sales Corporations'—Recourse to Arbitration by the United States under Article 22.6 of the DSU and Article 4.11 of the* SCM Agreement—*Decision of the Arbitrator* (30 August 2002) WT/DS108/ARB, para 6.10.

[32] On this, see V Di Comite, *Le sovvenzioni e le misure compensative nell'Organizzazione mondiale del commercio* (CEDAM 2009) 351, fn 316.

Furthermore, as concerns the role of substantial reciprocity in the WTO legal system, mention must immediately be made of the third recital of the Preamble of the Agreement Establishing the WTO (which reproduces the identical recital contained in the Preamble of the GATT 1947), according to which the achievement of the objectives described in the other recitals of the Preamble of the WTO will be pursued 'by entering into reciprocal and mutually advantageous arrangements' directed at the reduction of the barriers to trade and the elimination of discrimination in international trade. WTO adjudicating bodies have made reference to this reciprocity pact in their case law for interpretative purposes. In *European Communities—Frozen Chicken Cuts*, for instance, the Appellate Body upheld the panel's view that 'trade liberalization is achieved through negotiations for *mutual benefit*'.[33] That is to say that the expansion of trade and the reduction of tariffs cannot be sought outside a logic of mutually beneficial exchanges, namely over and beyond the equilibrium of reciprocal interests.

Seen from this perspective, the persisting doctrinal debate between those who support a 'contractual' vision of the WTO,[34] and those who adhere to a 'collectivist' vision (according to which WTO obligations should be construed as '*erga omnes partes*'),[35] seems essentially a debate between a descriptive and a normative conception of the system—a normative conception which the WTO dispute settlement practice still struggles or fails to confirm.

4. Reciprocity and the WTO dispute settlement mechanism: the issue of the *locus standi*

Let us now consider those aspects of the principle of reciprocity which are more strictly linked with the functioning of the WTO dispute settlement mechanism.

A first point is *locus standi* (ie the right to bring an action in a dispute) before the WTO dispute settlement bodies. This issue must be approached bearing in mind that according to Article 3.2 DSU '[t]he members recognize that it [the dispute settlement system of the WTO] serves to preserve the rights and obligations of members under the covered agreements', rights and obligations which the recommendations and rulings of the DSB cannot add to or diminish. Furthermore, according to Article 3.3 DSU 'The prompt settlement [...] is essential to [...] the maintenance of a proper *balance* between the rights and obligations of Members' (emphasis added), expression that clearly recalls the preservation of sinalagmatic relations between contracting parties.

However—although Article IX.2 Agreement Establishing the WTO attributes to the Ministerial Conference and the General Council 'the exclusive authority to adopt

[33] *European Communities—Customs Classification of Frozen Boneless Chicken Cuts—Report of the Appellate Body* (12 September 2005) WT/DS269/AB/R, WT/DS286/AB/R, para 243 (emphasis added).

[34] MJ Hahn, *Die einseitige Aussetzung von GATT-Verpflichtungen als Repressalie* (Springer 1996) 152; J Pauwelyn, 'A Typology of Multilateral Treaty Obligations: Are WTO Obligations Bilateral or Collective in Nature' (2003) 14 *European Journal of International Law* 907; J Pauwelyn, *Conflict of Norms in Public International Law. How WTO Law Relates to Other Rules of International Law* (CUP 2003) 52; RZ Lawrence, *Crimes and Punishment? Retaliation under the WTO* (Peterson Institute 2003) 19; Y Fukunaga, 'Securing Compliance through the WTO Dispute Settlement System: Implementation of DSB Recommendations' (2006) 9 *Journal of International Economic Law* 383; T. Gazzini, 'The Legal Nature of WTO Obligations and the Consequences of Their Violation' (2006) 17 *European Journal of International Law* 723; ME Footer, *An Institutional and Normative Analysis of the World Trade Organization* (Martinus Nijhoff 2006) 193–4; A von Bogdandy, 'Preamble WTO Agreement', in R Wolfrum et al. (eds), *WTO—Institutions and Dispute Settlement* (Martinus Nijhoff 2006), 1, 12.

[35] Y Iwasawa, 'WTO Dispute Settlement as Judicial Supervision' (2002) 5 *Journal of International Economic Law* 287, 295; NH Yenkong, 'Third Party Rights and the Concept of Legal Interest in World Trade Organization Dispute Settlement: Extending Participatory Rights to Enforcement Rights' (2004) 38 *Journal of World Trade* 757, 768; C Carmody, 'WTO Obligations as Collective' (2006) 17 *European Journal of International Law* 419; L Gradoni, Regime Failure *nel diritto internazionale* (CEDAM 2009), 153.

interpretations'—it must also be recalled that according to Article 3.2 DSU, the dispute settlement system serves also 'to clarify the existing provisions of those agreements in accordance with customary rules of interpretation of public international law', which in principle does not exclude the possibility of claims presented with the aim to obtain a clarification of the rules contained in the covered agreements. Accordingly, in June 2014 the EU filed a complaint against Indonesia, claiming to have '*a systemic interest* in the correct and consistent interpretation and application of the covered agreements'[36] (particularly with respect to the so-called 'sequencing problem' between compliance proceedings under Article 21.5 DSU and recourse to retaliation),[37] and that 'A WTO Member bringing a case under the DSU does not have to demonstrate any special interest over and above the fact of a WTO inconsistency',[38] citing the Appellate Body Report in *EC—Bananas III*. However, the EU also invoked a breach of *its* third party rights, and claimed to be itself involved in the production, trade, and regulation of clove cigarettes, and thus to have 'a close interest'[39] in compliance/arbitration proceedings from which it had been excluded as a third party (in the original panel proceedings and in the original Appellate Body proceedings) and upon request of Indonesia. Having been excluded from compliance proceedings, its 'substantial interest' (condition whose recurrence is requested in order to intervene as a third party pursuant to Article 10.2 DSU, but—oddly enough—which has not been deemed necessary in order to have standing and to initiate proceedings under the textual (but not very systematic) interpretation adopted by the Appellate Body in the *EC-Bananas III* case)[40] could not have been taken completely into account in breach of the prerogatives of third parties laid down in Article 10 DSU. For all these reasons, the EU argued that 'Indonesia's measures appear to nullify or impair *benefits* accruing to the European Union directly or indirectly'.[41] However, whether the EU had *locus standi* in this case and on what ground, will remain unknown since the EU's request for consultations has been withdrawn as a consequence of the settlement reached in the dispute on *Clove Cigarettes* between the US and Indonesia; accordingly the case has been terminated under a mutually agreed solution notified by the EU and Indonesia on 6 May 2015 prior to a panel report.[42]

[36] *Indonesia—Recourse to Article 22.2 of the DSU in the US—Clove Cigarettes Dispute—Request for Consultations by the European Union* (19 June 2014) WT/DS481/1, G/L/1072, 4 (emphasis added).

[37] The 'sequencing problem' first came up in the *EC—Bananas III* dispute, and relates to the question of how to coordinate requests for authorization to adopt countermeasures under Art 22 DSU and examination of the WTO-consistency of a measure taken to comply with the DSB's rulings and recommendations pursuant to Art 21.5 DSU. In fact, if a disagreement on implementation arises, Art 21.5 compliance proceedings would normally not be completed within the time limit of twenty days from the expiration of the reasonable period of time which is required under Art 22 DSU in order to introduce a request for authorization to suspend concessions or other obligations when no compensation has been agreed. In practice WTO Members have overcome the issue by concluding mutual agreements whereby the requests for suspension of concessions and referral to an Art 21.5 panel are made simultaneously, but the retaliation procedures are suspended until the Art 21.5 procedures are concluded. There is also a second type of agreement where the parties agree to preserve a Member's right to request authorization to suspend concessions until after the Art 21.5 process has been completed, even if this is after the expiry of the deadline foreseen in Art 22 DSU (see CM Valles and BP McGivern, 'The Right to Retaliate under the WTO Agreement – The 'Sequencing' Problem' (2000) 34 *Journal of World Trade* 63; SA Rhodes, 'The Article 21.5/22 Problem: Clarification through Bilateral Agreements?' (2000) 3 *Journal of International Economic Law* 553; PC Mavroidis, 'Proposals for Reform of Article 22 of the DSU: Reconsidering the 'Sequencing' Issue and Suspension of Concessions', in F Ortino, E-U Petersmann (eds), *The WTO Dispute Settlement System, 1995–2003* (Kluwer 2004) 61; A Yanovich 'The Evolving WTO Dispute Settlement System' in Taniguchi et al. (n 21) 248, 250.

[38] *Indonesia—Recourse to Article 22.2* (n 36). [39] ibid.

[40] *European Communities—Regime for the Importation, Sale and Distribution of Bananas—Report of the Appellate Body* (9 September 1997) WT/DS27/AB/R, para 132.

[41] *Indonesia—Recourse to Article 22.2* (n 36) 6 (emphasis added).

[42] *Indonesia—Recourse to Article 22.2 of the DSU in the US—Clove Cigarettes Dispute—Notification of a Mutually Agreed Solution and Withdrawal of a Request for Consultations* (11 May 2015) WT/DS481/5, G/L/1072/Add.1.

One possibility for tackling the issue of *locus standi* is to consider it resolved by Article 3.3 DSU (in accordance with the provisions of Article XXIII.1 GATT 1947), by referring primarily to the notion of nullification or impairment of benefits directly or indirectly enjoyed by the Members of the WTO. In this regard, however, it must be recalled that according to the Appellate Body in *EC—Bananas III (Article 21.5—US)* 'the notion of "standing" [...] is broader than the notion of "nullification or impairment"' to the extent that 'standing may also exist in cases which result in no finding of nullification or impairment'.[43] On the other hand 'the fact that nullification or impairment implies a higher standard than "legal standing" does not mean that "standing" cannot be found based on such higher standard'.[44] Accordingly, the question of standing does not automatically correspond to the question of knowing whether a violation of WTO obligations caused or did not cause a nullification or impairment of benefits, even if the existence of such a nullification or impairment implies standing to bring a complaint.

This also implies that the presumption dictated by Article 3.8 DSU—according to which a breach of a rule is presumed to constitute a case of nullification or impairment of benefits accruing to other Members parties to the agreements covered—is not in itself dispositive of the question of standing. In fact, even if according to some authors Article 3.8 DSU, rendering it 'easier to establish standing in the proceedings',[45] would strongly support 'action by Members against violation of agreements',[46] and would thus '*serve the common interest* in the security and predictability of the multilateral trading system',[47] the WTO dispute settlement bodies' case law (mentioned above) rather indicates that this provision covers a question which is *different* from that of standing, since it only shifts the burden of proof which in non-violation complaints primarily falls on the complaining party.[48]

Accordingly, in order to try to find a way out from this legal conundrum, some other elements must be borne in mind.

Firstly, the fact that, in *EC—Bananas III*, the Appellate Body has pointed out that 'a Member has broad discretion in deciding whether to bring a case',[49] and that 'a member is expected to be largely self-regulating in deciding whether any such action would be "fruitful"'[50] under the terms of Article 3.7 DSU, denotes a confusion between the concept of *locus standi* and the principle that—as observed by the Appellate Body in *Mexico—Corn Syrup (Article 21.5—US)*—'Members should have recourse to the WTO dispute settlement in good faith, and *not frivolously* set in motion the procedures contemplated in the DSU'.[51]

Second, and more importantly, what is actionable under the WTO is not so much a breach of obligations (in fact, 'non-violation' complaints are still admitted under Article 26 DSU), but the upsetting of the negotiated balance of benefits.[52] In this regard, it must be recalled that the concept of benefits relates not to export volumes but to competitive

[43] *European Communities—Regime for the Importation, Sale and Distribution of Bananas—Second Recourse to Article 21.5 of the DSU by Ecuador—Recourse to Article 21.5 of the DSU by the United States—Report of the Appellate Body* (26 November 2008) WT/DS27/AB/RW2/ECU, WT/DS27/AB/RW/USA, para 464.

[44] ibid, fn 538. [45] T Stoll, 'Article 3 DSU', in Wolfrum et al. (eds) (n 34), 281, 310.

[46] ibid. [47] ibid. (emphasis in the original text).

[48] *Japan—Measures Affecting Consumer Photographic Film and Paper—Report of the Panel* (31 March 1998) WT/DS44/R, para 10.32; *European Communities—Measures Affecting Asbestos and Asbestos-Containing Products—Report of the Panel* (18 September 2000) WT/DS135/R, paras 8.277–8.278.

[49] *European Communities—Regime for the Importation, Sale and Distribution of Bananas* (n 40), para 135.

[50] ibid.

[51] *Mexico—Anti-Dumping Investigations of High Fructose Corn Syrup (HFCS) from the United States—Recourse to Article 21.5 of the DSU by the United States—Report of the Appellate Body* (22 October 2001) WT/DS132/AB/RW, para 73 (emphasis added).

[52] J Pauwelyn, 'Enforcement and Countermeasures in the WTO: Rules are Rules - Toward a More Collective Approach' (2000) 94 *American Journal of International Law* 335, 340.

relationships,[53] and therefore not to actual trade but to *potential* trade. Benefits are nullified or impaired when the competitive relationship between domestic and imported products is upset.[54] Such a broad manner of construing the concept of 'harm' (which includes the notion of 'potential' harm) in the WTO system ends up in practice by 'cannibalizing' or at least marginalizing any attempt to reconstruct the existence of purely 'public' interests (ie detached from any individual interest) for the protection of which an *actio popularis* could be accepted.[55]

This is confirmed by the Appellate Body's report in the famous and already mentioned *EC—Bananas III* case, where (unlike cases of complaints raised in the interest of other Member States (and their nationals) in which, there being no contestation, the dispute settlement bodies found no difficulty in judging the merits),[56] the EC contested the right of the US to activate the dispute settlement mechanism by maintaining that the complainant was not an exporter of bananas. The Appellate Body, after having denied that 'the need for a "legal interest"' (ie the kind of interest whose recurrence characterises *erga omnes obligations*)[57] was 'implied in the DSU or in any other provision of the WTO Agreement',[58] rejected the objection since it considered the US to be *affected* by the EC banana regime. Indeed, the US was 'a producer of bananas, and a potential export interest by the United States cannot be excluded'.[59] Moreover 'the internal market of the United States for bananas could be *affected* by the EC banana regime, in particular, by the effects of that regime on world supplies and world prices of bananas'.[60] Finally—as already stated by the Panel—'with the increased interdependence of the global economy [...] Members have a greater stake in enforcing WTO rules than in the past since any deviation from the negotiated *balance* of rights and obligations is more likely than ever to *affect* them, directly or indirectly'.[61] What these three passages have in common is the reference to the fact that the US was directly or indirectly 'affected' by the EC's behaviour. The Appellate Body—unlike the panel, according to which standing was not dependant on the existence of an actual or potential trade interest, so that 'a Member's [...] interest in the determination of rights and obligations under the WTO Agreement [is] sufficient to establish a right to

[53] According to the GATT case law, reaffirmed under the WTO (see *European Communities—Regime for the Importation, Sale and Distribution of Bananas* (n 40), para 253), a GATT rule 'cannot be interpreted to protect expectations on export volumes; it protects expectations on the competitive relationship between imported and domestic products. A change in the competitive relationship contrary to that provision must consequently be regarded *ipso facto* as a nullification or impairment of benefits accruing under the General Agreement' (*United States—Superfund* (1987) GATT BISD 34S/136, para 5.1.9).

[54] *Japan—Measures Affecting Consumer Photographic Film and Paper* (n 48), para 10.82. In the legal scholarship, see T Stoll, 'Article XXIII', in R Wolfrum et al. (eds), *WTO—Trade in Goods* (Martinus Nijhoff 2011) 598, 604–5.

[55] See PJ Kuyper, 'The Law of GATT as a Special Field of International Law: Ignorance, Further Refinement or Self-Contained System of International Law?' (1994) 25 *Netherlands Yearbook of International Law* 227, 240–1; MI Papa, 'L'*actio popularis* nel sistema di risoluzione delle controversie dell'Organizzazione mondiale del commercio', in A Ligustro and G Sacerdoti (eds), *Problemi e tendenze del diritto internazionale dell'economia.* Liber Amicorum *in onore di Paolo Picone* (Editoriale Scientifica 2011) 575, 593. An *actio popularis* under international law can be defined as a 'right resident in any member of a community to take legal action in vindication of a public interest' (*South West Africa (Ethiopia v South Africa; Liberia v South Africa)* [1966] ICJ Reports 47).

[56] *United States—Section 211 Omnibus Appropriations Act of 1998—Report of the Appellate Body* (2 January 2002) WT/DS176/AB/R, paras 273–296; *United States—Definitive Safeguard Measures on Import of Circular Welded Carbon Quality Line Pipe from Korea—Report of the Appellate Body* (15 February 2002) WT/DS202/AB/R, paras 120–133. For a comment, see Pauwelyn, *Conflict of Norms* (n 34) 84–5.

[57] 'All States can be held to have a legal interest in their protection', *Case Concerning the Barcelona Traction, Light and Power Company, Limited* [1970] ICJ Reports 32.

[58] *European Communities—Regime for the Importation, Sale and Distribution of Bananas* (n 40) para 132.

[59] ibid, para 136. [60] ibid (emphasis added).

[61] ibid (emphasis added). However, the AB also affirmed that 'This does not mean, though, that one or more of the factors we have noted in this case would necessarily be dispositive in another case' (ibid, para 138).

pursue a WTO dispute settlement proceeding'[62]—ultimately thus referred to an alteration of the original *sinalagma* which had caused individual harm as the reason which fundamentally justified the existence of legal standing.

More recently, in the *Colombia—Ports of Entry* case, the panel recalled the conclusions reached by the Appellate Body in *EC—Bananas III* (and therefore, the notion of 'potential' interest and/or harm), by maintaining that the circumstance that Panama 'currently produces apparel for export, has stated its interest in exporting domestically produced footwear and other apparel in the future, and stated its potential to manufacture textiles in the future' represented 'a sufficient basis... for Panama to bring its claim'.[63] Accordingly, Panama had 'sufficiently demonstrated its interest in a determination of rights and obligations under the *WTO Agreement*'.[64]

As already noted, qualified exceptions from the recurrence of an individual interest criterion are provided by Article XXIII GATS and Article 4 Agreement on Subsidies and Countervailing Measures, provisions which do not require evidence of a subjective interest. Obviously, there would be no need for these special provisions if the opposite were not the rule.

On the other hand, it is true that the text of Article XXIII.1 GATT embodies the possibility of a sort of *actio popularis* when it admits of complaints if 'the attainment of any objective of the Agreement is being impeded', but it is also true that this provision has remained a sort of dead letter. The only complaint brought under this provision during the GATT period was rejected without considering its merits, since 'No detailed submission had been made [...] as to which objective of the General Agreement had been impeded, and the Panel did not consider these questions'.[65] Two other cases were initiated by the EEC against Japan as a *situation complaint*,[66] and by Australia against the EEC as a non-violation complaint, but were soon withdrawn.[67] It has been observed that these kinds of complaints are not exercised, probably, because it is difficult to link the achievement of the objectives of the GATT to a specific behaviour of certain parties.[68] On the other hand, as already said, the idea of individual interest which normally justifies the bringing of an action is so broad (as it also includes the notion of 'potential' interest and/or harm) that it ends up absorbing any other possible avenue provided by the GATT/WTO to initiate dispute settlement proceedings.

5. The lack of formal standing for individuals

The elements described in the previous paragraph, taken together, may be viewed as reflecting the reciprocity which informs the entire system, but also the fact that it operates only at inter-state level. The WTO dispute settlement mechanism may in fact be triggered only by the Member States, since—*unlike* the EU legal system—it does not include either (1) a control mechanism 'from above', operated *ex officio* by the DSB to protect the internal legality of the system; or (2) a control mechanism operable 'from below', by private individuals and legal entities directly affected in their interests.

[62] *European Communities—Regime for the Importation, Sale and Distribution of Bananas, Complaint by the United States—Report of the Panel* (25 September 1997) WT/DS27/R/USA, para 7.50.

[63] *Colombia—Indicative Prices and Restrictions on Ports of Entry—Report of the Panel* (20 May 2009) WT/DS366/R, para 7.329.

[64] ibid (emphasis in the original text).

[65] *European Communities—Refunds on Exports of Sugar* (1979) BISD 26S/290, para V (i).

[66] GATT, Analytical Index, Guide to GATT Law and Practice, vol 2, 654. [67] ibid, 655.

[68] See therefore A Ligustro, *Le controversie tra Stati nel diritto del commercio internazionale: dal GATT all'OMC* (CEDAM 1996) 253.

Evidently, this creates a discrepancy between the private nature of the interests immediately concerned by the WTO regulation and the public structure of international trade law. In this regard, we cannot but recall what was observed by the panel in the *US—Section 301 Trade Act* case, namely that 'it would be entirely wrong to consider that the position of individuals is of no relevance to the GATT/WTO legal matrix. Many of the benefits to members which are meant to flow as a result of the acceptance of various disciplines under the GATT/WTO depend on the activity of individual economic operators in the national and global market places. The purpose of many of these disciplines, indeed one of the primary objects of the GATT/WTO as a whole, is to produce certain market conditions which would allow this individual activity to flourish [...] The multilateral trading system is, per force, composed not only of States but also, indeed mostly, of individual economic operators [...] It is through improved conditions for these private operators that Members benefit from WTO disciplines'.[69]

Notwithstanding this recognition, in the WTO private parties participation manifests itself mainly in the form of the submission of '*amicus curiae*' briefs and indirectly through the work of private counsel as representatives of State parties to the dispute,[70] rather than by performing the role of 'private attorneys general' to ensure governments' respect of WTO obligations.[71]

Finally, it must be remembered that WTO norms are denied direct effect in the domestic legal orders of the WTO 'big players' (US, EU, Canada, Japan, China, Australia, India etc.). WTO rules cannot thus be invoked directly by private parties before their respective national courts. Consequently, the objective formulated with reference to the EC system by the ECJ in *Van Gend & Loos*,[72] namely that individuals might be involved as guardians of rule compliance by Member States (also at domestic level) has been widely disregarded in WTO law. This is no coincidence. In fact, according to the WTO panel in the *US-Trade Act of 1974* case, 'Neither the GATT nor the WTO has so far been interpreted by GATT/WTO institutions as a legal order producing direct effect. Following this approach the GATT/WTO did not create a new legal order the subjects of which comprise both Contracting Parties or Members and nationals'.[73]

This echo by contrast of *Van Gend & Loos*—where the ECJ had argued that: 'the Community constitutes a new legal order of international law [...] the subject of which comprise not only member States but also their nationals'[74]—was heard loud and clear.

From a wider perspective then, the choice of an exclusive horizontal control endowed to individually affected States reflects the circumstance that WTO trade obligations are still considered by their addressees not as *erga omnes partes* (or collective) in nature.[75] As was observed by the representative of the US before the DSB in the context of the *US-Foreign Sales Corporation* case 'the concept *erga omnes* was squarely at odds with the fundamentally bilateral nature of the WTO and GATT dispute settlement and with the notion that

[69] *United States—Sections 301-310 of the Trade Act of 1974—Report of the Panel* (22 December 1999) WT/DS152/R, paras 7.74 and 7.76.

[70] S Ohlhoff and H Schloemann, 'Transcending the Nation-State? Private Parties and the Enforcement of International Trade Law' (2001) 5 *Max Planck Yearbook of United Nations Law* 675; C-E Côté, *La participation des personnes privées au règlement des différends internationaux économiques: l'élargissement du droit de porter plainte à l'OMC* (Bruylant 2007) 385.

[71] See GC Shaffer, *Defending Interests: Public-Private Partnerships in the WTO Litigation* (The Brooking Institution Press 2003) 144.

[72] Case 26/62 *NV Algemene Transport—en Expeditie Onderneming van Gend & Loos v Netherlands Inland Revenue Administration* [1963] ECLI:EU:C:1963:1, para 13.

[73] *United States-Sections 310-310 of the Trade Act of 1974—Report of the Panel* (22 December 1999) WT/DS152/R, para 7.72.

[74] *NV Algemene Transport* (n 72) para 12.

[75] See Pauwelyn, *A Typology* (n 34) 907.

WTO disputes concerned nullification and impairment of negotiated benefits to a particular Member. WTO adjudicators were tasked with resolving disputes between specific complaining and defending parties. Adjudicators may not, through improper importation of the concept *erga omnes*, enforce WTO obligations on behalf of non-parties to a dispute'.[76] Nor are WTO obligations addressed to the WTO as an autonomous subject of international law, notwithstanding the fact that the multilateral system of trade regulation and dispute settlement hinges on an international organization endowed with legal personality.

6. Reciprocity and WTO remedies

As concerns the remedies provided by the WTO DSU in case of non-compliance (remedies whose purpose—as already noted—is to re-establish, though not retrospectively, the lost balance of reciprocal rights and obligations, and to induce compliance), it must be first remembered that—under Article 22.2 DSU—both compensation and countermeasures may be sought only by 'any party having invoked the dispute settlement procedures': that is, enforcement is not a collective business (except for the control exercised by the DSB on the implementation of the recommendations and rulings adopted by that same organ).

Second, and accordingly, the level of the suspension of the concessions which can be authorized at the demand of the winning party is governed by the principle of *equivalence*,[77] pursuant to Article 22.4 DSU. The notion of equivalence requires a calculation of the level of nullification and impairment of benefits suffered from the complaining party, which will then determine the maximum level of retaliatory measures to be applied. In the case of the *US-1916 Act*, the Arbitrators held that the limit of equivalence is *quantitative*.[78]

Furthermore, we have already seen that the dispute settlement system requires compliance *in rem* as a final result, in the sense that a Member must either withdraw or amend the WTO-inconsistent measure in order to bring its legal order into conformity with the agreements covered. In principle, no 'buy-option' or any other form of substantial restoration of reciprocity is permanently accepted as a substitute. However, notwithstanding the fact that the ultimate goal of the DSU is compliance *in rem*, and that alternative remedies may provide only a temporary solution, according to some authors the diplomatic inclination which was typical of the 'old' GATT still haunts the WTO legal system today.[79]

[76] Minutes of the DSB Meeting of 7 May 2003, WTO Doc. WT/DSB/M/149, para 20.

[77] Comparing the SCM standard of 'appropriateness' with the DSU's standard of 'equivalence', the arbitral panel in *EC—Bananas III (US) (Article 22.6—EC)* found that this latter 'implies a higher degree of correspondence, identity or stricter *balance* between the level of the proposed suspension and the level of nullification or impairment' (*European Communities—Regime for the Importation, Sale and Distribution of Bananas—Recourse to Arbitration by the European Communities under Article 22.6 of the DSU—Decision by Arbitrators* (9 April 1999) WT/DS27/ARB, para 6.5 (emphasis added)). On the other hand, the SCM standard of 'appropriateness' (terms which can be equated to 'not disproportionate' pursuant to two footnotes of the WTO Agreement on Subsidies and Countervailing Measures, see Arts 4.10, n 9, and 4.11, n 10) is somewhat more relaxed. In *United States—Tax Treatment for 'Foreign Sales Corporations'—Recourse to Arbitration by the United States under Article 22.6 of the DSU and Article 4.11 of the SCM Agreement* (30 August 2002) WT/DS108/ARB, para 5.18, the arbitrator held that it 'does not require exact equivalence – the relationship to be respected is precisely that of "proportion" rather than "equivalence"'. In other words, it is sufficient that 'there is no manifest imbalance or incongruity' (ibid, para 5.24).

[78] *United States—Anti-Dumping Act of 1916 (Original Complaint by the European Communities)—Recourse to Arbitration by the United States under Article 22.6 of the* DSU*—Decision by the Arbitrators* (24 February 2004) WT/DS136/ARB, para 5.23. See also ibid, paras 5.24–5.28, for further references to the relevant case law. More specifically, the Arbitrators held that the calculation of the level of nullification or impairment requires a quantification in monetary terms, and that this was 'the only way in which the arbitrators can determine "equivalence"'.

[79] JHH Weiler, 'The Rule of Lawyers and the Ethos of Diplomats' (2001) 35 *Journal of World Trade* 191.

If then '[t]he only sacred, inviolable aspect of the GATT was the overall balance of rights and obligations, of benefits and burdens, achieved among members through negotiations [...] The WTO substantially improved the GATT rules for settling disputes but did not alter the fundamental nature of the negotiated bargain among sovereign member States'.[80]

In summary, it is fair to say that the principle of substantial reciprocity still plays a fundamental (though not exclusive) role in the WTO legal system both at the stage of negotiation and enforcement.

Having said that, we turn now to examine another distinctive feature which characterizes the WTO implementation mechanism, and distinguishes it (among other things) from the EU legal system, namely the role played by negotiation in the post-adjudication phase of the dispute settlement procedure.

7. Post-litigation negotiations and the hybrid nature of the WTO dispute settlement mechanism

Given that the dispute settlement mechanism aims to secure a positive solution to a dispute, Article 3.7 DSU provides that '[a] solution mutually acceptable to the parties to a dispute and consistent with the covered agreements is clearly to be preferred'. The DSU thus expresses a clear preference for solutions mutually acceptable to the parties reached through negotiations. It is only 'in the absence of a mutually agreed solution', that the objective of the dispute settlement procedure becomes the withdrawal of the WTO-inconsistent measure. Accordingly, the negotiated settlement of WTO disputes has reached an important quantitative dimension so far. It has been estimated that of the first 450 cases formally brought before the WTO, over 200 were settled or are presumed to have been settled amicably by the disputing parties in different ways.[81]

The mutually agreed solution concluded in the framework of the WTO dispute settlement system must respect two requirements set out in Articles 3.5, 3.6, and 3.7 DSU. According to Article 3.5 (and 3.7), they shall be 'consistent' with the covered agreements, and 'shall not nullify or impair benefits accruing to any Member under those agreements, nor impede the attainment of any objective of those agreements'. On the other hand, according to Article 3.6, mutually agreed solutions 'shall be notified to the DSB and the relevant Councils and Committees, where any Member may raise any point relating thereto'.

Until the conclusion of the panel phase, the DSU accepts and aims at regulating the inherent tension between the consensual and the adjudicative method of dispute settlement. Indeed, its Article 4 provides for a compulsory preliminary phase based on consultations between the litigants. Mutually agreed solutions may be reached even during the panel procedure. After the presentation of the panel's and possibly the Appellate Body's report and their adoption by the DSB, the DSU appears to resolve the tension between consensual and quasi-jurisdictional dispute tools settlement in favour of the latter. In practice, however, the consensual dispute settlement tools continue to play a significant role even at the moment of the implementation of the panel's and the Appellate Body's reports adopted by the DSB, and thus after the stage at which the procedure has gone through the judicial channels.

[80] J Bello, 'The WTO Dispute Settlement Understanding: Less is More' (1996) 90 *American Journal of International Law* 416, 417.

[81] W Alschner, 'Amicable Settlements of WTO Disputes: Bilateral Solutions in a Multilateral System' (2014) 13 *World Trade Review* 65.

In this regard, it must be recalled that Article 19 DSU instructs the panel and the Appellate Body to recommend that the losing party bring the measure found inconsistent with the covered agreements into conformity with that agreement, not simply to withdraw the offending measure.[82] The word 'conformity' is ambiguous, since 'it does not invariably mean identity with the object being conformed to. Some deviation is hinted at'.[83] To bring the measure into conformity often entails an amendment of legislation or a change in administrative/judicial practices. In this regard, the WTO Appellate Body has pointed out that the DSU itself 'recognizes that a solution leading to compliance can be implemented in various ways'.[84] In some cases, in fact, the Appellate Body has found that the *application* of the measure, not the measure in itself, was WTO-inconsistent.[85] In this regard, the panel or the Appellate Body 'may suggest ways' in which the Member concerned could implement the recommendations. This has been interpreted in the WTO case law as meaning that panels have *discretion* to suggest ways but they are *not required* to do so.[86] Accordingly, in several instances, the Panels have declined to suggest ways to implement, because there was more than one way to comply,[87] or a request for a waiver was still pending.[88] Moreover, even if the panel suggests ways to implement its recommendation, even when implemented, this does not create a presumption of compliance[89] and it is not strictly binding, given that 'the choice of means of implementation is decided, in the first instance, by the Member concerned'.[90] As stated by the panel in *US-Section 301 Trade Act*, the enforcement of the obligation on Members to bring their laws into conformity with WTO obligations

[82] On the difference between a recommendation of withdrawal and a recommendation of conformity, see *United States—Measures Affecting Woven Wool Shirts and Blouses—Report of the Panel* (23 May 1997) WT/DS33/R, para 34. In the legal scholarship, see P Grané, 'Remedies Under WTO Law' (2001) 4 *Journal of International Economic Law* 755, 761–2.

[83] C Carmody, 'Remedies and Conformity Under the WTO Agreement' (2002) 5 *Journal of International Economic Law* 307, 316.

[84] *European Communities—Regime for the Importation, Sale and Distribution of Bananas—Second Recourse to Article 21.5 of the DSU by Ecuador* (n 43) para 212.

[85] *United States—Import Prohibition of Certain Shrimp and Shrimp Products—Report of the Appellate Body* (12 October 1998) WT/DS58/AB/R, para 115.

[86] *European Communities—Trade Description of Sardines—Report of the Panel* (29 May 2002) WT/DS231/R, para 8.3 ('the authority under Article 19.1 is one of discretion'); *United States—Final Dumping Determination on Softwood Lumber from Canada—Report of the Panel* (13 April 2004) WT/DS264/R, para 8.6. See also *Argentina—Definitive Anti-Dumping Duties on Poultry from Brazil—Report of the Panel* (22 April 2003) WT/DS241/R, para 8.5; *European Communities—Anti-Dumping Duties on Malleable Cast Iron Tube or Pipe Fittings from Brazil—Report of the Panel* (7 March 2003) WT/DS219/R, para 8.11; *United States—Definitive Safeguard Measures on Imports of Circular Welded Carbon Quality Line Pipe from Korea* (29 October 2001) WT/DS202/R, para 8.6.

[87] In *India—Patents (US)*, the panel rejected the US request to suggest the manner in which India should have implemented its obligation, since this would have impaired 'India's right to choose how to implement the TRIPS Agreement' (*India—Patent Protection for Pharmaceuticals and Agricultural Chemicals Products—Report of the Panel* (5 September 1997) WT/DS50/R, para 7.65). See also *United States—Anti-Dumping Duty on Dynamic Random Access Memory Semiconductors (DRAMS) of One Megabit or Above From Korea—Report of the Panel* (29 January 1999) WT/DS99/R, para 7.4 ('in light of the range of possible ways in which we believe the United States could appropriately implement our recommendation, we decline to make any suggestion in the present case'); *United States—Anti-Dumping and Countervailing Measures on Steel Plate from India—Report of the Panel* (28 June 2002) WT/DS206/R, para 7.110; *United States—Anti-Dumping Measures on Stainless Steel Plate in Coils and Stainless Steel Sheet and Strip from Korea—Report of the Panel* (22 December 2000) WT/DS179/R, para 7.10; *United States—Definitive Safeguard Measures on Imports of Circular Welded Carbon Quality Line Pipe from Korea—Report of the Panel* (29 October 2001) WT/DS202/R, para 8.6 ('there may be various other ways in which the United States could implement the Panel recommendation').

[88] *European Communities—Conditions for the Granting of Tariff Preferences to Developing Countries—Report of the Panel* (1 December 2003) WT/DS246/R, para 8.3.

[89] *European Communities—Regime for the Importation, Sale and Distribution of Bananas—Second Recourse to Article 21.5 of the DSU by Ecuador* (n 43), para 325.

[90] *United States—Anti-Dumping and Countervailing Measures on Steel Plate from India—Report of the Panel* (n 87) para 8.8. See also *United States—Countervailing Measures Concerning Certain Products From the European Communities—Report of the Panel* (31 July 2002) WT/DS212/R, para 6.43 ('Members have discretion in how to bring a measure found to be WTO-inconsistent into conformity with WTO obligations').

'must be done in the least intrusive way possible. The Member concerned must be allowed the maximum autonomy in ensuring such conformity and, if there is more than one lawful way to achieve this, should have the freedom to choose that way which suits it best'.[91]

The result is that the obligation to bring itself into compliance 'is progressively defined by the wrongdoer and its trading partners, who are left to articulate what the shape of the outcome will be'.[92]

Of course, it may be possible that the winning party is not satisfied with the implementation. It may then ask for a compliance review under Article 21.5 DSU. To avoid further recourse to litigation, parties may decide to conclude agreements on implementation.[93] In *Brazil—Aircraft (Article 21.5—Canada)*, the compliance panel stated that 'any agreement that WTO Members might reach among themselves to improve transparency regarding the implementation of WTO obligations can only be encouraged'.[94] Provided that these agreements are consistent with WTO law (pursuant to Article 3.5 DSU), their conclusion is just another way to implement DSB rulings (as pointed out by AG Tizzano in *Van Parys*).[95] However, as has been noted by AG Poiares Maduro in *FIAMM*, this outcome 'still constitutes freedom of choice'.[96]

At this point, it is interesting to see whether and how (temporary or permanent, partial or full) compliance has been achieved in the two long-standing WTO disputes which have been at the root of many of the cases brought before the EC/EU Courts: *Bananas* and *Beef Hormones*.

In the *Bananas* case, after more than twelve successive GATT and WTO panel reports, an Appellate Body report, and arbitration awards since 1993 on GATT and WTO inconsistencies concerning import restrictions on bananas, on 15 December 2009, two agreements setting conditions for the final settlement of the dispute were initialled by the EU and Latin American countries, and by the EU and the US.[97] On 8 November 2012, the parties notified the DSB of a mutually agreed solution pursuant to Article 3.6 DSU.[98] Accordingly, the EU has undertaken to cut its import tariff on bananas from Latin America in eight stages. This MFN duty, therefore, will fall only gradually, over at least eight years. This means that during this period, ACP bananas continue to enjoy a competitive advantage.

More generally, it seems that occasionally the 'big players' in the WTO system have gone so far as to 'contract out' of the obligations arising under the WTO covered agreements or the DSU. The agreements on bananas I just mentioned, enabling the ACP countries to continue to enjoy preferential treatment for some years, appear in fact to be—at least temporarily—not totally in line with primary and secondary obligations arising under the

[91] *United States—Sections 301–310 of the Trade Act of 1974—Report of the Panel* (22 December 1999) WT/DS152/R, para 7.102 (emphasis added).

[92] Carmody (n 83) 328.

[93] See for example the mutually agreed solutions on modalities for implementation concluded in *Japan—Taxes on Alcoholic Beverages—Mutually Acceptable Solution on Modalities for Implementation* (12 January 1998) WT/DS8/20 (Japan/EC), WT/DS10/20 (Japan/Canada), WT/DS11/18 (Japan/United States), and in *European Communities—Regime for the Importation, Sale and Distribution of Bananas—Notification of Mutually Agreed Solution* (2 July 2002) WT/DS27/58.

[94] *Brazil—Export Financing Programme for Aircraft—Recourse by Canada to Article 21.5 of the DSU—Report of the Panel* (9 May 2000) WT/DS46/RW, para 7.3.

[95] Case C-377/02 *Léon Van Parys NV v Belgisch Interventie- en Restitutiebureau (BIRB)* [2005] ECLI:EU:C:2005:121, para 57.

[96] Joined Cases C-120/06P and C-121/06P *Fabbrica italiana accumulatori motocarri Montecchio SpA (FIAMM) and Fabbrica italiana accumulatori motocarri Montecchio Technologies, Giorgio Fedon & Figli SpA and Fedon America, Inc. v Council of the European Union and Commission of the European Communities* [2008] ECLI:EU:C:2008:476, para 47.

[97] For further details, see *Geneva Agreement on Trade in Bananas*, WTO Doc. WT/L/784 of 15 December 2009.

[98] At http://www.wto.org/english/tratop_e/dispu_e/cases_e/ds27_e.htm, accessed 12 October 2016.

WTO, or, at least, an expression of that 'scope for manoeuvre' emphasized by the ECJ in its case law concerning the absence of direct effect of WTO law in the EU legal order.[99]

Another case in point, among others,[100] is provided by the provisional agreement concluded on 6 May 2009 by the US and the EC,[101] which allows the Community to maintain its ban on imports of hormone-treated beef from the US. In exchange, US beef which is free of hormones will be granted additional duty-free access to the EU market. Although today there is no final word on the compatibility with WTO obligations of the measures adopted by the EU to comply with the DSB rulings in the *Hormones* case, it should be pointed out that in the last paragraph of the report issued in *US—Continued Suspension of Obligations in the EC-Hormones Dispute*,[102] the Appellate Body confirmed that the recommendations and decisions adopted in the dispute over hormones remain fully 'operative'. If this is true, then the agreement of 2009 allows the EU to keep in place measures which remain in conflict with the EU's primary and secondary obligations. Furthermore, the compensation offered by the EU concerns exclusively the high quality beef imported from the US. For this reason, some of the States intervened in the DSB's meeting where the agreement was discussed emphasized the discriminatory character of the compensation agreed, and consequently its non-conformity with Article 3.5 DSU.[103] The discriminatory nature of the forms of compensation contained in mutually agreed solutions seems sometimes inherent in the decision to conclude these agreements. In this regard, reference is often made to the agreement concluded by Japan and Korea in the *Japan—Quotas on Laver* case,[104] since in that case Japan undertook to allocate exclusively to Korea its whole quota of imports of dried and seasoned laver (seaweed) used, inter alia, in the production of sushi. In this case, no contentious initiative appears to have been taken by other WTO Members in response to the conclusion of the said agreement.

The trend concerning the conclusion of post-judicial agreements whose terms are not completely in line with primary and/or secondary WTO obligations (and thus not in compliance with the requirement of substantive 'consistency' spelled out in Article 3.5 DSU), has been recently confirmed by the notification to the DSB of two agreements for the

[99] Case C-149/96 *Portuguese Republic v Council of the European Union* [1999] ECLI:EU:C:1999:574, para 46.

[100] Consider, for instance, the agreements concluded by the US and the EC in *the LIBERTAD ACT of 1996* (*Helms-Burton*) case; the 2006 agreement between Canada and the US on the *Softwood Lumber* dispute; or even the 2005 agreements between EC and China introducing voluntary export restraints for ten categories of textile products until December 2007 and therefore perpetuating the GATT 'grey area' understandings, in breach of Art 11.1 (b) WTO Agreement on Safeguards. For further analysis, see A Tancredi, 'EC Practice in the WTO: How Wide Is the 'Scope of Manoeuvre'?' (2004) 15 *European Journal of International Law* 933, and A Tancredi, 'Still Going "Grey" After All These Years? Export-Restraint Agreements and the WTO', in M Cremona et al., *Reflections on the Constitutionalisation of International Economic Law: Liber Amicorum for Ernst-Ulrich Petersmann* (Martinus Nijhoff 2014), 299.

[101] *Joint Communication from the European Communities and the United States* (30 September 2009) WT/DS26/28. On 14 April 2014, the US and the EU notified the DSB of a revised Memorandum of Understanding (*not* characterised as a 'mutually agreed solution' pursuant to Art 3.6 DSU) dated 21 October 2013 (WT/DS26/29 of 17 April 2014).

[102] *US—Continued Suspension of Obligations in the EC-Hormones Dispute—Report of the Appellate Body* (16 October 2008) WT/DS320/AB/R, para 737.

[103] See for instance the statement made by the Representative of Uruguay, in Minutes of Meeting Held in the Centre William Rappard on 19 June 2009, WTO Doc. WT/DSB/M/270, para 68, according to whom 'There was no justification for maintaining that this specific type of beef, which received preferential treatment, was different from other high quality beef. This constituted discriminatory treatment in favour of a certain origin [...] Uruguay and all other suppliers would be up against a competitor with a single and exclusive zero tariff preference'. 'Concern about consistency with the WTO Agreements' and in particular with the most-favoured-nation principle was also expressed by Australia (ibid, para 66), Argentina (ibid, para 67) and other countries.

[104] *Japan—Import Quotas on Dried Laver and Seasoned Laver*, Notification of a Mutually Agreed Solution (27 January 2006) WT/DS323/5. For a comment see J Nakagawa, 'No More Negotiated Deals? Settlement of Trade and Investment Disputes in East Asia' (2007) 10 *Journal of International Economic Law* 837, 856–8.

settlement of disputes which involved the US and Indonesia in the *US—Clove Cigarettes* case,[105] and the US and Brazil in the *US—Subsidies on Upland Cotton* case.[106] In both cases, the US managed to retain in force measures which were found WTO-inconsistent, or whose compatibility with the agreements covered remains doubtful, undertaking in exchange, and inter alia, not to bring complaints against voluntary export restraints prohibited under Article 11.1 (b) Agreement on Safeguards in the first case, and to pay monetary compensation to Brazil in the second.[107]

However, even admitting that these *inter se* agreements might prove to be *unlawful* vis-à-vis third States under Article 41(1)(b) Vienna Convention on the Law of Treaties (a provision which is substantially repeated in Article 3.5 DSU), they are *valid* as between the contracting parties,[108] as they deal with obligations which are regarded as non-peremptory and therefore, 'disposable' in nature.[109] In other words, ultimately the problem simply concerns the responsibility of the participants to the derogative agreement vis-à-vis the other WTO contracting parties whose rights may have been affected. If the other contracting parties do not feel damaged and/or do not activate the dispute settlement mechanism, the problem of responsibility does not arise.

In the light of this narrative, it seems clear how sometimes, especially for long-standing (sometimes politically loaded) disputes between the big stakeholders of the WTO system, the overall settlement of the dispute becomes the result of a complex process, made up of the adjudicative process and possibly an intermediate, provisional, *modus vivendi* agreement between the parties (which occasionally contains forms of ad hoc monetary compensation, not foreseen as such by the DSU which, as said, mandates compensation on a non-discriminatory basis),[110] plus, eventually, a final agreement which is not always notified as a 'mutually agreed solution', as requested by Article 3.6 DSU.

It could be argued that this evolution of the system, since 1995, was neither originally intended by the parties, nor compliant with the WTO dispute settlement system. I would partially disagree with both observations, and on purely descriptive grounds. A final, WTO-consistent, mutually agreed solution is exactly what is envisaged by Article 22.8 DSU as an *autonomous* method of settling disputes during the implementation phase, *alternative* (as clearly indicated by the use of the adversative 'or') to the simple removal of the WTO-inconsistent measure *or* to another kind of solution to the nullification and impairment of benefits. As observed by the Appellate Body in the *EC—Bananas III* cases, not only do '[w]e see nothing in Article 3.7 or elsewhere in the DSU that prevents parties to a dispute from reaching a settlement [...] after the adoption of recommendations and

[105] *United States—Measures Affecting the Production and Sale of Clove Cigarettes—Notification of a Mutually Agreed Solution* (28 October 2014) WT/DS406/17, G/L/917/Add.1, G/SPS/GEN/1015/Add.1, G/TBT/D/38/Add.1.

[106] *United States—Subsidies on Upland Cotton—Notification of a Mutually Agreed Solution* (23 October 2014) WT/DS267/46.

[107] For a short comment, see SJ Evenett and A Jara, 'Settling WTO Disputes without Solving the Problem: Abusing Compensation', available at: http://www.voxeu.org/article/settling-wto-disputes-without-solving-problem-abusing-compensation, accessed 12 October 2016.

[108] In fact, the commentary to Art 37 *Draft Articles on the Law of Treaties* adopted by the International Law Commission in 1966 (which later became Art 41 of the Vienna Convention on the Law of Treaties) points out that 'Under the present article [...] the main issue is the conditions under which *inter se* agreements may be regarded as *permissible*', Yearbook of the International Law Commission (1966) vol II, 235 (emphasis added). Furthermore, the Special Rapporteur Waldock, expressing a view upheld by the whole International Law Commission, pointed out that 'the later treaty is *valid* and *effective* as between the State parties to it' (see 'Sixth Report on the Law of Treaties', ibid, 76). The same position was later reaffirmed in the Opinion of Advocate General Saggio in Case C-149/96 *Portuguese Republic v Council* [1999] ECR I-8395, para 29.

[109] On this, see Pauwelyn, *A Typology* (n 34) 907.

[110] See for instance, *United States—Section 110(5) of the US Copyright Act—Notification of a Mutually Satisfactory Temporary Arrangement* (26 June 2003) WT/DS160/23.

rulings by the DSB', but it is precisely Article 22.8 DSU which 'clearly envisages' that possibility.[111]

Finally, as already hinted at, we must also take note of another emerging trend in the WTO dispute settlement practice, namely the spread of *provisional* agreements registered in the preceding few years. This type of agreement (often concluded in the form of a 'Memorandum of Understanding' or 'temporary arrangement'), does not bring about a *final settlement.* They are rather a precursor to a final solution to the dispute, since they normally limit themselves to envisaging the steps agreed between the parties in order to reach a final settlement and therefore—according to the relevant case law of the Appellate Body[112]—do not correspond to the concept of a 'mutually agreed solution' foreseen by Article 3.6 DSU. It is worth noting that such agreements, not having been expressly foreseen or regulated by the DSU, may be used to circumvent the obligations of compatibility with the agreements covered and transparency set out in Articles 3.5, 3.6, and 3.7 DSU with reference to any 'mutually agreed solution'. Their function is to provide temporary relief to the aggrieved WTO Member while awaiting a full implementation of the DSB's adopted reports by the losing party, without incurring the inconvenience inherent to the two remedies formally provided for by the DSU, i.e. the high costs of compensation granted on a MFN basis, and the negative impact of countermeasures on the domestic economy and on the consumers of the Member imposing them, something that often amounts to a self-inflicted wound. In essence, these agreements represent a sort of third remedy, alternative to the two foreseen in the DSU, which fills through practice what has probably been perceived by the contracting parties as a gap in the WTO dispute settlement mechanism.

8. (Sequitur) the hybrid nature of the WTO dispute settlement system and its consequences under a law-and-economics perspective

The result which can be drawn from the remarks previously made is that the WTO dispute settlement system has a *mixed* or *hybrid* nature.[113] In other words, the 'hard cases' of long-standing non-compliance—although rather limited in number—show that the WTO dispute settlement system is not exclusively judicial or quasi-judicial, because it combines the features of the *judicial* means of dispute settlement with elements typical of international *diplomatic* means based on negotiation aimed at reaching an agreement between the parties.[114] Negotiations take place during the whole procedure,[115] and therefore provisional or final agreements between the parties may or are concluded *at any stage* of the proceedings (including the quasi-jurisdictional part, since an agreed solution may be found both during the panel phase and the Appellate Body procedure).[116] In other words, WTO trade disputes often not only begin but also end with the use of diplomatic dispute

[111] *European Communities—Regime for the Importation, Sale and Distribution of Bananas—Second Recourse to Article 21.5 of the DSU by Ecuador* (n 43) para 215.

[112] ibid, para 219–20.

[113] I have already defended this thesis in Tancredi, "EC Practice in the WTO" (n 100) 946, and A Tancredi, 'On the Absence of Direct Effect of the WTO Dispute Settlement Body's Decisions in the EU Legal Order', in E Cannizzaro et al. (eds), *International Law as Law of the European Union* (Martinus Nijhoff 2011) 249.

[114] In this vein, see AF Lowenfeld, *International Economic Law* (OUP 2008) 172 ('The DSU retains some of the ambivalence about law versus diplomacy'); Marceau and Hamaoui (n 28) 209.

[115] See H Ruiz Fabri, 'The Relationship between Negotiations and Third-Party Dispute Settlement at the WTO, with an Emphasis on the EC-Bananas Dispute', in Boisson de Chazournes et al. (n 28) 87, 94–5.

[116] See the *Rule 30* of the *Working Procedures for Appellate Review.*

settlement means (at least to determine what measures should be adopted in order to implement the DSB's rulings). Within this 'realistic' picture, judicial means are only a component of a broader dispute settlement mechanism, 'punctuated' by the use of diplomatic means.[117]

The characterization of the WTO dispute settlement as a hybrid has consequences.

From a law-and-economics perspective, for instance, the WTO system of remedies has been depicted as a combination of an 'aspirational property rule operating through a temporary liability rule'.[118] As is well known,[119] a property rule system allows efficient breach, or deviation from a legal entitlement, only if the entitlement's holder consents. This will normally only happen if the benefit to the deviating party exceeds the value attached by the other party to specific performance. On the other hand, an entitlement protected by a liability rule may be taken without the holder's consent, provided that the holder receives an objectively determined value in compensation.[120] Now, the question is whether WTO rights and benefits are protected by property or liability, i.e. whether the WTO legal system permits deviation and the ensuing transfer of entitlement based on consent (by property) or on compensation (by liability). In this respect, it is generally believed[121] that protection by liability is employed in the case of the modification of the individual specific commitments of WTO Members under the GATT and GATS, and of certain WTO rules which explicitly permit unilateral adjustments in exchange for some sort of compensation (such as Article XXVIII GATT, Article XXI GATS, Article XIX GATT, Article 8 Agreement on Safeguards, Article 31(f) TRIPs, and Article 7.8 Agreement on Subsidies and Countervailing Measures). The question, however, remains open with respect to other norms not subject to specific rules of modification, and legal scholarship is divided on this issue.

Some authors emphasize that the WTO requires full and immediate compliance with a DSB ruling,[122] and thus support the existence of an inalienability rule. Others affirm that the DSU allows a provisional 'pay-option' which may give way to an 'efficient breach', where the parties can 'buy-out' their rights by concluding agreements with the complaining Member, thus characterizing the WTO dispute settlement system as a temporary liability rule and a final property rule.[123] Other authors in turn concede that the letter of the law requires specific performance, but take note that as a matter of practice, Members may disregard compliance *in rem* as long as they pay compensation or accept suspension of concession and other obligations.[124]

Now, since compensation and countermeasures are conceived only as temporary means of relief, or—in the words of the Appellate Body—as 'an abnormal state of affairs that is not meant to remain indefinitely', in the sense that 'Members must act in a cooperative manner so that the normal state of affairs, that is, compliance with the covered agreements and

[117] See L Boisson de Chazournes et al. Concluding Observations', in Boisson de Chazournes et al. (n 28) 335.

[118] Therefore see A Arcuri and S Poli, 'What Price for the Community Enforcement of WTO Law?' (2010) EUI Working Papers No 1, 28.

[119] G Calabresi, AD Melamed, 'Property Rules, Liability Rules, and Inalienability: One View of the Cathedral' (1972) 85 *Harvard Law Review* 1089.

[120] ibid, 1092.

[121] J Pauwelyn, *Optimal Protection of International Law: Navigating between European Absolutism and American Voluntarism* (CUP 2008), 134–6.

[122] J Jackson, 'International Law Status of WTO Dispute Settlement Reports: Obligation to Comply or Option to "Buy Out"' (2004) 98 *American Journal of International Law* 109.

[123] See WF Schwartz and A Sykes, 'The Economic Structure of Renegotiation and Dispute Resolution in the World Trade Organization' (2002) 31 *Journal of Legal Studies* S179, S181–3 and S191–2, where they argue that 'the WTO system contemplates departures from specified obligations when the costs of compliance exceed the associated benefits'.

[124] JP Trachtman, 'The WTO Cathedral' (2007) 43 *Stanford Journal of International Law* 127, 146, and 149.

absence of the suspension of concessions, may be restored as quickly as possible',[125] it must be concluded then no permanent shift of entitlement may be 'purchased' through compensation under the DSU. This is confirmed by the fact that under Article 22.8 DSU 'the DSB shall continue to keep under surveillance the implementation of adopted recommendations or rulings, including those cases where [...] concessions or other obligations have been suspended but the recommendations to bring a measure into conformity with the covered agreements have not been implemented'. Consequently, the DSU cannot be considered as endorsing a liability rule.

The second question is whether the DSU limits the contractual freedom for the disputing parties to conclude *inter se* agreements inspired to a property rule. And it is here that the hybrid nature of the WTO dispute settlement system seems to play a role.

Indeed, in *US—Continued Suspension*, the Appellate Body has clearly maintained that mutually agreed solutions, along with the other two conditions foreseen in Article 22.8 DSU 'concern the circumstances under which the suspension of concessions must be terminated because there has been a *final and substantive resolution* to the dispute',[126] where *final and substantive resolution* means that 'the inconsistency resulting from the measure [...] must be remedied'.[127] Accordingly, as a matter of principle and at least in the long run, the system is clearly inspired by an *inalienability* rule. In practice, however—as we have seen—parties sometimes agree to contract out of their WTO obligations, which may be said to imply a consensual shift of entitlement. Such mutually agreed solutions may be unlawful but are valid between the parties, as already noted. If no question of responsibility is raised by other WTO Members, then the dispute may find a final settlement inspired by a property rule.

The end result is that the DSU combines an inalienability rule in principle with a property rule in practice (a rule which, however, may give rise to responsibility towards other WTO Members)—thus reflecting its hybrid nature—while remedies partly inspired by a liability rule (partly, since no definitive transfer of entitlement takes place) may provide relief *only* on a temporary basis (even if sometimes it is '*a provisoire qui dure*').[128]

9. How long can the 'room for manoeuvre' be enjoyed?

The second question which we have to address to clarify the role played by negotiations in the framework of the WTO dispute settlement mechanism is whether negotiation is subject to a chronological term.

The ECJ in *Van Parys* made a realistic assessment of the WTO implementation process by noting that negotiation may even last after the expiry of the reasonable period of time, provided that the offending party is prepared to pay the costs.[129] To confirm this latter view, one should remember that firstly, the reasonable period of time which postpones compliance may always be extended if all the parties to the dispute agree to it.[130] Secondly,

[125] *United States—Continued Suspension of Obligations in the EC—Hormones Dispute—Report of the Appellate Body* (16 October 2008) WT/DS320/AB/R, para 310.

[126] ibid, para 304 (emphasis added). [127] ibid.

[128] CWA Timmermans, 'The Implementation of the Uruguay Round by the EC', in JHJ Bourgeois et al. (eds), *The Uruguay Round Results—A European Lawyer's Perspective* (European Interuniversity Press 1995) 501, 504.

[129] *Léon Van Parys* (n 95) para 45.

[130] *Canada—Measures Affecting the Importation of Milk and the Exportation of Dairy Products—Agreement under Article 21.3 (b) of the DSU* (7 January 2000) WT/DS103/10 (Canada/US) and WT/DS113/10 (Canada/New Zealand); *United States—Tax Treatment for 'Foreign Sales Corporation'—Request for Modification of the Time Period for Compliance* (2 October 2000) WT/DS108/11.

the DSU does not regulate the time frame for compensation or countermeasures.[131] Thirdly, even after an adverse ruling has been adopted and the reasonable period has elapsed, it is still possible to obtain a waiver (as happened to the Community in the *Bananas* dispute). Fourthly, Article 22.8 DSU, which is often invoked to provide the legal basis for agreements on implementation, *de facto* authorizes their conclusion at any time.

These remarks show that (1) the WTO dispute settlement mechanism is a living instrument; (2) since its functioning is not completely regulated by the DSU, the parties to the dispute often conclude agreements in order to fill its lacunae; and, therefore, (3) due regard must be had to the practice of its implementation. The practice then shows that there is always diplomatic room for manoeuvre to be enjoyed by the Member parties within the WTO dispute settlement system.

10. Conclusion

The reciprocal and bilateral nature of the WTO obligations and the possibility for the parties to a dispute to have recourse to negotiation (in ways not always foreseen and regulated by the DSU) in order to resolve the issue of the implementation in the post-adjudication phase of the dispute settlement procedure, are features which by-and-large differentiate the WTO legal system from that of the EU and also explain the differences between the remedies provided by the two systems.

Both elements denote the mixed or hybrid nature of the WTO dispute settlement system, which combines judicial and diplomatic dispute settlement means throughout its procedure. From a law-and-economics perspective, this mixture is reflected in the circumstance that the WTO system combines an inalienability rule in principle with a property rule in practice. At a different level of analysis, these elements render it difficult to conclude that the phenomenon of the legal fragmentation of trade relationships, which was a distinctive feature of the 'old' GATT *à la carte* (a mosaic of special schemes, exemptions and side-agreements that the creation of the WTO was intended to replace), has really or definitively been overcome. Accordingly, the uniformity of obligations arising under the WTO Agreements is not always guaranteed.

Considering however the high rate of compliance with the rulings of the DSB, the existence of a less centralized enforcement mechanism, having a hybrid 'legal-diplomatic' nature which leaves a significant role to consensual dispute settlement means, overall appears to be an appropriate solution to the legal nature of the multilateral trade obligations (mostly reciprocal and bilateral, unlike those created by the EU Treaties) whose implementation must be ensured.

[131] See Cottier (n 9) 325, 374.

21

Enforcement of UN Security Council Resolutions and of ICJ Judgments

The Unreliability of Political Enforcement Mechanisms

Irène Couzigou

Two types of binding measures may be adopted under the UN Charter towards its States parties: mandatory resolutions of the UN Security Council and judgments of the ICJ. Decisions of the Security Council must be implemented by Member States in conformity with Article 25 UN Charter. The Security Council is the principal organ of the UN which has primary responsibility for the maintenance of international peace and security. In particular, under Article 39 UN Charter, '[t]he Security Council shall determine the existence of any threat to the peace, breach of the peace, or act of aggression'. In doing so, the Council enjoys considerable discretion.[1] Once the Security Council has determined that the conduct of a State or even of a non-State actor constitutes a threat to the peace or more rarely, a breach of the peace or, concerning the behaviour of a State, an act of aggression, the Council can recommend to or order the State or non-State actor to cease its deviant conduct. It can also impose other obligations on the target State or non-State actor itself. Furthermore, the Security Council can adopt enforcement measures addressed to other UN Member States or sometimes to international organizations, asking them to take a particular action to compel a State or non-State actor to comply with demands made by the Security Council to counter a threat to or breach of the peace or, concerning a State, an act of aggression. Academia usually qualifies those measures as 'sanctions'.[2] The Security Council may also authorize States or international organizations to use armed force against the State or non-State actor whose conduct threatens or breaches international peace and security. Military intervention is conducted on a voluntary basis but is imposed on the State or non-State actor whose behaviour is qualified as a threat to the peace, breach of the peace or, concerning a State's behaviour, an act of aggression. The Security Council may also take coercive action to enforce a judgment of the ICJ in conformity with Article 94 (2) UN Charter.

The ICJ, the principal judicial organ of the UN, can also decide binding measures. In accordance with Article 94(1) UN Charter, Member States of the UN undertake to comply with the decisions of the ICJ in any case to which they are a party. This obligation is

[1] N Krisch, 'Article 39', in B Simma et al. (eds), *The Charter of the United Nations* (3rd edn, OUP 2012) vol II 1275.

[2] See for instance, M Shaw, *International Law* (7th edn, CUP 2014) 901–8. However, since enforcement measures under Chapter VII UN Charter are not always adopted as a reaction to a violation of the UN Charter, they are not always rightly qualified as sanctions. See H Kelsen, *The Law of the United Nations* (Stevens 1951) 732–5.

Enforcement of UN Security Council Resolutions and of International Court of Justice Judgments: The Unreliability of Political Enforcement Mechanisms. First Edition. Irène Couzigou © Irène Couzigou 2017. Published 2017 by Oxford University Press.

confirmed by the Statute of the ICJ to which all States parties to the UN Charter are party. The obligation to comply with judgments of the ICJ is extended to non-Member States of the UN which become parties to the Statute of the ICJ. Article 35(2) of the Statute provides that the conditions under which the Court is open to other States which are not parties to the Statute, will be laid down by the Security Council. The Security Council decided that any State not a party to the Statute could accept the jurisdiction of the Court by deposing a declaration whereby it 'undertakes to comply in good faith with the decision or decisions of the Court [. . .]'.[3] Article 35(2) of the Statute of the ICJ also refers to States which are not parties to the Statute but to which the Court is open by virtue of provisions contained in treaties in force. Compliance with judgments of the ICJ would then be governed by the relevant provisions of the treaty, or in case of the absence of such provisions, by customary international law. Indeed, under that law, it can be argued that States parties to a dispute are obliged to implement a judgment made at their request.[4]

Contrary to mandatory Security Council resolutions which may be addressed to several States and/or sometimes to international organizations, the judgments of the ICJ are enforced only on States parties to the legal dispute. Overall, States implement Security Council and ICJ measures in accordance with their international obligations. However, what can happen if this is not the case? Does the UN rely upon the good will of States to act on their legal obligations to implement Security Council and ICJ decisions? In the absence of action by States to comply with Security Council or ICJ provisions, is there any possibility to enforce the provisions? Since the international legal order is mostly decentralized, the answer to this question is not straightforward. Strangely, despite its socio-legal importance, the issue of the enforcement of binding Security Council resolutions in particular, has enjoyed relatively little doctrinal attention. This chapter intends to remedy this lack of doctrinal interest and will outline the different enforcement mechanisms of Security Council resolutions as well as of ICJ judgments. Overall, enforcement can take two forms: direct enforcement, when the content of the decision not implemented by the addressee is implemented by another actor; or indirect enforcement, when coercive measures are taken against the non-complying actor in order to compel compliance. This chapter is in three sections. Section 1 of this analysis will outline how binding Security Council measures are enforced. Security Council resolutions are implemented compulsorily or voluntarily, depending on their content. Generally, the Security Council itself supervises compliance with its resolutions. In case of non-compliance, there are no automatic compliance mechanisms. It will be showed that enforcement of Security Council resolutions is politically influenced and therefore inconsistent. Section 2 of this chapter will analyse the enforcement of ICJ judgments. ICJ judgments are normally complied with by the States which agree to submit their dispute to the Court. Where a State refuses to execute an ICJ decision, the other State in favour of which the decision was delivered can adopt countermeasures or have recourse to the Security Council or the General Assembly. These UN organs, however, take a political decision on whether to act and are thus not obliged to enforce ICJ judgments. Furthermore, other international or domestic actors provide for mechanisms to ensure compliance with a minority of ICJ judgments. I will demonstrate that enforcement of ICJ judgments is not done consistently, overall. Finally, section 3 will conclude on the enforcement of Security Council resolutions and of ICJ judgments. I will argue that such enforcement is mostly political, influenced by State sensitivities and thus,

[3] UNSC Res 6 (1946) UN Doc S/RES/6.

[4] G Guillaume, 'Enforcement of Decisions of the International Court of Justice', in N Jasentuliyana (ed), *Perspectives on International Law* (Kluwer Law International 1996) 277.

unreliable. I will therefore propose alternatives which improve the consistency of the enforcement of Security Council and ICJ measures.

1. Inconsistent enforcement of UN Security Council resolutions

Binding measures not involving the use of armed force, adopted by the Security Council, must be implemented by States, international organizations, and/or other non-State actors. Monitoring of the implementation of Security Council resolutions is generally done by the Council itself. In a situation where a resolution is not being complied with, the UN has several means at its disposal to ensure compliance. Politically influenced, it may or may not intervene, adopting a simple recommendation or a binding measure (section 1.a.). Contrary to the implementation of non-forcible coercive measures, the implementation of coercive measures involving the use of armed force is made on a voluntary basis by Member States or international organizations. Political considerations will determine participation in a military intervention. Though prosecuted voluntarily, it is however imposed on the target State or non-State actor. Whether Member States respect the terms of a Security Council delegation to use force is monitored by the Security Council itself, very often in broad terms (section 1.b.).

a. Political enforcement of coercive measures not involving the use of armed force

I. Compulsory implementation by States, international organizations, or other non-State actors

The Security Council can adopt three kinds of non-forcible coercive measures on the basis of Chapter VII UN Charter once it has qualified a situation as a threat to the peace or breach of the peace or an act of aggression. First, under Article 41, the Security Council may order the State whose conduct constitutes a threat to or a breach of the peace or an act of aggression, to cease its deviant conduct, or to a non-State actor to put an end to a threat to the peace or a breach of the peace. It may also impose other obligations on the target State or non-State actor itself.[5] Second, the Security Council may take provisional measures under Article 40 in order 'to prevent an aggravation of the situation'. These measures are normally addressed to specific States, for instance to those parties to a conflict. Third, under Article 41, the Security Council may also decide measures addressed to third States or non-State actors, calling upon them to take certain action with a view to obliging the State or the non-State actor responsible for a threat to the peace, a breach of the peace or, concerning the State, an act of aggression, to cease its deviant behaviour. Since Chapter VII binding measures need to be adopted by at least nine members of the Security Council, without a single negative vote of one of the five permanent members, injunctions or enforcement action will never be taken against one of the permanent members (China, France, Russia, the UK, and the US) or their allies.[6] The Security Council may also adopt binding measures under Article 94(2). This

[5] For example, the Security Council obliged Iraq to destroy different categories of weapons (UNSC Res 687 (1991) UN Doc S/RES/687); it ordered several States to surrender terrorist suspects or other criminals to foreign or international tribunals (UNSC Res 748 (1992) UN Doc S/RES/748 on Libya; UNSC Res 1267 (1999) UN Doc S/RES/1267 on Afghanistan).

[6] See Art 27 para 3 UN Charter and the interpretation made of it in practice in A Zimmermann, 'Article 27', in Simma et al. (eds) (n 1) vol I, 913–15.

provision deals with the enforcement of ICJ judgments and is analysed in section 2 of this chapter.

Since the early 1990s, Article 41 has been implemented with great creativity, going far beyond the indicative list of measures referred to by this provision. The Security Council has not only taken coercive measures against a State or non-State actor causing a threat to or breach of the peace or, concerning a State, an act of aggression. It created international criminal tribunals.[7] It adopted broader measures not addressed to any particular entity. Accordingly, in resolutions 1373 and 1540, the Security Council set out a range of abstract provisions of a general nature for all States to undertake in combating international terrorism and in preventing the proliferation of weapons of mass destruction, as well as their means of delivery, in the hands of non-State actors.[8]

According to Article 48(1) UN Charter, the Security Council can request all Member States collectively, or only some of them, to carry out its decisions. The Security Council usually addresses non-forcible binding measures to all States and sometimes emphasizes a particular group of States.[9] As stated in Article 48(2), such decisions can be carried out by the Member States directly or through 'international agencies' of which they are members, which includes international organizations and international institutions lacking international legal status.[10] It is then up to the Member States to ensure that the international organizations they are members of respect the Security Council measures. Under Article 53(1) UN Charter, the Security Council may require international organizations to enforce its Article 41 action.[11] Furthermore, the Security Council increasingly calls upon non-State actors, other than international organizations, to respect coercive measures. This practice did not elicit any objections from Member States and thus reveals a new, broad interpretation of Article 48.[12]

In conformity with the UN Charter, in the event that a mandatory Security Council resolution contradicts an obligation of a UN Member State under another treaty than the UN Charter, the State must give priority to the resolution.[13] Since there is no hierarchy between treaties and (non-peremptory) customary international law, the State should also give prevalence to a compulsory Security Council resolution over a (non-peremptory) customary international norm if they conflict with each other.[14] If some of the measures required for the implementation of Security Council resolutions need to be taken at the international level, such as the severance of diplomatic relations, others have to be implemented in the domestic legal order of the Member States. Generally, Security Council resolutions lack direct effect and, if necessary, are implemented in national law through the adoption of legislative, executive or administrative measures.[15] If there is a conflict between the provisions of a binding Security Council resolution and a national rule, a State cannot

[7] UNSC Res 827 (1993) UN Doc S/RES/827 on ICTY; UNSC Res 955 (1994) UN Doc S/RES/955 on ICTR.

[8] UNSC Res 1373 (2001) UN Doc S/RES/1373; UNSC Res 1540 (2004) UN Doc S/RES/1540.

[9] N Krisch, 'Article 48', in Simma et al. (eds) (n 1) vol II, 1379.

[10] ibid, 1380. The UN has also concluded agreements with specialized agencies as referred to in Art 57 UN Charter according to which the agencies have to cooperate in the implementation of Security Council decisions. ibid, 1381–2.

[11] C Walter, 'Article 53', in Simma et al. (eds) (n 1) vol II, 1497.

[12] O Corten, 'Article 48', in M Forteau (ed), *La Charte des Nations Unies* (3rd edn, Economica 2005) 1299.

[13] Art 103 UN Charter whose conflict rule covers conflicts between secondary norms derived from the Charter and obligations under other treaties than the UN Charter. *Questions of Interpretation and Application of the 1971 Montreal Convention Arising from the Aerial Incident at Lockerbie* (*Libyan Arab Jamahiriya* v. *United States of America*) (Order) [1992] ICJ Rep 126, para 42.

[14] R Bernhardt, 'Article 103', in B Simma (ed), *The Charter of the United Nations* (2nd edn, OUP 2002) vol II, 1299.

[15] V Gowlland-Debbas, 'Concluding Remarks', in V Gowlland-Debbas, *National Implementation of United Nations Sanctions* (Martinus Nijhoff 2004) 644.

invoke its domestic law to be relieved from the execution of the resolution. Indeed, Member States must implement mandatory Security Council action under the UN Charter. It is furthermore a principle of international law that a State cannot invoke its municipal law to exempt itself from the execution of international treaty obligations.[16] Any other rule would undermine the performance of treaties. A UN Member State could thus neither invoke a (non-peremptory) international obligation nor a national obligation to justify the non-implementation of a Security Council resolution.

II. *Variable monitoring of the implementation*

Monitoring the implementation of binding non-forcible Security Council resolutions can be done outside the Security Council, by the UN Secretary-General,[17] or sometimes by an international organization[18] on the basis of available information, in particular on the basis of periodic reports submitted by States on the implementation of the relevant resolutions. The Secretary-General must then prepare a report on such implementation to the Security Council.[19]

Monitoring compliance with Security Council resolutions is however often conducted by the Security Council itself, through one of its subsidiary organs established under Article 29 UN Charter, in particular through sanctions committees. These committees are often assisted by other subsidiary organs, bodies of independent experts whose denomination varies: panels of experts, groups of experts, committees of experts, teams of experts, monitoring mechanisms, monitoring teams, or monitoring groups.[20] Unfortunately, expert bodies are not as independent as they should be.[21]

Sanctions committees, among other duties, seek information by Member States on their implementation of sanctions.[22] They investigate and report violations of the Security Council resolutions on the basis of all available sources of information, using in particular regular reports States have to prepare on the implementation of the resolutions.[23] Such committees may remind States to submit their reports, request further information, and provide guidelines for their submission. The sanctions committees also provide guidance on the implementation of Security Council resolutions and recommend ways to improve the effectiveness of the sanctions regimes. They sometimes assist States in the

[16] *Greco-Bulgarian Communities* (Advisory Opinion) [1930] PCIJ Series B, no 17, 32; *Treatment of Polish Nationals in Danzig and Other Persons of Polish Origin or Speech in the Danzig Territory* (Advisory Opinion) [1932] PCIJ Series A/B, no 44, p. 24; *Applicability of the Obligation to Arbitrate under Section 21 of the United Nations Headquarters Agreements of 26 June 1947* (Advisory Opinion) [1988] ICJ Reports 12, 34–5. The Vienna Convention on the Law of Treaties that mostly codifies that law also acknowledges the primacy of treaties over domestic law. Art 27, 1155 UNTS 341.

[17] UNSC Res 1132 (1997) UN Doc S/RES/1132, para 13; UNSC Res 1210 (1998) UN Doc/RES/1210, para 4.

[18] UNSC Res 687 (1991) UN Doc S/RES/687, paras 12 and 13 concerning the role of the International Atomic Energy Agency.

[19] UNSC Res 1302 (2000) UN Doc S/RES/1302, para 5 on the report of the Secretary-General on the implementation of the resolution against Iraq; UNSC Res 1343 (2001) UN Doc S/RES/1343, para 12 on the report of the Secretary-General on the implementation of the resolution against Libya.

[20] JM Farrall, *United Nations Sanctions and the Rule of Law* (CUP 2007) 163–80; J Farrall, 'Should the United Nations Security Council Leave it to the Experts? The Governance and Accountability of UN Sanctions Monitoring', in J Farrall and K Robenstein (eds), *Sanctions, Accountability and Governance in a Globalised World* (CUP 2014) 197–201.

[21] Farrall, 'Should the United Nations Security Council Leave it to the Experts? (n 20) 205–6.

[22] E Lagrange and PM Eisemann, 'Article 41', in Forteau (n 12) 1235; GL Burci, 'Interpreting the Humanitarian Exceptions Through the Sanctions Committees', in V Gowlland-Debbas (ed), *United Nations Sanctions and International Law* (Kluwer Law International 2001) 144.

[23] In relation to the regime imposed against Southern-Rhodesia, the Security Council established a general duty to report to the sanctions committee, and referred to the task of the committee to report to the Council. UNSC Res 253 (1968) UN Doc S/RES/253, para 20. This model was applied to each subsequent sanctions committee.

implementation of the resolutions. Finally, sanctions committees may recommend measures appropriate to respond to violations of sanctions regimes.[24]

Furthermore, the Security Council can establish a specific commission to monitor the implementation of particular measures taken on the basis of Chapter VII. For instance, after the first Gulf war, the Council created the UN Special Commission (UNSCOM) to monitor and supervise the destruction, removal, or rendering harmless of Iraq's biological, chemical, and missile capabilities.[25] The Security Council may also recommend or decide to establish a peacekeeping operation whose mandate can include the supervision of the implementation of Security Council measures by Member States.[26]

Other committees established by the Security Council do not monitor the implementation of its resolutions, but assist Member States in their application and encourage international cooperation. This is the case of the counter-terrorism committee (CTC) and of the 1540 Committee concerning the implementation of resolutions 1373 and 1540.[27] It was thought that an overly coercive approach to enforcement could jeopardize the high level of cooperation needed to fulfil the mandates of those resolutions.

Overall, monitoring of the implementation of Security Council resolutions lacks independence, transparency, consistency, and precision. The monitoring is often done by the Security Council itself, through sanctions committees which reflect the composition of the Council. Their decisions are adopted by consensus and are politically influenced, as are those of the Security Council.[28] They tend to meet in closed sessions and records of those sessions are rarely made public. The decisions of the monitoring organs of Security Council resolutions are therefore not taken after a fair and independent procedure. Furthermore, the supervision of the compliance with Security Council measures is not consistent. The Security Council has sometimes established a subsidiary organ to monitor a sanctions regime, sometimes not, or only after several months or years.[29] Monitoring organs have taken various forms and sizes; they have been created for different periods and with a variety of tasks. Their workload differs considerably. In particular, sanctions committees do not meet and report to the Security Council on the same regular basis, and their reports vary in length and quality.[30] The monitoring of sanctions regimes is thus ad hoc and reactive.[31] Lastly, the State reports submitted to the monitoring organs of the Security Council are generally vague and the organs receiving them often only acknowledge their reception without asking for further information.[32]

III. Variable action to ensure compliance

How the Security Council should address non-compliance with its resolutions then arises. One possibility is to name States for their alleged role in the violation of Security Council resolutions. The same could be done with non-State actors not complying with Security

[24] A Kolliopoulos, 'Les comités des sanctions de l'Organisation des Nations Unies', in LP Forlati and L-A Sicilianos (eds), *Les sanctions économiques en droit international* (Martinus Nijhoff 2004) 593–5.

[25] UNSC Res 687 (1991) UN Doc S/RES/687, para 9. The UNSCOM was dissolved and replaced by another subsidiary organ in 1999: the United Nations Monitoring, Verification and Inspection Commission (UNMOVIC). UNSC Res 1284 (1999) UN Doc S/RES/1284, para 1.

[26] See for instance UNSC Res 816 (1993) UN Doc S/RES/816, para 3. Peace-keeping operations established by the Security Council are traditionally seen as subsidiary organs of the Security Council.

[27] UNSC Res 1373 (2001) UN Doc S/RES/1373; UNSC Res 1540 (2004) UN Doc S/RES/1540.

[28] J Charpentier, 'Les Comités des sanctions du Conseil de sécurité' in HR Fabri, L-A Sicilianos and J-M Sorel (ed), *L'effectivité des organisations internationales, mécanismes de suivi et de contrôle* (A Pedone 2000) 20.

[29] Farrall, *United Nations Sanctions* (n 20) 210–11.

[30] Farrall, 'Should the United Nations Security Council Leave it to the Experts? (n 20) 195.

[31] ibid, 192. [32] Kolliopoulos (n 24) 593.

Council measures. Thus the sanctions committees' reports are published and the identity of State actors not complying with sanctions revealed. The annual reports of the sanctions committees are annexed to the annual report of the Security Council.[33] The 'naming and shaming' of non-complying States is however not done consistently.

Furthermore, if a State or non-State actor does not comply with a Security Council injunction to stop conduct constituting a threat to the peace, breach of the peace or, concerning a State, an act of aggression, the Security Council could reinforce the sanctions adopted against it under Article 41 and, as a last step, authorize military action under Article 42.[34]

Article 40(3) UN Charter asks the Security Council to take account of failure to comply with provisional measures. This indicates that the Security Council could, provided it first qualifies the situation as a threat to or breach of the peace or act of aggression, also adopt sanctions against a State which does not comply with provisional measures even if that State is not the original target State.[35] The Security Council has at several occasions warned that, in case of non-compliance, further measures would be considered,[36] and has sometimes done so after provisional measures had been disregarded.[37] Similarly, if a State or a non-State actor does not implement coercive measures against the target State or the target non-State actor contrary to Article 41 UN Charter, the Security Council could also qualify the situation as a threat to or breach of the peace or, concerning a State, an act of aggression, and begin to sanction the non-complying actor itself.[38] This possibility is not often utilized.

Overall, the Security Council's practice is incoherent. Indeed, as a political organ, the Security Council has a discretionary power to intensify its sanctions against a State or a non-State actor whose conduct continues to threaten or breach international peace and security. The Security Council also has the discretion to decide that the non-execution by a State or a non-State actor of sanctions decided against another State or non-State actor constitutes in itself a threat to or a breach of the peace, which justifies coercive action for compliance against the State or the non-State actor.[39] Furthermore, logically, Security Council enforcement action is not open against the five permanent members, able to veto the adoption of Security Council measures, or against one of their allies.

The other principal organs of the UN can play useful roles in enhancing compliance with Security Council resolutions. In accordance with Article 10 UN Charter, '[t]he General Assembly may discuss any questions or any matters within the scope of the present Charter [...] and, except as provided in Article 12, may make recommendations to the Members of the United Nations [...] on any such questions or matters'. Non-compliance with a Security Council measure is a matter within the scope of the UN Charter. Under Article 12(1), the General Assembly shall not make recommendations while the Security Council exercises its functions under Chapter VI or VII UN Charter. In practice however, the General Assembly has interpreted Article 12(1) very narrowly and has made recommendations even on matters pending before the Council.[40] Thus, the General Assembly is hardly limited in its power to take action related to non-compliance with a Security Council

[33] Note by the President of the Security Council of 30 October 1998, UN Doc S/1998/1016, para 4 (a).

[34] See for instance, UNSC Res 678 (1990) UN Doc S/RES/678; UNSC Res 1973 (2011) UN Doc S/RES/1973. See section 2.b. below.

[35] N Krisch, 'Article 40', in Simma et al. (eds) (n 1) vol II, 1302.

[36] See for instance, UNSC Res 660 (1990) UN Doc S/RES/660, para 4.

[37] See for instance, UNSC Res 661 (1990) UN Doc/RES/661.

[38] See for instance, UNSC Res 1343 (2001) UN Doc S/RES/1343.

[39] Lagrange and Eisemann (n 22) 1238–9.

[40] E Klein and S Schmahl, 'Article 12', in Simma et al. (eds) (n 1) vol I, 516.

resolution, even if this non-compliance is dealt with by the Security Council under Chapter VI or VII.

Each Member State of the UN has one vote in the General Assembly and no State wields a veto. The General Assembly is thus a more democratic organ than the Security Council. A General Assembly resolution asking for compliance with a Security Council resolution simply needs to be adopted by a two-thirds majority of the States present and voting.[41] However, like the Security Council, the General Assembly is a political organ and will not necessarily react to non-compliance with a Security Council decision. Furthermore, it has less effective means than the Security Council to ensure compliance with a Security Council resolution and can only take action to bring about compliance in a recommendation. Although a General Assembly resolution is not binding, it may still exert political pressure on the recalcitrant State and cause the State to comply with a Security Council resolution.[42]

The Security Council and the General Assembly could combine their powers to act against a Member State which repeatedly fails to comply with Security Council enforcement action. In such a situation, as a last step, the General Assembly may suspend the State from the exercise of its rights and privileges of membership or even expel the State from the UN, by a two-thirds majority of the members present and voting in the General Assembly upon recommendation of the Security Council.[43] The General Assembly is not bound by the recommendation of the Security Council. Action by the Security Council and the General Assembly is discretionary, and will depend on the political will of both UN organs. Such joint political action is difficult to achieve and has never been done. Since permanent members of the Security Council can veto recommendations in favour of suspension or expulsion, they are effectively shielded from it as well as their allies. Furthermore, a suspension or expulsion would have little chance of having any persuasive effect on the repeatedly defaulting State.

b. Political enforcement of coercive measures involving the use of armed force

I. Voluntary implementation by states or international organizations

Article 42 envisages that the Security Council would take forcible measures to oblige a State or non-State actor responsible for a threat to the peace, a breach of the peace or, concerning a State, an act of aggression, to cease its deviant conduct. Recourse to forcible action conforms to Article 42 UN Charter only when non-forcible action proves inadequate or if the Security Council considers that non-forcible action would be inadequate. Chapter VII forcible measures must be necessary to counter or remove the threat to or breach of the peace or act of aggression, and must be adapted to this end. Recourse by the Security Council to military action is therefore guided by a principle of necessity and proportionality.[44] Article 43 UN Charter envisaged that Member States would agree to put troops at the disposal of the Security Council. However, such agreements have never been concluded. The Security Council is thus not able to enforce military measures itself or to oblige Member States to implement such measures. The Security Council instead resorts to the

[41] Art 18 (2) UN Charter.

[42] For instance, the General Assembly has at several times recommended to Member States to apply Security Council resolution 1373 related to the prevention and suppression of the financing of terrorist acts. See for example UNGA A/RES/58/136 of 2004, para 5.

[43] Arts 5 and 6 UN Charter respectively.

[44] A Orakhelashvili, *Collective Security* (OUP 2011) 226–7.

strategy of authorizing Member States to use armed force in sharply defined circumstances.[45] States have accepted the practice of the delegation of the use of armed force by the Security Council. It is therefore a well-established means of exercising the Security Council powers under Article 42.[46]

Military action is normally carried out against the will of the target State or non-State actor. It is however pursued freely by Member States which may choose whether and, unless specified by the Security Council, to what degree and how long to implement Security Council forcible measures. Political considerations determine the level of military participation by the Member States. The use of armed force is authorized by at least a majority of nine members of the Security Council. There has by now always been at least one member among those in favour of a military intervention which was ready to deploy armed force.

While not expressly providing that the Security Council may authorize individual Member States to use armed force, the UN Charter explicitly envisages instead, in Article 53, that the Council may authorize regional arrangements or regional agencies acting consistently with the principles and purposes of the UN Charter to take enforcement action under its authority. Even if not specified, the Security Council must have found a threat to or a breach of the peace or an act of aggression.[47] In practice, in order to avoid any controversy over the meaning of the notion of 'regional organization', the Security Council prefers to address Member States acting nationally or through regional organizations.[48]

II. *Broad monitoring of the implementation*

While participation in military action authorized by the Security Council is voluntary, the objectives of such action specified by the Council must be followed by the participating actors. Quite often, the Security Council has allowed the use of armed force to pursue general aims. For example, the Security Council authorised Member States to resort to force 'to uphold and implement resolution 660 (1990) and all subsequent resolutions and to restore international peace and security in the area'.[49] In other cases, the Security Council has set up more precise objectives to the military operation. For instance, in resolution 794 the Security Council authorized Member States 'to use all necessary means' to establish a secure environment for humanitarian relief operations in Somalia.[50]

When the UN Charter provides for centralized military enforcement action under the authority of the Security Council, it logically implies that a control by the Council should be organized in the case of a decentralized mode of implementation.[51] Article 53 of the Charter requires full information to be provided to the Security Council about the military activities undertaken by regional organizations with the authorization of the Council. Since military actions taken under Article 53 and Article 42 have the same aim, to maintain

[45] It is common practice for the Council to allow Member States to resort to force in authorizing them to use 'all necessary means' or 'all necessary measures'. See in particular UNSC Res 678 (1990) UN Doc S/RES/678, para 2; UNSC Res 1973 (2011) UN Doc S/RES/1973, para 4 respectively.

[46] N Krisch, 'Article 42', in Simma et al. (eds) (n 1) vol II, 1337–8.

[47] TM Franck, *Recourse to Force* (CUP 2002) 136–7.

[48] O Corten, *The Law Against War* (Hart 2012) 316.

[49] UNSC Res 678 (1990) UN Doc S/RES/678, para 2. See also UNSC Res 83 (1950) UN Doc S/RES/83; Res 1973 (2011) UN Doc S/RES/1973, para 4.

[50] UNSC Res 794 (1992) UN Doc S/RES/794, para 10. See also UNSC Res 221 (1966) UN Doc S/RES/221, para 5; UNSC Res 787 (1992) UN Doc S/RES/787, para 12; UNSC Res 929 (1994) UN Doc S/RES/1994, para 3.

[51] D Sarooshi, *The United Nations and the Development of Collective Security* (Clarendon 1999) 155.

international peace and security, the same obligation to report should apply to Member States acting individually or collectively under Article 42.[52]

In practice, the Security Council has asked Member States or international organizations for submission of regular reports in order to monitor the implementation of its resolutions authorizing the use of force.[53] It is doubtful whether the Security Council, a political organ, is the right organ to review the reports submitted to it on the authorized military operations. The reports remain often quite general without referring to any contemplated action. Indeed, Member States or international organizations wish to retain a broad margin of appreciation related to the necessity and nature of the means employed.[54] In other cases, the Security Council simply wanted to be informed within a specified period of time on the progress of actions undertaken.[55] Information is then provided by the State commanding the ad hoc multinational force or by the secretary-general of the organization coordinating the intervention.[56] Overall, the monitoring of the implementation of armed force authorized by the Security Council remains broad and ineffective.[57]

Some voices argue that States have overstepped the limits of Security Council authorizations to resort to force.[58] In such a situation, the Security Council could ask the relevant States to comply with its resolutions and sanction them if they do not follow the Council's requests, providing it qualifies the situation as a threat to or a breach of the peace or an act of aggression. In practice however, there is no known precedent where the Security Council has recognized that a Member State or an international organization exceeded the authority granted to use force. There has always been at least one permanent member in any military intervention authorized by the Security Council and each of them could veto any binding resolution of the Council disagreeing with the deployment of the military intervention.

2. An inconsistent enforcement of ICJ judgments

States parties to a judgment of the ICJ have an obligation to implement it (section 2.a.). If a State does not comply with an ICJ judgment, the State in favour of which the judgment was delivered has several means at its disposal to ensure compliance. First, it can resort to countermeasures (section 2.b.). Second, it can ask UN organs for action, in particular the Security Council (section 2.c.). The Security Council, however, can decide discretionarily if it wants to act and how. Third, concerning a minority of ICJ judgments, the State can have recourse to another international organization than the UN or to a domestic court. Indeed, the constitutive treaties of some international organizations provide for compliance mechanisms with ICJ judgments delivered in the framework of the dispute settlement mechanism of those treaties (section 2.d.).

[52] ibid, 161.

[53] See in particular, UNSC Res 84 (1950) UN Doc S/RES/84, para 6; UNSC Res 787 (1992) UN Doc S/RES/787, para 14; UNSC Res 794 (1992) UN Doc S/RES/794, para 18; UNSC Res 929 (1994) UN Doc S/RES/929, para 10.

[54] L-A Sicilianos, 'L'autorisation par le Conseil de sécurité de recourir à la force: une tentative d'évaluation' (2002) 106 *Revue générale de droit international public* 5, 22; T Christakis and K Bannelier, 'Acteur vigilant ou spectateur impuissant? Le contrôle exercé par le Conseil de sécurité sur les Etats autorisés à recourir à la force' (2004) 2 *Revue Belge de Droit International* 498, 507, and 517.

[55] See in particular, UNSC Res 678 (1990) UN Doc S/RES/678, para 4; UNSC Res 1973 (2011) UN Doc S/RES/1973, para 11.

[56] Sicilianos (n 54) 21.

[57] A de Guttry, 'How Does the UN Security Council Control States or Organizations Authorised to Use Force?' (2014) 11 *International Organizations Law Review* 251, 277.

[58] In the course of the recent crisis in Libya in 2012, several voices have argued that the NATO coalition overstepped the limits of the Security Council authorization. S Zifcak, 'The Responsibility to Protect after Libya and Syria' (2012) 1 *Melbourne Journal of International Law* 59, 87.

a. Compulsory implementation by the States parties to the judgments

Judgments of the ICJ are binding on the States parties to the legal disputes. ICJ judgments may concern only inter-State relationships. Sometimes however, they have to be applied in the national legal orders of States in conformity with their constitutional frameworks. If there is a conflict between ICJ measures and national legal measures of a State, the relevant State could not oppose its national law to justify the non-implementation of the ICJ provisions. Priority must be given to the obligation to implement an ICJ judgment. Indeed, Member States must implement ICJ judgments in accordance with the UN Charter and the ICJ Statute. And, in conformity with a principle of international law, a State cannot invoke its municipal law in order to derogate from the execution of international treaty obligations.[59]

Article 60 of the Statute of the ICJ provides that '[t]he judgment is final and without appeal'. Articles 60 and 61 of the Statute confer upon the Court exclusive competence over any dispute 'as to the meaning and scope of the judgment', as well as over proceedings for its revision. The only role the Court may play in the enforcement of its decisions is provided for by Article 61(3) stating that the Court can make compliance with the terms of a judgment a condition for admitting proceedings in revision, a provision never applied so far. It is not for the ICJ to indicate the mode of compliance with its judgments or to enforce its judgments.

Some judicial decisions are self-enforcing. This applies to judgments which reject the claims of an applicant State or which are purely declaratory, when for instance they establish that an action or a position adopted by a State conforms with international law. Other judgments need to be implemented. This is the case for judgments of the ICJ which order a State to behave in a certain way—for instance to proceed to a territorial delimitation or to pay compensation.[60]

As States have to express agreement to submit a dispute to the ICJ, they do so only after careful consideration of the pros and cons. States are thus generally ready to execute adverse judgments. Furthermore, ICJ judgments receive quite a lot of attention and public pressure plays a role in compliance with them. Only a minority of judgments have not been implemented at all. The non-execution of the following judgments are probably the most prominent: the judgment in the *Fisheries Jurisdiction* case, where the solutions decided by the ICJ were rapidly overtaken by the evolution of the law of the sea;[61] and the judgment in the *Nicaragua* case.[62]

b. Unilateral enforcement

If a losing State refuses to implement an ICJ judgment, that State violates its international obligation to execute the judgment. The winning State seeking execution of the judgment can, in the first instance, do so by having recourse to traditional diplomatic measures—negotiations, diplomatic protests, and ultimately a rupture in diplomatic relations.

[59] See (n 16).

[60] BA Ajibola, 'Compliance with Judgments of the International Court of Justice', in MK Bulterman (ed), *Compliance with Judgments of International Courts* (Nijhoff 1996) 17–18.

[61] *Fisheries Jurisdiction (United Kingdom v Iceland; Germany v Island)* [1973] ICJ Rep 1 and ICJ Rep 49.

[62] *Case concerning Military and Paramilitary Activities in and against Nicaragua* (*Nicaragua v United States of America*) [1986] ICJ Rep 14. Reference can also be made to the *Corfu Channel* case. Albania refused to pay the compensation awarded by the ICJ to the UK until the conclusion of an agreement between the parties more than forty years later, on 8 May 1992.

If these measures are ineffective, the successful litigant can then resort to countermeasures either to enforce the judgment or to persuade the unsuccessful litigant to comply with the judgment. The international legal system is decentralized. Under general international law, therefore, countermeasures are the primary means of enforcing rights. Countermeasures may in themselves be illegal acts but become justified by being a response to an earlier violation of international law.[63] The successful litigant may in particular use economic countermeasures, for example it may seize the assets of the unsuccessful litigant under its control in satisfaction of the ICJ judgment or to persuade it to comply with the ICJ judgment.[64]

c. Political enforcement by the UN

Any Member State of the UN and not only the State debtor of an ICJ judgment may notify the Security Council of non-compliance with an ICJ judgment which constitutes a threat to international peace and security. The Security Council, at the request of a Member State or autonomously, can then adopt the full range of measures under Chapter VII UN Charter, including military measures, to enforce compliance with the ICJ judgment. This has never happened.

Furthermore, the UN Charter has a specific provision dealing with the enforcement of ICJ decisions. In conformity with its Article 94(2), '[i]f any party to a case fails to perform the obligations incumbent upon it under a judgment rendered by the Court, the other party may have recourse to the Security Council, which may, if it deems necessary, make recommendations or decide upon measures to be taken to give effect to the judgment'. The procedure provided for in Article 94 cannot be initiated by a third State or by the Security Council.[65] Furthermore, Article 94 gives discretionary power to the Security Council to act. In considering the successful litigant's request, the Security Council may act or refrain from action. Finally, the Security Council action may be purely recommendatory. Only one case was referred to the Security Council on the basis of Article 94(2), by Nicaragua following the judgment of the Court on 27 June 1986 in the case between Nicaragua and the US *concerning military and paramilitary activities in and against Nicaragua*, when the US refused to execute the judgment.[66] In other cases, the parties had filed complaints with the Security Council but did not go further and did not request a Council meeting. Indeed, when the debtor State does not have the power to veto a Security Council resolution, the mere threat of Security Council action may be enough impetus for a State to comply with an ICJ judgment.[67]

According to Article 27 UN Charter, a Member of the Security Council which is also a party to a dispute should abstain from voting on a resolution which refers to the said

[63] Countermeasures can be adopted only if the responsible State has been called upon to fulfil its international obligation and after its notification of any decision to take countermeasures. They must be adopted to terminate the violation and not out of proportion to the violation. They cannot include the use of armed force. Draft Arts on the Responsibility of States for Internationally Wrongful Acts, Arts 49 to 52, at: http://legal.un.org/ilc/texts/instruments/english/commentaries/9_6_2001.pdf, accessed 20 October 2016.

[64] EK Nantwi, *The Enforcement of International Judicial Decisions and Arbitral Awards in Public International Law* (Sijthoff 1966) 137–43.

[65] The procedure can be initiated against a State debtor of an ICJ judgment that is neither a member of the UN nor a party to the ICJ Statute, but that has accepted the jurisdiction of the ICJ in pursuance of Security Council Res 6 (1946). Indeed, this State has accepted 'all the obligations of a Member of the United Nations under Article 94 of the Charter'. UNSC Res 6 (1946) UN Doc S/RES/6.

[66] UN Docs S/18230, S/18250 and S/18428; S/PV 2700, 2704, and 2718.

[67] AP Llamzon, 'Jurisdiction and Compliance in Recent Decisions of the International Court of Justice' (2008) 18 *European Journal of International Law* 815, 848.

dispute only when the resolution is based on Chapter VI. Article 94 does not belong to Chapter VI. Therefore, a State party to a case which was judged by the ICJ and which is also a member of the Security Council does not have to abstain from voting on a resolution adopted on the basis of Article 94(2), that addresses the non-execution of the Court's judgment. Article 27 distinguishes procedural matters discussed by the Security Council from other matters for which the veto of a permanent member can prevent a resolution from being adopted. A decision on action under Article 94(2) can lead to the adoption of enforcement measures against a State. It is not a matter related to the internal organization of the UN. A permanent member of the Security Council could thus veto a resolution adopted on the basis of Article 94(2).[68] This interpretation was confirmed in practice where the veto of the US was considered to have prevented the Security Council from adopting a resolution requiring that State to comply with the judgment in the *Nicaragua* case.[69] The Security Council has never actually adopted measures to enforce ICJ decisions under Article 94(2).

If the Security Council takes action, the question arises over the extent of its powers. Article 94(2) is not included in Chapter VII but in Chapter XIV, dedicated to the ICJ. The preparatory work indicates that the drafters of the Charter wanted to strengthen the enforcement mechanism for ICJ judgments and not simply to reiterate the coercive powers of the Security Council under Chapter VII.[70] Furthermore, if it is assumed that Article 94(2) has no independent significance, the article would be superfluous. Finally, the only basis of Nicaragua's request for a Security Council action to enforce compliance with the ICJ judgment in the *Nicaragua* case was Article 94(2) and there was no debate on the Council's jurisdiction. Therefore, it is argued that the powers of the Security Council in Article 94(2) are autonomous from the powers of the Council in Chapter VII.[71] The Security Council can adopt any kind of non-forcible measure needed to oblige a State to comply with an ICJ decision and proportionate to this aim. These measures could or could not be similar to the ones adopted by the Security Council on the basis of Chapter VII. In any case, any Security Council action to enforce compliance with an ICJ judgment would have to respect authority *res judicata* of the ICJ judgment.[72]

If non-compliance with an ICJ judgment does not represent a threat to international peace and security, the question arises whether the 'measures' referred to by Article 94(2) could also encompass military intervention. Given the importance of the prohibition on the use of inter-State armed force in international law, exceptions to this prohibition must be understood restrictively. The UN Charter contains explicit provisions on the use of force. Article 94(2) does not specifically mention military action. I therefore argue that Article 94 (2) cannot justify the adoption of military measures.[73]

Other principal organs of the UN than the Security Council may enforce ICJ judgments, especially the General Assembly. Non-compliance with an ICJ judgment is a matter within the scope of the UN Charter. Under Article 10 UN Charter, the General Assembly could thus recommend by a two-thirds majority, that a State comply with an ICJ judgment.[74] In

[68] A broad majority of commentators share this view. See C Schulte, *Compliance with Decisions of the International Court of Justice* (OUP 2004) 54–5 and the literature referred to at 54 fn 173.

[69] Guillaume (n 4) 284.

[70] *United Nations Conference on International Organization—Documents* (United Nations & Library of Congress 1945–1955) vol XIII, 266–9.

[71] The vast majority of commentators agree that Art 94(2) is an independent source of competence for the Security Council. See Schulte (n 68) 39–41 and the literature referred to at 40 fn 102.

[72] A Azar, *L'exécution des décisions de la Cour Internationale de Justice* (Bruylant 2003) 151–3.

[73] Schulte (n 68) 47; Azar (n 72) 161.

[74] See section 1.a.III. for the interpretation of Art 10 UN Charter.

the case of a serious contravention of an ICJ judgment, the General Assembly could recommend that diplomatic or economic measures are taken by third Member States to bring about compliance with the judgment. General Assembly resolutions would not be binding but could exert political pressure on the recalcitrant State. Like the Security Council, the General Assembly must abstain from action contrary to the judgment.[75] The *Nicaragua* case marks the furthest the General Assembly has gone to enforce compliance with an ICJ judgment. The General Assembly called on the US to comply with the ICJ decision delivered in that case.[76] However, the US did not respect the General Assembly resolutions.

d. Exceptional enforcement by other actors

I. By other international organizations than the UN

International organizations other than the UN can also play a role in the enforcement of ICJ decisions. Political considerations may not influence the measures of those organizations so acutely as they do with the measures of the Security Council and of the General Assembly. However, those organizations' enforcement measures are not always compulsory. Furthermore, they may be taken in very specific situations only. For instance, the constitutive act of the International Labour Organization (ILO) establishes mechanisms for the settlement of disputes relating to observance of ILO conventions. These mechanisms can include the enforcement of judgments by the ICJ. As stated in the Constitution of the ILO, '[i]n the event of any Member failing to carry out within the time specified the recommendations, if any, contained [...] in the decision of the International Court of Justice [...], the Governing Body [of the ILO] may recommend to the Conference such action as it may deem wise and expedient to secure compliance therewith'.[77] Enforcement action by the ILO has not yet been taken. The Convention on the International Civil Aviation Organization (ICAO) empowers the ICJ to give appeal rulings on decisions adopted by the Council of the ICAO in connection with disputes relating to the interpretation or application of the Convention. Articles 87 and 88 of the Convention provide for sanctions against airlines or States in the case of non-compliance by a State party with a decision of the Court.[78] It should be noted that Article 87 of the Convention applies automatically and therefore offers an effective enforcement procedure. Articles 87 and 88 have not yet been implemented. Furthermore, the Statute of the International Atomic Energy Agency confers jurisdiction on the ICJ for disputes concerning its interpretation or application. In case of non-compliance with obligations adjudicated upon by the Court, the Statute provides for the possibility to decide a suspension from the exercise of the privileges and rights of membership.[79] This has never occurred.

International organizations acting regionally might also provide for mechanisms to ensure compliance with ICJ judgments. At the regional level, there may be greater responsiveness on the part of the recalcitrant State to opinion and pressure from its own region than at the international level.[80] For instance, the American Treaty on Pacific Settlement states that: '[i]f one of the High Contracting Parties should fail to carry out the obligations imposed upon it by a decision of the International Court of Justice or by an arbitral award, the other party or parties concerned shall [...] propose a Meeting of Consultation of

[75] Schulte (n 68) 67.
[76] UNGA A/RES/41/31 of 1986, A/RES/42/18 of 1987, A/RES/43/11 of 1988 and A/RES/44/43 of 1989.
[77] Art 33, 15 UNTS 92. [78] Arts 87 and 88, 15 UNTS 354.
[79] Arts XVII and XIXB 276 UNTS 34 and 36–38 respectively. [80] Schulte (n 68) 76.

Ministers of Foreign Affairs to agree upon appropriate measures to ensure the fulfilment of the judicial decision or arbitral award'.[81] This provision was only applied with regard to the ICJ judgment concerning the *arbitral award* case between Honduras and Nicaragua.[82] A similar mechanism has been established under the European Convention for the Peaceful Settlement of Disputes. The Convention empowers the Committee of Ministers of the Council of Europe to make recommendations to ensure compliance with an ICJ decision rendered pursuant to the Convention.[83] This mechanism has not yet been implemented.

II. By domestic courts

The State creditor of an ICJ judgment could seek national judicial enforcement of the judgment through a domestic court of the State debtor of the judgment or even of a third State. In particular, if the judgment awards monetary compensation, the successful litigant could ask a domestic court of the unsuccessful litigant to attach assets of that latter litigant in order to satisfy the judgment. The debtor State's assets could be under the jurisdiction of a third State, whose executive is not willing to levy on the debtor State's assets at the request of the creditor State. The creditor State could then also launch judicial proceedings in the third State to obtain the attachment of the debtor State's assets.

There are however two possible obstacles to the domestic judicial enforcement of an ICJ judgment. First, the respondent State should not enjoy immunity from jurisdiction in the order of the State where the municipal court proceedings take place. Second, the domestic court must recognize and give effect to the international judgment, emanating from a non-domestic jurisdiction.[84] The ICJ rarely condemns a State to pay a precise indemnity. So far, therefore, no State creditor of an ICJ judgment has gone to the courts of another State in order to have the assets of the debtor State attached in satisfaction of the judgment.

3. Conclusion

In conclusion, enforcement of compulsory Security Council resolutions lacks independence, transparency, coherence, and efficiency. The monitoring of the implementation of Security Council coercive measures is not always organized and not always done according to the same scheme. If there is a monitoring mechanism, it is often conducted by the Security Council itself, whose working procedures lack independence. Furthermore, the monitoring is organized mostly on the basis of reports written by the monitored Member States or international organizations themselves. These reports are often vague and incomplete. In case of non-compliance with mandatory Security Council resolutions, action for enforcement is done by UN organs and in particular by the Security Council itself. As a political organ, the Security Council does not react consistently towards the non-implementation of one of its decisions. Its principal enforcement mechanism is to name and shame a State or an international organization which does not comply with its coercive action. However, the Council does so inconsistently. The Security Council has also, on occasion and more effectively, sanctioned a non-complying State. This alternative is also used without any coherent logic. Overall, the Security Council enforces its resolutions in a discretionary manner, depending on the political will of its members. Inevitably, since the

[81] Art L, 30 UNTS 102. [82] Nantwi (n 64) 171–2. [83] Art 39, 320 UNTS 262.

[84] O Schachter, 'The Enforcement of International Judicial and Arbitral Decisions' (1960) 54 *American Journal of International Law* 1, 12–13.

five permanent members have a right of veto, the Security Council will never be able to act against one of them or one of their allies.

The principal enforcement procedure of ICJ judgments is also political and therefore not applied fairly and consistently. It is indeed in the hands of a political organ, the Security Council. The Security Council is not obliged to act to enforce an ICJ judgment on the request of the State creditor of the judgment. Furthermore, if it decides to act, it again has discretion on how to act: it may only adopt recommendations and not necessarily binding measures. Furthermore, if the judgment debtor is also member of the Security Council, it is not nevertheless obliged to abstain from voting on whether and how to act. Finally, the five permanent members may use their veto and may therefore block the adoption of any resolution which sanctions them or one of their allies for non-compliance with an ICJ judgment.

International law efficiently provides for the prevalence of the obligation to comply with a binding Security Council resolution or with an ICJ judgment in the case of a conflict between the resolution or judgment and an international or domestic obligation. However, much should be done to improve the consistency and thus the efficiency of the enforcement of mandatory Security Council resolutions and of ICJ judgments. Such enforcement should be less dependent on political considerations. The evaluation of compliance with Security Council resolutions should be made by a court-like organ, independent from the Council, following a clear, transparent, and fair procedure. Ideally, only one permanent organ should be responsible for monitoring the implementation of Security Council resolutions. This organ should then be staffed flexibly so as to be able to respond to sanctions activity at it evolves. If there are several monitoring organs, they should harmonize their working standards. The monitoring of the implementation of Security Council coercive measures should be organized more coherently, each time the Council establishes a sanctions regime and along the same lines. The monitoring organ should ask for more precise reports on the implementation of Security Council resolutions by States or non-State actors. For the purpose of transparency, those reports should be publicly available, unless its author specifically requests that its report be kept confidential. The monitoring organ should be able to recommend compliance with Security Council action. Such a recommendation should be published and hopefully constitute enough impetus for the State or non-State actor to implement the relevant Security Council resolution. The Security Council would still be able to act under Chapter VII UN Charter if it decides that non-compliance with its resolutions constitutes a threat to or a breach of the peace or an act of aggression.

The UN procedure for enforcement of ICJ judgments should also be less politically influenced. First, an organ independent from the States parties to the dispute submitted to the ICJ should assess the non-execution of an ICJ judgment by the debtor State. This would avoid any controversy about compliance with the judgment. The ICJ could be empowered with such competence. Second, the main institutionalised enforcement process for ICJ judgments, through the UN, should be more independent from political interests. For the purposes of fairness, if an ICJ judgment debtor is a member of the Security Council, it should abstain from participating in a vote on any resolution under Article 94(2). Furthermore, the permanent members should not be able to use their veto when acting on the basis of Article 94(2). A less political and thus more reliable enforcement process of Security Council coercive measures and of ICJ judgments would increase the credibility of the Security Council and of the ICJ actions.

22

Securing Compliance with Democracy Requirements in Regional Organizations

Carlos Closa

1. Introduction

International organizations, and particularly organizations concerned with regional integration, have increasingly included provisions requiring member states to fulfil certain conditions in relation to the respect for democracy and the Rule of Law. These provisions are usually found alongside comprehensive instruments for the international protection of human rights. For instance, both the CoE and the Organization of American States (OAS) have provisions for suspending members who breach the democratic conditions of membership. Both also have mechanisms such as their respective charters of rights (the European Convention for the Protection of Human Rights and Fundamental Freedoms[1] and the American Convention on Human Rights,[2] respectively) enforced by independent supranational courts (the ECtHR and the IACHR). The protection of human rights is essentially conceived as a mechanism for protecting against breaches in individual or collective and in this respect is substantially distinct from the guarantee of democracy and Rule of Law. While breaches of the latter may affect human rights, more systemic aspects are at stake: general violation by state authorities of these basic principles.

Assuming that states yield sovereignty only very reluctantly, the question is why states commit themselves to respect democracy as a mechanism for regulating membership rights in regional organizations? Two concurrent lines of reasoning provide explanations: normative and functional.[3]

The normative approach would argue that democracy has become increasingly conceived of as a 'global good' that international, transnational, and supranational organizations ought therefore to guarantee, to counteract powerful domestic anti-democratic tendencies. This argument emerged strongly with the geopolitical changes in the 1990s,[4] when a significant number of new regional organizations sanctioned democracy and democracy protection. Additionally, older organizations (e.g. the OAS), adapted their own norms on democratic conditionality at this critical juncture. Although some have argued that post-war approaches to democratic protection do not contradict but build on

[1] Convention for the Protection of Human Rights and Fundamental Freedoms as amended by Protocols No 11 and No 14 (4 November 1950) CETS No 5.

[2] American Convention on Human Rights (12 November 1969) 1144 UNTS 123.

[3] See on this, C Closa, 'Institutional design of democratic conditionality in regional organizations' (2013) EUI Working Papers RSCAS No 45, http://cadmus.eui.eu/handle/1814/27462, accessed 12 October 2016.

[4] T Franck, 'The Emerging Right to Democratic Governance' (1992) 86 *American Journal of International Law* 1;GH Fox, 'The right to political participation in international law' (1992) 17 *Yale Journal of International Law* 539. As an illustration, The Harare Commonwealth Declaration, Twelfth Commonwealth Heads of Government Meeting (CHOGM) (Harare, 16–21 October 1991) refers explicitly to the change of the geopolitical context as justification for its promulgation.

old ideas about the role of respective regions as guarantors of democracy, the upsurge in different provisions in different organizations around different regions combined with burgeoning practice seems to suggest a substantial paradigm shift.[5]

A second explanation concurs with the normative one and points towards the functional aspect of conditionality provisions. On the one hand, democratizing countries have a vested interest in securing the irreversibility of newly-acquired democracy by means of supra-state commitments that domestic actors cannot easily alter.[6] On the other hand, securing democracy and the Rule of Law in the members of international organizations signals and guarantees their commitment to the objectives of the organization. This correlation is stronger if the organization commits itself to these principles (e.g. democracy and Rule of Law) as its own objectives. Also, the more complex the organization is (measured by its objectives), the more likely that it possesses such conditionality provisions. Indeed, democratic conditionality provisions are more common in integration organizations (e.g. EU, AU, Economic Community of West Africa (ECOWAS), Mercado Común del Sur (Mercosur), etc) (see Table 22.1 below).

In fact, both explanations are equally persuasive but both face the same difficulties to explain the enforcement problem, e.g. how regional organizations enforce suspension because of democratic breaches. My thesis is that international organizations and regional organizations respond to the enforcement dilemma by trading off democratic conditionality versus sovereignty and they reach an equilibrium point between the two by favouring institutional designs which grant a large margin for states' political discretion to decide whether or not breaches exist and to apply the accompanying sanctions provided. In order to discuss this thesis, sections 3 and 4 present the institutional configuration of suspension procedures because of democratic breaches and section 5 discusses the actual practice. Section 6 discusses the problems generated in the confluence of institutional design and practice. Before turning to institutional design, the analysis will first discuss the enforcement dilemma.

2. Enforcing democratic conditionality in regional organizations

Democratic conditionality provisions raise a key problem of institutional design: enforcement.[7] While conditional membership provisions scrutinize the democratic credentials of states at the moment of accession (and provide information on state's future behaviour) they cannot control deviation from the original fulfilment of conditions. International organizations and member states may therefore face an additional dilemma: how can they ensure that a current member honours the original conditions of membership, including respect for democratic principles? In order to resolve this dilemma, international organizations may create enforcement mechanisms which, in relation to membership, have two specific forms: expulsion and suspension.

Expulsion is a decisive act which terminates membership, while suspension will last until the circumstances that provoked its change.[8] To expel a member can be very costly, since it may harm the organization as much as it harms the offending member. Consequently,

[5] E Hellquist, 'Regional Organizations and Sanctions Against Members; Explaining the Different Trajectories of the African Union, the League of Arab States, and the Association of Southeast Asian Nations' (2014) Universität Berlin Kolleg-Forschergruppe Working Paper Series No 59.

[6] A Moravcsik, 'The Origins of Human Rights Regimes: Democratic Delegation in Postwar Europe' (2000) 54 (2) *International Organization* 217–52; JC Pevehouse, *Democracy from Above* (CUP 2005).

[7] B Koremenos et al., 'The Rational Design of International Institutions' (2001) 55 *International Organisations* 761.

[8] HG Schermers and NM Blokker *International Institutional Law* (Martinus Nijhoff 2011) 11.

expulsion is very uncommon both in terms of constitutional provisions and practice. In relation to formal legal provisions, only a limited number of international organization constitutions provide for the possibility of expulsion,[9] and as far as practice is concerned, prior to 1987, only four cases of expulsion from UN agencies occurred: Czechoslovakia was expelled from the IMF and the World Bank; and South Africa from the Universal Postal Union (UPU) and the International Telecommunication Union (ITU).[10] The number of cases may be greater if *voluntary withdrawal* is also considered, since the boundary between expulsion and withdrawal may become tenuous in certain cases in which states chose to withdraw rather than facing expulsion because of the reputational costs of the latter. For instance, Greece withdrew from the CoE in 1970 following the Colonels' coup,[11] but this was a result of the suspension procedure initiated within the Council.[12] Similarly, Fiji withdrew from the Commonwealth of Nations between 1987 and 1997, and Zimbabwe in 2003.[13] In both cases, these organizations had previously decided to suspend membership. Gambia withdrew in 2013 from the Commonwealth even though a suspension procedure was not initiated (although criticism was mounting against the Gambian authorities).[14] The limited number of cases only show that organizations rarely penalize deviation from compliance with democratic conditionality by expelling a member state. The scarce use of expulsion suggests the conclusion that enforcement through this mechanism is largely irrelevant.[15]

Suspension offers an attractive alternative to expulsion: offending states may be coerced into adapting their behaviour to the conditions set by the organization that they have violated. Naturally, expulsion can be easily converted into suspension if readmission applies. The slim difference between the two, and the one that leads presumably to states preferring suspension, is that it does not terminate membership and the offending state may engage with the organization's organs and other states for addressing the reasons for the suspension. In any case, suspension also presents an enforcement dilemma: on the one hand, states do not wish to restrict their unfettered sovereignty by creating supra-state commitments which they cannot control. Additionally, suspension clauses do not externalize costs: they potentially affect current members who may have to bear the costs, rather than exclusively externalizing them to third parties. Moreover, cost-bearers may be

[9] Art 6 Charter of the United Nations (signed on 26 June 1945) 1 UNTS 16; Art 26(2) and s 22 By Laws, Articles of Agreement of the International Monetary Fund (22 July 1944) 2 UNTS 39; Art VI (2) and s 21 By Laws, Articles of Agreement of the International Bank for Reconstruction and Development; Art 5(2)(a) and Art 18 By Laws, Articles of Agreement of the International Finance Corporation (25 May 1955) 264 UNTS 118; Art 7 (2)(a) Articles of Agreement of the International Development Association (24 September 1960); Art 8 Statute of the Council of Europe (5 May 1949) London, 5 V 1949 CETS no 001; Art 18 Charter of Arab League (22 March 1945); Art 32 Convention of the Asia-Pacific Space Cooperation Organization (28 October 2005); Art 13 Charter of the Shanghai Cooperation Organization (5 June 2002).

[10] In relation to Czechoslovakia, International Monetary Fund, Summary Proceedings of Ninth Annual Meeting (1954) 135 ff; International Bank for Reconstruction and Development, Tenth Annual Report of IBRD (1954–1955) 26; In relation to South Africa, Proposal 1012 91 UPUDoc Cg 1 Lausanne 1974 I, 23; Report on the Activities of the International Telecommunication Union in 1973, Resolution 31 (International Telecommunication Union Geneva 1973) 153.

[11] *Note verbale* from government of Greece to the Secretariat of the Council of Europe (12 December 1969); Resolution (70) 34 of the Committee of Ministers on the legal and financial consequences of the withdrawal of Greece from the organization (27 November 1970).

[12] Resolution 361 of the Consultative Assembly on the Situation in Greece (31 January 1968); Resolution 385 of the Consultative Assembly on the Situation in Greece (26 September 1968); Recommendation 547 of the Consultative Assembly on the Situation in Greece (30 January 1969); Resolution 18 of the Committee of Ministers on the Situation in Greece (6 May 1969); Resolution 51 of the Committee of Ministers on the Situation in Greece (12 December 1969).

[13] Ninth Commonwealth Heads of Government Meeting (CHOGM) (Vancouver, 15–17 October 1987).

[14] Seventeenth Commonwealth Heads of Government Meeting (CHOGM) (Coolum, 2–5 March 2002).

[15] B Koremenos et al., 'Rational Design: Looking Back to Move Forward' (2001) 55 *International Organisations* 1051.

undefined, since no state can calculate *a priori* who the cost-bearer will be (as evidenced by the case of the triggering of diplomatic sanctions against Austria in the EU in 1999. Austria had participated in the design of these provisions that were meant for new Central and Eastern European members[16]).

These arguments supply powerful reasons for states to resist such clauses but other equally persuasive arguments support the case for including them in the institutional design of organizations: a suspension clause guarantees an efficient enforcement mechanism for the initial democratic requirement and in this way, suspension clauses also contribute to reducing uncertainty about the future behaviour of a state by locking it into specific features consistent with the organization's objectives. Suspension clauses increase the costs for a given state if it resiles from its initial commitment. Reneging on conditions set out by an international organization can be costly for democratic states, therefore serving as a deterrent to influential groups within government which may have reason to derail liberal reforms: it thus increases the credibility of commitments to sustain such programmes.[17] In summary, suspension may be presented as a mechanism for enforcing conditional membership over time. I call this the 'temporal consistency expectation'.

The question of why states commit themselves to democratic conditionality suspension provision cannot be separated from the question of *how* these mechanisms are designed: states and organizations accept the trade-off between sovereignty, on the one hand, and commitment with principles or obtaining security for future behaviour, on the other, by means of the balance of suspension clauses (which fulfil the commitment to principles side), on the one hand, and carefully engineered implementation clauses (which permit states to retain control on these provisions and their application), on the other. Before revising institutional design, the next section presents a typology of provisions in different regional organizations.

3. Typology of suspension provisions in international organizations

Table 22.1 shows the three categories of suspension provisions. A dataset of eighty-five international organizations shows that treaties do not usually contain provisions on suspension and therefore the safest conclusion to be drawn that is this is not a very common provision.[18] Moreover, when suspension provisions do exist, they refer most commonly to the failure to comply with financial obligations (e.g. paying dues).

The first category, related to financial non-compliance, is not relevant for this chapter. The second refers to the possibility of suspension due to non-compliance with general obligations. Several organizations have used this as the legal basis for acting against members which commit breaches with respect to the Rule of Law, constitutionalism, or democracy. For instance, the Arab League enacted sanctions against Libya and Egypt applying this kind of provision.[19]

[16] Sadurski W, 'Adding a Bite to a Bark? A Story of Article 7, the EU Enlargement, and Jörg Haider' (2010) University of Sydney Law School Legal Studies Research Paper No 10/01.

[17] ED Mansfield and JC Pevehouse, 'Democratization and International Organizations' (2006) 60 *International Organization* 137.

[18] C Closa and L Casini, *Comparative Regional Integration Governance and Legal Models* (CUP 2016). See for a more elaborated discussion concerning Europe and Latin America, C Closa et al., *Regional Organisations and Mechanisms for Democracy Protection in Latin America, the Caribbean, and the European Union* (EU-LAC Foundation 2016). https://eulacfoundation.org/en/documents/regional-organisations-and-mechanisms-democracy-protection-latin-america-caribbean-and, accessed 12 October 2016.

[19] In relation to the 1979 sanctions against Egypt, see DW Bowett, *Law of International Institutions* (4th edn, Stevens & Sons 1982) 233. In relation to the 2011 suspension of Libya see, MH Aljaghoub et al., 'The Arab League' in G Zyberi (ed), *An Institutional Approach to the Responsibility to Protect* (CUP 2013), 293.

Table 22.1 Typology of suspension clauses

Suspension as a consequence of non-fulfilment of financial obligations	Suspension as a consequence of non-fulfilment of general obligations	Suspension as a consequence of offences against human rights, Rule of Law or democracy	No specific provision on suspension
AEC, AU, COMESA, CAN, CoE, ECCAS, IGAD, IAEA, IHO, ILO, IMO, IOM, INTERPOL, PICES, OPCW, OIC, SADC, UN, UPU, WIPO, WHO, UNWTO	AEC, Arab League, COMESA, CIS, CoE, EAC, ECOWAS, EAEC, EU, IAEA, IMF, IOM, OPCW , GUAM, SADC, SCO, UN, UNWTO	AU,* CAN, Commonwealth of Independent States, ECOWAS, EU, Mercosur, PIF, OIF, OAS, UNSAUR	AAEU, ACS, ASEAN, Benelux, CARICOM, GCC, ECO, EFTA, EPO, Helsinki Convention, IOR-ARC, ICES, IMSO, KEDO, LAIA, NAFTA, NATO, OECD, ODECA, OECS, OEI, OPEC, SICA, SAFTA, SAARC, SEATO, UMA, WAEMU, WAMZ, WCO, WEU, WTO

* The AU provision refers to overthrowing legitimate governments by unconstitutional means. This provision acts as a guarantor of the status quo rather than as protection for specific values.

Source: author's own elaboration.

Column three presents the central category for this study: organizations implementing suspension with specific provisions (in contrast to general ones) addressing breaches of democracy or the Rule of Law. As the 'expectation of temporal consistency' anticipates (e.g. the conditional accession provisions correlate with provisions on suspension because of breach of membership conditions), most international organizations with democratic conditional membership also have a suspension clause.

Several organizations have acquired *a posteriori* (i.e. as a result of a reform of the rules of the organization after this was created, its foundational members had adhered and the organization had worked for some time) a provision for suspending membership on the ground of a violation of democratic credentials. In fact, most of the organizations with instruments for democratically conditioned accession have additionally acquired the function of enforcing membership suspension because of democratic breaches. As mentioned, this evolution also occurred mainly in the 1990s and 2000s. Organizations in America, Africa, and Europe have displayed this development.

Regarding the Americas, the drafting of the OAS Charter reflected a certain ambivalence about the place of democracy and human rights in the institution.[20] Latin American states supported the inclusion of the principle of 'non-intervention' in the Charter, but they viewed democracy and human rights as 'ideals the ultimate consequence of which they were not prepared to accept, lest their protection or implementation would in some way interfere or jeopardise their sovereignty'.[21] Subsequent attempts to include a commitment to democracy in the Charter were also rejected. Once all American states had held democratic elections, the OAS formalized its commitment to 'democratic solidarity' via the Santiago Compromise[22] and the Washington Protocol.[23] Simultaneously with the

[20] OAS, *Charter of the Organisation of American States* (30 April 1948) 119 UNTS 3.

[21] A Duxbury, *The Participation of States in International Organizations. The Role of Human Rights and Democracy* (CUP 2011) 172. She quotes C Medina Quiroga, *The battle of human rights. Gross, systematic violations and the Inter-American system* (Martinus Nijhoff 1988) 39.

[22] OAS General Assembly Official Records, 21st Regional Session Organización de los Estados Americanos/Ser. P/AG document 2734/91 (4 June 1991).

[23] Protocol of amendments to the Charter of the Organization of American States, *Protocol of Washington* (25 September 1997) 1-E Rev Organización de los Estados Americanos Documentos Oficiales/SerA/2 Add 3 (SEPF), (1997) 33 *International Legal Materials* 1005.

Compromise, the OAS Assembly approved Resolution 1080 which provides a specific procedure for dealing with breaches of democracy and unconstitutional seizure of power.[24] The Protocol in turn amended Article 9 OAS Charter, which now permits suspending a member by a two-thirds majority of all members. Although almost all OAS members have ratified the amendment, Mexico has yet to do so and has even entered a reservation opposing the use of 'isolation, suspension or exclusion' as instruments for promoting democracy. The Mexican authorities argued that the punitive character assigned to the OAS has changed the original purpose of the organization. In 2001 the OAS added the Inter-American Democratic Charter (IADC),[25] which equally contains a provision for suspending membership because of democratic breaches (Article 21).[26] This provision served to suspend the participation of Honduras in the organization in 2009.[27] In 2001 the Summit of the Americas approved the *Declaration of Quebec*, establishing that any unconstitutional alteration or interruption of the democratic order in a state in the Hemisphere constitutes an insurmountable obstacle to the participation of that state's government in the summit of the Americas process.[28] The Summit does not form part of the OAS or any other organization but other American organizations have since developed similar instruments shortly afterwards, prompting the unavoidable conclusion that institutional mimesis has taken place in this process. Mercosur adopted the Protocol of Ushuaia I,[29] followed by the Protocol of Ushuaia II.[30] The Andean Community (CAN) adopted the Additional Protocol to the Cartagena Agreement, CAN Compromise with Democracy.[31] The UNASUR adopted in 2010 the Additional Protocol to the Constitutive Treaty of UNASUR on Compromise with Democracy.[32] Finally, the the Community of Latin American and Caribbean States (CELAC) adopted in 2011 a Special Declaration on Democracy and Constitutional Order which also contained a suspension clause (point 2).[33]

African organizations have shown the clearest and most radical evolution. Increasingly, a consensus emerged on the need to revise the original OAU concepts of sovereignty and

[24] Resolution 1080 of the General Assembly of the Organization of American States AG/RES 1080 (XXI-O/91). The procedure of Resolution 1080 was enforced in the cases of Haiti, Peru, Guatemala, and Paraguay in response to unconstitutional or anti-democratic situations.

[25] *Inter-American Democratic Charter*, Organización de los Estados Americanos Documentos Oficiales/SerP/AG/Resolution 1 (2001); 28th Special Session, Organization American States Documents Organización de los Estados Americanos Documentos Oficiales/SerP/AG/RES 1 (XXVIII-E/01) (OAS General Assembly, 11 September 2001), (2001) 40 *International Legal Materials* 1289.

[26] E Lagos and TD Rudy, 'In defence of democracy' (2004) 35 *University of Miami Inter-American Law Review* 304 argue that the OAS Democratic Charter is not a legally binding Treaty and it does not explicitly amend the OAS Charter. Instead, the Democratic Charter should be recognized as an aid to interpreting Art 9 OAS Charter rather than as a formal amendment. Duxbury has noticed the inconsistencies between the documents which in her opinion highlights the lack of precision in the circumstances which could give rise to one of a range of measures envisaged; Duxbury (n 20) 179.

[27] Suspension of the right of Honduras to participate in OAS (Adopted at the second plenary session, held on 4 July 2009, and reviewed by the Style Committee) AG/RES 2 (XXXVII-E/09). According to Duxbury, appeal to this legal basis happened mainly because the expelled President invoked it explicitly; Duxbury (n 20) 19.

[28] Third Summit of the Americas *Declaration of Quebec City* (22 April 2001).

[29] Ushuaia Protocol on the Democratic Commitment in the Southern Common Market and Mercosur, the Republic of Bolivia, and the Republic of Chile (open for signature 24 July 1998, entered into force 17 January 2002) 2177 UNTS 383.

[30] Montevideo Protocol on the Democratic Commitment in the Southern Common Market and Mercosur, *Ushuaia Protocol on the Democratic Commitment in the Southern Common Market II* (20 December 2011) (no UNTS publication).

[31] Additional Protocol to the Cartagena *Agreement Compromise of the Andean Community with Democracy* (signed on 20 June 2000).

[32] Additional Protocol to the Constitutive Treaty of UNASUR on Compromise with Democracy (adopted during 4th UNASUR summit in Georgetown on 26 November 2010).

[33] CELAC Special Declaration on Democracy and Constitutional Order (Caracas, 3 December 2011).

non-interference in line with the view of sovereignty as responsibility.[34] The Preamble of the OAU Charter committed to safeguard and consolidate the hard-won independence as well as the sovereignty and territorial integrity of African states. However, the Charter did not refer to democracy and human rights protection. The path towards formalization ran in parallel with the transformation of the OAU into the AU. First, the OAU Heads of State and Government approved a Decision on unconstitutional changes of government, which obliged governments which came to power by unconstitutional means to restore legality before the next summit.[35] Second, the OAU approved a Declaration on the Framework for an OAU response to unconstitutional changes of government.[36] The government concerned should be suspended from participating in OAU policy organs. The Declaration defines four situations which could be considered an 'unconstitutional change of government' and three of these referred to democratically elected governments and the fourth to non-recognition of elected authorities. Duxbury considers that these documents provide greater clarity than those of the OAS when describing the type of situations where membership could be invoked.[37] The third foundational document is the AU Constitutive Act itself, which recognizes explicitly the right of the AU to intervene with respect to very serious circumstances, namely, war crimes, genocide, and crimes against humanity.[38] The Act confirms the previous condemnation of unconstitutional rulers by excluding governments obtaining power through unconstitutional means from the AU's activities. The Act, however, does not provide a definition of 'unconstitutional' and therefore, the Declaration quoted above (adopted at the same summit) acts as an interpretative element for the Act. Finally, the African Charter on Democracy, elections and governance replicates, in Article 23, the four criteria contained in the Declaration and includes a fifth additional one referring to democracy.

Another African regional organization, ECOWAS, initially conceived as one of the regional building blocks of the AU itself, has developed probably the most ambitious and far reaching mechanisms for the protection of democracy via suspension of membership. Suspension here is, however, merely a by-product of the more ambitious role conceived for ECOWAS, which refers to crisis management and resolution, including peacekeeping. The initial Protocol on the issue was only later complemented by a more specific one, the supplementary protocol on democracy and good governance, which complemented the former on internal crisis prevention, democracy, good governance, Rule of Law, and individual rights.[39] The initial Protocol contained vigorous mechanism which the later subsequently subrogated.

The Commonwealth of Nations has followed a similar evolution to AU. Lacking specific formal instruments, the former has intervened only against its members in extreme situations—those of apartheid in South Africa and Uganda's massive rights violations. The

[34] Duxbury (n 20). W Lotze et al., 'An Early Spring? Regional Responses to Crisis in Côte d'Ivoire and Authoritarianism in Myanmar' (2012) *Paper prepared for the UNICRIS–UNECA Joint Conference 'After the Arab Spring' at Brussels 22–23 November 2012*; Hellquist (n 5).

[35] Assembly Heads of Government Decision Dec 150 XXXVI on Unconstitutional Changes of Government (CM/2166 LXXII).

[36] Assembly Heads of Government Declaration XXXVI, Lomé Declaration on the Framework for an Organization of the African Union Response to Unconstitutional Changes of Government (Lomé, 10–12 July 2000).

[37] Duxbury (n 20) 186.

[38] OAU, *Constitutive Act of the African Union* (Lomé, 1 July 2000) OAU Doc CAB/LEG/23 15, Art 4(h).

[39] OAU, Protocol relating the mechanism for conflict prevention, management and resolution, peacekeeping and security, Adopted by the 1st Ordinary Session of the Assembly of the African Union (Durban, 9 July 2002); and the Economic Community of West African States, Protocol on Democracy and Good Governance Supplementary to the Protocol relating to the Mechanism For Conflict Prevention, Management, Resolution, Peacekeeping and Security (Dakar, 21 December 2001) A/SP1/12/01.

Harare Declaration committed the Commonwealth to increase cooperation to promote democracy, democratic processes, and institutions which reflect national circumstances, as well as the Rule of Law.[40] However, the Declaration was not seen as a method of judging the behaviour of current Member States.[41] The 1995 Millbrook Action Programme included a number of mechanisms to implement the Harare Declaration, including suspension from participation in Commonwealth meetings and the removal of technical assistance.[42]

The trend towards formalization extends even to informal (e.g. non-Treaty-based) organizations. In Europe, the Organization for Security and Co-operation in Europe (OSCE) developed provisions on suspension on the grounds of democratic breaches even though this would appear to violate the organization's original emphasis on sovereign equality and consensus decision making.[43] Despite this, the OSCE Prague Document on Further Development of OSCE Institutions and Structures stated that 'action could be taken by either the Council or Committee of Senior Officials (CSO) to protect CSCE's capability to safeguard human rights, democracy and the rule of law'.[44] This was instrumental for suspending Yugoslavia. In America another informal organization, CELAC, created in 2010,[45] declared its essential objectives to be the preservation of democracy and democratic values and the permanence of institutions and the Rule of Law.[46] The later Declaration of Caracas restated that constructing democratic societies is a common aspiration of the Member States while, at the same time, recognizing the right of every state to construct its own political system and endorsing respect for self-determination, sovereignty, territorial integrity, and non-interference.[47] At the same time, CELAC approved a Special Declaration on the Defence of Democracy and Constitutional Order which foresaw two different situations: the first, when a constitutional government considered that there is the threat of rupture by an alternative to democratic order, it can notify the Presidency Pro-Tempore and member states can consider the adoption of specific concerted action.[48] The second refers to cases of rupture proper, for which the foreign affairs Ministers can decide in an extraordinary meeting the suspension of the state from its participation in the organs of CELAC and the rights and benefits derived from it. They can also decide to adopt diplomatic action aimed at restoring democracy. The existence of an urgent consultation mechanism gives teeth to these procedures.[49]

Finally, the fourth category, the most common, refers to organizations lacking specific suspension provisions. Of these organizations, the case of Association of Southeast Asian Nations (ASEAN) illustrates most clearly their distinctive features. ASEAN has never suspended or excluded a Member State, nor do any provisions in the Bangkok Declaration[50] or the Treaty on Amity and Cooperation create any such mechanism.[51] The

[40] The Harare Commonwealth Declaration (n 4).

[41] Duxbury (n 20) 205.

[42] Millbrook Commonwealth Action Programme on the Harare Declaration, Fourteenth Commonwealth Heads of Government Meeting (CHOGM) (Queenstown, 12 November 1995).

[43] Duxbury (n 20) 212.

[44] OSCE, Document of the Second Meeting of the Committee on Security and Cooperation in Europe (CSCE) Council of Ministers (Summary of Conclusions, Prague Document on Further Development of CSCE Institutions and Structures, Declaration on Non-Proliferation and Arms Transfers) (Prague, 31 January 1992).

[45] CELAC, Latin American and Caribbean Unity Summit Declaration (23 February 2010).

[46] CELAC, Declaration of Cancún (23 February 2010).

[47] CELAC, Declaration of Caracas (3 December, 2011).

[48] Secretaria General Iberoamericana, *Declaración especial sobre 'La defensa de la democracia y el orden constitucional en Iberoamérica'* (2011).

[49] The Pro-Tempore Presidency or any Member State may propose a draft declaration or communication which can be adopted after twelve hours if not explicitly rejected by a Member State. Procedures for organic functioning of the CELAC. This document reiterates also the commitment to democracy.

[50] ASEAN, The Asean Declaration/Bangkok Declaration (Bangkok, 8 August 1967).

[51] ASEAN, Treaty of Amity and Cooperation in Southeast Asia (Bali, 24 February 1976), (1988) 27 ILM 610.

drafting of the ASEAN Charter heralded the re-launch of South East Asian integration with renewed and more ambitious objectives.[52] In line with these ambitions, the Eminent Persons Group (EPG) which prepared the Charter proposed sanctions in case of non-compliance with democratic principles but the ASEAN governments eventually rejected the proposal.[53] Several provisions in the ASEAN Charter (e.g. Articles 1(7) and 2(2)(h–i) refer explicitly to the promotion and strengthening of democracy, human rights, and good governance. Some have concluded that ASEAN's conception of the principle of non-intervention continues to preclude either regional or external sanctions[54] and commentators are quick to attribute this unique characteristic to the ASEAN way. The dominant interpretation holds that unlike in Europe, regional institution-building in South East Asia is not founded on a shared commitment to liberal democracy.[55] According to Duxbury, the debate on Myanmar's membership marked a change in policy from the previous practice of non-interference in internal affairs.[56]

4. Institutional rules for implementing suspension clauses

Institutional design of suspension mechanisms and provisions does not demonstrate significant divergences. Similarities could be explained because of institutional mimesis or mimicry between organizations within the same region. For instance, all the provisions of American organizations have similar designs. Diffusion seems to have also operated between regions although these suspension provisions became 'translated' or adapted to regional specificity. According to McMahon, the AU 'copied and pasted' the OAS provision which Article 9 Washington Protocol had included in 1992.[57] However, it should be noted that the OAS provision actually differs substantially from the AU one: the former (Article 9 Charter of the OAS, as modified by the Washington Protocol) refers to overthrowing by force *democratically constituted governments*, whilst the later refers to the unconstitutional overthrow of governments (whether they are democratic or not). Institutional design responds to the following features:

a. Formalization

Some organizations do not contain formal provisions on suspension of membership but this has not precluded them from nonetheless taking action in respect of offending members. The cases of SICA in relation to Honduras and the Caribbean Community (CARICOM) in relation to Haiti provide examples of this. Equally, the OAS Charter as originally adopted, did not contain an explicit provision permitting membership sanctions

[52] ASEAN, Charter of the Association of Southeast Asian Nations (Singapore, 20 November 2007).

[53] The Report of the EPG on the ASEAN Charter (December 2006), http://www.asean.org/storage/images/archive/19247.pdf, accessed 17 October 2016, 31.

[54] Hellquist (n 5) 5.

[55] JI Dominguez, 'The Americas: Found, and then Lost Again' (1998) 112 *Foreign Policy* 125.

[56] Duxbury (n 20) 195.

[57] ER McMahon, 'Regional organizations and the promotion of democratic governance: the value of collective action' (2012) Discussion Paper prepared for the UNICRIS–UNECA Joint Conference 'After the Arab Spring' at Brussels 22–23 November, 2012, fn 12. This author writes that Malian President Alpha Oumar Konare, at the time also President of the Organization of African Unity, attended the 'Emerging Democracies Forum' in Sana'a, Yemen in June 1999. He learned there about the OAS provision on suspending governments which came to power through undemocratic means. He then asked his embassy in Washington DC to procure the exact language of the document from the OAS headquarters, from which he then drew in proposing the relevant OAU language. Also, ED Mansfield and JC Pevehouse, 'Democratization and International Organizations' (2006) 60 *International Organization* 137, fn 12.

against state parties. Nevertheless, OAS suspended Cuba in 1962. Despite these cases, explicit formal provisions commonly regulate the issue. Mercosur has the most developed set of provisions: the Protocol of Ushuaia was expanded by a Presidential Declaration on the Protocol, a Common Market Council decision which obliged the states willing to become associated with Mercosur to adhere to the Protocol.[58] In 2011 Mercosur approved the Protocol of Ushuaia II, which makes explicit the institutions and procedures involved in cases of suspension. Its entry into force is still pending Paraguay's ratification.[59]

I. Incomplete formalization: Implicit provisions.

In some cases, organizations have not explicitly and fully formalised either their commitment to protect democracy via membership suspension or otherwise the sanction itself is not clearly indicated. Some organizations possess this incomplete formalization, even though the degree of vagueness varies greatly. On the one hand, for cases in which protection of democracy is not clearly specified, reference to 'general obligations' provides a substitute. The absence of an explicit reference to suspension is rare and is restricted to the PIF which approved the Biketawa Declaration referring to 'other options including if necessary targeted measures' as the basis for the suspension of Fiji.[60]

II. Formalization in non-formal organizations.

Organizations lacking a formal foundational treaty may have developed alternative instruments, such as the Harare Declaration of the Commonwealth of Nations,[61] or the Charter of Paris for a New Europe of OSCE.[62]

b. Models of scrutiny: Incidental vs permanent scrutiny systems

The implementation of suspension clauses can follow a permanent scrutiny system or an incidental one. The former depends on periodic scrutiny of domestic compliance with conditionality requirements, while the latter is triggered ad hoc when specific events seem to threaten democracy in a member state. Being a routine exercise, the first mechanism treats all states equally, at least in terms of reporting. Incidental systems are reactive and hence their activation depending on circumstances and governmental preferences.

I. Permanent scrutiny systems

The CoE issues public reports on Member States' compliance with democracy requirements. However, the only practical case of suspension (involving Greece) happened before the CoE initiated its reports and it involved the Parliamentary Assembly, the European

[58] Mercosur CMC Decisión Nº 18/04 (XXVI CMC—Puerto Iguazú, 07/VII/04) Regimen de Participacion de los Estados Asociados al Mercosur.

[59] After its suspension from Mercosur in 2012, the Congress of Paraguay continued to reject the Protocol arguing that the implementation of the provisions of Ushuaia I was unlawful.

[60] Biketawa Declaration, PIF (28 October, 2000), http://www.forumsec.org/resources/uploads/attachments/documents/Biketawa%20Declaration,%2028%20October%2020002.pdf, accessed 17 October 2016.

[61] The Harare Commonwealth Declaration (n 4).

[62] OSCE, Second CSCE Summit of Heads of State or Government (Paris, 19–21 November 1990). Supplementary document to give effect to certain provisions contained in the Charter of Paris for a New Europe, http://www.osce.org/mc/39516?download=true, accessed 12 October 2016.

Commission for Human Rights, and the Committee of Ministers. Similarly, the *Organisation internationale de la Francophonie* (OIF) *Declaration of Bamako* introduced a permanent review of democratic practices and respect for human rights which could activate the suspension mechanism.[63] With only two occurrences, permanent systems do not appear to be the favourite procedure for scrutinizing compliance.

II. Incidental systems

Incidental systems are those which are activated only when and if an incident of breach is identified. Commonly, international organizations do not possess a procedure for continuous assessment of compliance with conditionality leading to eventual suspension for breach. Rather, organizations react on the spot in the case of serious breaches of democratic conditionality. In fact, all the organizations discussed in this study (with the exception of the former two) rely on incidental systems.

c. Institutional set up for enforcing compliance

The most important institutional feature is who are the bodies in charge of enforcing these provisions and, in particular, if they are solely designed in order to fulfill this function or not. Regardless whether specialized bodies exist, the procedures and decision making are intergovernmental in all cases, meaning that both the initiative and the decision are taken by government representatives.

I. Specialized bodies

Both the AU and the Commonwealth of Nations rely on specialised bodies. In the AU, the Peace and Security Council (PSC) (a delegated organ of the Executive Council made up of fifteen Member States at the ministerial level) has decision-making power concerning issues of breaches of democratic conditionality. The Commonwealth of Nations has a similarly appointed body, the Commonwealth Ministerial Action Group (CMAG), which meets regularly to address potential breaches of the Harare Declaration. The CMAG is composed by a rotating group of foreign ministers from eight countries and every Commonwealth Heads of Government Meeting reconstitutes it. The Commonwealth has continued to refine the functions and procedures of the CMAG.[64] ECOWAS also has a specialized body, the Mediation and Security Council (MSC), which is a delegated intergovernmental body of nine representatives of Member States with the authority to decide the deployment of its political and military missions.[65]

II. Non-specialized

Most systems rely on the organization's own institutions to deal with enforcement of conditionality. In all cases, intergovernmental bodies (and specifically the formation

[63] OIF, Declaration of Bamako (Bamako, 3 November 2000) 'Symposium international sur le bilan des pratiques de la démocratie, des droits et des libertés dans l'espace francophone'.

[64] Strengthening the Role of the Commonwealth Ministerial Action Group (CMAG), Report by CMAG as adopted by the Commonwealth Heads of Government Meeting (Perth, 2011), http://thecommonwealth.org/sites/default/files/news-items/documents/120131.pdf, accessed 12 October 2016.

[65] Protocol Relating to the Mechanism for Conflict Prevention, Management, Resolution, Peacekeeping and Security (n 38).

which brings together Presidents or Prime Ministers) are the leading ones in decision making. Secretary Generals play a certain role in several of the suspension procedures (e.g. in the AU, ECOWAS, or OAS). In general, the Secretary General acts as mere agents of the principal (e.g. national governments) without much autonomy of his or her own. As a clear example of this position, the Secretariat and the General Secretary of the Commonwealth of Nations are precluded from discussing Member States' internal affairs without that state's consent, or from interfering in the internal affairs of members.[66] However, some Secretariats have shown a significant degree of diplomatic entrepreneurship, such as in the case of OAS Secretary General Insulza vis-à-vis the suspension of Honduras.[67] Formally, the ECOWAS Commission (former Executive Secretary) has the largest panoply of powers: it can decide on fact-finding missions and actions for mediation, facilitation, negotiation, and reconciliation of parties in conflict. The Secretary General also appoints the Council of Elders and convenes both the Assembly and the MSC.[68] In like manner, the PIF grants significant powers to the Secretary General to assess the situation, take a judgment on the significance of the developments and consult the Forum Chair and the Leaders to secure approval to initiate further action. The Secretary General has several instruments and courses of action available.

III. Ad hoc bodies

In the absence of permanent bodies, regional organizations occasionally create ad hoc bodies to deal with specific crises. In 1999 following the crisis of Austria, the EU set up a Wise Men Group which produced a Report on the situation.[69] The PIF created an EPG, a Ministerial Contact Group, and a Joint Working Group to deal with the Fiji crisis.[70] The Terms of Reference of the latter clearly identify the procedures and courses of action which could be taken.[71]

d. Procedures: decision-making rule, fact finding, redress

Once a regional organization has decided on the inclusion of provisions for suspending a Member State because of a breach of democracy, the important issue is to decide on what kind of procedure will apply for implementing these provisions. Most organizations do not regulate this in detail or do not even have regulation at all. In fact, a procedural vacuum is not uncommon and this creates a wide margin for political discretion. Several procedural elements are relevant for the institutional design:

I. Fact finding

A key instrument for triggering the democracy protection mechanisms is assessment and scrutiny of the situation. Surprisingly, very few organizations provide explicit and specific

[66] Duxbury (n 20) 202 fn 107. [67] See above (n 26).

[68] Article 15 Protocol Relating to the Mechanism for Conflict Prevention, Management, Resolution, Peace-keeping and Security (n 38).

[69] P Alston and O de Schutter (eds), *Monitoring Fundamental Rights in the EU: The contribution of the Fundamental Rights Agency* (Hart 2005) 96.

[70] The EPG Review of the PIF, April 2004.

[71] PIF, Fiji Joint Working Group on the situation in Fiji Terms Of Reference, available at: http://www.forumsec.org/resources/uploads/embeds/file/tor_for_the_pif-fiji_joint_working_group_on_the_situation_in_fiji.pdf, accessed 12 October 2016.

mechanisms for establishing the facts of a case. Moreover, certain organizations are charged with both fact finding and diplomatic mediation missions.

II. Decision-making rule

Almost all international organizations and regional organizations apply either consensus or unanimity, the OAS being the only exception by requiring a majority of two-thirds of its members. This has not translated into a more active scrutiny of democratic conditionality. Needless to say, consensus/unanimity applies with the sanctioned state excluded from the vote, but it is also obvious that a veto guarantees strong state control over outcomes.

III. Right to be heard

Guaranteeing this right to the potential violator of an organization's democratic principles seems an obvious component of any procedure which adheres to strict observance of the Rule of Law. Yet few organizations regulate this explicitly (and in practice, several have ignored this requirement). An exception is the Commonwealth of Nations, whose High Level Review Group recommended that measures could only be instigated after the relevant member has been given an opportunity to respond to the allegations and the Secretary General has made use of his or her good offices role.[72] In the EU, the Austrian government proposed the inclusion of a hearing stage within the procedure of current Article 7 as a reaction to the improvised procedure activated against itself. The final shape of the provision does not however reflect this preoccupation.

IV. Redress

The enforcement of democratic conditionality via suspension is in all cases a political, not a judicial process. Accordingly, no judicial redress procedures exist in regional organizations, Mercosur being the only exception. Its Permanent Court (Tribunal Permanente de Revision) ruled, in the case of Paraguay, that the Protocol of Ushuaia is justiciable.[73] Whilst this would seem a big step forward towards a stricter application of the procedure, the ruling neutralized this interpretation: the Court rejected its automatic intervention without the previous consent of all Member States (as is in fact established in the Protocol which regulates its functioning).[74]

V. End of sanctions

Organizations do not by and large explicitly refer to when and how sanctions will end and this once again creates a significant margin for political discretion. CELAC declares that they will end when the circumstances which provoked the adoption of suspension are found to have been totally overcome, on the basis of periodic evaluation of a situation.[75]

[72] Report by the Commonwealth High Level Review Group to the Commonwealth Heads of Government (3 March 2002).

[73] Laudo No 1/2012 del Tribunal Permanente de Revisión en el marco de la presentación de la República del Paraguay bajo el procedimiento de urgencia. (Secretaría del Tribunal Permanente de Revisión del Mercosur, 9 July 2012).

[74] Mercosur, Olivos Protocol for the Settlement of Disputes in Mercosur (2003) 42 *International Legal Materials* 2, Art 23(1).

[75] CELAC, *Special Declaration on the defence of democracy and constitutional order* (Caracas, 3 December 2011).

e. Effects

The panoply of effects that suspension produces is indeed very broad. The central effect (and shared by almost all organizations) is suspension from the organization organs. However, in addition, there are other possible effects: suspension of participation in Mercosur organs, closure of borders and limitation of traffic, suspension of the rights and benefits of membership, the promotion of suspension in other international organizations and unspecified additional sanctions. Interestingly, Mercosur's Protocol of Ushuaia which lists the largest panoply of possible courses of action sets out very clear limitations on sanctioning activity: actions must respect sovereignty and territorial integrity and they must adhere to strict proportionality. More importantly, they should not endanger the welfare of the people and human rights. On other occasions, an open and unspecific wording opens up a wide range of courses of action. Thus the PIF Birketawa Declaration of 2002 refers to 'necessary targeted measures' to deal with democratic breaches. Leaders of the Forum agreed 'targeted measures' in January 2009, which included the suspension from participation of the Leader, Ministers, and officials of the Fiji Interim government in all forum meetings and events.[76]

5. Practice of suspension because of democratic breaches

The practice of suspension provides additional insights into institutional design. The practice of suspending membership has been traditionally restricted to cases of non-fulfilment of financial obligations.[77] However, the practice of suspension of membership because of breach of democratic commitments has increased significantly in the last twenty years and this extends even to regional schemes lacking specific provisions on the issue (Southern African Development Community (SADC) in relation to Madagascar in 2009,[78] or SICA in relation to Honduras also in 2009).[79] Even the Arab League, normally oriented towards sovereignty and non-intervention, applied suspension of membership in relation to Libya and Syria, both in 2011.[80]

The suspension practice is a relatively recent phenomenon: Hellquist notes that before the Cold War, organizations used sanctions only exceptionally, and never against members for events confined within their borders.[81] The few instances of regional sanctions against Member States were not seen as interference in domestic affairs but as reactions to events considered a threat from or to other states. OAS thus framed its suspension of Cuba within such terms.

After the end of the Cold War, only five (e.g. CAN, CoE, EAC, EU, andGUAM Organization for Democracy and Economic Development) out of the seventeen organizations possessing some form or other of suspension clauses have abstained from applying

[76] PIF Special Leaders' Retreat Leaders Decision (Port Moresby, 27 January 2009).

[77] The WHO has suspended the voting rights of eight members and is considering a further nine, while the IAEA has suspended fourteen others. In the past, the UN deprived Haiti (in 1963) and the Dominican Republic (in 1968) of voting rights, but in 2012 it accepted the voting rights of six member countries in arrears.

[78] Comuniqué Extraordinary Summit of SADC Heads of State and Government (30 March 2009), http://www.sadc.int/files/8213/5292/8385/SADC__Extraordinary_Summit-_March_2009.pdf, accessed 12 October 2016, para 16

[79] Declaración de Presidentes del SICA (Managua, 29 June 2009) http://www.sica.int/busqueda/Reuniones.aspx?IDItem=37551&IDCat=21&IdEnt=1&Idm=1&IdmStyle=1, accessed 12 October 2016.

[80] In 1979 the Arab League also suspended Egypt's membership as a sanction for signing a peace agreement with Israel. However, the constitution of the Arab League only provides for expulsion, not suspension. In 1989 the League re-admitted Egypt.

[81] Hellquist (n 5).

them, despite the fact that claims have been made in all cases. Continental (e.g. AU, CoE, and OAS) and identity-framing organizations (e.g. OIF and the Commonwealth) concentrate the cases of suspension of membership (forty-two) in relation to breaches of democratic principles. Significantly, most of the cases of suspension are concentrated in African organizations and/or with respect to African states, particularly after the 2000s (the OAU faced three cases of illegal seizure of power but it did not ultimately take action: Togo in 1963, Ghana in 1966, and Uganda in 1971).[82] Some countries have attracted more than one suspension, and/or suspension from more than one organization. The hyperactivity of the AU deserves some closer analysis: despite the later approval of the African Charter on Democracy, elections, and governance (adopted in 2007 and entered into force in 2012), the emphasis of conditionality is put on *unconstitutional changes* of government regardless of the character (e.g. democratic or not) of the regime.[83] This orientation reinforces, in fact, the defence of Member State sovereignty and favours the *status quo*. Additionally, the procedural mechanisms create a strong '*automatism*' in the activation of sanctions.[84] ECOWAS, on the other hand, started to intervene in crisis management (and from this in overseeing democratic conditionality) in the 1990s, well before acquiring formal instruments explicitly addressing these actions in legal form.[85] As mentioned, the ECOWAS approach is more ambitious in the sense that protection of democracy via membership suspension is merely a tiny element of a large and robust practice of crisis management involving direct intervention on the ground. Table 22.2 shows those international organizations suspended because of democratic conditionality.

Suspension patterns seem continent specific. Continent-wide organizations have been the most active in Europe, with the EU adopting a more reluctant role. Thus, the CoE suspended Greece in 1970 after a number of Recommendations and Decisions from the Parliamentary Assembly, and two Reports on the legality of the suspension of the constitutional order and torture from the European Commission of Human Rights.[86] NATO, whose covenant does not contain a suspension clause, took a restrained attitude. The CoE equally suspended Turkey in 1980 following a military coup and the country regained its right to vote in 1984, after democratic elections had taken place. Russia was suspended from the CoE's Parliamentary Assembly from 2000 to 2001 as a result of its policies in Chechnya. Later on, in relation to the Russian military occupation of part of Ukraine's territory, the threat to use military violence and the recognition of the illegal referendum and subsequent annexation of Crimea, the Parliamentary Assembly of the Council of Europe (PACE) suspended Russian delegation members.[87] These were deprived of their voting rights, their rights to be represented in PACE organs, and the right to participate in electoral observation. The Assembly, however, considered that full suspension of members would make political dialogue impossible and PACE believed that political dialogue should

[82] From the formation of the OAU in 1963 to the end of 1989, there were sixty-one successful coups in Africa, and more than half of all African states had at some point been governed by military regimes which had displaced civilian governments. MG Marshall, 'Conflict trends in Africa 1946–2004: A macro-comparative perspective', a report prepared for the Africa Conflict Prevention Pool (ACPP) (2005) Annex 2b: *coups d'État* in Africa, http://www.systemicpeace.org/africa/ACPPAnnex2b.pdf, accessed 12 October 2016. See further EY Omorogbe, 'A Club of Incumbents? The African Union and *coups d'État*' (2011) 44 *Vanderbilt Journal of Transnational Law* 123.

[83] OAU, African Charter on Democracy, Elections and Governance (30 January 2007) OAU Doc No Assembly/AU/Dec 147 (VIII).

[84] Hellquist (n 5).

[85] G Yabi, 'The Role of ECOWAS in Managing Political Crisis and Conflict: The Cases of Guinea and Guinea-Bissau' (2010) Friedrich-Ebert-Stiftung Peace and Security Series.

[86] See (n 11).

[87] PACE Resolution, Reconsideration on substantive grounds of the previously ratified credentials of the Russian delegation, Doc 13483 (8 April 2014).

Table 22.2 Suspension of membership in international organizations because of democratic conditionality

Organization	Suspension clause	Suspended members
AU (formerly OAU)	Y	12 Togo (2001); CAR (2003); Mauritania (2005, 2008), Madagascar (2009), Guinea (2009); Mali (2009; 2012), Niger (2010) Ivory Coast (2010), Guinea Bissau (2012), Egypt (2013)
CAN	Y	0*
CARICOM	N	1 Haiti (2004)
CoE	Y	3 Greece (1969), Turkey (1980), Russia (2000)
Commonwealth of Nations	Y	7 Fiji (1987–1997**; 2000, 2006, and 2009); Nigeria (1995); Pakistan (1999; 2007); Zimbabwe (2002)**
EAC	Y	–
ECOWAS	Y	6 Togo (2001); Guinea (2009); Mali (2009 and 2012); Niger (2009); Ivory Coast (2010)
EU	Y	–
Mercosur	Y	2 Paraguay (1996; 2012)
GUAM	Y	–
PIF	Y(implicit)	1 Fiji (2009)
OAS	N/Y	2 Cuba (1962); Honduras (2009)
OIF	Y	4 Mauritania (2008); Madagascar (2009); Guinea Bissau (2012); Mali (2012)
OSCE	Y	1 Yugoslavia (1992)
SADC	Y	1 Madagascar (2009)
SICA	N	1 Honduras (2009)
UNASUR	Y	1 Paraguay (2012)

* Chile withdrew unilaterally on 30 October 1970 because of disagreement with CAN Decision No 24 on the treatment of foreign capital which had a marked protectionist character.

** Fiji withdrew from the Commonwealth of Nations between 1987 and 1997, and Zimbabwe in 2003. Gambia withdrew in 2013.

remain the preferred way to find a compromise. Although PACE found that the former actions contradict the Statute of the Council of Europe (Preamble and Article 3) and the commitments that Russia accepted when it acceded to the CoE, Russia has not been suspended from membership. The EU in turn, has not applied its suspension clause even once, despite diplomatic skirmishes over Austria and reports on Hungary, Rumania, Bulgaria, and more recently Poland. In fact, some authors have called for a more militant EU approach to the defence of democracy in its Member States.[88]

The African cases show an unclear overlap between suspension in continental and regional communities. Each have their own protocols with detailed provisions on how to act in the event of human rights violations or unconstitutional changes of government. In practice, the regional and continental levels often work in parallel. However, discrepancies between the normative standards embedded in the AU and the regional organizations complicate this. The AU thus suspended members because of breaches of democratic conditions in ten cases between 2001 and 2012 and this has encouraged similar measures in African regional integration schemes: SADC (Madagascar); ECOWAS (Togo, Ivory Coast, and Mali) and OIF (Mauritania, Madagascar, and Guinea). ECOWAS has unilaterally suspended the membership of three countries: Guinea-Bissau, Niger, and Ivory Coast following either *coups d'état* or fraudulent elections. The Ivory Coast case illustrates the overlapping yet different approaches to suspension. While the AU initiated proceedings for

[88] See Müller in Chapter 13 of this volume.

suspension, ECOWAS moved much more quickly and suspended the Ivory Coast from all decision making in the organization until a transfer of power had been completed. As the crisis continued, the positions of the AU, ECOWAS, and the UN increasingly diverged. While the AU adopted a more conciliatory position, seeking to find a political solution to the conflict, ECOWAS and the UN prioritize human rights concerns above the need to find a political solution to the stalemate, thus adopting a more strongly interventionist approach to bring about an end to the conflict.

The practice of suspension of American organizations shows a similar pattern of divergence between continental and regional organizations. In 1962 the OAS decided to exclude Cuba from participation in the Inter-American System, arguing that 'the present government of Cuba, which has officially identified itself as a Marxist–Leninist government, is incompatible with the principles and objectives of the inter-American system'.[89] The US government lobbied hard to obtain the two-thirds majority required and six states abstained in the vote (Argentina, Bolivia, Brazil, Chile, Ecuador, and Mexico) since they questioned the authority of the OAS to take the decision in the absence of an explicit Charter provision. The OAS did not expel Cuba from the organization, but rather excluded the 'present government' and Cuba was this still considered a Member State. This phrasing underlined that the decision was not taken against the state or the people.[90] Cuban suspension terminated on 3 June 2009 after a vote by the foreign ministers of OAS member countries.[91] The only other case of suspension happened in 2009, when OAS suspended Honduras following a *coup d'État*. In three other cases (Haiti, Peru, and Guatemala), the OAS fell short of taking any action. Following a military coup in Haiti (1991), the OAS foreign affairs ministers called for Member States to suspend diplomatic relations with the military government and to suspend their economic and financial and commercial ties with Haiti. In relation to Peru's President Fujimori *autogolpe* (1992), foreign affairs ministers called for the re-establishment of democratic institutional order and invited the Inter-American Commission on Human Rights to investigate the situation. In the end, however, no sanctions followed. Finally, President Serrano suspended the constitution and dissolved the Supreme Court and the Congress in 1993. The OAS Permanent Council deplored the situation and announced a fact-finding mission but no sanctions were imposed.[92] Summarizing OAS performance up to the case of Honduras, Duxbury argues that until 2009, the OAS had shown a willingness to cite its democratic standards, to convene fact-finding missions and, in some cases, to recommend more stringent measures.[93]

American regional organizations have developed the practice of suspending membership independently of the umbrella of the OAS. Mercosur started this trend in 1996 when it applied pressure to attempt to prevent a military plot in Paraguay. Observers noticed the importance of Mercosur in enforcing its democracy conditions: for *The Economist*, 'But for Mercosur, Paraguay would this year almost certainly have gone back to military rule, setting a dangerous precedent for Latin America'.[94] Paraguay's case illustrates how practice, in fact, inspired the norm, since Mercosur Member States concluded the Commitment to Democracy a few months after the attempted coup and the Ushuaia Protocol two years later. In 2012 Mercosur members appealed to the Protocol to deal with the decision of the

[89] Resolution VI: Exclusion of the Present Government of Cuba from Participation in the Inter-American System, Eighth Meeting of Consultation of Ministers of Foreign Affairs, Punta del Este, January 1962. See http://www.cidh.oas.org/countryrep/Cuba79eng/intro.htm, accessed 12 October 2016.

[90] Duxbury (n 20) 175.

[91] Resolution on Cuba AG/RES 2438 (XXXIX-O/09) (San Pedro Sula, 9 June 2009).

[92] Duxbury (n 20) 180. [93] ibid, 181.

[94] M Reid, 'A Survey of Mercosur' (1996) 341 *The Economist* (12 October 1996), see also Dominguez (n 54).

Senate of Paraguay to oust President Lugo. Mercosur governments saw the decision as unlawful and undermining the country's constitutional order, and in response governments activated the provision which allowed the suspension of the offending state from attendance at block meetings. UNASUR, which had a similar clause albeit with greater scope, adopted the same measures as Mercosur.[95]

Organizations have also developed a practice of suspension without a specific treaty provision. CARICOM suspended Haiti in 2004 after the ousting of President Aristide. Suspension did not follow a specific procedure, and the ultimate solution arose from personal contacts between CARICOM leaders. SICA also suspended Honduras in 2009 despite the absence of a specific suspension provision, although the Framework Treaty on Democratic Security in Central America contains a number of undefined commitments on the promotion of democracy.

6. Assessing performance: when poor institutional design meets political practice

The lessons learnt from the implementation of suspension on the grounds of democratic breaches reveal quite a few significant problems. Questioning the legitimacy of the provisions is the most acute. Lack of legitimacy may derive, quite simply, from the absence of explicit provisions, creating a kind of 'legal uncertainty'. Equally, the uneven implementation of suspension provisions implies similar imperfection. The latter has two dimensions: unequal enforcement of provisions depending on the state and arbitrariness in the use of procedures.

a. Substantive issues

The precise and exact definition of the object of suspension is wanting in most organizations: what is a breach of democracy and the Rule of Law exactly? The EU Commission has referred to systemic breaches although the meaning of 'systemic' remains elusive.[96] When debating the strengthening of the procedures in its Resolution 1080, the OAS Permanent Council showed large differences of opinion among its members on the specific definition of the good to be protected (i.e. democracy).[97] In the case of the AU, Murray has suggested that the use of suspension as a sanction is confined to situations involving coups against elected governments and thus where action against a military regime is not unlawful.[98] For instance, the Council of Ministers of the AU did not condemn the ousting of the military regime in Sierra Leone which had earlier removed the elected president from power. In her seminal work, Duxbury considers this to be the main problem of suspension mechanisms. She argues that in practice, organizations have tended to restrict the use of suspension to a limited range of behaviour, suggesting a selective approach to rights enforcement. She also questions the appropriateness of using exclusion for organizations whose primary purpose

[95] Decisión 26/2012, Reunión Extraordinaria del Consejo de Jefas y Jefes de Estado y de Gobierno de UNASUR (2 July 2012). In fact, Paraguay had not ratified the *Protocolo Adicional sobre Compromiso con la Democracia* and furthermore, some of its parliamentarians had denounced it: 'Parlamentarios de Paraguay cuestionan cláusula democrática de la UNASUR'. Comunicado de prensa de la Delegación de Paraguay del Parlamento del Mercosur, http://www.parlamentodelmercosur.org/innovaportal/v/5656/1/secretaria/parlamentarios_de_paraguay_cuestionan_clausula_democratica_de_la_unasur.html, accessed 12 October 2016.

[96] Communication from the European Commission to the European Parliament and the Council, A new EU Framework to strengthen the Rule of Law, COM(2014)158 final, Brussels (11 March 2014).

[97] Duxbury (n 20) 183.

[98] AS Muller, *International Organizations and their Host States* (Kluwer 1995) 80.

is integration and cooperation. Here, however, the first objection is the most serious: by limiting the type of behaviour leading to suspension, the organizations are punishing only the most egregious (and also the most obvious) violations of democratic principles. Confirming this suspicion, the OAS, the AU, and the Commonwealth have focused their attention on military coups. The narrow range of circumstances in which organizations will consider suspending a state confirms that although the members are willing to articulate a broad definition of democracy, they are not altogether comfortable with enforcing such a wide definition.[99]

b. Legal uncertainty

Two situations in the practice of suspension of members for breaches of democratic requirements raise issues about legal certainty. The first refers to the absence of a clear, explicit provision granting specific powers to the organization for initiating suspension proceedings. This happened in the abovementioned cases of CARICOM, SICA, and OAS. Before their later formalization, these organizations took the view that states which no longer satisfy their criteria may be suspended even in the absence of an express Charter provision.[100] In relation to Cuba, Magliaveras considers its exclusion from OAS premature, since the organization merely decided that a Marxist–Leninist form of government was incompatible with the American system. At the time, no evidence yet existed that Cuba had infringed the Charter's provisions at the time of its exclusion.[101] Moreover, the decision was controversial from the perspective of OAS attributions: Mexico opined that the exclusion of a Member State was not legally possible unless the Charter was first amended.[102] On the other hand, legal certainty may be threatened when actors apply legal instruments which have not been validly enacted. UNASUR thus acted against Paraguay in 2012 by invoking its Protocol on Compromise with democracy, whose ratification and entry into force was only subsequently achieved in 2014.[103] To prevent legal formalism interfering with political decisions, Mercosur implemented the decision to suspend Paraguay from its membership in the organization. These cases of the absence of legal certainty lead to the associated problems of inequality and arbitrariness.

c. Unequal enforcement

The practice of suspension shows some cases of unequal enforcement of conditionality depending on the state involved, meaning that bigger states may be treated differently or geopolitical considerations may alter the automatic enforcement of democratic conditionality. The OAS exemplifies this situation perfectly: since 1948, only Cuba and Honduras have been suspended as members. This happened despite the fact that most of the Latin

[99] Duxbury (n 20) 214. [100] Schermers and Blokker (n 8) 117.

[101] MD Konstantinos, *Exclusion from Participation in International Organisations: The Law and Practice behind Member State Expulsion and Suspension of Membership* (Kluwer Law International 1999) 168.

[102] 'The Government of Mexico maintains that the preservation and strengthening of democracy in our region cannot be enhanced through isolation, suspension or exclusion, and hence believes that the wording on suspension of member states as approved here today, has changed the original purpose of our Organization'. Statement made at the time of adoption Protocol of amendments to the Charter of the Organization of American States, Protocol of Washington (n 22).

[103] Decisión 26/2012, Reunión Extraordinaria del Consejo de Jefas y Jefes de Estado y de Gobierno de Unasur (29 June 2012), http://www.iri.edu.ar/images/Documentos/documentos/126/unasur_decision_26_2012_jefas_jefes.pdf, accessed 17 October 2016.

American members of the organization had authoritarian regimes for a significant part of their membership history. During the Cold War, the OAS did not question undemocratic governments and did not react to coups against democratically elected governments. In other cases, it had a less passive, yet insufficient attitude: in 1979, the OAS denounced Nicaragua's revolution and in 1989, it also denounced the cancellation of electoral results by General Noriega in Panama. However, no action was taken in either case. The suspension of Cuba fitted with the geopolitical strategy of the USA for the continent, while the 2009 Honduras case attracted broad consensus, even though the strength of feeling came at the initiative of the ALBA governments, which were able to pursue their exclusion strategy in a number of other fora, e.g. SICA. Unsurprisingly, when the OAS suspended Honduras, its new President wrote to the OAS Secretary contesting the legitimacy of the organization—calling it a political organization, not a court—and arguing that it lacked the competence to pass judgment on the events in Honduras. The Commonwealth of Nations shows similar unequal practice: for all its activism after 1990, it failed to take earlier action in the cases of apartheid in South Africa and the massive violation of human rights in Uganda under Idi Amin Dada. Furthermore, even after formalizing its principles, the Commonwealth body in charge of the issue, the CMAG, has been criticized for failing to enforce the full range of principles encompassed within the Harare Declaration. The cases of the confrontation between India and Pakistan or the human rights abuses in the Sri Lankan civil war illustrate this criticism.

d. Procedural arbitrariness

Arbitrariness involves the biased use of the suspension procedures. The very instrumental way in which UNASUR and Mercosur handled the suspension of Paraguay illustrates arbitrariness very clearly: its suspension did not respect international norms and protocols. It was also used as a convenient solution to the Senate of Paraguay's blocking of Venezuela's accession to Mercosur.[104] Both organizations concurred on the case without a clearly delimitated distinction of functions but acting in concerted, synergetic fashion: UNASUR carried out the assessment and decided to suspend, but Mercosur implemented the sanctions following that assessment. The Presidents' Summit of 29 June 2009 suspended Paraguay of the right to take part in the organs of Mercosur and their deliberations, under the terms of Article 5 Ushuaia Protocol.[105] The same Summit decided simultaneously to conclude the process of the accession of Venezuela to Mercosur.[106] The concerted action of UNASUR and Mercosur thus had a clear political objective behind it. In fact, according to the OAS, the impeachment procedure complied with the Paraguayan constitution and therefore did not break the Inter-American Democratic Charter. Paraguayan officials also condemned Venezuela's accession without Paraguay's vote as a violation of treaties. As a consequence, the government of Paraguay even declared itself committed to annulling Venezuela's accession. At the same time, the government declared that all decisions taken by Mercosur had no legal validity and therefore did not bind the country.

[104] L Marsteintredet et al., 'Paraguay and the Politics of Impeachment' (2013) 24 *Journal of Democracy* 114.

[105] Decisión sobre la suspensión del Paraguay en el Mercosur en aplicación del Protocolo de Ushuaia sobre Compromiso Democrático, available at: http://www.dipublico.org/9410/cumbre-del-mercosur-mendoza-2012-decision-sobre-la-suspension-del-paraguay-en-el-mercosur-en-aplicacion-del-protocolo-de-ushuaia-sobre-compromiso-democratico/, accessed 17 October 2016.

[106] Declaración sobre la incorporación de la República Bolivariana de Venezuela al Mercosur, http://www10.iadb.org/intal/intalcdi/PE/CM%202012/10296.pdf, accessed 12 October 2016.

e. Fact finding and assessment mechanisms

The simultaneous suspension of Paraguay by UNASUR and Mercosur illustrates perfectly the potential flaws of the fact-finding and assessment procedures and their effects upon whether the legitimacy and legality of a given decision might be impugned. UNASUR foreign affairs ministers and permanent representatives travelled to Paraguay along with the Secretary General of UNASUR. They met Lugo and Franco on implementation of the mandate of the Heads of State of 21 June 2012. Foreign affairs ministers concluded that the situation could be framed within Article 1.5 and 6 UNASUR Compromise with Democracy Protocol (Communiqué 22 June 2012). The OAS also sent a fact-finding mission and it opted for not suspending membership of Paraguay. However, Mercosur did not do the same explicitly (note that the memberships of the two organizations are not linked). As a result, the Paraguayan government protested its suspension from Mercosur, arguing that it had been denied the right to defend itself as set out in the Ushuaia Protocol. Specifically, the Paraguayan government appealed to Article 4 Ushuaia Protocol, which requires that consultations be held with the affected state. Since no such consultations had taken place, the Paraguayan government considered the decision not only illegal but also illegitimate and a violation of the norms of due process. In the case of Honduras, the 40th OAS General Assembly (6–8 June 2010, Lima) had instructed the General Secretary to form a High Level Commission which should report back to the General Assembly by 30 July 2010. The resolution left open the details of the creation of the Commission and its work. Secretary General Insulza presented a Report to the General Assembly on the Diplomatic initiatives taken in accordance with Article 20 IADC.[107] The main OAS weaknesses are its failure to assess critical situations in their early stages, since action at this stage requires either consensus from the Member States or authorization from the national government.[108] A similar case illustrating such weakness is the Commonwealth of Nations involvement with Nigeria: since the Commonwealth did not have mechanisms to carry out investigations or to report on human rights breaches in its Member States, there was no formal or publicized investigation into the situation. The precise infringement of Commonwealth principles was not specified in the Auckland suspension communiqué.[109] Nonetheless, in 2002 a Commonwealth Observer Group sent to cover the Presidential election reported that the process did not allow the free expression of the will of electors.

f. Redress procedures

As a general rule, organizations do not contain redress procedures. In one case, Paraguay's suspension from Mercosur, the government sought to create a redress procedure: it appealed the decision to suspend its membership from Mercosur to the block Permanent Court. The Court, whilst establishing its competence on the issue, refused to rule on the matter since it did not have the prior consent of the state parties.[110]

[107] Resolution on the situation in Honduras AG/RES 2531 (XL-O/10), OAS 40th General Assembly (Lima, 6–8 June 2010).

[108] Latin America Advisor Staff, 'How Well is the OAS Handling the Coup in Honduras?' Daily Latin America Advisor Newsletter (22 July 2009).

[109] Duxbury (n 20) 207. [110] Laudo No 1/2012 (n 72).

7. Concluding remarks

Comparative experience shows that suspension provisions on the grounds of democratic breaches have become more common (but by no means universal). By and large, most international organizations have acquired democratic conditionality suspension provisions since 1989, the CoE and OAS being the early pioneers in this trend. In most cases, this happened *after* the creation of the international organization, at a time when geopolitical changes gave democratic ideals significant normative hegemony. Institutional design proves, however, that normative change is possible because of the adoption of mechanisms which do not relinquish national government control over the implementation of these provisions. Most of the systems for guaranteeing democratic conditions in member states via suspension thus rely on a very weak institutional structure of delegation. Organizations bodies (whether specialized, permanent, ad hoc etc) do not have the autonomy to implement these provisions. Nor do mechanisms work automatically or semi-automatically in the sense that no national government intervention is needed to activate the sanctioning procedure. Many organizations favour diplomatic bargaining as an alternative to sanctioning. Also, sanctioning has been mainly reputational rather than affecting a state materially, by and large.

Practice demonstrates the increasing willingness of international organizations and regional organizations to apply these measures. A closer look at both institutional design and practice, however, reveals a significant number of dubious cases in which several problems, such as legal uncertainty, inequality, procedural arbitrariness, and the dominance of political considerations through a purely intergovernmental decision-making process simultaneously diminish their efficiency and cast doubt on their legitimacy.

PART IV

CASE STUDIES IN THE CONTEXT OF EU LAW

23

Defiance by a Constitutional Court—Germany

*Franz C Mayer**

1. Introduction

Defiance by a court is a highly problematic phenomenon. Of all institutional players, courts are the ones we would expect to be the first to obey rules and to uphold the system. But in the context of European integration, defiance by national courts has happened again and again.[1] Is defiance a concept that captures the German Constitutional Court's approach to European integration? After all, the 1949 German Constitution (the *Grundgesetz*) appears to be more open for European and international cooperation than most other constitutions on the continent. As a first step it is thus necessary to take a closer look at the broader picture of the German constitutional landscape, in particular at the German Constitutional Court and its decisions on European integration (section 2). Based on that broader account of cases, it will be easier to assess the degree and motivations of defiance (section 3) and to reflect on possible future developments (section 4).

2. The German Constitutional Court and European integration—a closer look

The German Constitution of 1949 explicitly addresses European integration (section 2.a.). This is the legal framework for the German Constitutional Court's decisions (section 2.b.).

a. The German Constitution and its commitment to European integration

Most features of the 1949 *Grundgesetz*, the Constitution of the second German Republic, may be explained as a reaction to the Nazi dictatorship and the failures of the Weimar Republic.

* Professor, Dr jur, LLM (Yale), Chair of Public Law, European Law, Comparative Law, Law and Politics, University of Bielefeld, Faculty of Law. Contact: franz.mayer@uni-bielefeld.de. This chapter builds on my earlier work, in particular *Kompetenzüberschreitung und Letztentscheidung* (Beck 2000); 'Multilevel Constitutional Jurisdiction', in A von Bogdandy and J Bast (eds), Principles of European Constitutional Law (Hart 2010) 424; 'Rebels Without a Cause? A Critical Analysis of the German Constitutional Court's OMT Reference' (2014) 15 *German Law Journal* 111. I wish to thank Theresa Krampe, Bielefeld, for her assistance in finalizing this chapter. The chapter considers legal developments that happened until the end of 2015. Subsequent events, in particular the German Constitutional Court's final ruling on OMT in June 2016, are not addressed in detail.

[1] One of the more famous cases of court defiance is the French *Conseil d'Etat's Cohn-Bendit* decision (CE Ass 22 December 1978, Ministre de l'Intérieur c Sieur Cohn-Bendit, Recueil 524, Concl. Genevois; (1979) 15 *Revue Trimestrielle de Droit Européen* 157; (1980) 1 *Common Market Law Review* 543 (English translation)), establishing resistance to the direct effect of directives which was upheld for thirty years (until the *Perreux* case, CE Ass 30 October 2009, Emmanuelle Perreux, Recueil 407, Concl. Guyomar; (2009) Revue française de Droit administratif 1125). For an example for the Commission initiating a treaty infringement procedure against a Member State because of Member State court defiance, see Commission infringement proceeding 2003/2161 (against Sweden, non-reference of Swedish courts).

It comes as no surprise to find at the very beginning of the Constitution, in its preamble, a pledge to world peace and a 'United Europe'. This strong commitment to European and international cooperation was captured by the term 'offene Staatlichkeit'—literally: open statehood —in the early 1960s,[2] and this remains the mainstream narrative of post-war German constitutionalism to the present day. Elements of this openness include the commitment to human rights, the prohibition of aggression and war, and the possibility of transferring sovereign rights to supranational entities such as the EU. In part, this openness and the absence of references to 'sovereignty'—the word is never mentioned in the Constitution—were not a matter of choice but simply the only possible thing to do: In 1949 Germany was not a sovereign state, the *Grundgesetz* operated under a statute of occupation, and after the atrocities of the Nazis, Germany was the pariah among nations. At the same time there was a sincere determination among those political players who had rejected the Nazi regime to include the lessons of those dark times into the new constitutional settlement.

Although the 1949 Constitution was clearly drafted as a temporary legal order until reunification could be accomplished, Germany retained its *Grundgesetz* even after reunification, mostly because it was well-established and generally considered a good constitution. A major overhaul of the Constitution was carried out nonetheless, in the course of which the constitutional provisions governing Germany's membership in the EU were rewritten, without actually giving up the aim of a united Europe. But even though there remains no reference to German sovereignty in the text of the Constitution, formal sovereignty as a state was regained with the 2+4 Treaty in 1990,[3] and the reunification of Germany changed the constitutional options. The modification of the Constitution after reunification created the possibility to lay a greater emphasis on the limits to the Constitution's openness towards European and international integration. That the new Article 23—on European integration—focuses on German constitutional limits to membership in the EU can thus be read as foreshadowing future developments. Some of these limits were even linked to the 'eternity clause' in Article 79(3) of the German Constitution, so that the limits to European integration were joined to the provisions dealing with absolute limits to constitutional amendment. However, with the basic statements on openness remaining in the text of the Constitution,[4] the question of the newly reunified Germany's commitment to European and international cooperation is simply open. Its test had been running since 1949, it was reset in 1990, and the outcome depends on political action but also on how the Constitution is interpreted.

b. The case law of the German Constitutional Court in EU matters

One way to measure the degree of defiance or non-defiance of a Member State court vis-à-vis European integration is its record in the field of preliminary references to the ECJ (section 2.b.I). Beyond that, the relevant German case law can be divided into three distinct periods: the period before (section 2.b.II) and after the reunification of Germany (section 2.b.III), and a third period which began with the Euro-crisis (section 2.b.IV.).

[2] K Vogel, 'Die Verfassungsentscheidung des Grundgesetzes für eine internationale Zusammenarbeit' (1964) 292/293 *Recht und Staat in Geschichte und Gegenwart* 42.

[3] Treaty on the Final Settlement with Respect to Germany, 12 September 1990, 1696 UNTS 123.

[4] See the Preamble and Art 23(1) of the German Constitution.

I. The German Constitutional Court and the preliminary reference procedure

The German Constitutional Court was not exactly a front-runner in submitting preliminary references to the ECJ. The highest German courts started to make references as early as 1967.[5] It was only in 2014 that the German Constitutional Court submitted its first reference, arguably not even asking a real question but already giving the answers.[6]

On the other hand, it is also true that since 1987[7] the German Constitutional Court has not allowed ordinary German courts to practice defiance in a preliminary reference context. If an ordinary German court fails to submit a preliminary reference to the ECJ despite being obliged to, any citizen can file a constitutional complaint with the German Constitutional Court and invoke a fundamental right 'to have access to the lawful judge', the ECJ being such a judge (Article 101(1) German Constitution). In sum, the analysis of the preliminary reference case law of the German Constitutional Court indicates that the picture is neither all black nor all white. There is clearly defiance, as the German Constitutional Court has been reluctant to submit references to the ECJ. But at the same time, there is also a clear signal to the lower courts that they must submit preliminary references.

II. The pre-reunification case law

The early days of European integration are characterized by the total absence of the German Constitutional Court's voice. The Court never scrutinized the founding Treaties, and the ground-breaking decisions of the ECJ in Luxemburg of 1963 and 1964 establishing direct effect and the primacy of EU law[8] went completely unnoticed by the German Constitutional Court.

A decision of 5 July 1967[9] was the first to discuss Community law in some detail. There, the German Constitutional Court emphasized the central role of the 'act of assent' to the founding Treaties.[10] Later commentators likened this central role to that of a bridge[11] between EU law and national law in that—in the German view—the act of assent functions as the decisive 'order to give legal effect' (*Rechtsanwendungsbefehl*) to European law.

The tone of these early decisions was far from hostile or defiant. In 1967 the German Constitutional Court also expressed its view of the Community as a distinct public authority in a distinct legal order. This view continues to be held today. The German

[5] The *Bundessozialgericht* in 1967 (Case 14/67 *Welchner* [1967] ECLI:EU:C:1967:48); the *Bundesfinanzhof* also in 1967 (Case 17/67 *Neumann* [1967] ECLI:EU:C:1967:56); the *Bundesarbeitsgericht* in 1969 (Case 15/69 *Südmilch* [1969] ECLI:EU:C:1969:46 (German edn, no English translation available); the *Bundesverwaltungsgericht* in 1970 (Case 36/70 *Getreide-Import* [1970] ECLI:EU:C:1970:112); and the *Bundesgerichtshof* in 1974 (Case 32/74 *Haaga* [1974] ECLI:EU:C:1974:116). These courts have continued to use the preliminary reference procedure on a regular basis.

[6] *BVerfG*, 2 BvR 2728/13 (14 January 2014) (OMT).

[7] *BVerfGE* 75, 223—Kloppenburg.

[8] Case 26/62 *Van Gend en Loos* [1963] ECLI:EU:C:1963:1; Case 6/64 *Costa v ENEL* [1964] ECLI:EU:C:1964:66.

[9] *BVerfGE* 22, 134, 142.

[10] The *Zustimmungsgesetz*, a federally enacted law under Art 24 (now Art 23) of the German Constitution. Art 23 was introduced in December 1992 as the provision dealing specifically with European integration, replacing the old Art 23 which had served as the legal basis for German reunification. Both Art 23 and Art 24 foresee an act of assent for the transfer of public powers. Art 23 establishes two sets of limits; on the one hand, it institutes limits concerning the European construct, which for example has to guarantee a standard of fundamental rights protection essentially equal to that guaranteed by the German Constitution. On the other hand, Art 23(1) points to the limits of how European integration can affect Germany, as the principles mentioned in Art 79(3) are inalienable.

[11] This *Brückentheorie* is based on the metaphor suggested by the judge rapporteur in the German *Maastricht* case, P Kirchhof, for example, in 'Die Gewaltenbalance zwischen staatlichen und europäischen Organen' (1998) 53 *Juristenzeitung* 965, 966. On the European Communities Act as the British 'bridge', see N Bamforth, 'Courts in a Multi-Layered Constitution' in N Bamforth and P Leyland (eds), *Public Law in a Multi-Layered Constitution* (Hart 2003) 277, 288.

Constitutional Court qualified the EEC Treaty as a 'constitution, as it were, of this Community' and Community law as a 'distinct legal order, whose norms neither belong to public international law nor belong to the national law of the Member States', echoing the wording of the ECJ's *Van Gend en Loos* decision. The German Constitutional Court did also hint at constitutional limitations to the transfer of public authority rights (*Übertragung von Hoheitsrechten*) to the EC in the context of the German Constitution's guarantee of fundamental rights. But where exactly would the limits be? An answer to this question was not forthcoming at that stage.[12]

It is not without a sense of irony that the very case that the ECJ used in 1970 to confirm that the primacy of EU law included primacy over the Member States' constitutions[13] became the case which would be the first major act of resistance of the German Constitutional Court against the challenges of European integration: the *Solange I* case (section 2.b. II.*i*), settled by the *Solange II* decision (section 2.b.II.*ii*).

i. The German Constitutional Court awakens: *Solange I* (1974)

Fundamental rights are the cornerstones of the 1949 Constitution and the procedure which makes it possible for every citizen to ask the German Constitutional Court to protect his or her fundamental rights is probably the essential reason for the popularity of the German Constitutional Court with citizens. The importance of fundamental rights protection in today's Germany has historical reasons. With that in mind, one cannot be surprised that the first display of defiance from the German Constitutional Court emerged in the context of fundamental rights. In the *Solange I* decision of 29 May 1974,[14] the German Constitutional Court stipulated constitutional limits on the primacy of European law and reserved a right of judicial review of EU action in order to safeguard the fundamental rights guaranteed under the German Constitution by the German Constitutional Court, 'as long as' (*solange*) fundamental rights protection at the European level did not correspond to the level of protection under the German Constitution.

In a dissenting opinion,[15] three of the second senate's eight judges adopted a different position on the relationship between national constitutional law and European law, which is much closer to the ECJ's position than the majority opinion. The position adopted by the dissenting minority even went much further than the *Solange II* decision[16] twelve years later or any other subsequent decision by the German Constitutional Court: the minority considered the German Constitutional Court's reservation of a constitutional check on EC law—a reservation that the *Solange II* decision maintains—to be illegal. While it also stipulates a limit to the transfer of sovereign rights to the EC, the minority does not consider this limit to necessitate the reservation of a constitutional check.

ii. The German Constitutional Court in stand by-mode: *Solange II* (1986)

Twelve years after *Solange I*, the Court modified its approach. It acknowledged that in the meantime, the ECJ had built up a sufficient level of protection, so that 'as long as' (*solange*) that remained the case (thus '*Solange II*'),[17] the German Constitutional Court would not exercise its jurisdiction, insisting on the principle that they could still activate this

[12] *BVerfGE* 22, 293, 298 et seq. (EWG-Verordnungen).
[13] Case 11/70 *Internationale Handelsgesellschaft* [1970] ECLI:EU:C:1970:114.
[14] *BVerfGE* 37, 271, 282 (*Solange I*). [15] ibid. The dissenting opinion starts at p. 291.
[16] *BVerfGE* 73, 339 (*Solange II*) (English translation in Federal Constitutional Court (ed), *Decisions of the Bundesverfassungsgericht* (1992) vol 1 pt II, 613; and in A Oppenheimer (ed), *The Relationship between European Community Law and National Law* (CUP 1994) 461; see also (1987) 3 *Common Market Law Review* 225).
[17] *BVerfGE* 73, 339 (*Solange II*).

jurisdiction. *Solange II* is not exactly a U-turn, it is better understood as a supplement to the *Solange I* decision which—without renouncing the principle of a constitutional law check—defused the fundamental rights issue. The German Constitutional Court did insist in *Solange II* that the transfer of public authority to supranational institutions be subject to constitutional limits. There is no authorization, it held, to give up the identity of the German constitutional order[18] by means of transferring competences to supranational institutions with the result of an 'intrusion into the fundamental architecture, the constituting structures' of the Constitution.[19]

Later, the fundamental rights section of the 1993 *Maastricht* decision[20] and the 2000 *Banana* decision[21] basically confirmed the German Constitutional Court's statement of principle in *Solange II*.[22] The German Constitutional Court considers the standard of fundamental rights protection required by the German Constitution to be safeguarded at the European level.[23] Cases such as the data retention case (2010–2014) seem to indicate that sometimes the ECJ is even the stronger fundamental rights court compared to the German Constitutional Court.[24] In that case, the German Constitutional Court had not addressed the fundamental rights deficiencies of the data retention directive when the case was pending in Karlsruhe in 2010.[25]

From a procedural perspective, the German Constitutional Court contributes indirectly to safeguarding fundamental rights in an EU context by supervising the duty of the regular German courts to make references.[26] This appears to be a coherent and stable system: neither does the German Constitutional Court accept scrutiny of EU law with the fundamental rights yardstick of the German Constitution, nor will it submit a fundamental rights driven reference to the ECJ, but it will enforce the obligation of the other German courts to submit a case to the ECJ by means of the preliminary reference procedure in order to give the ECJ the opportunity to apply EU fundamental rights.

It remains an open question, however, whether it would not be even better for the development of a coherent fundamental rights protection system in Europe, at the same time enhancing the impact of German fundamental rights ideas, if the German Constitutional Court took a proactive stance by making fundamental rights-related references directly to the ECJ.[27]

Other open questions remain. The ECJ interpreted the reach of EU fundamental rights into the realm of the Member States extensively in the *Åkerberg Fransson* case.[28]

[18] Note that the issue of constitutional identity emerged as a major topic with the 2009 *Lisbon* decision, see section 2.b.III.*iii*.

[19] *BVerfGE* 73, 339, 375 et seq. (*Solange II*). Here, the Court refers to the jurisprudence of the Italian Constitutional Court.

[20] *BVerfGE* 89, 155, 175 as well as 3rd, 6th, and 7th sentence of summary No 5 (Maastricht).

[21] *BVerfGE* 102, 147 (*Banana* case).

[22] Any doubts that the *Maastricht* decision may have raised are resolved by the *Banana* decision of the *BVerfGE* 102, 147: the Court emphasized that an individual's constitutional complaint under Art 93(1) or a national court's reference under Art 100 of the German Constitution will simply be held inadmissible unless the individual/the referring court proves a complete erosion of fundamental rights in accordance with *Solange II*.

[23] *BVerfG*, Europäische Zeitschrift für Wirtschaftsrecht (2001) 255 (Non-reference by the Bundesverwaltungsgericht); see also *BVerwGE* 108, 289; see also the interim decision of the Bundesverfassungsgericht concerning the implementation of the data-retention directive, Europäische Grundrechte-Zeitschrift (2008) 257.

[24] Joined Cases C-293/12 and C-594/12 *Digital Rights Ireland* [2014] ECLI:EU:C:2014:238.

[25] *BVerfGE* 125, 260.

[26] See section 2.b.I.

[27] The German Constitutional Court submitted its first reference ever in 2014 only, in a case concerning the role of the ECB. Fundamental rights were not at the heart of this reference, it was about the limits of ECB competence, *BVerfG*, 2 BvR 2728/13 (14 January 2014) (OMT).

[28] Case C-617/10 *Åkerberg Fransson* [2013] ECLI:EU:C:2013:105.

This led to a particularly harsh reaction[29] from the first senate of the German Constitutional Court,[30] with an unconcealed threat to consider this kind of ECJ decision *ultra vires*: outside EU competence. This overreaction is quite stunning, as *Åkerberg Fransson* was neither a German case nor a hostile move directed against the German Constitutional Court. There are Member States where citizens would welcome an additional layer of fundamental rights protection. This incident shows that the fundamental rights issue is not completely settled between the German Constitutional Court and the European legal order. The element of defiance on display here is a reservation of jurisdiction, a 'we could if we wanted to'.

III. *After reunification: discovering sovereignty and parliament*

After German reunification, Germany's new situation in political and constitutional terms arguably required a recalibration of the German Constitutional Court's position on European integration. This recalibration process is still underway twenty-five years later. Landmark cases in this process before the Euro-crisis case law (see 2.b.IV.) are the *Maastricht* case 1993 (section 2.b.III.*i*.), the *European Arrest Warrant* case 2005 (section 2.b.III.*ii*.), the *Lisbon* case 2009 (section 2.b.III.*iii*) and the *Honeywell* case 2010 (section 2.b. III.*iv*.).

i. The *Maastricht* case (1993)

With the 1992 *Maastricht* Treaty, the German Constitutional Court scrutinized an important European integration treaty for the first time. Its *Maastricht* decision of 12 October 1993[31] established a constitutional law reserve of power over the exercise of competences by the EC/EU. The Court justifies its right of control over *ultra vires* acts[32] by pointing to the constraints of German constitutional law.

As far as ECJ 'acts' are concerned, the *Maastricht* decision remains unclear about how in practice to draw the line between the (permitted) development of the law by European judges and the (prohibited) development of judge-made European law, or between still acceptable alterations and substantial alterations of the European competence provisions.[33]

The legal consequences of deeming a European act *ultra vires* would be that this act would not be binding on Germany. This amounts to a German constitutional law-based reserve of power over European acts, a reserve that restricts the primacy of European law.

We could well say that the *Maastricht* decision is within a certain continuity of the German Constitutional Court's prior jurisprudence on fundamental rights, as far as the concept of a constitutional law reserve of control restricting the European law claim for

[29] *BVerfG*, 1 BvR 1215/07 (24 April 2013).

[30] The first senate is the senate dealing with fundamental rights, most of the decisions related to European integration stem from the second senate.

[31] *BVerfGE* 89, 155 (Maastricht). For English translations of the *Maastricht* decision, see Oppenheimer (n 16) 526; (1994) 22 *International Legal Materials* 388; I Winkelmann (ed), *Das Maastricht-Urteil des Bundesverfassungsgerichts vom 12. Oktober 1993: Dokumentation des Verfahrens mit Einführung* (Duncker & Humblot 1994), 751, also 751–99 for a French translation and 800–2 for a Spanish translation of the head notes; further references in FC Mayer, *Kompetenzüberschreitung und Letztentscheidung* (Beck 2000) 98 et seq.

[32] In the 1993 decision the Court said '*ausbrechende Rechtsakte*', literally 'acts breaking out'. This aggressive terminology was not upheld in the *Lisbon* and *Honeywell* decisions. For the terminology, see the earlier decision *BVerfGE* 75, 223, 242 (Kloppenburg). On the distinction between *ultra vires* acts in a narrow sense (i.e. overstepping competences defined according to area) and in a broad sense (i.e. the general illegality of an act), see Mayer (n 31) 24 et seq.

[33] See M Zuleeg, 'Die Rolle der rechtsprechenden Gewalt in der europäischen Integration' (1994) *Juristenzeitung* 1, 3; C Tomuschat, 'Die Europäische Union unter der Aufsicht des Bundesverfassungsgerichts' (1993) 20 *Europäische Grundrechte-Zeitschrift* 489, 494.

primacy is concerned. What is striking, though, is the aggressive tone of the decision when compared to previous decisions.[34]

On the other hand, we should also note a crucial difference between the fundamental rights issue (*Solange II*) and the competence issue (*Maastricht*): as for the competence issue, the reproach with which the European level is confronted in case of an *ultra vires* act goes beyond the bipolar relationship between the German constitutional order and the European legal order. The categories of an *ultra vires* act on the one hand and an act infringing upon the fundamental rights laid down in the German Constitution on the other hand are utterly different. The absence of a certain aspect of fundamental rights protection in the jurisprudence of the ECJ can already occur either for procedural reasons or because the range of a given fundamental right is defined differently at the European and national levels.

To uphold in principle the standard of fundamental rights protection guaranteed by the German Constitution does not necessarily imply a challenge of the European level. However, declaring an act *ultra vires* would also imply such a challenge and imply a critique of the ECJ. Moreover, challenging an *ultra vires* act would also concern the validity and/or application of European law in all other Member States, as an act cannot be *ultra vires* only in the bilateral relationship between one Member State and the EU.

The immediate effects of the *Maastricht* decision were limited. Nevertheless, at least one court, a Financial Court of the first instance (the *Finanzgericht Rheinland-Pfalz*)[35], declared an EC act to be *ultra vires*. In doctrinal writings, the German Constitutional Court's concept of *ultra vires* acts was immediately severely criticized by some[36] but welcomed by others, to the extent that it has been used as an argument against all kinds of alleged *ultra vires* acts stemming from the EC, in particular from the ECJ.[37] The topic keeps returning: in 2007 the intense German debate about the 2005 *Mangold* decision of the ECJ[38] was mainly about the question whether the ECJ decision was an *ultra vires* act.[39] In the 2010 *Honeywell* case the German Constitutional Court made it clear that an *ultra vires* statement would not result from each and every tiny competence issue, that the ECJ was even entitled to make errors in that context, and that the test question would be whether there was a structural shift of competences between the EU and Member State.[40] However, in 2013 the ECJ's *Åkerberg Fransson* case led the first senate of the German Constitutional Court openly to threaten the ECJ to consider an ECJ decision *ultra vires*.[41]

The 1993 *Maastricht* decision[42] marks a turning point in the Court's case law. The decision's core theme was not the 'openness' of the German Constitution, but rather the limits imposed by German statehood (*Staatlichkeit*), which was just another word for sovereignty. Although the Treaty as such turned out to be compatible with the Constitution,

[34] U Everling, 'BVerfG und Gerichtshof der Europäischen Gemeinschaften', in A Randelzhofer et al. (eds), *Gedächtnisschrift für Eberhard Grabitz* (Beck 1995) 72.

[35] Finanzgericht Rheinland-Pfalz, Entscheidungen der Finanzgerichte (1995) 378; see also Entscheidungen des Bundesfinanzhofs 180, 231, 236.

[36] JA Frowein, 'Kritische Bemerkungen zur Lage des deutschen Staatsrechts aus rechtsvergleichender Sicht' (1998) *Die Öffentliche Verwaltung* 806, 807 et seq.

[37] The term *ausbrechender Rechtsakt* is used, for example, by R Scholz, Art 12a(189) et seq, in T Maunz and G Dürig (eds), *Kommentar zum Grundgesetz*, loose-leaf (against the ECJ's *Kreil* decision as an ausbrechender Rechtsakt); F Schoch, '§ 80 paras 392–4 et seq.', in F Schoch et al. (eds), *Verwaltungsgerichtsordnung Kommentar*, loose-leaf (against the ECJ's Süderdithmarschen decision as *ultra vires* explicity stating that the ECJ decision should be disregarded in Germany).

[38] C-144/04 *Mangold* [2005] ECLI:EU:C:2005:709.

[39] See section 2.b.III.*iv*. on the German Constitutional Court's *Honeywell* decision, *BVerfGE* 126, 286.

[40] *BVerfGE* 126, 286 (*Honeywell*).

[41] Case C-617/10 *Åkerberg Fransson* [2013] ECLI:EU:C:2013:105.

[42] *BVerfGE* 89, 155 (*Maastricht*).

the decision established a significant number of red lines for the future. It emphasizes the German Constitution's limits to European integration—limits which are difficult to contest, as they are mentioned in the Constitution, and limits which are less obvious, as they derive from an interpretation of the Constitution by the Court. The decision also introduced the idea that the Constitutional Court could patrol the limits of the EU's powers and that it could declare any act overstepping the EU's competences inapplicable in Germany (*ultra vires*-control). The defiance of the Court is an indirect one, by means of interpretation of the domestic constitution.

It is probably no coincidence that merely three years after Germany attained full formal sovereignty with German reunification and the 2+4 Treaty, the Court began to emphasize the concept of statehood, a word which is nowhere to be found in the text of the 1949 Constitution. In line with that approach, the Court introduced the label of *Staatenverbund* for the EU, a 'compound of states' which evokes the concept of confederation (*Staatenbund*). It is also noteworthy that in the *Maastricht* case, the Court introduced the individual right 'to a Parliament with a say' under Article 38 of the German Constitution as a ruse to secure standing for the plaintiffs attacking EU law.

ii. Bringing in German parliament: the *European Arrest Warrant* decision (2005)

2005 brought another important development in the EU-related case law of the Court which foreshadowed core elements of the *Lisbon* and the *Euro* decisions. In a case concerning the German Parliament's proper involvement in the implementation of the European Arrest Warrant,[43] the Constitutional Court strengthened the role of the German Parliament vis-à-vis the German government. Although this outcome institutionally served Parliament well, the way the judges interrogated the parliamentarians at the hearings also caused a lasting rift with German parliamentarians, since the Court made them look as though they had no clue of what they were actually doing when dealing with the European Arrest Warrant. That episode is an early example of an antagonism in EU matters between the judges and the political players in Berlin which foreshadows clashes in the context of the Euro-crisis cases (see section 2.b.IV.). It is also an example of how a prima facie domestic constitutional issue turns out to be an element of defiance of European integration.

iii. The *Lisbon* decision (2009)

On 30 June 2009, the German Constitutional Court declared the Lisbon Treaty to be compatible with the German Constitution.[44] At the same time, the Court held that the German statute implementing the participatory rights of national Parliaments—rights the Lisbon Treaty provides—was insufficient. It emphasized that Germany could only deposit its ratification instrument after a new statute on the German Parliament's rights had been drawn up. Despite an upcoming electoral campaign in Germany, the statute on Parliament's rights was redrafted over the summer of 2009 and entered into force in September 2009.[45]

[43] *BVerfGE* 113, 273 (*European Arrest Warrant*).

[44] *BVerfGE* 123, 267 (*Lisbon*), available in German, English, and French at http://www.bverfg.de, accessed 12 October 2016. See for a report of the case containing the briefs of the parties, translations of the decision, and a transcript of the two days of hearings in February 2009, K Kaiser (ed), *Der Vertrag von Lissabon vor dem Bundesverfassungsgericht. Dokumentation des Verfahrens mit Einführung* (Springer 2013).

[45] Gesetz über die Wahrnehmung der Integrationsverantwortung des Bundestages und des Bundesrates, in Angelegenheiten der Europäischen Union (Integrationsverantwortungsgesetz – IntVG) (2009) I(60) *Bundesgesetzblatt* [Federal Official Journal], 3022.

After a final, futile attempt to have the Lisbon Treaty stopped by the German Constitutional Court,[46] Germany ratified it on 25 September 2009.[47]

The *Lisbon* decision marked the end of an intense constitutional battle which had started years earlier when the Treaty establishing a Constitution for Europe of 2004[48] was challenged by Eurosceptics before the German Constitutional Court in May 2005. The battle continued with the constitutional challenge of the Lisbon Treaty in 2008 which delayed German ratification for more than a year, a battle which saw hundreds of pages of legal argument being exchanged, two full days of oral hearings in February 2009, and ultimately a decision of 147 pages.

The decision triggered another debate on the message and the scope of the decision and, once again, on the role of the German Constitutional Court in European integration.[49]

Maastricht *reloaded*

To some extent, the 2009 Lisbon decision mirrors the 1993 *Maastricht* decision. Again, the treaty in question, the Treaty of Lisbon, turned out to be compatible with the German Constitution. And again, the decision primarily concerned the potential limits to European integration and future red lines. The concept of an *ultra vires*-control exercised by the German Constitutional Court, and the generous approach to standing of individuals under Article 38 of the German Constitution were confirmed. The decision also builds on the 2005 *European Arrest Warrant* decision and emphasizes the rights of Parliament. All this results in another example of defiance, again indirectly, through interpretation of the domestic constitution.

Identity control

But there is also a totally new element in that decision. The German Constitutional Court introduced '*Identitätskontrolle*,' i.e. identity review, as a new approach to the review of EU law, in addition to the already existing *ultra vires*-control.[50] The Court's test here is whether the core of the German Constitution, its 'identity' as enshrined in those provisions which indicate the Constitution's inalterable principles (Article 79(3) GG, protecting, inter alia, the core of the democracy principle, the Rule of Law and human dignity), is affected by EU law.[51]

The respect of national identity before the Lisbon *decision*

National identity appeared for the first time in the treaties in 1992 (*Maastricht*) in a provision which was modified by the Lisbon Treaty. According to Article 4(2) TEU, the

[46] *BVerfG*, Case 2 BvR 2136/09, Decision of 22 September 2009 (*Integrationsverantwortungsgesetz* – interim measures), BVerfGK 16, 230.

[47] The Treaty of Lisbon entered into force on 1 December 2009, following the second referendum in Ireland and the ratifications of Poland and the Czech Republic. Treaty of Lisbon amending the Treaty on European Union and the Treaty Establishing the European Community (signed 13 December 2007, entered into force 1 December 2009), consolidated version [2010] OJ C83.

[48] After the negative outcome of ratification referenda in France and in the Netherlands in 2005, the project of a Constitutional Treaty was given up.

[49] See the references listed in A Voßkuhle, 'Der europäische Verfassungsgerichtsverbund' (2010) 29 *Neue Zeitschrift für Verwaltungsrecht* 1; for an English version, see A Voßkuhle, 'Multilevel Cooperation of the European Constitutional Courts – Der Europäische Verfassungsgerichtsverbund' (2010) 6 *European Competition Law Review* 175. Since 2010, Andreas Voßkuhle has been the President of the German Constitutional Court and this article, based on a speech given in Brussels, suggests a differentiated reading of the Lisbon decision. See also FC Mayer, 'Rashomon in Karlsruhe – A reflection on Democracy and Identity in the European Union. The German Constitutional Court's Lisbon decision and the changing landscape of European constitutionalism' (2011) 9 *International Journal of Constitutional Law* 757.

[50] *BVerfGE* 123, 267, 353–5, para 240 (*Lisbon*).

[51] ibid.

EU shall respect the national identities of the Member States including their 'fundamental structures, political and constitutional'. This clarifies that national identity includes constitutional identity. This may indeed serve as a starting point on the European level to revoke the claim of the unconditional primacy of European law over Member States' constitutional identities.

It is hardly surprising that it was an Irish academic contribution which developed further the idea—inherent to Article 4(2) TEU, protecting fundamental national constitutional decisions— of attributing to national courts of last instance the role of determining the content of such choices, as recognized and protected by European law.[52] After all, it was the Irish protocol annexed to the Maastricht Treaty 1992[53] which conceptualized for the first time the idea of preserving the sacrosanctity of national constitutional provisions which are of particular importance to the relevant constitution. In the Irish case the provision at issue concerned the prohibition of abortion. The protocol itself, however, served as a kind of blueprint: the identity clause of the current EU Treaty takes the approach of the Irish protocol and generalizes the concept. It can be read more broadly as a revocation of European law's claim to primacy in respect of specific Member State interests of particular importance in a given case.[54] Member State courts had already begun to use the idea of national constitutional identity to build a bridge between European and national constitutional law before the Lisbon Treaty. The French *Conseil constitutionnel* stated implicitly in 2004 and explicitly in 2006[55] that national constitutional identity is a limit to the primacy of European law. A similar approach can also be found in a 2004 decision of the Spanish Constitutional Court.[56] Even the ECJ in 2010 began to turn to the concept of constitutional identity and to accept it as a limit to EU law.[57]

Note the fundamental difference between the categories of an *ultra vires* act on the one hand and an act impinging upon national constitutional identity on the other hand. The difference is reminiscent of the difference discussed earlier in this chapter between *ultra vires* acts and acts violating German fundamental rights.[58] To uphold, in principle, national constitutional identity does not go beyond the bipolar relationship between, e.g., the German and European legal orders.

Because the respective identity issue is a bipolar matter, the determination of what is part of national constitutional identity and thus a stop sign for EU law cannot be done unilaterally; it must be a joint effort of the respective national court and the ECJ.[59]

[52] DR Phelan, *Revolt or Revolution: The Constitutional Boundaries of the European Community* (Round Hall Sweet & Maxwell 1997), 416.

[53] Protocol 17 to the Treaty of Maastricht.

[54] See on this idea prior to the *Lisbon* decision, Mayer (n 31) 341; Mayer, 'Multilevel Constitutional Jurisdiction', in A von Bogdandy and J Bast (eds), *Principles of European Constitutional Law* (Hart 2010), 424, 425; see also A von Bogdandy and S Schill, 'Overcoming absolute primacy: Respect for national identity under the Lisbon Treaty' (2011) 48 *Common Market Law Review* 1417; M Wendel, *Permeabilität im europäischen Verfassungsrecht* (Mohr Siebeck 2011), 572–4; M Claes, 'Negotiating Constitutional Identity or Whose Identity is it Anyway?', in M Claes et al. (eds), *Constitutional Conversations in Europe: actors, topics and procedures* (Intersentia 2012), 205.

[55] CC, 2004-505 DC 19.11.2004, Traité établissant une Constitution pour l'Europe; CC, 2006-540 DC 27.7.2006, Loi relative au droit d'auteur et aux droits voisins dans la société de l'information.

[56] Tribunal Constitucional, DTC 1/2004 (13 December 2004).

[57] Case 208/09 *Ilonka Sayn-Wittgenstein* v *Landeshauptmann von Wien* [2010] ECR I-13693.

[58] See section 2.b.II.*i* and 2.b.II.*ii*, the *Solange I* and *II* context.

[59] See FC Mayer and M Wendel, 'Die verfassungsrechtlichen Grundlagen des Europarechts', in A Hatje and P-C Müller-Graff (eds), *Enzyklopädie des Europarechts Vol 1* (Nomos 2014); FC Mayer and M Wendel, 'Multilevel Constitutionalism and Constitutional Pluralism – querelle allemande or querelle d'Allemand?', in M Avbelj and J Komárek (eds), *Constitutional Pluralism in the European Union and Beyond* (Hart 2012) 127; Wendel (n 54) 573–5.

The Lisbon *decision as the all-time low of EU related cases?*

With the 2009 *Lisbon* decision, the German Constitutional Court probably pushed things too far. Although initial reactions in the media praised the decision, the reactions in the academic and the political world were mostly critical.[60] It was just too obvious that although far from perfect, the Lisbon Treaty did bring improvements to basically every aspect of constitutional law, from the protection of fundamental rights (introducing a binding Fundamental Rights Charter) to the control of European powers and competences (strengthening subsidiarity) and democracy (enhancing the role of national parliaments). Nevertheless, the German Constitutional Court elaborated in more than 100 pages on the potential dangers and risks and ultimate limits to European integration from the perspective of the German Constitutional order, emphasizing the relevance of German sovereignty—finally spelling out the term[61]—and displaying an underlying fear that Germany, after all the largest Member State, could be marginalized in the European political process.

That decision revealed much more clearly than ever before a major point of misunderstanding of European integration between most judges of the German Constitutional Court and the German political players: the latter know that there is no real risk of Germany being marginalized in European politics. Even the slightest insight into the actual workings of European politics will confirm that the largest Member State with its powerful economy is not in danger of being bullied. The German Constitutional Court has apparently not realized this yet. The *Lisbon* decision's overprotective language, repeatedly insisting on Germany's sovereign statehood, even turned out to be counterproductive, as this inward-looking perspective alienates other Member States, in particular the smaller ones.

iv. Stepping back: The *Honeywell* decision (2010)

One element of the *Lisbon* decision, the *ultra vires* doctrine, was the core topic of the 2010 *Honeywell* decision.[62] This decision can be read as a reaction to the critique of the *Lisbon* judgment, as it emphasized the pro-European elements in the German Constitution and confirmed the 'friendliness' of the German Constitution towards European integration as a constitutional principle. The Court also ruled that an *ultra vires* decision invalidating EU law in Germany depends on a number of preconditions, making it quite unlikely that the Court would actually declare an EU act *ultra vires*.

With this decision, the case law of the German Constitutional Court seemed to have reached a state of *modus vivendi* with the ECJ in matters of competence control. In principle, the German Constitutional Court insisted on the possibility of scrutinizing EU action. But the conditions for invalidating EU law in Germany set by the Court appeared rather hypothetical. In that, *Honeywell* and *Solange II* follow the same analytical plan: the possibility for the German Constitutional Court to intervene was not given up but at the same time, the conditions for this became so hypothetical that at that stage, it appeared quite unlikely that the German Constitutional Court would become active in matters of fundamental rights protection against EU activities or in an issue of European powers and competences (*ultra vires*).

And then the Euro-crisis emerged.

[60] See for example the contributions by C Schönberger, D Halberstam, C Möllers and C Tomuschat in the special section of the special issue on the Lisbon Judgment of the Federal Constitutional Court in (2009) 10 *German Law Journal* 1209, 1241, 1260.

[61] In the *Maastricht* decision, the concept was still being concealed by 'statehood' (*Staatlichkeit*), see section 2.b.III.*i*.

[62] *BVerfGE* 126, 286, 303–37, paras 58–66. See also FC Mayer and M Walter, 'Die Europarechtsfreundlichkeit des BVerfG nach dem Honeywell-Beschluss' (2011) 33 *Jura* 532.

IV. The Euro-crisis case law—towards open conflict?

i. Greece, EFSF, ESM (2010–2014)

As early as May 2010, with the very first measures initiated to help the Greek government, the German Constitutional Court was captured by the political forces which had already been reluctant to give up the Deutsche Mark, Germany's post-war currency.

An innocent observer of the ensuing series of decisions of the German Constitutional Court in the Euro-crisis context could be be led to think that there was no major problem. After all, the German Constitutional Court did not directly block any of the measures which were initiated to help members of the Eurozone: neither the measures taken to help Greece, nor the temporary mechanism set up as the EFSF, nor the permanent structure known as the ESM. Instead, the German Constitutional Court turned to the strategy of continuously strengthening the oversight and veto rights of the German Parliament in Euro matters. At the same time, the Court continued to be more than generous as far as standing for individuals bringing EU cases to the Court was concerned. The German Constitutional Court thus remained involved in the Euro rescue quasi-permanently, and with the continuous threat of invalidating measures taken to rescue the Euro, the German Constitutional Court did become a political player in the Euro-crisis, with a direct impact on the political process in adjudicating on what could be done and what could not.

What was likewise new in the Euro-crisis saga is that the German Constitutional Court increasingly seemed to be out of sync with the preferences of the other German political players as far as EU matters were concerned. In a critical reading of that development, the German Constitutional Court is even out of sync with German interests in the EU.

The active political role the Court took on became clearly visible with the German Constitutional Court's decision to ask the ECJ to scrutinize the legality of ECB action in the Euro-crisis in January 2014.[63]

ii. The German Constitutional Court and the ECB: The OMT case and the reference to the ECJ (2014–2016)

In September 2012, ECB President Draghi announced that the ECB would, if necessary, relieve the pressure on euro states in trouble by buying bonds on the secondary market issued by these states if they committed themselves to a EFSF/ESM-programme and strict conditions.[64]

The issue brought to the German Constitutional Court was whether this Outright Monetary Transactions (OMT) programme was compatible with the law of the EU and with German constitutional law.[65] This led to the first ever reference of the German Constitutional Court to the ECJ in January 2014. The reference turned out to be highly controversial, inside and outside the Court. Within the Court, two judges filed forceful dissenting opinions. According to the majority opinion supporting the reference, OMT was illegal.[66] Six judges of the Court believed that the OMT programme lay outside the ECB's mandate, exceeding the realm of monetary policy.[67] They also believed that the OMT programme violated the prohibition on monetary financing of the founding treaties.

[63] *BVerfG*, 2 BvR 2728/13 (14 January 2014).

[64] Available at: http://www.ecb.europa.eu/, accessed 12 October 2016.

[65] For more detail, see FC Mayer, 'Rebels Without a Cause? A Critical Analysis of the German Constitutional Court's OMT Reference' (2014) 15 *German Law Journal*, http://www.germanlawjournal.com/index.php?pageID=11&artID=1613, accessed 5 June 2015.

[66] *BVerfG*, 2 BvR 2728/13, paras 55–98 (14 January 2014).

[67] ibid, paras 63, 69.

The two dissenting judges stressed that the issue belonged to the realm of political questions (although in general, a political question doctrine is not openly endorsed by the Court) and that the Court should refrain from interfering. This is the better approach. It is quite stunning that the six majority judges believed they were able to decide a question which was—and remains—highly controversial, even among economists. The new dimension this case introduced was that the Court was trying to play in the playing field of central banks and economists. As one of the dissenting opinions states,[68] it was in fact the Constitutional Court which was overstepping the limits and boundaries of its powers and expertise.

Some of the majority judges of the German Constitutional Court, clearly in an effort to de-dramatize the case, tried to give that impression by speaking extra-judicially in the aftermath of the decision.[69] The unspectacular and sober confirmation of the September 2012 interim decision in March 2014[70]—that the ESM Treaty and the Fiscal Treaty are compatible with the German Constitution—is in line with this.

After the Opinion of the Advocate General dated 14 January 2015,[71] the ECJ's decision of June 2015 confirmed the legality of the OMT programme.[72] In a balanced and sober judgment, the Court emphasized that the ECB is operating under legal constraints and tried to address some but not all the concerns voiced in the German Constitutional Court's reference.

After this decision, the German Constitutional Court held another hearing in February 2016, which is rather unusual after a preliminary reference ruling. In its final decision of 21 June 2016, the German Constitutional Court basically accepted the ECJ's decision on the legality of the OMT programme. Under certain conditions programmes such as OMT are not *ultra vires*.[73]

The OMT reference saga reanimated two topics which had appeared settled, both related to defiance: the *ultra vires* issue (*Maastricht/Honeywell*) and identity control (*Lisbon*).

The ultra vires doctrine in action?

The majority of the court made it quite clear in the OMT reference that they believed the ECB's OMT action was *ultra vires*. A test for the soundness of an EU-related national court ruling could be whether it is conceivable that all other courts in the EU would adopt the same reasoning. This is clearly not the case with the *ultra vires* approach of the German Constitutional Court on display in the OMT reference. If all other supreme or constitutional courts in the EU took the same stance, the unity of EU law and the authority of the ECJ would be destroyed. EU law would become a pick-and-choose legal order. The six judges forming the majority opinion in the OMT reference seemed to think differently. They tried to depict their position as a position shared by many other courts in the EU and seemed to encourage other courts to join them.

The error in perception here is twofold. First, there is an erroneous assessment of the danger that the increasing number of national courts claiming to be the final arbiter of EU

[68] *BVerfG*, 2 BvR 2728/13, dissenting opinion of Judge Lübbe-Wolff, para 2 (14 January 2014).

[69] Judge Voßkuhle and Judge Huber both used similar wording in public appearances in Berlin in March 2014 stating that the German Constitutional Court would 'accept' (*akzeptieren*) a (sound) ECJ decision. This wording still leaves everything open and of course two judges cannot speak for the other judges on that matter. See on that point, M Steinbeis, 'OMT-Vorlage: Richter Huber signalisiert Demut gegenüber dem EuGH' (10 March 2014) Verfassungsblog, http://verfassungsblog.de/omt-vorlage-richter-huber-signalisiert-demut-geg, accessed 12 October 2016.

[70] *BVerfG*, 2 BvR 1390/12 (18 March 2014).

[71] Opinion of Advocate General Cruz Villalón, Case C-62/14 *Gauweiler and Others* [2015] ECLI:EU:C:2015:7.

[72] Case C-62/14 *Gauweiler and Others* [2015] ECLI:EU:C:2015:400.

[73] *BVerfG*, 2 BvR 2728/13 (21 June 2016).

law entails. There is also an error of perception as to the company the German Constitutional Court has on its *ultra vires* path. The six judges point to Danish, Estonian, French, Irish, Italian, Latvian, Polish, Swedish, Spanish, and Czech cases,[74] implying that the German approach is not isolated. This is not accurate. Firstly, ten out of the twenty-eight Member State legal orders would not even constitute a majority. Secondly, the Court is mixing different types of decisions motivated by all kinds of different arguments. Looking closer, only the Czech Constitutional Court with its *Landtova* ruling openly endorses the German *ultra vires* approach and comes close to actually applying an *ultra vires* review, which is arguably due to a specific domestic court dispute in the Czech Republic.[75] All other courts remain at the level of principle and theory, a much lesser degree of defiance, if defiance at all.

The way the six judges present other Member State courts as presumed 'allies' is also not in line with the rhetoric of cooperation and dialogue; it appears much more as though the Court is opening front lines against the ECJ. This may at some point go beyond defiance and cross the threshold into open conflict. In the final ruling on OMT it did not.

The protection of national constitutional identity according to the German Constitutional Court

The judges representing the majority opinion also brought up identity review in the OMT reference. This offers some insight into their concept of national constitutional identity.

Their claim is that the budgetary autonomy of the German *Bundestag* is part of German constitutional identity. They consider it possible that German budgetary autonomy and the overall budgetary responsibility of the German Parliament can be affected by the ECB action in question.[76]

So the argument appears to be that the OMT programme could lead to significant losses in the *Bundesbank*, which in turn could cripple the federal budget in Germany. This would render elections to Parliament meaningless to German voters, since a crippled budget deprives Parliament of any room for manoeuvre. This again affects the democracy in Germany to its core, which means that OMT could affect German constitutional identity. If you ever need an example of a far-fetched argument, there you have it.

While this line of argument is probably too absurd to discuss, the procedural remark the six judges made in this context is rather alarming.[77] They clearly do not accept that in the context of national constitutional identity, a preliminary reference to the ECJ would be needed to make sure that the legal argument in question falls under Article 4(2) TEU. A preliminary reference in the context of an 'identity review' effectuated by a national court would aim at the interpretation of Article 4(2) TEU by the ECJ. They seem to insist on unilaterally determining the meaning of Article 4(2) in a given case from their Member State perspective. Establishing national identity and national constitutional identity as a limit to EU law unilaterally is extremely dangerous for legal unity in the EU and is open to abuse.[78]

The idea of taking Article 4(2) TEU and the concept of national constitutional identity as a starting point to establish limits of EU law from the EU law perspective has a lot of

[74] *BVerfG*, 2 BvR 2728/13 para 30.

[75] See J Komarek, 'Playing With Matches: The Czech Constitutional Court's Ultra Vires Revolution' (22 February 2012) Verfassungsblog, http://verfassungsblog.de/playing-matches-czech-constitutional-courts-ultra-vires-revolution/, accessed 5 June 2015.

[76] *BVerfG*, 2 BvR 2728/13, para 102. [77] ibid.

[78] The next step would be for some German court to declare Volkswagen or Opel to be a part of German national identity, thus removing subsidies to core German industries from EU state aid control.

potential to improve how primacy is conceptualized. But this can only work in a genuine spirit of cooperation.

With a decision on a *European Arrest Warrant* case in December 2015,[79] the German Constitutional Court fused the fundamental rights protection issue and the identity issue. It is not clear yet if the Court repeals *Solange II* with this judgment, but it was not that surprising that the Court stated that the human dignity core of any fundamental right protected under the German Constitution is part of Germany's constitutional identity and can be invoked against EU law. In that decision, the Court also stressed that it would submit a preliminary reference to the ECJ before declaring a European act a violation of German constitutional identity.

V. The case law of the German Constitutional Court on European integration—a mixed bag

Again, very much like in the context of the preliminary references, the picture is not all white nor all black. In the field of fundamental rights protection, the decisions of the German Constitutional Court led to a *modus vivendi*: defiance in principle, but pragmatism in practice, with the potential of open conflict minimized. The same process seemed underway in the field of competence control (*ultra vires*), but then the Euro-crisis came along. It is also quite clear that the issue of sovereignty had particular relevance in the *ultra vires* context and in the context of safeguarding national constitutional identity. In the changing landscape of Europe after the end of the Cold War, with a reunified Germany, it still remains to be seen whether signals of defiance from the German Constitutional Court express a general change of Germany's view on European integration or whether at the end of the day, it is simply the more-or-less random appointment process of judges which leads to a given composition of the Court and to more or less defiance.

3. Rebels with or without a cause? Explaining and analysing the German Constitutional Court's defiance

If there is defiance in the case law of the German Constitutional Court when it comes to European integration, this raises the question of the motivations of and explanations for this defiance (section 3.a.). Whatever the reasons, it is possible to try better to understand the German Constitutional Court's defiance in terms of consistencies and inconsistencies (section 3.b.).

a. Explaining defiance

I. Euroscepticism?

The German Constitutional Court is a venerable institution which has served the Federal Republic for well over sixty years. It has helped establish a culture of democracy, Rule of Law, and fundamental rights protection in post-war West Germany and it has fostered a concept of values enshrined in the Constitution, with human dignity as the most important value of all.

However, decisions such as the majority opinion supporting the OMT reference[80] represent a Constitutional Court moving in the wrong direction. It is a direction which has the potential to damage the Court's authority,[81] its legacy, and its achievements, and to

[79] *BVerfG*, 2 BvR 2735/14 (14 December 2015). [80] See section 2.b.IV.*ii*.

[81] See Judge Lübbe-Wolff's dissent on this. *BVerfG*, 2 BvR 2728/13 (Lübbe-Wolff, dissenting at para 8).

divert it from the realm of domestic fundamental rights protection which it should focus on. Anti-Europeanism would be an easy explanation for the German Constitutional Court's defiance. Simplistic answers are not helpful, though. There is no evidence that any of the decisions on European integration were driven by a German Constitutional Court dominated by anti-Europeans. The self-image of the judges is better captured by the idea that in general, they truly believe that they are the last stand to defend and uphold the Constitution, even against European integration. One could argue that the path of Germany in European integration does not antagonize the Constitution, that it is part of its legacy since 1949. But this does not seem to be the prevailing view in Karlsruhe. From an outsider's perspective, there seems to be no general, ideological, or emotional hostility against European integration prevailing among judges and their staff. However, the standard view on European integration and thus EU law seems to be that it is something exterior and alien.

II. Power?

On Tuesday 12 September 2012, the German Constitutional Court could have brought the world economy down. That day, the Court published the decision on Germany's participation in the latest rescue efforts for troubled states within the euro system, the ESM.[82] With hundreds of media representatives from around the world observing a case which had been initiated by more than 40,000 plaintiffs, the case was the biggest in the history of the German Constitutional Court. Had the Court decided that for reasons of German constitutional law, Germany was not allowed to participate in the ESM, the repercussions on the financial markets in the EU and worldwide would have been dramatic. Not even the powerful US Supreme Court has ever been in a similar position. No court should have this amount of power.

The German Constitutional Court is a powerful institution. In the EU context this power has emerged over time, by means of decisions. At the same time, it is clear that there is a tension between this judicial power in Karlsruhe and the judicial power of the ECJ in Luxemburg. This is not only about judicial egos. Perhaps power and the attraction of power is part of an explanation for the decisions of the German Constitutional Court, because it is simply the human condition that giving up power is not easy, especially if the institutional narrative is that the power of the institution is benign and serves a higher purpose—here the safeguarding of constitutional values.

b. Understanding defiance—the consistency of the case law

To understand defiance better, it may also be helpful to look at consistencies and inconsistencies in the case law and at the dynamic elements which might indicate a direction or a trend.

I. Consistencies

The German Constitutional Court has always viewed the acts of assent to the respective Treaties, based on the German Constitution as the link between European law and national law, with the Member States remaining the 'Masters of the Treaties'.[83] Policing this link or,

[82] *BVerfGE* 132, 195 (12 September 2012). Other recent cases related to the Euro-crisis are *BVerfGE* 129, 124 (7 September 2011) (Greece and EFSF); *BVerfGE* 130, 318 (28 February 2012) (*Committee of Nine*); *BVerfGE* 131, 152 (19 June 2012). Older cases related to the EURO are *BVerfGE* 89, 155 (12 October 1993) (*Maastricht*); *BVerfGE* 97, 350 (31 March 1998) (*Euro*); *BVerfGE* 123, 267 (30 June 2009) (*Lisbon*).

[83] *BVerfGE* 75, 223 (Kloppenburg).

to return to the bridge-metaphor, controlling this bridge, enables the German Constitutional Court to effectuate far-reaching indirect control over the application of European law in Germany by applying the standard of German constitutional law under the guise of interpreting and controlling the act of assent to it. The German Constitutional Court thus consistently imposes constitutional law limits on the primacy of European law. The German Constitutional Court has never relinquished its claim to a right to decide the point at which it would leverage its constitutional control; it merely modified this threshold. This is especially visible in the *Solange I*/*Solange II* shift, where the Court reversed what it considered to be the principle and what the exception. For the *ultra vires*-control, there was a similar shift from *Lisbon* to *Honeywell*, loosening the grip on EU law, and then to the OMT reference, arguably tightening the grip again.

Only the dissenting opinion in *Solange I* indicated a willingness completely to abandon judicial review over the constitutionality of European law, albeit insisting on constitutional law limits.

II. Inconsistencies

There are also elements in the case law which appear inconsistent. A significant number of cases related to European integration were decided with split courts, and the respective dissenting opinions in *Solange I*, in the *European Arrest Warrant* case, in *Honeywell* and in the OMT reference are all about contradicting the respective majority and pointing to inconsistencies in the majority opinions.

There is one element of inconsistency which stands out: the alleged constitutional principle of 'friendliness' towards European integration (*Europafreundlichkeit*) emphasized in the 2010 *Honeywell* decision is not consistent with the threat to exercise a unilateral *ultra vires* or identity control. It is actually incompatible with any kind of unilateral defiance or hostility towards European integration. This begs the question why this idea finds its way into the arguably defiant case law of the German Constitutional Court in the first place. The simple answer is that it is just too obviously in the spirit of the Constitution. The *Grundgesetz* is not a constitution of defiance towards European integration.

III. Dynamic elements

The Euro cases added a new quality to the Court's role, a more political role in a EU-wide context. Several developments come together here. First, the topic of monetary union is simply so much more far-reaching in geopolitical terms and of much more political and even existential relevance and sensitivity than, say, the importation of mushrooms in the 1974 *Solange I* case.[84] Then there is also a more recent sensitivity about—often even a critique of—the German Constitutional Court's judges' extrajudicial 'political' behaviour'[85] which concerns judges acting like politicians.[86] The flip side of the Court appearing as a political player is that politicians increasingly try to anticipate the sensitivities of the

[84] With all due respect to the fundamental rights cases of the early period of European integration, most involved rather mundane issues of commerce and goods.

[85] In part this was triggered by an appearance of the Court's President at the *Bundespressekonferenz* (national press conference in Berlin): Hugo Müller Vogg, 'Voßkuhle spricht nicht nur durch seine Urteile' *Bayernkurier* (9 March 2013), http://www.bayernkurier.de/zeitung/artikel/ansicht/8522-voskuhle-spricht-nicht-nur-durch-seine-urteile.html, accessed 12 October 2016.

[86] Consider in this context the outburst of the then Interior Minister Friedrich in early 2013: 'If Constitutional Court judges want to make policy, then they should run as a candidate for parliament'. S Höll, 'Innenminister Friedrich rügt obersten Verfassungsrichter' (23 April 2013) *Süddeutsche Zeitung* http://www.sueddeutsche.de/

German Constitutional Court. Naturally, this is not to say that there is anything wrong with politicians trying to respect the framework of the Constitution. However, the reality of the Euro-crisis is that constitutional law arguments replace political arguments, which goes far beyond an attempt to respect the constitutional framework.

Part of the domestic critique of the Court is also related to a line of different, highly controversial judgments, such as the decisions invalidating the German rules governing elections to the EP and providing for a five and later for a three per cent threshold, decisions which appeared as anti-EP and as weakening the EP.[87]

The question raised in that context was whether the German Constitutional Court as an institution has a particular EU-related political agenda. We must consider the complexity of the institution, however, which makes it hard to imagine how a specific political agenda could be shaped in practical terms in a group of eight persons which keeps changing. Arguably, there is no such agenda beyond institutional self-interest and changing majorities and coalitions among the judges on specific issues.

4. Possible future developments

If the defiance of the German Constitutional Court towards European integration appears a problem, the question is how to solve it. If defiance reaches the point of open resistance and conflict, the EU treaties suggest an answer: at a legalistic level, Germany can be brought before the ECJ in a treaty infringement case if the German Constitutional Court openly ignores obligations flowing from the founding treaties. The ECB/OMT case, decided by the ECJ in June 2015[88] ultimately turned out not to be a test of the German judges' will to respect Germany's obligations under the founding treaties, which foresee that the ECJ rulings must be implemented.

Is there really a problem which needs to be solved? According to some, the German Constitutional Court is actually an institution in decline: in that reading, with judges feeling their power slip away in times of globalization and Europeanization, occasional judicial activism is just an expression of a desperate struggle against losing relevance and power. If that were true, the solution of real or perceived problems related to the Court would just be a matter of time. The alternate view considers the Court at a new height of its power, not only as the ultimate authority in Germany, but now also in the EU. This view is at least as plausible as the institution-in-decline view. Looking at the evolution of the German Constitutional Court's case law related to European integration over the last fifty years is equally inconclusive between a quantitative and a qualitative assessment: we may find defiance to be decreasing, while at the same time it could be said that where defiance remains, it appears increasingly serious.

If defiance by a constitutional court is used as an argument in European politics, this could create a certain dynamic. One possibility for the other EU Member States to counter the German argument of 'Our Court says [. . .]' is to establish corresponding capabilities at home. This may partly explain recent developments in France, where the *Conseil constitutionnel* now has a right to judicial review, or the UK, where a Supreme Court was introduced. This is an ongoing development and it is too early to assess these new institutional

politik/sicherheitsdebatte-innenminister-friedrich-ruegt-obersten-verfassungsrichter-1.1657163, accessed 12 October 2016.

[87] *BVerfGE* 129, 300 (five per cent); and *BVerfG*, 2 BvE 2/13 (26 Feb 2014) (three per cent).

[88] Case C-62/14 *Gauweiler and Others* ECLI:EU:C:2015:400. The German Constitutional Court accepted the decision in June 2016, see 2.b.IV.*ii.* for more detail.

emergences. However, if this leads to a political process where each Member State points to the respective defiant Constitutional or Supreme Court at home defending actual or perceived national interests, this would endanger the unity of EU law. On the other hand, if new judicial players demonstrate how to deal with EU-related legal issues constructively, this could also influence the German Constitutional Court and minimize defiance.

The German players have more options to influence the German Court than other Member States or EU institutions: they could modify their institution. Nevertheless, the US experience with court packing in the New Deal era indicates that not everything legally conceivable is also politically feasible.[89] The most comprehensive option, amending the Constitution to clarify the issues raised here and thereby forestall defiance, is thus probably not that easily done. Slightly more realistic is the option to amend the statute governing the German Constitutional Court's jurisdiction. But such a move would still have to deal with the foreseeable popular criticism that politicians would be trying to curb the court for selfish political reasons.

This points to the source of the German Constitutional Court's power, which ultimately also provides a deeper legitimation for any defiance of European integration: at least some of the judges may regard themselves in the role of giving a voice to an assumed silent popular majority beyond the 'Berlin elites', as an opposition to the mainstream. But the assumption of a silent majority can be misinformed. At the end of the day, if Court defiance is excessive, politicians will make a cost-benefit analysis of whether the political cost to curb the Court is worth the benefit. For the time being, given the Court's popularity, the cost of curbing it seems prohibitive.

Ultimately, change may come from within the Court. Dissenting opinions from *Solange I* to the OMT decision have been part of the EU case law of the German Constitutional Court many times, and most of them demonstrate an alternate approach to European integration. The German Constitution is sufficiently open to provide alternate narratives for the relationship between the European and the German legal orders. Such a narrative could emphasize that it is the German Constitution itself which opens up the domestic constitutional order, not some bridging act of assent. This would take one of the cornerstones of the German Constitutional Court's defiant case law away. It is a matter of interpretation. Ultimately, it depends on who is sitting on the bench.

[89] On court packing as the most dramatic measure and its limits, see FC Mayer, 'Kompetenzverschiebungen als Krisenfolge? Die US-Verfassungsentwicklung seit dem New Deal und Lehren für die Euro-Krise' (2014) *Juristenzeitung* 593.

24

Defiance for European Influence—the Empty Chair and France

Jacques Ziller

1. The crisis

As fifty years have elapsed since the 'Empty Chair' crisis, most readers will probably have a rather schematic knowledge of that paramount moment of European integration, if not a hackneyed one.[1] Let us recall the facts.[2]

Due to the rotation system of the Presidency of the EEC Council, France's Foreign Minister Maurice Couve de Murville chaired the last Council meeting of the first semester of 1965 on 30 June, before Italy was to take up the Presidency. France was represented by its ministers of agriculture Edgar Pisani and of finance Valéry Giscard d'Estaing. The issue to be solved in the latter meeting was that of the financing rules for the common agricultural policy (CAP), in application of the agreement reached at Stresa, in Italy, three years and a half earlier. France requested a permanent settlement while Italy wanted to go on with only a provisional arrangement until the CAP covered all products; Belgium's government, which had been recently defeated in parliament, could only deal with current business; Germany was far more interested in pressing forward with the free movement of industrial goods; and finally, although only very loosely connected to the issue under discussion, a number of initiatives were under way to reinforce the EP and the Commission (see section 2).

On 1 and 2 July 1965 the Permanent Representative of France to the European Communities Jean-Marc Boegner sent the following report[3] to the French Foreign Ministry, in which he recounted the Council's discussions during the previous night. It is worth quoting the entire text, as it is very precise on the facts and also conveys the atmosphere of the last Council meeting attended by France before the so called Luxembourg Compromise put an end to the crisis six months later. The decision-making rule at the Council was unanimity. Boegner wrote:[4]

> Yesterday's final act played out around the question whether the arrangements determining the regime of the transitional period of the Financial Regulation would cover the whole period or only two years. The discussion of this problem, which was raised late in the evening, showed that on this point, our partners' positions [were] distinct from each other.

[1] For more in-depth analyses of the crisis itself, see the best publication on the issue: J-M Palayret et al. (eds), *Visions, Votes and Vetoes—The Empty Chair crisis and the Luxembourg Compromise Forty Years On* (PIE–Peter Lang 2006) 15–19.

[2] This account is based on the excellent file available on the website of CVCE.eu—The research infrastructure on European integration, http://www.cvce.eu/en/collections/unit-content/-/unit/02bb76df-d066-4c08-a58a-d4686a3e68ff/62cd6534-f1a9-442a-b6fb-0bab7c842180/Resources, accessed 12 October 2016. NB the French language version of the site gives access to a far greater number of files (seventy-eight) than the English version (twenty five).

[3] Two telegrams, see (n 2).

[4] Translations and explanations in the footnotes are mine.

Defiance for European Influence—the Empty Chair and France. First Edition. Jacques Ziller. © Jacques Ziller 2017. Published 2017 by Oxford University Press.

The French delegation asserted that an agreement limited to two years was unacceptable both for legal reasons—abiding to the stipulations of the Financial Regulation, which provide that the rules to be defined should extend until the end of the transitional period—and for economic reasons—the impossibility to consider an irreversible system of regulation and of unified prices if one does not know how it would be funded.

After a rather confused debate which revealed the perplexity of some delegates and the ill-will of others, it appeared that our view was understood on the German, Belgian, and Luxembourg side, and that—subject to agreement on the detailed modalities—the principle of a solution for the entire transitional period would eventually be adopted. It was different for the Dutch and Italian delegations, which continued to stick to a two-year agreement.

Faced by this situation, Mr Couve de Murville decided at one o'clock in the morning to gather his colleagues[5] in restricted session to explain that the Council was facing a major difficulty which blocked the continuation of negotiations and that in the absence of an agreement on this vital topic, it was useless to continue debating.

Thus confronted by their responsibilities, other delegations naturally sought to evade and postpone the discussion. Mr Luns,[6] speaking first, said his government needed some time to consider all the proposals which had been made during the day and that his delegation was unable to decide immediately in the circumstances. As far as he was concerned, he was ready to return to Brussels as early as 8 July to resume discussions.

Mr Schmuecker, on behalf of the German delegation noted that following what Mr Luns said, it was impossible to make further progress and that it was indeed better to meet again very soon in order to achieve results.

Mr Fanfani[7] agreed with Mr Schmuecker and also referred to the need to consult his government and to study the suggestions and proposals which had been put forward from the different sides in the preceding hours.

Mr Couve de Murville, speaking on behalf of the French delegation, noted that what had been said confirmed to him that it was useless to continue to look for an agreement; he said that the French delegation was taking note that the solemn commitments adopted in the Financial Regulation on 14 January 1962 and confirmed since then in December and January past had not been honoured and that each party would therefore have to bear the ensuing consequences.

This statement by the head of the French delegation, which dispelled both ambiguities and illusions, instigated a final effort on the part of the other delegations to try to agree a fresh appointment in July to push the Commission to make fresh proposals. The Commission joined these efforts and recalled that it derived from the Treaty the right to make any proposal it deemed useful or to modify its earlier proposals. Mr Couve de Murville did enter this discussion and refused to make any commitment as to a date and to consent to a mandate for the Commission to make suggestions. As the question was raised whether the Council meeting already scheduled for 26 and 27 July could take place, Mr Couve de Murville did not deny that such an appointment had been made and that it should be maintained, but he doubted that the French delegation would be prepared to resume discussions on the Financial Regulation on that occasion. As for the Council of Ministers of Agriculture to be held on 12 and 13 July, Mr Couve de Murville said that the French delegation would not bring any positive contribution to the meeting. After that, it was suggested by various sides—and seemingly agreed—to postpone the meeting to a later date because of the situation.

Finally, some delegations referred to the possibility that contact be established between governments, either through diplomatic channels or through the Permanent Representatives, in order

[5] The General affairs Council.

[6] Foreign Minister of the Netherlands.

[7] Foreign Minister of Italy.

to consult on what was to be done. The matter ended there and the Council members separated at around two o'clock.

Boegner's first telegram ended here; in a second telegram the following day he went into greater detail:

Throughout the discussions, the Italian and Dutch delegations, and on several occasions the German delegation, or at least some of its members, had shown little willingness to achieve agreement.

Late in the afternoon, Mr Couve de Murville noted that attitude and questioned the usefulness of continuing discussions. At the same time, he reminded the Council that for the French government a Community which does not respect its commitments would stop truly being a community.

At that point Mr Spaak took the floor. He first strongly supported what Mr Couve de Murville had said and he stressed that if the Belgian delegation could not take on new commitments, it intended nevertheless to respect those that had been previously agreed. The delegation was therefore able to accept reasonable provisions on the financing of the common agricultural policy, subject to them being submitted to the new Belgian Cabinet as soon as it was be formed.

However, continued Mr Spaak, it was unclear why some felt the need to link these funding problems with a discussion of the powers of the Strasbourg Assembly. It would be appropriate to study democratic means by which the use of these revenues could be controlled once the Community had its own resources, something which would not happen before 1970, unless that process were accelerated. The issue, however, was not timely, and furthermore it was badly presented. Indeed, continued the Belgian minister, the issue of controlling the community budget, for which a technical solution could always be found, should not be confused with the issue of increased the powers of the Assembly, which some had raised. It would be quite unreasonable to grant powers to a 'parliament' which—*de jure* and *de facto*—is not and cannot be a real Parliament and which cannot in the current state of things, exercise responsibilities. What is usually called the European Parliament is only a consultative assembly whose members are not MPs responsible to their constituents, but delegates who are appointed by the national parliaments and who are also very imperfectly representative of political movements. A real Parliament, in addition to legislative powers, has the power to control government action; but, at European level, there was still no government.

For all these reasons, the Assembly should not acquire powers, and all should recognise that national parliaments, if confronted with reality, would be loath to relinquish some of their constitutional prerogatives in favour of an institution which is no doubt respectable, but which lacks the accountability and representativeness which are attached to the notion of a Parliament. At any rate, that would surely be the reaction of the Belgian Parliament.

In conclusion, Mr Spaak said that it was not the Belgian delegation which hindered an agreement, but those who were attaching conditions foreign to the issue under discussion.

This statement of the Foreign Minister of Belgium—in many ways remarkable—has obviously sowed disarray among the German, Dutch and Italian delegations. In an attempt to mitigate its effect, Mr Hallstein[8] said that the date of 30 June, set out in Regulation No 25, was not mandatory. He cited many instances where the Council had not been able to meet the deadlines it had set for itself, without anyone disputing that. That said, continued Mr Hallstein, the Commission was guardian of the Treaty and would take the necessary steps for it to be applied. Messrs Luns, Fanfani and Schröder[9] then spoke along the same lines. Mr Werner[10] did of course

[8] President of the EEC Commission.
[9] Minister of Foreign affairs of Germany.
[10] Minister of Foreign affairs of Luxembourg.

support the Belgian Minister, recalling his proposal to decide now what was required by Regulation No 25 and to adjourn the rest to the discussions on the merger of the Communities.[11] However, as Mr Schröder expressed his astonishment at Mr Spaak's statement, the latter took again the floor to confirm and clarify what he had said earlier about the Strasbourg Assembly, before which—he said—he did not fear to expose his views. He concluded his statement by regretting that some of his colleagues allowed themselves be impressed by the motions voted in their national parliaments, to the point of wanting to improvise in haste new formulas regarding the powers of the European Parliamentary Assembly. This was particularly directed at Mr Schröder who—as a matter of fact—had just reported a request from the Bundestag.

In my view, there is no other publication which permits our understanding of the events just described as clearly as the following comment, published forty years later by Etienne Davignon, who had been Spaak's Head of Cabinet.[12] The comment is a particularly balanced one, which departs from the standard account according to which the crisis was due to the sole initiative of France's President Charles De Gaulle, who had opposed the Treaties establishing the European Communities during his retreat from active political life, but had accepted the obligations deriving from them when he became Prime Minister on 3 June 1958, six months and two days after the entry into force of the Rome treaties.

Davignon's account is as follows:[13]

[...] The origins of the crisis brought together a fundamental difference of views on the future of the European Community, combined with an ordinary disagreement regarding opposing economic and financial interests and what was, in the end, a fairly childish spat about the trappings of the prestige which the President of the Commission considered his due.

Mr Walter Hallstein and his Commission seized the opportunity which presented itself at the end of the first phase of the introduction of the common market to propose a new stage of integration which included an increase in powers for the European Parliament. The Commission asked the Council of Ministers simultaneously to consider this formal proposal and the proposal concerning the common agricultural policy. The calculation was that De Gaulle could not oppose this political initiative as long as he was bent on achieving the common agricultural policy.

In order to bolster his position, Mr Hallstein departed from the usual procedure: rather than sending the proposal first to the Council of Ministers and then to the Parliament, he informed the European Parliament of his initiative first. His choice of procedure was unfortunate and revealed a misreading of the situation. If previous experience had taught us anything, it was that General De Gaulle was not in the least worried by seemingly stronger opponents and was wont to react strongly to provocation.

France therefore rejected the suggestion of simultaneous discussions, citing the Community's legal obligation to establish a common agricultural policy before the introduction of qualified majority voting in the Council of Ministers.

From this moment forward the Commission's 'strong arm' tactics were doomed to failure; such was the shock and tension engendered among the Member States that it proved impossible to achieve a decision on the common agricultural policy within the allotted time.

On 5 July the French Foreign Minister sent the following telegram to his Permanent Representative:[14]

1. You shall say to the Secretary General of the Councils that we will not participate in the EEC Council sessions; these will therefore not take place. For your information, we also request the

[11] See section 2. [12] Etienne Davignon, 'Foreword', in Palayret et al. (eds) (n 1) 15–19.
[13] See ibid. [14] See (n 2) and (n 4).

cancellation of the ECSC Council meeting scheduled for 13 July. Finally, the Minister of Finance will not attend the meeting of the six finance ministers scheduled for July 19 in Stresa.

2. Meetings of the Permanent Representatives have no purpose; you shall therefore not attend them.

3. We will not send an observer to the negotiations that the Commission, on the basis of the Council's mandate, has engaged or proposes to engage with third countries. With particular regard to tariff negotiations currently underway in Geneva, you shall inform the Commission that, in the absence of an agricultural policy in the Community, it cannot make any commitment to our partners in GATT.

4. We will not be represented on committees that make general studies or prepare projects for the establishment of common policies such as groups of experts for the medium-term policy, those who study the harmonisation of tax and social legislation, etc. You shall inform the secretariats of the Commission and the Council.

5. As regards certain technical committees that are working under the aegis of the Commission or the Council, our position has not yet been finalised: this is particularly the case for agricultural management committees. At any rate, we could only participate in current business. Instructions on this point will be sent later.

On 6 July, a press release was issued by the Councils of the European Communities where the Secretary General of the Council, Christian Calmes, announced that he had received Mr Maurice Ulrich, Deputy Permanent Representative of France to the European Communities at the latter's request, and that Ulrich told him, for the attention of the other members of the Council, that Ambassador Jean-Marc Boegner had been 'invited to return to Paris' and that Ulrich was in charge of managing the Permanent representation. The ECSC meeting scheduled later in July was postponed at the request of Belgium and Luxembourg, as it would be unable to make any decisions.

The 'Empty Chair' of the French delegations indeed meant that not a single Council decision could be adopted or even prepared usefully. The crisis finished more than six months later on 29 January 1966, with the adoption of the 'Luxembourg Compromise' by the six foreign ministers.

Davignon's account of those six months is as follows:[15]

For a brief period it was envisaged that the Five should provisionally continue to sit regardless. Where decisions were to be taken, the absence of France would legally be considered as an abstention. However, good sense prevailed after the summer break and so, in an effort to find a way out of the crisis, a return to the negotiation table was in order.

The first priority was the fundamental problem which lay behind the crisis. The Five met to decide the basic position to be adopted for resuming negotiations, to which France had discreetly made known that it was favourably disposed.

A negotiating position was agreed and two principles were established:

- there was to be no question of amending the Treaty; and
- the negotiations were to be collective in nature, between the Five on one side, and France on the other.

[...]

Once th[e] procedural [issue of the format of the meeting] has been resolved, the experts turned their attention to the question of whether it was possible to define a Member State's 'vital interest', which, if invoked, would lead the Council to seek unanimity, even where it would be

[15] See Davignon (n 12).

legally possible to proceed to a vote. Squaring this particular circle was to remain a stumbling block and these discussions led to a total impasse.

Even though no solution was in sight, it proved necessary to take the risk of meeting, in the hope that the group dynamic, on the one hand, and the economic necessity of agreeing a common agricultural policy, on the other, would allow the participants to find a way out.

Cracks appeared in the common position of the Five and during the second meeting of the Council, the German Minister for Foreign Affairs and, more surprisingly, Mr Luns, the Dutch Foreign Minister, were to put forward proposals of a questionable nature as regards the original mandate.

As a last resort, the ministers put forward the 'Luxembourg Compromise'.

The Council press release on the arrangements for cooperation between the Council and the Commission (29 January 1966)[16] needs to be quoted in full, as only its first part will already be known to most readers:

On the majority voting procedure in the Council of the EEC

I. Where, in the event of decisions which may be taken by majority vote on a proposal from the Commission, very important interests of one or more partners are at stake, the members of the Council will endeavour, within a reasonable time, to reach solutions which can be adopted by all the members of the Council while respecting their mutual interests and those of the Community, in accordance with Article 2 of the Treaty.

II. With regard to the preceding paragraph, the French Delegation considers that, where very important interests are at stake, the discussion must be continued until unanimous agreement is reached.

III. The six delegations note that there is a difference of opinion on what should be done in the event of a failure to reach complete agreement.

IV. The six delegations nevertheless consider that that difference of opinion does not prevent the Community's work from being resumed in accordance with the normal procedure.

V. The Council members intend to adopt the following decisions by mutual agreement unanimously:

- Agricultural Financial Regulation,
- Addition to be made to the fruit and vegetable market organizations,
- Regulation on the organization of the sugar market,
- Regulation on the market organization for fat,
- Setting common prices: beef, rice, sugar, olive oil, oilseeds, milk.

On the other hand, it was recognized that all issues regarding the Kennedy round would be considered as 'very important'.

On the collaboration between the Council and Commission of the EEC

Close cooperation between the Council and the Commission is essential for the functioning and development of the Community.

[16] English text from CVCE.eu (n 2). However, curiously, that text is incomplete: I have therefore added the subtitles of the document, section V of the first part, and the note to the second part, translated from the publication by La Documentation française: 'Traités et documents relatifs à la CEE' (1984) 4756 *Notes & Etudes documentaires* 131.

In order to improve and strengthen this cooperation at every level, the Council considers that the following practical methods should be applied, these methods to be adopted by joint agreement on the basis of Article 162 of the EEC Treaty without prejudice to the respective powers and remits of the two Institutions.

1. Before adopting a proposal of particular importance, the Commission should establish the appropriate contacts with the governments of the Member States, through the Permanent Representatives, without that procedure compromising the right to propose legislation which the Commission derives from the Treaty.
2. Proposals and all other official documents addressed by the Commission to the Council and to the Member States may not be made public until the recipients have had formal notice of them and are in possession of the texts.

   The Official Journal should be adjusted so as to show clearly which acts are binding. The methods to be employed for publishing texts whose publication is required will be adopted as part of the current work on the reorganisation of the Official Journal.
3. The letters of credence of Heads of Missions of non-member states accredited to the Community will be presented jointly to the President of the Council and to the President of the Commission, meeting together for that purpose.
4. The Council and the Commission will inform each other rapidly and in full of any approaches relating to fundamental questions made to either institution by the representatives of non-member states.
5. Pursuant to Article 162, the Council and the Commission will consult each other on the advisability of, the procedure for, and the nature of, any links which the Commission might establish with international organisations pursuant to Article 229 of the Treaty.
6. Cooperation between the Council and the Commission on the Community's information policy, which was the subject of the Council's discussions on 24 September 1963, will be strengthened in such a way that the programme of the Press and Information Service will be drawn up and carried out jointly in accordance with procedures which are to be determined at a later date and which may include the establishment of an ad hoc body.
7. Under the financial regulations relating to the drawing up and implementation of the Communities' budgets, the Council and the Commission will determine the means for more effective control over the commitment, authorisation and implementation of Community expenditure.

Note: A paragraph on the discretion to be observed by members of the Commission in their public statements was adopted. However it was not published because this should be treated discreetly between the President of the Council of Ministers and the President of the new Commission.

A careful reading of this press release shows that the 'Luxembourg Compromise' was not only an 'agreement to disagree' on the sole issue of resorting to majority voting. Indeed, the text contains a commitment not to resort to majority voting on a number of issues which all pertain to the field of the CAP. Furthermore, the text establishes a gentleman's agreement on the future behaviour of the Commission in its relation to the Council. Distinct from the 'Decision of the Heads of State and Government, meeting within the European Council, concerning certain problems raised by Denmark on the treaty on European union' annexed to the conclusions of the Presidency of the European Council of Edinburgh of 11–12

December 1992,[17] which did not create new provisions with respect to those already established in the Maastricht Treaty and its Protocols, there was no attempt to elevate the Luxemburg compromise into a binding document: the text of the press release has never been transformed into a binding instrument of primary law, and not even into a formal declaration,[18] which could have been added to the Merger Treaty which was to enter into force shortly afterwards.

2. The context

As appears from the previous section, the issue which triggered the Empty Chair crisis was the EEC's CAP, and especially its funding.

The CAP had been a major element of the Common Market for France since the negotiations which led to the signature of the Rome treaties on 27 February 1957. As a matter of fact, the main French political negotiator Maurice Faure, who signed the Treaty as State Secretary (ie junior minister) for Foreign Affairs along with the Minister Christian Pineau, was only able secure the necessary majority for ratification in the *Assemblée nationale* by getting the support of the farmers' unions. It would be wrong however to think that only France was interested in a CAP; all six member states, including Germany, had on the whole converging interests in establishing such a common policy[19]—very differently from the UK if it had joined the EEC at that time. That said, Germany was more interested than France in the free movement of industrial goods. Italy, for which a CAP was equally a priority, wanted however to make the best use of the transitional period provided for in the EEC treaty in order to protect some sectors, such as pig farming, and that explains the strong Franco-Italian opposition on the issue in question on 30 June 1965.

As a matter of fact, the establishment of the CAP, which was provided for in the EEC treaty, had been lagging behind schedule for more than two years, despite France's insistence. Furthermore, the EEC Commissioner for agriculture Sicco Mansholt had already presented the Commission's plans for the CAP to the public: those plans were based on demographic projections which were very realistic but hardly acceptable from a national political perspective—including in France, where the voting power of farmers was extremely strong, both because of the size of the rural population and because a large proportion of the inhabitants of urban areas had strong family ties to rural areas. Mansholt had explained the Commission's plans in a typically Dutch manner, very direct and without understatement, thus making himself the bête noire of French politics, along with the President of the EEC Commission, Walter Hallstein, whom the French President Charles De Gaulle thoroughly disliked as a typical European federalist of the same stripe as Jean Monnet.

That said, there was much more at stake in 1965 than the financing rules for the CAP; especially as the Commission, Italy, the Netherlands, and Germany had tried to peg the issue of the CAP to the institutional issues discussed in other fora, not realizing what De Gaulle's reaction to attempted blackmail would be.

[17] [1992] OJ C348, 1.

[18] On declarations, see A Toth, 'The legal status of the declarations annexed to the Single European Act' (1986) 23 *Common Market Law Review* 803–12.

[19] See K Patel (ed), *Fertile Ground for Europe? The History of European Integration and the Common Agricultural Policy since 1945* (Nomos 2009) 7–23.

Davignon's comment was as follows:[20]

> The conflict to be resolved went far beyond the intermittent problems associated with agricultural policy. It centred, more fundamentally, on the question of the governance of the Community (to use the modern phrase). The legal basis of the Commission's activities and its independence were both in the balance, as was the introduction of a right of veto—even in those instances where the Treaty [of Rome] allowed voting by qualified majority.
>
> It is not over-dramatic to say that the crisis touched on the very nature of the institutions established by the Treaty. Put simply, were we to change tack and opt for a form of governance which was typically intergovernmental, assisted by a Commission at the beck and call of the governments and with a parliament which was more virtual than real? Or were we to keep in place the original model, i.e. an independent Commission, mandated to define the European common good and possessing the sole right of initiative, tasked with putting forward suitable policies for the Council of Ministers to consider, under the qualified majority voting system?

In order to understand such a comment some more of the contextual elements need to be recalled here.

First, the Treaty establishing a Single Council and a Single Commission for the European Communities, the 'Merger Treaty', had been signed in Brussels on 8 April 1965 after more than four years of negotiation;[21] the French National Assembly—where De Gaulle had majority support—had approved ratification on 17 June, and the Senate on 26 June—while the German Bundestag gave its approval on 30 June—with the comments that are reported in the cited telegram of the French Permanent Representative.

The technical issue to be solved by that Treaty was the unification of two of the four Community institutions: whereas the Rome Treaties already established a single Court of Justice and a single parliamentary Assembly, the Councils of the three Communities remained formally separated, although a single common Secretariat of the Councils had been established since 1960, and there were three different independent institutions: the ECSC High Authority, the EEC Commission, and the Euratom Commission.

The Dutch government had put forward a proposal for the necessary treaty reform in January 1961, but the French government had opposed the reform until July 1963, as De Gaulle's priority in European matters was his effort to organize a common external policy on an intergovernmental basis with the Fouchet Plans,[22] which called for a 'Union of the European peoples', with institutions comprising a Council—which was to meet at the Heads of State or government level at least every four months, and at the level of Foreign Ministers at least once in the intervening session—a European Parliament with consultative powers, and a European Political Commission consisting of senior officials of the Foreign Affairs ministries of each Member State, presided over by the representative of the Member State which presided over the Council, and for the same period. As the reaction of the other Member States was at best lukewarm, the project was laid to rest—and was reactivated thirty years later with Part III of the Single European Act of 1986.

On 14 January 1963 De Gaulle vetoed the continuation of negotiations with the UK, whose government had presented an application for accession to the Communities the year before. Most historians agree that De Gaulle then agreed to negotiate on the Merger Treaty

[20] See Davignon (n 12).

[21] See F Laursen, 'The 1965 Merger Treaty: The First Reform of the Founding European Community Treaties', in F Laursen (ed), *Designing the European Union—From Paris to Lisbon* (Palgrave 2012) 77–97.

[22] See the file from CVCE.eu (n 2), http://www.cvce.eu/en/collections/unit-content/-/unit/02bb76df-d066-4c08-a58a-d4686a3e68ff/a70e642a-8531-494e-94b2-e459383192c9, accessed 12 October 2016.

in order to appease the other five governments.[23] As Laursen puts it: '"rational" concerns about efficiency dominated the debate. Issues of democratic accountability and legitimacy were largely kept off the agenda, only to re-emerge as important issues in the following treaty reforms relating to the budget in 1970 and 1975 as well as the decision to have the European Parliament elected directly from 1979. But those later reforms happened after the departure of General De Gaulle from French politics in 1969'.[24]

Second, a few other elements need to be recalled to understand the broader context. De Gaulle's priority agenda from mid-1958 to mid-1962 was the war in Algeria and more generally decolonization, as he had realized that far from being a jewel in the Crown, the colonies were an impediment to resuming France's role at an international level. The end of the war in Algeria came with the Evian Accords signed on 18 March 1962. Six months later the Cuban missile crisis gave De Gaulle the opportunity to show to the US that France was a reliable ally. A precondition was thus met for the establishment of the new course in French foreign policy, which was conceived of as independent from the US—especially insofar as attempts to 'de'-escalate the Cold War were concerned—and distinct from the position of the five other EC Member States and of the UK, which followed the US positions. As already mentioned, De Gaulle opposed the UK's entry into the Communities, mainly because he thought that the British could not share a common vision of European integration—whether along his preferred lines according to the Fouchet plan, or along the lines of the existing treaties—due to their interests as the centre of the Commonwealth and as the closest ally of the US. This international context is essential to understand De Gaulle's position, especially regarding the Commission as conceived of by Monnet, and developed by the latter and Hallstein from the Schuman Declaration of 9 May 1950 onwards.

Last but not least, the internal political context should also be recalled. De Gaulle, who had led the provisional government supported by the three French major political forces—the Communists, Christian Democrats, and Socialists—in 1945–1946, had withdrawn from French politics at a time when the European Communities were being established and had been unable to contribute to the definition of what was to become the major line of French foreign policy in the 1950s, i.e. European integration. He returned to power in June 1958 with the support of most political parties because he was perceived as the only protection against a possible military coup from Algeria; indeed, once the supporters of 'French Algeria' discovered that De Gaulle was not their representative but wanted to put an end to colonial wars, such a military coup was attempted in 1962. All in all, it was only from 1963 on that De Gaulle had the means to develop his own political line—both internally and internationally—with a view to the election of December 1965 where he hoped to gain confirmation of general popular support—which he had got in 1962 in the referenda on the end of the Algerian war and on the reform of the election of the Head of State. The Christian Democrats and Socialists had withdrawn their support for De Gaulle's government in 1962—the former in protest against his veto of the British candidacy to accession. More broadly it should be stressed that there had never been a broad consensus in French politics on the issues of European integration: the Communists and Gaullists were opposed to supranational institutions, but the other centre-right and centre-left parties had no unanimous line: the Christian Democrats had been the main Gaullist party in 1945, only to discover that De Gaulle did not share most of their preferences, and certainly not their views on Europe; and the Socialists were quite divided on European issues too.

[23] Laursen (n 21) 89. [24] ibid, 95.

3. The outcomes and aftermath of the Empty Chair crisis

It is not that easy to discern whether and to what extent the Empty Chair crisis had a clearly observable impact on the evolution of European integration, as nicely put by Hayes and Wallace: 'Changing the Course of European Integration – or Not?'.[25] A few points need to be stressed.

First, the crisis did not lead to any treaty change. On the contrary, according to Davignon,[26] the Luxembourg compromise 'was not included in the "*acquis communautaire*"[27] that was sent to the new member states at the time of the first enlargement of the Community in 1973'.[28] It was only with the Lisbon Treaty in 2007 that the remote descendant of the Luxembourg compromise, i.e. the adapted form of the Ioannina compromise, was inserted into Protocol No 36, thus acquiring the status of primary law.

Second, it is not possible to assert that it was the Empty Chair crisis that impeded majority voting for thirty years. The Council rules of procedure did not include any provision enabling any member other than the President to call for a vote until the reform that was adopted in 1987 in view of the entry into force of the Single European Act; and the rotating presidency of the Council naturally led its Presidents to be very cautious in calling to vote—at the end of the day, every Member State would have some 'vital interests' which needed the sword of Damocles of a veto. It has also to be stressed that there had been a few majority votes before 1 July 1987. The clearest case was the one recorded by Davignon,[29] when in spring 1982 shortly before the Council was due to fix the prices for the forthcoming agriculture price-fixing round:

> Mrs Thatcher, the British Prime Minister announced that the United Kingdom would no longer participate in any Community decision until her objections had been dealt with to her satisfaction. The Commission and the other member states had reached agreement, but the British Minister of Agriculture refused to give his approval on account of the disagreement regarding the level of the UK contribution to the Community budget. The Commission and the Belgian Presidency then took the initiative by proposing that the measures should be adopted by majority vote, noting that there was no reason to invoke a 'vital interest' since the United Kingdom had accepted the price agreement. The decision was duly agreed—in spite of the angry protestations of the British Minister, who voted against, joined by his Danish counterpart, whose government wished to retain the implicit power of veto.

Another important case was the decision to call for an intergovernmental conference, which was adopted by simple majority voting in conformity with the relevant treaty provisions during the Milan European Council of June 1985, against the strenuous protests of the British representative.

Third, it is not in my view possible to find a link between the Empty Chair crisis and the attitude of French institutions regarding the application of EC law. True, the *Conseil d'Etat*, as supreme administrative court, refused to permit Community law to prevail over French statutory instruments with its ruling in the *Syndicat général des fabricants de semoules de*

[25] F Hayes and H Wallace in Laursen (n 21) 301. [26] Davignon (n 12) 18.

[27] On the notion of 'acquis communautaire', see C Delcourt, 'The *Acquis Communautaire*: Has the Concept Had its Day?' (2001) 38 *Common Market Law Review* 829, who also refers to scholarly debates about the Luxembourg compromise being part or not of the acquis, 856–7.

[28] The Danish government, however, seems to have used the existence of the Luxembourg compromise as an argument to demonstrate that accession to the Communities would not diminish the Kingdom's sovereignty, see J Pedersen, 'Denmark and European law, 1973–1998' in M Rasmussen (ed), *Towards a New History of European Law*, forthcoming.

[29] Davignon (n 12) 18.

France case of 1 March 1968;[30] however, this attitude never descended to outright defiance: formally, the *Conseil d'Etat* based its reasoning on the fact that it had no competence to review the validity of French legislation, and therefore could not find such legislation to be incompatible with Community law nor 'disapply' it in favour of the latter; it took twenty-one years for the *Conseil d'Etat* to change its position with its ruling in the *Nicolo* case of 20 October 1989.[31] However, in the meanwhile, the *Cour de Cassation*, the other French Supreme Court, fully accepted the principle of primacy as expressed in the ECJ's case law, with its ruling of 24 May 1975 in *Société cafés Jacques Vabre*[32] which followed the *Conseil constitutionnel's* ruling on the statute on 'voluntary termination of pregnancy' of 15 January 1975:[33] The *Conseil constitutionnel* derived from Article 55 of the Constitution[34] that ordinary courts should set aside statutory provisions which contravene international treaty obligations—which includes secondary law derived from the EC treaties. All in all, if the word 'defiance' is to be used to characterize the Empty Chair crisis, it must be understood as 'defiance' of the EEC Commission of the time, presided over by Walter Hallstein, and as 'defiance' of other governments, i.e. mainly those of Germany, Italy, and the Netherlands. Defiance of governments and Community institutions, thus. At any rate, what was at stake in the Empty Chair crisis was not the enforcement of EU law against a Member State: if anything, it was the issue of enforcing Regulation No 25 on financing the CAP against Italy and the Netherlands, which was brought into play by the French delegation. . . .

4. Lessons to be learnt

Looking back at the Empty Chair crisis, I think it is interesting to underline how extremely simplistic it is to speak of the position of a Member State—in our case France—as if it were a deeply-shared position. France has been an essential driving force in Europe's integration since 1951, i.e. as instigator of the Community method and of functionalism, with Monnet and his collaborators, and champion of this method with Robert Schuman and a number of others. But France was also the first Member which expressed and tried to conceptualize a method of European integration different to the Community method: De Gaulle's very peculiar strong intergovernmentalism, which was certainly very far from the European federalist's method, which could be ascribed to Italy and championed by Altiero Spinelli, but which was also far from the far-right euroscepticism of Le Pen, UKIP and others. It might be interesting to reflect on how both methods—the Monnet method and the Gaullist method—have been woven into the structure and sociology of the French state as well as into the French concepts and methods of public law. Suffices it to say that the *Conseil d'Etat* is both the institution which gave us Maurice Lagrange,[35] who invented the 'general

[30] Decision of 1 March 1968 in *Syndicat Général de Fabricants de Semoules de France* (1970) *Common Market Law Reports* 395.

[31] Decision of 20 October 1989, *Nicolo*, N° 108243 ECLI:FR:CEASS:1989:108243.19891020 (xxxx) *Common Market Law Reports* 173.

[32] Decision of 24 May 1975, *Directeur général des douanes c. Socété cafés Jacques Vabre*, N° 73-13.556, no ECLI classification (xxxx) *Common Market Law Reports* 336.

[33] Decision 74-54 DC of 15 January 1975: English translation available on the website of the Conseil constitutionnel.

[34] 'Treaties or agreements duly ratified or approved shall, upon publication, prevail over Acts of Parliament, subject, with respect to each agreement or treaty, to its application by the other party.'

[35] First advocate general of the ECJ, but also legal counsel to Jean Monnet in the drafting of the ECSC treaty.

principles common to Member States'[36] as a tool which was destined to serve the enforcement of the principles of direct applicability and primacy, and the institution which resisted primacy until its *Nicolo* judgment of 1989. It is also quite tempting to try to show how the *Conseil d'Etat* and the *Conseil Constitutionnel* recognized that they would strengthen their position in France and in Europe by being supportive of and collaborative with the ECJ/CJEU, as opposed to the present-day attitude of the *Zweiter Senat* of the *Bundesverfassungsgericht*.[37]

That said, what do these considerations have to do with the Empty Chair crisis, which was clearly confined to the year 1965, while the *Conseil d'Etat*'s first sign of 'defiance' towards the ECJ case law can at best be dated to March 1968, with its ruling *Syndicat général des fabricants de semoules de France*? Is the Empty Chair crisis, which is obviously connected with defiance, a case study on enforcement? No, because the treaty rules on qualified majority voting were not yet applicable in 1965.

Nonetheless, there are lessons to be learnt from the Empty Chair crisis which are worth recalling. Let us quote Davignon again:[38]

> One final paradox comes to mind: the months of the crisis were to lead to a curious reinforcement of the trust between the various players involved in finding the solution. The Five, under the direction of Sig. Colombo (Italian Minister of Finance) remained united throughout. France, under the direction of Couve de Murville, with the active participation of his Deputy Permanent Representative, Maurice Ulrich, were to be part of a solution which respected the position of their European partners. It is fair to say that in the end no real attempt was made to return to the situation that prevailed before the signing of the Rome Treaty. The new President of the European Commission, Jean Rey, uncompromisingly took on the role allotted to his institution by the Treaty.

The main lesson of the Empty Chair crisis is thus fully in line with the Schuman Declaration of 9 May 1950: 'Europe will not be made all at once, or according to a single plan. It will be built through concrete achievements which first create a de facto solidarity. *The coming together of the nations of Europe requires the elimination of the age-old opposition* [...]'. However, the Declaration went on in its next paragraph: 'With this aim in view, the French Government proposes that *action be taken immediately on one limited but decisive point*' (emphasis added). What is striking in both the Schuman Declaration and the Empty Chair crisis is that legal issues were secondary, because none of the legal rules now expressed in Articles 2 TEU on values and 3 TEU on objectives were under contention in this crisis. The only legal rule in question was the rule still set out in Article 4(3), second and third indents TEU, which was already present in Article 5 EEC:

> The Member States shall take any appropriate measure, general or particular, to ensure fulfilment of the obligations arising out of the Treaties or resulting from the acts of the institutions of the Union.
>
> The Member States shall facilitate the achievement of the Union's [Community's] tasks and refrain from any measure which could jeopardise the attainment of the Union's [Community's] objectives.

[36] In his conclusions in Joined Cases 7/56, 3/57 to 7/57 *Dineke Algera, Giacomo Cicconardi, Simone Couturaud, Ignazio Genuardi, Félicie Steichen v Common Assembly of the European Coal and Steel Community* [1957] ECLI: EU:C:1957:6.

[37] For further developments on the attitude of French courts, see J Ziller, 'European Union Law in the Jurisprudence of French Supreme courts: Europe-friendliness with a French Touch' (2015) 21(4) *European Public Law* 765.

[38] Davignon (n 12) 18–19.

In the weeks leading to the Empty Chair crisis, and during the crisis itself, the President of the Commission and the governments of four of the six Member States had been playing with fire; only the interests of staying together saw the Belgian and Luxembourg governments play the roles they did, and drove the diplomats who came to terms with the need to find a compromise and to use a typical soft law instrument: the press release issued on 26 January 1986, which is worth reading and reading again in its entirety, as we just did.

25

Questioning the Basic Values—Austria and Jörg Haider

*Konrad Lachmayer**

1. The end of the grand coalition or the EU 14's measures

a. The different layers of the narrative

The EU 14's measures against Austria in 2000 are an interesting episode in the history of European integration. From today's perspective we get the impression that the whole response from the EU Member States to the Austrian situation was a failure and history today shows that Jörg Haider never threatened democracy and the Rule of Law in Austria. This chapter argues against this understanding by not only retracing the core part of the story but also extending the perspectives on the year 2000 to the past and the future.

In the first section, the historical dimension of Haider's Freedom Party and the political relevance of the developments in the year 2000 are analysed from an Austrian perspective. Moreover, the EU 14's measures and the effects on European integration are considered. The chapter argues that the EU did not learn effectively from the measures and failed to develop proper institutional and procedural mechanisms to deal with the questioning of basic values by a Member State.

Section 2 looks critically back on the participation of the Freedom Party in the Austrian government and the effects of Jörg Haider to Rule of Law and democracy in Austria. In contrast to the overall impression that the Freedom party's participation in the government had no negative effects, the chapter argues that Haider's approach to ethnic minorities in Carinthia significantly threatened the Rule of Law in Austria and the Carinthian model of corruption still threatens Austrian democracy and the federal state budget today. The EU 14's scepticism about governmental participation can be justified in retrospect. The EU and its Member States, however, did not monitor the Austrian situation after the developments in 2000 and failed to acknowledge the real questioning of basic values by Jörg Haider. In conclusion, it is necessary for us to acknowledge the different layers of the narrative on the EU 14's measures. The full picture enables us to re-evaluate the EU 14's measures and to draw conclusions for future challenges to European integration by problematic political and legal developments in the Member States.

* Dr Konrad Lachmayer holds a research chair at the Institute for Legal Studies at the Hungarian Academy of Sciences (Centre for Social Sciences), is a research fellow at Durham Law School, and an independent researcher in Vienna (http://www.lachmayer.eu, accessed 12 October 2016). The author is grateful to the participants of the International Workshop 'Enforcing EU Law Against Recalcitrant Member States' at the WZB Berlin Social Science Center in July 2014, where a former version of the chapter has been presented. The research regarding this paper is funded by ERC Grant Agreement n. 312304 of Robert SCHÜTZE on Neo-Federalism (see http://www.federalism.eu).

b. The Austrian political situation at the end of the twentieth century

I. The elections in 1999

In 1999 the elections for the first chamber of parliament[1] had a clear winner, the Social Democrats (SPÖ) with 33.2 per cent, although the party had lost almost five per cent of its representation. The real media sensation that day, however, was the second place for Jörg Haider's Freedom Party (26.91 per cent), which was a five per cent gain on their result at the previous elections. The Freedom Party defeated the conservative People's Party (ÖVP), although the results were very close (the conservative People's Party also gained 26.9 per cent of the votes, but fell short by a small number). This result was the best ever achieved by Haider's Freedom Party (FPÖ) in parliamentary elections at a federal level and remains the Freedom Party's best result. Moreover, the Liberal Party (which had split from the Freedom Party in the 1990s) did not reach the necessary 4 per cent needed for representation in Parliament (3.7 per cent).[2]

II. The historical dimension I: From the 1920s to 1986

We should look back on Austrian political history to understand the historical dimension of these elections.[3]

After the end of the Second World War and with the re-establishment of the Austrian state in 1945, the will to cooperation between the two major parties (the conservative People's Party and the Social Democrats) to reconceptualize Austrian political culture was paramount. It is important to recall that in the 1920s there was a huge political divide between these two parties.[4] This conflict of the 1920s led to the conservative party being taken over in 1933 and the establishment of the Austro-fascist regime (1933–1938).[5] A short civil war in February 1934 resulted in a ban of the social democratic party and the labour movement.[6] The Austrian 'Anschluss' in 1938, the Nazi regime, and Second World War made the leading political figures in both parties realize that it was necessary to overcome this political divide and to work together to get the country back on its feet.[7]

The post-Second World War political situation was characterized by a grand coalition government, which had a huge majority of up to 85 per cent in Parliament. The Communist Party never played an important role in Parliament, while the predecessor of the Freedom Party, the so-called 'Federation of Independents' which saw itself as the representative of former Nazis, expellees, and repatriated prisoners of war, gained up to 10 per cent in Parliament.[8] For twenty years after the Second World War, the grand coalition government was actually a great political success, rebuilding the country and

[1] The Austrian parliament consists of two chambers: the first is the National Council (*Nationalrat*), which represents the Austrian people, and the second, the Federal Council (*Bundesrat*), which represents the states (*Länder*) and only has limited powers: see M Stelzer, *The Constitution of the Republic of Austria* (Hart 2011).

[2] See the official results available at: http://www.bmi.gv.at/cms/BMI_wahlen/nationalrat/NRW_1999.aspx, accessed 12 October 2016.

[3] DM Wineroither, 'Dal conflitto al consenso: l'evoluzione dell'idea di consociativismo', in M Cau and G Pallaver (eds), *Il peso della storia nella gestione del consenso politico. L'Europa del second dopoguerra* (Il Mulino 2013) 121–67.

[4] P Berger, *Kurze Geschichte Österreichs im 20. Jahrhundert* (2nd edn, Facultas Verlags- und Buchhandels AG 2008) 98–113.

[5] E Tálos, *Das austrofaschistische Herrschaftssystem. Österreich 1933–1938* (2nd edn, Lit Verlag 2013).

[6] Tálos (n 5) 49–52. [7] Berger (n 4) 232–41.

[8] A Pelinka, 'Die geänderte Funktionalität von Vergangenheit und Vergangenheitspolitik. Das Ende der Konkordanzdemokratie und die Verschiebung der Feindbilder' (2001) 30 *Österreichische Zeitschrift für Politikwissenschaft* 35, 36–7.

establishing solid governmental structures and political stability, and it was viewed as the reason behind the stability of this small neutral country between Western and Eastern Europe during the Cold War.[9] Political debates about the country's own Nazi past seemed unpleasant and not necessary.

The subsequent twenty years (1966–1986) were mainly characterized by absolute majorities of one party in government. The main era was that of the Kreisky's Social Democratic government in the 1970s, which significantly contributed to the social liberalization of the country.[10] In the late 1970s the Green Party movement was started and entered Parliament in 1986. Moreover, in the early 1970s and 1980s, the Social Democrats cooperated in a minority government (1970–1971) or formed a coalition government (1983–1986) with the Freedom Party, which enjoyed broad politically support. These twenty years—even without a grand coalition government—stabilized the consensus policy between the two big parties, which cooperated regularly (e.g. regarding constitutional amendments). The political consensus was also part of the 'social partnership' between the Chamber of Commerce and the Chamber of Labour, designed to avoid social conflicts. This social partnership was and remains an integral part of Austrian politics.[11]

III. The historical dimension II: From 1986 to 1999

1986 marked a turning point in Austrian politics in a number of ways. Two scandals had rocked the political landscape, with fierce political debate centring on the election of Kurt Waldheim as president of the Austrian Republic. During the election campaign, the media revealed that Waldheim, who had been UN Secretary General in the 1970s, might have participated in Nazi war crimes in the Second World War. He denied all involvement[12] and was still elected President of the Republic by the people. As a suspected war criminal, he was put on the US watch-list and isolated in foreign politics. In Austrian politics the Waldheim scandal marked a turning point in Austrian public and political debate about the country's own Nazi past.[13]

The second scandal, less serious but still relevant, resulted from Jörg Haider becoming party chairman of the Freedom Party in 1986. With the support of the German-national wing of the Freedom Party, he succeeded in replacing the existing party chairman, who was a minister in the coalition government at the time.[14] This internal takeover by Haider led to the dissolution of the government and re-elections. Moreover, the Social Democrats had refused to form a coalition government with the Freedom Party since 1986 (and still do today).[15] This political stance by the Social Democrats limited the possibilities for a

[9] Berger (n 4) 276–86.

[10] O Rathkolb, *Die paradoxe Republik. Österreich 1945–2015* (Paul Zsolnay 2015) 196–207.

[11] See A Pelinka and G Bischof (eds), *Austro-Corporatism: Past, Present, Future* (Transaction Publishers 1995); Rathkolb (n 10) 93–7.

[12] H Lackner, 'Zeitgeschichte: Pflicht und Dunkel. Zum Tod des Altbundespräsidenten Kurt Waldheim' (23 June 2007) *profil*, http://www.profil.at/home/zeitgeschichte-pflicht-dunkel-zum-tod-altbundespraesidenten-kurt-waldheim-176122, accessed 12 October 2016.

[13] W Manoschek, 'Die Wehrmacht und die Ausstellung "Vernichtungskrieg. Verbrechen der Wehrmacht 1941 bis 1944" als Thema österreichischer Vergangenheitspolitik' (2001) 30 *Österreichische Zeitschrift für Politikwissenschaft* 61, 62.

[14] Berger (n 4) 372–86.

[15] E Gotsbachner, 'Normalisierungsstrategien in der Rhetorik der FPÖ: Die politische Alchemie, Kritik in Unterstützung zu verwandeln' (2003) 32 *Österreichische Zeitschrift für Politikwissenschaft* 457, 459–66. In 2015 the Social Democratic Party decided to form a coalition government with the FPÖ at a state level in Burgenland, which led to a huge internal upset in the party and debates about cooperating with the Freedom Party in general.

government coalition to just two options in the 1990s—a grand coalition government and a coalition between the conservatives and Haider's Freedom Party.[16]

The re-elections in 1986 led to a grand coalition government, which actually lasted from 1986 to 2000. With no realistic political alternative on the scene in the 1990s, the grand coalition was viewed with increasing scepticism by the Austrian people. After the end of the Cold War and the Fall of the Berlin Wall, there were new challenges for the government to confront. The consensus policy since the Second World War had led to huge privileges for certain groups in society and the government seemed unable to instigate significant reforms, appearing to be focused on administering its own privileges. The result was a decline in acceptance of the grand coalition government (1986: Social Democrats 43.1 per cent; People's Party 41.3 per cent—1999: Social Democrats 33.15 per cent; People's Party 26.91 per cent).[17]

Jörg Haider's populist approach seemed to appeal to certain parts of the population[18] but his political success (1986: Freedom Party 9.7 per cent—1999: Freedom Party 26.91 per cent) also related to the decreasing electoral turnout at the national elections (1986: 90.5 per cent—1999: 80.4 per cent).[19] In 1989 Haider was elected State Governor in Carinthia but lost his post because of a trivializing statement he made about the Nazi regime in 1991.[20] In 1999, however, he was re-elected as State Governor by a much larger majority. In the meantime, he had been a Member of Parliament and as such the leader of the largest opposition party. By criticizing the deficits of the grand coalition government, he gained increasing political importance.[21] The Freedom Party also became known for its xenophobic and racist election campaigns.[22] A real and explicit rejection of extreme right-wing political thought was absent.[23] On the contrary, certain FPÖ politicians, including Jörg Haider, made use of references to National Socialism.[24] Moreover, Haider attracted attention with the use of defamatory political tactics and his authoritarian political concepts (e.g. to establish a 'Third Republic').[25]

During the decline of the grand coalition government and the political growth of Haider's Freedom Party, Austria joined the EU in 1995 after a referendum in June 1994 (66.6 per cent majority).[26]

[16] Other parties such as the Green Party or the Liberal Party were too small in any event. See F Plasser and PA Ulram, 'Parteien ohne Stammwähler? Zerfall der Parteienbindungen und Neuausrichtung des österreichischen Wahlverhaltens', in A Pelinka, F Plasser, and W Meixner (eds), *Die Zukunft der österreichischen* Demokratie (Signum Verlag 2000) 169, 193–4.

[17] M Gehler, 'Die zweite Republik – zwischen Konsens und Konflikz. Historischer Überblick (1945–2005)' in H Dachs et al. (eds), *Politik in Österreich. Das Handbuch* (Manz 2006) 42–44.

[18] A Murphy, 'The rise of the Austrian Freedom Party in the 1990s: A culturalist approach' (2004) 33 *Österreichische Zeitschrift für Politikwissenschaft* 297.

[19] The turnout of voters is high in general in Austria. Today it is 74.9 per cent for the National Council elections. See S Kritzinger, MS Lewis-Beck et al., *The Austrian Voter* (V & R unipress 2013).

[20] Berger (n 4) 408–11.

[21] R Picker, B Salfinger, and E Zeglovits, 'Aufstieg und Fall der FPÖ aus der Perspektive der Empirischen Wahlforschung: Eine Langzeitanalyse (1986–2004)' (2004) 33 *Österreichische Zeitschrift für Politikwissenschaft* 263, 264.

[22] Jörg Haider also exploited opportunities to sue journalists and academics for libel. Because the ordinary courts did not consider the freedom of expression properly, he was actually successful in drawing people into long court proceedings. See AJ Noll, 'Die Freiheit der Wissenschaft im Lichte der Strafjustiz' 29 (2000) *Österreichische Zeitschrift für Politikwissenschaft* 381; AJ Noll, 'Die Arbeit der Strafjustiz im Lichte der Wissenschaft' 29 (2001) *Österreichische Zeitschrift für Politikwissenschaft* 233.

[23] F Marquart, 'Rechtspopulismus im Wandel. Wahlplakate der FPÖ von 1978–2008' (2013) 42 *Österreichische Zeitschrift für Politikwissenschaft* 353.

[24] A Peham, 'Die zwei Seiten des Gemeinschaftsdünkels. Zum antisemitischen Gehalt freiheitlicher Identitätspolitik im Wandel' (2010) 39 *Österreichische Zeitschrift für Politikwissenschaft* 467.

[25] http://www.zeit.de/2000/07/200007.assheuer_haider_.xml, accessed 12 October 2016.

[26] S Griller, 'Verfassungsfragen der österreichischen EU-Mitgliedschaft' (1995) *Zeitschrift für Rechtsvergleichung* 89, 100, 107.

IV. Post-electoral dynamics in 1999

Returning to the starting point, the parliamentary elections in 1999, it seemed obvious that the Social Democrats as the strongest party in Parliament would start to negotiate a grand coalition government again as a coalition with the People's Party was the only political possibility. The Freedom Party had been excluded by the Social Democrats as a possible coalition partner since 1986 and the Green Party was too small to provide a majority in Parliament. At this point, Vice-Chancellor and leader of the People's Party Wolfgang Schüssel made his move. The party had just lost the elections and was—for the first time in history—only the third biggest in the Austrian Parliament. By offering Jörg Haider a deal, Schüssel was able to become Austrian chancellor after having had no realistic chance of otherwise obtaining this position after the elections.[27] Although he had lost the elections, he claimed the position of chancellor, because he was the only one who could give Haider's Freedom party the chance to join the government.[28] Moreover, Jörg Haider himself—although leader of the Freedom Party—never actually joined the government but remained as State Governor in Carinthia. Schüssel's political move was a shock for the Social Democrats and ended an era of fourteen years of grand coalition government.[29]

c. The EU 14's measures[30]

I. The 'sanctions'

The coalition government between the People's Party and the Freedom Party was viewed internally as a political trick by the conservatives, but never understood as a real threat to Austrian democracy as a whole.[31] Obviously, the Social Democratic Party was disappointed and a part of the post-Second World War consensus was broken by this move of the conservatives. Various negative reactions from civil society groups resulted, such as a civil society movement which demonstrated against the coalition government every Thursday. The demonstrations continued for more than two years, starting with several thousand participants in 2000 and declining to 100 participants. The President of the Austrian Republic, Thomas Klestil, was also not impressed by the form of the government coalition and expressed his concern at the appointment procedure.[32]

The international perception of the Austrian political shift was much more dramatic and the reaction far greater than in Austria. While Austrians perceived Haider's party as a right-

[27] F Schorkopf, *Die Maßnahmen der XIV EU-Mitgliedsstaaten gegen Österreich: Möglichkeiten und Grenzen einer 'streitbaren Demokratie' auf europäischer Ebene* (Springer 2002) 15–23.

[28] Rathkolb (n 10) 218–22.

[29] KR Luther, 'Die Freiheitliche Partei Österreichs (FPÖ) und das Bündnis Zukunft Österreich (BZÖ)', in Dachs et al. (eds) (n 17) 364, 370.

[30] W Sadurski, 'Adding bite to a bark: The Story of Article 7, E.U. Enlargement, and Jörg Haider' (2010) 16 *Columbia Journal of European Law* 385–426; M Happold, 'Fourteen Against One: The EU Member States Response to Freedom Party Participation in the Austrian Government' (2000) 49 *International and Comparative Law Quarterly* 953; HB Freeman, 'Austria: The 1999 Parliamentary Elections and the European Union Members' Sanctions' (2002) 25 *BC International and Comparative Law Review* 109. M Merlingen et al., 'The Right and the Righteous? European Norms, Domestic Politics and the Sanctions Against Austria' (2001) 39 *Journal of Common Market Studies* 59; C Leconte, 'The Fragility of the EU as a "Community of Values": Lessons from the Haider Affair' (2005) 28 *West European Politics* 620.

[31] In contrast to the Jobbik party in Hungary today, Jörg Haider's party did not have a similar agenda. The Freedom Party did not begin to organize paramilitary groups in Austria or regularly to refer to Nazi imagery, nor did it openly argue in favour of abolishing democracy. However, this should not disguise the fact that the Freedom Party repeatedly used xenophobic rhetoric in its politics, sympathized with the Nazi past and had far-right supporters and politicians in its party base as well as authoritarian political ideas.

[32] M Welan, 'Regierungssystem unter Druck? Die gewendete Republik' in Pelinka, Plasser, and Meixner (n 16), *Die Zukunft der österreichischen Demokratie* (Signum Verlag 2000) 335–60.

wing populist party,[33] international media understood Haider as far-right,[34] which might be true for some parts of the party base, but which was definitely an inadequate description of the Freedom's Party members in government.

EU Member States increasingly began to react to the Austrian government developments and instigated certain diplomatic measures.[35] Describing these diplomatic measures as EU 'sanctions' against Austria can be considered a political success of the Austrian government.[36] The Austrian government was thereby able to make political capital out of the European measures by declaring them European 'aggression' against Austria, and pointing to the lack of understanding of the Austrian situation. The role of Austria as a victim of international misinterpretation of the country's situation was familiar, since the Waldheim scandal had been perceived similarly in Austria and had led to the election of Waldheim as President of the Republic in 1986.[37]

On 31 January 2000, the EU Council Presidency stated on behalf of the EU fourteen Member States that:

> Governments of the XIV Member States will not promote or accept any official bilateral contacts at political level with an Austrian government integrating the FPÖ;
>
> There will be no support for Austrian candidates seeking positions in international organizations;
>
> Austrian Ambassadors in EU capitals will only be received at a technical level.[38]

This statement was supported by the European Commission on 1 February 2000. The Commission stressed that 'The Commission will continue to fulfil its duty as guardian of the provisions and values set down in the Treaties, which provide that the Union is founded on the principles of liberty, democracy, respect of human rights and fundamental freedoms and the rule of law, as set out notably in Articles 6 and 7 of the Treaty on European Union'. The Commission never accused Austria, however, of violating the principles of the EU regarding Article 6 TEU.[39] The EP enacted a resolution on 3 February 2000,[40] in which the EP also expressed its concern.

[33] A Pelinka, 'Die FPÖ in der vergleichenden Parteienforschung. Zur typologischen Einordnung der Freiheitlichen Partei Österreichs' (2002) 31 *Österreichische Zeitschrift für Politikwissenschaft* 281.

[34] http://www.theguardian.com/world/2000/feb/04/austria.ianblack, accessed 12 October 2016. See also the analysis by C Bärenreuter et al., 'Zur Außenwahrnehmung der FPÖ: Der Mediendiskurs in Frankreich, Israel und Schweden über die Nationalratswahlen und die Regierungsbildungen in den Jahren 1999/2000 und 2002/2003' (2004) 33 *Österreichische Zeitschrift für Politikwissenschaft* 327.

[35] See B Bugarič, 'Protecting Democracy inside the EU: On Article 7 TEU and the Hungarian Turn to Authoritarianism', in C Closa and D Kochenov (eds), *Reinforcing the Rule of Law Oversight in the European Union* (CUP 2016 (forthcoming)).

[36] R Winkler-Hermaden, 'Als Österreich der Buhmann der EU war' (21 January 2010) Der Standard, http://derstandard.at/1263705581215/EU-Sanktionen-Als-Oesterreich-der-Buhmann-der-EU-war, accessed 12 October 2016.

[37] Rathkolb (n 10) 405–9.

[38] http://www.cvce.eu/en/unit-content/-/unit/3941c9b0-d6c4-4a2c-b842-34fc75add012/409e145f-2ebf-48a6-afb9-8432cb672286/Resources#8a5857af-cf29-4f2d-93c9-8bfdd90e40c1_en&overlay, accessed 12 October 2016.

[39] See also Besselink in Chapter 18 of this volume.

[40] '1. Condemns all the insulting, xenophobic and racist statements issued by the leader of the Austrian Freedom Party, Jörg Haider, over many years;
2. Believes that the admission of the FPÖ into a coalition government legitimises the extreme right in Europe;
3. Believes that such sentiments can play no part in the evolution of the political relations between Austria and the EU and in particular alerts Mr Schüssel, as leader of ÖVP, to his profound political responsibility to ensure that any government which he might lead must respect the spirit and the letter of the fundamental principles of the Treaty;
4. Welcomes the timely political intent of the statement of the Portuguese Presidency in so far as it reiterates Member States' common concern to defend common European values as an act of necessary heightened vigilance;

The newly-established Austrian Government was not expecting this European reaction and certainly felt itself misunderstood. It issued a declaration, including a statement, which stressed the negative attitude towards National Socialism and the overall commitment to the European project.[41] The Austrian Commissioner Franz Fischler issued a defensive response on 4 February 2000.[42]

The EU 14's measures in early 2000 fulfilled its political purpose as an immediate reaction to the Austrian situation but not as a long-term strategy.[43] The design of the sanctions was criticized and turned out to be ineffective.[44] The EU Member States' symbolic policy was an important step towards the EU creating a reaction mechanism to respond to anti-democratic developments (even if their potential was over-estimated). It forced the Austrian government, however, to clarify its own position and did not leave much leeway to depart from European values in the first months of the government. In May 2000 Jörg Haider, who was not part of the government, even resigned as party leader and Vice-Chancellor Susanne Riess-Passer became the formal leader of the Freedom Party.[45]

The country's new role as victimized and misunderstood by Europe seemed to provide political capital for the new government among the Austrian population. Austrian resistance against the sanctions increased and the Austrian government started to block

5. Trusts in the large majority of the Austrian people who did not vote for the FPÖ, and calls on the Council and Commission to give their full support to activities in Austria organised to counter racist, xenophobic and anti-immigrant views;
6. Welcomes the timely political intent of the statement of the Commission in so far as it reiterates Member States' common concern to defend common European values as an act of necessary heightened vigilance;
7. Calls on the Commission and the Council, together with the Parliament, to monitor developments especially regarding racism and xenophobia in Austria and throughout Europe;
8. Calls on the Council and Commission to be prepared, in the event of the existence of a serious and persistent breach by whatever Member State of principles mentioned in Article 6(1) of the Treaty on European Union, to take action under Article 7 of this Treaty and, following Parliament's assent, to suspend that State's rights deriving from the application of this Treaty;'

[41] 'The Federal Government is aware that the Austrian people must energetically continue to build on their great achievements of the past and develop Austria's strengths still further. Austria accepts her responsibility arising out of the tragic history of the 20th century and the horrendous crimes of the National Socialist regime. Our country is facing up to the light and dark sides of its past and to the deeds of all Austrians, good and evil, as its responsibility. Nationalism, dictatorship, and intolerance brought war, xenophobia, bondage, racism, and mass murder. The singularity of the crimes of the Holocaust which are without precedent in history are an exhortation to permanent alertness against all forms of dictatorship and totalitarianism.

The European Union's project for a broad, democratic and prosperous Europe, to which the Federal Government is unconditionally committed, is the best guarantee against a repetition of this darkest chapter of Austrian history. The Federal Government is committed to a self-critical scrutiny of the National Socialist past. It will ensure unreserved clarification, exposure of the structures of injustice, and the transmission of this knowledge to coming generations as a warning for the future. As regards the question of forced labor under the National Socialist regime, the Federal Government will endeavor to arrive at objective solutions in the light of the intermediate report by the Austrian commission of historians, while having regard to the primary responsibility of the companies concerned', http://www.prnewswire.com/news-releases/declaration-responsibility-for-austria—a-future-in-the-heart-of-europe-72387372.html?$G1Ref, accessed 12 October 2016.

[42] 'But another part of my responsibility, as I see it, is to help defend Austria's well-deserved reputation abroad. Austria is not a stronghold of fascism, of intolerance, but a functioning democracy. My fellow-countrymen, as the sovereign people of an independent state, naturally have every right to make up their own democratic mind. That is what has taken place, whether one likes the results or not. What would not be acceptable is any policy running counter to the essential and fundamental values of the European Union', http://www.cvce.eu/en/unit-content/-/unit/3941c9b0-d6c4-4a2c-b842-34fc75add012/409e145f-2ebf-48a6-afb9-8432cb672286/Resources#a71a8afa-c3ba-4d09-915f-834f46f4e1a3_en&overlay, accessed 12 October 2016.

[43] For a legal analysis of the EU 14's measures, see W Hummer and W Obwexer, 'Österreich unter "EU-Quarantäne". Rechtsfragen der Einflussnahme auf die Regierungsbildung eines Mitgliedstaates' (2000) 3 *ecolex* 250.

[44] G Falkner, 'The EU14's 'Sanctions' Against Austria: Sense and Nonsense' (2001) 14 *CSA Review (Journal of the European Union Studies Association)* 14–15 (available at: http://www.demokratiezentrum.org, accessed 12 October 2016).

[45] It remained, however, clear, that Jörg Haider had strong informal power in the Freedom Party.

decision-making in the EU in June 2000.[46] The Portuguese EU Presidency, which had led the EU 14 reactions, developed a strategy for finding a way out of the situation towards the end of the Portuguese Presidency.[47]

II. Finding a way out

As the procedure applied by the fourteen EU Member States neither followed any legal process nor any political routine, it was necessary to develop a new political strategy to end these diplomatic measures. After the EU summit of Heads of Government in mid-June 2000, the Portuguese Presidency created the idea of an expert report by 'three wise persons'. At the request of the Portuguese Prime Minister, Mr António Guterres, the President of the ECtHR Lucius Wildhaber appointed three experts for the reporting committee: Jochen Frowein, Martti Ahtisaari, and Marcelino Oreja.[48] The expert committee spoke not only to official representatives from the government and the parliament (including opposition parties) but also to many representatives from civil societies. They produced their reports very quickly and presented them in early September 2000.[49]

The mandate of the expert committee included an examination of the 'Austrian Government's commitment to the common European values, in particular concerning the rights of minorities, refugees and immigrants' and 'the evolution of the political nature of the FPÖ'.[50] The report[51] referred to the case law of the ECtHR and other international treaties as benchmarks.

With regard to the protection of minorities, the report concluded: 'The Austrian legal system has established a specific protection for the national minorities living in Austria. This protection is recognized at constitutional level. The Austrian legal system protects the existing national minorities in Austria to a greater extent than such a protection exists in many other European Union countries'.[52] Furthermore, the report concluded that the Austrian government followed its predecessors and did not introduce new policies with regard to refugees and immigrants and that 'the present Austrian Government is committed to continue the fight against racism, anti-Semitism, discrimination and xenophobia in

[46] Sadurski (n 30) 404.

[47] F Schorkopf, *Die Maßnahmen der XIV EU-Mitgliedsstaaten gegen Österreich: Möglichkeiten und Grenzen einer 'streitbaren Demokratie' auf europäischer Ebene* (Springer 2002) 39–44

[48] The following information was provided about the three experts:

'Mr Ahtisaari was born in 1937. He was President of Finland from 1994 to 2000. Since 1 March 2000, he has been active in several international institutions and foundations. He is, among other things, Co-Chair of the New York based EastWest Institute and Chair of the Brussels based International Crisis Group. Previous posts include United Nations Commissioner for Namibia, Under Secretary General at the United Nations and Special Adviser to the International Conference on the Former Yugoslavia, Secretary of State at the Ministry of Foreign Affairs.

Professor Frowein, who was born in 1934, has been Director of the Max-Planck Institute for Comparative and Public Law and International Law in Heidelberg since 1981. He was a member of the European Commission of Human Rights from 1973 to 1993 and its Vice-President from 1981 to 1993. He has held numerous academic appointments and is President of the German Association of Public-Law Teachers.

Mr Oreja was born in 1935. From 1976 to 1980 he was Spanish Minister of Foreign Affairs. From 1984 to 1989 he was Secretary General of the Council of Europe. From 1994 to 1999 he was a member of the Commission of the European Communities and in 1996 he represented the European Commission at the Intergovernmental Conference on the amendment of the Maastricht Treaty'.

[49] See Press Release 524 of the ECtHR, 12 July 2000.

[50] See Press Release 491 of the ECtHR, 29 June 2000.

[51] See Report by Martti Ahtisaari et al. adopted in Paris on 8 September 2000.

[52] See Report (n 51) Recital 29.

Austria.' The report, however, criticized the electoral campaign of the Freedom Party and statements by Jörg Haider.[53]

The expert report concluded that the EU 14 measures had 'heightened awareness of the importance of the common European values, not only in Austria but also in other Member States', 'intensified the efforts by the Austrian Government', and 'also energized the civil society to defend these values'. However, the continuation of the measures was considered to be counterproductive and thus the report concluded that the measures should be ended as 'they have in some cases been wrongly understood as sanctions directed against Austrian citizens.'[54] The report led to the end of the EU 14 measures the same year, in 2000.

d. The role of the EU 14's measures in European integration history

I. The values debate

The EU 14's measures against Austria finally became part of the history of European integration, something which should not be underestimated. Although the 'sanctions' were short-lived, ending after eight months, they had an impact on the Austrian governmental situation (at least for a number of months). In Austria the debate on the governmental developments strengthened civil society activities but also created the impression that the Austrian situation had been a misunderstood. The government could not be attacked legally on the basis of Article 7 TEU and made its commitment to the Union clear. A long-term political impact on the Austrian situation was not very likely and resistance at the political level from the Austrian government increased. The EU 14's measures generated political attention but only a limited political effect.

From a European perspective, they changed the EU's approach towards value questions in the Member States and ultimately affected the EU's political memory. The EU measures will remain an important reference case on Member State defiance.[55] The diplomatic and bilateral measures of the EU 14 against Austria have been criticized as inadequate and possibly ineffective, but they can be understood within the bigger picture with regard to the values debate behind the EU measures and the relevance for EU constitutionalism and the European constitutional network, as well as constitutional pluralism in general.[56]

II. The European context in the year 2000

Various observations can be made if we consider the overall situation in the EU in the year 2000.

First, the most significant event in 2000 was the ratification of the EU Charter of Fundamental Rights. The European Council initiated a drafting process for the Charter

[53] 'There are reasons why the description of the FPÖ as a right wing populist party with radical elements appears to still be correct. The FPÖ has exploited and enforced xenophobic sentiments in campaigns. This has created an atmosphere in which openly expressed remarks against foreigners became acceptable, causing feelings of anxiety. It is our opinion that the Federal Government should be as ready as the Federal President to condemn xenophobic or defamatory expressions. The FPÖ has also tried to suppress criticism by the continuous use of libel procedures. In contradiction with past FPÖ behavior and statements made by other FPÖ officials, the Ministers of the FPÖ have by and large worked according to the Government's commitments in carrying out their governmental activities so far. It is not excluded that with the passing of time new directions within the party may emerge. Whether this will happen remains to be seen'.

[54] See Report (n 51) Recital 116.

[55] The EU has nevertheless created more refined measures to deal with defiance but is still struggling with a coherent and comprehensive approach.

[56] With regard to EU constitutional pluralism, see Avbelj in Chapter 3 of this volume.

at the Cologne summit in 1999, to be prepared by a European Convention, which met especially in the first half of 2000 and presented its findings in October 2000. The enactment of an EU Charter of Fundamental Rights—although non-binding—was an important part of the European integration process and can definitely be understood as a core process debating European values. While the EU measures against Austria were being established, the EU was discussing which rights should be considered in a common text protecting values for its citizens.[57] The EU values debate must be understood in the context of the establishment of a Union of human rights.[58]

Second, the European Convention (establishing a Charter of Fundamental Rights) was the starting point of a new process of European constitutionalism intended to create an ever-closer Union, in apparent readiness for a constitutional treaty to be developed in another Convention (for the Future of Europe) in the coming years.[59] The political dimension of the Union and the interrelation between the Union and its Member States became crucial to the future of the Union in 2000. If the Union wanted to pursue a path of constitutionalism as a Union concept, a reaction was needed to the Austrian political developments. The Austrian situation became a test case for the limits of constitutional pluralism in European integration. The constitutional paradigm[60] is based on a certain coherence, reflected in the values debate.

Third, the Eastern European enlargement of the Union was already in preparation. The negotiations had begun in 1997 and finished in 2002. The Amsterdam Treaty introduced in Article 7 TEU the possibility to address a serious and persistent breach of the European values. Moreover, Article 49 TEU was replaced and it was made clear that only a European state which respects the European principles enshrined in Article 6 TEU could apply for membership of the EU. The Austrian case should also be viewed in the context of the looming EU enlargement. It showed the willingness of the Member States of the EU to act unanimously to defend European values, and that the EU would not accept a significant deviation from European values. The Austrian case however also showed that the Article 7 TEU procedure was unable to address the issue properly.[61]

Fourth, the EU measures against Austria occurred in an important economic transition period for the EU. The single European currency, the EURO, had already been established in 1999, but was not introduced as a real currency until 2002.[62] The full impact of the European Economic Union remained unclear before the economic crisis revealed the deep bonds created by a common currency. However, Austria was part of the overall process and thus deeply integrated within the European Economic Union (although it had only been a Member State for five years at that time). Political developments in a Member State leading to instability also have potential impacts on the country's economic situation. Although this element was not crucial in 2000, the

[57] See E de Smijter and K Lenaerts, 'A 'Bill of Rights' for the European Union' (2001) 38 *Common Market Law Review* 273–300.

[58] Regarding the ambivalence towards the Charter, see A Wiener, 'The Constitutional Significance of the Charter of Fundamental Rights' (2001) 2 *German Law Journal*, https://static1.squarespace.com/static/56330ad3e4b0733dcc0c8495/t/56bc534f1d07c01d7d30ad03/1455182671904/GLJ_Vol_02_No_18_Wiener.pdf, accessed 12 October 2016.

[59] See http://europa.eu/scadplus/european_convention/introduction_en.htm, accessed 12 October 2016; see also J Bruton, 'The Convention on the Future of Europe and its Draft Constitution for Europe' (2004) 15 *Irish Studies in International Affairs* 57–72.

[60] N Krisch, *Beyond Constitutionalism. A Pluralist Structure of Postnational Law* (OUP 2010).

[61] Sadurski (n 30).

[62] See http://eur-lex.europa.eu/legal-content/EN/TXT/?qid=1433717220275&uri=URISERV:ec0015, accessed 12 October 2016.

relevance of the interrelation between politics and economics regarding the values debate had become much more important in recent years.[63]

Fifth, the Austrian case occurred before 9/11 and the new security paradigm, which shook constitutional values across Europe.[64] European eyes were still focused on Europe, especially on increasing European integration and enlarging the Union.[65] In the post-9/11 paradigm the Austrian developments would possibly have been more relativized than in 2000. The Austrian threat might have been perceived as less relevant.

In conclusion, the values debate started by the Member States of the EU was a crucial part of the European integration process in 2000 and can be understood in the wider context of European integration at that time. The Austrian case exemplified but also sharpened parts of these debates and ultimately affected future steps towards European integration to a certain extent.

III. The impact of the EU 14's measures

The impact of the EU 14's measures on the European integration process were manifold.[66] To begin with, it is worth considering the experts' final recommendations in their report, which looked beyond the Austrian situation:

> We strongly recommend the development of a mechanism within the EU to monitor and evaluate the commitment and performance of individual Member States with respect to the common European values. We are therefore in favour of the introduction of preventive and monitoring procedures into Article 7 of the EU Treaty, so that a situation similar to the current situation in Austria would be dealt with within the EU from the very start. This would underline the fundamental commitment of the EU to common European values. Such a mechanism would also allow from the beginning an open and non-confrontational dialogue with the Member State concerned.
>
> Through this monitoring procedure the Council should be able to follow up, evaluate and take actions concerning the development of a specific situation in an EU country. Besides this monitoring procedure, a system of prevention should be put in place which would react through information and educational measures to any forms of direct or indirect discrimination or xenophobia.
>
> It is important that institutional arrangements within the Community institutions for furthering these aims are established. These may include the creation of a Human Rights office within the Council reporting to the European Council; the appointment within the Commission of a Commissioner responsible for human rights issues; and, particularly, the extension of the activities, budget, and status of the existing EU Observatory on racism and xenophobia, which is based in Vienna, in order to make possible the establishment of a full EU Agency on Human Rights.[67]

As a result of the EU 14 mechanism, the Union adopted a new Article 7 TEU mechanism with the Nice Treaty.[68] The suspension of the rights mechanism, which was introduced in the Amsterdam Treaty, was re-established in a more sophisticated and differentiated form.[69] Although the amended version of Article 7 TEU establishes more procedural

[63] See Maurice Adams, Federico Fabbrini, and Pierre Larouche (eds), *The Constitutionalization of European Budgetary Constraints* (Hart 2014).

[64] See e.g. C Murphy, *EU Counter-Terrorism: Pre-emption & Rule of Law* (Hart 2012).

[65] See the challenges faced by the EU in counter-terrorism: Murphy (n 64).

[66] A Williams, EU human rights policy and the convention on the future of Europe: a failure of design? (2003) 28 *European Law Review* 794–813.

[67] Report (n 51) Recitals 117–19.

[68] See the developments with regard to Art 7 TEU, Besselink (n 39).

[69] Sadurski (n 30) 385–426.

steps, it remained an emergency concept, giving the Union a tool to stop the violation of the Union's values, but only in very extreme situations and with complete political alignment among the Member States. The EU 14's measures against Austria had an impact on the TEU, but it only refined the emergency process instead of developing softer and more relevant monitoring procedures at the Treaty level. The Lisbon Treaty also missed the opportunity of creating explicit concepts to address the Union's concern with values and Member State defiance.

The expert committee furthermore recommended a monitoring procedure, which was actually introduced as a 'Network of Experts on Fundamental Rights'.[70] Based on a recommendation from the EP, the Network was established by the European Commission to monitor Member States with respect to their compliance with Article 7 TEU. The analysis of the Austrian country reports shows that the network focused on the provisions of the CFR and, within its scope, on the relevant case law in the country. The result is that, from an Austrian perspective, minority rights were only briefly considered and deeper structural problems with regard to the Rule of Law were not acknowledged.[71] Moreover, the fundamental rights perspective was not broad enough and only partly covered the European values considered in Article 7 TEU. With the establishment of the EU FRA in 2007, the network was re-established in the Agency. However, as Gráinne de Burca rightly criticizes, the newly established FRA no longer served the same function. Instead of monitoring the Member States with regard to Article 7 TEU, the FRA is supposed to provide assistance to the Member States in implementing Union Law.[72] The monitoring of Member States is thus not sufficiently provided for. In conclusion, the effect of the EU 14's measures was monitoring steps in the right directions. The monitoring reports, however, did not fully serve their purpose and were again limited after the establishment of the FRA.

The third expert committee recommendation was the establishment of a fully fledged FRA, which was introduced in 2007.[73] The FRA replaced the existing European Monitoring Centre on Racism and Xenophobia and has been criticized for various reasons, such as its limited mandate and its limited added value. It took quite a while to improve the Monitoring Centre and it is true that the competences of the FRA—especially in comparison to other EU agencies such as Frontex, Europol, or the European Food Safety Authority—are quite limited. Although some of the recommended extensions of its activities, budget, and status were realized through the establishment of the FRA, it is precisely 'the activities, budget and status' which continued to need extension to create a full partnership with the Member States in terms of monitoring and the interaction with Article 7 TEU.[74] The EU 14's measures contributed to the establishment of the FRA, though only half-heartedly.

In conclusion, the EU 14's measures against Austria and the ensuing actions, especially the expert report, had an impact on the development of European integration. Although most of the measures introduced in the ensuing years would perhaps have been established

[70] http://ec.europa.eu/justice/fundamental-rights/document/index_en.htm, accessed 12 October 2016.

[71] See eg http://ec.europa.eu/justice/fundamental-rights/files/cfr_cdf_synthesisrep2003_en.pdf, accessed 12 October 2016; http://ec.europa.eu/justice/fundamental-rights/files/cfr_cdf_synthrep_2004_en.pdf, accessed 12 October 2016.

[72] Gráinne de Búrca, 'The Evolution of EU Human Rights Law', in Paul Craig and Gráinne de Búrca (eds.), *The Evolution of EU Law* (2nd ed, OUP 2011) 465, 484–5.

[73] Council Regulation No 168/2007 of 15 February 2007 establishing a European Union Agency for Fundamental Rights [2007] OJ L53/1.

[74] See in an optimistic perspective, A von Bogdandy and J von Bernstorff, 'The EU Fundamental Rights Agency within the European and international human rights architecture: The legal framework and some unsettled issues in a new field of administrative law' (2009) 46 *Common Market Law Review* 1035.

anyway without the specific Austrian experience, it seems clear that the Austrian example contributed to certain developments. Judgment of these developments, however, cannot be overly enthusiastic: the Article 7 TEU procedure remained too rigid and impractical in political terms. The monitoring procedure, which had the biggest potential, was first too narrow in its scope from the very beginning, and second was converted into something different with the establishment of the FRA. Finally, the FRA itself was always limited and was never established with significant power or influence.

The results of this limited institutional learning became obvious in the EU's strategy for dealing with the Orbán government in 2010.[75] Although the EU had already developed more possibilities and strategies, it was not possible to form the impression that the Union was prepared with relevant institutions and effective procedures to react adequately to the Hungarian situation.[76] On the contrary, as with the Austrian situation, the EU had to create new political processes to deal with the Hungarian challenge from a European perspective. It was more than telling that the Venice Commission was ready to provide support while the European institutions seemed less focused.[77]

2. The story behind the story: evaluating the coalition government 2000–2006

a. Ignored Austrian developments

The EU response to the Austrian situation in 2000 was mainly based on the media reports on Jörg Haider and his Freedom Party and involved the election campaign in the reasoning of the report of the 'three wise men'. Moreover, it considered the information provided by Austrian NGOs and politicians about the threat Jörg Haider would pose for constitutional values in Austria. In the end, the EU measures seemed to be overambitious but missed their political target. Besides the EU 14's concrete measures and their limited impact on European integration with regard to European values, the concrete Austrian situation no longer seemed of particular importance. The EU 14's measures and their cessation in 2000 seemed to make it unnecessary to evaluate what happened in Austria, when the Freedom Party was part of the Austrian government.

It is however possible today to look back at the coalition government from 2000 to 2006 and to evaluate if the fears relating to the participation of the Freedom Party in the national government were realistic.[78] As a first approach, we could argue that Austria remained a democracy and the Rule of Law was and remains in force. I would like to argue that the coalition government indeed threatened the Austrian Rule of Law and the internal market of the EU significantly, a fact which has been overlooked by the Union since 2001.

After the EU measures were lifted, the EU was no longer concerned about the situation in Austria, since the matter seemed too closed and completed. There was still cause for concern and the EU (or its Member States) should not have been frustrated by the (possibly erroneous) form of the measures taken but rather concerned about the situation in

[75] For details with regard to the Hungarian situation, see Szente in Chapter 26 of this volume; see also R Uitz, 'Can you tell when an illiberal democracy is in the making?' (2015) 13 *International Journal on Constitutional Law* 279.

[76] See P Bard, The Hungarian Fundamental Law and related constitutional changes 2010–2013 (2013) *Revue des Affaires Européennes* 457–72.

[77] See, regarding the new Hungarian Basic Law, A Jakab and P Sonnevend, 'Continuity with Deficiencies: The New Basic Law of Hungary' (2013) 9 *European Constitutional Law Review* 102.

[78] See D Wineroither, *Kanzlermacht—Machtkanzler? Die Regierung Schüssel im historischen und internationalen Vergleich* (LIT 2009).

Austria. If consider the subsequent events in Austrian politics and economics more closely, we will clearly see that the questioning of EU values cannot be analysed on a point-by-point basis but must be considered from a permanent, holistic level.

b. The coalition government

After the lifting of the EU sanctions, the Austrian government seemed to return to business as usual. Jörg Haider remained in Carinthia and the Federal Government tried to return to a state of normalcy.[79] However, Haider did not prove to be a stable partner in the coalition government. Two ministers from the Freedom Party had already been replaced in 2000. The internal conflicts within the Freedom Party (moderate members of parliament versus Jörg Haider and others) led to the resignation of all the Freedom Party members of the government (the so-called Knittelfeld Putsch).[80] The internal struggles within the Freedom Party led to the withdrawal of all FPÖ members of government in 2002 and finally to the dissolution of Parliament. The following re-elections (only two years after the great debate on the EU measures) led to a huge loss of votes for the Freedom Party, which only got 10 per cent (2000: 26.91 per cent), while the People's Party reached a high of 42.3 per cent (2000: 26.91 per cent).[81] Federal Chancellor Schüssel continued his coalition with Haider's Freedom Party, but was already much more powerful than in 2000.[82]

The internal conflicts of the Freedom Party were far from over and in 2005 the party finally split into a more moderate right-wing populist part including Jörg Haider and a more extreme part. Haider founded a new party, which he called the 'Alliance for the Future of Austria'.[83] The more extreme right part remained as the Freedom Party under a new party leader called Heinz-Christian Strache, who remains party leader today. The split of the party affected every party level in all states and weakened both parts significantly over the following years.

There was no possibility for the conservative party to form a coalition with the new Haider party, which had gained only 4.11 per cent of the votes, nor with the old Freedom Party, which had gained 11 per cent, after the following elections in 2006. The Social Democrats won this election (35.34 per cent) and re-established the grand coalition with the conservatives (34.33 per cent).[84] Schüssel resigned as party leader and the experiment of the black-blue coalition between the People's Party and the Freedom Party (Alliance for the Future of Austria) was finished.

c. Threatening the Rule of Law: ethnic minorities in Carinthia

We need look more closely to see the cracks beneath the surface. The following narratives are deeply linked to Jörg Haider and Carinthia, but also are also relevantly connected to the Austrian government in which Haider's Freedom Party was involved. The first narrative

[79] Luther (n 29) 364, 370.

[80] M Gehler, 'Die zweite Republik – zwischen Konsens und Konflikt. Historischer Überblick (1945–2005)' in Dachs et al. (eds) (n 17) 47–51.

[81] R Picker, B Salfinger and E Zeglovits, 'Aufstieg und Fall der FPÖ aus der Perspektive der Empirischen Wahlforschung: Eine Langzeitanalyse (1986–2004)' (2004) 33 *Österreichische Zeitschrift für Politikwissenschaft* 263, 267.

[82] http://www.bmi.gv.at/cms/BMI_wahlen/nationalrat/2002/Broschuere.aspx, accessed 12 October 2016.

[83] Luther (n 29).

[84] http://www.bmi.gv.at/cms/BMI_wahlen/nationalrat/2006/start.aspx, accessed 12 October 2016.

relates to the Slovenian ethnic minority in Carinthia.[85] The tensions in Carinthia actually go back to the Carinthian plebiscite of 1920 after the First World War when according to the Treaty of Saint-Germain the border with the newly established Yugoslavia in Southern Carinthia was to be determined by plebiscite, in which a majority of the Slovenian Carinthians decided to remain with Austria.[86] The conflict escalated in the 1970s when, in 1972, Carinthians damaged bilingual road signs written in German and Slovenian.[87] Groups of German-nationalists and former National Socialists took to destroying bilingual road signs and other infrastructure. Road signs which were repaired were removed again. The statute requiring bilingual signs was ultimately not enforced.[88]

In 2001 the Austrian Constitutional Court reached a new decision with regard to bilingual road signs.[89] The case considered the re-evaluation of the 25 per cent rule (lowered to 10 per cent on the basis of Treaty of Vienna from 1955, which does not specify a percentage),[90] which regarded the percentage that a minority would have to represent in a population to require the erection of bilingual signs. Using newly-elaborated reasoning the Court argued that it was necessary from the perspective of international law and constitutional minority rights to erect bilingual road signs in more than 200 municipalities.[91] Jörg Haider as State Governor of Carinthia started a political campaign against this judgment, not only breaking the law but also attacking the Constitutional Court, whose authority had never been politically questioned in the Second Republic in such a manner.[92] Haider savagely attacked the President of the Constitutional Court, Ludwig Adamovich, publically.[93] The Constitutional Court actually reviewed the possibility of starting impeachment proceedings against its own president,[94] not to concede anything to Haider, but rather to create a forum to formally reject Haider's accusations.

Haider toyed with the judgment's enforcement using various legal arguments, such as by rearranging a village's signage and arguing that the signs were therefore not affected by the judgment, or he erected very small signs in Slovenian.[95] The result was an extensive body of case law for the Constitutional Court, initiated by the representatives of the Slovenian minority in Carinthia and the Austrian Ombudsman.[96] Haider's activities were politically

[85] J Marko, 'FOCUS: The Constitutional Framework of Minority Protection in Austria – Some Introductory Comments' (2008) *Vienna Journal on International Constitutional Law* 124–130.

[86] C Fräss-Ehrfeld, 'Zur Historie des Ortstafelstreits im Kontext der Kärntner Volksgruppenfrage' (2011) 4 *Europäisches Journal für Minderheitsfragen* 161.

[87] A Bender and K Lachmayer, 'Kampf ums Recht: Minderheitenschutz, Rechtsstaat und Verfassungsgerichtshof', in A Masát et al. (eds), *Der Donauraum in Europa* (Nomos Verlagsgesellschaft 2013) 336, 339.

[88] P Gstettner, '"... wo alle Macht vom Volk ausgeht". Eine nachhaltige Verhinderung. Zur Mikropolitik rund um den "Ortstafelsturm", in Kärnten' (2004) 33 *Österreichische Zeitschrift für Politikwissenschaft* 81.

[89] G Holzinger, 'Die Rechte der Volksgruppen in der Rechtsprechung des Verfassungsgerichtshofes' in B-C Funk et al. (eds), *Der Rechtsstaat vor neuen Herausforderungen. Festschrift Adamovich* (Verlag Österreich 2002) 193; J Marko, 'System des österreichischen Volksgruppenrechts und Minderheitenschutzes', in G Heißl (eds), *Handbuch Menschenrechte* (Facultas Verlagsgesellschaft 2009) 421, 432–5.

[90] Art 7 (3) Treaty of Vienna 1955: 'In the administrative and judicial districts of Carinthia, Burgenland and Styria, where there are Slovene, Croat or mixed populations, the Slovene or Croat language shall be accepted as an official language in addition to German. *In such districts topographical terminology and inscriptions shall be in the Slovene or Croat language as well as in German*' (emphasis added).

[91] Austrian Constitutional Court, 13 December 2001, VfSlg 16.404/2001; see M Salamun, 'Minority rights of the Slovene minority in Carinthia: Placement of bilingual signs for municipal units (Ortschaften) with 10 per cent (previously 25 per cent) minority population (2008) *Vienna Journal on International Constitutional Law* 135.

[92] Bender and Lachmayer (n 87) 336, 340–1.

[93] A Otti and MK Schulze, 'Die Gewalten auf Konfrontationskurs? Eine Fallstudie über das Verhältnis von VfGH und Regierung in den Anfängen der Wende' (2004) 33 *Österreichische Zeitschrift für Politikwissenschaft* 67, 72–5.

[94] See Austrian Constitutional Court, 6 January 2002, VfSlg 16.408/2002.

[95] See B-C Funk, 'Kärntner Ortstafelkonflikt – Zulässigkeit einer Volksbefragung?' (2006) *migraLex* 74.

[96] See V Leskovar, 'Rights of minorities and place name signs' (2008) *Vienna Journal on International Constitutional Law* 141; A Klingenbrunner, 'Bilingual Topography: Differences between German and Slovenian Place Names in Size are Unconstitutional' (2008) *Vienna Journal on International Constitutional Law* 146.

supported at least to a certain extent by ministers in the Federal Government who were members of the Freedom Party. Moreover, the Minister of Justice was a member of the Freedom Party and could prohibit any measures initiated by public prosecutors; the Minister for Transport, who could also have been involved in the installation of bilingual road signs, was also a member of the Freedom Party. Jörg Haider never enforced the judgment of the Constitutional Court before his death in 2008.

To conclude, the case of the bilingual road signs clearly showed that Haider was not willing to accept the Rule of Law when it did not suit his political strategies. He had the power and support of the Federal Government, which did not intervene, and things became particularly dramatic when Haider attacked the Constitutional Court, which represents a fundamental institution of the Austrian Constitution. It was possible to avert a deeper political crisis, but the non-enforcement of the judgment remained a legal and political statement by Haider which should have been relevant to the EU for two reasons: first, the clear violation of the Rule of Law, and second because of the negative effects on minority rights.[97] Although there was no direct link to EU competences, this situation clearly related to European values as stated in Article 6 TEU.[98] The topic of Austria's Freedom Party, however, seemed to be dead after the EU 14's measures in 2000 and the Austrian government seemed to be well-established from a European perspective.[99]

Finally, after Jörg Haider's death, the Federal Government and the newly elected state governor of Carinthia found a solution for the matter and established bilingual road signs in 164 villages. The Slovenian minority agreed to the compromise.[100] The compromise was implemented as a constitutional provision in the Austrian constitution, making it impossible for the Austrian Constitutional Court to review it. The judgment of 2001, which demanded bilingual road signs in more than 200 villages, was therefore never fully enforced in Austria.

d. Threatening the internal market: corruption

Haider and his Freedom Party, as well as his Alliance for the Future of Austria party, had another impact on the Austrian state which posed an even greater threat to the Rule of Law. The Haider System managed to undermine the country at its foundations without any significant visible effect between 2000 and 2006, but the dramatic results of his influence are more evident today. Haider's *modus operandi* as state governor, along with some members of the government (including the Minister of Finance), was based on corruption.[101] Particularly after the end of the participation of Haider's party in government in 2006, the number of corruption scandals was enormous and could not be compared to anything which had come before.

[97] See D Kochenov, 'A Summary of Contradictions: An Outline of the EU's Main Internal and External Approaches to Ethnic Minority Protection' (2008) 31 *Boston College International and Comparative Law Review* 1, 18.

[98] See, with regard to EU competences in minority policies, A Bender-Säbelkampf, *Demokratie der ethnischen Minderheiten* (Facultas Verlagsgesellschaft 2012) 127–59.

[99] The usual understanding of this sanction is that the Freedom Party committed no human rights violation, but there were concerns about Jörg Haider's political statements about national socialism; see Bugarič (n 35).

[100] See the amendment of the Ethnic Group Act, *Federal Law Gazette* I 46/2011; see also M Hiesel, 'Die Lösung des Kärntner Ortstafelstreites' (2011) *Europäisches Journal für Minderheitsfragen* 173; D Kolonovits, 'Die "Ortstafellösung" und Amtssprachenregelung in der Volksgruppengesetz-Novelle, BGBl I 2011/46' (2011) *migraLex* 62; Bender and Lachmayer (n 87) 336, 342–4.

[101] See http://derstandard.at/1342947561584/Steuerberater-Birnbacher-erweitert-Gestaendnis, accessed 12 October 2016.

The biggest scandal, which could have affected the European Monetary Union, is the so-called Hypo Scandal,[102] regarding the former state bank of Carinthia. Haider used this bank as his private slush fund to finance several prestigious projects and to finance his state party. The Hypo Alpe-Adria bank was found to have been secured by the state of Carinthia for liabilities of EUR 20 billion (!), although the overall annual state budget was only EUR 2 billion. Haider ultimately sold the bank to the Bavarian State Bank, which persuaded the Austrian government to renationalize it during the financial crisis in 2009 because of the Carinthian state liability and the overall effects on the banking landscape in Austria.

The Hypo scandal is the biggest finance scandal in Austrian criminal history. It includes falsification of balance sheets, breach of trust, corruption, and harmful speculation on international markets.[103] It was part of Haider's financing strategy and also had connections to authoritarian regimes, such as Gaddafi's regime in Libya. Between 2000 and 2006, the bank was able to act without any significant control and it was only the financial crisis which revealed the real extent of the Hypo disaster. Austrian Courts and a parliamentary commission of enquiry were busy trying to establish the political, economic, and legal background to the scandal.[104]

Although the Hypo scandal is the biggest, it was not the only one. Other scandals involved the website of the Minister of Finance,[105] government real-estate projects (the BUWOG Scandal—privatization of apartments owned by the government),[106] and the Telekom Scandal (involving illegal funding of political parties).[107]

To conclude, Haider ignored the legal and economic constraints of his position. Moreover, members of the government who belonged to Haider's party were also involved in various corruption scandals, though only partly convicted of this. First, this attitude threatened the Rule of Law in the country. The need to obey the law took a back seat to unjust enrichment. The corruption angle, however, has created a situation which the whole Federation will have to deal with for years. The EU as monetary, banking, and economic Union has had to deal with the affair and will have to contribute to stabilizing the Austrian economy.

e. European possibilities

In both cases, it is possible to argue that for competence reasons the EU was unable to react to developments regarding minority rights in Carinthia and that all the corruption affairs only indirectly affect the EU's internal market. Moreover, the EU could not have foreseen all these developments in 2000. The EU 14's measures could only react to developments in the past.

[102] See http://diepresse.com/home/wirtschaft/economist/4610315/Hypo_Versagen-auf-allen-Linien, accessed 12 October 2016.

[103] See Bericht der unabhängigen Untersuchungskommission zur transparenten Aufklärung der Vorkommnisse rund um die Hypo Group Alpe-Adria (2014), http://cdn.untersuchungskommission.at/pdf/BerichtHypo-UntersuchungskommissionKurzfassungEnglisch.pdf, accessed 12 October 2016, 1–20.

[104] http://www.parlament.gv.at/PAKT/VHG/XXV/A-USA/A-USA_00002_00383/index.shtml, accessed 12 October 2016.

[105] http://derstandard.at/1777793/Grasser-Homepage-ueber-220000-Euro-wert—Gerichtsverfahren-moeglich, accessed 12 October 2016.

[106] http://www.format.at/skandale/grasser/affaere-wie-karl-heinz-grasser-joerg-haider-buwog-deal-268641, accessed 12 October 2016.

[107] Rathkolb (n 10) 148–55.

These examples should however show the relevance of EU values in the Member States. The EU might be limited in its competences to react with infringement proceedings to certain problems; however, the Union can still monitor the Member States from a values perspective. The incidents in Austria described show that a more detailed and ongoing monitoring of the authoritarian developments in Member States would enable the Union to deal with Member State defiance more effectively. It would have been open to the Union politically to support the enforcement of the Constitutional Court's judgments and the protection of minority rights in Austria.

The link between authoritarian developments and corruption might not be direct, but it is also not far-fetched. Authoritarian regimes tend to limit the control powers, which usually opens the door to corruption. Limited control of political power and the possibility of unjust enrichment often go hand-in-hand. The impact of corruption on the Rule of Law and democracy is well known. The economic impact is also worse and crucial if the economic situation in a Member State is as closely linked to the other Member States as it is in an Economic Union. The corruption case also revealed a potential future direction, which the Union could use to foster its monitoring of the Member States.

In conclusion, the Union missed its opportunities in the Austrian case to continue its monitoring and interact in a debate on European values. Only half a year after the end of the EU 14 measures, the conflict over minority rights escalated without any significant European involvement. The lesson to be learned from the Austrian case is not only to review the involvement of an authoritarian party in a parliament punctually, but to evaluate developments on an ongoing basis and to keep a public dialogue alive. In most cases, value concerns cannot be linked to Article 7 TEU procedures and cannot be addressed sufficiently by infringement procedures but need ongoing supervision from the EU.[108] The possibilities are manifold and range from political dialogue and human rights monitoring to legal action.[109]

f. Haider's heritage

The end of the coalition government between the People's Party and the Freedom Party in 2006 led to the re-establishment of the old political system,[110] bringing back the grand coalition government between the Social Democrats and the People's Party, one which has lasted to the present. Jörg Haider remained State Governor until 2008, when he died in a car accident while driving under the influence of alcohol.[111] His death signalled the final decline of his political party (Alliance for the Future of Austria), which was split again into three parts: the first part returning to the Freedom Party, which is again on the rise; the second changing into a party run by Austro-Canadian billionaire Frank Stronach[112] whose political ambitions turned out to be a flash in the pan; and the third part remaining within the small group of Haider's Alliance. The only political party which will remain is the Freedom Party, which was able to regain power after Haider's death. In the 2013 election

[108] See with regard to the recent debate, C Hillion, 'Overseeing the rule of law in the EU: legal mandate and means', in Closa and Kochenov (n 35).

[109] See with regard to recent developments, Besselink (n 39).

[110] E Linhart and S Shikano, 'Die große Koalition in Österreich: Schwierigkeiten bei der Bildung, Stabilität und Alternativenlosigkeit' (2007) 36 *Österreichische Zeitschrift für Politikwissenschaft* 185.

[111] See http://derstandard.at/1231151779598/Joerg-Haider-1950—2008-Zweite-Blutuntersuchung-ergab-wieder-18-Promille, accessed 12 October 2016.

[112] S Pühringer and W Ötsch, 'Das Team Stronach. Eine österreichische Tea Party?' (2013) ICAE Working Paper Series No 19, http://www.jku.at/icae/content/e248904/e248907/e249185/e249193/wp19.pdf, accessed 12 October 2016.

the Freedom Party gained 20.5 per cent of the vote and the so-called grand coalition is consistently losing ground to it (Social Democrats 26.8 per cent; People's Party 24 per cent).[113] History seems to be repeating itself. People are again of the view that the grand coalition is not able adequately to address the challenges of our time and are looking for alternatives. The grand coalition government only has a 51 per cent absolute majority in Parliament.

The Freedom Party is getting stronger again. The party was able to convince the people that the split with Haider in 2005 meant that they were not involved in the corruption scandals of Jörg Haider. The Freedom Party has however not changed its political profile since the 1990s. The findings of the expert commission are just as relevant today. The party tends to attract media attention with its ambiguous statements[114] and the balance that the party leader, Heinz Christian Strache, strikes between a right-wing populist approach to appeal the wider public and a far-right approach for the party's extreme right-wing.[115] One example can be seen in the statements by Andreas Mölzer, who was a Member of the EP and the lead candidate for the Freedom Party in the electoral campaign for the EP in 2014. He stated in this campaign, that the EU is a 'negro-conglomerate', which is 'controlled by a gang of lobbyists' and that the EU is a 'paternalistic dictatorship, which instructed the people in everything' and that 'the old Soviet Union or the Third Reich was probably harmless and liberal'.[116] Mölzer finally resigned under pressure from his own party, which had to face a huge public uproar.

3. Conclusion

The participation of Haider's Freedom Party in the Austrian government was countered by the EU Member States at a time when the EU was focused on its internal integration process and on its own enlargement. Haider's Freedom Party was understood as a far-right party which threatened European values. The Austrian government had to react to the EU 14's measures but was able to extricate itself from its period of isolation with the help of the EU's expert group initiative.[117] The critical remarks of the experts about the Freedom Party seemed quickly forgotten. If the EU had monitored the situation in Austria further, they would have witnessed only one year later a huge conflict which threatened the Austrian Constitutional Court (i.e. the Rule of Law)[118] and saw the flagrant breach of minority rights (i.e. human rights).[119] The deeper structural problems with regard to corruption, e.g. in the context of illegal financing of political parties (i.e. threatening democracy) became evident much later.[120]

The EU itself used the debate on EU values further to improve its approach towards the constitutional values of the EU. In that context, the Austrian case may be just a marginal

[113] http://www.bmi.gv.at/cms/BMI_wahlen/nationalrat/2013/, accessed 12 October 2016.

[114] F Marquart, 'Rechtspopulismus im Wandel. Wahlplakate der FPÖ von 1978–2008' (2013) 42 *Österreichische Zeitschrift für Politikwissenschaft* 353.

[115] A Peham, 'Die zwei Seiten des Gemeinschaftsdünkels. Zum antisemitischen Gehalt freiheitlicher Identitätspolitik im Wandel' (2010) 39 *Österreichische Zeitschrift für Politikwissenschaft* 467.

[116] http://www.faz.net/aktuell/politik/europaeische-union/negerkonglomerat-fpoe-laesst-spitzenkandidaten-fuer-europawahl-nach-rassistischen-aeusserungen-fallen-12885718.html, accessed 12 October 2016.

[117] F Schorkopf, *Die Maßnahmen der XIV EU-Mitgliedsstaaten gegen Österreich: Möglichkeiten und Grenzen einer 'streitbaren Demokratie' auf europäischer Ebene* (Springer 2002).

[118] C Jabloner, 'Am Rande des Rechtsstaates'(2006) *Zeitschrift für Verwaltung* 426.

[119] A Bender-Säbelkampf, *Demokratie der ethnischen Minderheiten* (Facultas Verlagsgesellschaft 2012) 127–59.

[120] Obviously, Austrian politics had encountered economic difficulties before and other political scandals had also affected the Rule of Law in Austria in various ways. However, the intensity of the problems caused by the Freedom Party in government was particular and significant.

note in the history of European integration with regard to European values. The conclusions of the expert committee to reform Article 7 TEU to introduce a monitoring process and to establish a FRA were all considered; however, the implementation of all of these strategies seems incomplete. The further developments and debates on European values show clearly that the Union has not found a clear solution to approach these kinds of challenges properly, be it from a procedural, legal, or political perspective.[121] The challenges today, including the rise of populism in general and far-right parties in particular across Europe, make it even more necessary that the Union be able to formulate and defend its values.[122] Future narratives will reveal if the Union can meet the democratic challenges of its Member States.[123]

[121] See the proposal by A Von Bogdandy, M Kottmann et al., 'Reverse Solange–Protecting the essence of fundamental rights against EU Member States' (2012) 49 *Common Market Law Review* 489 and JW Müller, *Wo Europa endet: Ungarn, Brüssel und das Schicksal der liberalen Demokratie* (edition Suhrkamp 2013) to address the issue.

[122] See e.g. A von Bogdandy and P Sonnevend (eds), *Constitutional Crisis in the European Constitutional Area* (Hart 2015); see also B Bugaric, 'A crisis of constitutional democracy in post-Communist Europe: 'Lands in-between democracy and authoritarianism' (2015) 13 *International Journal of Constitutional Law* 219; V Perju, 'The Romanian double executive and the 2012 constitutional crisis' (2015) 13 *International Journal of Constitutional Law* 246.

[123] See the Communication of the Commission regarding 'A New Framework to strengthen the Rule of Law' COM(2014) 158 final/2, introducing an assessment by the Commission and the idea of the Council establishing a dialogue among the Member States within the Council (Council of the EU, Press Release No 16936/14, 3362nd Council meeting, General Affairs, Brussels, 16 December 2014, 20–1).

26

Challenging the Basic Values—Problems in the Rule of Law in Hungary and the Failure of the EU to Tackle Them

Zoltán Szente

1. Introduction

'A message to Brussels: respect for Hungarians'—the government parties, Fidesz and its satellite party the Christian Democrats could hardly have chosen a more expressive and characteristic slogan for their election campaign of the EP in 2014. Waging a 'freedom fight' against the dictats of the EU and comparing 'Brussels' to 'Moscow', the capital of the former Soviet Union, are not the catchwords of an extremist, anti-EU party, but utterances of Viktor Orbán, the Prime Minister of Hungary.[1] This might be considered astonishing from a country where more than ninety per cent of public investment is financed by EU funds.[2] But this is not the only ostensible paradox. Two others make understanding the current relationship between the EU and Hungary more difficult. First, it is puzzling that while from the early 1990s Hungary was a champion of the democratization process and was also a frontrunner of EU accession in the CEE region, today, constitutional democracy seems to be declining and there is growing Euroscepticism in government policy. If we review the political science literature before 2010, Hungary was always praised for its democratic achievement.[3] Even if many drew attention to the dangers of new authoritarianism in the post-communist countries very early on,[4] Hungary was never regarded as endangered by such a threat. The legal harmonization and institutional adaptation to EU requirements were also success stories. Although the level of corruption and the situation of Roma people emerged as Rule of Law problems,[5] no serious shortcomings in compliance with the Copenhagen criteria were raised during the accession process.

[1] See for example his oft cited speech, quoted in English by the *Guardian*, in which he said combatively that '[w]e will not be a colony!' and 'Hungarians will not live as foreigners dictate, will not give up their independence or their freedom'. I Traynor, 'Hungary Prime Minister Hits Out at EU Interference in National Day Speech' (15 March 2012) *Guardian*, http://www.theguardian.com/world/2012/mar/15/hungary-prime-minister-orban-eu, accessed 12 October 2016.

[2] T Szűcs, 'A magyar EU-tagság első évtizede az Európai Bizottság szemszögéből' in A Marján (ed), *Magyarország első évtizede az Európai Unióban 2004–2014* (Nemzeti Közszolgálati Egyetem Nemzetközi Intézet 2014) 200.

[3] See e.g. J Batt, 'The End of Communist Rule in East-Central Europe: A Four-Country Comparison' (1991) 26 *Government and Opposition* 368; S Saxonberg, *The Fall: A Comparative Study of the End of Communism in Czechoslovakia, East Germany, Hungary and Poland* (Harwood 2001); O Havrylyshyn, *Divergent Paths in Post-Communist Transformation Capitalism for All or Capitalism for the Few?* (Palgrave Macmillan 2006), 255–75; V Bunce, 'Political Transition' in SL Wolchik and JL Curry (eds), *Central and East European Politics. From Communism to Democracy* (Rowman & Littlefield 2011) 32.

[4] See e.g. DM Brissman and J Rupnik, 'The Post-Totalitarian Blues' (1995) 6 *Journal of Democracy* 61; and V Tismaneanu, *Fantasies of Salvation. Democracy, Nationalism, and Myth in Post-Communist Europe* (Princeton University Press 1998).

[5] TA Lane and E Stadtmüller (eds), *Europe on the Move: The Impact of Eastern Enlargement on the European Union* (LIT Verlag 2005), 95.

Challenging the Basic Values—The Problems of the Rule of Law in Hungary and the Failure of the European Union to Tackle Them. First Edition. Zoltán Szente. Published 2017 by Oxford University Press.

Despite all these antecedents, recent developments have changed this picture. The new Fundamental Law of Hungary adopted in 2011 drew wide international attention and attracted heavy criticism. A number of European institutions, human rights organizations and international newspapers equally expressed their doubts at whether certain principles and rules in the new basic law comply with European, or even purely democratic standards.

The other paradox is that while the number of Hungary's infringement procedures, which is a widely used and accepted indicator of the compliance with EU law,[6] is relatively low (see Chapter 1), there is a tense relationship between Hungary and the European Commission, the guardian of the EU law. Hungary is often regarded as the black sheep in the community, to the extent that some have even talked about excluding this country from the EU.[7]

I believe that understanding the reasons for these contradictions can provide useful insight into the relations between the EU and Hungary. It is certain that since 2010 there has been a new period in these relations. The Hungarian constitutional changes have challenged the EU, testing its capacity and ability to protect the Rule of Law in the Member States. Since 2000, when the far-right Freedom Party joined the government coalition in Austria, no such trouble has emerged.[8] Then, almost fifteen years ago, the problem was resolved, without any institutionalized solution. Now, when the challenge from the inside—that is from a Member State—to the democratic value system of the community is significantly greater than ever, the EU faces an unexpected obstacle. To work out an effective and long-term solution to a situation which has never occurred before, it is necessary to know the problem itself, in particular whether it threatens the foundations of EU law as a whole.

2. Non-compliance conflicts

From a conceptual perspective, Hungary's non-compliance problems can be classified into two groups: failures to implement secondary EU legislation and Rule of Law problems violating the basic values of EU law.

First, there are some conflicts which are quite usual between the EU and a Member State resulting from the failure of the domestic legal system to comply with EU law. If we use the number of infringement procedures to characterize the level of compliance with EU law, there were 44 such procedures brought against Hungary of the 1,347 infringement cases open at the end of 2014, and 38 of the total 1,368 open infringement procedures on 31 December 2015 (15th and 10th fewest among the 28 member states). It means that about three per cent of all procedures were instituted against this country.[9] Apart from the special Rule of Law cases, Hungary's record is not remarkably different from that of any other Member State, where most infringement procedures are instituted because of late

[6] See e.g. the annual reports of the European Commission on monitoring the application of EU law in the Member States.

[7] Ungarn, 'ein EU-Ausschlusskandidat' (2012), http://derstandard.at/1302745450901/Ungarn-ein-EU-Ausschlusskandidat, accessed 12 October 2016. 'Hungary could be expelled from the EU, former US Ambassador Palmer says' (2012) *Politics.hu*, http://www.politics.hu/20120102/hungary-could-be-expelled-from-eu-former-us-ambassador-palmer-says/, accessed 12 October 2016.

[8] See Lachmayer in Chapter 25 of this volume.

[9] European Commission, 'Monitoring the application of European Union law 2014 Annual Report' (2015) COM(2015) 329, 14; European Commission, 'Monitoring the application of European Union law 2015 Annual Report' (2016) COM(2016) 463, 24.

transposition of Union directives, and where transport, environment, and the internal market are the policy areas most frequently concerned.

However, the other type of non-compliance makes Hungary's case special. It is not usual for EU institutions to accuse a Member State of undermining the basic values of democracy and the Rule of Law. These values are entrenched in Article 2 TEU which declares that '[t]he Union is founded on the values of respect for human dignity, freedom, democracy, equality, the rule of law and respect for human rights, including the rights of persons belonging to minorities. These values are common to the Member States in a society in which pluralism, non-discrimination, tolerance, justice, solidarity and equality between women and men prevail'. Nevertheless, over the past few years, a number of compliance problems have been raised in this area in relation to Hungary, even if only a few of them were referred to the European Court of Justice by the European Commission. The country has been standing in the crossfire of criticism since it began to fundamentally transform its constitutional system in 2010. Sometimes it is difficult to distinguish between policy-related and value-laden non-compliance cases. In one example, when, in the summer of 2014, the national legislature introduced an advertisement tax for media companies,[10] disproportionately affecting one private broadcasting corporation, simply because it allegedly did not promote the government policy, the vice-president of the European Commission issued a statement warning against the undermining of free and plural media.[11] According to this law, the advertisement tax must be paid, unusually, after the revenues of the media companies, and not on their profit from advertising. The tax rates were structured so that the most tax revenues would be paid by RTL Klub, the most popular commercial TV channel, which was the only media outlet falling into the highest tax rate. The European Commission has opened an in-depth investigation into whether this new tax complies with EU state aid rules.[12] Although the case fell within the area of the competition regulation of the EU law, many have claimed that the imposition of the advertisement tax was an instrument of political pressure on the critical media and the freedom of the press.[13]

Other examples of the mixture of policy and Rule of Law issues are those policy objectives which aim to increase national property holdings in the banking sector, retail chain stores, or the public utility sector. The limitation on foreign land ownership is also a political aim, after the expiration of the moratorium on foreigners buying land. While these measures may appear to be policy (or non-compliance) problems for the EU institutions, the government tries to achieve these goals with public power tools, which might raise Rule of Law concerns, insofar as they intend to use public power to intervene in the right to property and the freedom of enterprise.

This study deals only with the second group of conflicts. I will call them constitutional conflicts, as they affect fundamental values and principles of the constitutional order of the EU.

[10] Law No XXII of 2014 on the Advertisement Tax.

[11] Commissioner Neelie Kroes, 'Media freedom remains under threat in Hungary' (2014) *europa.eu* (blog post), http://ec.europa.eu/commission_2010-2014/kroes/en/blog/media-freedom-remains-under-threat-hungary, accessed 12 October 2016.

[12] In the meantime, the Hungarian government indicated that it is open to reconsider the rates of this tax. Nevertheless, the investigation of the EC is still ongoing at the time of the closing of this study.

[13] When, for example, RTL Klub filed a complaint with the European Commission against the advertisement tax in 2014, it argued that 'the levy damages media pluralism and is a punitive and discriminatory [tax]'. 'RTL lodges Hungary complaint in Brussels' (2014) *Broadband TV News*, http://www.broadbandtvnews.com/2014/10/17/rtl-lodges-hungary-complaint-in-brussels/, accessed 12 October 2016. Eventually, the openly discriminative rules were eliminated from the law in 2015.

3. Threatening the basic values of the EU—the constitutional issues

The Hungarian constitutional changes which have been enacted since 2010[14] have brought about an unprecedented situation within the EU, in that an entire series of constitutional measures has never come under severe criticism by the EU institutions before. But it has been the case that since 2010, when the general elections saw an overwhelming victory for the former opposition parties, and a new conservative government coalition, based on a two-thirds (ie constitution-making) parliamentary majority, started to change the constitutional landscape of the country.

The objections of the EU institutions do not merely relate to a specific law or policy, but rather to the general direction of recent constitutional developments. Moreover, the criticism encompasses both the formal, procedural circumstances of the constitutional changes, and their substance.

a. The problems of the constitution-making process and of the subsequent legislation

The constitution-making process attracted considerable attention throughout Europe, but the EU institutions reacted to the new Fundamental Law of 2011 only after the intensive law making and its first amendments. This criticism, based in particular on the opinions of the Venice Commission of the Council of Europe, related not only to the content of the new constitution, but also to the manner in which it was drafted and adopted.

Whereas the various EU representatives recognised that the adoption of a new constitution and constitutional amendments fall within the scope of competences of the Member States, they emphasized that both the content of national constitutions and the constitutional processes must comply with the basic principles and standards of the TEU, that is, the common values of the EU. The Hungarian constitution-making process seemed not to have met these requirements, as it was extremely rapid and lacked transparency and openness. The non-consensual nature of the constitutional text, i.e. the lack of inclusiveness of the constitution-making procedure, was also condemned by various EU institutions and documents.[15]

The new basic law seems genuinely and likely irremediably defective in that it is a partisan constitution, in the sense that the basic rules of the game were set unilaterally by the government majority. These circumstances in the constitution-making process could on their own raise the issue of legitimacy,[16] even if the Fundamental Law was approved by the two-thirds majority of the National Assembly, as required by the prior constitution.

[14] For a more detailed description of this process in English, see K Kovács and GA Tóth, 'Hungary's Constitutional Transformation' (2011) 7 *European Constitutional Law Review* 183; M Bánkuti et al., 'Disabling the Constitution' (2012) 23 *Journal of Democracy* 138; I Pogány, 'The Crisis of Democracy in East Central Europe: The "New Constitutionalism" in Hungary' (2013) 19 *European Public Law* 341; JW Müller, 'The Hungarian Tragedy' (2011) 58 *Dissent* 5; M Bánkuti et al., 'From Separation of Powers to a Government without Checks: Hungary's Old and New Constitutions', in GA Tóth (ed), *Constitution for a Disunited Nation. On Hungary's 2011 Fundamental Law* (Central European University Press 2012), 237–68. For an apologetic presentation of the new Fundamental Law, see L Csink et al. (eds), *The Basic Law of Hungary. A First Commentary* (Clarus Press, National Institute of Public Administration 2012).

[15] See, for example, European Commission 'Statement of the European Commission on the Situation in Hungary on 11 January 2012' (2012) MEMO/12/9, http://europa.eu/rapid/press-release_MEMO-12-9_en.htm, accessed 12 October 2016; and EP, resolution of 3 July 2013 on the situation of fundamental rights: standards and practices in Hungary P7_TA(2013)0315, AB–AF.

[16] In contrast, some argue that the legitimacy of a constitution can be evaluated only after some time has lapsed, and on the basis of experience, that is, only the formal legality of the constitution-making process has a real

In sharp contrast to the government's political stability, the Constitution has been continuously in flux over the last five years, since the change of government following the general elections in 2010. Until the new Fundamental Law entered into force on 1 January 2012, the government majority had amended the previous constitution twelve times (three times after the formal passing of the new Fundamental Law in April 2011) concerning a number of its provisions. Shortly after the formation of the new government in May 2010, the new majority adopted a whole series of constitutional amendments that were made partly to fulfil its campaign promises and partly to clear the way for a radical change of government policy. In doing so, the number of members of Parliament was reduced from 386 to 199, and the *sui generis* parliamentary representation of the nationalities was realized. In addition, the serious limitation of the powers of the Constitutional Court to review the constitutionality of public finance laws was a first step towards dismantling the system of checks and balances. Finally, some amendments introduced only technical rules.

Interestingly, the new Constitution also seems to be an ever-changing basic law; already on the day of its entry into force a number of amendments were attached to the constitutional text by a dubious legal act named 'Transitional Provisions of the Fundamental Law',[17] containing a political manifesto condemning the communist dictatorship in Hungary before the system change, and the full responsibility of the largest opposition party, the Hungarian Socialist Party, for the communist crimes, as well as other provisions which gave constitutional rank to a number of rules to avoid their review against the Constitution.[18] Moreover, the text of the new Fundamental Law was amended five times within one and a half years, and a new, sixth amendment (introducing the 'state of terrorist threat' in the constitution) was adopted in June 2016. The Fourth Amendment to the Fundamental Law was particularly strongly criticized,[19] as it incorporated a number of rules into the constitutional text which had previously been declared unconstitutional by the Constitutional Court. The function of this amendment was to correct the constitutional defects of the Transitional Provisions attached to the constitutional text in a separate document, and of the parliamentary legislation, and to eliminate the possibility of their future constitutional review. The Fourth Amendment was thus viewed as introducing and perpetuating shortcomings in the constitutional system, as the relevant report of the Venice Commission said.[20]

The subsequent parliamentary legislation also inspired heavy criticism. The Hungarian Fundamental Law specifies twenty-six legislative subject areas to be defined only by

significance at the time of the adoption. See L Trócsányi 'The Creation of the Basic Law of Hungary', in Csink et al. (eds) (n 14) 9, 22.

[17] According to the relevant decision of the Constitutional Court, the legal nature and the place of the Transitional Provisions were uncertain. Z Szente, 'Az Alkotmánybíróság döntése Magyarország Alaptörvényének Átmeneti rendelkezései alkotmányosságáról. Az Alaptörvény integritása és az alkotmányozó hatalom korlátai' (2013) 4 *Jogesetek Magyarázata* 11.

[18] Most of the Transitional Provisions were repealed by the Constitutional Court in a year. Decision No 25/2012 (V 18) of the Constitutional Court.

[19] See e.g. I Vörös, 'The constitutional landscape after the fourth and fifth amendments of Hungarian Fundamental Law' (2014) 55 *Acta Juridica Hungarica* 1; M Bánkuti et al., 'Amicus brief a velencei bizottságnak az alaptörvény negyedik módosításáról' (2013) 17 *Fundamentum* 5. In contrast to these criticisms, for apologetic views, see F Delpérée et al., *Opinion on the Fourth Amendment of the Constitution of Hungary* (2013), an unpublished opinion prepared at the request of the government of Hungary now available at: http://vienna.io.gov.hu/download/1/ec/60000/alaptorveny_modositas_szakvelemeny_angol.pdf, accessed 12 October 2016; and L Trócsányi, *Az alkotmányozás dilemmái. Alkotmányos identitás és európai integráció* (HVG-Orac 2014), 153–222.

[20] Opinion on the Fourth Amendment to the Fundamental Law of Hungary Adopted by the Venice Commission at its 95th Plenary Session, Venice (14–15 June 2013) Opinion 720/2013 CDL-AD(2013)012.

so-called cardinal laws, requiring a two-thirds majority vote in Parliament.[21] While the institution of special laws has been known and used under various names since the system change in 1989–1990, a real innovation of the new Constitution is the requirement of a qualified majority for policy areas such as the pension and tax system or family law, which usually falls within the ordinary power of Parliament. According to these rules, after the adoption of the new constitution, the Parliament enacted a number of cardinal laws transforming not only the whole constitutional system, but also introducing fundamental changes to economic and social policy through accelerated legislative procedures. This process resembled 'revolutionary' law making; with most bills being introduced as individual member's bills without a transparent preparatory stage and public debate. The Parliament's amended standing orders enabled the governing parties to get their bills through the National Assembly in a few days, ignoring the views and proposals of the opposition. The so-called 'extraordinary urgent procedure', introduced in 2011, allowed the enactment of a new law the day following its introduction in Parliament; any bill could be amended fundamentally right up to the final vote: that is, after the closure of the plenary debate. Although these parliamentary contrivances were abolished in 2014, some new procedures were established instead, such as dispensing with the second reading of bills, depriving Parliament of the opportunity to debate on their detail. The frequent use the accelerated legislative procedure was criticized as opaque, unaccountable, and undemocratic,[22] because it undermines the rights of the opposition parties to participate effectively in the law-making process, and thereby reduces the legitimacy of the enacted laws, and ultimately negatively affecting the system of checks and balances.

b. Human rights issues

The authors of the new Fundamental Law chose a unique way of rewriting the catalogue of basic rights when they purportedly based this crucial part of the basic law on the Charter of Fundamental Rights of the EU.[23] The Venice Commission expressed its concerns about this idea, pointing out that some problems could arise from the different interpretation of the same provisions of the EU Charter by the European Court of Justice and the national Constitutional Court.[24]

The individual rights are mostly worded in a general and abstract way to allow a wide margin of appreciation for Parliament to regulate the specific rules for the scope and limitations to the respective rights, some of them (e.g. freedom of the press, the right to vote, freedom of religion, data protection, or the rights of the nationalities) in 'cardinal laws'. There was some concern that constitutional provisions might thus be eroded by special acts.[25] This proved not only to be a potential risk but an actual problem, when new media laws were enacted in 2011. The institutions of the EU harshly criticized the two laws. The EP adopted a resolution,[26] grounded on the reports of the Organisation for Security and Cooperation in Europe and the Council of Europe Commissioner for Human Rights,

[21] For a detailed report about this new law making, see P Smuk (ed), *The Transformation of the Hungarian Legal System 2010–2013* (Complex 2013).

[22] See e.g. Statement of the European Commission (n 15) II, 9.

[23] See the explanatory memorandum for the Fundamental Law, http://www.parlament.hu/irom39/02627/02627.pdf, accessed 12 October 2016, 32.

[24] Opinion on three legal questions arising in the process of drafting the new constitution of Hungary, Adopted by the Venice Commission at its 86th Plenary Session, Venice (25–26 March 2011) Opinion 614/2011 CDL-AD(2011)001, 6.

[25] See Traynor (n 1) 59.

[26] EP, resolution of 10 March 2011 on media law in Hungary P7_TA(2011)0094.

and the European Commission also started expert negotiations with the representatives of the Hungarian government. The extensive supervisory and sanctioning power of the central media authority, the composition of the powerful Media Council (which consisted exclusively of the government's candidates), the lack of independence of the media regulatory bodies, the registration requirements of the media companies, the content regulation of the printed press, and the exceptions to the protection of journalists' sources were particularly objected to by the Commission. After negotiations with the European Commission, and after the Hungarian Constitutional Court overturned many provisions of the media law in May 2012, the Hungarian Parliament amended the law at certain points. As the Council of Europe expressed its satisfaction with the changes, the European Commission removed this issue from the agenda. Nevertheless, some concerns have remained after the amendments regarded the continuing insufficient guarantees of the impartiality and independence of the public media, and exaggerated government interference with the freedom of the press.[27] In addition, new criticisms emerged when the Fourth Amendment of the Fundamental Law imposed strict restrictions on political advertisement on private television and radio channels. From that point on, the commercial media could publish political advertisements only free of charge, which practically eliminated these channels (as for-profit enterprises) from the election campaign. In this situation, the public media remained the main arena for the conduct of political campaigning, and which was repeatedly accused of pro-government bias. Later on, independent sources said these fears were confirmed during the election campaign in the parliamentary elections, where the Fidesz government, according to new electoral rules regained a two-thirds majority.[28]

Another issue attracting wide-ranging criticism was the freedom of religion and the recognition of churches.[29] The government coalition introduced a new regulation regime for churches, depriving all religious communities (more than 300 former churches) of their church status, and imposing new requirements for their recognition as churches. This legal re-registration was conditional on prior approval by the legislature by a two-thirds majority vote, although an exception was granted to 'historic churches' and some other religious associations which did not have to apply for recognition. It should also be noted that the new legislation did not provide any legal remedy for those religious associations whose applications were rejected by the Parliament without any reasoning being offered. The Venice Commission held that the new regulation limited the freedom of religion,[30] and the Hungarian Constitutional Court invalidated certain provisions of the Church Law in February 2013.[31] However, only two weeks later, the Fourth Amendment to the Fundamental Law incorporated the same rules into the text of the Constitution, so all the basic elements of the highly controversial regulation remained in effect. The ECtHR also

[27] Opinion of the Commissioner for Human Rights on Hungary's media legislation in light of Council of Europe standards on freedom of the media CommDH(2011)10, https://wcd.coe.int/ViewDoc.jsp?id=1751289, accessed 12 October 2016; PACE, 'The state of media freedom in Europe' (2013) Resolution 1920, http://assembly.coe.int/nw/xml/XRef/Xref-XML2HTML-en.asp?fileid=19474&lang=en, accessed 12 October 2016; Opinion on Media Legislation of Hungary, adopted by the Venice Commission at its 103rd Plenary Session (Venice, 19–20 June 2015), Opinion 798/2015 CDL-AD(2015)015.

[28] See OSCE ODIHR, 'Hungary Parliamentary Elections 6 April 2014: Limited Election Observation Mission Final Report (11 July 2014), http://www.osce.org/odihr/elections/hungary/121098?download=true, accessed 12 October 2016.

[29] See e.g. R Uitz, 'Freedom of Religion and Churches: Archaeology in a Constitution-making Assembly' in Tóth (n 14).

[30] Opinion on Act CCVI of 2011 on the right to freedom of conscience and religion and the legal status of churches, denominations and religious communities of Hungary adopted by the Venice Commission at its 90th Plenary Session (16–17 March 2012) Opinion 664/2012 CDL-AD(2012)004-e.

[31] Decision No 6/2013 (III 1) of the Constitutional Court.

stated that the relevant legislation does not treat the various religious communities as equals, and some measures, like the Parliament's decision on the recognition of churches or the absence of any right to appeal against the legislature's decision violates the corresponding provisions of the ECHR.[32]

Some other constitutional changes, such as the explicit exclusion of same-sex marriage,[33] the narrow constitutional definition of family, and the empowerment of public authorities to declare illegal homeless people remaining in public areas,[34] caused controversy, even if those regulations were not considered to violate any particular norm of EU law.

c. Decline of the system of checks and balances

The curious paradox of the new constitutional regulation of the exercise of public power is that while the state organization system changed only moderately, the changes introduced as a result of the introduction of the Fundamental Law have had significant political impact in practice. In general, the institutional restraints on executive power can be viewed as having been considerably weakened. Some of the politically neutral institutions with responsibility for counterbalancing the executive power have lost their independence[35] or some of their control powers.

One such institution which has seen its functions curtailed is the Constitutional Court, which for two decades was widely regarded as the most effective and strongest counterbalance to the executive.[36] Just a few months after its formation the new coalition government used its two-thirds majority to transform the process of nominating the judges of the Constitutional Court. Since then, the membership of the parliamentary committee responsible for the nomination has no longer been based on parity, but has reflected the party makeup of the National Assembly. Until the new regulation, the parliamentary majority and minority groups had been forced to compromise on new members of the Court, as the composition of the parliamentary committee responsible for nominating Constitutional Court judges had been based on parity between the government and opposition parties, thus, each candidate had to gain the support of both sides. According to the new rules, candidates are proposed by a parliamentary committee composed in proportion to the members of the parties represented in Parliament and they are elected by Parliament with a qualified majority of two-thirds. In addition, the number of judges, in order to be able to deal with an anticipated increase in its workload, was simultaneously raised from eleven to fifteen. The government coalition, over the next four years, was thus able to 'pack the Court', that is, replace retiring judges with its own allies and achieve a stable majority in the Court.

[32] *Magyar Keresztény Mennonita Egyház and Others v Hungary* App nos. 70945/11, 23611/12, 26998/12, 41150/12, 41155/12, 41463/12, 41553/12, 54977/12, and 56581/12 (ECtHR, 8 April 2014), paras 98, 112.

[33] Bánkúti et al. (n 14).

[34] K Gacs, 'Lakhatás helyett börtön – A hajléktalanság kriminalizációjának alkotmányossági problémái' (2014) 18 *Fundamentum* 22.

[35] For empirical research on the politicization of the Constitutional Court, see Z Szente, 'The Political Orientation of the Members of the Hungarian Constitutional Court between 2010 and 2014' (2016) 1 *Constitutional Studies* 123–49.

[36] See e.g. H Schwartz, *The Struggle for Constitutional Justice in Post-Communist Europe* (University of Chicago Press 2000) 87–108; L Sólyom and G Brunner, *Constitutional Judiciary in a New Democracy: The Hungarian Constitutional Court* (University of Michigan Press 2000); G Halmai, 'The Hungarian Approach to Constitutional Review: The End of Activism? The First Decade of the Hungarian Constitutional Court', in W Sadurski (ed), *Constitutional Justice, East and West. Democratic Legitimacy and Constitutional Courts in Post-Communist Europe in a Comparative Perspective* (Kluwer International Law 2000), 189–211.

Simultaneously, the governing majority abolished the institution of *actio popularis*, which made it possible for anybody to submit a petition to the Court to invalidate an unconstitutional legal act. Moreover, the Court was deprived of its *ex post* review power of budget-related laws. This means that the Court has only been able to review and annul budgetary laws, acts on taxes, duties, pensions, customs, or any kind of financial contributions to the state if they violate the right to life and human dignity, the right to the protection of personal data, freedom of thought, conscience and religion, and the rights related to Hungarian citizenship. This substantially limited the Court's jurisdiction, as it took the government's economic and financial policy out of major aspects of constitutional control, such as on grounds of anti-discrimination or protection of property.[37] The political motivation for this drastic measure was to prevent the constitutional review of the government's so-called 'unorthodox' economic policy, for example, the retroactive taxation of public sector staff severance payments or the nationalization of private pension fund savings in 2011.[38]

Despite the successful Court-packing in recent years, the Fourth Amendment to the Fundamental Law declares that the Constitutional Court's decisions prior to the entry into force of the new constitution are repealed, in an effort to force the Court to evolve a new jurisprudence based exclusively on the text of the new Fundamental Law.

The only new institution which emerged in the new constitution is the Budget Council,[39] an organ supporting Parliament's legislative activities and examining the feasibility of the state budget. However, it is not a purely advisory body, since its prior consent is required for the adoption of the state budget by Parliament. Although the Council may refuse to give consent only in specified cases (e.g. if the budget bill would allow state debt to exceed half of GDP), its decision may not be reviewed or annulled, so it will have a real veto right, which is an exceptional restriction of the Parliament's budgetary power. As a sanction for this jurisdiction, the President of the Republic was given a new power by the Fundamental Law to dissolve Parliament if it fails to adopt (and to get the Budget Council's approval) a state budget for the current year by 31 March. The Budget Council's absolute veto power can thus be a sword of Damocles over any possible leftist government in the future, because the conservative government was able to determine the composition of the Council for a long period. Although in theory this body consists of politically neutral persons, as the chairmen of the State Audit Office and the Hungarian National Bank are *ex officio* members, and its president is appointed by the Head of State (all members were appointed for nine years in 2011 and 2012), many claim that they are all only figureheads for the major government party.[40]

Another critical point was the independence of judiciary. The president of the Supreme Court was removed while he was still midway through his term of office by restructuring the organization of the judiciary,[41] and renaming the Court as 'Kúria' by the new

[37] The limitation was introduced by the legislature in 2011, but the Fundamental Law preserved and perpetuated it. This restriction of the Court's power will last as long as state debt exceeds half of GDP.

[38] For details see, Z Szente, 'Breaking and Making Constitutional Rules: The Constitutional Effects of the Financial Crisis in Hungary' in X Contiades (ed), *Constitutions in the Global Financial Crisis. A Comparative Analysis* (Ashgate 2013) 256–7.

[39] The Budget Council was established for the first time by law in 2008 but it had much weaker power than under the Fundamental Law.

[40] In fact, the chairman of the State Audit Commission (SAC), Mr László Domokos was a Fidesz MP between 1998 and 2010, while the president of the national bank, Mr György Matolcsy was also an MP, representing Fidesz from 2006 to 2013, and he was also the Minister for Economy for a while in the first and the second Orbán cabinet. The incumbent president of the Budget Council, Mr Árpád Kovács, was a former chairman of the SAC between 1997 and 2009, though without manifest political affiliation.

[41] Act CLXI of 2011 on the organization and administration of courts of Hungary.

Constitution.[42] The new legislation established the National Judicial Office (NJO), the highest administrative body of the judiciary, and conferred wide-ranging powers upon its president, such as the power to transfer any case to any court, even if the case should fall within the competence of another court. The president of the NJO's very wide powers and his or her lack of accountability also attracted international criticism.[43] It should be noted that the latter proved successful in this case, as the power of the NJO's president to transfer ongoing judicial cases from a trial court to another was abolished in 2013.

4. Rule of Law infringement procedures

Although a lot of problems arose in connection with the constitutional changes in Hungary, only a few of them led to formal infringement procedures initiated by the European Commission. The major problem was that the Commission did not find relevant EU legal norms on which to base a formal procedure. In the absence of effective sanctioning procedures and actions, the European Commission launched infringement procedures only in three Rule of Law cases. Even in these cases, the objections focused on a limited set of technical problems or on particular legal issues which were of only secondary importance, but the Commission could not find any relevant legal basis for action before the European Court of Justice. The removal of a number of judges by radically lowering the compulsory retirement age could thus not be litigated as a serious violation of the principle of judicial independence, as would have been obvious, but was challenged instead by the European Commission on the ground that the legislation discriminated against judges based on age.

So the EU institutions were not in a position to address directly most of the violations of the principles of the Rule of Law or human rights. In this context the European Commission preferred to have direct political consultations with the Hungarian government. As is usual, even in formal infringement procedures, the Commission tried to avoid open conflicts, that is, to avoid a legal dispute before the European Court of Justice, by means of letters and informal negotiations. Therefore, despite the recurrent objections of the Hungarian authorities relating to the 'double standards' used by the Commission against Hungary, infringement procedures took their usual course; after unsuccessful negotiations between the Commission and the national authorities, the EC started legal action against Hungary over the breach of Union law. It is another question whether the standard methods found and used for simple non-compliance cases are appropriate measures for handling Rule of Law problems.

a. Derogating the independence of the central bank

One of the three procedures launched against Hungary concerned the independence of the central bank, after the European Commission decided that the new Hungarian legislation of 2011 was in conflict with EU law by calling into question the independence of the Hungarian national bank. It is worth noting that the presidency of the central bank was, for

[42] The ECtHR in its judgment of 27 May 2014 declared that the removal of the president of the former Supreme Court violated the ECHR as Mr Baka's access to the courts had been impeded, and his freedom of expression was also violated as his dismissal was due to the criticism he had publicly expressed of government policy on judicial reform. See *Baka v Hungary* App no 20261/12 (ECtHR, 27 May 2014).

[43] Opinion on Act CLXII of 2011 on the Legal Status and Remuneration of Judges and Act CLXI of 2011 on the Organisation and Administration of Courts of Hungary, adopted by the Venice Commission at its 90th Plenary Session, Venice (16–17 March 2012) Opinion 663/2012 CDL-AD(2012)001-e.

a certain period, the only position of key political importance which had not been occupied by the governing coalition, as the mandate of the incumbent president of the national bank expired only in 2013. Since the central bank did not support the government's economic and financial policy unconditionally, the latter exerted political pressure on the leadership of the central bank, and by adopting new legislation, tried to gain greater influence over its activity. The European Commission raised some concerns regarding the potential violation of the independence of the central bank by some provisions of the Fundamental Law of 2011 and the new legislation. The Commission stated that the independence of national central banks is a cornerstone of the Lisbon Treaty, and the national authorities must refrain from seeking influence over their central banks.

Following a long process of negotiations at expert and political levels, the European Commission accepted the moderate amendments of the relevant law, and abandoned the infringement procedure.

b. The Judiciary

A proposal was submitted (and approved) at the last moment before the vote on the Fundamental Law, on applying a general retirement age to professional judges (except the President of the *Kúria*). As a result of lowering this age limit from 70 to 62,[44] about ten per cent of professional judges (almost 300 judges) had to retire. In fact, most leadership positions in the judiciary became vacant within a year, because most were filled by older judges.

The Constitutional Court ruled to overturn the lowering of the retirement age, stating that this could only be regulated by cardinal law, to respect the constitutional principle of the independence of the judiciary.[45] Since the government ignored the Court's ruling and did not replace the invalidated regulation, the Commission brought the case before the ECJ, which declared that 'the radical lowering of the retirement age for Hungarian judges constitutes unjustified discrimination on grounds of age', because this measure was 'not proportionate to the objectives pursued by the Hungarian legislature seeking to standardize the retirement age for the public-service professions and to establish a more balanced age structure in the area of the administration of justice'.[46]

In a formal sense, the EU succeeded through the ECJ's ruling in enforcing compliance with the relevant EU law (in this case, the prohibition of illegitimate discrimination based on age), as the Parliament amended the Judiciary Law, setting a new uniform retirement age (65) to be introduced gradually. The Commission was satisfied by the new regulation and closed the issue.

c. Data protection

The Fundamental Law abolished the position of the parliamentary ombudsman for personal data protection and freedom of information and replaced it with a National Authority for Data Protection and Freedom of Information. The ombudsman, elected by Parliament in 2008 for six years, was thus removed from his position on 31 December 2011 instead of 2014, and the Head of State appointed a new person as head of the authority for a term of nine years. The European Commission considered that the premature termination

[44] Law No CLXII of 2011. [45] Decision No 33/2012 (VII 17) of the Constitutional Court.
[46] Case C-286/12 *Commission v Hungary* [2012] ECLI:EU:C:2012:687.

of the parliamentary ombudsman violated Directive 95/46 on data protection,[47] which requires the Member States to ensure the independence of the relevant national authority. After the Hungarian government claimed that the premature removal of the ombudsman did not breach the institutional independence of the data protection authority, the Commission turned to the ECJ.

Hungary argued before the Court that the new law on the National Authority for Data Protection meets the requirements of the Directive, as it provides full independence for the Authority. Moreover, if the Court found that Hungary failed to fulfil its obligations, it could lead to the compulsory resignation of the head of the new Authority before the expiry of his term of office, which would be incompatible with the principle of the independence of the data protection authority. Paradoxically, the Hungarian government itself thus acknowledged that premature removal violated the institutional independence of the supervisor of data protection. But it did not matter, as the Court refused this argument, stating that a Member State cannot plead provisions prevailing in its domestic legal system to justify a failure to observe legal obligations arising under EU law. The ECJ also concluded that compulsory retirement or resignation, as a consequence of the new law, was an unlawful intervention in the independence of the former data protection authority (ie the parliamentary ombudsman), as the previous regulation did not permit this kind of interruption of the term of office.[48]

5. The legal arguments in the debate between the EU and the Hungarian government

a. Legal argumentation of the EU institutions

The general criticism of the constitution-making process—the use of constitutional amendments and cardinal laws to realize the short-term political ambitions of the governing parties—were basically of political nature. However, the European Commission has always refrained from publicly criticizing the political circumstances of the constitutional and legal changes. The European Commission did not want to step out of its neutral position as the guardian of EU law. Nevertheless, this policy strictly limited its room for manoeuvre in all cases when the Hungarian authorities observed formal rules. This did not pose difficulties for the Hungarian government, which enjoyed a qualified majority in Parliament between 2010 and 2015. The Commission could thus not intervene when party allies were appointed to almost every independent institution, including the Constitutional Court, the National Judicial Office, the State Audit Office, the State Prosecutor, the Budget Council, the National Election Board, and the National Media Council, or when independent journalists were purged from the public media, and serious efforts were made to strengthen the pro-government private broadcasters.

Not only the European Commission, but also the EP was, at least initially, reluctant to interfere with such a domestic affair as transforming the constitutional system. The EP has proved to be politically divided even in the most unambiguous matters on how to address these issues, and what actions would be the most effective to convince the Hungarian government to return to a more democratic line. The European People's Party, the centre-right political family at the European level to which Fidesz belongs, repeatedly defended the

[47] Directive 95/46/EC of the European Parliament and of the Council of 24 October 1995 on the protection of individuals with regard to the processing of personal data and on the free movement of such data [1995] OJ L281, 31–50.

[48] Case C-288/12 *Commission v Hungary* [2014] ECLI:EU:C:2014:237.

Hungarian government's constitutional policy. The governing coalition skilfully exploited this division in domestic politics, presenting the international criticism as simple political assaults against the Hungarian reform encouraged by the left-liberal opposition parties in Budapest or some multinational corporations whose economic interests were threatened by government policy.

As to the more formal or legal position of the EU institutions,[49] their common starting point was that the EU is founded on the values expressed by Article 2 TEU, highlighting the founding principles such as Rule of Law, pluralism, justice, and other values common to all Member States. In addition, the EU is based on the values of respect for basic human rights as enshrined in the Charter of the Fundamental Rights and Freedoms as well as the ECHR, as expressed by Article 6(1) and (3) respectively. Since the core values of these founding documents are addressed not only politically but are also legally binding principles,[50] both the EU institutions and the Member States must commit themselves clearly and unambiguously to them. In other words, the basic principles such as the Rule of Law or the respect of fundamental rights are unquestionable and enforceable parts of EU law. The respect and promotion of these values, the argumentation continues, is an explicit obligation deriving also from Articles 3(1) and (5) TEU, and it is an indispensable condition not only for becoming an EU member, but also for preserving membership itself.

The EU institutions sometimes also referred to the principle of cooperation as a special requirement, as a legal base for the EU to assess and verify the continuous compliance with EU law, including the common values by the Member States on a regular basis. In addition, Article 7(1) TEU grants the power to the EU institutions to determine if there is a clear risk of a serious breach of the values referred to in Article 2 by a Member State, and also defines a procedure for this assessment. This Article is of key importance to protecting the basic values of the EU, and can be invoked freely, as its scope is not limited to the policy areas covered by the EU law.

The very abstract nature of these values have repeatedly created difficulties for the EU institutions as to how to prove that particular national policy measures violate them. In the Hungarian cases in question, the EU regularly claimed that even if all of the challenged Hungarian action or legislation individually had equivalents in other Member States, the measures and policies as a whole are contrary to the basic values of the founding treaties. It should also be noted that even if the TEU acknowledges the Member States' right to establish and determine their own constitutional structures, since they have undertaken to respect the core values of the EU and their membership is based on constitutional traditions common to all member countries, there is a basic framework within which they must establish and preserve their own constitutional systems. Similarly, the fundamental principle of the EU to respect national identities and the different legal systems and traditions of the Member States as set out in Article 4(2) TEU and Article 67 TFEU, does not justify the violation of the principles of the Rule of Law and democratic values by the Member States. To sum up, if a member country such as Hungary wants to enjoy the privileges of EU membership, it has to comply with the basic values of this community of states, whatever constitutional structures and legal system it has.

The policy of the EU institutions in the Hungarian cases reflected the EU's overall argumentation strategy. First, the European Commission and the EP uniformly

[49] The legal arguments discussed here were used mainly by the European Commission in its informal actions (such as in its letters to the Hungarian government or the statements of its commissioners) and formal actions, and they emerged also in the resolutions of the EP cited above.

[50] See A von Bogdandy, 'Defining the Field of European Constitutional Law' in A von Bogdandy and J Bast (eds), *Principles of European Constitutional Law* (Hart/CH Beck 2011), 22.

represented the view that the EU is a community of values including the Rule of Law, democracy, and fundamental rights. These are not subsidiary but substantial principles underlying the EU.

Then, the deterioration of the Rule of Law and the backsliding in constitutional democracy in one or more Member States can lead to a lack of trust between the various members, which undermines not only their mutual relationships and recognition, but also the cooperative mechanisms of the whole EU and their effectiveness. This does not need more justification than that the disrespect or denial of the common values adversely affects the process of economic, political, and social integration in the future.

Furthermore, the EU, as an actor in world politics and a promoter of the Rule of Law in third countries, would lose credibility if it fails to preserve democratic principles in its own Member States.

b. The legal position of the Hungarian authorities

During the more-or-less informal consultations as well as the formal infringement procedures, the position of the Hungarian authorities was largely based on Article 4(2), according to which the EU must 'respect [...] the national identities, inherent in their fundamental structures, political and constitutional' of the Member States. As interpreted by Hungarian officials, constitutional issues simply do not fall within the competences of the EU. Its institutions may not thus launch any procedure or operate any control mechanism which is not explicitly recognized in the founding treaties. This approach is closely connected to the view that the obligations of respecting and guaranteeing the basic principles and values set out by Article 2 TEU impose explicit obligations, in the form of the Copenhagen criteria, only for candidate countries before their accession, also including control procedures, but such obligations are not formulated in the same form by the EU law for the Member States. Of course, this could only be an unspoken proposition, as the Hungarian government has always stressed that the recent constitutional changes meet the requirements of the basic values of the EU, and all criticisms are based on a lack of relevant information or misunderstandings.

Another direction taken in the Hungarian authorities' argumentation was that the criticism of the EU institutions was selective, because all the elements of the Hungarian constitutional changes can be found in the other EU Member States' legal systems. It was also a recurrent assertion that the 'assaults' against the 'Hungarians' were initiated by the leftist opposition and kept on the agenda by the European socialist parties. This allegation was particularly stressed in the debate over the 'Tavares report', adopted by the EP on the situation of fundamental rights, examining how far European standards and practices prevail in Hungary.[51] This kind of conspiracy theory was fuelled by the complaint that the same legal institutions, such as the very strong government control over the composition of the supervisory body of public and private media or the prohibition of same-sex marriage, are not criticized by the European Commission in other Member States.

In certain cases, special arguments were also used, such as active international lobbying by multinational corporations against the government's decision to decrease household costs.

But the basic strategy of the Hungarian government was to continue negotiations with the European Commission, and if necessary, to make some concessions without any

[51] EP, resolution of 3 July 2013 on the situation of fundamental rights: standards and practices in Hungary (pursuant to the EP resolution of 16 February 2012) (2012/2130(INI)).

substantial changes to the new constitutional and legal arrangements. This strategy proved successful at preserving the policy achievements of the Fidesz government, as the 'nuclear option', Article 7 TEU, was never invoked or even proposed by the Commission.

c. The state of affairs so far—striking a balance

Examining the outcome of the conflicts between Hungary and the EU so far, it is striking how little result has been achieved by the EU institutions. In fact, they have failed to achieve any real change in the issues debated.

Undoubtedly, as the guardian of EU law, the European Commission, has always had to limit itself to the legal dimension of the crucial problems, disregarding the real consequences of the controversial measures and policies of the Hungarian authorities. Although during the informal consultations the representatives of the EU probably also raised political concerns, the Commission did not discuss the political purge in the public media and in many public authorities, and it failed to prevent the practice of personalized legislation and many other worrisome events and developments. The Commission could not do anything, even with openly undemocratic rules and measures, such as the gerrymandering in the electoral law or the packing of the Constitutional Court. In particular, these failures are impressive with respect to those issues where the Commission launched formal infringement procedures: although the ECJ ruled that the compulsory retirement of judges violated EU law, not one removed judge was reinstated in his/her earlier position; the independence of the central bank was quickly removed from the agenda: subsequently, a very close ally of the Prime Minister, the former Minister for National Economy, was elected to be the president of the National Bank; and the parliamentary ombudsman for personal data protection did not get his mandate back (rather, he got financial compensation).

In fact, the European Commission was satisfied to declare that Hungary had returned to compliance with the relevant EU law after only minor changes in the contested legal regulations. The government was thus ready to change the media laws, the new regulation of the judiciary, and it was also willing to amend the Fundamental Law. However, none of these amendments, most of which were also minor technical changes, affected the substance of the original political effort and its effect on the relevant regulations. According to independent sources, the general situation of the Rule of Law and human rights has not improved in Hungary.[52]

In summary, it cannot be said that the EU institutions have succeeded in achieving substantial corrections to Hungarian constitutional policy or in restoring the previous level of protection of basic rights, and the quality of constitutionalism effective before 2010.

6. Explaining the recent Hungarian developments

At the moment, there is no consensual theory capable of sufficiently explaining the democratic deterioration in Hungary and for the new Eurosceptic political course in this country. We can only try to explain what has happened. One way of viewing this

[52] The most recent evaluations and discussions reported that the Rule of Law and human rights have deteriorated further. See e.g. Human Rights Watch 'World Report 2015, Events of 2014' (2015), http://www.hrw.org/sites/default/files/wr2015_web.pdf. 209-211, accessed 12 October 2016; and Freedom in the World 'Disregarding Democracy: Return to the Iron Fist' (2015) Freedom House, http://www.freedomhouse.org/report/freedom-world/freedom-world-2015, accessed 12 October 2016, 1, 13.

phenomenon is as an expression of widespread disappointment in EU membership. It is really surprising that the rate of economic convergence of Hungary to the EU average was faster in the pre-accession stage than after entry. The rate at which the country caught up fell significantly short of expectations; while Hungarian GDP was at 63 per cent of the EU average at the time of accession, after more than a decade of membership this rate is still only 67 per cent. In fact, since the beginning of the world financial crisis, the gap between the economic development of the EU average and the Hungarian economy has been widening continuously. The average standard of living in Hungary is greatly below that of Western European countries. This can contribute to the alleged disappointment in the achievement of the democratic era since the transition period. At least, the majority party in government readily relied on this argument to justify change to the constitutional framework.

Others argue that the elitist nature of the 'liberalization' of the country caused the trouble. According to this view, the economic liberalization was promoted at the expense of political liberalization. While the former was achieved through the successful establishment of a market economy, the political transformation has remained an elite-driven modernization, which 'could not sustain the goal of enhancing rights and freedoms inherent in political liberalization'.[53] As this model failed to deliver welfare for the masses, it was exposed to the populist position adopted by the Fidesz government after 2010, which promised a patriotic approach and the regaining of national sovereignty, emphasizing popular demands for welfare security rather than moral rights and abstract freedom. Another formulation of the same explanation attributes the recent decline in constitutional democracy to the exaggeration of legal constitutionalism at the expense of its civic form.[54] Whereas the system of the formal Rule of Law was carefully established, the elements of participatory democracy were overshadowed and ignored. The reason for this one-sided development is the vision of legal constitutionalism based on a distrust of the direct participation by citizens in the democratic decision-making process. This approach was supported by a 'perverse' impact of EU accession, strengthening the technocratic-instrumental view of democracy and the Rule of Law. Moreover, as this argumentation goes on, the transfer of power to the EU institutions eroded some of the bases of the constitutional democracy.[55] Hungary, like other post-communist countries, having just recently regained its sovereignty from the Soviet Union, suffering all the disadvantages of the oppressive domination of a foreign power, has lost a part of its sovereignty again as a consequence of EU accession.[56]

Although these theories have only little persuasive force and they might raise more questions than they answer,[57] it is a widely shared opinion that the constitutional culture of the democratic transition period in the early 1990s was not sufficiently appreciated by the people, who now might believe that the constitutional structures and values of the system change have contributed to the economic and social problems of today.

Many hold that the recent conflicts cannot be explained in the dimension of the EU and Hungary. The non-compliance problems do not thus derive from clashes between

[53] U Korkut, *Liberalization Challenges in Hungary. Elitism, Progressivism, and Populism* (Palgrave Macmillan 2012) 195–6.

[54] P Blokker, *New Democracies in Crisis? A comparative constitutional study of the Czech Republic, Hungary, Poland, Romania and Slovakia* (Routledge 2014) 79.

[55] ibid 136, 138.

[56] W Sadurski, *Constitutionalism and the Enlargement of Europe* (OUP 2012) 3.

[57] The new constitutional regime has not extended the forms of direct participation since 2010, and it is no less elitist than the old one, yet the conservative government coalition was able to repeat its electoral success in the parliamentary election of 2014. Furthermore, the transfer of public powers to the EU institutions has not led to any popular protest in the country since her accession in 2004.

European and national interests, but are rooted primarily in Hungarian domestic politics. Therefore, the intention of compliance cannot be modelled after the usual patterns of a cost-benefit analysis, according to which compliance is likely if the benefits outweigh the disadvantages. Instead, there is a new power politics at work here, aiming to replace the political, economic, and social elites and consolidate the current government's political power. If this is true, the price of non-compliance, except for in extreme cases, cannot be so high that it would encourage compliance with EU law, even if its basic values are at threat.

7. Lessons from the Hungarian case

From a European perspective, it is of great significance whether the change in Hungary's commitment to the European integration, as well as the deterioration of democracy in this country will be followed by other newcomers to the EU, or whether it remains an isolated, special case. Some argue that the Hungarian case, even though it might be the strongest challenge to the ability of the EU to protect democracy among its Member States, is not the only example of the deterioration of the Rule of Law. The political and legal transformations during the Law and Justice Party governments between 2005 and 2007 in Poland,[58] and the power politics of the Romanian government led by Victor Ponta between 2012 and 2015,[59] indicate that similar problems with liberal democracy can emerge in other countries in the Central and Eastern European region. Those who fear that Hungary is only the first country to diverge from the basic values of European constitutionalism argue that constitutional democracy in the post-communist countries is still vulnerable to populism and authoritarian tendencies caused by economic problems or financial crises. These presumptions seem to be confirmed in Poland where the government of the right-wing Law and Justice Party has followed the illiberal path of the Orbán government since it came to power in October 2015.

From the very beginning, EU institutions have tried to cooperate with other European organizations to exert pressure on the Hungarian authorities. The European Commission and the EP relied on the opinions of the Venice Commission, and frequently invoked the jurisprudence of the ECtHR. This itself shows that the EU institutions, including the ECJ, do not have far-reaching powers in Rule of Law or human rights issues.

Despite the strong arguments put forward by the EU institutions for recognizing the basic values entrenched in Article 2 TEU as a binding law with direct legal effects in the Member States, the European Commission has undertaken so far to bring these cases to the ECJ only if it found a relevant secondary source of EU law. The Commission probably did not feel that Article 2 TEU of itself was enough for a legal dispute. Instead, it carefully tried to find steady bases for any legal action against Hungary. The general explanation for this reticent attitude usually refers to the unavailability of appropriate instruments for the EU to enforce the respect of basic values, as the only possible sanction, the 'nuclear' Article 7(1) TEU, is widely held to be a disproportionate, politically undesirable, and dangerous weapon. Another possible argument is that the content of the fundamental values is not defined or specified in a manner necessary for the operation of any legal procedure. 'Human dignity', 'Rule of Law', 'democracy', 'pluralism', and other values are too vague as concepts, formulated generally and abstractly and without any further specification.

[58] EK Jenne and C Mudde, 'Hungary's Illiberal Turn: Can Outsiders Help?' (2012) 23 *Journal of Democracy* 147.

[59] U Sedelmeier, 'Anchoring Democracy from Above? The European Union and Democratic Backsliding in Hungary and Romania after Accession' (2014) 52 *Journal of Common Market Studies* 105; Blokker (n 54) 150.

Secondly, not only the legal instruments, but also the political intentions failed to exert any pressure on Hungary to force it to return to a more democratic way of government. There was not even an informal political boycott against the country. There is no doubt that the strong legitimacy of the Hungarian government made the situation more difficult for the European Commission; the Commission itself, at the peak in the debate on the legitimacy crisis of the EU, was struggling with a democratic deficit, and it had to represent the values and principles of constitutional democracy against a national government with extraordinarily wide popular support. Apart from its own legitimacy problems, the EU has a serious difficulty in arguing for democratic values in Hungary against the Fidesz government which came to power democratically in 2010, and which acquired a qualified majority in more-or-less free and democratic elections again in 2014.[60]

There are also other plausible explanations for the surprising incapacity of the EU institutions. First, it should be noted that the EU had to manage the negative effects of the world financial crisis during the same period, and it was in its primary institutional interest to minimize possible tensions or conflicts. The European Commission, for instance, has only a limited capacity to detect non-compliance with EU law in the Member States even in normal times, and, tackling the effects of the economic depression, it had even less attention to spare for the Hungarian constitutional shortcomings.

But the most important lesson of the Hungarian case undoubtedly is that it provided strong evidence for the weakness of EU law, in particular in the field of the Rule of Law.[61] The conclusion of the Charter of Fundamental Rights and Freedoms, and its recognition as a primary source of EU law was an important step towards improving EU level constitutional law, but, on account of its limited scope of application and the lack of the relevant jurisdiction, it was not an effective instrument in the hands of the European Commission in this specific case.

EU law is sketchy and rough-and-ready in this area, containing only abstract and general concepts and principles which are poorly suited to establishing the effective protection of the fundamental values of the EU. There is a blatant contradiction between the carefully elaborated and specified body of law in many other fields, and the EU level regulation of the Rule of Law and other key values. For example, while the Commission was able to act against the premature termination of the official term of the parliamentary ombudsman for data protection and freedom of information, it was incapable of doing anything against a similar removal of the president of the Supreme Court. From the perspective of European law, the only difference between the two cases is that the independence of the national authority for processing personal data is explicitly prescribed by a directive, while a similar safeguard for the courts or judges is absent from EU law.

Not only are the substantive provisions lacking, but effective legal sanctions as well. It is a widely shared view that the EU does not have any appropriate instruments by which it could enforce a recalcitrant Member State to comply with the EU law. Infringement procedures could lead to a financial penalty after a long process and a repeated procedure before the ECJ, if the Member State fails to implement the Court's ruling. But even this sanction had no deterrent effect in the Hungarian case, where the government majority passed a constitutional amendment which enabled the government to impose a special tax

[60] Nevertheless, the ODIHR found in its report on the parliamentary elections in Hungary in April 2014 that '[t]he main governing party enjoyed an undue advantage because of restrictive campaign regulations, biased media coverage and campaign activities that blurred the separation between political party and the State'. OSCE ODIHR (n 28).

[61] M Dawson and E Muir, 'Hungary and the Indirect Protection of EU Fundamental Rights and the Rule of Law' (2013) 14 *German Law Journal* 1959.

to cover the financial burdens of an ECJ judgment or a Constitutional Court ruling entailing payment obligations, if the state budget does not have sufficient funds available. Although this cynical provision in the Fourth Amendment was annulled by the Fifth Amendment to the Fundamental Law, it indicates the weakness of this sanction. In such special cases, the decentralized sanctioning through national courts, as encouraged by the European Commission, does not provide an effective instrument either, because systemic problems cannot be resolved by individual judicial cases, in particular when judicial independence itself is being threatened. The ultimate sanction in Article 7 TEU is, at the same time, an extremely severe penalty, which, because of its consequences, has never been used.

The only really effective means in the hands of the EU institutions to apply pressure on the Hungarian government was the suspension of payments from the EU structural funds, and the Council of Finance Ministers decided to do so, suspending EUR 495 million in March 2012 as a consequence of Hungary's failure to meet budget-deficit limits imposed by the EU after a long 'excessive deficit' procedure against the country. The withdrawal of this sanction that is the ending of the suspension, quickly became a top priority of government policy in Hungary to avoid any definitive loss of EU subsidies. But no matter how effective this instrument proved to be, it is not an available legal sanction against Rule of Law failures, and it is highly debatable whether it could be in the future.[62]

By all means, even if the EU has achieved certain successes in demanding fiscal discipline and stability and has a great influence over a number of technical matters from capacity-building for absorbing EU subsidies to legal harmonization, it appears to be powerless and ineffective in protecting the basic values of the whole Union. In fact, the Hungarian case has shown the limits of the EU legal domain in a field which is a new dimension in the ongoing integration, well beyond the market freedoms and economic cooperation among the Member States. Ten or twelve years ago it would not have been seen as a defect of the system of tools of European integration, but today, when the EU is held to be not only a close economic confederation of its Member States but appears also to be a community of values and commonly shared principles as Article 2 TEU declares, this raises the serious problem of its incapacity and failure to accomplish one of its fundamental functions.

The European Commission itself is aware of this weakness. Therefore, it issued a 'Communication' to the EP and the Council on 'A new EU Framework to strengthen the Rule of Law' in which the Commission proposes a new mechanism for resolving future threats to the Rule of Law in any Member State.[63] Through new preventive and sanctioning mechanisms the proposal seeks to solve the problem that the European Commission may launch an infringement procedure only if a Member State breaches a specific provision of EU law, by enabling the Commission to activate the procedures set out in Article 7 TEU when these instruments are ineffective, even if no particular EU legislation has been violated. Certainly, it is an open question whether a closer monitoring and assessment system to prevent any systemic breach of the Rule of Law in a Member State will be effective or not. However, it is worth noting that the clear political warnings or even pressure from the EU institutions have failed to achieve serious results in Hungary so far. In this situation, no positive changes can be expected for a long time. The Fidesz government managed to retain its two-thirds majority in Parliament after the general elections in 2014. Before the next parliamentary elections, many hoped that a period of consolidation would follow. But

[62] For such a proposal, see Jenne and Mudde (n 58) 153.

[63] European Commission, Communication from the Commission to the European Parliament and the Council. A new EU Framework to strengthen the Rule of Law (19 March 2014) COM(2014) 158 final 2.

the conservative coalition, owing to the highly disproportionate electoral system, acquired a two-thirds majority again, and is continuing its policy of further concentration of public power. The National Assembly has remained a rubber-stamp parliament, not only because of strong party discipline, but also because of the strict procedural rules adopted before the parliamentary elections. It is the only legislature in Europe which does not have the power to have a second reading to discuss the details of bills, losing all real influence over law making. In a new development in Hungary's internal politics, a comprehensive political campaign began in the summer of 2014 against non-governmental organizations, accusing many of them of being financed by foreign countries, and serving 'foreign interests'. The former and present Prime Minister Viktor Orbán, in a speech in July 2014 openly expressed his views about the policy objectives of his government. While praising Singapore, China, India, Turkey, and Russia for 'making [their] nations successful', and as the new 'stars of international analyses', he said that 'the new state that we are building is an illiberal state, a non-liberal state'.[64] The idea of the reestablishment of the death penalty and the government's harsh anti-immigration policy have attracted increasingly vociferous criticism from EU leaders and institutions.[65]

All in all, the chances of restoring constitutional democracy and returning to full compliance with the basic EU values are not very good. The partisan Constitution can be amended only by qualified majority. There is little hope of such a change in this country, where political populism has been so prevalent in the past few years. All public bodies are led by close party alliances of the current conservative (or right-wing populist) government, who did not raise their voices against any constitutional perversion in the past, and who would probably stand behind the constitutional regime of the Fundamental Law of 2011 in future. There is a greater likelihood that this illiberal form of democracy will be exported to other EU Member States. As a matter of fact, the first step has been taken in this direction: Mr Tibor Navracsics, the Minister of Justice between 2010 and 2014, *ex officio* responsible for many of the above criticized legislative and constitutional changes, was nominated by the Hungarian government to be a member of the new European Commission led by Jean-Claude Juncker, and he was confirmed in this position in the autumn of 2014.

[64] The whole speech can be found at: http://hungarianspectrum.wordpress.com/2014/07/31/viktor-orbans-speech-at-the-xxv-balvanyos-free-summer-university-and-youth-camp-july-26-2014-baile-tusnad-tusnadfurdo/, accessed 12 October 2016.

[65] See e.g. the EP's resolutions of 10 June 2015 on the situation in Hungary (P8_TA(2015)0227), and of 16 December 2015 on the situation in Hungary (P8_TA(2015)0461).

27

Weak Members and the Enforcement of EU Law

Michael Ioannidis

1. Introduction

The EU is based on the presumption that all Member States are effective in enforcing their law. Failures may occasionally occur due to the defiance of some state organs, a lack of administrative resources, or corruption, but they should be treated as isolated exceptions. The rule is that the law rules.

This chapter focuses on cases where this general presumption does not hold: when Member States show structural, persistent, and cross-sector ineffectiveness in enforcing their law.[1] Such problems might not have been an important concern when the EU was comprised of a comparatively small number of Member States with fairly similar structures and capacities. With the growth of the scope of EU law, however, and accession of new members from different governance traditions, such as the European South or the former Eastern bloc, enforcement problems resulting from widespread corruption, disproportionately long judicial proceedings, or a lack of necessary material resources have become more important.

In international law, states facing widespread problems of effectiveness are often described as weak, fragile, or failed. These concepts describe the persistent and cross-sector inability of the central authorities, government and parliament, to implement effectively their decisions, including their international and supranational commitments. This chapter borrows significantly from this literature and also relies on insights from the rich research on EU compliance[2] to develop three points. The first point is that on some occasions the EU might face a similar challenge to that of international law when dealing with weak states. To describe such cases of structural ineffectiveness, this chapter develops the concept of *weak member*. The second point is that these problems can be captured through the lens of EU constitutional law, and more specifically as Rule of Law problems. The third point is to present some of the measures taken during the Eurozone crisis to respond to this type of problems.

The remainder of this chapter treats each of these points in a separate section. Firstly, the concept of weak member is developed. Although we cannot speak of failed states or anything similar in the EU, there are cases where some Member States present such pervasive and persistent deficiencies that this places them in a different category to their European peers. A critical part of this argument is that these deficiencies are not assessed with reference to global, but European standards. Secondly, the chapter considers the

[1] In detail about this type of deficiency, see A von Bogdandy and M Ioannidis, 'Systemic deficiency in the Rule of Law: What it is, what has been done, what can be done.' (2014) 51 *ommon Market Law Review* 59. This chapter further develops some points made in this article.

[2] For an overview of the field, see E Mastenbroek, 'EU Compliance: Still a "Black Hole"?' (2005) 12 *Journal of European Public Policy* 1103; D Toshkov et al., 'Connecting the Dots: Case Studies and EU Implementation Research' (2010) Institute for European Integration Research Working Paper Series No 10.

impact of such weakness to the implementation of EU law. This cannot be an exhaustive account, and much of this research belongs to the field of empirical political science from which this chapter draws extensively. For presentational purposes, the case study of Greece is given more thorough attention. Finally, the third section of the chapter reflects on some potential reactions of the EU to this type of defiance. During the Eurozone crisis, when such problems became more obvious and more threatening, the EU tried to engage more actively in state-building actions in some Member States, and especially in Greece. Greece thus offers a good example for present purposes for two reasons: because it offers an indicative case of what might qualify as a weak Member State and because there new mechanisms to address this type of problem have been tried out.

2. Weak members

a. Weak statehood at the international level

The concept of weak statehood is often used at the international level to distinguish states which diverge considerably in terms of institutions, material resources or the ability to deliver certain public goods.[3] Treating some states as weak at the international level requires reflection on two questions: (I.) which elements of statehood should be relevant to distinguish between 'stronger' and 'weaker' states; and (II.) how much should a state diverge from its peers to allow (or even require) its qualification as 'weak'.

I. Criteria of weakness at the international level

State capacity is a concept which occupies an important place in economics, political science, and law. Depending on the focus, different criteria are employed to distinguish between stronger and weaker states. For present purposes, these criteria can be broadly distinguished into two categories.[4] The first is connected with the economic performance of the state or its ability to provide for a minimum of public goods. The second reflects effectiveness in implementing the law.

In an important part of the mostly economic-oriented literature, state strength is measured in terms of material capacity and economic success. Sometimes, the focus is on income, growth and other similar categories.[5] In other cases, economic performance is combined with other elements to measure military strength, capacity for self-defence and political influence.[6] A similar approach uses as a criterion a state's ability to offer certain public goods or carry out certain functions. The list of public goods relevant for distinguishing between stronger and weaker states diverges considerably from author to author.

[3] For a general overview, see D Kostovicova and V Bojicic-Dzelilovic, *Persistent State Weakness in the Global Age* (Ashgate 2009) 2; F Leidenmühler, *Kollabierter Staat und Völkerrechtsordnung: zur Aktualität der Westfälischen Ordnung, entwickelt an Fragen des Wegfalls effektiver Staatsgewalt* (Berliner Wissenschafts-Verlag 2011) 173 et seq.; C Richter, *Collapsed States: Perspektiven nach dem Wegfall von Staatlichkeit Zugleich ein Beitrag zu den Grundlagen des Selbstbestimmungsrechts der Völker und zur Struktur des völkerrechtlichen Staatsbegriffs* (Nomos 2011).

[4] For other categorizations, see U Schneckener, 'States at Risk – Zur Analyse fragile Staatlichkeit' in U Schneckener (ed), *States at Risk—Fragile Staaten als Sicherheits- und Entwicklungsproblem* (Stiftung Wissenschaft und Politik 2004) 12; Leidenmühler (n 3) 174 et seq.

[5] For one of the most recent influential accounts of that type, see D Acemoglu and JA Robinson, *Why Nations Fail: The Origins of Power, Prosperity and Poverty* (Profile Books 2012); D Acemoglou et al., 'Institutions as the Fundamental Cause of Long-Run Growth' in P Aghion and S Durlauf (eds), *Handbook of Economic Growth* (Elsevier 2005). See also RI Rotberg, 'Failed States, Collapsed States, Weak States. Causes and Indicators' in RI Rotberg (ed), *State Failure and State Weakness in a Time of Terror* (Brookings Institution Press 2003) 4.

[6] MI Handel, *Weak States in the International System* (2nd edn, Cass 1990) 48 et seq.

In some cases the accent is put on the existence of basic institutions, such as offering basic means for peaceful dispute resolution, while in other cases, the provision of some minimum degree of healthcare and education or more generally the ability of states to guarantee the 'welfare of their citizens' is added.[7]

The main problem with using these criteria in legal discourse is that their application presupposes value judgments in controversial issues. Whether GDP, income per capita, or the Gini coefficient should be definitive for classifying a state as strong or weak is contested among economists and requires a decision on whether equality or aggregate income should take precedence for a society—a decision which goes beyond what legal discourses can deliver. Similarly, defining which public goods are necessary to distinguish weak from strong states touches upon a polity's specific priorities. What level of healthcare should a state provide to its citizens is an issue too contingent upon policy preferences to serve as a tool for legal analysis.[8] As Max Weber noted with reference to the definition of state, all efforts to define statehood with reference to some alleged list of state-specific functions face the difficulty that there has been no function that states have not occasionally assumed.[9] For these reasons, the criterion which might serve best to qualify a state as strong or weak in a legal discourse is not its ability to deliver certain public goods, however important these might be deemed for modern societies, but *the capacity of a political entity to enforce its collective decisions, resorting to coercion if necessary*.[10] That is, the ability of a state to implement the law.

Indeed, in an important part of political science and legal discourses, the strength of states is assessed on the basis of their effectiveness in implementing decisions taken at the central level of governance. Effectiveness or strength, following this criterion, means the ability to 'make, implement, and enforce central decisions for a collectivity'.[11] This type of effectiveness requires in turn that central institutions, such as parliaments or governments, firstly, exist and secondly, command the necessary resources, material or otherwise, to implement the norms they set.[12] Adding the time factor to this approach, those states which dispose of a government and other organs with a long-term ability to implement their decisions throughout the realm are addressed as strong.

One of the reasons why this criterion serves well for a legal qualification of statehood is that it addresses effectiveness in a way familiar to constitutional theory. Following Hans Kelsen, what is typical of a legal order is its effectiveness 'by and large'.[13] According to this view, a legal order requires the existence of institutions which are 'by and large' capable of enforcing their decisions throughout a certain territory. Thus, entities which set norms but are unable to enforce them fail to constitute legal orders in the proper meaning of the term. What is, however, necessary is '*by and large*' effectiveness. Of relevance to this concept of

[7] See indicatively P Stewart, 'Weak States and Global Threats: Fact or Fiction?' (2006) 29 *The Washington Quarterly* 27, 29; E Ikpe, 'Challenging the discourse on fragile states' (2007) 7 *Conflict, Security and Development* 85, 86; E Newman, 'Failed States and International Order: Constructing a Post-Westphalian World' (2009) 30 *Contemporary Security Policy* 421, 422.

[8] These analytical hurdles become even more acute in those cases where standards of legitimacy are also added to measure state strength. See T Risse and U Lehmkuhl, 'Governance in Areas of Limited Statehood – New Modes of Governance?' (2006) SFB-Governance Working Paper Series No 1, 9–10.

[9] M Weber, *Wirtschaft und Gesellschaft: Grundriss der verstehenden Soziologie* (5th revised edn, Mohr 1972) 29.

[10] Weber (n 9) 29.

[11] T Risse, 'Governance in Areas of Limited Statehood: Introduction and Overview' in T Risse (ed), *Governance Without a State?* (Columbia University Press 2011) 4. See also RH Jackson and CG Rosberg, 'Why Africa's Weak States Persist: The Empirical and the Juridical in Statehood' (1982) 35 *World Politics* 1, 6.

[12] See Risse (n 11) 4; G Kreijen, *State Failure, Sovereignty and Effectiveness: Legal Lessons from the Decolonization of Sub-Saharan Africa* (Martinus Nijhoff 2004) 86.

[13] H Kelsen, *General Theory of Law and State* (trans A Wedberg, Harvard University Press 1949) 120, 152, 170, 173; H Kelsen, *Pure Theory of Law* (trans M Knight, University of California Press 1967) 46, 86, 210, 290.

law are structural, systemic, and persistent deficiencies in implementation—temporal or episodic failures in enforcement do not call into question the legal character of a coercive order. In sum, therefore, a minimum of state effectiveness—the structural capacity to implement centrally promulgated norms—is a conceptual requirement for the legal constitution of a polity.

This 'internal' connection between effectiveness and law is not the only reason why defining state weakness in terms of insufficient implementing capacity is preferable. State weakness not only has significant repercussions from a constitutional law perspective but also from that of international law. One of the preconditions for an operative system of international coordination is that the government which appears in international fora as the agent of a territorially organized collectivity and undertakes commitments in its name disposes of an organized system of authority able to give effect to these international responsibilities.[14] International law is largely based on the presumption that states are equally effective regarding their ability to exercise effective authority over their territories. Failure to live up to this expectation, due to the inability to give real effect to the laws, might thus also justify the qualification of statehood from the perspective of international law.

II. Setting a threshold

The second point which needs to be addressed when qualifying statehood is that of a threshold allowing for a meaningful distinction between strong, weak, failed, or other categories of statehood. Of course, this is not an exact science and distinctions depend on the analytical purpose of drawing them.[15] A variety of levels of weakness has thus emerged, pointing to different degrees of effectiveness in order to qualify statehood along the strong–weak continuum.[16]

At the one end of this spectrum is the ideal type of fully functioning state, where central institutions exist and are capable of enforcing their decisions and international commitments throughout the realm. At the other end, states are usually referred to as 'collapsed' or 'failed'. In these cases, central authorities have totally lost their ability to implement their decisions and do not even hold the monopoly of physical coercion.[17] Intermediate categories include states which fell short of fully functioning states without, however, the central public authority being totally irrelevant. A number of different subcategories have been distinguished here. For example, Thomas Risse distinguishes 'failed' from 'limited' statehood, which only refer to 'areas', namely 'territorial or functional spaces within otherwise functioning states'.[18] The focus on 'areas of limited statehood' has, however, the disadvantage of questioning the analytical and practical value of the concept of statehood as a useful generalization, covering the whole of a certain territory both spatially and functionally. Of course, capacity can be different in different fields of policy:[19] a state might be reasonably effective in organizing military operations but fail completely in setting up a system of healthcare or environmental protection. Nevertheless, qualifications

[14] Leidenmühler (n 3) 272. For international law, relevant government is the effective government, Kreijen (n 12) 21. This is reflected to the criterion of government being the most important of the criteria of statehood set by the Montevideo Convention.

[15] For an overview of relevant efforts, see R Koskenmäki, 'Legal Implications Resulting from State Failure in Light of the Case of Somalia' (2004) 73 *Nordic Journal of International Law* 1, 2; Newman (n 7) 426–7.

[16] C Clapham, 'Degrees of Statehood' (1998) 24 *Review of International Studies* 143 (focusing on Africa); M Brunazzo, 'The Variable Geometry of Policy Styles: Italy from Weak to Stronger State?' (2007) Paper presented to the European Union Studies Association Conference, Montreal, 17–19 May 2007.

[17] See Rotberg (n 5). [18] Risse (n 11) 5.

[19] L Weiss, *The Myth of the Powerless State* (Cornell University Press 1998).

of statehood are useful exactly in that they point to states which *do not simply* present incapacities in *specific* policy fields, but are rather characterized by *general, structural* deficiencies. For these states, 'weakness' can be reasonably used as an attribute of statehood rather than simply of some specific policy sectors. In short, the concept of weak statehood has an added value especially for the cases where it makes sense to speak of a *weak state* instead of a *state that is weak in a specific policy field.* To restate this idea in more general terms: the concept of weak statehood challenges the view that states can be addressed as an undiversified category, but it does accept that the state remains a useful generalization at the international level. The fact that many private and public institutions fund efforts to rank states along a weak–strong continuum[20] indicates that such a generalization remains useful for a variety of purposes, from guiding aid and investment decisions to offering an overview of potential security threats. For this reason, the threshold of weakness should not focus on specific policy areas but refer to the state as a whole; sectoral or spatially limited incapacities should not suffice for characterizing a state as 'weak'.

It thus appears that the most promising way to address state weakness is on the basis of *cross-sectoral ability to implement the law.* The degree of this ability or lack thereof is usually documented using reports from international organizations or indicators focusing on Rule of Law criteria and especially the ability to enforce the law. The World Bank criteria, as used in the Worldwide Governance Indicators (WGIs),[21] offer a good starting point as well as criteria developed by other institutions.[22] Additionally, the ad hoc reports of organizations such as the IMF or the EU often point to structural incapacities in the reviewed countries. To that extent they might also offer indications of weak states. The degree of weakness for qualifying a state as weak depends, however, on the specific purposes for using this concept. The following section will elaborate on the standards of weakness for the specific case of the EU.

b. Weak members in the EU

I. EU and the standard of weakness

The literature on qualified statehood has traditionally focused on rather extreme cases of state ineffectiveness, such as Somalia or Sierra Leone, and notions such as 'failed' or 'weak' state are usually associated with collapsed regimes in Africa or Asia. This might make similar references counterintuitive when speaking of developed EU Member States. Nevertheless, economic development, although usually the outcome of reliable institutions,[23] does not guarantee strong statehood. Economically developed nations might still suffer from persistent institutional weaknesses while less wealthy countries

[20] For a critical overview, see Newman (n 7) 426 et seq.

[21] http://info.worldbank.org/governance/wgi/index.asp, accessed 12 October 2016. See CR Apaza, 'Measuring Governance and Corruption through the Worldwide Governance Indicators: Critiques, Responses, and Ongoing Scholarly Discussion' (2009) 42 *Political Science & Politics* 139; MJ Kurtza and A Schrank, 'Growth and Governance: Models, Measures, and Mechanisms' (2007) 69 *The Journal of Politics* 538.

[22] See the Failed States Index (maintained by the Fund for Peace); Global Peace Index (maintained by the Vision for Humanity); Index of State Weakness in the Developing World (maintained by the Brookings Institution); State Fragility Index (maintained by the Center for Systemic Peace and Center for Global Policy at Maryland University); Human Development Index (maintained by the UN Development Programme).

[23] For the latest and most influential support for the connection between reliable and inclusive institutions with economic success, see Acemoglu and Robinson (n 5).

sometimes score better in good-governance listings than more prosperous nations. According to the WGIs, for example, developing and emerging economies, such as Chile, Uruguay, and Costa Rica have higher scores in governance effectiveness, the Rule of Law, and control of corruption than economically more developed countries such as Greece and Italy.[24]

At the EU level, 'weak statehood' has already been used as an analytical category to address some of the questions regarding the ability of the post-2004 and post-2007 enlargement members to meet their EU obligations.[25] Beate Sissenich, for example, used data from the World Values Survey and WGIs to distinguish a group of EU members which lag behind their peers to a significant extent.[26] But older members, mainly from the European South, have also been occasionally addressed as 'weak' in order to emphasize their structural deficiencies compared to some of their European peers.[27] More recently, during the 2010–2015 economic crisis, Greece was often referred to using the language of qualified statehood, namely as a 'failing developed state',[28] 'failing state',[29] or even 'failed state'.[30]

Of course, neither Greece nor any other EU Member State is failed within the meaning that the term has acquired in the international law and political science literature. Even crisis-laden Greece remains among the richest and most stable countries judged by global standards. At the European level, however, the threshold of effectiveness is set considerably higher than at the global level. EU Member States are not simply required to meet the standards of statehood indicated by a global average or simply the enforcement requirements of international law. Their capacity shall be judged with reference to their participation in the advanced project of European integration and the requirement to uphold EU law.[31] Membership in the EU thus sets *a higher threshold of state effectiveness for EU Member States*. This is the first reason why we should rather speak of weak *members* rather than weak *states* in the EU context: it is EU membership which determines the threshold of strength. This heightened threshold can be justified by reference to three categories of reasons: the closer interdependence of EU polities, the higher requirements set by EU law regarding the implementation of supranational norms, and the dual legitimatory basis of the EU.

[24] See WGIs, available at: http://info.worldbank.org/governance/wgi/index.aspx#reports, accessed 12 October 2016, selecting the respective indicators and countries as input. For the level of economic growth, see the data of the IMF World Economic Outlook (WEO), available at: http://www.imf.org/external/pubs/ft/weo/2015/02/weodata/index.aspx, accessed 12 October 2016, selecting gross domestic product based on PPP per capita and the respective countries.

[25] See B Sissenich, 'Weak States, Weak Societies: Europe's East-West Gap' (2010) 45 *Acta Politica* 11; TA Börzel, 'When Europeanization Hits Limited Statehood. The Western Balkans as a Test Case for the Transformative Power of Europe' (2011) KFG Working Paper No 30.

[26] See Sissenich (n 25). [27] See Brunazzo (n 16).

[28] H Mylonas, 'Is Greece a Failing Developed State? Causes and Socio-economic Consequences of the Financial Crisis' in KE Botsiou and A Klapsis (eds), *The Konstantinos Karamanlis Institute for Democracy Yearbook 2011* (2011) 77.

[29] K Featherstone, 'The JCMS Annual Lecture: The Greek Sovereign Debt Crisis and EMU: A Failing State in a Skewed Regime' (2011) 49 *Journal of Common Market Studies* 193; R Donadio, 'The Failing State of Greece' (25 February 2012) *The New York Times*, http://www.nytimes.com/2012/02/26/sunday-review/the-failing-state-of-greece.html?pagewanted=all, accessed 12 October 2016.

[30] N Malkoutzis, 'Is Greece a failed State?' (1 March 2012) *Foreign Policy*, http://www.foreignpolicy.com/articles/2012/03/01/is_greece_a_failed_state, accessed 12 October 2016. See also H-J Axt, 'Griechenland, Linkspopulisten und Euro' (2012) 60 *Südosteuropa* 321, 323 ('Staatszerfall, der nach einem neuen "state building" verlangt'). Critical to the use of the term is I Zelepos, 'Im Südosten nichts Neues?' (2012) 60 *Südosteuropa* 346, 354.

[31] Article 197 TFEU sets this idea in the rank of primary law, connecting domestic administrative capacity, the implementation of EU law, and the proper functioning of the Union.

i. Closer interdependence

Because of the closer territorial proximity of EU Member States, negative externalities owed to one member's weakness have greater impact upon the others, compared to the ineffectiveness of states located in more distant parts of the world. This is the other reason why we should rather speak of weak *members* rather than weak *states* in the EU context: to allude to the importance that the weakness of one 'limb' has for the 'body' as a whole. We could easily make this point by reference to contemporary European problems such as immigration and asylum, transnational criminality, or environmental risks. Regarding immigration and asylum, for example, the incapacity of some states to guard their borders may have consequences for the rest of the EU's Members. The 'Dublin III' Regulation[32] establishes a system for examining asylum claims by defining the criteria for deciding which member should be responsible for controlling immigration flows directed to Europe. The implementation of this system requires domestic authorities to develop an elaborate mechanism for processing applications which should meet the requirements of EU secondary and primary law, including respect of fundamental rights. The ineffectiveness of a Member State designated by Regulation 604/2013 in addressing immigration flows can have detrimental effects on other countries and it might even legally require them to shoulder the burden that the weak member is unable to discharge.[33] Another typical example of negative externalities is the inability to fight organized crime. As the Commission has noted on a number of occasions with regard to the 2007 accessions, grave inefficiencies in some Member States in adapting their criminal laws can become of legitimate concern for the other Members and require EU-coordinated action.[34]

ii. Legitimacy and mutual trust

In the debate about the legitimacy of the EU, the main focus is usually on the legitimacy of EU institutions, the European Commission, the Council, or the EP. Often, little attention is paid to the importance of the functioning of Member States to the overall legitimacy of the EU. That is the more surprising considering that Article 10(2) TEU clearly postulates that the EU stands on a double legitimatory basis.[35] On the one hand, there is legitimacy generated through the mechanisms which allow European citizens to exert direct control on European institutions, mainly through the elections to the EP, and on the other hand, the legitimate structuring and functioning of domestic legal orders.

The second component of the European legitimatory structure is of particular importance for the present purposes. Two dimensions of state weakness are relevant here. Firstly,

[32] Regulation (EU) No 604/2013 of the European Parliament and of the Council of 26 June 2013 establishing the criteria and mechanisms for determining the Member State responsible for an application for international protection lodged in one of the Member States by a third-country national or a stateless person (recast) [2013] OJ L180/31, 31.

[33] Joined Cases C-411 and 493/10 *NS v Secretary of State for the Home Department* [2011] ECLI:EU:C:2011:865. See S Lieven, 'Case Report on C-411/10, N.S. and C-493/10, M.E. and Others' (2012) 2 *European Journal of Migration and Law*, 223; I Canor, 'My Brother's Keeper? Horizontal Solange: 'An Ever Closer Distrust Among the Peoples of Europe" (2013) 50 *Common Market Law Review* 383.

[34] See European Commission, 'Decision establishing a mechanism for cooperation and verification of progress in Bulgaria to address specific benchmarks in the areas of judicial reform and the fight against corruption and organised crime, 13 December 2006' COM(2006) 6570 final; European Commission, 'Report from the Commission to the European Parliament and the Council on Progress in Bulgaria under the Co-operation and Verification Mechanism, Brussels, 28 January 2015' COM(2015) 36 final.

[35] See A Peters, *Elemente einer Theorie der Verfassung Europas* (Duncker & Humblot 2001) 209, 219; P Dann, 'The Political Institutions' in A von Bogdandy and J Bast (eds), *Principles of European Constitutional Law* (2nd edn, Hart/CH Beck 2009); A von Bogdandy, 'The European Lesson for International Democracy: The Significance of Articles 9 to 12 EU Treaty for International Organizations' (2012) 23 *European Journal of International Law* 315, 322.

weakness connected with the functioning and accountability of the government, which, according to Article 10(2) TEU, constitutes one of the pillars of EU legitimacy. Secondly, weak statehood might have a detrimental impact on the myriad of EU bodies comprised by national officials in their capacity as representatives of the Member States. States involved in European decision making through mechanisms such as comitology, but which display structural and persistent weakness regarding the capacity of their administrations, might compromise the overall effectiveness and legitimacy of those mechanisms.

The effects of weak statehood become more acute to the extent that the principle of mutual trust governs the relations between Member States. Trust in the effectiveness of domestic administrations and courts is presupposed by the principle of mutual recognition, which, by allowing products and services lawfully marketed in one Member State to enter the markets of other Member States,[36] amounts in effect to horizontal transfer of power to foreign domestic authorities.[37] Since it is only *lawfully* circulated products and services which should enjoy the privileges deriving from the principle of mutual recognition,[38] Member States need to trust each other's effectiveness when it comes to setting and enforcing their own rules. Considering that mutual recognition in the EU plays a much more important role than in other forms of economic integration, such as the WTO, the threshold of effectiveness is proportionately higher. This is even more true in the area of justice and security, where the mutual trust required is even higher. As Miguel Poiares Maduro notes in this regard, '[t]he mutual recognition of judicial decisions is not based simply on the mutual recognition of each applicable norm but on the assumption that the other's judicial and legislative decisions are legitimate *in systemic terms* [. . .] This involves the recognition of rules, goals and the processes and institutions through which they are adopted and implemented in another system'.[39] The Commission has also stressed this point on numerous occasions, pointing out that '[a] well functioning, independent judicial system, and respect for democratic institutions are indispensable for mutual trust within the European Union'.[40] It is exactly the premises of mutual trust and mutual recognition which are distorted in the cases covered by the concept of weak membership.

iii. Higher demands regarding the implementation of supranational law

The main reason why the weakness of a Member State might be of importance to the rest of the edifice has been alluded to before with reference to international law. The EU is a *Rechtsgemeinschaft*, setting norms in a broad spectrum of policy fields, but a *Rechtsgemeinschaft* that disposes only very limited capacities in directly implementing its own law. There is thus a divergence at the EU level between who sets the norms and who commands the resources that are necessary for their implementation—fiscal, material, or human resources. This is a fundamental point for the EU constitutional order and bears decisively on any discussion on effectiveness at the EU level. It essentially means that the effectiveness

36 This principle originates in the 'Cassis de Dijon' case law Case 120/78 *Rewe-Zentral AG v Bundesmonopolverwaltung für Branntwein* [1979] ECLI:EU:C:1979:42. See Regulation (EC) No 764/2008 European Parliament and of the Council of 9 July 2008 laying down procedures relating to the application of certain national technical rules to products lawfully marketed in another Member State and repealing Decision No 3052/95/EC (Text with EEA relevance) [2008] OJ L218, 21.

37 SK Schmidt, 'Mutual recognition as a new mode of governance' (2007) 14 *Journal of European Public Policy* 667, 672.

38 See Commission Working Document, Guidance Document. The concept of 'lawfully marketed' in the Mutual Recognition Regulation (EC) No 764/2008, COM(2013) 592 final.

39 MP Maduro, 'So Close and Yet so Far: The Paradoxes of Mutual Recognition' (2007) 14 *Journal of European Public Policy* 814, 823 (emphasis added).

40 Report from the Commission to the European Parliament and the Council, 'On Progress in Romania under the Cooperation and Verification Mechanism, Brussels', 18 July 2012, COM(2012) 410 final, 3.

of EU law relies on the implementing capacities of domestic governments and any subnational public entities. If a state lacks such capacities, the normativity of EU law is jeopardized.

This is true for any relatively decentralized legal order, and to that extent the problems which have been identified above with regard to the importance of state effectiveness in upholding the efficacy and validity of international law also apply to EU law. The major difference in the case of the EU supranational legal order is the higher demands it raises with regard to the enforcement capacities of its Member States. EU law, from product-safety norms to environmental-protection rules and asylum legislation, exerts far greater demands on domestic administrations and courts compared to international law. By raising the complexity and diversity of EU norms that Member States need to implement, the threshold of effectiveness they need to pass also rises. As will be discussed in greater detail in the following, the connection between institutional strength and the implementation of EU law is also supported by empirical research. Although there is a variety of reasons why Member States do not comply with EU law,[41] insufficient state capacity is among the most important.[42]

II. Weak members and the Rule of Law

Drawing an analogy between weak statehood at the international level and weak membership in the EU might sound intuitive. From a legal perspective, however, an important question is how the concept of a weak member fits into the constitutional vocabulary of the EU. It is argued here that weak members should be treated as an issue captured by the concept of the Rule of Law, one of the values that EU Member States need to uphold according to Article 2 TEU.[43] Treating weak members from this perspective allows bringing the problem under the lens of EU constitutional law.

Although the Rule of Law is a thoroughly contested concept,[44] there is general agreement regarding its minimum core: the Rule of Law certainly requires that the law actually *rules*. We can only speak of a polity governed by the Rule of Law when its public authorities act in accordance with constitutional norms and the general rules laid down by superior organs, usually a parliament, and when courts and administrative authorities are effective in ensuring that the law is generally observed by private actors. Essentially, this minimum content requires that there is a system in place to ensure that the law succeeds in structuring and upholding normative expectations, as the basic function of law is to offer the members of a society a reliable foundation upon which they can organize their activities and plan their conduct.[45] Only effective legal orders succeed in signalling that some actions

[41] See TA Börzel et al., 'Obstinate and Inefficient: Why Member States Do Not Comply With European Law' (2010) 43 *Comparative Political Studies* 1363, 1367.

[42] G Falkner et al., 'Non-Compliance with EU Directives in the Member States: Opposition through the Backdoor?' (2004) 27 *West European Politics* 452, 466; Börzel et al. (n 41) 1369–70.

[43] See D Kochenov et al., 'Reinforcing the Rule of Law Oversight in the European Union' (2014) EUI RSCAS Working Paper No 2014/15.

[44] The literature on the Rule of Law is voluminous, see indicatively C Grewe and HR Fabri, *Droits constitutionnels européens* (Presses Universitaires de France 1995) 22 et seq.; R Grote, 'Rule of law, rechtsstaat and état de droit', in Christian Starck (ed), *Constitutionalism, Universalism and Democracy: A Comparative Analysis* (Nomos 1999) 269; P Craig, 'Formal and Substantive Conceptions of the Rule of Law: An Analytical Framework' (1997) 21 *Public Law* 467; L Heuschling, *État de droit, Rechtsstaat, Rule of Law* (Dalloz 2002); M Krygier, 'Rule of law', in M Rosenfeld and A Sajó (eds), *The Oxford Handbook of Comparative Constitutional Law* (OUP 2012), 233. From a more theoretical perspective, see B Tamanaha, *On the Rule of Law* (CUP 2004) 7 et seq.; J Waldron, 'The Concept of Law and the Rule of Law' (2008) 43 *Georgia Law Review* 1, 6 et seq.; J Raz, *The Authority of Law* (2nd edn, OUP 2009) 210 et seq.

[45] N Luhmann, *Das Recht der Gesellschaft* (Suhrkamp 1993) 150–3; J Habermas, *Between Facts and Norms: Contributions to a Discourse Theory of Law and Democracy* (trans William Rehg, MIT Press 2008 (repr)) 144 et seq.; J Raz, *The Authority of Law* (2nd edn, OUP 2009) 222.

are more likely and acceptable than others, thus making it easier for persons to act within complex social environments.[46]

Law, however, can only accomplish this social function and generate reliable expectations when it is generally observed. In order to succeed in providing reliable information, rules must be 'socially shared': that is, they must be 'known to be generally applicable guides'.[47] General observance is not threatened by isolated, episodic infringements. In all systems there are cases of corrupt officials, unenforced judicial decisions, or agencies inefficient in enforcing certain rules. These instances of state ineffectiveness do not undermine people's general expectation that legal rules, courts, and administrative authorities have the power and ability to influence their incentives and disincentives when making socially relevant decisions. However, when an endemic inability to implement the law exists due to widespread corruption, unwillingness to enforce the law, institutional weakness, or lack of the necessary resources, the law fails to convey the information necessary to structure and support normative expectations. For example, in a system where obtaining a final judicial decision may take many years or where officials can be easily bribed, what the law requires is of secondary importance for social action. Once it has reached this threshold, a legal system fails to exercise its core function, to support reliable expectations. This systemic deficiency in the Rule of Law[48] is the defining element of what is described here as *weak members*. An EU Member State is thus weak if, due to widespread corruption, lack of resources, or bad organization, it fails to give real effect to its law, thereby falling short of the Rule of Law requirement set out in Article 2 TFEU.

3. Weak members and the enforcement of EU law: the case of Greece

a. Greece as a weak member?

Greece has always been treated as a 'critical case' in Europeanization studies.[49] The weakness of the Greek public administration and judiciary has been a recurring theme both in the literature and in the reports of many international institutions.[50] In the 1990s, inefficient government structure was already being blamed for the low EU law implementation rates.[51] The problem of weak institutions, however, gained new urgency during the economic crisis that began in 2010. The EU Task Force for Greece, the special Commission body established in 2011 to support Greek reform efforts and to assist the implementation of the EU/IMF adjustment programmes, referred to the structural ineffectiveness and non-implementation of policies as 'a major and debilitating weakness' of Greece.[52] In a similar

[46] N Luhmann, 'Positivität des Rechts als Voraussetzung einer modernen Gesellschaft' (1970) *Jahrbuch für Rechtssoziologie und Rechtstheorie* 175, 185.

[47] J Knight, *Institutions and Social Conflict* (CUP 1992) 17.

[48] Von Bogdandy and Ioannidis (n 1) 71 et seq.

[49] K Featherstone and D Papadimitriou, *The limits of Europeanization reform capacity and policy conflict in Greece* (Palgrave Macmillan 2008) 5.

[50] T Pelagidis, 'The Greek Paradox of Falling Competitiveness and Weak Institutions in a High GDP Growth Rate Context (1995–2008)' (2010) Hellenic Observatory Papers on Greece and Southeast Europe GreeSE Paper No 38, 13. For recent approaches to the causes of Greek failure in light of the crisis, see A Doxiadis, *The invisible rift: institutions and behaviors in Greek economy* (*Το αόρατο ρήγμα: θεσμοί και συμπεριφορές στην ελληνική οικονομία*) (2nd edn, Ikaros 2014) [in Greek], TS Pappas, 'Why Greece Failed' (2013) 24 *Journal of Democracy* 31; A Triandafyllidou et al., 'Introduction: Is Greece a Modern European Country?' in A Triandafyllidou et al. (eds), *The Greek Crisis and European Modernity* (Palgrave Macmillan 2013).

[51] See PC Ioakimidis, 'The EC and the Greek Political System: An Overview' in P Kazakos and PC Ioakimidis (eds), *Greece and EC Membership Evaluated* (St Martin's Press 1994).

[52] Task Force for Greece, First quarterly report (17 November 2011) SI(2011) 399/3, 14. On the connection between conditionality and Greek institutional weakness, see also K Featherstone, 'Conditionality, Democracy and Institutional Weakness: the Euro-crisis Trilemma' (2016) 54 *Journal of Common Market Studies* 48.

vein, in its 2011 comprehensive report on the Greek administration, the OECD noted the existence of systemic failures and functional weaknesses, pointing to the 'inadequate capacity of ministries to carry reforms into the implementation stage'.[53] The WGIs offer additional evidence of the divergence of Greece from its European peers in terms of administrative and judicial capacity. Greece ranks markedly below the EU average in terms of government effectiveness, control of corruption, and the Rule of Law.[54] Evidence of the systemic problems Greece faces in enforcement are also offered by the Bertelsmann Stiftung, which ranks OECD members using a list of Sustainable Governance Indicators which include the ability effectively to implement public policies.[55] According to this criterion, Greece falls in effect in the last category of countries where '[t]he government partly fails to implement its objectives or fails to implement several policy objectives'.[56] According to the 2016 report of the Bertelsmann Stiftung, Greece is not only weak in EU terms but is also in the bottom ranks internationally (fortieth) regarding executive capacity.[57]

It is not only the Greek administration which appears to face endemic problems, but also the other pole of law enforcement, the judicial system. Assessing the effectiveness of the judiciary is of course a difficult issue. Nevertheless, two types of argument can be used to assess weakness in this field: indicators developed by international institutions and decisions of international courts assessing the effectiveness of judicial remedies as a matter of observing fundamental rights requiring access to justice. One criterion often resorted to here is the duration of dispute settlement procedures. The 2014 Report of the Committee of Ministers of the Council of Europe identified the main structural problem of Greece as its 'failure or considerable delay in the enforcement of final domestic judgments and absence of effective remedies'.[58] This finding underlines a long series of judgments of the ECtHR which have also established the excessive delays in judicial procedures in Greece as a recurrent concern. In its decision in the case *Vassilios Athanasiou and Others v Greece* the Court examined the Greek incapacity to provide timely and efficient remedies under the pilot-judgment procedure, highlighting the existence of structural problems in this field.[59] In this case, the Court stressed the 'chronic and persistent nature'[60] of the problems in question and pointed out that the situation in Greece 'could in practice be regarded as a denial of justice'.[61] Other pilot judgments have also pointed to the systemic dimensions of the problem.[62] Despite efforts to address these deficiencies,[63] the problem remains significant. According to the Parliamentary Assembly of the Council of Europe, the delays in the execution of the Court's judgments, and especially those dealing with the excessive length

[53] OECD, 'Greece: Review of the Central Administration 2011' (2011) OECD Public Governance Reviews 27.

[54] Sissenich (n 25) 11, 22, 19–23.

[55] http://www.sgi-network.org/2016/, accessed 15 October 2016. For the latest OECD report, which approaches the Rule of Law focusing on the criteria of 'limited government powers' and 'fundamental rights', see OECD, 'Rule of law' in *Government at a Glance 2015* (OECD Publishing 2015), 160–1.

[56] http://www.sgi-network.org/2016/Governance/Executive_Capacity/Implementation/Government_Efficiency, accessed 15 October 2016.

[57] ibid.

[58] Council of Europe, Committee of Ministers, Supervision of the Execution of Judgments and Decisions of the European Court of Human Rights, 8th Annual Report of the Committee of Ministers (2015) 65.

[59] *Vassilios Athanasiou and Others v Greece* App no 50973/08 (ECtHR, 21 December 2010).

[60] ibid, para 44. [61] ibid, para 52.

[62] See also the pilot judgments in the cases *Michelioudakis v Greece* App no 54447/10 (ECtHR, 3 April 2012); *Glykantzi v Greece* App no 40150/09 (ECtHR, 30 October 2012).

[63] See A Arguros, *Just Satisfaction Due to Excessively Lengthy Court Proceedings (Η δίκαιη ικανοποίηση λόγω υπερβάσεως της εύλογης διάρκειας της δίκης)* (Sakkoulas 2015) [in Greek], discussing the remedies introduced by Law 4055/2012 and Law 4239/2014 in order to speed judicial proceedings.

of judicial proceedings,[64] are due to 'major structural problems' which amount to systemic/structural deficiencies in the Greek system.[65] The fact that these failings of the judicial system occur in an environment of generally weak institutions and low-quality laws makes their overall impact on the Rule of Law even more significant.[66]

These findings should be read together with those indicating very low levels of trust in public institutions and government in Greece. Trust in government and institutions is difficult to measure—also because respondents may interpret the relevant questions in narrow political terms[67] and the available data often do not differentiate between politicians and the bureaucracy.[68] Despite these limitations, data measuring trust do offer a valuable background for the questions investigated here, especially considering the connection between trust and the Rule of Law established in theoretical terms above. Indeed, Greece ranks close to the bottom when it comes to trust in public institutions among European countries.[69] Given the consistency of this finding, this is another element which can be taken into account when investigating weakness in its systemic form.

b. Weakness and the enforcement of EU law

Weakness of the kind described above is first and foremost an issue of domestic concern. It is domestic laws which remain ineffective when administrative authorities and courts fail to enforce them, and it is the domestic democratic rule that becomes suspended when parliament makes decisions which remain only in the books. In the case of EU Member States, however, the systemic inability to enforce domestic law often also translates into problems with enforcing EU law.

As noted above, the connection between domestic Rule of Law and the implementation of international obligations is well established. Both theoretical considerations and empirical research supports the view that states which submit to the Rule of Law at the domestic level are more likely to uphold the international Rule of Law as well. The same connection exists between domestic weakness and low enforcement of EU rules. The implementation of national legislation and EU law follows the same patterns and faces the same obstacles.[70] This would support the hypothesis that there are cases where Member States fail to comply with their supranational commitments, despite the fact that on the basis of a cost-benefit analysis or by virtue of norm internalization, compliance was to have been expected. Empirical studies support this hypothesis.

Already in their 1998 study, Siedentopf and Ziller indicated that administrative incapacity is an important factor to explaining problems with the application of EU law.[71] In a series of subsequent studies, weakness, in the form of inadequate institutions

[64] Parliamentary Assembly, Resolution 1787 (2011) Final version, Implementation of judgments of the European Court of Human Rights, 7.2.

[65] Parliamentary Assembly, Resolution 1914 (2013) Final version, Ensuring the viability of the Strasbourg Court: structural deficiencies in States Parties, 4.

[66] M Metsopoulos and TK Pelagides, *Understanding the Crisis in Greece: from Boom to Bust* (Palgrave Macmillan 2011) 103–4.

[67] OECD, *How's Life? 2015: Measuring Well-being* (OECD Publishing 2015) 126.

[68] OECD, 'Trust in government', in *Government at a Glance 2015* (OECD Publishing 2015), 156–7.

[69] OECD (n 67) 128. See also OECD (n 68) 156–7.

[70] H Siedentopf and C Hauschild, 'The Implementation of Community Legislation in the Member States: A Comparative Analysis', in H Siedentopf and J Ziller (eds), *Making European Policies Work: The Implementation of Community Legislation in the Member States. Vol. 1, Comparative Syntheses* (Sage 1988).

[71] S Heinrich and Z Jacques, *Making European Policies Work: The Implementation of Community Legislation in the Member States* (Sage 1998).

or insufficient resources, is identified as one basic reason for non-compliance.[72] Weakness in essential infrastructure such as public administration, labour inspectorates, courts, along with media and civil society institutions, have been connected with enforcement difficulties.[73] Falkner et al. describe domestic systems where the culture of compliance functions as a self-reinforcing social mechanism as the 'world of law observance'.[74] In such 'worlds', where the political and the administrative systems function on the stable premise that rules have to be observed, implementation of EU law is more timely and correct than in other cases.

Regardless of the differences in the focus of the various empirical studies, administrative capacity and coordination appear to have the greatest explanatory leverage when we consider the combined outcomes of the qualitative work undertaken on compliance in the EU[75]—even outweighing other variables, such as the relative wealth or relative political power of Member States.[76] For example, despite their differences in GDP and voting power within the EU, Greece and Italy are almost equally bad compliers due to lack of government capacity.[77] The importance of weakness for the implementation of EU law has also been tested and verified with regard to the performance of EU candidate countries in implementing the *acquis communautaire* prior to accession (pre-accession alignment).[78]

The connection between weakness and enforcement problems has been documented in particular with regard to Greece. As one would expect when considering its weak structures, discussed above, Greece is among the usual suspects when it comes to the enforcement of EU law, standing out in fines imposed for non-compliance with ECJ judgments.[79] This poor enforcement record is often associated with the weakness of the Greek state apparatus. Already in the country studies reported in the 1980s, Greece was among the countries presenting serious compliance problems owing to poor administrative infrastructure.[80] Later studies reinforce this connection, both in special fields of policy, such as environmental protection,[81] and in general.[82]

c. Addressing weak members as part of the Eurozone crisis-management

Different explanations for why states fail to comply with their international and EU obligations lead to different remedies for the problem.[83] Rationalists, who base their compliance theory on the paradigm of states as value-maximizing calculators, which make compliance decisions after rational cost-benefit analyses, recommend improvement to monitoring and sanctioning mechanisms. Norm-driven theorists, using shared worldviews as their basic variable of compliance, focus on the impact of socialization and norm-internalization by

[72] C Koutalakis, *Why are Laws not Enforced? (Γιατί δεν εφαρμόζονται οι νόμοι;)* (Gutenberg 2012) [in Greek] 111 et seq.; Börzel et al. (n 41) 1364.

[73] G Falkner, 'Is the EU a Non-Compliance Community? Towards "Compliance for Credibility" and EU Action for the Protection of Democracy in Europe' (2013) 1 *Les Cahiers Européens de Sciences Po*, 34.

[74] G Falkner et al., 'Worlds of Compliance: Why Leading Approaches to European Union Implementation are Only "Sometimes-True Theories"' (2007) 46 *European Journal of Political Research* 395, 406 (focusing on the transposition of directives). See also G Falkner, *Complying with Europe: EU Harmonisation and Soft Law in the Member States* (CUP 2005).

[75] Toshkov et al. (n 2) 5. See also Koutalakis (n 72) 111 et seq.; Börzel et al. (n 41) 1364; S Berglund, I Gange, and F van Waarden, 'Mass Production of Law. Routinization in the Transposition of European Directives: A Sociological-Institutionalist Account' (2006) 13 *Journal of European Public Policy* 692, 713; P Hille and C Knill, '"It's the Bureaucracy, Stupid"' (2006) 7 *European Union Politics* 531.

[76] Börzel et al. (n 41) 1380, 1381–2. [77] ibid, 1382. [78] Hille and Knill (n 75) 533 et seq.

[79] Falkner (n 4) 35. [80] Siedentopf and Hauschild (n 70). [81] Koutalakis (n 72) 340–1.

[82] Börzel et al. (n 41) 1342.

[83] On the different approaches, see K Raustiala, 'Compliance and Effectiveness in Regulatory Cooperation' (2000) 32 *Case Western Reserve Journal of International Law* 387, 399 et seq.

the actors critical to enforcement. Managerialists, who argue that non-compliance is typically non-volitional and often the outcome of administrative or financial incapacities, claim that sanctioning mechanisms may not always be effective.[84] When non-compliance is not the outcome of the rational calculation of costs and benefits but of weak institutions, sanctions lose much of their attractiveness as means to induce compliance.[85] On such occasions, the best response might be to resort to non-confrontational mechanisms and to assist the defiant state, often through technical and financial assistance.[86] However, capacity building through the mere transfer of resources to non-compliant states is usually not the preferred or more effective solution.[87] To foster bureaucratic efficiency and the Rule of Law, international organizations and the EU have developed a variety of mechanisms both at pre-accession and post-accession stages. The following briefly presents the responses offered during the crisis aimed at strengthening Greek enforcement capacities. This could be viewed as a new form of EU intervention when facing weak members.

I. Financial assistance conditionality

Conditionality has been a common element of all financial-assistance instruments since the beginning of the crisis in 2010.[88] All three bailout packages directed to Greece (2010, 2012, and 2015) were subject to 'strict conditionality',[89] reviewed and enforced at regular intervals. These conditions primarily focused on the attainment of budgetary targets and economic reforms aimed to ensure the ability of the recipient member to repay the financial assistance it received. It was already clear at the early stages of the crisis, however, that the weakness of the Greek state and the state of the Rule of Law in the country were additional issues of concern.[90]

Conditionality is not a new way to promote institutional strength and the Rule of Law. It has been one of the instruments used to address weaknesses and promote institution-building during the accession stage in many phases of EU enlargement.[91] Accession conditionality often has a significant Rule of Law component which requires aspiring members to strengthen their judicial and administrative systems. During the crisis, conditionality was used for the first time to address institutional weakness and poor enforcement in *current* EU Members in two different ways. Conditionality was firstly used as a means to induce compliance with certain norms which had been left unenforced by Greece, such as certain Directives which had not been transposed in time. In this case, financial assistance was used to alter the Member State's cost-benefit analysis. Instead of threatening sanctions ('stick'), however, the EU used the prospect of benefits ('carrot'). Secondly, conditionality has been used to require the establishment of strong institutions which would address weakness in the long term. Here, financial assistance was not made conditional upon the enforcement of specific provisions of EU law, but rather upon reforms in the administration and the judiciary.

[84] On the difference between the enforcement and management approaches, see J Tallberg, 'Paths to Compliance: Enforcement, Management, and the European Union' (2002) 56 *International Organization* 609, 611 et seq.

[85] Koutalakis (n 72) 97. [86] Raustiala (n 83). [87] Börzel et al. (n 41) 1383.

[88] On EU financial assistance conditionality, see M Ioannidis, 'EU Financial Assistance Conditionality after "Two Pack"' (2014) 74 *Zeitschrift für ausländisches öffentliches Recht und Völkerrecht* 61.

[89] See Art 136(3) TFEU. [90] Featherstone (n 29) 195 et seq.

[91] A Dimitrova, 'Enlargement, Institution-Building and the EU's Administrative Capacity Requirement' (2002) 25 *West European Politics* 171; D Kochenov, *EU Enlargement and the Failure of Conditionality: Pre-accession Conditionality in the Fields of Democracy and the Rule of Law* (Wolters Kluwer Law 2008). On accession conditionality law in general, see E Gateva, *European Union Enlargement Conditionality* (Palgrave Macmillan, 2015).

Regarding the first point, conditions required the transposition of non-implemented Directives on several occasions, such as Directive 2007/66/EC on public procurement regarding remedies and Directive 2009/81 on defence and security expenditure.[92] Special weight was given to key directives in the area of services, transport, and energy, including key electricity, gas and oil directives.[93] On some occasions, Greece was also directed to pay due attention to the relevant judgments of the ECJ. This was the case with the transposition of the Professional Qualifications Directive (Directive 2005/36/EC), 'including compliance with ECJ rulings'.[94]

Turning to the second point, in all three Greek programmes, a significant part of conditionality was directed to detailed requirements aiming at strengthening the state. The 2010 programme already noted that the Greek public administration did not always 'ensure that policies are implemented fully and efficiently once the legislation has been passed'.[95] As the continuing problems of Greece appeared to be closely connected to administrative and judicial ineffectiveness, subsequent conditions focused more closely on the reform and modernization of these sectors. For example, in the context of the second programme, Greece undertook the obligation to 'set up a high-level transformation steering group, chaired by the PM, that will supervise, monitor and ensure the implementation of administrative reforms'.[96] The creditors also focused on judicial reform, including the use of e-registration and e-tracking of the status of individual cases in all courts, the organization of the courts, the situation of court officials, and the effective and timely enforcement of contracts, competition rules, and judicial decisions.[97] The third programme, adopted in 2015, continued in the same direction. Greece undertook to 'propose by November 2015 and subsequently implement a three years strategic plan for the improvement of the functioning of the justice system' which would encompass actions aimed at enhancing judicial efficiency, speeding up judicial proceedings, and addressing shortcomings in the functioning of courts.[98] Corruption is also in focus[99] and the government is explicitly required to 'modernise and significantly strengthen the Greek administration, and to put in place a programme, in close collaboration with the European Commission, for capacity-building and de-politicizing the Greek administration'.[100]

Regardless of the actual success of these initiatives, which cannot be assessed here, the extent and detailed nature of these conditions seem to open a new chapter in EU intervention in the area of administrative and judicial reform in current Member States which goes far beyond the field traditionally covered by the Europeanization literature.[101] According to Featherstone, in the two first assistance packages, the conditions requiring administrative measures represented approximately forty per cent of the total number of reforms required,[102] with a rising trend over time.[103] These reforms touched upon several

[92] European Commission, 'The Economic Adjustment Programme for Greece' (May 2010) Occasional Papers No 61, 70.

[93] Commission (n 92) 23 and 155. [94] ibid, 69. [95] ibid, 23.

[96] European Commission, 'The Second Economic Adjustment Programme for Greece' (March 2012) Occasional Papers No 94, 130.

[97] ibid, 81–3.

[98] European Commission, 'Memorandum of Understanding Between the European Commission Acting on Behalf of the European Stability Mechanism and the Hellenic Republic and the Bank of Greece' (19 August 2015) 31.

[99] ibid. [100] ibid, 29.

[101] See E Ongaro, 'The Relationship between the New European Governance Emerging from the Fiscal Crisis and Administrative Reforms: Qualitatively Different, Quantitatively Different, or nothing New? A Plea for a Research Agenda' (2014) 15 *Administrative Culture* 10.

[102] K Featherstone, 'External Conditionality and the Debt Crisis: The 'Troika' and Public Administration Reform in Greece' (2014) 22 *Journal of European Public Policy* 295, 302.

[103] Featherstone (n 102) 303–4.

aspects of Greek administration and justice, with a focus on the better use of information technology, the strengthening of the autonomy of key parts of the administration—such as tax authorities—combating corruption, and the connection of the Greek administration with external technical advisors.[104] It seems that this is the first time that the EU has been involved in the organizational restructuring of national administrations in this way.[105]

Without explicitly saying so, therefore, EU financial assistance conditionality treated Greece as a *de facto* weak member. Greece's creditors have operated on the assumption that the Greek institutions did not conform to the paradigm of EU Member States and required special attention. This observation becomes even more justified if we compare the measures required of Greece with the conditions set for Ireland, where public administration reforms are hardly mentioned, and Portugal, where the requested reforms are much less intrusive.

II. *Technical assistance*

The third dimension of institution-building employed during the crisis was technical assistance. Article 197(2) TFEU provides that the EU 'may support the efforts of Member States to improve their administrative capacity to implement Union law' and clearly states that the support of administrative efficiency is a concern and competence of the Union. In 2011 the Commission established a special mechanism with the mandate actively to support capacity building in Greece, the so-called Task Force for Greece (TFGR). TFGR, was tasked with identifying and coordinating the technical assistance which Greece needed to deliver the structural reforms of the EU/IMF adjustment programme.[106] A significant part of its work focused on reforms to the public administration, combating corruption, and reform to the judicial system.[107] In June 2015 the Commission announced the creation of a new service, the 'Structural Reform Support Service'[108] aimed at assisting Member States to implement growth-enhancing administrative and structural reforms—such as the promotion of the Rule of Law and combating corruption.[109] It seems thus that the Greek experience resulted in the introduction of a general mechanism potentially relevant to all Member States. What is more interesting is that according to its agreement with the EU and the IMF, Greece is *required* to draw on the technical assistance offered by other EU Member States, the European Commission, the IMF, or other organizations in priority areas.[110] This reference to an obligation to make use of technical assistance is also reflected in Regulation 472/2013 governing the implementation of financial-assistance programmes.[111] Article 7(8) of this Regulation refers to capacity-building for members 'experiencing insufficient administrative capacity or significant problems in the implementation of its adjustment programme'. Such members 'shall seek technical assistance from

[104] ibid, 305. [105] ibid, 308.

[106] European Commission, 'The Task Force for Greece', http://ec.europa.eu/about/taskforce-greece/index_en.htm, accessed 12 October 2016.

[107] See the regular Reports of the TFGR, http://ec.europa.eu/about/taskforce-greece/reports/index_en.htm, and the 'Preliminary Evaluation of the Technical Assistance provided to Greece in 2011–2013 in the areas of Tax Administration and Central Administration Reform', prepared by Alvarez & Marsal Taxand and Adam Smith International for the European Commission (2014), http://ec.europa.eu/about/taskforce-greece/pdf/tfgr/evaluation_report_alvarez_july_2014_en.pdf, accessed 12 October 2016.

[108] European Commission, 'Speaking Points of Vice-President Dombrovskis on the Commission's New Structural Reform Support Service' (Statement, Brussels 17 June 2015), http://europa.eu/rapid/press-release_STATEMENT-15-5218_en.htm, accessed 12 October 2016.

[109] ibid. [110] Commission (n 96) 131.

[111] Regulation (EU) No 472/2013 of the European Parliament and of the Council of 21 May 2013 on the strengthening of economic and budgetary surveillance of Member States in the euro area experiencing or threatened with serious difficulties with respect to their financial stability [2013] OJ L140, 1.

the Commission', which will then explicitly outline the objectives and the means of that assistance and constitute a group of experts. Although it is difficult to imagine legal sanctions for violation of this provision, it clearly expresses the view that institutional weakness is a concern for the EU as a whole.

4. Conclusion

This chapter drew insights from international law, EU law, and Europeanization studies to develop three ideas. Firstly, it introduced the weak member concept as a concept of EU constitutional law, connecting it to the principle of the Rule of Law. A 'weak member', for this chapter, is a Member State which, due to widespread corruption, lack of resources, or bad organization, fails to give real effect to its law and thereby falls short of the Rule of Law requirement set out in Article 2 TEU. Secondly, this chapter connected the weak member concept with the field of EU law enforcement, the focus of the present volume. Revisiting some of the rich literature on compliance enables the establishment of a clear connection between poor implementation rates and weak domestic Rule of Law records. Thirdly, this chapter offered some insights into the state-building dimension of the measures adopted during the Eurozone crisis. It seems that Rule of Law deficiencies have been an important concern during the crisis, and especially that Greece has been treated in many respects as a weak member. Focusing on the institution-building aspects of the financial-assistance conditionality seems even more justified considering that these reforms could also contribute to better compliance with EU law. As the ongoing refugee crisis indicates, weak membership is one of the issues which connects the multifaceted crises the EU is currently experiencing. How to address this issue, both in political and legal terms, will be an important challenge to overcoming them.

28

Inside but Out? The UK and the EU

Adam Łazowski

The UK joined what were then the European Communities on 1 January 1973. From the start it was meant to be a marriage of convenience, not a relationship based on passion or deep affection. After over a decade in the European Free Trade Association and with the French dropping their veto, membership seemed to be the right option to take the relationship forward.[1] Obviously, it was for some but not for all, hence shortly after accession, the terms of membership were renegotiated and a referendum on withdrawal from the European Communities was held.[2] Arguably, a negative vote then would have led to a very early EC exit. It was one of the many idiosyncrasies of the UK's membership story; traditionally such referenda are held before but not right after the accession.[3] Norway may be a good example in this respect. Along with the UK, it was meant to be a part of the first wave of enlargement; however, negative results of a referendum forced the Norwegian authorities to drop their plans[4] before they ratified the Accession Treaty of 1972.[5] Since its accession, the UK has mastered the art of building coalitions, waving the veto card, threatening reforms and in the past six years, picking fights with little *raison d'être* behind them. When this volume went to print the UK was also—very likely—the first Member State to leave the EU.[6] Arguably, in the case of the UK, defiance was in the cards from the start. It is no secret that the UK has never been fully committed to the integration idea. This is reflected in an idiosyncratic approach to the EU, whether in everyday reality or purely in figurative terms. Quite symbolically, the political discourse is dominated by 'our relations with Europe' reasoning, which—as argued in this chapter—encapsulates the 'inside but out' school of thought. To put it differently, the debate is not about the UK's position in the EU but its relations with Europe, as if the Union was an external body. Against this background, it is fitting to ask three leading questions. Was the UK such a difficult Member State all the way long? Where does the defiance manifest itself the most? Will it exercise even more defiance as it leaves the EU?

[1] Membership of the UK in the EU is well documented in the academic literature. See e.g. D Nicol, *EC Membership and Judicialization of British Politics* (OUP 2001); C O'Neill and D Hannay, *Britain's Entry into the European Community: Report by Sir Con O'Neill on the Negotiations of 1970–1972* (Foreign & Commonwealth Office [FCO] Publications 2000).

[2] As D Lasok argued at the time: 'The United Kingdom has the unique but dubious distinction of having experienced renegotiations and a referendum subsequent to having bound herself internationally and according to her own constitution'. See further D Lasok, 'Some legal aspects of fundamental renegotiations' (1976) 1 *European Law Review* 375.

[3] See e.g. A Albi, 'Referendums in the CEE Candidate Countries: Implications for the EU Treaty Amendment Procedure' in C Hillion (ed), *EU Enlargement. A Legal Approach* (Hart 2004), 57–75.

[4] The same scenario was repeated in 1994. See further, e.g. C Archer, *Norway outside the European Union. Norway and European integration from 1994 to 2004* (Routledge 2005).

[5] OJ L73/1972, 5.

[6] Even though the new UK's Prime Minister Theresa May declared that the decision of voters will be respected it is not inconceivable that the continued political and economic turmoil that Brexit has already caused may lead to a reversal of the decision to leave the EU.

Inside but out? The United Kingdom and the European Union. First Edition. Adam Łazowski. Published 2017 by Oxford University Press.

The main argument of this chapter is that the approach pursued by the UK authorities was to fight for its own interests in the negotiations leading up to the adoption of legal acts, be it primary or secondary legislation. Once concessions and opt-outs were secured, the UK would stop being a difficult Member State and in general terms complied with the obligations undertaken. The number of infringement proceedings against it is rather average and so are its results on European Commission scoreboards. The UK does not therefore stand out when set against twenty-seven other Member States. Arguably, we are dealing here with a grand bifurcation between the political discourse and negotiations of *acquis*, on the one hand, and the application of EU law, on the other. However, following the political developments of the past six years the UK has, largely thanks to the anti-European sentiments of the Conservative Party, moved much closer to EU exit. On 23 June 2016 voters decided that the UK should leave the EU. Once Article 50 TEU is triggered the procedure for Brexit will commence.[7] The question is if the UK will feel bound by the principle of loyal cooperation until 'divorce will do us apart' or will the EU have to deal with a new type of defiance. It is worth noting that the Vote Leave manifesto envisaged steps that would amount to flagrant breaches of EU law.[8] If some of those ideas were to be implemented, which political and legal instruments would the EU have to deal with such a phenomenon? All the issues mentioned above are analysed in turn.

1. Defiance in action: the case of the UK

The evidence proves that the UK is willing and able to pick a genuine fight to protect its interests, irrespective of whether they are based on merits or political whim. However, once the rules are approved its record of implementation of EU law does not really differ much when compared to the other Member States, whether old, young, or new. Still, what for some is a genuine fight to protect their interests, to others—even the majority of Member States—may look like a case of defiance or in some cases outright obstruction. Bearing this in mind, it is interesting to delve into the methods of defiance employed by the UK, on the one hand and, the EU's *ex post* and *ex ante* methods of counteracting it, on the other. In the closing part of this section an attempt is made to set the score straight with a view to demonstrating that in terms of implementation of agreed rules, the UK is neither unique nor difficult by any stretch of imagination.

a. Political and legal tools of defiance

The UK, just like some other Member States, pushes the defiance button at the early stages of negotiations, be it on primary or secondary EU law. This is hardly surprising as the EU decision-making process is all about bargaining and finding a balance between the interests of the EU and its Member States. The latter's interests may vary, which is perfectly understandable in an organization comprising twenty-eight members.

The situation is the most complicated politically in case of the revisions of the Founding Treaties, which, as per Article 48 EU Treaty, always require the unanimity of the Member

[7] Following the Brexit referendum the UK government, despite the calls made by the EU institutions and some of the Member States, decided not to trigger Art 50 TEU with an immediate effect. When this volume went to print, Art 50 TEU was expected to be activated in early 2017.

[8] For a commentary, see A. Gostyńska-Jakubowska and A. Łazowski, 'Brexeteers' exit plans: an unrealistic folly?', http://blogs.lse.ac.uk/brexitvote/2016/06/22/the-brexiteers-exit-plan-legally-dubious-unfeasible-and-likely-to-antagonise-our-neighbours/, accessed 12 October 2016.

States.[9] Here the raising of a veto card by a single country, be it the smallest Malta or the biggest Germany, may ultimately block the approval of a new treaty. This is neither unheard of, nor is it a *spécialité de la maison* of the UK. For instance, in December 2003 Poland and Spain joined forces to block the approval of the Draft Treaty establishing a Constitution for Europe. This forced the others back to the negotiating table with the view of finding a compromise acceptable to all which eventually facilitated completion of negotiations of that Treaty, destined later to be rejected at the French and Dutch referenda in any event. However, in 2011 such a compromise proved impossible during the negotiations aimed at the strengthening of the Eurozone in the wake of the sovereign debt crisis. The UK refused to accept a revision of the Founding Treaties due to an alleged failure to obtain so-called safeguards to the Internal Market it had requested during the negotiations.[10] This forced the other Member States to step out of the EU framework and to conclude a treaty which, in technical terms, is not part of the EU legal order.[11]

There is far more room for manoeuvre when it comes to negotiations of secondary legislation. Various ways of securing acceptable solutions have been developed in practice, including the longer transposition of periods for selected Member States[12] or the adoption of optional provisions.[13] Nevertheless, such well-established practices may not be enough. If a unanimous agreement is not possible, recourse to voting in the Council is a standard way of adopting secondary legislation. Even though qualified majority voting has been in the Treaties for decades now, the Member States developed a consensus culture. The bottom line is that a vote, although prescribed by the Treaties as a norm, should be the last resort when all powers of persuasion fail.[14]

Interestingly enough, some of the key institutional decisions are now also taken by a qualified majority. Good examples in this respect are appointments of the Presidents of the European Council and of the European Commission as well as the High Representative for Foreign and Security Policy. No doubt, these appointments are of fundamental political importance and the result of heavy bargaining between the Member States, partly determined by the results of elections to the EP. Until the appointment of J-C Junker as the President of the European Commission for the 2014–2019 term, it had been politically unthinkable that a decision of such political weight could be adopted unless everyone agreed.[15] From that point of view, the QMV requirement looked more like an emergency break should a political deadlock occur. Alas, following a spectacular UK act of defiance, a vote was forced by Prime Minister David Cameron. As is well known, it led to an unprecedented situation whereby the new President of the Commission does not have

[9] See further on the revision procedures, e.g. B De Witte, 'Treaty revision procedures after Lisbon' in A Biondi et al. (eds), *EU Law after Lisbon* (OUP 2012) 107.

[10] For a detailed account, see House of Commons, *The future of the European Union: UK Government policy*. Vol 1, 2434.

[11] See further, e.g. M Gordon, 'The United Kingdom and the Fiscal Compact: past and future' (2014) 10 *European Constitutional Law* 28. For a more general analysis of the UK's position in respect of changes to the Economic and Monetary Union, see A Dashwood, 'The United Kingdom in a re-formed European Union' (2013) 38 *European Law Review* 737.

[12] See for instance, Art 18 of Council Directive 2000/78/EC of 27 November 2000 establishing a general framework for equal treatment in employment and occupation [2000] OJ L303, 16.

[13] See for instance, Directive 2004/18/EC of the European Parliament and of the Council of 31 March 2004 on the coordination of procedures for the award of public works contracts, public supply contracts and public service contracts [2004] OJ L134, 114.

[14] See e.g. F Hayes-Renshaw et al., 'When and Why the EU Council of Ministers Votes Explicitly' (2006) 44 *Journal of Common Market Studies* 161.

[15] QMV for the appointment of the European Commission was introduced by the Treaty of Nice.

the backing of all Member States.[16] It is a good demonstration of a simple truth that some acts of defiance may backfire and turn heavily against those who pursue such policies.

It is common wisdom that the art of negotiating EU legislation is something the Member States have been mastering for years. This includes the capacity to build coalitions with the view of pursuing a particular approach to a given piece of legislation or, should that be desired, building a blocking minority. Many authors argue that the UK has been very successful in this respect and thus able to make sure the EU secondary legislation meets its demands.[17] Taking this into account, it is interesting to analyse briefly the statistical data on voting patterns in the Council. For instance, the analysis conducted by VoteWatch Europe demonstrates that the UK is the Member State that voted against the majority most often in the recent years.[18] The number of votes against particular measures has proportionally increased ever since the government of David Cameron came into power in 2010.[19] In the case of its predecessor (27 June 2007–10 May 2010) a total of 115 votes were held in the Council. The UK voted three times against and abstained seven times.[20] The areas of particular concern for the then UK government were agriculture, economic affairs, employment, environment, and transport. Since 11 May 2010 the Council has voted in 549 cases. In thirty-seven instances the UK voted against, while in thirty-five the government abstained. It is noticeable that these acts of defiance were not limited to particular areas, as in the previous period, but rather spread across the board. The most contentious of all were budgetary matters with a total of twelve votes against and eleven abstentions. In six cases the UK voted against EU measures dealing with external relations.[21]

This data indicates that in the past years the EU adopted several pieces of legislation that the UK could not warm up to. The question is what legal tools of defiance it pursued when its power of persuasion or a simple veto failed. As argued above, the revisions of Treaties cannot be adopted without the consensus of all Member States. Hence, particularly as a result of strong opposition from the UK, the other Member States developed a number of methods of countering such acts of defiance. What recent experience demonstrates, however, is that if the other Member States step out of the EU legal framework to conclude a treaty, the UK is left empty-handed and has no legal tools at its disposal to exercise further defiance.

The situation is even more nuanced, however. To begin with, a Member State, which is outvoted in the Council, may proceed with action for annulment as per Article 263 TFEU. In recent years the UK has proven to be very active in this respect challenging EU secondary legislation it was against in the Council. This, for instance, includes a series of opt-out cases where the UK questioned the legal bases for decisions of the Council in the area of external relations. The first in line was case C-431/11 *United Kingdom v Council*[22] in which the UK challenged the legality of Council Decision 2011/407/EU on an update to

[16] In a dubious act of solidarity Hungary followed suit and also voted against the appointment of J-C Junker.

[17] See e.g. M Emerson (ed), *Britain's Future in Europe. Reform, renegotiation, repatriation or secession?* (CEPS 2015) 161–70.

[18] VoteWatch Europe. Annual Report 2012: 'Agreeing to Disagree. The voting records of EU Member States in the Council since 2009', 11–13, http://www.votewatch.eu/blog/wp-content/uploads/2012/07/votewatch-annual-report-july-2012-final-7-july.pdf, accessed 12 October 2016.

[19] See further, M. Kluger Rasmussen, '"Heavy Fog in the Channel. Continent Cut Off"? British Diplomatic Relations in Brussels after 2010' (2016) 54 *Journal of Common Market Studies* 709.

[20] See http://www.votewatch.eu/en/term8-council-minority-votes-term8-united-kingdom.html#/#6/0/2009-07-01/2010-05-10/CAB, accessed 12 October 2016.

[21] See http://www.votewatch.eu/en/term8-council-minority-votes-term8-united-kingdom.html#/#6/0/2010-05-11/2015-06-30/CAB, accessed 12 October 2016.

[22] Case C-431/11 *United Kingdom of Great Britain and Northern Ireland v Council of the European Union* [2013] ECLI:EU:C:2013:589.

EEA Agreement.[23] The UK argued that the legal basis chosen by the Council—Article 48 TFEU on free movement of workers—was incorrect and should have been replaced with Article 79(2)(b) TFEU. The latter provision falls under the Area of Freedom, Security and Justice (AFSJ), therefore the UK could have benefited from an opt-out as per Protocol 21 to the Founding Treaties.[24] Neither AG Kokott[25] nor the Court agreed with the applicant, hence the action was dismissed.[26] The same happened in cases C-656/11 *United Kingdom v Council*[27] and C-81/13 *United Kingdom v Council*.[28] In the first the legality of Council Decision 2011/863/EU was challenged.[29] In the second case the UK sought annulment of Council Decision 2012/776/EU.[30] In terms of substance, the legal issue at stake was just the same as in the EEA case. Therefore, it should not come as a surprise that neither of the actions was successful. These judgments triggered an unavoidable discussion about the actual scope of the JHA opt-outs and have led to a formal enquiry conducted by the EU Select Committee of the House of Lords.[31]

The challenges to several other pieces of secondary legislation, allegedly affecting the financial centre based in London, provide further good examples.[32] Case C-507/13 *United Kingdom v Council* is interesting for a number of reasons, not necessarily related to the substance of the dispute but to the shockwaves it created in the UK.[33] The request for annulment covered Directive 2013/36/EU[34] and Regulation 575/2013/EU.[35] The government argued that in both cases the EU legislator acted in breach of TFEU. AG Jääskinen presented his Opinion on 20 November 2014 and advised the Court to reject the action *in toto*.[36] For the ruling Conservative Party the timing was not very fortunate as the opinion was presented on the day of by-elections to the House of Commons, where it was expected

[23] Council Decision 2011/407/EU of 6 June 2011 on the position to be taken by the European Union within the EEA Joint Committee concerning an amendment to Annex VI (Social Security) and Protocol 37 to the EEA Agreement [2011] OJ 2011 L182, 12.

[24] The same would have applied to Ireland, which supported this action for annulment submitted by the UK.

[25] Opinion of Advocate General Kokott in Case C-431/11 *United Kingdom v Council* [2013] ECLI:EU:C:2013:187.

[26] For an academic appraisal, see e.g. N Rennuy and P van Elsuwege, 'Integration without membership and the dynamic development of EU law: United Kingdom v Council (EEA)' (2014) 51 *Common Market Law Review* 935–54.

[27] Case C-656/11 *United Kingdom of Great Britain and Northern Ireland v Council of the European Union* [2014] ECLI:EU:C:2014:97.

[28] Case C-81/13 *United Kingdom of Great Britain and Northern Ireland v Council of the European Union* [2014] ECLI:EU:C:2014:2449. See also Opinion of Advocate General Kokott [2014] ECLI:EU:C:2014:2114.

[29] Council Decision 2011/863/EU of 16 December 2011 on the position to be taken by the European Union in the Joint Committee established under the Agreement between the European Community and its Member States, of the one part, and the Swiss Confederation, of the other, on the free movement of persons as regards the replacement of Annex II to that Agreement on the coordination of social security schemes [2011] OJ L341, 1.

[30] Council Decision 2012/776/EU of 6 December 2012 on the position to be taken on behalf of the European Union within the Association Council set up by the Agreement establishing an association between the European Economic Community and Turkey, with regard to the adoption of provisions on the coordination of social security systems [2012] OJ L340, 19.

[31] The Report, the written evidence, as well as transcripts of oral evidence are available at: http://www.parliament.uk/business/committees/committees-a-z/lords-select/eu-law-and-institutions-sub-committee-e/inquiries/parliament-2010/the-uks-opt-in-and-international-agreements/, accessed 12 October 2016.

[32] See Case C-270/12 *United Kingdom of Great Britain and Northern Ireland v European Parliament and Council of the European Union* [2014] ECLI:EU:C:2014:18.

[33] Case C-507/13 *United Kingdom of Great Britain and Northern Ireland v European Parliament and Council of the European Union* [2014] ECLI:EU:C:2014:2394.

[34] Directive 2013/36/EU of the European Parliament and of the Council of 26 June 2013 on access to the activity of credit institutions and the prudential supervision of credit institutions and investment firms, amending Directive 2002/87/EC and repealing directives 2006/48/EC and 2006/49/EC [2013] OJ L176, 338.

[35] Regulation (EU) 575/2013 of the European Parliament and of the Council of 26 June 2013 on prudential requirements for credit institutions and investment firms and amending Regulation (EU) 648/2012 [2013] OJ L176, 1.

[36] Opinion of Advocate General Jääskinen delivered on 20 November 2014 Case C-507/13 (n 33).

to lose a seat to the heavily populist UK Independence Party (UKIP). To the surprise of many, having received the Opinion of AG Jääskinen, the government withdrew the action for annulment on the same day, arguing that it wished to save taxpayers money in a case it was certain to loose. If that is true, the question remains why the government submitted the action in the first place. In legal terms the withdrawal of this case makes little sense, however, if one looks at the timing of Court proceedings, and puts it against the electoral cycle in the UK, the answer is rather obvious. It was easier to swallow a bitter pill on the day of by-elections than it would have been in the heat of electoral campaign before the parliamentary elections of May 2015.

Another example worthy of attention is Case C-209/13 *United Kingdom v Council*.[37] This time the UK government challenged the legality of Council Decision 2013/52/EU.[38] The UK had been opposing the introduction of such a tax from the start, arguing a possible economic damage to the City. It was joined by a group of other countries which also refused their support for the proposal tabled by the European Commission in 2011.[39] The opposition was so fierce that the Member States had to accommodate a veto threat from the UK and some Member States and, at the same time, the pressure coming from other capitals to go ahead. The only way forward was to authorize enhanced cooperation.[40] The UK government took a decision to move from political to legal tools of defiance and challenged the legality of that decision. However, the Court unequivocally dismissed the action as premature and hence unfounded.[41]

b. Stepping up defiance? The European Union Act 2011

The European Union Act (EUA) 2011 was adopted shortly after the parliamentary elections of 2010, which, as is well known, brought back to power the Conservative Party. As it failed to gain enough seats in the House of Commons it was pushed into a coalition with the Liberal-Democratic Party. This was a proverbial marriage of convenience which, due to opposing views on EU integration, turned into a political dance macabre with the two parties running the country having simultaneously widely different views on the EU. The anti-EU credentials of the Conservative Party require no further explanation; one should note, however, that its coalition partner was by-and-large the only party on the UK political scene with a pro-EU agenda. Yet the Conservative Party managed to force its plan through, including the adoption of a highly contentious European Union Act 2011. It was pushed through both chambers of Parliament to the cheers of the Conservative backbenchers and, at the same time, fierce criticism from some parts of the academic community.[42] Since this piece of legislation has been thoroughly discussed in the literature, this analysis will be limited to some rudimentary issues only. First and foremost, the EUA imposes a referendum requirement largely on any future revision of TEU or TFEU, be it a fully-fledged revision based on Article 48(1–6) TEU

[37] Case C-209/13 *United Kingdom of Great Britain and Northern Ireland v Council of the European Union* [2014] ECLI:EU:C:2014:283.

[38] Council Decision 2013/52/EU of 22 January 2013 authorising enhanced cooperation in the area of financial transaction tax [2013] OJ L22, 11.

[39] Proposal for a Council Directive on a common system of financial transaction tax and amending Directive 2008/7/EC, COM(2011) 594 final.

[40] Council Decision 2013/52/EU of 22 January 2013 authorising enhanced cooperation in the area of financial transaction tax [2013] OJ L22, 11.

[41] See (n 37) paras 35–40.

[42] See S Peers, 'European integration and the European Union Act 2011: an irresistible force meets an immovable object?' (2013) 58 *Public Law* 119; P Craig, 'The European Union Act: locks, limits and legality' (2011) 48 *Common Market Law Review* 1915; M Gordon and M Dougan, 'The United Kingdom's European Union Act 2011: "who won the bloody war anyway?"' (2012) 37 *European Law Review* 3.

or a decision of the European Council adopted pursuant to the simplified treaty revision procedures laid down in Articles 48 (7–8).[43] Interestingly enough, it does not require a referendum for approval of a withdrawal agreement, which will be concluded between the EU and the UK, hence it will not be part of primary law. One has to agree with other authors that the increase of democratic control over the EU-related decisions of the UK government, either *qua* increased parliamentary control or plebiscite, is—at the level of principle—a much-desired step.[44] However, the extent to which the Act requires the use of referenda may translate into costly exercises devoted to technical matters of very little relevance for the UK, let alone its citizens.[45] Following the Brexit referendum the Act is unlikely ever to be used in practice. However, it is still fair to argue that with its locks and widespread introduction of direct democracy, the Act would have been a tool for defiance with a great potential to become a weapon of mass obstruction.[46]

c. Loyal cooperation after all? The grand bifurcation

As argued in the introduction, the transposition and implementation record of the UK does not measure up to its reputation of being a difficult Member State. To make a detailed assessment would definitely exceed the limits of this contribution; nevertheless, recourse to statistics allows one to draw academically sound, though generalist, conclusions. As is well known, the European Commission has several tools at its disposal. For data collection purposes the main instruments comprise annual reports on the application of EU law and annual scoreboards covering compliance with internal market *acquis*. In terms of enforcement machinery the infringement procedures are of outmost importance.

Neither the infringement statistics nor the Internal Market Scoreboards indicate that the UK is a master of defiance. On the contrary, the records prove it is often below average. According to one of the most recent Scoreboards, the UK's transposition deficit is 0.5 per cent, which is within the EU's average and 0.5 per cent target set for the Member States.[47] The average delay in transposition of directives is 11.3 months, which is a bit more than the general EU average of 10.1 months. However, according to the Commission, the UK in the last reporting period has decreased its backlog, which was still above the average due to two overdue directives. The transposition deficit has gone down since 1997, when it stood at 4.6 per cent (which was well below the average EU transposition deficit, peaking at 7 per cent at that time). The Scoreboard sometimes covers not only delays but also extends to cases of incorrect or incomplete transposition. In the case of the UK the compliance deficit enjoys a downward trend and it is also within reasonable limits. In May 2014 it stood at 0.7 per cent, which was the same as the EU average.[48]

A similar picture emerges also from the statistics of infringement proceedings. During 43 years of the UK's membership the European Commission submitted overall 139 infringement actions to the Court of Justice, a great majority of which led to judgments declaring the UK to be in breach of EU law. This figure, when contrasted with records of other Member States, proves the point made in this chapter. The worst performers are Italy, Greece, and Belgium with respectively 642, 400, and 383 infringements submitted to the

[43] See e.g. ss 2-6 of the Act. [44] For similar view, see Gordon and Dougan (n 42) 16.

[45] See for instance, Craig (n 42) 1932–3 and Gordon and Dougan (n 42) 19.

[46] For similar criticism, see Craig (n 42) 1932–3 and Gordon and Dougan (n 42) 19.

[47] Available at: http://ec.europa.eu/internal_market/score/index_en.htm, accessed 12 October 2016.

[48] See further, http://ec.europa.eu/internal_market/scoreboard/performance_by_member_state/united_kingdom/index_en.htm, accessed 12 October 2016.

Court. Only Croatia has a clean record, which, is hardly surprising taking into account that it joined the EU on 1 July 2013.[49] These statistics, however, may give a slightly misleading picture. To begin with, the available data covers only cases submitted to the Court. It includes neither cases where compliance was achieved during the administrative phase of the infringement procedure, nor infringement cases withdrawn from the Court. Furthermore, the available data does not include undetected infringements or those breaches which were present on the European Commission's radar, but for various reasons where not pursued.[50] More detailed statistics are available, however, for the preceding years. As we would expect, the number of opened infringement cases has been much higher than the actual volume of referrals to the Court. It is also interesting to note a considerable downward trend in this respect. In 2011 the European Commission had a total of seventy-six cases opened against the UK; this has gone down to forty-eight in 2016.[51] The great majority of those infringement cases ended during the administrative phase of proceedings, therefore only a small number reached the Luxembourg courtrooms and led to Court rulings. Since 2011 it declared the UK to be in breach of EU law seven times, while in two instances the actions were dismissed. Not a single judgment imposing penalties under Article 260 TFEU was rendered against the UK.

2. Methods of fighting defiance

Having looked at examples of defiance exercised by the UK it is worth turning to *ex ante* methods of fighting developed by the Member States over the years. It is also worth delving deeper into selected Court jurisprudence, particularly a few landmark cases where the judges found the UK to be in breach of EU law.

a. *Ex ante* methods of fighting defiance

The European integration project has developed rather dramatically since the accession of the UK. In those days the mandate of the European Communities was largely related to the common market and did not extend to such controversial areas as the AFSJ or the EMU. It was only when these issues were put on the negotiation agenda, along with the creation of the EU, that the UK—joined by Denmark and Ireland—made their objections vocally. The chosen option led to flexible integration or, as some prefer to call it, a Europe of different speeds. The opt-outs have become *ex ante* methods of accommodating requests made by defiant Member States and, by the same token, a necessary tool facilitating deeper integration within the EU. The practice proves, however, that opt-outs are good short-term solutions but that they then become troublesome, ending-up in further negotiations and—quite inevitably—litigation. These arguments are further elaborated on below.

I. Opt-out or not? Application of the Charter of Fundamental Rights to the UK

At the level of primary law one of the most noticeable features making the UK's position, at least prima facie, are the rules on the application of the Charter of Fundamental Rights. In

[49] See Annual Report of the Court of Justice of the European Union 2015, 100.

[50] See for instance, J Shaw and N Miller, 'When legal worlds collide: an exploration of what happens when EU free movement law meets UK immigration law' (2013) 38 *European Law Review* 137.

[51] European Commission, 'Monitoring the Application of European Union law' (2015) Staff Working Document Annual Report, SWD (2016) 231 final, 186.

this respect, the UK and Poland joined forces during the negotiations of the Treaty of Lisbon as both countries approached the Charter with a fair degree of trepidation. This is clearly reflected in a tailor-made Protocol No 30 attached to the Treaties. Article 1 of this Protocol is crucial and it provides that 'the Charter does not extend the ability of the Court of Justice of the European Union, or any court or tribunal of Poland or of the UK, to find that the laws, regulations or administrative provisions, practices or action of Poland or of the UK are inconsistent with the fundamental rights, freedoms and principles that it reaffirms.' The question was, however, whether this amounted to an opt-out or not. This was clarified by the Court in cases C-411/10 and C-493/10 *NS*,[52] where the judges ruled that the provision in question 'does not call into question the applicability of the Charter in the UK or in Poland'.[53] To put it differently, as per the third recital in the preamble to that Protocol, both the UK and Poland are required by means of Article 6 TEU to apply the Charter and interpret it accordingly. Furthermore, the Court ruled, 'the Charter reaffirms the rights, freedoms, and principles recognized in the Union and makes those rights more visible, but does not create new rights or principles.' The judges at Kirchberg ruled that the Protocol merely explains the rules inherent in Article 51 of the Charter and thus does not exempt these two countries from the obligation to comply with it. In this respect the Court followed the view expressed by the AG Trestenjak.[54]

II. Opt-outs

Opt-outs proved to be a preferred option forward for the very first time during the negotiations of the Treaty of Maastricht and then evolved through subsequent revisions of the Treaties. The main areas of contention were participation in the EMU and the AFSJ. Incorporation of Schengen *acquis* by the Treaty of Amsterdam also proved to be a stumbling block. As already mentioned, the UK was joined by Ireland and Denmark in its drive to secure opt-outs in these areas.

To begin with, Paragraph 1 of Protocol No 15 to the Treaties makes it unequivocally clear that the UK is under no obligation to adopt the Euro as its currency. Furthermore, Paragraph 3, in a similar fashion, clarifies that the UK retains its powers as far as monetary policy is concerned. At the same time, the UK may at any time decide to seek adoption of the EURO, however, this will be subject to compliance with the standard convergence criteria and dependent on positive (unanimous) decision of the Council. If that were to happen this opt-out regime would cease to apply. This solution meets the desires of the UK, which has expressed no intention to participate in the common currency so far. At the same time, however, it exacerbates tensions at the time when deeper integration within the Eurozone is inevitable. Being an opt-out country arguably reduces the UK's influence on measures that are developed and which in some ways may affect it.

The UK is also covered by opt-outs in respect of AFSJ, including the Schengen *acquis*. As per Article 4 of Protocol No 19 to the Founding Treaties, the UK may at any time express a desire to take part in some Schengen legislation. Article 5 of this Protocol lays down a *modus operandi* should the UK request participation (and also should it change its mind

[52] Joined Cases Case C-411/10 and C-493/10 *NS v Secretary of State for the Home Department* and *ME and Others v Refugee Applications Commissioner and Minister for Justice, Equality and Law Reform* [2011] ECLI:EU:C:2011:865. See also Opinion of Advocate General Trestenjak Case C-411/10 *NS* v *Secretary of State for the Home Department* [2011] ECLI:EU:C:2011:611.

[53] Para 119 of the judgment. [54] See, in particular, paras 165–77 of the Opinion.

during the negotiations). Furthermore, Protocol No 20 to the Treaties guarantees the UK's right to maintain border controls, including a separate visa regime for nationals of third countries. It also preserves the Common Travel Area between the UK and Ireland. Protocol No 21 regulates the position of the UK as far as the AFSJ is concerned. This extends to both measures dealing with border checks, asylum, immigration, as well as Judicial Cooperation in Civil and Criminal Matters. Unless the UK decides to opt-in, it remains largely immune to EU developments in these areas. Article 2 of Protocol No 21 makes it clear that no secondary legislation, international treaty concluded by the EU, or ruling of the Court is binding on the UK or affects its rights or obligations. A desire to opt in has to be presented, as per Article 3 of Protocol No 21, within three months of publication of particular measures. Interestingly enough, Article 3(2) of Protocol No 21 contains a provision clearly aimed at potential defiance which could be exercised by the UK (and equally Ireland) during negotiations of measures it expressed interest in during the early stages of the decision-making procedures. Mainly, it allows the Member States to go ahead without the UK and Ireland if they cannot be adopted after 'a reasonable period of time'. This solution is of advantage to both sides. It allows the EU to go ahead with secondary legislation the Member States wish to adopt and, at the same time, it will not force the UK to be bound by the adopted *acquis*. The latter would have been the case if a vote was triggered in those cases when TFEU requires qualified majority in the Council. It would also not allow the UK to veto secondary legislation that requires unanimous approval of all Member States (should it have a change of heart following a notification of intention to opt-in). Furthermore, Protocol No 21 provides for *modus operandi* applicable to negotiations of revisions of measures the UK had opted-in before. As per Article 4(a) of the Protocol, when the UK decides to exercise the right to opt-out in relation to a proposal for secondary legislation which amends an existing measure to which it had already opted in, the Council may 'urge' opt-out should application of amended rules make the original measures 'inoperable'. This, no doubt, is highly contentious matter.

Equally tricky in practice is determination of a correct legal basis when a proposed measure deals with a non-opt-out policy, yet it carries flavours of matters where the UK benefits from one of the regimes discussed in this section. A very good example to prove this point is Case C-43/12 *Commission v European Parliament and Council*.[55] The European Commission challenged the legality of Directive 2011/82/EU on transfer of data regarding road traffic accidents.[56] The Directive in question was based on Article 87(2) TFEU, allowing the UK (alongside Ireland and Denmark) to benefit from an opt-out. However, as the European Commission argued, a correct legal basis should have been Article 91(1)(c) TFEU dealing with transport. The latter belongs to non-opt-out areas and it should therefore not come as a surprise that the UK expressed a great interest in this litigation. The end result proved unsatisfactory for Whitehall as the Court annulled this Directive and held that the correct legal basis was transport, not AFSJ. This was certainly not the last case of that kind to reach the courtrooms at Kirchberg in Luxembourg. Arguably, more litigation is destined to follow even though the UK is on its way to EU withdrawal.

It should be also noted that Brexit will, inter alia, force the remaining Member States of the EU to proceed with a formal treaty revision in order to repeal/amend relevant parts of

[55] Case C-43/12 *European Commission v European Parliament, Council of the European Union* [2014] ECLI: EU:C:2014:298.

[56] Directive 2011/82/EU of the European Parliament and of the Council of 25 October 2011 facilitating the cross-border exchange of information on road safety related traffic offences [2011] OJ L288, 1.

the discussed Protocols in order to reflect the UK's departure from the EU. This cannot be done *qua* a withdrawal agreement, as it will not have the status of EU primary law.

III. The grand JHA opt-out from opt-in?

One of the main problems experienced by the Member States during subsequent rounds of treaty revisions was accommodation of further requests made by the 'opt-out' countries. The case of the UK's grand opt-out from EU criminal law is a very good example encapsulating the difficulties that may arise. On the one hand, in the period following the creation of the then Third Pillar of the EU (pre- and post-Amsterdam) the UK was, as discussed above, always given a choice of opting in or out. Quite frequently the former was preferred, and the UK had thus come to be bound by dozens of pieces of EU *acquis*, including EU criminal law.[57] However, during the negotiations of the Treaty of Lisbon one of the opening red lines of the UK government was a Treaty-based *modus operandi* for a complete opt-out from pre-Lisbon measures with a possibility of a subsequent 'box of chocolates' opt-in to some of them. A change in domestic political climate forced the government to make this move, which—allegedly—may have raised the eyebrows of negotiators from the other Member States. As is well known, the negotiations of the Treaty of Lisbon were largely about resuscitation of the defunct Treaty establishing Constitution for Europe and a request for such a blanket opt-out from measures the UK had already opted into was a considerable departure from the regime agreed to during the negotiations in the early years of this century. However, as argued in the literature, it was a political way out of the pledge made by the then Labour government to organize a referendum on the Constitutional Treaty. By securing the opt-out laid down in Protocol No 36 to the Treaties, it was entitled to argue that the Treaty of Lisbon was a different legal act altogether, hence the promise to organize a plebiscite no longer stood.[58] Whether the then government had a genuine intention to use the opt-out or treat it as a useful facade is a different matter. It has certainly been a welcome gift for the Conservative Party, which decided to make use of the possibility negotiated by its predecessors.

Under the terms of Article 10(4) of Protocol No 36 the UK was given five years from the date of entry into force of the Treaty of Lisbon to decide on the fate of JHA measures it had opted in before 1 December 2009. Arguably, in order to reduce the appetite for such an exercise, only an *en block* opt-out was made available with a possibility of opting in back to some of those measures. To put it differently, the complexity associated with such a move was supposed to force the UK authorities to think twice before employing this mechanism. Arguably, the possibility of opting in back again gave the UK an option of making domestic political gains by trumpeting the grand opt-out and then quietly opting in back again to those legal acts that were necessary or useful for all actors involved in the UK criminal justice system. The deterrent effect proved not to be strong enough for the government, which, after months of heated debates, decided to pull the trigger. As expected, the *en block* opt-out[59] was followed by opt-in to measures the UK had still a desire to adhere to.[60] The

[57] See House of Lords: *EU police and criminal justice measures: The UK's 2014 opt-out decision* (2013) 109 et seq.

[58] Gordon and Dougan (n 42) 5.

[59] See List of Union acts adopted before the entry into force of the Lisbon Treaty in the field of police cooperation and judicial cooperation in criminal matters which cease to apply to the UK as from 1 December 2014 pursuant to Art 10(4), second sentence, of Protocol (No 36) on transitional provisions [2014] OJ C430, 17.

[60] Council Decision 2014/857/EU of 1 December 2014 concerning the notification of the United Kingdom of Great Britain and Northern Ireland of its wish to take part in some of the provisions of the Schengen acquis which are contained in acts of the Union in the field of police cooperation and judicial cooperation in criminal matters

question is whether this decision was taken on purely political grounds or was it based on thorough knowledge of the subject matter. One would hope for the latter to be true. However, a quick look at an open letter published in the *Daily Telegraph*, signed by a large group of Conservative MPs, makes one wonder if the honourable members of the House of Commons are *au courant* with the EU law they so fiercely fight against. Misrepresentations and ignorance, painfully visible therein, speak for themselves.[61] The government, rather blindly and with a fair degree of populism, had pursued its agenda against suggestions of the House of Lords and some practitioners.[62] One of the main bones of contention was the European Arrest Warrant, which by some is perceived as a very useful tool to combat crime but for others it is a limitation of sovereignty and—at best—an unnecessary nuisance.[63] As argued in the literature, much of the debate was a Shakespearean 'much ado about nothing' as a lot of the legislation the UK eventually opted out from is already firmly present in the UK legal orders.[64] This conclusion only strengthens the argument that the entire ordeal was merely a political exercise, which, alas, has had serious legal implications.

IV. *Enhanced cooperation as a tool against defiance*

When it comes to negotiations of secondary legislation the UK often makes its position rather clear. As already mentioned, the Member States try to follow the consensus culture with the view of accommodating all needs of other counterparts. With the drive from unanimity to QMV in the Council the opposition of one Member State is not capable of stopping the others from giving a legislative development a green light. One of the contentious areas where, on the one hand, unanimity is still required and where, on the other hand, the UK has vital interests, is taxation. The clash about the financial transactions tax, discussed above, proves that the Member States are ready to use another *ex ante* tool to counteract a defiant member—the enhanced cooperation *modus operandi*. This is exactly what has happened in the case at hand.[65] Future will tell if a Europe of different speeds is the only and viable way forward. On the one hand, it makes development of integration possible. On the other hand, the variable geometry triggers myriads of political and legal issues, which make the entire system very complex indeed. One has to note, however, that enhanced cooperation is difficult to trigger as relevant provisions of TFEU impose several caveats. For instance, as per Article 326 TFEU, it may not undermine the internal market, constitute a barrier to trade, or provide for discrimination between the Member States.[66]

and amending Decisions 2000/365/EC and 2004/926/EC [2014] OJ L345, 1; Commission Decision 2014/858/EU of 1 December 2014 on the notification by the United Kingdom of Great Britain and Northern Ireland of its wish to participate in acts of the Union in the field of police cooperation and judicial cooperation in criminal matters adopted before the entry into force of the Treaty of Lisbon and which are not part of the Schengen acquis [2014] OJ L345, 6.

[61] The letter is reproduced in A Hinarejos et al., 'Opting out of EU Criminal law: What is actually involved?' (2012) CELS Working Paper, New Series, No 1.

[62] See further, House of Lords: EU police and criminal justice measures: The UK's 2014 opt-out decision, 2013.

[63] Council Framework Decision 2002/584/JHA of 13 June 2002 on the European arrest warrant and the surrender procedures between Member States [2002] OJ L190/1.

[64] See e.g. Hinarejos et al. (n 61).

[65] Two previous cases include: Council Decision 2010/405/EU of 12 July 2010 authorising enhanced cooperation in the area of the law applicable to divorce and legal separation [2010] OJ L189, 12; Council Decision 2011/167/EU of 10 March 2011 authorising enhanced cooperation in the area of the creation of unitary patent protection [2011] OJ L76, 53.

[66] See further for instance, F Amtenbrink and D Kochenov, 'Towards a More Flexible Approach to Enhanced Cooperation' in A Ott and E Vos (eds), *50 Years of European Integration. Foundations and Perspectives* (TMC Asser Press 2009).

Even a cursory reading of Articles 326–334 TFEU proves that it is the last resort, should lack of political compromise in the Council be faced with a prevalent desire of a group of Member States to go ahead regardless.

V. Non-EU Treaties as tools against defiance

Non-EU Treaties applicable among the Member States are not a new feature on the EU landscape. The history of Schengen *acquis* demonstrates that sometimes it may be a good option to develop deeper cooperation first between a small group of the Member States and then, when the time is fitting, incorporate it into the EU legal framework. Schengen, however, was not a clear-cut of defiance of minority but rather a natural stepping stone on the way to abolition of border controls. The situation was rather different with the Fiscal Compact Treaty,[67] where stepping outside of the EU legal framework was caused by an act of defiance, courtesy of the UK. As already argued, it eventually backfired. Not only that, but it left the UK isolated and also quite paradoxically allowed the other Member States to make entry into force of the Treaty subject to ratification by ten Member States only. This, of course, would not have been possible with a fully fledged revision of the Founding Treaties as per Article 48 TEU.

Such a short-term solution may also have implications for the future. To begin with, Article 16 of the Fiscal Compact Treaty provides that five years from its entry into force its incorporation into the EU legal order will come back to the table. If by then the UK is still a Member State and if so, it does not change its stance, the problems raised during the negotiations of this Treaty will return like a boomerang. Quite dangerously, stepping out of the EU framework may become an option which the Eurozone will return to should the UK, or any other Member State, exercise its defiance during negotiations of future treaty revisions. From that perspective, the decision taken in December 2011 may be perceived as a risky precedent, which under no circumstances should become the norm. More frequent recourse to such treaties would possibly undermine the uniformity of the EU legal order and erode the foundations of the EU as such. Subsequent incorporation into EU law of this species of treaty is a complex and a tricky exercise, to say the least. Experience with incorporation of Schengen *acquis* in the late 1990s is a very instructive example, indeed. One should also remember that although the Member States are the masters of the Treaties they are also bound by the principle of loyal cooperation laid down in Article 4(3) TEU. Arguably, this is an important barrier requiring such detours to non-EU treaties to be exercised with the highest degree of prudence, not to mention that they should serve as tools of deeper integration, not disintegration.

b. *Ex post* methods of fighting defiance

This section of the chapter has so far touched upon the *ex ante* methods of fighting defiance. The question is what sort of political and legal instruments the EU has at its disposal, should the UK fail to comply with its commitments. As argued earlier, the UK is difficult to satisfy during the negotiations of primary and secondary legislation; however, once it agrees to particular rules, it generally does not differ from other Member States.

[67] Treaty on Stability, Cooperation and Governance, D/12/2 Brussels, 1 February 2012. See further, e.g. P Craig, 'The Stability, Coordination and Governance Treaty: Principle, Politics and Pragmatism' (2012) 37 *European Law Review* 231; S Peers, 'The Stability Treaty: Permanent Austerity or Gesture Politics?' (2012) 8 *European Constitutional Law Review* 404.

Arguably, with the approval of measures, the defiance very often ends. In those cases when it does not the EU has the traditional tools at its disposal. They include political sanctions and Article 7 TEU as well as the infringement procedures laid down in Articles 258–260 TFEU. While the UK has never come near the first, it has had several cases at the Court when the judges declared the UK to be in breach of EU law. The statistical data presented earlier in this chapter proves this is not often the case, yet it does happen. It should be noted that the Court has never had an opportunity to impose on the UK one or both penalties as per Article 260 TFEU. Interestingly enough, two out of four cases ever submitted to the Court on the basis of Article 259 TFEU, involved the UK as a defendant.[68] To present all judgments where the UK was found to be in breach of EU law would exceed the limits of this chapter, therefore the analysis that follows will focus on two examples.

One of the early infringements targeting an alleged breach of EU law attributable to the UK was case 804/79 *Commission v United Kingdom*.[69] This case concerned Article 102 of the Act on Conditions of Accession, which was an inherent part of the Accession Treaty 1972.[70] It provided that within six years of accession of the UK, Ireland, and Denmark the Council would adopt measures determining conditions for fishing aimed at protection of fishing grounds and conservation of biological resources of the sea. Failure to adopt the prescribed measures made the UK argue that it would proceed with unilateral measures in this respect. The action submitted by the European Commission proved to be successful and the judgment of the Court was described by Weiler as'truly Solomonic'.[71]

In hindsight, there is no doubt that one of the examples where the infringement procedure proved to be an ultimate tool to fight defiance is the *Factortame* saga.[72] First and foremost, the European Commission challenged adoption of the Merchant Shipping Act 1988, which was approved by the UK Parliament as a reaction to, among other things, quota hopping exercised by the Spanish fishermen. The adopted measures were allegedly in breach of the then Articles 7, 52, and 221 of EEC Treaty, which guarantee the right of establishment. The breach was so profound that the European Commission requested from the Court interim measures before it actually adjudicated on the substance of the case. Not only was this request entertained[73] but the Court also ruled that the UK was in breach of the Treaty. As is well known, this act of defiance triggered more litigation at the national level and requests for preliminary ruling. It contributed quite considerably to strengthening of primacy of EU law[74] and one key tenet of the EU legal order: the doctrine of state liability.[75]

[68] Case 141/78 *French Republic v United Kingdom of Great Britain and Northern Ireland* [1979] ECLI:EU:C:1979:225; Case C-145/04 *Kingdom of Spain v United Kingdom of Great Britain and Northern Ireland* [2006] ECLI:EU:C:2006:543.

[69] Case 804/79 *Commission of the European Communities v United Kingdom of Great Britain and Northern Ireland* [1981] ECLI:EU:C:1981:93.

[70] OJ L73/1972, 5.

[71] JHH Weiler, 'Alternatives to Withdrawal from an International Organisation: the Case of the European Economic Community' (1985) 2 *Israel Law Review* 282, at 292.

[72] See Case C-246/89 *Commission of the European Communities v United Kingdom of Great Britain and Northern Ireland* [1991] ECLI:EU:C:1991:375.

[73] Case C-246/89R Order of the President of the Court of 10 October 1989: *Commission of the European Communities v United Kingdom of Great Britain and Northern Ireland* [1989] ECLI:EU:C:1989:368.

[74] Case C-213/89 *The Queen v Secretary of State for Transport, ex parte: Factortame Ltd and Others* [1990] ECLI:EU:C:1990:257.

[75] Joined Cases C-46/93 and C-48/93 *Brasserie du Pêcheur SA v Bundesrepublik Deutschland* and *The Queen v Secretary of State for Transport, ex parte: Factortame Ltd and Others* [1996] ECLI:EU:C:1996:79.

3. Looking ahead: how to secure enforcement of EU law in a politically hostile environment with a withdrawal looming on the horizon

a. Legal parameters of EU withdrawal

The anti-EU stance of the UK political parties and large parts of the public forced Prime Minister David Cameron to promise the voters an in-or-out referendum on the future of UK membership of the EU (though subject to several caveats). This, as already mentioned, led to a decision, though adopted with a slim majority, to leave the EU.[76] Bearing this in mind, it is fitting to take a closer look at a potentially explosive case of defiance of a departing Member State. It should be noted that the legal parameters of withdrawal are largely a *terra incognita*. Article 50 TEU provides a legal basis for an exit, however the provision in question is rather general and will have to be filled with practice and a proper legal framework. Once thing is certain, though. The UK will remain in the EU until the formal date of exit. Until then it may well be operating in a withdrawal mode, however, it will still be bound by EU law, including the principle of loyal cooperation based on Article 4(3) TEU.[77] This section of the chapter offers insight into some of the legal issues which may arise when Brexit is pursued.[78]

b. Unilateral exit: an ultimate act of defiance?

Article 50(1) TEU provides that a country expressing a desire to leave the EU shall submit a formal notification. Following the Brexit referendum two main questions emerge. The first is of a domestic constitutional nature, that is whether under UK's unwritten constitution, the government can file for EU divorce without involvement of the Parliament.[79] The second issue is closely related to Article 50 TEU itself. Mainly, the wording of its paragraph 1 makes it unclear what form should such a notification take. This author has already argued elsewhere that *mutatis mutandis* to application for EU membership the divorce notice should preferably take the form of a diplomatic letter.[80] Both issues are likely to be clarified in the second half of 2016 or in early 2017.

It should be noted that Article 50 TEU creates an obligation, but only for the EU, to negotiate a withdrawal agreement regulating terms of exit and taking account of framework for future relations between the divorcees. If such an agreement is not successfully concluded within two years of notification, the Treaties automatically cease to apply to such a country. This date, however, can be amended by a unanimous decision of the European Council (taken in agreement with a departing Member State). Many authors claim that Article 50 TEU allows the Member States to leave the EU unilaterally.[81]

[76] For a detailed account, see P Craig, 'Brexit: A Drama in Six Acts' (2016) 51 *European Law Review* 447.

[77] This was emphasized by the Heads of States and Governments in the wake of the Brexit referendum. See http://www.consilium.europa.eu/en/press/press-releases/2016/06/29-27ms-informal-meeting-statement/, accessed 12 October 2016.

[78] For a comprehensive analysis, see A Łazowski, *Withdrawal from the European Union. A Legal Appraisal* (Edward Elgar 2017).

[79] See a number of interesting posts available at: https://ukconstitutionallaw.org/blog/, accessed 12 October 2016.

[80] A Łazowski, 'Procedural steps towards Brexit', *CEPS*, http://www.ceps.eu/publications/procedural-steps-towards-brexit, accessed 12 October 2016.

[81] See for instance, J Herbst, 'Observation on the Right to Withdraw from the European Union: Who are the "Masters of the Treaties"'? (2005) 6 *German Law Journal* 1755; AF Tatham, '"Don't Mention Divorce at the Wedding, Darling!": EU Accession and Withdrawal after Lisbon' in Biondi et al. (eds) (n 9) 128.

Although such a proposition is legally sound it is rather inconceivable from the practical point of view. This author argued elsewhere that Article 50 TEU should be interpreted in a functional manner, bearing in mind the existing levels of economic and legal integration between the Member States.[82] Still, however, in theoretical terms, the UK may leave without any formal settlement with the EU. For the purposes of this chapter it is submitted that if that were to happen it would be an ultimate act of defiance and political vandalism. It is interesting to consider under what circumstances the UK could theoretically opt for such a radical move. For instance, one could imagine this happening if the negotiations of a withdrawal agreement were stalled or even blocked by the EU Member States (or other actors) and, at the same time, legal and economic uncertainty in the UK would push it to taking a radical decision. It is not unthinkable that the negotiations of a withdrawal agreement could stall due to the clashing interests of the UK and the remaining Member States. Exit talks are likely to be very complex, with a plethora of legal issues relating to withdrawal as well as future relations to be addressed. It suffices to mention the free movement of persons and an objective need to ensure post-divorce the rights acquired by EU citizens living in the UK and the latter's citizens living in other Member States to prove this point. Arguably, it would be in the interest of neither the UK, nor the EU to allow for unilateral withdrawal to happen, thus it is unlikely to materialize.

c. Defiance before the divorce?

A more likely scenario than a unilateral withdrawal is a consensual divorce based on a withdrawal agreement. Arguably, the negotiations between the UK and the EU will be far from easy, giving ample opportunities for the UK to demonstrate its defiance through various political and legal means. This may cover both negotiations of new EU legal acts, including primary legislation, as well as negotiations of the withdrawal agreement itself.

Formally speaking, a notification on the intention to leave triggers only the negotiations of a withdrawal agreement. It does not free such a country from the obligations of a Member State. What is unclear, however, is to what extent the UK should be involved in the daily business of the EU. Article 50 TEU is silent in this respect and without any practice at ones disposal, uncertainty prevails. A withdrawal is, no doubt, a reverse of the accession process. The question is if the vast experience with the latter offers any reasonable solutions to the matter at hand. The countries which apply for EU membership become *quasi* involved in EU decision making upon signature of their accession treaties in the capacity of observers and then they are fully engaged in the EU *modus operandi* as of the date of accession.[83] Clearly, one may distinguish two main phases: before conclusion of accession talks and between signature of an accession treaty and its entry into force. A phasing out model, based *mutatis mutandis* on the accession procedure, would look as follows. From the moment of notification of its intention to exit the EU, the UK would remain a fully fledged participant in the decision making until a formal signature of the withdrawal agreement. From that moment on until its actual exit from the EU the UK's status would be reduced to an observer. Such an arrangement may be a tempting proposition, yet unlikely to succeed. One has to bear in mind that, as far as this author is concerned, a

[82] A Łazowski, 'Withdrawal from the European Union and Alternatives to Membership' (2012) 37 *European Law Review* 523; A Łazowski, 'Unilateral withdrawal from the EU: realistic scenario or a folly?' (2016) *Journal of European Public Policy* 1294.

[83] For analysis of most recent practice in case of Croatia, see e.g. A Łazowski, 'EU do not worry, Croatia is behind you: A Commentary on the Seventh Accession Treaty' (2012) 8 *Croatian Yearbook of European Law and Policy* 1.

decision on withdrawal may change until the exit actually takes place, hence the UK should be allowed to participate as a fully fledged actor in the EU decision making if it were to stay in the EU.[84] Therefore, the reverse of the pre-accession phasing in is unlikely to work in the exit scenario and a more nuanced *modus operandi* would have to be developed at the early stages of negotiations of EU withdrawal.

Negotiating the terms of divorce is never an easy matter. The same will definitely apply to the EU. Arguably, both the Member States and now the UK are locked in, what may turn into a dance macabre. To balance the interests of both sides will be difficult to accomplish, but both sides will have as much to gain as they will have to loose. Still, defiance should not be excluded *ab initio*. Furthermore, it may have different faces. Based on the argument made above, it is likely that the UK, as a withdrawing country, will participate in EU decision-making procedures. By the same token, it is likely to be allowed to shape EU secondary legislation it ultimately wants to pull out from. Blocking meaningful reforms may turn into a tool for blackmailing with a view of securing more beneficial terms of withdrawal. Another aspect of possible defiance is a legal detachment preceding the actual exit from the EU. In the UK it would be enough for the Parliament to repeal the European Communities Act 1972. By this token it would close the doors of the UK's legal systems to EU law and preclude the application of doctrines of primacy, direct and indirect effect, as well as state liability by the national courts. Vote Leave in its pre-referendum manifesto even argued for unilateral limitation of the jurisdiction of the Court of Justice. Another way of showing defiance would be to repeal national law implementing unwanted parts of EU secondary legislation. In the case of the UK the obvious candidates would be EU free movement of persons legislation or EU *acquis* on the rights of third country nationals. Although such moves would backfire and undermine the position of the UK in the withdrawal negotiations, one has to be prepared for such steps. In purely theoretical terms one could also take these speculations even further and draw a hypothetical scenario whereby the UK completely ignores judgments of the Court based on Articles 258 and 260 TFEU. Although such extreme cases of defiance are rather unlikely, the EU should be prepared for a plethora of alternative scenarios. The question is if it is well equipped to face such developments.

d. Tools against defiance en route to Brexit

Should the UK decide to exercise defiance along the lines outlined above, the remaining Member States would have, first and foremost, political tools at their disposal. As already argued, it is in the interest of both sides to reach a reasonable settlement covering the terms of withdrawal and relations once the divorce materializes. It is questionable, however, if more institutionalized forms of political persuasion would be at the disposal of the EU. As is well known, Article 7 TEU can only be triggered when particular conditions are met and it is too Member State-driven to serve a meaningful purpose.[85]

If the UK decides to express its defiance by detaching itself from the EU legal order, the most effective way of counteracting it would be to employ Articles 258–260 TFEU. As long as the fast track procedure is used and, when necessary, interim measures are adopted by the Court, it could bring some positive results and stop the defying Member State from

[84] I concur with the authors who claim that the notification submitted as per Art 50(1) TEU can be withdrawn. See, for instance, P Craig (n 76).

[85] W Sadurski, 'Adding Bite to a Bark: The Story of Article 7, EU Enlargement, and Jörg Haider' (2010) 16 *Columbia Journal of European Law* 385; See also Besselink in Chapter 8 of this volume.

breaching the principle of loyal cooperation. A valid question is what the other Member States would do under such circumstances? Actions based on Article 259 TFEU should not be ruled out. Furthermore, some could resort to reciprocity, which—as a concept—is alien to EU law. Nevertheless, when faced with defiance on a large scale, some members of the club may seriously consider reintroducing it.

4. Conclusion

The participation of the UK in European integration was never meant to be an easy story and should this marriage of convenience come to an end it would likely leave a bitter aftertaste. Quite symbolically, the fortieth anniversary of accession largely went unnoticed and coincided with the Prime Minister's promise to hold a referendum on withdrawal. Judging by the amount of hard fought opt-outs, the UK is certainly one of a few Member States whose wishes are challenging to accommodate. To make things worse, ever since the coalition government took over the helm in 2010, it has become increasingly difficult to detect what its real wishes are. Politically, the UK painted itself into a *cul-de-sac*, which limited its political influence within the EU. Perhaps, had it had a stronger position it could have had further requests for opt-outs accommodated, *sans* a request for an opt-out from the weather.[86] Yet one has to bear in mind that the EU is arguably suffering from UK fatigue. As this chapter suggests, more adventures are possibly on the menu when the UK submits its EU withdrawal request. However, in purely legal terms, the UK has—at least so far—stayed within reasonable limits of defiance. As the Court statistics and Commission scoreboards prove, the implementation record is business as usual. This confirms the argument made in the introduction that the UK limits its exercises in defiance largely to the negotiation decision-making stages, regardless of whether primary or secondary legislation is at stake. However, once rules are adopted it is no different to the majority of the Member States. Whether this trend will continue once it negotiates the terms of its EU divorce and future relations with the EU is yet to be seen.

[86] Arguably, with the new settlement for the UK negotiated in early 2016 David Cameron has used all remaining political capital. See Decision of the Heads of State or Government, meeting within the European Council, concerning a New Settlement for the United Kingdom within the European Union, EUCO 1/16, Brussels 19 February 2016.

Index